Business, Government, and Society

**A Managerial Perspective,
Text and Cases**

Thirteenth Edition

John F. Steiner
*Professor of Management,
Emeritus California State
University, Los Angeles*

George A. Steiner
*Harry and Elsa Kunin
Professor of Business and
Society and Professor of
Management, Emeritus, UCLA*

McGraw-Hill
Irwin

BUSINESS, GOVERNMENT, AND SOCIETY:
A MANAGERIAL PERSPECTIVE, TEXT AND CASES
Published by McGraw-Hill/Irwin, a business unit of The McGraw-Hill Companies, Inc., 1221 Avenue of the Americas,
New York, NY, 10020.

Some ancillaries, including electronic and print components, may not be available to customers outside the United States.

This book is printed on acid-free paper.

1 2 3 4 5 6 7 8 9 0 DOC/DOC 1 0 9 8 7 6 5 4 3 2 1

ISBN 978-0-07-131663-7
MHID 0-07-131663-9

www.mhhe.com

We dedicate this book to the memory of
Jean Wood Steiner.

Brief Table of Contents

Table of Contents

v

Preface

This 13th edition continues a long effort to tell the story of how forces in business, government, and society shape our world. As always, a stream of events dictated the need for extensive revision. In particular, a major financial crisis and a new presidential administration altered parts of the subject matter in important ways. Accordingly, we have updated the chapters to include new ideas, events, personalities, and publications.

While current events move rapidly over the surface of our world, its underlying dynamics are largely undisturbed. As with every revision, we adapt to the flow of events, but we also continue the work of building insight into basic principles, institutions, and forces. So, while new events will doubtless erode the currency of the discussions, we believe that certain insights about the relationships between business, government, and society should endure.

In what follows, we summarize new elements in this edition.

THE CHAPTERS

Key revisions and additions in the chapters include these.

- Chapter 4, "Critics of Business," has a new discussion of the rise of free market ideas that came to be called the Chicago School and their interaction with, first, Keynesian thinkers and, later, progressive thinkers.

- Chapter 7, "Business Ethics," contains an expanded discussion of white-collar crime and criminal prosecution of both managers and corporations, including the growing use of deferred- and nonprosecution agreements. The chapter also has a new discussion of inner psychological processes interact that generate unethical behavior.

- Chapter 8, "Making Ethical Decisions in Business," adds a new section on the neural basis of ethical decisions. Studies of the brain using magnetic resonance imaging suggest that ethical decisions are fast, unconscious, and automatic processes. Their findings illuminate how individuals do (and should) make ethical decisions.

- Chapter 9, "Business in Politics," includes an expanded discussion of lobbying ethics, including a more thorough discussion of the nature of bribery and incidents to illustrate its boundaries. The section on corporate money in elections is revised to explain changes in election law following the *Citizens United v. Federal Election Commission* decision. The chapter case study is now the story of *Citizens United*.

- Chapter 10, "Regulating Business," adds a new fifth wave, "terrorism and financial crisis," to the four historical waves of regulatory growth. This new wave covers the federal government's aggressive expansion of regulation and changes in regulatory philosophy in the Barack Obama administration.

- Chapter 11, "Multinational Corporations," has a new discussion of the Organisation for Economic Co-Operation and Development's *Guidelines for Multinational*

Enterprises. It tells a story about how the guidelines were applied to a mining company that sought to develop a sacred tribal land in India.

- Chapter 12, "Globalization, Trade, and Corruption," introduces a new discussion of globalization. The section on trade now explains the rise of the modern trading system, including discussions of Bretton Woods, the International Monetary Fund, the World Bank, the General Agreement on Tariffs and Trade, and the World Trade Organization. The section on international corruption is revised to accommodate recent, more vigorous anti-bribery enforcement. It now relates more incidents and stories about bribery.
- Chapter 15, "Consumerism," has several new sections including a discussion of Henry David Thoreau and his principled rejection of materialism, a presentation of arguments defending consumerism, and a description of the consumer protection activities of the Federal Trade Commission.
- Chapter 17, "Civil Rights, Women, and Diversity," contains added emphasis on the nature and significance of diversity management programs in corporations.
- Chapter 18, "Corporate Governance," now tells the story of the Lehman Brothers bankruptcy that resulted from, among other factors, the lack of oversight by a poorly structured board of directors. It explains new governance reforms in the wake of the recent financial crisis.

CHAPTER-OPENING STORIES

As in past editions, we begin each chapter with a true story about a company, a biographical figure, or a government action. Five new stories appear in this edition.

- "David Geffen" is the story of a brash young man willing to compromise the truth to make his fortune. His career invites a timeless discussion of whether actions are always right and wrong in themselves, or whether their consequences should be considered.
- "Paul Magliocchetti and Associates" is the story of a bright young man who went to Washington, D.C., worked for a member of Congress, and set up a lobbying firm. He specialized in getting earmarks for corporations. His story reveals the hidden influence that characterizes politics in the nation's capital.
- "The Federal Aviation Administration" focuses on how this agency issues a license before each launch of a space vehicle by a private company. The story tells how the FAA goes about assessing risks to the public with each launch. The agency's actions are a small window into the work of a massive regulatory presence.
- "The Majestic Hudson River" reveals the details of the huge project to remove polychlorinated biphenyls from this waterway. More than half a century ago General Electric released the chemicals. Now it will pay as much as $2 billion to clean them out even as it protests that they do less harm if left undisturbed.
- "Mark Hurd" is about a former Hewlett-Packard CEO accused of sexual harassment. The board investigated, but found no violation of the company's sexual harassment policy. Still, when questioned by directors he had shaded the

truth about his friendship with a woman. The board lost confidence in his integrity. He was forced to resign.

THE CASE STUDIES

Every chapter, except Chapter 1, ends with a case study. The cases illustrate one or more central themes in the chapter. Five new cases appear in this edition.

- "Tangled Webs" is a story of temptation and transgression. A man and a woman meet on a Web site for adulterers and begin a fated game of insider trading. The case invites discussion of the business model used by the Web site and of the psychology of lying and ethical transgression.
- "*Citizens United v. FEC*" is the story of the Supreme Court decision that allowed corporations to contribute independently to federal political candidates. In a close five-to-four decision the Court's more conservative justices decided that parts of America's election law violated the First Amendment's guarantee of free speech.
- "Good and Evil on the Rails" invites debate about the benefits and costs of regulation. After a train crash in California killed 24 passengers, Congress passed a law mandating $13.3 billion of computerized controls to make trains safer. Unfortunately, the benefits, including the value of statistical lives saved, were less than $1 billion. Is the money well spent?
- "A World Melting Away" is the story of the polar bear endangered by warming of its habitat. What kind of measures can prevent its extinction?
- "A Tale of Two Raids" is a study of the dilemmas faced by corporations trying to comply with laws that prohibit hiring unauthorized workers. It tells of two raids, one a physical raid, the other a sudden, mass firing based on an audit. Both tore apart families and towns.

SUPPORT MATERIALS FOR INSTRUCTORS

The *Online Learning Center,* at www.mhhe.com/steiner13e, features resources for students and instructors. For students there are interactive exercises and self-quizzes designed to enhance understanding of text material.

For instructors there is an *Instructor's Resource Manual* with sample course outlines, chapter objectives, term paper topics for each chapter, and case study teaching notes with answers to the case questions. There also is a test bank covering chapters and case studies, including multiple-choice, true/false, fill-in, and essay questions.

Instructors will also find a set of *PowerPoint*© slides for each chapter to use for classroom lectures.

The *Computerized Test Bank* covers chapters and case studies. It includes multiple-choice, true/false, fill-in, and essay questions. In preparing exams instructors can view questions as they are selected; scramble questions and answers; add, delete, and edit questions; create multiple test versions; and view and save tests.

Acknowledgments

We are indebted to the long line of authors, extending from ancient Athens to the present, who have tutored and inspired us. We extend special thanks to the ranks of colleagues and friends within the Academy of Management who have worked to develop and expand the field over the years. Where appropriate we cite their work.

For this edition, the following reviewers have guided us. We are very appreciative of their efforts and have followed their recommendations.

Gwendolyn Yvonne Alexis	*Monmouth University*
Laura Curran	*California State University, Fullerton*
Jeanne Enders	*Portland State University*
Susan A. O'Sullivan-Gavin	*Seton Hall University*
Jaqueline G. Slifkin	*The College at Brockport, SUNY*
Dennis L. Slivinski	*California State University, Channel Islands*
Harry J. Taft	*Stetson University*
Robert E. Ward	*Baldwin-Wallace College*
George W. Watson	*Southern Illinois University, Edwardsville*
Aimee Lynn Williamson	*Suffolk University*

We thank also those in the world of affairs who were consulted along the way. Those who gave us new ideas, affirmed our interpretations, or verified our facts include Stephen E. Auslander; Jeff Ballinger, Press for Change; Ruthven Benjamin; Chris Banocy, General Electric Transportation; Jamie Yood, Google; Gordon Bennett, New Square Chambers; Bob Davis, Airgas Inc.; Warren Flatau, Federal Railroad Administration; Cheryl Gossin, Constellation Brands, Inc.; Maury Hendler; Kristi R. King, Talladega Speedway; George C. Nield, Office of Commercial Space Transportation, Federal Aviation Administration; Margaret L. Reilly, Office of Management and Budget, Executive Office of the President; Tracy Warner, *The Wenatchee World*; Tom Wasz, Yum! Brands, Inc.; and Jo Woodman, Survival International.

We are thankful for an outstanding editorial team at McGraw-Hill/Irwin, including especially managing development editor Laura Spell, whose guidance led to important and constructive changes in the book; editorial coordinator Jonathan Thornton, who responded to author suggestions while carefully putting all the elements of the effort in place; and lead project manager Christine Vaughan, who is exceptionally competent in the detailed work of turning an original manuscript into a printed book. Their patience and faith throughout the process were always welcome. We are grateful to copyeditor Nancy Dietz for schooling our style and adding clarity and consistency to the benefit of readers. We also express gratitude to marketing manager Jaime Halteman, designer Joanne Mennemeier, senior photo research coordinator Keri Johnson, and media project manager Suresh Babu. Finally, we express our appreciation for the very fine work of Rakhshinda Chishty and the composition team at Aptara, Inc.

This edition, like all previous editions, is an improbable, momentary, and partial triumph over an unruly, cosmic mass of information. That it occurred is due in significant part to those named here.

John F. Steiner

George A. Steiner

About the Authors

John F. Steiner

is Professor of Management Emeritus at California State University, Los Angeles. He received his B.S. from Southern Oregon University and received an M.A. and Ph.D. in political science from the University of Arizona. He has coauthored two other books with George A. Steiner, *Issues in Business and Society* and *Casebook for Business, Government, and Society*. He is also the author of *Industry, Society, and Change: A Casebook*. Professor Steiner is a former chair of the Social Issues in Management Division of the Academy of Management and former chair of the Department of Management at California State University, Los Angeles.

George A. Steiner

is one of the leading pioneers in the development of university curriculums, research, and scholarly writings in the field of business, government, and society. In 1983 he was the recipient of the first Sumner Marcus Award for distinguished achievement in the field by the Social Issues in Management Division of the Academy of Management. In 1990 he received the Distinguished Educator Award, given for the second time by the Academy of Management. After receiving his B.S. in business administration at Temple University, he was awarded an M.A. in economics from the Wharton School of the University of Pennsylvania and a Ph.D. in economics from the University of Illinois. He is the author of many books and articles. Two of his books received "book-of-the-year" awards. In recognition of his writings, Temple University awarded him a Litt.D. honorary degree. Professor Steiner has held top-level positions in the federal government and in industry, including corporate board directorships. He is a past president of the Academy of Management and cofounder of *The California Management Review*.

Chapter One

The Study of Business, Government, and Society

ExxonMobil Corporation

ExxonMobil is a colossus. In 2010 it had revenues of $370 billion and net income of $29 billion. To put this in perspective, it had five times the sales of Microsoft; its profits equaled the total sales of Nike. It paid $89 billion in taxes, a sum exceeding the combined revenues of Microsoft and Nike. ExxonMobil employs 84,000 people, most in the 143 subsidiaries it uses for its operations. Its main business is discovering, producing, and selling oil and natural gas, and it has a long record of profiting more at this business than its rivals.

The company cannot be well understood apart from its history. It descends from the Standard Oil Trust, incorporated in 1882 by John D. Rockefeller as Standard Oil of New Jersey. Rockefeller was a quiet, meticulous, secretive manager, a relentless competitor, and a painstaking accountant who obsessed over every detail of strategy and every penny of cost and earnings. He believed that the end of imposing order on a youthful, rowdy oil industry justified the use of ruthless means.

As Standard Oil grew, Rockefeller's values defined the company's culture; that is, the shared assumptions, both spoken and unspoken, that animate its employees. If the values of a founder such as Rockefeller are effective, they become embedded over time in the organization. Once widely shared, they tend to be exceptionally long-lived and stable.[1] Rockefeller emphasized cost control, efficiency, centralized organization, and suppression of competitors. And no set of principles was ever more triumphant. Standard Oil once had more than 90 percent of the American oil market.

Standard Oil's power so offended public values that in 1890 Congress passed the Sherman Antitrust Act to outlaw its monopoly. In 1911, after years of legal battles, the trust was finally broken into 39 separate companies.[2] After the breakup, Standard Oil

---

[1] See, for example, Edgar H. Schein, *The Corporate Culture Survival Guide,* rev. ed. (San Francisco: Jossey-Bass, 2009), part one.

[2] *Standard Oil Co. of New Jersey v. United States,* 221 U.S. 1 (1911).

of New Jersey continued to exist. Although it had shed 57 percent of its assets to create the new firms, it was still the world's largest oil company. Some companies formed in the breakup were Standard Oil of Indiana (later renamed Amoco), Atlantic Refining (ARCO), Standard Oil of California (Chevron), Continental Oil (Conoco), Standard Oil of Ohio (Sohio), Chesebrough-Pond's (a company that made petroleum jelly), and Standard Oil of New York (Mobil). In 1972 Standard Oil of New Jersey changed its name to Exxon, and in 1999 it merged with Mobil, forming Exxon Mobil.

The passage of time now obscures Rockefeller's influence, but ExxonMobil's actions remain consistent with his nature. It has a centralized, authoritarian culture. Profit is an overriding goal. Every project must meet strict criteria for return on capital. ExxonMobil consistently betters industry rivals in its favorite measure, return on average capital employed.

Unlike Southwest Airlines or Google, where having fun is part of the job, performance pressure at ExxonMobil is so intense that it "is not a fun place to work."[3] As Rockefeller bought competitors, he kept only the best managers from their ranks. Today managers at ExxonMobil face a Darwinian promotion system that weeds out anyone who is not a top performer. "We put them through a big distillation column," said a former CEO, and "only the top of the column stays there."[4] And oil industry competitors still find it a ferocious adversary. The company says simply that it "employs all methods of competition which are lawful and appropriate."[5]

Although ExxonMobil is a powerful corporation, it is no longer the commanding trust of Rockefeller's era. As in the old days, its power is challenged and limited by economic, political, and social forces. Now, however, these forces are more leveling.

Markets are more contested. ExxonMobil pumps only 8 percent of the world's daily output of oil and controls less than 2 percent of petroleum reserves. These figures are far lower than in the 1950s when Exxon was the largest of the Seven Sisters, a group of Western oil firms that dominated global production and reserves, including the huge Middle East oil fields.[6] Now its largest competitors are seven state-owned oil companies, often called the new Seven Sisters, whose output dwarfs that of today's privately owned companies.[7] The biggest, Saudi Aramco, is 3.5 times the size of ExxonMobil in daily crude oil output and has 32 times its reserves.[8] The rise of these state-owned companies reflects a new form of nationalism, one that rejects reliance on foreign firms to exploit natural resources.

[3] Fadel Gheit, a former employee and an oil industry analyst, quoted in Geoff Colvin, "The Defiant One," *Fortune,* April 30, 2007, p. 88.

[4] Lee Raymond, quoted in Tom Bower, *Oil: Money, Politics, and Power in the 21st Century* (New York: Grand Central Publishing, 2009), p. 162.

[5] Exxon Mobil Corporation, Form 10-K 2009, filed with the Securities and Exchange Commission, February 26, 2010, p. 1.

[6] The Seven Sisters were Exxon, Mobil, Shell, British Petroleum, Gulf, Texaco, and Chevron.

[7] The new Seven Sisters are Saudi Aramco (Saudi Arabia), Gazprom (Russia), China National Petroleum Company (China), National Iranian Oil Company (Iran), Petróleos de Venezuela S. A. (Venezuela), Petrobras (Brazil), and Petronas (Malaysia).

[8] Government Accountability Office, *Crude Oil,* GAO-07-283, February 2007, fig. 9; and Ian Bremmer, "The Long Shadow of the Visible Hand," *The Wall Street Journal,* May 22–23, 2010, p. W3.

ExxonMobil is on a treadmill, constantly searching for new oil and natural gas supplies to compensate for declining production in existing fields. Output from a mature field drops 5 to 8 percent a year. To maintain profitability the company pursues new reserves wherever they are, taking political risks and abiding unrest and corruption. Iran and Venezuela have expropriated its assets. In Indonesia, government troops guard its facilities against attacks by rebel forces. In Chad, Angola, Nigeria, and Equatorial Guinea, it has paid dictators for access to oil.

Governments are more active and relations with them, ranging from high-level diplomacy to mundane regulatory compliance, are more complex than in the past. In 2003 the company engaged in a high-stakes game of political intrigue trying to purchase Yukos Oil Company. Yukos was a technologically backward Russian company that controlled oil and gas deposits in Siberia so huge they would double Exxon-Mobil's reserves. ExxonMobil wanted it badly and offered $45 billion to the Russian capitalists who owned it. Their leader was billionaire Mikhail Khodorkovsky, a political rival of Russia's President Vladimir Putin. Khodorkovsky promised ExxonMobil that he would use his political influence to clear the deal, but when its top managers met with Putin he was guarded and said, "These details are for my ministers. You must deal with them."[9] Soon, Khodorkovsky's private jet was mysteriously delayed from taking off at a Siberian airfield and boarded by masked police, who arrested him on charges of fraud and tax evasion. He has been in jail ever since. Yukos soon merged with a state-owned oil company managed by one of Putin's close allies.

In more ordinary ways, webs of law and regulation dictate ExxonMobil's operations in each country where it does business. In the United States alone approximately 200 federal departments, commissions, agencies, offices, and bureaus, only a handful of which existed in Rockefeller's day, impose rules on the company. If the founder were alive, he might find this tight supervision unrecognizable—even incredible. For example, in 2009 the company paid a $600,000 fine to settle charges that 85 migratory birds in five states died of hydrocarbon exposure after landing in production and wastewater ponds. It agreed to a $2.5 million bird protection program. It will put nets over ponds and install electronic systems that turn on flashing lights and noisemakers when they detect incoming flights of birds.[10]

ExxonMobil also faces a demanding social environment. As a leader in the world's largest industry, it is closely watched by environmental, civil rights, labor, and consumer groups—some of which are actively hostile. For years the company agitated environmentalists by rejecting the scientific case for global warming. Alone among major oil companies, it refused to make significant investments in renewable energy. Its former CEO called such investments "a complete waste of money."[11]

In 2006 a new CEO, Rex Tillerson, tried to blunt criticism by granting publicly that the world is warming. But he made no changes in strategy. A group of John D. Rockefeller's heirs, believing that ExxonMobil no longer represented the "forward-looking" spirit of its great founder, wrote to Tillerson, welcoming him as the new

[9] Quoted in Tom Bower, *Oil: Money, Politics, and Power in the 21st Century,* p. 10.

[10] United States Attorney's Office, District of Colorado, "Exxon-Mobil Pleads Guilty to Killing Migratory Birds in Five States," press release, August 13, 2009.

[11] Lee Raymond, quoted in "The Unrepentant Oilman," *The Economist,* March 15, 2003, p. 64.

leader and requesting a meeting.[12] He would not meet with them. Subsequently, 66 Rockefeller descendants signed an initiative calling on the company to convene a climate change task force. The company refused to talk with the family members, who held only 0.006 percent of its shares.[13]

Besides using ethanol blends in gasoline, ExxonMobil's major investment in alternative energy is a $600 million research project to make biofuels from algae.[14] That investment pales in comparison with its $27 billion in capital and exploration expenditures in 2009 and a $30 billion project nearing completion to liquefy and ship natural gas from Qatar.

As a corporate citizen ExxonMobil funds worldwide programs to benefit communities, nature, and the arts. Its largest contributions, about 50 percent of the total, go to education. Other efforts range from $68 million to fight malaria in Africa to $5,000 for the National Cowgirl Museum in Fort Worth, Texas. In 2009 ExxonMobil gave $196 million to such efforts. This is a large sum from the perspective of an individual. However, for ExxonMobil it was seven-hundredths of 1 percent of its revenues, the equivalent of a person making $1 million a year giving $7 to charity. Does this giving live up to the elegant example of founder John D. Rockefeller, the great philanthropist of his era?

The story of ExxonMobil raises central questions about the role of business in society. When is a corporation socially responsible? How can managers know their responsibilities? What actions are ethical or unethical? How responsive must a corporation be to its critics? This book is a journey into the criteria for answering such questions. As a beginning for this first chapter, however, the story illustrates a range of interactions between one large corporation and many nations and social forces. Such business–government–society interactions are innumerable and complicated. In the chapter that follows we try to order the universe of these interactions by introducing four basic models of the business-government-society relationship. In addition, we define basic terms and explain our approach to the subject matter.

WHAT IS THE BUSINESS–GOVERNMENT–SOCIETY FIELD?

In the universe of human endeavor, we can distinguish subdivisions of economic, political, and social activity—that is, business, government, and society—in every civilization throughout time. Interplay among these activities creates an environment in which businesses operate. The business-government-society (BGS) field is the study of this environment and its importance for managers.

To begin, we define the basic terms.

Business is a broad term encompassing a range of actions and institutions. It covers management, manufacturing, finance, trade, service, investment, and other activities. Entities as different as a hamburger stand and a giant corporation are businesses. The fundamental purpose of every business is to make a profit by providing products and services that satisfy human needs.

business
Profit-making activity that provides products and services to satisfy human needs.

---

[12] Daniel Gross, "There Will Be Blood Orange Juice," *Slate,* April 30, 2008.

[13] Jad Mouawad, "Can Rockefeller Heirs Turn Exxon Greener?" *The New York Times,* May 4, 2008, p. B2.

[14] "ExxonMobil Invests in Algae for Biofuel," *Nature,* July 2009, p. 449.

government
Structures and processes in society that authoritatively make and apply policies and rules.

society
A network of human relations composed of ideas, institutions, and material things.

idea
An intangible object of thought.

value
An enduring belief about which fundamental life choices are correct.

ideology
A bundle of values that creates a particular view of the world.

institution
A formal pattern of relations that links people to accomplish a goal.

Government refers to structures and processes in society that authoritatively make and apply policies and rules. Like business, it encompasses a wide range of activities and institutions at many levels, from international to local. The focus of this book is on the economic and regulatory powers of government as they affect business.

A *society* is a cooperative network of human relations, organized by flows of power and relatively distinct in its boundaries from other, analogous networks.[15] Every society includes three interacting elements: (1) ideas, (2) institutions, and (3) material things.

Ideas, or intangible objects of thought, include values and ideologies. *Values* are enduring beliefs about which fundamental choices in personal and social life are correct. Cultural habits and norms are based on values. *Ideologies* are bundles of values that create a worldview. They establish the meaning of life or categories of experience by defining what is considered good, true, right, beautiful, and acceptable. Sacred ideologies, or theologies, include the great religions that define human experience in relation to a deity. Secular ideologies, such as democracy, liberalism, capitalism, socialism, or ethics, all of which will be discussed in this book as they relate to business, explain human experience in a visible world, a world ordered by values based on reason, not faith. The two kinds of ideology can overlap, as with ethics, an ideology rooted in both faith and reason. All ideologies have the power to organize collective activity. Ideas shape every institution in society, sometimes coming in conflict as when capitalism's practiced values of exploitation, ruthless competition, self-interest, and short-term gain abrade values of love, mercy, charity, and patience in Christianity.

Institutions are formal patterns of relations that link people to accomplish a goal. They are essential to coordinate the work of individuals having no direct relationship with each other.[16] In modern societies, economic, political, cultural, legal, religious, military, educational, media, and familial institutions are salient. There are multiple economic institutions such as financial institutions, the corporate form, and markets. Collectively, we call these business.

As Figure 1.1 shows, markets are supported by a range of institutions. Capitalism has wide variation in nations where it abides because supporting institutions grow from unique historical and cultural roots. In developed nations these institutions are highly evolved and mutually supportive. Where they are weak, markets work in dysfunctional ways. An example is the story of Russia, which introduced a market economy after the fall of communism in the early 1990s. In the old system workers spent lifetimes in secure jobs at state-owned firms. There was no unemployment insurance and, because few workers ever moved, housing markets were undeveloped. A free market economy requires a strong labor market, so workers can switch from jobs in declining firms to jobs in expanding ones. But Russia's labor market was undeveloped. Because the government did not yet

[15] See Michael Mann, *The Sources of Social Power,* vol. I: *A History of Power from the Beginning to A.D. 1760* (New York: Cambridge University Press, 1986), pp. 1–3.

[16] Arnold J. Toynbee, *A Study of History,* vol. XII, *Reconsiderations* (London: Oxford University Press, 1961), p. 270.

FIGURE 1.1   **How Institutions Support Markets**

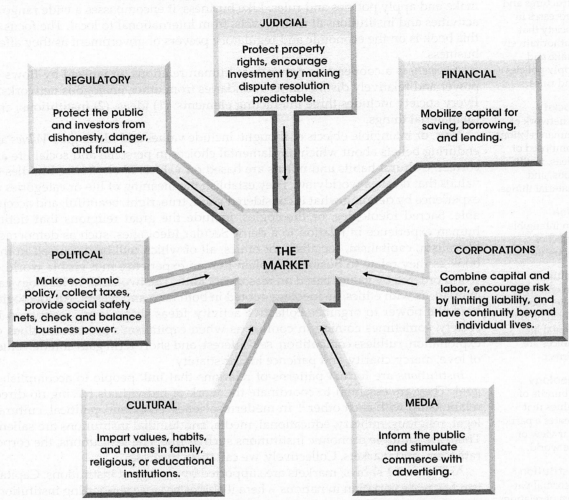

JUDICIAL

Protect property rights, encourage investment by making dispute resolution predictable.

REGULATORY

Protect the public and investors from dishonesty, danger, and fraud.

FINANCIAL

Mobilize capital for saving, borrowing, and lending.

POLITICAL

Make economic policy, collect taxes, provide social safety nets, check and balance business power.

THE MARKET

CORPORATIONS

Combine capital and labor, encourage risk by limiting liability, and have continuity beyond individual lives.

CULTURAL

Impart values, habits, and norms in family, religious, or educational institutions.

MEDIA

Inform the public and stimulate commerce with advertising.

provide unemployment benefits to idled workers, there was no safety net. And housing markets were anemic. Company managers, out of basic humanity, were unwilling to lay off workers who would get no benefits and who would find it difficult to move elsewhere.[17] As a result, restructuring in the new Russian economy was torpid. The lesson is that institutions are vital to markets.

Each institution has a specific purpose in society. The function of business is to make a profit by producing goods and services at prices attractive to consumers. A business uses the resources of society to create new wealth. This justifies its existence and is its priority task. All other social tasks—raising an army, advancing knowledge, healing the sick, or raising children—depend on it. Businesses must,

[17] Joseph E. Stiglitz, *Globalization and Its Discontents* (New York: W. W. Norton, 2002), p. 140.

therefore, be managed to make a profit. A categorical statement of this point comes from Peter Drucker: "Business management must always, in every decision and action put economic performance first."[18] Without profit, business fails in its duty to society and lacks legitimacy.

material things
Tangible artifacts of a society that shape and are shaped by ideas and institutions.

The third element in society is *material things*, including land, natural resources, infrastructure, and manufactured goods. These shape and, in the case of fabricated objects, are partly products of ideas and institutions. Economic institutions, together with the extent of resources, largely determine the type and quantity of society's material goods.

The BGS field is the study of interactions among the three broad areas defined above. Its primary focus is on the interaction of business with the other two elements. The basic subject matter, therefore, is how business shapes and changes government and society, and how it, in turn, is molded by political and social pressures. Of special interest is how forces in the BGS nexus affect the manager's task.

WHY IS THE BGS FIELD IMPORTANT TO MANAGERS?

To succeed in meeting its objectives, a business must be responsive to both its economic and its noneconomic environment.[19] ExxonMobil, for example, must efficiently discover, refine, transport, and market energy. Yet swift response to market forces is not always enough. There are powerful nonmarket forces to which many businesses, especially large ones, are exposed. Their importance is clear in the two dramatic episodes that punctuate ExxonMobil's history—the 1911 court-ordered breakup and the 1989 *Exxon Valdez* oil spill.

In 1911 the Supreme Court, in a decision that reflected public opinion as well as interpretation of the law, forced Standard Oil to conform with social values favoring open, competitive markets. With unparalleled managerial genius, courage, and perspicacity, John D. Rockefeller and his lieutenants had built a wonder of efficiency that spread fuel and light throughout America at lower cost than otherwise would have prevailed. They never understood why this remarkable commercial performance was not the full measure of Standard Oil. But beyond efficiency, the public demanded fair play. Thus, the great company was dismembered.

In Alaska, one of the company's massive tankers spilled 11 million gallons of crude oil when its captain, having consumed enough vodka "to make most people unconscious," quit the bridge during a critical maneuver. Left alone, an unlicenced third mate ran onto a reef in pristine, picturesque Prince William Sound.[20] The captain was an alcoholic, lately returned to command after a treatment program, but known to have relapsed, drinking in hotels, bars, restaurants, parking lots, and even with Exxon officials. Although the company had a clear policy against

---

[18] *Management: Tasks-Responsibilities-Practices* (New York: Harper & Row, 1973), p. 40.

[19] For discussion of this distinction see Jean J. Boddewyn, "Understanding and Advancing the Concept of 'Nonmarket,'" *Business & Society,* September 2003.

[20] *In re: the Exxon Valdez,* 270 F.3rd 1238 (2001).

use of alcohol by its crews, managers failed to monitor him. Years later, the United States Supreme Court would call this lapse "worse than negligent but less than malicious."[21]

The disaster brought acute legal, political, and image problems for the firm. It spent $2.4 billion to clean up the spill and another $2.2 billion to settle lawsuits that dragged on for 20 years, Congress passed a law barring its ship from ever again entering the area, and activists told motorists to get their gas from other companies.[22] Today ExxonMobil operates its 650 tankers with extreme care and randomly tests crews for drugs and alcohol. Remarkably, it is now so disciplined that it measures oil spills from its fleet in tablespoons per million gallons shipped. Between 2006 and 2009 it averaged fewer than five tablespoons lost per million gallons shipped.[23]

Recognizing that a company operates not only within markets but also within a society is critical. If the society, or one or more powerful elements within it, fails to accept a company's actions, that firm will be punished and constrained. Put philosophically, a basic agreement or *social contract* exists between economic institutions and other networks of power in a society. This contract establishes the general duties that business must fulfill to retain the support and acquiescence of the others as it organizes people, exploits nature, and moves markets. It is partly expressed in law, but it also resides in social values.

social contract
An underlying agreement between business and society on basic duties and responsibilities business must carry out to retain public support. It may be reflected in laws and regulations.

Unfortunately for managers, the social contract, while unequivocal, is not plain, fixed, precise, or concrete. It is as complex and ambiguous as the economic forces a business faces and no less difficult to comprehend. For example, the public believes that business has social responsibilities beyond making profits and obeying regulations. If business does not meet them, it will suffer. But precisely what are those responsibilities? How is corporate social performance to be measured? To what extent must a business comply with unlegislated ethical values? When meeting social expectations beyond the law conflicts with raising profits, what is the priority? Despite these questions, the social contract codifies the expectations of society, and managers who ignore, misread, or violate it court disaster.

FOUR MODELS OF THE BGS RELATIONSHIP

Interactions among business, government, and society are infinite and their meaning is open to interpretation. Faced with this complexity, many people use simple mental models to impose order and meaning on what they observe. These models are like prisms, each having a different refractive quality, each giving the holder a different view of the world. Depending on the model (or prism) used, a person

---

[21] *Exxon Shipping Company v. Baker*, 128 S.Ct. 2631 (2008).

[22] The $2.4 billion includes $303 million in voluntary payments to nearby residents for economic losses. The $2.2 billion figure includes criminal and civil fines, civil settlements, interest, and $500 million in punitive damages imposed by a federal jury. The law was a provision in the Oil Protection Act of 1990.

[23] "Changes ExxonMobil Has Made to Prevent Another Accident Like Valdez," at www.exxonmobil.com/Corporate/about_issues_valdez_prevention.aspx, accessed October 1, 2009.

will think differently about the scope of business power in society, criteria for managerial decisions, the extent of corporate responsibility, the ethical duties of managers, and the need for regulation.

The following four models are basic alternatives for seeing the BGS relationship. As abstractions they oversimplify reality and magnify central issues. Each model can be both descriptive and prescriptive; that is, it can be both an explanation of how the BGS relationship does work and, in addition, an ideal about how it should work.

market economy
The economy that emerges when people move beyond subsistence production to production for trade, and markets take on a more central role.

capitalism
An economic ideology with a bundle of values including private ownership of means of production, the profit motive, free competition, and limited government restraint in markets.

The Market Capitalism Model

The market capitalism model, shown in Figure 1.2, depicts business as operating within a market environment, responding primarily to powerful economic forces. There, it is substantially sheltered from direct impact by social and political forces. The market acts as a buffer between business and nonmarket forces. To appreciate this model, it is important to understand the history and nature of markets and the classic explanation of how they work.

Markets are as old as humanity, but for most of recorded history they were a minor institution. People produced mainly for subsistence, not to trade. Then, in the 1700s, some economies began to expand and industrialize, division of labor developed within them, and people started to produce more for trade. As trade grew, the market, through its price signals, took on a more central role in directing the creation and distribution of goods. The advent of this kind of *market economy*, or an economy in which markets play a major role, reshaped human life.

The classic explanation of how a market economy works comes from the Scottish professor of moral philosophy Adam Smith (1723–1790). In his extraordinary treatise, *The Wealth of Nations*, Smith wrote about what he called "commercial society" or what today we call *capitalism*. He never used that word. It was adopted later by the philosopher Karl Marx (1818–1883), who contrived it as a term of

FIGURE 1.2
The Market Capitalism Model

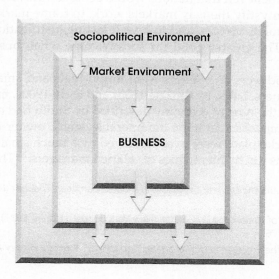

Full Production and Full Employment under Our Democratic System of Private Enterprise, ca. 1944, a crayon and ink drawing by Michael Lenson, an artist working for the Works Progress Administration Federal Art Project. Lenson focuses on the virtues of market capitalism. Source: The Library of Congress. © Barry Lenson, used with permission.

pointed insult. But it caught on and soon lost its negative connotation.[24] Smith said the desire to trade for mutual advantage lay deep in human instinct. He noted the growing division of labor in society led more people to try to satisfy their self-interests by specializing their work, then exchanging goods with each other. As they did so, the market's pricing mechanism reconciled supply and demand, and its ceaseless tendency was to make commodities cheaper, better, and more available.

The beauty of this process, according to Smith, was that it coordinated the activities of strangers who, to pursue their selfish advantage, were forced to fulfill the needs of others. In Smith's words, each trader was "led by an invisible hand to promote an end which was no part of his intention," the collective good of society.[25] Through markets that harnessed the constant energy of greed for the public welfare, Smith believed that nations would achieve "universal opulence." His genius was to demystify the way markets work, to frame market capitalism in moral terms, to extol its virtues, and to give it lasting justification as a source of human progress. The greater good for society came when businesses competed freely.

managerial capitalism
A market economy in which the dominant businesses are large firms run by salaried managers, not smaller firms run by owner-entrepreneurs.

In Smith's day producers and sellers were individuals and small businesses managed by their owners. Later, by the late 1800s and early 1900s, throughout the industrialized world, the type of economy described by Smith had evolved into a system of *managerial capitalism.* In it the innumerable, small, owner-run firms that animated Smith's marketplace were overshadowed by a much smaller number of dominant corporations run by hierarchies of salaried managers.[26] These managers

---

[24] Jerry Z. Muller, *The Mind and the Market: Capitalism in Modern European Thought* (New York: Knopf, 2002), p. xvi.

[25] Adam Smith, *The Wealth of Nations,* ed. E. Cannan (New York: Modern Library, 1937), Book IV, chap. II, p. 423. First published in 1776.

[26] Alfred D. Chandler, Jr., "The Emergence of Managerial Capitalism," *Business History Review,* winter 1984, p. 473.

had limited ownership in their companies and worked for shareholders. This variant of capitalism has now spread throughout the world.

laissez-faire
An economic philosophy that rejects government intervention in markets.

The model incorporates important assumptions. One is that government interference in economic life is slight. This is called *laissez-faire,* a term first used by the French to mean that government should "let us alone." It stands for the belief that government intervention in the market is undesirable. It is costly because it lessens the efficiency with which free enterprise operates to benefit customers. It is unnecessary because market forces are benevolent and, if liberated, will channel economic resources to meet society's needs. It is for governments, not businesses, to correct social problems. Therefore, managers should define company interests narrowly, as profitability and efficiency.

Another assumption is that individuals can own private property and freely risk investments. Under these circumstances, business owners are powerfully motivated to make a profit. If free competition exists, the market will hold profits to a minimum and the quality of products and services will rise as competing firms try to attract more buyers. If one tries to increase profits by charging higher prices, consumers will go to another. If one producer makes higher-quality products, others must follow. In this way, markets convert selfish competition into broad social benefits.

Other assumptions include these: Consumers are informed about products and prices and make rational decisions. Moral restraint accompanies the self-interested behavior of business. Basic institutions such as banking and laws exist to ease commerce. There are many producers and consumers in competitive markets.

The perspective of the market capitalism model leads to these conclusions about the BGS relationship: (1) government regulation should be limited, (2) markets will discipline private economic activity to promote social welfare, (3) the proper measure of corporate performance is profit, and (4) the ethical duty of management is to promote the interests of owners and investors. These tenets of market capitalism have shaped economic values in the industrialized West and, as markets spread, they do so increasingly elsewhere.

There are many critics of capitalism and the market capitalism model. Bernard Mandeville (1670–1733), an intellect predating Adam Smith, argued that markets erode virtue. The envy, avarice, self-love, and ruthlessness that energize them are base values driving out virtues such as love, friendship, and compassion.[27] Karl Marx believed that owners of capital exploited workers and promoted systems of rising inequality. The communist Vladimir Lenin (1870–1924) wrote that industrialists masterminded imperial foreign policies to effect a "territorial division of the whole world among the greatest capitalist powers."[28] Pope John Paul II (1920–2005) feared that markets place too much emphasis on money and material objects and cautioned against a "domination of things over people."[29]

[27] See George Bragues, "Business Is One Thing, Ethics Is Another: Revisiting Bernard Mandeville's *The Fable of the Bees,*" *Business Ethics Quarterly,* April 2005.

[28] V. I. Lenin, *Imperialism: The Highest Stage of Capitalism* (New York: International Publishers, 1939), p. 89.

[29] Ioannes Paulus PP.II, Encyclical Letter, *Centesimus annus* (May 1, 1991), no. 33.

Such critics see a long list of flaws that often, perhaps inevitably, appear in markets. Without correction the market amplifies blemishes of human nature and the result is conspiracies, monopolies, frauds, pollution, and dangerous products. Business models arise to satisfy vices such as adultery, gossiping, gambling, smoking, drug use, and prostitution. Calls for corporate social responsibility and more ethical managerial behavior stem from the inevitability of capitalism's flaws. As promised by its defenders, capitalism has created material progress. Yet its dark side is unremitting.

Denunciations of capitalism are pronounced today, but none are new. They carry on a regular attack that winds through the Western intellectual tradition. Adam Smith himself had some reservations and second thoughts. He feared both physical and moral decline in factory workers and the unwarranted idolization of the rich, who might have earned their wealth by unvirtuous methods. In his later years, he grew to see more need for government intervention. But Smith never envisioned a system based solely on greed and self-interest. He expected that in society these traits must coexist with restraint and benevolence.[30]

The ageless debate over whether capitalism is the best means to human fulfillment will continue. Meanwhile, we turn our discussion to an alternative model of the BGS relationship that attracts many of capitalism's detractors.

The Dominance Model

The dominance model is a second basic way of seeing the BGS relationship. It represents primarily the perspective of business critics. In it, business and government dominate the great mass of people. This idea is represented in the pyramidal, hierarchical image of society shown in Figure 1.3.

FIGURE 1.3
The Dominance Model

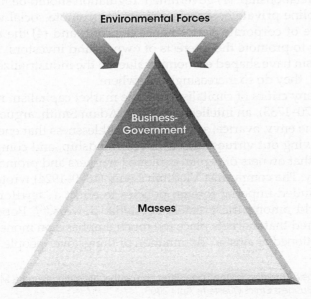

Environmental Forces

Business-Government

Masses

---

[30] E. G. West, ed., *The Theory of Moral Sentiments* (Indianapolis: Liberty Classics, 1976), pp. 70–72. Originally published in 1853.

Those who subscribe to the model believe that corporations and a powerful elite control a system that enriches a few at the expense of the many. Such a system is undemocratic. In democratic theory, governments and leaders represent interests expressed by the people, who are sovereign.

Proponents of the dominance model focus on the defects and inefficiencies of capitalism. They believe that corporations are insulated from pressures holding them responsible, that regulation by a government in thrall to big business is feeble, and that market forces are inadequate to ensure ethical management. Unlike other models, the dominance model does not represent an ideal in addition to a description of how things are. For its advocates, the ideal is to turn it upside down so that the BGS relationship conforms to democratic principles.

In the United States the dominance model gained a following during the late nineteenth century when large trusts such as Standard Oil emerged, buying politicians, exploiting workers, monopolizing markets, and sharpening income disparities. Beginning in the 1870s, diverse groups of plain people who found themselves toiling under the directives of rich capitalists rejected the market capitalism model and based a populist reform movement on the critical view of society implied in the dominance model.

populism
A political pattern, recurrent in world history, in which common people who feel oppressed or disadvantaged seek to take power from a ruling elite seen as thwarting fulfillment of the collective welfare.

Populism is a recurrent spectacle in which common people who feel oppressed or disadvantaged in some way seek to take power from a ruling elite that thwarts fulfillment of the collective welfare. In America, the populist impulse bred a sociopolitical movement of economically hard-pressed farmers, miners, and workers lasting from the 1870s to the 1890s that blamed the Eastern business establishment for a range of social ills and sought to limit its power.

This was an era when, for the first time, on a national scale the actions of powerful business magnates shaped the destinies of common people. Some displayed contempt for commoners. "The public be damned," railroad magnate William H. Vanderbilt told a reporter during an interview in his luxurious private railway car.[31] The next day, newspapers around the country printed his remark, enraging the public. Later, Edward Harriman, the aloof, arrogant president of the Union Pacific Railroad, allegedly reassured industry leaders worried about reform legislation, saying "that he 'could buy Congress' and that if necessary he 'could buy the judiciary.'"[32] It was with respect to Harriman that President Theodore Roosevelt once noted, "men of very great wealth in too many instances totally failed to understand the temper of the country and its needs."[33]

[31] "Reporter C.P. Dresser Dead," *The New York Times,* April 25, 1891, p. 7. In fairness to Vanderbilt, the context of the remark is elusive. It came in response to questioning by a reporter who may have awakened Vanderbilt at 2:00 a.m. to ask, perhaps insolently, if he would keep an unprofitable route in service to the public. Vanderbilt's response was magnified far beyond a cross retort to become the age's enduring emblem of arrogant wealth. See "Human Factor Great Lever in Railroading," *Los Angeles Times,* October 20, 1912, p. V15; and Ashley W. Cole, "A Famous Remark," *The New York Times,* August 25, 1918, p. 22 (letter to the editor).

[32] Quoted from correspondence of Theodore Roosevelt in Maury Klein, *The Life & Legend of E.H. Harriman* (Chapel Hill: University of North Carolina Press, 2000), p. 369.

[33] Ibid., p. 363.

This 1900 political cartoon illustrates a central theme of the dominance model, that powerful business interests act in concert with government to further selfish money interests. Although the cartoon is old, the idea remains compelling for many.
Source: © Bettmann/CORBIS

IN THE HANDS OF HIS PHILANTHROPIC FRIENDS.

The populist movement in America ultimately fell short of reforming the BGS relationship to a democratic ideal. Other industrializing nations, notably Japan, had similar populist movements. *Marxism*, an ideology opposed to industrial capitalism, emerged in Europe at about the same time as these movements, and it also contained ideas resonant with the dominance model. In capitalist societies, according to Karl Marx, an owner class dominates the economy and ruling institutions. Many business critics worldwide advocated socialist reforms that, based on Marx's theory, could achieve more equitable distribution of power and wealth.

In the United States the dominance model may have been most accurate in the late 1800s when it first arose to conceptualize a world of brazen corporate power and politicians who openly represented industries. However, it remains popular. Ralph Nader, for example, speaks its language.

> Over the past 20 years, big business has increasingly dominated our political economy. This control by corporate government over our political government is creating a widening "democracy gap." The unconstrained behavior of big business is subordinating our democracy to the control of a corporate plutocracy that knows few self-imposed limits to the spread of its power to all sectors of our society.[34]

Nader persists in the rhetoric of the dominance model. Running for president in 2008 he wrote that "the corporations . . . have become our government . . . [and]

Marxism
An ideology holding that workers should revolt against property-owning capitalists who exploit them, replacing economic and political domination with more equal and democratic socialist institutions.

[34] "Statement of Ralph Nader," in *The Ralph Nader Reader* (New York: Seven Stories Press, 2000), pp. 3 and 4.

FIGURE 1.4
The Counter-
vailing Forces
Model

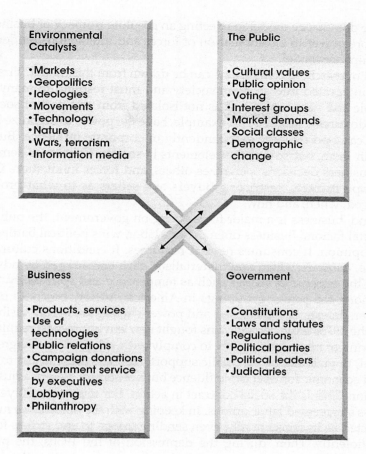

Environmental Catalysts

- Markets
- Geopolitics
- Ideologies
- Movements
- Technology
- Nature
- Wars, terrorism
- Information media

The Public

- Cultural values
- Public opinion
- Voting
- Interest groups
- Market demands
- Social classes
- Demographic change

Business

- Products, services
- Use of technologies
- Public relations
- Campaign donations
- Government service by executives
- Lobbying
- Philanthropy

Government

- Constitutions
- Laws and statutes
- Regulations
- Political parties
- Political leaders
- Judiciaries

both parties are moving deeper into the grip of global corporatism,"[35] later adding that "corporate power over our political economy and its control over people's lives knows few boundaries."[36]

The Countervailing Forces Model

The countervailing forces model, shown in Figure 1.4, depicts the BGS relationship as a flow of interactions among major elements of society. It suggests exchanges of power among them, attributing constant dominance to none.

This is a model of multiple forces. The power of each element can rise or fall depending on factors such as the subject at issue, the strength of competing interests, the intensity of feeling, and the influence of leaders. The countervailing forces model generally reflects a way of looking at the BGS relationship in the United States and other Western industrialized nations. It differs from the market capitalism model in opening business directly to influence by nonmarket forces. It differs

[35] Ralph Nader, "It's Not About Me. It's About Our Broken System," *USA Today,* March 5, 2008, p. 11A.
[36] Ralph Nader, "Time for Citizens to Convene," Common Dreams.org, September 28, 2009, at www.commondreams.org.

from the dominance model in rejecting an absolute primacy of business and crediting more power to a combination of forces and interactions rendered paltry by the dominance model.

What overarching conclusions can be drawn from this model? First, business is deeply integrated into an open society and must respond to many forces, both economic and noneconomic. It is not isolated from any part of society, nor is it always dominant. Markets, for example, have the power to organize human activity and can operate very independently of corporate influence. Business exerts power in them, but so do other elements in society. Consumer demand rewards some business decisions, penalizes others, and forces innovation. Governments also shape markets, restricting buyers and sellers as to what products can be exchanged, when, and how.

Second, business is a major force acting on government, the public, and environmental factors. Business often defeats labor, wins political battles, and shapes public opinion. It consumes natural resources. It conditions cultural values, for example, commercialism and materialism, each encouraged by advertising perhaps at the expense of values such as temperance and spirituality. Some believe that among the power groupings in American society business predominates. However, defeats, compromises, and power sharing are highly visible. For example, in the 1970s large corporations fought new environmental regulations only to see a string of major laws, costly to comply with, adopted by Congress.

Third, to maintain broad public support, business must adjust to social, political, and economic forces it can influence but not control. Faulty adjustment invites correction. This is the social contract in action. For more than 50 years American business suppressed labor unions. In keeping with the dominance model, government acted as its constant ally, even sending troops to end strikes forcibly, sometimes violently. Then, during the depression of the 1930s, the public blamed economic problems on corporate greed and excesses, electing President Franklin D. Roosevelt to bring reform. Sympathy for struggling workers was so strong that in 1935 Congress passed the National Labor Relations Act, protecting and easing union organizing, a colossal defeat for business and a bitter lesson about the social contract.

Finally, BGS relationships evolve as changes take place in the ideas, institutions, and processes of society. After the collapse of financial markets in late 2008, for example, the federal government took unprecedented actions, taking large ownership shares in big companies, firing the CEO of General Motors, and dictating executive salaries. Such actions altered the nature of capitalism as practiced in the United States in a way that reduced business power.

The Stakeholder Model

stakeholder
An entity that is benefitted or burdened by the actions of a corporation or whose actions may benefit or burden the corporation. The corporation has an ethical duty toward these entities.

The stakeholder model in Figure 1.5 shows the corporation at the center of an array of relationships with persons, groups, and entities called *stakeholders*. Stakeholders are those whom the corporation benefits or burdens by its actions and those who benefit or burden the firm with their actions. A large corporation has many stakeholders, all divisible into two categories based on the nature of the relationship. But the assignments are relative, approximate, and inexact. Depending

FIGURE 1.5
The Stakeholder Model

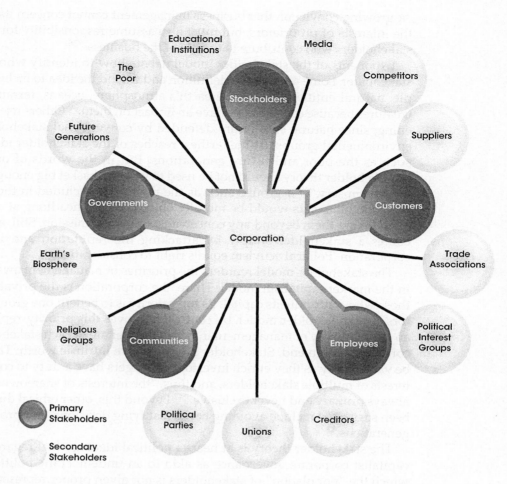

primary
stakeholders
Entities in a relationship with the corporation in which they, the corporation, or both are affected immediately, continuously, and powerfully.

secondary stakeholders
Entities in a relationship with the corporation in which the effects on them, the corporation, or both are less significant and pressing.

on the corporation or the episode, a few stakeholders may shift from one category to the other.

Primary stakeholders are a small number of constituents for which the impact of the relationship is mutually immediate, continuous, and powerful. They are usually stockholders (owners), customers, employees, communities, and governments and may, depending on the firm, include others such as suppliers or creditors.

Secondary stakeholders include a possibly broad range of constituents in which the relationship is one of less immediacy, benefit, burden, or power to influence. Examples are activists, trade associations, politicians, and schools.

This model is based on a growing body of work by academicians who follow the lead of R. Edward Freeman, a management scholar and ethicist whose seminal 1984 book consolidated rudimentary ideas into a cohesive theory.[37] Now the idea seizes the imagination of many, including Pope Benedict XVI who writes of

[37] R. Edward Freeman, *Strategic Management: A Stakeholder Approach* (Boston: Pitman Publishing, 1984).

"a growing conviction that business management cannot concern itself only with the interests of proprietors, but must also assume responsibility for all the other stakeholders who contribute to the life of the business."[38]

Exponents of the stakeholder model debate how to identify who or what is a stakeholder. Some use a broad definition and extend the idea to include, for example, natural entities such as the earth's atmosphere, oceans, terrain, and living creatures because corporations have an impact on them.[39] Others reject this broadening, since natural entities are defended by conventional stakeholders such as environmental groups. At the farthest reaches of the stakeholder idea lie groups such as the poor and future generations. But in the words of one advocate, "[s]takeholder theory should not be used to weave a basket big enough to hold the world's misery."[40] If groups such as the poor were included in the stakeholder network, managers would be morally obliged to run headlong at endless problems, taking them beyond any conceivable economic mission. Still, any group becomes a stakeholder simply by attacking the reputation and image of the corporation. Political activism equals right to consideration.

The stakeholder model reorders the priorities of management away from those in the market capitalism model. There, the corporation is the private property of those who contribute its capital. Its top priority is to benefit one group—the investors. The stakeholder model, by contrast, removes this priority, replacing it with an ethical theory of management in which the welfare of each stakeholder must be considered as an end. Stakeholder interests have intrinsic worth: They are not to be valued only as they enrich investors. Managers have a duty to consider the interests of multiple stakeholders, and thus, "the interests of shareowners . . . are not always primary and never exclusive."[41] Beyond this, other ethical duties that have been suggested include avoiding harm, justifying decisions, and protecting future generations.[42]

The stakeholder theory is at heart a political ideology that regards traditional capitalist corporate governance as akin to an undemocratic political system in which the "population" of stakeholders is not given proper representation. Without checks and balances autocratic managers will be tempted by greed into various degrees of economic oppression, treating the un- and underrepresented stakeholders unfairly. The ethical concept of duties introduces such a mechanism of representation. Stakeholder management creates duties toward multiple

---

[38] Benedictus PP.XVI, Encyclical Letter, *Caritas in Veritate* (2009), no. 40.

[39] See Edward Stead and Jean Garner Stead, "Earth: A Spiritual Stakeholder," *Business Ethics Quarterly*, Ruffin Series no. 2 (2000), pp. 321–44.

[40] Max Clarkson, *A Risk-Based Model of Stakeholder Theory* (Toronto: The Centre for Corporate Social Performance & Ethics, 1994), cited in Robert Philips, *Stakeholder Theory and Organizational Ethics* (San Francisco: Berrett-Koehler, 2003), p. 119. See also James P. Walsh, "Taking Stock of Stakeholder Management," *Academy of Management Review* 30, no. 2, p. 205.

[41] James E. Post, Lee E. Preston, and Sybille Sachs, *Redefining the Corporation: Stakeholder Management and Organizational Wealth* (Stanford, CA: Stanford University Press, 2002), p. 17.

[42] For a list of ethical duties toward stakeholders see Advisory Panel, Newmont Community Relationships Review, *Building Effective Community Relationships: Final Report of the Advisory Panel to Newmont's Community Relationship Review,* February 8, 2009, appendix 7.

entities of the corporation—duties not emphasized in the traditional capitalist firm, which tries to dominate its environment out of an obsessive focus on enriching stockholders. Management must raise its gaze above profits to see and respond to a spectrum of other values; it must manage to make each stakeholder "better off."[43] The stakeholder model is intended to "revitalize capitalism" with a "new conceptualization" of how the corporation should work.[44] It rejects the shareholder-centered view of the firm in the market capitalism model as "ethically unacceptable."[45]

Not everyone agrees. Critics argue that the stakeholder model is an unrealistic assessment of power relationships between the corporation and other entities. It seeks to give power to the powerless by replacing force with ethical duty, a timeless and often futile quest of moralists. In addition, it sets up too vague a guideline to substitute for the yardstick of pure profit. Unlike traditional criteria such as return on capital, there is no single, clear, and objective measure to evaluate the combined ethical/economic performance of a firm. According to one critic, this lack of a criterion "would render impossible rational management decision making for there is simply no way to adjudicate between alternative projects when there is more than one bottom line."[46]

In addition, the interests of stakeholders so vary that often they conflict with shareholders and with one another. With respect to corporate actions, laws and regulations protect stakeholder interests. Creating surplus ethical sensitivity that soars above legal duty is impractical and unnecessary.[47] And finally, a lasting conviction, going back to Adam Smith, is that even the most fanatical pursuit of profit, if guided by law and the invisible hand, creates greater lasting good for society than pursuit of profit tempered by compassion. If a new conception of capitalism redistributes decision-making power and resources to stakeholders it can only impair the efficiency of the firm in maximizing both profits and social benefits.[48]

Some puzzles exist in stakeholder thinking. It is not always clear who or what is a legitimate stakeholder, to what each stakeholder is entitled, or how managers should balance competing demands among a range of stakeholders. Yet its advocates find two arguments compelling. First, a corporation that embraces stakeholders prospers more, better sustaining its wealth-creating function with the support of a network of parties beyond shareholders. Put bluntly by an advocate of the stakeholder perspective, "[e]xecutives ignore stakeholders at the peril of the survival of their companies."[49] Second, it is the ethical way to manage because stakeholders have moral rights that grow from the way powerful corporations

---

[43] R. Edward Freeman, Jeffrey S. Harrison, and Andrew C. Wicks, *Managing for Stakeholders: Survival, Reputation, and Success* (New Haven: Yale University Press, 2007), p. 12.

[44] Freeman, Harrison, and Wicks, *Managing for Stakeholders*, pp. x and 3.

[45] Post, Preston, and Sachs, *Redefining the Corporation*, p. 16.

[46] John Argenti, "Stakeholders: The Case Against," *Long Range Planning*, June 1997, p. 444.

[47] Anant K. Sundaram, "Tending to Shareholders," *Financial Times*, May 26, 2006, p. 6.

[48] James A. Stieb, "Assessing Freeman's Stakeholder Theory," *Journal of Business Ethics*, 87 (2009), p. 410.

[49] R. Edward Freeman, "The Wal-Mart Effect and Business, Ethics, and Society," *Academy of Management Perspectives*, August 2006, p. 40.

affect them. Despite academic debates, in practice the stakeholder ideology has been powerful enough to change the way capitalist corporations are managed. Most of the largest global corporations now analyze their stakeholders and enter into dialogue with a wide range of them. This trend is discussed in Chapter 6.

OUR APPROACH TO THE SUBJECT MATTER

Discussion of the business-government-society field could be organized in many ways. The following is an overview of our approach.

Comprehensive Scope

This book is comprehensive. It covers many subjects. We believe that for those new to the field seeing a panorama is helpful. Because there is less depth in the treatment of subjects than can be found in specialized volumes, we suggest additional sources in footnotes.

Interdisciplinary Approach with a Management Focus

The field is exceptionally interdisciplinary. It exists at the confluence of a fairly large number of established academic disciplines, each of which contributes to its study. These disciplines include the traditional business disciplines, particularly management; other professional disciplines, including medicine, law, and theology; the social sciences, including economics, political science, philosophy, history, and sociology; and, from time to time, natural sciences such as chemistry and ecology. Thus, our approach is eclectic; we cross boundaries to find insight.

strategic management
Actions taken by managers to adapt a company to changes in its market and sociopolitical environments.

The dominant orientation, however, is the discipline of management and, within it, the study of *strategic management*, or actions that adapt the company to its changing environment. To compete and survive, firms must create missions, purposes, and objectives; the policies and programs to achieve them; and the methods to implement them. We discuss these elements as they relate to corporate social performance, illustrating successes and failures.

Use of Theory, Description, and Case Studies

theory
A statement or vision that creates insight by describing patterns or relationships in a diffuse subject matter. A good theory is concise and simplifies complex phenomena.

Theories simplify and organize areas of knowledge by describing patterns or regularities in the subject matter. They are important in every field, but especially in this one, where innumerable details from broad categories of human experience intersect to create a new intellectual universe. Where theory is missing or weak, scholarship must rely more on description and the use of case method.

No underlying theory to integrate the entire field exists. Fortunately, the community of scholars studying BGS relationships is building theory in several areas. The first is theory describing how corporations interact with stakeholders. The second is theory regarding the ethical duties of corporations and managers. And the third is theory explaining corporate social performance and how it can be measured. Theory in this last area focuses on defining exactly what a firm does to be responsible in society and on creating scales and rulers with which to weigh and measure its actions. Scholarship in all three areas shows increasing sophistication and wider agreement on basic ideas.

Despite the lack of a grand theory to unify the field, useful theories abound in related disciplines. For example, there are economic theories about the impact of government regulation, scientific theories on the risks of industrial pollution, political theories of corporate power, ethical theories about the good and evil in manager's actions, and legal theories on subjects such as negligence applied by courts to corporations when, for example, industrial accidents occur. When fitting, we discuss such theories; elsewhere we rely on descriptions of events. In each chapter, we also use stories at the beginning and case studies at the end to invite discussion.

Global Perspective

Today economic globalization animates the planetary stage, creating movements of people, money, goods, and information that, in turn, beget conflicts as some benefit more and others less or not at all. Viewing any nation's economy or businesses in isolation from the rest of the world is myopic. Every government finds its economic and social welfare policies judged by world markets. Every corporation has a home country, but many have more sales, assets, and employees outside its borders than within. For now, capitalism is ascendant. It brings unprecedented wealth creation and new material comforts, but it also brings profound risks of economic shocks, imposes burdens on human rights and the environment, and challenges diversity of values for those who stand aloof from the free market consensus. A fitting perspective on the BGS relationship must, therefore, be global.

Historical Perspective

history
The study of phenomena moving through time.

History is the study of phenomena moving through time. The BGS relationship is a stream of events, of which only one part exists today. Historical perspective is important for many reasons. It helps us see that today's BGS relationship is not like that of other eras; that current ideas and institutions are not the only alternative; that historical forces are irrepressible; that corporations both cause and adapt to change; that our era is not unique in undergoing rapid change; and that we are shaping the future now. In addition, the historical record is relatively complete, revealing more clearly the lessons and consequences of past events as compared with current ones that have yet to play out and show their full significance.

Despite appearances of novelty, the present is seldom unparalleled and is best understood as an extension of the past. So we often examine the origins of current arrangements, finding them both enlightening and entertaining. Readers of this book, many at the beginning of long business careers, can take heart from the words of Nicolò Machiavelli, a student of history who believed that "whoever wishes to foresee the future must consult the past; for human events ever resemble those of preceding times."[50]

---

[50] Niccolò Machiavelli, *Discourses on the First Ten Books of Titus Livius* (New York: The Modern Library, 1950), book 3, chapter 43, p. 530, written in 1513.

Chapter Two

The Dynamic Environment

Royal Dutch Shell PLC

Royal Dutch Shell is one of the world's largest companies. It operates in 130 countries. Each year it makes capital investments of between $30 billion and $40 billion, sums that exceed the annual revenues generated from Coca-Cola. Payoffs on these massive bets may come only after years or decades. Risks are large. Shell exists in an uncertain geopolitical environment stirred by forces it cannot dominate. Even a giant must bend to fortune. Are its investments right for the future?

To find out, Shell convenes teams of elite scholars and staff to write alternative versions of the future called scenarios.[1] A *scenario* is a plausible story of the future based on assumptions about how current trends might play out. Carefully written scenarios challenge managers to think in original ways. They are mental wind tunnels that shift environmental forces around the form of the company to see how it "flies."

scenario
A plausible story of the future based on assumptions about how current trends might play out.

Scenarios were first used in the 1960s by scholars studying the idea of a nuclear war between Russia and the United States. With no historical precedent for an exchange of atomic bombs, they drew up riveting alternatives about how such a battle might advance. In the 1970s, Shell pioneered the use of scenarios in corporate planning and they soon proved their worth. In 1971 its planners created a scenario in which oil-rich countries cut their oil exports to raise prices. Conventional wisdom at the time held this to be unlikely. Nonetheless, thinking about the possibility changed Shell's strategy, and when an oil embargo surprised the world in 1973 it was the only major oil firm prepared for the supply interruption.

liberalization
An economic policy of lowering tariffs and other barriers to encourage foreign trade.

Shell's reward was higher profits than its competitors for years afterward. Since then, it has continuously used scenarios to shape strategy. In the 1990s, its planners saw change in the global business environment caused by three dominant forces: globalization, technological change, and *liberalization* (meaning relaxation of trade restrictions and regulations). According to Shell, these forces made up "a rough,

---

[1] See Peter Cornelius, Alexander Van de Putte, and Mattia Romani, "Three Decades of Scenario Planning in Shell," *California Management Review,* Fall 2005.

impersonal game, involving stresses and pressures akin to those of the Industrial Revolution."[2] These three forces became the basis for multiple scenarios.

Now, Shell sees an emerging drama in the global energy system, with tensions building at the intersection of three powerful trends. First, developing nations with expanding populations are using policies of economic growth to alleviate poverty. China and India in particular will consume massive amounts of energy as they develop. Second, supplies of oil and gas cannot keep pace with rising demands for energy. Their shares in the global energy supply will shrink. Alternative sources of energy, including wind, solar, nuclear, and biofuels, will be insufficient to make up the difference. Coal remains abundant, but it is a pollution nightmare. Third, environmental stresses are growing. If fossil fuels maintain their current share of the global energy supply, atmospheric carbon dioxide, which has risen from about 280 parts per million (ppm) in 1800 to 390 ppm today, will bring climate warming that threatens the well-being of human society.

How will the tensions caused by the three trends play out? Shell explores the future in two new scenarios named Scramble and Blueprint.[3]

In Scramble the world fumbles its response to the energy challenge. A dwindling energy supply leads to price spikes and shortages, putting nations in competition with each other for access to fuels. Politicians are pressured to maintain economic growth, so they push the use of more coal and biofuels. Action on climate change is postponed, even as coal burning releases massive amounts of carbon dioxide into the atmosphere. Rising use of biofuels absorbs much of the world's corn crop. Soon, slowing economies, extreme weather events, and shortages of both energy and food cause political upheavals in several countries. Around 2030 advances in energy efficiency and the development of alternative sources bring energy shortages to an end. About this time a consensus on the need for a global greenhouse gas policy emerges. However, 20 years have passed and keeping carbon dioxide in the atmosphere below 550 ppm, a level that threatens human well-being, will be difficult.

In Blueprints the world is more prompt. As energy shortages emerge, a patchwork of responses appears in cities and regions around the world. New taxes and incentives promote energy efficiency. Carbon markets develop. A growing number of local actions bring calls by corporations for clarity and predictability in markets, so national governments act to harmonize policies. As they do, economies shift to less energy-intense footings. With predictability in markets, investment flows to alternative energy sources. Vehicles powered by new battery and fuel-cell technologies dominate transportation. International cooperation grows. Europe, the United States, Japan, China, and India join in establishing a carbon market. Their cooperation leads to an international framework for reducing carbon dioxide emissions with a chance of stabilizing greenhouse gas concentrations near 450 parts per million, a level that avoids catastrophic climate change.

Such story worlds may be more fantasy than prophecy. However, they show the importance that Shell places on understanding its dynamic external environment. In

---

[2] Shell International Limited, *Global Scenarios 1995–2020, Public Scenarios PX96-2* (London: Shell Center, May 1996), p. 2.

[3] Shell International BV, *Shell Energy Scenarios to 2050* (The Hague, The Netherlands: Royal Dutch Shell, 2008), pp. 12–41.

what follows we present a framework for understanding the forces that animate this environment. First, we identify deep historical forces that create change and risk. Then we identify key dimensions of the global business environment and describe major trends within them. Finally, we set forth a dynamic system that explains the interactions between business and its environment.

DEEP HISTORICAL FORCES AT WORK

Order exists behind the swirling patterns of current events. There is a deep logic in the passing of history. Change in the business environment results from the action of elemental historical forces moving in roughly predictable directions. Henry Adams defined a *historical force* as "anything that does, or helps to do, work."[4] The work to which Adams refers is the power to cause events. Change in the business environment is the work of nine deep historical forces or streams of related events. They are shown in Figure 2.1. As we will explain, they are part of a dynamic, interactive system that shapes the business environment.

FIGURE 2.1
Nine Deep Historical Forces

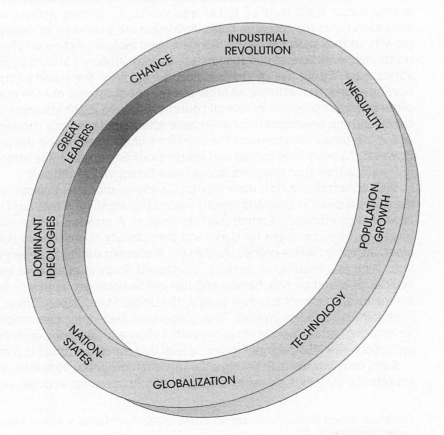

[4] In the essay "A Dynamic Theory of History (1904)," in Henry Adams, *The Education of Henry Adams* (New York: Modern Library, 1931), p. 474; originally published in 1908.

historical force

An environmental force of unknown origin and mysterious action that provides the energy for events. The discussion divides this force, somewhat artificially, into nine separate but related forces causing distinct chains of events.

The Industrial Revolution

An economic metamorphosis in England in the late 1700s. It occurred when certain necessary conditions were present and shifted the country from a simple agrarian economy into a growing industrial economy.

The Industrial Revolution

The first historical force is the drive for transformative economic change. It rose with the *Industrial Revolution* of the late 1700s, which turned simple economies of farmers and artisans into complex industrial societies, greatly increasing their wealth and national power. In thousands of years before this event, there had been no widespread, sustained economic growth to raise living standards. The vast majority of the world's population was mired in poverty.

The Industrial Revolution required specific conditions, including a sufficiency of capital, labor, natural resources, and fuels; adequate transportation; strong markets; and ideas and institutions that supported the productive blend of these ingredients. The right conditions first appeared in Great Britain. It was an open society that allowed social mobility and encouraged individual initiative. Its parliament embodied values of political liberty, free speech, and public debate. Perhaps consequently, Britain was the source of scientific advances and inventions such as the steam engine that liberated the energy in the nation's massive coal deposits. Its climate supported agriculture and its island geography put it at the hub of sea routes for world trade.[5]

After Britain's industrial takeoff, conditions for sustained economic growth arose in Western Europe and the United States during the late nineteenth century. Japan and Russia followed in the first half of the twentieth century, and other Asian nations, including Taiwan, South Korea, and China, followed in the second half. Industrialization continues to spread as less developed nations try to create the conditions for it.

Industrial growth remakes societies. It elevates living standards, alters life experience, and shifts values. Historically, material progress has been associated with moral progress; that is, in the words of one historian, it "fosters greater opportunity, tolerance of diversity, social mobility, commitment to fairness, and dedication to democracy."[6] Since institutions built on older ideas change more slowly than people's lives, industrialization generates huge strains in the social fabric even as it elevates civil life. The size and acceleration of economic growth in the twentieth century were astounding. The total amount of goods and services produced exceeded all that was produced in prior human history. As Figure 2.2 shows, output for just the half century from 1950 to 2000 exceeded all that came before. This growth continues today, generating enormous tensions in both developing and developed societies.

Inequality

From time immemorial, status distinctions, class structures, and gaps between rich and poor have characterized societies. Inequality is ubiquitous, as are its consequences—envy, demands for fair distribution of wealth, and doctrines to justify why some people have more than others. The basic political conflict

---

[5] See Jeffrey Sachs, *The End of Poverty: Economic Possibilities for Our Time* (New York: Penguin Press, 2005), chapter 2.

[6] Benjamin M. Friedman, *The Moral Consequences of Economic Growth* (New York: Knopf, 2005), p. 4.

FIGURE 2.2
World GDP Growth in 50-Year Intervals

Source: Bradford J. DeLong, "Estimating Worldwide GDP, One Million B.C.–Present," at http://econ161.berkeley.edu.

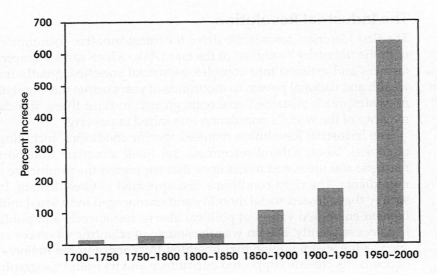

in every nation, and often between nations, is the antagonism between rich and poor.[7]

As the industrial revolution accelerated the accumulation of wealth, it worsened the persistent problem of uneven distribution. Explosive economic growth widened the gap between rich and poor around the globe. Global income inequality is measured by the *Gini index,* a statistic in which 0 percent stands for absolute equality, that is, a theoretical situation in which everyone has the same income, and 100 percent represents absolute inequality, where one person has all the income. Using this measure, inequality becomes greater as the percentage figure rises toward 100.

Figure 2.3 shows that by 1820, as the Industrial Revolution was spreading from England to Western Europe, global income inequality was already very high. The Gini index of 50 percent in 1820 climbed to 61 percent in 1910, as economies in industrializing nations rapidly expanded. After that, the rise continued, but more slowly, as populous Asian countries holding the bulk of the world's poor began to industrialize and catch up. The Gini index reached 64 percent in 1950 and continued its decelerating rise to 67 percent in 2007.[8] This represents an extreme level of inequality across the world population, so high it exceeds the inequality within any single nation. It reflects a situation in which the top 5 percent of people receive about 33 percent of all income and the bottom 5 percent receive 0.2 percent.[9] The cause of this striking gap is the diverging economic fortunes of nations.

Gini index
A statistical measure of inequality in which zero is perfect equality (everyone has the same amount of wealth) and 100 is absolute inequality (a single person has all wealth).

[7] This observation is as old as Plato, who observed that the Greek city-states were "not one, but of necessity two; one consisting of the poor, and the other of the rich, dwelling in one place and always plotting against one another." Plato, *The Republic,* trans. Harry Spens (New York: E. P. Dutton & Co., 1906), p. 263.

[8] Figures are from François Bourguignon and Christian Morrison, "Inequality among World Citizens: 1820–1992," *American Economic Review,* September 2002, pp. 731–32; and Rafael E. De Hoyos and Denis Medvedev, "Poverty Effects of Higher Food Prices: A Global Perspective," Policy Research Working Paper 4887, World Bank, March 2009, p. 4.

[9] Branko Milanovic, "Global Income Inequality: What It Is and Why It Matters," Policy Research Working Paper 3865, World Bank, March 2006, p. 16.

FIGURE 2.3
World Poverty and Income Inequality since 1820

Sources: François Bourguignon and Christian Morrison, "Inequality among World Citizens: 1820–1992," *American Economic Review*, September 2002, table 1; World Bank, *World Development Indicators: 2010* (Washington, DC: World Bank, April 2010); and Rafael E. De Hoyos and Denis Medvedev, "Poverty Effects of Higher Food Prices: A Global Perspective, Policy Research Work Paper 4887, World Bank, March 2009, table 1.

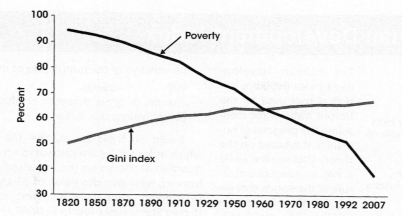

Contrary to popular opinion, economic growth itself does not increase income inequality within modernizing nations. During industrialization the incomes of the poorest people rise in proportion to the rise in average income for the country as a whole.[10] The cause of most of the rise in world income inequality is a growing gap between the peoples of rich and poor nations, not a growing separation of rich and poor within nations.

Today about 2.6 billion people live in poverty, defined as an income of less than $2 a day. About 1.4 billion live in extreme poverty with incomes below $1.25 a day.[11] This is more poor than at any time in history, an enormous pool of misfortune constituting 38 percent of the world population. Yet in 1820, near the beginning of the Industrial Revolution, 94 percent of the world's population lived in poverty. A great and steady retreat in the poverty percentage for almost two centuries, in the face of vaulting population growth, is testimony to the wealth-creating power of industrialization. Even as economic growth has widened the gap between rich and poor, it has dramatically reduced the proportion of the poor in the total population.

Although the Gini index trend line in Figure 2.3 seems to rise only modestly over the years, it in fact represents a striking confluence of progress and tragedy. If world distribution of income had not become more unequal after 1820, economic growth would have reduced the number of people living in poverty today by an estimated 80 percent.[12] Instead, as the wealth gap between nations widened with each passing year, the distribution of income grew more unequal. Yet even as inequality worsened, the drop in the poverty trend line shows how economic growth has led to a continuous, sharp reduction in privation.

Inequality is resilient. It is perpetuated by social institutions such as caste, marriage, land ownership, law, and market relationships. Arrangements and rules in these institutions are resilient, creating sinkholes of unequal opportunity. The vast majority of the world's 2.6 billion poor people live in nations not yet transformed

---

[10] David Dollar and Art Kraay, "Spreading the Wealth," *Foreign Affairs,* January/February 2002, p. 128.

[11] World Bank, *World Development Indicators: 2010* (Washington, DC: World Bank, April 2010), table 2.1.

[12] Bourguignon and Morrison, "Inequality Among World Citizens," p. 733. The $2-a-day figure represents what could be purchased in the United States for $2, not what could be purchased in local currency.

The Human Development Index

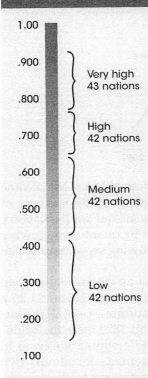

1.00

.900 } Very high
         43 nations

.800 }

.700 } High
         42 nations

.600 }

.500 } Medium
         42 nations

.400 }

.300 } Low
         42 nations

.200 }

.100

The Human Development Index (HDI) is a statistical tool used by the United Nations for measuring the progress of humanity. It is based on the theory that income alone is not an adequate measure of the standard of living, let alone a rich and fulfilling life. If this theory is correct, discussions of inequality based on income differences within and between nations do not give a complete picture of differences in human welfare.

The HDI scale is a scale running from 0 to 1, with 1 representing the highest human development and 0 the lowest. It measures the development of nations as an average of scores in three equally weighted categories.

- *Longevity,* or life expectancy at birth
- *Knowledge,* or the adult literacy rate plus the ratio of students enrolled in school as a percentage of the population of official school age.
- *Income,* or gross domestic product per capita (in equivalent U.S. dollars).

Based on their scores, the 169 nations for which index values are calculated are ranked into quartiles as shown on the index scale at the left. Norway, with an index value of 0.938, is the highest ranked. Zimbabwe is lowest at 0.140. The United States ranks fourth at 0.902.[13]

Historical HDI index values show enormous increases in human welfare. In 1970 the global average was 0.480. By 2010 it had risen to 0.680.[14] Inequality in living standards around the world, as measured by the HDI, is declining even while income inequality, as measured by the per capita GDP, is rising. Thus inequality is greater if measured only by monetary income and less if longevity and education, two traditional measures of a good life, are taken into consideration.

[13] United Nations Development Programme, *Human Development Report 2010* (New York: United Nations, 2010), table 1.
[14] Ibid, p. 25.

by industrial growth where entrenched inequities persist over generations. This situation creates expectations that ethical duties of global corporations include helping the poor and equitably distributing the fruits of commerce. The historical lesson of almost two centuries is that if capitalism is harnessed to create economic growth, the poor will benefit.

Population Growth

The basic population trend throughout human history is growth. As shown in Figure 2.4, world population inched ahead for centuries, then grew a little faster beginning about 1,000 years ago with the inception of large-scale crop cultivation. After eight more centuries, population growth began a rapid new acceleration in the late 1800s that turned into a skyrocketing rise through the twentieth century. It took until 1825 for the world population to reach 1 billion; then each billionth additional person was added faster and faster—first in 100 years, then in 35, then in 15,

FIGURE 2.4
Historical
World
Population
Growth and
Projections:
1 A.D. to 2300

Source: U.S. Bureau of the Census, "Historical Estimates of World Population," available at www.census.gov/ipc/www/worldhis.html; and United Nations, *World Population to 2300*, table A1.

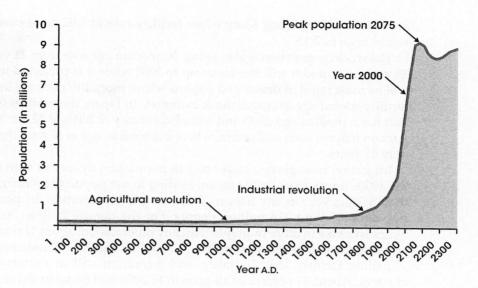

then in only 12.[15] This astonishing growth had two causes, both related to the Industrial Revolution. First, advances in water sanitation, hygiene, and scientific medicine reduced deaths from infectious disease, leading to rapid mortality decline. Second, mechanized farming expanded the food supply to feed record numbers.

World population reached 6.9 billion in 2011 and it continues to rise, but growth is predicted to slow and, for the first time in recorded history, end. Figure 2.4 shows United Nations projections that the world population will grow to a peak of 9.2 billion in 2075, then decline over a century to 8.3 billion in 2175 before slowly rising back to 9 billion in 2300.[16] This is an intriguing preview of the distant future, but for the near future, in the years up to 2050, rapid though slowing growth will characterize the business environment.

Growth will slow and eventually end as the world undergoes a transition from high to low fertility. In the initial stages of the Industrial Revolution economic progress encouraged population growth. Now this progress is a brake on fertility because having fewer children frees women to attend school, enter professions, and increase income. The world's total fertility rate, or the number of births per woman, dropped from 4.92 in 1950 to 2.56 in 2010 and is expected to drop as low as 2.02 by 2050. This would be below the *replacement fertility rate* of 2.1 births per woman, calculated as the number of children a woman must have on average to ensure that one daughter survives to reproductive age.

In theory, this number is sufficient to maintain a stable population. Fertility is declining on every continent, but the world average of 2.56 disguises wide variation. It is lowest in a group of 44 developed nations averaging 1.64 and highest in a group of 148 less developed nations averaging 2.73. The extremes

replacement fertility rate
The number of children a woman must have on average to ensure that one daughter survives to reproductive age.

[15] Clive Ponting, *A Green History of the World* (New York: Penguin Books, 1991), p. 240.

[16] United Nations, *World Population to 2300* (New York: United Nations Department of Economic and Social Affairs, 2004), medium variant, p. 2. Other figures in this section are extracted from the medium variant of the United Nation's "World Population Prospects: The 2008 Revision Population Database," at http://esa.un.org/unpp, August 2010.

are illustrated by Hong Kong's low fertility rate of 1.02 as opposed to Niger's world high of 7.15.

The world population is also aging. Its median age rose from 24 years in 1950 to 28 years now and it will rise faster up to 2050 when it is projected to be 38. Aging will be most rapid in developed nations where mortality rates are lowest. As with fertility, global age averages mask extremes. In Japan, the world's oldest population has a median age of 45 and a life expectancy at birth of 82, far higher than in African nations such as Zambia, where the median age is 17 and life expectancy is only 45 years.

Migration now plays a larger role in population dynamics than in the past. In the 1950s it was a negligible factor, leading to net population changes of no more than 5,000 a year in any nation. Today migrants constitute 3.1 percent of world population, about 214 million people. For the decade 2010 to 2020 the United States will take in more migrants than any other nation, about 11.6 million. Mexico and China will lose the most people, 3.7 million and 3.3 million, respectively.

Falling fertility, low mortality, and migration will drive future population changes. About 95 percent of all growth to 2050 will occur in developing and less developed countries, with only 5 percent in the developed world. Fertility will be lowest in Europe, and by 2050 its population will fall 6 percent or by 42 million people, reducing it from 11 percent of the world's population to only 8 percent. In North America the population will grow by 27 percent, but due to declining fertility rates in the United States (from 2.09 in 2010 to 1.85 in 2050) this growth will come from immigration. Africa, which contains many of the world's poorest nations, will grow fastest. Despite elevated mortality from the HIV/AIDS epidemic, by 2050 it will add almost 1 billion people, an increase of 93 percent from 2010.

These population trends have many implications. First, although global population growth is slowing, it will be highest in the least developed regions, further widening the wealth gap between high- and low-income countries. Second, growth will continue to strain the earth's ecosystems. Third, the West is in demographic decline compared with other peoples. Shrinking, aging populations may lead to slower GDP growth, putting more pressure on national welfare and pension policies. In the future, non-Western populations will be stronger economically, militarily, and politically and will push to expand their influence. Although Western market values and business ideology seem ascendant now, they may be less dominant in the future as the numerical basis of Western civilization declines. In such ways will population trends alter the business environment and create new societal expectations for corporate behavior.

Technology

Throughout recorded history new technologies and devices have fueled commerce and reshaped societies. In the 1450s the printing press was an immediate commercial success, but its impact went far beyond the publishing business. Over the next 100 years the affordable, printed word reshaped European culture by creating a free market for ideas that undermined the doctrinal monopoly of the Catholic Church. Printed pamphlets spread Martin Luther's challenge to its scriptural dogma and brought on the Protestant Reformation. Galileo was placed

FIGURE 2.5   **Waves of Innovation since the Beginning of the Industrial Revolution**

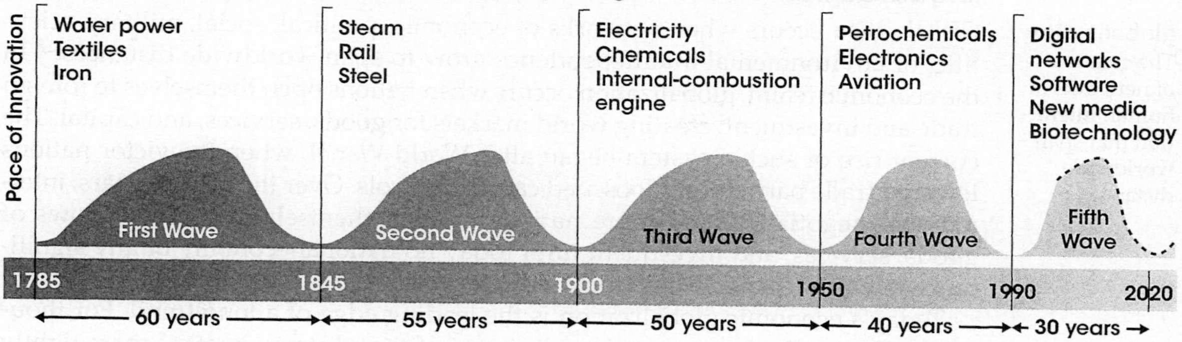

Pace of Innovation				
Water power Textiles Iron	Steam Rail Steel	Electricity Chemicals Internal-combustion engine	Petrochemicals Electronics Aviation	Digital networks Software New media Biotechnology
First Wave	Second Wave	Third Wave	Fourth Wave	Fifth Wave
1785	1845	1900	1950	1990 2020
← 60 years →	← 55 years →	← 50 years →	← 40 years →	← 30 years →

under house arrest in Florence for holding heretical views about astronomy, but his theories prevailed because they were published in Protestant Holland. A Europe opened to the exchange of new ideas based on experience and observation was primed for the scientific revolution.

The invention of the steam engine in the late 1700s and its widespread use beginning in the early 1800s, along with increased use of the waterwheel and new iron-making methods, triggered the Industrial Revolution. As Figure 2.5 shows, this was the first of five waves of technological revolution. With each wave innovations spread, stimulating economic booms of increased investment, rising productivity, and output growth. The shortening of successive waves reveals faster innovation.

New technologies foster the productivity gains that sustain long-term economic progress, and they promote human welfare. However, like the printing press, they also can agitate societies. For example, before the 1860s a trans-Atlantic voyage on a sailing ship took a month, cost a year's wages for a European worker, and was risky. About 5 to 10 percent of passengers died due to sinkings and shipboard transmission of diseases. Then steamship technology cut the cost of passage by 90 percent and reduced travel time to one week, cutting mortality to less than 1 percent. As a result, European immigrants poured into the American East, creating labor gluts that led to wage depressions and fueling political movements against big companies, financiers, and the gold standard.[17] In this way, steamship technology strained American political stability.

During the rise of industrial societies over more than two centuries, technology has altered human civilization by stimulating economic and population growth to sustained rises unimaginable in previous recorded history. New things have created many benefits, including higher living standards and longer life spans, but because technology changes faster than human beliefs and institutions, it also imposes strains.

[17] Robert William Fogel, *The Fourth Great Awakening & The Future of Egalitarianism* (Chicago: University of Chicago Press, 2001), p. 54.

Globalization

globalization
The creation of networks of human interaction that span worldwide distances.

Globalization occurs when networks of economic, political, social, military, scientific, or environmental interdependence grow to span worldwide distances.[18] In the economic realm, globalization occurs when nations open themselves to foreign trade and investment, creating world markets for goods, services, and capital. The current rise of such a system began after World War II, when the victor nations lowered trade barriers and loosened capital controls. Over the next 50 years, international negotiations led more nations to open themselves to global flows of goods, services, and investment until today no national economy of any significance remains isolated from world markets.

Today's economic globalization is the leading edge of a long trend. For thousands of years the human community has, in fits and starts, become more tightly knit. According to historians J. R. McNeill and William H. McNeill, in prehistoric times humans interacted in a loose worldwide web through which genes and inventions such as language and the bow and arrow were slowly exchanged by migrations between relatively isolated bands. Beginning about 12,000 years ago with the growth of agricultural societies, stable and expanding populations formed the first cities. Over time, these cities grew into nodes that tied regions together. Still, there was little interaction between civilizations on different continents. Then, about 500 years ago, China sponsored oceanic voyages to extend its power.[19]

Soon Portugal and Spain followed and over the next 250 years mariners connected even the most remote places to the great centers of civilization. By the late 1700s the world was knit together with the exchange of trade goods, currencies, and ideas. The consequences of this initial globalization are similar to those arising from the current globalization. Economic activity rapidly increased. Mines in Bolivia exported such quantities of silver that nations around the world adopted silver currencies, smoothing international trade. Trade expansion increased inequality among nations. Cultures changed, as when, for example, Spanish conquistadors introduced horses to the Plains Indians. Infectious diseases spread. In little more than a century microbes endemic to Europe killed 50 to 90 percent of the population of the Americas from Cape Horn to the Arctic.

Since this initial tying together of societies in the late 1700s, the trend toward integration has continued. Globalization has been accelerated by new technologies, particularly those based on electricity, but also sometimes slowed by national rivalries and wars.

Transnational corporations, especially a few hundred of the largest headquartered in developed nations, are the central forces of current economic globalization. Their rising levels of investment outside home countries make them the modern equivalents of the intrepid mariners who opened trade routes in the 1400s. However, globalization complicates their management. By operating in many countries they multiply the number and kind of stakeholders to which they must respond. Their actions create strains and anxieties that lead to heightened expectations of

[18] Joseph Nye, Jr., "Globalization's Democratic Deficit," *Foreign Affairs,* July–August 2001, p. 2.
[19] J.R. McNeill and William H. McNeill, *The Human Web* (New York: Norton, 2003), intro. and chap. VI.

responsible behavior. Not surprisingly, there is a strong anticorporate movement supported mainly by groups in rich nations that see the growing velocity of trade with alarm because it clashes with their values on the environment, human rights, and democracy. These groups seek to restrain and regulate the activities of transnational corporations and they have had some success.

Nation-States

nation-state
An international actor having a ruling authority, citizens, and a territory with fixed borders.

In the international arena, the *nation-state* is an actor formed of three elements, a ruling authority, citizens, and a territory with fixed borders. The modern nation-state system arose in an unplanned way out of the wreckage of the Roman Empire. The institution of the nation-state was well-suited for Western Europe, where boundaries were contiguous with the extent of languages. However, the idea was subsequently transplanted to territories in Eastern Europe, Southwest Asia, and the Middle East, partly by force of colonial empires and partly by mimicry among non-Western political elites for whom the idea had attained high prestige. Where it was transplanted, nations were often irrationally defined and boundary lines split historic areas of culture, ethnicity, religion, and language.

The nation-state is the unit of human organization in which individuals and cultural groups can influence their circumstances and future. This is its paramount function and the reason it has survived over centuries. Today the world is a mosaic of independent countries, and the dynamics of this system are a powerful force in the international business environment. Conflict between nations seeking to aggrandize wealth and power is frequent, though because of economic globalization its nature has changed.

In the past, nations increased their power by seizing territory. With more territory they acquired new natural resources, agriculture, and labor. Hence, in the 1930s Japan colonized South Asian countries to gain access to oil and bauxite. Now, however, the wealth of high-income nations is based on the operation of global corporations that use flows of capital and knowledge to provide goods and services in many nations. Seizing the headquarters or a few manufacturing facilities of one of these corporations would not enable the aggressor nation to take advantage of the value chain in the firm's worldwide operations, particularly where wealth creation was based on brainpower. So nations today increasingly prefer to aggrandize themselves through trade, where they can build wealth more efficiently than through traditional warfare.[20]

Even as world markets become new sources of national power, they also limit the power of regimes to control their economies. Freewheeling international competition penetrates borders. Nations have a choice. Either close borders to flows of goods, services, and capital, isolating their economies from the world, a move sure to stifle growth, or open borders, allowing free rein to disobedient market forces that quicken growth. No nation can choose isolation and still offer its citizens opportunity and prosperity. So governments are now deeply concerned about how international markets will interpret their domestic actions and policies.

---

[20] This thesis is elaborated in Richard Rosecrance, *The Rise of the Virtual State* (New York: Basic Books, 1999).

Market forces are just one force that penetrates nation-states and reduces their autonomy. Other forces are epidemics, climate change, terrorism, nuclear weapons, and potent ideas such as international norms of human rights. As intractable global forces, particularly market power, undercut the ability of national governments to protect their citizens, corporations may be called on to assume more of the responsibility.

Dominant Ideologies

ideology
A set of reinforcing beliefs and values that constructs a worldview.

Thought shapes history. An *ideology* is a set of reinforcing beliefs and values that constructs a worldview. The Industrial Revolution in the West was facilitated by a set of interlocking ideologies, including capitalism, but also constitutional democracy, which protected the rights that allowed individualism to flourish; progress, or the idea that humanity was in upward motion toward material betterment; Darwinism, or Charles Darwin's finding that constant improvement characterized the biological world, which reinforced the idea of progress; social Darwinism, or Herbert Spencer's idea that evolutionary competition in human society, as well as the natural world, weeded out the unfit and advanced humanity; and the Protestant ethic, or the belief that sacred authority called for hard work, saving, thrift, and honesty as necessary for salvation.

Ideologies are more than the sum of sensory perception and rational thought. They fulfill the human need for concepts and categories of meaning that explain daily life. Ideologies in accord with experience and current conditions often spread widely. Their belief systems lead adherents to feel a collective identity and to follow common norms that direct social behavior, thereby promoting cooperation and stability. And they give institutions that represent them, such as churches, governments, and corporations, the power to interpret events and resolve human problems.[21]

Ideologies are highly competitive and locked in a constant Darwinian struggle. Vibrant pluralism of belief existed for most of recorded history, but many doctrines have perished with globalization. As ideas diffuse through trade, travel, missionary work, and conquest, they often clash. A centuries-old culling process in the marketplace of ideas has eliminated and marginalized many historical belief systems and favored the ascendancy of a few.[22] Hundreds of local religions, unable to compete with the world salvation religions, have gone extinct. Cultural styles in entertainment, dress, sports, and food now converge in urban societies. In the political sphere, monarchy and dictatorship are fighting an endgame against democracy. After two centuries of contention, the economic ideology of capitalism has marginalized its rival socialism. This sifting of ideas accelerated in the twentieth century because of rising literacy and innovations that spread information, from magazines and radios in the early part of the century to jet aircraft and computers later.

[21] Michael Mann, *The Sources of Social Power,* vol. 1 (Cambridge: Cambridge University Press), 1986, pp. 20–23.
[22] McNeill and McNeill, *The Human Web*, pp. 269–76.

Great Leadership

Leaders have brought both beneficial and disastrous changes to societies and businesses. Alexander imposed his rule over the ancient Mediterranean world, creating new trade routes on which Greek merchants flourished. Adolf Hitler of Germany and Joseph Stalin in the Soviet Union were strong leaders, but they unleashed evil that retarded industrial growth in their countries.

There are two views about the power of leaders as a historical force. One is that leaders simply ride the wave of history. "Great men," writes Arnold Toynbee, "are precisely the points of intersection of great social forces."[23] When oil was discovered in western Pennsylvania in 1859, John D. Rockefeller was a young man living in nearby Cleveland, where he had accumulated a little money selling produce. He saw an opportunity in the new industry. His remarkable traits enabled him to domineer over a rising industry that reshaped the nation and the world. Yet is there any doubt that the reshaping would have occurred nonetheless had Rockefeller decided to stick with selling lettuce and carrots?

A differing view is that leaders themselves change history rather than being pushed by its tide. "The history of the world," wrote Thomas Carlyle, "is at bottom the History of the Great Men who have worked here."[24] It was John Jacob Astor of the American Fur Company who established a presence in the wild lands of the American continent, exploring them, knitting them together, and thwarting the efforts of other nations to occupy them. The United States map might today be different absent the effects of Astor's singular lust for fur riches. It was James B. Duke of the American Tobacco Company whose solitary marketing genius turned cigarette smoking from a local custom confined largely to the American South into a worldwide health disaster continuing now for more than a century.

Cases and stories in this text provide instances for debate about the role of business leaders in changing the world.

Chance

Scholars are reluctant to use the notion of chance, accident, or random occurrence as a category of analysis. Yet some changes in the business environment may be best explained as the product of unknown and unpredictable causes. No less perceptive a student of history than Niccolò Machiavelli observed that fortune determines about half the course of human events and human beings the other half. We cannot improve on this estimate, but we note it. Its significance is that managers must be prepared for the most unprecedented events and have faith in Machiavelli's counsel that when such episodes arrive those who are ready will prevail, as fortune "directs her bolts where there have been no defenses or bulwarks prepared against her."[25] No doubt Machiavelli would find Shell's scenarios praiseworthy.

[23] *A Study of History,* vol. XII, *Reconsiderations* (London: Oxford University Press, 1961), p. 125.

[24] In "The Hero as Divinity," reprinted in Carl Niemeyer, ed., *Thomas Carlyle on Heroes, Hero-Worship and the Heroic in History* (Lincoln: University of Nebraska Press, 1966), p. 1. This essay was originally written in 1840.

[25] Niccoló Machiavelli, *The Prince,* trans. George Bull (New York: Penguin Books, 1961), chap. XXV, p. 73. Originally published in 1532.

SIX EXTERNAL ENVIRONMENTS OF BUSINESS

Figure 2.6 adds a ring of six key external environments to the dynamic system that shapes the overall business environment. In each of these external environments, powerful forces create change in the relationships between business, governments, and societies. Here we give thumbnail sketches of each environment. We will dig more deeply into them throughout the book.

The Economic Environment

The economic environment consists of forces that influence market operations, including overall economic activity, commodity prices, interest rates, currency fluctuations, wages, competitors' actions, and government policies.

The global economy has recently experienced turbulence. Growth briefly slowed after 2001 from the economic repercussions of the September 11, 2001, terrorist attacks. However, after a contraction of several years, it picked up again, led by recovery in the United States and rapid expansion in China and India.

More recently, it has suffered a massive shock. The epicenter was the United States. By 2007 a bubble in U.S. housing prices fueled by easy credit had grown

FIGURE 2.6
Six Key External Environments

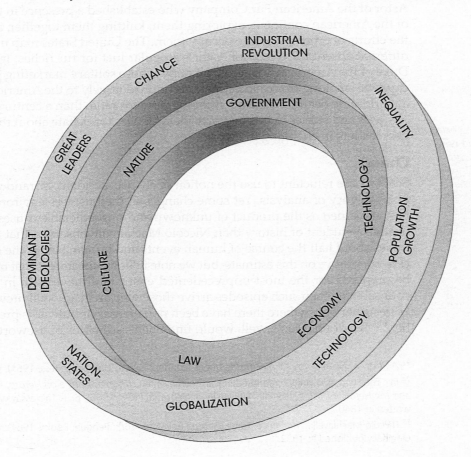

large. When it burst, credit tightened and the economy slowed, causing deterioration in asset prices. The default of Lehman Brothers, a large U.S. investment bank, brought a swift worsening of the situation. As demand for liquidity skyrocketed, credit markets froze and a severe economic contraction slowed the economies of every nation. It was the deepest global downturn in 75 years.

However, governments in developed economies acted decisively, using policy tools such as lower interest rates and stimulus spending to restore confidence. This led to a slow, uneven global recovery. Although risk is still present, it appears that the world economy will resume its long-term growth in output, consumption, and investment. This modern growth trend accelerated in the 1980s. World GDP increased 558 percent in the years between 1982 and its pre-crisis peak in 2008, rising from $10.9 trillion to $60.8 trillion.[26] It then fell 10 percent in 2009, but began to rise again in 2010. Underlying such strong and relatively continuous overall economic growth are two basic subtrends.

The first is rising trade. In 1948, three years after the end of World War II, the global sum of all exports was $58 billion. In 2008 it reached a peak of $16.1 trillion, an increase of 28,000 percent.[27] This spectacular rise has been enabled by a trading system created at the end of World War II. Nations within the system have been encouraged to lower tariffs and other trade barriers because other member nations promise to reciprocate this openness. The system has evolved into an institution called the World Trade Organization (WTO) that embodies an ongoing process of negotiation and *trade liberalization* in which 153 nations now participate. In addition, several hundred regional trade agreements promote freer exchange among countries that are parties to them.

The second subtrend underlying continued economic growth is a major expansion of foreign direct investment (FDI) by multinational corporations. *Foreign direct investment* is capital invested by private firms outside their home countries. Between 1982 and 2007 global FDI inflows (that is corporate investments moving into foreign countries) rose from $59 billion a year to $1.8 trillion, a 3,002 percent increase.[28] Figure 2.7 shows the long rise of FDI and how it has been affected by dips in the global economy.

Rising trade and consumer demand have rapidly expanded markets. To remain competitive, corporations have expanded with markets and restructured for efficiency. They invest to enter growing markets or to increase their power in established ones. Many multinationals have restructured by creating "global factories" in which production of goods or services occurs across geographically dispersed networks. These networks seek to duplicate at a global level the efficiencies of specialization and outsourcing often seen at the national level. They are now so extensive that nearly two-thirds of the world's exports move within them.

trade liberalization
A philosophy in which nations promote trade by easing restrictions, including both tariff and non-tariff barriers. This philosophy, sometimes called simply *liberalization,* is the bedrock of economic globalization.

foreign direct investment
Capital investment by private firms outside their home countries.

[26] United Nations Conference on Trade and Development (UNCTAD), *World Investment Report 2010* (New York: United Nations, 2010), table I.5.

[27] World Trade Organization Statistics Database, "Time Series on International Trade," at http:stat.wto.org.

[28] UNCTAD, *World Investment Report 2010,* table I.5.

FIGURE 2.7
Worldwide FDI Inflows: 1980–2009

Source: United Nations Commission on Trade and Development, *World Investment Reports*, various editions, annex table B.1 for 1980–2008, annex table 1 for 2010.

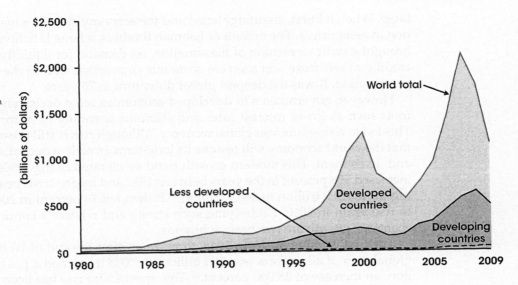

Since World War II, and especially since the early 1980s, the international economic environment has been favorable to the expansion of corporations. Although the world economy recently experienced two recessions, long-term growth is likely to continue.

The Technological Environment

Today new scientific discoveries create a business environment filled with mind-boggling technology. For example, *nanotechnology* allows manipulation of objects the size of atoms. New materials and tiny machines invisible to the naked eye can be engineered at the molecular level.

nanotechnology
Technology that is developed on the scale of a nanometer, which is one-billionth of a meter.

Semiconductor makers can now make microchips with components the size of a ten-millionth of a meter. When this ability is harnessed to practical manufacturing, it will create chips that operate on an atomic scale comparable to the photosynthesis process in plants. Users with such circuits could store all information in the Library of Congress in the space of a sugar cube.[29] Human genome mapping promises new biogenetic products that will cure intractable diseases. Methods of harnessing renewable energy may dramatically reduce use of fossil fuels.

Digital telecommunications technology now creates a global network of computers, software, and electronic devices. This network has led to radical innovations such as open sourcing, which allows numbers of individuals to participate in the creation of complex knowledge products. *Wikis*, or Web sites open to collaborative editing by multiple or innumerable parties, have been used to create browsers, encyclopedias, dictionaries, and news sites.

wiki
A Web site open to collaborative editing by multiple individuals.

The wiki principle is an example of how an innovation can be both an opportunity and a threat. It releases an open, Darwinian process in which knowledge emerges from the common pool of humanity and survives the meticulous scrutiny

[29] Philip Bond, quoted in Ronald Bailey, "The Smaller the Better," *Reason*, December 2003, p. 47.

of collective expertise rather than emanating from a single individual or small group to a passive audience. It promotes equality, but undermines hierarchical authority and attacks old business models of software firms and publishers. In fact, novel technologies are minefields for established firms, which often focus on the immediate commercial possibilities of a technology and miss, or underestimate, its ultimate defiance of their existing business model. An example is Western Union, the dominant communications company of the nineteenth century, which was so confident in the telegraph that it rejected the telephone.

When Alexander Graham Bell invented the telephone in 1876, it had only a three-mile range. Western Union considered hooking telephones into its lines, but decided such a short-range device was just a toy. So Bell formed his own company. When engineers lengthened the range of the phone by using wires made of copper instead of iron, Western Union saw its mistake and rushed into the business with a phone device of its own, but it lost a patent infringement suit brought by Bell's company and had to drop the business.[30]

The tiny Bell Telephone Company grew into AT&T, at one time in the twentieth century the world's largest corporation in revenues, a firm so creative that it gave birth to the transistor and the laser, so dominant that the U.S. government broke it up in 1984, so satisfied with success that it repeatedly failed to adapt. Stubbornly, it defined its business as providing voice conversation over wires, thus abiding with indifference as future competitors articulated new digital communication technologies such as wireless and cable networks, computers, and the Internet. Although AT&T is still a large corporation, it now scrambles through mergers and strategies, seeking a formula to restore past glory.

New technologies have unforeseen consequences for society when they are put in wide use for commercial gain. The cigarette-rolling machine was invented before the dangers of smoking were known. Manufacturing that mixed asbestos into hundreds of common materials came long before the morbid effects of asbestos fiber became clear. The World Wide Web is spreading into millions of lives before anyone has a full understanding of its implications for personal privacy. The lesson of the past is that corporations have an ethical duty to weigh carefully not only the strategic impact of technologies on their business models, but also the dangers they may impose on people.

The Cultural Environment

culture
A system of shared knowledge, values, norms, customs, and rituals acquired by social learning.

A *culture* is a system of shared knowledge, values, norms, customs, and rituals acquired by social learning. No universal culture exists, so the environment of a transnational corporation includes a variety of cultures, each with differing peoples, languages, religions, and values.

On one level, this variation causes conflicts of business custom, and managers in foreign countries must absorb both subtle and striking differences in employee loyalty, group versus individual initiative, the place of women in organizations, ethical values, norms of gift giving, attitudes toward authority, the meaning of time, and clothing worn in business settings.

[30] Page Smith, *The Rise of Industrial America*, vol. 6 (New York: Penguin Books, 1984), p. 115.

On a deeper level, although no uniform world culture exists, there is a fundamental divide between the culture of Western economic development and some other national cultures. The culture of the advanced West promotes a core ideology of markets, individualism, and democracy. It is sustained by Western nations that dominate international organizations, contain the most powerful corporations, and have the strongest militaries. Although developing nations tend to adopt elements of Western culture, some are resistant. Nations such as Iran, Pakistan, and China see spreading Western values as a form of cultural aggression. They resist adopting them.

Over the last half of the twentieth century, some cultural values in developed nations began to shift, creating changes in the global business environment. In these societies, beginning in the 1960s, traditional values based on historical realities of economic scarcity were transformed. In their place came *postmaterialist values*, or values based on assumptions of security and affluence.

postmaterialist values
Values based on assumptions of security and affluence, for example, tolerance of diversity and concern for the environment.

In older industrializing societies the drive for survival and material welfare dominated. People sacrificed other values such as leisure and environmental purity to make money and buy necessities, then luxuries. However, the generations after World War II grew up surrounded by affluence and the protections of welfare states. Because they felt material security, these generations began to rank individual autonomy over deference to authority, quality of life over mere survival, self-expression over conformity, and tolerance over prejudice.[31]

The World Values Surveys, a series of surveys in dozens of countries now spanning more than 50 years, show that the rise of postmaterialist values has uniformly shifted the social, political, economic, and sexual norms of rich countries. Despite greater resistance in some non-Western cultures, surveys report the rise of these norms in all modernizing nations where new generations experience feelings of secure prosperity. One survey found a "surprisingly high" support for values linked to democracy among the Chinese public."[32] In another support for democratic ideals in five Islamic countries was higher than in Western Europe.[33]

Postmaterialist values are a strong influence in the operating environments of multinational corporations. They support a powerful global movement to promote fundamental human rights by stamping out racism, sexism, authoritarianism, intolerance, and xenophobia. This movement is energized by West-dominated coalitions of individuals, advocacy groups, governments, and international organizations. Similar and interrelated movements have risen to promote sustainable development and humanitarian assistance to poor regions. This global tide of morality, based on postmaterialist values, elevates expectations about the behavior of multinational corporations. Increasingly, they must follow proliferating codes and rules developed by moral reformers and must define their strategies to promote both human welfare and net income.

[31] Ronald F. Inglehart, "Changing Values among Western Publics from 1970 to 2006," *West European Politics*, January–March 2008.

[32] Ronald F. Inglehart, "Globalization and Postmodern Values," *Washington Quarterly*, Winter 2000, p. 19.

[33] Ronald F. Inglehart, "The Worldviews of Islamic Publics in Global Perspective," in Mansoor Moaddel, ed., *Worldviews of Islamic Publics* (New York: Palgrave, 2005), fig. 14.

The Government Environment

Governments have simultaneously stimulated and constrained business. In this regard, two long-term global trends in government are central.

First, government activity has greatly expanded. One way of measuring this is by comparing a government's spending with the size of its economy. Around the world, the percentage of this spending has risen, from single digits in 1900 to an average of 28 percent in 2008.[34] In the United States, by 1930 spending was still only 3 percent of GDP, but by 2009 it had risen to 28 percent.[35] The percentages have risen highest, up to 40 percent and more, in European welfare states and are lower in developing countries, but broadly the trend is up because governments have taken on new functions. For one, they promote social welfare with a range of transfer payments to their citizens. This role grew in the twentieth century as many nations expanded their electorates. New voters included women and the less privileged, groups that voted to enlarge government assistance programs. Another source of government growth is expanded regulation. In the United States, for example, there is today practically no aspect of business that governments cannot and will not regulate if the occasion arises and popular support exists.

democracy
A form of government requiring three elements—popular sovereignty, political liberty, and majority rule.

The second long-term trend is rising democratization. In 1900 no nation was a full *democracy* with multiparty elections and universal suffrage. The United States and Britain were close, but both lacked female suffrage, and the United States additionally lacked black suffrage in practice. Yet by 1950 there were 22 democracies and by 2009 there were 89.[36] Figure 2.8 shows the dramatic rise—from 93 to 147—in the number of democratic and partially democratic regimes since 1975. Much of this rise came in the late 1980s and early 1990s after the breakup of the Soviet Union. When repressive socialist regimes no longer received external support from the Soviet bloc and the United States reduced its support for authoritarian regimes that were anticommunist, a wave of democratization swept over Southeast Asia, Latin America, and Africa.

However, a more fundamental cause of expanding democracy is the rise of postmaterialist values in countries that have undergone a socioeconomic rise. These values undermine hierarchical authority and create expectations for more political participation and autonomy. For business, the consequence of more openness to popular majorities is that governments increasingly respond to public demands for corporate social performance and these demands reflect postmaterialist values promoting human rights, the environment, aesthetics, and ethics.

---

[34] World Bank, *World Development Indicators,* table 4.10.

[35] Census Bureau, "Federal Government-Receipts and Outlays: 1900–2003," table HS-47 at www.census.gov/statab/hist/HS-47.pdf, accessed August 2010; and Census Bureau, *Statistical Abstract of the United States: 2010,* 129th ed. (Washington, DC: Census Bureau, 2009), table 457.

[36] Figures are from *Democracy's Century: A Survey of Global Political Change in the 20th Century* (Washington, DC: Freedom House, 2001), p. 2 and Figure 2.7; and Freedom House, *Freedom in the World 2010: Erosion of Freedom Intensifies* (Washington, DC: Freedom House, 2010), "Global Data, 1972–2009," p. 6 at www.freedomhouse.org.

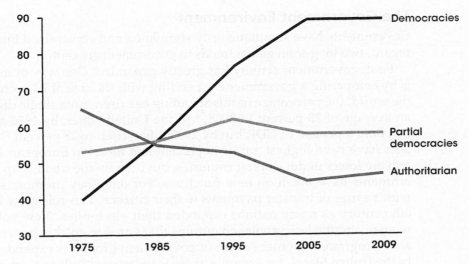

FIGURE 2.8
The Rise of Democratic Regimes

Source: Freedom House. Data based on combined measures for democracy and civil liberty.

The Legal Environment

The legal environment consists of legislation, regulation, and litigation. Five enduring trends in this environment work to constrain business behavior.

First, laws and regulations steadily grow in number and complexity. As governments become more active and more participatory they respond to citizens' calls for restraining corporate power with new statutes and heightened regulatory activity.

Second, legal duties to protect the rights of stakeholders, such as employees, consumers, and the public, have expanded. These rights derive from the steady flow of laws and court decisions on, for example, discrimination, sexual harassment, advertising, antitrust, the environment, product liability, and intellectual property.

Third, globalization has increased the complexity of the legal environment by exposing corporations to international law and the laws of foreign nations. In addition, advocacy groups promoting human rights, labor, and environmental causes push corporations to adopt so-called *soft law*, or guidelines for conduct based on emerging norms and standards in international codes, declarations, and conventions. These guidelines can exceed requirements in the laws of some nations.

soft law
Voluntarily adopted guidelines for corporate behavior derived from emerging norms and standards in international codes, declarations, and conventions.

Fourth, although requirements of ethical behavior and corporate social responsibility go beyond legal duty, they are continuously plucked from the voluntary realm and encoded into law. Actions that once elicited debate over the nature of corporate responsibility continuously move into regulatory regimes that reduce or eliminate managerial freedom. Until the early 1970s pollution control in the United States was largely a matter of corporate conscience. Now the Environmental Protection Agency, a corps of 17,000 regulators, including a staff of criminal investigators, enforces more than 1 million pages of laws, rules, and guideline documents that define, sometimes down to a few molecules, what managers can do.

Finally, the law is constantly evolving. Because of technological change, for example, corporations need to anticipate emerging causes of liability. In this respect, the old *T. J. Hooper* case is still good reading for corporate counsel. On a sunny day in March 1928 the tugboat *T. J. Hooper* hauled a coal barge out to sea. Two days

FIGURE 2.9   Measures of Human Impact on Nature

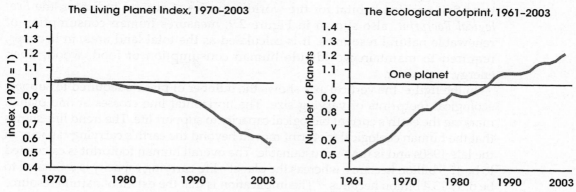

later it hit stormy weather off New Jersey, and the barge sank with its load of coal. The owners of the cargo sued, claiming that the tug was unseaworthy because it had no receiving radio. Lacking a radio, the *T. J. Hooper* missed a weather broadcast that caused other ships to put into harbor before the gale hit. Although no law required a radio and there was no industry custom of installing them, the eminent judge Learned Hand held that "there are precautions so imperative that even their universal disregard will not excuse their omission."[37]

The tug owners were found negligent and paid for the coal cargo because they had not adopted a cutting-edge technology. Moving ahead to the present, a parallel example is the existence of electrically charged table-saw blades that can detect contact with a human finger and stop rotation within thousandths of a second. No law or industry standard now requires manufacturers to use this technology, but its availability opens employers who do not use it to charges of negligence by workers who lose fingers and hands.

The Natural Environment

Economic activity is a geophysical force with power to change the natural environment. Just as it has strained the ability of human institutions to adapt, so also has it sometimes overwhelmed the ability of ecosystems to cleanse and regenerate. Spectacular economic growth has come at a high cost to the planet. It has depleted mineral resources, reduced forest cover, killed species, released artificial molecules, and unbalanced the nitrogen and carbon cycles.

Two measures used by the World Wildlife Fund exhibit global trends for the overall burden of human activity on nature. The *Living Planet Index*, shown in Figure 2.9, combines in one measure thousands of population trends among terrestrial, freshwater, and marine vertebrate species. It fell 28 percent between 1970 and 2005.[38] This decline of biodiversity reflects deteriorating conditions in

[37] *In re the* T. J. Hooper *et al.*, 60 F.2d 737 (1932), at 740.
[38] World Wide Fund for Nature, *Living Planet Report 2008* (Gland, Switzerland: WWF International, 2008), table 2.

the forests, grasslands, deserts, savannahs, and freshwater and marine ecosystems that provide habitat for the world's species. A second indicator, the *Ecological Footprint*, also shown in Figure 2.9, measures human consumption of renewable natural resources. It is calculated as the total land area, in hectares, required to maintain worldwide human consumption of food, wood, fiber, energy, and water.

In the figure, the vertical axis shows the number of planets required to support ecological footprints of varying size. The horizontal line crosses at one planet, marking the earth's current biological capacity to support life. The trend line shows that the human ecological footprint moved beyond the earth's carrying capacity in the late 1980s and is now unsustainable. The overall human footprint is calculated to be 17.5 billion hectares, whereas the planet's life-carrying capacity is estimated to be only 13.4 billion hectares.[39] The implication is that the extent of natural resource use encouraged by current forms of economic activity is unsustainable.

Attitudes about the human relationship with nature are now rapidly changing. When the twentieth century began, dominating and consuming nature was justified by a variety of doctrines, not the least being capitalism, which values nature as a production input. At its end, thinking moved toward preservation of nature. Managers in the twenty-first century must adapt to this changed thinking. With growing frequency environmental criteria enter their decisions.

The Internal Environment

Besides external environments, corporations also have internal environments that shape their actions. Figure 2.10 adds this internal environment to the dynamic environmental system developed throughout this chapter. The internal environment consists of four groups: managers, owners or shareholders, employees, and boards of directors.

In the United States and other developed nations, the duties of these groups to one another are defined in bodies of laws and regulations. Each group has both separate and common objectives. Managers must harmonize them to achieve overall company goals. The interplay of internal groups occurs in the atmosphere of a corporate culture, added as an element in Figure 2.10. These cultures, unique to each company, are bundles of assumptions, beliefs, and values that may be as significant in coordinating activity as formal policies and procedures.

Forces in external environments affect the power of these internal groups in complex ways. For example, growth of regulation has limited the power of managers over employees, who are entitled to a growing list of employment rights. On the other hand, technological change allows managers to globalize production of goods and services, exposing employees to competition with low-wage foreign labor markets. In the United States, new financial regulations designed to protect shareholders from dishonest managers have given boards of directors, which represent shareholders, more power and greater independence from top management. However, there is also some erosion of shareholder power caused by the demands of external groups for socially responsible actions that conflict with profit maximization.

---

[39] A hectare is an area of 10,000 square meters, equivalent to 2.47 acres.

FIGURE 2.10
The Internal Environment

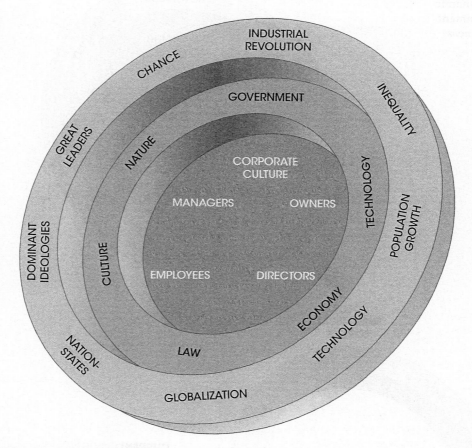

CONCLUDING OBSERVATIONS

The environments of business, and the historical forces that shape them, have profound implications for managers. Figure 2.11 summarizes the chapter discussion by illustrating how these historical forces, forces in current environments, and forces in corporations form a dynamic system of mutual influence. The deep historical forces act to shape the six external environments, and both act to shape the internal environment. Simultaneously, the actions of companies and industries shape not only their external environments but also the deeper course of history.

Business is not simply a passive entity that reacts to historical and environmental forces like a billiard ball pushed by the strike of a cue. On the contrary, although strongly constrained by its environment, business has a powerful capacity to shape society and change history in ways large and small.

For example, when Eastman Kodak wanted to display the speed of its fast film and Flashmatic shutter in 1940, it ran magazine ads showing pictures of "Kodak Moments" when people blew out candles on birthday cakes. The ads so popularized this charming rite that it became universal among Americans.[40] In contrast to

[40] James B. Twitchell, *Lead Us Not into Temptation* (New York: Columbia University Press, 1999), p. 26.

FIGURE 2.11
The Dynamic
Environment
of Business

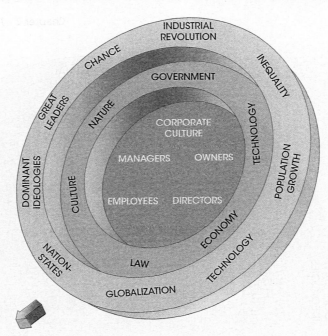

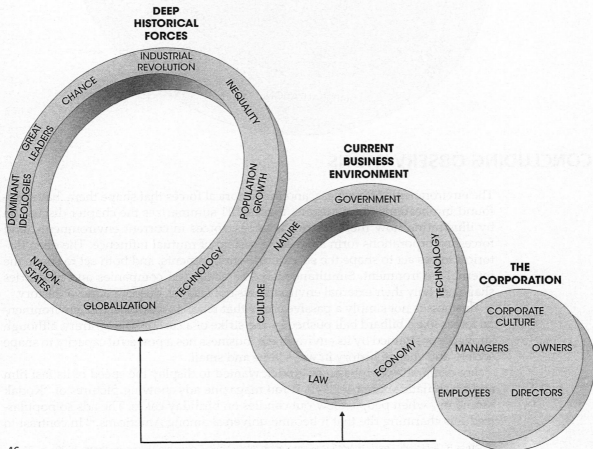

**DEEP
HISTORICAL
FORCES**

**CURRENT
BUSINESS
ENVIRONMENT**

**THE
CORPORATION**

such a slight cultural change, the story of the automobile illustrates how industries can rearrange whole societies. No twentieth century industry created more intentional and unintentional change. It was a prime mover of the American economy and once accounted directly or indirectly for one of every eight jobs. It encouraged an expansive highway system, accelerated the decline of railroads, depleted oil reserves, created suburbs, fouled urban air, entrenched the idea that status was conferred by ownership of material objects, and changed patterns of courtship and crime. In the next chapter we will focus on how business power has shaped societies.

The American Fur Company

The American Fur Company was a relentless monopoly built in the climactic era of the fur trade. It was created in 1808 by John Jacob Astor, a striving German immigrant, in an environment so favorable that over vast North American territories it had more power than the fledgling American government. In its time, this company shaped the destiny of a young nation. It made Astor the richest American of his day. Yet by the 1830s its situation had so changed that it and the 300-year-old trade in furs collapsed.

ASTOR ARRIVES IN A YOUNG NATION

In 1763 Astor was born to a butcher and his wife in the German village of Waldorf. In childhood he met hardship. The family was poor and often hungry, his mother died and a new step-mother was hostile. He spent much time alone but grew into a strong, diligent young man. Finding no joy in his father's butchering work, at the age of 15 he left the village for London, working four years there to save money for an ocean voyage to the New World. In 1783, at the age of 20, with no education, little money, and speaking poor English, he set sail on a merchant ship. During the long voyage, a fur trader taught him how to appraise and handle skins. These lessons gave Astor knowledge he needed for an occupation. He would soon show himself an apt student.

At this time, the fur trade on the North American continent was almost 300 years old. It had begun early in the sixteenth century after Spanish and French explorers made contact with native forest dwellers, and it soon included the British. The Europeans wanted beaver, martin, ermine, mink, otter, bear, deer, muskrat, wolf, raccoon, and other animal skins for fashionable hats and clothing. The Native Americans, who had not yet entered the age of metal, were eager to get even the simplest manufactured goods such as knives, mirrors, ornaments, and buttons. This simple mutual advantage proved durable over time.

Indians were the fur industry's production workers. Fur traders depended on them to trap animals. Indian women skinned and prepared the hides. Overhead costs for traders were low. Instead of collecting wages, Indians traded the pelts for goods worth a fraction of a fur's ultimate value. Since furs were light, they could be transported economically by mules, barges, and ships to Eastern ports and thence to Europe. The fur companies' profits were enormous.

Fur trading had transforming effects on society because it promoted settlement. Traders worked on the edges of Euro-American habitation. Over time, fur production in these frontier areas always declined. Populations of fur-bearing animals such as beaver, having slow breeding cycles, were steadily depleted. The reliability of Indian trappers fell as their tribal cultures buckled under the strains of new values and diseases. When productivity in an area fell, fur traders pushed over the horizon. In their wake came settlers using fresh maps and trails. Farms and towns sprouted. Indians were killed or dislodged. This unsentimental cycle of the fur trade, repeated over and over, generated waves of migration that settled much of the United States.

ASTOR ENTERS THE FUR BUSINESS

Astor made his way to New York, then a city of 25,000, where he got a job selling bakery goods. He invested most of his $2-a-week pay in small trinkets and in his spare time prowled the waterfront for Indians who might have a fur to trade. Within a year he picked up enough skins to take a ship back to London, where he established connections with fur-trading houses. This was a phenomenal achievement for an immigrant lad of 21 who had been nearly penniless on his arrival in America, and it revealed Astor's deadly serious and hard-driving personality.

Astor worked briefly with a fur dealer in New York City during which time he trekked into the forests of upstate New York to bargain for furs. He soon left his employer and by 1787 was working solely for himself. He demonstrated sharp negotiating skills in trading trinkets for furs and quickly built up an impressive business. One neighbor said:

> Many times I have seen John Jacob Astor with his coat off, unpacking in a vacant yard near my residence a lot of furs he had bought dog-cheap off the Indians and beating them out, cleaning them, and repacking them in more elegant and salable form to be transported to England and Germany, where they would yield him 1,000 percent on the original costs.[1]

Astor made great profits and expanded his business but, like other Americans, he was blocked from harvesting furs in the forests of the Northwest Territory. The Northwest Territory was the huge unsettled area between the Ohio River and the Mississippi River bounded on the north by the Great Lakes. After the Revolutionary War, Great Britain ceded this area to the United States but continued to maintain forts and troops there because the American government was too weak to enforce its rights. British fur-trading companies exploited the area and incited Indians to attack American traders and settlers who dared enter.

This audacity pushed Congress near to declaring war. To avoid hostilities, England agreed to a treaty in 1794 that required removal of British troops and gave both British and Americans trading rights in the Northwest Territory.[2] "Now," said Astor on hearing this news, "I will make my fortune in the fur trade."[3]

But he was stunned when President George Washington proposed befriending the Indians by setting up government fur-trading posts to be run with benevolent policies. These posts would compete with Astor and other private traders. Congress approved the plan, which required that trade goods be sold at cost, prohibited the use of liquor, and ordered payment of fair prices for furs.

The government trading posts infuriated Astor, who moved quickly to undercut them. He saturated the territory with his agents, instructing them to buy every fur they could get their hands on before competitors did. He bought trade goods in huge quantities to lower the cost, and his agents paid for furs with these trinkets. And he allowed liquor to flow freely during trade negotiations, creating an advantage the government could not match.

Astor had great success with these tactics. The government lacked his nimbleness and commitment, and he outwitted other rivals. In less than 10 years he was the second-richest man in America (after only Stephen Girard, the shipping magnate and banker). Having accumulated deep resources, the Astor juggernaut turned toward the West.

THE LOUSIANA PURCHASE

In 1803 the territory of the United States more than doubled with the Louisiana Purchase. President Thomas Jefferson agreed to purchase from France for $15 million approximately 800,000 square miles of land between the Mississippi River and the Rocky Mountains and running north from New Orleans to the 49th parallel, which is now the Canada–U.S. boundary. At the time, little was known about the area called the Louisiana Territory. No accurate or complete maps existed; even its exact boundaries were vague. But Louisiana was beautiful in its mystery.

Some geographers thought it was largely an arid desert. Others predicted a lush, fertile land. Rumors of geological wonders, horrific animals, and strange natives circulated, including the story of a tribe of

---

[1] A "Gentleman of Schenectady," quoted in John Upton Terrell, *Furs by Astor* (New York: Morrow, 1963), p. 55.

[2] The treaty was negotiated for the United States by John Jay and is known as Jay's Treaty.

[3] Terrell, *Furs by Astor*, p. 93.

bow-hunting, man-hating female savages in which the archers had their right breasts removed to keep them from interfering with the bowstrings.[4]

Jefferson himself had a clear vision of how to use the new territory. In his 1803 message to Congress, he proposed to relocate into Louisiana eastern tribes getting in the way of American settlers, and over the next 50 years this occurred many times.[5] He also ordered an Expedition of Discovery headed by Meriwether Lewis and William Clark to explore on foot the unknown territory.

A primary purpose of the Lewis and Clark expedition was to determine the suitability of Louisiana for the fur trade. The adventurers set out on a round-trip march between St. Louis and the Pacific Ocean, going where no white American had gone before, and on their return in 1806 reported a wondrous land "richer in beaver and otter than any country on earth."[6] They also reported that most Indian tribes in the territory were friendly to Americans and the fur trade. These discoveries were not lost on fur traders, among them John Jacob Astor.

THE AMERICAN FUR COMPANY IS BORN

The Lewis and Clark expedition was a catalyst for fur trading in the new territory. Beaver production in the Northwest Territory was already beginning to fall off. The North West Company, Astor's main competitor, began to move down from Canada, intent on harvesting the Louisiana Territory as rapidly as possible.

However, it would reckon with Astor, who wanted the prize himself. In his distant New York City study, Astor pored over maps of the fur-rich areas discovered by Lewis and Clark, hatching a vast and daring plan for a new company that would string trading posts over a 2,000-mile route.

In those days, state legislatures had exclusive power to create a company by issuing a charter that listed the conditions of its existence. So he approached the governor and legislature of New York seeking to charter a company to be known as the American Fur Company.

To sell the idea, he cloaked his mercenary scheme with a veil of patriotism. He argued that most of the furs taken from the Louisiana territory went to Canadians and British, thereby depriving America of trade revenue. His new company would drive the foreigners out. He would join with 10 or 12 other wealthy entrepreneurs to capitalize the new company, which would then issue stock to others. The new company would enhance U.S. security by establishing a strong presence of American citizens over unpopulated areas. And finally, Astor promised that his company would deal honestly with the Indians and drive out smaller, irresponsible traders. The legislators of New York, responding more to Astor's open pocketbook than to the credibility of his arguments, passed a charter setting up the American Fur Company. Soon President Jefferson wrote a letter to Astor giving his blessing to the new company also.

Astor proceeded to take on four partners and establish a board of directors as the charter required. However, he retained 99.9 percent of the stock, elected himself president, and subsequently declared dividends whenever he wanted to compensate himself. The partnership was a fiction; Astor never intended to share either the proceeds of the company or any portion of the fur trade that he could control.

In 1810 he made his first move. His ship, the *Tonquin,* sailed to the mouth of the Columbia River on the Pacific Coast and set up a trading post named Astoria. At this time, Britain and the United States contested the wild area known as Oregon territory, consisting of present-day Oregon and Washington. Astor got diplomatic support for his trading post by arguing that its presence established an American claim to the territory. Secretly, however, he hoped to form a new nation called Astoria and make himself king.

Meanwhile, he would make Astoria one end of a vise that would squeeze competitors out of the new fur areas. Furs taken in the West would come to Astoria and then be shipped to China, which was a major fur market, or to New York. By this time, Astor owned a fleet of ships with which to do this. The other end of the vise would be St. Louis. Furs from Astor's planned string of trading posts on the eastern slopes of the Rocky Mountains would come down

[4] Ben Gilbert, *The Trailblazers* (New York: Time-Life Books, 1973), p. 18.

[5] For a list of 24 relocations, see Cardinal Goodwin, *The Trans-Mississippi West (1803–1853)* (New York: Appleton, 1922), plate following p. 88.

[6] Quoted in David J. Wishart, *The Fur Trade of the American West (1807–1840): A Geographical Synthesis* (Lincoln: University of Nebraska Press, 1979), p. 19, citing the original journals of the trip.

the Missouri River system to St. Louis and from there go overland to New York or on to the port of New Orleans to be shipped to Europe. It was a megalomaniac scheme, and no one but Astor had both the nerve and the resources even to attempt it. But it was too grandiose. Only part of it was to work, and the rest worked only until the fur trade fell apart.

THE ROAD TO MONOPOLY

In 1813 Astor's plan suffered a great reversal when he was forced to sell Astoria to the British during the War of 1812. He sold out at a fraction of its value because British soldiers were in a position to seize it as a war prize. Without Astoria as a foothold in the Oregon territory, he was unable to compete with British and Canadian fur companies. And 61 of Astor's employees died pursuing the settlement, along with hundreds of natives they came in conflict with.[7] Unbowed, Astor later commissioned Washington Irving, the best-selling author of the day, to write a book about the intrepid adventurers and himself as the great mind behind them.[8]

Despite the loss of Astoria, Astor nonetheless predominated. In 1816 his lobbying succeeded in getting Congress to pass a law forbidding foreigners from trading furs in U.S. territories. This prevented Canadian and British companies from operating in the Northwest Territory, and Astor immediately bought out their interests, giving him a monopoly in furs east of the Missouri River. Blocked from the Pacific Coast trade by the British presence, he turned his attention to the upper-Missouri fur trade.

Astor bided his time as other fur companies pioneered trading in the northern Great Plains and then, after discovery of rich valleys of beaver, in the Rocky Mountains. By 1822 Astor had established a presence selling trade goods and buying furs in St. Louis, but he waited as other companies sent expensive expeditions of traders and mountain men up the Missouri, absorbing heavy losses of men and money. These pioneering companies found tremendous reserves of beaver in Rocky Mountain valleys, mapped new routes, and discovered advantageous locations for trading posts.

Portrait of John Jacob Astor. Source: © Getty Images.

Then Astor crushed the competition. In 1826 he merged with Bernard Pratte & Company, an established firm, using it as an agent. He bought out and liquidated another competitor, Stone, Bostwick & Company. In 1827 he broke the Columbia Fur Company by building his own trading posts next to every one of theirs, engaging in cutthroat price competition for furs, and plying Indians liberally with whiskey. His trappers shadowed its trapping parties to learn where the beaver were, then muscled in. Using similar tactics, he bankrupted Menard & Valle. Now, according to Astor's biographer Terrell:

> Competition on the Missouri River was all but nonexistent. What remained was inconsequential, and might have been likened to a terrier yapping at a bear. The bear lumbered on, ignoring the noise until it became aggravating. Then with the sudden swipe of a paw, the yapping was forever stilled.[9]

Astor made astonishing profits. He would buy, for example, a 10-pound keg of gunpowder for $2, or 20 cents a pound, in London and transport it to his trading posts using his ships. He paid himself a

[7] Axel Madsen, *John Jacob Astor: America's First Multimillionaire* (New York: John Wiley & Sons, 2001), p. 163.

[8] *Astoria; or, Enterprise beyond the Rocky Mountains* (New York: The Century Co., 1909); originally published in 1839.

[9] Terrell, *Furs by Astor*, p. 391.

2 percent commission for buying the trade goods, or $0.04 cents on the keg of gunpowder.

He paid himself a freight charge for carrying the gunpowder on his ship to New Orleans. From there the keg was transported up the Missouri using the inexpensive labor of his hired trappers and traders. The gunpowder was valued at $4 a pound to the Indians, who were not allowed to pay money for it but got it only by exchanging furs or on credit. In the 1820s Astor charged one 2-pound beaver skin for each pound of gunpowder, getting 10 skins weighing 20 pounds for the keg of gunpowder. These skins were transported back to London, where they were worth $7 a pound or $140. From the $140 Astor deducted a 5 percent commission, or $7, for brokering the sale of the furs. Astor also subtracted 25 percent, or $35 from the $140, for the estimated costs of transportation and wages.

All told, this left a net profit for the American Fur Company of $97.96, or 4,900 percent on the original $2 investment.[10] And Astor owned over 99 percent of the company's shares. This profitable arithmetic was repeated on a wide range of trade goods.

The value of trade goods lay not in their utility but in Indian beliefs. Indians coveted them so much that they considered whites foolish to exchange even the smallest trinkets for beaver skins that were abundant in the forests. The idea of material acquisition beyond basic needs was foreign to Indian cultures. The Arikaras, for example, believed a person who had more possessions than needed to survive ought to give the excess to others. Offering money to Indians did not motivate them to trap and process furs; they were indifferent to accumulating currency.

Trade goods such as rifles, knives, clothing, blankets, beads, and trinkets were useful, but native-made equivalents were often just as good. Trade goods, however, had mystical significance beyond their utility or monetary value. Their allure lay in magical, spiritual qualities.

Indians believed the future could be seen by looking in a reflection of the self. Because manufactured mirrors gave a clearer reflection than water they were a wondrous advance in prophecy. They thought guns had supernatural properties, because they created thunder, an event associated with the spirit world.

They thought pots and kettles were alive, because they rang or sang out when hit. Thus, Indians found in trade goods supernatural qualities that were lost on Europeans.[11]

Astor encouraged Indians to take trade goods on credit. As a result, some tribes—the Winnebagos, Sacs, Foxes, Cherokees, Chickasaws, and Sioux—were hopelessly mired in debt, owing the American Fur Company as much as $50,000 each. Since trinkets had sky-high markups, Astor could not lose much even if tribal debts grew, but indebtedness forced tribes to trade furs with him rather than with competitors.

His traders and trappers fared no better. He marked up trade goods heavily before selling them to traders. Often, traders were in debt to Astor or had mortgaged their trading posts to him and were forced to mark up goods heavily themselves before selling them to Indians and trappers.

Trappers employed by the American Fur Company were ruthlessly exploited. They worked unlimited hours in hazardous conditions and extreme weather, but when Astor achieved dominance in an area, he cut their salaries from $100 a year to $250 every three years. They had to buy trade goods and staples at markups that were higher than those charged Indians to get furs. Whiskey costing 30 cents a gallon in St. Louis was diluted with water and sold to them at $3 a pint. Coffee and sugar costing 10 cents a pound was sold for $2 at trading posts up the Missouri. Clothing was marked up 300 to 400 percent.

Astor had contrived a lucrative, pitiless system that amplified his fortune by diminishing those caught in its workings. Though never venturing out West, he was in touch, working long hours, his shrewd mind obsessed with the most minor details and with squeezing out the smallest unnecessary expenses. In 1831 his son William estimated American Fur Company revenues of "not less than $500,000" yearly.[12] Astor was by now the richest man in America. He began to buy real estate in and around New York City.

[11] Richard White, "Expansion and Exodus," in Betty Ballantine and Ian Ballantine, eds., *The Native Americans: An Illustrated History* (Atlanta: Turner, 1993), chap. 14.

[12] Gustavus Myers, *History of the Great American Fortunes* (New York: Modern Library, 1936), p. 102; originally published in 1909.

[10] These calculations are based on figures in Terrell, *Furs by Astor,* pp. 397–98.

ASTOR RACES ON

In the early 1830s it seemed nothing could slow Astor. Men who hated the American Fur Company started competing firms, but few lasted. Astor destroyed them by underbidding for furs and debauching the Indians with alcohol.

In 1832 Congress prohibited bringing alcohol into Indian territories, but the law was mostly ignored. Astor never favored using alcohol. It raised costs. However, many competitors saw inebriation as their only hope of seducing Indians with furs away from him. Astor, obsessed with defeating his rivals, let the spirits flow despite sad consequences.

Alcohol was unknown in native cultures; Indians developed a craving for it only after European traders introduced intoxication into fur price negotiations. Some thought that spirits occupied their bodies when they drank. Among Indians who took to whiskey, a new desire was created, a desire that motivated them to produce furs. A few tribes, notably the Pawnee, Crow, and Arikara, never imbibed. Most did, however, and some were so debilitated that their fur production fell and traders moved on.

Astor smuggled liquor as needed past Indian agents. He ordered construction of a still at the confluence of the Yellowstone and Missouri rivers, producing enough spirits to keep tribes in several states in a constant drunken state. Congress could not enforce its will because the federal government had almost no presence in vast areas of the West. Statutes were meaningless where no authorities stood to enforce them. In Indian country, the only law was the will of leaders of trading companies and brigades of trappers who wore self-designed, military-style uniforms and could rob, cheat, and murder both Indians and whites with impunity. An 1831 report to Lewis Cass, secretary of War, stated:

> The traders that occupy the largest and most important space in the Indian country are the agents and engagees of the American Fur Trade Company. They entertain, as I know to be the fact, no sort of respect for our citizens, agents, officers of the Government, or its laws or general policy.[13]

Government officials such as Cass were disinclined to thwart Astor in any case since they were frequently in his pay. Cass, who was the federal official in charge of enforcing the prohibition law, was paid $35,000 by the American Fur Company between 1817 and 1834.[14] At one time, Astor even advanced a personal loan of $5,000 to President James Monroe. Over the years, the Astor lobby achieved most of its objectives in Washington, D.C., and state capitals, including heavy tariffs on imported furs and abolition of the government fur-trading posts so beloved to Washington and Jefferson. Under these circumstances, it is not surprising that the government failed to regulate the fur trade.

In 1831 Astor introduced a new technological innovation, the steamboat *Yellowstone*, which could travel 50 to 100 miles a day up the Missouri, transporting supplies to his posts. Keelboats used by competitors made only 20 miles upriver on a good day and exposed men pulling them with ropes from the bank to hostile Indian fire. Upriver Indians were awestruck by the *Yellowstone* and traveled hundreds of miles to see the spirit that walked on water. Some tribes refused to trade with the Hudson Bay Company any longer, believing that because of the *Yellowstone* it could no longer compete with the American Fur Company.

THE ENVIRONMENT OF THE FUR TRADE CHANGES

Although the American Fur Company was ascendant, unfavorable trends were building that would bring it down. Demand for beaver was falling as the fashion trends that made every European and American gentleman want a beaver hat waned. Silk hats became the new rage. Also, new ways of felting hats without using fibrous underhair from beaver pelts had developed, and nutria pelts from South America were entering the market.

These were not the only problems. In 1832 trade came to a near standstill during a worldwide cholera epidemic because many people thought the disease was spread on transported furs. Beaver populations were depleted by overtrapping. The fur companies made no conservation efforts; the incentive was rather to trap all beaver in an area, leaving none for competitors. In the 1820s the Hudson Bay Company tried to prevent Astor from moving into Oregon

---

[13] Report of Andrew S. Hughes, quoted in Myers, *History of the Great American Fortunes*, p. 99.

[14] Myers, *History of the Great American Fortunes*, p. 103.

territory by exterminating beaver along a band of terrain to create a "fur desert" that would be unprofitable for Astor's trappers to cross.

Losses of human life rose as mountain men entered the shrinking areas where beaver were still abundant, leaving behind somewhat friendly Indians such as the Snake and Crow to encounter more hostile tribes such as the Blackfeet, who poisoned their arrows with rattlesnake venom and conducted open war against trappers.[15] One study of 446 mountain men actively trapping between 1805 and 1845 found that 182, or 41 percent, were killed in the occupation.[16]

Astor knew that the fur industry was doomed. Beaver pelts that had fetched $6 a pound in 1830 brought only $3.50 a pound by 1833. In that year he liquidated all his fur-trading interests. He spent the rest of his life accumulating more money in New York real estate. For a time, the American Fur Company carried on under new owners, but the industry environment continued to worsen. In 1837 the firm's steamboat *St. Peters* carried smallpox up the Missouri, killing more than 17,000 natives, and an agent observed that "our most profitable Indians have died."[17] By 1840 the firm had withdrawn from the Rocky Mountains and focused on buffalo robes, which remained profitable for some time.

ASTOR'S LAST YEARS

Astor lived on in New York, wringing immense profits from rents and leases as the city grew around his real estate holdings. By 1847 he had built a fortune of $20 million that towered above any other of that day. In 1998 this sum was estimated to be the equivalent of $78 billion, at the time more than the wealth of Microsoft's Bill Gates.[18] In his last years he was weak and frail and exercised by having attendants toss him up and down in a blanket. Yet despite his physical deterioration, he remained focused on getting every last penny from his tenants, poring over the rents for long hours behind the barred windows of his office.

Astor gave little to charity. An early biographer found "no trustworthy evidence of a single instance" in which he bestowed even a small sum of charity beyond his family and close friends and concluded:

> To get all that he could and to keep nearly all that he got—those were the laws of his being. He had a vast genius for making money, and that was all that he had.[19]

Social critics attacked him for his stinginess. When he died in 1848, his major gift to society was $460,000 in his will for building an Astor Library. In addition, he left $50,000 to the town of Waldorf, Germany, his birthplace; $30,000 for the German Society of New York; and $30,000 to the Home for Aged Ladies in New York City. This totaled, in the words of one commentator, less than "the proceeds of one year's pillage of the Indians."[20] The rest of his wealth went to his heirs. As to how America felt about him, one obituary minced no words.

> No doubt he had many fine, noble qualities, but avarice seemed to hold an all-conquering sway.... [W]hat a vast amount of good he might have rendered the world! But how reverse is the case—he dies and no one mourns! His soul was eaten up with avarice. Charity and benevolence found not a congenial home in his cold and frigid bosom![21]

THE LEGACY OF THE FUR TRADE

For 300 years the fur trade shaped the economic, political, and cultural life of both native and European inhabitants of the raw North American continent.

Its climactic era has often been depicted as a progressive and romantic period when trading posts

[15] Trappers also attacked Blackfeet without provocation. See Osborne Russell, *Journal of a Trapper* (Lincoln: University of Nebraska Press, 1955), pp. 52, 86.

[16] William H. Goetzmann, "The Mountain Man as Jacksonian Man," *American Quarterly,* Fall 1963, p. 409.

[17] Jacob Halsey, a clerk at Fort Pierre, quoted in Wishart, *The Fur Trade of the American West,* p. 68.

[18] This is the estimate of Michael Klepper and Robert Gunther in "The American Heritage 40," *American Heritage,* October 1998, p. 56.

[19] James Parton, *Life of John Jacob Astor* (New York: The American News Company, 1865), pp. 72 and 52.

[20] Myers, *History of the Great American Fortunes,* p. 149.

[21] "John Jacob Astor," *Appleton's Journal of Literature, Science and Art,* June 1, 1848, p. 116.

represented "civilization which was slowly mastering the opposition of nature and barbarism."[22] According to historian Dan Elbert Clark:

> The fur traders, with all their faults and short-comings, were the pathfinders of civilization. They marked the trails that were followed by settlers. They built trading posts where later appeared thriving towns and cities. They knew the Indians better than any other class of white men who came among them.[23]

The American Fur Company and its competitors greatly advanced geographical knowledge and blazed trails. The fur industry reinforced central American values such as rugged individualism, the frontier spirit, and optimism about the inevitability of progress. Yet there is also a dark side to the story. Traders undermined Indian cultures by introducing new economic motivations. Tribal societies were destroyed by alcohol, smallpox, and venereal disease. "The fur trade," according to Professor David J. Wishart of the University of Nebraska, "was the vanguard of a massive wave of Euro-American colonisation, which brought into contact two sets of cultures with disparate and irreconcilable ways of life."[24]

The industry also left extensive ecological damage in its wake. It slaughtered animal populations and denuded riverside forest areas to get steamboat fuel. Astor's mentality of pillage set a destructive standard. Argues Wishart: "The attitude of rapacious, short-term exploitation which was imprinted during the fur trade persisted after 1840 as the focus shifted from furs to minerals, timber, land, and water."[25]

---

[22] Arthur D. Howden Smith, *John Jacob Astor: Landlord of New York* (Philadelphia: Lippincott, 1929), p. 131.

[23] Dan Elbert Clark, *The West in American History* (New York: Thomas Y. Crowell, 1937), p. 441.

[24] Wishart, *The Fur Trade of the American West*, p. 215.

[25] Ibid., p. 212.

The American Fur Company, now largely forgotten, was the main actor in a global industry with enormous geopolitical power. The firm's operation was like a test-tube experiment on the social consequences of raw, unrestrained capitalism. It would be many years before the American nation gave thought to the lessons.

Questions

1. How would you evaluate Astor in terms of his motive, his managerial ability, and his ethics? What lesson does his career teach about the relationship between virtue and success?

2. How did the environment of the American Fur Company change in the 1830s? What deep historical forces are implicated in these changes?

3. What were the impacts of the fur trade on society in major dimensions of the business environment, that is, economic, cultural, technological, natural, governmental, legal, and internal?

4. Who were the most important stakeholders of the nineteenth century fur industry? Were they treated responsibly by the standards of the day? By the standards of today?

5. On balance, is the legacy of the American Fur Company and of the fur trade itself a positive legacy? Or is the impact predominantly negative?

6. Does the story of the American Fur Company hint at how and why capitalism has changed and has been changed over the years?

7. Do one or more models of the business–government–society relationship discussed in Chapter 1 apply to the historical era set forth in this case? Which model or models have explanatory power and why?

Chapter Three

Business Power

James B. Duke and the American Tobacco Company

On December 23, 1856, cries of new life swelled from a North Carolina farmhouse, their source a baby boy named James Buchanan Duke. The lad would have far more impact on the world than the failed president his name honored.

Soon, the Civil War displaced the Duke family from its land. On returning home in 1865 little James's father built a small factory to make a brand of chewing tobacco named Pro Bono Publico (a Latin phrase meaning "for the public good"). James helped. He was a precocious, energetic boy, diligent, gifted at sales and, at the age of 14, an overseer of 20 workers.

By his late teens, James had lost interest in attending college, his love of the business being so great. He had visions of grandeur for the little factory, but the presence of a rival firm, the Bull Durham Co., thwarted them. Its chewing tobacco was so dominant that head-on competition seemed hopeless. Taking a major gamble, he committed the company to a then-novel product—the cigarette. This was a venturesome move, because at the time few people smoked them. Most tobacco users were rural men who associated cigarettes with degenerate dudes and dandies in big cities.

Nonetheless, in 1881 Duke brought 10 Russian immigrant cigarette rollers to his North Carolina factory and set them to work. Each made about 2,000 per day. At first there was no demand. Tobacco shops refused to order his Duke of Durham brand since customers never asked for them. But Duke was a merchandising genius. In Atlanta, he took out a full-page newspaper ad of a famous actress holding Duke cigarettes in her outstretched hand. This use of a woman to advertise cigarettes created a sensation and, along with it, demand. In St. Louis, Duke confronted extreme prejudice against cigarettes. Tobacco shop proprietors simply would not place orders. He had his agents hire a young, redheaded widow to call on the tobacconists, and she got 19 orders on her first day.

By this time a Virginia engineer, James Bonsack, had invented a machine capable of rolling 200 cigarettes per minute. He offered it first to the largest tobacco companies, but they turned him down, believing that smokers would reject newfangled, machine-rolled cigarettes. Duke saw the significance of the technology and jumped at it.[1] In 1883 he negotiated an exclusive agreement to operate the device, and his

---

[1] Patrick G. Porter, "Origins of the American Tobacco Company," *Business History Review,* Spring 1969, pp. 68–69.

Duke lured men to try his new cigarette brands by putting picture cards in packs. The first cards were stage actresses in poses that were provocative for that day. Later card series included Indian chiefs, perilous occupations, ocean and river steamers, coins, musical instruments, flags, fish, ships, and prize fighters. Source: Tobacco Advertising Collection—Database #D0047, D0059. Emergence of Advertising On-Line Project, John W. Hartman Center for Sales, Advertising & Marketing History. Duke University Rare Book, Manuscript, and Special Collections Library. http://library.duke.edu/digitalcollections/eaa/

competitors never recovered. With the new Bonsack machines, Duke simultaneously cut manufacturing costs from $0.80 per thousand to $0.30 and multiplied factory production by many times.[2]

To find new markets for this swollen output, Duke next went to New York City, where he rented a loft and set up a small cigarette factory. Then he moved to create demand. He was tireless, working 12 hours a day in the factory, then making the rounds of tobacco shops at night. He gave secret rebates and cash payments to friendly dealers. He hired people to visit tobacco shops and demand his new machine-rolled Cameo and Cross Cut brands. Immigrants were welcomed with free samples as they emerged from the New York Immigration Station to set foot in America for the first time. Ingeniously, he put numbered cards with glamour photos of actresses in his cigarette packs, encouraging men to complete a collection. Late at night he haunted the streets, picking up crumpled cigarette packs from sidewalks and trash cans, creating a crude sales count.

Overseas, Duke's minions were also at work. One great conquest was China. At the time a few Chinese, mostly older men, smoked a bitter native tobacco in pipes. Cigarettes were unknown. Duke sent experts to Shantung Province with bright leaf

[2] John K. Winkler, *Tobacco Tycoon: The Story of James Buchanan Duke* (New York: Random House, 1942), p. 56.

from North Carolina to cultivate a milder tobacco. His sales force hired "teachers" to walk village streets showing curious Chinese how to light and hold cigarettes. He installed Bonsak machines in four new manufacturing plants that soon ran 24 hours a day. And he unleashed on the Chinese a full range of promotional activities. At one time his cigarette packs contained pictures of seminude American actresses, which were a big hit with Chinese men. In this way, Duke turned China into a nation of smokers.

Back home his tactics wore down competitors. He carefully observed John D. Rockefeller's conquest of the oil industry and saw that Rockefeller's methods could be applied to the tobacco industry. In 1884, at the age of 26, he engineered a combination of his firm and other large firms into a holding company known as the American Tobacco trust. As president, Duke built the trust into a monopoly that controlled 98 percent of the domestic cigarette market by 1892, a year in which 2.9 billion cigarettes were sold.[3] Not content with domination alone, he worked tirelessly to expand the tobacco market. By 1903, more than 10 billion cigarettes were sold in the United States.[4] Over two decades his combination ruthlessly swallowed or bankrupted 250 firms until it dominated the cigar, snuff, and smoking tobacco markets too.

Duke used a simple method to strangle competitors. Instead of selling its output at wholesale prices, Duke's company "consigned" its products to dealers. The dealers had to pay full retail price for tobacco goods sent to them "on consignment" and do so within 10 days of receipt. Three months later, the company paid the dealer a "commission," which was the dealer's profit. Dealers who sold competitors' brands were not eligible to receive this "commission," so they could not make a profit on brands the vast majority of their customers wanted. Duke enforced the scheme using detectives to spy on dealers. Many dealers disliked this arrogant, coercive system, but they had to play along or wither away.

Duke's monopoly lasted until 1911, when the Supreme Court ordered it broken up.[5] Duke himself figured out how to divide the giant firm into four independent companies: Liggett & Myers, P. Lorillard, R. J. Reynolds, and a new American Tobacco Company. After the breakup he retired from the tobacco industry to start an electric utility, Duke Power & Light. He also gave money to a small North Carolina college, which became Duke University. He died of complications from pernicious anemia in 1925.

Duke's career illustrates the power of commerce to shape society. He made the cigarette an acceptable consumer product and spread it around the world. His monopoly destroyed rivals and defined the structure of the tobacco industry. His bribes to legislators blocked antismoking laws and checked the early efforts of antitobacco leagues to publicize health hazards. And, owing largely to Duke's ingenuity, a surging tobacco trade revived the crippled post-Civil War Southern economy. Eventually, he ran into a hard check on power when the Supreme Court dismantled his colossus, but his work endures in the roll call of smokers across 120 years.

[3] "Iron Heel of Monopoly," *The New York Times,* December 28, 1892, p. 10.

[4] "The Caesar of Tobacco," *The Wall Street Journal,* June 27, 1903, p. 6.

[5] *United States v. American Tobacco Company,* 221 U.S. 106 (1911).

THE NATURE OF BUSINESS POWER

Business has tremendous power to change society, and the extent of this power is underappreciated. Companies in ascending industries change societies by altering all three of their primary elements—ideas, institutions, and material things. This effect is visible in the stories of dominant companies such as the American Tobacco Company, the American Fur Company, and the Standard Oil Trust. The cumulative power of all business is a massive, irrepressible shaping force. In this chapter we explain the underlying dynamics of this power to change society. We then discuss its limits.

WHAT IS POWER?

power
The force or strength to act or to compel another entity to act.

Power is the force or strength to act or to compel another entity to act. In human society it is used to organize and control people and materials to achieve individual or collective goals. It exists on a wide spectrum ranging from coercion at one extreme to weak influence at the other. Its use in human society creates change. Although power is sometimes exerted to prevent change, such resistance is itself a force that alters history. The many sources of power include wealth, position, knowledge, law, arms, status, and charisma. Power is unevenly distributed, and all societies have mechanisms to control and channel it for wide or narrow benefit. These mechanisms, which are imperfect, include governments, laws, police, cultural values, and public opinion. Also, multiple, competing formations of power may check and balance each other.

business power
The force behind an act by a company, industry, or sector.

Business power is the force behind an act by a company, industry, or sector. The greater this force, the more the action creates change or influences the actions of other entities in society. Its basic origin is a grant of authority from society to convert resources efficiently into needed goods and services. In return for doing this, society gives corporations the authority to take necessary actions and permits a profit. This agreement derives from the social contract.

legitimacy
The rightful use of power. Its opposite is tyranny, or the exercise of power beyond right.

The social contract legitimizes business power by giving it a moral basis. *Legitimacy* is the rightful use of power. The power of giant corporations is legitimate when it is exercised in keeping with the agreed-upon contract. The philosopher John Locke wrote that for governments the opposite of legitimacy is tyranny, defined as "the exercise of power beyond right."[6] Corporations breach the social contract, exercising "power beyond right," when they violate social values, endanger the public, or act illegally.

Business power is legitimate when it is used for the common good. The grounds of legitimacy vary between societies and over time. Child labor, once widespread in the United States, is no longer permitted, but it exists in other nations. As we will see in subsequent chapters, the definition of the common good that business must serve has expanded throughout American history and is now expanding globally.

---

[6] John Locke, *The Second Treatise of Government* (New York: Bobbs-Merrill, 1952), p. 112; originally published in 1690.

LEVELS AND SPHERES OF CORPORATE POWER

Business power, like any form of social power, is intangible, its exercise not subject to direct or exact calibrations. Having no physical state to be observed, it is known to be great or small solely by its effects on the world. In this respect, corporate actions have an impact on society at two levels, and on each level they create change.

On the *surface level*, business power is the direct cause of visible, immediate changes, both great and small. Corporations expand and contract, hire and fire; they make and sell products. On a *deep level*, corporate power shapes society over time through the aggregate changes of industrial growth. At this level we encounter an intangible realm of social networks, time, and physical space, a realm crossed by complex chains of cause and effect that converge and interact, shaping and reshaping society. Here the workings of corporate power are unplanned, unpredictable, indirect, and irregular, but they are constant and far more significant. Corporate power "is something more than men," wrote John Steinbeck. "It's the monster. Men made it, but they can't control it."[7] This is a poetic but accurate description of business power at a deep level.

On both the surface and deep levels, business power is exercised in spheres corresponding to the seven business environments set forth in Chapter 2.

- *Economic power* is the ability of the corporation to influence events, activities, and people by virtue of control over resources, particularly property. At the surface level, the operation of a corporation may immediately and visibly affect its stakeholders, for example, by building or closing a factory. At a deeper level, the accumulating impact of corporate economic activity has sweeping effects. For example, over many years corporations have created enough wealth to raise living standards dramatically in industrialized nations.

- *Technological power* is the ability to influence the direction, rate, characteristics, and consequences of physical innovations as they develop. On a surface level, in 1914, assembly lines run by new electric motors allowed Henry Ford to introduce transportation based on the internal combustion engine. Using this method, he turned an expensive luxury of the rich into a mass consumer product. But at a deeper level, as the auto took hold in American society it created unanticipated consequences. One juvenile court judge in the 1920s called the automobile a "house of prostitution on wheels," something that the puritanical Henry Ford doubtless never intended to create.[8]

- *Political power* is the ability to influence governments. On the surface, corporations give money to candidates and lobby legislatures. On a deeper level, around the world industrialization engenders values that radiate freedom and erode authoritarian regimes.

- *Legal power* is the ability to shape the laws of society. On the surface, big corporations have formidable legal resources that intimidate opponents. On a deeper

---

[7] *The Grapes of Wrath* (New York: Viking Press, 1939), p. 45.

[8] Frederick Lewis Allen, *Only Yesterday: An Informal History of the 1920s* (New York: Harper & Brothers, 1931), p. 100.

American Landscape, a 1930 oil painting, depicts Ford Motor Company's mighty River Rouge plant, which took in raw materials such as sand and iron ore at one end and turned out finished autos at the other. In its day, the plant was regarded as a wonder and people traveled from around the world to see it. Here artist Charles Sheeler evokes the power of business to change and shape society. On the surface, this vista seems to beautify and ennoble the architecture of production, making it seem almost pastoral. Yet on a deeper level the painting provokes anxiety. Factory buildings run nature off the scene, dominating a landscape that is now, but for the sky, entirely artificial. A tiny human figure in the middle ground is overwhelmed and marginalized by the massive complex; its movement limited and regimented by the surrounding industrial structure. Here, then, art reveals emotions and insights about business power. Other Sheeler paintings and photographs are open to the same interpretation. He never revealed his intentions, leaving art critics to debate whether he was, in fact, sanguine or dispirited about how business power was shaping the "American landscape." Source: Digital Image © The Museum of Modern Art/Licensed by SCALA/Art Resource, NY.

level, the laws of the United States—including constitutional, civil, and criminal laws—have been shaped by the consequences of industrial activity.

- *Cultural power* is the ability to influence cultural values, habits, and institutions such as the family. John Wanamaker, founder of a department store chain and a master of advertising, started Mother's Day in the early 1900s. He ran full-page ads in the *Philadelphia Inquirer* about a woman mourning for her mother, creating the sentiment that gratitude for mothers should be expressed by a gift on a special day.[9] At a deeper level, the cumulative impact of ads has altered American society by reinforcing values selectively, for example, materialism over asceticism, individualism over community, or personal appearance over inner character.

- *Environmental power* is the impact of a company on nature. On the surface, a power plant may pollute the air; on a deeper level, since the seventeenth century, emission of gases in the burning of wood, coal, and oil to power industry has altered the chemistry of earth's atmosphere. One study found that since 1882 the Standard Oil Trust and its successor companies have contributed between 4.7 and 5.2 percent of worldwide carbon dioxide emissions.[10]

- *Power over individuals* is exercised over employees, managers, stockholders, consumers, and citizens. On the surface, a corporation may determine the work life and buying habits of individuals. At a deeper level, industrialism sets the pattern of daily life. People are regimented, living by clocks, moving in routes fixed by the model of an industrial city with its streets and sidewalks. Their occupation determines their status and fortune.

Activity in the economic sphere is the primary force for change. From this, change radiates into other spheres. The story of the railroad industry in the United States illustrates how an expanding industry with a radical new technology can change its environments.

THE STORY OF THE RAILROADS

When small railroads sprang up in the 1820s, most passengers and freight moved by horse and over canals. The railroad was a vastly superior conveyance and was bound to revolutionize transportation. Tracks cost less to build than canals and did not freeze in winter. Routes could be more direct. For the first time in history, people and cargo traveled overland faster than the speed of a horse. The trip from New York to Chicago was reduced from three weeks to just three days. And the cost of moving goods and passengers was less; in a day a train could go back and forth many times over the distance that a canal boat or wagon could traverse once.

The initial boom in railroading came at midcentury. In 1850 trains ran on only 9,021 miles of track, but by 1860 30,626 miles had been laid. During that decade, 30 railroad companies completed route systems, which had significant consequences for the financial system. Tracks were expensive, and each of these enterprises was a giant for its day. Many needed $10 million to $35 million in capital, and the smallest at least $2 million. Companies in other industries did not approach this size; only a handful of textile mills and steel plants required capitalization of more than $1 million.[11]

---

[9] Richard Wolkomir and Joyce Wolkomir, "You Are What You Buy," *Smithsonian,* May 2000, p. 107.

[10] Friends of the Earth International, *Exxon's Climate Footprint* (London: FOEI, January 2004), p. 5. See also Richard Heede, *Exxon Mobil Corporation Emissions Inventory: 1882–2002* (London: Friends of the Earth Trust Ltd., December 17, 2003).

[11] Alfred D. Chandler, Jr., *The Visible Hand: The Managerial Revolution in American Business* (Cambridge, MA: Belknap Press, 1977), pp. 83, 86, and 90.

The call for this much money transformed capital markets. The only place such huge sums could be raised was in large Northeastern cities. Since interest rates were a little higher in Boston at the time, New York became the center of financial activity and has remained so to this day. Railroads sold bonds and offered stocks to raise capital, and a new investment banking industry was created. The New York Stock Exchange went from a sleepy place, where only a few hundred shares might change hands each week, to a roaring market. Speculative techniques such as margin trading, short-selling, and options trading appeared for the first time. Later, the financial mechanisms inspired by railroad construction were in place when other industries needed more capital to grow. This changed American history by accelerating the industrial transformation of the late 1800s. It also put New York bankers such as J. P. Morgan in a position to control access to capital.

At first the railroads ran between existing trade centers, but as time passed and track mileage increased, they linked ever more points. The 30,626 miles of track in 1860 increased to 93,267 miles by 1880 and 167,191 miles by 1890.[12] This required enormous amounts of wood, and whole forests were downed to make ties and stoke fires in early steam locomotives. A deeper consequence of extending the tracks was a society transformed.

Before tracks radiated everywhere, the United States was a nation of farmers and small towns held together by the traditional institutions of family, church, and local government. Since long-distance travel was time-consuming and arduous, these towns often were isolated. Populations were stable. People identified more with local areas than with the nation as a whole. Into this world came the train, a destabilizing technology powered by aggressive market capitalism.

Trains took away young people who might have stayed in rural society but for the lure of wealth in distant cities. In their place came a stream of outsiders who were less under the control of community values. Small-town intimacy declined, and a new phenomenon appeared in American life—the impersonal crowd of strangers. Trains violated established customs. Sunday was a day of rest and worship, so many churchgoers were angered when huffing and whistling trains intruded on services. But new capital accounting methods used by railroad companies dictated using equipment an extra day each week to increase return on investment. This imperative trumped devoutness. In early America, localities set their own time according to the sun's overhead transit, but this resulted in a patchwork of time zones that made scheduling difficult. An editorial in *Railroad Age* argued, "Local time must go."[13] For the convenience of the railroads, a General Time Convention met in 1882 and standardized the time of day, though not without resistence from holdouts who felt that "[s]urely the world ran by higher priorities than railroad scheduling."[14]

---

[12] Bureau of the Census, *Statistical Abstract of the United States,* 77th ed. (Washington, DC: Government Printing Office, 1956), table 683.

[13] Bill Kauffman, "Why Spring Ahead," *The American Enterprise,* April–May 2001, p. 50.

[14] Ibid., p. 50, quoting Michael O'Malley, *Keeping Watch: A History of American Time* (Washington, DC: Smithsonian Institution Press, 1996).

As the railroads grew, they spread impersonality and an ethic of commerce. Towns reoriented themselves around their train stations. Shops and restaurants sprang up nearby so that strangers would spend money before moving on. The railroads gave more frequent service to cities with commercial possibilities and bypassed small towns or let them wither from less frequent service. This speeded urbanization and the centralization of corporate power in cities. Rural areas were redefined. Once the cultural heartland, they now were seen as backward and rustic—places best used for vacations from urban stress.

The railroads also changed American politics. On the surface, their lobbyists could dominate legislatures. On a deeper level, the changes were more profound. Congress had always selected nominees before presidential elections, but now trains brought delegates to national party nominating conventions, changing the way candidates were picked. Trains enabled all sorts of associations to have national meetings, and the rails spread issues that might in an earlier era have remained local. The movement to give women the vote, for example, succeeded after Susan B. Anthony took trains to all parts of the country, spreading her rhetoric and unifying the cause.[15]

At first government encouraged and subsidized railroads. All told, federal and state governments gave them land grants of 164 million acres, an area equal to the size of California and Nevada combined.[16] But later the challenge was to control them. When Congress passed the Interstate Commerce Act in 1887 to regulate railroads, the design of the statute set the example for regulating other industries later.

Many other changes in American society are traceable to the railroads. They were the first businesses to require modern management structures. The need for precise coordination of speeding trains over vast reaches caused railroads to pioneer professional management teams, division structures, and modern cost accounting—all innovations later adopted in other industries.[17] Railroads lay behind Indian wars. For the Plains Indians, tracks that divided old hunting grounds were the main barrier to peace.[18] Thousands of laborers came from China to lay rail, and their descendants live on in communities along the lines. Railroads changed the language. The word *diner*, meaning a place to eat, appeared after the introduction of the Pullman Palace Car Company's first dining car in 1868. The expression "hell on wheels" originally described the raucous body of prostitutes, gambling cars, and saloons that rolled along with construction crews as tracks spread west. The phrase "off again, on again" derives from discussions about train derailments.[19] And social values changed. Big-city commercial values rumbled down the tracks, jolting traditions along rural byways.

[15] These and other social and political changes are treated at length in Sarah H. Gordon, *Passage to Union* (Chicago: Ivan R. Dees, 1996).

[16] Page Smith, *The Rise of Industrial America*, vol. 6 (New York: Viking Penguin, 1984), p. 99.

[17] Chandler, *The Visible Hand*, chap. 3.

[18] Smith, *The Rise of Industrial America*, p. 89.

[19] Rudolph Daniels, *Trains across the Continent: North American Railroad History,* 2nd ed. (Bloomington: Indiana University Press, 2000), pp. 53 and 78.

FIGURE 3.1 Railroad Track Miles in Operation: 1830–2010

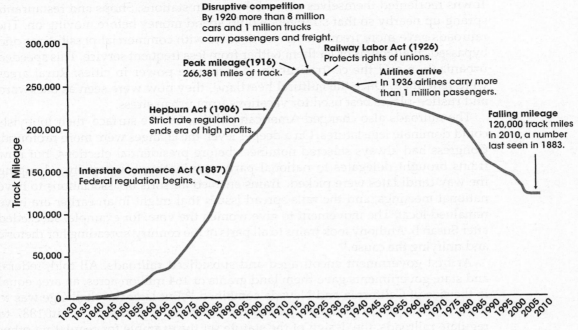

Source: *Statistical Abstract of the United States*, various editions 1878–2010.

As the track system swelled so did the power of railroads to shape the sociopolitical and the physical landscapes. Figure 3.1 shows how track mileage fell after 1916, reflecting a decline in the fortunes of the industry. Government regulation hardened, making rate hikes more difficult and strengthening the hand of unions. In addition, railroads came into competition with new transportation technologies, first autos, buses, and trucks, then aircraft. As the importance of rails receded, these rising technologies hastened to reshape American life, converting the nation from one that ran on steam to one that ran on oil.

TWO PERSPECTIVES ON BUSINESS POWER

dominance theory
The view that business is the most powerful institution in society, because of its control of wealth. This power is inadequately checked and, therefore, excessive.

There is agreement that business has great power. But there is considerable disagreement about whether its power is adequately checked and balanced for the public good. Views about business power cover a wide spectrum, but there are two basic and opposing positions.

On one side is the *dominance theory*, which holds that business is preeminent in American society, primarily because of its control of wealth, and that its power is both excessive and inadequately checked. Corporations can alter their environments in self-interested ways that harm the general welfare. This was the thesis of Karl Marx, who wrote that a ruling capitalist class exploited workers and dominated other classes. The dominance theory is the basis of the dominance model of the business–government–society relationship set forth in Chapter 1.

pluralist theory
The view that business power is exercised in a society where other institutions also have great power. It is counterbalanced and restricted and, therefore, not excessive.

On the other side the *pluralist theory* holds that business power is exercised in a society in which other institutions such as markets, government, labor unions, advocacy groups, and public opinion also have great power. Business power is counterbalanced, restricted, controlled, and subject to defeat. Adam Smith was convinced that largely through market forces, business power could be disciplined to benefit society. The pluralist theory is the basis of the countervailing forces model in Chapter 1.

The Dominance Theory

In industrializing societies, business organizations grow in size and concentrate wealth. According to the dominance theory, business abuses the power its size and wealth confer in a number of ways. The rise of huge corporations creates a business elite that exercises inordinate power over public policy. Asset concentration creates monopoly or oligopoly in markets that reduces competition and harms consumers. Corporations wield financial and organizational resources unmatched by opposing interests. For example, they use campaign contributions to corrupt politicians, hire lobbyists to undermine the independence of elected officials, employ accountants and lawyers to avoid taxes, and run public relations campaigns that shape opinion in their favor.

Moreover, large corporations achieve such importance in a nation's economy that elected officials are forced to adopt probusiness measures or face public wrath. "If enterprises falter for lack of inducement to invest, hire, and produce," writes one advocate of the dominance theory, "members of the political elite are more likely than those of the entrepreneurial elite to lose their positions."[20] We will discuss further the growth in size and wealth of corporations and the presence of elites.

Corporate Asset Concentration

The idea that concentration of economic power results in abuse arose, in part, as an intellectual reaction to the awesome economic growth of the late nineteenth century. Until then, the United States had been primarily an agricultural economy. But between 1860 and 1890, industrial progress transformed the country. Statistics illustrating this are striking. During these 30 years, the number of manufacturing plants more than doubled, growing from 140,433 to 355,415; the value of what they made rose more than 400 percent, from $1.8 billion to $9.3 billion; and the capital invested in them grew 650 percent, from $1 billion to $6.5 billion.[21]

This growth did more than create wealth; it also concentrated it. At the end of the century, between 1895 and 1904, an unprecedented merger wave assembled dominant firms in industry after industry. Since then, there have been other great merger waves, but this was the first. It made a definitive impression on the American mind, and its legacy is an enduring fear of big companies.

[20] Charles E. Lindblom, *The Market System: What It Is, How It Works, and What to Make of It* (New Haven: Yale University Press, 2001), p. 247.
[21] Figures in this paragraph are from Arthur M. Schlesinger, *Political and Social Growth of the United States: 1852–1933* (New York: Macmillan, 1935), pp. 132–44.

Merger waves are caused by changes in the economic environment that create incentives to combine. The main stimulus for the 1895–1904 wave was growth of the transcontinental railroads, which reduced transportation costs, thereby creating new national markets. Companies rushed to transform themselves from regional operations to national ones. Combinations such as James Duke's American Tobacco Company gorged themselves, swallowing competitors, crowding into formerly isolated markets, and wiping out small family businesses. The story was repeated in roughly 300 commodities, including oil, copper, cattle, smelting, and such items as playing cards and tombstones. A 1904 study of the 92 largest firms found that 78 controlled 50 percent of their market, 57 controlled 60 percent or more, and 26 controlled 80 percent or more.[22]

At the time, the public failed to see the growth of huge firms as a natural, inevitable, or desirable response to the new economic incentives. Instead, it saw them as colossal monuments to greed. Companies of this size were something new. They inspired a mixture of awe and fear. In 1904, when the United States Steel Corporation became the first company with more than $1 billion in assets, people were astounded. Previously, such numbers applied in the realm of astronomy, not business.

In the twentieth century, corporations continued to grow in size, but the marked rise in asset concentration slowed and leveled off. By 1929 the 200 largest nonfinancial corporations in the United States (less than 0.7 percent of all nonfinancials) controlled nearly 50 percent of all corporate wealth. But by 1947 the nation's top 200 corporations had only 46 percent of corporate wealth, and this was reduced to 36 percent in 1996.[23] Although no continuing data series exists to provide a current figure, a recent study reveals that asset concentration in the top 200 firms on the Fortune 500 declined by 8 percent between 1995 and 2004.[24]

With economic globalization, the number of multinational firms and the scale of their activity has grown. There are approximately 82,000 multinationals, up from only about 34,000 as recently as 1990. Asset s and sales of the largest of these firms are rising. Between 1990 and 2008, assets of the 100 biggest multinationals increased by 336 percent and sales by 269 percent.[25] Yet even with heightened global merger activity, the largest global firms show no signs of concentrating foreign assets the way that large American firms have concentrated domestic assets. In fact, the foreign assets of the largest 100 multinationals fell from 13 percent of estimated global assets in 1999 to 9 percent in 2008.[26] And these 100 firms are still only a small part of world economic activity. For the decade 1990–2000,

[22] John Moody, *The Truth about Trusts: A Description and Analysis of the American Trust Movement* (New York: Greenwood Press, 1968), p. 487; originally published in 1904.

[23] J. Fred Weston, Kwang S. Chung, and Juan A. Siu, *Takeovers, Restructuring, and Corporate Governance,* 2nd ed. (Upper Saddle River, NJ: Prentice Hall, 1998), p. 116. These figures allow rotation of new firms into the top 200 firms. If the same 200 firms had been followed over the years, asset concentration would have fallen even faster.

[24] Edward Nissan, "Structure of American Business: Goods versus Services," *Southwestern Economic Review* (online), Spring 2006, table 1.

[25] United Nations Conference on Trade and Development (UNCTAD), *World Investment Report 2010* (New York: United Nations, 2010), table I.11; and UNCTAD, *World Investment Report 1993* (New York: United Nations, 1993), table I.11.

[26] UNCTAD, *World Investment Report 2009* (New York: United Nations, 2009), p. xxi.

their output as a share of world GDP grew from 3.5 percent to only 4.3 percent, then fell back to 4 percent by 2008.[27]

Despite this, adherents of the dominance theory believe that the increasing size and financial power of global corporations will be converted into the same old abuses. But the link between market power and abuse remains to be seen. Multinationals with growing assets and sales do not necessarily have increased market power. They face formidable competitors, emerging competition from new industries, geographically enlarged market boundaries, and, in the European Union, more aggressive antitrust enforcement. In the social dimension, these firms face growing global pressures to act responsibly.

Also, no corporation, no matter how large, is assured of prospering. Over time competition, strategic errors, and, most important, technological changes have continuously winnowed the roster of America's biggest companies. Looking back at lists of the top 200 industrial corporations by assets, one study found that of 543 corporations that appeared on the lists between 1900 and 2000 only 28 "persistent giants," or 5 percent of the total number that drifted on and off the list, survived for 100 years.[28] The rest came and went, primarily due to the rise of disruptive technologies. Early in the century railroads and metal companies were dominant, but fell away as new entrants in electrical equipment and chemicals went to the top. By midcentury oil and auto companies appeared, then later, computer-related firms. For the largest companies in each era, economies of scale and oligopoly in markets led to high profits and may have prolonged their dominance, yet these advantages were no shield from the technological changes that dislodged them from the top. Based on this century of evidence, the authors predict that "[t]urbulence is the future, just as it is the past of these giant firms."[29]

Other studies confirm the low survival rate at the top of the asset roster. Of the 100 largest corporations in 1909, only 36 remained on the list until 1948. Between 1948 and 1958, only 65 of the top 100 held their place. Only 116 company names remained on the Fortune 500 list of industrial corporations from its inception in 1955 to 1994 when it was revised to included service industries.[30] Many firms dropped from the list were, of course, acquired by other firms. Among the 100 largest transnational corporations there were 28 American firms in 1990, but that number had declined to 18 by 2008.[31] The lesson in all these numbers is that, with very few exceptions, the power of technology-based market forces exceeds the power of even the largest corporations to maintain their dominance.

[27] UNCTAD, *World Investment Report 2002* (New York: United Nations, 2002), box table IV.1.2; and UNCTAD, *World Investment Report 2009* (New York: United Nations, 2009), p. xxi. These figures are based on a value-added calculation (the sum of salaries, pretax profits, and depreciation and amortization) for transnational corporations.

[28] Francisco Louçã and Sandro Mendonça, "Steady Change: The 200 Largest U.S. Manufacturing Firms Throughout the 20th Century," *Industrial and Corporate Change,* August 2002, pp. 818 and 825.

[29] Ibid., p. 840.

[30] Figures in this paragraph are from Neil H. Jacoby, *Corporate Power and Social Responsibility* (New York: Macmillan, 1973), p. 32; John Paul Newport, Jr., "A New Era of Rapid Rise and Ruin," *Fortune,* April 24, 1989, p. 77; and Carol J. Loomis, "Forty Years of the 500," *Fortune,* May 15, 1995, p. 182.

[31] UNCTAD, *World Investment Report 2010,* table I.8.

The Rise and Decline of Corporate Giants

When the New York Stock Exchange was young ordinary investors had trouble making sense of daily trading. Some stocks went up, others went down, and the gyrations hid trends. In 1896 journalist Charles H. Dow created a list of 12 companies as an index of stock market performance. Now investors could see the market's direction by watching a daily sum of these company's share prices. At the time a great merger wave was reshaping the economy by creating giant firms, and Dow filled his index with them. Each was a leader in an important industry and represented its fortunes.

As the years passed America's economy changed, companies came and went; and the index, today called the Dow Jones Industrial Average, grew from 12 to 30 companies by 1928. The most recent additions and deletions were made in 2010.

The leading firms in 1896 reflect a different world. Farming was much more prominent, and four firms dealt in agricultural products. They were James B. Duke's American Tobacco Company, cotton and sugar producers, and a company that made livestock feeds. Two firms represented the centrality of technologies based on iron, lead, and coal. Another, U.S. Leather, made a product in the shadow of imminent obsolescence, leather belts used for power transmission in factories. General Electric, which built electric motors, was the high technology company of that era. Chicago Gas and Laclede Gas Light of St. Louis supplied natural gas for new streetlamps in booming cities. North American operated streetcars.

1896	2010	
American Cotton Oil	3M	Intel
American Sugar Refining	Alcoa	IBM
American Tobacco	American Express	Johnson & Johnson
Chicago Gas	AT&T	JPMorgan Chase
Distilling & Cattle Feeding	Bank of America	Kraft Foods
General Electric	Boeing	McDonald's
Laclede Gas Light	Caterpillar	Merck
National Lead	Chevron	Microsoft
North American	Cisco Systems	Pfizer
Tennessee Coal & Iron	Coca-Cola	Procter & Gamble
U.S. Leather	DuPont	Travelers
U.S. Rubber	Exxon Mobil	United Technologies
	General Electric	Walmart
	Hewlett-Packard	Walt Disney
	Home Depot	

The 2010 list registers the rise of new technologies and of economic sectors providing services and consumer products. General Electric is the only company that was on the 1896 list, and it was removed for nine years between 1898 and 1907. Of the other 11 original firms, 2 (American Tobacco and North American) were broken up by antitrust action, 1 (U.S. Leather) was dissolved, and 8 continue to operate as less important companies or as parts of other firms that acquired their assets.

As a biography of American industry, the index dramatizes the rise and fall of powerful companies and industries. Over more than a century, 100 different firms have been listed. The index teaches that dominance of even the largest firms is transient.

Elite Dominance

Another argument that supports the dominance theory is that there exists a small group of individuals who, by virtue of wealth and position, control the nation. Members of this elite are alleged to act in concert and in undemocratic ways. There is a long history of belief in an economic elite dominating American society. In debates preceding adoption of the Constitution in 1789, some opponents charged that the delegates were wealthy aristocrats designing a government favorable to their businesses. Later, farmers suspected the hand of an economic elite in the probusiness policies of Alexander Hamilton, George Washington's secretary of the treasury, who had many ties to wealth and commercial power. Since the Colonial era, charges of elitism have surfaced repeatedly in popular movements opposed to big business.

The modern impetus for the theory of elite dominance comes from the sociologist C. Wright Mills, who wrote a scholarly book in 1956 describing a "power elite" in American society. "Insofar as national events are decided," wrote Mills, "the power elite are those who decide them."[32] Mills saw American society as a pyramid of power and status. At the top was a tiny elite in command of the economic, political, and military domains. Mills was never specific about its numbers, but said it was small. Just below was a group of lieutenants who carried out the elite's policies. They included professional managers of corporations, politicians beholden to the elite for their election, and bureaucrats appointed by the politicians. The large base of the pyramid was composed of a mass of powerless citizens, including feeble groups and associations with little policy impact. This image of a pyramid corresponds to the dominance model in Chapter 1.

Mills did not see America as a democracy and thought the elite simply used government "as an umbrella under whose authority they do their work."[33] Although he never stated that the economic segment of the elite was dominant over the political and military, he noted, "The key organizations, perhaps, are the major corporations."[34]

power elite
A small group of individuals in control of the economy, government, and military. The theory of its existence is associated with the American sociologist C. Wright Mills.

The Power Elite is a book in which there is more speculation than substantiation. It is based on cursory evidence and included none of the statistical research that would be required to support such sweeping generalizations in a similar work of sociology today. Yet it contained a powerful new explanation of economic power and came out just as many American leftists were becoming disenchanted with Marxism. Mills's vision of a small ruling elite caught on and has been popular with the anticorporate left ever since. Mills would have been pleased. In correspondence, he once expressed indignation about the power of "the sons of bitches who run American Big Business."[35]

Scholars inspired by Mills continue to study elites and are less reluctant to suggest business dominance. One is G. William Domhoff, who, in a series of books extending over 40 years, argues the existence of a cohesive American upper class based on

[32] C. Wright Mills, *The Power Elite* (New York: Oxford University Press, 1956), p. 18.

[33] Ibid., p. 287.

[34] Ibid., p. 283.

[35] In a letter to his parents quoted by John B. Judis, "The Spiritual Wobbly," *The New York Times Book Review,* July 9, 2000, p. 9.

wealth, socialization in private schools, membership in exclusive clubs, and occupancy of high positions in business, government, and nonprofit institutions. Within this upper class lies a smaller leadership group, a controlling core of leaders in the corporate community. According to Domhoff, this core is a power elite.

> The power elite is made up of those people who serve as directors or trustees in . . . institutions controlled by the corporate community through stock ownership, financial support, involvement on the board of trustees, or some combination of these factors. [It has] . . . the power to shape the economic and political frameworks within which other groups and classes must operate.[36]

Domhoff does not quantify the power elite. Its power can be measured by the maintenance of a pro-corporate environment. Using foundation money, think tanks, lobbying, and campaign contributions it is consistently able to defeat the policy preferences of liberals and progressives who favor income redistribution and greater equality of opportunities.

In an effort that extended over 25 years, political scientist Thomas R. Dye tried to identify precisely which individuals made up an American elite. Believing that power comes from leadership in organizations, he identified an "institutional elite" of individuals who occupied the top positions in 10 sectors–industrial, banking, insurance, investments, mass media, law, education, foundations, civic and cultural organizations, and government. Applying this method, Dye identified an elite of 5,778 individuals.[37] This is a much larger elite than that suggested by Mills, but it is still only a speck of the population.

Another scholar, David Rothkopf, writes that with globalization, a transnational power elite or "superclass" has emerged, operating across borders through "networks of individuals and organizations."[38] Rothkopf calculates a superclass membership of about 6,000, which is 0.0001 percent of the world population, or a member for each 1 million people. The largest group, 17 percent, is Americans and another third come from European nations. They resemble national power elites in their origins and acculturation. Members attend elite universities. Harvard, Stanford, and the University of Chicago have produced the most. They join exclusive groups such as the Council on Foreign Relations, have memberships on overlapping boards of directors, and meet at events such as the World Economic Forum in Davos, Switzerland. Because multinational corporations, global banks, and hedge funds are "the largest and most significant transnational actors" their leaders dominate, working together "in clusters knit together by business deals, corporate boards, investment flows, old school ties, club memberships, and countless other strands that transform . . . into groups that are proven masters at advancing their aligned self-interests."[39] The new superclass eclipses the power of national elites. According to Rothkopf, it does not rule or conspire,

[36] G. William Domhoff, *Who Rules America?* 6th ed. (New York: McGraw-Hill, 2010), p. 114.

[37] Thomas R. Dye, *Who's Running America? The Bush Restoration,* 7th ed. (Upper Saddle River, NJ: Prentice Hall, 2002), p. 205; emphasis in the original.

[38] David Rothkopf, *Superclass: The Global Power Elite and the World They are Making,* (New York: Farrar, Straus and Giroux, 2008), p. 84.

[39] Ibid., pp. 33 and xvii.

but its dominant business subset, having "vastly more power than any other group on the planet," abets an agenda of oil dependence, free markets, free trade, and military spending.[40]

Elites formed from some combination of wealth, ability, position, and social status are timeless and inevitable. They challenge the logic of democratic ideology because a few citizens, acting in the shadows of electoral mechanisms, pilot a vast majority. Yet elites are not necessarily sinister, oppressive, or conspiratorial. They can be sources of talent, expert leadership, and cultural stability. American and global business elites spring from the pinnacles of corporate, government, religious, and cultural institutions, having arrived at such positions based overwhelmingly on ability.

However, those who move into elites come from a thin range of backgrounds. Every study finds that disproportionately they are male, white, and Christian; come from upper-class families; and attend a short list of prestigious schools. The inclusion of blacks, Latinos, and women is based on their similarity in background and thinking to the existing elite.[41] Rothkopf finds that only 6.3 percent of the global superclass is women.[42] At least in the United States, the idea of a power elite, one perhaps dominated by business interests, troubles citizens with a deep commitment to equality. Yet some argue that its actions are adequately checked and balanced. This view is taken up in the next section.

Pluralist Theory

pluralistic society
A society with multiple groups and institutions through which power is diffused.

A *pluralistic society* is one having multiple groups and institutions through which power is diffused. Within such a society no entity or interest has overriding power, and each may check and balance others. The countervailing forces model in Chapter 1 illustrates how, in such a society, business must interact with constraining forces in its environment. It may have considerable influence over some of them; but over most it has limited influence, and over a few none at all. Several features of American society support this thesis of pluralism.

First, it is infused with democratic values. Unlike many nations, America has no history of feudal or authoritarian rule, so there is no entrenched deference to an aristocracy of wealth. In Colonial days, Americans adopted the then-revolutionary doctrine of natural rights, which held that all persons were created equal and entitled to the same opportunities and protections. The French aristocrat Alexis de Tocqueville, who toured America and wrote an insightful book about American customs in the 1830s, was forcibly struck by the "prodigious influence" of the notion of equality. Belief in equality, he wrote, ran through American society, directing public opinion, informing the law, and defining politics. It was, he wrote, "the fundamental fact from which all others seem to be derived."[43] Thus, in America

---

[40] Ibid., p. xiii.

[41] Richard L. Zweigenhaft and G. William Domhoff, *Diversity in the Power Elite: Have Women and Minorities Reached the Top?* (New Haven: Yale University Press, 1998).

[42] Rothkopf, *Superclass*, p. 290.

[43] Alexis de Tocqueville, *Democracy in America* (New York: New American Library, 1956), p. 26; originally published as two volumes in 1835 and 1850.

J. P. Morgan and the Panic of 1907

In the first decade of the twentieth century, J. P. Morgan (1837–1913), head of J. P, Morgan & Co. in New York, was often called the most powerful man in the country. He specialized in buying competing companies in the same industry and merging them into a single, monopolistic firm. He joined separate railroads into large systems. He combined smaller electrical concerns into General Electric in 1892 and then pulled a collection of manufacturers into the International Harvester Company, which started with 85 percent of the farm machinery market. In 1901 he created the first billion-dollar company when he merged 785 separate firms to form the United States Steel Company with capitalization of 11.4 billion.

Morgan and two of his close associates together held 341 corporate directorships. His power was very independent of government controls since at the time antitrust laws were little enforced, there was no national bank to regulate the money supply, and existing securities and banking laws were rudimentary. One awestruck biographer said that Morgan "was a God" who "ruled for a generation the pitiless, predatory world of cash.[44] His critics were less kind. Senator Robert W. La Follette once called him "a beefy, red-faced, thick-necked financial bully, drunk with wealth and power."[45]

In October 1907 panic swept Wall Street and stocks plummeted as frantic investors sold shares. Soon banks suffered runs of withdrawals and were on the verge of failure. Liquidity, or the free flow of money, was fast vanishing from financial markets, and the nation's banking system teetered on the verge of collapse. So influential was Morgan that he commanded the New York Stock Exchange to stay open all day on October 24 to maintain investor confidence. To support it, he raised $25 million of credit.

The federal government could do little to ease the crisis. President Theodore Roosevelt was off hunting bears in Louisiana, an ironic pursuit in light of the crashing stock market. Without a national bank, the government had no capacity to increase the money supply and restore liquidity. Powerless, Secretary of the Treasury George B. Cortelyou traveled to New York to get Morgan's advice

On the evening of October 24, Morgan gathered members of the New York banking elite at his private library. He played solitaire while in another room the assembled bankers discussed methods for resolving the crisis. Periodically, someone came to him with a proposal, several of which he rejected. Finally, a plan was hatched in which $33 million would be raised to support the stock exchange and failing banks. Where would this money come from? The secretary of the treasury was to supply $10 million in government funds, John D. Rockefeller contributed $10 million, and Morgan the remaining $13 million.

This action stabilized the economy. Perhaps it demonstrates that elite power may be exercised in the common good. It should be noted, however, that the panic of 1907—and other panics of that era—came after Morgan and other titans of finance repeatedly choked the stock exchange with the colossal stock offerings needed to finance their new combinations.

Morgan was widely criticized for his role in ending the panic of 1907. Conspiracy theorists, suspicious of so much power resident in one man, attacked him. Upton Sinclair, for example, accused him of inciting the panic for self-gain, a wildly erroneous accusation. In 1912 Morgan was the focus of congressional hearings which concluded that he led a "money trust" that controlled the nation's finances and that this was bad for the nation. Death claimed him in 1913 just before Congress passed the Federal Reserve Act to set up a central bank and ensure that no private banker would ever again be sole caretaker of the money supply.

[44] John K. Winkler, *Morgan the Magnificent* (New York: Doubleday, 1950), p. 3; originally published in 1930.

[45] Jean Strouse, *Morgan: American Financier* (New York: Random House, 2000), p. x.

laws apply equally to all. All interests have the right to be heard. To be legitimate, power must be exercised for the common good.

Second, America encompasses a large population spread over a wide geography and engaged in diverse occupations. It has a great mixture of interests, more than some other countries. Economic interests, including labor, banking, manufacturing, agriculture, and consumers, are a permanent fixture. A rainbow of voluntary associations (whose size, longevity, and influence vary) compete in governments at all levels.

Third, the Constitution encourages pluralism. Its guarantees of rights protect the freedom of individuals to form associations and freely to express and pursue interests. Thus, business is challenged by human rights, environmental, and other groups. The Constitution diffuses political power through the three branches of the federal government and between the federal and state governments and to the people. This creates a remarkably open political system.

In addition, business is exposed to constraining market pressures that force a stream of resource allocation decisions centered on cost reduction and consumer satisfaction, forces that can fell even the mighty. Henry J. Kaiser seemed unerring in business. The son of German immigrants, he worked his way up from store clerk to owner of 32 companies, including seven shipyards that launched one finished ship a day during most of World War II. When he started an auto company in 1945, nobody thought he could fail. Eager customers put down thousands of deposits before a single car was built.[46] But his cars, the Kaiser and the Frazier, were underpowered and overpriced, and the market eventually rejected them. Kaiser never got costs under control; he had to negotiate the prices of many parts with competing auto companies that made them. Toward the end, he built a model that was sold at Sears as the Allstate. This was a terrible mistake because it gave the car a low-quality image with consumers. The venture failed.

In sum, predictable and strong forces in a pluralistic, free market society limit business power. Wise managers anticipate that, despite having considerable influence on governments, markets, and public opinion, their power can be restricted, challenged, or shared by others. Overall, as illustrated in Figure 3.2, there are four major boundaries on managerial power.

1. *Governments and laws* in all countries regulate business activity. Governments are the ultimate arbiters of legitimate behavior and can act forcefully to blunt the exercise of corporate power that harms the public. Laws channel and regulate operations.

2. *Social interest groups* represent every segment of global society and have many ways to restrict business, including boycotts, lawsuits, picket lines, media campaigns, and lobbying for more regulation. Historically, labor has been the great antagonist and counterweight to business power, but also prominent in recent years are environmental, human rights, religious, and consumer groups. Increasingly, groups form coalitions with other groups, governments, and international institutions.

---

[46] Robert Sobel, "The $150 Million Lemon," *Audacity,* Winter 1997, p. 11.

FIGURE 3.2
Boundaries of Managerial Power

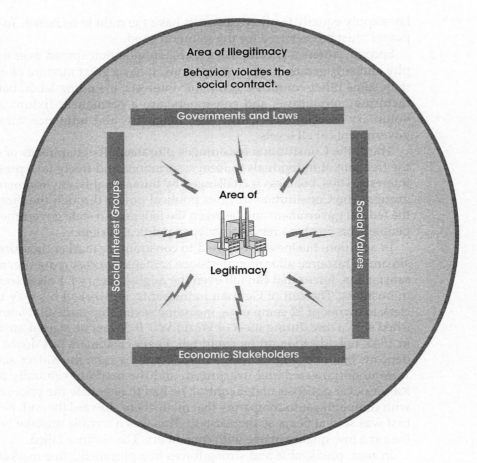

Area of Illegitimacy

Behavior violates the social contract.

Governments and Laws

Social Interest Groups

Social Values

Area of

Legitimacy

Economic Stakeholders

3. *Social values* are transmitted across generations, reflected in public opinion, and embedded in the law. Managers internalize them in schools and churches. Social values include norms of duty, justice, truth, and piety that can direct a manager's behavior as powerfully as laws. For example, in the 1960s shifting generational values gave film studios license to experiment with brazen nudity and violence, but Walt Disney never did. No financial incentive was enough to make him forsake his own values about the importance of morality, family life, and the small-town decency he saw in his Kansas boyhood.[47]

4. *Markets and economic stakeholders* impose strong limits. Stockholders, employees, suppliers, creditors, and competitors influence corporate decisions. The market also registers the great waves of technological change that can sweep away even the largest corporations.

According to the theory of pluralism, these are the boundaries of managerial power. Just as in the solar system the planets move freely within but cannot escape

[47] Richard Schickel, *The Disney Version*, 3rd ed. (Chicago: Ivan R. Dee, 1997), p. 39.

their gravitational fields, so major corporations in American society move within orbits constrained by plural interests.

CONCLUDING OBSERVATIONS

In a recent poll, 87 percent of Americans believed that "big companies . . . have too much . . . power and influence."[48] Are they correct? The answer requires perspective and judgment. In this chapter we break down the idea of corporate power into patterns, categories, and theories to allow critical thinking. We explain how corporate power is a strong force for change and how, at a deep level, economic growth shapes society in sweeping, unplanned ways.

We also set forth two opposing perspectives. The dominance theory holds that inadequately restrained economic power is concentrated in large corporations and in the hands of a wealthy elite. The pluralist theory holds that many restraints in an open society control corporate power. These theories are locked in perpetual conflict. Both are molds into which varieties of evidence must be fitted. Both contain insights, but neither has a lock on accuracy. And both attract adherents based on inner judgments about whether market capitalism moves society in the right direction.

If corporate power remains generally accountable to democratic controls, society will accord it legitimacy. If rule by law and a just economy exist, corporate power will broadly and ultimately be directed toward the public welfare, this despite the habitual breakouts of deviltry that inflame critics.

[48] The Harris Poll, "Business Divides: Big Companies Have Too Much Power and Influence in DC, Small Business Has Too Little," April 1, 2010, table 2, at www.harrisinteractive.com.

John D. Rockefeller and the Standard Oil Trust

This is the story of John D. Rockefeller, founder of the Standard Oil Company. It is the story of a somber, small-town boy who dominated the oil industry with organizational genius, audacity, and ruthless, methodical execution. He became the richest man in America and, for a time, the most hated.

Rockefeller's life spanned nearly 98 years. At his birth Martin Van Buren was president and settlers drove covered wagons over the Oregon Trail. He lived to see Franklin Roosevelt's New Deal, watch the rise of the Nazi party in Germany, and hear Frank Sinatra and *The Lone Ranger* on radio.

The historical backdrop of this lifetime is an economy gripped by the fever of industrial progress. Rockefeller built his fortune in an era that lacked many of today's ethical norms and commercial laws,

an era in which the power of a corporation and its founder could be exercised with fewer restraints.

THE FORMATIVE YEARS

John Davison Rockefeller was born July 8, 1839, in a small village in southern New York. He was the second of six children and the oldest boy. His father, William Rockefeller, was an itinerant quack doctor who sold worthless elixirs. He was jovial, slick, and cunning and made enough money to keep the family in handsome style until he had to flee and live away from home to avoid arrest for raping a local woman. After that, he visited only in the dark of night. But he taught young John D. and his brothers lessons of business conduct, especially that sentimentality should not influence business transactions. "I cheat my boys every chance I get," he once said. "I want to make 'em sharp."[1]

John D.'s mother was a somber, religious woman who gave the children a strict upbringing, emphasizing manners, church attendance, and the work ethic. She preached homilies such as "Willful waste makes woeful want." And she taught charity to the children; from an early age John D. made regular contributions to worthy causes.

Young John D. was not precocious in school. In high school he was an uninspired student, little interested in books and ideas, but willing to work hard. He grew into a somber, intense lad nicknamed "the Deacon" by his classmates because he faithfully attended a Baptist church and memorized hymns. In the summer of 1855 he took a three-month course at a business college in Cleveland, Ohio, and then set out looking for a job. In addition to his formal schooling, he carried the contradictory temperaments of his parents—the wily, self-assured boldness of his father and the exacting, pietistic character of his mother. He internalized both, and the combination was to prove formidable. Here was a man with the precision of an accountant and the cunning of Cesare Borgia.

EARLY BUSINESS CAREER

Rockefeller's first job was as a bookkeeper at a Cleveland firm where he meticulously examined each bill submitted and pounced on errors. He also recorded every cent he earned and spent in a personal ledger. Its pages show that he was parsimonious and saved most of his $25-a-month salary, but that he still gave generously to the Baptist church and the poor.

In 1859 he formed a successful partnership with two others in the produce business in Cleveland and proved himself an intense negotiator, described by an acquaintance as a person "who can walk right up on a man's shirt bosom and sit down."[2] The business boomed from supplying food to the Union army during the Civil War. Although in his early 20s at the time, the steady, unemotional lad was never touched by patriotic fervor. In those days, the law permitted

any man of means to pay someone else to serve in his place, and this he did.

BEGINNINGS OF THE OIL BUSINESS

Profits from the produce business were high, and John D. looked around for a promising new investment. He soon found one—a Cleveland petroleum refinery in which he invested $4,000 in 1863. At the time, petroleum production and refining was an infant industry. A new drilling technology had led to an 1859 oil strike in nearby Pennsylvania, followed by a frenzied boom in drilling and refining.

Soon Rockefeller devoted himself to the oil business, and he began to apply his principles of parsimony. One basic principle was to avoid paying a profit to anyone. For example, instead of buying barrels and paying the cooper $2.50 each, Rockefeller set up his own barrel-making factory and made them for $.96. He purchased a forest to make staves from his own trees. Another basic principle was methodical cost cutting. Lumber for barrel staves was kiln-dried before shipment to the cooperage plant. Water evaporated from the wood, making it lighter and lowering transportation costs.

Though obsessed with details and small economies, Rockefeller also proved aggressive in larger plans. He borrowed heavily from banks to expand the refinery. The risk scared his partners, so he bought them out. In 1865 he borrowed more to build a second refinery. Soon he incorporated an export sales company in New York, making the world his market.

DYNAMICS OF THE OIL INDUSTRY

During this early period, the new industry was in a chaotic state. A basic cause was overproduction in the Pennsylvania oil regions, which were the only source of crude oil. The price of crude fluctuated wildly, but was in long-term decline. Each drop in the price of crude oil encouraged construction of new refineries and by the late 1860s refining capacity was three times greater than oil production. This caused vicious price wars. Some refiners tried to stay in business by selling products at a loss to raise cash for continued debt payments. In doing so, they dragged down profit margins for all refiners.

---

[1] David Freeman Hawke, *John D.: The Founding Father of the Rockefellers* (New York: Harper & Row, 1980), p. 13.

[2] Jules Abels, *The Rockefeller Billions* (New York: Macmillan, 1965), p. 35.

Rockefeller had the insight to invest in large-scale refineries and, because he cut costs relentlessly, his refineries made money. Yet despite disciplined cost control, the market forces of a sick industry ate away at his net earnings. He believed it was time to "rationalize" the entire industry and stop destructive competition.[3] His method for doing this would be monopoly, his tactics hard-nosed.

ROCKEFELLER'S COMPETITIVE STRATEGIES

Rockefeller used a range of competitive strategies. He was a low-cost, high-volume producer. He used debt financing to expand. He attempted to make his refined petroleum products of high and consistent quality, since fly-by-night refiners turned out inferior distillates. Cheap kerosene with a low ignition point had burned many a home down after exploding in a wick lamp. When he incorporated the Standard Oil Company of Ohio in 1870, the name suggested a "standard oil" of uniformly good quality. He engaged in vertical integration by making wooden barrels. As time when on, he also bought pipelines, storage tanks, and railroad tank cars.

Critical to his success, however, was the art of strong-arming the railroads. In this, Rockefeller was the master. Transportation costs paid to railroads were important to refiners, who shipped in crude oil and then shipped out products such as kerosene or lubricating oil. In the 1860s railroads were highly competitive and often altered shipping rates to attract business. No law prohibited this, and published rates were only the starting point of negotiations.

Railroads often granted *rebates* to shippers; that is, they returned part of the freight charge after shipment. These rebates were usually secret and given in return for the guarantee of future business. Large volume shippers, including oil refineries, got the biggest rebates. Standard Oil was no exception.

At this time, Rockefeller has been described by biographers as a prepossessing man with penetrating eyes who drove a hard bargain. He would take the measure of a person with a withering stare, and few were his match. He was formidable in negotiations, being invariably informed in detail about the other's

business. And he was still a pious churchgoer who read the Bible nightly before retiring.

Late in 1870 Rockefeller hatched a brazen plan for stabilizing the oil industry at the refining level. In clandestine meetings, he worked out a rebate scheme between a few major refiners and the three railroads going into the Pennsylvania oil regions. They gave this scheme an innocent-sounding name, the South Improvement Plan. In it, the railroads agreed to increase published rates for hauling oil. Then Rockefeller's Cleveland refineries and a few others would get large rebates on each barrel shipped. For example, the regular rate between the oil regions and Cleveland would be $.80 a barrel and between Cleveland and New York $2.00 a barrel. It would cost a total of $2.80 per barrel for any other refinery in Cleveland to bring in a barrel of crude oil and ship a barrel of refined oil to New York for sale or export. Rockefeller and his accomplices, on the other hand, would be charged $2.80 but then get a rebate of $.90.

In addition, the refineries participating in the South Improvement Plan received *drawbacks* or payments made on the shipment of oil by competitors! Thus, Rockefeller would be paid $.40 on every barrel of crude oil his competitors shipped into Cleveland and $.50 on every barrel of refined oil shipped to New York. Under this venal scheme, the more a competitor shipped, the more Rockefeller's transportation costs were lowered. While competitors were charged $2.80 on the critical route (Pennsylvania oil regions–Cleveland–New York), Rockefeller paid only $1.00. Moreover, the railroads agreed to give the conspirators waybills detailing competitors' shipments; a better espionage system would be hard to find.

Why did the railroads agree to this plot? There were several reasons. First, it removed the uncertainty of cutthroat competition. Oil traffic was guaranteed in large volume. Second, the refiners provided services to the railroads including tank cars, loading facilities, and insurance. And third, railroad executives received stock in the participating refineries, giving them a stake in their success.

The consequences of the South Improvement Plan were predictable. Nonparticipating refiners faced bloated transportation costs and would be uncompetitive. They had two choices. Either they could sell to Rockefeller and his allies, or they could stand on principle and go bankrupt. When they sold, as they must, the flaw in industry structure would be corrected. Rockefeller intended to acquire them, then

[3] Ron Chernow, *Titan: The Life of John D. Rockefeller, Sr.* (New York: Random House, 1998), pp. 130 and 149–52.

close them or limit their capacity. This would give him market power to stabilize the price of both crude oil and refined products. And the rebates would be a formidable barrier to new entrants.

THE CONSPIRACY PLAYS OUT

In February 1872 the new freight rates were announced. Quickly, the full design was revealed, causing widespread, explosive rage in the oil regions. Although it broke no laws, it overstepped prevailing norms. People believed that since railroads got their right-of-ways from the public they had a duty to serve shippers fairly. Volume discounts might be justified, but this shakedown was extortionate. Producers and refiners in the oil regions boycotted the conspirators and the railroads.

Rockefeller, seen as the prime mover behind the South Improvement Plan, was vilified in the industry and the press. His wife feared for his life. Yet he never wavered. "It was right," he said of the plan. "I knew it as a matter of conscience. It was right between me and my God."[4] As journalist Ida Tarbell noted, Rockefeller was not squeamish about such business affairs.

> Mr. Rockefeller was "good." There was no more faithful Baptist in Cleveland than he. Every enterprise of that church he had supported liberally from his youth. He gave to its poor. He visited its sick. He wept with its suffering. Moreover, he gave unostentatiously to many outside charities . . . Yet he was willing to strain every nerve to obtain himself special and unjust privileges from the railroads which were bound to ruin every man in the oil business not sharing them with him.[5]

Within a month, the weight of negative public opinion and loss of revenue caused the railroads to cave in. They rescinded the discriminatory rate structure. All appearances were of a Rockefeller defeat, but appearances deceived. Rockefeller had moved quickly, meeting one by one with rival refiners, explaining the rebate scheme and its salutary effect on the industry, and asking to buy them out. He offered the exact value of the business in cash or, preferably, in Standard Oil Company stock.

By the time the railroads reset their rates, Rockefeller had bought out 21 of his 26 Cleveland competitors. Some acquisitions were simply dismantled to reduce surplus capacity. He now dominated Cleveland, the country's major refining center, and controlled more than a quarter of U.S. capacity. In secrecy, he negotiated a new rebate agreement with the Erie Railroad. Of these actions, Ida Tarbell noted sardonically: "He had a mind which, stopped by a wall, burrows under or creeps around."[6]

Regardless of methods, he had, indeed, corrected structural flaws in the oil industry. It would attract more capital. If any circumstance cast a shadow over this striking victory, it was that public opinion had turned against him. From then on, he was reviled as an unfair competitor, hatred of him growing apace with his burgeoning wealth. He never understood why.

ONWARD THE COURSE OF EMPIRE

Rockefeller, now 33, was wealthy. Yet he drove on, compelled to finish a grand design, to spread his pattern over the industry landscape, to conform it to his vision.

He continued the strategy of horizontal integration at the refinery level by absorbing more and more of his competitors. As the size of Standard Oil increased, Rockefeller gained added leverage over the railroads. Like an orchestra conductor he played them against each other, granting shares of the oil traffic in return for rebates that gave him a decisive advantage.

Some competitors stubbornly clung to their businesses, partly out of hatred for Rockefeller. He made them "sweat" and "feel sick" until they sold.[7] The fleets of tank cars that he leased to railroads were often "unavailable" to ship feedstock and distillates to and from such refiners. Rockefeller concealed many of his acquisitions, disguising the full sweep of his drive to monopoly. These companies were the Trojan horses in his war against rival refiners. They seemed independent but secretly helped to undermine Standard's competitors. Often they were at the center of elaborate pricing conspiracies involving code words in telegrams such as "doubters" for

[4] Peter Collier and David Horowitz, *The Rockefellers: An American Dynasty* (New York: New American Library, 1976), p. 11.

[5] Ida M. Tarbell, *The History of the Standard Oil Company*, vol. 1 (Gloucester, MA: Peter Smith, 1963), p. 43.

[6] Ibid., p. 99.

[7] Abels, *The Rockefeller Billions*, p. 35.

refiners and "mixer" for railroad drawbacks. The phantoms bought some refiners who refused in principle to sell out to Standard Oil. Their existence confronted independents with a dark, mysterious force that could not be brought into the light and fought.

THE STANDARD OIL TRUST

By 1882 Rockefeller's company was capitalized at $70 million and produced 90 percent of the nation's refining output. Its main product, illuminating oil, was changing the way people lived. Before the sale of affordable illuminating oil of good quality, most Americans went to bed with darkness. They could not afford expensive candles or whale oil and feared using the unstable kerosene made by early, small refiners. With the rise of Rockefeller's colossus, they had reliable, inexpensive light and stayed up. Their lives, and the life of the nation, changed.

Rockefeller reorganized Standard Oil as a trust.[8] His purpose was to make state regulation more difficult. Soon other large companies followed his lead, adopting the trust form to avoid government restrictions. Inside Standard Oil, Rockefeller's organizing skills were extraordinary. Working with a loyal inner circle of managers, he directed his far-flung empire from headquarters at 26 Broadway in New York City. As he absorbed his competitors, so had he co-opted the best minds in the industry and much of Standard's success is attributable to this stellar supporting cast. Though dominant, Rockefeller delegated great responsibility to his managers.

High-level committees controlled business operations. He circulated monthly cost statements for each refinery, causing fierce internal competition among their managers that led to high performance. He set up a network of informants around the globe. Critics called them spies, but they functioned as a well-organized information system.

A perfectionist, he insisted on having a statement of the exact net worth of Standard Oil on his desk every morning. Oil prices always were calculated to three decimals. He was so dogged about efficiency and recycling that his Standard Oil plants might win

environmental awards were they operating today. At night he prowled the headquarters turning down wicks in oil lamps.

His management style was one of formal politeness. He never spoke harshly to any employee. Once, when a manager leaked information to the press, Rockefeller said to his secretary: "Suggest to Mr. Blank that he would do admirably as a newspaper man, and that we shall not need his services after the close of this month."[9] Compared with other moguls of that era, he lived simply. He had two large estates, in Cleveland and New York, but neither was too ostentatious. He read the Bible daily, continued regular attendance at a Baptist church, and gave generously to charities.

Rockefeller's organizing skills were critical to his success. Discussions often focus on his ethics, but the key to Standard Oil's long-term domination lay elsewhere. The company was an immense, organized force opposed only by smaller, less united adversaries. Its success came from centralized, coordinated effort. Compromising methods, to the extent they were used, were of far less importance.[10]

EXTENDING DOMINATION

By the 1880s Standard Oil had overwhelming market power. Its embrace of refining activity was virtually complete, and it had moved into drilling, pipelines, storage tanks, transportation, and marketing of finished products. By now the entire world was addicted to kerosene and other petroleum products, and Standard's international sales grew.

Rockefeller's dominating competitive philosophy prevailed. His marketing agents were ordered to destroy independent suppliers. To suppress competition, his employees pioneered fanatical customer service. The intelligence-gathering network paid competitors' employees to pass information to Standard Oil. Railroad agents were bribed to misroute shipments. Standard Oil workers climbed on competitors' tank cars and measured the contents. Price warfare was relentless. A stubborn competitor often

---

[8] A trust is a method of controlling a number of companies in which the voting stock of each company is transferred to a board of trustees. The trustees then have the power to coordinate the operations of all companies in the group. This organizing form is no longer legal in the United States.

[9] Quoted in "A Great Monopoly's Work: An Inner View of the Standard Oil Company," *The New York Times,* February 27, 1883, p. 1.

[10] David M. Chalmers, ed., "Introductory Essay," in Ida M. Tarbell, *The History of the Standard Oil Company, Briefer Version* (Mineola, NY: Dover, 2003), pp. xvii–xviii.

found Standard selling kerosene to its customers at a price substantially below production cost.

Rockefeller himself was never proved to be directly involved in flagrant misconduct. He blamed criminal and unethical actions on overzealous subordinates. His critics thought the strategy of suffocating small rivals and policies such as that requiring regular written intelligence reports encouraged degenerative ethics among his minions.

Rockefeller saw Standard Oil as a stabilizing force in the industry and as a righteous crusade to illuminate the world. How, as a good Christian devoted to the moral injunctions of the Bible, was Rockefeller able to suborn such vicious behavior in commerce? One biographer, Allan Nevins, gives this explanation:

> From a chaotic industry he was building an efficient industrial empire for what seemed to him the good not only of its heads but of the general public. If he relaxed his general methods of warfare . . . a multitude of small competitors would smash his empire and plunge the oil business back to chaos. He always believed in what William McKinley called "benevolent assimilation"; he preferred to buy out rivals on decent terms, and to employ the ablest competitors as helpers. It was when his terms were refused that he ruthlessly crushed the "outsiders." . . . It seemed to him better that a limited number of small businesses should die than that the whole industry should go through a constant process of half-dying, reviving, and again half-dying.[11]

THE STANDARD OIL TRUST UNDER ATTACK

Standard Oil continued to grow, doubling in size before the turn of the century and doubling again by 1905.[12] Eventually its very size brought a flood of criticism that complicated operations. Predatory monopoly was at odds with prevailing beliefs about individual rights and free competition. The states tried to regulate Standard Oil and filed antitrust suits against it. Overwrought muckrakers lashed out at Rockefeller. Because of him, wrote one, "hundreds and thousands of men have been ruined."[13] He was the personification of greed in political cartoons. Politicians not suborned by his bribery lambasted him.

Rockefeller, by now the richest American, was shaken by public hatred. He hired bodyguards and slept with a revolver. Pinkerton detectives were present at church on Sundays to handle gawkers and shouters. He developed a digestive ailment so severe that he could eat only a few bland foods, and upon his doctor's advice he stopped daily office work. By 1896 he appeared only rarely at 26 Broadway. Soon he was afflicted with a nervous disorder and lost all his hair.

As attacks on Rockefeller grew, the vise of government regulation tightened on his company. A swarm of lawsuits and legislative hearings hung about it. Finally, in 1911, the Supreme Court ordered its breakup under the Sherman Antitrust Act, holding that its monopoly position was an "undue" restraint on trade that violated the "standard of reason."[14] The company was given six months to separate into 39 independent firms. The breakup consisted mainly of moving the desks of managers at 26 Broadway and was a financial windfall for Rockefeller, who received shares of stock in all the companies, the prices of which were driven up by frenzied public buying. Before the breakup kerosene sales had buoyed the company. However, just as electric lightbulbs were replacing oil lamps, the automobile jolted demand for another petroleum distillate—gasoline. Rockefeller, who was 71 at the time of the breakup and would live another 26 years, earned new fortunes simply by maintaining his equity in the separate companies.

Rockefeller remained a source of fascination for the American public. As *The Wall Street Journal* noted, "The richest man in a world where money is power is necessarily a fascinating object of study."[15] This being so, it was his enduring misfortune that muckraking journalist Ida Tarbell turned her gaze on him.

Tarbell wrote two unflattering character studies and a detailed, two-volume biography of Rockefeller, all serialized in the widely read *McClure's Magazine* between 1902 and 1905. Her unsentimental words were no less ruthless than the actions of the old man himself. Although admitting that Rockefeller and Standard Oil

---

[11] Allan Nevins, *Study in Power: John D. Rockefeller,* vol. 2 (New York: Scribner, 1953), p. 433.

[12] Ibid., app. 3, p. 478.

[13] Henry Demarest Lloyd, "Story of a Great Monopoly," *The Atlantic,* March 1881, p. 320.

[14] *Standard Oil Company of New Jersey v. United States,* 31 U.S. 221. It was an 8–1 decision.

[15] "Incarnate Business," *The Wall Street Journal,* June 26, 1905, p. 1.

had some measure of "legitimate greatness," she was obsessed with his flaws. In one essay she found "something indefinably repulsive" in his appearance, writing that his mouth was "the cruelest feature of his face," and that his nose "rose like a thorn."[16] Such ad hominem attacks lacked merit but, in addition, Tarbell delved deeply into Rockefeller's career, producing narratives of exquisite detail. The thesis she conveyed to the public was that by his singular example, Rockefeller was responsible for debasing the moral tone of American business. She believed his story incited legions of the ambitious to use cold-blooded methods, teaching them that success justifies itself. Like the master, the junior scoundrels often cited biblical verse to support their actions.

Few public figures have a nemesis such as Ida Tarbell. Her relentless pen, along with others, deprived him of some public adulation he may have craved and her scholarship permanently defined him. Her intricate period research cannot be duplicated and subsequent biographers, even more friendly ones, must go to it for insight. Rockefeller may or may not have deserved such a definitive hand. He called her a "poisonous woman."[17]

THE GREAT ALMONER

Since childhood Rockefeller had made charitable donations and, as his fortune accumulated, he increased them. After 1884 the total was never less than $100,000 a year, and after 1892 it was usually over $1 million and sometimes far more. In his mind, these benefactions were linked to his duty as a good Christian to uplift humanity. To a reporter he once said:

> I believe the power to make money is a gift from God—just as are the instincts for art, music, literature, the doctor's talent, yours—to be developed and used to the best of our ability for the good of mankind. Having been endowed with the gift I possess, I believe it is my duty to make money and still more money and to use the money I make for the good of my fellow-man according to the dictates of my conscience.[18]

Over his lifetime, Rockefeller gave gifts of approximately $550 million. He gave, for example, $8.2 million for the construction of Peking Union Medical College in response to the need to educate doctors in China. He gave $50 million to the University of Chicago. He created charitable trusts and endowed them with millions. One such trust was the General Education Board, set up in 1902, which started 1,600 new high schools. Another, the Rockefeller Sanitary Commission, succeeded in eradicating hookworm in the South. The largest was the Rockefeller Foundation, established in 1913 and endowed with $200 million. Its purpose was "to promote the well-being of mankind throughout the world." Rockefeller always said, however, that the greatest philanthropy of all was developing the earth's natural resources and employing people. Critics greeted his gifts with skepticism, thinking them atonement for years of plundering American society.

In his later years, Rockefeller lived a secluded, placid existence on his great Pocantico estate in New York, which had 75 buildings and 70 miles of roads. As years passed, the public grew increasingly fond of him. Memories of his early business career dimmed, and a new generation viewed him in the glow of his

John D. Rockefeller at age 65. This photograph was taken shortly after a disease, generalized alopecia, caused him to lose his hair. Source: The Library of Congress.

[16] Ida Tarbell, "John D. Rockefeller: A Character Study," *McClure's*, August 1905, p. 386.

[17] Chernow, *Titan: The Life of John D. Rockefeller, Sr.*, p. xxii.

[18] Quoted in Abels, *The Rockefeller Billions*, p. 280.

huge charitable contributions. For many years, he carried shiny nickels and dimes in his pockets to give to children and well-wishers.

On his 86th birthday he wrote the following verse.

> I was early taught to work as well as play,
> My life has been one long, happy holiday;
> Full of work and full of play—
> I dropped the worry on the way—
> And God was good to me every day.

He died in 1937 at the age of 97. His estate was valued at $26,410,837. He had given the rest away.

Questions

1. With reference to the levels and spheres of corporate power discussed in the chapter, how did the power of Standard Oil change society? Was this power exercised in keeping with the social contract of Rockefeller's era?

2. How does the story of Standard Oil illustrate the limits of business power? Does it better illustrate the dominance theory or the pluralist theory discussed in the chapter?

3. Did Rockefeller himself ever act unethically? By the standards of his day? By those of today? How could he simultaneously be a devout Christian and a ruthless monopolist? Is there any contradiction between his personal and business ethics?

4. In the utilitarian sense of accomplishing the greatest good for the greatest number in society, was the Standard Oil Company a net plus or a minus? On balance, did the company meet its responsibilities to society?

5. Did strategies of Standard Oil encourage unethical behavior? Could Rockefeller's vision have been fulfilled using "nicer" tactics?

Chapter Four

Critics of Business

Mary "Mother" Jones

In the early years of the twentieth century Mary Jones (1837–1930), known as Mother Jones, was one of the most notable women in America. Emerging from personal tragedy, she created a singular persona and hurled herself against big corporations and the capitalist system that sustained them. Hers was an era of great change, dissent, and conflict. It was the ideal stage for a defiant performance.

She was born in 1837 as Mary Harris in Cork, Ireland. When she was eight years old, a fungus blighted the nation's potato crop, causing a terrible famine. She emigrated with her family to Toronto and there grew up, graduated from a convent school, and became a schoolteacher. Eventually she moved to Memphis and married an iron molder named George Jones. Between 1862 and 1867 they had four children. She devoted herself to cooking, cleaning, and sewing for the family. Then yellow fever struck.

The deadly epidemic came in the fall of 1867. As mortality rose, rich families left town, leaving those who could not afford travel to become victims. The sounds of death carts taking bodies away filled neighborhoods. Mary Jones describes what happened to her.

> All about my house I could hear weeping and the cries of delirium. One by one, my four little children sickened and died. I washed their little bodies and got them ready for burial. My husband caught the fever and died. I sat alone through nights of grief. No one came to me. No one could.[1]

She nursed the sick until the plague ended, then returned to Chicago to set up a dressmaking business. She often worked for wealthy society matrons.

> I had ample opportunity to observe the luxury and extravagance of their lives. Often while sewing for the lords and barons who lived in magnificence on the Lake Shore Drive, I would look out of the plate glass windows and see the poor, shivering wretches, jobless and hungry, walking along the frozen lake front. The contrast of their condition with that of the tropical comfort of the people for whom I sewed was painful to me. My employers seemed neither to notice nor to care.[2]

---

[1] Mary Field Parton, ed., *The Autobiography of Mother Jones* (Chicago: C. H. Kerr, 1925), p. 12.
[2] Ibid., chap. 1, p. 13.

Several years passed, then in 1871 the Great Chicago Fire burned her business and left her destitute. After the fire she attended evening meetings of the Knights of Labor, an early union, becoming absorbed in the fight of industrial workers for better wages and conditions. The perspective of class war began to dominate her view of society. She felt that workers were enslaved by corporate employers and by the corrupt politicians and judges who did their bidding. She believed that only by overthrowing capitalism could the laboring class end its bondage and usher in a new day of socialism, so she joined a small socialist political party.

For almost two decades Mary Jones worked in obscurity for labor causes and during this time she created the persona that would make her powerful and famous. Mary Jones became Mother Jones. The loss of her own family had freed her to take on another, to adopt the downtrodden. In an era when women had no vote, held no leadership positions, and received no encouragement to speak up, she would use this metaphor of motherhood to give her power.

She rose to prominence as an organizer for the United Mine Workers. Horrible working conditions prevailed in coal mines. Miners worked 10- and 12-hour days in damp, dusty, cramped, dangerous tunnels. Wages were so low that mining families put their children to work to get by. Boys as young as eight years old toiled six or seven days a week, some spending so many hours in cramped shafts that their bones grew irregularly and they could not stand straight as adults. Textile mills were built near mining towns to employ the miners' wives and daughters. The United Mine Workers wanted to unionize the miners, but the coal companies viciously resisted. Organizers were followed and observed. Miners who shook an organizer's hand were fired. Hired thugs beat up troublemakers. Companies had friendly judges convene lunacy hearings and commit prounion employees to asylums. The miners wanted unions, but they were intimidated.

In the late 1890s Mother Jones arrived in Pennsylvania coal country. At 60 years old she looked like a grandmother. She stood five feet tall with silver hair and sharp blue eyes. With great energy she worked the coal towns. She was an explosive orator with a vocal range from shrill cries to a forceful, low pitch that mesmerized listeners. She knew the miners' language and spoke in colorful terms, calling mine owners "a crew of pirates," "a gang of thieves," and "cowards." She called the men her "boys" and as their "mother" told them to stand up to the companies.

During a bitter strike in 1900 when some miners were losing their nerve, she organized marches of the miners' wives. The women paraded to work sites wearing aprons, waving mops, and banging pans. Laughing company guards saw no danger from the comical processions and let them through, not realizing how Mother Jones had cleverly dramatized the role of aggrieved wives and mothers fighting for the welfare of their families. She scolded the men, telling them they were shamed if their wives stood up to the companies and they did not.

Mother Jones used ironic wit to puncture establishment pretensions. In 1902 she was arrested in West Virginia after the coal companies got an injunction against union organizing. In court, the judge suspended her sentence, but advised her that as a woman it would be "better far for her to follow the lines and paths which the Allwise Being intended her sex should pursue." She appreciated the advice, she said, adding that it was no surprise he was taking the company's side, since

Mary "Mother" Jones. Source: Library of Congress.

experience had taught her that "robbers tend to like each other."[3] When asked by a Princeton professor to address his class, she brought with her a stooped and pale 10-year-old boy. "Here's a textbook on economics," she said. "He gets three dollars a week . . . [working] in a carpet factory ten hours a day while the children of the rich are getting higher education."[4] She had a favorite story for audiences: "I asked a man in prison once how he happened to get there. He had stolen a pair of shoes. I told him that if he had stolen a railroad he could be a United States Senator."[5]

Eventually, Mother Jones fell out with the United Mine Workers because she was more militant than its leadership. She became a lecturer for the Socialist Party, but in time she renounced socialism. She was a doer, not an ideologue, and she lacked patience with hairsplitting doctrinal debates among intellectuals who led comfortable lives. However, in 1905 she helped launch the International Workers of the World (IWW), a radical union dedicated to overthrowing American capitalism. By 1911 she had returned to the front lines in mining regions. Later, she marched with striking

[3] Gene R. Nichol, Jr., "Fighting Poverty with Virtue," *Michigan Law Review,* May 2002, p. 1661.

[4] Quoted in Marilyn Jurich, "The Female Trickster—Known as Trickstar—As Exemplified by Two American Legendary Women, 'Billy' Tipton and Mother Jones," *Journal of American Culture,* Spring 1999, p. 69.

[5] "Mother Jones Speaks to Coney Island Crowd," *The New York Times,* July 27, 1903.

garment and streetcar workers in New York City. In 1916 she started a riot by 200 wives of streetcar workers with an inflammatory speech, telling them: "You ought to be out raising hell."[6]

By the 1920s Mother Jones had grown disillusioned with unions. She quit the IWW saying it was more interested in symbolic displays than in concrete victories. Other unions had grown comfortable with the corporate establishment. She had contempt for union leaders motivated by their own importance and called John L. Lewis, president of the United Mine Workers, a "pie counter hunter."[7] She retired from public life, speaking out now and then, and died in 1930 at the age of 92.

Today Mother Jones is little remembered. Her time passed, and the specific labor abuses that enraged her are mostly ended. Perhaps her invective is unmatched today. She defined "monster capitalism," as a "robber system" supported by the "national gang of burglars of Wall Street." The corporations she attacked had "snake brains" and were run by "idiots" and "commercial pirates." But her ideas live on. Although her life was unique in its tragedy and drama, her attacks were based on enduring values that recycle through time. We may forget Mother Jones, but we hear her in today's business critics. In this chapter we explore the birth and life of these values.

ORIGINS OF CRITICAL ATTITUDES TOWARD BUSINESS

There are two underlying sources of criticism of business, one ancient and the other modern. The first is the belief that people in business place profit before more worthy values such as honesty, truth, justice, love, piety, aesthetics, tranquility, and respect for nature. The second is the strain of economic development. During industrialization and later, when market economies grow large and complex, business has a range of problematic impacts on societies. We will discuss both fundamental sources of criticism. We begin in the ancient Mediterranean world.

The Greeks and Romans

agrarian society
A society with a largely agricultural economy.

The earliest societies were agrarian in nature. An *agrarian society* is a preindustrial society in which economic, political, and cultural values are based on agricultural experience. In these societies, most people worked the land for subsistence. No industrial centers or mass markets existed, so business activity beyond barter and exchange was a tiny part of the economy. The activities of merchants were often thought unprincipled because their sharp trading practices clashed with the traditional, more altruistic values of family and clan relations among farmers. Merchants typically had lower class status than officials, farmers, soldiers, artisans, and teachers.

The extraordinary civilizations of ancient Greece and Rome were based on subsistence agriculture. Economic activity by merchants, bankers, and manufacturers was limited. The largest factory in Athens, for example, employed 120 workers making shields.[8] Commercial activity was greater in Rome, but it was still mainly

---

[6] "Car Riot Started by 'Mother' Jones," *The New York Times,* October 6, 1916, p. 1.

[7] Quoted in Elliot J. Gorn, *Mother Jones: The Most Dangerous Woman in America* (New York: Hill and Wang, 2001), p. 249.

[8] Will Durant, *The Life of Greece* (New York: Simon & Schuster, 1939), p. 272.

an agrarian society. Perhaps because industry was so limited in both societies, in-accurate economic doctrines arose to explain commercial activity.[9] For example, the desire for riches was suspect due to the popular belief that the amount of wealth was fixed. If so, an individual accumulated wealth only by subtracting from the share of others. This is believable logic in an agrarian society because the land on which the economy is based is fixed in amount.

Philosophers moved into this realm of intellectual error, reasoning that profit seek-ing was an inferior motive and that commercial activity led to excess, corruption, and misery. Their views are of lasting significance because, as with many topics of dis-course in Western civilization, they first defined the terms of debate over the ranking of profit relative to other values. In particular, both Plato and Aristotle articulated the fundamental indictment that casts an everlasting shadow over business.

Plato believed that insatiable appetites existed in every person. These could be controlled only by inner virtues painstakingly acquired through character devel-opment. The pursuit of money was one such appetite, and Plato thought that when people engaged in trade they inevitably succumbed to the temptation of excess and became grasping. In a society, as with an individual, wealth spawned evils, including inequality, envy, class conflict, and war. "Virtue and wealth," he argued, "are balanced against one another in the scales."[10] Rulers of the utopian society he conceived in *The Republic* were prohibited from owning possessions for fear they would be corrupted and turn into tyrants. So troubled was he about this that they were forbidden even to touch gold or silver.

Aristotle believed there was a benign form of acquisition that consisted of get-ting the things needed for subsistence. This kind of acquisition was natural and moderate. However, after trading and monetary systems arose, the art of acquisi-tion was no longer practiced this simple way. Instead, merchants studied the tech-niques of commerce, figuring out how to make the greatest profit, seeking not the necessities, but unlimited pools of money. Aristotle thought this was a lower form of acquisition because it was activity that did not contribute to inner virtue.

For Aristotle, happiness is the ultimate goal of life. It comes to those who de-velop character virtues such as courage, temperance, justice, and wisdom. He called these virtues "goods of the soul" and held them superior to "external goods," which he defined as possessions and money. Aristotle believed that the amount of happiness a person gained in life was equal to the amount of virtue ac-cumulated in the soul. Since material possessions beyond those needed for sub-sistence added nothing to the store of virtue in the soul, it followed that they contributed nothing to happiness; thus, it was a waste or "perversion" of any vir-tue to apply it toward the acquisition of excess. "The proper function of courage, for example, is not to produce money but to give confidence," he wrote.[11]

Thus, both Plato and Aristotle relegated the profit motive to the sphere of lower or base impulses, a place from which it would not escape for centuries and then

---

[9] John Kenneth Galbraith, *Economics in Perspective* (Boston: Houghton Mifflin, 1987), pp. 9–10.

[10] *The Republic,* trans. F. M. Cornford (New York: Oxford University Press, 1945), p. 274.

[11] In *Politics,* trans. Ernest Barker (New York: Oxford University Press, 1962), book I, chap. X, sec. 17. See also book VII, chap. 1, secs. 1–10.

only partially. Soon, Roman law would forbid the senatorial class from making business investments (and the law would be widely circumvented). Likewise, the Stoic philosophers of Rome, including Epictetus and Marcus Aurelius, taught that the truly rich person possessed inner peace rather than capital or property. "Asked, 'Who is the rich man?' Epictetus replied, 'He who is content.'"[12] These sages looked down on merchants of their day as materialists who, in pursuit of wealth, sacrificed character development. Of course, this did not deter the merchants from accumulating fortunes and neglecting the study of ideals. The scornful ethos of the philosophers, though potent enough to endure and to beget perennial hostility, has never had enough power to suppress the tide of commerce.

The Medieval World

During the Middle Ages, the prevailing theology of the Roman Catholic Church was intolerant of profit seeking. As the Christian religion arose, its early practitioners had been persecuted by the wealthy and corrupt ruling class of Rome. The church, then, rejected a focus on wealth and sought special status for the poor. Saint Augustine, the towering figure of early church doctrine, accepted the idea that material wealth was fixed in supply. To become rich, a person necessarily sinned by accumulation that violated the natural equality of creation. Moreover, the love of material things was a snare that pulled the soul away from God.[13]

just price
A price giving a moderate profit; one inspired by fairness, not greed.

The Roman Catholic Church's most definitive theologian, St. Thomas Aquinas, was greatly influenced by the ideas of Aristotle when he set forth church canon about the ethics of profit making and lending money. Merchants were exhorted to charge a *just price* for their wares, a price that incorporated a modest profit just adequate to maintain them in the social station to which they were born. The just price stands in contrast to the modern idea of a *market price* determined by supply and demand without any moral dimension. Today we hear echoes of medieval theology when consumers complain that high prices for a scarce product are unjust. Catholicism also condemned *usury*, or the lending of money for interest. By the twelfth and thirteenth centuries, however, the money supply and economic activity had greatly expanded and interest-bearing loans were common. "Commercial activity," notes historian Will Durant, "proved stronger than fear of prison or hell."[14] In time, the church backed away from the dogma of just price and usury. It was a slow process. Not until 1917 did the Catholic church officially renounce the teaching that lending money for interest was a sin.

market price
A price determined by the interaction of supply and demand.

usury
The lending of money for interest.

The Modern World

As business activity accelerated during the Renaissance, new theories arose to justify previously condemned practices. Two are of great importance. First, is the rise of the *Protestant ethic* in the sixteenth century. The Protestant reformers Martin Luther

Protestant ethic
The belief that hard work and adherence to a set of virtues such as thrift, saving, and sobriety would bring wealth and God's approval.

[12] *The Golden Sayings of Epictetus,* trans. Hastings Crossley, in Charles W. Eliot, ed., *Plato, Epictetus, Marcus Aurelius* (Danbury, CT: Grolier, 1980), p. 179.

[13] Saint Augustine, *The City of God,* trans. Gerald G. Walsh et al. (New York: Image Books, 1958), book XIX, chap. 17. This work was completed in A.D. 426.

[14] *The Age of Faith* (New York: Simon & Schuster, 1950), p. 631.

and John Calvin believed that work was a means of serving God and that if a person earned great wealth through hard work it was a sign of God's approval. This confronted the church's antagonism toward commerce with a new doctrine that removed moral suspicion of wealth. It contradicted the belief that pursuit of money corrupted the soul. Second, in 1776 Adam Smith published his theory of capitalism, writing that free markets harnessed greed for the public good and protected consumers from abuse. This defied the church's insistence on the idea of a just price. Moreover, visible wealth creation in expanding economies forcefully countered the notion that only a more or less fixed amount of wealth existed in a society. These developments ended the domination of doctrines that made business activity seem faintly criminal and released new energies into commerce. But the broom of doctrinal reform failed to make a clean sweep, and many business critics clung to the old approbations of the Greek philosophers and of the Roman Catholic Church.

In addition, just when old strictures were loosening, the Industrial Revolution created new tensions that reinforced critical attitudes about business. These new tensions arose as inventions and industries transformed agrarian societies and challenged traditional values with modern alternatives. During industrialization, rural, slow-paced, stable societies are swiftly and dramatically altered. They become urban and fast-paced. More emphasis is placed on material things and people's values shift. Wealth creation overwhelms self-restraint. Consumption supplants thrift and saving. Conquest of nature replaces awe of nature.

THE AMERICAN CRITIQUE OF BUSINESS

As societies modernize, the antiquarian values of Greece live on in the charges of critics who are troubled by these changes. Always, the fundamental critique is altered to fit current circumstances. We will see how this happened in the United States.

The Colonial Era

The American nation was colonized by corporations. The colonists who landed at Jamestown, Virginia, in 1606 were sponsored by investors in the London Company, who hoped to make a fortune by discovering gold in the New World. Instead, the colonists found a mild strain of native tobacco that caused a sensation in England (and became the basis for the plantation economy that would rise in the South). The Pilgrims who came in the *Mayflower* to Cape Cod, Massachusetts, in 1620 had fled persecution to set up a religious colony. But their voyage was financed by the Plymouth Company, whose backers sought to make a profit. To repay their debt and to buy manufactured goods they exported furs and forest products such as timber, tar, and turpentine. In this way the early colonists became lively traders.

As international trade in coastal regions expanded, settlers moved inland, creating a broad agrarian base for the economy. These frontier farms seethed with profit-oriented activity. Unlike European peasants, American farmers owned their land and this turned them into little capitalists. Most tried to make money by raising crops for market. Some were land speculators. Others built and ran grain mills and in other ways employed their capital like the traders and merchants in towns.

The popular theoretician of the rising capitalist spirit was Benjamin Franklin (1706–1790). Franklin began a business career at the age of 22 by opening a printing shop. He then bought several newspapers and retired rich at the age of 42. During travels in Europe he became acquainted with Adam Smith, who shared parts of the manuscript for *Wealth of Nations* with him. Franklin came to accept Smith's then-radical views on the superiority of laissez-faire markets. Writing prolifically, he gave form to a new American business ethos.

In 1732 Franklin published the first annual *Poor Richard's Almanack,* an eclectic book of facts, information, and self-help advice. Over many years the *Almanack* carried aphorisms and maxims about the road to success in business, a road open to all who practiced virtues such as hard work, thrift, and frugality. "The sleeping Fox catches no Poultry." "Lost Time is never found again." "Diligence is the Mother of Good Luck." "The Art of getting Riches consists very much in Thrift."[15]

Unlike the Old World theologians who taught that commercial success was slightly sinful, Franklin taught that God would approve the pursuit of self-interest and wealth. "God gives all things to Industry."[16] He made business activity synonymous with traditional virtues and released it from moral suspicion. His teaching resonated with the American condition, and he became the prophet of a vibrant economy. Not surprisingly, his *Almanacks* were best sellers.

The Young Nation

The amalgam of a new land, a new people, and a new thinking generated an early emphasis on business activity and material progress. Yet not everyone felt this was either inevitable or proper and dissent soon emerged. After independence in 1783, business interests were important in the new nation but not to the extent that they would be in time. There were few large companies. The economy was 90 percent agricultural, so the interests of farmers and planters dominated those of infant industry. A major debate arose over the direction of the economy, one that would define subsequent debate between business and its critics in America. It was played out in a bitter rivalry between two members of President George Washington's cabinet who differed both in temperament and ideas.

Alexander Hamilton (1755–1804), the first secretary of the treasury, was young, ambitious, brilliant, and inclined to action. He believed that industrial growth would increase national power and designed a grand scheme to promote manufacturing and finance. He was an arrogant, aloof leader who mistrusted the wisdom of common citizens. Having once said "the people is a great beast," he favored rule by an economic elite.[17] Hamilton got Congress to approve his plans for taxation, debt financing, tariffs to protect infant industry, and creation of a national bank, setting a policy of industrialization in motion.

---

[15] Quotations are in *Poor Richard's Almanack,* 1749, and "The Way to Wealth," Preface to *Poor Richard Improved,* 1758, in Nathan G. Goodman, ed., *The Autobiography of Benjamin Franklin and Selections from His Other Writings* (New York: Carlton House, 1932), pp. 198, 206, 207.

[16] Ibid., "The Way to Wealth," p. 207.

[17] Quoted in Vernon Louis Parrington, *Main Currents in American Thought,* vol. 1 (New York: Harcourt, Brace, 1958), p. 300; originally published in 1927.

He was opposed by Secretary of State Thomas Jefferson (1743–1826), one of America's most original and philosophical minds. Jefferson was a shy man who avoided conflict. His thinking achieved great depth, but he was less a man of action than Hamilton. His weakness as a manager is summed up in a revealing statement. "We can only be answerable for the orders we give, and not for their execution."[18] He had grown up in sparsely populated frontier areas of Virginia, never having seen a village of more than 20 houses until he was 18 years old. Awed by the common sense and resourcefulness of the settlers he knew, he formed the opinion that an agrarian economy of landowning farmers was the ideal social order.

Reading books as much as 15 hours a day, he gathered arguments to reinforce his convictions. According to Jefferson, America should aspire to spread farming over its immense, unsettled territory. He wrote that God placed "genuine virtue" in farmers, His chosen people. Manufacturing as an occupation "suffocates the germ of virtue," leads to venality, and corrupts the "manners and principles" of those who work at it.[19] He believed that an agrarian economy would prevent the rise of subservience to the wealthy and bring a state of equality, basic justice, and concern for the common good. Jefferson was well-read in Greek philosophy, and it was no coincidence that he echoed the admonitions against commerce found in Plato and Aristotle. Even as he restated the Greeks, he laid the ground for more than two centuries of American business critics to follow.

Jefferson did not prevail. His agrarian ideal was fated to exist in the shadows of industrial growth. His theory of a nation of small farmers was somewhat nebulous and idealistic. As a policy it was no match for the more concrete design that Hamilton sold to Congress with great energy, a design that was surely more in tune with economic forces afoot in the young nation. With the support of business leaders, Hamilton carried out a bold, visionary program to stimulate the growth of manufacturing. His actions prepared the ground for the unexampled industrial growth that roared through the next century. He so angered Jefferson that the two rarely spoke even as they served together in George Washington's cabinet. Each had many followers and the conflict between their positions created not only the basis for subsequent criticism of business, but the basic cleavage that has prevailed in the American two-party system to the present.

1800–1865

The first half of the nineteenth century saw steady industrial growth. This aroused critics who clung to the values and life of the agrarian society that was fading before their eyes. Early in the century banking and manufacturing expanded. Markets were opened by tens of thousands of miles of new turnpikes. Completion of the 350-mile-long Erie Canal in 1825 inspired another 4,400 miles of canals to transport goods over water.[20] Railroads started to run in the 1830s. Immigrants arrived and cities grew. Business boomed.

[18] Letter to Baron F. W. von Stueben, March 10, 1781, quoted in Stanley Elkins and Eric McKitrick, *The Age of Federalism* (New York: Oxford University Press, 1993), p. 206.

[19] Quotes are from *Notes on Virginia*, in Adrienne Koch and William Peden, *The Life and Selected Writings of Thomas Jefferson* (New York: Random House, 1944), p. 280; first published in 1784.

[20] James Oliver Robertson, *America's Business* (New York: Hill and Wang, 1985), p. 81.

As the force of events put capitalism in control, agrarian romantics were pushed to the side, having only the power to object as cherished values were eroded. "Commerce," complained Ralph Waldo Emerson in 1839, "threatens to upset the balance of man and establish a new, universal Monarchy more tyrannical than Babylon or Rome."[21] Later, his friend Henry David Thoreau wrote to belittle a society in which this commerce smothered the poetry and grace of everyday life.

> This world is a place of business. What an infinite bustle! I am awakened almost every night by the panting of the locomotive. It interrupts my dreams. There is no sabbath. It would be glorious to see mankind at leisure for once. It is nothing but work, work, work. I cannot easily buy a blank-book to write thoughts in; they are commonly ruled for dollars and cents . . . I think that there is nothing, not even crime, more opposed to poetry, to philosophy, ay, to life itself, than this incessant business.[22]

utopia
A socially engineered model community designed to correct faults in the world so its members can find happiness.

Among those who rejected capitalism, some tried to create alternative worlds. Beginning in the 1820s there was a frenzy of *utopia* building. Small bands of people who disdained the values prized in industrial society—materialism, competition, individualism, and tireless labor—built model communities intended to act as beacons for a better way. The largest was New Harmony, Indiana, founded in 1825 by Robert Owen (1771–1858), an English industrialist. Owen ran a large cotton mill in Scotland that had become a model for fair treatment of workers. Yet he believed that human values were corrupted by factory work and life in capitalist societies. He aspired to show that a society based on principles of equality, charity, cooperation, and moderation could flourish. At New Harmony, money was abolished and the residents shared the fruits of communal labor.

Owen called his creation a "socialist" system and in the 1820s the term *socialism* first came into widespread use as a reference to Owen's philosophy. He started several other socialist communities and his ventures inspired others to form utopias based on socialist principles. More than 100 such communities appeared between 1820 and 1850.[23] A few were successful. The Oneida Community in New York lasted 31 years from 1848 to 1879. But most floundered, on average in less than two years.[24]

New Harmony emptied after only four years. Like other utopias it required businesslike activities for subsistence, but it attracted more loafers than skilled farmers and artisans who, in any case, could command higher material rewards in the outside world. After their initial zeal wore off, the sojourners tired of spartan living, regimentation, and rules to enforce cooperation. Most communes had programs to infuse socialist values into human natures tainted by capitalist schooling. Rarely did this work. One indication is that pilfering of supplies from common storehouses was common.

---

[21] Quoted from Emerson's *Journals,* vol. V, pp. 284–86, in Parrington, *Main Currents in American Thought,* vol. I, p. 386.

[22] "Life without Principle," *The Atlantic Monthly,* October 1863, pp. 484–85.

[23] W. Fitzhugh Brundage, *A Socialist Utopia in the New South* (Urbana: University of Illinois Press, 1996), p. 6.

[24] Joshua Muravchik, *Heaven on Earth: The Rise and Fall of Socialism* (San Francisco: Encounter Books, 2002), p. 51.

The agrarian and socialist communes failed utterly as alternatives to the bustling capitalism beyond their margins. Although a few new ones appeared as late as the 1890s, by the 1850s the idea had run its course. It failed in practice because it was based on romantic thinking, not on sustaining social forces. A series of withered utopias and a growing consensus on capitalist values adjourned the experiments. Socialism would return, but it awaited a new day and new ideas.

Populists and Progressives

At the end of the Civil War in 1865, America was still a predominantly rural, agrarian society of small, local businesses. But explosive industrial growth rapidly reshaped it, creating severe social problems in the process. Cities grew as farmers left the land and immigrants swelled slum populations. Corrupt political machines ran cities but failed to improve parlous conditions. Companies merged into huge national monopolies. These changes were the raw material of two movements critical of big business.

populist movement
A political reform movement that arose among farmers in the late 1800s. Populists blamed social problems on industry and sought radical reforms such as government ownership of railroads.

The first was the *populist movement,* a farmers' protest movement that began in the 1870s and led to formation of a national political party, the Populist Party, which assailed business interests until its decisive defeat in the presidential election of 1896. The movement arose soon after the Civil War, when farmers experienced falling crop prices. The declines were due mainly to overproduction by mechanized farm machinery and to competition from foreign farmers exploiting new transport technologies. Farmers overlooked these factors and blamed their distress on railroad companies, the largest businesses of the day, which frequently overcharged for crop hauling, and on "plutocrats" such as J. P. Morgan and other Eastern bankers who controlled the loan companies that foreclosed on their farms.

In a typical tirade, Mary Lease, a populist orator who whipped up crowds of farmers at picnics and fairs, explained:

> Wall Street owns the country. It is no longer a government of the people, by the people and for the people, but a government of Wall Street and for Wall Street. The great common people of this country are slaves, and monopoly is the master. The West and South are bound and prostrate before the manufacturing East.[25]

To solve agrarian ills, the populists advocated government ownership of railroads, telegraph and telephone companies, and banks, a policy dagger that revealed their fundamental rejection of capitalism. They demanded direct election of U.S. senators, who at the time were picked by state legislatures corrupted with money from big business. And to ease credit they sought to abandon the gold standard and expand the money supply.

Historian Louis Galambos believes that despite the populist critique, there existed a great reservoir of respect for and confidence in business until the late 1880s.[26] After that, analysis of newspaper and magazine editorials shows mounting hostility

[25] In John D. Hicks, *The Populist Revolt* (Minneapolis: University of Minnesota Press, 1931), p. 160.

[26] Louis Galambos, *The Public Image of Big Business in America, 1880–1940* (Baltimore: Johns Hopkins University Press, 1975), chap. 3. Galambos examined 8,976 items related to big business that were printed in newspapers and journals between 1879 and 1940, using content analysis to reconstruct rough measures of opinion among certain influential groups.

Was President McKinley the Wizard of Oz?

The Wonderful Wizard of Oz is one of the all-time best-selling children's books.[27] It was written by Lyman Frank Baum (1856–1919), an actor, sales-clerk, and small-town newspaper editor who loved creating stories for children. On the surface, the book is a magical adventure in a fairyland where children are as wise as adults. However, the book has a deeper dimension. It is a parable of populism.[28]

The Wonderful Wizard of Oz satirizes the evils of an industrial society run by a moneyed elite of bankers and industrialists. "Oz" is the abbreviation for ounce, a measure of gold. It and the Yellow Brick Road allude to the hated gold standard. The main characters represent groups in society. Dorothy is the common person. The Scarecrow is the farmer. The Tin Woodsman is industrial labor. His rusted condition symbolizes factory closings in the depression years of the 1890s, and his lack of a heart hints that factories dehumanize workers. The Cowardly Lion is William Jennings Bryan, the defeated Populist Party candidate, whom Baum

regarded as lacking sufficient courage. The Wicked Witch of the East is a parody of the capitalist elite. She kept the munchkins, or "little people," in servitude. At the end of the Yellow Brick Road lay the Emerald City, or Washington, D.C., where on arrival the group was met by the Wizard, representing the president of the United States. At the time Baum wrote the book, William McKinley was president, having defeated Bryan in 1896. Populists reviled McKinley because he had the backing of big trusts and he supported the hated gold standard.

At the conclusion, Dorothy melted the Wicked Witch of the East, the Wizard flew off in a balloon, the Scarecrow became the ruler of Oz, and the Tin Woodsman took charge of the East. This ending is the unrealized populist dream.

Baum's first motive was to be a child's storyteller, not to write political satire for adults. He never stated that the book contained populist themes, leading to debate over whether finding such symbolism is fair. Yet Baum lived in South Dakota while populism was emerging and he marched in Populist Party rallies. *The Wonderful Wizard of Oz* was written in 1898, at the height of ardor for reform. Therefore, it seems reasonable to think that Baum's tale was inspired by the politics of the day.

[27] L. Frank Baum (Chicago: Reilly & Britten, 1915), first published in 1900.

[28] The classic interpretation of symbolism is by Henry W. Littlefield, "The Wizard of Oz: Parable on Populism," *American Quarterly,* Spring 1964.

toward large trusts. Soon the populists succeeded in electing many state and local officials, who enacted laws to regulate the railroads and provided the political groundswell behind creation of the Interstate Commerce Commission in 1887 to regulate railroads.

The populist movement was a diverse, unstable coalition of interests, including farmers, labor, prohibitionists, antimonopolists, silverites, and suffragists. These groups were held together for a time by a common, deep-seated hostility toward big companies. Ultimately, the populists failed to forge an effective political coalition and the movement was moribund after 1900 when William Jennings Bryan, the Populist Party's presidential candidate, was decisively defeated for a second time.

However, the populists refined a logic and lexicon for attacking business. They blamed adverse consequences of industrialization on monopoly, trusts, Wall Street, "silk-hatted Easterners," the soulless "loan sharks" and shameless "bloodhounds of money" who foreclosed on farms, and on corrupt politicians who worked as errand boys for the "moneybags" in a system of "plutocracy" (or rule by the wealthy).

Their criticisms were harsh and colorful. "The James Brothers and the Daltons were limited in their methods," thundered Mary Lease to a cheering crowd. "If they had operated on as large a scale as the millionaires of the country they could have built universities like Rockefeller. . . ."[29] In an essay on the virtues of farming as an occupation, Bryan wrote that for farmers "even the dumb animals are more wholesome companions than the bulls and bears of Wall Street."[30] Thomas Jefferson would likely have applauded.

It was, of course, too late for America to be a nation of farmers. This did not diminish the appeal of the populist message to large segments of the population. On the contrary, continued industrial growth has caused this message to resurface time and again up to the present, each time its vocabulary recycled and its content refined to fit current circumstances.

progressive movement
A turn-of-the-twentieth-century political movement that associated moderate social reform with progress. Progressivism was less radical than populism and had wider appeal.

The second critical movement was the *progressive movement*, a broader reform effort lasting from about 1900 until the end of World War I in 1918. Fueled by wide moral indignation about social problems caused by industry, it had strong support from the urban middle class and professionals. Although a short-lived Progressive Party was formed and unsuccessfully ran Theodore Roosevelt for president in 1912, both the Democratic and Republican parties had powerful progressive wings. Unlike populism, progressivism was a mainstream political doctrine. Like populism, it was at root an effort to cure social ills by using government to control perceived abuses of big business.

Because of broad popular support, Progressives were far more effective than populists in their reform efforts, and during their era a cleansing tide washed over business. "Turn the waters of pure public spirit into the corrupt pools of private interests," wrote Ernest Crosby, editor of *Cosmopolitan* magazine, "and wash the offensive accumulations away."[31] Progressives broke up trusts and monopolies, outlawed corporate campaign contributions, restricted child labor, passed a corporate income tax, and regulated food and drug companies and public utilities. With the Seventeenth Amendment in 1913 requiring direct election of senators they completed part of the Populist agenda.

Socialists

socialism
The doctrine of a classless society in which property is collectively owned and income from labor is equally divided among members. It rejects the values of capitalism.

The full story of the Progressive movement's success lies in the counterpoint it provided to the socialist movement of that era. *Socialism* is a classless social system in which property is collectively owned and income from labor is equally and indiscriminately divided among members. When wealth is shared, want and conflict are eliminated. Socialism poses a revolutionary challenge to capitalist society because it requires a change in property relationships that destroys bedrock arrangements.

Although elements of socialist thinking are ageless, the originator of modern socialist doctrine is Francois-Noël Babeuf (1764–1797), a minor French official and writer who wanted to fulfill the promise of equality for all made during the French

[29] Quoted in "Furor over Mary Lease," *The New York Times*, August 11, 1896, p. 3.
[30] "Farming as an Occupation," *Cosmopolitan*, January 1904, p. 371.
[31] Ernest Crosby, "The Man with the Hose," *Cosmopolitan*, August 1906, p. 341.

Art Young, a radical cartoonist of the Progressive era, had an impish ability to highlight the excesses of the industrial age. This cartoon, typical of many then drawn by Young and others, first appeared in 1912. Source: Art Young, *The Best of Art Young,* New York: Vanguard Press, 1936, p. 89).

CAPITALISM

Revolution of 1789. He advocated seizing the possessions of the wealthy and giving them to the masses. Following this seizure, Babeuf envisioned a new communal economy. Private property would be abolished. Citizens would be required to work based on their trade or skill. The government would receive their output and distribute to everyone the basic material necessities of life. To eliminate individual desire for wealth and power, schools would teach egalitarian principles. Babeuf pushed for a violent overthrow of the French regime to achieve his vision and for this he was imprisoned, then beheaded in 1797. But his ideas took hold and circulated throughout Europe. One convert was Robert Owen, who was inspired to set up his tiny utopia in Indiana.

For a half century after Babeuf, socialist thought was splintered and muddied in a ferment of competing schools. Then, in 1848, Karl Marx (1818–1883) and his lifetime collaborator, Friedrich Engels (1820–1895), published *The Communist Manifesto* and put socialism on a new foundation.[32] Marx and Engels argued that the basis for socialism was an inevitable process of class struggle underlying and explaining the history of human society. Under capitalism the working class is exploited by the owners of capital, who pay low wages for dehumanizing work and then usurp for themselves the value of what workers toil to create. Marx often used metaphors in which capitalists became vampires and werewolves, sucking the lifeblood from labor.

Like Babeuf and others, Marx and Engels envisioned an equalitarian society that abolished private ownership of capital and instituted wealth-sharing among all members. Workers would no longer be alienated by miserable, meaningless labor. With class distinctions ended, people would live in harmony, their basic needs fulfilled. While Marx and Engels repeated many of the timeless criticisms of capitalism as characterized by barbaric competition, corruption of values by money, and meaningless work, they made socialism more compelling when they discovered a theory of history to explain it. Class warfare was the underlying dynamic that changed society. Workers in all nations had the duty to rise and overthrow the capitalist class. The last sentence of the *Manifesto* reads: "WORKINGMEN OF ALL COUNTRIES UNITE!"[33]

Meanwhile, in the United States of 1850 to 1900, rapid industrial growth was taking place within a coarse, little-regulated capitalist system that in many ways seemed to bear out the socialist's nightmare of exploitation. Child labor was widespread; factories injured and wore down workers; wealth and power were concentrated in great banks, trusts, and railway systems; inequality between rich and poor seemed obscene; and the masses suffered through financial panics and unemployment. Also, industrial growth was taking people away from agrarian occupations and creating a new class of employed Americans. In 1860 about 1.3 million people worked for the trusts, mines, and railroads, but by 1890 there were 4.3 million so occupied.[34] The rise of this new social class formed the soil in which labor unions could grow, and given widespread labor abuses, these unions might be attracted to socialism. As it turned out, this attraction would be limited.

As unions sprang up employers fought them. Most early unions were tied to single companies or locations. A few were radical and avowedly socialist, especially those with many European immigrants who brought Marxist thinking with them. The first big national union was the Knights of Labor, set up in 1869. Its constitution recognized exploitation of labor by owners of capital, but it called for

[32] According to Paul Sweezy, Marx chose to use the word *communist* rather than *socialist* because the meaning of the word *socialist* had become muddled. The term *communist*, in use for centuries to denote pooled property, more clearly conveyed his theory. See *Socialism* (New York: McGraw-Hill, 1949), pp. 8–9.

[33] Karl Marx and Friedrich Engels, *Manifesto of the Communist Party,* in Lewis S. Feuer, ed., *Marx & Engels: Basic Writings on Politics & Philosophy* (New York: Anchor Books, 1959), p. 41.

[34] Arthur M. Schlesinger, *Political and Social Growth of the United States: 1852–1933* (New York: MacMillan, 1935), p. 203.

reforms to protect labor rather than for overthrow of the capitalists. However, the union movement soon struck fear in the capitalist heart.

In the summer of 1877 a wave of violent strikes hit the railroads, then rolled on to other industries as it spread across the nation. Fighting and killing between strikers and the hired armies of employers was widespread. President Rutherford B. Hayes called his cabinet into a continuous session. He was so terrified that the country would fall to a workers' revolution that, rather than using federal troops to restore order in major cities, he gathered them in Washington, D.C., to protect the government. The strikes eventually ran their course, and although there was never again such a violent cluster, from this time until the end of the century the number, size, and violence of strikes only increased.

In this climate of unrest, the socialist movement was surprisingly slow to blossom. The largest union, the American Federation of Labor, formed in 1886, disdained Marxism and elected to work with employers for higher wages and better working conditions. As time passed and the union movement grew, many workers still wanted radical change. They eventually found a home when the Industrial Workers of the World (IWW) was formed in 1905. The IWW proposed to represent all workers of both sexes and all races and in every industry in the fight to overthrow the capitalist system. Its platform was clear.

> We are here to confederate the workers of this country into a working-class movement that shall have for its purpose the emancipation of the working-class from the slave bondage of capitalism. . . . The aims and objects of this organization shall be to put the working-class in possession of the economic power, the means of life, in control of the machinery of production and distribution, without regard to the capitalist masters.[35]

Although the IWW was not as large as other unions, its unmitigated rejection of the system scared mainstream America and it was severely repressed. Laws were passed to prevent IWW members from speaking or assembling and it defied them, sometimes violently.

Working alongside the IWW was a young Socialist Party with growing power. It had been formed in 1901 with the avowed purpose of overthrowing capitalism. At the peak of its popularity in 1912 it had 118,000 members and its presidential candidate, Eugene V. Debs, got 6 percent of the popular vote. More than 1,000 socialists had been elected to state and local office.[36] This moment was the high mark of socialism in the United States. From then on, its appeal rapidly declined and it never recovered meaningful power.

There were four immediate reasons. First, because of its electoral successes the Socialist Party chose to make itself less radical to appeal to more voters. This breached socialist unity by alienating firebrand IWW leaders. Second, moderate reforms of the Progressive movement stole much of the socialists' thunder. Arguably, these reforms came only because the threat of growing socialist popularity put pressure on the capitalist elite. Third, socialist unions made a huge tactical

[35] Quoted in Howard Zinn, *A People's History of the United States: 1492–Present*, rev. ed. (New York: HarperCollins, 2003), p. 330.

[36] Irving Howe, *Socialism and America* (New York: Harcourt, Brace, Jovanovich, 1985), p. 3.

mistake (though not a doctrinal error) when they labeled World War I (1914–1918) an imperialist war and said that labor would refuse to shed its blood for wealthy capitalists. In 1917 the government put 101 leaders of the IWW on trial for violating sedition laws and all were convicted. Almost half of them got prison sentences of from 10 to 20 years. Others got shorter terms. This decapitated the IWW and crippled the socialist labor movement going forward. Fourth, as time passed the lot of most workers simply improved. Between 1897 and 1914 real wages rose 37 percent and the average 60-hour workweek declined to 50 hours.[37] Again, the irony is that much of this improvement undoubtedly came out of fear of socialism.

The Great Depression and World War II

With the decline of socialism, capitalism had pushed back its most radical critics. After the triumph of progressive reforms, there was a period of high public confidence in big business during the prosperous, expansive 1920s. This rosy era ended abruptly with the stock market crash of 1929, and business again came under sustained attack. During the 1920s, the idea that American capitalism would bring perpetual prosperity had been widely accepted. The catastrophic Depression of the 1930s disproved this and, in addition, brought to light much ineptness, criminal negligence, and outright fraud by prominent executives. There was a popular feeling that the economic collapse would not have occurred if business leaders had been more honest.

As the Depression deepened, anger at business grew and the old rhetoric of populism reemerged. In the Senate, for example, Huey Long, a colorful populist Democrat from Louisiana who claimed to be the advocate of the poor against the rich, rose to condemn a "ruling plutocratic class."[38]

> The 125 million people of America have seated themselves at the barbecue table to consume the products which have been guaranteed to them by their Lord and Creator. There is provided by the Almighty what it takes for them all to eat: yea, more. . . . But the financial masters of America have taken off the barbecue table 90 percent of the food placed thereon by God, through the labors of mankind, even before the feast begins, and there is left on that table to be eaten by 125 million people less than should be there for 10 million of them.
>
> What has become of the remainder of those things placed on the table by the Lord for the use of us all? They are in the hands of the Morgans, the Rockefellers, the Mellons, the Baruchs, the Bakers, the Astors, and the Vanderbilts—600 families at the most either possessing or controlling the entire 90 percent of all that is in America. . . . I hope none will be horror-stricken when they hear me say that we must limit the size of the big man's fortune in order to guarantee a minimum of fortune, life and comfort to the little man.[39]

These remarks echo the ancient Greek view that wealth in a society is limited and the accumulation of one person is a taking from all others—that great material

---

[37] Louis B. Wright et al., *The Democratic Experience: A Short American History* (Chicago: Scott Foresman, 1963), p. 302.

[38] *Congressional Record*, 73d Cong., 2d sess., 1934, p. 6081, speech of April 5.

[39] Radio speech broadcast March 7, 1935, inserted in the *Congressional Record*, March 12, 1935.

FIGURE 4.1
Production of .30 and .50 Caliber Machine Guns by General Motors: 1941–1944

Source: Based on data in James Truslow Adams, *Big Business in a Democracy* (New York: Scribner's Sons, 1945), p. 251.

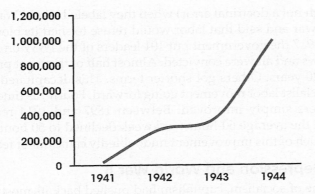

wealth reflects greed. Long used these views to gain moral authority for his radical proposals. In 1934 he introduced a plan to redistribute wealth by collecting annual taxes on corporate assets and large fortunes and then giving every family a $5,000 initial gift followed with a guaranteed annual income of $2,500. In a collapsed economy, this populist-like plan had tremendous appeal, and Long attracted millions of followers. However, he was assassinated before it could be enacted, leaving the milder reforms of President Franklin D. Roosevelt's New Deal to carry the day.

During World War II, support for business rebounded. Industry wrapped itself in patriotism, and its high output proved essential to Allied victory. For example, General Motors converted itself almost entirely to war production. The company made 3,600 war items, including ball bearings, bullets, rifles, torpedoes, trucks, tanks, bombers, and fighter airplanes. In a remarkable effort, it doubled its output of war material between 1942 and 1944. Figure 4.1 shows the production record for one item, machine guns.

Because of similar efforts by many corporations, the war years washed away the populist/socialist/depression era image of the corporation as a bloated plutocracy. It was instead the source of miraculous industrial production. In a radio address President Franklin Roosevelt labeled American business the "arsenal of democracy" that would turn the tide against evil dictatorships that sought to control the world.[40] The wartime performance was spectacular and in a postwar poll, only 10 percent of the population believed that where "big business activity" was concerned "the bad effects outweighed the good."[41] This renascence of respect lasted into the 1960s before the populist seed again sprouted.

The Collapse of Confidence

Strong public support for business collapsed in the mid-1960s. The nation was growing more affluent, but four strong social movements—for civil rights, consumer rights, and the environment and against the Vietnam War—attacked business

[40] Radio address, Washington, D.C., December 29, 1940. U.S. Department of State, *Peace and War: United States Foreign Policy, 1931–1941* (Washington, DC: U.S. Government Printing Office, 1943), pp. 598–607.
[41] Burton R. Fisher and Stephen B. Withey, *Big Business as the People See It* (Ann Arbor: University of Michigan Microfilms, December 1951), p. xiii.

FIGURE 4.2
Percentage of American Public Expressing "A Great Deal of Confidence" in Leaders of Major Companies: 1966–2010

Source: Annual Harris Poll Confidence Index.

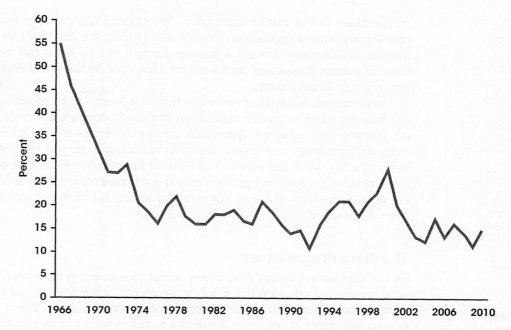

for contributing to a range of social ills including racism and sexism, consumer fraud, dangerous and alienating work, political corruption, and war profiteering. These attacks coincided with a negative trend in public opinion toward business. While in 1968, 70 percent of Americans agreed that business tried to strike a fair balance between profits and the public interest, by 1970 the number had declined to 33 percent, and by 1976 to 15 percent. This astonishing drop of 55 points took only eight years.[42]

Scholars who studied the polls theorized that turmoil in American society in the 1960s created a "confidence gap," or a gap between public expectations about how corporations *should* act and public perceptions of how they actually *did* act. Such gaps are perennial. They widened during the populist and Progressive eras and during the Great Depression years. This new gap has now persisted for almost 40 years and continues to define the climate of public opinion.

Figure 4.2 shows the long-term trend for the percentage of Americans expressing "a great deal of confidence" in "people in charge of running major companies." In 1966, 55 percent of the public expressed such confidence, but over the next decade the percentage fell to 16 percent. Since then the confidence trend has bumped along a low road for more than 40 years, recovering to 28 percent in 2000 near the peak of a great bull market, but sinking again to a low of 11 percent in 2009 after banks, insurers, and loan companies led the nation into a financial crisis.[43]

[42] Seymour M. Lipset and William Schneider, "How's Business: What the Public Thinks," *Public Opinion*, July–August 1978.

[43] Figures are based on Harris polls asking this question: "As far as people in charge of running . . . major companies . . . are concerned, would you say you have a great deal of confidence, only some confidence, or hardly any confidence in them?" See Harris Poll, "Virtually No Change in Annual Harris Poll Confidence Index from Last Year," March 9, 2010, table 1, at www.harrisinteractive.com.

The steep fall of public trust after 1966 opened the door for reformers to increase government regulation dramatically. During the late 1960s and early 1970s, liberals in Congress affected a spectacular run of new laws and agencies in defense of nature, consumers, and workers. However, by the mid-1970s business had organized to blunt reform.

Corporations funded conservative think tanks and used advertising to spread the message that excessive regulation imposed unnecessary costs and burdens on companies, reducing American competitiveness in the global economy. Although business was unsuccessful in restoring basic public trust, it did alter key attitudes. With the election of Ronald Reagan in 1980 a tide of Republican conservatism swept through the federal government, frustrating liberal reformers whose ideology of using government to control business was diminished—even discredited.

The New Progressives

Out of this liberal defeat rose a new leftist movement with a new ideology. The new movement adopted the label "progressive" after the turn-of-the-twentieth-century movement that sought a broad range of social and political reforms. Both movements have in common the desire to restrain corporate power in the public interest, but major differences exist between them. The *old Progressives* had moderate wings in both the Democratic and Republican parties, so a wide span of politicians, from the left through the middle, often supported reforms. Support for the *new Progressives'* agenda has moved to the left of both the old Progressives and the New Deal liberals.

Unlike the old Progressives and liberals, who wanted to enact reforms through government, the new Progressives have abandoned efforts to build majority coalitions in the mainstream, instead seeking to carry out radical change through direct action. And while the old-timers applied new scientific, legal, and management theories of the day to smooth the harsh edges of capitalism, the obsession of the new Progressives has been attacks on big corporations and the values and laws that support them. Largely blocked from the avenue of reform legislation by conservative, antiregulatory trends that they see as corporate dominance of government, activists confront corporations and industries directly, trying to alter their behavior, even in the absence of laws against what the corporations are doing. Their actions derive from three basic beliefs.

First, corporations have too much power. Free markets do not force them to serve the public interest. Governments cannot control them. They use their wealth to undermine democracy by corrupting politicians. Like entrenched oligarchs, they escape accountability for their self-interested exercise of power.

Second, corporations have inordinate legal rights. In the colonial era the state charters that authorized corporations carefully restricted them to ensure that they acted for the common welfare. For example, they defined the company's business and limited its existence to a fixed number of years. Today, instead of restricting corporations, state charters are very permissive. They allow branching out to new lines of business and grant their creations perpetual life. Over the years legislatures,

old Progressive Members of a broad political and social reform movement in the early years of the twentieth century.

new Progressive Members of contemporary left-leaning groups who advocate more radical corporate reform than did old-time Progressives. New Progressives seek to avoid being branded as liberals and try to take advantage of favorable connotations in the word *progressive*.

courts, and trade agreements have regularly added more rights, including the granting of "personhood" to corporate entities, entitling them to many constitutional rights of flesh-and-blood citizens.[44]

Third, corporations are inherently immoral. If often run or staffed by good people, their actions are perverted by an implacable master force, the very logic of the corporation itself. Corporations act to make money. They seek market expansion, sales growth, short-term financial results, and regulatory lenience. They value nature only as a production resource, workers only as costs, and human needs only as demand. Strong corporate cultures inculcate these values, pressuring and ultimately coercing the wills of even the most ethical employees, turning them into witting or unwitting agents of an antisocial institution.

The Progressive network has no single leader, but in the United States a prominent figure and senior diplomat is Ralph Nader. Nader began his activist career more than 30 years ago by writing *Unsafe at Any Speed*, a book that attacked the auto industry for putting styling ahead of safety.[45] The popularity of the book prodded Congress to pass auto safety legislation. Based on this success and his desire to seek change through government, Nader created more than 50 organizations to articulate consumer issues and lobby for protective laws. Over time, his hostility toward corporations deepened and his desire to seek moderate reforms lessened.

Announcing his candidacy for president of the United States in 2000, Nader said he was running to challenge "rampaging corporate titans" and "global corporations . . . astride our planet."[46] He declined to seek nomination as either a Republican or a Democrat because, he explained, both parties "feed at the same corporate trough."[47] Instead, he ran as a candidate for the progressive Green Party. Although he got only 2.7 percent of the popular vote, he prevented Democrat Al Gore from winning the electoral votes of key states, allowing Republican George W. Bush, the more probusiness candidate, to win. This angered many Progressive allies.

GLOBAL CRITICS

**nongovern-
mental
organization**
A term for
voluntary,
nonprofit
organizations
that are not
affiliated with
governments.

Corporate power grows in the world economy. And with it opposition, which is mostly found in an emerging global civic culture shaped by eruptive growth of *nongovernmental organizations* (NGOs), or voluntary, nonprofit organizations that are not part of governments. There are now more than 47,000 NGOs, almost 90 percent of them created since 1970.[48] The variety of NGOs that operate over

[44] For enumeration see Ted Nance, *Gangs of America: The Rise of Corporate Power and the Disabling of Democracy* (San Francisco: Berrett-Koehler, 2003), table 1.1.

[45] Ralph Nader, *Unsafe at Any Speed* (New York: Grossman, 1965).

[46] "Closing the Democracy Gap," *The Progressive Populist,* October 15, 2000, pp. 13 and 14.

[47] Ibid., p. 14.

[48] Michael Edwards, *Civil Society* (Cambridge, England: Polity Press, 2004), p. 23; and World Association of Non-Governmental Organizations, "Worldwide NGO Directory," at www.wango.org, accessed October 30, 2009, showing 47,535 listings.

civil society
A zone of ideas, discourse, and action, dominated by progressive values, that transcends national societies and focuses on global issues.

global justice movement
A coalition of groups united by opposition to economic globalization dominated by corporate capitalism.

neoliberalism
A word denoting both the ideology of using markets to organize society and a set of specific policies to free markets from state intrusion.

liberalism
The philosophy of an open society in which the state does not interfere with rights of individuals.

economic liberalism
The philosophy that social progress comes when individuals freely pursue their self-interests in unregulated markets.

national boundaries encompasses business, cultural, educational, environmental, human rights, social service, health, and religious entities. They animate a global zone of ideas, discourse, and action that has come to be called *civil society*. Although civil society is a vast churning of interests, it is dominated by intellectuals, NGOs, grass roots movements, and institutions with progressive values critical of corporate capitalism. These actors, linked by electronic communications, engage in advocacy and struggle to advance a leftist design that includes global income redistribution, sustainable development, gender equity, and protection of human and labor rights.

In the 1990s a *global justice movement* evolved within civil society. It coalesced around resistance to a global economy directed by markets, corporations, trade agreements, and capitalist-dominated international organizations. It was especially united in rejecting the economic ideology seen as inspiring it all, a doctrine it labeled *neoliberalism*.[49] To understand neoliberalism, it is necessary to know the history of liberalism, an idea that has profoundly shaped Western civilization.

The Story of Liberalism

Liberalism arose in Europe as a social philosophy in the 1500s. It promoted a free and open society in which the power of government to interfere with individual rights such as speech, association, conscience, and occupation was limited. Liberals[50] had great faith in human reason and believed this freedom would lead to social progress. For example, as freedom of speech allowed multiple opinions to be aired, truth would drive out falsehood, allowing progress toward enlightenment. Liberalism proved compelling. It spread over centuries until it came to define the essence of a good society in much of the West.

A natural extension of liberalism was a philosophy of *economic liberalism* that sanctified the pursuit of individual self-interest in markets free from state interferences. According to economic liberals, the market was a natural, self-correcting mechanism. If left alone, free from state interference, forces of supply and demand would maintain a perpetual, automatic, self-correcting balance, continuously elevating material welfare. Adam Smith's vision of *laissez-faire* capitalism defined the essence of economic liberalism.

Economic liberalism seized hold in the West. It was a critical ideology underlying the Industrial Revolution in England. Later, in the United States, it was used to justify the predatory capitalism of the 1800s and early 1900s that so aggravated Mary Lease, Mother Jones, and Huey Long. No matter the market was pitiless to

---

[49] This movement is usually called the "antiglobalism movement" in the press, but its advocates reject that label because it is not opposed to global expansion of economic and political ties, only the current, corporate-dominated expansion suspected of putting profit before human welfare. Some in the movement prefer the name "alter-globalization."

[50] The word *liberal* is used here in its original, classical sense where it refers to freedom from government interference, a *negative freedom*. It should not be confused with the term *liberal* as it is applied in contemporary politics to those who want state power to restrain business, a situation of *positive freedom*, meaning that government acts positively to create a just, free society.

children, miners, farmers, and debtors, it was an inviolate work of nature, a benevolent cosmic design best freed of human meddling.

But classical liberalism perished in the world depression of the 1930s. To end the Depression and make economies perform for the public good, governments began to intervene in markets. A British economist, John Maynard Keynes (1883–1946), argued the then-radical view that, far from being self-correcting, markets could be managed to dampen business cycles and promote full employment. Keynes' ideas, which became known as *Keynesianism*, spread and in the United States and Europe, states dropped the hands-off-the-market philosophy, embracing forms of "mixed economy" to promote stability, full employment, and social welfare. Liberalism changed. Although economic freedoms were important, it was no longer assumed that free markets always produced moral outcomes. They required state supervision. An era of growing market regulation followed.

Keynesianism
An economic philosophy of active state intervention to stabilize the economy and stimulate employment.

The Rise of Neoliberalism

Meanwhile, old beliefs about the virtues of laissez-faire hibernated. While Keynes' ideas dominated around the world, in the late 1940s a small, elite group of intellectuals began composing a new free market ideology, readying it for a day when the world would call. They believed that government intrusion in markets menaced human freedom. Left alone, competitive forces and price signals were the most effective way to coordinate individual efforts. And the power of free markets would offset political power. When government regulated markets, it infringed on free choice by individuals and, by intruding, fused economic and political power, removing a counterbalance essential to free society. Such interference was, in the words of the group's founding leader, Austrian philosopher Friedrich Hayek (1899–1992), "the road to serfdom."[51]

Convening just after the end of World War II, the group had before it the terrible specters of fascism in Germany and Stalinism in Russia, both based on state control of the economy, both leading to human misery. What leaped out at them was the importance of the market as a counterbalance to government authority. They would work to promote individual liberty by keeping the state out of markets. In practice, their theories would unchain corporate power.

Another member in the group was Milton Friedman (1912–2006), the leader of free market thinking in the Department of Economics at the University of Chicago. There, he and other like-thinking faculty used statistical models to test free market theories. Like Hayek, Friedman saw markets as bulwarks against tyranny. "Every act of government intervention," he wrote, "limits the area of individual freedom directly."[52] Friedman advocated policies to maximize the market's role, even extending its reach into areas traditionally occupied by government. He wanted to abolish the minimum wage, end Social Security, eliminate tariffs, let for-profit companies compete with the post office, turn America's national parks over to corporations, and end detailed regulation of industries. Friedman, his colleagues,

---

[51] Friedrich A. Hayek, *The Road to Serfdom* (Chicago: University of Chicago Press, 1944), see p. 37.
[52] Milton Friedman, *Capitalism and Freedom* (Chicago: University of Chicago Press, 1962), p. 32.

University of Chicago economist Milton Friedman.
Source: © Time & Life Pictures/ Getty Images

Chicago School
The name given to a group of economists and to the free market doctrine they taught. It is synonymous with neoliberalism.

and their free market ideas came to be called the *Chicago School*, a shorthand term for a doctrine of privatization, free trade, and deregulation.

In the lore of the global justice movement, the Chicago School, encouraged by funding from corporations, incubated neoliberalism. For decades the doctrine abided within academia as, outside, global prosperity seemed to confirm Keynesian policies. Then, in 1973 it was put into practice in Chile. There, American corporations and the Central Intelligence Agency backed a coup against a democratically elected government with socialist leanings. The economic policies of the new government, which relied on terror to suppress its opponents, were created by graduates of the Chicago School, who opened the country to corporate exploitation by selling state-owned corporations, lowering protective trade barriers, and privatizing social security. Eventually, their efforts led to an economic boom, though it ended abruptly in a 1982 global currency crisis.

Meanwhile, economies in developed countries had become mired in "stagflation," a condition of high unemployment with weak growth. In England, Prime Minister Margaret Thatcher moved in the direction of privatization and deregulation to cure this, as did Ronald Reagan in the United States. The eventual prosperity of these nations led to the further spread of neoliberal ideas. Friedman and his colleagues traversed the globe advising leaders. Graduates of the Chicago School staffed economic ministries, agencies, and international institutions. As economic globalization accelerated in the 1990s neoliberalism was a major force behind it.

Agenda of the Global Justice Movement

Critics in the global justice movement saw neoliberalism as a new doctrine of Western, particularly American, colonialism and imperialism, opening poor nations and indigenous peoples to plunder by corporations advancing on the laissez-faire tide. Exaggerating the movement's anger at what came to pass is hard. One of its leading reporters, Naomi Klein, saw "the rise of disaster capitalism" because neoliberal ideas were frequently imposed after "shocks" such as coups, wars, economic collapse, and natural disasters.[53] In Iraq, for example, the U.S.-dominated coalition in 2003 ordered the government to privatize national companies, allow foreign firms to own Iraqi companies and banks, and eliminate most trade barriers.[54] Another critic calls the process of neoliberal conquest "necrocapitalism," or the creation of death zones that subjugate life to wealth creation, as when nations send their armies to repress indigenous populations on lands being drilled or mined for profit or when poor farmers commit suicide after removal of protective tariffs lowers the price of their crops.[55]

The movement is populated by progressive-leaning actors including labor unions, human rights groups, environmentalists, religious bodies, farmers, socialists, indigenous people's movements, feminists, animal rights activists, Neo-Luddites,[56] and anarchists opposed to any overarching world order. It has little unity. Politely, it is called a movement of movements, more unerringly, "multitudes on the edge of chaos."[57] It first achieved high visibility in 1999 when 50,000 activists gathered to protest World Trade Organization meetings in Seattle and street riots broke out. Two years later at a *Group of Eight* summit in Genoa, Italy, as many as 100,000 came to protest as heads of state from the wealthiest nations met to discuss the global economy. Rioting followed and police killed one activist.

Since then, the movement has created less visible turbulence. Concerns about terrorism made street protests more difficult and protests against trade became awkward after the September 11, 2001, attacks on the World Trade Center, a symbol of free trade. But outside the limelight it has proved durable, growing in numbers and connectivity. With the global economic crisis in 2008 it found vindication. In the words of one adherent, "While eyes were on the absurd charade of the 'threat of Islamist terrorism to western civilization, the real doomsday scenario . . . was gathering pace right next to Ground Zero, in Wall Street."[58]

For now, debate and confrontation often center on the actions of multinational corporations seen as mechanisms of dominance by capital. The struggle against them excites many in the movement. Managers have come to fear clashes between market logic and the moral agenda of civil society. One estimate is that 6,000 of the

Group of Eight
Formerly an annual meeting where eight leaders of large industrial democracies met to discuss economic issues, since replaced by an expanded group of the wealthiest nations called the Group of 20, or G20.

---

[53] Naomi Klein, *The Shock Doctrine: The Rise of Disaster Capitalism* (New York: Henry Holt, 2007), chap. 2.

[54] David Harvey, *A Brief History of Neoliberalism* (New York: Oxford University Press, 2005), p. 6.

[55] Subhabrata Bobby Banerjee, "Necrocapitalism," *Organization Studies* 29, no. 12 (2008), p. 1542.

[56] The Luddites (1811–1816) were English textile workers who blamed unemployment and low wages on new steam-powered textile machines. The name comes from a mythical figure, Ned Ludd. They wrecked the machines and violently attacked their builders before being suppressed.

[57] Graeme Chesters and Ian Welsh, *Complexity and Social Movements: Multitudes on the Edge of Chaos* (London: Routledge, 2006).

[58] Madeleine Bunting, "Faith. Belief. Trust," *The Guardian,* October 6, 2008, p. 31.

world's NGOs are of the variety that attack corporations.[59] A leading scholar within civil society issues the call to battle.

> [We are in] . . . a struggle between two globalizations grounded in sharply contrasting visions of human possibility—one imperial and the other democratic. It pits an alliance of state and corporate power devoted to a vision of global Empire against an alliance of people power devoted to a vision of Earth Community. Empire holds the edge in institutional power; Earth Community holds the edge in the moral power of the authentic cultural values of a mature consciousness.[60]

Today, the antiglobalism movement remains a cacophony of voices, so ascribing to it a specific goal or platform is difficult. It is broadly against capitalism, corporate power, deregulation, privatization, sweatshops, child labor, trade agreements, consumerism, colonialism, imperialism, racism, sexism, and militarism. Again broadly, it favors *inter alia* popular democracy, horizontalism (the opposite of hierarchical power relationships), subsidiarity (local control of affairs as opposed to control by a centralized power from afar), human rights, sustainability, equality, and, as expressed in one of the movement's catchphrases, "a world in which many worlds fit."

Global Activism

Activists, by definition, take action. Progressive elements have spun unique webs of advocacy to correct perceived problems or abuses. A recent example is the International Campaign to Ban Landmines, composed at its height of 800 groups in 50 countries. Activists from groups such as Human Rights Watch attacked corporations making antipersonnel mines. As a result, Raytheon stopped making the mines, and others, including Motorola, and General Electric, quit selling parts used to make them.[61] Similar advocacy networks have formed to fight sweatshop contracting by clothing makers and environmental abuses by energy and mining companies.

Such efforts are not new. In the early 1800s a remarkably similar advocacy network led the global antislavery campaign.[62] In the 1970s international campaigns forced Nestlé and other infant-formula makers to change the way formula was sold in developing countries. And in the 1980s a fierce human rights coalition pushed foreign corporations out of very profitable markets in apartheid-era South Africa.[63]

---

[59] George Lodge and Craig Wilson, *A Corporate Solution to Global Poverty* (Princeton, NJ: Princeton University Press, 2006), p. 46.

[60] David C. Korten, *The Great Turning: From Empire to Earth Community* (Bloomfield, CT: Kumarian Press, 2006), p. 12.

[61] Christina Del Valle and Monica Larner, "A New Front in the War on Land Mines," *BusinessWeek*, April 28, 1997, p. 43.

[62] Margaret E. Keck and Kathyrn Sikkink, *Activists Beyond Borders* (Ithaca, NY: Cornell University Press, 1998), pp. 8–22.

[63] S. Prakash Sethi and Oliver F. Williams, *Economic Imperatives and Ethical Values in Global Business: The South African Experience and International Codes Today* (South Bend, IN: University of Notre Dame Press, 2001).

Attacks on corporations marshal a range of devices that create pressure. Following is a list, hardly exhaustive, of tactics.

- *Consumer boycotts.* A boycott is a call to pressure a company by not buying its products and services. Perhaps the first global boycott, against white sugar, was called in 1792 by radical groups in England protesting brutal slavery in the British East Indies. It halved sugar sales in England and may have been crucial in ending the slave trade within the British Empire.[64] In recent years, advocacy groups have called hundreds of boycotts. Here are some current examples. Animal Liberation Victoria, an Australian group, is leading a worldwide boycott of Adidas for using the skins of inhumanely killed kangaroos for soccer boots. War on Want, a British group that fights global poverty, has called a boycott of Caterpillar, Volvo, and Daewoo for supplying Israel with the bulldozers used to demolish Palestinian homes. In the effort with perhaps the broadest international base and the most recent success, 115 groups in 20 countries have joined in the Burma Campaign UK boycott of a "Dirty List" of hundreds of companies that do business in Myanmar, thereby supporting a regime accused of flagrant human rights violations.

- *Shareholder attacks.* In European nations and the United States rules permit shareholders of public companies to sponsor resolutions on which all shareholders may vote at annual meetings. Most are on governance issues such as procedures for electing directors, but many are attempts to impose progressive political and social values on corporate action. In this effort, religious organizations take the lead, usually working through the Interfaith Center on Corporate Responsibility in New York, a group that coordinates about 300 religious orders, denominations, and pension funds representing many faiths. Here are examples of some of the 390 resolutions planned through it in 2009. Two orders of nuns, a Catholic hospital, a social responsibility fund, and the United Methodist Church asked Nucor, the nation's second-largest steel company, to stop buying pig iron made with charcoal produced by slaves in Brazil. It got 27 percent of the vote. And seven orders of nuns asked PepsiCo to report to shareholders about the dangers of using genetically engineered corn, rice, and sugar in its products. It got 8.4 percent. Each resolution was opposed by the company. Few such proposals get a majority vote, but they create bad publicity and may damage brand images.

- *Harassment, ridicule, and shaming.* Forms of harassment are limited only by the imagination. Activists bring lawsuits based on clever charges such as racketeering. They disrupt the lives of executives and their families by picketing their homes, protesting at their children's schools, and interrupting services at their churches. They climb corporate buildings to unfurl banners. Some groups hand out mock awards. Corporate Accountability International regularly inducts corporations into its Hall of Shame. Each year on the eve of the World Economic Forum in Davos, a meeting of global corporate and political elites, a progressive jury hands out Public Eye "awards" to corporations nominated by NGOs

---

[64] "Sick with Excess of Sweetness," *The Economist*, December 23, 2006, p. 93.

around the world for exceptional irresponsibility.[65] Past "winners," including Shell, Walt Disney, Walmart, and Dow Chemical, have declined to send anyone to pick up the statuette that goes with the recognition.

- *Corporate campaigns.* A corporate campaign is a broad, sustained attack, usually by a coalition of groups that mobilizes activists for coordinated warfare and employs a wide range of tactics.[66] The campaign depicts the firm as engaging in antisocial behavior to make a profit while portraying the advocacy groups as moral crusaders for truth and fairness. Multinational corporations have enormous financial resources, strong influence in governments, and trusted brand names. Activists typically have slender financing, little political power, and low name recognition. However, a key source of strength is the public's willingness to see environmental, religious, or human rights groups as selfless and acting for justice. Using this perception, activists seize the ethical high ground and engage the corporation with an assault that might be likened to warfare because the action sometimes stretches or breaks the bonds of civility. A recent example is the campaign of ForestEthics to get Victoria's Secret, a subsidiary of Limited Brands, to stop using pulp from virgin Canadian forests in its catalogs. The company agreed to use recycled paper after enduring two years of a "Victoria's Dirty Secret" campaign that included store picketing by chain-saw-wielding women in lingerie, civil disobedience in shopping malls, and shareholder meetings picketed by hecklers in bear costumes.

The activism of global civil society challenges traditional notions of democracy. Advocacy groups have limited memberships. Unlike representative legislatures, they are not accountable to a broad base of voters even as they claim that their ideas about everything from sustainable forests to healthy diets represent the public interest. They are unwilling to accept corporate behavior guided merely by laws, trade agreements, or the choices of consumers in markets as responsible behavior. Instead, they argue that because corporations have corrupted governments and manipulated consumers, the groups are justified in taking action to impose standards of "responsibility," "justice," "equity," and "rights" as defined by the progressive vision. This vision is not uncontroversial. Once into a campaign, progressive advocates tap the deep cynicism in public opinion to build anger against the corporate target. If the company capitulates and changes its policies, the activists have, in effect, appropriated its power and assets to further their policy agenda.

CONCLUDING OBSERVATIONS

We have narrated a history in which basic criticisms of business are repeated over and over. Each era brings new personalities, new targets, and some new issues, but the fundamental substance endures. The story is one of endless debate between critics and defenders of capitalism. Figure 4.3 shows two timelines that

---

[65] Gustavo Capdevila, "World Economic Forum: Davos Under Fire," Inter Press Service, January 31, 2009, at http://ipsnews.net/news.asp?idnews=45618.

[66] For an extended discussion, see Jarol B. Manheim, *The Death of a Thousand Cuts: Corporate Campaigns and the Attack on Corporations* (Mahwah, NJ: Lawrence Erlbaum, 2001).

FIGURE 4.3   Timelines of Ideological Conflict in the United States

		Alexander Hamilton				John D. Rockefeller	J.P. Morgan		Henry Ford		Ronald Reagan	George W. Bush
Capitalists	Federalists	Classical liberalism	Republican party		Laissez-faire			Great Depression		Neoliberalism	

			Robert Owen and New Harmony	Emerson and Thoreau		Mary Lease	Mother Jones	Huey Long	FDR	Ralph Nader		Global Justice Movement
		Thomas Jefferson										
Critics	Antifederalists	Democratic party		Populism		Old Progressives		Radicals		Liberals		New Progressives

1790   1810   1830   1850   1870   1890   1910   1930   1950   1970   1990   2010

The two timelines show how a debate between business and its critics moves through American history. Each timeline represents the sweep of people and ideas associated with one side of this enduring debate.

represent this exchange. Imagine a dinner party at which Aristotle, Saint Augustine, Thomas Jefferson, and Ralph Nader sit at one table, while Adam Smith, Benjamin Franklin, Alexander Hamilton, and Ronald Reagan sit at another. Now imagine the harmony among tablemates as contrasted with the gulf between the two groups.

Philosophically, the difference between the two groups is profound. Economic liberals believe that uncontrolled, laissez-faire markets give humans freedom to follow laws of nature leading to the rise of the Good Society. Progressives have a different vision. They believe that people in society should be managed according to a human plan, based on their vision what will create the Good Society. For them, true human liberty is not freedom from government, but the freedom to fulfill human potential in a society unmarked by vices including sexism, racism, homophobia, colonialism, wars, obesity, smoking, and corporate manipulation.

In contrast, the conservative capitalist vision is one of material progress. It sees industrial capitalism as a historical force for continuous, turbulent social change; it is, as the economist Joseph Shumpeter wrote years ago, "a perennial gale of creative destruction" that strains institutions and challenges existing authority.[67] The defense of capitalism is that, for the most part, the changes it brings represent progress, a condition of improvement for humanity. All the while that critics have been objecting, it has steadily improved living standards for billions of people. As against promoting greed, it has promoted positive cultural values such as imagination, innovation, cooperation, hard work, and the interpersonal trust necessary for numberless daily business transactions.

In the end, a broad spectrum of criticism is an important check on power. Legitimate criticism exists and demands attention. If criticism is properly channeled, it can preserve the best of the business institution and bring wide benefit.

[67] *Capitalism, Socialism and Democracy* (New York: Harper & Row, 1976), p. 143; originally published in 1942.

A Campaign against KFC Corporation

Peyton Hull, a 12-year-old middle school student in Pittsburgh, loves animals and hopes to be a veterinarian. One day while volunteering at a shelter she learned that People for the Ethical Treatment of Animals (PETA) was boycotting KFC. Later, at her home computer, she watched actress Pamela Anderson narrate a "Kentucky Fried Cruelty" video showing mangled, abused chickens at facilities supplying KFC.

Peyton organized a dozen friends. Helped by her mother, she stayed up all night with markers and poster paper making signs, and the next day, Saturday, she and her friends stood vigil at a KFC restaurant with their signs. People inside waved their chicken. Some teenagers in the parking lot yelled, "KFC is good. Get a life," and threw chicken at them. However, one older woman approached the girls, talked to them, then decided not to go in. Peyton was pleased and told her mother: "Mom, we saved one person from going to KFC."[1]

The incident is just one skirmish in a larger battle between PETA and KFC. War was declared on January 6, 2003. In a press release, People for the Ethical Treatment of Animals announced the start of a campaign against KFC Corporation, the world's largest chicken restaurant chain. PETA held KFC responsible for "cruel treatment" of poultry raised and slaughtered for its restaurants.[2] It demanded that the company force more humane practices on its suppliers. KFC responded with a statement dismissing such "allegations," saying the birds in its meals were treated humanely.

KFC does not raise any chickens. In the United States it buys them from independent companies in the poultry processing industry, a $40 billion a year business that sells to supermarkets, restaurants, and institutions. Its pieces of fried chicken emerge from a supply chain of hatcheries, feed mills, "grow-out" farms, processing plants, and cold storage buildings. This industry is very competitive. With average net profit after tax a slim 0.8 percent, operations are highly automated and focused on efficiencies that reduce cost.[3]

PETA is angry about how chickens are handled in this supply chain, but the maze of facilities, owned by more than 500 corporations, is out of public view, fragmented, and largely anonymous. In contrast, KFC is vulnerable to PETA's basic strategy of tarnishing a brand by associating it with animal cruelty. By threatening the value of KFC's brand, PETA hopes to make the company use its market power as the world's largest buyer of chickens to force reform on growers and slaughter plants. If this occurs, PETA will have harnessed a reluctant giant to further its agenda.

Going into the chicken war, PETA had a record of success. Its initial effort was a campaign against McDonald's in 1999. After less than a year of exposure to a boycott, restaurant demonstrations, and the group's mccruelty.com Web site the company succumbed, imposing stricter animal welfare standards on its suppliers as a condition for ending the assault. It forced changes on reluctant growers, including roomier cages for hens and surprise slaughterhouse inspections. After McDonald's capitulated, its smaller rivals followed. Burger King adopted animal welfare guidelines after a five-month campaign. Then Wendy's buckled. Safeway lasted only three months. Albertsons and Kroger were subdued by campaigns of only one week each.

INITIAL SKIRMISHES

KFC learned of PETA's intentions in 2001, when Cheryl Bachelder, its president, received a letter from Bruce Friedrich, director of the group's restaurant campaigns. The letter asked why KFC, knowing of PETA's actions against its competitors, was doing "nothing at all" to improve the lives of chickens raised for its restaurants. Friedrich asked what KFC intended to do, offered to put the company in touch with animal welfare experts, and added, "We are looking ahead to our next target."[4]

---

[1] Quotes in this paragraph are from Dev Meyers, "Seventh-Grader Organizes Animal-Rights Protest," *Pittsburgh Post-Gazette*, February 24, 2008, p. W1.

[2] "Company Stonewalls on Animal Welfare Reforms," press release, People for the Ethical Treatment of Animals, January 6, 2003, at www.peta.org.

[3] First Research, "Industry Profile: Poultry Processing, Quarterly Update," October 12, 2009, pp. 2 and 9.

[4] The letter is at www.kfccruelty.com/letter-042501.asp.

Over the next several weeks Friedrich had a series of phone calls and meetings with Bachelder and David Novak, CEO of KFC's parent corporation Yum! Brands. Yum! Brands was created in 1997 when PepsiCo spun off its KFC, Pizza Hut, and Taco Bell chains as a separate corporation. Subsequently, the new firm bought the Long John Silver's and A&W chains. Today, Yum! is the world's largest quick-service restaurant corporation with 36,500 restaurants worldwide. The KFC brand traces its origins to the Kentucky Fried Chicken franchise started by the avuncular Colonel Harlan Sanders in 1952. It has 15,580 restaurants in 109 countries and serves about 12 million customers a day.

The dialogue revealed a wide gulf between the company and its interlocutor. KFC told Friedrich that it included humane treatment guidelines in its poultry supplier contracts. He accused the company of using only inadequate industry standards permitting ghastly treatment of chickens and considering their welfare only at the point where deaths from abuse lowered profits. He stated that the suffering of chickens was an ethical issue going beyond financial considerations.[5] KFC said it would review its guidelines and promised to keep PETA informed.

In the months that followed, KFC took several actions. It convened an Animal Welfare Advisory Council composed of outside academic and industry experts. It began unannounced audits of growers and slaughterhouses. And it worked with industry associations to develop new poultry welfare guidelines. However, its efforts were unsatisfactory to PETA because they did not lead to specific, more radical changes including the following.

- *Gas killing.* KFC chickens are stunned by electrical shock before immersion in scalding water (to loosen feathers) and then exposed to mechanical blades that slit their throats. PETA believes that gas killing is preferable because it ensures that chickens are insensate before these painful procedures, whereas electrical stunning is less reliable.
- *Cameras in slaughterhouses.* Cameras would supplement audits and make oversight more reliable.

- *Mechanized chicken-catching.* Hand-catching crews gather KFC chickens from grower buildings. PETA believes that the crews treat the birds roughly and that mechanical catching systems are less likely to result in bruises and broken bones.
- *New genetic strains of chickens.* The chickens eaten in KFC restaurants, known as "broilers," are bred to gain weight rapidly over their brief lives. However, the "broiler breeders" used to produce the flocks of chickens slaughtered for restaurant meals live longer. They exhibit the rapid weight gain characteristic of all broiler strains, but their skeletons and joints do not grow commensurate with their overall weight and they are prone to painful joint conditions as they age. PETA requested introduction of leaner genetic strains that did not exhibit skeletal deficiencies.
- *Elimination of forced growth.* Broiler strains bred for rapid weight gain under forced growth regimens suffer from metabolic pathologies and excess mortality. Slowing growth means longer upkeep of chickens before slaughter, but it reduces premature deaths.
- *More room for birds to move around.* PETA requests that KFC give its chickens at least two to three times more space per bird and give them sheltered areas and perches in the warehouselike buildings where they are raised.
- *Allowance for instinctive behavior of chickens.* PETA believes that birds raised in captivity suffer from chronic stress and boredom induced by suppression of natural behaviors. Among other measures, it suggests that they get whole green cabbages to peck and eat.[6]

Debate between the antagonists was dysfunctional. PETA addressed the corporation in the tone of a parent scolding an errant child. It was "extremely concerned" that the firm "has no interest in making real progress to stop animal cruelty," adding that "we have pressed you to take action on this issue, yet you have done nothing."[7] KFC, on the other hand, wrote to PETA "[i]n the spirit of open communications," but kept it at arm's length, giving only brief and general information about

---

[5] Letter of May 14, 2001, from Bruce G. Friedrich to Jonathan D. Blum, senior vice president, Tricon Global Restaurants, at www.kfccruelty.com/letter-052401.asp. Yum! Brands was formerly named Tricon Global Restaurants.

[6] Letter of August 6, 2002, from Bruce G. Friedrich to Jonathan D. Blum, at www.kfccruelty.com/letter-080602.asp.
[7] Ibid.

conducting audits, holding meetings, and working on animal welfare standards with industry groups.[8] PETA thought that KFC was dragging its feet.

A LOOK AT PETA

PETA is dominated by its founder, Ingrid Newkirk, who became an animal rights activist after a formative experience. Living in Maryland in 1972, she was training to be a stockbroker. A neighbor moved, abandoning cats that soon bred litters of kittens nearby. She gathered them up and took them to a nearby animal shelter to be cared for. Yet a short time later she learned they had been killed. The episode changed her. With no desire to become a stockbroker remaining, she talked her way into a job at the shelter. Observing brutal treatment of animals, she began to arrive early in the morning to kill them in a humane way before others came. "I must have killed a thousand of them," she says, "sometimes dozens every day."[9]

From the shelter Newkirk moved on to work as a deputy sheriff on animal cruelty investigations, then headed a commission to control animal disease. She was inspired to form PETA after reading a book, *Animal Liberation,* by philosopher Peter Singer.[10]

In the book, Singer argues that animals have moral rights. Moral rights are strong entitlements to dutiful treatment by others—in this case human beings. He asserts that the traditional, absolute dominion of humans over animals is an unfair exploitation. Because animals are living, sentient beings capable of suffering, their interests are entitled to equal consideration with human interests. In his words: "No matter what the nature of the being, the principle of equality requires that its suffering be counted equally with the like suffering . . . of any other being."[11] Thus, he argues, animals have an unalienable right to have their needs accommodated by humans. Denial of this right is speciesism, or the prejudicial favoring of one species over another. Speciesism, according to Singer, is an evil akin to racism and sexism because it restricts moral rights to one species just as racism and sexism have restricted them to one race or sex. The PETA Mission Statement, Exhibit 1, reflects the inspiration Newkirk found in this philosophy.

Newkirk has a combative attitude about animal rights. "The animals are defenseless," she says. "They can't talk back, and they can't fight back. But we can. And no matter what it takes, we always will."[12] After reading about a Palestinian bomb put on a donkey and detonated by remote control she wrote to Yasir Arafat requesting that innocent animals be left out of the Arab–Israeli conflict. Her will stipulates that when she dies the meat on her body is to be cooked for a human barbeque, her skin used to make leather products such as purses, and her feet made into umbrella stands.[13]

PETA is creative. Since most people give no thought to animal rights, its actions are designed to attract attention, even at the cost of offending some. Perhaps the mildest attention-getting tactic is the use of theater. For example, PETA demonstrators have dragged themselves down streets with their feet in leg traps to publicize the evils of fur trapping. Another tactic is that of the outrageous act. To protest pictures of women wearing fur in *Vogue,* activists went to the chic Manhattan restaurant where its editor was having lunch and threw a dead raccoon on her plate. Young ladies at county fairs are crowned as pork queens only to have pies thrown in their faces by PETA activists. The group has asked Wisconsin, the "Dairy State," to change its state beverage from cows' milk to soy milk.

PETA freely uses sexuality to get attention. When the American Meat Institute puts on its Annual Hot Dog Lunches for government officials in Washington, D.C., former *Playboy* Playmates wearing bikinis made of lettuce hand out "veggie dogs" outside. It recruits celebrities to present its message. Fame and glamour attract. Their presence endows a view that might otherwise be disregarded with the celebrity's aura of success and legitimacy. PETA also uses the Internet to get its message out. It has multiple Web sites for issues such as zoos, circuses, and animal testing. The network of sites is easy to navigate, informative in depth, and often entertaining. There are facts, games, pictures,

[8] Letter of July 17, 2002, from Jonathan Blum to Bruce G. Friedrich, at www.kfccruelty.com/petakfc.asp.

[9] Quoted in Michael Specter, "The Extremist," *The New Yorker,* April 14, 2003, p. 56.

[10] Peter Singer, *Animal Liberation* (New York: Avon Books, 1975).

[11] Ibid., p. 8.

[12] Quoted in Specter, "The Extremist," p. 54.

[13] Ibid., pp. 57 and 58.

EXHIBIT 1
PETA's
Mission
Statement

Source: Courtesy
of People for the
Ethical Treatment
of Animals (PETA).

People for the Ethical Treatment of Animals (PETA), with more than 1.2 million members and supporters, is the largest animal rights organization in the world.

PETA focuses its attention on the four areas in which the largest numbers of animals suffer the most intensely for the longest periods of time: on factory farms, in laboratories, in the clothing trade, and in the entertainment industry. We also work on a variety of other issues, including the cruel killing of beavers, birds and other "pests," and the abuse of backyard dogs.

PETA works through public education, cruelty investigations, research, animal rescue, legislation, special events, celebrity involvement, and protest campaigns.

video clips, humor, and celebrities. PETA makes a special effort to influence children. One comic brochure, "Your Mommy Kills Animals" shows a crazed woman wielding a bloody knife over a rabbit. "Ask your mommy," it suggests, "how many animals she killed to make her fur coat."[14]

All these tactics, and more, have been employed in the fight against KFC.

THE CHICKENS

At the center of the conflict are the chickens. Chickens are a species of the order Galliformes, which includes turkeys, pheasants, grouse, and partridges. Galliformes are heavy-bodied, short-duration fliers that feed on insects and seeds, nest on the ground, and hatch precocial (self-caring) young. They are social birds that communicate with each other and establish complex hierarchies in flocks.

The earliest wild chickens, members of the species *Gallus gallus*, inhabited jungles of Southeast Asia. About 4,000 years ago they were domesticated. From Asia the domesticated chicken, *Gallus domesticus*, spread across the globe. In ancient Greece they were valued for the sport of cockfighting, and in imperial Rome prophets read the future in their entrails. Chickens had such a hold on the superstitious Romans that generals kept special flocks in the belief that their behavior could foretell victory or defeat in battle. In the hours before combat, hardened legionnaires crowded around these flocks seeking portents. As the legions marched, they spread *Gallus domesticus* across the empire. Centuries later, the earliest European settlers brought chickens to North America.

In the United States, large-scale chicken production developed slowly. As late as the 1920s chicken

farms had flocks of only about 500 free-ranging birds. Today the industry is highly specialized, with some farms in egg production and others raising broilers (or chickens slaughtered for meat; literally, chickens for broiling—or baking or frying). Flocks are now raised in long, windowless, buildings with automated equipment to maintain as many as 100,000 birds. Consumption of chicken has risen. In 1955 only a little more than 1 billion broilers were raised, or 6.5 chickens for each American; by 2009 there were 9 billion raised, or 30 per American.[15]

Chickens, like other animal species, adapted for survival in an ecological niche. In doing so, certain behaviors became instinctive. They live in flocks of approximately 10 and establish dominance hierarchies called pecking orders. The dominant bird in a flock can peck any other bird, and that bird will yield. Status in the pecking order is conveyed by sounds such as crowing or cackling, aggressive or passive postures, spacing, use of more or less desirable nesting sites, and running at or away from rivals. In mixed-sex flocks there are two pecking orders, one for cocks and one for hens, but the hen hierarchy is subordinate. All hens yield to even the lowest cock. This is a genetically predisposed trait essential for species survival because a cock will not mate with a dominating hen. Pecking orders have survival value. Once dominance is established, fighting ceases and energy is used in socially productive ways.

In nature, chickens are omnivorous, eating plants, insects, and small animals such as lizards. Hens are secretive and build hidden nests, preferably on the ground. During the day chickens spread out to

---

[14] At www.furissdead.com.

[15] Bureau of the Census, *Statistical Abstract of the United States 1956,* 77th ed., tables 1 and 857; and Bureau of the Census, *Statistical Abstract of the United States 2010,* 129th ed., tables 2 and 846.

forage, but at dusk they reduce the spaces between them. At night they often roost in trees. According to PETA, chickens are "inquisitive and interesting animals" and "as intelligent as mammals like cats, dogs, and even primates."[16] In nature, they are individuals with "distinct personalities" that "form friendships and social hierarchies, recognize one another, love their young, and enjoy a full life, dust-bathing, making nests, roosting in trees, and more."[17]

Life in high-density growing environments frustrates these natural behaviors. Cages or crowding prevent division into flocks with established pecking orders. Without a complete pecking order, individuals may not yield to threat displays, and physical attacks occur as birds compete over space, food, and water.[18] Weaker animals have no place to hide and may be assaulted repeatedly until they die. In addition, crowded chickens are unable to engage in a range of ordinary foraging, grooming, nesting, brooding, and roosting behaviors. Critics claim that such deprivation violates the right of an animal to satisfy its needs through natural behaviors.

THE CAMPAIGN

At the start of the campaign, PETA activists descended on KFC outlets worldwide, conducting hundreds of demonstrations in the first months. Members handed out "Buckets of Blood" containing "Psycho Col. Sanders" figures and toy chickens with slit throats. When Yum! Brands CEO David Novak appeared at the opening of a restaurant in Germany, two activists doused him with fake blood and feathers. According to campaign leader Friedrich: "There is so much blood on this chicken-killer's hands, a little more on his business suit won't hurt."[19]

KFC issued a statement calling the attacks "corporate terrorism" that "crossed the line from simply expressing their views to corporate attacks and personal

Yum! Brands CEO David Novak after being splattered with fake blood at a PETA demonstration in Hanover, Germany, on June 23, 2003. Source: © AP Photo.

violence."[20] In Paris, Ingrid Newkirk and celebrity musician Chrissie Hynde led activists who stormed into a busy KFC restaurant at the noon hour, smearing the front window with red paint symbolic of chicken blood and lecturing diners until guards threw them out. Outside, the protest blocked traffic on a boulevard for two hours. Back in the United States, PETA put up roadside billboards depicting Col. Sanders hacking a chicken with a bloody knife under the words "Kentucky Fried Cruelty. We do chickens wrong."[21]

Although the main effort was directed toward publicly associating the KFC brand with cruelty to chickens, another focus was on pressuring KFC and Yum! Brands executives at a personal level. Several months into the campaign KFC President Cheryl Bachelder failed to keep what Ingrid Newkirk thought was a commitment to call her. So Newkirk phoned Bachelder at home on a Saturday evening.

[16] "Chickens," at www.peta.org.

[17] "PETA Reveals Shocking Cruelty to Animals at KFC Factory Chicken Farm," press release, October 2, 2003, at www.peta.org.

[18] T. R. O'Keefe et al., "Social Organization in Caged Layers: The Peck Order Revisited," *Poultry Science,* July 1988, p. 1013.

[19] Quoted in Jay Nordlinger, "PETA vs. KFC," *National Review,* December 22, 2003, p. 28.

[20] Cited in "Animal Rights Activists Spray KFC Chief with Fake Blood and Chicken Feathers," The Associated Press State & Local Wire, June 23, 2003.

[21] "Finger-Lickin' Foul," *Houston Press,* December 18, 2003, p. 2.

When Bachelder objected to being called at home, Newkirk responded with a letter that read, in part:

> Of course you would rather not be disturbed in the privacy of your own home, but the animals you torture and slaughter pay for that home with their misery and their very lives yet have nothing remotely like a life or even a nest of any kind. . . . It is merely an accident of birth that you are not one of them.[22]

Newkirk wrote to both Bachelder and CEO Novak at their homes in Louisville, Kentucky, posting the letters with their home addresses on PETA's kentuckyfriedcruelty.com Web site. It enlisted former Beatle Paul McCartney to write to Novak. His letter, which requested an end to "the egregious forms of abuse endured by chickens," ran as a full-page ad in the Louisville *Courier-Journal*. A KFC spokesperson responded that "PETA should follow one of Sir Paul's songs and just 'Let It Be.'"[23] Other celebrities were recruited. The Rev. Al Sharpton asked the black community to boycott KFC. His Holiness the Dalai Lama asked KFC to stop its plans for a restaurant in Tibet.

Taking advantage of Securities and Exchange Commission rules, PETA gained entry to the Yum! Brands 2003 annual shareholders' meeting in Louisville. After activists spoke, CEO Novak called for an end to the campaign saying, "We don't want to be abused, just like you don't want the chickens to be abused." In 2004 PETA qualified a shareholder resolution asking for a company report on actions to reduce cruelty toward chickens. Only 7.6 percent of shareholders voted for it. PETA would go on to introduce similar resolutions each year, getting only single-digit support each time.

A MUTED CORPORATE DEFENSE

Throughout the PETA campaign, KFC and Yum! Brands have maintained a low media profile while working to elevate animal welfare standards. When contacted by reporters a typical response is: "We don't comment on PETA's activities and publicity stunts, which speak for themselves."[24] This reticence is characteristic of the animal agriculture, food, and restaurant industries generally when animal welfare becomes an issue. In mass growing and slaughter, some pain is inevitable. Altering production to address chicken discomfort, injury, and behavior deprivation raises costs.

Most consumers are ignorant of factory farming methods and fail to entertain the link between a KFC meal and the life experience of the creature in it. Despite PETA's efforts, there is no groundswell of demand for more humane treatment of chickens. Reacting to a protest going on outside a restaurant in Israel, a KFC customer said: "There's nothing to do. This is life and it is all part of the food chain. I have to eat."[25]

This vacuum of interest and concern sustains industry calculations balancing poultry welfare against costs. For example, industry guidelines that KFC helped develop and now follows stipulate that corrective action be taken if the number of "DOA" [dead-on-arrival] chickens at a plant exceeds 0.5 percent, if the number of broken or dislocated wings from handling to place chickens on the stun line exceeds 5 percent, and if less than 98 percent of chickens are effectively stunned before having their throats cut by automatic knife.[26] These standards may be defined as humane, but for every 500 chickens they are met if 3 arrive dead, 25 get their wings broken by handlers, and 10 are conscious when plunged into a tank of scalding water to loosen their feathers before further "processing." Magnified to the scale of KFC operations, assuming each of its claimed 720 million annual diners consumes the equivalent of only one-tenth of a chicken, the standard could allow 360,000 dead-on-arrival chickens, 3.6 million broken wings, and 1.4 million live throat cuttings.

Such compromises in chicken welfare to avoid higher costs are tacitly accepted by KFC diners, but difficult to defend in a media debate. PETA's greatest source of power is the desire of average people to see themselves as humane and decent.[27] The impossibility of defending a standard that lets chickens be boiled

[22] Letter of March 24, 2003, from Ingrid E. Newkirk to Cheryl Bachelder, at www.kentuckyfriedcruelty.com/pdfs/letter-032.

[23] Mark Naegele, "McCartney Accuses KFC of Fowl Play," *Columbus Dispatch*, July 25, 2003, p. 2C.

[24] Rick Maynard, manager of public relations at KFC, quoted in Keith Edwards, "These Protesters Aren't Chicken," *Portland Press Herald*, December 17, 2008, p. B1.

[25] Yitchak Mokitada, quoted in Jenny Merkin and Yael Wolynetz, "KFC Diners Remain Unflappable in Face of Chicken Cruelty Protest," *The Jerusalem Post*, July 4, 2006, p. 5.

[26] National Chicken Council, *National Chicken Council Animal Welfare Guidelines and Audit Checklist*, (Washington, DC: National Chicken Council, January 28, 2010), pp. 7–8.

[27] Eric Dezenhall, *Nail 'Em* (Amherst, NY: Prometheus Books, 2003), p. 80.

EXHIBIT 2
Yum! Brands Animal Welfare Guiding Principles

Source: www.yum.com (2004).

Food Safety: Above all else, we are committed to providing our customers with safe, delicious meals and ensuring that our restaurants are maintained and operated under the highest food safety standards. This commitment is at the heart of our entire operations and supply chain management, and is evident in every aspect of our business—from raw material procurement to our restaurant food preparation and delivery.

Animal Treatment: Yum! Brands believes treating animals humanely and with care is a key part of our quality assurance efforts. This means animals should be free from mistreatment at all possible times from how they are raised and cared for to how they are transported and processed. Our goal is to only deal with suppliers who provide an environment that is free from cruelty, abuse and neglect.

Partnership: Yum! Brands partners with experts on our Animal Welfare Advisory Council and our suppliers to implement humane procedures/guidelines and to audit our suppliers to determine whether the adopted guidelines are being met.

Ongoing Training and Education: Yum! Brands recognizes that maintaining high standards of animal welfare is an ongoing process. Training and education has and will continue to play a key role in our efforts. Yum! Brands will continue to work with experts to ensure our quality assurance employees and suppliers have the training and knowledge necessary to further the humane treatment of animals.

Performance Quantification & Follow-up: Yum! Brands' animal welfare guidelines are specific and quantifiable. Yum! Brands measures performance against these guidelines through audits of our suppliers on a consistent basis.

Communication: Yum! Brands will communicate our best practices to counterparts within the industry and work with industry associations such as the National Council of Chain Restaurants and the Food Marketing Institute to implement continuous improvement of industry standards and operations.

---

alive makes cautious nonconfrontation a better policy than frontal assault on PETA.

Therefore, in response to attacks, the company sidesteps discussing welfare to cost trade-offs and regularly makes four other points. First, it is justified in selling chickens by the morality of the market in which meeting customer demand is a positive duty. Hence, it says, "We support our customers' preference to eat meat—a preference that represents the viewpoint of the majority of Americans."[28] Second, it is the target of false claims by PETA, a "radical organization" that deceptively hides its real goal, the advent of a vegetarian world. Third, it complies with

and usually goes beyond all laws in countries where it has restaurants. And fourth, it is only a purchaser and does not own chicken production facilities where abuses may occur; nevertheless, it accepts that its size as a chicken buyer gives it responsibility and the power to lead in humane treatment of chickens and it is taking a range of actions.

Since 2000 KFC has followed the Yum! Brands set of principles for animal welfare shown in Exhibit 2 and since 2004 it has carried out a more comprehensive set of KFC Poultry Welfare Guidelines covering breeding, growing houses, catching, transport, holding, stunning, and slaughter. KFC calls these guidelines "industry leading" because they exceed standards set by industry groups such as the National Chicken Council, but PETA rejects them because they do not require the changes it demands.

Yum! Brands set up an Animal Welfare Advisory Council of outside experts. When it was set up, PETA recommended people acceptable to it as

[28] KFC, "Animal Welfare Program: Facts," 2009, at www.kfc.com/facts/. A 2007 survey found that 91 percent of respondents had eaten chicken in the past two weeks, averaging 4.5 times combined. Paul Prekopa, "2007 Consumer Chicken Survey," WATT Poultry USA, at www.wattpoultry.com/market_survey2007.aspx.

members and the company appointed four of them. In 2005 three of these panel members submitted a set of recommendations for the welfare of chickens, calling for actions that would have satisfied all of PETA's demands.[29] KFC refused these recommendations and two of the panel members resigned. Currently the advisory group has six members, four academics and two managers from major suppliers, and meets twice a year to "align practices with the latest research and thinking in the field of animal welfare."[30]

KFC ABIDES, PETA IS UNRELENTING

As the campaign moved into its seventh year, KFC stood firm. Although surely it has lost some customers and its executives have been harassed, it has not, on the whole, suffered much from PETA's boycott. Between 2003 and 2010 KFC added more than 4,600 new outlets, an increase of 37 percent, and sales per outlet grew 7 percent despite a severe recession.[31] The performance of its parent, Yum! Brands, has also been strong. Anyone who bought its stock at the beginning of the boycott saw its share price outperform the Dow, the Standard & Poor's 500, and McDonald's since then.

PETA, now joined by more than a dozen other groups, including the Humane Society of the United States, continued its assertive campaign. Demonstrations, of which there have been more than 10,000, remained a staple. A favorite stunt is planting young women in yellow bikinis at KFC outlets where, especially in cold weather, they attract attention. During the winter of 2008–2009 PETA's bikini maidens held signs in below-freezing weather at KFCs in Michigan, Wisconsin, New York, and Maine. Newspapers described scenes where the women trembled uncontrollably as distracted drivers ran their cars over curbs. "It's a little bit chilly," said a protester in 20 degree Kalamazoo weather, "but it's really nothing compared to what the animals go through."[32]

In Louisville PETA set up its KFCruelty campaign headquarters across the street from KFC's flagship restaurant. It continues to visit the neighbors of KFC executives, handing out "bloody" chicken figures, asking them to prevail on their friends to end the cruelty. When Yum! Brands unknowingly tried to buy a building owned by PETA in Norfolk, Virginia, the group offered to give it the property for nothing in return for meeting the campaign's demands.

When KFC gave $3,000 grants of asphalt for cities to fix potholes, PETA offered to double them if it could put chalk marks on the patches reading "KFC Tortures Animals."[33] The offers were rejected. When KFC sponsored an effort at the Talladega Superspeedway to get in the *Guinness Book of World Records* for the most people simultaneously doing the chicken dance, Ingrid Newkirk wrote to Guinness officials, pointing out that records for killing animals are against its rules and asking them to "go a step further" and reject records from companies that subject animals to "needless suffering."[34] The attempt went on, but no record was set.

A PHILOSOPHICAL IMPASSE

Although the campaign against KFC could end if the company adopted specific practices, the plain issue between PETA and the corporation would remain. What is the proper relationship between humans and food animal species? The sides are polarized.

Richard Martin, editor of the industry magazine *Nation's Restaurant News,* says PETA errs in its "rejection of the animal kingdom's remorseless food chain paradigm" and in its "repudiation of the world-wide

[29] "Animal Welfare Recommendations and Proposed Plan of Action for Implementation at KFC Suppliers," memo from Dr. Iam Duncan, Dr. Temple Grandin, and Dr. Mohan Raj to Harvey Brownlee, chief operating officer, KFC, March 11, 2005, at www.kentuckyfriedcruelty.com/pdfs/March11document.pdf.

[30] KFC, "Animal Welfare Program: Latest News," 2009, at www.kfc.com/about/animalwelfare_news.asp.

[31] Sources of figures are Yum! Brands, Inc., annual reports and Form 10-Ks, various years.

[32] Quoted in "Protester Doesn't Chicken Out," *Kalamazoo Gazette,* January 27, 2009. See also Erin Richards, "PETA Protesters Give Milwaukee KFC the Cold Shoulder," *The Milwaukee Journal Sentinel,* January 24, 2009.

[33] See John Horton, "PETA Asks Cities to Reject KFC Pothole Fix," *Plain Dealer,* April 4, 2009, p. B2; and Cliff Hightower, "PETA Doubles Ante on Pothole Patches," *Chattanooga Times Free Press,* May 1, 2009, p. A9.

[34] Quoted in Dustin Long, "NASCAR, PETA Officials Playing a Game of Chicken," *News & Record,* April 22, 2009, p. C3.

acceptance of meat eating as a proper option for descendants of hunters. . . ."[35]

This position is entirely at odds with the values of animal rights activists, including one who writes, "if we cannot imagine how chickens must feel . . . perhaps we should try to imagine ourselves placed helplessly in the hands of an overpowering extraterrestrial species, to whom our pleas for mercy sound like nothing more than bleats and squeals and clucks—mere 'noise' to the master race in whose 'superior' minds we are 'only animals.'"[36]

Questions

1. Do you support KFC Corporation or People for the Ethical Treatment of Animals in this controversy? Why?

2. What are the basic criticisms that PETA makes of KFC? Are they convincing? Are its criticisms similar to timeless criticisms of business mentioned in the chapter?

3. What methods and arguments has KFC used to support its actions? Is it conducting the best defense?

4. Is the range of PETA's actions acceptable? Why does the group use controversial tactics? What are its sources of power in corporate campaigns?

5. Is it proper for PETA to pressure KFC for change when the company is following the law and public custom? Does PETA represent so compelling a truth or enough people to justify attacks on, and perhaps damage to, major corporations supported by and supporting millions of customers, employees, and stockholders?

6. Do animals have rights? If so, what are they? What duties do human beings have toward animals? Does KFC protect animal welfare at an acceptable level?

[35] Richard Martin, "Game of Chicken: Critics Say Capitulation to PETA Will Worsen Animal Rights Reprisals," *Nation's Restaurant News,* July 28, 2003, p. 31.

[36] Karen Davis, "Animal Suffering Similar to Human Slaves," *Chicago Sun-Times,* September 6, 2005, p. 50.

Chapter **Five**

Corporate Social Responsibility

Merck & Co., Inc.

Corporate social responsibility takes many forms. The following story stands out as extraordinary.

For ages, river blindness, or onchocerciasis (on-ko-sir-KYE-a-sis), has tortured humanity in tropical regions. Its cause is a parasitic worm that, in its adult form, lives only in humans. People are infected with the worm's tiny, immature larvae when bitten by black flies that swarm near fast-moving rivers and streams. These larvae settle in tissue near the bite and form colonies, often visible lumps, where adults grow up to two feet long. Mature worms live for 7 to 18 years coiled in these internal nodes, mating, and releasing tens of thousands of microscopic new larvae that migrate back to the skin's surface, causing welts, lumps, and discoloration along with a persistent itch that drives some sufferers to suicide. Eventually, the parasites move to the eyes, causing blindness. The cycle of infection is renewed when black flies take a blood meal from an infected person, ingesting tiny larvae, then bite an uninfected person, passing on the parasite.

People suffer in many ways. For Amarech Bitena of Ethiopia, the cost of river blindness is a broken heart. The parasites came in childhood. Now, at 25, her skin is hard and dark, her vision blurred. She has not married. "When I think about the future," she says, "I feel completely hopeless. . . . My vision can't be restored. My skin is destroyed. I would have liked to be a doctor."[1] Almost 18 million people suffer from onchocerciasis in tropical areas of Africa, South America, and Yemen.[2] About 500,000 have impaired vision and 270,000 are blind. It saps economies by enervating workers and driving farmers from fertile, riverside land.

Until recently, no treatment for river blindness existed, and little was done. It is only one of many tropical diseases affecting millions in developing nations. Critics said that big drug companies ignored these epidemics to focus on pills for the diseases of people in rich nations. Years ago the World Health Organization began pesticide spraying to kill the black fly, but it was a frustrating job. Winds carry flies up to

---

[1] Claudia Feldman, "River Blindness: A Forgotten Disease," *The Houston Chronicle,* October 9, 2005, p. 5.

[2] "Fighting River Blindness and Other Ills," *The Lancet* 374, no. 9684 (2009), p. 91.

In countries ravaged by river blindness, the blind sometimes hold sticks and follow the lead of children. Merck commissioned this bronze sculpture for the lobby of its New Jersey headquarters, where top executives pass by each day. It symbolizes Merck's commitment to make medicine for the good of humanity. Because of Merck's unprecedented donation of a river blindness drug, such scenes are no longer common. Source: Photo courtesy of Merck & Co., Inc.

100 miles from breeding grounds. And scientists estimate that the breeding cycle must be suppressed for at least 14 years to stop reinfections.

In 1975 scientists at Merck & Co. discovered a compound that killed animal parasites. By 1981 they had synthesized it and marketed it for deworming dogs, cattle, sheep, and pigs. Ivermectin, as it was called, was a blockbuster hit and would be the best-selling veterinary drug worldwide for two decades. Merck's researchers had a strong hunch it also would be effective in humans against *Onchocerca volvulus,* the river blindness parasite.[3]

Merck faced a decision. It would be very expensive to bring a new drug to market and manufacture it. Yet people with the disease were among the world's poorest. Their villages had no doctors to prescribe it, no drugstores to sell it. Should Merck develop a drug that might never be profitable?

George W. Merck, son of the firm's founder and its leader for 32 years, once said: "We try never to forget that medicine is for the people. It is not for the profits. The profits follow, and if we have remembered that, they have never failed to appear."[4] This advice was still respected at Merck; it lived in the corporate culture. Merck's scientists were motivated by humanitarian goals and restraining them was awkward. The decision to go ahead was made. The cost would be $200 million.

Clinical trials of ivermectin confirmed its effectiveness. A single yearly dose of 150 micrograms per kilogram of body weight reduced the burden of tiny worms migrating through the body to near zero and impaired reproduction by adult parasites, alleviating symptoms and preventing blindness.[5]

Eventually, it became clear that neither those in need nor their governments could afford to buy ivermectin. So in 1987 Merck committed itself to manufacture and ship it at no cost to where it was needed for as long as it was needed to control river blindness. The company asked governments and private organizations to help set up distribution.

Since then, Merck has given away more than 2.5 billion tablets in 37 countries at a cost of $3.9 billion. Estimates are that treatment has prevented 40,000 cases of blindness each year; returned to use 62 million acres of farmland, an area the size of Michigan; and added 7.5 million years of adult labor in national workforces.[6] A study

---

[3] David Bollier, *Merck & Company* (Stanford, CA: Business Enterprise Trust, 1991), p. 5.

[4] Roy Vagelos and Louis Galambos, *The Moral Corporation* (New York: Cambridge University Press, 2006), p. 171.

[5] Mohammed A. Aziz, et al., "Efficacy and Tolerance of Ivermectin in Human Onchocerciasis," *The Lancet,* July 24, 1982.

[6] "Merck MECTIZAN® Donation Program: Priorities and Goals," at www.merck.com, accessed December 8, 2009.

of economic effects for two areas in Africa estimated $573 million in net benefits over 40 years.[7]

By 2012 the transmission of onchocerciasis in six Latin American countries is predicted to end. No end is in sight for Africa, but infection rates are falling in the most afflicted areas. In Benin, for example, infection rates in 51 areas ranged from 25 percent to 98 percent in the mid-1990s. Now the highest rate anywhere in the country is 3 percent.[8]

For a drug company to go through the new drug development process and then give the drug away is unprecedented. Merck's management believes that although developing and donating ivermectin has been expensive, humanitarianism and enlightened self-interest vindicate the decision. Few corporations have such singular opportunities to fight evil as did Merck, but every corporation must fulfill a range of obligations to society and many can apply unique commercial competencies to global problems. In this chapter we define the idea of social responsibility and explain how it has expanded in meaning and practice over time. The next chapter explains more about the management methods corporations use to execute social actions.

THE EVOLVING IDEA OF CORPORATE SOCIAL RESPONSIBILITY

corporate social responsibility
The duty of a corporation to create wealth in ways that avoid harm to, protect, or enhance societal assets.

Corporate social responsibility is the duty of a corporation to create wealth in ways that avoid harm to, protect, or enhance societal assets. The term is a modern one. It did not enter common use until the 1960s, when it appeared in academic literature. It often goes by other names, including its abbreviation CSR, corporate citizenship, stakeholder management, sustainability, and, in Japan, *kyosei*, a word that translates as "living and working together for the common good." Whatever it is called, there is no precise, operational meaning. It is primarily a political ideology, because its central purposes are to control and legitimize the exercise of corporate power. As an ideology, it is a worldview of how a corporate should act. In addition, it can be defined more narrowly as a management practice, specifically as the use of special tools and procedures to make a corporation responsible. This practical aspect is the subject of the next chapter.

The fundamental idea is that corporations have duties that go beyond lawful execution of their economic function. Here is the reasoning. The overall performance of a firm must benefit society. Because of market imperfections, the firm will not fulfill all its duties, and may breach some, if it responds only to market forces. Laws and regulations correct some shortcomings, more in developed countries, fewer in less developed. Beyond the law, firms must voluntarily take additional actions to meet their full obligations to society. What additional actions must they take? These have to be defined in practice by negotiation with stakeholders and they change over time.

Advocates of social responsibility, who occupy a very broad middle band of the political spectrum, justify it with three basic arguments. First, it is an ethical duty

---

[7] H. R. Waters, et al., "Economic Evaluation of Mectizan Distribution," *Tropical Medicine and International Health*, April 2004, p. A16.

[8] "Benin: The End of River Blindness," *Africa News*, May 8, 2008.

FIGURE 5.1   The CSR Spectrum

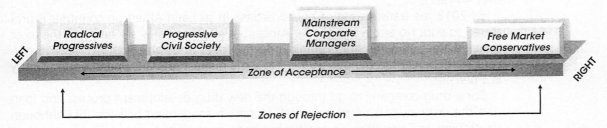

to promote social justice. A timeless principle is that power should be used fairly. If it harms or fails society, it is badly used. Second, social responsibility is practical. It has concrete benefits. It motivates employees and creates loyal customers. It leads to innovative products and strategies. It strengthens surrounding communities. It protects reputations and avoids regulation. In short, there is a "business case" beyond ethical duty. Third, it is necessary because other forces do not force full responsibility on corporations, particularly multinational corporations that operate across borders in a global arena of weak governance.

Opponents of corporate social responsibility are found toward the left and right edges of the political spectrum shown in Figure 5.1. On the far left, it is seen by radical Progressives as an insufficient doctrine, one that substitutes only poorly for tougher laws and regulations, allowing corporations to form a smoke screen of virtue behind which their "inviolable core" of profit seeking behavior is untouched.[9] On the far right, it is seen as a pernicious doctrine, draining and enervating the strength of the corporate institution. Conservative economists see it as an unwarranted cost. It creates administrative expenses, distracts executives, confuses economic goals with other goals, and subtracts from social welfare when the corporation is less efficient.[10] Corporations are owned by shareholders and the primary responsibility of managers is acting lawfully to maximize profits for them, thereby producing maximum value and surplus wealth for society.

Conservatives see capitalism as a natural, venerable, practical, and beneficent institution that has developed over centuries and led to rising global prosperity. They dislike CSR for thwarting natural market dynamics. They reject the agenda of corporate social responsibility, seeing it as centered in progressive ideology and based, therefore, on the goals of a movement at heart dubious of capitalism. Markets, not politics, should direct corporations. When markets fail, they should be corrected by the policies of representative government, not by unelected executives or activists.

Between these fringes there is wide acceptance of CSR. More moderate progressives are willing to work with responsible corporations. And corporate managers occupy a middle ground. Most now accept the idea as a practical necessity even as they often harbor doctrinal reservations. Years ago, most managers were on the

---

[9] Marjorie Kelly and Allen L. White, "From Corporate Responsibility to Corporate Design," *Journal of Corporate Citizenship,* spring 2009, p. 25. See also Subhabrata Bobby Banerjee, *Corporate Social Responsibility: the Good, the Bad and the Ugly* (Cheltenham: Edward Elgar Publishing, 2007).

[10] See, for example, "The Good Company: A Survey of Corporate Social Responsibility," *The Economist,* January 22, 2005.

right side of this spectrum. Why did they move left? As we will explain, the doctrine of corporate responsibility has evolved over time to require more expansive action by companies largely because stakeholder groups gained more power to impose their agendas, but also because the ethical and legal philosophies underlying it matured to support broader action by managers. In fact, corporate social responsibility is a profoundly durable and successful ideology. All through an era when free market principles were ascendant, it coiled more and more tightly around the corporation to restrain excesses and direct behavior to the public good. The story of corporate social responsibility begins with Adam Smith.

Social Responsibility in Classical Economic Theory

Throughout American history, classical capitalism, which is the basis for the market capitalism model in Chapter 1, has been the basic inspiration for business. In the classical view, a business is socially responsible if it maximizes profits while operating within the law, because an "invisible hand" will direct economic activity to serve the good of the whole.

This ideology, derived from Adam Smith's *Wealth of Nations,* is compelling in its simplicity and its resonance with self-interest. In nineteenth century America, it was elevated to the status of a commandment. However, the idea that markets harness low motives and work them into social progress has always attracted skeptics. Smith himself had a surprising number of reservations about the market's ability to protect human welfare.[11] Today the classical ideology still commands the economic landscape, but, as we will see, ethical theories of broader responsibility have worn down its prominences.

The Early Charitable Impulse

The idea that corporations had social responsibilities awaited the rise of corporations themselves. Meanwhile, the most prominent expression of duty to society was the good deed of charity by business owners.

Most colonial era businesses were very small. Merchants practiced thrift and frugality, which were dominant virtues then, to an extreme. Benjamin Franklin's advice to a business acquaintance reflects the penny-pinching nature of the time: "He that kills a breeding sow, destroys all her offspring to the thousandth generation. He that murders a crown, destroys all that it might have produced, even scores of pounds."[12] Yet charity was a coexisting virtue, and business owners sought respectability by giving to churches, orphanages, and poorhouses. Their actions first illustrate that although American business history can be pictured as a jungle of profit maximization, people in it have always been concerned citizens.[13]

Charity by owners continued in the early nineteenth century and grew as great fortunes were made. Mostly, the new millionaires endowed social causes as

---

[11] Jacob Viner, "Adam Smith and Laissez-Faire," *Journal of Political Economy,* April 1927.

[12] In "Advice to a Young Tradesman [1748]," in *The Autobiography of Benjamin Franklin and Selections from His Other Writings,* ed. Nathan G. Goodman (New York: Carlton House, 1932), p. 210. A crown was a British coin on which appeared the figure of a royal crown.

[13] Mark Sharfman, "The Evolution of Corporate Philanthropy, 1883–1952," *Business & Society,* December 1994.

Andrew Carnegie (1835–1919).
Source: The Library of Congress.

individuals, not through the companies that were the fountainheads of their wealth.

One of the earliest was Steven Girard, a shipping and banking tycoon. When he died in 1831, the richest person in the nation, he made generous charitable bequests in his will, the largest of which was $6 million for a school to educate orphaned boys from the first grade through high school.[14] This single act changed the climate of education in the United States because it came before free public schooling, when a high school education was still only for children of the wealthy.

Following Girard, others donated generously and did so while still living. John D. Rockefeller systematically gave away $550 million over his lifetime. Andrew Carnegie gave $350 million during his life to social causes, built 2,811 public libraries, and donated 7,689 organs to churches. He wrote a famous article titled "The Disgrace of Dying Rich" and argued that it was the duty of a man of wealth "to consider all surplus revenues . . . as trust funds which he is called upon to administer."[15]

social Darwinism
A philosophy of the late 1800s and early 1900s that used evolution to explain the dynamics of human society and institutions. The idea of "survival of the fittest" in the social realm implied that rich people and dominant companies were morally superior.

However, Carnegie's philosophy of giving was highly paternalistic. He believed that big fortunes should be used for grand purposes such as endowing universities and building concert halls such as Carnegie Hall. They should not be wasted by paying higher wages to workers or giving gifts to poor people; that would dissipate riches on small indulgences and would not, in the end, elevate the culture of a society. Thus, one day when a friend of Carnegie's encountered a beggar and gave him a quarter, Carnegie admonished the friend that it was one of "the very worst actions of his life."[16]

In this remark, Carnegie echoed the doctrine of *social Darwinism*, which held that charity interfered with the natural evolutionary process in which society shed its less fit to make way for the better adapted. Well-meaning people who gave to charity interfered with the natural law of progress by propping up failed examples of the human race. The leading advocate of this astringent doctrine, the English philosopher Herbert Spencer, wrote the following heartless passage in a best-selling 1850 book.

---

[14] The school became known as Girard College, which one of the authors of this book, George Steiner, attended. It still exists in Philadelphia.

[15] Andrew Carnegie, *The Gospel of Wealth* (Cambridge, MA: Harvard University Press, 1962), p. 25; originally published in 1901.

[16] Quoted in Page Smith, *The Rise of Industrial America,* vol. 6 (New York: Penguin Books, 1984), p. 136.

Herbert Spencer (1820–1903). Spencer attempted a synthesis of human knowledge based on the unifying idea of evolution. When he visited the United States in 1882 a grand dinner attended by 200 leading Americans was held for him at Delmonico's in New York.
Source: © Hulton-Deutsch Collection/CORBIS.

It seems hard that a laborer incapacitated by sickness from competing with his stronger fellows should have to bear the resulting privations. It seems hard that widows and orphans should be left to struggle for life or death. Nevertheless, when regarded not separately, but in connection with the interests of universal humanity, these harsh fatalities are seen to be full of the highest beneficence—the same beneficence which brings to early graves the children of diseased parents and singles out the low-spirited, the intemperate, and the debilitated as the victims of an epidemic. [17]

Spencer approved of some charity, though only when it raised the character and superiority of the giver. Still, the overall effect of Spencer's arguments was to moderate charity by business leaders and retard the growth of a modern social conscience.

More than just faith in markets and social Darwinism constrained business from undertaking voluntary social action. Charters granted by states when corporations were formed required that profits be disbursed to shareholders. Courts consistently held charitable gifts to be *ultra vires,* that is, "beyond the law," because charters did not expressly permit them. To use company funds for charity or social works took money from the pockets of shareholders and invited lawsuits. Thus, when Rockefeller had the humanitarian impulse to build the first medical school in China, he paid for it out of his own pocket; not a penny came from Standard Oil. Although most companies took a negative view of philanthropy, by the 1880s the railroads were an exception. They sponsored the Young Men's Christian Association (YMCA) movement, which provided rooming and religious indoctrination for rail construction crews. Yet such actions were exceptional.

As the twentieth century approached, classical ideology was still a mountain of resistance to expanding the idea of business social responsibility. A poet of that era, James Russell Lowell, captured the spirit of the day.

> Not a deed would he do,
> Nor a word would he utter
> Till he'd weighed its relations
> To plain bread and butter. [18]

Social Responsibility in the Late Nineteenth and Early Twentieth Centuries

Giving, no matter how generous, was a narrow kind of social responsibility often unrelated to a company's impacts on society. By the late 1800s it was growing apparent to the business elite that prevailing doctrines used to legitimize business defined its responsibilities too narrowly. Industrialization had fostered social

[17] Herbert Spencer, *Social Statics* (New York: D. Appleton and Company, 1890), p. 354; first published in 1850.
[18] "A Fable for Critics," *The Complete Poetical Works of James Russell Lowell,* Cabinet Edition (Boston: Houghton, Mifflin and Company, 1899), p. 122.

problems and political corruption. Farmers were in revolt. Labor was increasingly violent. Socialism was at high tide. Average Americans began to question unfettered laissez-faire economics and the doctrine of social Darwinism.

As Rockefeller, Carnegie, and other barons of wealth gave away large sums, public doubt about their motives grew. They were accused of cloaking their greed with gifts that confused the eye, diverting it from the coarse origins of their money. As one of Carnegie's workers asked, "What use has a man who works twelve hours a day for a library, anyway?"[19] Thus the criticism that corporate responsibility is a smoke screen first emerged in this bygone era. It has never lost a following.

By now, business feared a growing clamor for more regulation. It was terrified of socialist calls for appropriation of assets. So it sought to blunt the urgency of these appeals by voluntary action.

During the Progressive era, three interrelated themes of broader responsibility emerged. First, managers were *trustees*, that is, agents whose corporate roles put them in positions of power over the fate of not just stockholders, but also of others such as workers, customers, and communities. This power implied a duty to promote the welfare of each group. Second, managers had an obligation to *balance* these multiple interests. They were, in effect, coordinators who settled competing claims. Third, many managers subscribed to the *service principle*, a near-spiritual belief that individual managers served society by making each business successful; if they all prospered, the aggregate effect would eradicate social injustice, poverty, and other ills. This belief was only a fancy reincarnation of classical ideology. However, many of its adherents conceded that companies were still obligated to undertake social projects that helped, or "served," the public.[20] These three interrelated ideas—trusteeship, balance, and service—expanded the idea of business responsibility beyond simple charity. But the type of responsibility envisioned was still paternalistic, and the actions of big company leaders often showed an underlying Scroogelike mentality.

One such leader was Henry Ford, who had an aptitude for covering meanness with a shining veneer of citizenship. In the winter of 1914 Ford thrilled the public by announcing the "Five-Dollar Day" for Ford Motor Co. workers. Five dollars was about double the daily pay for manufacturing workers at the time and seemed very generous. In fact, although Ford took credit for being big-hearted, the $5 wage was intended to cool unionizing and was not what it appeared on the surface. The offer attracted hordes of job seekers from around the country to Highland Park, Michigan. One subzero morning in January, there were 2,000 lined up outside the Ford plant by 5:00 a.m.; by dawn there were 10,000. Disorder broke out, and the fire department turned hoses on the freezing men.

The few who were hired had to serve a six-month apprenticeship and comply with the puritanical Ford Motor Co. code of conduct (no drinking, marital discord, or otherwise immoral living) to qualify for the $5 day. Many were fired on pretexts

trustee
An agent of a company whose corporate role puts him or her in a position of power over the fate of not just stockholders, but also of others such as customers, employees, and communities.

service principle
A belief that managers served society by making companies profitable and that aggregate success by many managers would resolve major social problems.

[19] Quoted in Margaret F. Byington, *Homestead: The Households of a Mill Town* (Philadelphia: William F. Fell Co., 1910), p. 178.

[20] Rolf Lunden, *Business and Religion in the American 1920s* (New York: Greenwood Press, 1988), pp. 147–50.

Inventor and industrialist Henry Ford (1863–1947). The public made him a folk hero and saw him as a generous employer. But he manipulated workers to lower costs.
Source: The Library of Congress.

before the six months passed. Thousands of replacements waited outside each day hoping to fill a new vacancy. Inside, Ford speeded up the assembly line. Insecure employees worked faster under the threat of being purged for a younger, stronger, lower-paid new hire. Those who hung on to qualify for the $5 wage had to face greedy merchants and landlords in the surrounding area who raised prices and rents.

Ford was a master of image. In 1926 he announced the first five-day, 40-hour week for workers, but with public accolades still echoing for this "humanitarian" gesture, he speeded up the line still more, cut wages, and announced a program to weed out less-efficient employees. These actions were necessary, he said, to compensate for Saturdays off. Later that year, Ford told the adulatory public that he had started a program to fight juvenile delinquency. He proposed to employ 5,000 boys 16 to 20 years old and pay them "independence wages."[21] This was trumpeted as citizenship, but as the "boys" were hired, older workers were pitted against younger, lower-paid replacements.

A few business leaders, however, acted more consistently with the emerging themes of business responsibility. One was General Robert E. Wood, who led Sears, Roebuck and Company from 1924 to 1954. He believed that a large corporation was more than an economic institution; it was a social and political force as well. In the Sears *Annual Report* for 1936, he outlined the ways in which Sears was discharging its responsibilities to what he said were the chief constituencies of the company—customers, the public, employees, suppliers, and stockholders.[22] Stockholders came last because, according to General Wood, they could not attain their "full measure of reward" unless the other groups were satisfied first. In thought and action, General Wood was far ahead of his time. Nevertheless, in the 1920s and after that, corporations found various ways to support communities. Organized charities were formed, such as the Community Chest, the Red Cross, and the Boy Scouts, to which they contributed. In many cities, companies gave money and expertise to improve schools and public health. In the 1940s corporations began to give cash and stock to tax-exempt foundations set up for philanthropic giving.

1950 to the Present

The contemporary understanding of corporate social responsibility was formed during this period. An early and influential statement of the idea was made in 1954 by Howard R. Bowen in his book *Social Responsibilities of the Businessman.*[23] Bowen said that managers felt strong public expectations to act in ways that went beyond profit-maximizing and were, in fact, meeting those expectations. Then he laid out the basic arguments for social responsibility: (1) managers have an ethical

[21] Keith Sward, *The Legend of Henry Ford* (New York: Rinehart & Company, 1948), p. 176.

[22] James C. Worthy, *Shaping an American Institution: Robert E. Wood and Sears, Roebuck* (Urbana: University of Illinois Press, 1984), p. 173.

[23] Howard Bowen, *Social Responsibilities of the Businessman* (New York: Harper, 1954).

duty to consider the broad social impacts of their decisions; (2) businesses are reservoirs of skill and energy for improving civic life; (3) corporations must use power in keeping with a broad social contract, or lose their legitimacy; (4) it is in the enlightened self-interest of business to improve society; and (5) voluntary action may head off negative public attitudes and unwanted regulations. This book, despite being almost 60 years old, remains an excellent encapsulation of the current ideology of corporate responsibility.[24]

Not everyone accepted Bowen's arguments. The primary dissenters were conservative economists who claimed that business is *most* responsible when it makes money efficiently, not when it misapplies its energy on social projects. The best-known advocate of this view, then and now, is Nobel laureate Milton Friedman.

> There is one and only one social responsibility of business—to use its resources and engage in activities designed to increase its profits so long as it stays within the rules of the game, which is to say, engages in open and free competition, without deception or fraud. . . . Few trends could so thoroughly undermine the very foundations of our free society as the acceptance by corporate officials of social responsibility other than to make as much money for their stockholders as possible. This is a fundamentally subversive doctrine.[25]

Friedman argues that managers are the employees of a corporation's owners and are directly responsible to them. Stockholders want to maximize profits, so the manager's sole objective is to accommodate them. If a manager spends corporate funds on social projects, he or she is diverting shareholders' dollars to programs they may not even favor. Similarly, if the cost of social projects is passed on to consumers in higher prices, the manager is spending their money. This "taxation without representation," says Friedman, is wrong.[26] Furthermore, if the market price of a product does not reflect the true costs of producing it, but includes costs for social programs, then the market's allocation mechanism is distorted.

The opposition of Friedman and other adherents of classical economic doctrine proved to be a principled, rearguard action. In theory the arguments were unerring, but in practice they were inexpedient. When the great tides of consumerism, environmentalism, civil rights, and feminism rose in the 1960s, leftist critics wanted to control rip-offs, pollution, employment discrimination, and other perceived excesses of capitalism with new regulations. In this power struggle Friedman's position seemed cold and indifferent, an abstract calculus aloof from costs in flesh and blood. It incited critics and invited retaliation and more regulation should the business community openly agree. Moreover, the idea that corporations could undertake expanded social responsibility was useful for business. If corporations volunteered to do more it would calm critics, forestall regulation,

---

[24] See, for example, Rosabeth Moss Kanter, *Supercorp* (New York: Crown Business, 2009), the result of three years of research and 350 interviews in 20 countries by the author and her team, leading to the discovery that "vanguard," or socially progressive, companies accept Bowen's basic arguments.

[25] *Capitalism and Freedom* (Chicago: University of Chicago Press, 1962), p. 133.

[26] "The Social Responsibility of Business Is to Increase Its Profits," *The New York Times Magazine*, September 13, 1970, p. 33.

and preserve their legitimacy. Not surprisingly, Friedman's view was decisively rejected by business leaders, who soon articulated a new vision.

In 1971 the Committee for Economic Development, a prestigious voice of business, published a bold statement of the case for expansive social responsibility. Society, it said, has broadened its expectations outward over "three concentric circles of responsibilities."[27]

- An *inner circle* of clear-cut responsibility for efficient execution of the economic function resulting in products, jobs, and economic growth.
- An *intermediate circle* encompassing responsibility to exercise this economic function with a sensitive awareness of changing values and priorities.
- An *outer circle* that outlines newly emerging and still amorphous responsibilities that business should assume to improve the social environment, even if they are not directly related to specific business processes.

Classical ideology focused solely on the first circle. Now business leaders argued that management responsibilities went further. The report was followed in 1981 by a *Statement on Corporate Responsibility* from the Business Roundtable, a group of 200 CEOs of the largest corporations. It said:

> Economic responsibility is by no means incompatible with other corporate responsibilities in society . . . A corporation's responsibilities include how the whole business is conducted every day. It must be a thoughtful institution which rises above the bottom line to consider the impact of its actions on all, from shareholders to the society at large. Its business activities must make social sense.[28]

Friedmanism
The theory that the sole responsibility of a corporation is to optimize profits while obeying the law.

After these statements from top executives appeared, the range of social programs assumed by business expanded rapidly in education, the arts, public health, housing, the environment, literacy, employee relations, and other areas. However, although the business elite formally rejected *Friedmanism,* corporate cultures, which change only at glacial rates, still promoted a single-minded obsession with efficiency and financial results. The belief that a trade-off existed between profits and social responsibility was (and still is) widespread and visible in corporate actions.

BASIC ELEMENTS OF SOCIAL RESPONSIBILITY

The three elements of social responsibility are market actions, externally mandated actions, and voluntary actions. Figure 5.2 illustrates the relative magnitude of each, how that magnitude has changed over historical eras, and how change will progress if the trend toward expansion of the idea of corporate responsibility continues. To be socially responsible, a corporation must fulfill its duties in each area of action.

Market actions are responses to competitive forces in markets. Such actions have always dominated and this will continue. When a corporation responds to

---

[27] Committee for Economic Development, *Social Responsibilities of Business Corporations* (New York: CED, 1971), p. 11.

[28] *Statement on Corporate Responsibility* (New York: Business Roundtable, October 1981), pp. 12 and 14.

FIGURE 5.2
Motives for Social Responsibility and Their Evolving Magnitudes

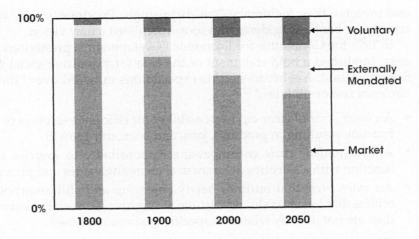

markets, it fulfills its first and most important social responsibility. All else pales before its economic impact. Recently the giant Unilever Group cooperated with Oxfam International, a confederation of progressive NGOs fighting world poverty, to study the overall impact of its branch company in Indonesia. Oxfam is suspicious of corporations and had "ruthlessly challenged" Unilever's profit-seeking actions.[29] Yet the final report detailed a wondrous economic effect in a country where half the population lives below $2 a day.

Unilever Indonesia (UI) is the 13th-largest company in the country. Like its global parent, it sells personal and home products such as Kleenex, Pepsodent, and Lux soap, along with a variety of foods. Over five years ending in 2006, UI made a net profit of $212 million. But the surprise was that its operations created total monetary value of $633 million along its *value chain*. A value chain is the sequence of coordinated actions that add value to a product or service. For Unilever it includes economic actors outside the corporation in both its backward supply chain and forward distribution channels.

Of the $633 million total, only 34 percent was captured by UI; the rest went to others: 4 percent to farmers for their crops, 12 percent to several hundred suppliers, 6 percent to product distributors, and 18 percent to as many as 1.8 million retailers, among them tiny shops and street vendors selling "sachets," or small packets of Unilever products made especially for low-income consumers who could not afford regular sizes. From its share, UI put the majority back into the Indonesian economy, reinvesting 25 percent in its local business, giving 30 percent to the government in taxes, and paying 7 percent in dividends to Indonesian shareholders.[30] Unilever Indonesia employed about 5,000 workers, but the study found that the entire value chain created 300,764 full-time jobs, an important contribution in a nation with more than 9 percent unemployment.

value chain
The sequence of coordinated actions that add value to a product or service.

---

[29] Jason Caly, *Exploring the Links Between International Business and Poverty Reduction: A Case Study of Unilever in Indonesia* (Eynsham, UK: Oxfam GB and Unilever PLC, 2005), p. 10.

[30] The other 38 percent was paid as dividends to overseas shareholders. Figures in this paragraph are from ibid., pp. 14, 82, and 83.

Figures such as these illustrate how the greatest positive impact of a corporation on society is economic and why maximizing that impact is a corporation's greatest social responsibility. From the study, Oxfam concluded that tremendous potential for poverty alleviation existed in UI's routine profit-seeking actions. It absolved Unilever of draining Indonesian society by profiting on the backs of poor people.

Mandated actions are those required either by government regulation or civil regulation. Government, or public, regulation is rooted in the authority of the state and its mandates are enforceable by law. Government mandates have multiplied rapidly in developed countries. *Civil regulation* is regulation by nonstate actors based on social norms or standards enforced by social or market sanctions. Civil regulation, sometimes called private regulation, has many faces. It is imposed when activists, consumers, investors, lenders, shareholders, or employees make demands on a company and failure to comply will lead to reputational or financial damage. Such mandates are enforced by the power of the market, not the power of law.[31] As we will see later in this chapter, mandates based on civil regulation are now expanding rapidly in the global economy.

civil regulation
Regulation by nonstate actors based on social norms or standards enforced by social or market sanctions.

The third element is *voluntary actions* that go beyond those compelled by law or regulation. Some voluntary actions can be called "legal plus" because they exceed required mandates. After the deadly Bhopal, India, gas leak in 1984, the subject of a case study in Chapter 11, the chemical industry introduced plant safety standards that went beyond the requirements of any nation. Other actions are unrelated to mandates, but respond to public consensus. Charitable giving, which is expected of every corporation though not legally required, is an example. Still other actions may be strategic initiatives where the firm seeks to profit from solving a social problem as does GE when it sells energy-saving hybrid locomotives.

GENERAL PRINCIPLES OF CORPORATE SOCIAL RESPONSIBILITY

What must a corporation do to be socially responsible? Many actions are possible. One meticulous study classified CSR into seven main areas with 31 categories containing 147 specific CSR activities.[32] Each company must choose a range of appropriate economic, mandated, and voluntary actions to fulfill its total obligations to society. No precise formula determines these choices. However, the following broad principles are widely accepted.

- *Corporations are economic institutions run for profit.* Their greatest responsibility is to create economic benefits. They should be judged primarily on economic criteria and cannot be expected to meet purely social objectives without financial incentives. Corporations may incur short-run costs on social initiatives that promise long-term benefits. And they should seek ways to solve social problems at a profit.

[31] See David Vogel, "The Private Regulation of Global Corporate Conduct," in Walter Mattli and Ngaire Woods, eds. *The Politics of Global Regulation* (Princeton, NJ: Princeton University Press, 2009).

[32] Ashridge Centre for Business and Society, *A Catalogue of CSR Activities* (Berkhamsted: Ashridge Centre for Business and Society, 2005). The areas are (1) leadership, vision, and values, (2) the marketplace, (3) the workforce, (4) supply chain activities, (5) stakeholder engagement, (6) the community, and (7) the environment.

- *All firms must follow multiple bodies of law*, including (1) corporation laws and chartering provisions, (2) the civil and criminal laws of nations, (3) legislated regulations that protect stakeholders, and (4) international laws, including treaties and trade agreements.

- *Managers must act ethically.* They must respect the law and, in addition, conform their behavior to ethical principles; model ethical values such as integrity, honesty, and justice; and set up codes, policies, and procedures to elevate behavior within the firm.

external cost
A production cost not paid by a firm or its customers, but by members of society.

- *Corporations have a duty to correct adverse social impacts they cause.* They should try to internalize negative *external costs*, or adverse costs of production borne by society. A factory dumping toxic effluent into a stream creates costs such as human and animal disease imposed on innocents, not on the company or its customers. Increasingly, this duty to correct radiates outward to include taking responsibility for adverse impacts along global supply chains.

- *Social responsibility varies with company characteristics* such as size, industry, products, strategies, marketing methods, locations, internal cultures, and external demands. Thus, a global pharmaceutical company such as Merck has a far different impact on society than a local insurance company, so its responsibilities are different and greater.

- *Managers should try to meet legitimate needs of multiple stakeholders.* Although corporations have a fiduciary duty to shareholders, it is not legally required, desirable, or possible, to manage solely in their interest. Consumers, employees, governments, communities, and other groups also have important claims on the firm.

- *Corporate behavior must comply with an underlying social contract.* To understand this contract and how it changes, managers can study the direction of national policies and global norms as evidenced in legislation, regulations, treaties, conventions, trade agreements, and public opinion.

- *Corporations should be transparent and accountable.* They should publicly report on their social performance in addition to their financial performance. This social reporting should cover major social impacts and, like financial reporting, be verifiable; that is, audited and checked by independent parties.

ARE SOCIAL AND FINANCIAL PERFORMANCE RELATED?

Scholars have done at least 127 studies to see if companies that are more socially responsible are also more profitable.[33] Most report a positive correlation between responsibility and profitability. Yet many have mixed, inconclusive, or negative findings. A review of 95 such studies over 30 years found that a majority (53 percent) showed that socially responsible behavior was related to higher profits. However, 24 percent found no relationship, 19 percent a mixed relationship, and 5 percent a negative relationship.[34]

[33] Joshua Daniel Margolis and James Patrick Walsh, *People and Profits: The Search for a Link between a Company's Social and Financial Performance* (Mahwah, NJ: Lawrence Erlbaum, 2001), p. 394.
[34] Ibid., p. 10.

Inconsistent results from study to study are not surprising given the difficult problems of method that researchers face. To begin, if social performance is defined as including economic performance, then any effort to separate the two elements to assess their relationship is doomed. Even if social performance is not defined to include economic performance, profit or loss does not solely depend on virtue, being also determined by market forces oblivious to the grade in a CSR report card. Also, no fixed, neutral definition of social responsibility exists, making it impossible objectively to rank corporations as more or less responsible. Many studies have used corporate responsibility ratings done by progressive analysts who evaluate companies based on whether they fulfill the left's social agenda. Others rely on rankings of reputation made by executives of Fortune 500 companies, who have a more conservative perspective.

As opposed to the subjectivity of a corporation's social performance it might seem that financial performance can be gauged more objectively, but there are many ways to measure profitability. Should researchers use accounting measures such as net income or market measures such as stock price appreciation?

In the above review of 95 studies, the authors report that researchers drew on 27 information sources to rate social performance and used 70 methods to calculate financial performance. This makes it difficult to compare the findings of one study to the findings of others. However, a fresh analysis of 52 studies took advantage of a statistical technique that allows correlations in individual studies to be compared. The authors found that the overall correlation between social and financial performance was "moderately positive," rising to "highly positive" for some combinations of performance measures.[35] Still, confounding results persist. A more recent study looked at companies that made *Business Ethics* magazine's annual list of 100 top corporate citizens four years in a row. It found that most were less profitable than direct competitors in their industries, suggesting to the authors that "higher profitability is associated with less corporate social responsibility."[36]

Overall, the majority of academic studies find that companies rated as notably responsible are at least as profitable, and often more so, than companies rated as less responsible. However, the results are mixed and there are such significant methodological questions that reservations are warranted. The best conclusion is that socially responsible behavior contributes to better financial performance for some companies, but evidence that it does so broadly for most companies is weak. If the evidence were stronger, there would be little need for activists and NGOs to force a CSR agenda on hesitant corporations.

CORPORATE SOCIAL RESPONSIBILITY IN A GLOBAL CONTEXT

In the early twenty-first century the doctrine of corporate responsibility is widely accepted in industrialized nations. Although its early development was strongest in the United States, sometime in the 1990s leadership passed to Europe, where

[35] Marc Orlitzky, Frank L. Schmidt, and Sara L. Rynes, "Corporate Social and Financial Performance: A Meta-Analysis," *Organization Studies* 24, no. 3 (2003).

[36] Arthur B. Laffer, Andrew Coors, and Wayne Winegarden, *Does Corporate Social Responsibility Enhance Business Profitability?* (San Diego: Laffer Associates, 2005), p. 5.

welfare state systems have nurtured some of the most powerful social justice NGOs and consumers are more inclined to purchase goods from companies they see as responsible. Until this time American corporations took the lead in evolving voluntary responses to societal demands because, relative to Europe, American markets were more laissez-faire and government regulation was looser, leaving more of the company's total responsibility in the voluntary category.

In Europe, social welfare states intervened more in markets and mandated extensive protections for workers, consumers, and the natural environment. While American companies volunteered to give health benefits to workers and make recyclable products, for example, their counterparts in the European Union were legally required to do so. So European companies never needed the spectrum of voluntary social actions that American companies did. Then, in the 1990s, Europe reacted to the rise of global competition, engaging with neoliberal ideas, deregulating markets, grinding away protections for workers, and shrinking other legal mandates on companies. In response, leading activist groups pressured firms to engage in more voluntary CSR activity and the stronger social welfare expectations in European nations gave birth to a robust, creative, and expansive design of corporate responsibility that now dominates and defines Western practice.

Corporate responsibility has strong roots elsewhere in both the developed and developing world and, as in Europe, its practice often diverges from the U.S. experience. In Japan, for example, it means paternalism toward workers and there is little tradition of philanthropy. In Australia voluntary CSR is actively encouraged by the government. In India it has risen on the teaching of Mohandas Gandhi that those who accumulate wealth hold it in trust for society.

Global CSR is now defined and dominated by the progressive ideology of Western civil society and the practices of Western multinationals. It has little foundation in some rapidly growing non-Western nations and as their businesses gain power in the world economy the consequences for CSR practice are unknown. The primary mystery is China, where a communist regime plans economic growth as it smothers dissent. Chinese corporations respond to social interests as directed by this unrepresentative, one-party government, and they adopt voluntary codes, standards, and social programs mainly to ease access into Western export markets. Although Confucian ethics teach harmony and reciprocity as central virtues and the basis of Buddhism is the interdependence of a person with the larger community and with nature, the Western idea of stakeholder engagement is lifeless in a Stalinist world.[37]

THE PROBLEM OF CROSS-BORDER CORPORATE POWER

While there is no consensus on the meaning and extent of CSR from nation to nation, the idea has taken on new and novel international dimensions in response to economic globalization. As governments deregulated markets and lowered

---

[37] See, for example, Po Keung Ip, "Is Confucianism Good for Business Ethics in China," *Journal of Business Ethics* 82 (2008); and "From CSR in Asia to Asian CSR," in Jem Bendell, Chew Ng, and Niaz Alam, "World Review," *Journal of Corporate Citizenship*, Spring 2009, pp. 19–22.

trade barriers in the 1980s, cross-border trade and investment began a steep rise. Dominant corporations grew larger and more active. As they did, critics and observers perceived the exercise of too much power and too little restraint, particularly of Western corporations in developing nations.

The perception that transnational corporations elude proper controls is rooted in a group of observations. First, international law, as found in treaties, conventions, and trade agreements, is weak in addressing social impacts of business. It strongly protects commercial rights, but norms protecting labor, human rights, nature, indigenous cultures, and other social resources are far less codified. Second, transnational corporations are subject to uneven regulation in developing nations, where institutions may be rudimentary and enforcement feeble. Some governments have overly bureaucratic agencies riddled with corruption. And some are undemocratic, run by elites that siphon off the economic benefits of foreign investment and neglect public needs. Third, in adapting to global economic growth, corporations use strategies of joint venture, outsourcing, and supply chain extension that create efficiencies, but sometimes also distance them from direct accountability for social harms. And fourth, significantly more government regulation of transnational firms is unlikely. No global government exists and no nation-state has the power (or the wish) to regulate international commerce. Developing nations fear, correctly, that stricter rules will deter foreign investment.

In a world where regulation is uneven, some corporations, such as Merck, have operated with high standards across nations. But others have compromised their standards in permissive host country environments. By the early 1990s, critics of multinational corporations began calling for new standards of responsibility. One by-product of globalization was the growing number, international reach, and networking of nongovernmental organizations (NGOs). Many of these groups developed a close association with the United Nations (UN), which, besides its peacekeeping function, promotes international human rights and interests of poorer, developing nations in the global South. During the 1990s, coalitions of NGOs pushed for a series of conferences sponsored by the UN for member nations. Conferences were held on environmental sustainability (Rio de Janeiro, 1992), population (Cairo, 1993), human rights (Vienna, 1994), social development (Copenhagen, 1995), and gender (Beijing, 1995).

THE RISE OF NEW GLOBAL VALUES

A defining moment came at the Rio conference on sustainability in 1992, when NGOs arrived demanding regulation of corporations. Their agenda failed, in part because the philosophy of economic liberalization driving the world economy was inhospitable to restrictions on business and in part because corporations and business groups that lobbied against regulation promoted an expanded, international doctrine of voluntary corporate responsibility. NGOs, unable to secure the hard regulations they wanted, were forced to work with business groups in developing new, innovative CSR mechanisms.

soft law
Statements of philosophy, policy, and principle found in nonbinding international conventions that, over time, gain legitimacy as guidelines for interpreting the hard law in legally binding agreements.

In hindsight, these conferences led to several important changes in the operating environments of multinational corporations. First, they generated a series of declarations, resolutions, statements of principle, guidelines, and frameworks under UN auspices that shaped international norms for the conduct of both nations and corporations. These documents created what international legal scholars call *soft law*. In the realm of international law, hard law, found mainly in treaties, creates binding rights, prohibitions, and duties. While soft law creates no binding obligations or duties for corporations, if its contents are widely accepted as expressing international norms it can, over time, become the basis for interpreting treaties. Second, the conferences provided occasions for NGOs to interact and develop influence strategies for confronting corporations. And third, they set the stage for further, this time global, expansion of the CSR ideology.

GLOBAL CORPORATE RESPONSIBILITY

The new, global dimension of CSR makes it the duty of a multinational corporation voluntarily to compensate for international and developing country regulatory deficits. It should do this, first, by extending its home country standards outward to its foreign operations and to its supply chain, and, second, by following a growing body of international norms enforced by various mechanisms of civil regulation. This new dimension of CSR flourishes because it has value across much of the CSR political spectrum. It appeals to activists as a substitute for the new laws they would prefer but cannot get and as a way to overcome the failure of weak governments to fight human rights abuses, corruption, ecological insult, and poverty. It also appeals to enlightened corporations as a way to forestall more traditional and formal regulation and to placate belligerent NGOs. As a result, the world seethes with activity pushing the idea along.

Figure 5.3 shows the range of entities and elements in an evolving system of global CSR. This system, solidifying now out of a less mature patchwork, organizes values, principles, rules, institutions, and management tools in support of voluntary corporate actions. Simultaneously, it has grown into a framework of civil regulation that can often command corporate behavior. We illuminate its structure by discussing the elements set forth in Figure 5.3, moving clockwise from the top right. In subsequent chapters we discuss some of them at greater length.

norm
A standard that arises over time and is enforced by social sanction or law.

principle
A rule, natural law, or truth used as a standard to guide conduct.

Development of Norms and Principles

A *norm* is a standard that arises over time and, as agreement on it becomes widespread, is enforced by social sanction or law. It is similar to a *principle*, which is a rule, natural law, or truth used as a standard to guide conduct. The norms and principles that direct global CSR are derived in part from timeless accretions of civilization, but international conventions to codify and interpret them are increasingly influential. The United Nations is a ringleader. An early codification of norms is the *Universal Declaration of Human Rights*, adopted by the UN in 1948,

FIGURE 5.3
A Global
System of
CSR Activity

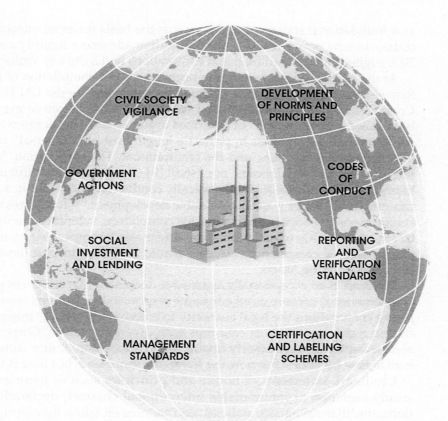

which spells out a "common standard" of "inalienable rights," that are specified in 30 articles.[38] The rights in this document are now widely accepted and it is the foundation for many of the human rights standards in corporate and NGO conduct codes. It requires, for example, equal rights for men and women, and corporations following such codes must meet this standard, often by imposing it on suppliers in less developed nations where no legislation requires it.

A second milestone in the development of norms is the *Tripartite Declaration of Principles concerning Multinational Enterprises and Social Policy,* adopted by an agency of the UN in 1977. The Tripartite Declaration, so-called because unions, governments, and industry collaborated in its creation, came in response to the rising power of multinational corporations in the 1960s. It sets forth a long list of "guidelines" related to worker rights, for example, that multinational corporations should not offer wages and benefits less than those offered for comparable work elsewhere in a country.[39] Over the years, the *Tripartite Declaration* has been accepted

[38] *Universal Declaration of Human Rights,* G.A. res. 217 A (III), UN Doc. A/810, December 10, 1948, Preamble.

[39] *Tripartite Declaration of Principles concerning Multinational Enterprises and Social Policy,* 3rd ed. (Geneva: International Labour Office, 2001), p. v and p. 7, para. 33. First edition published in 1977.

as a foundational statement and it now is the basis for most international labor codes. As new norms solidify, additions are made, most recently a new entry in 2006 suggesting that multinational corporations had a duty to abolish child labor.

At the leading edge of emerging norms is a draft compilation of *Norms on the Responsibilities of Transnational Corporations*, advanced by the UN Human Rights Commission in 2004 and discussed for several years before dying in what has been called a "train wreck" of polarized arguments.[40] The *Norms* would obligate multinational corporations to protect a lengthy list of "universal" rights of peoples, consumers, workers, and the environment. The corporation "shall not use forced or compulsory labour," nor "shall [it] . . . advertise harmful or potentially harmful products" and it "shall generally conduct [its] activities in a manner contributing to the wider goal of sustainable development."[41] It requires transnational corporations to adopt internal rules for compliance, submit to monitoring by the UN in which NGOs would participate, and make "prompt reparation" for injuries due to lack of compliance. Nations would be asked to pass laws to legalize enforcement of the *Norms*.

The draft is an exceptionally aggressive document that advances past the edge of international consensus on corporate responsibility. Nations were skeptical of giving corporations the legal authority to enforce "universal," meaning Western, human rights standards in countries with diverging values. Corporations, with some exceptions, were bitterly hostile to the imposition of new duties and exposure to new liabilities. For now the *Norms* are moribund, but time is their ally.

Landmark statements of norms and principles such as these arise from the steady accretion of innumerable international charters, declarations, conventions, multilateral agency policies, and treaties on labor, human rights, corruption, migratory birds, and other issues that, by their sheer numbers, promote broad acceptance of progressive, developed-country values as universal norms. These norms are the basis for proliferating codes of conduct that target corporate behavior.

Codes of Conduct

Codes of conduct are formal statements of aspirations, principles, guidelines, and rules for corporate behavior. They arise from many sources. Corporations write them. In addition, there are hundreds of codes created by industry associations, NGOs, governments, and international organizations such as the UN. Many codes result from collaborative processes by multiple parties; these are called *multistakeholder initiatives*. Any large multinational corporation will follow more than one code. It will have its own code or codes and, in addition, will be a signatory of multiple codes developed by other actors, likely including an industry code and specialized codes focused on labor, human rights, environmental

codes of conduct
Formal statements of aspirations, principles, guidelines, and rules for corporate behavior.

multistakeholder initiative
A code-based form of civil regulation created by some combination of corporate, government, NGO, or international organization actors.

---

[40] Spoken remarks of J. Ruggie, the Secretary General's Special Representative on Business and Human Rights, quoted in David Kinley, Justine Nolan, and Natalie Zerial, "The Politics of Corporate Social Responsibility: Reflections on the UN Human Rights Norms for Corporations," *Company and Securities Law Journal* 25, no. 1 (2007), p. 31.

[41] *Norms on the Responsibilities of Transnational Corporations and Other Business Enterprises with Regard to Human Rights,* U.N. Doc. E/CN.4/Sub.2/2003/12/Rev.2 (2003), secs. D(5), F.(13), and G.(14).

protection, corruption, and other matters. Here are examples of codes from different sources.

- Samsung Electronics Company has a *Global Code of Conduct* based on five aspirational principles: legal and ethical behavior, a "clean organization culture" (which means a culture free of discrimination, sexual harassment, insider trading, and similar misbehaviors), respect for stakeholders, care for the environment, and social responsibility. Brief, descriptive statements in each category give more specific guidance to employees.[42]

- The *Electronic Industry Code of Conduct* is intended to protect the safety and rights of workers in overseas plants that do computer assembly and component manufacturing. The 11-page code requires participants, who sign on voluntarily, to "go beyond legal compliance" in enforcing its standards for labor, health and safety, environmental protection, and ethical behavior.[43] It explicitly incorporates standards in the *Universal Declaration of Human Rights* and other codifications of international norms.

- In the 1990s a small band of activists within Amnesty International UK, a human rights NGO, began to work with companies, resulting in a checklist of human rights principles that evolved into a code titled *Human Rights Guidelines for Companies*. Although no companies adopted the Guidelines in their entirety, their appearance altered a widespread belief of executives at that time that only governments, not corporations, had responsibility for human rights. They were the template for a wave of changes written into corporate codes and policies.[44]

- The Ethical Trading Initiative is an alliance of companies, unions, and NGOs based in the United Kingdom. It has a *Base Code* setting standards for working conditions in overseas supplier firms. Its 50 member companies agree to conform their own codes to the *Base Code,* apply the standards across their international supply chains to almost 40,000 contractors with 8.6 million workers, and allow independent monitoring for compliance. Although the entity can discipline and even expel member companies for noncompliance, it does not publicly report such actions or any information about individual companies.

No matter what the source of a code, the target is the corporation. A code's effectiveness depends on how the corporation carries it out. Codes written by corporations themselves often lack rigor. Codes created by other parties usually require companies to sign compliance agreements that require some form of monitoring, and these are more effective, if uneven in result, leading to a growing focus on ways of monitoring corporations to verify code compliance.

---

[42] Samsung Electronics Co., *Global Code of Conduct* (Seoul, Korea: Samsung, 2006).

[43] Electronic Industry Citizenship Coalition, *Electronic Industry Code of Conduct,* v3.0 (2009), p. 1, at www.eicc.info/EICC%20CODE.htm.

[44] Sir Geoffrey Chandler, "The Amnesty International UK Business Group," *The Journal of Corporate Citizenship,* Spring 2009, p. 33.

Reporting and Verification Standards

sustainability
reporting
The practice of
a corporation
publishing in-
formation about
its economic,
social, and
environmental
performance.

There is growing demand for accurate information about CSR performance. This has led more companies to issue public reports that describe and measure their actions, a practice often called *sustainability reporting*. The reports take many forms. Information may be part of the annual report or appear in separate publications. It is costly to collect data and compile such reports, but they have benefits. They protect corporate reputation and they are a management tool for measuring performance and progress.

Two problems with sustainability reporting are, first, that defining and measuring social performance is difficult and, second, that the reports are not comparable from company to company. But uniformity is growing. In 2000, an organization in the Netherlands, the Global Reporting Initiative (GRI), released a model reporting framework that lists specific performance indicators and methods for doing the reports. Adoption of the GRI format has been so rapid that now 77 percent of the 250 largest global corporations are using it.[45]

Because of deep cynicism about corporate candor, institutions that independently verify reports have arisen. A nonprofit group, AccountAbility, has created a widely used "assurance standard" for independent parties that audit corporate reports for reliability. Reporting is further discussed in Chapter 6.

Certification and Labeling Schemes

Labels are symbols displayed on or with a product to certify that it, or its production process, meets a set of social or environmental criteria. Such schemes try to create a market for social responsibility by influencing consumers to prefer marked products. Criteria for labels are set by the labeling body, which is often a cooperative project of industry, NGOs, unions, and governments. Certified companies must usually allow independent auditors to inspect and monitor their activities. Typically the process is funded with licensing fees paid by producers, importers, and retailers. Here are several examples from dozens of such schemes.

- The *Kimberley Process Certification Scheme* is a device to stop the flow of so-called "blood" diamonds, which are rough diamonds from parts of Africa where sales to exporters fund civil wars and rebellions. Its governing body consists of 74 member nations, including all major diamond producing and importing nations, representatives from the diamond industry, and human rights groups. Each participating country is required to enforce trade rules. Companies export diamonds only in sealed, tamper-proof containers tagged with compliance certificates. Smuggling around the scheme persists, but after its inception in 2003 the share of "blood diamonds" in world markets dropped from 15 percent to 0.1 percent.[46]

- The *Forest Stewardship Council* sets standards to certify that forests are managed sustainably and certifies to mills, wholesalers, and retailers that wood

[45] KPMG, *International Survey of Corporate Responsibility Reporting 2008* (Amstelveen, the Netherlands: KPMG, 2008), p. 35.

[46] These percentages are in Vivienne Walt, "Diamonds Aren't Forever," *Fortune*, December 11, 2006, p. 89; and "Kimberley Process: Frequently Asked Questions," at www.kimberleyprocess.com/faqs/index_en.html, accessed December 5, 2009.

they buy is responsibly grown and harvested. It is an international body with 800 members, including timber companies, foresters, and NGOs ranging from Greenpeace Russia to the East Sepik Council of Women in Papua New Guinea. Members make decisions in a fastidiously democratic assembly where weighted counting gives the global North and South each 50 percent of votes. Because the Council's standards are high, it must compete with rival and less costly forest certification schemes created by industry that confuse consumers who are largely ignorant of differences between standards. The Council certifies only 5 percent of the world's timber harvest.[47]

fair trade
The idea that ethical consumers will pay a premium for commodities from producers in developing nations who use sustainable methods.

- Many certifications promote *fair trade*, or the idea that small, marginal producers in Africa, Asia, and Latin America should be paid a "fair," that is, a stable, guaranteed, and sometimes above-market price for crops so they can make a living and engage in sustainable farming practices. *Transfair USA*, a coalition of religious, human rights, labor, and consumer groups, offers the trademarked *Fair Trade Certified* term and logo on agricultural products such as coffee, tea, cocoa, honey, rice, and flowers exported to the United States. With coffee, for example, it audits sales of beans by farmers to companies. Its black-and-white logo depicting a farmer in front of a globe certifies that coffee farmers were paid a guaranteed minimum price.

Management Standards

management standard
A model of the methods an organization can use to achieve certain goals.

A *management standard* is a model of the methods an organization can use to achieve certain goals. The use of quality standards is widespread. Now, actors in the global CSR network have established standards for social responsibility or elements of social responsibility such as health and safety or environmental protection.

- The *EcoManagement and Audit Scheme* (EMAS) is a standard that rises above legal requirements for environmental performance in European nations that already have some of the world's strictest regulations.[48] Companies that join this voluntary initiative must reduce emissions, energy use, and waste beyond legal requirements. They also agree to publish regular statements of their environmental performance and have them checked for accuracy by outside auditors. More than 4,000 firms participate. They are allowed to use the EMAS logo in ads that make green claims for their products. EMAS is run by representatives of governments, industries, unions, and NGOs.

- The *International Organization for Standardization* (ISO), which has already created widely used standards in other areas, for example, ISO 9000 on quality and *ISO 14000* on the environment, is developing a broad new social responsibility standard named *ISO 2600* intended to set forth underlying principles, core subjects, and methods for integrating social performance in the plans, systems, and processes of organizations. The standard is now in draft form.[49]

[47] Tom Arup, "Timber Standard Pleases Union but Fails to Impress Greens," *Sydney Morning Herald,* November 30, 2009, p. 2.

[48] The standard is set forth in "Regulation (ED) No. 761/2001 of the European Parliament and of the Council of 19 March 2001," *Official Journal of the European Communities,* April 24, 2001, p. L114/1.

[49] International Organization for Standardization, *Draft International Standard ISO/DIS 2600: Guidance on Social Responsibility* (Geneva: ISO, 2009).

Social Investment and Lending

Equity capital and borrowing are critical to corporate financial strategies. Knowing this, actors in the international CSR movement have tried to introduce social criteria into capital markets. Initiatives such as these threaten to raise the cost of capital for corporations that dodge evolving norms.

- Under the auspices of the United Nations, a coalition of institutional investors and civil society groups created a set of voluntary *Principles for Responsible Investment*. Its signatories, about 560 banks, pension funds, hedge funds, and insurers with, collectively, $18 trillion in assets, must consider a company's environmental, social, and governance performance when they evaluate investments.[50] They also must accept a duty to pressure corporations in the direction of responsible behavior.

- The *FTSE4Good Global Index* is intended to set the world standard for those wanting to invest in companies following "good standards of corporate responsibility." The index was started by a British company in 2001. Scanning a universe of about 2,000 companies on 23 world stock exchanges, it first excludes companies producing tobacco, nuclear weapons, nuclear power, and major weapons systems. From what remains, it includes approximately 650 companies that meet somewhat stringent criteria for the practice of CSR. Since its inception it has delisted more than 200 companies for lapses in meeting its standards.

Government Actions

Governments advance corporate responsibility mainly with binding national regulation. Some also promote voluntary actions. European nations lead. The European Commission and European Parliament generate a stream of communications and reports encouraging codes, labels, and forums. The Belgium government set up the *Belgium Social Label*, a brown-and-blue cartoon of a person with arms uplifted in exultation, presumably because the company that made the product saw to it that its entire production chain followed basic International Labor Organization standards. Sweden requires its 55 state-owned companies to produce a yearly sustainability report based on Global Reporting Initiative guidelines. Denmark requires several thousand companies to report annually on their efforts to reduce environmental impacts.

Elsewhere there is also encouragement. The United States does far less than most European governments, but one study found 50 federal activities that could be classified as promoting CSR.[51] However, most were awards or programs with tiny budgets. In Australia the legislature published a study of global CSR initiatives and recommended "greater uptake" of the idea by Australian companies.[52]

[50] PRI, "New Data Signals Growing 'Culture Change' Amongst Significant Portion of Global Investors," media release, July 16, 2009, p. 1.

[51] General Accountability Office, *Globalization: Numerous Federal Activities Complement U.S. Business's Global Corporate Social Responsibility Efforts*, GAO-05-744, August 2005.

[52] Parliamentary Joint Committee on Corporations and Financial Sectors, *Corporate Responsibility: Managing Risk and Creating Value* (Canberra: Senate Printing Unit, Parliament House, June 2006).

Although the governments of developing nations where human rights abuses, corruption, and ecosystem destruction are targeted sometimes resist or ignore efforts to impose Western-based schemes of civil regulation, the Chinese commission that manages state-owned firms for the central government recently issued a set of CSR guidelines for the companies it oversees. Calling CSR "an unavoidable pathway" that "has become a key criteria worldwide," these guidelines call on the firms to "develop in a people-centered, scientific way and make profits," and emphasize energy conservation, philanthropy, and jobs creation as core CSR duties.[53] Since the commission appoints, removes, disciplines, and sets the salaries of managers at state-owned firms, the guidelines are unlikely to be ignored. Some companies have already set up internal "CSR work commissions" to implement them.

Civil Society Vigilance

NGOs watch multinational corporations and police actions they see as departing from emerging global norms. A direct action campaign by experienced activists is unpleasant and, if it carries any element of validity, very dangerous to brand reputation. The abiding threat of attack inspires entry into various code, labeling, reporting, and standards schemes.

- The force behind the Electronic Industry Code of Conduct noted earlier is the Catholic Agency for Overseas Development. When the group issued a report on "computer factory sweatshops" and began a "Clean Up Your Computer" campaign, it galvanized Hewlett-Packard, IBM, Dell, and others in the industry to create a protective code of conduct.[54]

- In 2000, the Rainforest Action Network (RAN) began a campaign against Citigroup, alleging that the bank's loans funded socially and environmentally disruptive pipelines, mines, dams, and other projects in developing countries. RAN was the sharp edge of a coalition of more than 100 NGOs opposed to bank lending that failed to take deforestation, pollution, and disruption of indigenous peoples into account. Three years of artful attack on the bank's reputation and harassment of its executives went by until Citigroup tired. Working with other banks it adopted industry lending guidelines based on sustainability guidelines then in use by the World Bank. Today, largely due to pressure by RAN, 69 of the world's largest banks, making 95 percent of the world's private development loans, subscribe to these "voluntary" principles, now called the *Equator Principles*.[55] The *Principles* divide projects into high, medium, and low social and environmental risk and compel borrowers to meet standards for ecological protection and to consult with native peoples. In effect, this is a global environmental regulatory scheme for the banking, mining, forestry, and energy industries.

[53] State-Owned Assets Supervision and Administration Commission, *CSR Guideline for State-Owned Enterprises (SOE)*, January 4, 2008, trans. Guo Peiyuan, 1(a) and 1(d).

[54] CAFOD, *Clean Up Your Computer: Working Conditions in the Electronics Sector* (London: CAFOD, January 2004); and Peter Burrows, "Stalking High-Tech Sweatshops," *BusinessWeek*, June 19, 2006, p. 62.

[55] International Finance Corporation, Treasury Department, *Funding Operations* (Washington, DC: World Bank Group, July 2009), slide 5.

ASSESSING THE EVOLVING GLOBAL CSR SYSTEM

In sum, a perceived shortage of regulation over multinational corporations has been countered mainly by action within civil society to create private regulatory schemes. Elements of civil society, often working through the United Nations, came together on statements and conventions that congealed global norms, raising expectations of corporate behavior and opening miscreants to the reputation risks of activist "name and shame" campaigns. As this dynamic unfolded over 20 years, regulatory leadership flowed from nations to other actors, particularly to multiparty alliances combining NGOs, UN agencies, unions, and corporations. These bodies, novel at first, but now duplicating endlessly, direct corporate adherence to the CSR standards they create using tools such as codes, labels, audits, and certifications. So prolific is the device that one or more standards are now established for almost every industry and commodity.

The growth of civil regulation invites reflection. First, it reveals that for much of civil society constructive engagement with corporations has become more important than hostility and attack. There is a realization that business has unique organizational and financial capacities that can be brought to bear on global problems. Second, the multinational corporation is slowly and reluctantly being redefined as a stakeholder entity. In the new world of international civil regulation it has duties toward the environment, human rights, and social development as real as its duties to shareowners. Third, civil regulation is a pragmatic solution to the regulatory vacuum. It has partially, but not fully, compensated for lack of binding global regulation. Though piecemeal, experimental, partial, and subject to enforcement failures it is a forceful presence.

Finally, because it is an extra-state phenomenon, civil regulation raises issues of representation. Conservatives find the new system undemocratic because it relies heavily for monitoring and compliance on progressive NGOs that are self-constituted communities of belief, unelected and not clearly or formally representative even of their membership rolls, let alone of the people in developing countries affected by transnational corporations.[56] Goals are dominated by the muses/anxieties of Western activists.

CONCLUDING OBSERVATIONS

In this chapter we focused on defining and explaining the idea of corporate social responsibility and its evolution. Figure 5.4 summarizes this evolution.

Historically, corporations have been motivated primarily by profit. However, as they have grown in size and power they have been exhorted and pressured to alter this single-minded focus. This is because (1) the ideology of corporate social responsibility has gradually evolved an expanded ethical duty and (2) the power of stakeholders to enforce this duty has increased.

[56] Larry Cata Backer, 'Multinational Corporations, Transnational Law: The United Nations' Norms on the Responsibilities of Transnational Corporations as a Harbinger of Corporate Social Responsibility in International Law," *Columbia Human Rights Law Review,* Winter 2006, pp. 386–88.

FIGURE 5.4 The Evolution of Corporate Social Responsibility

Although the term corporate social responsibility is of relatively recent use, the idea it represents has been under construction for more than two centuries. These timelines show how its elements have evolved.

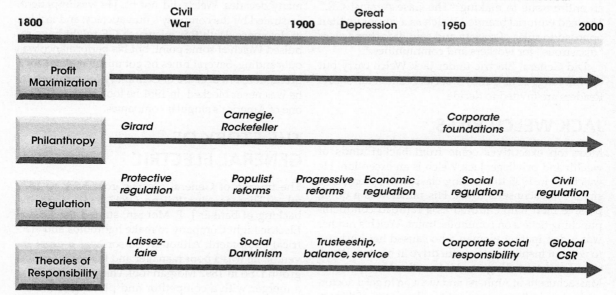

Doubts about CSR remain. In the progressive community there is cynicism about its limits. On the conservative side, elaborate CSR schemes might just be abandoned, replaced by nothing, allowing the natural grace of laissez-faire room to work. Debates over its proper nature will continue. Yet no radical changes are likely; the evolved CSR ideology that now exists is entrenched. No corporation of any size can afford to ignore the range of social obligations beyond market activity. In the next chapter, we will discuss specific management practices used to carry out corporate responsibility.

Jack Welch at General Electric

In April 1981 John Francis "Jack" Welch, Jr., became chief executive officer of General Electric. He held the position for 20 years until retiring in September 2001. During that time, he transformed GE, turning a solidly profitable manufacturing company into an exceptionally profitable conglomerate dominated by service businesses. If you had invested $100 in GE stock when Welch took the reins and held it for 20 years, it would have been worth $6,749.

Welch is lauded for his creative management style and became a national business hero. A fawning *BusinessWeek* article called him "America's #1

Manager."[1] *Fortune* magazine gushed that GE under Welch was "the best-managed, best-regarded company in America."[2] Yet the intense, aggressive Welch made fortunes for GE shareholders using methods that had mixed impacts on employees, unions, communities, other companies, and governments. As a result, not everyone sees the GE performance as a

[1] John A. Byrne, "Jack: A Close-Up Look at How America's #1 Manager Runs GE," *BusinessWeek,* June 8, 1998, p. 91.

[2] Jerry Useem, "It's All Yours, Jeff. Now What?" *Fortune,* September 17, 2001, p. 64.

model for corporate social responsibility. Upon Welch's retirement, the *Multinational Monitor,* a progressive magazine founded by Ralph Nader, devoted an entire issue to making "The Case Against GE." The lead editorial branded Welch as a corporate titan opposed to rules of society and said his actions were "disastrous" for workers and communities.[3]

Did General Electric under Jack Welch carry out the full range of its duties to society? Did it fall short? Readers are invited to decide.

JACK WELCH RISES

Most top executives come from backgrounds of wealth and privilege. Jack Welch is an exception. He was born in 1935 to working-class Irish parents in a small Massachusetts town. His father was a quiet, passive man who endured as a railroad conductor punching tickets on commuter trains. Welch's mother was a dominating woman who caused her husband to wilt but instilled a powerful drive in her son. Welch was an outstanding student at the University of Massachusetts at Amherst and went on to get a doctorate in chemical engineering at the University of Illinois.

After graduating, he started working at a GE plastics factory in 1960. His tremendous energy and ambition were very apparent. He was so competitive in weekend softball games that his aggressive play alienated co-workers and he stopped going. After one year, he threatened to quit when he got the same $1,000 raise as everyone else. His boss cajoled him into staying and as the years and promotions flashed by he never again wavered.

As he rose, Welch exhibited a fiery temperament and expected those around him to share his intensity. He was blunt, impatient with subordinates, and emotionally volatile. He loved no-holds-barred discussions in meetings but frequently put people on the spot, saying, "My six-year-old kid could do better than that."[4] With every promotion, he sized up his new staff with a cold eye and purged those who failed to impress him. "I'm the first to admit," he says, "I could be impulsive in removing people during those early days."[5]

This was just preparation for the big leagues to come. GE had a polished corporate culture reflecting the Eastern establishment values of its leadership over many decades. Welch did not fit. He was impatient, frustrated by the company's bureaucracy, and lacking in deference. With this mismatch GE might have repulsed Welch at some point, but his performance was outstanding. Several times he got mixed reviews for a promotion, but because of exemplary financial results he was never blocked. In 1981 he took over as CEO of one of America's singular companies.

THE STORY OF GENERAL ELECTRIC

The lineage of General Electric goes back to 1879 when Thomas Alva Edison (1847–1931), with the backing of banker J. P. Morgan, started the Edison Electric Light Company to make lightbulbs and electrical equipment. Although Edison was a great inventor, he was a poor manager and the company lost ground. So in 1892 Morgan took charge, engineering a merger with a competitor and plotting to reduce Edison to a figurehead in the new company.

Morgan disposed of Edison's top managers and dropped the word Edison from its name so that the firm became simply General Electric Company. Morgan sat as a commanding figure on the new company's board. Although Edison was also a director, he attended only the first meeting and never returned.[6]

After the merger, GE built a near-monopoly in the incandescent bulb market. Over the years, great things emerged from the company. Early in the twentieth century, its motors worked the Panama Canal locks, powered battleships, and ran locomotives.[7] GE's research labs bred a profusion of new electrical appliances, including fans, toasters, refrigerators, vacuum cleaners, ranges, garbage disposals, air conditioners, and irons. At first these new inventions were very expensive, but as more people purchased them, production costs fell and they became commodities within the reach of every family. By 1960 GE was credited with a remarkable list of other inventions, including

---

[3] "You Don't Know Jack," *Multinational Monitor,* July–August 2001, p. 5.

[4] Jack Welch, *Jack: Straight from the Gut* (New York: Warner Books, 2001), p. 43.

[5] Ibid., p. 43.

[6] Thomas F. O'Boyle, *At Any Cost: Jack Welch, General Electric, and the Pursuit of Profit* (New York: Knopf, 1998), p. 55.

[7] For more on the early history of GE see John Winthrop Hammond, *Men and Volts: The Story of General Electric* (Philadelphia: J. B. Lippincott, 1948).

the X-ray machine, the motion picture with sound, fluorescent lighting, the diesel-electric locomotive, the jet engine, synthetic diamonds, the hard plastic Lexan, and Silly Putty.[8]

As it added manufacturing capacity to build these inventions, GE grew. By 1981, when Jack Welch took the reins, the company had $27 billion in revenues and 404,000 employees. It was organized into 50 separate businesses reporting to a layer of six sector executives at corporate headquarters in Fairfield, Connecticut, who in turn reported to the CEO. To make it run, a large, almost imperial staff of researchers and planners created detailed annual plans setting forth revenue goals and other objectives for each business.

THE WELCH ERA BEGINS

Welch believes that managers must confront reality and adapt to the world as it is, not as they wish it to be. As he studied GE's situation in the early 1980s, he saw a corporation that needed to change. GE's manufacturing businesses were still profitable, but margins were shrinking. The wages of American workers were rising even as their productivity was declining. International competition was growing, particularly from the Japanese, who had cost advantages because of a weak yen. Although GE seemed healthy at the moment, ominous forces were gathering. In addition, Welch saw GE bloated with layers of bureaucracy that infuriated him by slowing decisions and frustrating change. The company, as currently operated, could not weather the competitive storms ahead. It would have to change.

Welch articulated a simple guiding vision. Every GE business would be the number one or number two player in its industry. If it failed this test it would be fixed, closed, or sold. In addition, Welch said all GE businesses would have to fit into one of three areas—core manufacturing, technology, or services. Any business that fell outside these three hubs was a candidate for sale or closure. This included manufacturing businesses that could not sustain high profit margins.

In the next five years, Welch executed his strategy by closing 73 plants, selling 232 businesses, and eliminating 132,000 workers from GE payrolls.[9] As he conformed GE to his vision, he also bought hundreds of

Jack Welch (1935–). Source: © Bob Daemmrich/CORBIS.

other businesses large and small. Within GE businesses he eliminated jobs through attrition, layoffs, and outsourcing. In the largest acquisition of that period, Welch acquired RCA in 1985. RCA was a giant electronics and broadcasting conglomerate with a storied history as the company that had developed radio technology. After paying $6.7 billion for RCA, Welch chopped it up, keeping NBC and selling other businesses one by one, in effect, destroying the giant company as an organizational entity. As jobs vanished, Welch got the nickname "Neutron Jack," comparing him with a neutron bomb that left buildings standing but killed everyone inside.

Welch also attacked the GE bureaucracy. One problem was its size. There were too many vice presidents, too many layers, and too many staffs with authority to review and approve decisions. A second problem was the bureaucratic mentality in which headquarters staff practiced a "superficial congeniality" that Welch interpreted as smiling to your face and getting you behind your back.[10] He demolished the hierarchy by laying

---

[8] Thomas F. O'Boyle, "'At Any Cost' Is Too High," *Multinational Monitor,* July–August 2001, p. 41.

[9] Frank Swoboda, "GE Picks Welch's Successor," *Washington Post,* November 28, 2000, p. E1.

[10] Welch, *Jack,* p. 96.

EXHIBIT 1
The Vitality Curve

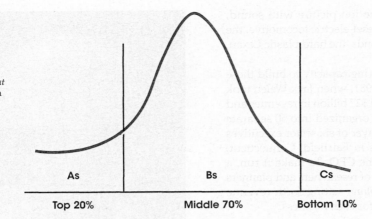

As	Bs	Cs
Top 20%	**Middle 70%**	**Bottom 10%**

off thousands of central staff in strategic planning, personnel, and other areas. Then he set out to change GE's culture by promoting the notion of a "boundary-less" organization, or one in which ideas were freely exchanged so that organizational learning could rapidly occur. Welch compared GE to an old house:

> Floors represent layers and the walls functional barriers. To get the best out of an organization, these floors and walls must be blown away, creating an open space where ideas flow freely, independent of rank or function.[11]

Later, Welch introduced the practice of "workout" sessions in which employees in every GE business had an opportunity to confront their bosses to express frustration with bureaucratic practices and suggest more efficient alternatives. Managers in these sessions sat in front of a room filled with subordinates and had to agree or disagree on the spot to carry out suggestions. Thousands of such sessions were held to drive out the bureaucratic mentality.

Welch also used Crotonville, the company's training center on the Hudson River, to meet with managers and instill his vision. He invited candid discussions, and gradually the company culture became more informal and open.

DIFFERENTIATION

Welch is convinced that having the right people in management positions is the single most important cause of success in a business. Early in his career, he developed a colorful vocabulary to differentiate

between players. Inept managers were "turkeys" and "dinks," standouts were called "all-stars." As CEO he reinforced strategic initiatives with a system of "differentiation" that generously rewarded managers who achieved performance goals and got rid of those who missed them. In this system, every year each GE business was forced to evaluate its managers and rank them on a "vitality curve" that differentiated among As, Bs, and Cs. The As were committed people, filled with passion for their jobs, who took initiative and exceeded performance goals. They had what Welch called "the four Es of GE leadership":

> very high *energy* levels, the ability to *energize* others around common goals, the *edge* to make tough yes-and-no decisions, and finally, the ability to consistently *execute* and deliver on their promises.[12]

The vitality curve was Darwinian. The As were the top 20 percent, Bs were the middle 70 percent, and Cs were the bottom 10 percent (see Exhibit 1). The As received salary increases, promotions, and stock options. Welch followed their careers closely. He kept large loose-leaf notebooks containing evaluations of the top 750 of GE's 4,000 managers. Bs were considered vital to the success of the company and were coached so that some would become As. Cs were not worth wasting time on and were dismissed. The process was repeated annually, and each time the bottom 10 percent had to go. The curve applied to every GE business. No business leader could claim that his or her group was an exception, though some tried. Filling the A, B, and C categories forced difficult decisions. If 20 managers were evaluated, 2 had

[11] Welch, *Jack*, p. 162.

[12] Welch, *Jack*, p. 158.

to be placed at the bottom and their careers at GE ended. After several years of getting rid of low performers, the leaders of GE businesses resisted classifying anyone as a C, but Welch was relentless. If they didn't identify the bottom 10 percent, he refused to carry out stock option and salary recommendations for the entire group until they did. In this way, the bar of performance was continually raised.

Welch compared people to plants. "If they grow, you have a beautiful garden," he said. "If they don't, you cut them out."[13] He disagreed with those who found the system heartless:

> Some think it's cruel or brutal to remove the bottom 10 percent of our people. It isn't. It's just the opposite. What I think is brutal and "false kindness" is keeping people around who aren't going to grow and prosper . . . The characterization of a vitality curve as cruel stems from false logic and is an outgrowth of a culture that practices false kindness.[14]

AN ASSESSMENT OF THE WELCH YEARS

With Jack Welch at the helm GE sustained exceptionally high rates of profitability, and shareholders were enriched. Even with five stock splits, earnings per share rose from $0.46 in 1981 to $1.07 in 2000, his last full year as CEO, and total return on GE shares averaged 21.5 percent.[15] In 2000 GE reported a net operating margin of 19 percent and earned 27 percent on invested capital.[16] These are high figures for a large multinational corporation.

Welch also reshaped GE. He continuously bought and sold businesses both large and small. During his last four years alone he made more than 400 acquisitions. One underlying reason for the increasing profitability of GE is that through this churning of businesses GE's center of gravity shifted from manufacturing to services. The GE he inherited earned 85 percent of its revenues from manufacturing; the GE he created got 70 percent of its revenues from services.[17]

Welch wrung profits from GE by creating a performance culture. Managers were energized. Plants grew more efficient. For instance, when Welch became CEO, GE's locomotive plant in Erie, Pennsylvania, needed 7,500 hourly employees to make 350 locomotives a year. By 2000 productivity had improved so much that only 4,000 workers could make 900 locomotives a year.[18]

The story of the Welch years has the elements of legend. An ambitious son of working-class parents rises through hard work to command a mighty company, inspire managers everywhere, and become rich along with other company shareholders. To reward Welch for the shower of wealth he created, in his last year the GE board awarded him a special bonus bringing his yearly compensation to $174 million.[19] At this time he held more than 22 million shares of GE stock and options worth almost $1 billion, as shown in Exhibit 2. This is astronomical compensation for one person, but his $972 million in stock is only four-hundredths of 1 percent of the $460 billion in equity value created during his tenure.

Exhibit 2 shows how directors shared in the GE equity windfall. When they joined the board, each outside (nonemployee) director was given 5,000 shares of GE stock and a $150,000 life insurance policy. Thereafter, each year directors were given $75,000, $2,000 for each of the 10 meetings they were required to attend, and options on 18,000 more shares of GE stock. If they retired at age 65 with five years of service, they were eligible to receive the $75,000 annual retainer for life. There were other rewards. One GE business sold diamonds and directors could buy them at cost for their personal use or for spouses. The year that Welch retired, the group purchased $975,595 worth of diamonds and must have looked very good at the kinds of parties to which laid-off workers were not invited.[20]

While the board feted Welch, not everyone saw his leadership as something to admire or emulate. Early in his career, he was compared to a speedboat

---

[13] Quoted in Carol Hymowitz and Matt Murray, "Raises and Praise or Out the Door—How GE's Chief Rates and Spurs His Employees," *The Wall Street Journal,* June 21, 1999, p. B1.

[14] Welch, *Jack,* p. 162. See also Jack and Suzy Welch, "The Case for 20-70-10," *BusinessWeek,* October 2, 2006, p. 108.

[15] Swoboda, "GE Picks Welch's Successor," p. E1; Julie Schlosser, "Jack? Jack Who?" *Fortune,* September 17, 2001, p. 52.

[16] General Electric Company, *GE Annual Report 2000* (Fairfield, CT: General Electric Company, 2001), p. 42.

[17] James Flanigan, "New Boss's Challenge: To Keep GE Together," *Los Angeles Times,* August 26, 2001, p. C1.

[18] "Dignity and Defiance: An Interview with John Hovis," *Multinational Monitor,* July–August 2001, p. 35.

[19] *General Electric Company, Notice of 2001 Annual Meeting* and *Proxy Statement,* March 9, 2001, pp. 22 and 27.

[20] Ibid., p. 14.

EXHIBIT 2   The 2001 GE Board of Directors: Market Value of Total Holdings in GE Stock (shaded entries are inside directors)

Director	Value	Director	Value
James I. Cash Professor, Harvard Business School	$3,719,059	Sam Nunn Former U.S. Senator from Georgia	$4,516,975
Silas S. Cathcart CEO, Illinois Tool Works(ret.)	$34,601,060	Roger S. Penske Chairman, Penske Corp.	$6,844,896
Paolo Fresco Chairman, Fiat	$111,700,043	Frank H. T. Rhodes President Emeritus, Cornell University	$10,931,672
Ann M Fudge Vice President, Kraft Foods	$1,667,828	Andrew C. Sigler CEO, Champion International (ret.)	$5,820,301
Claudio X. Gonzalez CEO, Kimberly-Clark de Mexico	$9,871,797	Douglas A. Warner Chairman, J. P. Morgan Chase & Co.	$8,323,021
Andrea Jung CEO, Avon Products	$2,733,352	Dennis. D. Dammerman Chairman, GE Capital	$187,238,259
Kenneth G. Langone CEO, Invamed Associates	$14,805,848	Jeffrey R. Immelt President, General Electric	$130,853,846
Rochelle B. Lazarus CEO, Ogilvy & Mather Worldwide	$877,690	John F. Welch, Jr. Chairman and CEO, General Electric	$972,022,731
Scott G. McNealy CEO, Sun Microsystems	$2,089,684	Robert Wright Vice Chairman of GE, President, NBC	$229,777,982
Gertrude Michelson Former Senior V.P., Macy's	$14,381,950		

Source: General Electric Company, *Proxy Statement*, March 9, 2001, p. 12. Total holdings include common stock, option holdings, deferred compensation, restricted stock units, and stock appreciation rights.

going down a narrow canal, leaving considerable turbulence in its wake.[21] His detractors say that once Welch was at the master controls of GE he piloted the mammoth organization through global straits the same way. There is no denying that he created wealth. But what were the costs to people, communities, and society? The flaws in the Welch performance, according to critics, include the following.

Loss of Jobs

Early on, Welch was caricatured as a ruthless job cutter. When he became CEO in 1981, the corporate culture reinforced loyalty. People went to work at GE

directly out of college, stayed for 40 years, retired in communities of GE people, and attended GE alumni clubs until rigor mortis set in.

As Welch remodeled GE there were mass layoffs. Within a few years, one of every four employees was gone. Welch believed that the idea of loyalty in GE's culture retarded change, so he rooted it out. At meetings he told employees it was out of fashion. He instructed staff never to use the word *loyalty* in any company handbook or other document. He wanted all GE managers to prove their value every day and said people who knew they could be fired worked harder.

In the Welch years there was tumultuous change in the workforce. No total number exists for workers who lost jobs. When he took over there were 404,000 GE employees; when he left there were 313,000. In

[21] O'Boyle, *At Any Cost,* p. 59.

between, tens of thousands came and went. Union leaders estimate that in his last 15 years GE eliminated 150,000 jobs in the United States through layoffs, subcontracting, and outsourcing to foreign countries.[22] Welch expressed his feelings about these layoffs in his memoirs:

> Removing people will always be the hardest decision a leader faces. Anyone who "enjoys doing it" shouldn't be on the payroll and neither should anyone who "can't do it." I never underestimated the human cost of those layoffs or the hardship they might cause people and communities.[23]

Welch stressed globalization of production to lower costs. Many jobs still existed, but they left the United States. In 1985 the electrical worker's union had 46,000 members working at GE, but by 2001 the number had declined to 16,000. Ed Fire, the union's president, estimates that two-thirds of the 30,000 lost jobs were simply transferred to low-wage countries.[24] GE eliminated additional jobs in the United States by pressuring suppliers to migrate along with it. After moving production to Mexico, for example, GE Aircraft Engines held a conference for supplier companies and told them to cut costs by moving their facilities (and jobs) to Mexico's low-wage labor market or face inevitable loss of their GE business.[25] Says Fire:

> GE is the quintessential American corporation that has engaged in what has been referred to as the "race to the bottom"—finding the lowest wages, the lowest benefit levels and most intolerant working conditions . . . I don't think they have given enough consideration to the consequences, particularly the human consequences, of the decisions they make. In my opinion, the decisions are designed too much to increase the company's profitability at the expense of the employees.[26]

A Flawed Evaluation System

The vitality curve rating method is controversial. Critics argue that forced ranking hurts the morale of employees who are not placed on top. At first, GE ranked employees in five categories instead of three, but it was soon discovered that everyone who failed to land in the top category was demoralized. Hence, three categories were combined into one to create the "vital" 70 percent of Bs in the middle. Disheartening classifications as 2s, 3s, and 4s were abolished.

The system can also hurt teamwork by pitting people against each other. It may encourage backstabbing behavior. Its inflexibility produces unfair results when high-performing and low-performing units must classify managers the same way. The bottom 10 percent in an outstanding business may be better than middle- or top-ranked managers on a weaker team. If the axing of the bottom 10 percent goes on for many years, people who were once in the middle range may find themselves lopped off. Of course, the curve calls the recruiting system into question if recent hires are lost.

Forced ranking was just one source of pressure on GE managers, who were expected to meet high profit goals and knew that if there were too many mistakes or misjudgments Welch would get rid of them. His confrontational style reduced some to tears. He reportedly believed that overweight people were undisciplined. Some GE businesses hid these people when he visited for fear they would catch Welch's eye and lose their jobs. One large manager trying to save his career had surgery to staple his colon.[27] Working at GE was also hard on marriages because of the long hours required to be a player. Welch himself divorced in 1987 and remarried in 1990.

Because of Welch's status as a management icon, his approach to forced ranking has spread widely, imposing the practice on many managers at other corporations. Even small businesses have picked up the idea. The manager of a Fifth Avenue clothing store once took Welch aside and explained that he had 20 sales workers. "Mr. Welch," he asked, "do I really have to let two go?" "You probably do," replied Welch, "if you want the best sales staff on Fifth Avenue."[28]

[22] "GE Fast Facts," GE Workers United, May 7, 2001, at www.geworkersunited.org/news/fast_facts.asp.

[23] Welch, *Jack*, p. 128.

[24] Ed Fire, president of the International Union of Electronic, Electrical, Salaried, Machine and Furniture Workers– Communications Workers of America, the Industrial Division of CWA, "Resisting the Goliath," *Multinational Monitor*, July–August 2001, p. 31.

[25] Robert Weissman, "Global Management by Stress," *Multinational Monitor*, July–August 2001, p. 20.

[26] Fire, "Resisting the Goliath," pp. 31 and 33.

[27] O'Boyle, *At Any Cost*, p. 76.

[28] Welch, *Jack*, p. 434.

No Diversity at the Top

Using the vitality curve Welch created a high-performance management team, but failed to create diversity. The year before Welch retired *The New York Times* reported that although women and minorities were 40 percent of GE's domestic workforce, white men dominated its top leadership. The paper ran a photo collage of the top 31 executives, including heads of the 20 businesses responsible for 90 percent of corporate earnings. All were male and all but one were white.[29]

Diversity was never a priority for Welch. Later, he would explain why not. "Winning companies are meritocracies . . . [that] practice differentiation" and "this is the most effective way for an organization to field the best team." He argued, "Quotas artificially push some people ahead, independent of qualifications" and that slows the rise of star performers, puts "unprepared people" into important jobs, and "doesn't do much for results."[30] In the subhead for its story *The New York Times* challenged Welch with this question: "Can Only White Men Run a Model Company?"

Pollution in the Hudson River

For 35 years several GE manufacturing plants in New York released polychlorinated biphenyls (PCBs) into the Hudson River. They followed permits that set release levels and stopped in 1977 when PCBs were outlawed because of evidence they were toxic to humans and animals. PCBs cause cancer in test animals and probably cause cancer and other illnesses in humans.

More than 100,000 pounds of PCBs released by GE still lay on the riverbed. Although the biggest deposits were covered by new sediments, slowing their release into the river, the fishing industry had been destroyed, fish were unsafe for children or women of childbearing age to eat, and the chemicals gradually spread downstream from hot spots of contamination, flowing down 200 miles of river to the ocean, from there migrating around the planet.

The Environmental Protection Agency (EPA) studied the river, concluding that dredging the

bottom was necessary to remove the dangerous deposits. This would be expensive, and GE was liable for the cost. Welch objected. During his last year as CEO he ordered an extensive campaign of radio and print ads in the Hudson River region to convince residents that dredging would be an ineffective nuisance. It succeeded in dividing them to such an extent that people began to shop only at stores where the owners supported their position and children teased classmates over their parents' views.[31] GE hired 17 lobbyists, including a former senator and six former House members, to fight an extended political battle against the cleanup.[32] Eventually, the company agreed on a cleanup plan, but only after Welch retired.[33]

The GE Pension Fund

During Welch's tenure the GE pension fund covered approximately 485,000 people, including 195,000 who were retired. As the stock market rose in the 1990s, the fund also rose, and by 2001 it totaled $50 billion. Its liabilities, the future payments it must make to retirees, were only $29 billion, leaving a surplus of $21 billion. GE's retirees and their unions requested increased benefits and cost-of-living increases for pensioners, but the company rejected their demands. By law, it did not have to meet more than the original obligations.

Welch understood that there were several benefits in leaving the pension plan overfunded. First, it generated bottom-line profits. Under accounting rules, a company can put interest earned by the pension fund on the balance sheet as revenue, and during the Welch years these earnings increased GE's net by as much as 13.7 percent.[34] Second, these "vapor profits" increased the income of top GE executives, whose bonuses were tied to corporate profits. And third, the excess funding made it easier for GE

---

[29] Mary Williams Walsh, "Where G.E. Falls Short: Diversity at the Top," *The New York Times*, September 3, 2000, sec. 3, pp. 1 and 13.

[30] Jack Welch with Suzy Welch, *Winning* (New York: HarperCollins, 2005), p. 346.

[31] John Glionna, "Dredging Up Ill Will on the Hudson," *Los Angeles Times*, October 1, 2001, p. A17.

[32] Charlie Cray, "Toxins on the Hudson," *Multinational Monitor*, July–August 2001.

[33] "GE's New Image: The Company Offers to Cooperate in Dredging the Hudson of PCBs," *The Times Union*, April 11, 2002, p. A12.

[34] Rob Walker, "Overvalued: Why Jack Welch Isn't God," *The New Republic*, June 18, 2001, p. 22. See *GE Annual Report 2000*, Notes to Consolidated Financial Statements, 6, "Pension Benefits."

to acquire companies with underfunded pension plans. This eased deal making, but involved sharing funds set aside for GE workers and retirees with people who got a windfall coming in after careers in other companies.

After being pressured by unions and pensioners, GE announced increases of 15 to 35 percent in 2000. But since 1965 prices had risen by 60 percent, so retirees were still losing ground.[35] Helen Quirini, 81, was part of a group protesting GE's failure to be more generous. After working 39 years at a GE factory, one year less than Welch's 40-year tenure, she retired in 1980 and was receiving $737 a month, or $8,844 a year. She believed that GE management was "out all the time trying to figure out how to screw us" using "accounting gimmicks."[36]

Welch's GE pension is $357,128 a month. Court documents filed in proceedings when Welch divorced his second wife in 2002 revealed that he spent an average of $8,982 a month on food and beverages, slightly more than Helen Quirini's yearly pension income.[37] A 1996 retention agreement between Welch and the GE board also granted him nonmonetary perquisites in retirement. He got lifetime use of a spacious apartment owned by GE at the Trump International Hotel and Tower on Central Park West in New York, including a cook, a housekeeper, and a wait staff plus flowers, laundry, dry cleaning, newspaper and magazine subscriptions, and front-row seats at sporting and entertainment events.[38] He was allowed unlimited use of GE's corporate jets. Criticism of these arrangements arose when they were detailed during the divorce. Although he felt there was nothing improper, he elected to pay GE "between $2 and $2.5 million a year" for continued use of the apartment and the planes.[39]

Criminality at GE

Pressure for performance tempts employees to cut corners. Welch knew this and tried to fuse high performance and integrity in the GE culture.[40] In his own words:

> If there was one thing I preached every day at GE, it was integrity. It was our No. 1 value. Nothing came before it. We never had a corporate meeting where I didn't emphasize integrity in my closing remarks.[41]

Yet during his tenure, GE committed a long string of civil and criminal transgressions. The *Multinational Monitor* compiled a "GE Rap Sheet," listing 39 law violations, court-ordered remedies, and fines in the 1990s alone.[42] Many are for pollution hazards from GE facilities. Others are for consumer fraud, including a $165,000 fine for deceptive advertising of lightbulbs and a $100 million fine on GE Capital for unfair debt-collection practices. Still others are for defense contracting fraud, including a $69 million fine for diverting fighter contract funds to other purposes and other fines for overcharging on contracts.

Since GE is such a large company, technical violations of complex regulations and incidents of wrongdoing by individual managers are inevitable. The *Multinational Monitor* sees "a consistent pattern of violating criminal and civil laws over many years."[43] The key question is whether GE's malfeasance increased because of relentless performance pressure on its managers.

THE WELCH ERA AND WHAT FOLLOWED

General Electric in the Welch era fulfilled its primary economic responsibilities to society. It was remarkably profitable. It paid taxes. Shareholders, including pension and mutual funds, were enriched. Many of its directors and managers became multimillionaires

[35] "GE Pension Fund Story: Workers Pay, GE Benefits," *GE Workers United*, April 1, 2001, at www.geworkersunited.org/pensions/index.asp?ID_61.

[36] Vincent Lloyd, "Penny Pinching the Retirees at GE," *Multinational Monitor*, July–August 2001, p. 23.

[37] "Here's the Retirement Jack Welch Built: $1.4 Million a Month," *The Wall Street Journal*, October 31, 2002, p. A1.

[38] Geraldine Fabrikant, "G.E. Expenses for Ex-Chief Cited in Filing," *The New York Times*, September 6, 2002, p. C1.

[39] Jack Welch, "My Dilemma and How I Resolved It," *The New York Times*, September 16, 2002, p. A14.

[40] For a description of his efforts see a book by GE's senior vice president for public affairs during the Welch years, Ben W. Heineman, Jr., *High Performance with High Integrity* (Boston: Harvard Business Press, 2008).

[41] Welch, *Jack*, pp. 279-80.

[42] "GE: Decades of Misdeeds and Wrongdoing," *Multinational Monitor*, July–August 2001, p. 26.

[43] Ibid., p. 30.

in GE stock. Welch believed he was acting for the greater good.

> I believe social responsibility begins with a strong, competitive company, only a healthy enterprise can improve and enrich the lives of people and their communities . . . That's why a CEO's primary social responsibility is to assure the financial success of the company. Only a healthy, winning company has the resources and the capability to do the right thing.[44]

In September 2001 Welch was succeeded by a new CEO, Jeffrey Immelt, a carefully groomed Harvard MBA drawn from GE's stable of stars. The new leader proved to have different values. Shortly after taking over he reversed Welch's two decades of opposition to cleaning up the Hudson River and agreed to a cleanup that would cost GE more than $1 billion.[45] He retained the ranking process for managers, but loosened rigid Welch-era guidelines. Now the bottom 10 percent could be 5 percent or 15 percent, but did not have to be exactly 10 percent. He joined the board of directors of Catalyst, a New York organization that promotes progress of women in management through research about sexism. And he appointed a new vice president for corporate citizenship.

But his real love was the environment. In 2002 a Catholic group filed a shareholder's proposal asking the company to measure its global warming gas emissions. It got only 20 percent of the vote at the annual meeting, but Immelt ordered an inventory anyway, then, over objections by subordinates who doubted global warming, pledged to cut GE's emissions. In 2005 Immelt launched GE's "eco-imagination" initiative based on a strategy of profiting from efforts to stop climate change. It focused the corporation on energy-saving, less polluting technologies, moving it into solar panels, wind turbines, coal gasification, recyclable plastics, and hybrid locomotives. Again, some hard-bitten, profit-focused managers resisted, but Immelt pushed on.

Immelt was more visibly alert to GE's social and environmental impacts than Welch. By 2008 the company was the second most socially responsible company among the largest 100 global corporations in one

prominent ranking by NGOs.[46] Yet for shareholders, his leadership was bad news.

If you had invested $10,000 in GE on the day Welch retired in 2001, counting dividends your investment shrank to $4,648 at the end of 2010, a loss of 54 percent. It was, of course, a difficult period. Four days after Immelt took over terrorists in jets with GE engines destroyed World Trade Center buildings insured by GE, leading to a global recession. Late in 2008 a global financial crisis caused the stock market to plummet. Nevertheless, over Immelt's tenure, GE underperformed the Dow Jones Industrial Index, a benchmark of large peer corporations. If you had put $10,000 into the Dow the day Welch retired you would have had $11,578 at the end of 2010, even with GE weighing down the index, a meager return for nine years, but 82 percent better than GE's return alone.

Questions

1. Corporate social responsibility is defined in Chapter 5 as the corporate duty to create wealth by using means that avoid harm to, protect, or enhance societal assets. Did GE in the Welch era fulfill this duty? Could it have done better? What should it have done?

2. Does GE under Welch illustrate a narrower view of corporate social responsibility closer to Friedman's view that the only social responsibility is to increase profits while obeying the law?

3. How well did GE conform with the "General Principles of Corporate Social Responsibility" set forth in the section of that title in the chapter?

4. What are the pros and cons of ranking shareholders over employees and other stakeholders? Is it wrong to see employees as costs of production? Should GE have rebalanced its priorities?

5. Was GE a more socially responsible corporation in the Welch era or the Immelt aftermath? In which era did it give the most benefit to society? What lesson(s) can be learned from the differences?

---

[44] Welch, *Jack*, pp. 381–82.

[45] See the story of "The Majestic Hudson River," in Chapter 13.

[46] This was the "Accountability Rating 2008: Full G100 Ranking," by the AccountAbility and Two Tomorrows networks, at http://www.accountabilityrating.com/latest_overview.asp. Vodafone was ranked first.

Chapter **Six**

Implementing Corporate Social Responsibility

The Bill & Melinda Gates Foundation

Growing up in Seattle, William H. Gates III was a slender, intense boy with a messy room and a dazzling mind. At age seven or eight he read the entire *World Book Encyclopedia*. At his family's church the minister challenged young congregants to earn a free dinner by memorizing the Sermon on the Mount, a passage covering Chapters 5, 6, and 7 in the Book of Matthew. At age 11 young Bill became the only one, in 25 years of the minister's experience, ever to recite every word perfectly, never stumbling, never erring.[1] Yet Christianity itself never attracted Gates. Years later he would remark, "There's a lot more I could be doing on a Sunday morning," an incongruous conviction for one who would become devoted to serving the poor.[2] His brilliance, however, was lasting.

At private Lakeside prep school he was a prodigy, often challenging his teachers in class. Obsessed with computers in their then-primitive form, he stayed up all night writing code, a routine that would stay with him. He also read biographies of great historical figures to enter their minds and understand how they succeeded. After high school he attended Harvard University hoping to find an atmosphere of exciting erudition. Instead, he grew bored and left to pursue a fascination with computers. At age 19, Gates founded Microsoft Corporation with his Lakeside School friend Paul Allen. As its leader he was energetic, independent, and confrontational. He developed the reputation of a fanatical competitor willing to appropriate any technology and crush market rivals. He built a dominant business and by 1987, at age 31, he was a billionaire.

Microsoft's stock took flight, making more billions for Gates. However, even as he became the world's richest man he remained absorbed in running the corporation.

[1] James Wallace and Jim Erickson, *Hard Drive: Bill Gates and the Making of the Microsoft Empire* (New York: HarperBusiness, 1992), pp. 6–7.

[2] Garrison Keillor, "Faith at the Speed of Light," *Time,* July 14, 1999, p. 25.

Bill Gates at 31, already a billionaire.
Source: © Ed Kashi/CORBIS.

He put little energy into charity, thinking it could wait until he grew old. But the world expected more. Requests for good deeds and contributions poured in. Gates responded with the help of his father, who worked in a home basement office handling his son's donations.

In 1994, Gates formalized his giving by creating the William H. Gates Foundation and endowing it with $94 million. His father agreed to manage it from the basement. Eventually, this arrangement evolved into the Bill & Melinda Gates Foundation, which included the name of his wife and was run by a professional staff from its new headquarters in Seattle. A foundation is essentially an organization with a pool of money for giving to nonprofit and charitable causes. It is not taxed if it gives out at least 5 percent of its funds each year. Bill Gates gave his foundation $16 billion in Microsoft stock in 2000. Since then he has given more.

Today the Foundation is endowed with $37 billion, making it the world's largest. It has two parts. One part decides what projects to fund. So far, more than $25 billion has been given out. The other part manages the endowment by investing the money to make it grow. The Gateses are deeply involved in the foundation's work, which is based on a pair of "simple values" that inspire them. One is that "all lives—no matter where they are being led—have equal value," and the other is that "to whom much is given, much is expected." Giving is tightly focused on three areas—global health, poverty in developing nations, and U.S. public education.

Because the foundation's endowment is unprecedentedly large, more than the gross domestic products (GDPs) of 107 countries, its goals are ambitious. One is to correct market signals that cause modern medicine to neglect diseases of the poor, thus failing to value all lives equally. Pursuing this goal, the foundation has spent more than $3.8 billion on basic vaccinations for newborns in countries with low GDPs, preventing so far an estimated 3.4 million deaths.[3] It purchases such massive amounts of vaccines that prices fall, allowing doses for millions more children. It spends billions more to create new vaccines for tropical parasitic diseases and to fight a resurgence of polio in Africa.

Bill Gates is characteristically intense, impatient, and direct in the quest to save lives. Learning that the global health staff was paying big travel grants for people to fly to meetings, he issued a curt memo about "rich people flying around to talk to other rich people." He lectured the staff: "Our net effect should be to save years of life for well under $100, so, if we waste even $500,000, we are wasting 5,000 years of life."[4]

[3] Statement of Helen Evans, "State of the World's Vaccines and Immunization Report 2009," GAVI Alliance, October 31, 2009, at www.gavialliance.org.

[4] Quoted in Andrew Jack, "Gates Foundation: Smaller Funds, Hard Decisions," FT.com, September 30, 2009, at www.ft.com.

In 2006 Bill Gates' friend Warren Buffett, chairman of Berkshire Hathaway and, at the time, the world's second-richest man, decided to give most of his wealth away and made a bequest of 10 million shares of Berkshire Hathaway to the Gates Foundation. He believed Bill and Melinda Gates were doing such a superior job he could do no better and, rather than manage billions of dollars of giving on his own, he left his legacy in their hands. At the time, his gift was worth $31 billion, a sum that roughly doubled the Gates endowment. It arrives in annual installments of between $1 billion and $2 billion.

The Gates Foundation confronts enormous social problems. Poverty and disease defy solution. Spending large sums in poor nations is a challenge. Corruption diverts funds. Agencies lack capacity. When infant lives are saved by vaccination, more people live to seek ordinary care. Some nations struggle to provide even the most basic care due to shortages of doctors and nurses. Thus, children are saved from diphtheria only to die in large numbers from common diarrhea.[5] Improving education is another nightmare. After spending $1 billion over six years to make small high schools better, an analysis showed that attendance, graduation rates, and test scores on basic subjects were lower than at similar schools not funded by the Gates Foundation.[6]

Despite its magnificence, the Gates Foundation attracts critics. It is directed by only three trustees—Bill and Melinda Gates and Warren Buffet—putting its multibillion-dollar expenditures in the hands of just two families.[7] It has been called an elitist, antidemocratic institution subsidized by taxpayers (through its tax exemptions) but having no accountability to society.[8] Suspicions are raised that its grants, being so big, shape the world's health agenda and distort research priorities, for example, by over-emphasizing vaccines for tropical diseases as opposed to other forms of treatment.[9]

However, the Gateses and Warren Buffet want to extend the example set by their philanthropy. In 2009 they arranged a series of small, confidential dinners attended by fellow billionaires. Guests were asked to pledge the majority of their wealth to charity, either during their lifetime or at death, each one determining which causes to fund. Over the next year this initiative was formalized in a "Giving Pledge" joined by 40 billionaires.[10] Their pledges are moral commitments; they are not monitored or enforced as legal contracts. The Gateses and Buffet hope to spread the initiative to other nations. Their goal is to divert wealth from the very rich to enlarge the scope of global philanthropy for generations to come.

---

[5] Laurie Garrett, "The Challenge of Global Health," *Foreign Affairs,* January/February 2007.

[6] The National Institutes of High School Transformation, *Evaluation of the Bill & Melinda Gates Foundation's High School Grants Initiative: 2001–2005 Final Report* (Washington, DC: American Institutes for Research, 2006), pp. 9–10.

[7] Pablo Eisenberg, "The Gates-Buffett Merger Isn't Good for Philanthropy," *Chronicle of Philanthropy,* July 20, 2006, p. 33.

[8] "Philanthropic World Voices Mixed Reaction on Buffett's Gift to Gates Fund," *Chronicle of Philanthropy,* July 20, 2006, p. 12, comment of Rick Cohen.

[9] David McCoy, et al., "The Bill & Melinda Gates Foundation's Grant-Making Programme for Global Health," *The Lancet,* May 9, 2009, p. 1652.

[10] Carol J. Loomis, "The $600 Billion Challenge," *Fortune,* July 5, 2010.

Philanthropy is one method for converting wealth to social value. Bill Gates and Warren Buffet follow a long tradition of rich capitalists who make fortunes, then later in life spend their wealth on works of kindness. In this chapter we will expand on the subject of philanthropy. First, however, we look at how managers implement social responsibility efforts within their firms. Social responsibility, like any other corporate goal, must be systematically planned, organized, and carried out. We will set forth a model of how this can be done.

MANAGING THE RESPONSIVE CORPORATION

Corporations must and do undertake a range of social initiatives. Whatever management's opinion about corporate social responsibility (CSR)—its desirability and its affect on profits—companies must respond to multiple sources of pressure for social actions. There is no alternative. Figure 6.1 shows sources of these pressures on corporations. Each source can generate many demands, some conflicting. We begin here a discussion about how CSR actions may be defined and implemented. First, we look at two elements that can determine the CSR orientation of a firm—its business model and its leadership.

LEADERSHIP AND BUSINESS MODELS

business model
The underlying idea or theory that explains how a business will create value by making and selling products or services in the market.

Founders and top managers set the tone for a company's social response. Their perspective on corporate responsibility is reflected throughout the organization. A *business model* is the underlying idea or theory of how a business will create value by making and selling something in the market. The theory is validated if the business makes a profit. In the universe of business models, there are two distinct types as they relate to corporate responsibility, the progressive model and the traditional model.

A traditional business model is one in which the central strategy for creating value is based on meeting market demands while complying with the law. A progressive business model differs. It creates value by meeting market demands

FIGURE 6.1
Sources of Pressure for Social Responsibility

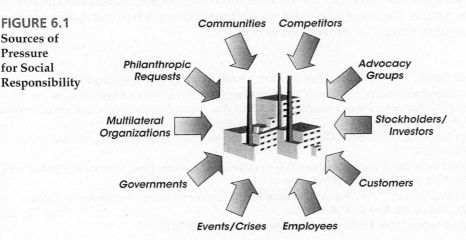

and, in the process, mitigating social problems or improving society in some way. The value proposition is based on actions that would be considered voluntary responsibilities in more traditional companies. Anita Roddick devised The Body Shop to be a beacon of ethical and social activism in a world darkened with capitalist greed. She saw cosmetics as "an industry dominated by men trying to create needs that don't exist" by selling false, unattainable notions of female beauty. So she devoted herself to "harnessing commercial success to altruistic ideals."[11] Her business model predicted that women would buy from an honest company that used natural ingredients, made realistic product claims, and supported feminist causes. The company's ads encouraged women to accept their natural appearance. One read: "There are 3 billion women who don't look like supermodels and only 8 who do."

Progressive business models are rare, the basis of only a few companies. Other examples include Ben & Jerry's, the ice cream company founded to support Vermont farmers and promote world peace; Patagonia, Inc., a clothing firm that built protection of nature into its strategy; Stonyfield Farm, an organic yogurt maker; and Seventh Generation, which makes nontoxic household cleaning products.[12] The validity of a business model is determined by profit or loss. Each of these businesses has succeeded, at least for an extended time, though each has faced tensions between social visions and market realities. Some have suffered financial difficulties and been absorbed by larger firms run on more traditional business models.

The Body Shop was acquired by L'Oreal, Stonyfield Farm by Groupe Danone, and Ben & Jerry's by Unilever. In each case absorption of the mouse by the elephant has been hard, as the progressive culture clashed with the traditional one. At Unilever, for example, Ben & Jerry's business was subjected to cost-cutting pressures and the social code in its brand was very hard for the big company to decipher, as when it failed to see a problem with using eggs from factory-farmed chickens even as activists were protesting their use.[13]

A rare variant of the progressive model is the large corporation where a founder with noble impulses left a culture inclined to corporate responsibility. The German media conglomerate Bertelsmann was founded in 1835 to publish hymnals by Carl Bertelsmann, a Protestant inspired by the Great Awakening. He believed the primary goal of his company should be to make society better. He shared half the firm's profits with the workers and gave them pensions and other benefits long before other German companies. Bertelsmann has grown into the third-largest global media conglomerate owning, among other brands, BMG Music, Random House, and RCA, but it is still controlled by descendants of the founder. A revealing flash of the old corporate virtue showed when the family fired Bertelsmann's chief

[11] Anita Roddick, *Business as Unusual* (London: Thorsons, 2000), pp. 97 and 172.

[12] For other examples see David Y. Choi and Edmund R. Gray, *Values-Centered Entrepreneurs and Their Companies* (New York: Routledge, 2011).

[13] Philip H. Mirvis, "Can You Buy CSR?" *California Management Review*, Fall 2008, p. 114. See also James E. Austin and Herman B. "Dutch" Leonard, "Can the Virtuous Mouse and the Wealthy Elephant Live Happily Ever After?" *California Management Review,* Fall 2008.

executive, in part because he bought Napster, a business they believed was unethical.[14] Another example is Johnson & Johnson, where Robert Wood Johnson, a member of the founding family, wrote "Our Credo" in 1943, just before the company sold stock to the public. Over the years this credo, which required Johnson & Johnson to model a stakeholder firm, became central to the company's culture and helped make major decisions.[15]

Most companies, however, including nearly all of the largest multinationals, begin with no founding impulse for truth, justice, and the stakeholder way. Their social performance is based on responses of their management teams to pressures in the operating environment. Such companies vary in their reaction to these pressures across a spectrum from reluctance to enthusiasm. At the left of this spectrum (see Figure 6.2), companies focus on making a profit and resist demands to go beyond the minimum duty of obeying the law. For them, the extent of citizenship is determined by the power of stakeholders over their behavior. In the middle, companies accept social obligations and may work to mitigate adverse impacts on society before regulations can be passed. And at the right, companies seek to be proactive by anticipating demands and resolving problems before they arise. Companies today are moving to the right, becoming more responsive.

A MODEL OF CSR IMPLEMENTATION

Companies can manage their corporate responsibility efforts by creating an implementation process. Figure 6.3 illustrates a model sequence or method for assessing the societal environment, defining responsibilities, creating a CSR strategy, and

FIGURE 6.2
A Spectrum of Responses to Social Demands

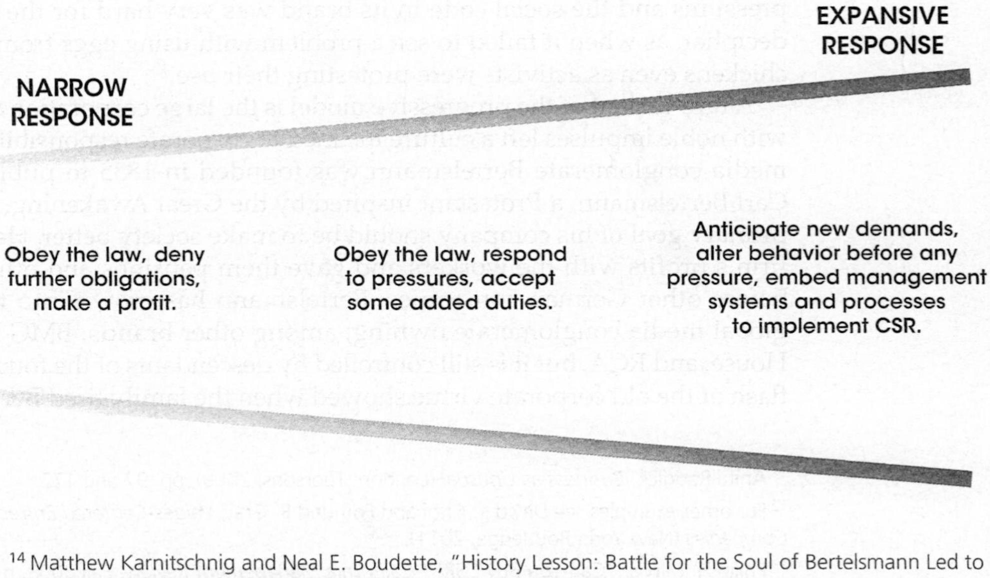

NARROW RESPONSE

EXPANSIVE RESPONSE

Obey the law, deny further obligations, make a profit.

Obey the law, respond to pressures, accept some added duties.

Anticipate new demands, alter behavior before any pressure, embed management systems and processes to implement CSR.

[14] Matthew Karnitschnig and Neal E. Boudette, "History Lesson: Battle for the Soul of Bertelsmann Led to CEO Ouster," *The Wall Street Journal*, July 30, 2002, p. A1.
[15] Read "Our Credo" at www.jnj.com/connect/about-jnj/jnj-credo/.

FIGURE 6.3 **A Model Process of CSR Implementation**

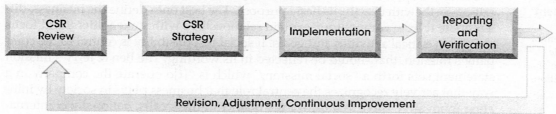

taking action. The sequence implied in this basic model is an ideal.[16] It depicts a more systematic approach than likely exists in practice. Beginning at the left with CSR assessment, we discuss each stage and illustrate related company actions.

CSR Review

To begin, a corporation should assess its current situation and activities. No single responsibility formula fits all. Each business must be systematically reviewed to discover its range of societal impacts and the societal expectations that bear on it. Finding these requires looking at factors such as its size, financial structure, products, production processes, employees, culture, geographic location(s), supply chain, and leader's views. The review should be expansive. It can begin with a definition of CSR to focus thinking. Then it might explore legal or regulatory standards, inventory existing CSR projects, and examine competitor's actions. Two other important steps are discovery of core values and engagement of stakeholders.

Discovering Core Values

Core values, the central beliefs that guide decisions, reside deep in the company's culture. Once formed they are very persistent. There are many ways to find them. In 1995 Fujitsu Group, a Japanese information technology corporation, created its "Fujitsu Way," a philosophy of corporate purpose and responsibility, by finding its "corporate DNA" in the speeches of past presidents going back to its origins in the 1930s. Similarly, the origin of a statement of "purpose, values, and principles" that guides social missions at Procter & Gamble was a project by top managers to write down basic beliefs in the company's culture.[17] At other companies, core values are found in existing mission, vision, and values statements, charters, credos, and codes of governance or conduct. Responsibility initiatives taken by a firm should harmonize with core goals and values. If these basic documents do not reference goals and values that facilitate CSR, support for action may be weak.

[16] The model is inspired by models and process standards elsewhere, including Business Leaders Initiative on Human Rights, et al., *A Guide for Integrating Human Rights into Business Management* (New York: Global Compact Office, February 2007); International Organization for Standardization, *Draft International Standard ISO/DIS 26000: Guidance on Social Responsibility* (Geneva: ISO, 2009), chap. 7; and Government of Canada, *Corporate Social Responsibility: An Implementation Guide for Canadian Business* (Ottawa: Public Works and Government Services Canada, March 2006).

[17] Rosabeth Moss Kanter, *Supercorp* (New York: Crown Business, 2009), p. 73.

mission statement
A brief statement of the basic purpose of a corporation.

For any corporation a key source of values is the *mission statement,* a document setting forth, with brevity, its basic purpose. The best ones define the business, differentiate it from competitors, explain relationships with stakeholders, and focus energy on critical activities and goals. If social responsibility is central to the company's mission, that should be reflected in its wording. The Ben & Jerry's mission statement sets forth a "social mission," which is "[t]o operate the company in a way that actively recognizes the central role that business plays in society by initiating innovative ways to improve the quality of life locally, nationally & internationally." The idea of "initiating innovative ways" led over the years to specific actions such as planting trees to replace the wood used in popsicle sticks and donating a percentage of Peace Pops sales to fund research on world peace.

In the past, most mission statements centered on profits and products. Many still limit themselves to this narrow focus. AutoNation aspires "[t]o be America's best run, most profitable automotive retailer." AGCO Corporation, a tractor manufacturer, aims for "[p]rofitable growth through superior customer service, innovation, quality, and commitment." National City Corp., a Cleveland bank, plans to "achieve superior levels of financial performance as compared to our peers and provide stockholders with an attractive return on their investment over time." These are firms with traditional business models.

However, many formerly traditional companies have revised their missions to include a social purpose. PepsiCo seeks "to provide financial rewards to investors as we provide opportunities for growth and enrichment to our employees, our business partners and the communities in which we operate." And Pfizer says: "We will become the world's most valued company to patients, customers, colleagues, investors, business partners and the communities where we work and live."

Engaging Stakeholders

Many companies now engage in formal or informal dialogue with a range of stakeholders, those entities that can affect or are affected by their activities. They are driven less by an ethical duty to be open than by a desire to avoid disruption of operations. In the process, they protect their "social license to operate" and can get new ideas. A simple way to identify stakeholders is a *stakeholder map,* a diagram that sketches stakeholders in basic categories and depicts their relationship to the firm. Figure 6.4 shows the basic map of stakeholders used by ArcelorMittal, a global steel manufacturer. Such a map is only the beginning. Figure 6.5 shows how just one category, government and regulators, might be articulated into a more complete picture.

Choosing which stakeholder to engage is an art. In stakeholder theory the corporation has an ethical duty of fairness toward all of them, including, perhaps especially, those it imposes burdens on though they may be powerless. In practice, corporations seriously engage only stakeholders with power to affect operations.

With stakeholders identified, a plan of engagement is constructed. Each company must decide what closeness of engagement, from very structured and frequent to informal and infrequent, is appropriate. Stakeholders can be categorized in many ways, for example, by orientation to the firm (confrontational, neutral, or supportive), by power to affect its business (high, medium, or low influence), or

FIGURE 6.4
Basic Stakeholder Map for ArcelorMittal

Adapted from *Corporate Responsibility Report 2009: Our Progress towards Safe Sustainable Steel* (Luxembourg: ArcelorMittal, 2010), p. 8.

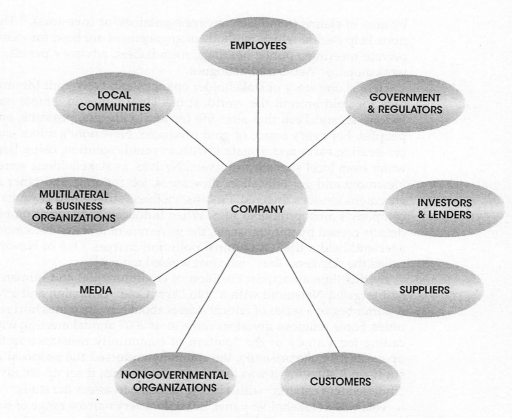

This basic map is used by ArcelorMittal to classify global stakeholders, beginning the company's process of engagement.

FIGURE 6.5
Stakeholder Map Articulated to Show Government Stakeholders

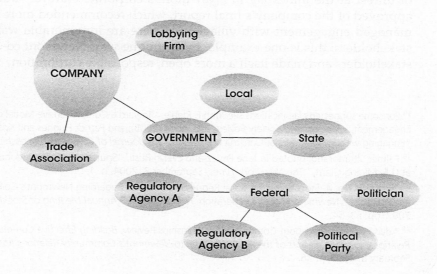

by area of claims (feminists, environmentalists, or investors).[18] These classifications help decide which methods of engagement are best, for example, surveys, private meetings, public hearings, roundtables, advisory panels, focus groups, workshops, or Web-based dialogues.

Here is one story of stakeholder engagement. Newmont Mining Corporation digs for gold around the world. It has large mines in remote parts of Ghana, Indonesia, and Peru that alter life for local villagers, peasants, and indigenous peoples. For every ounce of gold produced, Newmont's mines excavate tons of ore-bearing earth and irrigate it with a cyanide solution, using large volumes of water from local streams and rivers. Natives, as stakeholders, were consulted by Newmont and got relocation allowances, job training, and other assistance, yet enormous tensions lingered. Protests, violence, strikes, and lawsuits hung over the company's most profitable sites. When Indonesian villagers complained of birth defects caused by mining waste, the government arrested Newmont's local manager and held a trial on criminal pollution charges. One of Newmont's lawyers called the villagers "liars" who just wanted money.[19]

By this time an activist coalition of environmental and human rights groups had targeted Newmont with a "No Dirty Gold" campaign and a *New York Times* reporter began a series of critical stories about how its mines hurt remote communities. Some religious investors came to its 2007 annual meeting with a resolution calling for a study of the "pattern of community resistance to the company's operations."[20] Surprisingly, the company endorsed the proposal and began the study and, showing it was learning some lessons, it set up an advisory panel of "independent experts" with a broad mandate to assess the study.

This was a stakeholder panel, but with a very narrow range of stakeholders. Of the seven members, all had roots in progressive activism, and two were former heads of groups in the anti-Newmont advocacy campaign. In the end, this panel, in its own words, "encountered a degree of institutional resistance and defensiveness" in the company as it tried to do its work and suggested that the "root causes" of unrest at the mines lay in "Newmont's corporate culture." But it generally approved of the company's final report, which recommended more active, better managed engagement with villagers.[21] There are innumerable ways to engage stakeholders; this is one example. In its unique way, Newmont co-opted critical stakeholders and made itself a more open, responsible corporation.

---

[18] For some suggested classifications see John F. Preble, "Toward a Comprehensive Model of Stakeholder Engagement," *Business and Society Review* 110, no. 4 (2005); and Patrick Hughes and Kristin Demetrious, "Engaging with Stakeholders or Constructing Them?" *The Journal of Corporate Citizenship,* Autumn 2006.

[19] Palmer Situmorang, quoted in Jane Perlez and Evelyn Rusli, "Spurred by Illness, Indonesians Lash Out at U.S. Mining Giant," *The New York Times,* September 8, 2004, p. 1.

[20] "Proposal No. 4–Stockholder Proposal Requesting a Report Regarding Newmont's Community Policies and Practices," Newmont Mining Corporation, *Notices of 2007 Annual Meeting of Stockholders,* March 5, 2007, pp. 53–54.

[21] Advisory Panel, Newmont Community Relationships Review, *Building Effective Community Relationships: Final Report of the Advisory Panel to Newmont's Community Relationships Review,* February 8, 2009, p. 35.

CSR Strategy

The next stage in Figure 6.3 is the development of an overall strategy for corporate responsibility. A *strategy* is a basic approach, method, or plan for achieving an objective. A company with a strategy is like a traveler with a map showing the city of destination and a plan to reach it by taking the morning train. Like this traveler, a company defining its CSR strategy must first find an objective, or a vision of what it will achieve, then create a method for reaching it.

To establish its CSR objective a company can consider the profile it constructed in the CSR review stage, analyzing it to find strengths and weaknesses in its social response and threats and opportunities in its environment. Then the company can list a range of possible social initiatives. At a minimum, these actions must meet legal requirements. Beyond that, voluntary actions can be listed. Then, a few actions should be given priority. These become the firm's strategic CSR objectives.

For large firms the task of setting priorities is complex. Multiple, even conflicting, stakeholder demands exist. Along the value chain there are potential adverse impacts to correct. More broadly, difficult social problems in the firm's environment may demand attention. To which tasks should the firm assign priority? Companies must respond to some stakeholder demands or risk damage to their reputations and businesses. Ethical duty requires that where the firm has influence it should seek to mitigate value chain activities that damage society. Yet beyond such imperatives there are many options.

Michael Porter and Mark Kramer suggest an "essential test" for the worthiness of any additional social initiative, that is, "whether it presents an opportunity to create shared value—that is, a meaningful benefit for society that is also valuable to the business."[22] According to them, companies should distinguish between a wide range of generic social issues and a much narrower range of social issues that affect their competitive advantage. Generic social issues, such as the need to reduce crime, poverty, and disease, are important in society, but are not affected by and do not affect the company's business. Competitive social issues are those related to factors that influence success in the marketplace. The importance of specific issues to each firm will vary. Greenhouse gas emissions are a generic social issue for Tiffany's, but a competitive factor for General Motors and Toyota, which sell low-emission vehicles. Poverty may be a generic social issue for Lockheed, but a competitive issue for Unilever and Nestlé, which market small, inexpensive, single-use product packages.

An example of how a company can prioritize a social issue to competitive advantage is General Electric's "ecomagination" strategy. Ecomagination is a neologism created to denote concern for the environment and the imagination residing in GE's research labs. As a strategy, it is simultaneously a plan for revenue growth and a social program.

So far, GE has marketed 80 ecomagination products including wind turbines, generators powered by landfill gas, and filters that recycle wastewater without

strategy
A basic approach, method, or plan for achieving an objective.

---

[22] Michael E. Porter and Mark R. Kramer, "Strategy and Society," *Harvard Business Review*, December 2006, p. 84.

chemicals. To fulfill strategic intent each product must meet a dual test. It has to improve the customer's operating performance measurably. It has to be better for the environment. One example is the Trip Optimizer, a throttle control for freight locomotives. It reads train weight and length, track conditions, elevation, temperature, and engine power, then calculates the most efficient route and throttle movements for on-time arrival with least fuel used, eliminating human variation between locomotive engineers. Depending on terrain, it cuts diesel fuel consumption by 6 to 10 percent and raises the ton-miles-per-gallon ratio railroads use to measure productivity. It also eliminates several hundred tons of polluting emissions per locomotive each year.[23]

Implementation of CSR Strategy

To be carried out, a strategy must be translated into specific goals and performance objectives, embedded in policies and procedures, reinforced with processes, and supported by both the formal structure and the corporate culture. If the structure, culture, and processes of a company are misaligned with its strategic goals, those goals will be slighted. A range of actions that facilitate implementation is discussed.

Organization Structure

An initial step in implementation is to create an effective CSR decision-making structure. Many companies create elements of formal structure at top levels to ensure leadership and overall coordination. Examples of companies with corporate responsibility committees on their boards of directors are Altria, Hasbro, H. J. Heinz, Kellogg, McDonald's, Lockheed Martin, and Occidental Petroleum. Below the board, many companies assign an executive to oversee the action. Companies with staff vice presidents of corporate responsibility include British Petroleum, Chiquita Brands, Campbell Soup, General Electric, Hershey, Nike, Walmart, and Walt Disney.

However, the growing number of board committees and vice presidents implies more centralization than usually exists in practice. At most companies CSR is still supplemental, and largely incidental, to core business strategies. Elements of CSR are isolated in parts of the organization. Charitable giving is in the foundation. Human rights and diversity are managed by the human resources staff. The code of conduct is in the legal department. Environmental impacts are left to operations managers. The CSR agenda is fragmented. To wit:

> Citizenship has many rooms but no home. Rarely is corporate citizenship organized across the business. Many organizational functions touch some piece of the elephant but each unit is generally responsible . . . to a particular part of citizenship. . . . [O]rganizational silos are created and frustrate any overall organization strategy where all units are pulling together around a common vision. . . .[24]

---

[23] "GE's Fuel Autopilot Software Set for 200 Locomotives," *GE Reports*, December 19, 2009, at www.gereports.com.

[24] Bradley K. Googins and Steven Rochlin, "Corporate Citizenship Top to Bottom: Vision, Strategy, and Execution," in Marc J. Epstein and Kirk O. Hanson, eds. *The Accountable Corporation: Corporate Social Responsibility,* vol. 3 (Westport, CT: Praeger, 2006), p. 117.

To centralize oversight, some companies, for example, Coca-Cola, Pfizer, Time Warner, and Vodafone have cross-functional CSR committees made up of managers from different departments or business units. Such organizational forms are still the minority.

Action Planning

When a strategy and decision-making structure are in place, transforming intent into action is still necessary. An action plan sets forth the multitude of tasks that, together, will bring the strategy to fruition. Such tasks include revising or creating policies, budgeting resources, and assigning work.

An illustration of the effectiveness of an action plan is found within Denmark's Novo Nordisk, a pharmaceutical corporation with 24,000 employees in 81 countries. After a CSR review in the late 1990s it decided to focus its corporate responsibility strategy on fighting all forms of discrimination. The strategy turned into three actions. First, employees were trained in national regulations against discrimination. Second, informal barriers to advancement within Novo Nordisk were found and removed. Third, managers were encouraged to turn employee diversity into a business advantage.

Each Novo Nordisk business unit set up its own action plan. In South Africa, where physicians are predominantly white, the company sales representatives were white also, but after a new action plan most of the sales force became black and mixed-race. A strict policy excluded as customers doctors who disliked visits from nonwhite salespersons.

Performance Goals and Timelines

A strong action plan sets performance goals and timelines for their accomplishment. To be effective, goals must be specific and progress toward them should be measurable. Such goals and measures create a common language and focus efforts across organizational units. Examples of time-based, quantitative objectives, desirable for their clarity, are those set by General Electric in 2005 for its ecomagination strategy. By 2008 it would reduce its ratio of greenhouse gas emissions per dollar of revenue by 30 percent. By 2010 it would invest $1.5 billion in ecomagination product research and raise revenues to $25 billion. And by 2012 it would reduce its water use by 20 percent and reduce its absolute emissions of greenhouse gases by 1 percent. It exceeded all but one of its goals by 2009, the exception being revenues from ecomagination products, which were only $18 billion, and set new, more ambitious goals for 2015.[25] Its new revenue goal is to grow ecomagination sales at a rate two times that of sales for the overall company.

One of Procter & Gamble's social strategies is "to improve children's lives." In 2007 it set a goal for 2015 of preventing "160 million days of disease and saving 20,000 lives by delivering 4 billion liters of clean water" to children in areas where diarrheal illness is common. It acts by donating sachets of a product that treats contaminated water, making it drinkable. By 2009 it had delivered 930 million

[25] General Electric Company, *2009 Ecomagination Annual Report* (Fairfield, CT: General Electric Company, 2010), pp. 3–9.

liters of clean water, preventing an estimated 39 million days of disease and 5,200 deaths.[26]

The design of metrics is limited only by the imagination. Many companies use sustainability indicators recommended by an international standard-setting body called the Global Reporting Initiative. We will discuss these later in the chapter. Others design their own. Software vendors sell sustainability software to adapt a company's information system so it collects data on sustainability from dispersed units and even from independent firms in the supply chain.[27] Precise measurement of actions toward goals can be a challenge, but even approximations are helpful since, in the words of one consultant, "ignoring those impacts that are difficult to measure implicitly assigns a value of zero."[28]

Incentives and Accountability

Job descriptions that include sustainability duties encourage accountability. Incentives further encourage meeting goals. Performance evaluations, pay, and promotions are linked to targeted actions. Executive pay is linked to environmental performance at British Petroleum and Dow Chemical. At Alcoa 10 percent of the incentive pay for managers at each business unit is based on achieving diversity.[29] When the board of directors at Johnson & Johnson sets compensation for its top executives, it evaluates whether they modeled core values of responsibility and citizenship in its guiding Credo.[30] But this is exceptional. Formulas for CEO compensation are almost universally focused on attaining specific financial goals.

Business units and facilities can also be rewarded or punished based on sustainable performance. For example, Dow Chemical built a waste landfill in Michigan for its plants to use, but instead of allowing each plant to dump freely, it charged a fee based on how much material was brought for disposal. The fee penalized more polluting plants by, in effect, charging an internal tax on them. To avoid the fee, facilities changed their production processes to reduce waste. Dow now estimates the landfill will last until 2034, instead of filling by 2007 as originally estimated.[31]

Alignment of Strategy and Culture

Corporate culture must be aligned with strategic intent. Where the culture contains deep-seated, informal values that conflict with official CSR policies, those policies are likely to be ignored. If managers who meet financial goals but neglect "soft" sustainability goals are promoted, it indicates that formal policy is inconsistent with underlying beliefs about requirements for career advancement. For example, Timberland Co. executives backed a program allowing

[26] Procter & Gamble, *Designed to Matter: 2009 Sustainability Report*, Procter & Gamble 2009, at www.pg.com/en_US/sustainability/reports.shtml.

[27] Chris McClean, "CSR Management Needs Drive Application Revolution," *CRO*, July/August 2008.

[28] Marc J. Epstein, *Making Sustainability Work* (San Francisco: Berrett-Koehler, 2008), p. 256.

[29] Alcoa, *Notice of 2009 Annual Meeting and Proxy Statement*, March 16, 2009, p. 26.

[30] Johnson & Johnson, *Notice of Annual Meeting and Proxy Statement*, March 11, 2009, p. 23.

[31] Epstein, *Making Sustainability Work*, p. 135.

employees to take one week a year at full pay to work at local charities. However, line managers felt pressured to meet production goals and resisted giving workers time off.[32]

transparency
The state in which company social strategies, structures, and processes are visible to external observers.

sustainability reporting
Documentation and disclosure of how closely corporate operations conform to the goal of sustainable development.

sustainable development
Economic growth that meets current needs without social and environmental impacts that harm future generations.

triple bottom line
An accounting of a firm's economic, social, and environmental performance.

Reporting and Verification

To complete the cycle of CSR implementation, as shown in Figure 6.3, companies can assess and report information about their social performance. Publishing such reports serves two main purposes. First, by informing stakeholders they create *transparency;* that is, they lift the veil, revealing the internal strategies, structures, and processes that explain social performance. The opposite of transparency is opacity, or an inability to see inside the organization to know how it works and acts. Openness is increasingly necessary to protect a firm's reputation and to establish trust with stakeholders. Second, aggregating data in a report allows both managers and outsiders to appraise the firm's social performance.

A pioneering fad of social reporting appeared during the 1960s and 1970s in the United States, when a few large firms produced reports called social audits, a term that differentiated them from traditional financial audits. Bank of America, Exxon, and Philip Morris assessed their social impacts, and for a few years in the 1970s Atlantic Richfield Company published an annual social balance sheet that candidly weighed the multiple pluses and minuses of its social performance, an eccentric act of corporate candor that stopped when the company was acquired by British Petroleum. A 1974 survey found that 76 percent of 284 large companies did some form of social auditing.[33]

Early interest in social audits waned in the 1970s after American companies were hit by a massive increase in environmental and social regulation. The new regulations had strong reporting requirements that were, in effect, government-mandated social reports. However, as time passed and large corporations became more globalized, these requirements were less and less adequate. An information gap between companies and stakeholders opened wide.

To fill this gap, the international progressive community created a new reporting format called the Global Reporting Initiative (GRI). The GRI is a set of uniform standards for *sustainability reporting,* or the measurement and disclosure of corporate impacts to inform stakeholders how closely operations conform to the goal of *sustainable development.* Sustainable development is an ideal of economic growth that can "meet the needs of the present without compromising the ability of future generations to meet their own needs."[34] Using GRI guidelines, companies show how closely they conform to this ideal by explaining their performance on a *triple bottom line* of economic, social, and environmental results (see Figure 6.6).

---

[32] Joseph Pereira, "Doing Good and Doing Well at Timberland," *The Wall Street Journal,* September 9, 2003, p. B1.

[33] John J. Corson and George A. Steiner, *Measuring Business's Social Performance: The Corporate Social Audit* (New York: Committee for Economic Development, 1974), pp. 24–25.

[34] Global Reporting Initiative, *Sustainability Reporting Guidelines,* version 3.0 (Amsterdam: GRI, 2000–2006), p. 2, citing World Commission on Environment and Development, *Our Common Future* (Oxford: Oxford University Press, 1987), p. 43.

FIGURE 6.6
The Prism of the Triple Bottom Line

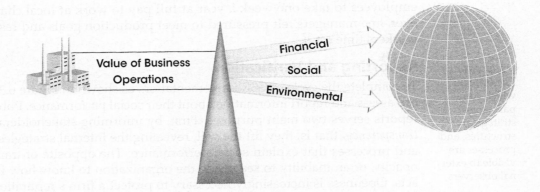

The triple bottom line is an idea attributed to John Elkington, a progressive scholar/activist who first wrote of it in the late 1990s.[35] Its essence is to appraise the total impact of a firm's operations, accounting for the full range of costs and value, by combining nonfinancial measures—social and environmental—with financial ones. It is now the consensus approach to sustainability reporting, not because it is an elegant calculation, but because it indulges a range of demanding stakeholders.

According to GRI guidelines, a good social report also meets certain format criteria. Its content is useful to stakeholders—clear, timely, comparable to past reports, reliable, and verifiable. It should include a statement of management's CSR vision and strategy, an extensive factual profile of the company, a description of its governance structure, policies for matters such as executive pay and stakeholder engagement, and data on a series of 71 performance indicators spanning the triple bottom lines (see the box for a sample). Forty-nine of these are called core indicators because they generally apply to all companies. Another 30 are additional indicators that may or may not be material to every reporter. For instance, additional indicator HR9 (the ninth human rights indicator) requires reporting the "[t]otal number of incidents of violations involving rights of indigenous people," and is only for companies having contacts with such peoples. The indicators span a range of complexity. Many require reporting of multiple measures, so a full report requires expensive data collection.

Additional indicators are set forth in more than a dozen "sector supplements" for specific industries. One of these, for food processing companies, adds eight industry-specific core indicators, for example FPSS4 (the fourth food processing sector supplement indicator) requires reporting the "[p]ercentage of consumer products sold, by product category, that are lowered in saturated fat, trans fats, sodium and added sugars."[36] This is justified, the *Guidelines* state, because the World Health Organization says a global epidemic of obesity exists and companies have a

[35] See John Elkington in *Cannibals with Forks: The Triple Bottom Line of 21st Century Business* (Oxford: Oxford University Press, 1997), chap. 3.

[36] Global Reporting Initiative, *Sustainability Reporting Guidelines & Food Sector Supplement*, version August 24, 2009, p. 46.

A Sample of GRI Core Performance Indicators

Here is a random, illustrative sample of 15 of the total of 49 core performance indicators in the *Global Reporting Guidelines,* five from each of the three "bottom lines."

ENVIRONMENTAL

- Materials used by weight or volume.
- Total water withdrawn by source.
- Description of significant impacts of activities, products, and services on biodiversity in protected areas and areas of high biodiversity value outside protected areas.
- Total direct and indirect greenhouse gas emissions by weight.
- Percentage of products sold and their packaging materials that are reclaimed by category.

SOCIAL

- Total number of incidents of discrimination and actions taken.
- Percentage of employees covered by collective bargaining agreements.
- Ratio of basic salary of men to women by employee category.

- Percentage and total number of business units analyzed for risks of corruption.
- Public policy position and participation in public policy development and lobbying.

ECONOMIC

- Direct economic value generated and distributed, including revenues, operating costs, employee compensation, donations and other community investments, retained earnings, and payments to capital providers and government.
- Financial implications and other risks and opportunities for the organization's activities due to climate change.
- Coverage of the organization's defined benefits plan obligations.
- Significant financial assistance received from government.
- Policy, practices, and proportion of spending on locally-based suppliers of significant locations of operation.

Source: Global Reporting Initiative, *Sustainability Reporting Guidelines,* Version 3.0 (Amsterdam: GRI, 2000–2006).

---

assurance
Verification by audit that information in a corporate sustainability report is reliable.

duty to report whether their products contribute to it. New indicators are frequently added to the *Guidelines.*

Finally, the GRI strongly suggests providing *assurance,* that is, verification for readers, that a report is reliable. The most effective assurance is provided by independent, outside auditors who assess the reporting process and verify accuracy of information. Only a minority of companies that issue a social report also choose to provide assurance. Of those that do, most hire one of the Big Four accounting and auditing firms that apply a professional assurance standard.[37]

Many of the rest use a standard created by AccountAbility, a civil society entity that provides a free, open-source assurance standard, licensing and training smaller consulting services to evaluate reports based on their inclusiveness, completeness, and transparency.[38] In either case, assurance requires certain steps,

---

[37] This standard is ISAE (for International Standard on Assurance Engagements) 3000, International Federation of Accountants, *Assurance Engagements Other than Audits or Reviews of Historical Financial Information* (New York: IFA, 2004).

[38] This standard is AA1000AS, AccountAbility, *AA1000 Assurance Standard 2008* (London: AccountAbility, 2008).

including interviews with managers and reviews of policies, processes, documents, and data samples. These audits are expensive, costing $1 million to $2 million for companies in single industries and much more for conglomerates, so some companies provide a more limited assurance by inviting stakeholder panels or academic experts to review their reports and make public statements. Around the world, sustainability reporting is now a mainstream activity.

HOW EFFECTIVELY IS CSR IMPLEMENTED?

In this section we have set forth model process for implementing CSR. If a company navigates this process, it can embed CSR as a countervailing force to the risks of bad behavior in its pursuit of profit. There is a trend, especially among the world's largest corporations, to adopt the elements of this model. A recent survey found that 62 percent of the 250 largest firms in the *Fortune* Global 500 formally engage stakeholders, 73 percent have created a sustainability strategy, 66 percent link performance indicators to strategic objectives, and 60 percent report data for these indicators. Also, 79 percent produce a corporate responsibility report, with 77 percent of these reporters following the Global Reporting Initiative guidelines and 40 percent including third-party assurance statements.[39] These numbers reflect the civil society pressures on the largest, most exposed global firms. Smaller and less-international firms reported far less adoption of model CSR actions in the survey.

A question is whether corporations, especially the largest and most exposed, use mostly ritual, bare compliance with the codes, certifications, and reporting requirements in the new civil regulation to innoculate against activism and more stringent forms of legislated regulation. John Elkington, the early champion of triple-bottom-line reporting, now believes corporations show an "almost willful avoidance of the social dimension."[40] Whatever its advances, social responsibility is still frequently seen as a superfluous activity only indirectly, if that, related to the bottom line, one that costs money, takes time, and reduces efficiency. Within many companies it is still bolted onto, not integrated with, core business strategies, its pieces fragmented in separate departments with no central oversight, and its spirit smothered by cultures of revenue. As one manager notes: "While I may be encouraged to participate in [a CSR event] on the weekend to support the company's CSR initiative, on Monday morning, it is business as usual, and all that really matters is how many cases I've pushed out the door."[41]

[39] Survey figures are from KPMG, *KPMG International Survey of Corporate Responsibility Reporting 2008* (Amstelveen: The Netherlands: KPMG Sustainability Services, 2008).

[40] Quoted in Adam Werbach, *Strategy for Sustainability: A Business Manifesto* (Boston: Harvard Business Press, 2009), p. 112.

[41] An anonymous interview subject quoted in Ida P. Berger, Peggy H. Cunningham, and Minette E. Drumwright, "Mainstreaming Corporate Social Responsibility: Developing Markets for Virtue," *California Management Review*, Summer 2007, p. 142. Brackets in the original.

Four Costly Errors of CSR Implementation

In practice, most companies fall short of the model process for CSR action set forth in this section because they make one of these errors.

1. They give no coherent, systematic thought to CSR.
2. They allow CSR strategy to be reactive by not aligning it with major social impacts, core competencies, or business strategies.

3. They fragment responsibility for CSR initiatives by assigning them to separate areas without central oversight.
4. They do not issue credible reports of CSR actions for stakeholders and fail the test of transparency.

CORPORATE PHILANTHROPY

philanthropy
Charitable giving of money, property, or work for the welfare of society.

Philanthropy, meaning literally love of mankind, is charity carried out by business with gifts of money, property, or work given to the needy or for social welfare activities. Large philanthropic contributions by American corporations are relatively recent. Until about 50 years ago courts held that corporate funds belonged to shareholders; therefore, managers had no right to give money away, even for noble motives. This restrictive doctrine made sense in the distant past when businesses were small and charity came mainly from their owners. However, as businesses grew and professional managers took control from their rich founders, the public started to expect giving from corporations, too.

The first major break from legal restrictions on corporate philanthropy was the Revenue Act of 1935, which allowed charitable contributions to be deducted from taxable earnings up to 5 percent of net profits before taxes (raised to 10 percent in 1981). Still, the legality of corporate giving remained doubtful, and managers were tight with charity dollars because they feared stockholder lawsuits. Eventually, the *A. P. Smith* case in 1953 (see the box) cleared away outdated rigidities in the law, freeing companies to be more generous. Now, corporations give $14 billion to $15 billion a year to worthy causes ranging from disaster relief to support for local orchestras. Conservative opponents of corporate social responsibility still argue that such giving is theft, like Robin Hood stealing from stockholders and giving to the poor. However, they no longer receive support from the law.

Patterns of Corporate Giving

Charitable giving is now a traditional dimension of corporate responsibility. Even so, most firms do not give a significant amount compared with their potential. In 2008, for example, corporations gave $14.5 billion, a large sum, but only 0.12 percent of worldwide sales and 1 percent of pretax income. Since the 1950s, overall corporate contributions have been remarkably consistent, hovering around 1 percent of pretax income. This is far less than the 10 percent that is tax deductible. Contributions rise as firms get larger, with the largest firms in one study giving

A. P. Smith Manufacturing Company v. Barlow et al., 13 N.J. 145 (1953)

A. P. Smith was a New Jersey corporation set up in 1896. It made valves and hydrants. In 1951 the firm gave $1,500 to Princeton University's annual fund-raising drive. This was not its first charitable contribution. It gave to a local community chest fund and had donated to other nearby colleges.

These contributions were made in a legal environment clouded by inconsistency. On the one hand was the law of corporate charters. These charters were issued by states, and corporations were not allowed to act beyond the powers expressly granted in them. The assumption in the charters was that the corporation's duty was to maximize profits for shareholders. A. P. Smith's incorporation papers, like those of most firms at the time, did not grant specific authority to make charity gifts. On the other hand was a statute. New Jersey passed a law in 1930 giving its corporations the right to make such donations if they did not exceed 1 percent of capital.

Ruth Barlow and four other angry owners of common and preferred stock thought the company had no right to give away any amount of money, because it was rightfully theirs as share-holders. They sued and in due course a trial was held. Luminaries from the business community appeared as witnesses for A. P. Smith to assert the merits of corporate charity. A Standard Oil of New Jersey executive argued that it was "good business" to show the kind of citizenship the public demanded. A U.S. Steel executive said that maintaining universities was essential to preserving capitalism. Nevertheless, the judge ruled against A. P. Smith, saying that the company had acted beyond its legitimate power.

A. P. Smith appealed. In 1953 the Supreme Court of New Jersey overturned the lower court, holding that rigid interpretation of charters to restrict charitable giving was no longer fitting since, unlike the old days when corporations were small and had limited assets relative to individuals, they now had enormous assets and it was reasonable for the public to expect generosity from them.

The *Smith* case settled the legal question of whether corporations could give to charity. After it, the legal cloud of acting *ultra vires* dissipated, clearing the way for greater corporate giving.

2.38 percent of pretax income. Large drug companies were the most generous, averaging 5.77 percent; aerospace and defense firms gave the least, only 0.45 percent.[42]

Corporate philanthropy is a small part of overall philanthropy in the United States; in 2009 it was only 4.6 percent. Figure 6.7 displays the 10-year trend in giving and segments sources into their relative proportions. During this time total giving rose from $203 billion to a high of $314 billion in 2007, then fell to $304 billion in 2009. As the segmented bars show, individuals gave by far the largest proportion, followed by foundations, charitable bequests, and, finally, corporations (including corporate foundations). In the years shown, corporate giving rose from $10.7 billion to a high of $15.2 billion in 2007, then fell to $14.1 billion in 2009. Corporate giving was consistently about 5 percent of total giving.

Corporations that contribute do so in many ways, including cash, products, services, volunteered employee time, and use of facilities. Cash giving is only about half of all giving. Among the largest corporations, about 42 percent of giving goes to United Way campaigns and grants to health and human service agencies such as the Red Cross and the American Cancer Society. Another 23 percent

[42] Figures in this paragraph are from Carolyn Cavicchio and Judit Torik, *The 2009 Corporate Contributions Report* (New York: The Conference Board, December 2009), pp. 4–10.

FIGURE 6.7
The Trend
in Private
Philanthropy:
1999–2009

Source: U.S. Census
Bureau, *Statistical
Abstract of the United
States: 2009*, 129th ed.
(Washington, DC:
U.S. Census Bureau,
2009), table 561; and
Giving USA Foun-
dation, "U.S. Chari-
table Giving Falls
3.6 Percent in 2009,"
news release, June 9,
2010, pp. 2–3.

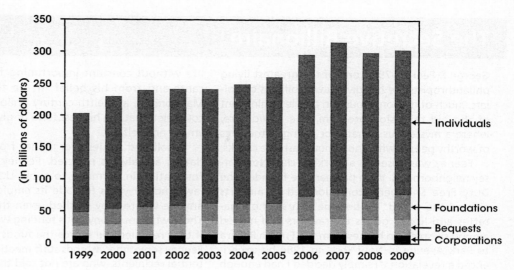

flows to education, about 13 percent goes to civic groups such as YMCA/YWCAs and to local governments, about 6 percent to culture and arts causes, and a tiny amount, less than 3 percent, to environmental groups.[43]

Strategic Philanthropy

With historical roots in religious teachings, the act of philanthropy presumes a selfless motive of giving out of moral duty to benefit the needy or to advance society. Traditionally, corporate philanthropy conformed to such ideals of altruism and magnanimity. Companies and their foundations gave to help the destitute while funding social goods such as education and the arts. Some self-benefit resided in these donations since the elevating deed often raised corporate reputations, created goodwill, or improved the economy by strengthening society.

As corporations gained experience with philanthropy, some concluded that the traditional approach of diffuse giving to myriad worthy causes was noble but flawed. Over time, the number of causes grew. As charity recipients proliferated, the shrinking sums given to each had less and less impact. Executives and their spouses diverted funds into pet artistic and cultural projects unimportant to the firm's main stakeholders. In Detroit, a city hollowed out by race riots and loss of its tax base as whites ran to the suburbs, Ford Motor gave millions of dollars to the Michigan Opera Theater because Jennifer Nasser, the wife of its CEO, was a patron.[44] As vacant downtown buildings sat with broken windows she had Ford employees refurbish the theater. Such an impulsive approach to philanthropy, often called *checkbook philanthropy*, leads to awards, plaques, and honors for executives but lacks an underlying business logic.

checkbook philanthropy
A traditional form of corporate giving in which donations go to multiple worthy causes without any link to business strategy.

Most large corporations still engage in some checkbook philanthropy. However, more and more convert their philosophy of giving from one of pure, if

[43] These figures are from Cavicchio and Torik, *The 2009 Corporate Contributions Report*, p. 49. The 13 percent remainder goes to miscellaneous recipients outside these main categories of giving.
[44] Keith Bradsher, "A Horn of Plenty for Opera in Detroit," *The New York Times*, October 28, 1999, p. E1.

The Secretive Billionaire

George F. Feeney, 79, is one of the greatest living philanthropists. He has given away billions of dollars, much of it anonymously in a style reminiscent of the old television program, *The Millionaire*, where a mysterious benefactor changed the lives of worthy people with anonymous cashier's checks.

Feeney was raised in a working-class New Jersey neighborhood. With partners, he founded the Duty Free Shoppers stores located in airports around the world. He became rich selling cigarettes and luxury goods to travelers and moved among six splendid homes from the French Riviera to Park Avenue in New York. In 1984 he experienced a revelation. "I simply decided I had enough money," he told a reporter.[45]

Without even informing his three partners he set up a foundation in Bermuda. Then he irrevocably transferred his ownership interest in Duty Free Shoppers to it. At the time, this was worth about $500 million. More followed. Over the years, the foundation has given away more than $5 billion.

If Feeney had kept the money he could now be worth as much as $10 billion, but his personal assets may be only about $5 million. He does not own a house and lives in a one-bedroom San Francisco rental. He has no car, preferring to get around by bus. He has no briefcase and brings papers to meetings in a plastic bag. He wears a $15 watch, prefers casual clothes, and doubts the need for more than one pair of shoes.[46] He also has a passion for secrecy coming from a desire to live life without constant importuning from supplicants and from his belief in the teachings of Maimonides, a twelfth century philosopher who counseled that the highest form of giving is anonymous and selfless.

Unsolicited requests for money from the foundation are always rejected. Feeney located his foundation in Bermuda to avoid U.S. disclosure laws and for years forbade its employees to tell anyone where they worked, even their families. Those who got anonymous funding were told that if they revealed the source the funds would stop. Feeney sometimes attends staff meetings with potential recipients, who are not told the identity of the quiet observer.

The existence of the foundation, called Atlantic Philanthropies, became public when Duty Free Shops was sold in 1997. Since then, it has become much more open. It lists its mission as "fostering lasting changes in the lives of disadvantaged and vulnerable people" and to that end it funds projects large and small, from building hospitals in Vietnam to repairing broken windows in South African schools.

Most foundations give away only limited sums each year, allowing them indefinitely to maintain large endowments. But Feeney has instructed Atlantic Philanthropies to exhaust its remaining funds by 2016. He believes his money should start doing good as soon as possible, not in some distant future.

strategic philanthropy
A form of corporate philanthropy in which charitable activities reinforce strategic business goals.

scattered and unplanned generosity to one that aligns giving with commercial objectives. This is known as *strategic philanthropy,* or the alignment of charity with business strategy.

General Mills was a pioneer. It has always been a generous company, giving an unusually high 5 percent of its pretax domestic profits to charity. For years it emphasized funding of prestigious cultural and arts programs in its Minneapolis headquarters area. In the late 1990s it began to redirect giving to projects on youth nutrition, schools, and social services in 20 cities where it had facilities. Then it

[45] Quoted in Judith Miller, "He Gave Away $600 Million, and No One Knew," *The New York Times,* January 23, 1997, p. A1.

[46] Conor O'Clery, *The Billionaire Who Wasn't* (New York: Perseus Books, 2007), pp. 321–22.

moved to align its brands with philanthropic causes. In its Spoonfuls of Stories campaign it gave millions of dollars to buy new books for children in low-income families and it put children's books in millions of Cheerios boxes. These efforts better matched charity giving with the concerns of average grocery shoppers who buy Cheerios. There are many similar examples.

- Mattel donated $25 million to put its name on the children's hospital at UCLA, now called Mattel Children's Hospital. The company has no role in running the facility, although it gives toys to patients. Adding the company name to the hospital increases brand recognition and contributes to a compassionate corporate image among toy buyers. These benefits reinforce the commercial goals of a toy company while also helping sick children.[47]

- Since 1995 Home Depot has partnered with a nonprofit named KaBOOM! to build playgrounds. The KaBOOM! vision is "a great place to play within walking distance of every child." In 2005 Home Depot gave it $25 million and pledged more support in materials and employee time to build 1,000 playgrounds in 1,000 days. That goal was met and playgrounds are still forthcoming. Home Depot faces strong competitors, including Lowe's and Walmart. It believes that its work on playgrounds, while helping children, differentiates its brand, creates appreciation in local store markets, and underlines the expertise of its staff with building materials.[48]

Cause Marketing

cause marketing
A form of strategic philanthropy in which charitable contributions are based on purchases of a product.

Cause marketing is a variant of strategic philanthropy in which charitable contributions are based on purchases of a product. It links a brand to a social cause so both benefit. Marketers use branding to differentiate products, especially mass-produced products that consumers might see as interchangeable commodities if they lack brand attributes. Companies spend heavily to endow brands with these attributes so they can charge a price premium. Traditional branding creates attributes in two dimensions to influence buying decisions. One is an impression of the product's positive qualities directed to the logical mind. The other is an emotional association with the product that allows consumers to fulfill emotional needs by using it. Marketers have learned that if their brand is connected to a charitable cause a third attribute is created, one that appeals to the consumer's conscience. In cause-related marketing the corporation calculates it will add this benevolent dimension to its brand while also doing a philanthropic good deed.

Cause marketing is a powerful sales tool. In a recent survey 75 percent of consumers said they would try a new brand if it supported a cause and 64 percent said they would be willing to pay more for it if the cause were important to them.[49] In the United Kingdom, for example, Mars Inc. made a donation to animal rescue

[47] Julie Edelson Halpert, "Dr. Pepper Hospital? Perhaps, for a Price," *The New York Times*, February 18, 2001, sec. 3, p. 1.

[48] Sandra O'Loughlin, "Tools for Tots," *Brandweek*, July 10–17, 2006, p. 18.

[49] "Struggling Consumers Say Companies Connect," *Marketing Weekly News*, November 21, 2009, p. 62, citing a 2009 PR Week/Barkley Public Relations Cause Survey.

charities for each of its Pedigree brand dog food products sold. In just three months the campaign raised $778,000 for homeless dogs, increased sales by 6 percent, and led to an 8 percent rise in consumers who identified the brand as having "dogs at its heart."[50] Here are two other examples:

- In the early 1990s restaurant owners felt that American Express card fees were too high. Enough restaurants refused the cards that, rather than face rejection, many cardholders used a competing card instead. To counteract this, American Express started a cause marketing campaign called "Charge Against Hunger" in which it donated 3 cents per transaction to nonprofit anti-hunger groups during the holiday months of November and December each year. The campaign created a clear link between using the card to pay for restaurant meals and fighting hunger. It raised $21 million in four years for donations to 600 anti-hunger groups. It also increased the charge volume by 12 percent and raised the opinion of restaurant owners about the card.[51]

- Avon Products sells more beauty products than any other company. Most of its revenues come from direct sales through 5.4 million part-time, predominantly female sales representatives in 100 countries. In the early 1990s Avon's brand image was deteriorating because its direct-selling strategy carried an old-fashioned, down-market connotation. The company decided to burnish its name using cause-related marketing. The vast majority of Avon's sales are to women. Research showed that fighting breast cancer was important to them, so Avon developed a line of affordable "pink ribbon" products and donated a specified amount from the purchase price to breast cancer research. Its brand has benefited so much that the cause-related "crusade" continues uninterrupted. Since 1992 Avon has collected more than $640 million for breast cancer research, detection, and treatment.[52]

Cause-related marketing raises big sums for worthy causes but, like other forms of strategic philanthropy, its mixture of altruism and self-interest attracts criticism. Skeptics call it "consumption philanthropy" that promotes wasteful materialism and suggest that people simply give directly to causes.[53] They note that companies pick causes based on research into what consumers care about, instead of trying to find the most acute needs. Heart disease is the leading killer of women and the leading fatal cancer in women is lung cancer. However, because the fight against breast cancer resonates more with high-spending female consumers ages 30 to 55, more than 300 companies have copied Avon's marketing innovation. Other causes languish from this convergence.

There is plenty of cynicism about corporate motives. One woman who has had breast cancer complains that "companies are making money off my disease—even

---

[50] "Golden Jubilee Awards 2009: Cause-related Marketing," *Marketing*, June 10, 2009, p. 28.

[51] Shirley Sagawa and Eli Segal, *Common Interest, Common Good* (Boston: Harvard Business School Press, 2000), p. 15.

[52] "Avon Breast Cancer Crusade," at www.avoncompany.com/women/avoncrusade/index.html.

[53] Angela M. Eikenberry, "The Hidden Costs of Cause Marketing," *Stanford Social Innovation Review*, Summer 2009, p. 51.

if they're giving an amount to charity, they're making so much more in profit. . . . [I]t's like getting hit in the face."[54] In current breast cancer campaigns Avon donates $6.24 of the $10 price of its Crusade Tote Bag, and Coach gives $60 for each "awareness watch" it sells. Others are less generous. Duraflame gives 10 cents for each pink color log sold, only 2 percent of the $4.99 price. Yoplait donates 10 cents per yogurt container, but makes customers put their container lids in an envelope and return them by mail before it makes a contribution, imposing the cost of a stamp that exceeds the donation amount on people with fewer than five lids. Corporations, however, do not see commercial interest as an ethically inferior motive and believe that concrete benefits to both companies and causes far outweigh the importance of abstract arguments about base motives.

New Forms of Philanthropy

In traditional philanthropy, foundations and corporations give grants to nonprofit organizations that then spend the money to meet stated goals, for example, increasing literacy or buying medicines for the poor. The donor expects no financial return, in effect losing 100 percent of the capital invested, and may follow up at intervals or at the end of a project to see if objectives were met. Much good has come from this model, including such triumphs as the "green revolution," led by the Rockefeller Foundation's support for research in agriculture that led to new varieties of wheat, maize, and rice, increasing crop yields and saving an estimated 1 billion lives since the 1960s.[55] Nevertheless, it has shortcomings. Large foundation offices and staffs create administrative expenses. Committees slow decisions. Grant officers become conservative, rejecting innovation for fear a mistake will hurt their career. Grant recipients spend much of what they get on overhead, especially the costs of fund-raising necessary to continue their work. Some do not achieve what they promise, and monitoring their performance burdens donors.

Now, another model of philanthropy is emerging based largely, but not entirely, on the philosophies and examples of new billionaires from technology industries. In distinctive ways, new philanthropists such as Bill Gates of Microsoft, Pierre Omidyar and Jeffrey Skoll of eBay, Larry Page and Sergey Brin of Google, and Steve Case of AOL, either themselves or through their companies, apply the business methods that made them rich to the field of philanthropy, blurring the line between charity and business, seeking to harness market forces. This new philanthropy, or *philanthrocapitalism* as it is often called, covers a range of actors and approaches but it is bold, entrepreneurial, results-oriented, closely engaged, and impatient.

philanthro-capitalism
An emerging form of philanthropy that relies on market forces to achieve results.

Here are some examples of philanthrocapitalism at work, all different, but having in common the use of market incentives.

- Before the initial public offering of Google, its founders, Larry Page and Sergey Brin, told investors that 1 percent of equity, 1 percent of annual profits, and 1 percent of employee time would be set aside for "active philanthropy." This

[54] Jeanne Sather, quoted in Kris Frieswick, "Sick of Pink," *The Boston Globe*, October 4, 2009, magazine section.

[55] "A Scholar's Analysis of Grant-Making Successes—and Failures," *Chronicle of Philanthropy*, December 7, 2006, p. 3.

work is done within an entity named Google.org, which is a business unit of the parent company. Within Google.org the company's technologists attack three priority threats—climate change, emerging pandemics, and energy shortages. They bring to bear the engineering skills and information-gathering expertise that are core strengths of Google. One project is an online technology to measure spacial changes in the world's forests. Projects are developed as businesses and any profits accrue to Google.

- Around the world 3 billion of the world's poor cook with wood, dung, and coal, filling their dwellings with dangerous smoke causing 1.5 million deaths a year, most of women and children. In the past, aid groups gave away small stoves that reduced indoor pollution, but often they were not used. Many people thought smoke was harmless. Others put no value on what they got free. Some stoves were unsuited for local fuels. The charity model was failing. But this problem fit the mission of the Shell Foundation, set up by the oil company to apply market principles in solving problems of poverty and the environment. It committed $25 million in grants to a small, nonprofit corporation in Colorado named Envirofit that would design, manufacture, and sell stoves in the developing world using a business model. The foundation injected "business DNA" into the company by giving it advice on how to operate as a business. So far, Envirofit has sold more than 120,000 of the small stoves in India.[56] Its vans travel dirt roads in rural areas selling stoves for the equivalent of $17.50 to $55.60 in local currency. They reduce particle emissions by 80 percent, but customers like them because they reduce fuel use by 60 percent and can pay for themselves in months. Envirofit sells stoves as a business, not as a subsidized charity. It reinvests net income to expand the business.

- The Robin Hood Foundation was started by billionaire hedge fund manager Paul Tudor to better the lives of the poor in New York City. It funds programs that attack poverty. Of hundreds of such programs offered by agencies and nonprofits in the city, which should it fund to get the most poverty reduction per dollar spent? In a corporation, managers would compare return on capital invested to allocate funds between various business units. Robin Hood uses the same approach, modified to its charitable goals. It calculates a benefit-cost ratio for each grant program by monetizing the results of its work and comparing these with the cost of the grant. If a program has a benefit-cost ratio of 6:1, it creates $6 of benefits to the poor for every $1 of Robin Hood's funds. Measuring benefits requires estimates, for example, that an adolescent's future earnings increase $5,000 a year by avoiding a first arrest.[57] By using this benefit-cost metric Robin Hood disciplines its investment, cutting support for programs with low ratios to move dollars where they purchase more poverty reduction.

The new philanthropy is now small in relation to total philanthropy. Some are skeptical of any impact. Market solutions may be too superficial for bottomless

---

[56] Shell Foundation, *Annual Report and Accounts, 2008*, at www.shellfoundation.org; and Jeffrey Ball, "Small Energy-Saving Steps Can Make Big Strides," *The Wall Street Journal*, November 27, 2009, p. A16.
[57] Michael M. Weinstein, *Measuring Success: How Robin Hood Estimates the Impact of Grants* (New York: Robin Hood Foundation, 2009), p. 34.

social problems such as violence, corruption, bad government, and inequality. Success stories may be limited to initiatives such as indoor stoves, with dimensions that lend themselves to the application of market forces. Also, the pitfall of greed is there. Muhammad Yunus, who won a Nobel Prize for his creative work with *micro-finance,* or small loans to the poor, once criticized Banco Compartamos, a Mexican bank that makes micro-loans, for giving priority to profit over social good. The bank made a 23 percent profit, a fine return for a normal business but, it seems, a questionable one for a social enterprise.[58] According to Yunus, "Social businesses should not make a profit off the poor."[59]

micro-finance
Small loans given to poor people.

CONCLUDING OBSERVATIONS

Good intentions are worth little if not reflected in actions. If a corporation hopes to be socially responsible, it must do the hard work of building its aspirations into its operations. To implement CSR strategies it must use the same methods it uses to implement business strategies. No CSR initiative of any significance will succeed without their application.

Corporate philanthropy is a basic, widely accepted dimension of social responsibility. Traditionally, it was practiced as a form of charity, but today that is changing. Often, corporations align their giving with their profit goals. And both corporations and new billionaires with corporate fortunes are now using business methods to attack social problems. Optimism that capitalist tools can solve social problems as easily as they made people rich is natural, but not yet verified. Still, the new philanthropy in all its variations already shows promise of increasing the power of charity to do good.

[58] Gregory M. Lamb, "Charities Borrow For-Profit Strategies To Do Good," *Christian Science Monitor*, January 5, 2009, p. 14.

[59] Quoted in Steve Hamm, "Capitalism with a Human Face," *BusinessWeek*, December 8, 2008, p. 50.

Marc Kasky versus Nike

Marc Kasky of San Francisco sees his world as a community and has a long history of caring about the others in it. He got early lessons in business ethics from his father, who ran a car repair business.

> The customer would bring his car in and say there's something horribly wrong in my car: I think I need a new transmission. . . . My father would call them back an hour later and say, "Come get your car, there was a loose screw here and there; I fixed it. What does it cost? Nothing." I saw how that affected our family. It impressed me a great deal.[1]

After graduating from Yale University in 1969, he volunteered to work in poor Cleveland neighbor-

hoods. Moving to San Francisco, he headed a nonprofit center for foundations that funded schools. He involved himself in civic and environmental causes. He also became an avid jogger and ran marathons.

Over the years Kasky wore many pairs of Nike shoes and considered them a "good product."[2] But he stopped buying them in the mid-1990s after reading

[1] Quoted in Jim Edwards, "Taking It to the Big Guys," *Brandweek*, August 12, 2002, p. 1.

[2] Steve Rubenstein, "S. F. Man Changes from Customer to Nike Adversary," *San Francisco Chronicle*, May 3, 2002, p. A6. Kasky stated his ownership of Nike shoes in the interview for this article. However, his lawyer told the Supreme Court that he had "never bought any Nikes." *Nike v. Kasky*, No. 02–575, Oral Argument, April 23, 2003 (Washington, DC: Alderson Reporting Company, 2003), p. 30, lines 21 and 22. We give priority to Kasky's story, but this is a remarkable contradiction.

Marc Kasky. Source: © AP Photo/Denis Poroy.

stories about working conditions in overseas factories where they were made. By then Nike, Inc., had become the main focus of the anti-sweatshop cause, accused of exploiting low-wage workers who made its shoes and clothing. The more Kasky read about Nike, the more convinced he was that it was not only victimizing workers, but lying about it too. Kasky sought the help of an old friend, Alan Caplan, an attorney who had achieved fame in progressive circles by bringing the suit that forced R. J. Reynolds to stop using Joe Camel in its ads.

With Caplan's help, Kasky sued Nike in 1998 for false advertising, alleging it had made untrue statements about its labor practices. This was not Kasky's first lawsuit. Previously, he had sued Perrier over its claim to be "spring water" and Pillsbury Co. for labeling Mexican vegetables with the words "San Francisco style." Both suits were settled.[3] Nike sought dismissal of Kasky's suit, arguing that the statements he questioned were part of a public debate about sweatshops and protected by the First Amendment.

[3] Roger Parloff, "Can We Talk?" *Fortune*, September 2, 2002, p. 108.

NIKE

Nike, Inc., is the world's largest producer of athletic shoes and sports apparel. It grew out of a handshake in 1962 between Bill Bowerman, the track coach at the University of Oregon, and Phil Knight, a runner he had coached in the 1950s. Knight had just received an MBA from Stanford University, where in a term paper he had written about competing against established athletic shoe companies by importing shoes made in low-wage Asian factories. Now he was ready to try it. He and Bowerman each put up $550 and Knight flew to Japan, arranging to import 300 pairs of Onitsuka Tiger shoes.

After seven years, Knight and Bowerman decided to stop selling the Japanese company's brand and create their own. So they designed a shoe and subcontracted its production to a factory in Japan. By now Bowerman and Knight had incorporated, and an employee suggested naming the company Nike, for the Greek goddess of victory. Knight paid a design student at Portland State University $35 to create a logo. She drew a "swoosh." The elements of future market conquest were now in place and the company rapidly grew.

Nike succeeded using two basic strategies. First, its product strategy is to design innovative, fashionable footwear and apparel for affluent markets, then have contractors in low-wage countries manufacture it. This way Nike avoids the cost of building and managing factories. At first, it made most of its shoes in Japan (some were made in the United States until 1980), but as wages rose there it moved contracts to plants in South Korea and Taiwan. When wages rose in these countries, Nike again shifted production, this time to China, Indonesia, and Thailand, and later to Vietnam.

Second, its marketing strategy is to create carefully calculated brand images. Advertising associates the Nike brand with a range of ideas. Prominent among them is the idea of sport. Endorsements by professional athletes and college teams endow the swoosh with a high-performance image. Campaigns with the "just do it" slogan add connotations of competition, courage, strength, and winning. Other advertising associates the brand with urban culture to make it "street cool." In this way Nike transforms shoes and T-shirts that would otherwise be low-cost commodities into high-priced, high-fashion items that generate positive emotions when they are worn.

THE SWEATSHOP LABOR ISSUE

By 1980 when the company went public, it had seized half the world's athletic shoe market. But the outsourcing and advertising strategies that propelled it to the top put it on a collision course with a force in its social environment. This force, the sweatshop issue, would gain power and cause considerable damage.

In 1988 an Indonesian union newspaper published a study of bad working conditions in a plant making Nike footwear.[4] Soon other critical articles appeared in the Indonesian press. The AFL-CIO decided to investigate how workers were being treated in plants that manufactured for American firms and sent an investigator named Jeffrey Ballinger to Indonesia. Ballinger focused on Nike contractors, gathering detailed information.

In 1992 he published a clever indictment of Nike in *Harper's Magazine* by exhibiting the monthly pay stub of an Indonesian woman named Sadisah who made Nike running shoes. Sadisah worked on an assembly line 10-and-a-half hours a day, six days a week, making $1.03 per day or about $0.14 an hour, less than the Indonesian minimum wage. She was paid only $0.02 an hour for 63 hours of overtime during the pay period. Her home was all she could afford, a rented shanty lacking electricity and plumbing. The Nikes she made sold for $80 in the United States, yet the cost of her labor per shoe was only $0.12. If anyone missed the point, Ballinger noted that the year before Nike had made a profit of $287 million and signed Michael Jordan to a $20 million advertising contract, a sum that Sadisah would have had to work 44,492 years to earn.[5]

Ballinger's article appeared with a flurry of other negative stories, but the issue did not immediately heat up. Nevertheless, Nike elected to show more responsibility for the welfare of foreign workers. In 1992 it adopted a "Code of Conduct" requiring its contractors to certify compliance with local minimum wage, child labor, health, safety, workers' compensation, forced labor, environmental, and discrimination laws. In 1994, it hired the accounting firm Ernst & Young to audit code compliance by making spot checks at factories.

These developments suggest that at some point CEO Philip Knight came to believe that even if Nike did not directly employ foreign workers, it benefited from their labor and so had an ethical duty toward their welfare. But Nike would not escape damage from the issue. The code and spot checks were not enough. Negative stories about its contract factories grew more numerous.

Finally, the issue exploded after April 1996 congressional testimony by the leader of a human rights group, who said clothing for Walmart's Kathie Lee apparel line was made at a Honduran factory where children worked 14 hours a day. Daytime television viewers saw talk show host Kathie Lee Gifford reduced to tears as she responded, "You can say I'm ugly, you can say I'm not talented, but when you say that I don't care about children . . . How dare you?"[6] Now the issue had emotional content for American consumers.

Soon after the Gifford spectacle anti-sweatshop activists decided to focus on Nike, and attacks heated up. Nike was an industry leader. If it could be reformed, other clothing companies and retailers would fall into line. It was also vulnerable to a brand name attack. Advocacy groups joined forces to inform the public of what they saw as a gap between the inspiring images in Nike's advertising and the grim reality of its labor practices. This alarmed Nike because bad publicity could rub away the image magic that made its brand cool.

NIKE AT WAR WITH ITS CRITICS

The war over Nike's image would be fought in the media. An early skirmish came when Bob Herbert at *The New York Times* wrote the first of what became a yearlong series of columns berating Nike. After describing a climate of atrocities in Indonesia, including government-condoned killings and torture, he accused Nike of using "the magnificent image of Michael Jordan soaring, twisting, driving, flying" to divert attention from its exploitation of Indonesian workers. "Nike executives know exactly what is going on in Indonesia. They are not bothered by the cries of the oppressed. It suits them. Each cry is a signal that their investment is paying off."[7]

---

[4] Cited in Jeffrey Hollender and Stephen Fenichell, *What Matters Most* (New York: Basic Books, 2004), p. 190.

[5] Jeffrey Ballinger, "The New Free-Trade Heel," *Harper's*, August 1992, pp. 46–47.

[6] Rob Howe et al., "Labor Pains," *People Magazine*, June 10, 1996, p. 58.

[7] Bob Herbert, "Nike's Bad Neighborhood," *The New York Times*, June 14, 1996, p. A29.

EXHIBIT 1
Rise of Negative News Stories about Nike's Labor Practices, 1988–1999

Source: From S. Prakash Sethi, *Setting Global Standards*, 2003. Table 9.2. Reprinted with permission of John Wiley & Sons, Inc.

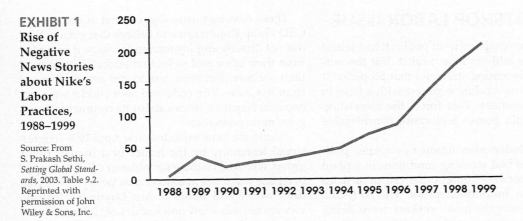

CEO Philip Knight quickly responded with a letter to the editor, citing ways that Nike tried to help workers, and noting that it paid "double the minimum wage" and "had an oversight system that works." He accused Herbert of trying to "sacrifice enlightenment for hype."[8] Herbert's response was a second column rebuking Nike for running theme ads about women's empowerment while most of its shoes were produced "by grossly underpaid women stuck in utterly powerless and often abusive circumstances."[9]

Over the next two years, negative stories about Nike appeared with increasing frequency (see Exhibit 1). An inspection report by the human rights group Vietnam Labor Watch reported that young women working in a Nike factory were paid subminimum wages. A supervisor had forced 56 women to run twice around the 1.2-mile factory boundary under a hot sun for failing to wear regulation shoes. Twelve of them fainted and required hospitalization.[10] Gary Trudeau drew a series of *Doonesbury* cartoons based on these allegations.

Activists urged people to return Nike sneakers during "shoe-ins" at Niketown outlets. A disgruntled Ernst & Young employee leaked a confidential spot inspection report on a Vietnamese shoe factory. It showed violations of Vietnamese labor law and said

that 77 percent of the employees suffered respiratory problems from breathing toxic vapors at levels that violated both Vietnamese and U.S. standards.[11] Another group, the Hong Kong Christian Industrial Committee, released a study of Nike factories in China documenting long workdays, forced overtime, pay below minimum wages, and unsafe levels of airborne dust and toxic chemicals.[12] *The Oregonian*, the paper in Portland where Nike is headquartered, called Nike "an international human rights incident."[13]

Now Nike found itself at the center of a worldwide debate over sweatshops. The company expanded efforts to stop workplace abuses and started a public relations campaign. At great expense it became the only shoe company in the world to eliminate the use of polyvinyl chloride in shoe construction, ending worker exposure to chlorine compounds. It revised its conduct code, expanding protections for workers. It set up a compliance department of more than 50 employees. Its staff members were assigned to specific Asian plants or to a region, where they trained local managers and did audits assessing code compliance.[14]

Working with Kathie Lee Gifford, other apparel companies, human rights and labor groups, and universities that buy school clothing, Nike helped to

[8] "Nike Pays Good Wages to Foreign Workers," *The New York Times*, June 21, 1996, p. A26.

[9] "From Sweatshops to Aerobics," *The New York Times*, June 24, 1996, p. A15.

[10] Vietnam Labor Watch, "Nike Labor Practices in Vietnam," March 20, 1997, available at www.saigon.com/~nike/reports/report1.html#summary; and Ellen Neuborne, "Nike to Take a Hit in Labor Report," *USA Today*, March 27, 1997, p. 1A.

[11] Steven Greenhouse, "Nike Shoe Plant in Vietnam Is Called Unsafe for Workers," *The New York Times*, November 8, 1997, p. A1.

[12] *Kasky v. Nike*, 93 Cal. Rptr. 2d 856.

[13] Jeff Manning, "Nike's Global Machine Goes on Trial," *The Oregonian*, November 9, 1997, p. A1.

[14] S. Prakash Sethi, *Setting Global Standards* (New York: John Wiley & Sons, 2003), p. 167.

EXHIBIT 2
The Nike Code of Conduct

Source: Nike.com.

The Code of Conduct has been revised and articulated since its introduction in 1992. Listed below are its seven "core standards." Another document, the Code Leadership Standards, elaborates 51 specific labor, safety, health, and environmental standards. The Code is translated into local languages and today is posted in more than 900 contract factories making Nike products.

1. **Forced Labor.** The contractor does not use forced labor in any form—prison, indentured, bonded, or otherwise.

2. **Child Labor.** The contractor does not employ any person below the age of 18 to produce footwear. The contractor does not employ any person below the age of 16 to produce apparel, accessories or equipment. If at the time Nike production begins, the contractor employs people of the legal working age who are at least 15, that employment may continue, but the contractor will not hire any person going forward who is younger than the Nike or legal age limit, whichever is higher. To further ensure these age standards are complied with, the contractor does not use any form of homework for Nike production.

3. **Compensation.** The contractor provides each employee at least the minimum wage, or the prevailing industry wage, whichever is higher; provides each employee a clear, written accounting for every pay period; and does not deduct from employee pay for disciplinary infractions.

4. **Benefits.** The contractor provides each employee all legally mandated benefits.

5. **Hours of Work/Overtime.** The contractor complies with legally mandated work hours; uses overtime only when each employee is fully compensated according to local law; informs each employee at the time of hiring if mandatory overtime is a condition of employment; and on a regularly scheduled basis provides one day off in seven, and requires no more than 60 hours of work per week on a regularly scheduled basis, or complies with local limits if they are lower.

6. **Environment, Safety and Health (ES&H).** From suppliers to factories to distributors and to retailers, Nike considers every member of our supply chain as partners in our business. As such, we've worked with our Asian partners to achieve specific environmental, health and safety goals, beginning with a program called MESH (Management of Environment, Safety and Health).

7. **Documentation and Inspection.** The contractor maintains on file all documentation needed to demonstrate compliance with this Code of Conduct and required laws; agrees to make these documents available for Nike or its designated monitor; and agrees to submit to inspections with or without prior notice.

start a voluntary CSR initiative called the Fair Labor Association to enforce a code of conduct and monitoring scheme to end sweatshop labor. It hired Andrew Young, a former U.S. ambassador to the United Nations, to visit Asian plants and write an inspection report. Young toured 12 factories over 15 days and found that conditions "certainly did not appear to be what most Americans would call sweatshops."[15]

[15] Dana Canedy, "Nike's Asian Factories Pass Young's Muster," *The New York Times,* June 25, 1997, p. D2.

Nike purchased full-page editorial advertisements in newspapers to broadcast his generally favorable findings, saying the report showed it was "operating morally" and promising to act on his recommendations for improvement.

Finally, Nike ran a public relations counteroffensive. Unlike some rival firms that lay low, it chose to confront critics. It hired an experienced strategist to manage the campaign. Nike responded to every charge, no matter how small or what the source. Allegations were countered with press releases, letters

At work in a Vietnam plant making Nike footwear.
Source: © Steve Raymer/CORBIS.

to the editor, and letters to presidents and athletic directors of universities using Nike products. In these communications Nike sought to portray itself as a responsible employer creating opportunity for thousands of workers in emerging economies. CEO Knight expressed the Nike philosophy, saying, "This is going to be a long fight, but I'm confident the truth will win in the end."[16]

THE KASKY LAWSUIT

While Knight thought he was fighting for truth, Marc Kasky perceived something less noble—a fraud conducted to sell shoes and T-shirts. He believed that Nike knowingly deceived consumers, who relied on the company's statements for reassurance that their purchases did not sustain sweatshops. Under an unusual state law, any California citizen can sue a corporation on behalf of the public for an unlawful business practice. Kasky took advantage of this provision, alleging that Nike had engaged in negligent misrepresentation, fraud and deceit, and misleading advertising in violation of the state's commercial code. The code prohibits "any

unlawful, unfair, deceptive, untrue or misleading advertising."[17]

In his complaint, Kasky accused Nike of using a "promotional scheme," including its code of conduct, to create a "carefully cultured image" that was "intended . . . to entice consumers who do not want to purchase products made in sweatshop . . . conditions."[18] He set forth six classes of misleading claims.

- In its Code of Conduct (see Exhibit 2) and in a "Nike Production Primer" pamphlet given to the media, Nike stated that its contracts prevent corporal punishment and sexual harassment at factories making Nike products. But the Vietnam Labor Watch report told of workers forced to kneel in the hot sun and described frequent complaints by female employees against their supervisors.

---

[16] Quoted in Tony Emerson, "Swoosh Wars," *Newsweek,* March 12, 2001, p. 35.

[17] The law is California's Unfair Competition Law, which is codified as §17200 (source of the quotation) and §17500 of the California Business & Professions Code. Kasky also alleged violations of California Civil Code §1572 (which defines fraud) and §1709 and §1710 (which define deceit).

[18] First Amended Complaint of Milberg, Weiss et al., *Kasky v. Nike,* Superior Court, San Francisco County, No. 994446, July 2, 1998, pp. 5, 6, and 10.

- In a range of promotional materials Nike asserted that its products were manufactured in compliance with laws and regulations on wages and overtime. But evidence from a report by the Hong Kong Christian Industrial Committee and the leaked Ernst & Young audit showed that plants in China and Vietnam violated such laws.

- At the Nike annual shareholder meeting in 1997 CEO Knight said that the air in Nike's newest Vietnam shoe factory was less polluted than the air in Los Angeles. But the Ernst & Young report documented exposures to excessive levels of hazardous air pollutants.

- In his letter to the editor of *The New York Times,* Knight stated that Nike paid, on average, double the minimum wage to workers worldwide. But this was contradicted by data from pay stubs in the Vietnam Labor Watch report. He also said that Nike gave workers free meals, but an article in the *Youth Newspaper* of Ho Chi Minh City reported that workers paid for lunches.

- In its paid editorial ads discussing Andrew Young's report on its factories, Nike made the claim that it was "doing a good job" and "operating morally." But the report was deficient because it failed to address central issues such as minimum wage violations.

- In a press release Nike made the claim that it guaranteed a "living wage for all workers." But the director of its own Labor Practices Department had written a letter defining a "living wage" as income sufficient to support a family of four, then stated that the company did not ask contractors to raise wages that high.[19]

Kasky sought no monetary gain for himself. Instead, he asked for an injunction against further deception, a court-approved public information campaign forcing the company to correct misrepresentations, disgorgement of Nike profits from California sales, and payment of his legal expenses.

However, Superior Court Judge David A. Garcia threw the case out. There was no trial to decide whether any of the statements made by Nike were misleading. The judge simply accepted Nike's claim that the statements in question were part of an ongoing public debate and, therefore, entitled to broad protection.

[19] Ibid., pp. 10–25.

COMMERCIAL SPEECH OR PROTECTED EXPRESSION?

Freedom of speech is a central value in American culture. It derives from a long philosophical tradition, exemplified in John Stuart Mill's classic essay *On Liberty.* Mill believed that freedom of opinion and expression were necessary to maintain a free society, the kind of society that could protect liberty and promote happiness. He wrote that a natural tendency existed to silence discomfiting, doubtful, or unorthodox views. But this is wrong, because no person is in possession of unerring truth.

Restricting debate deprives society of the opportunity to find new ideas that are more valid than prevailing ones. Even bizarre or incorrect comments should be valued. The former may contain partial truth and the latter make the truth more compelling because of its contrast to the falsehood. Censorship of any kind is wrong because no person, society, or generation is infallible. It is better to leave open many avenues for expression of views so that error and pretention can be opposed. Truth, said Mill, needs to be "fully, frequently, and fearlessly discussed."[20]

The First Amendment was intended to protect public debate that is critical to the functioning of democracy. It prohibits government from "abridging the freedom of speech, or of the press."[21] A complicating factor is the efforts of courts over many years to distinguish between commercial speech and other speech. Commercial speech, or advertising, receives less protection from restriction by government than speech in the broad marketplace of ideas. Ordinary speech, including political, scientific, and artistic expression, is entitled to strong protection. Laws restricting expression of opinion are regarded as invalid on their face and justified only in extreme circumstances. Commercial speech, however, is often restricted by federal and state laws to prevent consumer deception and fraud.

[20] John Stuart Mill, *On Liberty,* ed. Currin V. Shields (Indianapolis: Bobbs-Merrill, 1956), p. 43. Originally published posthumously in 1907.

[21] The amendment originally applied only to actions by the federal government, but the Supreme Court has held that it also limits state government's infringement on speech.

Over many years, courts have struggled to come up with a clear definition of commercial speech.[22] The Supreme Court has defined it as "speech proposing a commercial transaction," but this still begs clarification.[23] An ad that said "Buy Nike shoes" would be commercial speech under this definition. But what about an ad picturing athletes with the statement "Just Do It," in which there is no literal sales proposal? Elsewhere in the same case, the Supreme Court also defined commercial speech as "expression related solely to the economic interests of the speaker and its audience."[24] Would Nike's statements on sweatshops meet this standard?

The focal point of Kasky's suit would become whether or not Nike's communications were, in fact, commercial speech. At a Superior Court hearing in early 1999, his lawyers argued that they were, therefore, they should be required to meet standards of truth and honesty enforced in California law. They were not entitled to the deference that would be given under the First Amendment to, for example, statements of political candidates or poets. Nike disagreed, saying that its statements about shoe and garment factories were part of a broader public debate and thus were speech entitled to strong First Amendment protection.[25] The judge agreed with Nike and dismissed the case.[26] Kasky appealed, but a year later the appeals court again rejected his argument. Kasky then appealed to the California Supreme Court.

There he won. In a 4–3 decision the California Supreme Court held that Kasky's case should go to trial.[27] In reaching its decision, the majority created a novel, three-part definition of commercial speech and applied it to Nike's messages. For speech to be commercial it had to (1) come from a business, (2) be intended for an audience of consumers, and (3) make representations of facts related to products. Nike's statements fit each requirement. The majority conceded that commercial and noncommercial speech were intermingled in the communications, but argued, "Nike may not 'immunize false or misleading product information from government regulation simply by including references to public issues.'"[28] That put Nike in the position of a used car dealer falsely advertising "none of our cars has ever been in an accident," but evading prosecution for fraud by adding a political opinion such as, "our city should budget more for traffic safety."

Dissenting opinions revealed serious disagreement among the justices. Justice Ming Chin attacked the majority for unfairly tilting the playing field against Nike. "While Nike's critics have taken full advantage of their right to 'uninhibited, robust, and wide-open' debate," he wrote, "the same cannot be said of Nike, the object of their ire. When Nike tries to defend itself from these attacks, the majority denies it the same First Amendment protection Nike's critics enjoy."[29]

A second dissent came from Justice Janice R. Brown, who found Nike's commercial and noncommercial speech inseparable. In her view, "Nike's commercial statements about its labor practices cannot be separated from its noncommercial statements about a public issue, because its labor practices *are* the public issue."[30] She admonished the majority for creating a test of commercial speech that was unconstitutional because it made "the level of protection given to speech dependant on the identity of the speaker—and not just the speech's content."[31]

The consequences of the decision went far beyond Nike. Now any company doing business in California had to be careful about expressions of fact or opinion that reached consumers in the state. The sharpest and most ideological critics of a corporation could take issue with its statements, bring it to court, and force a trial about the accuracy of its claims. The decision was as unwelcome in the business community as it was unexpected. Nike would seek to overturn it.

---

[22] Samuel A. Terilli, *"Nike v. Kasky* and the Running-But-Going-Nowhere Commercial Speech Debate," *Commercial Law and Policy* 10 (2005).

[23] *Central Hudson Gas & Electric Corp. v. Public Service Commission,* 447 U.S. 562 (1980).

[24] Ibid., at 561.

[25] Nike also asserted speech protections under Article I, section 2(a) of the California Constitution which reads: "Every person may freely speak, write and publish his or her sentiments on all subjects, being responsible for the abuse of that right. A law may not restrain or abridge liberty of speech or press."

[26] *Kasky v. Nike,* 79 Cal. App. 4th 165 (2000).

[27] *Kasky v. Nike,* 27 Cal. 4th 939 (2002).

[28] At 966, quoting *Bolger v. Youngs Drug Prods. Corp.,* 463 U.S. 68 (1983).

[29] At 970–971, quoting *Garrison v. Louisiana* 379 U.S. 75 (1964).

[30] At 980. Emphasis in the original.

[31] At 978.

IN THE UNITED STATES SUPREME COURT

Nike appealed to the United States Supreme Court, which accepted the case. In its brief, Nike asked that the California Supreme Court's definition of commercial speech be struck down to remove its unconstitutional, chilling effect on public debate. Kasky argued once again that statements emanating from Nike's public relation's campaign fell into the category of free speech. He asserted that the First Amendment gave no shelter to false statements by a company about how its products were made.

Strangely, no decision would ever be made. The nine justices heard oral argument in April 2003. Then, late in June, they dismissed their consideration of the case as "improvidently granted."[32] In a brief opinion Justice John Paul Stevens said the Court had erred in accepting it before trial proceedings in California were finished. The Court would wait.

This view was not unanimous. Three justices dissented. They saw no reason to wait and hinted that they were ready to strike down any restriction on Nike's speech.

> In my view . . . the questions presented directly concern the freedom of Americans to speak about public matters in public debate, no jurisdictional rule prevents us from deciding these questions now, and delay itself may inhibit the exercise of constitutionally protected rights of free speech without making the issue significantly easier to decide later on. . . . [A]n action to enforce California's laws—laws that discourage certain kinds of speech—amounts to more than just a genuine, future threat. It is a present reality—one that discourages Nike from engaging in speech. It thereby creates "injury in fact." Further, that injury is directly "traceable" to Kasky's pursuit of this lawsuit. And this Court's decision, if favorable to Nike, can "redress" that injury.[33]

SETTLEMENT AND AFTERMATH

With the Supreme Court dismissal, Kasky's specific charges against Nike could go to trial in California. The company would now be forced to defend the alleged misrepresentations about its labor practices. Its antagonists relished the prospect.

However, late in 2003 Kasky and Nike announced a settlement. In return for Kasky dropping the case, Nike agreed to give $1.5 million to an industry-friendly factory monitoring group. It may have paid Kasky's legal fees. This was not a tough settlement for Nike.

Supporters on both sides were disappointed. Activists lost their grand show trial putting the corporate devil on display. Industry was disappointed that Nike did not stay the course because settlement left standing the California Supreme Court's broad definition of commercial speech. This definition still stands.

NIKE TURNS A NEW LEAF

Meanwhile, Nike was moving through a process of CSR review and implementation. In 2005 it published a *Corporate Responsibility Report* stating three strategic CSR goals.[34] First, it would seek to create industry-wide, systemic change for the better in contractor shoe and apparel factories. Second, it would promote sustainability by eliminating toxic chemicals in shoe-making and using more recycled materials. Third, it would improve society by promoting the idea of sport with its benefits of healthy exercise and keeping young people out of trouble.

Nike learned that its business processes and culture were in tension with the policies in its code for contractors. Many of its own actions triggered violations. For example, it rewarded its buyers for meeting price, quality, and delivery date targets, giving them a financial incentive to push contractors hard. That undermined code policies to limit workweeks and hours in the factories. Nike products were often seasonal and ordered in response to rapidly shifting fashion trends. This led Nike to adopt a low inventory policy, but in consequence the factories it contracted with were often pressured to meet last-minute production goals. Sometimes their managers responded by cheating on labor guidelines. Changing Nike's internal processes to align them with its CSR goals meant slowing its reaction to consumer trends and risking loss of revenue. It also violated the spirit of Nike's

---

[32] *Nike v. Kasky,* 539 U.S. 654 (2003), *per curiam.*

[33] Ibid., at 667, 668. The three dissenters were Anthony Kennedy, Stephen Breyer, and Sandra Day O'Connor.

[34] Nike, Inc., *FY04 Corporate Responsibility Report* (Beaverton, OR: Nike, April 2005).

aggressive procurement culture and met with internal resistance.[35]

Nike's main tactic for improving labor conditions is factory monitoring to check compliance with the Nike Code of Conduct. Its self-run monitoring program has two parts. One is a labor audit of factories requiring inspectors to check off boxes for requirements in areas such as work hours, wages, and grievance systems. The other is an environmental health and safety audit on compliance with rules on chemical management, fire safety, and protective equipment. These audits take 48 working hours to complete and result in letter grades from A to F. Experts say their design is exemplary.[36] Their results are reviewed all the way up to Nike's board of directors. Yet they have failed to end very significant labor problems.

Nike uses about 700 factories in 56 countries employing 800,000 workers. It cannot hope to monitor them all, so it focuses its audits on roughly 20 percent that do most of its production or are high risk, trying to check on them once every three years. For example, in China it has 57 so-called "focus factories," and in 2007 audited 22 of them, handing out five As, six Bs, eight Cs, and three Ds.[37] Other factories are monitored by voluntary responsibility alliances, such as the industry-funded Fair Labor Association. A few pay for their own audits. It is an expansive effort, but bad reports keep coming in.

In Vietnam, 20,000 workers walked off the job for two days at a plant making Nike shoes. They were asking for a 20 percent raise, but received only 10 percent and free lunches. On their return they were in a violent mood and the plant had to be closed for another three days.[38] This was just one of 720 strikes at factories in Vietnam in 2008.[39]

When management at a Nike hat plant in Bangladesh learned that workers had attended a labor rights seminar, the personnel manager interrogated a woman who had attended, threatening to reinjure a hand she had badly injured in the past unless she gave up the names of other attendees. She refused, but management intimidated another person into revealing the names and those named were fired. Nike investigated the situation and got the workers rehired.[40]

An Australian TV reporter posed as a fashion buyer to get inside a Malaysian garment factory making Nike T-shirts where he discovered parlous conditions. It employed immigrant workers who paid large recruiting fees to get their jobs, then had to surrender their passports to plant management, which held them until the recruiting fees were repaid, an unlikely event given the low wages paid. They lived in crowded, malodorous rooms. Nike admitted many code violations, rectified the problems, and called in managers from all of its 37 factories in that country for training.[41]

These are more than isolated episodes. A scholarly analysis of 800 Nike audits concluded that despite years of effort, working conditions at its factories remained highly variable. While conditions improved in some plants, in others they stayed the same, and in many they deteriorated, leaving "little evidence that this system of private voluntary regulation is at all an effective strategy for improving labor standards."[42] And an in-depth report by a global coalition of more than 100 unions and human rights groups concluded this:

> Despite more than 15 years of codes of conduct adopted by major sportswear brands such as Adidas, Nike, New Balance, Puma and Reebok, workers making their products still face extreme pressure to meet production quotas, excessive, undocumented and unpaid overtime, verbal abuse, threats to health and safety related to the high quotas and exposure to toxic chemicals, and a failure to provide legally required health and other insurance programs.[43]

[35] Simon Zadek, "The Path to Corporate Responsibility," *Harvard Business Review,* December 2004, pp. 129–30.

[36] John Ruwitch, "Nike's Chinese Suppliers Defy Labour Laws," *National Post,* March 15, 2008, p. FP16.

[37] Nike, Inc., *Innovate for a Better World: Nike China 2008 Corporate Responsibility Reporting Supplement* (Beaverton, OR: Nike, 2008).

[38] "Nike Strike Ends, Violence Begins," *The Toronto Star,* April 3, 2008, p. B2.

[39] Jeff Ballinger, "Finding an Anti-Sweatshop Strategy that Works," *Dissent,* Summer 2009, p. 6.

[40] Worker Rights Consortium, *Case Summary: Dada Dhaka and Max Embo* (Washington, DC: WRC, November 1, 2008).

[41] Eugenia Levenson, "Citizen Nike," *Fortune,* November 24, 2008, p. 165. The report can be viewed at http://tinyurl.com/63vvpq.

[42] Richard M. Locke and Monica Romis, "The Promise and Perils of Private Voluntary Regulation: Labor Standards and Work Organization in Two Mexican Garment Factories," MIT Sloan School Working Paper 4734–09, January 13, 2009, p. 2. Richard M. Locke, Fei Qin, and Alberto A. Brause, "Does Monitoring Improve Labour Standards? Lessons from Nike," *Industrial & Labour Relations Review,* October 2007.

[43] Play Fair 2008, *Clearing the Hurdles: Steps to Improving Wages and Working Conditions in the Global Sportswear Industry* (Play Fair 2008 Campaign, April 2008), p. 6.

UNDERLYING PROBLEMS

Why do such problems still exist? Nike's 700-factory supply chain is too big to monitor. Its business model invites labor exploitation. When wages rise in one country, it seeks a lower-wage alternative. Factories are still faced with tight deadlines, sudden shifts in orders, and late design changes. They have insufficient power in supply chains to push back against global brands such as Nike. But they often have great power over workers eager for jobs. If timely order fulfillment is threatened, the easiest way to catch up is forced overtime or elimination of days off.[44]

According to Jeffrey Ballinger, monitoring by Nike and groups such as the Fair Labor Association is a prime example of voluntary corporate responsibility being used to avoid real reform.[45] Audits focus on the accuracy of wage slips, worker-to-toilet ratios, and placement of fire extinguishers. They avoid securing core global labor rights such as collective bargaining. Part of the problem is that many nations do not adequately enforce their labor laws.

International Labor Organization Convention No. 81 requires countries to inspect workplaces for compliance, but most countries with low-wage labor markets do not do so, in part because they want to attract foreign investment. They welcome voluntary corporate responsibility inspection regimes that make it look like action is being taken, even if the action is light. Corporations, in turn, prefer voluntary action to strict regulation. So governments and corporations unite in supporting CSR as a cosmetic touch to cover fundamental problems. In nations where labor laws are feebly enforced it is hard for workers to help themselves. They are often uninformed about their rights; they have no examples of successful unionizing before them. Until workers are empowered, forced work in poor conditions will lead to more scandals, violence, and reputation damage for global brands.

Ballinger suggests a solution for Nike.

> My research shows that about 75 cents per pair of shoes to the worker would be needed to fix problems that workers have been complaining about since the 1980s. That is roughly 80 percent more to workers, or $1.80 on a $70 pair of shoes at Foot Locker. If Nike, instead, paid workers that 75 cents more per pair of shoes, the cost to Nike would be $210 million a year. . . .[46]

Questions

1. What responsibility does Nike have for conditions of work at foreign factories making its products?

2. Could Nike have better anticipated and more effectively handled the sweatshop issue? What did it do right? What was ineffective or counterproductive?

3. Has Nike created and implemented an effective approach to social responsibility? Does it address root causes of problems in Nike's supply chain? Should it now do more or do something different?

4. Did the California Supreme Court correctly decide the *Kasky* case? Why or why not?

5. How should the line between commercial and noncommercial speech be drawn?

[44] Richard Read, "Nike Gets What It Pays For, Critics Say," *The Oregonian,* August 5, 2008, p. A1.

[45] Jeff Ballinger, "No Sweat? Corporate Social Responsibility and the Dilemma of Anti-Sweatshop Activism," *New Labor Forum,* Spring 2008.

[46] Ibid., pp. 95–96.

Chapter Seven

Business Ethics

Bernard Ebbers

September 27, 2006. At 9:00 a.m. on this Tuesday morning Bernard J. Ebbers, former CEO of WorldCom, pulled away from his home just outside Jackson, Mississippi. At 1:09 p.m. he arrived at a federal prison near Oakdale, Louisiana, drove through the gate, and surrendered himself to begin a 25-year sentence. The trip was 200 miles, far enough to end one life and begin another.

There is no parole for a federal sentence. Time can be reduced up to 15 percent for good behavior, but even with this Ebbers will serve 21 years and 4 months. Since he was 65 when he entered prison, he would be 86 on his projected release date of July 4, 2028. However, he has a serious heart condition. Besides his freedom, Ebbers

Former WorldCom chief Bernard Ebbers drives through the gates of a federal prison in Oakdale, Louisiana, to begin a 25-year sentence for his role in a massive accounting fraud. Source: © AP Photo/Rogelio V. Solis.

also lost his fortune. Once a billionaire, he forfeited all assets except a home and $50,000 to be used by his wife, Kristie.

Ebbers built WorldCom from a small phone company into a global telecommunications giant. His rise began in 1984. After investing in a local long-distance company he was asked to manage it. He made it grow with mergers that were audacious in their reach. Eventually, it became a publicly traded corporation with annual revenues of $39 billion. As WorldCom grew so did Ebbers' wealth, but extravagant spending forced him to use his stock as collateral for loans to pay his debts. If share prices fell too far he would be lost.

Fate is uncaring and about this time the 1990s dot-com investment bubble burst. WorldCom's revenues declined and expenses for its fiber optic network rose more than anticipated. In 2000 the chief financial officer began to report false quarterly revenues, using accounting tricks to disguise rising expenses. The share prices held. However, internal auditors discovered the deceit and reported it to the Securities and Exchange Commission (SEC), which began an investigation.

The revenue manipulations became known to investors, and WorldCom shares lost 90 percent of their value. WorldCom's board of directors forced Ebbers to resign. In 2002 the company set a record in failure, breaking Enron's previous total for the largest bankruptcy in American history. Although it ultimately survived, 17,000 workers lost their jobs and investors lost billions of dollars.

Federal prosecutors charged Ebbers with nine counts of criminal conspiracy, securities fraud, and filing false documents with the SEC.[1] He refused to plead guilty, claiming that his chief financial officer had duped him. At his trial in 2005 he testified that he had no knowledge of the fraud.

Q: Did you ever believe that any of the statements contained in those public filings were not true?

A: No, sir.

Q: Did you ever believe that WorldCom had reported revenue that it was not entitled to report?

A: No, sir. . . .

Q: Did you ever believe that WorldCom was putting out bad numbers in its financial statements in any way at all?

A: No.[2]

Five of Ebbers' subordinates, including the chief financial officer, had pled guilty to related charges and agreed to cooperate with prosecutors. They testified that Ebbers not only knew about the conspiracy, but also actively directed it. A jury convicted him on all counts. It was a big victory for federal prosecutors. "Today's verdict is a triumph of our legal system," declared Attorney General Alberto Gonzalez.[3]

---

[1] *United States v. Bernard J. Ebbers,* Indictment, S3 02 Cr. 1144 (BSJ), 2004.

[2] *United States v. Bernard J. Ebbers,* 458 F.3d 124 (2006).

[3] Department of Justice, *Statement of Attorney General Alberto R. Gonzales on the Bernard Ebbers Conviction,* press release 05–122, March 15, 2005.

Ebbers "wept and sniffled" at his sentencing.[4] Victims of the fraud were invited to speak. One was a former WorldCom sales representative whose retirement money evaporated from a company 401(k) plan. "My life was destroyed by the greed of Bernard Ebbers," he said. "He can't ever repay me or the tens of thousands like me whose lives disintegrated in the blink of an eye."[5]

Federal sentencing guidelines called for a sentence of 30 years based on the presence of certain aggravating factors. Direct losses to investors were estimated to be $2.2 billion, there were thousands of victims, and as a CEO Ebbers had abused a position of public trust. Judge Barbara Jones decided to subtract five years. She was moved by 170 letters from Ebbers' friends and neighbors asking for mercy. That left the sentence at 25 years. Ebbers requested further leniency because he suffers from cardiomyopathy, an inflammation of the heart. The judge rejected the relevance of this condition to sentencing. "Although I recognize . . . this is likely to be a life sentence for Mr. Ebbers," she said, "I find anything else would not reflect the seriousness of the crime."[6]

The judge recommended that Ebbers serve his time in a low-security facility. However, the Federal Bureau of Prisons bases assignments on the length of sentences, assuming that a long sentence signals its bearer is more likely to pose an escape risk and to endanger fellow inmates. Because Ebbers' sentence was 25 years, he was put in a medium-security facility. There, he lives with violence-prone inmates, sleeps in a cell rather than a dormitory, and encounters many locks and fences.

Ebbers' wife, who was making the 400-mile round-trip to visit him on weekends, filed for divorce 19 months into his sentence. Ebbers still maintains his innocence and petitioned President George W. Bush for clemency in 2008. He was denied.

Criminal sentences are intended to punish individuals and deter future crime. Ebbers' sentence inspires rumination. Was it fair retribution for his actions? Was its length necessary to deter more accounting fraud? And how did Ebbers' 25 years compare with the sentences of violent criminals? It exceeded the 20 years given to Salvatore Gravano, a Mafia hit man who confessed to 19 murders.[7] It exceeded the average of 24.4 years served by first-degree murderers in California.[8]

Ebbers is exposed now as unethical, a criminal, and deficient as a leader. In this chapter we add perspective to each of these dimensions. We discuss the sources of ethical values in business, including truth telling, a basic virtue that Ebbers neglected. Then we discuss prosecution of corporate crime. Finally, we look at factors shaping ethical climates in organizations and discuss the managerial tools leaders can use to elevate behavior.

[4] Carrie Johnson, "Ebbers Gets 25-Year Sentence for Role in WorldCom Fraud," *Washington Post,* July 14, 2005, p. A1.

[5] Quoted in Leonard Greene and Richard Wilner, "Bawling Bernie Smacked," *New York Post,* July 14, 2005, p. 3.

[6] Quoted in Johnson, "Ebbers Gets 25-Year Sentence for Role in WorldCom Fraud," p. A1.

[7] Andy Newman, "Mafia Turncoat Gets 20 Years for Running Ecstacy Ring," *The New York Times,* September 7, 2002, p. 3.

[8] Department of Corrections and Rehabilitation, *Time Served on Prison Sentence* (Sacramento, CA: DCR, March 2006), table 1.

WHAT ARE BUSINESS ETHICS?

ethics
The study of good and evil, right and wrong, and just and unjust.

business ethics
The study of good and evil, right and wrong, and just and unjust actions in business.

Ethics is the study of what is good and evil, right and wrong, and just and unjust. *Business ethics,* therefore, is the study of good and evil, right and wrong, and just and unjust actions in business. Ethical managers try to do good and avoid doing evil. A mass of principles, values, norms, and thoughts concerned with what conduct *ought* to be exists to guide them. Yet in this vaporous mass, the outlines of good and evil are at times shadowy. Usually they are distinct enough, but often not. So, using ethical ideas in business is an art, an art requiring judgment about both the motivations behind an act and the act's consequences.

Discussions of business ethics frequently emphasize refractory and unclear situations, perhaps to show drama and novelty. Although all managers face difficult ethical conflicts, applying clear guidelines resolves the vast majority of them. The Eighth Commandment, for example, prohibits stealing and is plainly violated by taking tools home from work or the theft of trade secrets. Lies in advertising violate a general rule of the Western business world that the seller of a product must not purposely deceive a buyer. This general understanding stems from the Mosaic law, the Code of Hammurabi, Roman law, and other sources and is part of a general ethic favoring truth going back at least 3,000 years.

Overall, ethical traditions that apply to business support truth telling, honesty, protection of life, respect for rights, fairness, and obedience to law. Some beliefs in this bundle of traditions go back thousands of years. Others, such as the idea that a corporation is responsible for the long-term health of its workers, have emerged more recently. In keeping with this long and growing ethical heritage, most business actions can be clearly judged ethical or unethical; eliminating unethical behavior such as bribery or embezzlement may be difficult, but knowing the rightness or wrongness of actions is usually easy.

This does not mean that ethical decisions are always clear. Some are troublesome because although basic ethical standards apply, conflicts between them defy resolution.

> In the mid-1970s Lockheed Aircraft Corp. faced default on government loans. It paid $12 million ($48 million today) in bribes to politicians and business executives in Japan, selling 120 warplanes and 21 civilian airliners, protecting its future, and saving thousands of jobs. Making the payments broke no U.S. laws, but they broke a Japanese law. Sixteen people there were convicted of a crime, including a former prime minister and a likely future prime minister. Carl Kotchian, Lockheed's president, had no regrets. Bribes were tangled with foreign sales. "Even when offering a better product," he said, "we would lose out if we did not also make the required payments."[9] Competing in the industry meant slighting ethical norms. When the bribes came out, politicians and publics in both countries went into a dither. Kotchian retired to run an alfalfa farm saying, "I'd do it again."[10]

[9] Quoted in Donald E. Fink, "New Lockheed Management Studying Impact of Payments," *Aviation Week & Space Technology,* February 23, 1976, p. 15.

[10] Quoted in Peter Pae, "Ex-Lockheed Chief Told of Paying Bribes," *Los Angeles Times,* December 22, 2008, p. B10.

Daniel Drew (1797–1879), speculator in railroad stocks and an exponent of the theory of amorality.
Source: © Picture History/Napoleon Sarony.

Some ethical issues are hidden, at least initially, and hard to recognize.

A. H. Robins Co. began to market its Dalkon Shield intrauterine device through general practitioners while competitors continued selling them only through obstetricians and gynecologists. This strategy was wildly successful in getting market share for Robins and did not, initially, seem to raise ethical issues, but when dangerous side effects with the device appeared, the general practitioners were slower to see than the specialists. Robins' failure to make extra efforts in tracking the safety of the device then emerged as an ethical shortcoming. It cost women their lives.

TWO THEORIES OF BUSINESS ETHICS

In the ageless debate about whether ethics in business may be more permissive than general societal or personal ethics, there are two basic views.

theory of amorality
The belief that business should be conducted without reference to the full range of ethical standards, restraints, and ideals in society.

The first, the *theory of amorality,* is that business should be amoral, that is, conducted without reference to the full range of ethical standards, restraints, and ideals in society. Managers may use compromising ethics because competition distills their selfish actions into benefits for society. Adam Smith noted that the "invisible hand" of the market assures that "by pursuing his own interest [a merchant] frequently promotes that of the society more effectively than when he really intends to promote it."[11]

The apex of this view came during the latter half of the nineteenth century. It was widely believed that business and personal ethics existed in separate compartments, that business was a special sanctuary in which less idealistic ethics were permissible.[12] Daniel Drew, who made a fortune in the 1860s by manipulating railroad stocks

[11] *The Wealth of Nations,* ed. Edwin Cannan (New York: Modern Library, 1937), p. 423; originally published in 1776. Smith also believed that merchants must abide by prevailing societal ethics.

[12] This was the conviction of social Darwinist Herbert Spencer, who believed in two sets of ethics. *Family ethics* were based on the principle of charity and benefits were apportioned without relation to merit. *State ethics* were based on a competitive justice and benefits were apportioned strictly on merit. Family ethics interjected into business or government by well-meaning people interfered with the laws of nature and would slowly corrupt the workings of Darwinian natural selection. See "The Sins of Legislators," in *The Man versus the State* (London: Watts, 1940); originally published in 1884.

James Cash Penney (1875–1971), son of a Baptist minister and an exemplar of the theory of moral unity.
Source: © Oscar White/CORBIS.

without scruple, summed up the nineteenth century compartmentalization of business decisions in these words:

> Sentiment is all right up in the part of the city where your home is. But downtown, no. Down there the dog that snaps the quickest gets the bone. Friendship is very nice for a Sunday afternoon when you're sitting around the dinner table with your relations, talking about the sermon that morning. But nine o'clock Monday morning, notions should be brushed aside like cobwebs from a machine. I never took any stock in a man who mixed up business with anything else. He can go into other things outside of business hours, but when he's in the office, he ought not to have a relation in the world—and least of all a poor relation.[13]

The theory of amorality has far less public acceptance today, but it lives on quietly. Many managers still allow competitive pressures to justify acts that would be wrong in private life. The theory of amorality releases them from feelings of guilt.

The second basic ethical view is the *theory of moral unity*, in which business actions are judged by the general ethical standards in society, not by a special set of more permissive standards. Only one basic ethical standard exists, so business actions are judged by the same principles as actions in other areas of life.

theory of moral unity
Business actions are judged by the general ethical standards of society, not by a special set of more permissive standards.

Many managers take this position today, and some did even in the nineteenth century. An example is James Cash Penney. We remember Penney for building a chain of department stores, but his first enterprise was a butcher shop. As a young man, Penney went to Denver, where, finding the shop for sale, he wired his mother for $3,000 to buy it. The departing butcher shop owner warned him that his success depended on orders from a nearby hotel. "To keep the hotel for a customer," the butcher explained, "all you have to do is buy the chef a bottle of whiskey a week." Penney regularly made the gift and business was good, but he soon had second thoughts. Resolving no longer to do business that way, he stopped the bribe, lost the hotel's business, and went broke when the shop failed. He was 23 years old.

Penney later started the Golden Rule Department Store in Denver and always believed that principles of honesty led to its ultimate success. In contrast to the unsentimental lone wolf Daniel Drew, Penney reflects his focus on ethics in this little story.

---

[13] Bouck White, *The Book of Daniel Drew* (New York: Doubleday, Page & Company, 1910), pp. 120–21.

It seems that the manager of a chain store had run out of a certain line of goods and had appealed to the manager of another store in the chain for a share of the supply which this second man had on hand. This man consented—but sent some goods of poor quality which *he* had not been able to sell. He thought he was being very shrewd. But if I had the chance I would fire that man. He was not being square. He hadn't the instinct of fair dealing. You can't build a solid, substantial house with decayed planks, no matter what kind of a veneer is put over their rottenness. That man's action was rotten, even though it was veneered with temporary shrewdness.[14]

To J. C. Penney, and other exemplars of the theory of moral unity, desire to succeed is never an excuse to neglect principled behavior. Actions are not moral just because they make money. Ethical conflicts cannot be avoided simply because they arise in the course of business.

MAJOR SOURCES OF ETHICAL VALUES IN BUSINESS

reciprocity
A form of social behavior in which people behave supportively in the expectation that this behavior will be given in return.

Four great repositories of ethical values influence managers. They are religion, philosophy, cultural experience, and law (see Figure 7.1). A common theme, the idea of *reciprocity*, or mutual help, is found in each of these value systems. This idea reflects the central purpose of ethics, which is to bind individuals into a cooperative social whole. Ethical values are a mechanism that controls behavior in business and in other areas of life. Ethical restraint is more efficient with society's resources than are cruder controls such as police, lawsuits, or economic incentives. Ethical values channel individual energy into pursuits that are benign to others and beneficial to society.

FIGURE 7.1
Major Sources of Ethical Values in Business

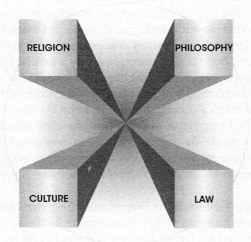

[14] J. C. Penney, "It Is One Thing to Desire—and Another to Determine," in Peter Krass, ed., *The Book of Business Wisdom* (New York: John Wiley & Sons, 1997), p. 89. Reprinted from *American Magazine*, August 1919. Emphasis in the original.

Religion

The great religions, including the Judeo-Christian tradition prominent in American history, converge in the belief that a divine will reveals the nature of right and wrong behavior, including in business. Despite doctrinal differences, major religions agree on ideas forming the basic building blocks of ethics in every society. For example, the principle of reciprocity is found, encapsulated in variations of the Golden Rule, in Buddhism, Confucianism, Hinduism, Islam, Judaism, and Christianity. These religions also converge in emphasizing traits such as promise keeping, honesty, fairness, charity, and responsibility to others.

Christian managers often seek guidance in the Bible. Like the source books and writings of other main religions, the Bible was written in a premodern, agricultural society, and many of its ethical teachings require interpretation before they can be applied to problems in the modern workplace. Much of the ethical teaching in the Bible comes from parables. The parable of the prodigal son (Luke 15:11–32) tells the story of an unconditionally merciful father—an image applicable to ethical conflicts in corporate superior–subordinate relationships. The story of the rich man and Lazarus (Luke 16:19–31) teaches concern for the poor and challenges Christian managers to consider the less privileged, a fitting admonition in a world where billions of people survive on less than $1 a day.[15]

In Islam the Koran is a source of ethical inspiration. The Prophet Muhammad said, "Every one of you is a shepherd and everyone is responsible for what he is shepherd of."[16] In a modern context, the Muslim manager is like a shepherd and the corporation is like a flock. The manager has a duty to rise above self-interest and protect the good of the organization.

In the Jewish tradition, managers can turn to rabbinic moral commentary in the Talmud and the books of Moses in the Torah. Here again, ancient teachings are regarded as analogies. For example, a Talmudic ruling holds that a person who sets a force in motion bears responsibility for any resulting harm, even if natural forces intervene (*Baba Qamma* 60a). This is discussed in the context of an agrarian society in which a person who starts a fire is responsible for damage from flying sparks, even if nature intervenes with high winds. In an industrial context, the ethics lesson is that polluting companies are responsible for problems caused by their waste.[17] Another passage comments on a situation in which laborers are hired to dig in a field, but a nearby river overflows, preventing the work (*Bava Metzia* 76b–77a). The Talmud counsels that if the employer knew the river was likely to overflow then the workers should be paid, but if the flood was unpredictable then the workers should bear the loss. This teaching may inform thinking about modern layoffs. In highly cyclical industries, workers can anticipate

[15] See Oliver F. Williams and John W. Houck, *Full Value: Cases in Christian Business Ethics* (New York: Harper & Row, 1978), for discussion of these and other biblical sources of inspiration for managers.

[16] Quoted in Tanri Abeng, "Business Ethics in Islamic Context: Perspectives of a Muslim Business Leader," *Business Ethics Quarterly,* July 1997, p. 52.

[17] Moses L. Pava, *Business Ethics: A Jewish Perspective* (New York: Yeshiva University Press, 1997), pp. 72–73.

the risk of layoffs, but in more stable industries management may bear greater responsibility for job security.[18]

Parables and stories in the literature of ancient worlds can seem so innocent as to have little value for modern managers. However, as one rabbinic scholar notes, "Our world has undergone tremendous technological changes, but the issues stay the same—egotism, jealousy, greed, among others."[19] Thus, the central wisdom remains. When Confucius told Chinese merchants that "He who acts with a constant view to his own advantage (*li*) will be much murmured against," he exposed a speck of truth visible in any era.[20]

Philosophy

A Western manager can look back on more than 2,000 years of philosophical inquiry into ethics. This rich, complex tradition is the source of many notions about what is right or wrong in business. Every age has added new ideas, but it is a mistake to regard the history of ethical philosophy as a single debate that, over centuries, has matured to bear the fruit of growing wisdom and clear, precise standards of conduct. Even after two millennia, there remains considerable dispute among ethical thinkers about the nature of right action. If anything, standards of ethical behavior were arguably clearer in ancient Greek civilization than they are now.

In a brief circuit of milestones in ethical thinking, we turn first to the Greek philosophers. Greek ethics, from Homeric times onward, were embodied in the discharge of duties related to social roles such as shepherd, warrior, merchant, citizen, or king. Expectations of the occupants of these roles were clearer than in contemporary America, where social roles such as those of business manager or employee are more vague, overlapping, and marked by conflict.[21]

Socrates (469–399 BC) asserted that virtue and ethical behavior were associated with wisdom and taught that insight into life would naturally lead to right conduct. He also introduced the idea of a moral law higher than human law, an idea that activists use to demand supralegal behavior from transnational corporations. Plato (428–348 BC), the gifted student of Socrates, carried this doctrine of virtue as knowledge further by elaborating the theory that absolute justice exists independently of individuals and that its nature can be discovered by intellectual effort. In *The Republic,* Plato set up a 50-year program for training rulers to rule in harmony with the ideal of justice.[22] Plato's most apt pupil, Aristotle, spelled out virtues of character in the *Nicomachean Ethics* and advocated a regimen of continuous learning to improve ethical behavior.[23]

[18] See Robert H. Carver, "If the River Stopped: A Talmudic Perspective on Downsizing," *Journal of Business Ethics* 50 (2004), pp. 144–45.

[19] Meir Tamari, quoted in Gail Lichtman, "Ethics Is Their Business," *The Jerusalem Post,* May 25, 2001, p. 13.

[20] *Analects,* book IV, chap. XII. Cited in Stephen B. Young, "The CRT *Principles for Business* as an Expression of Original Confucian Morality," *Caux Roundtable Newsletter,* Fall 2000, p. 9.

[21] Alasdair MacIntyre, *After Virtue: A Study in Moral Theory* (South Bend, IN: University of Notre Dame Press, 1981), p.115.

[22] Plato, *The Republic,* F. M. Cornford, trans. (New York: Oxford University Press, 1945).

[23] *Nicomachean Ethics,* J. A. K. Thomson, trans. (New York: Penguin Books, 1982), p. 51.

The Stoic school of ethics, spanning four centuries from the death of Alexander to the rise of Christianity in Rome, furthered the trend toward character development in Greek ethics. Epictetus (AD 50–100), for instance, taught that virtue was found solely within and should be valued for its own sake, arguing that this inner virtue was a higher reward than external riches or worldly success.

In business, the ethical legacy of the Greeks and Romans lives on in the conviction that virtues such as truth telling, charity, obeying the law, justice, courage, friendship, and the just use of power are important qualities. Today when a manager trades integrity for profit, we condemn this on the basis of the teachings of the ancient Mediterranean world.

Ethical thinking after the rise of Christianity was dominated by the great Catholic theologians St. Augustine (354–430) and St. Thomas Aquinas (1225–1274). Both believed that humanity should follow God's will; correct behavior in business and in all worldly activity was necessary to achieve salvation and life after death. Christianity was the source of many ethical teachings, including specific rules such as the Ten Commandments.

Christian theology created a lasting reservoir of ethical doctrine, but its command of ethical thought weakened during the historical period of intellectual and industrial expansion in Europe called the Enlightenment. Secular philosophers such as Baruch Spinoza (1632–1677) tried to demonstrate ethical principles with logical analysis rather than ordain them by reference to God's will. So also, Immanuel Kant (1724–1804) tried to find universal and objective ethical rules in logic. Kant and Spinoza, and others who followed, created a great estrangement with moral theology by believing that humanity could discover the nature of good behavior without reference to God. To this day, there is a deep divide between Christian managers who look to the Bible for divine guidance and other managers who look to worldly writing for ethical wisdom.

Other milestones of secular thinking followed. Jeremy Bentham (1748–1832) developed the idea of utilitarianism as a guide to ethics. Bentham observed that an ethical action was the one among all alternatives that brought pleasure to the largest number of persons and pain to the fewest. The worldly impact of this ethical philosophy is almost impossible to overestimate, because it validated two dominant ideologies, democracy and industrialism, allowing them first to arise and then to flourish. The legitimacy of majority rule in democratic governments rests in large part on Bentham's theory of utility as later refined by John Stuart Mill (1806–1873). Utilitarianism also sanctified industrial development by legitimizing the notion that economic growth benefits the majority; thus the pain and dislocation it brings to a few may be ethically permitted.

realist school
A school of thought that rejects ethical perfection, taking the position that human affairs will be characterized by flawed behavior and ought to be depicted as they are, not as we might wish them to be.

John Locke (1632–1704) developed and refined doctrines of human rights and left an ethical legacy supporting belief in the inalienable rights of human beings, including the right to pursue life, liberty, and happiness, and the right to freedom from tyranny. Our leaders, including business leaders, continue to be restrained by these beliefs.

A *realist school* of ethics also developed alongside the idealistic thinking of philosophers such as Spinoza, Kant, the utilitarians, and Locke. The realists believed that both good and evil were naturally present in human nature; human behavior inevitably would reflect this mixture. Since good and evil occurred naturally, it was futile to try to teach ideals. Ideals could never be realized because evil was a permanent human trait. The realist school developed ethical theories that shrugged off the idea of perfect goodness. Niccolò Machiavelli (1469–1527) argued that important ends justified expedient means. Herbert Spencer (1820–1903) wrote prolifically of a harsh ethic that justified vicious competition among companies because it furthered evolution—a process in which humanity improved as the unfit fell down. Friedrich Nietzsche (1844–1900) rejected the ideals of earlier "nice" ethics, saying they were prescriptions of the timid, designed to fetter the actions of great men whose irresistible power and will were regarded as dangerous by the common herd of ordinary mortals.

Nietzsche believed in the existence of a "master morality" in which great men made their own ethical rules according to their convenience and without respect for the general good of average people. In reaction to this master morality, the mass of ordinary people developed a "slave morality" intended to shackle the great men. For example, according to Nietzsche, the mass of ordinary people celebrate the Christian virtue of turning the other cheek because they lack the power to revenge themselves on great men. He felt that prominent ethical ideals of his day were recipes for timidity and once said of utilitarianism that it made him want to vomit.[24] The influence of realists on managers has been strong. Spencer was wildly popular among the business class in the nineteenth century. Machiavelli is still read for inspiration. The lasting influence of realism is that many managers, deep down, do not believe that ideals can be achieved in business life.

Cultural Experience

Every culture transmits between generations a set of traditional values, rules, and standards that define acceptable behavior. In this way, individuals channel their conduct in socially approved directions. Civilization itself is a cumulative cultural experience consisting of three stages; in each, economic and social arrangements have dictated a distinct moral code.[25]

For millions of generations in the *hunting and gathering stage* of human development, ethics were adapted to conditions in which our ancestors had to be ready to fight, face brutal foes, and suffer hostile forces of nature. Under such circumstances, a premium was placed on pugnacity, appetite, greed, and sexual readiness, since it was often the strongest who survived. Trade ethics in early civilizations were probably deceitful and dishonest by our standards, and economic transactions were frequently conducted by brute force and violence.

Civilization passed into an *agricultural stage* approximately 10,000 years ago, beginning a time when industriousness was more important than ferocity, thrift paid greater dividends than violence, monogamy became the prevailing sexual custom because of the relatively equal numbers of the sexes, and peace came to be valued over wars, which destroyed crops and animals. These new values were

[24] His exact words were "the general welfare is no ideal, no goal, no remotely intelligible concept, but only an emetic." In *Beyond Good and Evil* (New York: Vintage Books, 1966), p. 157; originally published in 1886.

[25] Will Durant and Ariel Durant, *The Lessons of History* (New York: Simon & Schuster, 1968), pp. 37–42.

codified into ethical systems by philosophers and founders of religions. So the great ethical philosophies and theologies that guide managers today are largely products of the agricultural revolution.

Three centuries ago, society entered an *industrial stage* of cultural experience, and ethical systems began to reflect changed institutions, ideologies, and ecosystems. Powerful forces such as electricity, capitalism, constitutional democracy, population growth, and nuclear weapons have appeared. Industrialism has begun to create a distinct ethic, as its impacts put stress on ethical values that evolved in ancient, agriculture-based worlds, altering people's judgments about good and evil. For example, the copious outpouring of material goods from factories encourages materialism and consumption at the expense of older, scarcity-based virtues such as moderation and thrift. The old truism that nature exists for human exploitation is less compelling when reexamined in a cloud of industrial gases.

Ethical Variation in Cultures

Ethical values differ among nations as historical experiences have interacted with philosophies and religions to create diverging cultural values and laws. Where differences do exist, are some cultures correct about proper business ethics and others wrong? There are two answers to this question.

The school of *ethical universalism* holds that in terms of biological and psychological needs, human nature is everywhere the same. Ethical rules are transcultural because behavior that fulfills basic human needs should be the same everywhere; for example, basic rules of justice must be followed. Basic justice might be achieved, however, by emphasizing group welfare or by emphasizing individual rights, leaving room for cultural variation.

The school of *ethical relativism* holds that, although human biology is everywhere similar, cultural experience creates widely diverging values, including ethical values. Ethical values are subjective. There is no objective way to prove them right or wrong as with scientific facts. Truth is not a property inherent within them. They are ideas that work in their cultural setting. It is wrong, therefore, for one society to claim that its ethics are superior to those of another.

We cannot settle this age-old philosophical debate. However, ethical variation is a practical and urgent issue. Because of globalization, corporations extend their values into foreign markets where they are sometimes inimical. Google is on a mission to make the world's information accessible to everyone across all borders. Its search engine is based on a "democratic" algorithm that registers "votes" on Web pages. Its ethics code is summed in the phrase "Don't be evil." This bundle of values is dear to Google, but alien to the Chinese communist government, which employs Internet police to monitor and suppress dissent. Eventually, Google refused to compromise its strategic and ethical principles by remaining in the Chinese market.

What guidelines exist for companies that want flexibility in their ethical codes? Some scholars argue that at a high level of abstraction, the ethical ideals of all cultures converge to basic sameness. Thomas Donaldson and Thomas W. Dunfee see a deep social contract underlying all human societies. This contract is based on what they call *hypernorms*, or principles at the root of all human ethics. Examples include basic rights such as life, liberty, and the priority of the community over its

ethical universalism The theory that because human nature is everywhere the same, basic ethical rules are applicable in all cultures. There is some room for variation in the way these rules are followed.

ethical relativism The theory that ethical values are created by cultural experience. Different cultures may create different values and there is no universal standard by which to judge which values are superior.

hypernorms Master ethical principles that underlie all other ethical principles. All variations of ethical principle must conform to them.

individual members. These hypernorms validate other ethical norms, which can differ from nation to nation but still be consistent with the hypernorms. For example, many U.S. corporations prohibit people from hiring their relatives. In India, however, tradition places a high value on supporting family and clan members, and some companies promise to hire workers' children when they grow up. Although these practices are inconsistent, neither violates any universal prohibition. They exist in what Donaldson and Dunfee call "moral free space" where inconsistent norms are permitted if they do not violate any hypernorms.[26]

Law

Laws codify, or formalize, ethical expectations. They proliferate over time as emerging regulations, statutes, and court rulings impose new conduct standards. Corporations and their managers face a range of mechanisms set up to deter illegal acts, punish offenses, and rehabilitate offenders. In particular, they face civil actions by regulatory agencies and private parties and criminal prosecution by governments. We will discuss these mechanisms to illustrate how legal controls and sanctions work.

Damages

For seven years Joseph Kelly managed "roll-off" operations in Burlington, Vermont, for Browning-Ferris Industries, a national waste disposal corporation. Roll-off waste is collected in long containers trucked to and from industrial and construction sites. Browning-Ferris had all of the city's roll-off business until Kelly resigned to start a competing company. Soon he had 47 percent of the market and a Browning-Ferris executive in Boston called the local manager, telling him to "[p]ut [Kelly] out of business. Do whatever it takes. Squish him like a bug."[27] The local manager, violating antitrust laws, used predatory pricing, slashing roll-off prices below cost. Even so, Kelly's market share climbed to 56 percent, but he sued Browning-Ferris for antitrust violations anyway.

compensatory damages
Payments awarded to redress actual, concrete losses suffered by injured parties.

A Vermont jury awarded Kelly $51,146 in *compensatory damages*, which are payments to redress actual, concrete losses suffered by injured parties due to wrongful conduct. Then, after Kelly's attorney told the jury Browning-Ferris had a net worth of $1.3 billion, it awarded Kelly an additional $6 million in *punitive damages*, which are payments in excess of a wronged party's actual losses, awarded when corporate conduct is not only damaging, but reprehensible. Punitive damages are intended to punish and deter similar actions in the future.

punitive damages
Payments in excess of a wronged party's actual losses to deter similar actions and punish a corporation that has exhibited reprehensible conduct.

Such awards raise questions of fairness. In this case punitive damages were 115 times greater than compensatory damages. Is it fair to impose such a penalty based on a defendant's status as a large corporation? Is a misdeed to be punished more harshly because the perpetrator is rich? Although Browning-Ferris was guilty, was its conduct so reckless, malicious, and harmful that retribution of $6 million was required?

The company appealed to the Supreme Court, arguing that the $6 million sum violated the Eighth Amendment's prohibition against "cruel and unusual

---

[26] Thomas Donaldson and Thomas W. Dunfee, "When Ethics Travel: The Promise and Peril of Global Business Ethics," *California Management Review,* Summer 1999, p. 61.

[27] *Browning-Ferris Industries v. Kelko Disposal,* 429 U.S. 257 (1989), at 260.

punishment." Although the Court dismissed this appeal on narrow technical grounds, the justices were concerned about capricious punitive damages against large corporations, which were frequent, and in subsequent cases set increasingly strict guidelines. Since the *Browning-Ferris* decision the Court has spent more than 20 years working to limit punitive awards against corporations, not because it considers them too large, but because it believes they can be unpredictable, arbitrary, and disproportionate to the wrongdoing.

It started to rein them in with the case of an Alabama physician, Dr. Ira Gore, Jr., who bought a BMW for $40,751 and drove it for nine months without noticing any problem. After an auto detailer told him that part of the car had been repainted, Gore learned that BMW North America secretly repainted cars with shipping damage and sold them as new. Gore set his damages at $4,000 and sued, charging BMW with malicious fraud. A jury awarded him $4 million in punitive damages—1,000 times his actual loss.

On appeal, the Supreme Court held that such a big award for retouching paint was unconstitutionally excessive.[28] It said punitive damages must be reasonably related to the degree of reprehensibility in the company's conduct and proportionate to the size of actual damages. Thus, the Alabama Supreme Court reconsidered the case and awarded Gore only $50,000.[29]

In a subsequent case, the Court suggested rough guidelines for the ratio of punitive damages to compensatory damages. In it, a jury awarded $1 million in compensatory damages to a Utah couple for emotional distress suffered when State Farm Insurance mishandled their accident claim. Then, believing State Farm had schemed to cheat other customers as well, jurors decided to take away several weeks of its profits with $145 million in punitive damages—a ratio of 145:1. The Supreme Court found this award "neither reasonable nor proportionate to the wrong committed" and suggested that a ratio greater than 4:1 is suspect and a ratio of 10:1 or higher probably could never be justified.[30] The Utah Supreme Court then reduced the award to $9 million, a 9:1 ratio, just below the unjustifiable maximum.[31]

Most recently, the Court dramatically cut the punitive damages award against ExxonMobil for the *Exxon Valdez* oil spill. In 1993 an Alaska jury had given residents near the spill compensatory damages of $500 million, then imposed a $5 billion punitive award on the company. An appeals court subsequently halved this to $2.5 billion. When the Supreme Court got the case it further reduced the award to $500 million, a 1:1 ratio. In its opinion it suggested that the company's actions were not intentionally malicious and, absent extraordinary malice, the 1:1 ratio was sufficient to punish and deter in most cases.[32] Unless the Court backs away from this line of decisions, it is unlikely that corporations will suffer punitive damages exceeding this 1:1 ratio in the future. However, the most important factor in punitive

---

[28] *BMW of North America, Inc., v. Gore,* 116 S.Ct. 1589 (1996). The Court based its decision on the Due Process Clause of the Fourteenth Amendment, which prohibits excessive or arbitrary punishment.

[29] *BMW of North America, Inc. v. Gore,* 701 So. 2d 507 Ala. (1997).

[30] *State Farm Mutual Automobile Insurance Company v. Campbell,* 123 S. Ct. 1513 (2003).

[31] *Campbell v. State Farm Mutual Automobile Insurance Company,* 98 P.3d 409 (Utah, 2004).

[32] *Exxon Shipping Co. v. Baker,* 128 S. Ct. 2605 (2008).

damages continues to be the reprehensibility of corporate behavior and in cases of egregious, willful, or reckless conduct, exceptional awards are still likely.[33]

Criminal Prosecution of Managers and Corporations

Crimes are offenses against the public prosecuted by federal and state governments. Corporate crimes impair lawful competition in markets and harm consumers, investors, and the public. They include managerial wrongdoing that falls in the category of *white-collar crime*, or nonviolent economic offenses involving cheating and deception done for personal or corporate gain in the course of employment. These crimes are often difficult to detect, being hidden or disguised to look like legal activity. Unlike an armed robbery or murder there is no crime scene or body. Evidence may exist only in a perplexing maze of documents and conspiratorial decisions.

Both individuals and corporations are prosecuted for crimes. Both kinds of prosecutions can be complicated, but it is easier to prosecute corporations because criminal law evolved in the twentieth century in ways that make organizations especially vulnerable. Under the doctrine of *respondeat superior*, (rez PON' day aht superior), created by the Supreme Court in 1909, corporations are liable for the actions of employees who commit a crime in the course of their employment when their act is for the benefit of the company.[34]

To establish guilty intent when crimes have occurred, the law assumes that a corporation has the aggregate knowledge of all its employees. Unlike with an individual, prosecutors do not have to prove that a corporation had criminal intent, only that an employee committed a crime intended to benefit it. If so, the corporation is guilty of that crime, even if the employee's action was against company rules and higher management had no knowledge of wrongdoing. And, unlike individuals, corporations are not allowed to invoke the Fifth Amendment right against self-incrimination when prosecutors ask them to turn over documents related to a crime.

Prosecutors find it easier to impose penalties on corporations because they are reluctant to go to trial. Juries are more inclined to convict corporations than individuals. When Royal Caribbean Cruise Lines was indicted for criminal violations of the Clean Water Act it decided to fight and put together an all-star defense team including two former U.S. attorneys general. It still lost the case. For corporations in many industries, criminal prosecution risks catastrophe. A conviction can lead to a drop in share price, higher cost of capital, reputational damage, and loss of federal contracts and licenses. These secondary consequences punish not only the company, but also its employees, pensioners, shareholders, and communities, all innocent of any crime.

Arthur Andersen is a cautionary example. Its auditors failed to deter Enron from stating false earnings. While federal investigators were looking into Enron's books Andersen shredded some germane documents, believing it had the right to do so. Indicted for obstruction of justice, it went to trial, and in 2002 a jury found

white-collar crime
A nonviolent economic offense of cheating and deception done for personal or corporate gain in the course of employment.

[33] Note that the Court let pass an $80 million award by an Oregon jury against Philip Morris USA where actual damages were $522,000, a ratio of 153:1. See *Philip Morris USA v. Williams* 129 S. Ct. 1436 (2009), *per curium*.

[34] The Supreme Court established this precedent for liability in *New York Central & Hudson River Railroad Co. v. United States*, 212 U.S. 481 (1909).

Charging Factors

These factors are used by federal prosecutors to decide when a corporation should be charged with a crime. All factors must be weighed, although in some cases, such as the nature of the offense, a single factor could be of overriding importance. Note that the seventh factor requires reflection about consequences for innocent parties, a concern that leads to many deferred and nonprosecution agreements.

1. Nature and seriousness of the offense, including risk of harm to the public.
2. Pervasiveness of wrongdoing within the corporation, including management complicity or involvement.
3. The corporation's history of similar misconduct.
4. The corporation's timely and voluntary disclosure of wrongdoing and its willingness to cooperate in the investigation.
5. Existence and effectiveness of a preexisting compliance program.
6. Remedial actions, including starting or improving a compliance program, replacing management, and disciplining wrongdoers.
7. Consequences for shareholder, pension holders, employees, and other innocent parties as well as the public.
8. Adequacy of prosecuting individuals responsible for the crimes.
9. Adequacy of other remedies such as civil lawsuits or enforcing regulations.

Source: "Principles of Federal Prosecution of Business Organizations," *United States Attorney's Manual,* Title 9 §928.800(B), at 15-16, August 28, 2008 (the Filip Memorandum).

deferred prosecution agreement
An agreement between a prosecutor and a corporation to delay prosecution while the company takes remedial actions.

nonprosecution agreement
An agreement in which U.S. attorneys decline prosecution of a corporation that has taken appropriate steps to report a crime, cooperate, and compensate victims.

it guilty. The judge imposed a $500,000 criminal fine, affordable enough, and put Andersen on five years' probation, but the company was moribund, its clients fleeing from an auditor whose name was now synonymous with scandal. Still, Andersen appealed and three years later a unanimous Supreme Court overturned the conviction, saying flawed jury instructions allowed the guilty verdict.[35] It was too late, Andersen had expired.

The Department of Justice, which controls all criminal prosecutions in which the United States has an interest, weighs nine factors (see the accompanying box) in deciding whether or not to indict a corporation and, depending on the outcome, allows U.S. attorneys to enter *deferred prosecution agreements* (DPAs) and *nonprosecution agreements* (NPAs) in which the government will delay or not prosecute if the corporation takes steps to compensate victims and prevent future wrongdoing. Since 1993 there have been more than 150 DPAs and NPAs, most with well-known companies including Aetna, Boeing, Chevron, Fiat, Monsanto, Pfizer, and Sears.

When a company signs a DPA or NPA it is not indicted. It agrees to a set of terms, typical among them being to set up or improve an internal compliance program, to pay restitution to victims, to forfeit income from criminal activity, to cooperate with an investigation, to fire guilty executives, and to hire a *monitor* who will oversee its compliance with the DPA or NPA and report at intervals to prosecutors. It must fulfill these terms in a specific time, usually three to five years.

[35] *Andersen v. United States,* 544 U.S. 696 (2005).

monitor
A person hired by a corporation to oversee fulfillment of conditions in an agreement to avoid criminal indictment.

Because corporations are so fearful of indictment, even when they are innocent of wrongdoing or the wrongdoing is confined to a few rogue employees, they are drawn into DPAs and NPAs. Some critics believe the agreements let corporate criminals off too easily. Others think managers of basically innocent companies make rational decisions to avoid trials, but their firms are then unfairly branded as criminals and federal prosecutors gain power to dictate their affairs.

Executives are more often prosecuted than corporations, though harder to convict. Unlike a corporation, where evidence that an employee committed a crime is sufficient for conviction, the government must prove beyond a reasonable doubt that an executive either had specific knowledge of a crime and acted to abet it or realized the probable existence of a crime and consciously avoided inquiring into it. Unlike corporations, executive defendants do not have to produce information, so pretrial investigation can be lengthy and expensive. And cases are complex. At Pfizer the FBI spent four years going through boxes of documents, scanning them into computers, and doing name and keyword searches trying to reveal how a regional sales manager directed kickbacks to doctors who prescribed its drugs.[36] White-collar crimes such as accounting frauds require prosecutors to educate lay juries about intricate financial transactions that even experienced auditors find hard to follow. This was a problem in the trial of Richard Scruchy, former CEO of HealthSouth, who was tried on 36 counts of conspiracy, fraud, and money laundering. After sitting through five months of testimony, fossilized jurors acquitted him of all wrongdoing.

After a cluster of corporate frauds, including the Enron and WorldCom collapses, President George W. Bush set up a Corporate Fraud Task Force to prosecute managers. A separate Enron Task Force was created to concentrate on the labyrinthine Enron fraud. To pierce the veil of culpability, its prosecutors methodically pressured lower-level managers into cooperating as witnesses. In return for guilty pleas and testimony against their former bosses, they received lighter sentences. It was ruthless work. To get the cooperation of former Chief Financial Officer Andrew S. Fastow, prosecutors charged his wife, Lea, a former assistant treasurer at Enron, with defrauding the company for personal enrichment.[37] Both Fastows then agreed to a reduction of charges in return for his testimony. As managers caved in, the task force moved up the chain of responsibility to the very top where former CEOs Kenneth L. Lay and Jeffrey K. Skilling maintained ignorance of any wrongdoing.

Eventually, the task force triumphed in a 17-week trial in which jurors convicted both Lay and Skilling on multiple counts of conspiracy and fraud. After inculpating testimony by almost two dozen former subordinates, jurors simply did not believe that Lay and Skilling lacked knowledge of any schemes.[38] Although Lay died of a heart attack before sentencing, Skilling was sentenced to 24 years and 4 months in prison.[39] Because Andrew Fastow cooperated with the government, his sentence was only six years. Lea Fastow served five months in prison.

[36] Federal Bureau of Investigation, "Pfizer $2.3 Billion Settlement," press release, September 3, 2009.

[37] *United States v. Lea W. Fastow*, Indictment, U.S.D.C., S. Dist. Texas, Cr. No. H-03.

[38] Department of Justice, "Prepared Remarks of Deputy Attorney General Paul J. McNulty at the Corporate Fraud Task Force Fifth Anniversary Event," Washington, DC, July 17, 2007, p. 1.

[39] Skilling has since won an appeal to have his sentence recalculated.

The government's record in prosecuting executives is mixed. The Enron Task Force was disbanded in 2006 after bringing criminal charges against 27 executives and obtaining 20 convictions. The larger Corporate Fraud Task Force investigated more than 400 corporate fraud cases and obtained more than 1,300 convictions, including 350 senior executives, before merging into a 25-agency financial fraud task force in 2009.[40]

Such large conviction numbers are impressive, but most offenders have pleaded guilty. Corporate criminals remain extremely difficult to prosecute. When cases with high-level executives go to trial, prosecutors struggle. A study of 17 major corporate fraud prosecutions over four years, including Enron trials, shows that government prosecutors failed to convict most of the defendants. Of 46 executives, 20 were convicted but 11 were acquitted and juries deadlocked on 15 others.[41]

Sentencing and Fines

In 1991 the U.S. Sentencing Commission, a judicial agency that standardizes penalties for federal crimes, released guidelines for sentencing both managers and corporations. These guidelines are not mandatory, but most judges follow them.[42] When managers are convicted of a crime, their prison sentences are based on a numerical point system. Calculations begin with a base score for the type of offense. Points are then added or subtracted because of enhancing or mitigating factors. A sentence for fraud, for example, begins with a base level of 6, then 15 factors are considered, including the number of victims and their losses. As losses to victims rise on a scale from $5,000 to $400 million or more, between 2 and 30 points are added. As the number of victims rises from 10 to 250 or more, between 2 and 6 points are added.[43] Downward adjustments are made if the manager has no criminal history or cooperated with authorities. The point total is then converted into a prison sentence using a table. Besides prison terms, managers may also be fined, put on probation, given community service, asked to make restitution to injured parties, or banned from working as corporate officers or directors.

Corporations cannot be imprisoned, but they can be fined. Criminal fines are intended to punish, to deter future lawbreaking, to cause disgorgement of wrongful gains, and to remedy harms where possible. As with the prison sentences of managers, judges base their fine calculations on a point system in the federal sentencing guidelines. The calculation begins with a fine range based on the type of offense, then adds or subtracts points based on aggravating or mitigating factors such as top-management involvement and cooperation during the investigation. If, for example, management "willfully obstructed" authorities, three points are added. Up to five points may be subtracted if top managers immediately reported the crime.[44]

---

[40] Government Accountability Office, *Corporate Crime: DOJ Has Taken Steps to Better Track Its Use of Deferred and Non-Prosecution Agreements, but Should Evaluate Effectiveness*, GAO-10-110, December 2009, p. 36.

[41] Kathleen F. Brickey, "In Enron's Wake: Corporate Executives on Trial," *Journal of Criminal Law & Criminology*, Winter 2006, pp. 401–07. Convictions of K. Lay and J. Skilling are included in the figures.

[42] See *United States v. Booker*, 125 S.Ct. 738 (2005).

[43] United States Sentencing Commission, *Guidelines Manual*, §2B1.1 (November 2009).

[44] Ibid.

A cynical public doubts that fines are large enough to hurt. The Environmental Protection Agency once threatened to impose a $27,500 fine on General Electric each day it failed to clean up toxic waste at a factory. Based on GE's revenues it was the equivalent of trying to intimidate a person making $1 million a year with a fine of three cents a day. Another time, the government fined GE $50 million to settle accounting fraud charges.[45] It was the equivalent of a $2.74 fine for the hypothetical millionaire.

The largest fine ever levied is a $2.5 billion civil penalty by the Securities and Exchange Commission against WorldCom in 2003. The record for a criminal fine is $1.2 billion. It was imposed on Pfizer in 2009 for paying kickbacks to doctors who prescribed its drugs for uses not allowed by the Food and Drug Administration. This was 15 percent of its net income for the year, an amount that affected Pfizer's operations. Corporate fines are frequent. In 2009, for example, 177 companies were sentenced for crimes. Of these 131 were fined. The mean fine was $14,861,234.[46]

FACTORS THAT INFLUENCE MANAGERIAL ETHICS

Strong forces in organizations shape ethical behavior. Depending on how they are managed, these forces elevate or depress standards of conduct. We discuss here four prominent and interrelated forces that shape conduct: leadership, strategies and policies, organization culture, and individual characteristics (see Figure 7.2).

Leadership

The example of company leaders is perhaps the strongest influence on integrity. Not only do leaders set formal rules, but by their example they also reinforce or undermine right behavior. Subordinates are keen observers and quickly notice if

FIGURE 7.2
Four Internal
Forces
Shaping
Corporate
Ethics

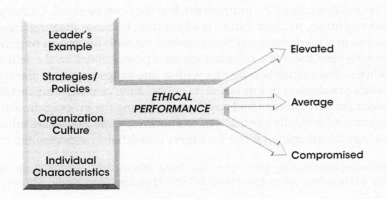

[45] Securities and Exchange Commission, "SEC Charges General Electric with Accounting Fraud," *Litigation Release No. 21166,* August 4, 2009.

[46] United States Sentencing Commission, *2009 Sourcebook on Federal Sentencing Statistics* (Washington, DC: USSC, 2009), table 52.

standards are, in practice, upheld or evaded. Exemplary behavior is a powerful tool available to all managers. It was well used by this executive.

> When Paul O'Neill arrived as CEO at Alcoa, a secretary put papers in front of him to join an expensive country club. His dues would be paid by the company. He was expected to join because other senior executives could not continue their paid memberships unless the CEO was a member. Before signing, he looked into the club and realized that it had a discriminatory membership policy. He was urged just to go along and join, like others before him. Since he was new, he ought to wait a while before disturbing Alcoa custom. However, he refused to join. His thoughts were: "What excuse am I going to use 6 or 12 months from now? I've just discovered my principles? They were on vacation . . . when I first came?"[47] He then set up a policy against reimbursing executives for dues in discriminatory clubs.

A common failing is for managers to show by their actions that ethical duties may be compromised. For example, when managers give themselves expensive perks, they display an irreverence for the stewardship of money that rightly belongs to investors as owners, not to management. An executive at one large corporation describes how arrogant behavior sends the wrong signals.

> Too often through my career I've been at management dinners—no customers—and I see $600 bottles of wine being ordered. Think about the message that sends out through the whole organization. And don't ever think such attitudes don't spread and infect the whole firm. Leadership, after all, is about communicating values. And deeds trump words any day.
>
> The message in that bottle is this: Some sales representative and a couple of technicians, supported by others, busted their butts to get that $600 to the bottom line. And their work, as evaluated by the guy who bought the wine, was worth a couple of tasty swallows.
>
> If money is the way we keep track of the good things our employees accomplish for our customers, then who do we think we are spilling it?[48]

Many employees are prone to cynicism. Diverting blame for mistakes, breaking small promises, showing favoritism, and diversion of even trivial company resources for personal use are ill-advised—because if the leader does it, an opportunistic employee can rationalize his or her entitlement to do it also. According to Sherron Watkins, a whistle-blower at Enron, Andrew Fastow was such a shrewdly observant subordinate. As Enron's chief financial officer, he created a warren of complex and deceitful investments that not only contributed nonexistent revenue, but also diverted corporate funds into his and his wife's pockets. What inspired Fastow to act as he did? According to Watkins, it may have been the example set by CEO Ken Lay.

---

[47] Quoted in Linda K. Treviño and Katherine A. Nelson, who tell this story in their book, *Managing Business Ethics: Straight Talk about How to Do It Right,* 5th ed. (New York: John Wiley & Sons, 2011), p. 161.

[48] Betsy Bernard, President AT&T, "Seven Golden Rules of Leadership," *Vital Speeches of the Day,* December 15, 2002, p. 155.

Ken Lay had Enron . . . use his sister's travel agency. That gave millions of dollars to that agency and it was a wretched travel agency. The service wasn't even good and I can speak to that because I have some horror stories about their travel scheduling. This went on for years and years and years. Now, if you take someone like Andy Fastow who does not appear to have a good sense of right and wrong, that's telling him that "hey, my partnerships are helping Enron meet their financial statement targets so why shouldn't I carve some out for myself because Ken Lay has been carving some out for his sister?"[49]

He also abused the corporate jet in really onerous ways. He moved a stepdaughter back and forth to France—furniture, not her! . . . [O]nce again that sent a message to executives that when you get to the top, the company is there for you versus you being there to serve the company.[50]

Strategies and Policies

A critical function of managers is to create strong competitive strategies that enable a company to meet strategic goals without encouraging ethical compromise. In companies with deteriorating businesses, managers have great difficulty meeting performance targets and may feel pressure to compromise ethical standards. Even in strong companies, strategies must be executed with policies that reinforce honest achievement. Of special concern are unrealistic performance goals that pressure those who must make them work.

At Lucent Technologies CEO Richard McGinn made the company's shares rocket by promising 20 percent yearly sales growth. Twice he missed quarterly targets and each time the stock plummeted. He could not miss again. Warned by subordinates that fourth quarter sales might fall short, he "went ballistic."[51] Under intense pressure to meet the revenue goal, the sales force reacted. It first offered legitimate discounts to customers, but the goal was still unmet. Other tactics then emerged from the shadows. Customers were given credits toward future purchases and these were booked as revenue in the fourth quarter. Revenues were booked when products were sold to distributors, not final customers, an unoriginal trick known as "channel stuffing." Told again by the head of sales that the revenue target was hopeless, McGinn said he would not take no for an answer. Ultimately, the target was missed. McGinn was fired. Lucent had to report that $679 million in fourth quarter revenue was unallowable. One sales agent lost his job for falsifying sales documents. McGinn later rationalized that he "never asked anyone to do anything untoward."

Reward and compensation systems can also expose employees to ethical compromises.

Ads for the Laser Vision Institute stated a fee of $499 per eye for laser surgery, although small type warned that the "price may vary according to RX and astigmatism." When prospects arrived they did not see physicians at first; instead, they met

[49] Sherron S. Watkins, "Ethical Conflicts at Enron: Moral Responsibility in Corporate Capitalism," *California Management Review,* Summer 2003, p. 17.

[50] Sherron Watkins, "Pristine Ethics," *Vital Speeches of the Day,* May 1, 2003, p. 435.

[51] Quotes in this paragraph are from Dennis K. Berman and Rebecca Blumstein, "Behind Lucent's Woes: All-Out Revenue Goal and Pressure to Meet It," *The Wall Street Journal,* March 29, 2001, pp. A1 and A8.

with counselors who decided what type of surgery the person needed and collected a deposit. What patients did not realize was that the counselors worked on an incentive system. They made yearly base salaries of $40,000 but added to their income with bonuses paid when patients were upgraded to more expensive surgeries. For the $499 procedure they got a per-eye bonus of only $1. But the amount rose with the surgery's price—$2 for a $599 surgery, $6 for the $799 procedure, $16 for $999, and so forth, up to $40 for patients paying $1,599. To be eligible for these bonuses the counselors had to have a 75 percent close rate on people who came in. It is no surprise, then, that prospects were subjected to aggressive tactics similar to those faced by car buyers and that, in the end, 88 percent paid more than $499.[52] Eventually, customers sued over "bait and switch" tactics and the Federal Trade Commission ordered the company to stop making false claims.

When companies adopt policies that put employees under pressure, they should build in strong ethical rules too. When the tide of money runs high, shore up the ethical dikes.

Corporate Culture

corporate culture
A set of values, norms, rituals, formal rules, and physical artifacts that exists in a company.

Corporate culture refers to a set of values, norms, rituals, formal rules, and physical artifacts that exists in a company. Corporate cultures are powerful and deep. In the words of one scholar, they are "like water around fish." They evolve as companies cope with recurring stresses in their competitive environments. Over time, attitudes and behaviors that solve problems and bring success are reinforced and become permanent parts of the culture. Often the influence of a founder is important and lasting. Henry Ford's early philosophy of brutal labor policies endured so strongly that more than 50 years after his death Ford Motor had to root out pervasive authoritarianism in its management ranks before it could adapt more flexible manufacturing methods to compete with Japanese rivals.

According to a pioneering researcher, Edgar Schein, a corporate culture can be understood by separating it into three levels and reflecting on their relationship.[53] The first level is one of *artifacts*, which include both physical expressions of culture and visible behaviors. Physical elements include ways of dressing, office layouts, and symbolic displays such as picture walls of former executives. Visible behaviors include patterns of interaction, for example, the use of first or last names as an indication of formality, and the kinds of decisions made.

At the second level are the organization's *espoused values*, that is, formal statements of belief and intention. Espoused values are found in documents such as mission statements, codes of ethics, and employee handbooks. They state what the organization officially stands for. Often, inconsistencies are observed between the physical and behavioral artifacts on the first level and the espoused policies on the second level.

When such inconsistencies arise they are explained by the hidden influence of a third cultural level of *tacit underlying values*. At this level reside the deep, shared assumptions in the organization's culture about how things really work. These are the

---

[52] Marc Borbely, "Lasik Surgery Sales Tactics Raise Eyebrows," *Washington Post,* September 4, 2001, p. A1.
[53] Edgar H. Schein, *The Corporate Culture Survival Guide, rev. ed.* (San Francisco: Jossey-Bass, 2009), pp. 21–27.

unspoken, unwritten beliefs about the nature of the company and what behaviors bring success. Though often unarticulated, these silent assumptions are usually the cause of deviation from nice-sounding espoused values.

A simple example of such an inconsistency is a company with a mission statement that emphasizes teamwork, but in which a visible artifact, a prominently placed employee-of-the-month award plaque, seems to contradict the official emphasis on teamwork. This may indicate that at the level of tacit underlying assumptions employees understand individual achievement as the route to promotion despite the mission statement's endorsement of teamwork.

All corporate cultures have ethical dimensions. When the behavior of employees fails to match the values in a written ethics code, it can be a reflection of silent assumptions lying deep in the culture that confute the code. For example, recent graduates of the Harvard MBA program who were interviewed about the ethical atmosphere in their organizations revealed the strong presence of four informal but powerful "commandments" conveyed to them early in their careers.

> First, performance is what really counts, so make your numbers. Second, be loyal and show us that you're a team player. Third, don't break the law. Fourth, don't overinvest in ethical behavior.[54]

These "commandments" clearly strain the spirit of any strong corporate ethics code. When the contradictions between espoused values and underlying tacit assumptions grow too wide trouble is not far ahead. The story of Fannie Mae illustrates the point.

> Franklin D. Raines was a suave and exceptionally talented manager who became CEO of Fannie Mae, the giant mortgage company. Fannie Mae had a strong Ethical Responsibility Policy that called for "a corporate culture characterized by openness, integrity, responsibility, and accountability."[55] Raines often espoused these values of honesty and openness in talks to employees.
>
> However, in his first few months on the job, he discovered that Fannie Mae would miss earnings per share (EPS) targets that triggered maximum executive bonuses. Raines told the firm's controller to prepare a list of "alternative" accounting methods and in a meeting with senior managers it was agreed to use them to meet the targets. This action overrode the advice of both internal and external auditors and sent the message to the organization that meeting EPS goals was what mattered, not the way they were met.
>
> Next Raines set in motion a five-year plan to double EPS from $3.23 to $6.46 and again tied bonuses to meeting yearly EPS goals. He pushed the plan hard. What happened to the culture is encapsulated in a speech to Fannie Mae's internal auditors by their boss.
>
> "Be objective, be fair but tough . . . [and] never compromise or dilute your conclusions . . . By now every one of you must have 6.46 branded in your brains. You must be able to say it in your sleep, you must be able to recite it forwards and backwards, you must have a raging fire in your belly that burns away all doubts, you

[54] Joseph L. Badaracco, Jr., and Allen P. Webb, "Business Ethics: A View from the Trenches," *California Management Review,* Winter 1995, p. 11.

[55] Warren B. Rudman, ed., *A Report to the Special Review Committee of the Board of Directors of Fannie Mae* (Washington, DC: Paul, Weiss, Rifkind, Wharton & Garrison, February 23, 2006), p. 439.

must live, breath and dream 6.46, you must be obsessed on 6.46 . . . Remember Frank has given us an opportunity to earn not *just* our salaries . . . but substantially over and above if we make 6.46 . . . It is our *moral obligation* to . . . have made tangible contributions to Frank's goals."[56]

The mixed message in this speech typified the pervasive conflict between espoused values of openness and honesty and the tacit underlying assumption that meeting EPS targets in any way possible was the road to success. The result was years of questionable accounting. Eventually, probes by regulators forced Raines and other top executives to resign and the company had to restate $6.3 billion in earnings.[57]

Cultures are resilient. Observers are always puzzled when corporations with strong ethics programs founder. Why after years of formal effort to make Shell Oil a more responsible corporation was the CEO caught leading other executives in a conspiracy to lie about the company's oil reserves? Why was the CEO of Boeing, an experienced executive brought out of retirement to elevate the company's ethics, forced to resign over an affair with a subordinate? Why, after years of effort to elevate its ethics, did Chiquita Brands' top executives and board of directors covertly approve illegal bribes, not once, but many times? One explanation is that these are simply perverse actions by a few bad apples. But a better explanation, insofar as humans can know the source of evils in their nature, likely lies deeper, in the persistence of contradictions in corporate cultures. As the story of Consolidated Edison illustrates, cultures are extremely resistant to change.

After a steam explosion that killed three people and sprayed asbestos over a Manhattan neighborhood, Consolidated Edison pleaded guilty to four federal environmental crimes. Only two weeks later in a state court it accepted guilt for 319 environmental violations over many years. It entered an agreement for broad reform "from the chairman to the lineman" and the court appointed a monitor to supervise its efforts during three years of probation.[58]

Edison's leadership rolled out a program of environmental responsibility. A new senior vice president for environmental affairs was put in charge. Two high-level environmental committees were formed to review progress. Every employee was made personally responsible for environmental safety and encouraged to raise problems openly. Any worker had the power to stop a job immediately on seeing a problem.

However, violations continued. More than a year later the court-appointed monitor reported that workers who spoke out were being intimidated. When one employee complained about pollutants leaking into the Hudson River, a supervisor called him a "snake" and a "troublemaker."[59] Another was transferred from his job. The monitor believed the company nurtured a "destructive corporate culture" that inhibited environmental responsibility.

[56] Quoted in Office of Federal Housing Enterprise Oversight, *Report of the Special Examination of Fannie Mae* (Washington, DC: OFHEO, May 2006), p. 42.

[57] Eric Dash, "Ex-Officers Sued by U.S." *The New York Times,* December 19, 2006, p. 1.

[58] Joe Sexton, "Con Edison Agrees to $9 Million Fine for Contamination," *The New York Times,* November 16, 1994, p. A1.

[59] Dan Van Natta, Jr., "Con Ed Cited in Intimidation of Employees," *The New York Times,* December 19, 1995, p. B1.

This was correct. Although the espoused values of Consolidated Edison had been quickly elevated, tacit underlying assumptions were much slower to change. For decades its workers shared the assumption that keeping power on was the top priority. They went to heroic lengths to fix problems, often ignoring formal procedures to speed the job. The work culture required unquestioned obedience to supervisors. Group loyalty was strong. No one confronted co-workers about environmental hazards and no one ratted outside the group. Anyone who did was ostracized.[60] These underlying values endured, leading to repeated violations of the new environmental policies.

Individual Characteristics

Researchers try to discover what individual qualities are associated with ethical behavior. Demographic factors seem to explain little.[61] Some studies show that women are more ethical than men, but results are mixed.[62] No studies find men to be more ethically sensitive than women, but some show no difference. A few studies suggest that people with more education are more ethical, but others do not. Similarly, some studies find that religious belief leads to more ethical attitudes, but many others fail to discover any relationship.[63] There are indications that higher ethics come with advancing age and longer work experience.[64] Personality traits may be more important, but are less studied in the literature of ethics. The only personality trait extensively studied and correlated with unethical behavior is Machiavellianism, the tendency of an individual to use self-centered, immoral, manipulative behavior in a group. However, the correlations tend to be modest and some studies fail to find a relationship.[65]

Many companies now use integrity tests to predict whether job applicants are inclined to antisocial, counterproductive behaviors such as rule breaking, fraud, cheating, and theft. Over many years these tests have been shown to work well. Some of them simply ask test takers to admit antisocial behaviors such as stealing. They also ask about attitudes toward theft. For example: "When you read about a robbery in the newspaper do you ever hope the thief gets away with it?" or "At your previous job did you think about ways you could have gotten away with stealing if you wanted to?" Using many such questions an integrity test can separate those more inclined to steal from more honest people because thieves think more about stealing and justify it more easily. Other kinds of integrity tests predict a broader range of counterproductive work behaviors by measuring traits such as

[60] Schein, *The Corporate Culture Survival Guide,* pp. 153–63.

[61] Liane Young and Rebecca Saxe, "Innocent Intentions: A Correlation Between Forgiveness for Accidental Harm and Neural Activity," *Neuropsychologia* 47 (2009), p. 2070.

[62] See the discussion in Steven Kaplan, Kurt Pany, Janet Samuels, and Jian Zhang, " An Examination of the Association Between Gender and Reporting Intentions for Fraudulent Financial Reporting, *Journal of Business Ethics* 87 (2009), p. 17.

[63] Gary R. Weaver and Bradley R. Agle, "Religiosity and Ethical Behavior in Organizations: A Symbolic Interactionist Perspective," *Academy of Management Review,* January 2002, p. 79.

[64] Terry W. Low, Linda Ferrell, and Phylis Mansfield, "A Review of Empirical Studies Assessing Ethical Decision Making in Business," *Journal of Business Ethics,* June 2000, p. 185.

[65] Kibeom Lee, et al., "Predicting Integrity with the HEXACO Personality Model," *Journal of Occupational and Organizational Psychology* 81 (2008), p. 155.

dependability, conscientiousness, thrill seeking/risk taking, conformity, hostility, response to authority. Although these tests predict integrity, it is not clear exactly what they measure. Experts believe they work by measuring a complex, multilevel hierarchy of personality components that is not fully understood.[66]

While there is limited evidence that fixed traits determine whether a person makes ethical decisions, there is overwhelming evidence that individuals are influenced to be more or less ethical by the situations they are in. Employees, for example, are more ethical when the company has an ethics code. Salespeople are more ethical when the sales manager clearly defines boundaries of ethical behavior.[67] Alternately, in a corporation with a dreary ethical climate, corrupt leaders, or performance pressures, otherwise honest individuals may buckle. This situational variation is due to the work of what sociologist Philip Zimbardo calls "dynamic psychological processes," or innate, predictable, and powerful tendencies in "ordinary" good people. They include obedience to authority, need to belong, desire to conform, self-justification, and rationalization. Consider the Rybergs.

> Nick Ryberg, an ambitious manager, was hired to direct human resources for a large company. He, his wife, Carolyn, and their two daughters moved to the Twin Cities area in Minnesota to begin. They sought status, using material displays to exhibit a lifestyle of success.
>
> Soon, Nick suggested that Carolyn start an executive search firm to find job candidates for his company. It would help the company and bring in a little extra money for their family. In an initial job she submitted some résumés for engineers and billed the company. This was legitimate work, but though legal it was a conflict of interest for Nick. Therefore, he asked her to send the invoice in her maiden name.
>
> Over time the scheme changed. Carolyn started two more companies in her maiden name for invoicing Nick's company.[68] At times Nick and Carolyn worried they had become criminals, but the work was authentic. Gradually, Nick began to submit invoices where little work, then no work, was done. The shadow over their lives darkened.
>
> Besides the human resources department, he also supervised accounting, security, records management, and IT. This was a management mistake. It reduced checks and balances on him. He set the recruiting budget and stayed within it. No one questioned the invoices. The family got luxury cars, expensive vacations, and a $200,000 kitchen remodel. He felt in control. It was hard to stop.
>
> Eventually, they made an error by submitting an invoice with an address that did not match one of Carolyn's companies. An audit led to fraud charges. They pled guilty and agreed to pay $964,265 in restitution. Nick was sentenced to 30 months in federal prison and Carolyn to 24 months.[69] They lost all but 15 boxes of personal belongings. Their high-school-age daughters went to separate homes. Their thoughts turned to shame and remorse. After prison they pursued theology studies and spoke on campuses about the need to avoid ethical traps.

[66] Christopher M. Berry, Paul R. Sackett, and Shelly Wiemann, "A Review of Recent Developments in Integrity Test Research," *Personnel Psychology,* Summer 2007, p. 276.

[67] Jay P. Mulki, Jorge Fernando Jaramillo, and William B. Locander, "Critical Role of Leadership on Ethical Climate and Salesperson Behavior," *Journal of Business Ethics* 86 (2009).

[68] Paul Gallagher, "Lessons from the Dark Side," *Human Resource Executive,* July 2009.

[69] "Two Residents of Minnesota Sentenced for Defrauding Flint Hills Resources," *States News Service,* February 2, 2005.

The story of the Rybergs illustrates many situational dynamics. They started with a small first step, then advanced. They wanted to fit in with an affluent status group. They admit to growing arrogance and sense of entitlement. They rationalized to justify wrongdoing. Also, because of poor management, there was opportunity. According to Zimbardo, situational factors such as these are so powerful, that "any deed, for good or evil, that any human being has ever done, you and I could also do–given the same situational forces."[70]

HOW CORPORATIONS MANAGE ETHICS

Years ago, little thought was given to formal management of ethics. One pioneer was James Cash Penney, who introduced a company conduct code in 1913. His effort was a lonely one. Until the 1980s, most companies gave more thought to managing petty cash than to elevating ethics. Since then, more and more companies have set up *ethics and compliance programs,* or systems of structures, policies, procedures, and controls designed to prevent lawbreaking and promote ethical behavior. In general, these programs originated in scandal and they continue to grow from it. Although a few companies voluntarily adopted them years ago, more put them in place after being ordered to by courts as part of their restitution for corporate wrongdoing. Now, the vast majority of law-abiding companies use them as protection against criminal indictment.

ethics and compliance program
A system of structures, policies, procedures, and controls used by corporations to promote ethical behavior and ensure compliance with laws and regulations.

The wider movement to ethics and compliance programs began in the 1980s. In response to a run of billing frauds and cost overruns, military contractors started the Defense Industry Initiative, a project requiring firms to adopt ethics codes and train employees to obey laws. More scandal-spawned ethics programs came in the mid-1990s, when the federal government cracked down on hospitals and nursing homes for Medicare billing fraud. Corporations in the health care industry rushed to follow the defense industry model.

The need to manage ethics was driven home to other industries in the 1996 *Caremark* case. Caremark International, a health care company, was caught giving kickbacks to physicians who referred patients to its clinics. After being indicted, the company set up a compliance program, but it was too late to prevent a $250 million fine. Angry shareholders sued its directors for breach of duty because they had failed to set up an ethics program earlier and this omission exposed the firm to a big fine. Caremark's directors narrowly escaped paying damages from their own pockets after a settlement. However, the judge who approved this settlement made it plain that if directors fail to set up a compliance program they can be sued for a breach of duty.[71]

Meanwhile, the U.S. Sentencing Commission in 1991 established the first sentencing guidelines. As previously explained, these guidelines set forth imprisonment and fine calculations for managers and corporations, allowing reductions in

---

[70] Philip Zimbardo, *The Lucifer Effect: Understanding How Good People Turn Evil* (New York: Random House, 2007), p. 320.

[71] *In re Caremark International Inc. Derivative Litigation,* 698 A2d 970 (1996).

Seven Steps for an Ethics Program

The U. S. Sentencing Commission sets forth these seven steps as minimally required to prevent criminal behavior and promote an ethical corporate culture. For federal prosecutors and regulators they define an acceptable effort by managers to ensure that companies and their employees follow the law.

1. Establish standards and procedures.
2. Create high-level oversight.

3. Screen out criminals.
4. Communicate standards to all employees.
5. Monitor and set up a hotline.
6. Enforce standards, discipline violators.
7. Assess areas of risk, modify the program.

Source: *Guidelines Manual,* §8B2.1, effective November 1, 2004.

---

both if companies had ethics and compliance programs. These reductions are a major incentive.

After the turn-of-the-century fraud scandals Congress created requirements for antifraud mechanisms with the Sarbanes-Oxley Act in 2002, including a code of ethics for financial officers, an internal process for reporting illegal behavior, and protection for employees who reveal wrongdoing. The Department of Justice and the Securities and Exchange Commission adopted new guidelines for making the presence of ethics and compliance programs a factor in the decision to prosecute. And both the New York and NASDAQ stock exchanges require that listed companies have in place codes of conduct and procedures to enforce them.[72]

Because of these actions all listed public corporations now have at least some elements of a comprehensive program in place, though the efforts differ in their vigor and their aims. Ethics and compliance programs may combine two distinct approaches to prevent wrongdoing. A *compliance approach* teaches employees to meet legal and regulatory requirements and emphasizes following rules. An *ethics approach* teaches values such as integrity, truth, fairness, and respect for others, preparing workers to separate right from wrong in moral spheres of work life. Most companies focus on compliance, but many put effort into both.

While there is no standard format, the U.S. Sentencing Commission's *Guidelines Manual* sets forth seven minimum steps that define a diligent effort (see the box). Many companies explicitly follow these steps, which have a strong compliance orientation, and others create processes that meet their general requirements in a variety of ways. The seven steps are a convenient framework for explaining the basic elements of programs.

1. *Establish standards and procedures to prevent and detect criminal conduct.* Companies meet this requirement with a variety of written documents. The centerpiece is often a short statement of guidelines at a high level of abstraction. An example

compliance approach
Training employees to follow rules in laws, regulations, and policy.

ethics approach
Training employees to make decisions based on ethical values.

---

[72] New York Stock Exchange *Listing Manual,* §503 A.10, "Code of Business Conduct and Ethics," amended November 25, 2009; and *NASDAQ Stock Market Listing Rules,* Rule 5610, adopted March 12, 2009.

THE GE Code of Conduct

- Obey the applicable laws and regulations governing our business conduct worldwide.
- Be honest, fair and trustworthy in all your GE activities and relationships.
- Avoid all conflicts of interest between work and personal affairs.
- Foster an atmosphere in which fair employment practices extend to every member of the diverse GE community.

- Strive to create a safe workplace and to protect the environment.
- Through leadership at all levels, sustain a culture where ethical conduct is recognized, valued and exemplified by all employees.

Source: General Electric Company, *Integrity: The Spirit & Letter of Our Commitment,* January 2008, p. 3.

is GE's (see the accompanying box). Most companies also set forth an expanded code of conduct, often in a booklet of 20 to 50 pages with graphic designs and stock photos of well-groomed people at work. Simple writing is used to make the standards clear. Cisco Systems once revised its code to an eighth-grade reading level. Many begin with a list of basic values such as honesty, integrity, fairness, respect for others, and upholding the law and the spirit of the law that should characterize employee behavior. Then they set forth brief guidance in a range of problem areas, including conflict of interest, bribery, gifts, insider trading, antitrust violations, trade secrets, political contributions, and discrimination. These relatively brief treatments are usually backed by separate, detailed compliance policies, so that the complete "code of ethics" of a large company can include dozens of documents running hundreds of pages.

Conduct codes contain typical elements, including introductions by CEOs, ways to report wrongdoing, tips for making ethical decisions, and disciplinary procedures. There is inexhaustible sameness in their content and format. They are saturated with similar principles, cover much the same compliance issues, and contain virtually identical guides for reporting concerns. Creativity comes at the margins. Accenture's graceful *Code of Business Ethics* is filled with photographs of trees and contains simple cases in question-and-answer format. Here is an example from the section titled "Integrity."

Q: My supervisor asked me to prepare a purchase order for services costing $30,000. Her spending authority is only $25,000. Can I break the request into two purchase orders to avoid getting higher level approval? She says that is savvy business practice. What should I do?

A: Not getting the proper approvals violates Accenture policy, which is to ensure that adequate internal accounting controls are maintained and operating effectively. If you are uncomfortable telling your supervisor, alert your local Finance lead.[73]

---

[73] Accenture, *Code of Business Ethics: Our Core Values in Action* (New York: Accenture, August 1, 2007, ver. 4.11), p. 32.

Codes are usually distributed to all employees. Many companies ask them to sign an annual form certifying compliance. Multinational companies translate them into many languages. Dow's booklet is translated into 20, PepsiCo's 30, Abbott Labs' 35, and Merck's 55.

2. *Give oversight of the program to the board of directors and assign responsibility for it to a high-level executive who, in turn, will assign day-to-day responsibility to a specific manager.* The *Guidelines Manual* requires that the board of directors exercise "reasonable oversight" over an ethics and compliance program, that one or more top executives take responsibility for it, and that specific managers be assigned day-to-day supervision. An example of a structure that meets these requirements is the Abbott Laboratories program shown in Figure 7.3. This structure is the result of a strengthened compliance effort coming after the FBI uncovered a 10-year fraud to cheat customers and Abbott paid $614 million in fines.[74]

At Abbott a chief ethics and compliance officer takes day-to-day responsibility for running the program. This ethics chief reports directly to Abbott's top executive, the chairman and CEO, and also reports directly to the board of directors through periodic reports to its Public Policy Committee and annual reports to the full board. This reporting relationship strengthens the ethics effort.[75] In some companies the ethics chief reports to the director of human resources or the legal department, but at Abbott the ethics program is independent and must answer only to the board, which has ultimate responsibility for ethics, and to the CEO, so its actions carry greater credibility. In addition, the ethics officer chairs a Business Conduct Committee that includes the heads of Abbott's business divisions and other top executives.

Below the chief ethics and compliance officer the program structure reaches down into the organization. Each business division has an ethics and compliance officer who reports to a divisional vice president of ethics and compliance, who in turn reports back to the corporate ethics chief. In this way the program parallels Abbott's operating structure. Note how a reporting chain for ethics staff is created separately from the line chain of command all the way up to the board of directors. This separation is an important check and balance. If ethics officers reported only to division managers, without a separate reporting channel, they would have less independence.

3. *Exclude individuals with a history of illegal or unethical conduct from positions of substantial authority.* Criminal background checks are inexpensive. Companies that fail to conduct them can be surprised, as was Smith & Wesson Holding Corp. on discovering that its chairman was the notorious "Shotgun Bandit" who had terrorized victims in a string of armed robberies years before.[76] He resigned.

[74] Raymond V. Gilmartin, *Ethics and the Corporate Culture* (Waltham, MA: Bentley College Center for Business Ethics, November 10, 2003), p. 12.

[75] Martin T. Biegelman, *Building a World-Class Compliance Program* (New York: John Wiley & Sons, 2008), pp. 155 and 178; and Michael D. Greenberg, *Perspectives of Chief Ethics and Compliance Officers on the Detection and Prevention of Corporate Misdeeds* (Santa Monica, CA: Rand Corporation, 2009), p. 29.

[76] Vanessa O'Connell, "How Troubled Past Finally Caught Up with James Minder," *The Wall Street Journal*, March 8, 2001, p. A1.

FIGURE 7.3 **Oversight Structure of Abbott Laboratories' Ethics and Compliance Program**

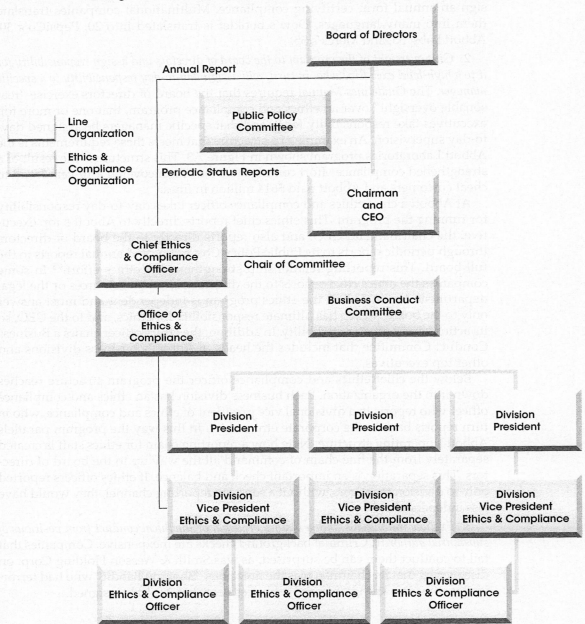

Companies also check for false claims about education and job experience on résumés. Again, failure to check can lead to surprises. In 2006 the chief executive of RadioShack was forced to resign after claiming a bachelor's degree in psychology from a small Baptist college that never offered degrees in that subject.[77] More recently, *The Wall Street Journal* checked the degree claims of 358 senior executives and directors at publicly traded companies and found seven cases of false claims.[78]

Even if an executive candidate's claims are accurate, it is hard to measure their inner character. Some psychologists believe that integrity can be tested in interviews. One expert recommends building rapport with the subject, then eliciting comments on ethical issues late in an interview. He suggests these inquiries. "Give me an example of an ethical decision you have had to make on the job?" "Have you ever had to bend the rules or exaggerate a little bit when trying to make a sale?" and "Tell me about an instance when you've had to go against company guidelines or procedures to get something done."[79]

4. *Periodically communicate standards and procedures to all employees from the lowest up to the board of directors.* Companies reinforce standards using everything from T-shirts to posters to newsletters. At one Kaiser Permanente facility the ethics and compliance staff held a fair with candy, popcorn, and a "Wheel of Compliance" that employees could spin and win prizes if they correctly answered a question about ethical standards.[80] However, training is the key to communicating ethics and compliance knowledge.

Generally, such training is most effective when company managers do it, not outsiders, and when it steers away from abstract philosophy to focus on the work lives of attendees. A few companies offer in-depth seminars lasting one to three days with discussion of policies and case studies. Briefer sessions are more typical. One-to-three-hour yearly sessions in which employees watch a video and discuss cases are common. Most popular are interactive sessions on a company intranet in which employees read short cases and try to pick the correct or most ethical responses from multiple-choice alternatives.

At Lockheed Martin employees attend one- or two-hour training sessions where they discuss incidents enacted on a video. Here are examples.

On his way to lunch, Charlie cuts his leg on a desk drawer that was not completely closed. Charlie's supervisor has been talking for weeks that the group's injury performance had not been good but one more incident would break the Target Zero goal for the department. Chloe, a co-worker, notices that Charlie hurt himself. Charlie asks her not to say anything.[81]

[77] Gary McWilliams, "RadioShack CEO Agrees to Resign," *The Wall Street Journal,* February 21, 2006, p. A3.

[78] Keith J. Winstein, "Inflated Credentials Surface in Executive Suite," *The Wall Street Journal,* November 13, 2008, p. B1.

[79] William C. Byham, "Can You Interview for Integrity?" *Across the Board,* March/April 2004, pp. 36–37.

[80] Elizabeth Schainbaum, "The Wheel of Compliance," *Compliance Today,* March 2008, p. 31.

[81] Lockheed Martin, *The 2005 Ethics Effect: Leader's Guide* (Marietta, GA: Lockheed Martin, 2005), p. 5.

Vivian, a factory employee, and her supervisor, Rhomeyn, notice that test data is missing from a part already stamped as inspected. Rhomeyn goes to speak with Burt, the employee who stamped the paperwork indicating that the part was inspected. Burt, however, is nowhere to be found. It turns out his co-worker, Chris, has been covering for him. Burt's perception is that he is being harassed. Burt also tells Chris that he didn't do the testing, but it isn't a big deal—he will just do it now.[82]

5. *Monitor the organization for criminal conduct, and set up a system for reporting of suspicious conduct without fear of retaliation.* Monitoring entails collection of data that can indicate suspicious activity. For example, some companies require reports of unusual financial transactions. Ethical audits can also detect problems. HCA Healthcare Corp. conducts two-day ethical compliance audits to reveal strengths and weaknesses at its hospitals. Employees are interviewed randomly as auditors cover a 53-page checklist.

All programs now have 24-hour toll-free telephone and e-mail hotlines for reporting suspected wrongdoing. To protect users' identities, they usually allow anonymous contacts. Whistle-blowers fear revenge, so hotlines must be supported with strong policies against retaliation. On average, between 2 and 4 percent of U. S. employees use hotlines each year.[83]

Hotlines create an enormous amount of work for ethics offices. Many callers seek advice: "Would it be a conflict of interest for me to work in the evening?" Others have trivial complaints, such as "My supervisor came back an hour late from lunch." Allegations must be investigated; for instance, "I think one of my team members gave confidential papers to a client." Although few calls reveal criminal wrongdoing, hotlines open a critical channel of communication. Here is an example of a hotline contact and how it was handled at KPMG.

A hotline report was filed alleging business integrity issues, such as over-stating credentials to a client, about a professional. Additional concerns of unprofessional conduct, such as demeaning team members, were raised by other reporters shortly thereafter. An investigation by the Ethics and Compliance Group substantiated the allegations. Firm and area functional leadership demoted the professional, issued a written reprimand, appointed a coach, and reduced the professional's annual performance rating for the purposes of determining compensation.[84]

6. *Enforce standards by providing both incentives to reward compliance and discipline to deter criminal conduct.* It has been objected that doing the right thing should require no incentive; however, many companies link ethics to performance reviews, promotions, and compensation. This seems like a powerful incentive, but in practice it is difficult and awkward to rate ethical performance. Tenet Healthcare tried to tie the bonuses of its top 800 managers to a numerical ethics score between −5 and +5, with each point changing the bonus by 5 percent. Managers felt

---

[82] Lockheed Martin, *Leader's Guide: A Culture of Trust 2009,* at www.lockheedmartin.com/aboutus/ethics/, p. 12.

[83] Andrew Singer, "Cisco Transmits Ethics to a 'Wired' Work Force," *Ethikos,* September/October 2009, p. 1.

[84] KPMG, *Ethics and Compliance Report 2009* (New York: KPMG LLP, 2009), p. 24.

humiliated, however, when they received negative scores, called "dings" in company slang.[85]

When Boeing made compliance with the company's ethics code part of every employee's evaluation it ran into the same problem. According to a report on Boeing's ethics program, it almost never affected the outcome.

> Managers perceive pressure (often self-imposed) not to rate any employee as below average in ethics. There is also resistance against rating any employee above average, as that implies that other employees are not doing as well with ethical conduct. The strong tendency, therefore, is to award all employees an average score for this component, effectively rendering it meaningless.[86]

Written disciplinary policies are widespread. Discipline is usually based on factors such as seriousness of the violation, the organizational level or leadership role of the violator, extent of cooperation with the investigation, prior misconduct, and willfulness of the action. A progressive range of disciplinary options—counseling, oral reprimand, probation, suspension, salary reduction, termination—can be used as fits the case. Xerox, for example, uses disciplinary guidelines that specify minimum and maximum penalties by type of infraction for first and second offenses but "[t]here are no guidelines for third offenses because there are no options at that point."[87]

7. *If criminal conduct occurs, modify the program to prevent repeat offenses. Periodically assess the risks of criminal conduct and try to reduce them.* Unless lawbreaking is the isolated failure of one person, the program is not working. It should be modified by changing or adding elements, restructuring responsibilities, or reappraising the culture in which it operates.

Some companies use ethical risk assessment to predict areas of ethical and legal risk in their businesses. General Electric, for example, formed a risk committee of top executives that meets quarterly to assess changing global ethical standards. This committee then decides whether GE should alter existing standards or adopt new ones.[88]

ETHICS AND COMPLIANCE PROGRAMS: AN ASSESSMENT

Nearly all large U.S. corporations now have at least some ethics and compliance mechanisms centered on a code of conduct. Fewer have full, comprehensive programs. In a recent survey only 23 percent of human resource managers reported a full range of program elements, comparable to the seven steps discussed above,

[85] Andrew W. Singer, "At Tenet Healthcare: Linking Ethics to Compensation," *Ethikos,* January–February 2001, pp. 4–5.

[86] Warren B. Rudman, et al., *A Report to the Chairman and Board of Directors of the Boeing Company Concerning the Company's Ethics Program and Its Rules and Procedures for the Treatment of Competitors' Proprietary Information* (Washington, DC: Paul, Weiss, Rifkind, Wharton & Garrison LLP, November 3, 2003), p. 36.

[87] Xerox, "Overview of Xerox Business Ethics & Compliance Office," at www.xerox.com, accessed February 12, 2010.

[88] Ben W. Heineman, Jr., "Avoiding Integrity Land Mines," *Harvard Business Review,* April 2007, p. 104.

in their organizations. However, 67 percent reported having at least four of these elements.[89]

The main incentive is almost universally the desire to avoid lawbreaking and reduce sanctions for corporations terrified of criminal indictment. One way to look at these programs is that they extend the reach of federal regulators and prosecutors who must police corporations in the public interest. In effect, ethics and compliance programs recruit corporations and their employees to police themselves. Codes of conduct almost always make it the duty of employees to report violations, and some impose discipline for failure to report even suspected illegal behavior, in effect, turning the entire workforce into an army of snitches working for the Department of Justice or, put more politely, "a corporate system of espionage to ferret out wrongdoing."[90]

Do the programs work? Surveys of employees reporting misconduct suggest their effectiveness in reducing unethical or illegal behavior is "modest and/or mixed."[91] Weak effect can result when companies fail to commit resources to the program. Sometimes ethics managers are marginalized in the hierarchy and have inadequate influence. Top executives who fail to lead by example undermine formal efforts. In such cases silent assumptions deep in the corporate culture work to undermine official intentions.

CONCLUDING OBSERVATIONS

Ethics is the study of good and evil. These are understood to be separate due to religious and philosophical teachings at the foundation of social norms and the law. Although it is naively thought that business requires ethical compromise, it does so no more or less than any other part of life. Not everyone can achieve their goals in business because success depends on more than forces the individual can control. It depends also on overcoming competition, economic conditions, and other rudiments of fortune. So there are sometimes strong motives and pressures to reach goals by lying, deceiving, and cheating. But doing evil is never right.

In this chapter we focused on the dynamics of ethics in organizations. The single most important factor in good corporate ethics is the example of leaders, who shape strategies and cultures. In recent years highly standardized ethics and compliance programs have emerged to fight bad conduct in corporations. They still depend heavily on effective leadership to work. Their effectiveness in reducing evil in practice has so far been mixed, but they are promising. In the next chapter we move from a focus on organizations to a focus on individuals and how they make ethical decisions.

[89] Society for Human Resource Management, *The Ethics Landscape in American Business* (Alexandria, VA: SHRM, 2008), p. 10.

[90] Miriam Hechler Baer, "Governing Corporate Compliance," *Boston College Law Review,* September 2009, p. 962.

[91] See Nicole Andreoli and Joel Lefkowitz, "Individual and Organizational Antecedents of Misconduct in Organizations," *Journal of Business Ethics,* 2009, pp. 314–15 and 320–21.

The Trial of Martha Stewart

From indictment to sentencing, the case of Martha Stewart was a matter of intense public interest. Some thought that her misdeeds, if any, were slight. Cynics believed the government was prosecuting a celebrity for a minor infraction to show it was tough on business crime. An indignant *Wall Street Journal* complained that innocent employees and shareholders of Martha Stewart Living Omnimedia were paying the price for the government's zeal.[1] Feminists argued that she was picked on for being a successful woman. "It's hard to imagine a male in precisely this spot," said Mary Becker, a DePaul University law professor. "Targeting a successful woman is very consistent with dominant cultural values."[2]

Others believed that her prosecution was justified. "I don't buy any of it," wrote Scott Turow, a criminal defense lawyer and the author of best-selling legal fiction. "What the jury felt Martha Stewart did—lying about having received inside information before she traded—is wrong, really wrong."[3]

This is the story.

DECEMBER 27

On the morning of Thursday, December 27, 2001, Douglas Faneuil was on duty at the mid-Manhattan office of Merrill Lynch. Faneuil, 24, who had been in his job only six months, assisted a stockbroker named Peter Bacanovic. It was two days after Christmas and Bacanovic was on vacation. Staffing was thin and Faneuil expected a slow day with light trading.

Soon Faneuil took a call from Aliza Waksal. Aliza was the daughter of Samuel Waksal, co-founder of ImClone Systems, a biopharmaceutical company. She wanted to sell her ImClone shares. Faneuil executed the order and by 9:48 a.m. her 39,472 shares had been sold for $2,472,837. Then Faneuil had a call from Samuel Waksal's accountant requesting that another 79,797 shares held in his Merrill Lynch account be transferred to Aliza's account and then

sold. The call was followed by a written direction saying that making the transfer and sale that morning was imperative.

Faneuil sought help on the transfer and called Peter Bacanovic in Florida. Bacanovic, 39, was an old friend of Waksal's. He had worked at ImClone for two years before coming to Merrill Lynch, and he handled the personal accounts of Waksal and his daughter. When Bacanovic learned that the Waksals were selling, he instructed Faneuil immediately to call another of his clients, Martha Stewart, while he remained on the line.

Bacanovic, who was active in New York social life, first met Martha Stewart in the mid-1980s when they were introduced by her daughter Alexis. Stewart was one of his most important clients. He handled her pension and personal accounts. He also handled accounts for her company, Martha Stewart Living Omnimedia, Inc.

At 10:04 a.m. Faneuil dialed Stewart, but reached her administrative assistant Ann Armstrong, who said Stewart was on an airplane. Bacanovic left a brief message, asking Stewart to call back when she became available. In her phone log, Armstrong wrote, "Peter Bacanovic thinks ImClone is going to start trading downward." Bacanovic instructed Faneuil that when Stewart called back he should tell her that the Waksals were selling all their shares. At this time ImClone was priced at $61.53 a share.

This instruction from Bacanovic bothered Faneuil. Merrill Lynch had a written policy (see Exhibit 1) that required its employees to hold client information in strict confidence. But he was very busy and working under a sense of urgency, handling calls from the Waksals, and making calls to Merrill Lynch staff in several offices arranging the transfer of Sam Waksal's shares to his daughter.

Several hours later, Stewart's plane landed in San Antonio to refuel. She went into the airport and on her cell phone called Ann Armstrong to check for messages. At 1:39 p.m. she phoned Merrill Lynch, reaching Faneuil, who told her that Sam Waksal and his daughter had sold all of their shares. She asked for the current price of ImClone. Faneuil quoted approximately $58 a share. Stewart told him to sell all 3,928 shares she owned.

---

[1] "The Trials of Martha," *The Wall Street Journal*, February 13, 2004, p. A12.

[2] Quoted in Jonathan D. Glater, "Stewart's Celebrity Created Magnet for Scrutiny," *The New York Times*, sec. 1, p. 1.

[3] Scott Turow, "Cry No Tears for Martha Stewart," *The New York Times*, May 27, 2004, p. 29.

EXHIBIT 1
Client
Information
Privacy Policy

Merrill Lynch protects the confidentiality and security of client information. Employees must understand the need for careful handling of this information. Merrill Lynch's client information privacy policy provides that—

...

- Employees may not discuss the business affairs of any client with any other employee, except on a strict need-to-know basis.
- We do not release client information, except upon a client's authorization or when permitted or required by law.

She hung up and immediately put in a call to Sam Waksal. The two were close friends who had been introduced by Stewart's daughter Alexis in the early 1990s. Unable to reach him, she left a message that his assistant took down as "Martha Stewart something is going on with ImClone and she wants to know what."[4] By 1:52 p.m. Stewart's ImClone shares had been sold at an average price of $58.43, for a total of approximately $228,000.

THE PUZZLE OF THE WAKSAL TRADES

What *was* going on with ImClone? For almost 10 years Waksal had put ImClone's resources into the development of a promising new colon cancer drug named Erbitux. Two months earlier, ImClone had submitted a licensing application for approval of Erbitux to the Food and Drug Administration (FDA). On December 26, Waksal learned from an ImClone executive that, according to a source within the FDA, on December 28 ImClone would receive a letter rejecting the Erbitux application. When the FDA's action was publicly announced ImClone's share price was sure to plummet.

Waksal was in possession of material insider information. It was material because any reasonable investor would find it important in deciding to buy or sell ImClone stock. It was insider information because it was not yet known to the public. Since the FDA application was so critical, ImClone's general counsel had declared a "blackout period" after December 21 when employees should not trade ImClone shares. The purpose of the blackout was to guard against illegal insider trading.

Despite being informed of the blackout and despite possessing knowledge of the law with respect to insider trading, Waksal elected to sell. This was exceptionally foolish. His motive was to escape the unpleasant consequences of debt. He had obligations of $75 million, most of which was margin debt secured by shares he owned in ImClone. Servicing this debt was costing him $800,000 a month. He knew that if ImClone's share price slipped very far, many of his shares would be sold, dramatically lowering his net worth. He also tipped family and friends to sell on December 27. Besides his daughter Aliza, his father sold 135,000 shares, his sister Patti sold 1,336 shares, and another daughter, Elana, sold 4,000 shares. Waksal also tipped an investment adviser who sold all of her 1,178 shares on December 27 and passed the tip to a physician on one of ImClone's advisory boards, who sold more than $5 million in shares—all he owned—on the same day.

On Friday, December 28, the FDA faxed ImClone a "refusal to file" letter at 2:55 p.m. Later in the afternoon, after the market closed with ImClone trading at $55.25 a share, the company issued a press release disclosing the FDA's action. On December 31, the next trading day, ImClone opened at $45.39 a share. If Martha Stewart had waited until then to sell her shares, she would have gotten about $178,292 or $49,708 less than she received by selling on the afternoon of December 27. ImClone closed on December 31 at $46.46. It had dropped about 16 percent on the news of the FDA's action.

AN UNSETTLED AFTERMATH

Four days later a supervisor at Merrill Lynch questioned Faneuil about the ImClone trades. Afterward, Faneuil called Bacanovic, who was still vacationing in Florida. Bacanovic told him that Martha Stewart sold her shares because of a prearranged plan to

---

[4] Complaint, *Securities and Exchange Commission v. Martha Stewart and Peter Bacanovic*, 03CV 4070 (NRB)(S.D.N.Y.), June 4, 2003, p. 7.

reduce her taxes. He told Faneuil about a December 20 telephone call in which he and Stewart had gone down a list of the stock holdings in her account deciding which ones to sell at a loss to balance out capital gains from other sales during 2001.

Soon, however, Faneuil had a call from Eileen DeLuca, Martha Stewart's business manager, who demanded to know why the ImClone shares had been sold, since the sale had resulted in a profit that disrupted her tax-loss selling plan. Again he called Bacanovic. This time, Bacanovic told him that Stewart had sold because they had a preexisting agreement to sell ImClone if the price fell below $60 a share.

Merrill Lynch contacted the Securities and Exchange Commission (SEC) to report suspicions of insider trading in ImClone. On January 3, 2002, SEC attorneys called Faneuil to interview him. Faneuil told them Stewart had sold because the price of ImClone fell below $60 a share. He did not tell them that he had conveyed news about the Waksals' sales to her. On January 7, SEC attorneys interviewed Bacanovic on the telephone. He told them he had spoken to Martha Stewart on the day she traded and recommended that she sell based on their preexisting $60 sell agreement.

On January 16, Martha Stewart and Peter Bacanovic had a breakfast meeting. Their conversation is unrecorded. According to Faneuil, after the meeting Bacanovic told him, "I've spoken to Martha. I've met with her. And everyone's telling the same story . . . This was a $60 stop-loss order. That was the reason for her sale. We're all on the same page, and it's the truth."[5] In at least five subsequent conversations, Bacanovic reassured Faneuil of the need to stick to this story. If he did, Bacanovic promised to give him extra compensation.

On January 30, in response to a request for documents by the SEC, Bacanovic turned over the worksheet that he said was used in his December 20 tax sale conversation with Martha Stewart. It was a single-page printout listing approximately 40 securities in her account and noting the number of shares and the purchase price. The notation "@60" appeared near the entry for ImClone,

On January 31, Martha Stewart had a lengthy conversation with a criminal attorney. Following the conversation she went to her assistant Ann Armstrong

asking to see the telephone log. Sitting at Armstrong's computer, she changed Bacanovic's December 27 phone message from "Peter Bacanovic thinks ImClone is going to start trading downward," to "Peter Bacanovic re imclone."[6] Then, thinking better of it, she told Armstrong to restore the original wording and left.

INTERVIEWS

On February 2, Martha Stewart was interviewed in New York by attorneys from the SEC, the Federal Bureau of Investigation (FBI), and the U.S. Attorney's Office. Asked to explain her ImClone transaction, she said she and Bacanovic had decided to sell if ImClone fell below $60 a share. On December 27 she had spoken to Bacanovic, who told her it had fallen below $60 and inquired if she wished to sell. She had assented, in part, because she was on vacation and did not want to worry about the stock market. She did not recall speaking to Faneuil on that day. She denied knowledge of the December 27 phone message from Bacanovic, even though only two days before she had gone to her assistant's computer to alter its wording. According to one attorney present, at the end of the interview Stewart asked in a "curt, annoyed" tone, "Can I go now? I have a business to run."[7]

On February 13, Bacanovic was subpoenaed by the SEC to testify under oath in New York. He reported a December 20 phone call with Stewart in which he recommended the sale of ImClone if it fell below $60. The worksheet he turned over to the agency had notes of this conversation. He also stated that he had not discussed the ImClone stock sale with Stewart since December 27. Yet records of calls between Bacanovic's and Stewart's cell phones show that by this time they had spoken often, including once on the day of Stewart's interview in New York. The content of their conversations is unrecorded.

On March 7, Douglas Faneuil was interviewed by SEC attorneys. Details of this session have not been made public, but his subsequent indictment alleges that he failed to fully and truthfully disclose all he

---

[5] Brooke A. Masters, "Stewart Ordered Sale, Says Witness," *The Washington Post*, February 5, 2004, p. E1.

[6] Matthew Rose and Kara Scannell, "Dramatic Flourishes at Stewart, Tyco Trials," *The Wall Street Journal*, February 11, 2004, p. C1.

[7] Thomas S. Mulligan, "Jurors Hear of Attempt by Stewart to Alter Phone Log," *Los Angeles Times*, February 11, 2004, p. C7.

knew about the events of December 27.[8] Following the interview, Bacanovic offered Faneuil an extra week of vacation and airfare for a trip as a reward for sticking to Bacanovic's script.[9]

On April 10, Stewart was interviewed again on the telephone by investigators. She told them she had spoken with Bacanovic on December 27, but she could not remember if Bacanovic had mentioned the Waksals. She said again that the two had set up a $60 sell order on ImClone.

TURMOIL

After these interviews, government investigators continued the painstaking work of gathering, verifying, and interpreting details. Meanwhile, the main actors in the ImClone trades struggled in the backwash of their actions. In late May, Samuel Waksal resigned as the CEO of ImClone. In early June, the Associated Press broke the story that Martha Stewart was being investigated, setting off a three-week decline in the share price of Martha Stewart Living Omnimedia. Merrill Lynch suspended Peter Bacanovic without pay.

When Waksal was arrested and charged with criminal insider trading on June 12, shares in Stewart's company fell 5.6 percent. Waksal would eventually plead guilty to insider trading charges, receive a prison sentence of 87 months, and pay a fine of $4 million. The family members were forced to disgorge the profits from their trades, with interest, and the two other tippees—the investment adviser and the physician—paid disgorgement of profits, interest, and civil fines totaling $112,000 and $2.7 million, respectively.

Stewart issued a statement saying she and her broker had agreed on a $60 sell order in October 2001, that he had called her on December 27 and told her ImClone was trading under $60, and that she had told him to sell in line with their prior understanding. She denied having nonpublic information at the time. Later in the month she repeated this story at a conference for securities analysts and investors. Her intent was to halt the decline in her company's shares. At this time she held 61,323,850 shares and had suffered paper losses of more than $462 million over three weeks.

Douglas Faneuil's conscience bothered him. In late June he went to a manager at Merrill Lynch and volunteered what he believed was the complete and accurate story of December 27 and its aftermath. Subsequently, he spoke again to government investigators, who then subpoenaed both Stewart and Bacanovic to testify at an investigative hearing. This time, both declined, invoking their Fifth Amendment privilege against self-incrimination. Faneuil pled guilty to a misdemeanor charge of accepting money from Bacanovic in return for not informing federal investigators of illegal conduct. Merrill Lynch fired Bacanovic.

INDICTMENTS

It took the government a year and a half, but on June 4, 2003, in a "coordinated action," both the U.S. Attorney's Office and the SEC filed indictments against Martha Stewart and Peter Bacanovic.

The U.S. Attorney's Office filed a criminal complaint with multiple counts under the basic charges of, first, conspiracy, and second, obstruction of justice and making false statements.[10] The two were charged with conspiring to conceal evidence that Bacanovic had given nonpublic information about ImClone to Stewart. And they were accused of lying to government attorneys to hamper the investigation. In addition, only Martha Stewart was charged with securities fraud. The charge was that she had made a series of false statements about her innocence to mislead investors and prop up her company's share price. Conviction on all counts could bring a maximum of 30 years in prison and a fine of $2 million. Bacanovic alone was additionally charged with perjury for altering the worksheet that listed Stewart's stocks by adding "@60" near ImClone to fool investigators. He faced a maximum of 25 years in prison and a $1.25 million fine.

In its separate civil action, the SEC charged Stewart and Bacanovic with insider trading.[11] It sought disgorgement of illegal gains and the imposition of a fine. In addition, it sought to bar Stewart from acting as a director or officer of a public company.

---

[8] Misdemeanor Information, *United States v. Faneuil*, 02 Cr. 1287, S.D.N.Y. (2002), pp. 7–8.

[9] Ibid., p. 8.

[10] *United States v. Martha Stewart and Peter Bacanovic*, 03 Cr. 717 (MGC)(S.D.N.Y.), 2003.

[11] *Securities and Exchange Commission v. Martha Stewart and Peter Bacanovic*, 03 CV 4070 (NRB)(S.D.N.Y), 2003.

Martha Stewart's lawyers immediately issued a statement challenging the government's case. "Martha Stewart has done nothing wrong," they said. They accused the government of making an "unprecedented" interpretation of the securities laws when it charged her with fraudulent manipulation simply because she spoke out publicly to maintain her innocence. And they questioned the government's motive for the other charges, raising themes that would course through the media during the subsequent trial.

> Is it for publicity purposes because Martha Stewart is a celebrity? Is it because she is a woman who has successfully competed in a man's business world by virtue of her talent, hard work and demanding standards? Is it because the government would like to be able to define securities fraud as whatever it wants it to be?[12]

A week later, Martha Stewart went to the FBI's Manhattan office for processing. She was given a mug shot, fingerprinted, and released without bail. She also resigned her positions as director and chief creative officer of Martha Stewart Living Omnimedia, taking on the nonofficer position of founding editorial director. She continued to receive her annual salary of $900,000 and in 2003 she was awarded a $500,000 bonus.

THE TRIAL OPENS

On January 20, 2004, Martha Stewart and Peter Bacanovic appeared in the Manhattan courtroom of the Hon. Miriam Goldman Cedarbaum, a federal district court judge with 18 years' bench experience. They entered pleas of not guilty and jury selection began. Potential jurors were given 35 pages of questions designed to detect biases. One question was, "Have you ever made a project or cooked a recipe from Martha Stewart?"[13] Eight women and four men were picked.

The trial began January 27. The lead prosecutor was Assistant U.S. Attorney Karen Patton Seymour. In her opening argument she told the jury that Martha Stewart sold ImClone after a "secret tip" from Bacanovic that the Waksals were selling. Then, she and Bacanovic tried to cover it up. Stewart's motive, she argued, was a desire to protect her multimillion-dollar business empire. Seymour pointed out that every $1 decline in the stock price of Martha Stewart's company decreased her net worth by $30 million. "Ladies and gentlemen," she said, "lying to federal agents, obstructing justice, committing perjury, fabricating evidence and cheating investors in the stock market—these are serious federal crimes."[14]

In his opening argument Stewart's attorney, Robert G. Morvillo, pronounced her "innocent of all charges" and tried to offer reasonable explanations for her actions. He pointed out that the ImClone shares she sold were less than 1 percent of her net worth. He told the jury that December was a busy month for her and she gets worn out. When she called Faneuil about the trade she was in a noisy airport on her cell phone and thought she was talking to Bacanovic. She had no way of knowing that insider trading was taking place. "How," he asked, "was she supposed to figure out the broker, who has always been honorable, was asking her to commit a crime?" If, indeed, she had been told that Waksal and his daughter were selling, it meant that Merrill Lynch was making the sales, which it would not do if it believed them to be illegal.

Morvillo explained that Stewart and Bacanovic had established a $60 sell agreement the week before her trades. And he called Stewart's alteration of her assistant's entry in the phone log "much ado about nothing." He said that she was changing it "to be consistent with what she recalled," but then quickly realized that her change "might be misconstrued." He concluded his opening statement by asking the jury to "decide the case based upon what is correct and just."[15]

TESTIMONY

Key witnesses for the government were Helen Glotzer, an SEC attorney, and Catherine Farmer, an FBI agent. Both had been present at interviews of Stewart and

[12] Robert G. Morvillo and John J. Tigue, "Press Statement," June 4, 2003, at www.marthatalks.com/trial.

[13] Thomas S. Mulligan, "Stewart Case Poses Challenges for All Parties as Trial Begins Today," *Los Angeles Times,* January 20, 2004, p. C1.

[14] Kara Scannel and Matthew Rose, "Early Sparks at the Stewart Trial," *The Wall Street Journal,* January 28, 2004, p. C1.

[15] Quotations of Morvillo are from "Opening Argument on Behalf of Martha Stewart," January 27, 2004, at www.marthatalks.com/trial.

Bacanovic and both testified about apparent false statements, including Stewart's denial that she spoke with Faneuil on December 27 and her denial that she knew that the Waksals were selling.

The government's star witness, however, was Douglas Faneuil. Under questioning by Seymour, Faneuil described his morning phone call to Bacanovic on December 27. On learning that the Waksals were selling Bacanovic said: "Oh my God, you've got to get Martha on the phone!" Faneuil said that he then asked Bacanovic, "Can I tell her about Sam? Am I allowed to?" "Of course," replied Bacanovic, "That's the whole point."[16] When Martha Stewart called in that afternoon, she asked, "What's going on with Sam?" Faneuil said that he told her, "We have no news about the company, but we thought you might like to act on the information that Sam is selling all his shares." He described her end of the conversation as a series of "clipped demands."

Faneuil also recounted how Bacanovic had tried to pull him into a cover-up. He described a scene at a coffee shop near their office in which he told Bacanovic, "I was on the phone. I know what happened." In response Bacanovic put an arm around him and said, "With all due respect, no, you don't."[17]

During cross-examination Bacanovic's attorney, David Apfel, tried to tarnish Faneuil as an unreliable witness. He called Faneuil an admitted liar who had changed his story seeking leniency from prosecutors. He brought out Faneuil's use of recreational drugs. And he introduced e-mail messages by Faneuil to show that he disliked Martha Stewart and might have held a grudge against her. One read: "I just spoke to MARTHA! I have never, ever been treated more rudely by a stranger on the telephone." Another was: "Martha yelled at me again today, but I snapped in her face and she actually backed down! Baby put Ms. Martha in her place!!!"[18] Faneuil also testified about a time when he put Martha Stewart on hold. When he came back on the line she threatened to pull her account from Merrill Lynch unless the hold music was changed. Jurors laughed.

Faneuil's testimony took 13 hours over six days. On his last day he was cross-examined by Stewart's attorney Morvillo, who tried to depict him as overwhelmed by the rush of events on December 27. He pointed out that Faneuil had taken 75 phone calls that day and some e-mails. He questioned why his memory of Stewart's call was sharp, in contrast to some other calls about which he was less clear. He got Faneuil to admit that he suspected the Waksals of insider trading, but said nothing to Bacanovic.

Following Faneuil, Stewart's administrative assistant Ann Armstrong was called to testify about how Stewart altered the message of Bacanovic's call. Taking the stand, she began to sob. After getting a glass of water from the defense table she tried to resume, but could not. Judge Cedarbaum recessed the trial to the next day, when Armstrong recounted how Stewart first altered, then instructed her to restore, the wording of the phone message.

Maria Pasternak was a friend who had been traveling with Martha Stewart on December 27. Pasternak related conversations with Stewart at a resort in Los Cabos over the following days. She said Stewart told her that the Waksals were trying to sell all their shares in ImClone and that she had sold all her shares. She testified that Stewart remarked, "Isn't it nice to have brokers who tell you those things?" But under cross-examination she vacillated about the clarity of her recall. The judge instructed jurors to disregard the remark.

An expert ink analyst with the U.S. Secret Service was called for his analysis of Bacanovic's tax sale worksheet. Larry Stewart, who is not related to Martha Stewart, testified that tests he conducted showed two pens had been used on the worksheet. All the notations on it, except "@60," were made by a "cheap" Paper Mate pen. The "@60" was written with a second, unidentified pen. The second pen did not match any of 8,500 ink samples on record, so he concluded it was either foreign or very rare.[19] This was important evidence for the prosecution, which argued that the "@60" had been added only after December 27, when the defendants constructed a cover-up.

After the prosecution finished its case, Martha Stewart's lawyers elected to use a minimal defense. They called only one witness, a former Stewart lawyer

[16] Brooke A. Masters, "Broker's Aide Says He Was Told to Tip Off Stewart," *The Washington Post,* February 3, 2004, p. E1.

[17] Testimony quoted in Constance L. Hays, "Witness Describes Stewart Cover-Up," *The New York Times,* February 5, 2004, p. C4.

[18] Brooke A. Masters, "Broker's Assistant, Stewart Clashed," *The Washington Post,* February 5, 2004, p. E1.

[19] Matthew Rose and Kara Scannell, "Stewart Trial Gets Testimony of a Broker's Tip," *The Wall Street Journal,* February 20, 2004, p. C3.

and note-taker at the February 4 meeting with investigators, who testified for only 15 minutes. There was much speculation about whether Martha Stewart would take the stand in her own defense. If she did, prosecutors would push her, try to trap her in inconsistencies and provoke her temper. If she did not, the intense curiosity of the jurors to learn what she could say to them would be unfulfilled. In the end, she did not take the stand.

Late in the trial Judge Cedarbaum dismissed the government's allegations of securities fraud. This charge had met with wide skepticism from the beginning. How could a defendant exercise her right to speak out in self-defense if doing so could be construed as criminal manipulation of share prices? Cedarbaum held that, given the evidence, no reasonable juror could find her guilty beyond a reasonable doubt.[20]

After the defense called its single witness, there had been 27 witnesses during 19 days of testimony. Closing arguments came on March 2. Prosecutor Michael Schachter told jurors that Stewart and Bacanovic believed they would never be caught. But mistakes they made trying to deceive left a trail of damning inconsistencies. He carefully listed contradictions in their stories. Bacanovic's lawyer gave a closing argument trying once again to undermine the credibility of Douglas Faneuil's testimony.

In his closing argument for Martha Stewart, Morvillo ridiculed the conspiracy charge, saying the events alleged by the government amounted to "a confederation of dunces."[21] Nobody, he argued, "could have done what Peter Bacanovic and Martha Stewart are alleged to have done and done it in a dumber fashion." He asked the jurors to consider that if the two had really conspired they would have been much more consistent in their stories. Their inconsistencies were a sign of innocence. This was a dangerous argument, because it conceded some contradictions in testimony.

Morvillo then made the case for Stewart's innocence. She had no evidence that anything was wrong with the trade. She had no reason to suspect that Waksal would behave so foolishly as to trade during a blackout period. She had a preexisting agreement with her broker to trade ImClone if it fell below $60. She could not hear well enough on the phone to know she was talking to Faneuil, not Bacanovic. The amount of the trade was too small to tempt jeopardizing her future. Her change in Ann Armstrong's telephone log was insignificant. Faneuil was an untrustworthy witness. Finally, he explained that she did not take the stand because she twice testified on the record at investigative hearings two years before and "her recollection [of the events] hasn't gotten any better." He concluded with this.

> This has been a two-year ordeal for this good woman. It's an ordeal based on the fact that she trusted her financial adviser not to put her in a compromising position. It's an ordeal based on the fact that she voluntarily submitted to a government interview. And it's an ordeal that is in the process of wiping out all the good that she has done, all her contributions, all her accomplishments . . . Martha Stewart's life is in your hands . . . I ask you to acquit Martha Stewart. I ask you to let her return to her life of improving the quality of life for all of us. If you do that, it's a good thing.[22]

THE VERDICT

The jury deliberated for 14 hours over three days. On March 5 one female juror wept as the verdicts were announced. Stewart and Bacanovic were each found guilty on four counts of lying and conspiring to lie to conceal the fact that she had been tipped with insider information. However, the jury could not agree that the government had proved beyond a reasonable doubt its allegation that Stewart and Bacanovic fabricated the $60 sale agreement and it acquitted them on those counts.

Jurors described their deliberations as calm. They found Faneuil credible and gave much weight to his testimony. Ann Armstrong was also an important witness because she cried. "We feel that she knew that something was wrong," said the forewoman. Jurors were also suspicious of the January 16 breakfast meeting between Stewart and Bacanovic and they felt cynical about Stewart hiring a criminal defense lawyer even before she was contacted by government investigators. They put little stock in the

[20] *United States v. Martha Stewart and Peter Bacanovic,* 305 F. Supp. 2d 368, February 27, 2004.

[21] "Closing Argument on Behalf of Martha Stewart," March 2, 2004, at www.marthatalks.com/trial, p. 1.

[22] Ibid., p. 10.

Martha Stewart outside the Manhattan courthouse after hearing the verdict. Source: © AP Photo/Julie Jacobson.

"conspiracy of dunces" argument. "We felt that she was a smart lady who made a dumb mistake," said the forewoman.[23]

A juror named Chappell Hartridge characterized the verdict as "a victory for the little guys who lose money in the market because of these kinds of transactions."[24] After looking into Hartridge's background, Stewart's legal team believed he had not been completely honest on his jurors' questionnaire. When asked about contacts with law enforcement, he did not disclose an arrest for assaulting a former girlfriend, and several other problems. Arguing that they would have exercised a challenge to keep Chappell off the jury had they known, her lawyers moved for a new trial. Judge Cedarbaum ruled that the allegations were little more than hearsay and there was no evidence that bias in Chappell affected the verdict.[25]

Meanwhile, prosecutors had filed a criminal complaint against Larry Stewart, the ink expert who testified at the trial. Stewart was accused of perjury for saying that he had conducted the ink tests after a co-worker came forward saying that, in fact, she had done them. Again Stewart's attorneys filed a motion for retrial. Again Cedarbaum denied the motion, because "there was no reasonable likelihood that this perjury could have affected the jury's verdict, and because overwhelming independent evidence supports the verdict . . ."[26] Subsequently, Larry Stewart was tried and, based on evidence that his co-worker had a history of harassment, acquitted of perjury.[27]

SENTENCING

On July 16, 2004, Martha Stewart appeared before Judge Cedarbaum. Addressing the judge, she appealed for leniency, saying, "Today is a shameful day. I ask that in judging me, you remember all the good I've done and the contributions I've made." Prosecutor Seymour countered, arguing that Stewart was "asking for leniency far beyond" that justified for "a serious offense with broad implications" for the justice system. Judge Cedarbaum responded, "I believe that you have suffered, and will continue to suffer, enough."[28] Her sentence was five months' imprisonment followed by five months' of home confinement. She was fined $30,000. This set of penalties was at the light end of what could have been imposed under federal sentencing guidelines and showed that Judge Cedarbaum was using what discretion she had to avoid a harsh sentence.

After the sentencing, Martha Stewart emerged from the courthouse to read a less contrite statement. "I'm just very, very sorry that it's come to this, that a small personal matter has been able to be blown out of all proportion, and with such venom and such gore—I mean, it's just terrible."[29]

At a separate hearing that day, Peter Bacanovic received a nearly identical sentence of five months in prison, five months of home confinement, and a $4,000 fine. A week later Daniel Faneuil appeared before Judge Cedarbaum. Tearfully, he apologized for

[23] Kara Scannell, Matthew Rose, and Laurie P. Cohen, "In Stewart Case, Reluctant Jurors Found Guilt after Skimpy Defense," *The Wall Street Journal*, March 8, 2004, p. A1.

[24] Constance L. Hays, "Martha Stewart Seeks New Trial, Saying a Juror Lied," *The New York Times*, April 1, 2004, p. C3.

[25] *United States v. Martha Stewart and Peter Bacanovic*, 317 F. Supp. 2d 426, May 5, 2004.

[26] *United States v. Martha Stewart and Peter Bacanovic*, 323 F. Supp. 2d 606, July 8, 2004.

[27] "Jurors Acquit Stewart Witness," *Los Angeles Times*, October 6, 2004, p. C3.

[28] Thomas S. Mulligan, "Stewart Gets 5 Months in Prison, Then Delivers a Plug for Her Firm," *Los Angeles Times*, July 17, 2004, p. A4.

[29] Ibid., p. A1.

his actions. His cooperation with federal prosecutors saved him from going to prison. His sentence was a $2,000 fine.

On October 8, Martha Stewart reported to a minimum-security prison camp in West Virginia to begin her incarceration. She had appealed her case, but the appeal was expected to take two years. Therefore, she elected to serve her sentence. Doing so would end much of the speculation and tumult affecting both her and her company.

She served her time. In prison she worked in the garden and cleaned the warden's office for 12 cents an hour. She disliked the food but made some friends among the other women. She gave them yoga lessons and a seminar on entrepreneurship. Her last day of home confinement (extended three weeks due to a violation that was not publicly explained) ended on September 1, 2005. In 2006 a federal appeals court turned down her request to overturn her conviction.[30] Then she settled with the SEC, which had brought a civil case of insider trading against her in 2003. In the settlement, she neither admitted nor denied guilt. She agreed to a five-year ban on serving as an officer or director of her company and a $195,081 fine. In the same settlement,

Bacanovic agreed to a fine of $75,645.[31] Stewart's legal troubles were finally over with the end of court-ordered probation in March 2007.

Questions

1. Did Martha Stewart commit the crime of insider trading when she sold her ImClone shares on December 27, 2001?

2. Did the U.S. attorneys and the Securities and Exchange Commission use good judgment in indicting Martha Stewart? Do you believe that her indictment was based on evidence of a serious crime, or do you believe that prosecutors consciously or unconsciously had additional motives for pursuing the case?

3. Do you agree with the jury that she was guilty beyond a reasonable doubt of the conspiracy and obstruction of justice charges?

4. Was her punishment, including both imprisonment and fines, appropriate? Were the punishments of Peter Bacanovic and Douglas Faneuil appropriate?

---

[30] *U.S. v. Martha Stewart and Peter Bacanovic,* 433F. 3d 273 (2006).

[31] See Securities and Exchange Commission, Litigation Release No. 19794, *SEC v. Martha Stewart and Peter Bacanovic,* 03 Civ. 4070 (RJH) (S.D.N.Y.), August 7, 2006.

Chapter Eight

Making Ethical Decisions in Business

David Geffen

David Geffen entered the world in 1943, the son of poor Russian immigrants. His father, Abe, was without ambition or talent, a passive man, often unemployed, who deferred to life. His mother, Batya, a bustling, pugnacious woman, supported the family making brassieres and corsets in their small apartment. She doted over young David, teaching him worldly lessons as she went about her business. Among them, apparently, was integrity. "She taught me to tell the truth," he would later say.[1]

Batya accepted and praised David even as he turned into a brash young boy. His elementary school teachers found him voluble, impulsive, and hard to discipline. He was also adventurous. At 10 he took trains into Manhattan by himself, getting off at the Times Square station and walking to see Broadway musicals. Show business was another world. It fascinated him. At home he filled out applications in different names for the CBS Record Club, joining it about 50 times to build a collection of show tunes from free sign-up offers. Meanwhile, on Broadway, he bought tickets for shows, then scalped them outside the theaters.[2]

Although Geffen was coming of age as an entrepreneur, he still had to face school. His grades were poor in junior high, and he sometimes forged his parents' signatures on report cards so they would not see. In high school he was enthusiastic about the drama club and involved himself in plays, but in class he rejected authority. An English teacher characterized him this way: "Rather talkative, self-centered, ignores teachers' orders and instructions. Is fresh, at times, and conceited, as well. Is not as good as he thinks he is."[3]

Geffen graduated from high school wanting to get rich in show business. Adversity, its source in his nature, lay ahead. He immediately went to Los Angeles, where he found a menial job and attended night classes at a junior college, telling friends he was going to UCLA. Soon he dropped out of school and returned to New York

---

[1] Quoted in John Duka, "The Ego and the Art of David Geffen," *The New York Times,* October 3, 1982, sec. 3, p. 1.

[2] Tom King, *The Operator* (New York: Random House, 2000), p. 23.

[3] Quoted in King, *The Operator,* p. 32.

because his father was ill. He attended evening classes for a while, then, when his father died, left to attend the University of Texas at Austin. But he was impatient, unsuited for classrooms and libraries, and made little progress before dropping out, abandoning further efforts at formal education, and returning to Los Angeles. This time he found a job in entertainment, working as an usher at CBS Television City. But he was soon fired for trying to hit an audience member. Lacking funds, he went back to New York.

There Geffen got a job with a production company, but he was fired after two weeks. On his untimely departure a casting director suggested a good place to start in the entertainment industry was the mailroom of a talent agency. With résumé in hand, he applied to one agency where his lack of a college degree and irregular job history brought rejection. Geffen learned quickly, just not from textbooks. He telephoned a second agency, the William Morris Agency, saying he was a cousin of famous record producer Phil Spector. This was not true, although he had met Spector. However, the claim got him an interview. He appeared in a suit and tie, his résumé revised to show a theater arts degree from UCLA. He got the job.

In his first week a tremor went through the mailroom. A new trainee had been fired for lying on his application. Now knowing that the agency would check on his degree, Geffen came an hour early every day, going through each mailbag until, after several weeks, he found the letter from UCLA. Conspiring with his brother, a UCLA law school graduate, he counterfeited a confirming letter that saved his job.

From the mailroom a 21-year-old Geffen launched the career that made him "the richest man in Hollywood."[4] He worked harder and faster than others. He read everything that passed through the mailroom to learn how deals were done and even learned to read documents upside down when he stood at agents' desks. He stayed late and skipped vacations. Told that the agency's president, Nat Lefkowitz, worked on Saturdays, he came in too, lingering by the lobby elevators to run into him and impress him on the ride up. Soon Geffen had a mentor and Lefkowitz made him the secretary to an agent, the first step out of the mailroom. But another misadventure lay between Geffen and his destiny.

One day the agent Geffen worked for talked an employee of a rival agency into mailing a list of that agency's clients. This was a precious gem of competitor espionage. When it arrived, Geffen intercepted it in the mail, gave it to Lefkowitz, and took credit for it. The agent, Geffen's boss, was infuriated and fired him.

deontological ethics
The idea that actions are right and wrong in themselves independently of any consequences.

Geffen ran to Lefkowitz, begging to stay, later telling his brother he had said their mother had cancer and he needed the job to pay for her operation.[5] Geffen not only stayed, but Lefkowitz promoted him to assistant agent.

A lie is a false statement made with intent to deceive. It steals from others the power to make decisions that protect their rights or interests. Lies are condemned by those who believe that ethical rules such as telling the truth must always be followed, that actions are right or wrong in themselves, no matter the consequences. In moral philosophy this position is called *deontological* (dēŏn tĕ logical) *ethics* from the Greek word *deont,* meaning that which is binding.

[4] Bernard Weinraub, "David Geffen, Still Hungry," *The New York Times Magazine,* May 2, 1993, p. 28.
[5] King, *The Operator,* pp. 56–57.

Irrespective of moral admonitions Geffen was now on his way. His extraordinary qualities—a work ethic, audacity, and shrewdness—prevailed in a business that rewards such traits. He became an agent representing talent such as Janis Joplin and Bob Dylan, started record labels that produced 50 gold and 31 platinum albums, produced Broadway shows, including "Cats" and "Dreamgirls," and co-founded DreamWorks film studios. He would know presidents; own homes in Manhattan, Malibu, and Beverly Hills; fly in his own Gulfstream jet; and sell a painting by Jackson Pollock for more than a painting had ever sold for before. Along the way he joined Henry Ford, Thomas Edison, Steve Jobs, Bill Gates, and others who have prevailed without a college degree. In recent years *Forbes* has listed his wealth at between $4 billion and $5 billion.

In 1980, in an act reflecting ignorance, disregard, or pardon of Geffen's earlier degree claim, Governor Jerry Brown appointed him to the University of California Board of Regents, the governing body that presides over UCLA and the other system campuses. He served for seven years and was subsequently generous with his make-believe alma mater. To support the UCLA theater arts program he donated $5 million for a theater building, which was named the Geffen Playhouse. Later, saying "each of us has a responsibility to give back in some way," he gave $200 million to UCLA's medical school, which was renamed the David Geffen School of Medicine.[6]

consequentialism
The idea that actions are right or wrong, in part or whole, based on their consequences.

Looking back, Geffen's achievements and atonements can be weighed against his early indiscretions. A school of moral philosophy called *consequentialism* holds that actions are right or wrong based on their consequences. This perspective is less majestic than its deontological competitor. It affirms the simple maxim: the greatest good for the greatest number. His career has brought countless hours of entertainment

David Geffen in 1993. Source: Lynn Goldsmith/ CORBIS.

[6] Quoted in Jill Feiwell, "Geffen Gives UCLA $200 Million," *Daily Variety,* May 8, 2002, p. 1.

to millions around the world, employment to tens of thousands, and, through his philanthropic gifts, advances in medicine and the arts.

Geffen's actions challenge moral philosophy. If ethical rules must without exception be followed and doing wrong is never right, his legacy is flawed. If ethical thinking must judge not just the action, but also its consequences for the overall good, if what happens later counts, then the balance tips to a moral outcome.

In this chapter we will discuss a wide range of principles and approaches to making ethical decisions. These include intuitive judgment, principles great and small, procedures that corporations suggest to their employees, and practical tips.

PRINCIPLES OF ETHICAL CONDUCT

We begin with a compendium of ethical principles—some ancient, some modern. There are many such principles in the philosophical and religious traditions of East and West.

From a larger universe, we set forth 14 principles that every manager should know and think about. (See the accompanying box and discussion that follows.) The 14 principles here are fundamental guides or rules for behavior. Each of them has strengths and weaknesses. Some were created to be universal tests of conduct. Others have a more limited reach and apply only in certain spheres of human relations. Some are ideals. Others accommodate balancing of interests where perfection is elusive. A few invite compromise and can be used to rationalize flawed behavior. One principle, might equals right, is a justification for ignoble acts, but we include it here because it has been a basis of ethical reasoning since time immemorial.

These principles distill basic wisdom from 2,000 years of ethical thought. To the extent that they offer ideas for thinking about and resolving ethical dilemmas, they are not vague abstractions but useful, living guides to analysis and conduct.[7] We present them alphabetically.

The Categorical Imperative

categorical imperative
Act only according to that maxim by which you can at the same time will that it should become a universal law.

The *categorical imperative* (meaning, literally, a command that admits no exception) is a guide for ethical behavior set forth by the German philosopher Immanuel Kant in his *Foundations of the Metaphysics of Morals,* a tract published in 1785. In Kant's words: "Act only according to that maxim by which you can at the same time will that it should become a universal law."[8]

In other words, one should not adopt principles of action unless they can, without inconsistency, be adopted by everyone. Lying, stealing, and breaking promises, for example, are ruled out because society would disintegrate if they replaced

---

[7] T. K. Das asked managers to rank the favorability of these principles for use in business decisions in "How Strong Are the Ethical Preferences of Senior Business Executives," *Journal of Business Ethics,* January 2005. Among the 14 ethical principles discussed in this chapter, they ranked the Golden Rule most favorably and the Conventionalist Ethic least favorably.

[8] Immanuel Kant, *Foundations of the Metaphysics of Morals,* trans. Lewis White Beck (Indianapolis: Bobbs-Merrill, 1969), p. 44; written in 1785.

Fourteen Ethical Principles

The Categorical Imperative   Act only according to that maxim by which you can at the same time will that it should become a universal law.

The Conventionalist Ethic   Business is like a game with permissive ethics and any action that does not violate the law is permitted.

The Disclosure Rule   Test an ethical decision by asking how you would feel explaining it to a wider audience such as newspaper readers, television viewers, or your family.

The Doctrine of the Mean   Virtue is achieved through moderation. Avoid behavior that is excessive or deficient of a virtue.

The Ends–Means Ethic   The end justifies the means.

The Golden Rule   Do unto others what you would have them do unto you.

The Intuition Ethic   What is good or right is understood by an inner moral sense based on character development and felt as intuition.

Might-Equals-Right Ethic   Justice is the interest of the stronger.

The Organization Ethic   Be loyal to the organization.

The Principle of Equal Freedom   A person has the right to freedom of action unless such action deprives another person of a proper freedom.

The Proportionality Ethic   A set of rules for making decisions having both good and evil consequences.

The Rights Ethic   Each person has protections and entitlements that others have a duty to respect.

The Theory of Justice   Each person should act fairly toward others in order to maintain the bonds of community.

The Utilitarian Ethic   The greatest good for the greatest number.

---

truth telling, property rights, and vow keeping. Using this guideline, a manager faced with a moral choice must act in a way that he or she believes is right and just for any person in a similar situation. Each action should be judged by asking: "Could this act be turned into a universal code of behavior?" This quick *test of universalizability* has achieved great popularity.

test of universalizability
Could this act be turned into a universal code of behavior?

Kant was an extreme perfectionist. He walked the same route each day at the same time, appearing at places along the route so punctually that neighbors set their clocks by him. Before leaving his house he attached strings to the top of his socks and connected them to a spring apparatus held by his belt. As he walked, the contraption would pull the slack out of his socks. To no one's surprise, his ethical philosophies are perfectionist also, and that is their weakness. Kant's categorical imperative is a deontological ethic of the kind discussed in the story about David Geffen. It commands ethical action now; it weighs no future consequences. In this it is dogmatic and inflexible, a general rule that must be applied in every specific situation. There are no exceptions. But real life challenges the simple, single ethical law. If a competitor asks whether your company is planning to sell shirts in Beijing next year, must you answer the question with the truth?

The Conventionalist Ethic

This is the view that business is analogous to a game and special, lower ethics are permissible. In business, people may act to further their self-interest so long as

conventionalist ethic
Business is like a game with permissive ethics and actions that do not violate the law are permitted.

they do not violate the law. The *conventionalist ethic*, which has a long history, was popularized some years ago by Albert Z. Carr in *Business as a Game.*[9] "If an executive allows himself to be torn between a decision based on business considerations and one based on his private ethical code," explained Carr, "he exposes himself to a grave psychological strain."[10]

Business may be regarded as a game, such as poker, in which the rules are different from those we adopt in personal life. Assuming game ethics, managers are allowed to bluff (a euphemism for lie) and to take advantage of all legal opportunities and widespread practices or customs. Carr used two examples of situations in which game ethics were permissible. In the first, an out-of-work sales agent with a good employment record feared discrimination because of his age—58. He dyed his hair and stated on his résumé that he was 45. In the second, a job applicant was asked to check off magazines he read, but decided not to check off *Playboy, The Nation,* or *The New Republic.* Though he read them, he did not want to be labeled controversial. He checked the *Reader's Digest* instead. [11]

The conventionalist ethic is criticized by those who make no distinction between society's ethics and business ethics. They argue that commerce defines the life chances of millions and is not a game to be taken lightly. As a principle, the conventionalist ethic is a thin justification for deceptive behavior at the office.

The Disclosure Rule

disclosure rule
Test an ethical decision by asking how you would feel explaining it to a wider audience such as newspaper readers, television viewers, or your family.

Using the *disclosure rule*, a manager faced with an ethical dilemma asks how it would feel to explain the decision to a wider audience. This simple idea appears in many company ethics codes. Here are two examples.

- Google: When faced with a potential conflict of interest, ask yourself: Would this relationship or situation embarrass me or Google if it showed up on the front page of a local newspaper or the top of a blog?[12]
- Western Union: When faced with a tough situation, ask yourself which course of action . . . [w]ould look better if it were printed in your local newspaper? Would you feel more comfortable explaining to your family? A judge?[13]

The disclosure rule is a mental exercise that invokes the potential for emotional distress. Censure by a community or family members brings shame, humiliation, guilt, and regret. This imaginary test screens out base conduct such as lying and theft, which are unacceptable if disclosed, but it does not always give full guidance for ethical dilemmas in which decent arguments exist for alternative actions. Also, an action that sounds acceptable if disclosed may not, upon reflection, always be the most ethical.

---

[9] Albert Z. Carr, *Business as a Game* (New York: New American Library, 1968).

[10] "Is Business Bluffing Ethical," *Harvard Business Review,* January–February 1968, p. 149.

[11] Carr, *Business as a Game,* p. 142.

[12] Google, "Google Code of Conduct," April 8, 2009, at http://investor.google.com/conduct.html.

[13] Western Union Company, *Code of Conduct* (Englewood, CO: Western Union Company), 2006, pp. 2–3.

The Doctrine of the Mean

doctrine of the mean
Virtue is achieved through moderation. Avoid behavior that is excessive or deficient of a virtue.

This ethic, set forth by Aristotle in the *Nicomachean Ethics* and sometimes called the *golden mean,* calls for virtue through moderation.[14] Right actions are found in the area between extreme behaviors, which are labeled as excess on the one hand and deficient on the other. Facing an ethical decision, a person first identifies the ethical virtue at its core (such as truthfulness) and then seeks the mean or moderate course of action between an excess of that virtue (boastfulness) and a deficiency of it (understatement).

At ITT, Harold Geneen pushed managers to extraordinary personal sacrifices. Their time, energy, loyalty, and will were bent to corporate purposes. Obsessive work led to remarkable business successes. During his tenure earnings increased for an incredible 58 consecutive quarters. And 130 of the managers he trained went on to take top positions at other companies.[15] Yet, it also led to personal difficulties such as marital problems. While the work of ITT was constructive and ethical, its demands led some to sacrifice a balanced life.[16] To Aristotle, this would have been wrong.

The doctrine of the mean is today little recognized, but the underlying notion of moderation as a virtue lingers in Western societies. The doctrine itself is inexact. To observe it is simply to act conservatively, never in the extreme. The moderate course and specific virtues such as honesty, however, are defined as aspects existing between and defined in relation to polar extremes. What they are is open to wide interpretation.

The Ends–Means Ethic

ends–means ethic
The end justifies the means.

This principle is age-old, appearing as an ancient Roman proverb, *existus acta probat,* or "the result validates the deeds." It is often associated with the Italian philosopher Niccolò Machiavelli. In *The Prince* (1513), Machiavelli argued that worthwhile ends justify efficient means, that when ends are of overriding importance or virtue, unscrupulous means may be employed to reach them.[17] When confronted with a decision involving an ethically questionable act, a person should ask whether some overall good—such as the survival of a country or business—justifies cutting corners.

In the 1980s Oracle Corporation grew rapidly. To get this growth, founder and CEO Lawrence J. Ellison pressed his sales managers to double revenues every year. Methods used by the frenzied sales force were watched less closely than its ability to hit targets. In 1993 the Securities and Exchange Commission fined Oracle for overstating earnings by double-billing customers, invoicing companies for products never sold, and violating accounting standards by recording sales

[14] *Nicomachean Ethics,* J. A. K. Thomson, trans. (New York: Penguin Books, 1982), book II, chap. 6.

[15] Alvin Moscow, "Introduction," in Harold Geneen, *Managing* (New York: Avon Books, 1984), pp. 5 and 13.

[16] Manuel Velasquez and Neil Brady, "Catholic Natural Law and Business Ethics," *Business Ethics Quarterly,* March 1997, p. 95.

[17] Niccolò Machiavelli, *The Prince,* trans. T. G. Bergin, ed. (New York: Appleton-Century-Crofts, 1947); written in 1513 and first published in 1532.

revenue before it was received.[18] However, by then Oracle had crushed its early competition in the relational database market. Today Oracle is a $27 billion corporation and Ellison is a billionaire. Oracle employs 105,000 people and has made many of them millionaires. Its software makes governments, businesses, and universities more productive. It pays taxes in 60 countries. It has a wide range of social responsibility programs. Did belief in this end result justify the competitive tactics used to build the company?

Any manager using unscrupulous means concedes the highest virtue and accepts the necessity of ethical compromise. In solving ethical problems, means may be as important, or more so, than ends. In addition, the process of ethical character development can never be furthered by the use of expedient means.

The Golden Rule

Golden Rule
Do unto others as you would have them do unto you.

An ideal found in the great religions and in works of philosophy, the *Golden Rule* has been a popular guide for centuries. Simply put, it is: "Do unto others as you would have them do unto you." It includes not knowingly doing harm to others. A manager trying to solve an ethical problem places him- or herself in the position of another party affected by the decision and tries to figure out what action is most fair from that perspective.

practical imperative
Treat others as ends in themselves, not as means to other goals. This principle prohibits selfish manipulation of other people.

A related principle called the *practical imperative* was set forth by Immanuel Kant. It is: "Act so that you treat humanity, whether in your own person or in that of another, always as an end and never as a means only."[19] This principle admonishes a manager to treat employees as ends in themselves, not to manipulate them simply as factors of production for the self-interested ends of the company.

Around 1900, when E. H. Harriman owned the Southern Pacific railroad, train accidents killed between 5,000 and 6,000 people a year. One day on an inspection tour, his train hit a rough section of track and nearly derailed because a work crew had neglected to post a flagman. Instead of firing the crew chief, Harriman insisted on firing the whole crew. A top executive spoke up, arguing it was cruel to punish them all. "Perhaps," responded Harriman, "but it will probably save a lot of lives. I want every man connected with the operation to feel a sense of responsibility. Now, everybody knew that the man hadn't gone back with the flag."[20] Harriman used this crew of workers to send a message to all other crews. The workers were not treated as individuals; they were punished en masse to signal others in the company.

test of reversibility
Would you be willing to change places with the person or persons affected by your actions?

A manager may comply with both the practical imperative and the Golden Rule by using the *test of reversibility*, that is, by asking if he or she would change places with the person affected by the contemplated action. A problem with the Golden Rule is that people's ethical values differ, and they may mistakenly assume that their preferences are universal. In addition, it is primarily a perfectionist rule for

[18] Mike Wilson, *The Difference between God and Larry Ellison* (New York: William Morrow, 1997), p. 239.
[19] Kant, *Foundations of the Metaphysics of Morals*, p. 54.
[20] Quoted in Maury Klein, *The Life & Legend of E. H. Harriman* (Chapel Hill: University of North Carolina Press, 2000), p. 266.

interpersonal relations. So applying it in business life where the interests of individuals are subordinated to the needs of the firm is sometimes hard.

The Intuition Ethic

intuition ethic
What is good or right is understood by an inner moral sense based on character development and felt as intuition.

The *intuition ethic*, as defined by philosophers such as G. E. Moore in his *Principia Ethica*, holds that what is good is simply understood.[21] That is, people are endowed with a moral sense by which they intuitively know the difference between right and wrong. The solution to an ethical problem lies in what you sense or understand to be right or wrong without resort to conscious reasoning.

People facing an ethical decision can experience a rapid, emotional reaction before they make any conscious effort to search for facts, weigh evidence, and reach a conclusion. The situation just bothers them, even if they are not sure why in the instant. Something is wrong. This ethical intuition, according to philosophers, is not simply ungrounded opinion. A person's ethical instincts are the product of socialization, role expectations, education, and experience. Everyone carries a lifetime of moral lessons that can well up in an instant emotional reaction. Though fallible, intuition is usually accurate. As we will see later in this chapter, the idea of an ethical intuition is more than speculative; it has a solid basis in the physiology of the brain.

Many companies recognize the intuition ethic in their conduct codes and offer it as a simple guideline for employees. At Cummins Inc., for example, employees are told to ask, "Do I feel uncomfortable with this particular course of action? If the answer is yes, don't do it."[22] At Dow Chemical Company employees are to ask: "What feels right or wrong about the situation or action?"[23]

Ethical intuition is reliable, but not infallible. Self-interest can be confused with ethical insight. No standard of validation exists outside the individual. It is unpersuasive to others for a manager to say, "It's wrong because I just think so."[24] Also, intuition may fail to give a clear answer when ethical norms are in conflict.

The Might-Equals-Right Ethic

might equals right
Justice is the interest of the stronger.

The classic statement of this ancient ethic is that of Thracymachus (thră-sǐm'-ă-cǔs), an Athenian teacher of rhetoric who argued with Socrates that justice is "nothing but what is the interest of the stronger."[25] No era since has been without both its expression and its practice. In business this thinking is expressed in some competitive strategies and marketing tactics. What is ethical is what a stronger individual or company has the power to impose on a weaker one. When faced with an ethical decision, people should seize what advantage they are strong enough to take, without regard for lofty sentiments.

[21] G. E. Moore, *Principia Ethica* (Cambridge: Cambridge University Press, 1903).

[22] *Cummins Code of Business Conduct* (Columbus, IN: Cummins Inc., undated), p. ii.

[23] Dow Chemical Company, *Code of Business Conduct* (Midland, MI: Dow Chemical Company, September 2006), p. 2.

[24] For an excellent discussion of intuition in managers' decisions, see Joseph L. Badaracco, Jr., *Defining Moments* (Boston: Harvard Business School Press, 1997), chap. 4.

[25] *The Republic*, F. M. Cornford, trans. (New York: Oxford University Press, 1966), p. 18.

In the 1860s Ben Holladay, owner of the Overland Stage Line, perfected a competitive strategy based on overbearing power. He entered new routes with lowball coach fares, subsidizing this service with profits from monopoly routes, waiting until local competitors failed. In 1863 a small stage line between Denver and Central City in Colorado charged $6 per run. Holladay put an elegant new Concord Coach with a leather interior on the line and charged only $2. The competitor soon folded, then Holladay replaced the new stagecoach with a primitive vehicle resembling a freight wagon and raised the fare to $12.

The weakness of the might-equals-right ethic lies in its confusion of ethics with force. Exercising power is different than acting from ethical duty. An ethical principle that can be invalidated by its foundation (e.g., physical force) is not consistent, logical, or valid. Might equals right is not a legitimate approach in civilized settings. It invites retaliation and censure, and it is not conducive to long-term advantage. Seizure by power violates the bedrock ethical duty of reciprocity on which all societies are based.

The Organization Ethic

organization ethic
Be loyal to the organization.

Simply put, this principle is: "Be loyal to the organization." It implies that the wills and needs of individuals are subordinate to the overall welfare of the organization (be it a corporation, government, university, or army). A member should act consistent with the organization's goals. This ethic leads to cooperation and mutual trust.

Many employees have such deep loyalty to an organization that it transcends self-interest. Some Americans jeopardize their health and work excessively long hours without pay out of devotion to the employer. In Asian societies, which have strong collectivist values, identification with and commitment to companies is exceptionally strong. In Japan, workers are so afraid of letting down their work group or employer that they come to work despite broken limbs and serious ailments. This behavior is so common that a word for death from overwork, *karoshi,* has entered the Japanese language.

The ethical limits of obedience are reached when duty to the organization is used to rationalize wrongdoing. The Nuremberg trials, which convicted Nazis of war crimes, taught that Western society expects members of organizations to follow their conscience. Just as no war criminal argued successfully that taking orders in a military chain of command excused his behavior, so no business manager may claim to be the helpless prisoner of corporate loyalties that crush free will and justify wrongdoing.

You are sailing to Rome (you tell me) to obtain the post of Governor of Cnossus. You are not content to stay at home with the honours you had before; you want something on a larger scale, and more conspicuous. But when did you ever undertake a voyage for the purpose of reviewing your own principles and getting rid of any of them that proved unsound?

Source: Epictetus, *The Discourses* (circa. AD 120).

The Principle of Equal Freedom

principle of equal freedom
A person has the right to freedom of action unless such action deprives another person of a proper freedom.

This principle was set forth by the philosopher Herbert Spencer in his 1850 book *Social Statics*. "Everyman may claim the fullest liberty to exercise his faculties," said Spencer, "compatible with the possession of like liberty by every other man."[26] Thus, a person has the right to freedom of action unless such action deprives another person of a proper freedom. Spencer believed this was the first principle of ethical behavior in society because only when individual liberty was protected against infringement by others could human progress occur.

To use the principle, a person asks if an action will restrict others from actions that they have a legitimate right to undertake. Most people know the colloquial version: "Your right to swing your fist ends where my nose begins."

The principle of equal freedom lacks a tiebreaker for situations in which two rights conflict. Such situations require invocation of some additional rule to decide which right or freedom has priority. Ethically permissible management decisions may abridge the rights of some parties for the benefit of others. For example, all employees have broad privacy rights, but management invades them when it hires undercover detectives to investigate theft.

The Proportionality Ethic

proportionality
A set of rules for making decisions having both good and evil consequences.

Proportionality, an idea incubated in medieval Catholic theology, applies to decisions having both good and evil consequences. For instance, a maker of small-caliber, short-barreled, handguns that are irreverently called Saturday Night Specials has a dual impact on society. It makes available cheap, easily concealable weapons for criminals. Yet it also creates a supply of affordable self-defense weapons for poor people in crime-ridden areas who cannot afford high-quality handguns costing $1,000 and more. In this and similar cases, where a manager's action has a good effect but also entails a harm, the idea of proportionality fits.

principle of proportionality
Managers can risk predictable, but unwilled, harms to people after weighing five factors: type of good and evil, probability, urgency, intensity of influence, and alternatives.

A classic formulation of proportionality into a specific principle is Thomas M. Garrett's *principle of proportionality*. It states that managers are responsible for the consequences when they create situations leading to both good and evil effects. The principle allows them to risk predictable, but unwilled, harms to people (for example, innocent victims being shot by handguns) if they correctly weigh five factors.

First, managers must assess the *type of good and evil* involved, distinguishing between major and minor forms. Second, they should calculate the *urgency* of the situation. For example, would the firm go out of business unless employees were laid off? Third, they must estimate the *probability* of both good and evil effects. If good effects are certain and risks of serious harm are remote, an action is more favorable. Fourth, the *intensity of influence* over effects must be considered. In considering handgun injuries, for instance, manufacturers might assume that criminal action was an intervening force over which they had no control. Fifth, the existence of *alternatives* must be considered. If, for instance, an advertisement subtly encourages product misuse, the most ethical action might be to change it. Garrett

---

[26] Herbert Spencer, *Social Statics* (New York: Robert Schalkenbach Foundation, 1970), p. 69; first published in 1850.

principle of double effect
When both good and evil consequences result from a decision, a manager has acted ethically if the good outweighs the evil, if his or her intention is to achieve the good, and if there is no better alternative.

rights ethic
Each person has protections and entitlements that others have a duty to respect.

natural rights
Protections and entitlements that can be inferred by reason from the study of human nature.

legal rights
Protections and entitlements conferred by law.

theory of justice
Each person should act fairly toward others in order to maintain the bonds of community.

believed that taking these five factors into consideration would reveal fully the ethical dimension of a decision.[27]

An alternative formulation of the idea of proportionality is the *principle of double effect*, which is that in a situation from which both good and evil consequences are bound to result, a manager will act ethically if (1) the good effects outweigh the bad, (2) the manager's intention is to achieve the good effects, and (3) there is no better alternative.

These are intricate principles, requiring consideration of many factors. They force a manager to think about and weigh these factors in an organized way.

The Rights Ethic

Rights protect people against abuses and entitle them to important liberties. A strong philosophical movement defining *natural rights,* or rights that can be inferred by reason from the study of human nature, grew in Western Europe during the Enlightenment as a reaction against medieval religious persecutions. Over time, many such rights were given legal status and became *legal rights.*

Basic rights that are now widely accepted and protected in Western nations include the right to life; personal liberties such as expression, conscience, religious worship, and privacy; freedom from arbitrary, unjust police actions or unequal application of laws; and political liberties such as voting and lobbying. In Eastern societies, especially those transfused by the collectivist values of ancient Chinese culture, there is far less recognition of individual rights.

Rights imply duties. Because individuals have rights, many protected by law, other people have clear duties to respect them. For example, management should not permit operation of a dangerous machine because this would deprive workers of the right to a safe workplace. This right is based on the natural right to protection from harm by negligent actions of others and is legally established in common law and the Occupational Safety and Health Act. If some risk in operating a machine is unavoidable, workers have the right to be given an accurate risk assessment.

Theories of rights have great importance in American ethical debates. A problem caused by our reverence for rights is that they are sometimes stretched into selfish demands or entitlements. Rights are not absolute and their limits may be hard to define. For example, every person has a right to life, but industry daily exposes people to risk of death by releasing carcinogens into the environment. An absolute right to life would require cessation of much manufacturing activity (for example, petroleum refining). Rights, such as the right to life, are commonly abridged for compelling reasons of benefit to the public.

The Theory of Justice

A *theory of justice* defines what individuals must do for the common good of society. Maintaining the community is important because natural rights, such as the right to life, are reasonably protected only in a well-kept civil society. A basic principle of justice, then, is to act in such a way that the bonds of community are

---

[27] Thomas M. Garrett, *Business Ethics* (New York: Appleton-Century-Crofts, 1966), p. 8.

maintained. In broad terms, this means acting fairly toward others and establishing institutions in which people are subject to rules of fair treatment. In business life, justice requires fair relationships within the corporate community and using policies that treat its members fairly.

In society, a person's chances for justice are determined by basic economic and political arrangements. The design of institutions such as business corporations and political constitutions has a profound effect on the welfare and life chances of individuals. A contemporary philosopher, John Rawls, has developed an influential set of principles for the design of a just society. Rawls speculates that rational persons situated behind a hypothetical "veil of ignorance" and not knowing their place in a society (i.e., their social status, class position, economic fortune, intelligence, appearance, or the like) but knowing general principles of human society (such as those in political, economic, sociological, and psychological theories) would deliberate and choose two rules to ensure fairness in any society they created. First, "each person is to have an equal right to the most extensive basic liberty compatible with a similar liberty for others," and second, "social and economic inequalities are to be arranged so that they are both (a) reasonably expected to be to everyone's advantage, and (b) attached to positions and offices open to all."[28] In general, inequality would be allowed only if it would make better the lot of the most disadvantaged members of the society.

distributive justice
The benefits and burdens of company life should be distributed using impartial criteria.

The impartiality and equal treatment called for in Rawls' principles are resplendent in theory and could even inspire some business decisions, but they are best applied to an analysis of broad societal issues. Acting justly in daily business life, on the other hand, requires the application of maxims that more concretely define justice. Managers can find such guidelines in three basic spheres of justice, as shown in Figure 8.1.

Distributive justice requires that the benefits and burdens of company life be distributed using impartial criteria. Awarding pay raises based on friendship

FIGURE 8.1
Three Spheres of Justice

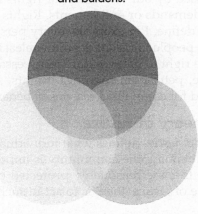

Distributive Justice
The distribution of benefits and burdens.

Compensatory Justice
Compensation for victims of injury.

Retributive Justice
Imposition of blame and punishment for wrongdoing.

[28] John Rawls, *A Theory of Justice* (Cambridge, MA: Harvard University Press, 1971), pp. 60–71.

retributive justice
Punishment should be evenhanded and proportionate to transgressions.

compensatory justice
Victims should receive fair compensation for damages.

utilitarian ethic
The greatest good for the greatest number.

rather than performance criteria is unfair. All laws, rules, and procedures should apply equally to each employee. *Retributive justice* requires punishment to be evenhanded and proportionate to transgressions. A cashier should not be fired for stealing $5 if an executive who embezzled $10,000 is allowed to stay on the job and pay it back. And *compensatory justice* requires fair compensation to victims. A corporation that damages nearby property must restore it to its original state; one that hurts a customer must pay damages. The general idea of fairness in such maxims of justice supports orderly communities and organizations in which people secure human rights and meet human needs.

The Utilitarian Ethic

The *utilitarian ethic* was developed between the late eighteenth century and the mid-nineteenth century by a line of English philosophers, including Jeremy Bentham and John Stuart Mill. The principle of utility, on which this ethic is based, is that actions that promote happiness are right and actions that cause unhappiness are wrong. The utilitarians advocated choosing alternatives that led to the greatest sum of happiness or, as we express the thought today, the greatest good for the greatest number.

In making a decision using this principle, one must determine whether the harm in an action is outweighed by the good. If the action maximizes benefit, then it is the optimum choice over other alternatives that provide less benefit. Decision makers should try to maximize pleasure and reduce pain, not simply for themselves but for everyone affected by their decision. Utilitarianism requires comparison of the ethical consequences for each alternative in a decision. It is a popular principle. Cost-benefit studies embody its logic and its spirit.

Utilitarianism illustrates the ethical perspective of consequentialism discussed in the story about David Geffen. It can permit violation of an ethical rule if, in the sequel, that leads to the greatest good. One problem is that in practice it invites self-interested reasoning. Since the exact definition of the "greatest good" is subjective, its calculation has often been a matter of expediency. A second problem is that because decisions are to be made for the greatest good of the community, utilitarian thinking may permit the abridgment of individual or minority group rights. It does not relate individual and community ends in a way that necessarily protects both.[29]

REASONING WITH PRINCIPLES

The use of ethical principles, as opposed to the intuitive use of ethical common sense, may improve reasoning, especially in complex situations. Say a bank teller pockets $20 at the end of the day. The person's supervisor strongly feels that stealing

[29] See, for example, Mortimer Adler, *Desires: Right and Wrong* (New York: Macmillan, 1991), p. 61. John Stuart Mill's *Utilitarianism* (London: George Routledge & Sons, 1895) deals directly and brilliantly with these and other criticisms. It was originally published in 1863.

is wrong and fires the teller. Ethical common sense is all that is needed in this situation, but the following situation defies a simple solution.

> I was working as a manager in a division that was going to be closed. The secret clock was ticking away to the surprise mass layoff. Then a co-worker approached. He was thinking of buying a house. Did I think it was a good time to get into real estate?
>
> The man's job was doomed and I knew it. But spilling the secret, I believed, would violate my integrity as a corporate officer and doom the company to a firestorm of fear and rumor. There was no way to win and no way out.
>
> I considered it my fiduciary responsibility to the business to keep my mouth shut, and yet here was this person coming for advice as a friend and a business acquaintance and I had material information that would affect him. For someone with a sense of empathy and sympathy, which I like to think I have some of, it was very, very hard.
>
> In the end I swallowed my anguish and kept silent. The man bought the house and lost his job. The secret held. But now 10 years later I have many times relived the story and second-guessed what I did that day.[30]

This is a vexing situation, and one created by the complexities of modern organizational life. The last paragraph finds the narrator alerted by emotion to the presence of an ethical conflict. Something in the situation causes anguish. In this predicament, however, simple moral homilies such as "tell the truth" or "be fair" are insufficient to resolve conflicts. Let us apply to this case three ethical principles, each of which offers a distinct perspective—utilitarianism, the rights ethic, and the theory of justice.

The *utilitarian* ethic requires the manager to calculate which course of action, among alternatives, will result in the greatest benefit for the company and all workers. A frank response here might disrupt operations. People could resign, take days off, work less efficiently, and engage in sabotage. Keeping the secret will cause hardship for a single employee about to buy a house and perhaps others in a similar situation. On balance, the manager must protect the broader welfare of customers, stockholders, and remaining employees.

From the standpoint of *rights*, the employee is entitled to the truth and the manager has a duty to speak honestly. It would be truthful to say, "As a manager my duty is always to keep such matters confidential," yet this comment veils the full truth. On the other hand, rights are not absolute. The corporation has a competing right to protect its property, and this right must be balanced against the right of an employee to honest treatment. In addition, the manager, in effect, promised to keep the secret and has a duty of promise keeping.

With respect to *justice*, corporations are required to promote fair, evenhanded treatment of employees. Distributive justice demands giving out benefits and burdens impartially. It would be partial to signal the layoff to one worker and not others.

Based on the application of utility, rights, and justice, the manager's decision to remain silent is probably acceptable. Some judgment is required in balancing

---

[30] Paraphrased and quoted from Kirk Johnson, "In the Class of '70, Wounded Winners," *The New York Times,* March 7, 1996, p. A12.

rights, but the combined weight of reasoning with all three principles supports the manager's decision. Yet the manager's moral intuition was not wrongly aroused. The situation offends the rules of deontological ethics. It exacts, by commission or omission, a lie, and it violates the practical imperative by treating the employee as expendable while achieving a corporate goal. Both good and evil result here. In such cases, application of the principle of double effect is appropriate. Here the welfare of the company outweighs the welfare of one employee, the manager's intention is not to hurt the employee but to help the company, and no better alternative presents itself. So the consequentialist principle of double effect confirms the manager's action.

CHARACTER DEVELOPMENT

virtue ethic
Ethical behavior stems from character virtues built up by habit.

Character development is a source of ethical behavior separate from the use of principled reasoning. The idea that character development is the wellspring of ethical behavior is known as the *virtue ethic*. It originated with the Greek philosophers. Aristotle wrote that moral virtue is the result of habit.[31] He believed that by their nature ethical decisions require choice, and we build virtue, or ethical character, by habitually making the right choices. Just as we learn to play the piano through daily practice, so we develop virtues by constant practice, and the more conscientious we are, the more accomplished we become. In a virtuous person ethical behavior comes from inner disposition, not from obeying external rules or applying abstract principles. Plato identified four fundamental traits—justice, temperance, courage, and wisdom—that have come to be called the *cardinal virtues*. Many other virtues have been mentioned over the years, including prudence, reverence, charitableness, hopefulness, and integrity.[32]

cardinal virtues
The four most basic traits of an ethical character—justice, temperance, courage, and wisdom. They were identified by Plato.

The virtue ethic requires conscious effort to develop a good disposition by making right decisions over time. Then acts are generated by inner traits ingrained from repetition and they reflect the disposition of a virtuous character. When Sholom Menora, CEO of Tri-United Technologies, moved out of Chicago, he sent a check for $25 to the city to compensate it for his periodic failure to put coins in parking meters.[33] This act reveals a trait of obsessive integrity, not an exercise of grand principles. However, such flashes of inner virtue are not a rejection of the study and use of philosophical principles, which can still inspire and delight the moral imagination.

THE NEURAL BASIS OF ETHICAL DECISIONS

The traditional view in moral philosophy is that ethical decisions, particularly right ones, come from deliberate reasoning that relies on principles and maxims. However, evidence from study of the brain casts doubt on this assumption. It

---

[31] *Nicomachean Ethics,* p. 91.

[32] Dennis J. Moberg, "The Big Five and Organizational Virtue," *Business Ethics Quarterly,* April 1999, p. 246.

[33] "Chicago Businessman Does Right by Jewish Law," *Ha'aretz,* October 6, 2000.

suggests that a fast, unconscious, and automatic process in neural circuits causes ethical judgments to appear in our awareness without any feeling of having gone through a reasoning process.

There is no specific part of the brain that makes ethical decisions. Rather, imaging shows that ethical problems simultaneously activate arrays or networks of neural circuits in some areas of the brain.[34] These neural circuits operate in parallel, coursing through regions associated with both social emotions and logical thinking, and they compete to dominate without any central control. A judgment is reached when one circuit is amplified over others, causing the decision maker to become conscious of a moral conviction. Although neural circuits involved with both emotions and reasoning are activated when a person considers an ethical dilemma, evidence suggests that emotional circuits tend to dominate the process and that they are needed to reach good moral judgments.

Probing Ethical Decisions

functional magnetic resonance imaging
A method used to map activity in neural networks during ethical decision making.

Researchers use *functional magnetic resonance imaging*, or fMRI, to study the brains of people making ethical judgments. An fMRI test detects and measures changes in blood flow and blood oxygen content related to neural activity. Neurons, the nerve cells in the brain, do not store oxygen, so they require increased blood supply as soon as they activate. An fMRI test measures cognitive function as it arises and spreads in the brain by detecting and mapping these changes in as little as one second after the neurons become active. It works by detecting shifts in magnetic properties of hemoglobin, a protein that carries oxygen in the blood. With a strong enough magnetic field, fMRI can pinpoint neural activity to within 1 millimeter in the brain.

Researchers have asked subjects in fMRI settings to consider ethical dilemmas, for example, these two situations involving trolleys.

You are standing by a track when you notice a runaway trolley that will kill five workers standing down the track if it continues on its path. If you flip a nearby switch you will divert the trolley to an alternate track, but it will kill one worker on that track. Is it appropriate for you to flip the switch?

You are standing on a footbridge when you notice a runaway trolley that will kill five workers standing on the track below if it continues on course. You can prevent the trolley from hitting them by pushing an overweight stranger standing next to you down onto the track, killing that person, but stopping the trolley. Is it appropriate for you to push the bystander in front of the trolley?

Both dilemmas could be resolved with utilitarian logic, since in each case the subject can act to save five lives by sacrificing one life. However, they differ in emotional engagement. The first version requires the more remote, impersonal act of flipping a switch. The second version contemplates a hands-on, repugnant, murderous act that will kill an innocent person. Such actions are forbidden in rule-based, deontological thinking. Over many experiments, large majorities of every

---

[34] Chadd M. Funk and Michael S. Gazzaniga, "The Functional Brain Architecture of Human Morality," *Current Opinion in Neurobiology*, December 2009, p. 678.

demographic and cultural background solve the dilemmas in the same way, choosing to flip the switch but refusing to push the bystander.[35] These dilemmas may seem remote from business life, but they allow study of how the brain processes situations in which there is a conflict between deontological rules and utilitarian balances. Business life teems with such situations.

In a defining experiment, brain imaging showed that when subjects made a decision about the more personal footbridge dilemma they engaged four brain regions associated with social emotions. But when deciding about the impersonal track-switching situation they activated three regions associated with working memory (conscious reasoning) and they responded more slowly.[36] Another fMRI study found that subjects with lesions on the ventromedial prefrontal cortex, a brain region needed to produce normal social emotions, were more likely than normal subjects to push the bystander off the footbridge. They lacked neural circuits that generated social emotions such as guilt, shame, and fear of punishment, the feelings that inhibit unimpaired subjects.

The study shows that areas of the brain associated with emotion are necessary to make "normal" distinctions in ethical judgment.[37] All the subjects calculated the 5:1 utilitarian equation correctly, but those with emotional deficits made more cool, calculating decisions. As expected, both the normal and impaired subjects approved of flipping the switch in the first dilemma. However, in the second, those with emotional deficits were far more willing to push the stranger.

Other studies have identified neural circuits activated by different species of ethical decisions. The maxims of retributive justice are one example. Subjects were given multiple scenarios in which a person was more or less blameworthy for a crime. In an fMRI setting they were asked for each scenario, first, to assess the person's blameworthiness, and second, to calculate appropriate levels of punishment. The first decisions, about guilt or innocence, activated neural circuits in the right dorsolateral prefrontal cortex, a region associated with deliberate reasoning. The second decisions, about the level of punishment, activated the amygdala, medial prefrontal cortex, and posterior cingulate cortex, a set of regions linked with unconscious social intuition and emotional processing.[38]

[35] John Mikhail, "Universal Moral Grammar: Theory, Evidence and the Future," *TRENDS in Cognitive Sciences,* April 2007, p. 144. See, for example, Joshua D. Greene, et al., "Cognitive Load Selectively Interferes with Utilitarian Moral Judgment," *Cognition,* June 2008, supplementary materials, pp. 6 and 19, showing that 82 percent would flip the switch and 79 percent would refuse to push a stranger.

[36] Joshua D. Greene, et al., "An fMRI Investigation of Emotional Engagement in Moral Judgment," *Science,* September 14, 2001, fig. 1. Areas associated with emotion were the bilateral medial frontal gyrus, the bilateral posterior cingulate gyrus, the left angular gyrus, and the right angular gyrus. Areas associated with working memory were the right middle frontal gyrus, the left parietal lobe, and the right parietal lobe.

[37] Michael Koenigs, et al., "Damage to the Prefrontal Cortex Increases Utilitarian Moral Judgments," *Nature,* April 19, 2007, p. 908.

[38] Joshua W. Buckholtz, et al., "The Neural Correlates of Third-Party Punishment," *Neuron,* December 2008, pp. 935–36.

Emotions and Intuition

Emotions have a central role in ethical thought because of their importance to adaptive behavior. The extensive cooperation between genetically unrelated individuals that characterizes human society is rare in the rest of the animal kingdom.[39] It is possible only because of strong social norms, including ethical norms. These norms enable cooperation among humans if they are adhered to and if deviation is punished. So the human brain has evolved to generate feelings that motivate fair exchanges with others.

Emotions such as guilt, shame, remorse, contempt, outrage, and disgust are reactions to moral violations. Normal individuals find it emotionally painful to act unethically. A person who creates reproving emotions in others risks punishment, shunning, and loss of relationships, all of which confer disadvantage. So these social emotions enforce and motivate moral conduct, reduce cheating, and promote mutual trust, allowing the large-scale cooperation in human society that confers a survival advantage.[40] Natural selection is the evolutionary basis of ethics.

In sum, evidence suggests that ethical decisions have a basis in brain architecture. They derive from the activation of parallel neural circuits in areas associated with both social emotions and logical reasoning. In the absence of any central control, these parallel circuits compete to lead the decision. Research supports the existence of a moral intuition, driven mainly by rapid activation of neural circuits that process social emotions. This moral intuition creates awareness of a moral judgment without any memory of having gone through a step-by-step reasoning process.[41] Thus, neuroscience provides a basis for the intuition ethic set forth by philosopher G. E. Moore more than a century ago.

Moral intuition is a form of social intuition that is adaptive to the social environment and predominates in individual ethical decisions, more so when they are immediate, personal, and emotional. There is more room for conscious reflection in decisions that are further off, abstract, less emotionally loaded, or amenable to decision regimes such as corporate policies or conduct codes. When subjects in fMRI experiments face more complex dilemmas and engage areas of the brain used for cognitive reasoning they take more time to respond, suggesting reflection beyond simple emotional response.[42]

In addition, although ethical stories and dilemmas activate the same regions of experimental subject's brains, there is considerable individual variation in perceptions of right and wrong. Evidence suggests that the sensitivity of neural pathways is based on social experience and learning. Life experience can bias one circuit over another, leading to a better ethical decision. Young children, for example,

---

[39] Ibid., p. 930.

[40] Bryce Huebner, Susan Dwyer, and Marc Hauser, "The Role of Emotion in Moral Psychology," *Trends in Cognitive Sciences,* December 2008.

[41] James Woodward and John Allman, "Moral Intuition: Its Neural Substrates and Normative Significance," *Journal of Physiology—Paris* 101 (2007), p. 186.

[42] Joshua D. Greene, et al., "The Neural Bases of Cognitive Conflict and Control in Moral Judgment," *Neuron,* October 2004, p. 397.

have a less-developed capacity for empathy and they have difficulty distinguishing between an accident and an intentionally evil action when both have the same outcome.[43]

At first glance, evidence for the importance of unconscious processes seems to reduce the relevance of reasoning with ethical principles. However, that conclusion is incorrect. Brain research discussed here confirms the existence of neural circuits activated by the deontological or consequentialist (utilitarian) approaches found in several principles and by problems of retributive justice. The effectiveness of the disclosure rule—the idea of revealing your action to your family or the world—is shown to rest on emotions such as shame and remorse.

Research into neural sensitivity also affirms the virtue ethic if it is defined as moral intuition enlightened by experience and ethical education. Character development, or the learning of specific virtues such as prudence or honesty, can amplify some neural circuits, biasing the outcome of a competition with other neural circuits in their favor. This explains the rise of a moral habit. Efforts to be more virtuous bias some neural circuits over others.

So neuroscience, as it removes physiological mysteries, reinforces the ethical teachings of centuries. It confirms that principles, at least the noble ones, are still enlightened, practical guides. We follow them unconsciously when we rely on intuition. And, when we have the luxury of reflection, they guide our reason.

PRACTICAL SUGGESTIONS FOR MAKING ETHICAL DECISIONS

Here are practical steps to better define and resolve ethical problems in business.

First, pay attention to your ethical intuition. Ethical intuition is a form of social intuition. Like social intuition it has evolved to protect us by making fast, automatic, unconscious, adaptive judgments in complex situations where risks may be high. Our initial gut reactions are as helpful or more so than judgments we make after lengthy thought. However, it can be wise and reassuring to confirm instant decisions with deliberate.

Second, consider tactics that illuminate alternatives. The philosopher Bertrand Russell advocated imaginary conversations with a hypothetical devil's advocate as an antidote for certitude. Seek out a more experienced, ethically sensitive person in the company as an adviser. This person can be of great value in revealing the ethical climate of a firm or industry. Divide a sheet of paper with columns to enter the pros and cons for various alternatives. Such balance sheets organize information and discipline scattered, agitated thinking. Also, the process of entering all relevant factors sometimes brings hidden considerations to light.

critical questions approach
A method of ethical reasoning in which insight comes from answering a list of questions.

Another tactic is the *critical questions approach.* Ask yourself questions about the ethical implications of an action. This approach is often suggested in corporate

---

[43] Liane Young and Rebecca Saxe, "Innocent Intentions: A Correlation Between Forgiveness for Accidental Harm and Neural Activity," *Neuropsychologia,* August 2009, p. 2071.

conduct codes. At International Paper, employees are given a wallet card with these questions to ask if they are in doubt.

- Are my actions legal?
- Am I being fair and honest?
- Will my action stand the test of time?
- How will I feel about myself afterward?
- How will it look in the newspaper?
- Will I sleep soundly tonight?
- Can I explain my action to the person I admire most?[44]

These critical questions are shorthand for a variety of approaches to ethical reasoning. Some invoke maxims such as "obey the law" and "tell the truth." Others rest on the disclosure ethic and the intuition ethic.

Third, sort out ethical priorities early. Serious ethical dilemmas can generate paralyzing stress. However, clear values reduce stress by reducing temptation and easing conscience as a source of anxiety. For example, when being honest means sacrificing a sale, it helps to clarify in advance that integrity is more important than money. Publicly commit yourself on ethical issues. Tell your co-workers you are opposed to taking office supplies home or price fixing, or any other action that could be an issue. They will now be disinclined to approach you with corrupt intentions, and public commitment forces you to maintain your standards or suffer shame.

Fourth, set an example. This is a basic managerial function. An ethical manager creates a morally uplifting workplace. An unethical manager can make money, but he or she pays the price, and the price is the person's integrity. Employees who see unethical behavior by their supervisor always wonder when that behavior will be directed at them.

Fifth, thoughts must be translated into action, and ethical deeds often require courage. Reaching a judgment is easier than acting. Ethical stands can provoke anger in others, strain relationships, and cost a company business, and there are risks of job loss.

Sixth, cultivate sympathy and charity toward others. The question "What is ethical?" is one on which well-intentioned people may differ. Marcus Aurelius wrote: "When thou art offended by any man's fault, forthwith turn to thyself and reflect in what like manner thou dost err thyself; for example, in thinking that money is a good thing, or pleasure, or a bit of reputation, and the like."[45]

Ethical perfection is illusory. We live in a morally complex civilization with endless rules, norms, obligations, and duties that are like road signs, usually pointing in the same direction but sometimes not. No decision ends conflicts, no principle penetrates unerringly to the good, no manager achieves sainthood.

---

[44] International Paper Company, *Code of Business Ethics,* 3rd ed. (Memphis, TN: International Paper Company, 2008), p. 27.

[45] *The Meditations of Marcus Aurelius Antoninus,* George Long, trans. (Danbury, CT: Grolier, 1980), p. 281; originally written circa AD 180.

Warning Signs

Lockheed Martin gives this list of phrases to all employees, telling them that when they hear one they are "on thin ethical ice."

- "It doesn't matter how it gets done as long as it gets done."
- "No one will ever know."
- "We didn't have this conversation."
- "It sounds too good to be true."
- "Shred that document."
- "I deserve it."

- "It's all for a good cause."
- "Well, maybe just this once."
- "Everyone does it."
- "This will destroy the competition."
- "What's in it for me?"
- "It's okay if I don't gain personally."
- "No one will get hurt."
- "This is a non-meeting."

Source: Lockheed Martin, *Setting the Standard*, October 2008, p. 32.

There is an old story about the inauguration of James Canfield as president of Ohio State University. With him on the inaugural platform was Charles W. Eliot, president of Harvard University for 20 years. After receiving the mace of office, Canfield sat next to Eliot, who leaned over and whispered, "Now, son, you are president, and your faculty will call you a liar." "Surely," said Canfield, "your faculty have not accused you of lying." Replied Eliot, "Not only that son, they've proved it."

CONCLUDING OBSERVATIONS

There are many paths to ethical behavior. Not all managers have studied the repertoire of principles and ideas that exist to resolve ethical problems of business life. One who did was J. C. Penney, who believed they had great value.

> I believe today and shall to the end of my days, that when a man truly works with a principle, such as the golden rule, that principle makes him the representative of a great and positive working force. Then a creative force of the universe is back of him, for the principle is doing the work, while he merely attends to the details.[46]

This is an inspiring quotation. Here Penney offers hope for managers to find a just order in the universe and act with it. Modern science locates this just order not in the universe, but inside each manager, in neural circuits that evolved to facilitate social cooperation. Either way, attending to the details, as Penney puts it, is a difficult art. By reflecting on principles, a person becomes more sensitive to the presence of ethical issues and more resolute in acting with integrity.

---

[46] J.C. Penney, *Fifty Years with the Golden Rule* (New York: Harper, 1950), p. 78.

Short Incidents for Ethical Reasoning

The following situations contain ethical conflicts. Try to define the ethical problems that exist. Then apply ideas, principles, and methods from the preceding two chapters to resolve them.

A CLOUDED PROMOTION

As chairman of an accounting firm in a large city, you were prepared to promote one of your vice chairmen to the position of managing partner. Your decision was based on a record of outstanding performance by this person over the eight years she has been with the firm. A new personnel director recently insisted on implementing a policy of résumé checks for hirees and current employees receiving promotions who had not been through such checks. Unfortunately, it was discovered that although the vice chairman claimed to have an MBA from the University of Michigan, she dropped out before completing her last 20 units of course work. Would you proceed with the promotion, retain the vice chairman but not promote her, or fire her?

THE ADMIRAL AND THE THIEVES

When Admiral Thomas Westfall took command of the Portsmouth Naval Shipyard, theft of supplies was endemic. It was a standing joke that homes in the area were painted gray with paint stolen from the Navy. Admiral Westfall issued an order that rules related to supply practices and forbidding theft would be strictly enforced. Within a few days, two career petty officers were apprehended carrying a piece of Plexiglas worth $25 out of the base. Westfall immediately fired both of them and also a civilian storeroom clerk with 30 years' service, who lost both his job and his pension. According to Westfall, "The fact that I did it made a lot of honest citizens real quick." Did the admiral act ethically?

SAM, SALLY, AND HECTOR

Sam, Sally, and Hector have been laid off from middle-management positions. Sam and Hector are very upset by their misfortune. They are nervous, inarticulate, and docile at an exit meeting in the personnel department and accept the severance package offered by the company (two weeks' pay plus continuation of health benefits for two weeks) without questioning its provisions. Sally, on the other hand, manifests her anxiety about job loss by becoming angry. In the exit meeting, she complains about the inadequacy of the severance package, threatens a lawsuit, and tries to negotiate more compensation. She receives an extra week of pay that the others did not get. Has the company been fair in its treatment of these employees?

A PERSONALITY TEST

You are asked by a potential employer to take a psychological profile test. A sample segment includes the items shown in Exhibit 1.

Because you have read that it is best to fit into a "normal" range and pattern of behavior, and because it is your hunch that the personnel office will weed out unusual personalities, you try to guess which answers are most appropriate for a conservative or average response and write them in. Is this ethical?

EXHIBIT 1

	Yes	No	Can't Say
It is difficult to sleep at night.			
I worry about sexual matters.			
Sometimes my hands feel disjointed from my body.			
I sometimes smell strange odors.			
I enjoyed dancing classes in junior high school.			
Not all of my friends really like me.			
Work is often a source of stress.			

AL

The CEO of a Midwestern manufacturing company tells the following story.

I was looking over recent performance reviews in the household products division and one thing that struck me was the review of a star sales rep named Al. I know Al because he handles our Walmart account. Al had the highest annual sales for the past five years and last year nearly doubled the next highest rep's total. The sales manager's written evaluation was highly laudatory as expected, but cautioned Al to adhere strictly to discount policy, shipping protocol, and billing protocol. I got curious.

A conversation with the division manager revealed that Al ingratiated himself with workers on the loading dock, socializing with them, sending them birthday cards, and giving them small gifts such as tickets to minor-league ball games. The loading dock supervisor complained that Al was requesting and sometimes getting priority loading of trucks for his customers despite the formal first-in, first-out rules for shipping orders. Second, Al had given several customers slightly deeper discounts than authorized, although the resulting orders were highly profitable for the company. And finally, late in December, Al had informally requested that one big account delay payment on an order by a week so that the commission would be counted in the next year. This would have gotten him off to a running start had not an accountant for the purchaser paid promptly and written to Al's manager in refusing the request.

The division head stuck up for Al. I didn't press or request that any action be taken. Did I do the right thing?

How would you answer the CEO's question?

A TRIP TO SEAWORLD

A sales representative for a large manufacturer of consumer electronics equipment headquartered in Los Angeles, California, has courted a buyer from a nationwide chain of 319 retail stores for more than a year. At company expense the buyer was flown to Los Angeles from Trenton, New Jersey, with his spouse, for a three-day sales presentation. The company is paying all expenses for this trip and for the couple to attend a Los Angeles Dodgers baseball game and dine at fine restaurants.

During the second day of meetings, the buyer discusses a one-year, $40 million order. The chain that the buyer represents has not sold the company's products before, but once it starts, reorders are likely. At dinner that evening, the buyer mentions that he and his wife have always wanted to visit SeaWorld in San Diego. While they are in Southern California and so close, they would like to fly down. It is clear that he expects the company to pay for this trip and that he will delay making a commitment for the $40 million order until he gets a response.

The company has already spent $4,200 for the buyer's trip to Los Angeles. The San Diego excursion would cost about $500. The marketing manager estimates that the company can make a 9 percent gross profit on the sale. The sales representative stands to receive a 0.125 percent commission over base salary.

What should the sales representative do?

MARY AND TOM

Mary P., an aerospace engineer, tells about a difficult career experience in which her friend Tom plays a central role.

My friend Tom and I are employed by Republic Systems Corporation. We started about the same time after graduating from engineering school five years ago. The company does a lot of defense work, mostly for the Air Force, and it's big. Tom and I worked on project teams doing tests to make sure that electronics shipped to customers met specifications. We have very similar backgrounds and job records, and there has always been a little competition between us. But neither one of us pulled ahead of the other on the corporate ladder. That is until last winter.

At that time, we were assigned a special project to modify the testing protocol on certain radar components. The success of the projects was critical; it had to be done before Republic bid for two more years on its big radar systems contract. About 40 percent of our people work radar.

We rolled up our sleeves and put in long hours. After a month, though, Tom volunteered to be on a companywide task force developing a new employee privacy policy. Privacy is a big deal to Al Manchester, our CEO.

Tom continued to work with me, but he gradually put more and more of his energy into the privacy project. I had to start taking up some of the slack. He enjoyed the task force meetings. They met in the dining room at the Kenthill Country Club and he could hobnob with Al and some of the other big shots. He worked overtime to impress them.

We finally finished the testing project and it was a success. But toward the end I did the lion's share of it. One day, Tom made me angry by ending a capacitor test at 94 hours instead of the 100 hours you really have to have for validity. He did it because he was late for a privacy task force meeting. Overall, I guess Tom helped a lot, but he didn't do his share all the way through.

Last month the assistant manager of the radar project left the company and Tom and I both applied for the position. It was a pay raise of several grades and meant getting a lot of recognition. They chose Tom. The announcement in the company newsletter said that he was a "strong team player" and mentioned both the testing project and the privacy task force as major accomplishments.

I don't think it was fair.

Was Tom fair to Mary? Was Tom's promotion fair to Mary? Was the company wrong to promote Tom?

THE HONDA AUCTION

Dave Conant co-owned and managed Norm Reeves Honda in Cerritos, California. Naturally, he worked closely with Honda marketing executives to get cars for his dealership. One day, one of these executives, Dennis Josleyn, the new zone sales manager, approached him, asking him to submit a bid on 64 company cars. These were near-new cars previously driven by corporate executives or used to train mechanics. Company policy called for periodic auctions in which Honda dealers submitted competitive bids, and the high bidder got the cars to sell on its lot. It was Josleyn's job to conduct the auction.

"I want you to submit bids on each car $2,000 below wholesale market value," Joselyn told Dave Conant. Conant dutifully inspected the 64 cars and submitted the asked-for bids. Meanwhile, Josleyn busied himself creating fake auction papers showing that other Honda dealers bid less than Conant. Of course, others bid near the wholesale price, so their bids were higher. Completing the phony auction, Josleyn announced the winner—Conant's dealership. The next day he showed up there and handed Conant an envelope.

"I have a little invoice for you," he said.

Conant went to his office, opened it, and found a bill for $64,000 payable to an ad agency co-owned by Josleyn and his brother. The message was clear. Josleyn wanted a 50–50 split with the dealer on the $2,000 windfall each car would bring, so he was billing Conant for half the extra $128,000 the entire batch of cars would bring in.

Conant faced a decision. If the invoice was paid, the dealership would make a $64,000 windfall. If he refused to pay, the cars would be rerouted to a dealer who was a "player" and future shipments of new Hondas might be slower. He decided to pay the invoice. In his own words: "I believed I had no choice. If I hadn't paid the amount, I would have incurred the wrath of Dennis Josleyn and possibly some of the other Honda gods, and I believe they would have taken our store down."[1]

Conant was not alone. Honda dealers around the country faced a dilemma. After investing large sums to build new showrooms and facilities and hire employees, they soon found themselves having to choose between two paths. If they gave bribes and kickbacks to Honda executives, they secured a copious flow of cars and made a fortune. On average, a favored dealer made almost $1 million a year in personal income. However, if they stayed clean, no matter how modern their dealership and well trained its sales force; they received fewer cars and less profitable models. If they went bankrupt, and many did, the Honda executives arranged for less scrupulous owners to take over their dealerships.

Many an honest dealer short on cars drove across town to see a rival's lot packed with fast-selling models in popular colors. Over time, it also became clear that the highest Japanese executives at Honda knew what was going on but chose to do nothing.

Did Conant make the right decision? What would you do in his position?

THE TOKYO BAY STEAMSHIP COMPANY

The Tokyo Bay Steamship Company operated a tourist ship between Tokyo and the volcanic island of Oshima 50 miles offshore. It also had a restaurant on the island. It was a modest business until February 1933, when Kiyoko Matsumoto, a 19-year-old college student, committed suicide by jumping into the crater of the volcano, which bubbled with molten lava. Ms. Matsumoto left a poetic suicide note and, through newspaper stories, the Japanese public became obsessed with her story.

[1] Quoted in Steve Lynch, *Arrogance and Accords: The Inside Story of the Honda Scandal* (Dallas: Pecos Press, 1997), p. 106.

Soon other Japanese emulated Ms. Matsumoto. In the next 10 months, 143 people threw themselves into the crater. Many more came to watch. One Sunday in April, for example, 31 people tried to jump; 25 were restrained, but 6 succeeded. People crowded around the edge of the crater waiting for jumpers. Shouts of "Who's next?" and "Step right this way. Lots of room down in front" could be heard.[2]

The Tokyo Bay Steamship Company capitalized on the volcano's popularity. It increased its fleet to 30 ships and added 19 more restaurants. Meanwhile, the Oshima police chief met the boat and tried to weed out potential suicides using a crude behavioral profile (was someone too happy or too sad?). A police officer stood at the rim of the volcano. The Japanese government made purchase of a one-way ticket to Oshima a crime. Many suicides were prevented; others succeeded. Twenty-nine people who were stopped at the volcano killed themselves by jumping into the ocean on the return boat to Tokyo.

In the meantime, Tokyo Bay Steamship Company prospered. Its shares rose on the Tokyo exchange. But did it meet basic standards of ethics?

TIGER WOODS

In the early morning hours of November 26, 2009, golf star Tiger Woods drove from his Florida mansion, hitting a fire hydrant and a tree. The media soon revealed infidelities, destroying his image as a dedicated husband and parent of two small children.

Before this, Woods was one of the world's most popular athletes. Corporations used him as an endorser with global appeal and his income from this was as high as $100 million a year. When the scandal broke, corporate sponsors needed to reassess the relationship.

AT&T, which has a *Code of Ethics* requiring "[e]ach director, officer, and employee . . . to act with integrity . . . including being honest and ethical" was the first to act.[3] It ended an agreement paying Woods to carry its logo on his golf bag.

Two weeks later Accenture, which used Woods in its ads because his golf skills reinforced its slogan, "high performance delivered," chose to end its ties. In its *Code of Business Ethics* the global consulting firm says, "We conduct our personal activities . . . in the same way we conduct our business activities: with the utmost integrity" and it defines integrity as "recognizing right from wrong and understanding the ethical implications of our choices."[4]

Three of Woods' most prominent sponsors, Nike, Gatorade, and Gillette, affirmed their support for him. However, within several months Gatorade, a PepsiCo brand, broke off its sponsorship and the CEO of Procter & Gamble said the company would not use Woods again in its Gillette brand commercials. Nike continued to support Woods. On its Web site Nike says the company was "founded on a handshake" and was "based on trust, teamwork, honesty, and mutual respect." "Our task," it says, "has been to maintain this same ethic across our operations."[5] Nike's code, *Inside the Lines*, sets criteria for employees' behavior.

> Nike's good name and reputation result in large part from our collective actions. That means the work-related actions of every employee must reflect standards of honesty, loyalty, trustworthiness, fairness, concern for others, and accountability. We are expected to be sensitive to any situations that can adversely impact Nike's reputation and are expected to use good judgment and common sense in the way we all conduct business.[6]

Nike was not the only sponsor that stuck with Woods. Electronic Arts continued to feature him on its Web site and in a video game. NetJets, TLC Laser Eye Centers, and Upper Deck made no changes. Tag Heuer reduced, but did not eliminate, his presence in its advertising.

The events here raise many questions, most prominent among them, should corporate sponsors apply their ethics standards to celebrity endorsers?

---

[2] "Profits in Suicide," *Fortune*, May 1935, p. 116.

[3] AT&T Inc., "AT&T Inc. Code of Ethics," at www.att.com/gen/investor-relations?pid=5595, accessed March 6, 2010.

[4] Accenture, *Code of Business Ethics: Our Core Values in Action* (New York: Accenture, August 2007, ver. 4.11), pp. 11 and 12.

[5] "Nike Responsibility Governance" at www.nikebiz.com/responsibility/cr_governance.html, accessed March 6, 2010.

[6] Nike, *Inside the Lines: The Nike Code of Ethics* (Beaverton, OR: Nike, 2008), p. 23.

Tangled Webs

Through the ages philosophers, poets, leaders, teachers, and scholars have spoken on the merits of truth. Yet lying lives on. Here we relate two stories from the business world that, each in a different way, invite discussion of lies.

Years ago philosopher Sissela Bok defined a lie as "an intentionally deceptive message in the form of a *statement*."[1] A lie takes power from others. It allows the person speaking an untruth to manipulate another by withholding information, depriving that person of the ability to make an informed choice.

Lies harm others by causing them to act against their interest. Even small lies can carry a price for the people who tell them. They might pay a conscience penalty. Their resistance to telling other, bigger lies can gradually wear down. They can complicate their lives by having to remember the original lie and cover it with additional lies. And, if found out, they lose the trust of others and have less power in the end.

***

James E. Gansman was an affluent, successful, highly competent, curious, and partly unfulfilled man. In the winter of 2004 he joined Ashley Madison, a social networking site that connects people seeking extramarital affairs. Gansman was a senior partner and an attorney in the New York office of Ernst & Young. His job was to advise client companies about the cost of paying severance and other compensation to executives of firms they targeted for takeovers. However, on Ashley Madison he sought a more gentle form of combination.

***

At Ashley Madison the motto is, "Life is Short, Have an Affair." Users, who must be over 18, go to its Web site, ashleymadison.com, and sign up as members. After that, they create profiles, post photos, and interact with others on the site. Revenue for the company comes when users buy credits needed to initiate chat sessions, post messages, and send virtual gifts. Members can search for amorous contacts by location, age, and descriptive characteristics, compile lists of favorites, and give contacts a special "key" to their personal photo collection.

When members feel comfortable with new acquaintances, they graduate to in-person relationships.

The site provides advice. It recommends safe ways to arrange initial meetings in public locations such as restaurants and coffee shops, and cautions the adventurers to tell friends when they expect to return home. It discusses the risks of sexually transmitted diseases from 20 kinds of sexual activity.

In 2008 Ashley Madison introduced an "Affair Guarantee Program." For $249 a member receives 1,000 credits and a guarantee of finding a willing partner in three months or getting a refund. To qualify, seekers must follow rules that require specific numbers and types of actions on the site.

***

Gansman found a willing companion. She was Donna Murdoch, 40, a consultant, securities broker, and investment adviser living near Philadelphia. The two began to exchange phone calls and text messages and met in luxury hotels in New York and Philadelphia. As the relationship advanced, Gansman tried to impress Murdoch by bragging about his role in a few corporate mergers that appeared in the media.

In time the pair settled into a routine of daily phone calls and started playing a teasing game. With both of them at a computer, looking at the same Yahoo! Finance screens, Gansman would drop clues about deals on which he was working. "The game was," she said, "I wouldn't be looking and he would give me hints: the market cap of $2 billion or market cap of $400 billion and here's what they do, and he'd read it to me, and ultimately make sure I guessed."[2] Eventually, the games stopped and he just told her company names. One day he revealed an upcoming takeover to help one of Murdoch's children with a stock market simulation exercise at school.[3]

These disclosures were indiscreet. Ernst & Young had written confidentiality policies. As an Ernst employee Gansman was "prohibited from disclosing nonpublic information regarding clients or other entities to anyone other than for authorized firm business, or using it for any personal purpose."[4] Each of

---

[1] Sissela Bok, *Lying: Moral Choice in Public and Private Life* (New York: Vintage Books, 1978), p. 16.

[2] Donna Murdoch, quoted in Dennis K. Berman, "Insider Affair: An SEC Trial of the Heart," *The Wall Street Journal*, July 28, 2009, p. C1.

[3] Ibid., p. C1.

[4] Grand Jury Indictment in *United States v. James Gansman and Donna Murdoch*, U.S.D.C., S.D.N.Y, 1:08-cr-00471, May 27, 2008, pp. 2–3.

the 13 years he had worked for Ernst he also had signed a statement of compliance with a second policy that forbade trading securities based on confidential information. It read, in part:

> It is the firm's longstanding policy that partners . . . may not purchase or sell securities while in possession of material, non-public information and may not disclose such information to anyone except on a strict "need-to-know" basis. Violations of this policy can result in immediate dismissal from the firm.[5]

Gansman's indiscretions were Murdoch's temptations. She and her husband were in debt and struggling to make payments on a $1.45 million home mortgage. Public announcements of big mergers can trigger rapid, large, price movements in the shares of target companies. She began to act on Gansman's tips.

***

Gansman and Murdoch were one of Ashley Madison's success stories. Since its founding in 2000, the site has expanded from North America to Great Britain, Australia, and New Zealand. It claims more than 6 million active members, defined as those who have logged on at least once in the past six months. Among those who sign up, men outnumber women by 7: 3; however, many men are not very active and among those who buy credits women outnumber men by 3:1.[6]

The site grows with amazing rapidity and, unlike most businesses, flourishes during periods of economic hardship when couples face added financial problems and divorce is less of an option. Between 2008 and 2010 its membership rose from 2.2 million to 6 million. At one point in 2008 it got one new member every 20 seconds.[7] In 2010 it opened new sites in Australia and New Zealand. After one month it had 205,224 members in the former and 2,832 in the latter.[8] In Canada its membership rose 79 percent between 2009 and 2010, from 362,086 to 649,509. The fastest growth, 291 percent, came in "female newlyweds," defined by the site as female members married three years or less.[9]

***

In June 2006 Gansman learned that Blackstone Group, a private equity firm, planned to acquire Freescale, a Texas semiconductor company listed on the New York Stock Exchange. Blackstone wanted the matter treated with utmost confidentiality. "Do not breathe the name of the target outside of [the] team," a colleague told him, "and please advise all others who assist you."[10] Nonetheless, Gansman told Murdoch the news. On July 18 she began trading in Freescale, buying contracts for 50 August $30 call options. The next day she bought 20 more of the same contracts.

Call options allow buyers to speculate on securities they do not own. Each option contract allows the holder to buy 100 shares of a company's stock at a specific price, called the strike price, on the day the option expires. So the 50 contracts she bought on July 18 gave her the right to buy 5,000 shares of Freescale on August 18 at $30 a share. If Freescale were selling below $30 a share she was not obligated to buy the shares. The calls would be worthless because she could buy shares of Freescale on the open market for less than $30. If Freescale were selling above $30 on August 18, for example at $40, she could buy 5,000 shares at $30, taking a profit of $10 a share, or $50,000 (minus the price of the option contracts). Options are priced based on risk. The further they are "out-of-the-money," that is, priced below the current market price of the company's shares, and the closer the expiration date, the lower their price. Buying call options allowed Murdoch to speculate on price movements with less invested than if she had bought common shares of Freescale and paid the full price at the time of purchase.

No matter how adept their calculation, Murdoch's trades violated the written policies of her employer. On her hiring, she received a policy manual and later

[5] Ernst & Young, "Policies Regarding Trading of Securities While in Possession of Confidential or Non-Public Information ("Insider Trading")"; and Grand Jury Indictment in *United States v. James Gansman and Donna Murdoch,* p. 4.

[6] Ashley Madison, "Frequently Asked Questions," at ashleymadison.com, September 1, 2010.

[7] "AshleyMadison.com," *Marketing Weekly News,* November 22, 2008, p. 79.

[8] "Adultery Site Aims to Hook New Zealanders," *The New Zealand Herald,* May 9, 2010.

[9] Shannon Proudfoot, "Adulterous Website Gets More Canadian Hits and More Women," *Nanaimo Daily News,* April 24, 2010, p. C1.

[10] E-mail from an Ernst & Young partner, quoted in Complaint, *Securities and Exchange Commission v. Gansman, Murdoch, and Brodsky,* U.S.D.C., S.D.N.Y., No. 08-cv-4918. May 29, 2008, p. 12.

certified that she had read and understood it. The following two statements were in this manual.

> SEC Rule 10b-5 under the Securities Exchange Act of 1934 generally makes it unlawful for any person to use . . . material inside information that has not been publicly disseminated in connection with the purchase or sale of securities.
>
>   It is the policy of [the company] that no personnel . . . may trade . . . any security of any issuer about which the individual possesses material non-public information at or prior to the time such information is publicly disclosed and available in the marketplace.[11]

When Murdoch bought her call options, Freescale shares were selling between $26.09 and $27.89. The options would expire August 18. The discussions between Blackstone and Freescale continued and on August 10 Murdoch sold all of her contracts at a price that allowed her to break even. Late in August, she resumed trading in Freescale options. Between August 30 and September 7, as Freescale's stock hovered between $30.01 and $31.62, she purchased 610 Freescale September $35 call options. She also bought 50 October $30 call options, but suddenly sold them on September 8 and purchased another 80 September $30 contracts.

On the next trading day, Monday, September 11, *The New York Times* reported the possibility that Freescale would be bought and its stock jumped 20 percent, up $6.31 to $37.06. Murdoch sold all her options for a profit of $158,970.

Others also profited. Earlier, Murdoch had met another man through the Ashley Madison site, Richard Hansen, managing director of an investment banking firm near her home. The firm had hired her and was now her current employer. Hansen was her supervisor. She never revealed her relationship with either man to the other. Yet she tipped Hansen. On the same day Murdoch first traded in Freescale, he bought 2,000 shares of the company's common stock in accounts registered to each of his two daughters. On September 11, he sold these shares for a total gain of $45,820.

Murdoch also tipped her father, Gerald L. Brodsky, 73, a man with a past conviction for securities fraud. Years before, as president of a company that sold medical newsletters, he had reported millions of dollars in false income to shareholders. In 1993 he pled guilty to one criminal count of defrauding share-

holders. He was sentenced to a year and a day in prison and had to pay $1,318,864 in restitution.[12] Brodsky was clever in his trading. He asked an old friend to buy 370 September $35 call options. On September 11 he told this friend to sell them, netting a profit of $63,400.

And so it went. For more than a year Murdoch traded in the options of 18 target companies, sometimes tipping others, who traded too. She had made approximately $390,000, but she had been imprudent. Acting with foreknowledge, she at times bought seldom-traded contracts. On some days her trading was all or most of the activity in those contracts. By early 2007 she had appeared on watch lists at the Securities and Exchange Commission (SEC). The SEC monitors trades to identify any that appear suspicious because of their size, their timing, or the individuals who made them. In May an investigator from the agency called her on the telephone. She concealed her actions and denied trading on inside information, then told Gansman about the call. He suggested she get an untraceable cell phone for their calls.[13]

Murdoch continued trading options into November until she learned an SEC investigation was under way. Soon the Department of Justice launched a criminal investigation. Trying to hide her relationship with Gansman, she took her laptop computer to a store and asked a technician to erase the hard drive beyond restoration. The technician accepted the job without question, but did not succeed. Later, when an FBI agent interviewed her, she gave deceptive answers and turned over false documents. Gansman was also named in the investigations. When word of them got to Ernst, it put him on administrative leave. "We are going to jail," he told Murdoch and accused her of ruining his life.[14]

***

Ashley Madison faces continuous criticism. "It's like dumping raw sewage into the culture," states the head of a pro-marriage group.[15] According to Noel

[11] Grand Jury indictment, pp. 4–5.

[12] *United States v. Gerald L. Brodsky,* No. 93-cr-10 (E.D. Pa. 1993), judgement entered April 26, 1994: Securities and Exchange Commission, "Gerald Brodsky Enters Guilty Plea," *News Digest,* Issue 93–213, November 4, 1993, pp. 3–4.

[13] Berman, "Insider Affair: An SEC Trial of the Heart," p. C1.

[14] Ibid., p. C1.

[15] Charmaine Yoest, president of Americans United for Life, quoted in Kelly Jane Torrance, *Washington Times,* September 5, 2008, p. B1.

Biderman, 38, the founder of Ashley Madison, such comments are misguided. Biderman is a former sports attorney who shifted his career into online commerce. He married in 2002. He and his wife have two children. He says his marriage is happy and characterized by fidelity. "I do not cheat, no. I've been faithful to date," he says. Once when asked how he would feel if his wife cheated he replied: "I'd be devastated." However, he said, "I wouldn't blame a Web site."[16]

Biderman believes that humans are genetically disposed to philander, that monogamy is unnatural. Equating marriage with monogamy is a "broken paradigm."[17] People naturally stray. Ashley Madison does not persuade anyone to abandon a happy, fulfilling matrimonial bond. Rather, it protects anyone who has already decided to have an extra-marital affair.

> [I]f you're predisposed to having an affair, don't have it in the workplace, because someone's going to lose their job. Or don't go on a singles dating site and pretend to be something you're not, because that's unfair to the other person—that's going to end badly for you as well, don't go and break the law and visit an escort.[18]

Dislike of Ashley Madison often manifests itself in resistance to its advertising. "I feel I should have the right, as long as I'm following the regulations, to advertise my product," argues Biderman.[19] Broadcast television networks have rejected its commercials, but it has placed them on CNN, ESPN, Fox News, and MSNBC. In 2009, NBC and the National Football League refused to run its ad during the Super Bowl. A few months later, when it saw a spike in new members from Utah, it placed ads on two Salt Lake City radio stations. However, when the owner of one station heard it on his morning commute, he ordered it stopped.[20] And later in the year the Toronto Transit

Commission turned down $200,000 to put the company's ads in its subways, buses, and streetcars. Biderman disagreed with the commission. "I just think they're mistaken about the average . . . rider's willingness to accept these kind of ads in exchange for cheaper fares," he said.[21]

***

In May 2008 a New York grand jury charged Gansman and Murdoch with 1 count of conspiracy for furthering an insider trading conspiracy and 11 counts of securities fraud based on Murdoch's trades.[22] Murdoch alone faced two additional charges. She was charged with one count of making false statements for lying to the FBI and one count of obstruction of justice for paying an individual to erase evidence from her hard drive. The government collected voluminous evidence of the scheme, about 280,000 pages altogether. A criminal case against the two began. Instead of plotting together, though, their paths would now separate.

The case went to the federal courthouse in Manhattan, where it was assigned to Judge Miriam Goldman Cedarbaum, the same jurist who presided over the trial of Martha Stewart. Gansman pled not guilty. Murdoch initially pled not guilty. Then she decided to change her plea to guilty on all counts and to cooperate with the government for a lighter sentence. At the time she was taking medication for depression. Instead of sticking by her benefactor, she would testify against him.

Before Gansman's trial began, his attorney entered a motion to dismiss the charges. It argued that Gansman never traded on insider knowledge, never knew of Murdoch's trades, and never benefitted financially from her trades. It was correct that Gansman had never traded on confidential information himself. Yet it strained credulity to believe he

---

[16] Quotations are from Zosia Bielski, "His Not-So-Cheatin' Heart," *The Globe and Mail,* November 6, 2009, p. L1.

[17] Noel Biderman, quoted in Proudfoot, "Adulterous Website Gets More Canadian Hits and More Women," p. C1.

[18] Noel Biderman, quoted in Frank Dobrovnik, "2,000 Spouses Looking for Action, Ashley Says," *Sault Star,* April 23, 2010, p. A1.

[19] Ibid.

[20] Sean P. Means, "Infidelity Ad Dumped by Salt Lake City Radio Station," *The Salt Lake Tribune,* April 16, 2009.

[21] Quoted in Don Peat, "Cheating Ad Nixed," *The Toronto Sun,* December 12, 2009, p. 4.

[22] The law prohibits insider trading, defined as buying or selling a security when in possession of significant information not yet available to the public when those purchases or sales violate a duty to keep that information confidential. It also prohibits "tipping," where a person with "material, nonpublic information" breaches a duty of confidence to share that information with a person not covered by such a duty. And if the tipped person buys or sells securities based on the information those transactions also violate the law. See 15 USC §78j and 78ff, 71 CFR §240.10b-5 and 240.10b5-2, and 18 USC §2.

had no knowledge of Murdoch's trades. The government produced records of more than 7,000 phone calls and text messages between the two. Murdoch's testimony also undermined his claim of ignorance. This exchange from the hearing on her plea agreement is an example.

> JUDGE CEDARBAUM: But because of your work you were familiar with the serious consequences of trading on inside material non-public information, isn't that correct?
>
> DONNA MURDOCH: Yes, your honor.
>
> JUDGE CEDARBAUM: All right. What is it that you agreed with Mr. Gansman to do?
>
> DONNA MURDOCH: Well, I knew that he was violating a duty of confidentiality that he owed to these companies and I knew that I was trading based on those terms. I did discuss sometimes with him and sometimes not, not what exactly the specific amounts I was trading, but many times it was discussed with him.[23]

It was also correct that Gansman had received no financial benefit from Murdoch's trades. However, the government argued that the definition of benefit under the law was broader than pecuniary gain. It also included the reputational enhancement to the tipper from benefiting a friend or relative who receives the tip. Still, even with Murdoch's testimony, it proved difficult to pin down Gansman's motive with precision.

> JUDGE CEDARBAUM: Did you [and Gansman] have an agreement of some kind? Did you share money at all?
>
> MS. MURDOCH: Money, no, your honor.
>
> JUDGE CEDARBAUM: Well, did he receive something in exchange for this agreement?
>
> MS. MURDOCH: He received a gift or two. He received—I don't know what he received himself for sharing the information.[24]

Here Murdoch's attorney Paul Schechtman stepped in to offer an explanation.

> MR. SCHECHTMAN: Judge, I think it is fair to say that the arrangement here was . . . an arrangement of a personal nature. I think it is that relationship that Mr. Gansman hoped to foster by giving this information. It was a personal relationship and not a monetary relationship.
>
> JUDGE CEDARBAUM: So in exchange he hoped to gain a closer relationship?
>
> MR. SCHECHTMAN: Or to cement a closer relationship, I think. A close relationship. I think that is right, your Honor.
>
> JUDGE CEDARBAUM: Now [Ms. Murdoch], did you tell Mr. Gansman if he gave you these tips you would give him more affection than you otherwise would?
>
> MS. MURDOCH: Absolutely not, your Honor.
>
> JUDGE CEDARBAUM: It is a puzzling agreement to me.[25]

Murdoch's testimony that Gansman knew about her trades was enough for Judge Cedarbaum to turn down his motion for dismissal. His trial went forward in May 2009. It lasted for eight days and included additional testimony by Murdoch. In the end the jury convicted him of six counts of insider trading.

In February 2010 Judge Cedarbaum sentenced Gansman to one year and one day in federal prison followed by six months of supervised release. In March he was disbarred because of the conviction and no longer can practice law in New York.[26] In August he settled a concurrent civil case brought by the SEC, agreeing to a judgment of $250,000 to disgorge a share of the profits made from Murdoch's trades.[27] In the same settlement Murdoch agreed to a final judgment of $404,054, which was waived based on her inability to pay. Earlier, her father had agreed to a penalty of $265,924, equal to three times his illegal profits plus interest.[28]

Murdoch has yet to be sentenced in the criminal case.

---

[23] Transcript of Plea Allocation of Donna Murdoch *United States v. Donna Murdoch,* U.S.D.C., S.D.N.Y, 08-cr-471, December 23, 2008, p. 16–17.

[24] Ibid., p. 17.

[25] Ibid., pp. 19–20.

[26] *In the Matter of James E. Gansman,* 898 N.Y.S.2d 18 (2009).

[27] *Securities and Exchange Commission v. Gansman, Murdoch, and Brodsky,* U.S.D.C., S.D.N.Y., No. 08-cv-4918 (2010); Securities and Exchange Commission, litigation release No. 21629, August 18, 2010.

[28] Securities and Exchange Commission, litigation release No. 21059, May 27, 2009.

A Family of Brands

Avid Life Media is the parent company for six brands. Each is a social networking site for a separate niche in the dating universe.

> **Ashley Madison:** A brand described as "the world's leading infidelity service." It targets people who want to break the monotony of their marriage by having an affair.

> **Hot or Not:** A site where "hot singles age 18 to 34" post photographs, rate each other, and contact other members.

> **Established Men:** A site designed to help "rich, successful men and sexy sugar babies" find each other and verify the relationship is what they seek.

> **Cougar Life:** A place for "strong, successful, sexy older women" and "vibrant, ambitious young men" to come together.

> **Man Crunch:** A community for gay men seeking long-lasting relationships. Its motto is: "Putting the MAN back in romance."

> **Swappernet:** A site for "real couples" seeking other couples, singles looking for threesomes, and "wife-swapping adventurers."

> **Eroticy:** An adult personal ad site with erotic photos and videos. It allows members to have "no strings attached fun."

Source: Avid Life Media at www.avidlifemedia.com/brands.html.

Ashley Madison is only one brand in a larger stable. Its parent company is Avid Life Media, headquartered in Ontario, Canada. Avid Life markets six other "targeted niche brands," as shown in the box, each with a Web site of its own. Its mission is: "To hook up like-minded individuals who share the same passions and desires; regardless of their lifestyle preferences."[29] In 2009, the company had earnings of $8 million on sales of $30 million. Ashley Madison accounted for only 15 percent of its sales. The rest came from its other sites.[30]

In 2010 Avid Life proposed a merger with a much larger media advertising firm, Moxey Media, after which the company would make a public stock offering, allowing average investors to buy its shares. The merger made strategic sense. A combination of two profitable firms, one with a network of popular, expanding, recession-proof Web businesses and the other with sophisticated advertising tools, should have charmed investors. It did not. An investment banking firm hired to find partners willing to fund the deal made no progress. Fund managers who might ordinarily have seen an attractive risk showed no interest. One Canadian billionaire whom they approached as a potential investor had this to say.

> I don't mind investing in liquor because without it, you'd miss something in life. I tell friends to stop smoking, and I still buy tobacco companies. But Ashley Madison shouldn't be a public venture, because it can destroy families. And there is nothing worse than the effect of divorce on children. There are thousands of other stocks to buy, so why bother with this crap?[31]

Eventually, Avid Media's banker ended its efforts, attributing the withdrawal of support to economic conditions. A Canadian magazine reported that the firm backed away when its top executive read this user posting on Ashley Madison.

> To be honest I'm really looking for a sugar daddy, so if that isn't you I wouldn't waste your time replying. I'm looking for a generous man that loves to take care of a younger lady, i am 18 and have just started university and my parents aren't paying a cent for it . . . So if there is a nicer gentlemen on here that really gets off on helping a young woman with some bills, taking stress of her shoulders while receiveing the same back both emotionaly and physically please msg me.[32]

[29] www.avidlife.com/about.html.

[30] Andrew Willis and Boyd Erman, "Avid Life IPO Could Be an Affair to Remember," *The Globe and Mail,* January 25, 2010, p. B1.

[31] Stephen Jarislowski, quoted in Thomas Watson, "Abandoned at the Altar," *Canadian Business,* March 2010, p. 47.

[32] Ibid., p. 47.

***

As noted in Chapter 7, otherwise honest individuals can be drawn into evil by circumstances. In this story the Gansman–Murdoch alliance was born in temptation. As time passed James Gansman's early restraint gradually wore away. If, at first, he would not have betrayed his employer, during an interval of growing weakness he gradually abandoned his fidelity and came to lack any limit. Was he simply a fallible man? His attorney seemed to think so. "This is a good person who made a bad decision," he told Judge Cedarbaum just before she sentenced his client.[33]

Donna Murdoch believed she was a good person too. As if in a dream she was granted knowledge of the future that could be turned into gold. At first she resisted temptation, but in the end she went into its snare. Her testimony before Judge Cedarbaum is a window into how she rationalized.

> Your honor, I've, I really have tried to live a good life. I have wonderful children and I've been trying to take care of them, both my husband and my children, and our financial situation was really, really bad, really bleak. I thought I could bail us out. I thought I could keep my kids the way they were, in the schools they were in, and our house from being foreclosed on and whatnot. What I did was wrong. It was wrong. It was wrong. And I'm so sorry, and I wish . . . I could make it disappear.[34]

***

Noel Biderman is comfortable with his labors, which, unlike the actions of Gansman and Murdoch,

are legal. "I sleep well at night," he states.[35] His wife Amanda, 34, believes "he's a great husband and father." "Neither of us condones infidelity," she explains, "and we separate our personal beliefs from Noel's business." Yet Amanda Biderman is troubled, saying, "I do feel really bad for the people who are being cheated on as a result of their partners becoming members of the Web site." And she anticipates social opprobrium.

> I'm going to struggle when the children are older. That will be the first major conflict of interest for me. I'm preparing myself for the fact that there are likely to be parents at my children's school and nursery who will point the finger at us if they find out what Noel does.[36]

Questions

1. What lies are present in the "tangled webs" considered here? How were they used? How were they justified by those who executed them? Who was harmed by them? Which lies were most harmful?

2. Were the punishments for James Gansman, Donna Murdoch, and Gerald Brodsky fair?

3. Is Ashley Madison based on an ethical business model?

4. How does Noel Biderman, the founder of Ashley Madison, explain and justify the business? Does he fulfill his ethical duties to all those affected by his actions?

5. What do the events in this story teach us about business ethics? About capitalism?

---

[33] Barry Bohrer, quoted in Chad Bray, "Gansman Sentenced in Insider Case," *The Wall Street Journal,* February 9, 2010, p. C2.

[34] Waiver of Indictment by Donna Murdoch, *United States v. Donna Murdoch,* U.S.D.C., S.D.N.Y., 08-cr-00471 (December 23, 2008), p. 30.

[35] Quoted in Bielski, "His Not-So-Cheatin' Heart," p. L1.

[36] Quotations of Amanda Biderman are in "I Feel Guilty But He's Just Trying to Help People," *The Express,* April 30, 2010, p. 37.

Chapter **Nine**

Business in Politics

Paul Magliocchetti and Associates

Once upon a time there was a bright young man from Pittsburgh named Paul. He went to Washington, D.C., becoming an aide to an important legislator from his state, Rep. John P. Murtha (D-Pennsylvania). Rep. Murtha chaired the powerful House Appropriations Subcommittee on Defense, a small group of legislators that approves the annual military budget. The young man worked on the subcommittee's staff, forming ties with its members, learning the budget process, paying his dues as an apprentice to power.

After nine years he left to follow a well-worn career path in the nation's capital. He set up a lobbying firm, locating it not far from the Pentagon, and naming it after himself—Paul Magliocchetti and Associates Group (PMA Group). It flourished. He specialized in helping defense contractors get project funding through insertions in defense spending bills. These insertions are called earmarks.

earmark
An amount of money for a project added into an appropriations bill by any member of the Senate or House of Representatives.

An *earmark* is a line item appropriation a legislator puts into a bill allotting, or "earmarking," a specific sum for a project. Although the federal budget comes to Congress from the president, Article I, Section 8 of the Constitution gives Congress the power of the purse. It alone allocates the taxpayers' money from the U.S. Treasury, and any representative or senator can set aside funds for projects even if the president does not request them.

When Paul Magliocchetti set up shop in 1989 earmarking was an infrequent practice, but it grew. By 1991 there were 564 earmarks, by 1999 there were 2,838, and by 2005 the number reached an all-time high of 13,997.[1]

Legislators mostly do earmarks for programs that create jobs in their districts and states. There were 1,100 earmarks in the 2010 defense spending bill. It included an extra destroyer the Navy never asked for, 10 cargo planes the Air Force did not request, and five deluxe presidential helicopters ridiculed by Secretary of Defense Robert Gates as costing "nearly half a billion dollars each" so the president could "cook dinner while in flight under nuclear attack."[2] Most earmarks were for much smaller programs. Among them, were some for tiny defense contractors—clients of PMA Group.

[1] Based on information compiled by Citizens Against Government Waste, www.cagw.org/reports/pig-book/#trends, accessed on April 10, 2010.

[2] Quoted in R. Jeffrey Smith, "House Seems To Be Set on Pork-Padded Defense Bill," *Washington Post*, July 30, 2009, p. A1.

Magliocchetti was a pioneer in the art of earmarking. He was "bright, blunt, and ambitious."[3] He knew the mazes of defense appropriations so well that members of Congress often relied on his knowledge. When defense firms hired him, he coached them on earmark proposals and told them which lawmaker to contact. He advised them to open facilities in the sponsoring member's districts to create jobs there when earmarks were funded. And he encouraged large campaign contributions. Over the years, he gave $434,000 in all. Members of his family gave another $1.2 million and lobbyists in his firm $2 million more.[4]

His client list grew to include Northrop Grumman, General Dynamics, Boeing, and Lockheed Martin along with many smaller defense contractors. The firm expanded to 35 lobbyists, most recruited from congressional staffs and the Pentagon. They crossed Washington in a fleet of Lexus automobiles. Eventually the firm's revenues put it in the top 10 among Washington lobby shops.

Paul Magliocchetti prospered with the firm. He took a $1 million annual salary and had a $2 million home. He entertained legislators and their staffs at the Capital Grille, a steak house with a view of the Capitol dome. Although he hired lawyers to train his lobbyists on congressional ethics rules, he was adept at finding loopholes. One was an exception in the House gift policy that allowed him to send food to the appropriations committee office when staff worked after hours.[5]

After almost two decades of lobbying stardom, Magliocchetti prepared to sell his firm, move to Florida, and start an Italian restaurant. Alas, one day FBI agents surprised him at his home seeking records of his campaign giving. They were probing contributions from his ex-wife's parents, a couple, both in their 80s, who lived in an unpretentious house Magliocchetti bought for them, had modest assets, rarely voted, and yet gave $83,000 over five years. Until suddenly taking an interest in reelecting members of the defense appropriations subcommittee, they had never made a political contribution. Magliocchetti's children and some friends were making similar, large donations.[6]

Using other people as conduits to exceed contribution limits is a crime. If Magliocchetti gave money to others, reimbursing them for contributing, he could be subject to five years in prison and fined triple the amounts involved. The FBI investigation marked the end of his firm. Its lobbyists swarmed from the tainted hive and it collapsed. Magliocchetti fell to earth. His private wine locker at the Capital Grille gathered dust and he needed medication for stress.

The House of Representatives investigated seven members of the defense appropriations subcommittee, recipients of the curious contributions, looking into their links with Magliocchetti. His clients had given these seven members $834,000 in contributions and, over time, received $245 million in earmarks.[7] It is a crime for a

[3] Dennis B. Roddy, "Former Pittsburgher in Middle of Earmark Scandal," *Pittsburgh Post-Gazette,* April 5, 2009, p. A7.

[4] Chuck Neubauer, "Lobbyist's Kin Unlikely Campaign Contributors," *Washington Times,* December 23, 2009, p. 1.

[5] "Earmarks of Scandal," *The New York Times,* April 2, 2009, p. 26.

[6] Neubauer, "Lobbyist's Kin Unlikely Campaign Contributors," p. 1.

[7] R. Jeffrey Smith, "Thin Wall Separates Lobbyist Contributions and Earmarks," *Washington Post,* March 7, 2010, p. A6.

representative to exchange an official act, such as sponsoring an earmark, for a campaign contribution.

In the inquiry, led by congressional staff, five of the seven committee members "credibly articulated a process that separates . . . legislative activities from campaign fund-raising activities."[8] For example, between 2008 and 2010 Rep. Jim Moran (D-Virginia) sponsored earmarks for 13 companies represented by PMA and received a combined $180,200 from the companies. Rep. Moran said all earmark requests were first reviewed by a staff member, who ranked them on three criteria—the military's interest in the project, the company's record, and the number of jobs created in his district. Then he reviewed the list, often changing rankings and amounts requested.

Moran, a 19-year incumbent, said he raised about $600,000 to $1 million for each reelection campaign. A professional finance director did the fund-raising, not a staff member in his office. Invitations to regular fund-raising breakfasts and dinners went to a list of Democratic donors and to anyone who had attended a fund-raiser or contributed in the past. He also spent two or three afternoons a week making phone calls to raise money. However, unless the contribution came through one of his calls, "he did not know who made donations or what amounts were made to his campaign and . . . he did not want to know."[9] He felt it was improper to have that information and he never wanted to abstain from a vote or action because of a contribution. The staff aide who analyzed the earmarks rarely attended the fund-raisers. When he did, the aide told anyone who brought up business with the congressman to schedule a meeting at the office.[10]

The other two members under investigation aroused more suspicion. One was Rep. Peter Visclosky (D-Indiana), who received more money from PMA Group and its clients than any of the others—$270,000 since 1989.[11] Visclosky refused to cooperate, but the ethics investigators found "probable cause" to believe he had sponsored earmarks in exchange for contributions.[12]

Rep. Visclosky invited earmarks. On January 15, 2008, a staff member in his office sent e-mails to companies that had requested earmarks in the past, telling them that requests for the 2009 appropriations bill had to be in by February 15. An earmark proposal form was attached. Then, on February 27, his campaign manager sent invitations for a March 12 fund-raising dinner to all the lobbyists and companies seeking earmarks. In Washington society a fund-raising dinner is worded as an occasion to "honor" a legislator, but it is actually a request for a contribution. In the etiquette of that society you must write a check to attend. "Please make checks payable to 'Visclosky for Congress,' noted the event flyer.[13]

[8] Report of the Committee on Standards of Official Conduct, *In the Matter of Allegations Relating to the Lobbying Activities of Paul Magliocchetti and Associates Group, Inc. (PMA),* House of Representatives Report 111–423, February 26, 2010, p. 93.

[9] Ibid., p. 92.

[10] Ibid., p. 105.

[11] David D. Kirkpatrick, "Indiana Lawmaker's Name Is Said to Surface in Inquiry Into Lobbying," *The New York Times,* April 4, 2009, p. 11.

[12] Report of the Committee on Standards of Official Conduct, p. 230.

[13] Ibid., Exhibit 2, p. 238.

Representative Peter Visclosky (D-Indiana)
Source: ©Congressional Quarterly/Getty Images.

The fund-raiser brought in contributions of $35,300 from PMA Group lobbyists, its political action committee, the employees of client companies seeking earmarks, and those companies' political action committees. Only a week after the dinner, on March 19, Rep. Visclosky approved $14,400,000 in earmarks for six PMA Group clients. The timing here was truly awkward. Visclosky had solicited contributions from people seeking his official action and did so very close to the time he took that action. Was this a corrupt exchange? Members of Congress are cautioned to avoid even the appearance of a connection between the receipt of anything of value and acting to benefit the giver.

Moreover, the contributors believed they were buying influence. In one company's internal e-mails an executive had asked the director of its political action committee, "Can you give me some justification for giving $20K to Visclosky?" The answer was that it was the amount PMA had suggested and they should do it because Visclosky "has been a good supporter" and "[w]e have gotten over 10M in adds from him."[14] At a second company, the political action committee director bragged that "generous contributions" to Visclosky the previous year had purchased seats at the head table where its executives discussed earmark requests with Visclosky and his staff.[15]

The perception of contributors that they were buying access did not necessarily mean that Rep. Visclosky had knowledge of their intent or cooperated with it. However, the investigators thought it was likely. Yet, when they turned their evidence over to the House ethics committee, it quickly issued a brief, final report exonerating all seven representatives.[16] It stated: "[S]imply because a Member sponsors an earmark for an entity that also happens to be a campaign contributor does not, on these two

[14] Ibid., Exhibit 7, p. 249.

[15] Ibid., p. 224.

[16] In addition to Moran and Visclosky those investigated were Reps. Norman Dicks (D-Washington), Marcy Kaptur (D-Ohio), John Murtha (D-Pennsylvania), Bill Young (R-Florida), and Todd Tiahrt (R-Kansas).

facts alone, support a claim that a Member's actions are being influenced by campaign contributions."[17] Indeed.

Paul Magliocchetti was not as lucky. In 2010 he was charged with 11 criminal counts of illegal campaign contributions and false reporting.[18] In a plea agreement, his son Mark, who with his wife made more than $120,000 in straw donations for his father, agreed to cooperate with federal prosecutors. When a new Congress was elected later in that year both the Senate and House Republicans agreed to a two-year moratorium on earmarks. House Democrats agreed only to stop earmarks for companies. These decisions will be revisited in the next Congress.

Politics is mostly opaque. Its hidden action and subtlety invite cynicism and simple judgments. Now and then a window opens to reveal how corporate influence works. It is not clear if this story is typical. Its lessons for a working democracy are uncertain. This chapter goes into more detail about subjects raised in this story including the influence of business in politics, how lobbying works, the role of corporate money in politics, laws on lobbying and campaign contributions, and the nature of business influence both past and present.

THE OPEN STRUCTURE OF AMERICAN GOVERNMENT

federal system
A government in which powers are divided between a central government and subdivision governments. In American government, the specific division of powers between the national and state governments is set forth in the Constitution.

supremacy clause
A clause in the Constitution, Article VI, Section 2, setting forth the principle that when the federal government passes a law within its powers, the states are bound by that law.

Business seeks and exercises political power in a government that is extraordinarily open to influence. Its power is exercised on constitutional terrain created by the Founding Fathers more than 200 years ago. The Constitution of the United States, as elaborated by judicial interpretation since its adoption in 1789, establishes the formal structure and broad rules of political activity. Its provisions create a system predisposed to a certain pragmatic, freewheeling political culture in daily political life.

Several basic features of the Constitution shape American politics. Each stands as a barrier to the concentrated power that the founders feared would lead to tyranny. Each has consequences for corporate political activity.

First, the Constitution sets up a *federal system*, or a government in which powers are divided between a national government and state governments. This structure has great significance for business, particularly for large corporations with national operations. These corporations are affected by political actions at different levels and in many places.

The *supremacy clause* in Article VI, Section 2 stipulates that when the federal government passes a law within its powers, that law preempts, or takes precedence over, state laws on the same subject. For example, Congress passed the Telecommunications Act of 1996 to speed the growth and lower the cost of cell phone use. Later, San Diego County passed a zoning law that set height, color, and camouflage requirements for cellular towers to reduce their "visual impact." Sprint sued, claiming the law raised costs and slowed the expansion of its wireless network and was, therefore, in conflict with the Telecommunications Act. A federal court agreed and ordered the county to stop enforcing the tower requirements.[19]

[17] Report of the Committee on Standards of Official Conduct, p. 4.

[18] Indictment in *United States v. Magliocchetti,* No 10CR286, U.S.D.C., East. Dist. Va. (2010).

[19] *Sprint Telephony PCS v. County of San Diego,* 479 F.3d 1061 (2007).

separation of powers
The constitutional arrangement that separates the legislative, executive, and judicial functions of the national government into three branches, giving each considerable independence and the power to check and balance the others.

The federal system has many implications for the regulation of business. Sometimes business prefers federal regulation, so it must follow one law instead of as many as 50 different state laws. In the 1960s, for instance, several states tried to pass laws requiring warning labels on cigarette packs. If states had been allowed one by one to require labels, the tobacco companies would have had to print specially worded cigarette packs for sale in each state. So they supported a bill in Congress that, when passed, preempted that area of regulation and required a uniform warning label across the country. Unlike the tobacco industry, the insurance industry fights national regulation, preferring instead oversight by state insurance commissions. Insurance companies are big employers and heavy campaign contributors in many states. They tend to receive gentle treatment from these commissions and fight all efforts to pass national regulations.

Second, the Constitution establishes a system of *separation of powers*, under which the basic functions of government—legislative, executive, and judicial—are set up in three branches of the federal government. Each branch has considerable independence and has the power to check and balance the others. The states mimic these power-sharing arrangements in their governments. For business, it is significant that the actions of one branch do not fully define policy. For example, if Congress passes a law despite business opposition, corporations can lobby regulatory agencies in the executive branch to get favorable application of its provisions or they can go to the judicial branch to challenge its constitutionality.

judicial review
The power of judges to review legislative and executive actions and strike down laws that are unconstitutional or acts of officials that exceed their authority.

Third, the Constitution provides for *judicial review* by giving judges the power to review legislative and executive actions and to strike down laws that are unconstitutional or acts of officials that exceed their authority. A classic example of judicial review came in the spring of 1952 when a steelworkers strike threatened to stop steel production while hard-pressed U.S. troops in Korea were desperate for supplies and equipment. To support the war effort, President Harry Truman issued an order for the government to take control of and run the steel industry. Steel companies sued to stop him and the Supreme Court held that Truman had exceeded his constitutional powers.[20]

The government structure created by the Constitution is open. It diffuses power, creates multiple points of access, and invites business and other interests to attempt influence. Because no single, central authority exists, government action often requires widespread cooperation between levels and branches of government that share power. This characteristic also makes the system particularly vulnerable to blockage and delay. When important actions require the combined authority of several elements of government, special interests can block action by getting a favorable decision at only one juncture. To get action, on the other hand, an interest such as business must successfully pressure many actors in the political equation. Thus, there has developed a style in the American system in which interests are willing to bargain, compromise, and form temporary alliances to achieve their goals rather than stand firm on rigid ideological positions.

[20] *Youngstown Sheet & Tube Co. v. Sawyer*, 343 U.S. 579. The basis for the Court's ruling was that Congress had once considered giving presidents the power to seize industries in similar circumstances but had not done so.

First Amendment
An amendment to the Constitution added in 1791 as part of the Bill of Rights. It protects the rights of free speech, a free press, freedom to assemble or form groups, and freedom to contact and lobby government.

The *First Amendment* is an additional element of the Constitution critical to business. It protects the right of business to organize and press its agenda on government. In its elegantly archaic language is stated the right "to petition the Government for a redress of grievances." The First Amendment also protects rights of free speech, freedom of the press, and freedom of assembly—all critical for pressuring government. Without these guarantees, the e-mail campaigns, speeches, editorials, and ads that business orchestrates could be suppressed. Imagine how different the system would be if the public, agitated by a corporate scandal, could pressure Congress to restrict the lobbying rights of some industry.

While corporate speech is expansive, it is restricted in one area. The Supreme Court years ago defined monetary campaign contributions as a form of speech and allowed them to be limited because of fears that corporate money corrupts elections.[21]

A HISTORY OF POLITICAL DOMINANCE BY BUSINESS

Though not ordained in the Constitution, the preeminence of business in politics is an enduring fact in America. The Revolutionary War of 1775–1783 that created the nation was, according to some historians, fought to free colonial business interests from smothering British mercantile policies.[22] The founders who drafted the Constitution were an economic elite. John Jay and Robert Morris, for example, were among the wealthiest men in the colonies. It comes as no surprise that the government they designed was conducive to domination by business interests. The noted historian Charles Beard argued that the Constitution was an "economic document" drawn up and ratified by propertied interests, for their own benefit.[23] His thesis is controversial, in part because it trivializes the importance of philosophical, social, and cultural forces in the politics of constitutional adoption.[24] Yet the record since adoption of the Constitution in 1789 is one of virtually unbroken business ascendancy.

Laying the Groundwork

Business interests were important in the new nation but did not dominate to the extent that they soon would. There were few large companies. The economy was 90 percent agricultural, so farmers and planters were a major part of the political elite. Their interests balanced and checked those of infant industry. The fledgling government was a tiny presence. Economic regulation was virtually nonexistent.

---

[21] *Buckley v. Valeo,* 424 U.S. 1 (1976).

[22] See, for example, Clarence L. Ver Steeg, "The American Revolution Considered as an Economic Movement," *Huntington Library Quarterly,* August 1957.

[23] Charles Beard, *An Economic Interpretation of the Constitution of the United States* (New York: Macmillan, 1913).

[24] See, for example, Robert E. Brown, *Charles Beard and the Constitution* (Princeton: Princeton University Press, 1956); and Forrest McDonald, *We the People: The Economic Origins of the Constitution* (Chicago: University of Chicago Press, 1963).

Nevertheless, under the leadership of Secretary of the Treasury Alexander Hamilton the new government was soon turned toward the promotion of industry. With the support of business leaders, Hamilton pursued his visionary policies, laying the groundwork for the unprecedented industrial growth that roared through the next century. As the young nation's economy expanded, so also did the political power of business.

Ascendance, Corruption, and Reform

During the nineteenth century, commercial interests grew in strength. When the Civil War between 1861 and 1865 decimated the power base of Southern agriculture, a major counterweight to the power of Northern industry vanished. In the period following the war, big business dominated state governments and the federal government in a way never seen before or since. It was a time of great imbalance, in which economic interests faced only frail obstacles.

Companies commonly manipulated the politics of whole states. West Virginia and Kentucky were dominated by coal companies. New York, a number of Midwestern states, and California were controlled by railroads. Montana politics was engineered by the Anaconda Copper Mining Company. In Ohio, Texas, and Pennsylvania, oil companies predominated; the noted critic of Standard Oil, Henry Demarest Lloyd, wrote, "The Standard has done everything with the Pennsylvania legislature, except refine it."[25]

Business was also predominant in Washington, D.C. Through ascendancy in the Republican party, corporations had decisive influence over the nomination and election of a string of probusiness Republican presidents from Ulysses S. Grant in 1868 to William McKinley in 1900.[26] In the Congress, senators were suborned by business money; some even openly represented companies and industries. One observer noted that in 1889,

> a United States senator . . . represented something more than a state, more even than a region. He represented principalities and powers in business. One senator, for instance, represented the Union Pacific Railway System, another the New York Central, still another the insurance interests of New York and New Jersey . . . Coal and iron owned a coterie from the Middle and Eastern seaport states. Cotton had half a dozen senators. And so it went.[27]

Under these circumstances, corruption was rampant. Grant's first term, for example, was stained by the famous "whiskey ring" scandals in which liquor companies cheated on their taxes and a member of Grant's cabinet solicited bribes in exchange for licenses to sell liquor to Indian tribes. In Grant's second term, the Crédit Mobilier Company gave members of Congress shares of its stock to avoid investigation of its fraudulent railroad construction work.

[25] "The Story of a Great Monopoly," *The Atlantic*, March 1881, p. 322.

[26] The exception was the election of the Democrat and reformer Grover Cleveland in 1884. But even Cleveland had strong business supporters, Andrew Carnegie and James J. Hill among them. His administration never threatened business interests.

[27] William Allen White, *Masks in a Pageant* (New York: Macmillan, 1928), p. 79.

Nineteenth-century political cartoonist Joseph Keppler (1838–1894) was a critic of big business who particularly resented the ascendancy of moneyed interests in politics. This cartoon appeared in the magazine *Puck* on January 23, 1889. Source: © CORBIS.

The soaring political fortunes of business in the post-Civil War era invited reaction. A counterbalancing of corporate power began that continues to this day. Late in the century, farmers tried to reassert agrarian values through the Populist party. They foundered, but not before wresting control of several state legislatures from corporations and forcing through legislation to control the railroads, the biggest companies of that day. More important, the Populist movement was the beginning of a long-lived democratic reform tradition opposed to big business power.

Two other formidable business adversaries emerged. One was organized labor, which was destined to be the strongest single element opposing industry over the following century. The other was the powerful Anti-Saloon League, which advocated prohibition of alcohol. Like labor, the Anti-Saloon League became a strong national adversary of business. Brewers and distillers were not its only adversaries. Big corporations in many industries worked against Prohibition because they opposed the principle and onset of more government regulation.

After 1900, reforms of the Progressive movement curtailed overweening corporate power. For example, the Seventeenth Amendment in 1913 instituted the direct election of senators by voters in each state. Corporations fought the amendment. Before, state legislatures had chosen senators, a practice that invited corrupting influence by big companies. For example, in 1884 representatives of Standard Oil called members of the Ohio legislature one by one into a back room where $65,000 in bribes was handed out to obtain the election of Henry B. Payne to the Senate. One witness saw "canvas bags and coin bags and cases for greenbacks littered and scattered around the room and on the table and on the floor . . . with something green sticking out."[28]

Big business also fought suffrage for women. The battle was led by liquor companies that feared women would vote for Prohibition. However, there was broader fear of women voters. It was widely believed by businessmen that women would vote for radical and socialist measures. The powerful Women's Christian Temperance Union, which had as many as 10,000 local chapters by 1890, frightened business by standing against liquor, child labor, and income inequality. Yet after adoption of the Nineteenth Amendment in 1920 giving women the vote, no strong shifts in voting patterns appeared.

The great political reforms of the Progressive era were reactions to corruption in a political system dominated by business. It would be a mistake, however, to conclude that because of reforms and newly emerged opponents, the primacy of economic interests had been eclipsed. While business was more often checked after the turn of the century, it remained preeminent. Corruption continued. In 1920 Warren G. Harding, a backroom candidate picked by powerful business interests at a deadlocked Republican nominating convention, was elected president. His vice president was Calvin Coolidge, the rabidly antilabor ex-governor of Massachusetts. Harding's administration was so beset by scandals in which officials accepted money for granting favors to corporations that Congress was considering impeaching him when he died of a stroke in 1923. The worst scandal involved Secretary of the Interior Albert B. Fall, who accepted bribes from oil company executives in return for the right to pump oil from government reserves in Teapot Dome, Wyoming. The Teapot Dome affair came to light only after Harding's death, but so besmirched his reputation that it was eight years before his grand tomb in Marion, Ohio, could be dedicated.

Business Falls Back under the New Deal

By the time Harding was officially laid to rest, the stock market had crashed and catastrophic economic depression racked the country. Conservative business executives argued that the Depression would correct itself without government action. After the election of Franklin D. Roosevelt in 1932, corporations fought his efforts to regulate banking and industry, strengthen labor unions, and enact Social Security. Business lobbyists in opposing Social Security argued that children would no longer support aging parents, that the required payroll tax would discourage workers and they would quit their jobs, and that its protection would remove the "romance of life." Leaders of DuPont, General Motors, Standard Oil, U.S. Steel, J. C. Penney, Heinz, and other firms formed the anti-Roosevelt American Liberty League to campaign against "unconstitutional" and "socialistic" New Deal measures.

[28] Quoted in Henry Demarest Lloyd, *Wealth Against Commonwealth* (New York: Harper, 1898), pp. 377–78.

Many executives hated Roosevelt. They said he was bringing communism to the United States and called him names such as "Stalin Delano Roosevelt."[29] But business had lost its way. Corporate opposition to New Deal measures ran counter to public sentiment. It became ineffective and was sometimes disgraceful. In 1935, for example, utility lobbyists sent Congress 250,000 fake letters and telegrams in a losing effort to stop a bill. Subsequently they ran a whispering campaign saying Roosevelt was insane.

Much New Deal legislation was profoundly egalitarian and humanitarian and reasserted the tradition of agrarian idealism. Because business lacked a positive philosophy for change, its political power was greatly diminished. According to Edwin M. Epstein, "Corporate political influence reached its nadir during the New Deal."[30] Roosevelt was hurt by all the hate and believed that through his major New Deal programs, he had saved capitalism despite the capitalists.

The New Deal was a political sea change born out of the Great Depression. One lasting legacy of the era was the philosophy that government should be used to correct the flaws of capitalism and control the economy. Government would also be used to create a "welfare state" to protect citizens from want. Whereas, in the past, government had kept its hands off corporations, now it would actively use interest rates, regulation, taxes, subsidies, and other policy instruments to control them. Whereas, in the past, most domestic spending had been for infrastructure programs that promoted business, spending would increasingly focus on social programs such as Social Security. These changes laid the groundwork for an increasingly large, powerful, and activist federal government.

Postwar Politics and Winds of Change

In the 1940s, industry's patriotic World War II production record and subsequent postwar prosperity quieted lingering public restiveness about corporate political activity. During the 1950s, corporations once again predominated in a very hospitable political environment. In the years between 1952 and 1960, Dwight D. Eisenhower was a probusiness president with a cabinet dominated by political appointees from business. A probusiness conservative coalition of Southern Democrats and Republicans in Congress ensured legislative support. Corporations could promote their policy agendas by influencing a small number of leaders. Charls E. Walker, an official in the Eisenhower administration and later a business lobbyist, recalls how only four men shaped economic policy.

> These four officials were President Eisenhower, Treasury Secretary Robert Anderson, Speaker of the House Sam Rayburn, and Senate Majority Leader Lyndon B. Johnson. These four men would get together every week over a drink at the White House and the President would say, "I think we ought to do this or that." Then Mr. Sam or LBJ might say, "Well, that's a real good idea; send it up and we'll get it through." And they would. They could deliver because at that time they had great influence in Congress, partly because of the seniority system.[31]

[29] William Manchester, *The Glory and the Dream*, vol. 1 (Boston: Little, Brown, 1973), p. 126.

[30] *The Corporation in American Politics* (Englewood Cliffs, NJ: Prentice Hall, 1969), p. 31.

[31] Quoted in Gene E. Bradley, "How to Work in Washington: Building Understanding for Your Business," *Columbia Journal of World Business,* Spring 1994, p. 53.

However, changing political trends soon led business into more sophisticated methods of political intervention. During the 1960s and 1970s, national politics became dominated by a liberal reform agenda. New groups rose to defy corporations, internal reforms made Congress more openly democratic and responsive to business's foes, business was bridled with expensive new regulatory schemes, and government swelled with new tiers of authority. Business suffered unaccustomed defeats at the hands of public interest groups and agency staffs in government, defeats that encouraged more aggression from companies.

THE RISE OF ANTAGONISTIC GROUPS

During the late 1960s, the climate of pressure politics changed with the rise of new groups focused on consumer, environmental, taxpayer, civil rights, and other issues. Some, including Ralph Nader's Public Citizen, the Natural Resources Defense Council, and the Consumer Federation of America, grew to have many members and enough power to push an agenda of corporate regulation.

The presence of these groups changed the political arena for business. A decade earlier, corporations had dominated Washington politics with quiet, behind-the-scenes influence over key leaders. Now they faced hostile groups that used a favorable climate of public opinion to wrest control of the policy agenda away from business. The result was a remarkable period, lasting roughly from the late 1960s to the late 1970s, during which the antagonists of business pressured Congress to enact one massive regulatory program after another.

The rise of groups hostile to business is part of a broader trend in which new groups of all kinds, including business groups, have been stimulated by growth of government. Government growth is reflected by fast-rising federal spending. After adjusting for inflation, federal outlays nearly doubled in the 20 years between 1960 and 1980, rising 95 percent. And the trend continued as outlays rose another 304 percent between 1980 and 2009.[32] Figure 9.1 shows the rise of federal spending and extends back to 1940. As government grows, interest groups proliferate around policy areas. By the 1990s there were an estimated 23,000 organized interests, roughly 400 percent more than in the 1950s.[33]

The heyday of the public interest movement was short-lived. By the late 1970s business interests had mobilized to fight back in more sophisticated ways and never again did the movement win great legislative victories. It remains an institutionalized enemy of business power, but its focus, as suggested in Chapter 5, is now on forms of civil regulation, not on legislation.

---

[32] Bureau of the Census, *Statistical Abstract of the United States: 2010,* table 459, at www.census.gov/compendia/statab/2010/tables/10s0457.pdf. Calculations are based on constant 2000 dollars.

[33] Burdett A. Loomis and Allan J. Cigler, "Introduction: The Changing Nature of Interest Group Politics," in *Interest Group Politics,* 5th ed. (Washington, DC: Congressional Quarterly Press, 1998), p. 11.

FIGURE 9.1 **Growth of the Federal Budget: 1940–2010**

The tremendous spending increase shown is a key measure of government's growth. This growth made government more complex, caused proliferation of interest groups, and increased its impact on industries, markets, and competition. Historically, growth of government is the major stimulant to political activity by business. Throughout the period shown here, progressives and liberals used government more and more to solve social problems and regulate business. As they built government bigger with expensive programs, they strengthened the incentive for corporations to influence it.

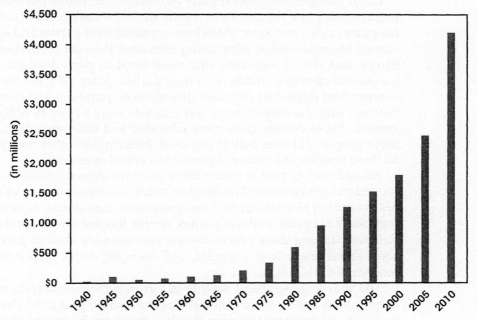

Source: *Statistical Abstract of the United States,* various editions. Figures are constant dollars.

DIFFUSION OF POWER IN GOVERNMENT

Another change in the climate of politics, besides new groups and expanding business advocacy, has been the diffusion and decentralization of power in Washington, D.C. Three major reasons for this are (1) reforms in Congress, (2) the decline of political parties, and (3) increased complexity of government.

Traditionally, a few party leaders and powerful committee chairs ran the House and Senate autocratically. But the stubborn resistance of Southern Democrats to civil rights legislation in the 1960s eventually led in 1974 to an uprising of junior legislators, who passed procedural reforms to democratize Congress, taking power from the party leaders and spreading it widely. After 1974, subcommittees could hold hearings on any subject they wished; they developed large staffs and often became small fiefdoms of independent action. Instead of an institution dominated by a few leaders, one observer described Congress as "like a log floating down a river with 535 giant ants aboard, and each one thinks he or she is steering."[34]

Now business lobbyists had to contact nearly every member of a committee or subcommittee to get support for a measure, rather than just the chair. A veteran lobbyist mused about the change this way: "On a tax issue if you had the agreement of the chairman of Ways and Means, you could go out and play golf," but "these days you can't rest easy unless you've worked all the members."[35]

Other changes also eroded party authority. The media, particularly television, began to supplant the parties as a source of information about candidates. Using television, more and more politicians bypassed their parties and spoke directly to voters. More television advertising increased the cost of elections. In the past, Senate and House members who were loyal to party leaders could count on substantial campaign funds from their parties. After 1974, however, increasingly independent legislators appealed directly to corporations and interests for contributions. And the corporations and interests were happy to oblige. In the background, the electorate grew more educated and independent than in past eras. More people split their ballots and used decision cues other than party labels. For all these reasons, the power of parties has ebbed over time.

An additional cause of power diffusion is the growth in size and complexity of the federal government. Washington today is a maze of competing power centers, including elected officials, congressional committees, cabinet departments, regulatory agencies, political parties, courts, interest groups, and lobbying firms. Relations among these power centers continuously shift as partisan tides, personal ambitions, power struggles, and emerging issues glide across the political landscape.

The sum of government activity has growing significance to business, and so corporations are far more politically active than in past eras. The expanded size and scope of government mean that its actions can be critical to company operations. Many bills passed by Congress directly affect earnings. Legislation affects taxes, interest rates, import/export rules, antitrust policy, defense spending, regulatory compliance costs, health care costs, the dollar exchange rate, uses of information, and much more.

THE UNIVERSE OF ORGANIZED BUSINESS INTERESTS

peak association
A group that represents the political interests of many companies and industries.

Literally thousands of groups represent business. What follows is a summary of this universe.

The most prominent groups are *peak associations* that represent many companies and industries. Their strength lies in representing a large expanse of the business community. Their weakness is that many issues divide their members, so they lobby aggressively only on broad issues that unite diverse company interests.

[34] Bradley, "How to Work in Washington," p. 55.
[35] Charls E. Walker, quoted in Jill Abramson, "The Business of Persuasion Thrives in Nation's Capital," *The New York Times*, September 29, 1998, p. A23.

The largest and most powerful peak association is the U.S. Chamber of Commerce, which was founded in 1912. The Chamber is a federation of 3,000 local and state chapters, 830 trade associations, and 3 million companies, 96 percent of which have fewer than 100 employees. The Chamber is the largest and most aggressive business lobby. In 2009 it spent $145 million, five times as much as ExxonMobil, the second highest spender, to push its agenda of free trade, low taxes, and limited regulation.[36] It is also antilabor, its president having once suggested that "somebody's got to go hit [the president of the AFL-CIO] in the mouth."[37] Such causes unite its diverse membership.

Several other peak associations are also powerful. The National Association of Manufacturers (NAM), founded in 1895, represents a membership of 10,000 companies and 350 trade associations. Its interests generally align with those of the Chamber. The National Federation of Independent Businesses (NFIB), founded in 1943, represents about 350,000 small businesses, most with five or fewer employees and less than $500,000 a year in sales. It pursues a lobbying agenda of easing compliance with government rules, reducing taxes, and keeping a lid on the minimum wage. It is the most partisan of the groups. In the 2008 elections, for example, it gave 83 percent of its campaign contributions to Republican candidates.[38] Though not as powerful or aggressive as the Chamber, it sometimes takes extreme positions. The president of the Chamber once said, "I love the NFIB, the way they get out there on the edge, like when they said, 'Get rid of the IRS.' They make us sound reasonable."[39]

Finally, the Business Roundtable is the organization that speaks for big corporations. It was founded in 1972 and consists of about 160 CEOs whose companies' dues support it. Each year it confines its advocacy to a few initiatives critical to the largest multinational firms. Its great strength is that its member CEOs are its lobbyists. They go to Washington carrying its message. It is the least partisan, most low-key of the four groups discussed here. It often takes no stand on legislation but simply provides data on how new laws will affect Companies. Some believe the Business Roundtable, in an unspoken way, counts on the Chamber of Commerce's brass knuckles to fix certain legislative problems while its CEOs stand above the fray.

trade association
A group representing the interests of an industry or industry segment.

Besides these peak associations, more than 6,000 *trade associations* represent companies grouped by industry. Virtually every industry has one or more such associations. Illustrative are the American Boiler Manufacturers Association, the Soap and Detergent Association, the Institute of Makers of Explosives, the Indoor Tanning Association, and the National Turkey Federation. Beyond lobbying for the industries they represent, these trade groups identify emerging issues, track bills in Congress, hold conferences, set industry standards, and publish data.

[36] Tom Hamburger, "New Lobbying Force Taking Shape in D.C.," *Los Angeles Times*, March 9, 2010, p. A11.

[37] Albert Eisele, "Business Leader Stirs Archer Wrath," *The Hill*, July 2, 1997, p. 1.

[38] Bara Vaida, "Steering Small Business Left," *National Journal*, January 9, 2010, p. 10.

[39] Thomas Donohue, quoted in Jeffrey H. Birnbaum, "Power Player," *Fortune Small Business*, October 2001, p. 56.

Trade associations of powerful industries, such as the American Petroleum Institute, have deep financial resources and are among the most influential players in Washington. Corporations with diverse business lines often belong to many trade associations.

Hundreds of corporations have staffs of government relations experts in Washington. These *Washington offices* are set up mainly by big companies. A recent survey of 80 of them found that on average they employed three lobbyists and spent $900,000 on lobbying.[40] General Electric, for example, has a staff organized into teams that specialize in lobbying for the needs of GE's business segments. Some specialize in contacting Republicans; others work with Democrats. When a federal stimulus bill was passed by Congress in 2009, GE's lobbyists worked to get $4.4 billion for modernizing city electrical grids included in it.[41] GE makes the equipment used in these grids. Then experts in its Washington office helped GE customers work with government agencies that gave out the money, adding hundreds of millions of dollars in revenues over many years as a result of spending $26 million for lobbying during 2009.[42]

Most firms supplement their Washington offices by hiring lobbyists from independent lobbying firms. There are dozens of such firms in Washington, D.C. Paul Magliocchetti and Associates Group was one example. The most prominent employ former legislators, officials, and congressional staff members from both parties to offer a potent mix of access, influence, and advice. Few small firms can afford to have Washington outposts, so they contract with lobbying firms or work through trade associations.

Business interests also form *coalitions* to create broader support. There are dozens of business coalitions in Washington at any time. These groupings of instant allies are ephemeral. Most form around a single issue and break up when that issue loses urgency. The advantage of membership in a coalition is that lobbying with allies can enhance impact. Sometimes, allies in one coalition find themselves on opposite sides in another.

Business gains strength when it is united, but there is chronic disunity. Longstanding tensions exist between domestic and foreign firms, truckers and railroads, manufacturers and retailers, and raw material producers and end-product manufacturers. To illustrate, for years the American Sugar Alliance, the trade association for sugar growers and refiners, has fought to preserve a federal program that inflates prices of raw cane and beet sugar by limiting sugar imports. Its political power is based on the desire of legislators in sugar producing states to preserve jobs. Big corporations such as Mars and Coca-Cola oppose it because higher sugar prices raise the cost of candy, cookies, and soft drinks. However, they

Washington office
An office in Washington, D.C., set up by a corporation and staffed with experts in advocating the firm's point of view to lawmakers and regulators.

coalition
A combination of business interests— including corporations, trade associations, and peak associations— united to pursue a political goal.

---

[40] Public Affairs Council, *2009 Corporate Government Relations Washington Office Benchmarking Report: Summary of Key Findings* (Washington, DC: Public Affairs Council, 2009), p. 3.

[41] The American Recovery and Reinvestment Act of 2009, P.L. 111-5.

[42] Elizabeth Williamson and Paul Glader, "General Electric Pursues Pot of Government Stimulus Gold," *The Wall Street Journal*, November 17, 2009, p. A18; and OpenSecrets.org, "Federal Lobbying Climbs in 2009 as Lawmakers Execute Aggressive Congressional Agenda," February 10, 2009, at www.opensecrets.org/news/2010/02/federal-lobbying-soars-in-2009.html.

have never had enough political power to defeat the sugar lobby and, ultimately, the artificially high cost of sugar is passed to consumers.

There are two broad areas of business involvement in politics. One is government relations, or lobbying, in which business exercises influence by advocating positions to lawmakers and officials. The other is electoral activity, in which business works to elect or defeat candidates. These two areas are intertwined, but if considered separately, corporations spend about 20 times as much on lobbying as they do on all forms of campaign spending.[43] We will discuss both.

LOBBYING

lobbying
Advocating a position to government.

Lobbying is advocating a position to government. A lobbyist is the person who tries to influence members of Congress, their staffs, or executive branch officials—from the president to administrators in regulatory agencies—on behalf of corporations, interest groups, trade associations, or other clients who employ or contract with them. This activity carries negative connotations. Business lobbyists, in particular, are caricatured as pleading selfish interests, ignoring the public interest, and corrupting officials with trips, gifts, and campaign contributions. Although sainthood escapes the profession, most in it work honestly and their craft is an essential political art, the exercise of which lubricates the machinery of representative government.

Lobbyists perform a crucial function; they articulate diverse interests in the great sweep of American pluralism. They do this in two ways. First, they inform and assist government. For example, members of Congress and their staffs have limited resources and knowledge. They cannot research each of 20,000 or more bills introduced every session or the hundreds of issues swirling in the political arena. Whatever the issue, somewhere in the lobbying community is an expert who has spent decades living with it and becoming an authority in that narrow, finely specialized subject. That lobbyist can brief the elected officials, educating them about a legislative proposal. Will it contribute to global warming, cause inflation, create jobs? In addition, lobbyists provide political intelligence. How are the lawmaker's colleagues voting? Will the measure pass? How will it affect the lawmaker's district or state?

According to the former chief of staff of two Senate committees, the best lobbyists are effective because they are good at this informational role.

> Good lobbyists tell you something you don't know—say, why teaching hospitals need more money for doctor training. They tell you what they think you should do about it, how to pay for it, and, most important, who opposes it and why. They know their opposition is going to be lobbying you too, so they don't say anything that can be proved wrong in your next meeting.[44]

[43] Hui Chen, David Parsley, and Ya-Wen Yang, "Corporate Lobbying and Financial Performance," MPRA Paper No. 21114, March 2010, p. 4 and table 2.
[44] Lawrence O'Donnell, "Good Lobbyists, Good Government," *Los Angeles Times,* January 13, 2006, p. B11.

And according to a former member of the House of Representatives:

> When I was in office, if I could ask a lobbyist, "So what's the other side?" and they would be willing to respect and acknowledge that there were two sides of the argument, it helped me understand the issue better . . . It also enhanced their credibility a great deal. It showed they were relying on data and facts and good solid reasoning as opposed to relying on influence and rhetoric and implied threats.[45]

Lobbyists could try to mislead a lawmaker with bias and falsehood, but this is counterproductive. A former member of Congress explains the consequences.

> There is a proper term for a lobbyist who lies or misleads or distorts, and that proper term is *former lobbyist.* When you are dealing with each other . . . the truth is your . . . real capital. Once you mislead, once you exaggerate, once you fail to give an accurate picture, you'll never be allowed in the office again.[46]

A lobbyist who lacks integrity loses access to the very people he or she earns a living trying to influence. In addition, effective corporate lobbyists must defend their proposals based at least in part on public benefit, since legislators and regulators, as a rule, cannot justify acting simply to promote corporate self-interest. The exception is small provisions that mean something primarily, and perhaps only, to the industry or company sponsoring them. Lobbyists have been called the "detail men and women" of government.[47] They have little power over broad liberal and conservative tides and headline issues to which the public is attentive. But backstage they orchestrate the small, precise actions that, cumulatively, determine how great political shifts play out. As government has grown, particularly since the 1960s, the role of the lobbyist has expanded in another direction. They are now essential guides for corporations and other clients who, standing before the immense, overwhelming edifice of power, need help to find its entrances and penetrate its mysterious processes.

Lobbying Methods

contact lobbying
Direct interaction with government officials or staff in meetings, phone calls, or e-mail.

The art of persuasion admits of many approaches. Figure 9.2 summarizes the main paths of influence used by corporations.

Direct contact with officials through oral or written communication, sometimes called *contact lobbying*, is the gold standard. Presenting the client's case in a face-to-face meeting is often the most effective way to get action. Access to decision makers is a precious commodity. Members of Congress typically have appointments booked at 5- to 10-minute intervals. An unwritten rule is that campaign contributions entitle the corporations or lobbyists who make them to access. A

---

[45] Former Rep. David Skaggs (D-Colo.), quoted in Sara Jerome, "When Lobbying Goes Wrong," *National Journal,* February 6, 2010, p. 23.

[46] Michael Watkins, Mickey Edwards, and Usha Thakrar, *Winning the Influence Game: What Every Business Leader Should Know about Government* (New York: John Wiley & Sons, 2001), p. 173; emphasis in original.

[47] Anthony J. Nownes, *Total Lobbying* (New York: Cambridge University Press, 2006), p. 208.

FIGURE 9.2   Paths of Pressure
A corporation can directly lobby for its interests or it may lobby indirectly with a grassroots campaign aimed at the public or certain groups and interests within the public. It may be assisted in both efforts by independent lobbying firms.

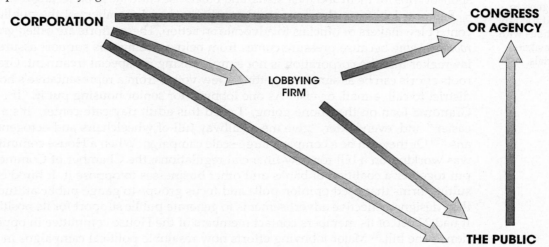

Texas legislator explains how he thinks about situations in which two lobbyists want to talk to him.

> One [is] a person you've never seen before [and] the other person helped "bring you to the dance" [i.e., contributed money to your campaign]. Who are you going to listen to? You come back to your office and there are 30 phone messages. You go through, you recognize five of them because they helped bring you to the dance. Which five are you going to return your calls to?[48]

Lobbyists often meet with a legislator's staff or committee staff. Working with staff they sometimes draft legislation. They testify at rule-making hearings in agencies and legislative hearings in the House and Senate. During subcommittee markup sessions when bills are put together, it is not uncommon for them to catch a legislator's eye and give a thumbs-up or thumbs-down signal as amendments come to a vote. Unless they are former senators or representatives, they are not allowed on the floor of either chamber, but they can stand in hallways and confer with passing lawmakers. A former senator once described the press of supplicants.

> On several occasions when we were debating important tax bills, I needed a police escort to get into the Finance Committee hearing room because so many lobbyists were crowding the halls, trying to get one last chance to make their pitch to each senator. Senators generally knew which lobbyist represented the interests of which large donor.[49]

Most advocacy work is done away from legislative chambers. Lobbyists read documents, monitor agency actions, and write papers to support their positions. Much

[48] Anonymous quotation in Knownes, *Total Lobbying*, p. 81. Brackets in original.

[49] Former Sen. David L. Boren (D-Oklahoma), quoted in *McConnell v. Federal Election Commission*, 124 S. Ct. 751.

background lobbying
Indirect lobbying activity designed to build friendly relations with lawmakers, officials, and staff.

additional time is spent on *background lobbying*, when lobbyists cultivate relationships rather than present a direct case. Corporations and lobbying firms sponsor fundraisers for senators and representatives, work in their campaigns, buy meals and sponsor trips for them and their staffs, and otherwise cultivate good feelings.

Business lobbyists also encourage constituents and members of the public to contact lawmakers or officials to advocate an action. These efforts are called *grassroots lobbying* because pressure comes from below. Seeing this support assures a lawmaker that the corporation is not simply asking for special treatment. Grassroots efforts can be as simple as getting a few voters from a representative's home district to call, e-mail, or visit. As one lobbyist for senior housing put it, "If I get Grandma Joan on the phone going, 'I need this adult day care center,' it's a lot easier," and, even better, "give me a hallway full of wheelchairs and octogenarians."[50] Or they can be a complex, large-scale campaign. When a House committee was working on a bill for new financial regulations, the Chamber of Commerce put together a coalition of banks and other businesses to oppose it. It hired consulting firms that used opinion polls and focus groups to gauge public attitudes, then designed effective advertisements to generate public support for its position. It had 22,000 of its members contact members of the House committee in opposition to the bill.[51] Major lobbying efforts now resemble political campaigns in the way they combine a broad range of methods, including direct contact, public relations, polling, policy analysis, videos, Web forums, and social networking.

Power and Limits

grassroots lobbying
The technique of generating an expression of public, or "grassroots," support for the position of a company, industry, or any interest.

Washington, D.C., is described by a veteran *Washington Post* reporter as "the center of a vast industry devoted to influencing the American government on behalf of big business."[52] His newspaper and others regularly report stories that associate heavy corporate lobbying and campaign contributions with government actions that open markets, create subsidies, lower taxes, and limit competition. In 2007, for example, the chair of a House committee proposed closing a loophole that capped taxes on the income of hedge fund executives at only 15 percent. The industry responded by increasing its lobbying expenses from $3.8 million in the previous year to $21.4 million in the next. It raised campaign contributions to House members from less than $3 million to almost $11 million. The proposal never came to a vote.[53]

Beyond such anecdotal evidence, a recent study of publicly held corporations found that heavy spending on lobbying was positively correlated with both profitability and share price.[54] Companies that spent the most on lobbying had excess market returns of 5.5 percent over peer companies that spent less. The appearance

---

[50] David Wenhold of Miller/Wenhold Capitol Strategies, quoted in Sara Jerome, "When Lobbying Goes Wrong," p. 23.

[51] Peter H. Stone, "Finance Lobby Still Opposed to New Agency," *National Journal,* October 3, 2009, p. 17; and Eliza Newlin Carney, "K Street All A-Twitter," *National Journal,* March 21, 2009, p. 9.

[52] Robert G. Kaiser, *So Damn Much Money* (New York: Vintage Books, 2010), p. 345.

[53] Robert G. Kaiser, "Obama Had a Special Interest in Curbing K-Street. Can He Do It?" *Washington Post,* February 1, 2009, p. B1.

[54] Chen, Parsley, and Yang, "Corporate Lobbying and Financial Performance," pp. 22 and 26 and table VII, panel B.

is that, using their wealth, companies bypass democratic routines, carefully exchanging gifts and contributions for action, avoiding the legal line of corruption, but routinely working at its border. A few step over. Currently, several former House members, congressional staff, agency officials, and lobbyists live in federal prisons after violating federal bribery laws.

Based on such evidence it is effortless to accept the consensus that corporate money dominates Washington. Other evidence suggests caution. An expansive four-year study of victory and defeat in efforts to influence the federal government fails to confirm that corporations translate their wealth into power and get their way more often than other interests. In this study researchers examined 98 specific issues worked on by 1,244 Washington lobbyists for corporations, unions, professional, and public interest groups.

Using interviews among these lobbyists and more than 800 government officials the researchers tracked the issues carefully, looking to see who got what they wanted, then correlating the outcomes with corporate and group resources. These resources included lobbyists employed, lobbying firms hired, former government officials used, spending on lobbying, and political contributions made. It was clear that there was a "general imbalance of resources in favor of business."

When "political success" was correlated with each of these resources, it was discovered that "businesses with high levels of resources are slightly more likely to achieve preferred policy positions," but the correlations were "very weak" and the impact of resources on outcomes was so close to zero that the researchers concluded the outcomes were "a wash."[55] Almost half the time, businesses failed to get what they wanted. Unions, professional groups, and environmental or other public interest groups did about as well. The authors concluded, "The relationship between money and power is not simple, and the richest side does not always win."[56]

Lobbying is highly competitive. Corporations often face coalitions, in which weaker opponents form alliances to build strength. Many issues are affected not just by lobbyists, but also by great partisan shifts in power between Democrats and Republicans. So the conclusion that corporate power dominates the American political system may be accurate in specific cases but is unconvincing on the whole.

Regulation of Lobbyists

Lobbyists have been regulated since 1946, when they were first required to register with the clerks of the House and Senate. Periodic, scandal-driven efforts to tighten the rules have had mixed success. Restraints on them are problematic because the First Amendment protects both the right of speech and the right of citizens to contact government officials. Still, at the federal level there are three imperfect checks on their activities.

First, the Lobbying Disclosure Act requires individuals and corporations engaged in lobbying to register with Congress and fill out quarterly forms on

---

[55] Frank R. Baumgartner, Jeffrey M. Berry, Marie Hojnacki, David C. Kimball, and Beth L. Leech, *Lobbying and Policy Change: Who Wins, Who Loses, and Why* (Chicago: University of Chicago Press, 2009), pp. 203 and 204.

[56] Ibid., p. 208.

whom they contacted, their issue objectives, and their fees or expenses. Twice a year, they must disclose political contributions to candidates, parties, and committees. These disclosures far underreport activity because only lobbyists who spend more than 20 percent of their time lobbying and make two or more written or oral contacts with lawmakers or officials must register. The rest do not, meaning coverage excludes an important range of influence activities, such as those associated with grassroots lobbying.

Second, both the House and the Senate have adopted similar rules to prevent the appearance of impropriety. These rules are reinforced in the Lobbying Disclosure Act, which prohibits individuals and corporations registered as lobbyists from giving gifts to members of Congress or congressional staff when such gifts would violate House and Senate rules.[57] For the most part, the rules are carefully followed, but are nonetheless riddled with exclusions and only loosely enforced. The House, for instance, explains its *Code of Official Conduct* in a 444-page ethics manual that strains with complexity and exceptions. Although it is forbidden for a registered lobbyist to buy a meal for a legislator at a restaurant—not even at a McDonald's— every evening trade associations sponsor lavish receptions overflowing with food. Lawmakers are permitted to attend if there are no forks with the food! According to an interpretation of House rules, if forks are present, the reception is a meal. Bagels are acceptable, but not hot dogs. To avoid stumbling over such arbitrary minutia some organizations have attorneys study their reception menus.[58]

Here are two examples from the ethics manual used to clarify when gifts may be accepted. The first example illustrates the House rule that members and their staffs can accept gifts from persons who are not registered lobbyists, but only if their value is $50 or less.

> **Example 9.** A staff person is offered four tickets to a baseball game, each having a value of $15. The staff person may accept three of the tickets, but he must either decline or pay the full price of the fourth ticket.[59]

The second interprets an exception to the gift rule allowing acceptance of a commemorative plaque or trophy presented to the representative at a public event.

> **Example 38.** An aircraft manufacturer in a Member's district sends the Member, through the mail, a high-quality model of one of the airplanes it builds. While the Member probably could have accepted the model as a commemorative item had it been presented to him in person, he may not accept it under this provision since it was merely mailed to him.[60]

bribery
An agreement to exchange something of value for an official act.

Third, it is a criminal act for public officials to ask for or receive any gift or gratuity tied to an official act. Lobbyists must avoid two crimes defined in federal law. *Bribery* occurs when a lawmaker or official asks for, is offered, or receives something valuable

---

[57] P.L. 104–65 (1995) as amended by the Honest Leadership and Open Government Act of 2007, P.L. 110–81.

[58] Cynthia Dizikes, "New Ethics Rules Won't Spoil Parties," *Los Angeles Times,* August 25, 2008, p. A8.

[59] Committee on Standards of Official Conduct, *House Ethics Manual,* 2008 ed. (Washington, DC: Government Printing Office, 2008), p. 36.

[60] Ibid., p. 54.

in return for being influenced to perform an official act. Bribery requires the existence of an agreement, or *quid pro quo*, that a gift will elicit an action. It is punishable by up to 15 years in prison and a fine up to three times the value of the bribe. The lesser offense of *illegal gratuity* occurs when a lawmaker or official seeks or receives anything of value because of an official action taken in the past or to be performed in the future. In this situation, the action might have been or might be taken even in the absence of the gift. It is punishable by a sentence of up to two years. Two examples from the Senate's ethics manual illustrate the difference between these crimes.

illegal gratuity
The exchange of a gratuity for an official action in the past or future when that action might have been or might be taken even without the exchange.

Example 44. Lobbyist U offers Senator H a substantial campaign contribution if H will introduce certain legislation. U has violated the bribery law, as will H if H accepts.

Example 45. Senator I introduces S. 007 and manages the bill through passage solely because I believes the legislation will be good for the country. Lobbyist T also favors the legislation because it will benefit his clients. Lobbyist T sends Senator I a color television set, with a note saying, "In appreciation for your good work on S. 007." The television is an illegal gratuity.[61]

The crime of bribery can be hard to define and prosecute. Whether something is a bribe depends heavily on context and situation. The exchange of money or a gift must be closely linked in time with the official act, be designated for a specific action, or be part of a pattern of exchanges associated with performance of official acts.[62] A campaign contribution, unless it involves a clear *quid pro quo*, that is, an agreed upon exchange, one thing for another, is not a bribe.[63] Therefore, ordinary contributions given to curry general favor, even if very large, are not prosecuted.

To avoid signs of bribery, political etiquette requires that lobbyists and lawmakers speak about campaign contributions and legislative favors in separate conversations. When lobbyists entertain legislators at receptions or, through various loopholes, pay for their meals, trips, and rounds of golf, they do not engage in criminal bribery unless a tight, specific link to official favor exists. Naturally, such links are elusive and bribery convictions are rare. Implicit and unspoken understandings are perhaps less rare.

Limits on campaign contributions also restrain lobbyists. We now discuss the presence of and limits on business money in elections.

THE CORPORATE ROLE IN ELECTIONS

In the first presidential campaign, George Washington did little campaigning and spent only £39 on "treats" for voters.[64] Since then, the cost of campaigns for federal offices—president, vice president, senator, and representative—has risen steadily, at first because the rise of political parties increased competitiveness, then because

---

[61] Select Committee on Ethics, United States Senate, *Senate Ethics Manual*, 2003 ed. (Washington, DC: Government Printing Office, 2003), p. 58.

[62] United States Department of Justice, *Criminal Resource Manual* (Washington, DC: DOJ, looseleaf with multiple dates), title 9 §2041, "Bribery of Public Officials," October 1997.

[63] See *United States v. Brewster*, 506 F2d. 62 (1974).

[64] James V. DeLong, "Free Money," *Reason*, August–September 2000, p. 42.

modern campaigns required more travel and advertising, and more recently, because television dramatically inflated costs. It has now been more than a century since Congress passed the first law to limit corporate money in elections. Over that time the law has evolved, billowing into a giant mass of hair-splitting distinctions that few understand in full, but never completely succeeding in its goal. The best way to appreciate this body of law is to go back to its beginnings and watch it grow.

Efforts to Limit Corporate Influence

Throughout the nineteenth century, companies gave money directly to candidates. As companies grew and large trusts emerged the amounts given grew also. Eventually, excess invited reaction. After the Civil War, business money went disproportionately to the Republican party, which promoted a doctrine of laissez-faire capitalism. Corporate giving reached an early peak in the presidential campaigns of William McKinley. The election of 1896 matched the probusiness Republican McKinley against the radical populist William Jennings Bryan, who ran as the Democratic candidate. Bryan, a spellbinder on the stump, terrified Eastern bankers by advocating an end to the gold standard, a radical change that they opposed.

federal elections
Elections for president, vice president, senator, and representative. The 435 representatives are elected every two years, the president and vice president every four years, and the 100 senators every six years (with one-third of the senators up for election biennially). Elections are held on the first Tuesday after the first Monday of November in even-numbered years.

McKinley's campaign manager, Marcus Hanna, capitalized on their fright by establishing recommended levels of dollar contributions to the McKinley campaign. He assessed 0.25 percent of the assets of each bank from the trembling financiers and, overall, raised about $3.5 million.[65] This inflated McKinley's campaign funding to double that of any prior election and he was victorious.

In 1900 Bryan again ran against McKinley, this time on a platform of breaking up trusts. So Hanna assessed big trusts such as Standard Oil and U.S. Steel amounts based on their assets. He raised a new record sum, estimated as high as $7 million, an astronomical amount for that day. McKinley won again, by an even wider margin.

Hanna believed his assessment scheme elevated the ethics of fund-raising above the borderline bribery and petty extortion that had long characterized it. Companies did not give wanting special favors in return; instead, each put in a fair amount and in return would share in the general economic prosperity of a McKinley administration. In fact, the success of Hanna's formula created public hostility toward corporate money as the greatest threat of corruption in American elections. An effort at reform was inevitable, and it came after the election of 1904, when Republican Theodore Roosevelt, who campaigned as a reformer, was embarrassed by his opponent, Democrat Alton B. Parker, for taking large cash contributions from corporations.

Progressive reformers sought to derail the business juggernaut. In 1907 they passed the Tillman Act, making it a crime for banks and corporations to directly contribute to candidates in *federal elections,* and this is still the law today.[66] The law was sponsored by Sen. Benjamin R. "Pitchfork Ben" Tillman (D-S. Carolina). Tillman was not an idealist seeking fair elections. He was a racist with a vicious hatred of the Republicans who had freed the slaves and given them the right to

---

[65] See Herbert Croly, *Marcus Alonzo Hanna: His Life and Work* (New York: Macmillan, 1912), p. 220. A grateful McKinley engineered Hanna's appointment to the U.S. Senate.

[66] Its formal title is Act of January 26, 1907, now codified as 2 U.S. Code §441b(a).

vote in his state. He bragged on the Senate floor about riding with vigilantes and shooting freed slaves at polling places. His purpose was to break Republican party dominance by stopping the gusher of corporate money that flowed to it.

Tillman's venom is now a historical artifact. What endures from that era is fear of corporate money in politics. American political culture is shaped by egalitarian ideals. Large campaign contributions from business strained popular belief in a rough equality among interests. The Tillman Act was the first of many efforts to protect the electoral system from lopsided corporate influence. But money, especially corporate money, plays an essential role in funding elections. It is a resource that can be converted to power. Candidates use it to persuade voters. Contributors use it to buy access, influence, and favors. Because money is elemental, new conduits for giving arise when old routes are closed.

After 1907 the spirit of the Tillman Act was quickly and continuously violated. Forbidden from giving directly, companies found clever, indirect ways to put their dollars to work in campaigns. They lent money to candidates and later forgave the debts, paid lavish sums for ads no bigger than postage stamps in political party booklets, assigned employees to work for campaigns, and provided free services such as rental cars and air travel. Since the Tillman Act did not limit individual contributions, wealthy donors stepped in. These "fat cats," who included corporate executives, legally gave unlimited sums. And many companies paid salary bonuses to managers for use as campaign contributions. The history of election law after the Tillman Act has been one of trying to limit corporate influence by blocking circumventions. But, as each channel is blocked a new one quickly opens. And, as we will see, recently the direction of policy has changed, and for the first time in a century corporations are being freed of some restraint.

The Federal Election Campaign Act

In the years following the Tillman Act, Congress added to the body of election law from time to time, requiring candidates to disclose contributions, prohibiting elected officials from using federal employees in their campaigns, and barring direct contributions from labor unions to candidates.[67] Besides being riddled with loopholes, none of these measures limited the influence of what continued to be the main source of campaign funding—corporations.

In 1968, Republican Richard Nixon outspent his Democratic opponent Hubert Humphrey largely because of contributions from wealthy business magnates. One was W. Clement Stone, an insurance company executive, who set a record by giving $2.2 million to Nixon through a maze of committees. Angry Democrats passed the Federal Election Campaign Act (FECA) of 1971 to stiffen disclosure requirements on campaign contributions and expenditures. Immediately after its passage, the election of 1972 again made corporate money in politics a major reform issue. Investigations related to the Watergate scandals found that 21 corporations had violated the Tillman Act by giving direct contributions totaling $842,000 to the Nixon campaign.

---

[67] The laws were, respectively, the Publicity Act of 1910, the Federal Corrupt Practices Act of 1925, the Hatch Act of 1939, and the War Disputes Act of 1943 (a temporary measure made permanent by provisions in the Labor-Management Relations Act of 1947, better known as the Taft-Hartley Act).

In reaction to this illegality, Congress extensively amended the FECA in 1974 (the first of five amending acts over a decade). As revised, the FECA curbed wealthy donors by placing ceilings on both campaign contributions and expenditures. Instead of giving as much as they wanted, individuals could contribute only $1,000 per election to a candidate and only $25,000 a year in total to any combination of candidates or political committees. The Tillman Act's prohibition on direct corporate contributions continued. In an attempt to put more enforcement power behind election law, the amendments created a new regulatory agency, the Federal Election Commission. The intent of the amendments was to limit corporate influence. However, over the 30 years that this legal framework remained in force it failed to do so. There were three reasons.

First, in 1976 the Supreme Court severely compromised the law's design for controlling campaign money. In *Buckley v. Valeo,* the Court held that giving and spending money in political campaigns are forms of expression protected by the First Amendment guarantee of free speech.[68] The Court upheld the FECA's *contribution* limits, saying the government had a legitimate interest in avoiding corruption and the appearance of corruption that unlimited contributions invited. But it struck down overall *expenditure* limits as too great a restraint on political speech. This badly compromised the law's ability to limit campaign spending.

Second, the proliferation of interest groups caused by the growth of government created more organized interests to fund campaigns. Because the FECA—even after the *Buckley* decision—limited individual contributions, the era of fat cats seemed to be over, though as we will see, only temporarily. So corporations raced to set up devices called political action committees (PACs), which could legally contribute to candidates in their name. The number of PACs grew rapidly, and with them the sums of money entering politics.

Third, corporations and lobbyists adapted to the new FECA regime by learning how to exploit, avoid, and live with its regulations. Their machinations over 30 years paralleled those that followed the Tillman Act in 1907 and showed again that political money is like water in a stream; dammed up in one place, it flows around and over in another. The two most important maneuvers around the spirit of the law were (1) the use of political action committees and (2) the rise of soft money used for issue advertising. We will explain each one.

Political Action Committees

political action committee
A political committee carrying a company's name formed to make campaign contributions. The money it gives to candidates comes from individual employees, not from the corporate treasury.

When Congress limited individual contributions, it left open a loophole permitting corporations to set up *political action committees,* or political committees carrying a company's name. These committees make campaign contributions, not with corporate money, but with money put in by employees. Although corporations previously had not formed PACs, unions had used them since the 1940s and already had more than 200. When the new FECA contribution limits went into effect in 1974, corporations started forming PACs too. The number rose steadily, peaking at 1,816 in 1988, then slowly declining and stabilizing at around 1,600. The primary reason

68 421 U.S. 1. ·

FIGURE 9.3
Contributions to Candidates by Corporate and Labor Political Action Committees in Two-Year Election Cycles: 1986–2008

Source: Federal Election Commission.

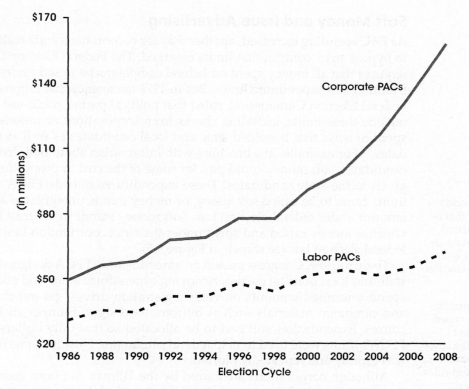

for the decline was that some companies wearied of politicians who pressured them for money.

Other interests also use PACs; in 2009 there were 4,611, including 1,598 corporate PACs, 272 union PACs, and 995 trade association PACs.[69] As Figure 9.3 shows, despite stability in numbers, contributions by corporate PACs more than tripled between 1986 and 2008. Union PACs contribute only a little more than corporate PACs did two decades ago.

Money in a PAC is spent based on decisions made by its officers, who must be corporate employees. Their decisions are aligned with corporate political goals. Currently, PACs are allowed to give up to $5,000 per election to candidates, but most contributions are smaller ones of $500 to $2,000. In 2010 a $2,000 contribution was less than one-hundredth of 1 percent of the cost of an average Senate race and less than one-tenth of 1 percent of the cost of an average House race. Company lobbyists know that even these minor contributions create an expectation of access, or a hearing of the corporation's position, after the candidate is elected.

election cycle
The two-year period between federal elections.

There are no dollar limits on the overall amounts that PACs can lawfully raise and spend. Most corporate PACs contribute less than $50,000 during a two-year *election cycle*, although in the 2007–2008 cycle, 19 contributed more than $1 million to candidates. AT&T's PAC topped the list at $3.1 million.[70]

[69] "Semiannual PAC Count 2000–Present," *Federal Election Commission Record,* April 2009, p. 9.

[70] Federal Election Commission, "Growth in PAC Financial Activity Slows," news release, April 24, 2009, table 14.

Soft Money and Issue Advertising

As PAC spending increased, another way for corporations and wealthy executives to bypass strict contribution limits emerged. The Federal Election Campaign Act requires that all money spent on federal campaigns be raised under its strict contribution and expenditure limits. But in 1978 the agency that enforces the law, the Federal Election Commission, ruled that political parties could use money raised outside these limits, including checks from corporations or unions, when it was spent in ways that benefited state and local candidates as well as federal candidates.[71] For example, in a brochure with information about both federal and state candidates, soft money could pay for some of the cost in proportion to the space given to the state candidates. These expenditures outside FECA's contribution limits came to be called *soft money*, or money that is unregulated as to source or amount under federal election law. Soft money stands in contrast to *hard money*, which is money raised and spent under the strict contribution limits and rules in federal election law (as shown in Figure 9.5).

Then, in 1979, Congress passed an amendment to FECA designed to encourage state and local political parties, removing expenditure limits and allowing them to spend unlimited amounts on voter registration drives, get-out-the-vote efforts, and campaign materials such as buttons, yard signs, bumper stickers, and brochures. Expenditures still had to be allocated so that only dollars raised under FECA's limits were used to help federal candidates. However, this fine distinction was rapidly and repeatedly blurred.

Although corporations are barred by the Tillman Act from contributing from their treasuries to federal campaigns, a series of advisory opinions by the Federal Election Commission opened the door for them to give unlimited soft money contributions to the national Democratic and Republican parties. The national parties then disbursed the money to state and local parties, which used it in inventive ways, not to buy lawn signs, but more and more to promote the election of federal candidates. Figure 9.4 shows how soft money receipts ballooned from $87 million to $495 million in a decade. Corporations were virtually unrestrained. AT&T, the largest soft money donor in the 2002 election cycle, gave $2.3 million to the Republican party and $1.5 million to the Democratic party.[72]

Most of the flood came after 1996, when the Supreme Court held that soft money could be used for a certain kind of political ad aimed at influencing federal races.[73] The Court distinguished between *issue advocacy*, which presents a political view or comment on an electoral race, and *express advocacy*, which suggests the election or defeat of a candidate using specific words such as "vote for," "defeat," or "support." Soft money could be used for issue ads that tiptoed around direct electioneering by avoiding the use of these words, even if the intent to support or oppose a candidate was clear to voters. Within a few years most soft

soft money
Money that is unregulated as to source or amount under federal election law.

hard money
Money raised and spent under the strict contribution limits and rules in federal election law.

---

[71] Federal Election Commission, Advisory Opinion 1978–10, 1 Fed. Election Camp. Fin. Guide (CCH) ¶5340 (Aug. 29, 1978).

[72] Common Cause, "Top Soft Money Donors," www.commoncause.org. Figures include contributions by the corporation, its subsidiaries, and its executives.

[73] *Colorado Republican Federal Campaign Committee v. FEC,* 116 S. Ct. 2390 (1996).

FIGURE 9.4
Soft Money
Receipts by
Democratic
and
Republication
National Party
Committees:
1992–2002
Election
Cycles

Source: Federal Election Commission.

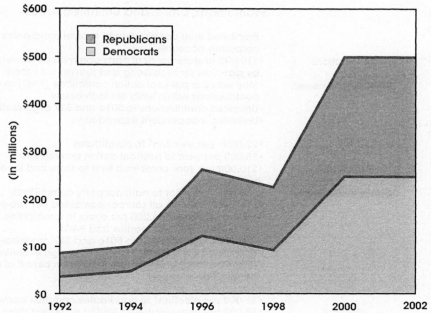

money was buying issue ads on television. Corporations wrote big checks to the national Democratic and Republican parties, which forwarded the money to state and local parties, which used it to pay for thinly disguised electioneering targeted at federal races.

Reform Legislation in 2002

By the election of 2000, the spectacle of corporations giving soft money in unlimited amounts mocked the spirit of election law. Finally, Congress passed the Bipartisan Campaign Reform Act of 2002 (BCRA).[74] The new reform tried to limit the use and influence of soft money contributions by corporations, unions, and wealthy individuals. It had three main provisions.

First, it prohibited the national parties from raising and spending soft money. It also imposed strict rules forcing state and local parties to use only hard money for activities that benefited federal candidates. Instantly and effectively this closed the soft money loophole, ending the bonanza of corporate money the parties had used for election ads that were thinly disguised as advocacy of an issue when, in fact, they were advocating election or defeat of a federal candidate, not expressly but by implication.

Second, to compensate for the loss of soft money funds, contribution limits for individuals were raised. Since they were first set in 1976, contribution limits had never been raised and they were unrealistically low. Now they were more than quadrupled and indexed for inflation. The new limits, shown in Figure 9.5 as

[74] The BCRA is better known as the McCain-Feingold Act after Senators John McCain (R-Arizona) and Russell Feingold (D-Wisconsin), its principle sponsors. Technically, it is a set of amendments to the Federal Election Campaign Act of 1971.

FIGURE 9.5
Current Contribution and Expenditure Rules in Federal Elections

Source: Federal Election Commission.

Prohibitions, Limits, and Unlimited Areas

Corporations

- Prohibited from contributing to federal candidates using corporate accounts
- $10,000 to state political party committees where permitted by state law for registering and turning out voters
- May set up a political action committee (PAC) to make contributions within limits set forth below
- Unlimited contributions to 501c and 527 organizations
- Unlimited independent expenditures

Individuals

- $2,500* per election† to candidates
- $5,000 per year to political action committees
- $10,000 per year combined limit to state and local party committees
- $30,800* per year to national party committees
- $117,000* total to all sources combined per two-year election cycle as follows: $46,200 per cycle to candidates and $70,800 per cycle to national parties and PACs
- Unlimited contributions to 501c and 527 organizations
- Unlimited expenditures to own campaign if running for office
- Unlimited independent expenditures on behalf of or against candidates or causes

Political Action Committees

- $5,000 per election† to candidates and their committees
- $5,000 per year combined limit to state and local parties
- $15,000 per year to national party committees
- $5,000 per year to other political committees
- Unlimited independent expenditures

*These limits are indexed for inflation. Figures are for 2010–2011 election cycle.
†Primary elections, general elections, special elections, and nominating conventions or caucuses are all separate elections, and individuals or committees may contribute up to the legal limit in each.

currently in effect, let individuals give $2,400 per election and up to $115,500 per two-year election cycle.

Third, the BCRA prohibited corporations and unions from directly funding "issue ads." However, it was still legal for them to make contributions from their treasuries to advocacy groups, ranging from trade associations to political committees set up for the sole purpose of running issue ads. To prevent such circumventions, the new law prohibited issue ads funded by corporate independent expenditures within 30 days before a primary election and 60 days before a general election. Only ads funded by hard dollars, that is, dollars contributed by individuals or corporate PACs under the limits and rules shown in Figure 9.5, could run during these blackout periods. The law set up a test for which ads could be blacked out. They had to clearly identify a federal candidate, be communicated by broadcast, cable, or satellite (newspaper, magazine, and Internet ads were permitted), target a relevant audience of 50,000 or more voters, and be paid for, in whole or part, by a corporation. If all this, including Figure 9.5, seems complicated, it is. Federal election law had become an unduly complex, nearly incomprehensible system of partial censorship.

In 2009 the Supreme Court struck down this blackout rule and held the BCRA's prohibition against corporations funding issue ads unconstitutional. It also held

FIGURE 9.6   The Fundamental Vision of Election Law
The challenge to the courts and to Congress with respect to election law is to balance the guarantee of free speech in the First Amendment against an implied duty to maintain elections free of corruption and the appearance of corruption.

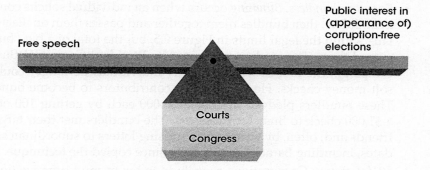

unconstitutional the FECA's prohibition against corporations making independent expenditures that expressly advocated election or defeat of federal candidates. The Court decided that both rules were a "ban on speech" in violation of the First Amendment.[75] Its decision in *Citizens United v. Federal Election Commission* freed corporations to pay for political ads, that is, to "speak," with general treasury funds. Because the Tillman Act's prohibition of direct corporate contributions to candidates is still in force, corporations cannot coordinate their electioneering activities with candidates. However, they can independently advocate their choice in any federal race for office. The *Citizens United* decision is examined in the case study at the end of this chapter.

Citizens United abraded a cardinal principle in American election law—that Congress may restrict corporate speech to insure the fairness of elections. This principle resolves the tension between two strong values in the American political system, freedom of speech and political equality (see Figure 9.6). But it did not reject the principle entirely and so today corporations, their executives and owners, are still limited in their advocacy of candidates or measures in elections. In the next section, we explain the openings for business money seeking to influence elections.

HOW BUSINESS DOLLARS ENTER ELECTIONS

Despite more than a century of efforts by reformers to limit business influence, corporations continue to inject large sums into elections. How do they do it? Here are the basic conduits for both hard and soft dollars.

- *Political action committees.* Corporate PACs raise unlimited amounts of hard money that can be contributed to candidates, other political committees, and political parties in amounts as specified in Figure 9.5. As mentioned, some corporate PACs contribute millions of dollars to candidates.

---

[75] *Citizens United v. Federal Election Commission*, 130 S. Ct. 876 (2009), at 899.

- *Individual contributions.* Wealthy corporate executives contribute hard money up to the individual contribution limits shown in Figure 9.5. They contribute to candidates in state and local races according to state law. And they contribute soft money to the 501(c) and 527 nonprofit groups described below.

bundling
Fund-raising by an individual who solicits multiple contributions for a candidate, then "bundles" the checks and passes them on.

- *Executive bundlers. Bundling* occurs when an individual solicits contributions for a candidate, then bundles them together and passes them on. Each contribution falls within the legal limits in Figure 9.5, but the total of a big "bundle" can far exceed them. The model was created by President George W. Bush in his 2004 campaign, the first in which wealthy individuals no longer could write large soft money checks. He asked major contributors to become bundlers instead. These bundlers pledged to raise $100,000 each by getting 100 others to write a $1,000 check to Bush for President. The bundlers met their targets by calling friends and, often, by writing fund-raising letters to subordinates. Other candidates, including Barack Obama, have since copied the technique.

- *501(c) groups.* Corporations contribute to tax-exempt organizations set up under section 501(c) of the Internal Revenue Code. These groups are allowed to engage in political activity so long as that is not their primary purpose. For example, Americans for Job Security is one of many probusiness 501(c)(4) "social welfare" organizations. It has raised more than $40 million from corporations and wealthy executives to run issue ads on television and radio. Business leagues such as the Chamber of Commerce and trade associations such as the American Petroleum Institute are organized under section 501(c)(6). Dues from their corporate members support annual expenditures of hundreds of millions of dollars on lobbying and election activities. These 501(c) groups are not required to report political expenditures to the Federal Election Commission, but must otherwise obey election laws.[76]

- *527 groups.* Groups organized under section 527 of the tax code are "political organizations" set up primarily to influence elections. If they advocate the election or defeat of specific candidates they must register with the Federal Election Commission. They can take in unlimited amounts of soft money from any source to conduct voter drives or create advertising to influence elections. Many companies contribute to them. For example, between 2004 and 2010 Altria Group gave them $2.8 million and AT&T gave them $1.4 million.[77] Much spending by 527 advocacy groups is unreported, but one estimate of the total in the 2008 elections is $245 million, only part of which came from corporations.[78]

independent expenditure
A message of express advocacy to voters that is not coordinated with a candidate.

- *Independent expenditures.* The *Citizens United* decision invalidated the long-standing prohibition against corporations paying for ads or actions that expressly advocate election or defeat of a federal candidate. Now, they can fund *independent expenditures* for communications that are made independently, that

---

[76] Erika Lunder, *Tax-Exempt Organizations: Political Activity and Disclosure Requirements,* Congressional Research Service, Report RL33377, April 20, 2006, pp. 13–15.

[77] See Center for Political Accountability, "Political Transparency and Accountability Reports," at www.politicalaccountability.net.

[78] Center for Responsive Politics, "527s: Advocacy Groups in the 2010 Elections," www.opensecrets.org/527s/index.php, accessed March 25, 2010.

FIGURE 9.7
History of Efforts to Suppress Corporate Money in Politics
When the flow of political money into elections is blocked by reform, the money flows around the barrier through loopholes in the regulations. In the long run, each milestone effort to stem the tide has failed.

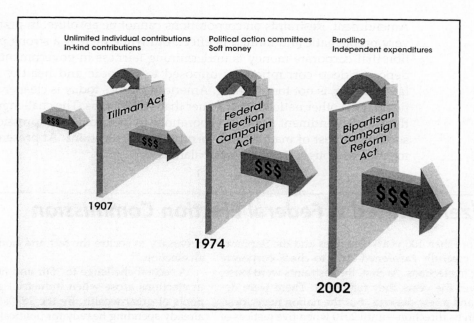

is, not coordinated in any way with candidates. In other words, the corporation can run an ad asking voters to elect a candidate, but it cannot consult with the candidate. It violates the law if it creates the ad at the request of a candidate or if "substantial discussion" has occurred with the candidate about the ad.[79]

- *State and local elections.* Corporate contributions to candidates are banned in 23 states and many cities. Corporations are not required to report their giving at the state and local levels and reporting by candidates and parties varies, so the total is unknown. But it is large and will grow. To give two examples, in 2008 state-level contributions totaled $4.8 million for AT&T and $840,000 for Union Pacific.[80] These figures include both contributions from corporate treasuries and corporate PACs and are likely incomplete.

In sum, although corporations may not use money from their treasuries to contribute to federal candidates directly, corporate money flows through many other channels into federal, state, and local elections. Figure 9.7 summarizes the century-old effort to suppress corporate money in politics. As it shows, each time reformers set up new legal barriers, business finds a way around them.

CONCLUDING OBSERVATIONS

Corporations have a long history of participation in the nation's political life. In this chapter we discussed the nature of this participation in two areas, lobbying and elections. In each area the rights of corporations are protected by the First

---

[79] "Notice of Proposed Rulemaking on Coordinated Communications," *FEC Record*, March 2010, p. 8.

[80] Center for Political Accountability, "Political Transparency and Accountability Reports."

Amendment. Restraints on corporations cannot be absolute. In practice, they are very problematic and limited in effect. But while there is a strong public perception that corporate money is undermining fairness in government, specific evidence of deep corruption, as opposed to periodic and healthy exposures of lawbreaking, is not forthcoming. American politics today is cleaner than the politics of most other nations and cleaner than in past eras. The challenge is to balance the First Amendment right of corporations to free political expression against the societal interest of maintaining corruption-free elections. At present, our society maintains a rough, if not perfect, balance.

Citizens United v. Federal Election Commission

For more than 100 years Congress and the Supreme Court carefully fashioned laws to check corporate power in elections. At first, the restraints were loose, but over the years they tightened. There were debates and a few dissents, but the nation never hesitated in its direction—until 2010 when five justices of the Supreme Court decided to reverse course. This is the story of their decision. It begins in the nation's youth.

CONGRESS PROTECTS ELECTIONS

In the American philosophy of self-government, free elections are an indispensable bulwark against tyranny. The founders believed all citizens should have the right to vote, that their votes should count equally, and that a majority should prevail. The rules in the Constitution bound the young nation to these ideals. The Founding Fathers also believed that if citizens were to vote wisely, they needed full, open debate on candidates and issues. The central purpose of the First Amendment, which directs that "Congress shall make no law . . . abridging the freedom of speech," is to protect this debate.

In the early years of the republic the practice largely accorded with the ideal. The first challenge came right after the Civil War when violence and intimidation kept freed slaves from the polls. Congress passed two Enforcement Acts in 1870 and 1871 to protect the freed slaves' right to vote and these were the first election laws. The Supreme Court eventually upheld "the [constitutional] power of [C]ongress to make such provisions as are

necessary to secure the fair and honest conduct of an election."[1]

A second challenge to "fair and honest conduct" in elections arose when industrial growth created pools of great wealth. By the 1870s railroads were already spending heavily for political favors. In 1873 Jay Gould, owner of the Erie Railroad, explained his businesslike approach to elections.

> It was the custom when men received nominations to come to me for contributions, and I made them and considered them good paying dividends for the company; in a republican district I was a strong republican, in a democratic district I was democratic, and in doubtful districts I was doubtful; in politics I was an Erie railroad man every time.[2]

As time passed, the amounts of business money in elections grew. So did public perception of corruption, real and imagined. Standard Oil is reported to have given a check for $250,000 (about $6.4 million in current dollars) to reelect McKinley in 1900. In 1905 an investigation of New York insurance companies inflamed the nation. It revealed they had spent hundreds of thousands of dollars electing state and national politicians. A prominent Republican boss, when asked if these contributions bought favors, replied: "That's naturally what would be involved."[3] The investigation also revealed a $50,000 ($1.2 million in today's dollars) donation from New York Life

---

[1] The case is *ex parte Coy*, 127 U.S. 731 (1888), at 752.

[2] Quoted in Maury Klein, *The Life and Legend of Jay Gould* (Baltimore: Johns Hopkins, 1986), p. 97.

[3] Thomas Platt, quoted in Thomas Fleming, "The Long, Stormy Marriage of Money and Politics," *American Heritage*, November 1998, p. 45.

to President Theodore Roosevelt in 1904. Roosevelt, who had said he would reject money from the trusts and fund his campaign with contributions from average citizens, was so embarrassed that he called on Congress to forbid "all contributions by corporations to any political committee or for any political purpose."[4] In 1907 it did so with the Tillman Act, which prohibited banks, corporations, and insurance companies from contributing money to presidential and congressional candidates.

ELECTION LAW EXPANDS, TIGHTENS RESTRAINTS ON CORPORATIONS

The Tillman Act was the first effort by Congress to protect the institution of free elections by restricting the entry of corporate wealth. Although the Tillman Act applied only to federal elections—that is, elections for president, vice president, senator, and representative—about half the states eventually passed similar laws. One was Montana, where copper interests had corrupted elections for sheriffs, judges, county commissioners, and state legislators. Its citizens, weary of vote buying, passed a 1912 initiative making it illegal for a corporation to "pay or contribute in order to aid, promote or prevent the nomination or election of any person . . . political party or organization."[5]

The Tillman Act and its progeny in the states turned out to be more loophole than law. Corruption continued. In 1925, after the Teapot Dome scandal, Congress passed the Federal Corrupt Practices Act to strengthen restrictions on campaign contributions and spending. In 1939 it passed the Hatch Act banning contributions from federal employees so that presidents could not make campaign giving a condition of holding a job. In 1947 the Taft-Hartley Act extended the ban on contributions to labor unions and prohibited independent expenditures by banks, corporations, and unions for messages that asked for the election or defeat of candidates. Congress intended to prevent these entities from

going around the Tillman Act's contribution ban and spending money from their treasuries to elect or defeat candidates on their own. President Truman vetoed the law, expressing concern that banning independent spending was "a dangerous intrusion on free speech, unwarranted by any demonstration of need."[6] Congress overrode the veto.

When the United Auto Workers tested the Taft-Hartley law by spending union dues on television ads in the 1954 elections, the Supreme Court upheld the independent expenditure ban in a close 5–4 decision. This drew a spirited dissent from Justice William O. Douglas.

> Until today political speech has never been considered a crime . . . [I]t costs money to communicate an idea to a large audience . . . Yet [the Taft-Hartley law] . . . makes criminal any "expenditure" by a union for the purpose of expressing its views on the issues of an election and the candidates. Some may think that one group or another should not express its views in an election because it is too powerful . . .
>
> But [this does not justify] withholding First Amendment rights from any group—labor or corporate.[7]

Although corporate spending on campaigns continued to flow through loopholes and grow, for the next quarter century Congress took no action. It acted again in 1971 by passing the Federal Election Campaign Act (FECA) to compel more disclosure of contributions and expenditures. Then, following the Watergate scandal, it amended and strengthened this law in 1974 to close longtime loopholes for corporate money. It set contributions limits of $1,000 per election per candidate and $25,000 a year total giving for individuals and limited their independent expenditures to only $1,000 a year. Wealthy executives could no longer contribute at will. It also set strict contribution limits for political committees. It expanded the Tillman Act's ban on corporate contributions to include giving anything of value. Corporations could no longer abet campaigns with gifts of staff and services. It continued the Taft-Hartley Act's ban on independent expenditures for election advocacy by corporations (see the accompanying box for the wording).

[4] Quoted in Nancy Lammers, ed., *Dollar Politics,* 3rd ed. (Washington, DC: Congressional Quarterly, 1982), p. 41.

[5] Cited in testimony of Montana Attorney General Steve Bullock, Hearing on *Corporate America v. the Voter: Examining the Supreme Court's Decision to Allow Unlimited Corporate Spending,* U.S. Senate, Committee on Rules and Administration, 111th Congress, 2nd Session, February 2, 2010, p. 2.

[6] Cited in Allison R. Hayward, "Revisiting the Fable of Reform," *Harvard Journal on Litigation* 45 (2008), p. 459.

[7] *United States v. International Union United Automobile, Aircraft and Agricultural Implement Workers of America,* 77 S. Ct. 529, at 543 and 595.

With passage of the Federal Election Campaign Act the ban on independent expenditures by corporations from the Taft-Hartley Act was codified in 2 U.S.C. §441b. It read, in part:

§441b Contributions or expenditures by national banks, corporations, or labor organizations

(a) It is unlawful for any national bank, or any corporation organized by authority of any law of Congress, to make a contribution or expenditure in connection with any election to any political office . . .

(2) For purposes of this section . . . "contribution or expenditure" . . . includes any direct or indirect payment, distribution, loan, advance, deposit, or gift of money, or any services, or anything of value . . . to any candidate, campaign committee, or political party . . . but shall not include

(A) communications by a corporation to its stockholders and executive[s] . . .

(B) nonpartisan registration and get-out-the-vote campaigns by a corporation aimed at its stockholders and executive[s] . . .

(C) . . . contributions to a separate segregated fund* to be utilized for political purposes by a corporation . . .

* A "separate, segregated fund" is a political action committee, which must by law keep its funds set apart from general treasury funds.

But it opened a loophole. It permitted corporations to set up political action committees (PACs). These PACs could not be funded by corporate treasuries, only by individual contributions from employees up to a limit of $5,000 per employee per two-year election cycle. Using this money, PACs could engage in advocacy, for example, by running television ads for or against candidates. With PACs, corporations had a political voice, one muted by the limited amounts employees would contribute, but a voice nonetheless. With this provision Congress tried to narrow its remedy for the corruption potential in corporate spending, taking away most, but not all, of the corporation's potential voice, abridging its speech only as much as necessary out of deference to the First Amendment.

The FECA also created a new agency to enforce election laws. The Federal Election Commission (FEC) is an independent regulatory agency with six commissioners, no more than three of whom can be from one political party. Candidates and committees must register with it and file periodic finance reports. It writes rules, issues guidance, files reports from candidates and donors, and keeps records.

And to underline its resolve, Congress added criminal penalties. Now "knowingly and willfully" violating the law by an aggregate amount more than $25,000 in a year was a felony subject to imprisonment of up to five years and a fine or both. Lesser violations were misdemeanors with sentences up to one year and fines up to triple the amount of illegal contributions or expenditures.

Election law now was more complex. Essentially, the government had created a censorship regime that, in carefully calculated ways, would protect elections by prohibiting speech here, reducing it there, and allowing it elsewhere.

TESTS OF CONSTITUTIONALITY

Forthwith, opponents disputed the constitutionality of the new contribution and expenditure limits. In 1976 the Supreme Court said campaign contributions and spending were speech protected by the First Amendment. But it held that preventing "the reality or appearance of improper influence stemming from the dependence of candidates on large campaign contributions" was so important that it justified abridging some speech rights.[8] It upheld the FECA limits on individual contributions. The prohibitions on corporate contributions and independent expenditures remained in place. However, the Court struck down limits on independent expenditures by individuals,

---

[8] *Buckley v. Valeo,* 96 S. Ct. 12 (1976), at 58. Lead plaintiff James L. Buckley was a Republican senator from New York. Francis R. Valeo was secretary of the U. S. Senate, whose duties included administering aspects of the campaign finance laws.

holding that because they were not prearranged or coordinated with a campaign they did not present the same danger of real or apparent corruption. The case was *Buckley v. Valeo*.

After *Buckley*, regulation of elections under the FECA expanded. Congress twice more amended the law. The Federal Election Commission wrote rules and issued hundreds of advisory opinions about its application, supporting some methods of advocacy, denying others, creating tests, and parsing reporting requirements. Its voluminous output added to the complexity already present in election law. Candidates and corporations needed to consult attorneys before speaking out. Yet the regulatory scheme failed to slow the rise of money in elections, eliminate episodic corruption scandals, subdue corporate influence, or restore public confidence in government.

In cases coming before it, the Supreme Court generally upheld the government's right to limit direct contributions and independent election spending by corporations (and unions). The Michigan Chamber of Commerce brought one such case. It wanted to support a state candidate with an ad in a local newspaper. This would be an independent expenditure made apart from any control or direction by the candidate's campaign. The Chamber, a nonprofit corporation funded by dues from its corporate members, wanted to pay for the ad with general treasury funds.

However, like the federal government, Michigan's election law prohibited corporations from using their own funds to advocate election or defeat of a candidate. The Chamber challenged the constitutionality of the Michigan law as a violation of its First Amendment speech rights. This was the first time the constitutionality of the government ban on independent expenditure by corporations had come before the Supreme Court. In *Austin v. Michigan Chamber of Commerce* the Court upheld the Michigan law. In doing so it invented a new justification for limiting corporate speech. The year was 1990.

When the Court inspects speech restrictions of any kind it submits them to *strict scrutiny*, a term with specific meaning. To survive strict scrutiny, a speech law must pass two tests. First, it must serve a compelling government interest, not simply respond to a passing need or solve a minor problem, but address a matter of highest importance. In *Austin* the majority found that compelling interest in the "distorting effects" of corporate wealth that reflects only

the economic decisions of consumers and investors. It was a novel argument that implied it was the government's business to referee the relative strength of ideas in political debate.

> Michigan's regulation aims at . . . the corrosive and distorting effects of immense aggregations of wealth that are accumulated with the help of the corporate form and that have little or no correlation to the public's support for the corporation's political ideals . . . Corporate wealth can unfairly influence elections when it is deployed in the form of independent expenditures, just as it can when it assumes the guise of political contributions.[9]

Second, a speech regulation must be *narrowly tailored*, that is, it must restrict only as much expression as is necessary to achieve its objective. By analogy, a swatter is the narrowly tailored solution for a fly on the wall, not fumigation of the building. The Michigan law passed this part of the test because it was not an absolute ban on corporate speech. Even if corporations could not spend money from their treasuries, they could still make political expenditures through PACs.

CLOSING THE SOFT MONEY LOOPHOLE

The *Austin* decision confirmed that the ban on independent expenditures by corporations was constitutional. However, corporations found their way around this ban, exploiting a loophole in the FECA and several advisory opinions of the Federal Election Commission that, together, allowed them to give unlimited amounts of soft money to national party committees. Soft money is simply money raised outside the rules of the FECA. Not falling under the law, it could come from corporate treasuries. Corporations began writing large checks to national party committees, which gave the money to state party committees that used it to broadcast ads for and against candidates. These ads were flimsily disguised as "issue ads." They purported to address broad issues but in fact promoted specific candidates. Instead of saying "Vote for Smith" at the end, they would say something such as, "Call Smith, tell her what you think."

As corporate funding for "issue ads" skyrocketed, their pretense wore thin with the American public.

[9] *Austin v. Michigan Chamber of Commerce*, 110 S. Ct. 1391 (1990), at 1411.

When the Bipartisan Campaign Reform Act (the McCain-Feingold Act) was passed §203 on "electioneering communications" was codified as 2 U.S.C. §434. It read, in part:

§434 (3) *Electioneering communication*. For purposes of this subsection–

(A) *In general.*

(i) The term 'electioneering communication' means any broadcast, cable, or satellite communication which—

(I) refers to a clearly identified candidate for Federal office:

(aa) 60 days before a general, special, or runoff election for the office sought by the candidate; or

(bb) 30 days before a primary or preferential election, or a convention or caucus of a political party that has authority to nominate a candidate . . .

(III) in the case of a communication which refers to a candidate for office other than President or Vice President, is targeted to the relevant electorate.

(C) . . . a communication which refers to a clearly identified candidate for Federal office is 'targeted to the relevant electorate' if [it] can be received by 50,000 or more persons—

(i) in the district the [House] candidate seeks to represent . . .

(ii) in the State the [Senate] candidate seeks to represent . . .

Congress then passed a new law to protect elections from the dangers of corruption posed by soft money. It was the Bipartisan Campaign Reform Act of 2002, better known as the McCain-Feingold Act after its sponsors Sen. John R. McCain (R-Arizona) and Sen. Russ Feingold (D-Wisconsin). The new law amended the FECA, banning soft money contributions to reduce the influence of corporations. It raised contribution limits for individuals to give them more influence in elections. And it attempted to reduce the influence of "issue ads" funded with corporation's independent expenditures by setting up blackout periods just before elections when they were prohibited.

In the arcane lexicon of McCain-Feingold a banned "issue ad" became an "electioneering communication." The term meant any broadcast, cable, or satellite communication that referred to a clearly identified federal candidate made within 60 days before a general election or 30 days before a primary and targeted to the relevant electorate (see the accompanying box). To meet the definition, the potential audience for an ad that referred to a candidate for president or vice president had to be 50,000 or more. If it referred to a candidate for the House or Senate, it had to be 50,000 or more persons in the relevant congressional district or state.[10] Electioneering communications did not include news stories or editorials from media corporations or ads paid for by corporate PACs, since the FECA allowed them to pay for advocacy with money raised from individual contributions, or "hard money."

That at this point the law was confusing, even baffling, was the result of an underlying dynamic at work in election law. Congress was struggling to make good on its constitutional duty to ensure "fair and honest" elections. As in the past, each time it tried to shut another door for corporate money, the rules grew more complex. It is a winless, endless game between two players. Corporations, blocked by election laws, work continuously and successfully to find new loopholes. As they do, Congress has to work around the speech protections in the First Amendment to close them. Both parties are clever innovators. The public provides an audience and federal courts and regulators serve as arbiters.

Inevitably, the constitutionality of McCain-Feingold's restrictions on speech was challenged. If the intricacy of the law was ever in question, the 1,700-page district court decision upholding its major elements confirmed that.[11] Likewise, when the case,

---

[10] 2 U.S.C. §434(3).

[11] *McConnell v. Federal Election Commission*, 251 F. Supp. 2d. 176 (2003). The lead plaintiff was Sen. Mitch McConnell (R-Kentucky).

McConnell v. Federal Election Commission, was appealed to the Supreme Court, the justices upheld the soft money and electioneering provisions. Their close 5–4 decision was 272 pages and contained six separate opinions.[12]

Years of accumulated complexity in the law invited uncertainty. Was something illegal or not? Advisory opinions rolled in waves from the Federal Election Commission. For example, a Wisconsin corporation that owned 22 auto dealerships was unsure if it could advertise on television before a primary. Its owner, Russ Darrow, was running for the Senate and his name was part of each dealership. It requested an advisory opinion from the commission on a batch of ads.

One said: "Stop into Russ Darrow Cadillac on Highway 18 in Waukesha and see what Cadillac style is really all about." Another: "We'll prove to you that Toyotas cost less in West Bend at Russ Darrow." Did these ads violate the ban on electioneering communications by referring to a clearly identified federal candidate? In a five-page opinion letter the commission said no, the ads referred to a dealership, not to the candidate.[13] It was a fine distinction. Had the company been wrong, it would have been guilty of a crime.

ENTER CITIZENS UNITED

Citizens United is a political advocacy group founded in 1988 to promote a conservative agenda. It is funded mainly by individuals, but about 1 percent of its budget comes from corporate contributions. Its mission is to educate the public about issues and to support conservative candidates and causes. It produces a stream of partisan editorials, reports, and books with titles such as *Intelligence Failure: How Clinton's National Security Policy Set the Stage for 9/11.*[14]

In 2008 it made a 90-minute documentary titled *Hillary: The Movie* to show during the presidential primaries as Hillary Rodham Clinton campaigned for the Democratic presidential nomination. The

movie was very negative, containing comments such as "[s]he is steeped in controversy, steeped in sleaze" and "[s]he is the expert at not saying what she believes," and "we must never forget the fundamental danger that this woman [poses] to every value that we hold dear."[15]

Citizens United released *Hillary* in January 2008. Seven theaters across the country showed it. The group's Web site sold DVDs for $23.95. Since no "broadcast, cable, or satellite communication" took place, these actions were not an "electioneering communication" that violated the law. But Citizens United also wanted to make *Hillary* available on a nationwide video-on-demand channel named "Elections '08" and run short ads for the film on TV stations.

The group believed that the Federal Election Commission would define these actions as electioneering communications. It filed a complaint in federal district court asking for an injunction to stop the commission from enforcing the law. Then, it could show *Hillary* while it challenged the application and constitutionality of provisions in the McCain-Feingold law. The case was *Citizens United v. Federal Election Commission.*

IN FEDERAL DISTRICT COURT

This litigation was more than a straightforward effort to broadcast the movie. It was a principled challenge. Citizens United had two main arguments.

First, the ban on corporate expenditures for electioneering communications was an unconstitutional abridgement of speech guaranteed by the First Amendment. This is a *facial challenge*, which the court must resolve by a ruling that a law is or is not consistent with the intent of the Constitution. If it is unconstitutional, it is struck down from any application. The district court rejected this facial challenge, pointing out that the Supreme Court had previously upheld the constitutionality of the ban on electioneering communications.

Second, Citizens United argued that even if this provision were constitutional it was wrongly applied to *Hillary*, which was a journalistic documentary that nowhere explicitly asked the audience to vote for or against Hillary Clinton. It was a genuine

[12] *McConnell v. Federal Election Commission,* 124 S. Ct. 619 (2003).

[13] Federal Election Commission, A.O. 2004-31, September 10, 2004.

[14] David N. Bossie, *Intelligence Failure: How Clinton's National Security Policy Set the Stage for 9/11* (Nashville, TN: Thomas Nelson, 2004).

[15] Quoted in *Citizens United v. Federal Election Commission,* 530 F. Supp. 2d 274 (2008) at 280.

discussion of issues, not an electioneering communication. This is an *as-applied challenge*, which is resolved by determining if a constitutionally valid law is invalid in part or in a specific set of circumstances. The court rejected this as-applied argument too, noting that the film "is susceptible of no other interpretation than to inform the electorate that Senator Clinton is unfit for office."[16] So the law applied. It could not show the film.

Finally, Citizens United had also challenged certain disclosure and disclaimer requirements in McCain-Feingold. It planned to televise several ads for *Hillary* and the law required a spoken statement naming Citizens United as the group responsible for their content. The same statement had to appear in print on-screen for at least four seconds. The group also had to include its name, address, and phone number. Two of the ads were only 10 seconds long and it argued these inclusions were an unconstitutional burden on speech. Here is the script of one 10-second ad.

> [Image(s) of Senator Clinton on screen]
> "First, a kind word about Hillary Clinton: [Ann Coulter Speaking & Visual] She looks good in a pant suit."
> "Now, a movie about everything else."
> [Film Title Card]
> [Visual Only] www.hillarythemovie.com[17]

The district court upheld the disclosure requirements and permitted televising of the ads.

IN THE SUPREME COURT

Citizens United appealed to the Supreme Court, which accepted the case. Oral argument before the nine justices was scheduled for March 24, 2009. During oral argument the time, usually one hour, is divided equally, giving each side a chance to make its case. Sessions are lively. The justices show little deference to the presenting attorneys, interrupting frequently to challenge them and to test their own ideas.

Theodore Olsen, a former U.S. solicitor general, represented Citizens United. The primary duty of the Office of the Solicitor General is to represent the interests of the government in the Supreme Court. He was an experienced hand, but this day he represented not the government, but the group that challenged its laws. "Participation in the political process is the First Amendment's most fundamental guarantee," he began. "Yet that freedom is being smothered by one of the most complicated, expensive, and incomprehensible regulatory regimes ever invented by the administrative state."[18] He was quickly and frequently challenged by the Court's liberal justices, who wanted to know why the law, in their eyes a good law, should be interpreted to allow Citizens United to broadcast *Hillary: The Movie*.

"So how would we draw the line?" asked Justice David Souter.[19] Olsen tried to portray the film as ordinary journalism. It was "a long discussion of the record, qualifications, history, and conduct of someone who is in the political arena," and not the kind of "short, punchy" advocacy ad that Congress intended to prohibit.[20] The liberals were skeptical. Justice Souter characterized its contents: "She will lie about anything. She is deceitful. She is ruthless, cunning, dishonest, [will] do anything for power, will speak dishonestly, reckless, a congenital liar, sorely lacking in qualifications, not qualified as commander in chief. I mean, this sounds to me like campaign advocacy," he said.[21]

Next, Malcolm L. Stewart, the government's lawyer, rose to defend the election laws. It would not go well. He suggested that if there was "no reasonable interpretation" of a movie or ad other than "as an appeal to vote for or against a specific candidate" it was an electioneering communication.[22] Quickly, the conservatives rose like wasps. "If," asked Chief Justice John Roberts, "Walmart airs an advertisement that says we have candidate action figures for sale, come buy them, that counts as an electioneering communication?" "If," replied Stewart, "it's aired at the right place at the right time, that would be covered."[23] It made the law sound ridiculous.

---

[16] 530 F. Supp. 2d 279.

[17] Ibid. at 276.

[18] *Citizens United v. Federal Election Commission*, No. 08-205, oral argument transcript, March 24, 2009 (Alderson Reporting Co.), p. 3.

[19] Oral argument, p. 5.

[20] Oral argument, p. 11.

[21] Oral argument, p. 11.

[22] Oral argument, p. 24.

[23] Oral argument, p. 26.

Then Justice Samuel Alito asked if the Constitution would permit restricting access to a book with contents similar to *Hillary*. "I think," replied Stewart "the Constitution would have permitted Congress to apply the electioneering communications restrictions . . . to additional media as well."[24] This was a huge blunder. The government's position now embraced book banning, a timeless metaphor for the evils of censorship. "That's pretty incredible," responded Justice Alito.[25] Justice Anthony Kennedy asked if satellite downloads to a Kindle could be prohibited, and Stewart was forced to admit that the electioneering statute applied to satellite communications. The book ban metaphor hung over the rest of the argument like a dark cloud. It was a turning point in the case and for American election law.

Citizen's United had a good day. At the end of the argument, the case was submitted for the Court's opinion. However, three months later the Court surprised both sides with an unusual call for the case to re reargued.[26] This time, it asked the parties to focus on whether the ban on independent expenditures by corporations upheld in *Austin* and the ban on electioneering communications upheld in *McConnell* were constitutional under the First Amendment. This signaled that the Court's conservatives were ready to find that the founders words in the First Amendment disallowed restrictions on independent expenditures. If so, a venerable pillar of congressional efforts to limit corporate money in elections would fall.

REARGUMENT

Reargument was held on September 9, 2009. Again, Theodore Olsen rose on behalf of Citizens United with strong, resounding, principled words. "Robust debate about candidates for elective office is the most fundamental value protected by the First Amendment's guarantee of free speech," he said. "Yet that is precisely the dialogue that the government has prohibited if practiced by unions or corporations."[27]

The Court's liberals tried to tone down his argument. Justice Ruth Bader Ginsburg remarked that corporations were not prohibited from advocacy in elections, they could always speak using political action committees. Justice Stephen Breyer warned against making "a hash of this statute."[28] Justice John Paul Stevens said it was possible to draw lines between permissible and impermissible corporate advocacy. They wanted to save the law from a fatal date with First Amendment ideals. Olsen held his ground.

Next, Solicitor General Elena Kagan, a future Supreme Court justice, rose to speak for the government. "For over 100 years," she began, "Congress has made a judgment that corporations must be subject to special rules when they participate in elections and this Court has never questioned that judgment."[29] She got no farther. "Wait, wait, wait, wait," interjected Justice Antonin Scalia. "We never questioned it, but we never approved it either."[30] Technically this was correct. The Supreme Court must wait for cases to come before it; it cannot make law except out of a controversy duly brought before it. And no prior case had directly raised the question of the constitutionality of corporate independent expenditures.

Scalia's correction was just the beginning. The other conservatives swarmed in with sharp, dogged questions and stinging rebukes. When asked if the statute could be used to ban a book, Kagan answered, "The FEC has never applied this statute to a book." But, scolded Chief Justice Roberts, "we don't put our First Amendment rights in the hands of bureaucrats."[31]

No evidence or argument swayed the conservatives. Not even the prospect of corruption phased them. Justice Alito noted that "more than half the States . . . permit independent corporate expenditures," and asked, "Now have they all been overwhelmed by corruption?" "I think," replied Elena Kagan, "the experience of some half the States cannot be more important than the 100-year-old judgment of Congress that these expenditures would corrupt the Federal system."[32] But she would win no converts this day.

[24] Oral argument, p. 27.

[25] Oral argument, p. 27.

[26] *Citizens United v. Federal Election Commission,* 129 S. Ct. 2893 (2009).

[27] *Citizens United v. Federal Election Commission,* No. 08-205, reargument transcript, March 24, 2009 (Alderson Reporting Co.), p. 3

[28] Reargument, p. 23.

[29] Reargument, p. 35.

[30] Reargument, p. 35.

[31] Reargument, pp. 65–66.

[32] Reargument, p. 50.

THE DECISION

On January 21, 2010, the Court issued its decision, striking down as unconstitutional the bans on independent expenditures and electioneering communications by corporations. It was a split 5–4 decision set forth in 187 pages with five separate opinions including a 57-page majority opinion, a 90-page dissent, and three shorter concurring opinions.

Justice Anthony Kennedy wrote the majority opinion in which Chief Justice Roberts and Justices Alito, Scalia, and Thomas joined. It began by explaining why no exception from the government's ban on independent expenditures for advocacy could be made for *Hillary*. The film was an electioneering communication because there were 34.5 million cable subscribers and it would reach 50,000 or more voters. It was "in essence . . . a feature-length negative ad," not a journalistic documentary.[33] And the Court refused to make an exception for it just because only a small fraction of the film's budget came from corporations. It would put the Court on a road to endless drawing and redrawing of constitutional lines.

In short, the Court could not save the statute by narrowing its application "without chilling political speech, speech that is central to the meaning and purpose of the First Amendment."[34] There were too many problems. If it made an exception for *Hillary* it would extend a situation where speakers were often uncertain if their speech was or was not a crime under the law. It would take time to examine claims for exceptions, thus chilling speech just before elections. And the existing campaign finance rules, made up of 568 pages of regulations, 1,278 pages of guidance, and 1,771 FEC advisory opinions were, essentially, a complex censorship scheme that acted as a prior restraint on speech. Put this way, the body of election law that had grown over more than 100 years was no longer the edifice supporting free and fair elections, but a menace to the founders' ideals.

[33] *Citizens United v. Federal Election Commission*, 139 S. Ct. 876 (2010) at 890.

[34] 139 S. Ct. 893.

The *Citizens United* Court. Standing, from left, are Justices Samuel Alito Jr., Ruth Bader Ginsburg, Stephen Breyer, and Sonya Sotomayor. Seated, from left, are Justices Anthony Kennedy and John Paul Stevens, Chief Justice John Roberts, and Justices Antonin Scalia and Clarence Thomas. Not pictured is Justice David Souter, who retired after the initial oral argument and was replaced by Justice Sotomayor. Source: ©Doug Mills/*The New York Times*.

From here the majority marched to its conclusion. "The law before us is an outright ban, backed by criminal sanctions," wrote Kennedy.[35] First Amendment protection extends to corporations. Speech has never been and should not be banned based on the identity or wealth of the speaker. Allowing corporations to speak through political action committees restricts their speech because such committees are burdensome and expensive to administer. Finally, there is no evidence that independent expenditures by corporations, unlike direct contributions to candidates, leads to quid pro quo corruption of officials.

Therefore, the Court struck down as unconstitutional the part of §441(b) of the Federal Election Campaign Act (see the previous box) that prohibited corporate independent expenditures. That forced it to overrule the 1990 *Austin* decision, which had upheld the constitutionality of a ban on independent expenditures by corporations.

It also struck down §434 (see the previous box), the ban on electioneering communications added by the McCain-Feingold amendments. That required overruling the part of its 2003 *McConnell* decision upholding §434's constitutionality. However, the Court kept the disclosure and disclaimer requirements in the law that Citizens United disliked.

It was a principled opinion that sought to remove inroads on free, unlimited political debate. With their intrusive restrictions, well-meaning legislators had created an annoying censorship regime posing greater and more fundamental dangers to American democracy than any unproved evil of corruption. In consequence, corporations and unions are now free to make independent expenditures, spending as much as they wish on any form of political advertising anytime. They can "speak" more freely.

THE DISSENT

Justice John Paul Stevens wrote the dissent in which Justices Ginsburg, Breyer, and Sotomayor joined. Stevens was the Court's oldest justice at age 89 and its most senior, having served 35 years since President Gerald Ford nominated him in 1975. The 87-page dissent was the longest he had ever written. That was one measure of his displeasure with the majority.

Justice Stevens began by observing that Citizens United had been free to show *Hillary* as much as it wanted anytime except 30 or 60 days before elections. Using its political action committee, it could even have shown it at those times. So there was no speech ban.

Next, he attacked the majority for its belief that the First Amendment prohibited government from restricting speech based on a speaker's identity as a corporation. "Absurd," he wrote. "Such an assumption would have accorded the propaganda broadcasts to our troops by 'Tokyo Rose' during World War II the same protection as speech by Allied commanders."[36] He argued that corporations are artificial entities, "not members of We the People," and not the individuals whose self-expression the First Amendment was written to protect. "Corporations," he wrote, "have no consciences, no beliefs, no feelings, no thoughts, no desires."[37] They participate in elections solely based on their economic self-interest.

He believed the decision was "a radical departure," a "dramatic break from our past," that "threatens to undermine the integrity of elected institutions across the Nation." It "makes a hash" of the "delicate and interconnected regulatory scheme" created by Congress.[38]

It threatened to produce corruption. "Our lawmakers," he wrote, "have a compelling constitutional basis, if not also a democratic duty to take measures designed to guard against the potentially deleterious effects of corporate spending in local and national races."[39] There are many kinds and degrees of corruption. Corporations have large sums to spend buying access and buying votes. Evidence showed that issue ads bought significant influence.

> The sponsors of these ads were routinely granted special access after the campaign was over; candidates and officials knew who their friends were . . . Many corporate independent expenditures, it seemed, had become essentially interchangeable with direct contributions in their capacity to generate quid pro quo arrangements . . . politicians who fear that a certain corporation can make or break their reelection chances may be cowed into silence about that corporation.[40]

---

[35] 139 S. Ct. 898.

[36] 139 S. Ct. 947.
[37] 139 S. Ct. 972.
[38] 139 S. Ct. 940.
[39] 139 S. Ct. 929.
[40] 139 S. Ct. 965 and 974.

It was an impassioned dissent, rich with the wisdom of 35 years on the bench and he crowned it with a jewel of sarcasm: "While American democracy is imperfect, few outside the majority of this Court would have thought its flaws included a dearth of corporate money in politics."[41]

THE REACTION

President Barack Obama was displeased. "With its ruling today, the Supreme Court has given a green light to a new stampede of special interest money in our politics."[42] Sen. John McCain was "disappointed" and Rep. Russ Feingold saw it as "a terrible mistake."[43] The liberal press portrayed it as a disaster. A headline in *The New York Times* read, "Lobbies' New Power: Cross Us, and Our Cash Will Bury You."[44] A columnist in the *Washington Post* imagined the worst.

> Think of this rather persuasive moment in a chat between a corporate lobbyist and a senator: "Are you going to block that taxpayer bailout we want? Well, I'm really sorry, but we're going to have to run $2 million worth of really vicious ads against you."[45]

The progressive community felt threatened. Ralph Nader predicted that "[b]ig business domination of Washington will now intensify,"[46] and *The Nation* saw "a dramatic assault on American democracy."[47] But conservatives disagreed. Columnist George Will was glad to see that "the decades when the court was derelict in its duty to actively defend the Constitution" had ended and it had overturned "a censorship regime."[48] "Freedom had its best week in many years," editorialized *the Wall Street Journal*, "Congress's long and misbegotten campaign-finance crusade has reached a Constitutional dead end."[49]

THE FUTURE

The full consequences of *Citizens United* will not be known for years. Corporations may not react as cynics fear. For instance, conspicuous support or opposition for candidates could backfire. Both Republicans and Democrats buy cars, soft drinks, and computers, shop in department stores, eat at fast food chains, and select airlines and hotels. Few corporations would risk partisan labels. They may, however, push their advocacy through trade associations and front groups with innocuous names.

In his 2010 State of the Union address, President Obama looked down at the justices and, expressing distaste for their decision, called on Congress to correct the "problems" the Court had created. Since then, the following actions have been considered.[50]

Pass a constitutional amendment. Several have been suggested including (a) giving Congress the power to regulate corporate expenditures, (b) prohibiting corporations from using general treasury funds in elections, (c) prohibiting all corporate political activity, and (d) defining a corporation as an artificial entity to which First Amendment rights do not apply. To go into effect, an amendment would require two-thirds approval in both the Senate and the House and ratification by three-fourths of state legislatures within seven years.

Require shareholder approval, by majority vote, of all corporate political expenditures over a certain amount. It is likely in the wake of the decision that progressive shareholder activists will push for such a policy.

Create public funding for elections. Candidates would receive government funds for their campaigns. If these funds were sufficient, candidates could rely on them for election or reelection and would not need or fear expenditures by corporate interests.

[41] 139 S. Ct. 979.

[42] The White House, Office of the Press Secretary, "Statement from the President on Today's Supreme Court Decision," January 21, 2010.

[43] Quoted in Robert Barnes and Dan Eggen, "Court Rejects Corporate Political Spending Limits," *Washington Post,* January 22, 2010, p. A1.

[44] David Kirkpatrick, "Lobbies' New Power: Cross Us, and Our Cash Will Bury You," *Washington Post,* January 22, 2010, p. A1.

[45] E. J. Dionne Jr., "Supreme Court Ruling Calls for a Populist Revolt," *Washington Post,* January 25, 2010, p. A17.

[46] Ralph Nader and Robert Weissman, "The Case Against Corporate Speech," *The Wall Street Journal,* February 10, 2010, p. A19.

[47] "Democracy Inc.," *The Nation,* January 15, 2010, p. 3.

[48] George Will, "Campaign Finance: A 'Reform' Wisely Struck Down," *Washington Post,* January 28, 2010, p. A25.

[49] "A Free Speech Landmark," *The Wall Street Journal,* January 22, 2010, p. A18.

[50] See L. Paige Whitaker, et al., *Legislative Options After Citizens United v. FEC: Constitutional and Legal Issues,* Congressional Research Service Report R41096, March 8, 2010.

Ban foreign contributions. Critics say the decision would permit foreign corporations or U.S. corporations with foreign owners to influence elections. Election law prohibits foreign nationals from contributing to candidates or directing expenditures, but U.S. citizens in foreign-owned or controlled firms could direct political activity.

Questions

1. Was *Hillary: The Movie* a disguised campaign ad or a journalistic documentary? Should the Court have created an exception in the law to permit its broadcast? What could it have done?

2. Should the First Amendment protect corporate political expression? If not, where should the line be drawn for corporations between freedom and restrictions? Should First Amendment protections apply only to individual citizens?

3. If you were on the Supreme Court would you have voted in the majority or joined the dissent? Why?

4. After *Citizens United* are the rules for corporate participation in elections still too strict, about right, or too relaxed? Why?

5. Should Congress legislate in response to *Citizens United*? If so, what should it do?

Chapter Ten

Regulating Business

The Federal Aviation Administration

On December 8, 2010, a two-stage rocket rose from Cape Canaveral, Florida. Atop the 18-story Falcon 9 sat a Dragon capsule, a spacecraft capable of carrying seven astronauts or an inanimate payload into orbit and returning to earth for reuse. Both rocket and capsule were built by SpaceX, a privately held company. It was a historic moment. Only five countries and one intergovernmental agency had ever launched an object into orbit and recovered it after reentry.[1] SpaceX would join this elite band.

The Falcon 9's first stage burned for 255 seconds, its second stage for 345 seconds, taking the launch vehicle to a speed of 17,000 miles per hour and inserting the Dragon capsule into an orbit 186 miles up. After almost two earth orbits the capsule reentered the atmosphere, firing thrusters to position itself for an exact landing. At 45,000 feet small parachutes stabilized its attitude. At 10,000 feet main parachutes deployed and it splashed down in the Pacific Ocean about 500 miles off the Southern California coast. "If there had been people sitting in Dragon today," said the company's founder, "they would've had a nice ride."[2]

The SpaceX projectile may have shed the bonds of earth's gravity, but it could not escape federal regulators. Every commercial suborbital flight or reentry of a spacecraft from orbit must be licensed by the Federal Aviation Administration (FAA). The FAA is one of 14 regulatory boards and offices in the huge regulatory conglomerate known as the Department of Transportation. It writes and enforces rules to ensure the safety of civil aviation, sets standards for aircraft, inspects them, certifies pilots, operates the nation's air traffic control system, and monitors aircraft noise. It gives drug tests to flight attendants, verifies the qualifications of parachute riggers, and imposes flight restrictions over Super Bowls. As regulatory agencies go, it is moderately large, with an annual budget of $7.3 billion and 41,700 employees, including 16,000 air traffic controllers. Its administrator is appointed by the president and reports to the Secretary of Transportation.

Within the FAA, launch licenses are issued by a unit named the Office of Commercial Space Transportation, a group of 70 people, mostly engineers and scientists, who regulate the commercial launch industry with a dual mission (see the box). Their top

[1] These are the United States, Russia, China, Japan, India, and the European Space Agency.
[2] Elon Musk, quoted in W. J. Hennigan, "Successful Test Flight Is Giant Step for SpaceX," *Los Angeles Times*, December 9, 2010, p. B4.

Office of Commercial Space Transportation Mission

To ensure the protection of the public, property, and the national security and foreign policy interest of the United States during commercial launch and reentry activities, and to encourage, facilitate, and promote U.S. commercial space transportation.

priority is to protect public safety during commercial launches and reentries. A second priority is to promote the industry. So far, the FAA has licensed 21 launches.

A launch license application is a major paperwork project for a company such as SpaceX. The FAA enforces codified license requirements covering hundreds of pages. A launch vehicle is a device for controlled release of energy from highly explosive fuels. If anything goes wrong, it is a potential bomb endangering populations below its trajectory. To assess the risks, the agency collects a massive load of information in the applications. Much of it is proprietary, so it is not made public.

Requirements begin with a description of the launch vehicle including detailed diagrams of hardware, electrical circuits, software designs, and logic circuits. Each subsystem electronic component must be described. Radioactive parts must be identified. Flight information includes the launch location, schedule, flight azimuth at liftoff, motor ignition and burn times, orbital parameters, and a list of objects to be put in orbit. The path of the rocket over populated areas is precisely calculated. After launch, as operators track the rocket, an icon projecting its impact point on earth, should it fail, must move ahead of it on the radar screen. If the rocket is malfunctioning when that icon is about to enter a populated area, then it must immediately be destroyed.

Before issuing a launch license the FAA makes elaborate use of statistical models. Its rules prohibit a launch if the flight poses a risk greater than 0.00003 (30 in 1 million) public casualties from the impact of inert and explosive debris and blast overpressure greater than 1 pound per square inch.[3] To predict where debris might fall it calculates as many as 10,000 random malfunction turns from nominal flight trajectories. Then, using information in the license application about flight geometry, vehicle mass, propulsion, aerodynamics, and winds, it estimates the size and type of debris that might impact terrain. Finally, based on the locations and densities of populations below potential trajectories, it calculates the risk to members of the public.[4]

The detail in these calculations is amazing. Figure 10.1 shows the casualty area for a piece of inert debris such as a metal bracket that falls vertically. A casualty is defined as a death or serious injury. This area is a circle whose radius is the sum of the radius of a human being and the radius of a circle drawn around the largest area of a debris piece. In FAA models a human being is a cylinder six feet tall and one foot wide. A second

[3] 14 CFR §417.107(b)(1) and (c).

[4] See, for example, Steven Millard, "Risk Considerations for the Launch of the SpaceX Falcon 1 Rocket," paper, American Institute of Aeronautics and Astronautics, Honolulu, Hawaii, August 18–21, 2008.

FIGURE 10.1
**Casualty Area
for a Piece of
Debris Falling
Vertically**

Source: Federal
Aviation
Administration.

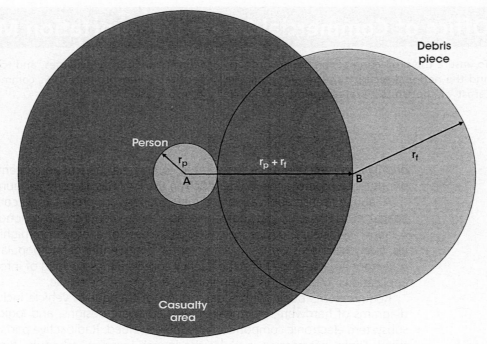

Area of casualty (A_c) equation:

$$A_c = 2[r(p) + r(f)]d + \pi[r(p) + r(f)]^2$$

Where r(p) = radius of person (1 foot)
r(f) = radius of the fragment
d = height of person (6 feet)/tangent (impact angle)

method is used to calculate the casualty area for debris that falls diagonally.[5] A similarly sized piece of debris falling diagonally covers a larger area due to the angle of its fall and its potential to bounce or ricochet along hard surfaces such as rock or concrete. A third method is used to calculate casualty areas for blasts from explosive debris.

So far, the commercial space industry is tiny. In 2009 it generated economic activity of only $828 million, less than 1 percent that of the commercial aviation industry.[6] But it will grow. As it does, federal regulation will grow with it. Already the FAA is developing regulations in areas such as liability insurance, physical exams for space tourists, and control panel designs in spaceships. So far, it has written fewer than a thousand pages of rules on commercial space transport, hardly a handful by Washington standards. However, more will come.

Some challenges are already visible. The FAA's dual mission of ensuring launch safety and promoting the launch industry is a dangerous, time-proven formula for

[5] Federal Aviation Administration, "Expected Casualty Calculations for Commercial Space Launch and Reentry Missions," *Advisory Circular*, No. 431.35–1, August 30, 2000, pp. 13–14.

[6] Federal Aviation Administration, *The Economic Impact of Commercial Space Transportation on the U.S. Economy in 2009* (Washington, DC: FAA and The Tauri Group, LLC), September 2010, app. II.

scandal and failure. It invites a cozy bond between regulators and companies that threatens objectivity. A second concern is that while the FAA can regulate suborbital flights, orbital insertions, and reentries, it has, with one exception, no authority over payloads in orbit. The exception is "obtrusive space advertising." Congress gave the agency power to prohibit any ad in space "capable of being recognized by a human being on the surface of the Earth without the aid of a telescope or other technological device."[7]

The story of the FAA and its regulation of commercial space transport is the beginning of a new chapter in the long story of federal regulation. Now we turn to that story to discuss the reasons for regulation, its rise, its legal basis, how it is carried out, its costs and benefits, and how it works in other countries.

WHY GOVERNMENT REGULATES BUSINESS

Two circumstances justify regulation of the private sector: first, when flaws appear in the market that lead to undesirable consequences, and second, when sufficient social or political reasons for regulation exist.

Flaws in the Market

When functioning freely, the competitive market mechanism determines which of society's resources can be used most efficiently in producing goods and services that people want. It yields the "best" answer to questions of what should be produced, when, and how. Although highly efficient, the free market is not flawless. Some market failures that justify regulation are these.

- *Natural monopoly.* When a firm can supply the entire market for a good or service more cheaply than a combination of smaller firms, it has a natural monopoly. Examples are local public utilities that, absent government regulation, could restrict output and raise prices without fear of competition.

- *Destructive competition.* When companies dominate an industry, they may engage in unfair or destructive competition. For example, they may cut prices until competitors leave the market, then raise prices. Large firms may conspire to fix prices. Without laws to make such behavior illegal, consumers can be harmed.

externalities
Costs of production borne not by the enterprise that causes them but by society.

- *Externalities. Externalities* are costs of production borne not by the enterprise that causes them but by society. For example, a factory that dumps waste into a river pollutes the water. It costs the factory nothing, but the community will have to pay dearly for the cleanup. Competition inhibits the factory from reducing its waste because buying expensive pollution-control equipment would put it at a cost disadvantage to its competitors. Regulation can remove this disadvantage by forcing all factories to bear the cost. The same principle applies to a wide range of similar external costs, from worker safety practices to jet noise.

[7] 49 USC §70102(9).

- *Inadequate information.* Competitive markets operate more efficiently when producers and consumers have enough information to make informed choices. To the extent that such information is not available, government finds justification for regulating the knowledge in question. Thus, regulators require that consumers be told about product quality, warranty, and content; employees be warned of work hazards; and investors be given financial data.

Social and Political Objectives

Social regulation is used to promote the broad public interest. Some regulation is also adopted to help politically powerful special interests. The two kinds of regulation can blend when the public interest is defined in ways that benefit some interests at the expense of others. Some objectives that justify social and political regulations are the following.

- *Socially desirable goods and services.* Regulation is used to ensure production of safe products. For example, the Department of Agriculture sets standards for and inspects foods entering the production process. The Department of Transportation requires seat belts and air bags in vehicles.
- *Socially desirable production methods.* Some regulations stop firms from making products in harmful ways, for example, by exposing workers to danger or by releasing pollutants. Regulation is also used to protect civil rights at work. The Equal Employment Opportunity Commission enforces rules prohibiting workplace discrimination.
- *Resolution of national and global problems.* As the nation grew, the federal government took on more responsibility to solve national problems not resolvable by state and local governments or individuals. Examples are regulation of railroads, banks, and natural resources.
- *Regulation to benefit special interests.* Some regulations protect special interests that have the political strength to pressure lawmakers for favorable laws and rules. Many such regulations apply narrowly to single companies, but industries such as the steel industry and big agricultural sectors such as cotton, peanuts, sugar cane, and tobacco benefit from protectionist rules and subsidies.

WAVES OF GROWTH

Regulation grew from the beginning. It inched ahead in the nation's first century, when laissez-faire economic doctrines restrained government controls. It sped up and barreled ahead in the second century, as a consensus for controlling markets emerged. Figure 10.2 shows that volume growth in regulation displays a wavelike pattern punctuated by spikes. The waves are triggered by popular demand for action to solve contemporary problems. The spikes mark brief intervals when the federal government exercised emergency wartime controls over production, consumption, and prices then abandoned them after the war.

After each new growth wave, the rate of regulation has tapered off. But the long trend is relentlessly up because each wave adds new authorities that live on to

FIGURE 10.2   Historical Waves of Government Regulation of Business

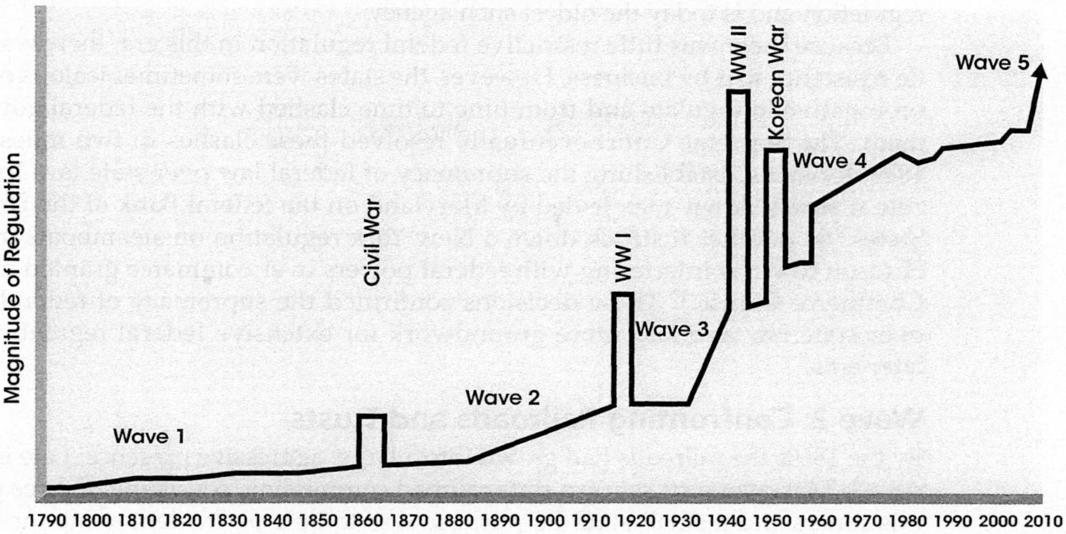

write regulations year after year. The scale on the left of Figure 10.2 is our estimate of the relative volume and impact of federal regulation of business. Following are highlights of events in each of five waves.

Wave 1: The Young Nation

In the dawn of its creation the federal government was tiny and regulation was a modest function. However, the basis for aggressive regulation existed in the U.S. Constitution. In particular, Article I, Section 8 gave Congress wide powers, including the power "to regulate Commerce . . . among the several States." This key phrase in the *Commerce Clause* would eventually become the legal grounds for imposing extensive regulation on business. But that was far in the future.

At first regulation was predominately promotional for business. The government gave vast financial subsidies and huge grants of land to private interests for the building of turnpikes, canals, and railroads. These actions facilitated the building of a much-needed infrastructure. There were also tariffs to protect "infant" industries.

As the years passed, a few offices that performed regulatory functions were established, including the Patent and Trademark Office (1836), the Copyright Office (1870), and the Bureau of Fisheries (1871), but they also were primarily promotional. The exception was the Comptroller of the Currency, set up in 1863 to charter

Commerce Clause
A clause in Article I, Section 8 of the Constitution that gives Congress the power "to regulate Commerce with foreign Nations, and among the several States, and with the Indian Tribes."[8] It has been interpreted to give the federal government wide power to regulate business.

[8] Other powers in Article I, Section 8 also gave a basis for the exercise of federal power over business. They include the power to provide for "the general welfare of the United States," to levy and collect taxes, to provide for the common defense, to borrow money, to establish bankruptcy laws, to promote science and useful arts by granting patents, and "[t]o make all Laws which shall be necessary and proper for carrying into Execution the foregoing Powers . . ."

and regulate national banks. It was the first federal agency exercising control-like regulation and is today the oldest such agency.

Because there was little restrictive federal regulation in this era, there was little resistance to it by business. However, the states were sometimes jealous of the prerogative to regulate and from time to time clashed with the federal government. The Supreme Court eventually resolved these clashes in two milestone 1819 decisions, establishing the supremacy of federal law over state law. In one case it struck down a tax levied by Maryland on the federal Bank of the United States.[9] In another it struck down a New York regulation on steamboats in the Hudson River as interfering with federal powers over commerce granted in the Commerce Clause.[10] These decisions confirmed the supremacy of federal law over state law and laid more groundwork for extensive federal regulation in later eras.

Wave 2: Confronting Railroads and Trusts

By the 1860s the railroads had grown into a large, aggressive presence. Late in the decade Massachusetts set up a state railroad commission, consisting of three commissioners and a small staff. Its purpose was to be a permanent arena for legal resolution of the conflicts that continuously arose over trains.[11] Other states soon copied this innovation. However, as railroad routes grew to span the continent, it made less and less sense for state entities to regulate them. So in 1887 Congress built the prototype of the modern federal regulatory authority when it created the Interstate Commerce Commission (ICC). The ICC shifted railroad regulation from the states to the federal government. It was an *independent commission* run by five commissioners, serving staggered six-year terms, who were nominated by the president and confirmed by the Senate. The president was to designate one commissioner as chair. No more than three of the five were to be of any one political party.

By the 1880s large, dominant trusts in many industries grew by absorbing competitors, colluding in cartels, and choking competition in other ways. The public was offended. When state laws against monopolistic practices proved ineffective, Congress passed the Sherman Antitrust Act in 1890. In 1914 it set up a second independent regulatory commission, the Federal Trade Commission (FTC), to further define and prohibit unfair means of competition. The FTC was modeled after the ICC, headed by five commissioners serving seven-year terms, no more than three from one party. Congress also passed more regulations in other areas, and by the early 1930s there were seven more new federal agencies and commissions regulating business.[12]

These steps marked a significant increase in both the volume and force of regulation, and now business began to fight for its freedom. Its biggest ally turned out to be the Supreme Court. Early in the era the Court seemed to clear the way for

independent commission
A regulatory agency run by a small group of commissioners independent of political control.

[9] *McCulloch v. Maryland,* 4 Wheaton 316 (1819).
[10] *Gibbons v. Ogden,* 9 Wheaton 316 (1819).
[11] Thomas K. McCraw, *Prophets of Regulation* (Cambridge, MA: The Belknap Press, 1984), see chap. 2.
[12] *Federal Regulatory Directory,* 14th ed. (Washington, DC: CQ Press, 2010), p. 5.

more regulation. It upheld state laws regulating railroads and in one 1877 decision made the seminal, sweeping, and noble statement that "When private property is devoted to a public use, it is subject to public regulation."[13] But soon the Court began to slow and limit regulation in decisions that, beneath the legal language, glowed with conservative economic philosophies of the day. For example, in 1905 it refused to allow a state law limiting bakers to 10 working hours a day because the law unreasonably meddled with the liberty of the bakers and their employers to make a contract on working conditions.[14] When Congress passed a 1916 law taxing products made by factories using child labor, the Court struck it down, saying the power to regulate commerce extended only to the movement of goods in interstate transportation, not to their production in factories.[15] A national crisis would be required to enlighten such cramped reasoning. It arrived in the 1930s.

Wave 3: The New Deal

When Franklin D. Roosevelt was elected in 1932, the economy was sunk in depression. The gross national product had fallen from $103 billion in 1929 to $58 billion in 1932. Roosevelt proposed the New Deal, a series of programs to bring "Relief, Recovery, and Reform." Congress responded by passing new economic regulations pushed by the new president. As a result, the federal government for the first time assumed responsibility for stimulating business activity out of a depression. It undertook to correct a wide range of abuses in the nation's economic machinery, amassing more far-reaching laws to this end in a shorter time than ever before or since.

The Supreme Court, filled with aging, conservative justices, was still a roadblock. It struck down as beyond federal power a series of regulations designed to relieve the economic catastrophe. In 1936 it unanimously struck down the National Industrial Recovery Act, a centerpiece of Roosevelt's recovery program that regulated activity in many industries. It was unconstitutional, said the justices, because the Commerce Clause did not give the federal government power to regulate business activity within the states, which is where most of the NIRA's regulations applied. Again, the Court thought that government could regulate only *interstate* commerce, which it defined as the movement of products across state lines. Otherwise, said the Court, "there would be virtually no limit to federal power, and for all practical purposes we should have a completely centralized government."[16]

Roosevelt was infuriated. Since his election in 1932 he had not had a chance to appoint even a single justice. In 1936 he was reelected in a landslide and believed that the Supreme Court was out of step with the mandate given him by American voters.

---

[13] *Munn v. Illinois*, 94 U.S. 113 (1877), at 130.

[14] *Lochner v. New York*, 198 U.S. 45 (1905).

[15] *Hammer v. Dagenhart*, 247 U.S. 251 (1918).

[16] *A. L. A. Schechter Poultry Corp. v. United States*, 295 U.S. 495 (1935), at 548.

"Man Controlling Trade" is one of two monumental limestone sculptures outside the Federal Trade Commission building in Washington, D.C. At the ceremony for laying the building's foundation, President Franklin Roosevelt directed the commission "to insist on a greater application of the golden rule to the conduct of corporations."[19] The allegorical sculpture depicting a muscular man restraining a wild horse symbolizes the power of government regulation to restrain exuberant markets. It was completed by artist Michael Lantz in 1942. Just as its Art Deco style fits the New Deal era, so does the message it represents. Source: © Elliot Teel.

executive agency
A regulatory agency in the executive branch run by a single administrator.

At the time, six of the nine justices were more than 70 years old. None suggested plans to retire. So Roosevelt sent Congress a scheme to change the Court by appointing one new justice for every justice over age 70, up to a membership of 15. This formula would have allowed him to appoint enough pro–New Deal justices to overcome the deadweight of the Court's aging conservatives. However, it was never acted upon.

Right away, the Court got the message. In its first decision in 1937 it surprised everyone by reversing its position on the Commerce Clause, upholding the new National Labor Relations Act that regulated labor organizing. The justices said the federal government could order a Pennsylvania steel plant to allow unionizing because the plant shipped steel out of the state in interstate commerce.[17] From then on, the Court saw factories and other business facilities as within a "stream of commerce" and held that the Commerce Clause gave the government power to regulate them.[18] This opened a door and new federal regulations rushed through it. The Court's changed constitutional interpretation is a good lesson that broad wording often ends up meaning what those with the most power want it to.

Wave 4: Administering the Social Revolution

There was little new regulation in the 1940s and 1950s. Then, in the late 1960s and early 1970s, a groundswell of interest in improving the quality of life created the fourth wave of government regulation. The result was a sudden burst of new controls designed to achieve broad social objectives.

The outpouring came in approximately 100 new statutes imposing regulation of consumer protection, environmental quality, workplace safety, and energy production.[20] There were several new independent commissions—the Equal Employment Opportunity Commission (1964) to protect civil rights in the workplace, the Consumer Product Safety Commission (1972) to protect the public from unsafe products, and the Nuclear Regulatory Commission (1974) to regulate nuclear facilities.

However, most of the new authorities went to a different kind of agency, the *executive agency,* or an agency within the executive branch run by a single administrator. This person is nominated by the president and confirmed by the Senate, but unlike the commissioners in independent commissions, who can be removed

---

[17] *National Labor Relations Board v. Jones & Laughlin Steel Corp.*, 301 U.S. 1 (1937).

[18] Ibid., at 36.

[19] Franklin D. Roosevelt, "Address at the Cornerstone Laying Ceremonies for the New Federal Trade Commission Building," July 12, 1937, in John Woolley and Gerhard Peters, *The American Presidency Project* [online]. Santa Barbara, CA: University of California (hosted), Gerhard Peters (database), at www.presidency.ucsb.edu/ws/?pid=15436.

[20] *Federal Regulatory Directory,* 14th ed., p. 6.

only for cause (such as incompetence or violating the law) agency heads can be removed by the president for any reason. These agencies are, therefore, more exposed to political winds than the independent commissions. Examples of executive agencies are the Environmental Protection Agency (1970), the Occupational Health and Safety Administration (1970), and the National Highway Traffic Safety Administration (1970).

deregulation
The removal or substantial reduction of the body of regulation covering an industry.

In this era, the voluminous buildup of regulations to achieve social objectives existed simultaneously with a *deregulation* movement that focused on removing or streamlining older economic regulations. While economic regulation was welcomed during the Great Depression as necessary to make markets work fairly, subsequent prosperity brought renewed faith in the efficiency of markets free from government interference. The objective of the movement was to cut regulations that limited competition within industries so that the free market could work.

In the first such experiment in 1976 all regulation of routes and fares was removed from the airlines. Financial institutions, cable television, and natural gas followed. Then railroads, trucking, and shipping were deregulated, leaving the original model of regulatory authority, the Interstate Commerce Commission, with so little to do that it was eventually abolished in 1995. Most deregulation seemed to benefit consumers, bringing more competition and lower prices, but not all of it ended happily. Reduction in federal oversight of the savings and loan industry led to corruption and fraud costing taxpayers more than $100 billion.

Wave 5: Terrorism and Financial Crisis

At the end of the fourth wave the idea that regulation had grown into excess and should be trimmed back was deeply entrenched. However, two events in the next decade brought on a new surge of activity.

First, the terrorist attacks in 2001 led to creation of a mammoth regulator for protecting American security. The George W. Bush administration combined 22 agencies with 60,000 employees into a new Department of Homeland Security. It is a giant. It has grown to 145,000 employees. Its budget is almost five times that of the next largest agency, the EPA. Though not primarily a business regulator, it issues rules affecting every industry. These include hiring rules for employers, import and export restrictions, customs inspection standards for plants and animals, rules for design and operation of commercial airports, and rules for shipping by air, rail, sea, truck, and pipeline.

Second, a crisis in financial markets led to federal intervention in the economy on a scale not seen since the Roosevelt administration in the 1930s. In 2007 housing prices collapsed and mortgage debt held by banks and insurance companies lost value. Lending froze and banks had too little capital to cover losses. Many failed. Businesses began to lay off workers. Falling stock markets destroyed personal wealth.

Two regulators, the Federal Reserve Board and the Department of the Treasury, intervened to prevent panic and system collapse. When the investment bank Bear Stearns was about to fail, they pledged $29 billion to cover its failing assets and it merged with JPMorgan Chase. To prevent failure of insurer A.I.G. they gave an emergency loan of $85 billion.

Troubled Asset Relief Program
A program that gave federal regulators power to exchange funds for an ownership interest in banks and corporations.

Late in 2008 Congress passed the Emergency Economic Stabilization Act to restore financial stability. The law set up a *Troubled Asset Relief Program* (TARP), authorizing the Treasury Department to buy $700 billion of deflated mortgage-backed securities from banks in exchange for equity. It also authorized purchase of stock in other corporations. Essentially, regulators were injecting new capital into banks and corporations in exchange for part ownership. Through this program the government purchased shares in the nation's largest financial institutions including A.I.G., Bank of America, Goldman Sachs, Morgan Stanley, GMAC, and American Express, and in hundreds of smaller banks. It also came to own 61 percent of General Motors and 10 percent of Chrysler. This intervention was justified with the argument that collectively, and in a few cases individually, these businesses could not fail without risking collapse of the nation's economy.

In return for its support, the government imposed conditions. Under authority of the TARP program and an early 2009 spending bill designed to stimulate the economy, corporations receiving TARP funds had to limit senior executive compensation, restrict dividends, limit lobbying, follow certain governance guidelines, report their performance to regulators, and comply with other specific conditions.[21] Chrysler, for example, agreed to produce 40 percent of its cars in the United States.

To administer the TARP program Congress created a new agency, the Office of Financial Stability (OFS), in the Treasury Department. It soon had a staff of 200 and began writing rules.[22] Regulators did not run day-to-day operations in TARP companies, but they intervened in many ways. The Obama administration fired one CEO of General Motors, then appointed a board to oversee it that soon fired a second CEO. At Bank of America, Kenneth Lewis, a successful, long-term CEO, seethed under the restrictions. Late in 2008 regulators pressured him into merging with Merrill Lynch to save it from failure. Secretary of the Treasury Henry Paulson threatened to fire Lewis and the bank's board of directors if they refused. Nine members of the bank's board resigned; six new ones approved by regulators replaced them. Although the merger was completed, another regulator, the Securities and Exchange Commission, brought a civil action against the bank for failing to inform shareholders fully of the merger's risks. Lewis eventually resigned, saying, "This is not my company any more and it's not my board."[23]

Other companies also felt the bridle of control. When General Motors agreed to accept TARP funds, its CFO called James Lambright, the chief regulator at OFS, seeking to negotiate some details. Lambright would have none of it. "You're our third-biggest deal of the day," he said. "So if you don't want to do this now, we

---

[21] Government Accountability Office, *Troubled Asset Relief Program: The U.S. Government Role as Shareholder in AIG, Citigroup, Chrysler, and General Motors and Preliminary Views on its Investment Management Activities,* Testimony before the Subcommittee on Domestic Policy, Committee on Oversight and Government Reform, House of Representatives, GAO-1-325T, December 16, 2009. The spending bill was the American Recovery and Reinvestment Act of 2009.

[22] See, for example, Department of the Treasury, "TARP Standards for Compensation and Corporate Governance," 74 FR 28394, June 15, 2009.

[23] Quoted in Carrick Mollenkampf and Dan Fitzpatrick, "With Feds, B of A's Lewis Met His Match," *The Wall Street Journal,* November 9, 2009, p. A16.

have plenty else to do. Call us later."[24] Another recipient of TARP funds was GMAC. Part of its recovery strategy was to offer high interest rates on savings accounts and lend aggressively to low-income car buyers. This brought in many customers. Then, the Federal Deposit Insurance Corporation, stepped in, forcing GMAC to lower rates and restrict its lending.[25]

This fifth wave of regulation may have crested, but government intervention is unlikely to subside to former levels. Unlike previous wars that led to temporary surges in regulation, the already long war on terrorism is a low-intensity, asymmetrical conflict that can continue for many more years. Although the wave of direct federal intervention to counteract market failures will recede as banks and corporations repay TARP loans, it leaves new regulatory authority in its wake. For example, the Dodd-Frank Act of 2010 was passed to control risk in financial markets. It is the biggest surge in economic regulation since the New Deal, a fountain of new rules that will gush for a decade. It creates five agencies and mandates hundreds of specific controls on financial activity.

War Blips

As Figure 10.2 shows, wars have brought sudden increases in government controls. During the Civil War, there was little control over production and prices, but the North created a National Bank to help finance the war, and this had lasting impact on the financial system. World War I brought substantial controls over industry, but ended before the controls began to bite. The federal government exercised complete control over the economy during World War II and to a lesser but still substantial extent during the Korean War. After both wars, the wartime controls were abandoned. No comparable increase in regulation came during the Vietnam War or the two Gulf wars. However, the war on terrorism declared by President George W. Bush began the fifth wave of regulation described above.

HOW REGULATIONS ARE MADE

regulation
Government activity that guides the behavior of citizens, groups, and corporations to reach economic or social goals.

Regulation is a government activity that guides the behavior of citizens, groups, and corporations to reach economic or social goals. In the United States, federal regulation is carried out by rules created in a mazelike process that follows complex guidelines. Figure 10.3 shows a simplified, visual overview of this process, which we will describe.

Regulatory Statutes

Federal regulation originates in an act of Congress. When a bill containing regulatory authority is passed by both houses and signed by the president, that new authority is assigned to a regulatory agency, either an independent commission or an executive branch agency. This agency then creates binding rules to carry out the

[24] Quoted in Deborah Solomon, "Bailout Man Turns the Screws," *The Wall Street Journal,* April 7, 2009, p. A1.

[25] Dan Fitzpatrick and Damien Paletta, "U.S. Turns Screws on Bailed-Out GMAC," *The Wall Street Journal,* November 1, 2009, p. A1.

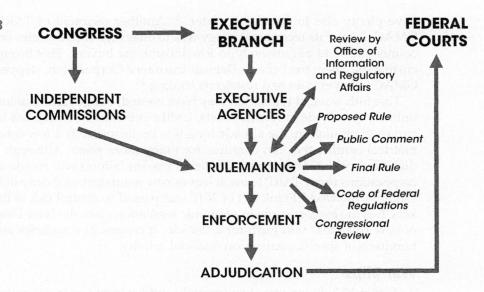

FIGURE 10.3
The
Regulatory
Process

new law. Statutes rarely contain all the specific rules needed to achieve their intended purpose. It is the agency's job to develop the necessary body of more detailed regulation.

Some statutes give broad grants of authority to the implementing agency. The Federal Reserve Act of 1913, for example, gave the Federal Reserve Board complete authority to set interest rates. The Clean Air Act of 1970 granted the Environmental Protection Agency the authority to set air quality standards that protect public health "allowing an adequate margin of safety."[26] The phrase "an adequate margin" allows the EPA to define how much of a specific pollutant can be emitted by factories and vehicles. Other statutes, however, are very specific. The Department of Transportation has little leeway in setting weight limits for trucks because Congress legislated an equation to calculate exact legal weights based on number of axles and their distance apart.[27]

Early in the New Deal era, Congress in its rush passed regulatory laws written with spacious and even vague wording. This capacious language was challenged by companies growing restive with the blizzard of rules emanating from bureaucrats in Washington. Business argued that delegating so much legislative power to the executive branch was unconstitutional. Congress' duty to make the laws could not be delegated to unelected drones in agencies. The Supreme Court resolved this issue, holding that broad delegation of legislative power to executive branch regulators was constitutional, but only if Congress put clear principles and guidelines for using that power into the enabling statutes.[28]

[26] Clean Air Act, as amended 1990, Title I, Part A, §109(B)(b)(1).

[27] Vehicle Weight Limitations–Interstate System," 23 U.S.C. §127(a).

[28] *Panama Refining Co. v. Ryan,* 293 U.S. 388 (1935). The Court did strike down some New Deal laws, wholly or in part because they delegated too much power to the executive branch. See, for example. *A. L. A. Schechter Poultry Corp. v. United States,* 295 U.S. 495 (1953).

Although the trend today is toward more specific laws, the great bulk of federal regulation is still created and administered in agencies based on broad grants of authority. This is inevitable, because Congress depends on the technical and scientific expertise of regulators to carry out its intent. Despite some early reticence, federal courts generally allow considerable leeway when agencies undertake to fill in the blanks in rulemaking.[29] However, as we will see, the courts keep a tight rein on regulators to ensure their actions are reasonable.

Rulemaking

rule
A decree issued by an agency to implement a law passed by Congress.

Regulatory agencies promulgate rules that have the force of law. A *rule* is a decree issued by an agency to implement a law passed by Congress.[30] There are many types of rules. For example, some rules command a business to do something or stop doing something. Some ask only for information, some set prices, some set standards for business to meet, some prescribe how such standards will be met, some license business activity, and some subsidize business.

Rules are created in a complex, formal rulemaking process. This process is designed to protect the public from arbitrary and capricious acts of government. Its basic steps were set forth in the Administrative Procedures Act in 1946, but since then more and more requirements have been added, making the process rigid and cumbersome.[31] Rulemaking for lesser regulations can be completed in several months, but major rules often take years. In what follows, we describe the basic steps.

Federal Register
A daily government publication containing proposed rules, final rules, notices of public meetings by regulatory agencies, and presidential executive orders.

When an agency decides to promulgate a rule it may already have gone through lengthy research, deliberation, and consultation with affected parties. When a draft is ready, the agency publishes it as a proposed rule in the *Federal Register*. The *Federal Register* is a daily publication of the federal government started during the New Deal years as an official source for all agency notifications. It is published every working day and has never missed a day since its first issue on March 14, 1936. Publication of a proposed rule opens a period, usually 30 to 60 days, during which the public can comment to the agency. For rules affecting business, comments usually come from lobbyists, corporate lawyers, and trade associations; however, anyone can submit a comment.[32]

Proposed rules are also sent by executive branch agencies to the Office of Information and Regulatory Affairs, a small office in the Office of Management and Budget, a White House group that provides central oversight of regulation for the president.

---

[29] See, for example, *Whitman v. American Trucking Associations,* 531 U.S. 457 (2001), upholding the EPA's right to fill in meaning to phrases in the Clean Air Act Amendments of 1990.

[30] The legal definition of a rule in the Administrative Procedure Act of 1946, 5 U.S.C. II §551(4), is "an agency statement . . . designed to implement, interpret, or prescribe a law or policy."

[31] In addition to guidelines in executive orders discussed later in this section, the most important of these additional requirements include environmental impact statements, if required under the National Environmental Policy Act of 1969; analysis of impacts on small businesses as required in the Regulatory Flexibility Act of 1980; minimization of paperwork under the Paperwork Reduction Act of 1995; appraisal of impacts on states and cities as required by the Unfunded Mandates Act of 1995; and following data guidelines set up under the Information Quality Act of 2000.

[32] The act of commenting is centralized on a Web site, www.regulations.gov.

significant regulatory action
A rule with an annual effect on the economy of $100 million or more.

Within the OIRA, spoken of as "oh-EYE-ruh," a staff of about 50 scrutinizes the proposed rule to see if it is really needed, if all alternatives have been examined, and whether its costs are justified.[33] If it is a *significant regulatory action*, that is, one having an annual impact of $100 million or more on the U.S. economy, it must be accompanied by an analysis that details its full impact, including monetary benefits and costs.[34] Such studies can be a big hurdle for agencies. They are time-consuming and expensive. For example, when the EPA decided to require new emission controls on diesel locomotives the regulatory analysis took years and finally weighed in at 1,568 pages.[35]

The Office of Information and Regulatory Affair's presence serves as a check on the agencies. Aggressive agencies may propose regulations that enhance their power. Agencies that are unduly influenced by the industries they regulate may slight the public interest. In theory, OIRA provides "a dispassionate and analytical 'second opinion' on agency actions."[36] In OIRA there is a general presumption against new rules, so agencies must present a strong justification for action. Since its creation in 1980 growing power over regulation has centered in OIRA.[37] Some believe its tiny staff usurps the authority and expertise of agencies.[38]

In the 20 years between 1990 and 2010 OIRA undertook 19,102 reviews of rules in various stages from 68 executive-branch agencies, including 8,844 final rules. As shown in Figure 10.4, the majority, 54 percent, came from five departments and agencies. However, only executive-branch agencies have to submit proposed and final rules to OIRA. Independent regulatory commissions must follow procedures in the Administrative Procedures Act, but are not at any stage required to submit

FIGURE 10.4
Big Rule Makers: 1990–2010

Source: Office of Information and Regulatory Affairs.

	Final Rules	Economically Significant Rules
Department of Agriculture	1,253	312
Health and Human Services	1,238	516
Department of Transportation	796	187
Environmental Protection Agency	770	328
Department of Commerce	753	47
68 Executive Branch Agencies Combined	8,844	1,960

[33] Guidelines for the analysis that agencies must comply with are in OIRA's Circular A-4, a 48-page memorandum on "Regulatory Analysis" sent to the heads of executive agencies on September 17, 2003, www.whitehouse.gov/omb/circulars/a004/a-4.pdf.

[34] Executive Order 12866, "Regulatory Planning and Review," October 4, 1993, 58 FR 51738, §3(f).

[35] *Final Regulatory Analysis: Control of Emissions from Nonroad Diesel Engines,* EPA420-R-04-007 (Washington, DC: EPA Office of Transportation and Air Quality, May 2004).

[36] Susan E. Dudley, "Lessons Learned, Challenges Ahead," *Regulation,* Summer 2009, p. 8.

[37] Anthony Vitarelli, "Happiness Metrics in Federal Rulemaking," *Yale Journal on Regulation,* Winter 2010, p. 116.

[38] See, for example, Gary D. Bass, et al., *Advancing the Public Interest Through Regulatory Reform* (Washington, DC: OMB Watch, November 2008), p. 16.

rules for White House review. As a result, the analysis underlying their regulations has, overall, been less disciplined.

After the comment period ends regulators must reconsider and rewrite the regulation to incorporate public comments. Executive-branch agencies then resubmit the final rule to OIRA for a last check to see if the agency fully complied with all regulatory principles and procedures. When ready, rules in their final wording are printed in the *Federal Register*. They usually take effect 60 days after this printing.

Pages in the *Federal Register* are a crude gauge of regulatory activity. By law it prints all proposed and final rules, executive orders, and notices of agency meetings and hearings. Pages are printed in three columns with a small font and average more than 1,000 words. Daily issues vary in size but some are more than 300 pages, making them equivalent to the length of this textbook. Figure 10.5 shows how the rise and fall of *Federal Register* pages reflects long-term regulatory growth.

Code of Federal Regulations
A reference work that compiles regulations of all agencies in a series of volumes.

After publication in the *Federal Register* final regulations are codified in another government publication, the *Code of Federal Regulations*. The code is divided into 50 titles containing final regulations from all federal agencies. The titles are divided into volumes, chapters, parts, and sections with all rules from an agency generally found in one title or subpart of a title. For example, regulations from the EPA are contained in Title 40, "Protection of the Environment," covering 32 volumes containing 1,068 sections. Each title is updated and republished each year.[39] In print it

FIGURE 10.5
Annual Page Count in the *Federal Register*: 1936–2010

Source: Office of the Federal Register.

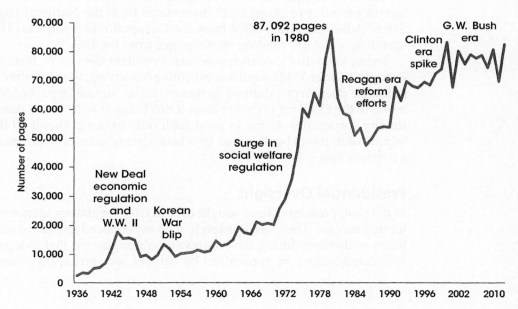

[39] The *Code of Federal Regulations* is published in printed volumes and on the Government Printing Office Web site at www.gpoaccess.gov/cfr/.

covers 157,974 pages in 218 volumes and costs $1,664 for a full set. It grows with every revision.

Even if corporations followed every regulation as it appeared in the *Federal Register* and the *Code of Federal Regulations,* full compliance would still elude them. This is because, in addition to regulations, agencies issue even larger volumes of *guidance* in documents such as memoranda, circulars, compliance manuals, and advisory opinions. Such guidance is intended as clarification for regulated parties. In reality, it often changes and adds to existing rules. The agency's motive may be to assist the regulated, or it may be to bypass the increasingly petrified rulemaking process. A federal appeals court once explained how billows of guidance arise.

guidance
Information in nonbinding documents intended to clarify official regulations.

> Congress passes a broadly worded statute. The agency follows with regulations containing broad language, open-ended phrases, ambiguous standards, and the like. Then as years pass, the agency issues circulars or guidance or memoranda, explaining, interpreting, defining, and often expanding the commands in the regulations. One guidance document may yield another and then another and so on. Several words in a regulation may spawn hundreds of pages of text as the agency offers more and more detail regarding what its regulations demand of regulated entities. Law is made, without notice and comment, without public participation, and without publication in the *Federal Register* or the *Code of Federal Regulations.*[40]

Although guidance is not supposed to be legally binding, the regulated ignore it at their peril. Its volume is astounding. When a congressional committee asked three agencies to submit guidance documents from a three-year, nine-month period it received 1,225 documents from the National Highway Traffic Safety Administration, 3,374 from the Occupational Safety and Health Administration, and 2,653 totaling 96,906 pages from the EPA.[41]

Trying to control guidance practices, President George W. Bush in 2007 issued Executive Order 13422 requiring executive branch agencies to submit "significant" guidance documents, defined as those with an annual impact of $100 million or more, to the OMB for review.[42] Even if this helps, it will remain nearly impossible for any corporation acting in good faith fully to comprehend all that regulators require of it. It will be thwarted by a bewildering mass of instructions growing at a fantastic rate.

Presidential Oversight

In the past, presidents have sought control over regulatory agencies, but met with limited success. Theodore Roosevelt, who experienced growth of major new regulatory authorities during the Progressive era, suggested that independent regulatory commissions be supervised by cabinet secretaries, but Congress took no

[40] *Appalachian Power Company v. Environmental Protection Agency,* 341 U.S. App. D.C. 46 (2000), at 1020.
[41] Committee on Government Reform, *Non-Binding Legal Effect of Agency Guidance Documents,* 106th Congress, 2d Session, H. Rep. 106-1009, October 26, 2000, p. 5.
[42] 72 FR 2763, January 23, 2007.

action. Franklin D. Roosevelt repeated this proposal, again to no avail. In 1949 former President Herbert Hoover, then head of a blue-ribbon commission to review government regulation, again made the suggestion. No action was taken.

Absent such formal authority over independent commissions, recent presidents have sought to impose their will on regulators in other ways. President Ronald Reagan took office in 1980 determined to stem the rising tide of regulation. He began by cutting agency budgets. Although presidents have no formal control over rulemaking by independent agencies, since 1939 they have had the authority to review and revise budget requests sent to Congress. Over the next four years Reagan cut agency budgets an average of 37 percent, forcing both independent and executive-branch agencies to lay off staff and curtail their activities.[43]

President Reagan also issued Executive Order 12291 in 1981 giving OIRA authority to review proposed rules from executive-branch agencies and to request changes if they were inconsistent with the administration's philosophy.[44] "Significant" rules, those with an annual economic impact of $100 million or more, had to be supported by massive analytical studies that included benefit–cost calculations. Early in the Reagan years, the output of new regulations sharply declined. His effort to take control, particularly by requiring centralized review, was unprecedented and would be continued. However, regulation itself was irrepressible, and by the end of his second term in 1988, growth resumed.

The George H. W. Bush administration (1988–1992) focused more on foreign events than on domestic issues, including regulation, yet it continued the mandates in Reagan's Executive Order 12291 and made one additional effort to slow regulatory growth. President Bush appointed a special commission headed by Vice President Dan Quayle and gave it authority to review existing and proposed regulations. It rejected and repealed a modest number of minor rules.

President Bill Clinton continued efforts to control regulatory excess. In 1993 he issued Executive Order 12866, which replaced Reagan's earlier order but retained the requirement of centralized review for executive agencies.[45] In addition, Clinton asked agencies to consider nonregulatory alternatives to rules and to write regulations in simple, easily understood language. He appointed Vice President Al Gore to head a working group of agency heads, which invented an ambitious but ultimately quixotic crusade to end "regulatory overkill" by eliminating outdated, overlapping, and unnecessary regulations.[46] Despite this, agencies busied themselves with new rules up to the last days of the Clinton administration.

President George W. Bush came into office in 2001 committed to again nipping growth. Immediately he imposed a 60-day delay on 3,512 pages of new regulations agencies had submitted to the *Federal Register* on the last Friday of the Clinton presidency. Although most of these rules eventually went into effect, he checked regulators in other ways. He created offices to review rulemaking in each agency and

---

[43] *Federal Regulatory Directory,* 14ed., p. 26.

[44] "Improving Government Regulations," 46 FR 13193, February 17, 1981.

[45] "Regulatory Planning and Review," 58 FR 5173, October 4, 1993.

[46] Albert Gore, *Creating a Government That Works Better & Costs Less, Report of the National Performance Review* (Washington, DC: Government Printing Office, September 7, 1993), p. 32.

staffed them with political czars who sympathized with his desire to reduce regulatory burdens. The Office of Information and Regulatory Affairs adopted tougher review procedures. The net result was a small drop in new regulation early in Bush's presidency followed by a major surge in response to terror attacks and an economic crisis. In the end, his administration issued more than 2,000 significant final regulations imposing annual costs estimated at more than $50 billion.[47]

When President Obama took office in 2009, he immediately issued Executive Order 13497 to revoke the changes in regulatory oversight adopted by his predecessor, abolishing the political officers in agencies and loosening OIRA's overview requirements.[48] Early in his first term he announced an initiative to promote "transparency, participation, and collaboration" and encourage "greater openness in the regulatory process."[49] He had no desire to reduce the flow of regulations, rather, he sought an expansive legislative agenda for creating new regulatory authority in health care, finance, the environment, and consumer protection.

In sum, presidents have used many administrative devices to control and slow regulation. Restraints have included executive orders, moratoriums, appointments of obliging agency administrators, budget cutting, and central review of regulations in the White House. Yet the tide still rises. Congress continues to create more agencies and laws mandating regulation. Rules from independent agencies remain largely outside presidential oversight. And within all agencies lurks an inclination to act.

> As anyone who has worked on regulatory issues knows, government agencies are not staffed with objective bureaucrats. The sympathies and paths to career advancement and outside pressures tend to go in one direction, toward more regulation.[50]

Congressional Oversight

Congress has many ways to influence and control regulatory agencies. Besides passing or amending laws, it approves presidential nominees as head regulators and makes appropriations to agencies. Both House and Senate committees have oversight jurisdiction over specific areas of regulation and may request information or summon regulators to testify at hearings. For example, the House Energy and Commerce Committee has jurisdiction over consumer protection, telecommunications, air quality, energy, and food and drug safety. It has a culture of tenacious oversight of agencies in these areas. Yet, overall, committee oversight is inconsistent, sometimes nonexistent. Jurisdiction is often fragmented among several or more committees that do not coordinate their actions. Also, most committees lack sufficient staff to investigate agency actions in depth.

In 1996 Congress added to its oversight capacity by passing the Congressional Review Act. This law mandates that most new rules cannot go into effect until

---

[47] Dudley, "Lessons Learned, Challenges Ahead," p. 10.

[48] "Revocation of Certain Executive Orders Concerning Regulatory Planning and Review," 74 FR 6113, February 4, 2009.

[49] See, for example, Office of Management and Budget, Memorandum from Cass R. Sunstein, "Increasing Openness in the Rulemaking Process–Use of the Regulation Identifier Number (RIN)," April 7, 2010, p. 1.

[50] Ike Brannon, "Treating the Unserious Seriously," *Regulation*, Winter 2005–2006, p. 51.

60 days after they have been sent to Congress for review. If, within that time, a resolution of disapproval is introduced, passed by both Houses, and signed by the president, the rule is nullified. Since this process began, more than 50,000 new regulations have passed into law. Although 37 joint resolutions of disapproval were introduced, only one passed—a rejection of an ergonomics rule from the Occupational Safety and Health Administration.[51]

In sum, congressional oversight is an important influence on agency actions. However, the formal checks that exist are used sparingly.

Challenges in the Courts

As they enforce rules, agencies are beset by conflicts with regulated parties. Formal conflicts are resolved in two ways. First, the Administrative Procedure Act requires each agency to set up an adjudication process leading to trial before an administrative law judge. Second, if the judge's decision fails to resolve the dispute, federal courts can review agency actions.

Usually, federal courts defer to the judgment of agencies when their rules are based on reasonable interpretations of statutes. The case that solidified this deference arose when a rule on factory pollution from the Environmental Protection Agency provoked environmental groups. A section of the Clean Air Act Amendments of 1977 required the EPA to cut emissions from "stationary sources" of air pollution at industrial plants. It issued a regulation that put all single emission sources at a plant under an imaginary plantwide "bubble" and required that total emissions within the bubble be reduced. This allowed companies to meet plantwide emission limits by cutting emissions more from some sources than others based on control costs. Angry environmentalists claimed the statute's mandate to control "stationary source" pollution required permits and reductions for each stack, oven, engine, and valve, not a plantwide aggregate of sources.

In *Chevron v. National Resources Defense Council* the Supreme Court set the guiding precedent on deference to regulatory agencies. It held that a court should look first to see if a statute's direct wording revealed congressional intent. If it did not, as was the case here, then the court should decide whether the agency had made a "permissible" interpretation of wording. Unless the agency's interpretation was "arbitrary, capricious, or manifestly contrary to the statute," it should be held "reasonable" and "permissible."[52] This 1984 decision created the *Chevron doctrine,* or the general rule that courts should defer to agency rules that are based on reasonable interpretations of ambiguous statutes. Citing the *Chevron* doctrine, the courts now reject most challenges to agency rules.

Although the standard for judging agency actions is a lenient one, judicial oversight is vigilant. Congress has given federal courts the power to hold unlawful agency actions that are arbitrary, capricious, unconstitutional, in excess of agency

Chevron doctrine
The general rule that federal courts should defer to agency rules that are based on reasonable interpretations of ambiguous statutes.

---

[51] In 2010 it was discovered that over a decade agencies had neglected to submit more than 1,000 final rules to Congress before making them law. Walter J. Oleszek, *Congressional Oversight: An Overview* (Washington, DC: Congressional Research Service, Report R41079, February 22, 2010), p. 8 and fn. 25.

[52] *Chevron U.S.A v. Natural Resources Defense Council,* 467 U.S. 837 (1984).

jurisdiction, or unsupported by evidence.[53] In this sampling of cases, rules were rejected for the following reasons.

- *The agency misinterpreted congressional intent.* General Dynamics and a labor union agreed that, henceforth, only workers who were already age 50 or older would get health benefits when they retired. However, the deal violated an EEOC rule prohibiting age-related discrimination of any kind against workers over age 40. The Supreme Court struck down the agency's rule saying that "beyond reasonable doubt" its underlying authority, the Age Discrimination in Employment Act of 1967, was never intended by Congress to prohibit favoring the old over the young. Congress intended only to stop discrimination against older workers in favor of younger ones.[54]

- *The agency lacked convincing evidence for its action.* When the Environmental Protection Agency banned commercial uses of asbestos a federal appeals court struck down the rule because it was not based on "substantial evidence." The main problem was that the agency's cost–benefit studies never evaluated the risks of substitute materials likely to be used in place of asbestos.[55]

- *The agency ignored guidelines in the law.* The Energy Policy Act of 1992 directed the EPA to set human health standards for disposal of nuclear waste at a Yucca Mountain, Nevada, site. The statute directed the agency to base its standards on data from the National Academy of Sciences (NAS), which predicted high levels of radiation peaking after 100,000 years and lasting 2 million to 17 million years. Eventually, the EPA promulgated a standard that protected a hypothetical person living near the site for 10,000 years. Opponents of the site challenged this standard for ignoring the NAS prediction that radiation danger would be greatest in tens of thousands to 100,000 years. The EPA argued it had acted reasonably because regulating more than 10,000 years in the future was unrealistic. However, a federal appeals court held that the EPA had ignored its statutory mandate and struck down the rule.[56]

Finally, courts may force reticent agencies to act. Environmental groups petitioned the EPA to regulate auto emissions of gases implicated in global warming, including carbon dioxide. The EPA refused, saying carbon dioxide did not fit the definition in the Clean Air Act of an "air pollutant" as "any physical, chemical, biological, [or] radioactive . . . substance" posing a danger to people.[57] However, the Supreme Court held that the definition was "unambiguous" in including "any" airborne substance that threatened public health and welfare, including natural molecules such as carbon dioxide.[58] It ordered the EPA to initiate regulatory actions. This case illustrates the power of the judiciary to force a reluctant agency to act.

[53] The scope of judicial review comes under the authority of the Administrative Procedures Act and is set forth in 5 U.S.C. §706(2)(A).

[54] *General Dynamics Land Systems v. Cline,* 540 U.S. 581 (2004).

[55] *Corrosion Proof Fittings v. EPA,* 947 F.2d 1201 (1991).

[56] *Nuclear Energy Institute v. EPA,* 362 U.S. App. D.C. 204 (2004).

[57] 42 U.S.C. §7602(g).

[58] *Massachusetts v. EPA,* 127 S.Ct. 1438 (2007).

COSTS AND BENEFITS OF REGULATION

Rulemaking has significant and growing impact on consumers, corporations, and the economy. A way of analyzing this impact is to measure and compare the benefits of regulation with its costs. Both are difficult to measure in precise and comparable ways.

The Regulatory Burden

We can characterize the cost of regulation in many ways. One way is the total dollar cost. A study of the overall compliance burden calculated that the total cost of federal regulation was $876 billion in 2000, or 8.6 percent of GDP.[59] This is how much money business spent to follow all the rules imposed by federal agencies. An extrapolation from this study estimated that by 2009 the overall compliance cost rose to $1.187 trillion.[60]

Another measure of the burden is the cost of administering the regulatory process. This is revealed in the growth of spending by regulatory agencies as shown in Figure 10.6. Agency budgets are a rough indication of the extent of regulatory

FIGURE 10.6
Total Administrative Costs of Regulation: 1960–2010
Note: Economic regulations include those for finance and banking, industry-specific regulations, and general business. Social regulations include those for consumer safety and health, homeland security, working conditions, environment, and energy. Figures are constant 2000 dollars. Totals for 2009 and 2010 are estimates.

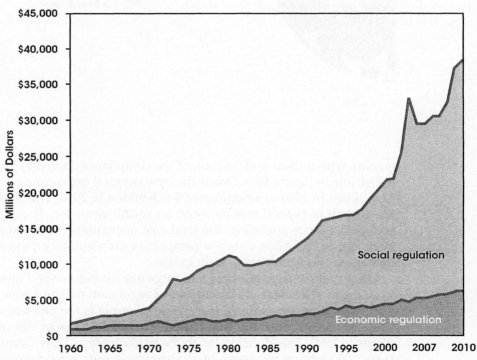

Source: Veronique de Rugy and Melinda Warren, *Regulators' Budget: Fiscal Year 2010 Annual Report*, table A-5.

[59] W. Mark Crain and Thomas D. Hopkins, *The Impact of Regulatory Costs on Small Firms* (Washington, DC: Small Business Administration, SBAHQ-00-R-0027, 2001), p. 3.

[60] Clyde Wayne Crews Jr., *Ten Thousand Commandments: 2010* (Washington, DC: Competitive Enterprise Institute, April 2010), p. 7.

FIGURE 10.7

If Agencies Were Planets

The size of regulatory agencies is shown here relative to fiscal 2010 budgets.

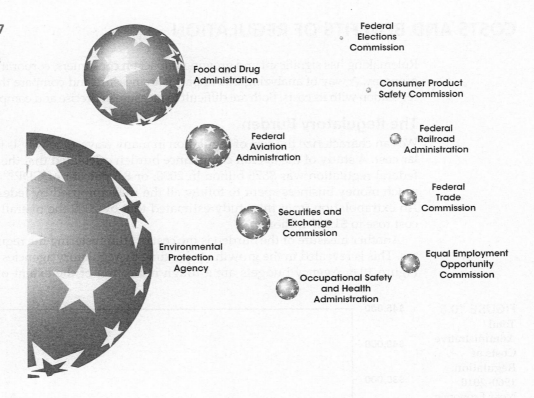

activity within them and, in turn, of the compliance costs they create. Two trends are visible in Figure 10.6. One is the upward total expenditure trend, rising from $2.6 billion in 1960 to an estimated $44.8 billion in 2010. The other is that most of the growth in expenditure has been for social regulation. If compliance costs are added to agency spending, the total cost of regulation rises to $1.23 trillion for 2009. Figure 10.7 adds a second perspective on regulatory expenditures showing that agency budgets vary greatly in size.

Other costs of regulation are also large but are indirect and much more difficult to quantify. These include the impact of regulation on employment, productivity, and innovation. An extreme but telling example is the decision of the Food and Drug Administration to order a moratorium on the use of silicone gel breast implants in 1992. This decision led to the bankruptcy of Dow Corning, loss of more than 1,000 jobs, evaporation of shareholder equity, and dampening of research into new uses of silicone body parts. Eventually, medical research exonerated silicone, but not before a robust industry had been crippled. And arrested innovation meant consumers had fewer choices of silicone medical devices. In another example, regulators have slowed the growth of the U.S. crop-biotechnology industry. New genetically modified crops must be cleared for sale by three agencies, the

FDA, the EPA, and the USDA.[61] In this official maze, approval times have passed three years, reducing DuPont's and Monsanto's competitiveness with corporations in Brazil, Argentina, and China where regulators act more quickly.

Benefits of Regulation

Measuring the benefits of federal regulation is far more difficult than calculating costs. At an aggregate level, business could not operate easily and society could not prosper without certain types of regulation. Regulation has reduced discrimination, improved the environment, freed competition, reduced corruption, banned dangerous products, strengthened the banking system, cut workplace fatalities, helped the elderly, controlled communicable diseases, and much more. These benefits are enormous and incalculable.

When proposals for "significant" rules are made to OIRA, they must be accompanied by estimates of benefits and costs. Critics of regulation believe that agencies sometimes bias their assumptions and calculations in favor of a rule. However, these studies often provide needed discipline. Here is one example.

By studying aircraft accidents the Federal Aviation Administration (FAA) concluded that more passengers and crew would survive crash landings if seats could withstand forces 16 times the force of gravity before collapsing rather than the existing 9 times the force of gravity. It wrote a rule requiring all seats in new airplanes to meet this standard beginning in 2009. It calculated the cost of stronger seats at $35 million between 2009 and 2034, but the benefits in lives saved and injuries averted were much greater, $79 million. Still more lives could be saved if the FAA required retrofitting existing passenger planes with the stronger seats, but the agency's benefit–cost analysis showed the cost would be $512 million, far higher than even the most optimistic benefit estimates. Therefore, the FAA issued the rule without a retrofitting requirement.[62] Absent the benefit–cost study, it might have imposed a net cost on society.

While the net benefits of specific rules can be clear, estimates of aggregate benefits of regulation to society have little credibility given the deficiencies of available data. A partial effort is that of the Office of Management and Budget to calculate total benefits and costs of 99 "major rules" it reviewed between 1998 and 2008. During this decade benefits were $126 billion to $663 billion, far greater than costs that were $51 billion to $60 billion.[63] This left a net benefit (benefit minus cost) of $75 billion to $603 billion. If these estimates are accurate, the benefits of these major rules over a decade were as much as eight times greater than their costs. Overall, the figures, which are based on inconsistent assumptions across 99 benefit–cost studies, provide no basis for any assumption regarding all regulation in the aggregate.

---

[61] Scott Kilman, "Biotech Firms Seek Speedier Reviews of Seeds," *The Wall Street Journal,* April 28, 2010, p. A8.

[62] Cindy Skryzcki, "FAA Updates Rule on Airline Seats," *Washington Post,* October 18, 2005, p. D1.

[63] Office of Management and Budget, *2009 Report to Congress on the Benefits and Costs of Federal Regulations and Unfunded Mandates on State, Local, and Tribal Entities* (Washington, DC: OMB, 2009), table 1-1.

REGULATION IN OTHER NATIONS

In varying form, quantity, and quality, regulation of business exists in every national economy. It is a basic institution underlying markets and, as the following stories suggest, it can impair or support them.

Tawanda owns a restaurant in Zimbabwe. Business has declined and she needs to lay off three workers, but under the country's labor laws if she does she must pay each one more than eight years' salary. So instead of reducing her payroll, Tawanda abandons her business and flees across the border to Malawi. Meanwhile, 5,000 miles to the east in Singapore, Chek takes a call and learns her small advertising agency has lost a major account. That afternoon she lays off the account representative and two graphic artists, paying each four weeks' salary as required by law.[64]

Poorer countries generally have heavier regulation. Rules tend to be badly, often corruptly, enforced. The result is that many small- and medium-sized businesses operate underground. In Bolivia, for example, regulation is so burdensome that on average 80 percent of private business activity takes place in the informal economy.[65] Workers have no paid vacations or maternity leave. Small businesses have difficulty getting credit, and enforcing contracts is hard. The infrastructure deteriorates because underground businesses pay no taxes, limiting government revenue. Businesses try to remain small in the hope of avoiding inspectors and tax collectors, crimping economic growth.

In 2004 the World Bank began an ambitious, long-term effort to catalog, classify, compare, and evaluate regulations on the ease of doing business in every nation. This study is now in its eighth year and covers 183 nations. Each year the World Bank revises its country rankings on the overall ease of doing business and the efficiency of rules in 10 categories from starting a business to going out of business. Figure 10.8 shows the highest- and lowest-ranking nations in 2011. These rankings have had surprising consequences. Nations now compete to reform their rules and move higher. In 2010 the World Bank reported 314 regulatory changes, 287 it defined as easing business and only 27 that raised obstacles, the most positive record since the effort began. The top reformer was Rwanda, with seven reforms that jumped its rank from 143 to 67.

Early in the study, the World Bank made four basic findings.

- Regulation varies widely around the world. For example, starting a business in Bolivia requires 15 steps that take 51 days and paying fees equal to 99 percent of the country's average per capita annual income. In Europe, the average is 6 steps over 13 days and fees near 5 percent of per capita income. In the easiest country, New Zealand, all it takes is one day to get a $160 permit.[66]
- Poor countries regulate the most. And heavier regulation brings bad outcomes, including delays, higher costs, more corruption, lower productivity, and less investment.

[64] World Bank, *Doing Business 2010: Reforming through Difficult Times* (Washington, DC: The World Bank, 2009), pp. 150 and 163.

[65] Ibid., p. vii.

[66] See annually updated World Bank indicators at www.doingbusiness.org, "Rankings."

FIGURE 10.8
Ease of Doing Business Rankings
This list ranks the best and the worst regulatory environments for doing business in 183 nations. Rankings are based on the sum of average percentile rankings for 10 performance measures.

Source: World Bank Group, "Doing Business," http://www.doingbusiness.org/rankings.

Top 10	Bottom 10
1. Singapore	174. Timor-Leste
2. Hong Kong, China	175. Congo, Dem. Republic
3. New Zealand	176. Guinea-Bissau
4. United Kingdom	177. Congo, Rep.
5. United States	178. São Tomé and Principe
6. Denmark	179. Guinea
7. Canada	180. Eritria
8. Norway	181. Burundi
9. Ireland	182. Central African Republic
10. Australia	183. Chad

- Rich countries regulate business in a consistent manner. Poor countries do not. Rich countries regulate less on all aspects of business activity.
- Developed countries engage in continuous regulatory reform to improve the business environment. There is much less reform in developing countries.[67] For example, the top 10 countries in Figure 10.8 made a total of 10 reforms over the previous year compared with only 4 reforms in the bottom 10.

The World Bank concluded that the same principles of effective regulation work well in both rich and poor nations. It set forth five "principles of good regulation."

- Simplify and deregulate in competitive markets.
- Focus on enhancing property rights.
- Expand the use of technology (particularly the Internet and information systems).
- Reduce court involvement in business matters.
- Make reform a continuous process.[68]

Not everyone likes the World Bank's approach. Progressive critics condemn it for spreading free market principles that "restrict the ability of developing countries to determine their own policies" and reward them for "scrapping regulations" that might be needed to make sure "markets function fairly."[69] However, research shows a strong correlation between regulation that follows these principles and overall economic growth. One study of the World Bank's data found that in the year after making one or more reforms poor countries raised their gross domestic

---

[67] World Bank, *Doing Business 2004: Understanding Regulation* (Washington, DC: World Bank and Oxford University Press, 2004), pp. xiii–xvii and pp. 83–90.

[68] Ibid., p. 92.

[69] Christian Aid, *Getting Back on the Rails: The Private Sector and Development* (London: Christian Aid, October 2009), p. 2.

products about 0.4 percent over countries that did not reform, and reforming countries elevated their investment rates by 0.6 percent in the next year.[70]

CONCLUDING OBSERVATIONS

Federal regulation of business is a tool used to achieve public goals. It has expanded over time. There have been ups and downs, but the basic direction has been up, with respect to both volume and complexity. Successive efforts of presidents over the past 40 years have not succeeded in slowing the expansion, but have produced needed discipline including centralized reviews, greater transparency, benefit–cost analysis, and deregulation of some industries. The cost of federal regulation to industry and consumers is huge but is offset by many benefits to society as a whole, individuals, companies, and industries.

[70] Benjamin P. Eifert, "Do Regulatory Reforms Stimulate Investment and Growth? Evidence from the Doing Business Data, 2003–07," Center for Global Development, Working Paper No.159, January 2009.

Good and Evil on the Rails

As a child Robert M. Sanchez counted the cars on passing trains. One day when he was seven he ran to an idling locomotive and the engineer took him into the wondrous machine, let him blow the horn, and, unwittingly, set his course for life. As he grew up he often visited nearby railyards, never losing his fascination with trains.

After high school he drove Greyhound buses for a time and then found work with Union Pacific on a maintenance crew. After several years he worked his way up, fulfilling his dream of becoming an engineer. Soon Amtrak hired him. He and his partner, a waiter, bought a home near Los Angeles. Neighbors described Sanchez as relentlessly cheerful, buoyant, and passionate about trains. Yet trouble was there too. He was caught shoplifting at Costco, pleaded guilty, and served 90 days in jail on weekends. He argued with his partner and suggested they break up. On February 14, 2003, his partner hung himself in their garage, leaving a note that read: "Rob, Happy Valentine's Day. I love you."[1]

Two years later Sanchez became an engineer for Metrolink, a commuter rail system crossing six Southern California counties. Metrolink carries about 40,000 passengers a day on a busy 388-mile track network shared with freight traffic. He loved his job though he worked a tiring split shift. Soon he bought a modest suburban house where he lived with four miniature greyhounds. Again, neighbors described him as cheerful, spirited, and exhilarated by railroading, but some saw him as a recluse who kept to himself and avoided revealing his past. He abided with a dirt yard that stood out in a neighborhood of tended landscapes.[2]

Although friends said Sanchez found joy in his work, there were a few difficulties. He received five informal discipline letters for absences and failure to follow rules. Twice he was counseled orally about use of his cell phone while on duty. In July 2008 a suicidal man sidestepped a crossing arm and ran in front of the train he was operating. Under Metrolink's policy he took some days off before returning to work, but, according to his family, he was forced to go back before his emotional recovery was complete.[3]

[1] David Kelly and Sam Quinones, "Engineer Led Solitary Life Marked By Tragedy," *Los Angeles Times,* September 17, 2008, p. A1.

[2] Rachel Uranga, "Engineer Had Lifelong Love of Trains," *Daily News of Los Angeles,* September 16, 2008, p. A3.
[3] Molly Hennessy-Fiske, "A Burden of Grief on Their Shoulders," *Los Angeles Times,* September 30, 2008, p. B1.

Metrolink engineer Robert M. Sanchez holding an Italian greyhound. Source: © AP Photo/Courtesy of Lilian Barber.

FRIDAY, SEPTEMBER 12, 2008

On this day, Robert Sanchez was up before dawn. He reported at 5:30 a.m. and worked four hours, rested four hours, then returned to work in the afternoon. At 3:03 p.m. he took train 111, a diesel-electric locomotive and three passenger cars, on a commuter route out of Union Station. After five stops he approached the Chatsworth station 33 miles northwest, passing a solid yellow light indicating he should be prepared to stop at the next signal. He failed to radio the dispatcher and call it out as required. It was a beautiful day there with clear skies, calm winds, and a mild 73 degrees.

After stopping for 57 seconds the train departed the station, a random assembly of 225 souls with perhaps the most troubled in the lead. At exactly 4:20:07 p.m. Sanchez shifted the throttle from the idle position to position 2 and released the train's air brakes. As it moved, he pushed the throttle to its maximum 8 position. Rapidly, the train increased speed to 42 mph. At 4:20:20 he sounded the locomotive's bell and horn for the Devonshire Road crossing.[4]

At 4:21:03 he received a short text message from a teenage rail fan: "I would like that too. We already need to meet 796. That would be best." This was about a plan for Sanchez to sneak him aboard the locomotive later that day and let him take the controls for fun. At 4:21:23 Sanchez again activated the bell and horn for the Chatsworth Street crossing. By 4:21:35 the train's speed was 54 mph and he moved the throttle back to position 4 and braked, slowing it to 44 mph in preparation for a curve. At 4:21:56 the train passed a red signal light ahead of the curve. It was a command to stop. Sanchez failed to radio in the signal and did not stop.

At 4:22:01 Sanchez sent a text in reply to the teenager: "yea . . . usually @ north camarillo." At 4:22:02 the train passed over a power switch turned to move a local freight train coming in the opposite direction off on a siding.

The freight train was Union Pacific LOF65-12 consisting of two locomotives and 17 cars. It entered the curve eastbound at 41 mph as Sanchez came on at 43 mph from the west. Closing at a combined 84 mph, each locomotive became visible to the engineer in the other only when they were 540 feet apart and four to five seconds from impact. In that instant the Union Pacific engineer and the conductor, who was also in the cab, saw the Metrolink locomotive. The engineer hit an emergency brake and started to run out the cab's rear door. Seeing there was too little time he "just stood there and watched it happen in disbelief."[5] The conductor froze on his feet, uttering an epithet. In the other locomotive, Sanchez did nothing with the controls.

At 4:22:23 the trains collided. The lead Union Pacific locomotive crushed Sanchez before pushing the massive bulk of his locomotive back 52 feet into the first coach. The compression killed 23 passengers. Another person died in the second coach. A sheriff's deputy described the scene. "I saw locomotives engulfed in flames . . . and . . . I saw numerous people, maybe a dozen, walking in various means, I don't know, delusioned, like they were zombies waking with various types of injuries with their hands out and saying help . . ."[6] Rescue workers needed four hours to extricate all the victims from wreckage. Hospitals took in 102 injured including the engineer and conductor from the freight train.

---

[4] This complied with a federal regulation that the horn sound for 15 to 20 seconds before a train comes to a rail-highway crossing. See Federal Railroad Administration, "Use of Locomotive Horns at Highway-Rail Grade Crossings: Final Rule," 70 FR 21844, April 27, 2005.

[5] Interview of Steven D. Cousino, National Transportation Safety Board, DCA-08-MR-009, p. 6.

[6] Interview of Deputy William Lynch, Deputy Brad Johnson, National Transportation Safety Board, DCA-08-MR-009, September 16, 2008, p. 7.

THE INVESTIGATION

The National Transportation Safety Board (NTSB) was called in. The NTSB is a small, independent federal agency established by Congress in 1967 to investigate transportation accidents and make safety recommendations. It did a detailed analysis of the collision, interviewing witnesses, holding hearings, and examining physical evidence such as the signal switch wiring and even fasteners on the track's wooden crossties.

An autopsy found that Sanchez had adult-onset diabetes, high blood pressure, and an enlarged heart. He met the clinical definition of obesity. And he was HIV positive. His use of prescription drugs kept these conditions under control. The Union Pacific conductor's blood and urine tested positive for marijuana use, though this was not relevant to the cause of the accident.

The investigation also focused on management. Metrolink is organized as a regional association with a governing board of representatives from five Southern California counties. It was formed in 1992 to improve mobility and reduce traffic congestion in densely populated areas. Most of its operations are outsourced. Sanchez was hired and supervised by Connex, the subsidiary of a French corporation that ran Metrolink's trains under a contract worth about $25 million a year.

Under the contract Metrolink retained overall responsibility for its operations. As one top Connex manager noted, "We run the railroad the way they want it run."[7] However, much was delegated, including the supervision of train crews. Connex conducted the "efficiency tests" required of every railroad.[8] These tests are done by supervisors who observe trains, monitor radio traffic, and analyze data from recorders in locomotives to check rules compliance. For example, they use stopwatches to make sure engineers blow horns for 15 seconds before entering a street crossing. They use radar guns to check train speeds. They stop trains for surprise inspections.

Connex supervisors performed about 1,000 such tests monthly. During his three years with Metrolink Sanchez had only a few failures on them. In 2006,

when a rule against cell phone use on duty went into effect, a safety manager arranged for someone to call Sanchez' number, then stopped his train and boarded the locomotive. As they were talking, Sanchez' phone rang. The phone was not supposed to be in the operator's compartment or turned on, but it was stowed away in a bag and Sanchez said he had forgotten about it. The supervisor accepted this and simply counseled him about the policy. No more calls were made to his phone to test his compliance.

In 2007 he twice was cited for failing to call out a wayside signal. Engineers are supposed to radio the Metrolink operations center to acknowledge each lighted signal they encounter. Still, his supervisor said Sanchez was frequently tested on calling signals and his performance was "above average."[9] Earlier that year Sanchez also got a written warning for neglecting to light a marker at the end of his train. And about a month before the collision a conductor saw him using a cell phone as his train was ready to leave a station. Sanchez told him he knew he should put the phone away and did. The conductor reported this to their Connex supervisor, who spoke to Sanchez again about the policy and did two observations of him in the next two weeks. He was confident that Sanchez understood the policy. However, the supervisor said it was hard to enforce.

> It's almost impossible . . . [T]he engineer, first of all, is going to have the door locked. You've got to unlock the door to get up on it. He's probably going to hear you coming—he or she, and, you know, it would be almost impossible to surprise somebody, you know, to inspect it . . . [O]f all the times I've gone up on a locomotive, I've never seen anybody with a cell phone or talking on a cell phone.[10]

In themselves, these incidents on Sanchez' record were not damning. The Connex safety manager had a subjective faith in him. "[He] was a competent engineer," he told investigators, "[a]nd I felt comfortable putting people with him."[11] Several weeks before his final shift Sanchez even got an award for "safety and rules compliance."

[7] Interview of Gregg Kunstler, assistant general manager, Connex, National Transportation Safety Board, DCA-08-MR-009, September 25, 2008, p. 5.

[8] "Railroad Operating Rules," 49 CFR-217.

[9] National Transportation Safety Board Hearing, Richard Dahl, manager of safety and operating practices, Connex Railroad, Washington, DC, March 3, 2009, p. 97.

[10] Ibid., p. 11.

[11] Interview of Richard Dahl, September 25, 2008, National Transportation Safety Board, DCA-08-MR-009, p. 37.

However, his behavior on the day of the accident showed brazen deceit and disrespect for rules. He failed to call out two signals. And Verizon Wireless records showed he made four phone calls, sent 21 text messages, and received 21 text messages while operating the train. It was habitual behavior. On each of seven working days preceding the accident he had made calls and sent and received between 30 and 125 text messages while operating trains.[12] Most of the texting was with teenage rail fans. Interviews revealed he had once before let a teenager sneak on to run a locomotive.

In its accident report the NTSB stated the probable cause of the collision as Sanchez' inattention to the red signal light because texting in violation of company rules distracted him. It made one new recommendation, that railroads put audio and video devices in locomotive cabs to monitor train crews. It repeated a previous recommendation for installing a crash- and fire-protected cab voice recorder similar to those in commercial airliners. And it noted that an automatic system called positive train control would have intervened to prevent the collision by taking control of the train when Sanchez failed to stop at the red signal.

POSITIVE TRAIN CONTROL

Positive train control is an old idea in railroading. It had been on the NTSB's "Most Wanted List of Transportation Safety Improvements" for 18 years at the time of the accident. Now, thanks to Robert Sanchez, it would become a reality. Briefly explained, it is an interconnected network of digital data and controls. It allows remote operators to take control of trains from on-board engineers if necessary. It includes these basic elements.

- Global positioning system receivers on trains to continuously track movement.
- Computers on trains that record data and send information to displays in locomotive cabs about train position, speed, length, and weight; route speed limits; actual and recommended throttle and brake settings; sensor readings on cars; signal and switch settings; and more.

- Wayside devices that monitor signals, switches, and track alignment, and can detect overheated brakes, cracked wheels, rock slides, and other problems.
- Wireless interfaces on throttle and brake controls that allow remote control.
- Computers and displays in railroad operations centers that show the schedule, position, speed, and control settings of each train in the network and allow remote command of train and track functions.[13]

Modern train control is technically complex, but the basic invention, electro-mechanical automatic braking, came around 1900. In 1920 the Interstate Commerce Commission (ICC) ordered 49 railroads to install it on passenger lines to reduce accidents and fatalities. Though effective, the systems were very expensive to put in and maintain.

When interstate highways spread in the 1950s, rail traffic faced more competition from trucking. Revenues fell, tracks were abandoned, railroads failed or merged, and the ICC let companies discard the controls. After that, human error regularly led to avoidable fatalities from train collisions, overspeed derailments, and runaway locomotives in work zones. Periodic headline accidents that killed passengers led to regular calls for reinstating automatic controls. However, little was done because the railroads argued it was unaffordable.

CONGRESS ACTS

When the National Transportation Safety Board placed positive train controls on its "Most Wanted" list in 1990 it revived the issue. Congress considered action, but retreated when the Federal Railroad Administration (FRA) did a study showing that the cost of controls far outweighed safety benefits.[14] The FRA is part of the Department of Transportation. As an executive branch agency its administrator is nominated

---

[12] National Transportation Safety Board, *Collision of Metrolink Train 111 With Union Pacific Train LOF 65-12 Chatsworth, California, September 12, 2008: Accident Report* (Washington, DC: NTSB, 2010), p. 55.

[13] Steven R. Ditmeyer, "Network-Centric Railroading Utilizing Intelligent Railroad Systems," paper presented at the 10th International Command and Control Research and Technology Symposium, McLean, Virginia, June 2005, p. 16.

[14] Federal Railroad Administration, *Railroad Communications and Train Control* (Washington, DC: FRA, 1994). It was in this report that the FRA coined the term *positive train control*. It also embraced specifications for such systems developed by the railroad industry.

by the president and approved by the Senate and, when appointed, reports to the Secretary of Transportation. Congress created the agency in 1966 to regulate railroad safety. It also administers federal programs that support railroads and promote passenger service, giving it close ties with the industry it regulates. Most of its 900 employees have worked for railroads.

After the early 1990s there were short bouts of Congressional interest in train controls after major rail accidents. In 2003 Congress asked the FRA for an updated benefit–cost study. It showed that the costs still far outweighed safety benefits.[15] In 2005 the agency issued a rule to encourage voluntary use of train controls.[16] Lacking a mandate, railroads installed automatic systems on only about 4,000 track miles, most in the Northeast.

A few legislators remained interested in train controls. When the Metrolink crash occurred, there were two moribund bills in Congress, a House bill requiring controls on several high-risk routes and a Senate bill seeking only further study. Neither was headed to passage because of opposition from railroad lobbyists.

The Metrolink fatalities mobilized California's two Democratic senators, Dianne Feinstein and Barbara Boxer, who zoomed in like superheroes on a mission. Within a week they introduced an amendment to the House bill, which had already passed, ordering railroads to install positive train control. In remarks on the Senate floor, Senator Feinstein grew irate and accused the railroads of "criminal negligence."

> The accident happened because of a resistance in the railroad community in America to utilizing existing technology to produce a fail-safe control of trains . . . Over the years the railroads resisted, saying these systems are too expensive. Well, how expensive is the loss of human life? The cost of any system doesn't come close to the cost of the lives that were lost this past Friday. [17]

A week later she and Senator Boxer invited Joseph H. Boardman, administrator of the FRA, to a public hearing. Senator Feinstein opened the hearing by saying she was upset with "lobbying behind the scenes to prevent an early date" for installation of train controls. Boardman explained to the two senators why "progress has not been faster," namely because of "limited availability of needed radio spectrum," concerns about "interoperability," and "braking algorithms that need refinement."[18] These technicalities must have sounded like excuses to Senator Boxer and they drew a sharp rebuke.

> What powers do you have? What's your job? You're sitting there saying you can't tell them to do anything? . . . You have the power, you don't want to do it, you'd rather work for the railroads.[19]

After the hearing Senator Feinstein called the FRA "an old boys club." "I think they sit down and talk to the railroads," she said. "I think they do what the railroads want."[20] In floor remarks she tried to stir her Senate colleagues to action with a moral argument.

> When we know there is global positioning that can be in place to shut down the freight train and the passenger train before they run into each other and we do nothing about it, then I believe this body is also culpable and negligent.[21]

This idea echoes Aristotle, who held that ethical decisions are a matter of choice and only ignorance of facts or lack of freedom to act excuses a person from choosing the ethical action.[22] Senator Feinstein deprived the senators of either excuse. But many Senate Republicans were unmoved and still tried to stop the bill, believing it imposed a net economic burden on society. Their effort to thwart its passage

---

[15] Federal Railroad Administration, *Benefits and Costs of Positive Train Control: Report in Response to Request of Appropriations Committees* (Washington, DC: U.S. Department of Transportation, August 2004).

[16] Federal Railroad Administration, "Standards for Development and Use of Processor-Based Signal and Train Control: Final Rule," 70 FR 11052, March 7, 2005.

[17] "Statements on Introduced Bills and Joint Resolutions," 154 CR S8858, September 16, 2008.

[18] "Statement of Joseph H. Boardman, administrator, Federal Railroad Administration," September 23, 2008, p. 4, www.fra.dot.gov.

[19] Quoted in Steve Hymon and Cynthia Dizikes, "Accord Reached on Rail Bill," *Los Angeles Times,* September 24, 2008, p. B1.

[20] Ibid., p. B1.

[21] 154 CR S8859, September 16, 2008.

[22] Aristotle, *The Nicomachean Ethics,* J. A. K. Thomson, trans. (New York: Penguin Books, 1955), Book III [IIIOa16-IIIIa18-b5].

Sen. Dianne Feinstein (D-California) opens the hearing on positive train controls on September 23, 2008. At right is Sen. Barbara Boxer (D-California). Source: © AP Photo/Manuel Balce Ceneta.

with a filibuster was defeated, and on October 1, 2008, just 19 days after the Metrolink accident, the Rail Safety Improvement Act of 2008 became law.[23] The roll call was 74 to 24. Every Democrat voted for it and all the "nay" votes were Republicans. These are the main provisions of the 123-page statute.

- Mandatory installation by 2015 of positive train control on rail lines shared by freight and passenger trains, on "main lines" carrying more than 5 million tons of freight yearly, and on any stretch of track carrying substances such as ammonia and chlorine that pose toxic inhalation hazards.

- Rules designed to prevent crew fatigue, including prohibition of train crews working more than 12 hours a day or 266 hours a month.

- A long list of new mandates for the Federal Railroad Administration including certifying conductors, monitoring locomotive radio traffic, and

studying the safety of antique locomotives used for rides at railroad museums.

- Measures to improve safety at railroad–highway crossings.

- Assistance to families of victims of passenger train accidents.

- A program of annual $50 million grants to railroads for safety improvements.

REGULATORS GO TO WORK

Like many laws passed by Congress, the Rail Safety Improvement Act is a mixture of specifics and generalities. It was very precise in dictating work-hour rules for train crews under varying circumstances, even prohibiting companies from telephoning or paging crew members at home during mandatory 10-hour rest periods. Yet it also set broad new requirements such as positive train control that left much to the discretion of the Federal Railroad Administration. In fact, it gave the agency so much to do it authorized hiring 200 new employees. Quickly, the agency went to work.

Within a week of the bill's passage it issued an emergency order prohibiting use of wireless electronic

[23] The cloture motion passed 69 to 17. It was signed by President George W. Bush on October 16, 2008, and the National Archives & Records Administration designated it as Public Law 110-423, indicating that it was the 423rd created by the 110th Congress.

devices in locomotive cabs and elsewhere on or near operating trains.[24] It cited seven accidents besides the Metrolink collision where cell phone use distracted engineers. Two led to fatalities. It also listed examples of unsafe behavior observed by its staff. Some of the stories were incredible.

> An FRA deputy regional administrator was conducting an initial preemployment interview over the telephone with a locomotive engineer who was applying for an FRA operating practices inspector position. The deputy regional administrator heard a train horn in a two long, one short, and one long pattern and asked the candidate if he was operating a locomotive. The candidate replied that he was, and the deputy regional administrator terminated the telephone call. The candidate was not selected.[25]

The agency also set to work on a rule for implementing positive train controls. It began late in 2008 by convening a working group with representatives from 18 organizations including railroads, unions, suppliers, and the FRA. This group met five times. Between meetings it broke into task forces. Disagreements between participants were resolved by FRA decisions. The agency also began a new benefit–cost study.

Within six months it submitted a proposed rule to the Office of Information and Regulatory Affairs (OIRA) along with its benefit–cost study. The 167-page study revealed a stunning excess of costs over benefits. Depending on net present value assumptions, the costs of positive train controls over 20 years were estimated at between $10 billion and $14 billion. The safety benefits were only $608 million to $931 million. Under either assumption the cost of controls was more than 15 times the benefits.

Although OIRA's job is to make sure regulations have a net benefit for society, its hands were tied because of the congressional mandate. It approved the proposed rule and the FRA published a 79-page Notice of Proposed Rulemaking in the *Federal Register*.[26] This opened a 30-day comment period. Written comments from anyone could be entered on the Federal eRulemaking Portal mailed, faxed, or hand-delivered

to the agency. During this comment period the FRA also held a one-day hearing at a Washington hotel to give railroads, unions, and state transportation officials a chance to comment before regulators.

When all comments were in, the agency reconvened its working group to review them and consider changes to the proposed rule. It took six more months. The final rule was published in the *Federal Register* on January 15, 2010, and later entered in the *Code of Federal Regulations*.[27] It set standards for the design, functioning, certification, and maintenance of positive train control systems.

It also responded to comments. For example, large railroad companies objected to a requirement for dual displays in locomotive cabs for both engineers and brakemen. The agency responded that both were necessary to ensure safety. General Electric, which sells equipment to the railroads, objected to the agency's insistence on approving entire systems and asked it to approve individual parts or components instead. The agency rejected this suggestion as complicating and more expensive. Chemical shippers asked to exclude rail lines from controls if they carried fewer than 100 tank cars of toxic chemicals a year. The agency refused, saying that was contrary to the safety mission Congress had given it.

The final rule also revised the 20-year benefit–cost projection, making it even less favorable. Depending on net present value assumptions, the costs would be $9.6 billion to $13.3 billion and the benefits $440 million to $674 million, a ratio of more than 20:1 in either case.

WORTH IT?

America now has another expensive regulatory program, one that will raise shipping rates, consumer prices, and rail passenger fares. Railroads are now more heavily regulated in their operations and employee relations. The Federal Railroad Administration grows larger and more powerful. On the other hand, rail passengers are safer, and the railroads may see some efficiency gains. Was the Rail Safety Improvement Act of 2008 justified?

Trains are dangerous. Exhibit 1 shows an annual total of between 700 and 950 railroad fatalities over the past decade, but few of them were passengers killed in train accidents—only 85 over the 10-year

---

[24] Federal Railroad Administration, "Emergency Order to Restrict On-Duty Railroad Operating Employees' Use of Cellular Telephones and Other Distracting Electronic and Electrical Devices," 73 FR 58702, October 7, 2008.

[25] 73 FR 58705.

[26] Federal Railroad Administration, "Positive Train Control Systems: Proposed Rule," 74 FR 3590, July 21, 2009.

[27] "Positive Train Control Systems: Final Rule," 75 FR 2598, January 15, 2010 and 49 CFR Parts 229, 234, 235, and 236.

EXHIBIT 1   Railroad Fatalities: 1999–2009

During this decade there were between 700 and 950 deaths each year due to train operations. Total deaths are the sum of the lines for trespasser fatalities, rail worker fatalities, highway crossing fatalities, and passenger fatalities. More than 90 percent of all railroad fatalities are trespassers on railroad rights-of-way and motorists killed in crossing accidents.

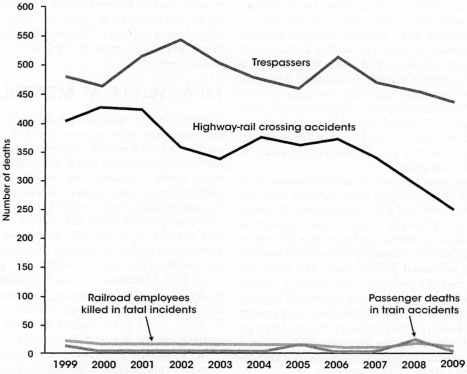

Source: Federal Railroad Administration.

period. Most fatalities are trespassers who ride trains or enter track corridors. Hundreds more are motorists hit at crossings.

In 2009, for example, there were 713 train fatalities. Of these only three were passengers killed in accidents. Of the rest, 446 were people trespassing on tracks,[28] 248 were motorists at rail crossings, and 16 were on-duty railroad employees. A nationwide system of train

controls might have saved the three passengers and some of the 16 railroad workers killed on duty, but would have done nothing to save the other 697 people.

In absolute numbers, motor vehicles kill far more people than passenger trains, to be exact 33,960 more in 2009, but they are safer per mile traveled. In 2009 the fatality rate per 100 million miles traveled was 6.07 for passenger trains compared with 1.10 for motor vehicles.[29]

[28] Trespasser fatalities are predominantly people walking, sleeping, lying, or standing on tracks or riding bicycles, motorcycles, and ATVs on them. They are, on average, 38 years old and 87 percent male. Eighty-one percent are under the influence of either alcohol or drugs or both. Federal Railroad Administration, *Rail Trespasser Fatalities: Developing Demographic Profiles* (Washington, DC: FRA, March 2008), pp. 13–19.

[29] Figures in this paragraph are from the Federal Railroad Administration, Office of Safety Analysis, "1.01 Accident Incident Overview," at http://safetydata.fra.dot.gov/officeofsafety/; and National Highway Transportation Safety Administration, "Early Estimate of Motor Vehicle Traffic Fatalities in 2009," DOT HS 811 291, March 2010.

In the FRA's benefit–cost calculations, the safety benefits of positive train controls were $440 million to $674 million over 20 years. It assumed that train controls would lead to a 60 percent reduction in rail accident costs including casualties, train delay, emergency response, and track and equipment damage.[30] A statistical life was valued at $6 million. The study also noted other potential benefits but did not monetize them. Possible business benefits for the railroads include the ability to run more trains, greater reliability, and diesel fuel savings; a possible benefit for society is reduced pollution from diesel exhaust. However, the agency concluded that such benefits were uncertain and, even if they appeared, would not fill the gap between costs and benefits for 20 to 25 years. For example, trains may have to run more slowly for years as systems are introduced.[31]

The expense to railroads is greater because final cost estimates for positive train controls were between $9.6 billion and $13.3 billion over 20 years. These include primarily wayside and locomotive components and continuing maintenance. For example, the railroads must equip roughly 30,000 locomotives at an estimated $55,000 each. The FRA also predicted that the railroads will spend 1,729,848 hours each year completing new paperwork requirements.[32] Altogether this is a formidable cost burden and an expansion of the regulatory burden on an industry that often struggles for profitability, all for a safety rule where, as the FRA concludes, "the cost-to-benefit comparison . . . is not favorable."[33]

Congress required swift installation of train controls on roughly 69,000 miles of track. Suppliers such as Lockheed Martin and General Electric have to rush component design. Railroads must make massive, unanticipated shifts in capital expenditures. In the past they were criticized for rejecting investments in train controls because capital returns were higher for expenditures on mergers and track equipment. Now there is no choice. One company, CSX Transportation, expects to spend $1.2 billion to comply with the new rule.[34]

MEANWHILE AT METROLINK

Metrolink made changes after the accident. It issued an emergency order against crew use of electronic devices, added a second engineer in locomotives, installed brighter signal bulbs, and reduced speeds in some zones. It enlarged its supervisory structure, adding four new managers to oversee operations and rules compliance, and it asked Connex to add a new vice president for safety. Efficiency testing of crews was stepped up. Eventually, it replaced its chief executive and ended its contract with Connex, giving its operations to Amtrak instead.

In 2009 Metrolink installed automatic braking equipment at 43 locations along its routes. This is an interim measure until it puts positive train controls in place, which it has agreed to do by 2012, three years before the federal 2015 deadline.

It also put inward-looking video cameras in its locomotive cabs, making it the only railroad to respond to the NTSB's recommendation. The Brotherhood of Locomotive Engineers and Trainmen, which represents Metrolink engineers, sued but could not stop the action. The union said cameras were "punitive in nature" and breached the right to privacy found in the California constitution.[35] It recommended equipment to jam cell phones instead, but Metrolink continues to use the cameras. In 2010 Metrolink took delivery of 117 new coaches designed to protect passengers by absorbing energy.

---

[30] The assumption was that other measures already taken by the FRA such as banning cell phone use would reduce accident costs by 25 percent and that train controls would eliminate 80 percent of remaining costs, yielding a 60 percent overall total cost reduction. See Frank D. Roskind, *Positive Train Control Systems: Economic Analysis* (Washington, DC: Federal Railroad Administration, July 10, 2009), pp. 139–40.

[31] The American Association of Railroads, an industry trade group, also commissioned an analysis of potential business benefits. Its study concluded the upper limit was $413 million over 20 years. Oliver Wyman, *Assessment of the Commercial Benefits of Positive Train Control* (New York: Oliver Wyman, Inc., April 23, 2010), p. 5.

[32] "Positive Train Control Systems: Final Rule," 75 FR 2598 at 2693–95.

[33] Roskind, *Positive Train Control Systems: Economic Analysis*, p. 146.

[34] John D. Boyd, "CSX Hikes Crash Avoidance Costs to $1.2 Billion," *Journal of Commerce Online*, April 14, 2010, p. WP.

[35] Tim Smith of the Brotherhood of Locomotive Engineers and Trainmen, quoted in Rich Connell, "Metrolink Seeks to Film Its Engineers," *Los Angeles Times*, December 25, 2008, p. B1; and Phil Willon, "Union Sues Over Cameras on Trains," *Los Angeles Times*, October 21, 2009, p. A12.

Since the Chatsworth Station accident there have been no Metrolink passenger fatalities from train accidents.

Questions

1. What were the causes of the Metrolink accident?
2. What could have been done to prevent the accident? Was management deficient? Were regulators deficient? Should either have been doing anything differently?
3. Is the cost of positive train control justified by the likely safety gains for passengers?
4. Did the Federal Railroad Administration fairly value a statistical life at $6 million?
5. Is money spent to regulate railroad safety being spent in the most efficient way to reduce risks of death and injury in society?
6. Were the railroads justified in opposing legislation to mandate train controls?
7. Is video recording in locomotive cabs an invasion of privacy? Should unions oppose it?

Chapter **Eleven**

Multinational Corporations

The Coca-Cola Company

John S. Pemberton, an Atlanta pharmacist, invented Coca-Cola in 1866. After some experiments to create a headache remedy, he found a formula that pleased him and named it Coca-Cola, after two of its ingredients, namely, "coca," the dried leaf of a South American shrub, and "cola," an extract of the kola nut. It became popular after local druggists began mixing it with soda water at their store fountains. When Pemberton became ill his formula moved into the hands of an Atlanta druggist named Asa Candler. Candler revised the formula, promoted it as a soft drink, and founded The Coca-Cola Company in 1892.[1]

Coca-Cola was the first soft drink to become a national brand. Candler's strategy was to manufacture the syrup, selling it to fountains, and let others add sparkling water and bottle it for the mass market. It made him rich. The company still follows this basic strategy, although its execution has grown far more complex.

The Coca-Cola Company is now an international giant with revenues of $35 billion from more than 200 countries in 2010. Its headquarters are still in Atlanta, but America is no longer its dominant market. It gets 75 percent of its sales in 200 other nations where 86 percent of its 92,800 employees live and work. Its global strategy is to expand by licensing more and more bottlers to make and sell its brands. It produces only about 21 percent of its "unit case volume," the measure it uses to calculate output, in its own syrup manufacturing and bottling plants. The rest comes from licensed bottlers with whom it has a wide range of business relationships. Some, about 23 percent, are from independent bottlers in which Coca-Cola has no ownership. Another 45 percent are bottlers partly owned but not controlled by Coca-Cola, and 11 percent are bottlers it partly owns and controls.[2]

---

[1] The exact nature of the formula is a trade secret. Years ago food and drug regulators accused the company of adulterating its product with a "poisonous" ingredient—caffeine. Coca-Cola denied any health danger and the dispute went to court. When the Supreme Court overturned a lower court ruling in the company's favor, its opinion divulged that Coke syrup contained extracts from coca shrub leaves and cola tree nuts, water (42.63 percent), sugar (52.64 percent), caffeine (1.21 grains per ounce), glycerine, and lime juice. See *United States v. Coca Cola,* 36 S.Ct. 573 (1916), at 574 and 579.

[2] The Coca-Cola Company, *Form 10-K 2010,* February 28, 2011, p. 33.

While some multinational corporations try to project a uniform product and "company way" around the world, Coca-Cola Company adapts to foreign business climates. Its organization structure divides the world into five operating groups—Eurasia and Africa, Europe, Latin America, North America, and the Pacific—reflecting a focus on regional markets. International experience is a key criterion for selecting members of its board of directors. Eight of 14 current directors are noted for strength in this area.

Acting within this structure and through more than 300 bottlers, the company is "a global business that operates on a local scale."[3] Instead of trying to market the same beverages everywhere, it finely adapts its portfolio to local tastes, selling 3,300 products based on 500 brands. It markets Georgia Coffee in Japan, Matte Leao herbal beverages in Brazil, Tian Yu Di (Heaven & Earth) teas in China, Cappy Lemonade in Turkey, and Mazoe peach juice in Ghana. Per capita consumption of its products is highest in Mexico, where the average citizen drinks 665 company beverages a year, far more than the 399 average in the United States.[4]

Around the world 1.6 billion Coca-Cola brand drinks are consumed daily. Yet satisfied customers do not insulate the company from vicious critics. In India, for example, environmental activists released data purporting to show the company's soft drinks harbored pesticides. Although Coca-Cola produced laboratory data certifying the safety of its products, several Indian states prohibited their sale. Indian courts have since reversed these bans.

In Columbia, a widow backed by activist lawyers alleged Coca-Cola was complicit in the murder of her husband, a union leader at a bottling plant. This charge has persisted despite a series of court decisions dismissing the case for lack of evidence that the company had any knowledge of, or control over, events at the independently owned plant.[5] In the United States, legendary labor activist Ray Rogers launched a "Killer Coke" campaign broadening accusations against the company to include condoning torture and kidnapping of union organizers at bottling plants, using child and prison labor, exploiting water resources, and overselling products that cause obesity. At the company's 2010 annual meeting Rogers rose to confront management, charging that the company operated "like a criminal syndicate" and asking the directors to make sure it "reins in its greed [and] cleans up its act."[6] CEO Muhtar Kent dismissed his accusations as having "no merit."[7]

One way Coca-Cola protects its brand is to set rising standards for corporate citizenship. It is spending $6 million to plant 30 million trees in Mexico and $30 million to supply 2 million Africans with clean water. If any of the 60,000 African workers for Coca-Cola and its bottlers or their family members contract HIV/AIDS, the company

---

[3] The Coca-Cola Company, "The Coca-Cola System," at www.thecoca-colacompany.com, September 19, 2010.

[4] The Coca-Cola Company, "Per Capita Consumption of Company Beverage Products," at www.thecoca-colacompany.com/ourcompany/ar/pdf/2009-per-capita-consumption.pdf, 2010.

[5] See, most recently, *Sinaltrainal v. Coca-Cola,* 578 F.3d 1252 (2009).

[6] Quoted in *Stop Killer Coke Newsletter,* May 6, 2010, at www.killercoke.org/nl100506.htm, at 1.

[7] Quoted in Jeremiah McWilliams, "Mixed Emotions at Coca-Cola Annual Meeting," *Atlanta Journal-Constitution,* April 21, 2010, p. A15.

provides medical coverage. It builds playgrounds in the Ukraine and organized thousands of volunteers to clean parks in Russia. It has global programs to reduce its energy use and replace the water it takes from nature.

Along with other multinational corporations Coca-Cola has embraced schemes of civil regulation that promote responsibility in emerging economies. To protect against accusations of bad behavior it is awash in codes. It has adopted a "Code of Business Conduct," a "Workplace Rights Policy," a "Human Rights Statement," an "Anti-Bribery Policy," and "Supplier Guiding Principles." As a signatory of the United Nations Global Compact it pledges to follow a set of 10 corporate responsibility principles. A statement on its Web site reads: "The Coca-Cola Company and our bottling partners are committed to making a lasting, positive difference in the world."[8]

In this chapter we discuss the nature of multinational corporations, their strategies for internationalization, the impacts of their foreign investment, and their efforts to show responsibility using a range of devices, from voluntary codes of conduct through collaborations with multiple stakeholders. Elements of the Coca-Cola story illustrate all these themes.

THE MULTINATIONAL CORPORATION

multinational corporation
An entity headquartered in one country that does business in one or more foreign countries.

The *multinational corporation* (MNC) is an entity headquartered in one country, its home country, that does at least part of its business in one or more foreign, or host, countries. The universe of MNCs is one of exceptional diversity. Most are private enterprises, but some are cooperatives or state-owned. A few MNCs have the majority of their assets, sales, or employees in foreign countries. Most are primarily domestic businesses with some foreign activity. While some global giants have made a visible impact for good or ill in foreign societies, most MNCs are only medium or small in size and hardly make a ripple. The oldest, largest, and most-powerful ones are based in rich countries. However, those based in China, India, Malaysia, South Africa, and other developing countries now challenge the global leaders, especially in emerging markets.

MNCs also vary widely in their organizational structures and operations. In general, however, there are five tiers of internationalization as shown in Figure 11.1. These tiers are not stages, though they might be for a given company. Rather, they represent options to extend business activity into foreign markets. Each tier is best seen as a theory, model, or ideal. Many of the largest MNCs defy categorization. They have so much structural and strategic variation that they simultaneously use the methods in all five tiers.

1. Export sales to foreign countries.
2. Establish foreign sales offices.
3. License franchises, brands, the use of patents, or technology to foreign firms that make or sell the MNC's products. For example, McDonald's restaurants outside

---

[8] The Coca-Cola Company, *2008/2009 Sustainability Review*, at www.thecoca-colacompany.com/citizenship/index.html, p. ii.

FIGURE 11.1
Five Tiers of Internationalization

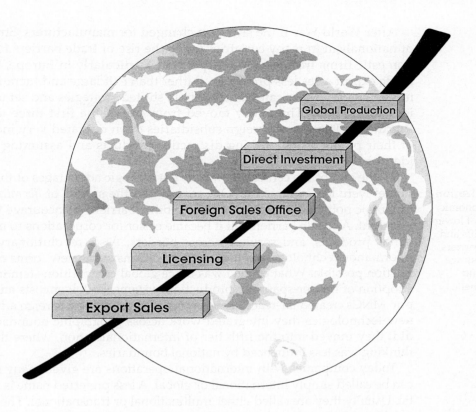

Global Production

Direct Investment

Foreign Sales Office

Licensing

Export Sales

the United States are franchises run by foreign entrepreneurs. Coca-Cola licenses foreign bottlers to make almost all of its beverages in some 200 countries.

4. Buy or create facilities in another country for producing in local markets. Such facilities may become hubs for regional or global sales. The company operates as a group of country-based business units or subsidiaries.

5. Practice global production in which a value chain spans two or more countries. Work on one or more tasks—research, design, manufacturing, logistics, distribution, marketing, sales, or support services—that would be confined to a single country in the fourth-tier model now is done in two or more countries. Organization and control of these cross-border processes are centralized in the parent company's headquarters.

Companies have strategic reasons for moving across these tiers. Through much of the previous century, firms limited themselves to the first four tiers. Before World War II, only a handful of large companies, such as Ford Motor, Singer, and Bayer, had moved into the fourth tier by operating foreign production facilities. Most manufacturers exploited foreign consumer markets through exports and foreign sales offices. The bulk of foreign investment was made in poor countries by multinationals engaged in plantation agriculture, mining, or petroleum extraction.[9]

[9] Jeffry A. Frieden, *Global Capitalism* (New York: Norton, 2006), p. 293.

After World War II the situation changed for manufacturers. Strong feelings of nationalism in many countries led to the rise of trade barriers for protecting domestic firms from import competition. Particularly in Europe, rising tariffs made export sales less profitable. Rather than exit large and lucrative domestic markets there, American manufacturers shifted strategies and set up subsidiaries within them. Thus, they moved from one of the first three tiers into the fourth tier. These new foreign subsidiaries often operated very independently of their parent firms, making distinctive products and assuming strong local identities.[10]

By the end of the century, however, the strategic advantages of this fourth-tier model were less compelling. One reason was the spread of *liberalization,* or the economic policy of lowering tariffs and other barriers to encourage trade and investment. As trade barriers fell it became easier for corporations to move components, products, and services across borders. Also, revolutionary changes in information technology and telecommunications made new forms of global production possible. What ensued was fierce global competition stemming from the adoption of border-spanning production systems. To lower costs and speed output, MNCs created far-reaching networks of suppliers and foreign affiliates. Using new technologies they integrated work across geographic boundaries. As they did, they moved into the fifth tier of internationalization, where their strategic thinking was less influenced by national boundaries.

Today companies with international operations are given many names. They can be called simply international or global. A less preferred name is multidomestic. Usually they are called either multinational or transnational. These names are used loosely, but they occasionally signify diverging beliefs about the nature of these corporations. Sometimes those using the name *multinational* mean to imply that these companies have erased national allegiances, becoming itinerant firms that move investment and activity from nation to nation in search of profits. The name *transnational* is sometimes intended to suggest that rather than becoming stateless entities, large global firms are best understood as invariably and unalterably national companies that have simply extended their reach over borders. The distinction is impractical. There are so many variations of MNCs that either definition fails if applied to the whole universe. Therefore, in this book, we prefer the traditional and long-standing name *multinational* used loosely and interchangeably with transnational, global, and international.

A Statistical Perspective

Multinational corporations have flourished so spectacularly that if they were a natural species ecologists would inspect their environment for the explanation. One trend is a rapid rise in numbers. The United Nations calculated that in 2008 there were 82,000 *transnational corporations* (TNCs), which it defines as parent firms that control the assets of affiliated entities in foreign countries including branches, subsidiaries, and joint ventures. It estimated that these parent TNCs controlled

liberalization
The economic policy of lowering tariffs and other barriers to encourage trade and investment.

transnational corporation
As defined by the United Nations, a parent firm that controls the assets of affiliated entities in foreign countries.

---

[10] Geoffrey G. Jones, "Nationality and Multinationals in Historical Perspective," Working Paper 06-052, Harvard Business School, 2005, p. 23.

FIGURE 11.2
The Dominance of the Largest Transnational Corporations
The United Nations reports there are now 82,000 transnational corporations. Of these, the largest 100 nonfinancial corporations are 12 percent of the number but have a disproportionately great impact on the global economy. All but 10 are from the United States, Europe, and Japan.

Source: Data from United Nations Conference on Trade and Development, *World Investment Report 2009* (New York: United Nations, 2009), p. 17; and United Nations Conference on Trade and Development, *World Investment Report 2010* (New York: United Nations, 2010), annex table 26.

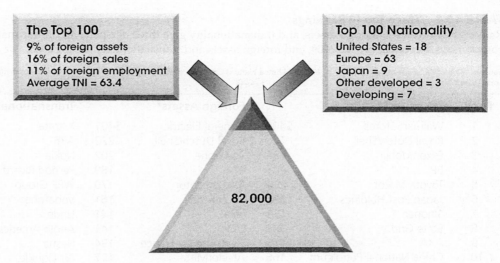

The Top 100
9% of foreign assets
16% of foreign sales
11% of foreign employment
Average TNI = 63.4

Top 100 Nationality
United States = 18
Europe = 63
Japan = 9
Other developed = 3
Developing = 7

82,000

807,000 such *foreign affiliates*.[11] This is more than double the 37,000 TNCs in the United Nations' first estimate of their numbers back in 1991 and more than seven times the 10,700 estimated to exist in 1969.[12] The ranks of parent TNCs are dominated by those from developed nations, but the number from developing countries has risen to 28 percent of the total, up from only 8 percent in 1992.[13]

If the largest firms are any indication, transnational firms have also grown in size. In the decade from 1998 to 2008, the assets, sales, and employment of the largest 100 transnational firms increased by 131 percent, 107 percent, and 20 percent, respectively. As they grew, a larger part of their activities became international. During the same decade, the foreign assets, foreign sales, and foreign employment of these top 100 firms grew faster than their overall growth, going up 217 percent, 153 percent, and 35 percent, respectively.[14] On average, each of these big firms operates in 41 countries and 70 percent of their affiliates are in foreign countries.[15]

Figure 11.2 sketches the universe of TNCs and hints at the dominance of the 100 largest firms. Their origins reflect the commanding position in the global economy of the United States, Europe, and Japan, which are home to 90 of the top 100. TNCs

foreign affiliates
Business entities in foreign countries controlled by parent transnational corporations.

[11] This 2008 estimate is from United Nations Conference on Trade and Development, *World Investment Report 2009* (New York and Geneva: United Nations, 2009), annex table A.I.8.

[12] The 1990 estimate is from United Nations Conference on Trade and Development, *World Investment Report 1993* (New York: United Nations, 1993), table I.6. The 1969 estimate is extrapolated from data in fn. 7 and table I.6.

[13] United Nations Conference on Trade and Development, *World Investment Report,* 2010, p. 17 and figure I.12.

[14] United Nations Conference on Trade and Development, *World Investment Report 2000* (New York: United Nations, 2000), table III.2; and United Nations Conference on Trade and Development, *World Investment Report 2009,* table I.7. Figures are based on an annual list of nonfinancial companies ranked by foreign assets.

[15] United Nations Conference on Trade and Development, "Largest Transnational Corporations Pursued further Expansion Abroad in 2007," press release, September 24, 2008.

TABLE 11.1   Three Top 10 Rankings

Rankings by revenues, foreign assets, and transnationality give three perspectives on transnational corporations. Revenues are for 2009, and foreign assets and transnationality are for 2008.

Source: "Global 500," *Fortune*, July 26, 2010, p. 131; and United Nations Conference on Trade and Development, *World Investment Report 2010* (New York: United Nations, 2010), annex table 26.

Rank	Revenues*		Foreign Assets*		Transnationality	TNI
1	Walmart Stores	$408	General Electric	$401	Xstrata	93.2%
2	Royal Dutch/Shell	285	Royal Dutch/Shell	222	ABB	90.4
3	ExxonMobil	285	Vodafone	202	Nokia	90.3
4	BP	246	BP	189	Pernod Ricard	89.1
5	Toyota Motor	204	Toyota Motor	170	WPP Group	88.9
6	Japan Post Holdings	202	ExxonMobil	161	Vodafone	88.6
7	Sinopec	188	Total	141	Linde	88.3
8	State Grid	185	E.On	141	Anglo American	87.5
9	AXA	175	Electricite De France	134	Nestlé	87.1
10	China National Petroleum	166	ArcelorMittal	127	Air Liquide	86.9

*Revenues and assets are rounded in billions of dollars.

from developing countries occupy only 7 spots in the top 100, but their importance is growing. They account for 28 percent of all TNCs, up from only 8 percent in 1992 and their foreign assets are about 10 percent of all TNC foreign assets.[16] Table 11.1 shows several dimensions of the top 10 firms—their sales, assets, and rank on an index of internationalization to be explained in the next section.

How Transnational Is a Corporation?

One way of gauging the largest TNCs is by measuring the degree to which they have extended critical elements of their operations into foreign countries. Corporations vary in a range of international dimensions. These include the ratio of domestic to foreign operations; the number of foreign countries entered; the size of foreign direct investment; the geographic span of operations; the extent of global integration in the production chain; and the extent of national diversity among shareholders, employees, managers, and directors. Since TNCs differ greatly in these dimensions, no single measure can capture the definitive meaning of "transnational."

Yet measures have been created. The most widely used is the *transnationality index*, or TNI, used by the United Nations to rank corporations based on the relative importance of their domestic and foreign operations. The TNI is calculated as the average of three ratios: (1) foreign assets to total assets, (2) foreign sales to total sales, and (3) foreign employment to total employment. Table 11.2 looks at the TNI index for two of the largest 100 multinational corporations, General Electric, a diversified conglomerate headquartered in the United States, and Philips Electronics of the Netherlands, a global manufacturer of electronic equipment.

transnationality index (TNI)
The average of three ratios: foreign assets to total assets, foreign sales to total sales, and foreign employment to total employment.

[16] UNCTAD, *World Investment Report 2010*, p. 17.

TABLE 11.2 Calculating the Transnationality Index (TNI) for General Electric and Philips Electronics

Source: Data from United Nations Conference on Trade and Development, *World Investment Report 2010* (New York: United Nations, 2010), annex table 26. Figures are for 2008.

General Electric		Ratio	Philips Electronics		Ratio
Foreign assets	$401,290		Foreign assets	$ 32,675	
Total assets	797,769	50.3	Total assets	45,986	71.1
Foreign sales	97,214		Foreign sales	37,122	
Total sales	182,515	53.3	Total sales	38,603	96.2
Foreign employees	171,000		Foreign employees	83,946	
Total employees	323,000	52.9	Total employees	121,398	69.2
		TNI = 52.2%			TNI = 78.8%

Although GE ranks first in assets among the largest 100 nonfinancial TNCs, it is tied for 80th in its transnationality score. Philips, on the other hand, ranks 65th in assets but 24th in TNI, making it one of the most internationalized of the 100. Although Philips is a much smaller company, its foreign activities are larger in proportion to the whole.

In the eyes of some corporate critics, it is possible for an MNC to become too transnational. Eventually, some MNCs are said to be stateless in a pejorative sense, meaning that not only do foreign operations dominate strategy, but they also structure themselves to elude national controls. This stateless incarnation is more theoretical than operational. The typical MNC remains national rather than international.

Corporations are formed under national incorporation laws. In the United States, for example, each company must be chartered by a state. Most employees at company headquarters are home country nationals. Boards of directors are dominated by home country majorities. It is still rare for top executives to be foreign citizens. Most shareholders are usually in the home country. Record keeping is done in the home country currency. These ties are part of the culture of the company, which is not easily modified. Finally, in many fifth-tier companies there is a strong trend toward more centralized authority rather than more "statelessness."[17] Sprawling global production networks require a strong, controlling hand at headquarters.

For all these reasons, escaping its nationality of origin is awkward for an MNC. Most remain national firms with international operations. Despite these generalizations, a few MNCs find strategic advantage in breaking home country bonds. Consider the odyssey of Weatherford International.

Breaking the Bonds of Country: Weatherford International

Weatherford makes machinery used for oil and natural gas drilling and provides services to energy companies ranging from flushing pipes on drill rigs to cooking meals for crews. It was founded in 1972 in Texas and until the 1990s it operated mostly in the United States. Then it decided to expand into oil fields around the world. It has grown into a company of 53,000 employees with $10 billion in

[17] Geoffrey G. Jones, "The Rise of Corporate Nationality," *Harvard Business Review*, October 2006, p. 21.

FIGURE 11.3
Weatherford
International:
1972–2002

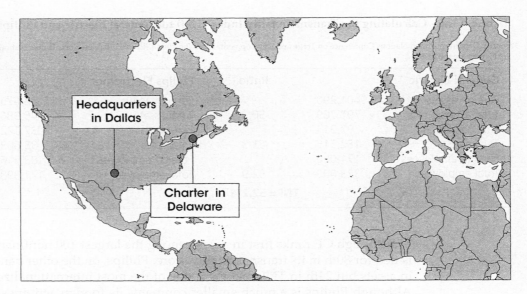

Headquarters
in Dallas

Charter in
Delaware

revenues, 62 percent coming from outside the U.S. It operates through about 300 foreign affiliates, including 30 wholly owned subsidiaries and another 250-plus entities in which it has a controlling or noncontrolling interest.

Weatherford was incorporated in Delaware in 1972. Although its headquarters were in Houston, Texas, it could legally charter itself in any state (see Figure 11.3). It picked Delaware because incorporation laws there are business-friendly. In 2002, however, Weatherford decided to restructure and incorporate in Bermuda (see Figure 11.4). It saw several advantages in this. Bermuda law makes it hard for shareholders to sue directors. Hostile takeovers are more difficult. And, most important, corporate taxes are lower because Bermuda has no tax treaty with the United States. By moving there Weatherford could lower its tax rate from 35 percent in the United States, one of the world's highest rates, to about 11 percent.[18] So Weatherford created a new Bermuda corporation, then "reorganized" by making its U.S. corporation a subsidiary of the Bermuda parent. Its headquarters were still in Texas. It remained on the Standard & Poor's 500 index of leading U.S. corporations.

This action irritated some lawmakers. Sen. Max Baucus (D-Montana) was offended that Weatherford and several dozen other U.S. corporations that went to Bermuda were still being run in the United States. "Their executives and employees enjoy all the privileges afforded to honest U.S. taxpayers," he noted.[19] "If companies don't have their hearts in America, they ought to get out," said Sen. Charles Grassley, (R-Iowa)[20] The two senators introduced a tax code amendment to strip Weatherford of its favorable tax treatment.

[18] David Cay Johnston, "Tax Treaties with Small Nations Turn into a New Shield for Profits," *The New York Times,* April 16, 2002, p. 1; and Duanjie Chen and Jack Mintz, "U.S. Effective Corporate Tax Rate on New Investments: Highest in the OECD," *Tax & Budget Bulletin,* May 2010, p. 1.

[19] *Congressional Record-Senate,* April 11, 2002, p. S2594.

[20] Ibid., p. S2592.

FIGURE 11.4
Weatherford
International:
2002–2009

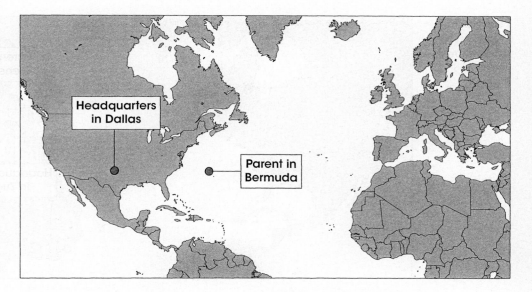

Headquarters
in Dallas

Parent in
Bermuda

It did not pass, but after the election of President Barack Obama in 2008, Democratic majorities in Congress targeted corporations moving to tax haven countries. Seeing the danger, Weatherford took itself out of reach again. In 2009 it completed a "redomestication" to Switzerland, another tax-friendly country. It did this by making its Bermuda corporation the subsidiary of a new Swiss parent corporation (see Figure 11.5). Switzerland has a low corporate tax rate and, unlike the United States, does not tax revenue from foreign subsidiaries. By 2009 Weatherford had reduced its tax rate to 6.5 percent.[21]

To put itself out of the reach of Congress, the company relocated its headquarters to Zug, Switzerland, and its top executives moved there. As in the prior Bermuda move, management saw other advantages in Swiss incorporation law. For example, although it allows shareholders to remove directors, it makes the process very complicated. And by holding annual meetings in Switzerland it will be more difficult for its majority of U.S. shareholders to attend. Weatherford will not escape all its U.S. bonds by this reflagging. It still keeps its records in U.S. dollars. Seven of its 10 directors, including Nicholas Brady, a former secretary of the Treasury, are U.S. citizens. Unless directors and executives renounce U.S. citizenship they remain subject to many U.S. laws. An example is the antibribery statute, the Foreign Corrupt Practices Act, which makes it illegal for U.S. citizens anywhere in the world to bribe foreign officials.

Weatherford, now a Swiss corporation run by Americans, continues to expand its international operations. It projects that by 2014 it will get only 20 to 25 percent of its sales in North America.[22] It has been removed from the S&P 500 index.

---

[21] Weatherford International, *2009 Annual Report* (Geneva: Weatherford International, Ltd., 2010), p. AR-25.

[22] Barclays Capital, 2010 CEO Energy-Power Conference, "Weatherford," p. 21, at http://phx.corporate-ir.net/.

FIGURE 11.5
Weatherford
International:
2009 to
Present

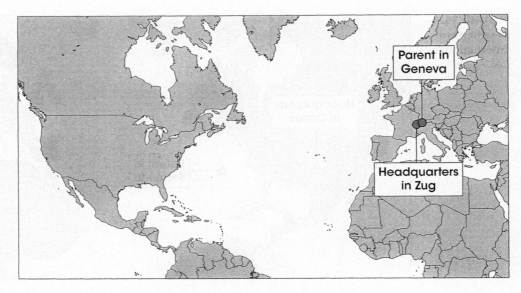

FOREIGN DIRECT INVESTMENT

foreign direct
investment
Funds invested
by a parent
MNC for start-
ing, acquiring,
or expanding
an affiliate in a
foreign nation.

portfolio
investment
The limited,
speculative
purchase of
stocks and
bonds in a for-
eign company
by individuals
or equity funds.

The single measure that best captures the cross-border activity and power of MNCs is how much capital they inject into foreign economies. This capital is called *foreign direct investment,* or FDI, and is measured as the dollar value of funds invested by a parent corporation for starting, acquiring, or expanding an enter-prise in a foreign nation. As a form of investment, FDI stands in contrast to *portfo-lio investment*, or the purchase of stocks and bonds of a foreign company by individuals or equity funds. Compared with FDI, portfolio investment is limited and speculative. Unlike FDI, it does not confer any degree of control over the com-pany and it can be a short-term position sold any time. FDI is the means by which a corporation takes partial or total control of foreign assets with the intention of a long-term presence. Usually, this is defined as an investment of 10 percent or more in a foreign enterprise.

FDI can come through cross-border mergers and acquisitions of existing busi-nesses; through the purchase of property such as factories, mines, or real estate; as earnings reinvested in an affiliate; or from the transfer of funds within a corpora-tion to a foreign affiliate. Almost all FDI comes from multinational corporations. About 1 percent comes from private equity and hedge funds. Tiny fractions of a percent come from individuals and sovereign wealth funds. A *sovereign wealth fund* is a government entity that invests the savings of a nation. FDI by such funds has sometimes raised suspicion because unlike private investors, state-run actors can have geopolitical motives. Although they are emerging as sources of FDI, they so far have little impact. In 2009 they were the source of less than a hundredth of one percent of global FDI.[23]

[23] United Nations Conference on Trade and Investment, *World Investment Report: 2010,* p. 14.

FIGURE 11.6
Where Foreign Direct Investment Flows

Source: UNCTAD, *World Investment Report 2010* (New York: United Nations, 2010), annex table 1.

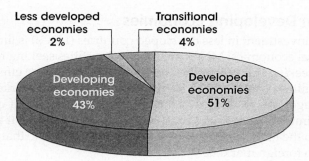

Less developed economies 2%

Transitional economies 4%

Developing economies 43%

Developed economies 51%

sovereign wealth fund
A government entity that invests the savings of a nation. Since it is state-owned, its investment goals may be different from those of private equity funds.

Annual flows of FDI from parent MNCs to foreign affiliates are in a long-term rise, growing from $202 billion in 1990 to $1.1 trillion in 2009, an increase of 537 percent. Over the same period, these annual flows elevated the total assets of foreign affiliates from $6 trillion to $77 trillion, an increase of 1,283 percent.[24]

Corporations make foreign direct investments for many reasons. Three are most common. First, they seek access to new markets. After World War II, for example, European countries had high tariffs on imported goods. American companies jumped over the tariff walls by starting European subsidiaries. Second, companies in nations with small domestic markets enter foreign markets to grow. Nestlé began in the 1860s as a powdered milk company in Switzerland. Now only 1.9 percent of its sales are in the Swiss domestic market. And third, some companies create efficiencies and lower their costs by moving production across borders. By doing so they can use low-wage workers, own sources of critical material, and acquire skills that confer advantages over competitors in, for example, advertising, branding, logistics, or the use of new technologies.

Figure 11.6 shows the distribution of FDI inflows. About half the $1.1 trillion FDI in 2009 moved into 38 developed nations. The United States was the top recipient with $130 billion. European Union countries took in $362 billion collectively. Most of the other half of total FDI, 43 percent, went to 75 developing nations. China took in $95 billion, which was second only to the United States among all nations. Together, China, Brazil, India, and Russia took in 41 percent of developing nation FDI.

Only small portions of FDI entered the world's weakest economies. The 18 transitional economies of South-East Europe and the Commonwealth of Independent States received only 4 percent. A group of 50 least developed countries, the majority in Africa, took in just 2 percent. The $28 billion in FDI entering these poorest of nations was far less than the $51 billion in development aid they received from the world community.[25] Nations with struggling economies are unattractive to investment for a variety of reasons, including weak currencies, political instability, the presence of trade barriers, bad regulatory climates, corruption, unskilled workforces, deficient infrastructure, and tiny domestic markets.

[24] Ibid., table I.5.

[25] Development aid includes both loans and grants from multilateral agencies and donations from donor countries. See World Bank, *World Development Indicators 2010* (Washington, DC: World Bank, April 2010), tables 6.13 and 6.16.

Investment in Developing Economies

Although MNC investment in less developed countries (LDCs) is limited, it can be significant in local economies. MNCs are for-profit entities seeking return on capital invested. In seeking this return they can have many positive effects. They may build or buy facilities, contract with local suppliers, and hire workers. They may bring new management skills and technologies to the region. If conditions are right, FDI can stimulate growth of a local economic "ecosystem." If a local affiliate is integrated into the MNC's international production network, that then links the local economy to foreign markets.

Botswana is an example. On independence from Britain in 1966 it was a poor nation where the average citizen earned $76 a year. The country had little domestic capital to exploit its large deposits of copper, nickel, and diamonds, but foreign mining firms did. The government adopted FDI-friendly policies, giving companies long leases, low tax rates, and freedom to operate. MNCs from England, Australia, Canada, Russia, and South Africa invested in mines and with them roads, airstrips, power stations, waterworks, rail lines, schools, and hospitals. At a time when South African giant De Beers dominated global diamonds, its trading company connected Botswana to world markets, bringing monopoly profits back to the country.

Other MNCs used aerial detectors to chart minute shifts in gravitational fields caused by ore deposits.[26] This technology identified more mineral deposits. Because of foreign investment, Botswana has one of the fastest-growing economies in the world. Per capita annual income rose to $14,100 in 2008. It is now classified as a middle-income country. It is not yet a paradise. It has the highest rate of HIV/AIDS in the world and more than 30 percent of its people live in poverty. Nevertheless, mining is not the cause of these problems and the country is better off from its receptivity to FDI.

Such stories motivate poor nations to alter their trade and investment policies courting FDI. Other actors in the international community have moved from a hostile attitude toward MNCs to embrace a new pragmatism about the presence of FDI. In the United Nations, international aid groups, and progressive NGOs, longstanding suspicion has been replaced by calculated acceptance of a role for MNCs in development. The United Nations now advises developing nations to set up a "stable and enabling regulatory environment" that indulges the "concern of the business sector for national policies that are enabling but not overly regulating."[27]

Negative effects of FDI are also visible. They are the basis of enduring fear of MNC power. In 1974 two progressive authors of a popular book, *Global Reach*, wrote that "a few hundred" multinational corporations "are making daily business decisions which have more impact than those of most sovereign governments."[28] As trade liberalization produced a more global economy in the 1990s, critics expressed more anxiety over corporate power. One leading progressive, David C. Korten,

---

[26] Keith Jefferis, "The Role of TNCs in the Extractive Industry in Botswana," *Transnational Corporations,* April 2009, p. 63.

[27] United Nations Conference on Trade and Development, *World Investment Report 2010,* p. 117.

[28] Richard J. Barnet and Ronald E. Müller, *Global Reach: The Power of the Multinational Corporations* (New York: Simon and Schuster, 1974), p. 15.

argued that power on earth was being "transferred from national governments . . . to transnational corporations . . . which by their nature serve only the short-term interests of citizens."[29] A subsequent manifesto of progressive theorists said that "several hundred global corporations and banks" held "a concentration of economic and political power that is increasingly unaccountable to governments, people, or the planet."[30] Such statements focused activists on the sins of MNCs, not their promise.

To say that MNCs have so much power is artful. Their economic and social power comes primarily from the impact of FDI. And although FDI has grown, and grown faster than domestic investment, the gross product of all foreign affiliates of all MNCs was only 11 percent of world GDP in 2009.[31] So the economic activity generated by foreign investment is small compared with domestic economic activity. The social impact of this investment, both positive and negative, cannot be measured precisely, but should not be vastly exaggerated. The power of global corporations is closely tied to their foreign investments and cannot too greatly exceed this base. Giant corporations may arguably wield excessive power, but their transnational activities are insufficient in themselves to constitute the excess.

Still, negative economic and social effects of FDI exist. First, we discuss potentially negative economic effects. Although competition from a new foreign affiliate can stimulate local firms, the new entry can also overwhelm them and, in a lax regulatory climate, come to monopolize a domestic market. Governments protect weak or politically powerful industries with patchworks of control. India, for example, forbids foreign investment in retail stores and the manufacture of cigarettes, cheroots, or cigars. It limits investment in FM radio stations to 20 percent of ownership.[32] Russia limits foreign investors to a 10 percent interest in oil, gas, gold, and copper. And China allows officials to reject foreign acquisitions of Chinese companies when "economic security" is threatened.[33]

Multinational corporations are criticized for repatriating profits to home countries, so that local residents get limited benefit from their presence. In Africa, global mining and energy firms own much of the continent's vast stores of oil, natural gas, gold, diamonds, uranium, copper, and platinum. Yet, using intrafirm money transfers, much of the economic value they generate moves out of impoverished nations. Production taxes and royalties paid to African governments are often pocketed by corrupt elites. Critics say this kind of FDI amounts to a "recolonization" that leaves average citizens as poor as they were before its arrival.[34]

[29] David C. Korten, "The Limits of the Earth," *The Nation,* July 15/22, 1996, p. 16. See also Korten's book, *When Corporations Rule the World* (San Francisco: Kumarian Press and Barrett-Koehler, 1995).

[30] The International Forum on Globalization, *Alternatives to Economic Globalization* (San Francisco: Barrett-Koehler, 2002), p. 17.

[31] See United Nations Conference on Trade and Development, *World Investment Report 2010,* table I.5.

[32] Government of India, Ministry of Commerce and Industry, *Consolidated FDI Policy (Effective from October 1, 2010),* Circular 2 (2010), pp. 39 and 54.

[33] Government Accountability Office, *Laws and Policies Regulating Foreign Investment in 10 Countries,* GAO-08-320, February 2008, pp. 10–12.

[34] Jeffrey Gogo, "Vast Mineral Wealth Sparks New 'Scramble for Africa,'" *The Herald* (Zimbabwe), February 27, 2007, p. 1.

Even without making direct investments in a nation, powerful MNCs can shake its economy. For example, about 30 large supermarket and food corporations are now the gatekeepers in global markets for fruits and vegetables. Buyers for Walmart, Carrefour, Royal Ahold, Tesco, and others seek low price, rapid delivery, and uniform quality when they source produce. Their intense pressure pushes low prices all the way back to small farmers growing crops for export. They prefer to contract with a few big export companies rather than with multitudes of small farmers. In the past decade, most of Kenya's small farmers abandoned their livelihoods as more and more produce was purchased from large farms owned by export companies. So, although Walmart and the others made no direct investment in the Kenyan economy, their market power reshaped its agricultural sector.[35]

Social impacts often accompany the economic impacts of multinational corporations. Where the material standard of living is raised, these are positive. But, especially where social regulation is rudimentary, they can be negative. Recurrently there are charges that mining and drilling facilities in remote areas harm the environment and disrupt native peoples. MNCs in manufacturing are accused of exploiting factory workers. And MNCs selling consumer products such as entertainment, fast food, and apparel are suspected of tainting local cultural values with Western indulgence and materialism.

Even as their power builds or distorts, the companies themselves frequently take a beating. Recently, for example, IKEA decided to suspend investment in Russia because of what it called the "unpredictable character of administrative procedures."[36] This was a polite reference to corruption. One problem was a ministry that refused to approve a shopping mall not built to withstand hurricane force winds, though such winds are unknown in the region. Officials hinted the problem would be solved if IKEA hired a certain firm to reinforce the structure. In Thailand, where foreign corporations live with airport closures, mass protests, and threatened military coups, a court suddenly froze $12 billion in foreign investment projects for an unknown time to study its environmental consequences. Ford Motor Company, which exports vehicles from Thailand to 50 other countries, is considering relocation.

A new law in Indonesia shortens the time of exploration licenses for mining MNCs, gives local authorities more power over mining, and prohibits shipping ore away from mines for smelting. Such a law strengthens the hand of towns affected by mines and could lead to smelter investment and employment for Indonesians. However, big miners such as Rio Tinto and BHP Billiton now rate Indonesia's investment climate the worst of any mineral-rich country and may reduce their FDI.[37] In Bolivia the government issued a decree nationalizing four power companies 50 percent-owned by French and British corporations. The next day it took over a metals plant owned by a Swiss company. In nearby Venezuela the president threatened to seize a Toyota Motor assembly plant unless it was converted to

---

[35] United Nations Development Programme, *Human Development Report 2005* (New York: UNDP, 2005), pp. 142–43.

[36] "Courting Disaster," *The Economist,* July 4, 2009, p. 63.

[37] Tom Wright, "Indonesian Mining Law Adds Obstacles for Foreign Investors," *The Wall Street Journal,* December 17, 2008, p. A14.

advanced manufacturing technology and made inexpensive vehicles designed for rough roads.[38]

Nevertheless, fear of MNC power, especially its exercise in LDCs, has led to an international movement promoting responsible behavior. The result is a global web of norms, codes, standards, labels, audits, and certifications already described in Chapter 5. In what follows, we discuss several additional efforts to control MNCs' behavior. We begin with the story of the Sullivan Principles, a pioneering effort that set the stage for further efforts.

INTERNATIONAL CODES OF CONDUCT

international codes of conduct
Voluntary, aspirational statements by MNCs that set forth standards for foreign operations.

Sullivan Principles
A 1977 code of conduct that required multinational corporations in South Africa to do business in a nondiscriminatory way.

International codes of conduct are aspirational statements of principles, policies, and rules for foreign operations that a multinational corporation voluntarily agrees to follow. The first such code to engage a large number of corporations was the *Sullivan Principles.*

In 1977 the Rev. Leon Sullivan, a Baptist minister and civil rights activist who sat on General Motors' board of directors, set forth six broad principles for the conduct of MNCs in South Africa. At the time, South African law decreed an elaborate system of *apartheid,* or separation of the races, in which the civil rights of black, Indian, and mixed-race citizens were restricted by a government of *Afrikaners,* descendants of white Europeans who had settled that part of Africa more than 300 years earlier. Human rights activists charged MNCs that invested in South Africa with complicity in a repressive, racist regime. General Motors, which was the largest employer of black South Africans, sold vehicles to the police and the military. Polaroid, for a time, sold the film used for pictures in official passbooks the government used to classify citizens by race and restrict their movements.

Reverend Sullivan rose to prominence as a civil rights activist and minister at a large Baptist church in Philadelphia. In 1971 General Motors put him on its board of directors, and he became the first black director of a major U.S. corporation. As a director he led GM to hire more black workers and set up more black dealerships. But when he would argue that GM should leave South Africa to protest racism there, other directors were unconvinced. In time, they even began turning in their seats to show him their backs.[39] It was a trip to South Africa, however, that pushed him into more direct action. Years later, he told a reporter what happened.

> When I was getting on the plane to go home, the police took me to a room and told me to remove my clothes. A man with the biggest .45 I'd ever seen said, "We do to you what we have to."
>
> I stood there in my underwear, thinking, "I'm the head of the largest black church in Philadelphia and I'm on the board of directors of General Motors. When I get home, I'll do to you what I have to."[40]

---

[38] Dan Molinski and Norihiko Shirouzu, "Venezuela's President Threatens Toyota, GM," *The Wall Street Journal,* December 26, 2009, p. A1.

[39] Claudia Levy, "Civil Rights Crusader Leon Sullivan Dies," *Washington Post,* April 26, 2001, p. B7.

[40] Quoted in Jan Hoffman, "A Civil Rights Crusader Takes On the World," *The New York Times,* November 3, 1999, p. B2.

The Rev. Leon H. Sullivan (1922–2001). The Sullivan Principles demonstrated that codes of conduct could promote corporate responsibility on a global scale. Source: © Bettmann/CORBIS.

The Sullivan Principles required MNCs in South Africa to integrate workplaces, provide equal pay, and promote nonwhites to supervisory roles. In effect, they turned foreign corporations into civil disobedients, since these requirements violated South African employment law. This was an early instance when a code called on MNCs to enforce international norms in a host country. Additionally, companies were to improve housing, schools, and health care for nonwhite workers and their families.

The principles remained in place until a change in government ended apartheid in 1994. During this time more than 100 firms became signatories and spent $350 million to carry out their commitments.[41] The results were mixed. The principles helped overcome apartheid, but failed to satisfy global antiapartheid activists whose vicious attacks and domestic boycotts drove many signatory corporations out of South Africa. Coca-Cola, for example, argued that as a signatory it could have a constructive presence in South Africa. However, activists believed that the very presence of Coca-Cola, no matter how principled its operations, gave the regime legitimacy. They called a boycott. As black consumers emptied Coke bottles onto the streets around its Atlanta headquarters, the company sold its facilities to South African entrepreneurs.

The Sullivan Principles inspired more efforts to enumerate and codify international standards of corporate conduct. Code making exploded in the 1990s as a response to expanding FDI. By 2001, one study identified 246 voluntary codes for MNCs, including 118 company codes, 92 from business or industry groups, and

[41] Oliver F. Williams, "Shaping a High-Trust Society: The Crucial Role of Codes of Conduct," *Business Ethics Quarterly* 14, no. 2 (2004), p. 342.

32 from partnerships of stakeholders.[42] Today the global total of conduct codes, sets of principles, and standards of operation for MNCs is doubtless higher. The overall structure of this code-based civil regulation of CSR was discussed in Chapter 5. Here we will take a narrower, case-oriented focus, examining in depth two of the most prominent international schemes to encourage responsible MNC behavior, one a code of conduct backed by governments, the other a set of aspirational principles backed by the United Nations. Neither is, strictly speaking, enforceable. But each, in its own way, has encouraged better MNC citizenship. Then, we discuss an additional element of the global CSR system, the Alien Tort Claims Act.

THE *OECD GUIDELINES FOR MULTINATIONAL ENTERPRISES*

This is the only comprehensive global code of corporate conduct promoted by governments. The Organisation for Economic Co-operation and Development (OECD) is a group of 33 nations that works to further economic growth by expanding trade. It formed in 1961 as an outgrowth of cooperation to rebuild Europe after World War II. At first it was a select group of advanced economies, including only the United States and 19 European nations. Since then, membership has grown to include Japan, Australia, and some developing countries.

The *OECD Guidelines for Multinational Enterprises* are "recommendations" from OECD governments to multinational corporations that operate within or from their borders. Along with the 33 OECD member nations another 11 nonmember nations now adopt them.[43] The *Guidelines* are an extensive, detailed code of conduct grounded in 11 general policies, as set forth in the accompanying box. These are further articulated in eight chapters of more detailed policies for specific areas—disclosure, employment, environment, bribery, consumers, science and technology, competition, and taxation. Standards in each area are derived from the mesh of hard and *soft law* in international treaties, conventions, covenants, and norms.

soft law
Statements of philosophy, policy, and principle found in nonbinding international agreements that, over time, gain legitimacy as guidelines for interpreting the "hard law" in legally binding agreements.

How the *OECD Guidelines* Work

Observance of the guidelines is voluntary; they are nonbinding. There are no sanctions or penalties for violations. However, a formal process exists to "encourage" observance. Each government that joins in the guidelines sets up an office, called a "national contact point." Any individual or group can file a complaint at one of these offices alleging violations by a corporation. The office then goes through a three-step process. First, it assesses the complaint. Second, if there is merit, it offers to mediate the dispute between the parties. Then, if mediation is rejected or fails, it can issue a "final statement" about the matter, including recommendations to the disputants.

Complaints come primarily from activists and labor unions. In the decade between 2000 and 2010 there were 96 complaints from NGOs and 117 from unions. The complaint process is imperfect. Of 96 complaints from NGOs, for example,

---

[42] Organisation for Economic Co-operation and Development, "Corporate Codes of Conduct: Expanded Review of their Contents," *Working Papers on International Investment,* No. 2001/6, May 2001, p. 31.

[43] These are Argentina, Brazil, Egypt, Estonia, Latvia, Lithuania, Morocco, Peru, and Romania.

The *OECD Guidelines for Multinational Enterprises*

GENERAL POLICIES

Enterprises should take fully into account established policies in the countries in which they operate, and consider the views of other stakeholders. In this regard, enterprises should:

1. Contribute to economic, social and environmental progress with a view to achieving sustainable development.

2. Respect the human rights of those affected by their activities consistent with the host government's international obligations and commitments.

3. Encourage local capacity building through close co-operation with the local community, including business interests, as well as developing the enterprise's activities in domestic and foreign markets, consistent with the need for sound commercial practice.

4. Encourage human capital formation, in particular by creating employment opportunities and facilitating training opportunities for employees.

5. Refrain from seeking or accepting exemptions not contemplated in the statutory or regulatory framework related to environmental, health, safety, labour, taxation, financial incentives, or other issues.

6. Support and uphold good corporate governance principles and develop and apply good corporate governance practices.

7. Develop and apply effective self-regulatory practices and management systems that foster a relationship of confidence and mutual trust between enterprises and the societies in which they operate.

8. Promote employee awareness of, and compliance with, company policies through appropriate dissemination of these policies, including through training programmes.

9. Refrain from discriminatory or disciplinary action against employees who make *bona fide* reports to management or, as appropriate, to the competent public authorities, on practices that contravene the law, the *Guidelines* or the enterprise's policies.

10. Encourage, where practicable, business partners, including suppliers and sub-contractors, to apply principles of corporate conduct compatible with the *Guidelines.*

11. Abstain from any improper involvement in local political activities.

Source: Organisation for Economic Co-operation and Development, *OECD Guidelines for Multinational Enterprises* (Paris, France: OECD, 2008). Reprinted with permission.

only 27 percent were concluded with a settlement or final statement.[44] According to OECD Watch, a network of 80 activist groups that reports on the effectiveness of the *Guidelines,* the code has potential but so far it has "a poor track record in dealing with the social, environmental, and economic problems that matter most."[45] The potential lies in its singular joining of international standards with oversight by governments.

The shortcomings are multiple. Activists lack confidence in favorable outcomes. Doing the research and preparation for filing a complaint is costly. National offices often fail to find merit or decline to pursue the matter. Mediated resolutions are rare. And even when the offices issue final statements, they cannot enforce their

[44] OECD Watch, *10 Years On: Assessing the Contribution of the OECD Guidelines for Multinational Enterprises to Responsible Business Conduct* (Amsterdam: OECD Watch, June 2010), p. 9.
[45] Ibid., p. 8.

FIGURE 11.7
Vedanta
Resources
2010

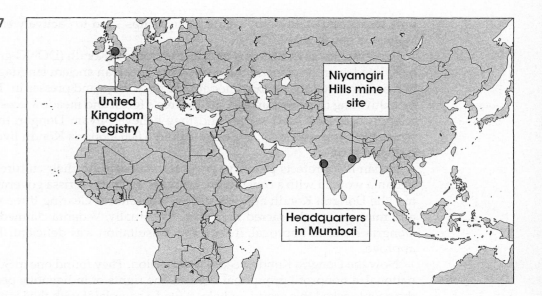

recommendations or apply penalties. They can only ask for follow-up reports from both parties. Lack of cooperation by companies is another obstacle. They often assign junior staff to work with national offices, ignore timetables, and refuse to comply with recommendations.[46] The following story of one complaint shows the *OECD Guidelines for Multinational Enterprises* at work and reveals their strengths and weaknesses.

Vedanta Resources

Vedanta is the largest mining corporation in India. It is officially registered in the United Kingdom so as to be listed on the London Stock Exchange, but it has only an office there. Its headquarters are in Mumbai and it operates through subsidiaries in India, Zambia, and Australia. In 2010 it had 27,000 employees and revenues of almost $8 billion. Most of its assets are in India. Its basic strategy is to "capitalise on attractive growth opportunities arising from India's large mineral reserves."[47]

It seized one such opportunity in 2003, entering an agreement with the State of Orissa to construct a bauxite mine and an aluminum refinery in the Niyamgiri Hills of northeast India (see Figure 11.7). Ore from the mine was to supply the refinery for 25 years. Vedanta first built the refinery, which ran on bauxite ore from other locations. Then it began to secure approvals for the mine, which was to be on top of a nearby mountain. Vedanta claims to be an environmentally responsible company and promises not only to minimize any damage from its projects, but also "to make a net positive impact on the environment."[48] It also promises to work

[46] OECD, *Annual Report on the Guidelines for Multinational Enterprises 2009* (Paris: OECD Publishing, 2010), p. 85.

[47] Vedanta Resources, "About Us," at www.vedantaresources.com/about-us.aspx.

[48] Vedanta Resources, "Mission and Values," at www.vedantaresources.com/mission%20values.aspx.

with local communities, to "create partnerships" and to "actively enter into dialogue and engagement."[49]

For centuries an indigenous people, the Dongria Kondh (DONG-gree-ah cond), have lived near the planned mine site. They speak an ancient language and maintain a unique culture, even as modern life rings them and presses in. They survive by cultivating crops and animals in the area's forest and meadow ecosystem. Their religion holds the land sacred and they believe Niyam Dongar, the mountain where the mine would sit, is a deity. About 8,000 Dongria Kondh live around the god-mountain.

Indian law protects primitive peoples, safeguarding their cultures and lands. Vedanta worked with a consultative body set up by the Orissa government to contact the Dongria Kondh and obtain their consent for clearing three square miles and mining atop the sacred mountain. Eventually, Vedanta claimed to have the Dongria Kondh's approval. In fact, the consultation was deficient. They did not approve.

Now the Dongria Kondh needed a champion. They found one in Survival International, a nonprofit group that defends the rights of indigenous peoples. When the people asked this group for help, it filed a complaint with the United Kingdom OECD office alleging that Vedanta had acted against the OECD *Guidelines*. It said the company had no human rights policy and had barely consulted the Dongria Kondh, citing, for example, the experience of a villager in a group approached by Vedanta's representatives.

> They asked us "do you support Vedanta?" and "Do you want to mine bauxite?" We said no, we do not want to give our mountain.
>
> Then they said everyone from [another village] has agreed to mine bauxite. That's why they have a school, roads, and . . . are getting machines. If you complain to us, then we can't provide anything to you again. You have to say "yes."
>
> . . . Then I said yes! I am really against Vedanta . . . In my heart I have never supported Vedanta. They offered me these temptations, that's why I was tempted. But all our people in the area don't want this company and don't want to mine.[50]

The complaint charged that Vedanta had violated not only the *Guidelines*, but also several international covenants and declarations on which they are based. Even if it created economic growth and jobs, a mine on a sacred mountain operating 24 hours a day, making noise, polluting streams, and scarring a virgin ecosystem intruded too far on the rights of an indigenous people. "The nearest equivalent," said the brief, "might be the demolition of Durham Cathedral to allow access to the rich seam of coal that lies beneath it."[51]

When the UK office received the complaint, it did an initial assessment. Its staff met with members of Survival International. Vedanta did not come to meetings

[49] Vedanta Resources plc, *Sustainable Development Report 2008* (London: Vedanta Resources, 2009), p. 40.

[50] Sahadev Kadraka, quoted in Survival International, *Vedenta Resources plc (UK): Complaint to the UK National Contact Point under the Specific Instance Procedure of the OECD Guidelines for Multinational Enterprises,* December 19, 2008, p. 15.

[51] Ibid., p. 20.

but engaged in an exchange of e-mails and letters. Soon, the office offered to mediate the dispute, but Vedanta declined. Thus, the office moved to examine the merits of the complaint, asking both parties for evidence to support their positions. Survival International submitted "a great deal" of material. Vedanta submitted no specific evidence, only a copy of its most recent sustainability development report.

Vedanta claims to be a socially responsible corporation and its sustainability reports seem to confirm this. Its actions fight poverty, disease, and famine. It feeds lunches to 200,000 schoolchildren in poor villages and aspires to feed 1 million. It has built 2,387 public toilets where sanitation is a problem. It plants foliage to protect watersheds. It runs hundreds of health care centers to vaccinate children. It teaches farmers methods that raise crop yields. It funds a charitable cancer hospital.

Yet its benevolence seemed to take a holiday from the mining project. The British OECD office concluded that Vedanta "failed to put in place an adequate and timely consultation mechanism fully to engage the Dongria Kondh."[52] In fact, it verified only three public meetings in six years. Two meetings were attended by 10 people and 30 people, respectively, but there was no evidence of Dongria Kondh in the audience. They might not have known, since the meetings were announced only in English and few know the language. A third meeting was attended by 400 people, but it was unclear if any Dongria Kondh were there and only the aluminum refinery was discussed, not the mine.

Convention on Biological Diversity
A treaty that requires nations to preserve biological diversity by promoting sustainable economic activity. It emerged from the UN-sponsored Earth Summit in 1992 and has been signed by 163 nations.

The "final statement" of the British office concluded Vedanta had offended three sections of the *Guidelines*.[53] It also stated the company had acted against several international conventions and covenants that define norms for treatment of peoples such as the Dongria Kongh.[54] It made two recommendations to Vedanta. First, it should "immediately and adequately engage with the Dongria Kondh," respecting the outcome of this consultation. Second, it should always analyze the human rights impact when its projects affect an indigenous people. To carry out these recommendations Vedanta was referred to the "Akwe: Kon Guidelines," a set of voluntary principles for studying the social impact of industrial projects on indigenous peoples. These principles issued from the *Convention on Biological Diversity*, a treaty to which India is a signatory. It was also encouraged to develop a human rights policy and referred to a UN Web site on business and human rights for inspiration.

---

[52] *Final Statement by the UK National Contact Point for the OECD Guidelines for Multinational Enterprises: Complaint from Survival International against Vedanta Resources plc,* URN: 09/1373 (London: UK National Contact Point, September 25, 2009), p. 1.

[53] These were Chapter V(2)(b) encouraging MNCs to "engage in adequate and timely communication and consultation with the communities directly affected by the environmental, health and safety policies of the enterprise and by their implementation," Chapter II(7) that encourages them to "develop and apply effective self-regulatory practices and management systems that foster a relationship of confidence and mutual trust between enterprises and the societies in which they operate," and Chapter II(2) that encourages them to "respect the human rights of those affected by their activities." See Organisation for Economic Co-operation and Development, *OECD Guidelines for Multinational Enterprises* (Paris: OECD, 2008), pp. 14 and 19.

[54] These included the UN International Covenant on Civil and Political Rights, the UN Convention on the Elimination of All Forms of Racial Discrimination, the Convention on Biological Diversity, the UN Declaration on the Rights of Indigenous People, Convention 138 of the International Labour Organisation, and the UN Convention on the Rights of the Child.

Dongria Kondh tribal women listen to an Indian politician speak about the plan to build a mine on top of their sacred mountain.
Source: © AP Photo.

Finally, both parties were asked to send the office an update in three months.

To provide this update, Survival International sent a team to the Niyamgiri Hills, but it reported harassment by Vedanta. It believed the company paid some villagers to object to its presence. Someone told local police the group was going to stir up trouble. Its motorcycle was vandalized. However, after interviews with Dongria Kondh in six villages, it found no evidence of systematic consultation on the mine by Vedanta.

The British office's report was quite a load of guilt for any company to bear, but Vedanta stood unbowed. A top executive rejected the authority of the OECD procedure, saying it violated Indian sovereignty.[55] Nonetheless, the company submitted an update to the British office saying construction of the mine was proceeding in accord with applicable laws and regulations in India. It noted an agreement approved by the Indian Supreme Court requiring 5 percent of the mine's profits each year go to improving health services, water quality, and education in the area. It denied hindering the Survival International team.

The final action of the British office was to summarize each side's update. It made no further analysis of claims. It only encouraged the two parties "to engage with each other in order to achieve a mutually satisfactory outcome."[56] This was unlikely, but the *Guidelines* permitted no stronger action. However, the inquiry by the British office prodded the Indian government. One observation in its report was that although India was a signatory to certain relevant treaties and conventions, it was not assuring Vedanta's compliance with them. The report was publicized in India, fueling resistance to the mine.

Subsequently, an Indian ministry sent a team of investigators from New Delhi to examine the Niyamgiri Hills project. The team's report stopped the mine cold. Along with inadequate consultation of the Dongria Kondh, the investigators believed the company had violated Indian laws protecting the environment and indigenous peoples. They also hinted at the presence of corruption or conflict of interest between the company and local officials. Overall, they characterized the mine project as "an act of total contempt for the law on the part of the company and an appalling degree of collusion on the part of the concerned officials."[57]

Late in 2010 the Indian ministry rescinded permits for expansion of the aluminum refinery and construction of the mine. Vedanta's share price fell by 5 percent.

---

[55] Mukesh Kumar, chief operating officer, quoted in "Vedanta's Orissa Bauxite Mine Plan Under Scrutiny," *Metal Bulletin Weekly,* January 4, 2010, p. 2.

[56] *Follow up to Final Statement by the UK National Contact Point: Complaint from Survival International against Vedanta Resources plc,* URN 10/778 (London: UK National Contact Point, March 12, 2010), p. 1.

[57] N. C. Saxena, et al., *Report of the Four Member Committee for Investigation into the Proposal Submitted by the Orissa Mining Company for Bauxite Mining in Niyamgiri* (New Delhi: Ministry of Environment & Forests, August 16, 2010), p. 14.

It denied breaking any laws and called the accusations against it "lies and hoax."[58] Its chairman argued that the economic benefits of the project far outweighed any harm to the Dongria Kondh or the mountain ecosystem.

The story teaches several lessons. First, multinational corporations can use claims of corporate responsibility as a veneer to disguise corporate cultures that exploit lax regulation in developing economies. Voluntary CSR is not, and can never be, the full corrective for flaws in markets. Second, international codes such as the *Guidelines* effectively wield the soft-law bible to challenge corporations acting outside international norms. Although the *Guidelines* could not be enforced on Vedanta, when its violations came to light they became untenable. Third, although these norms, codes, and agreements are an important force, they have major limitations. Ultimately, only governments can force compliance on defiant MNCs. Vedanta was brought to heel only when the Indian government invoked statute-based regulations.

THE UNITED NATIONS GLOBAL COMPACT

The single most conspicuous effort to promote MNC social responsibility and to harness FDI for economic development is the Global Compact. It started in 2000 when UN Secretary-General Kofi Annan challenged global corporations to collaborate with UN agencies, labor unions, NGOs, and governments in embracing a set of "universal values." He called on MNCs to carry out a set of 10 principles (see the box) in four areas. The Global Compact is not a code of conduct. It does not enforce the principles. Rather, it advances them as an "aspirational" set of "shared values."

The 10 principles condense basic ideas from international declarations and conventions made under UN auspices over the years. They seem simple, broad, and aspirational. However, this rudimentary appearance is deceptive. Their meaning is articulated in voluminous and more specific guidance materials such as reports, handbooks, case studies, best-practice digests, online assessments, and learning tools. And they push boundaries. Principle 6, for example, calls for the "elimination of discrimination," which, as articulated in the Global Compact documents, includes that based on sexual orientation, a protection not found in labor laws of many nations, including the United States. Principle 9 urges a precautionary approach to environmental risks, a philosophy rising from the *Rio Declaration* and accepted by regulators in Europe, but less so in the United States.

Other principles are layered on. For example, working with another UN agency, in 2010 the Global Compact launched the Women's Empowerment Principles as a "gender lens" for corporations to use in evaluating their actions (see the box on page 377). In fact, the Global Compact is a fountain of principles. Cooperating with other UN agencies it has developed additional sets of principles for "responsible investment," "responsible management education," and "children's principles" that direct MNCs to support children's rights.

Rio Declaration
A set of 27 principles for sustainable development that emerged from the 1992 Earth Summit, a UN Conference of 172 nations and 2,400 NGOs held in Rio de Janeiro.

---

[58] Alistair Dawber, "Vedanta's Failure to Speak Out Earlier Could Cost It Dearly," *The Independent*, August 25, 2010, p. 8.

The Global Compact Principles

Human Rights

1. Businesses should support and respect the protection of internationally proclaimed human rights; and

2. Make sure that they are not complicit in human rights abuses.

Labour Standards

3. Businesses should uphold the freedom of association and the effective recognition of the right to collective bargaining;

4. The elimination of all forms of forced and compulsory labour;

5. The effective abolition of child labour; and

6. The elimination of discrimination in respect of employment and occupation.

The Environment

7. Businesses should support a precautionary approach to environmental challenges;

8. Undertake initiatives to promote greater environmental responsibility; and

9. Encourage the development and diffusion of environmentally friendly technologies.

Anti-Corruption

10. Businesses should work against all forms of corruption, including extortion and bribery.

The Global Compact is administered within the United Nations Secretariat. Participation by all parties is voluntary. Its central purposes are to (1) promote responsible corporate behavior that (2) advances central UN goals such as world peace, protection of human rights, poverty reduction, and sustainable markets. Only 47 corporations were aboard when it started in 2000, but by 2010 there were 6,210. This is a large number, and more than any other global corporate responsibility initiative, but less than 8 percent of the total number of MNCs. In addition, about 2,400 NGOs and labor organizations participate.[59]

Companies joining the Global Compact commit themselves to breathe life into the principles, writing them into mission statements, using them to guide strategy, applying them in daily operations, and extending them over their spheres of influence to subsidiaries, partners, and suppliers. There is a modest fee scale for participating; only $10,000 a year for companies with revenues of $1 billion or more. Also, each year, the company must post a progress report on the Global Compact Web site.[60]

communication on progress
The required annual report of a company participating in the Global Compact. It explains how the company is implementing the 10 principles.

These reports, called *communications on progress* in Global Compact jargon, must have three elements. First, the top executive of the company must endorse the Global Compact. Second, the company describes its actions. In the first five years it needs to act on principles in at least two of the four issue areas. After five years it must report action in all four areas. Third, it must measure results using appropriate yardsticks. Companies failing to report are listed as "non-communicating" after the first year. After a second year of silence they are delisted. So far, 1,535 companies,

---

[59] "News & Updates," *UN Global Compact Bulletin,* October 2010, p. 2.

[60] These reports are posted at www.unglobalcompact.org/COP/analyzing_progress.html.

Women's Empowerment Principles

1. Establish high-level corporate leadership for gender equality.

2. Treat all women and men fairly at work—respect and support human rights and nondiscrimination.

3. Ensure the health, safety and well-being of all women and men workers.

4. Promote education, training and professional development for women.

5. Implement enterprise development, supply chain and marketing practices that empower women.

6. Promote equality through community initiatives and advocacy.

7. Measure and publicly report on progress to achieve gender equality.

These principles are the result of collaboration between the United Nations Global Compact and the United Nations Development Fund for Women. Their development included a process of consultation with governments, NGOs, business, and labor groups.

mostly smaller ones, have met this fate. The Global Compact also delists firms that ignore charges of egregious irresponsibility.

The reports reveal a wide range of CSR activity. Since the Global Compact is not a binding code it does not evaluate or judge them. Here is a sampling of actions reported.

- Nikon Corporation joined the Global Compact in 2007. Since then it has written a CSR plan that requires carrying out the 10 principles worldwide. It set up a high-level CSR committee and a department to organize its response. All employees receive training in the 10 principles and take a mandatory online exam about them. The company requires each of its 70 subsidiaries in 23 countries to report on how the principles are carried out. It defines performance indicators, measures outcomes, and reports results for all of the principles.[61]

- In pursuit of Principle 8, which asks companies "to promote greater environmental responsibility," Levi Strauss requires factories in its supply chain to meet a set of "global effluent guidelines."[62] All wastewater from the manufacture of jeans, shirts, zippers, and buttons anywhere in the world must meet standards for 19 measures of water quality and metals residue. In some locations the limits are stricter than local pollution laws. Factories in its supply chain must test discharges and send reports to Levi Strauss.

- As part of the Global Compact companies are asked to promote development in poorer economies. Land in some war-torn nations lies fallow when land mines are not cleared. Komatsu Ltd., a Japanese company that makes construction equipment, built a bulldozer-like machine that removes antipersonnel land

[61] See Nikon Corporation, *CSR Report 2010* (Tokyo: Nikon Corporation, September 2010).

[62] Levi Strauss & Co., *Environment, Health and Safety Handbook,* v. 2.0 (San Francisco: Levi Strauss & Co., April 2007), appendix V.

mines. In Cambodia it donated the machine to clear mines from around a village, allowing the land again to be used for vegetable farming.[63] Then the company improved roads into the village and rebuilt its school, creating a newly vibrant community. Komatsu is now clearing mines in Angola.

- Sexual exploitation of children in tourism is a persistent human rights problem. Tourists from the United States make up 25 percent of customers in a global sex trade involving as many as 2 million children. Carlson Companies, headquartered in Minneapolis, operates hotels and travel services. A centerpiece of its efforts to uphold Principles 1 and 2 is a policy to fight child prostitution. Its Radisson hotels are located in 77 countries, including several—Brazil, Costa Rica, and Thailand—where the child sex trade thrives. Carlson trains hotel staff to observe and report suspicious use of rooms. It acts to discourage demand for sex with children by educating travelers, telling American travelers, for example, that if they have sex with children under age 18 abroad they can be prosecuted under U.S. laws after they return home.

These meritorious examples, taken from hundreds of "noteworthy" reports showcased by the Global Compact, suggest its promise. However, most participating MNCs report less ambitious or less specific accomplishments. A typical communication on progress lists the 10 principles on a chart, with references to pages in a company sustainability report where actions said to be undertaken in support of a particular principle are discussed. It is not clear that the activities referenced were done to further the principles or for unrelated reasons. And many activities, such as setting up a committee to investigate the company's performance with respect to X, Y, or Z responsibility, may or may not have significance.

Criticism of the Global Compact

The Global Compact experiment started slowly. Companies, especially the largest MNCs, were skeptical of the need for another code and feared being sued by NGOs for violating its principles. Cynical NGOs saw it as toothless because the principles were not enforced. To this day, critics believe that MNCs indulge in *bluewashing*, a word that references the color of the UN flag, a worldwide symbol of peace and justice. In bluewashing, the prestige of the United Nations is exploited by insincere corporations that sign onto the principles but fail to fulfill their spirit.

bluewashing
The act of a corporation cloaking its lack of social responsibility by insincere membership in the UN Global Compact.

After a decade of the Global Compact, progressives have mixed feelings about its achievements. They see a rapidly growing initiative in which corporations more or less, and sometimes remarkably, act on affirmative principles. A recent survey of CEOs reported that 67 percent believed participation in the Global Compact helped their companies advance CSR performance.[64] The compact is now rapidly evolving and expanding. Its principles contain the potent seed of ideals. An ideal with momentum, which the Global Compact has, generally works to elevate behavior and shame laggards.

---

[63] "Komatsu Contributing to Safe and Revitalized Communities," *Komatsu Views,* no. 1 (2010), pp. 18–19.
[64] *United Nations Global Compact Annual Review–Anniversary Edition* June 2010, pp. 10 and 16.

However, skeptics think the emphasis is on building the rolls, not on fundamental change, that business is made to feel comfortable, not challenged. Most large MNCs already have broad CSR programs. After joining the Global Compact they simply report what they already do and go on unchanged. Now, say critics, the compact needs to demand more. It must convert itself from a platform for bluewashing to a leadership force that challenges MNCs with a more ambitious agenda.[65] It could, for example, require that top executives link their pay to the achievement of social responsibility goals.[66] Such changes are far in the future, so skepticism about the effort is likely to continue.

A perceived shortcoming of both the *OECD Guidelines* and the Global Compact is the lack of a hard fist behind their normative codes. We turn now to the realm of law for another effort to ensure responsible MNC behavior, one that promises hard sanctions.

THE ALIEN TORT CLAIMS ACT

Alien Tort Claims Act
A 1789 law permitting foreign citizens to litigate, in a federal court, wrongful actions occurring anywhere in the world that violate international law or U.S. treaties.

Critics suspect that in the obscurity of distant places some MNCs behave badly. The docket of cases brought under a singular law, the *Alien Tort Claims Act*, opens a window into some serious allegations. This law allows foreign citizens to sue individuals and corporations of any nation in U.S. courts for wrongful acts committed anywhere in the world violating the law of nations or U.S. treaties. It allows lawsuits against individuals and corporations of any nation.

The original intent of the Alien Tort Claims Act, an old law from 1789, was to protect the rights of ambassadors and to try pirates.[67] Long in disuse, it was rediscovered in the 1990s by progressive and labor lawyers seeking to prosecute MNCs for wrongful actions anywhere in the world. Since then, it has been the basis of more than 125 cases against corporations and their executives for actions occurring in 60 countries. Most cases are eventually dismissed, but they often wind through interminable appeals. Several corporations have tired after more than a decade and settled, while continuing to deny guilt. Only two cases have reached trial and in both federal juries acquitted the corporate defendants.

The initial wave of Alien Tort Claims Act suits alleged human rights abuses by corporations. In one, a group of Indonesian villagers accused ExxonMobil of directing soldiers guarding its natural gas fields to kidnap, rape, and murder villagers who opposed its activities, then providing bulldozers to help the troops dig

---

[65] See, for example, Jem Bendell, "What If We are Failing? Towards a Post-Crisis Compact for Systemic Change," *Journal of Corporate Citizenship,* Summer 2010; and James Epstein-Reeves, "Critics of the UN Global Compact Sound Off," *Citizen Polity,* November 11, 2009; http://citizenpolity.com/2009/11/11/critics-of-the-un-global-compact-sound-off/.

[66] Lifeworth Consulting, "From Global Compact to Global Impact," August 2010, at www.lifeworth.com/consult/2010/08/from-global-compact-to-global-impact/.

[67] The entirety of this statute is a brief clause in the Judiciary Act of 1789 providing that "the district courts shall have original jurisdiction of any civil action by an alien for a tort only, committed in violation of the law of nations or a treaty of the United States."

mass graves.[68] In another, Chevron was charged with helping to repress native activists who opposed oil drilling. It had supplied helicopters to government troops, who flew to a Chevron drilling rig and shot at protesters , killing two and wounding others.[69]

In time, suits appeared based on labor abuses. Relatives of 23 people killed and tortured in Argentina during the years of its military dictatorship have sued Daimler. They accuse its Mercedes-Benz subsidiary of collaborating with the regime by identifying union leaders who were then abducted.[70] Adults and children aged 6 through 16 working at a rubber plantation in Liberia have sued tiremaker Bridgestone Corporation. The workers believe that through unfair labor practices the Japanese company turned them into "modern day slaves, forced to work by the coercion of poverty."[71]

A few suits allege environmental crimes. Residents of New Guinea say that as Rio Tinto worked a gold mine on the island of Bougainville it forced natives to toil in "slavelike" conditions and dumped 200,000 tons of waste rock into waterways each day. The damage caused "environmental devastation" that "undermined the physical and mental health of the island's residents."[72] In another case, DynCorp International was accused of erratic herbicide spraying in Colombia that missed targeted cocaine and heroin fields, hitting a town where it made 89 percent of the people sick and killed four.[73] At the time it was acting as a contractor for the U.S. State Department, which sought to interrupt the flow of illegal narcotics from the country by destroying poppy plantations.

The future of Alien Tort Claims Act cases is uncertain. So far, federal courts have been highly skeptical of legal theories extending an archaic eighteenth century law to the actions of modern corporations.[74] Yet it is an area of law under development as plaintiffs probe with various theories, appealing repeatedly, seeking the key to victory. As the cases go on, opinion about them is divided. Business groups say they victimize the world's poor "by imposing an enormous tax on investment in developing countries at a time the world desperately needs such investment."[75] Progressives believe they bring justice for the oppressed, giving "people in foreign countries comfort that U.S. corporations and officials will abide by international standards and not go to different corners of the globe and exploit the local populations."[76]

[68] *Doe v. ExxonMobil Corporation,* 473 F.3d 345 (2007).

[69] *Bowoto v. Chevron Corp.,* C99-02506 SI, N. Dist. Cal. (2007).

[70] *Bauman v. DaimlerChrysler AG,* 579 F.3d 1088 (2009).

[71] *Roe v. Bridgestone Corporation,* 492 F.Supp. 2d 988 (2007), at 995.

[72] *Sarei v. Rio Tinto Ltd.,* 487 F.3d 1193 (2007), at 1198.

[73] *Arias v. DynCorp.,* 517 F. Supp. 2d 221 (2007).

[74] In *Kiobel v. Royal Dutch Petroleum,* 2010 U.S. App. LEXIS 19382, for example, the Second Circuit held that corporations are not subject to liability under international human rights law. Executives, as individuals, could still be sued.

[75] Curtis A. Bradley and Jack L. Goldsmith, "Rights Case Gone Wrong," *Washington Post,* April 19, 2009, p. A19.

[76] Katherine Gallagher, attorney with the Center for Constitutional Rights, quoted in Nathan Koppel, "Arcane Law Brings Conflicts From Overseas to U.S. Courts," *The Wall Street Journal,* August 27, 2009, p. A11.

FIGURE 11.8
Drummond
Company
2010

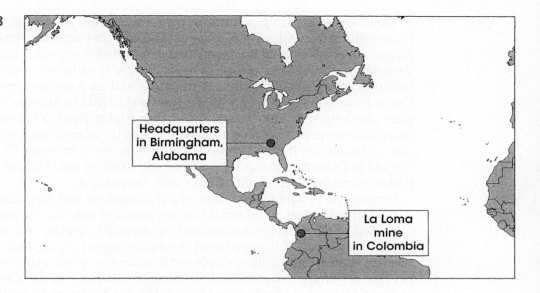

The Drummond Company on Trial

The Drummond Company, a coal mining firm headquartered in Birmingham, Alabama, was the target of the first Alien Tort Claims Act case to go to trial. It was sued by the widows of three murdered union leaders in Colombia. They alleged that the president of its Colombian subsidiary, acting with the knowledge of top U.S. executives, ordered their husbands killed.[77] They requested compensation for these deaths.

Drummond was founded in 1935 to mine coal in Alabama. The company gradually moved across tiers of internationalization. First, it began exporting coal from its Alabama mines to Europe. Then it made its first direct foreign investment by building a mine in northeast Colombia. When it entered Colombia in the late 1980s, it was aware of the country's violence. A shadowy, ongoing civil war persists between the government, Marxist guerillas, and right-wing paramilitary groups. Nevertheless, Drummond put $1 billion into its La Loma mine, a huge facility that ships 25 million tons of coal to Europe and the United States each year (see Figure 11.8). A new subsidiary headquartered in Alabama ran the mine.

In 2001, paramilitaries pulled two La Loma union leaders from a company bus carrying shift workers. Witnesses said the paramilitaries identified the two by name, forced them to show identification, and told both men they "had a problem with Drummond." Outside the bus, in view of its passengers, they shot one victim several times in the head. The other was abducted and found dead several hours later, having been tortured, then shot in the head. Five months later, a third union leader was taken from a public bus on his way home, tortured, and shot twice in the head.

[77] *Complaint, Rodriquez v. Drummond,* CV-02-BE-0665-W, N. D. Ala., March 2002. See also *Rodriquez v. Drummond,* 256 F. Supp. 2d 1250 (2003).

Their widows, using attorneys with the United Steelworkers union in Pittsburgh, filed an Alien Tort Claims Act lawsuit. They sued Drummond in a U.S. district court alleging its managers had committed a wrongful act, aiding and abetting the murders in violation of both "the law of nations," which upholds the fundamental right to associate and organize, and an American law, the Torture Victim Protection Act of 1991, which prohibits extrajudicial killings.[78] The widows were also helped by the International Labor Rights Fund, a Washington, D.C., group that supports Alien Tort Claims Act cases to "address the fundamental human rights abuses that unfettered capitalism leaves in its wake."[79] Its members worked in Colombia, gathering evidence and handing out "Wanted for Murder" posters picturing Drummond's CEO, Garry Drummond.

Drummond "emphatically" denied the allegations and filed slander charges against an individual in Colombia who accused it of ordering the murders. It was "appalled by the vicious, relentless and unfathomable attacks" and refused to settle with the widows.[80] It emphasized its positive impact in Colombia, where it had invested more than $1 billion, employed thousands, created a coal export market, paid the government hundreds of millions of dollars in royalties and taxes, and improved living standards around the mine. Yet for its trade union opponents these benefits meant little.

In 2007 the case came to trial in Alabama. Several witnesses testified that Drummond made covert payments to local paramilitaries for security services and secretly employed their members. Regular Colombian soldiers guarded its property. The Colombian military has a shadowy, cooperative relationship with paramilitaries, and the lawsuit alleged those forces were allowed on the mine property. One former paramilitary said the president of Drummond's Colombia subsidiary met with one of the private army's leaders, paying him $200,000 to "neutralize" the first two union leaders. This and other evidence was hearsay and circumstantial. Much of the testimony came from other paramilitaries who submitted affidavits while in Colombia jails. Drummond questioned the honesty of witnesses with criminal histories. One of its lawyers argued that, "Nobody at Drummond . . . believes that the rules don't apply to them just because they are doing business in Colombia."[81]

[78] Specifically, the company's actions violated the "law of nations" found in International Labour Organization Conventions 87 and 98, which protect the right of labor to associate and bargain collectively; Article 8 of the International Covenant on Economic, Social, and Cultural Rights, which protects the right to associate and organize; Article 22 of the International Covenant on Civil and Political Rights, which protects the right to freely associate; the Universal Declaration of Human Rights, which protects *inter alia* rights to associate, organize, and bargain collectively; and the Geneva Conventions, which codify the law of war and prohibit murder by combatants.

[79] International Labor Rights Fund, *Annual Report 2006* (Washington, DC: ILRF, 2006), p. 1.

[80] Drummond Ltd., "Drummond Does Not Negotiate with Illegal Groups," press release, Bogotá, Colombia, March 21, 2007.

[81] William H. Jeffress, quoted in Kyle Whitmire, "Suit in U.S. over Murders in Colombia," *The New York Times,* July 13, 2007, p. A4.

After only a day of deliberation the jury returned a verdict of not guilty, clearing Drummond. Nonetheless, like other Alien Tort Claims Act cases targeting corporations, its backers refuse to let it die, preferring to sink their teeth into the company and hold on. Appeals to reopen the case ended in failure a year later.[82] Then, in 2009, Colombian authorities arrested and convicted the men responsible for the murders. However, the United Steelworkers believed that Drummond executives, the "intellectual authors" of the murders, were still fugitives from justice. It now sued on behalf of the murdered men's children, claiming new evidence that Drummond was involved.[83] When a judge dismissed this case, it sued again on behalf of 252 relatives of 67 union members and farm workers killed by paramilitaries in areas near the Drummond mine, accusing Drummond of paying the paramilitaries to conduct a reign of terror.[84] That case is ongoing. Drummond has announced it will sell its Colombian property and leave the country—if it can find a buyer.

The story of the Drummond litigation illustrates how one law can be used to check, limit, and harass MNCs. To date its main effect has been to harass, but it may develop into a more powerful check with time.

CONCLUDING OBSERVATIONS

Multinational corporations are highly variable entities. They differ in size, strategy, structure, geographic reach, and extent of foreign investment. These variables interact with forces in as many as 200 host economies—poor, developing, and advanced—making generalization about MNC behavior difficult.

It is too great a leap to argue that MNCs dominate and define the global economy. They are better understood as entities reacting to forces of globalization along with governments, NGOs, and international agencies. They can be understood as reacting to change and opportunity with an inner business logic.

While MNCs are widely mistrusted and still act badly at times, the progressive community now has more appreciation of the need to bring them into the fold of cooperation with governments and NGOs to address issues such as poverty, fresh water shortages, and climate warming. In the past two decades a firmament of norms, codes, principles, and citizenship schemes has appeared to guide MNCs. It is too early to say these efforts have caused much increase in MNC responsibility. However, their direction is clear. It is now impossible for the largest, most powerful MNCs to avoid joining at least some collaborative CSR initiatives. Corporate actions are being compared with the principles, reporting standards, and UN-generated "universal" norms that drive arrangements such as the Global Compact. To retain long-term legitimacy, MNCs must show acceptable performance.

---

[82] *Romero v. Drummond,* 552 F.3d 1303 (2008).

[83] *Baloco v. Drummond,* 09-CV-00557, N. D. Ala. (2009).

[84] *Jane Doe v. Drummond,* 09-CV-01041, N. D. Ala. November 9, 2009.

Union Carbide Corporation and Bhopal

On December 3, 1984, tragedy unfolded at the Union Carbide pesticide plant in Bhopal, India. Water entered a large tank where a volatile chemical was stored, starting a violent reaction. Rapidly, a sequence of safety procedures and devices failed. Fugitive vapors sailed over plant boundaries, forming a lethal cloud that moved with the south wind, enveloping slum dwellings, searing lungs and eyes, asphyxiating fated souls, scarring the unlucky.

Bhopal is the worst sudden industrial accident ever in terms of human life lost. Death and injury estimates vary widely. The official death toll set forth by the Indian government for that night is 5,295, with an additional 527,894 serious injuries. Greenpeace has put the death toll at 16,000.[1]

The incredible event galvanized industry critics. "Like Auschwitz and Hiroshima," wrote one, "the catastrophe at Bhopal is a manifestation of something fundamentally wrong in our stewardship of the earth."[2] Union Carbide was debilitated and slowly declined as a company after the incident. The government of India earned mixed reviews for its response. The chemical industry changed, but according to some, not enough. And the gas victims endure a continuing struggle to get compensation and medical care.[3]

UNION CARBIDE IN INDIA

Union Carbide established an Indian subsidiary named Union Carbide India Ltd. (UCIL) in 1934. At first the company owned a 60 percent majority interest, but over the years this was reduced to 50.9 percent. Shares in the ownership of the other 49.1 percent traded on the Bombay Stock Exchange. This ownership scheme was significant because although UCIL operated with a great deal of autonomy, it gave the appearance that Union Carbide was in control of its operations. By itself, UCIL was one of India's largest firms. In 1984, the year of the incident, it

had 14 plants and 9,000 employees, including 500 at Bhopal. Most of its revenues came from selling Eveready batteries.

Union Carbide decided to build a pesticide plant at Bhopal in 1969. The plant formulated pesticides from chemical ingredients imported to the site. At that time, there was a growing demand in India and throughout Asia for pesticides because of the "green revolution," a type of planned agriculture that requires intensive use of pesticides and fertilizers on special strains of food crops such as wheat, rice, and corn. Although pesticides may be misused and pose some risk, they also have great social value. Without pesticides, damage to crops, losses in food storage, and toxic mold growth in food supplies would cause much loss of life from starvation and food poisoning, especially in countries such as India. Exhibit 1 shows a Union Carbide advertisement from the 1960s that describes the company's activities in India.

The Bhopal plant would supply these pesticides and serve a market anticipated to expand rapidly. The plant's location in Bhopal was encouraged by tax incentives from the city and the surrounding state of Madhya Pradesh. After a few years, however, the Indian government pressured UCIL to stop importing chemical ingredients. The company then proposed to manufacture methyl isocyanate (MIC) at the plant rather than ship it in from Carbide facilities outside the country. This was a fateful decision.

Methyl isocyanate, CH_3NCO, is a colorless, odorless liquid. Its presence can be detected by tearing and the burning sensation it causes in the eyes and noses of exposed individuals. At the Bhopal plant it was used as an intermediate chemical in pesticide manufacture. It was not the final product; rather, MIC molecules were created, then pumped into a vessel where they reacted with other chemicals. The reaction created unique molecules with qualities that disrupted insect nervous systems, causing convulsions and death. The plant turned out two similar pesticides marketed under the names Sevin and Temik.

In 1975 UCIL received a permit from the Ministry of Industry in New Delhi to build an MIC production unit at the Bhopal plant. Two months before the

[1] "Has the World Forgotten Bhopal?" *The Lancet,* December 2, 2000, p. 1863.

[2] David Weir, *The Bhopal Syndrome* (San Francisco: Sierra Club Books, 1987), p. xii.

[3] Rama Lakshmi, "Justice for Bhopal Victims," *The Economic Times,* February 18, 2011.

EXHIBIT 1
Union Carbide
Advertisement
This ad
appeared
in *Fortune*
magazine in
April 1962.

Source: Courtesy
of Union Carbide
Corporation.

Science helps build a new India

Oxen working the fields . . . the eternal river Ganges . . . jeweled elephants on parade. Today these symbols of ancient India exist side by side with a new sight—modern industry. India has developed bold new plans to build its economy and bring the promise of a bright future to its more than 400,000,000 people. ▷ But India needs the technical knowledge of the western world. For example, working with Indian engineers and technicians, Union Carbide recently made available its vast scientific resources to help build a major chemicals and plastics plant near Bombay. ▷ Throughout the free world, Union Carbide has been actively engaged in building plants for the manufacture of chemicals, plastics, carbons, gases, and metals. The people of Union Carbide welcome the opportunity to use their knowledge and skills in partnership with the citizens of so many great countries.

UNION CARBIDE

A HAND IN THINGS TO COME

WRITE *for booklet B-3 "The Exciting Universe of Union Carbide", which tells how research in the fields of carbons, chemicals, gases, metals, plastics and nuclear energy keeps bringing new wonders into your life.*
Union Carbide Corporation, 270 Park Avenue, New York 17, N.Y.

issuance of this permit, the city of Bhopal had enacted a development plan requiring dangerous industries to relocate in an industrial zone 15 miles away. Pursuant to the plan, M. N. Buch, the Bhopal city administrator, tried to move the UCIL pesticide plant and convert the site to housing and light commercial use. For reasons that are unclear, his effort failed, and Buch was soon transferred to forestry duties elsewhere.

The MIC unit was based on a process design provided by Union Carbide's engineers in the United States and elaborated by engineers in India.

The design required storage of MIC in big tanks. An alternative used at most other pesticide plants would have been to produce small amounts of MIC only as they were consumed in pesticide production. The decision to use large storage tanks was based on an optimistic projection that pesticide sales would grow dramatically. Since an Indian law, the Foreign Exchange Regulation Act of 1973, requires foreign multinationals to share technology and use Indian resources, detailed design work was done by an Indian subsidiary of a British firm. Local labor using Indian equipment and materials built the unit.

In 1980 the MIC unit began operation under UCIL's management. During the five years of design and construction, densely populated shantytowns sprang up nearby, inhabited mainly by impoverished, unemployed people who had left rural areas seeking their fortunes in the city. A childlike faith that the facility was a benevolent presence turning out miraculous substances to make plants grow was widespread among them.

In fact, when the MIC unit came on line the plant began to pose higher risk to its neighbors; it now made the basic chemicals used in pesticides rather than using shipped-in ingredients. One step in the manufacture of MIC, for example, creates phosgene, the lethal "mustard gas" used in World War I. The benighted crowd by the plant abided unaware.

In 1981 a phosgene leak killed one worker, and a crusading Indian journalist wrote articles about dangers to the population. No one acted. A year later, a second phosgene leak forced temporary evacuation of some surrounding neighborhoods. Worker safety and environmental inspections of the plant were done by the state Department of Labour, an agency with only 15 factory inspectors to cover 8,000 plants and a record of lax enforcement.[4] Oversight was not vigorous.

Meanwhile, the Indian economy had turned down, and stiff competition from other pesticide firms marketing new, less expensive products reduced demand for Sevin and Temik. As revenues fell, so did the plant's budget, and it was necessary to defer some maintenance, lessen the rigor of training, and lay off workers. By the time of the incident, the MIC unit operated with six workers per shift, half the number anticipated by its designers.

UNION CARBIDE'S RELATIONSHIP WITH THE BHOPAL PLANT

What was the organizational relationship of Union Carbide Corporation in the United States to its subsidiary, Union Carbide India Ltd., and ultimately to the Bhopal plant? How much direction and control did the corporate parent half a world away in Danbury, Connecticut, exercise over the facility?

The Bhopal plant fit into the Union Carbide management hierarchy as shown in the chart in Exhibit 2. Although Carbide employees from the United States managed the plant in its early years, in 1982, under pressure from the government, it was turned over to Indian managers. The experience of colonial rule in India created a strong political need for leaders to put on shows of strength with foreign investors. Indians felt a burning desire to avoid any appearance of subjugation and demanded self-sufficiency. This is what had led to passage of the law requiring foreign investors to use Indian firms and workers in certain ways—and to put pressure on Union Carbide to turn the plant completely over to its Indian subsidiary.

The Bhopal plant was but one of 500 facilities in 34 countries in the Union Carbide Corporation universe. There was no regular or direct reporting relationship between it and Union Carbide's headquarters in Connecticut. At the request of UCIL, employees of Union Carbide had gone to India twice to perform safety inspections on the plant. Other than those occasions, managers in the United States had received information or reporting about the plant only infrequently and irregularly when major changes or capital expenditures were requested. Thus, the Bhopal plant was run with near total independence from the American corporation. In litigation to determine where victims' lawsuits should be tried, a U.S. court described its autonomy in these words:

> [Union Carbide Corporation's] participation [in the design and construction of the plant] was limited and its involvement in plant operations terminated long before the accident . . . [It] was constructed and managed by Indians in India. No Americans were

---

[4] Sheila Jasanoff, "Managing India's Environment," *Environment*, October 1986, p. 33.

EXHIBIT 2
Union Carbide's Organization Structure as Related to the Bhopal Plant

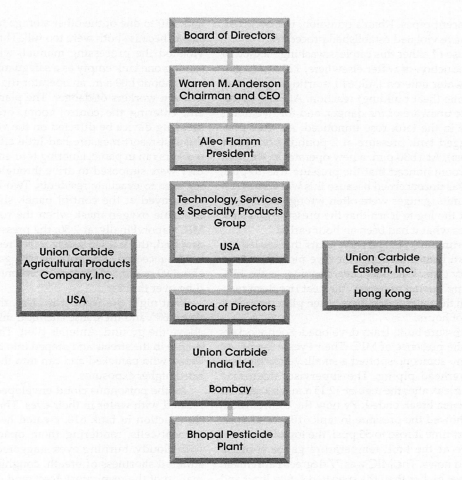

Board of Directors

Warren M. Anderson
Chairman and CEO

Alec Flamm
President

Technology, Services & Specialty Products Group

USA

Union Carbide Agricultural Products Company, Inc.

USA

Union Carbide Eastern, Inc.

Hong Kong

Board of Directors

Union Carbide India Ltd.

Bombay

Bhopal Pesticide Plant

employed at the plant at the time of the accident. In the five years from 1980 to 1984, although more than 1,000 Indians were employed at the plant, only one American was employed there and he left in 1982. No Americans visited the plant for more than one year prior to the accident, and during the 5-year period before the accident the communications between the plant and the United States were almost nonexistent.[5]

Thus, the Bhopal plant was run by UCIL with near total independence from the American corporation. Despite this, shortly after the gas leak Chairman Warren M. Anderson said that Carbide accepted "moral responsibility" for the tragedy.

[5] *In re Union Carbide Corporation Gas Plant Disaster at Bhopal*, 809 F.2d 195 (1987), at 200.

THE GAS LEAK

On the eve of the disaster, tank 610, one of three storage tanks in the MIC unit, sat filled with 11,290 gallons of MIC. The tank, having a capacity of 15,000 gallons, was a partly buried, stainless-steel, pressurized vessel. Its purpose was to take in MIC made elsewhere in the plant and hold it for some time until it was sent to the pesticide production area through a transfer pipe, there to be converted into Sevin or Temik.

At about 9:30 p.m. a supervisor ordered an operator, R. Khan, to unclog four filter valves near the MIC production area by washing them out with water. Khan connected a water hose to the piping above the clogged valves but neglected to insert a slip blind, a device that seals lines to prevent water leaks into adjacent pipes. Khan's omission, if it occurred, would have violated established procedure.

Because of either this careless washing method or the introduction of water elsewhere, 120 to 240 gallons of water entered tank 610, starting a powerful exothermic (heat building) reaction. At first, operators were unaware of the danger, and for two hours pressure in the tank rose unnoticed. At 10:20 p.m. they logged tank pressure at 2 pounds per square inch (ppsi). At 11:30 p.m. a new operator in the MIC control room noticed that the pressure was 10 ppsi, but he was unconcerned because this was within tolerable limits, gauges were often wrong, and he had not read the log to learn that the pressure was now five times what it had been an hour earlier.

Unfortunately, refrigeration units that cooled the tanks had been shut down for five months to save electricity costs. Had they been running, as the MIC processing manual required, the heat rise from reaction with the water might have taken place over days instead of hours.

As pressure built, leaks developed. Soon workers sensed the presence of MIC. Their eyes watered. At 11:45 p.m. someone spotted a small, yellowish drip from overhead piping. The supervisor suggested fixing the leak after the regular 12:15 a.m. tea break. At 12:40 the tea break ended. By now the control room gauge showed the pressure in tank 610 was 40 ppsi. In a short time it rose to 55 ppsi, the top of the scale. A glance at the tank temperature gauge brought more bad news. The MIC was 77 degrees Fahrenheit, 36 degrees higher than the specified safety limit and hot enough to vaporize. Startled by readings on the gauges, the control room operator ran out to tank 610. He felt radiating heat and heard its concrete cover cracking. Within seconds, a pressure-release valve opened and a white cloud of deadly MIC vapor shot into the atmosphere with a high-decibel screech.

Back in the control room, operators turned a switch to activate the vent gas scrubber, a safety device designed to neutralize escaping toxic gases by circulating them through caustic soda. It was down for maintenance and inoperable. Even if it had been on line, it was too small to handle the explosive volume of MIC shooting from the tank. A flare tower built to burn off toxic gases before they reached the atmosphere was also off line; it had been dismantled for maintenance and an elbow joint was missing. Another emergency measure, transferring MIC from tank 610 to one of the other storage tanks, was foreclosed because both were too full. This situation also violated the processing manual, which called for leaving one tank empty as a safeguard.

At about 1:00 a.m. an operator triggered an alarm to warn workers of danger. The plant superintendent, entering the control room, ordered a water spraying device be directed on the venting gas, but this last-resort measure had little effect. Now most workers ran in panic, ignoring four emergency buses they were supposed to drive through the surrounding area to evacuate residents. Two intrepid operators stayed at the control panel, sharing the only available oxygen mask when the room filled with MIC vapor. Finally, at 2:30, the pressure in tank 610 dropped, the leaking safety valve resealed, and the venting ceased. Roughly 10,000 gallons of MIC, about 90 percent of the tank's contents, was now settling over the city.

That night the wind was calm, the temperature about 60°, and the dense chemical mist lingered just above the ground. Animals died. The gas attacked people in the streets and seeped into their bedrooms. Those who panicked and ran into the night air suffered higher exposures.

As the poisonous cloud enveloped victims, MIC reacted with water in their eyes. This reaction, like the reaction in tank 610, created heat that burned corneal cells, rendering them opaque. Residents with cloudy, burning eyes staggered about. Many suffered shortness of breath, coughing fits, inflammation of the respiratory tract, and chemical pneumonia. In the lungs, MIC molecules reacted with moisture, causing chemical burns. Fluid oozed from seared tissue and pooled, a condition called pulmonary edema, and its victims literally drowned in their own secretions. Burned lung tissue eventually healed, creating scarred areas that diminished breathing capacity. Because MIC is so reactive with water, simply breathing through a wet cloth would have saved many lives. However, people lacked this simple knowledge.

UNION CARBIDE REACTS

Awakened early in the morning, CEO Warren M. Anderson rushed to Carbide's Danbury, Connecticut, headquarters and learned of the rising death toll. When the extent of the disaster was evident, a senior management committee held an urgent meeting.

It decided to send emergency medical supplies, respirators, oxygen (all Carbide products), and an American doctor with knowledge of MIC to Bhopal.

The next day, Tuesday, December 5, Carbide dispatched a team of technical experts to examine the plant. On Thursday, Anderson himself left for India. However, after arriving in Bhopal, he was charged with criminal negligence, placed under house arrest, and then asked to leave the country.

With worldwide attention focused on Bhopal, Carbide held daily press conferences. Christmas parties were canceled. Flags at Carbide facilities flew at half-staff. All of its nearly 100,000 employees observed a moment of silence for the victims. It gave $1 million to an emergency relief fund and offered to turn its guesthouse in Bhopal into an orphanage.

Months later, the company offered another $5 million, but the money was refused because Indian politicians trembled in fear that they would be seen cooperating with the company. The Indian public reviled anything associated with Carbide. Later, when the state government learned that Carbide had set up a training school for the unemployed in Bhopal, it flattened the facility with bulldozers.

CARBIDE FIGHTS LAWSUITS AND A TAKEOVER BID

No sooner had the mists cleared than American attorneys arrived in Bhopal seeking litigants for damage claims. They walked the streets signing up plaintiffs. Just four days after the gas leak, the first suit was filed in a U.S. court; soon cases seeking $40 billion in damages for 200,000 Indians were filed against Carbide.

However, the Indian Parliament passed a law giving the Indian government an exclusive right to represent victims. Then India sued in the United States. Union Carbide offered $350 million to settle existing claims (an offer rejected by the Indian government) and brought a motion to have the cases heard in India. Both Indian and American lawyers claiming to represent victims opposed the motion, knowing that wrongful death awards in India were small compared with those in the United States. However, in 1986 a federal court ruled that the cases should be heard in India, noting that "to retain the litigation in [the United States] . . . would be yet another example

of imperialism, another situation in which an established sovereign inflicted its rules, its standards and values on a developing nation."[6] This was a victory for Carbide and a defeat for American lawyers, who could not carry their cases to India in defiance of the government.

In late 1986 the Indian government filed a $3.3 billion civil suit against Carbide in an Indian court.[7] The suit alleged that Union Carbide Corporation, in addition to being majority shareholder in Union Carbide India Ltd., had exercised policy control over the establishment and design of the Bhopal plant. The Bhopal plant was defective in design because its safety standards were lower than similar Carbide plants in the United States. Carbide had consciously permitted inadequate safety standards to exist. The suit also alleged that Carbide was conducting an "ultrahazardous activity" at the Bhopal plant and had strict and absolute liability for compensating victims regardless of whether the plant was operating carefully or not.

Carbide countered with the defense that it had a holding company relationship with UCIL and never exercised direct control over the Bhopal plant; it was prohibited from doing so by Indian laws requiring management by Indian nationals. In addition to the civil suit, Carbide's chairman, Warren Anderson, and several UCIL executives were charged with homicide in a Bhopal court. This apparently was a pressure tactic, since no attempt to arrest them was made.

On top of its legal battle, Carbide had to fight for its independence. In December 1985, GAF Corporation, which had been accumulating Carbide's shares, made a takeover bid. After a suspenseful monthlong battle, Carbide fought off GAF, but only at the cost of taking on enormous new debt to buy back 55 percent of its outstanding shares. This huge debt had to be reduced because interest payments were crippling. So in 1986 Carbide sold $3.5 billion of assets, including its most popular consumer brands—Eveready batteries, Glad bags, and Prestone antifreeze. It had sacrificed stable sources of revenue and was now a smaller, weaker company more exposed to cyclical economic trends.

---

[6] *In re Union Carbide Corporation Gas Plant Disaster*, 634 F. Supp. 867 (S.D.N.Y. 1986).

[7] *Union of India v. Union Carbide Corp. and Union Carbide India Ltd.*, Bhopal District Court, No. 1113 (1986).

INVESTIGATING THE CAUSE OF THE MIC LEAK

In the days following the gas leak, there was worldwide interest in pinning down its precise cause. A team of reporters from *The New York Times* interviewed plant workers in Bhopal. Their six-week investigation concluded that a large volume of water entered tank 610, causing the accident.[8] The *Times* reporters thought that water had entered when R. Khan failed to use a slip blind as he washed out piping. Water from his hose simply backed up and eventually flowed about 400 feet into the tank. Their account was widely circulated and this theory, called the "water washing theory," gained currency. However, it was not to be the only theory of the accident's cause.

Immediately after the disaster, Union Carbide also rushed a team of investigators to Bhopal. But the team got little cooperation from Indian authorities operating in a climate of anti-Carbide popular protest. It was denied access to plant records and workers. Yet the investigators got to look at tank 610 and took core samples from its bottom residue. These samples went back to the United States, where more than 500 experimental chemical reactions were undertaken to explain their chemical composition. In March 1985 Carbide finally released its report. It stated that entry of water into the tank caused the gas release, but it rejected the water washing theory.

Instead, Carbide scientists felt the only way that an amount of water sufficient to cause the observed reaction could have entered the tank was through accidental or deliberate connection of a water hose to piping that led directly into the tank. This was possible because outlets for compressed air, nitrogen, steam, and water were stationed throughout the plant. The investigators rejected the water washing hypothesis for several reasons. The piping system was designed to prevent water contamination even without a slip blind. Valves between the piping being washed and tank 610 were found closed after the

accident. And the volume of water required to create the reaction—1,000 to 2,000 pounds—was far too much to be explained by valve leakage.

The Carbide report gave a plausible alternative to the water washing theory, but within months an investigation by the Indian government rejected it. This study, made by Indian scientists and engineers, confirmed that the entry of water into the MIC tank caused the reaction but concluded that the improper washing procedure was to blame (see Exhibit 3).

There matters stood until late 1985, when the Indian government allowed Carbide more access to plant records and employees. Carbide investigators sought out the plant's employees. More than 70 interviews and careful examination of plant records and physical evidence led them to conclude that the cause of the gas leak was sabotage by a disgruntled employee who intentionally hooked a water hose to the tank.

Here is the sequence of events on the night of December 2–3 that Carbide set forth. At 10:20 p.m. the pressure gauge on tank 610 read 2 ppsi. This meant that no water had yet entered the tank and no reaction had begun. At 10:45 the regular shift change occurred. Shift changes take half an hour, and the MIC storage area would have been deserted. At this time, an operator who had been angry for days about his failure to get a promotion stole into the area. He unscrewed the local pressure indicator gauge on tank 610, hooked up a rubber water hose, and turned the water on. Five minutes would have sufficed to do this.

Carbide claimed to know the name of this person, but it has never been made public. Its investigative team speculated that his intention was simply to ruin the MIC batch in the tank; it is doubtful that this worker realized all that might happen. The interviews revealed that the workers thought of MIC chiefly as a lacrimator, a chemical that causes tearing; they did not regard it as a lethal hazard.

Now the plot thickens. A few minutes after midnight, MIC operators noted the fast pressure rise in tank 610. Walking to the tank, they found the water hose connected and removed it, then informed their supervisors. The supervisors tried to prevent a catastrophic pressure rise by draining water from tank 610. Between 12:15 and 12:30 a.m., just minutes before the explosive release, they transferred about 1 metric ton of the contents from tank 610 to a holding tank. Water is heavier than MIC, and the transfer was made through a drain in the tank's bottom; thus, the

---

[8] The team wrote a series of articles. See Stuart Diamond, "The Bhopal Disaster: How It Happened," *The New York Times,* January 28, 1985; Thomas J. Lueck, "Carbide Says Inquiry Showed Errors but Is Incomplete," *The New York Times,* January 28, 1985; Stuart Diamond, "The Disaster in Bhopal: Workers Recall Horror," *The New York Times,* January 30, 1985; and Robert Reinhold, "Disaster in Bhopal: Where Does Blame Lie?" *The New York Times,* January 31, 1985.

EXHIBIT 3 Two Theories Clash on Water Entry into MIC Tank

According to the water washing theory of the Indian government, water was introduced through a hose into bleeder A at filter pressure safety valve lines. As the hose kept running, water proceeded through the leaking valve in that area and rose up into the relief valve vent header line (RVVH). It took a turn at the jumper line, B, and moved into the process vent header line (PVH), filling it in the reverse direction all the way to the slip blind, C. When PVH was completely filled, water rose at line D and proceeded into MIC storage tank 610.

On February 8, 1985, two months after the leak, India's Central Bureau of Investigation drilled a hole in the PVH line at point E to drain any water left in the line. No water emerged. Carbide says this fact alone disproves the water washing theory. The fact that various valves in the pathway to the tank were closed also disproves the theory, according to Carbide.

Carbide espouses an alternative theory: The company says it has proof that water was introduced by a "disgruntled employee" who removed pressure gauge F, attached a hose to the open piping, and ran water into the MIC tank. Gas then escaped through a rupture disk and proceeded through the RVVH and out the vent gas scrubber.

Source: Courtesy of Union Carbide.

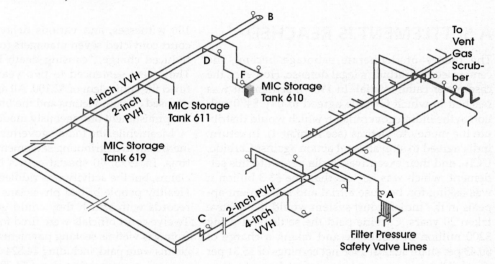

supervisors hoped to remove the water. They failed, and within 15 minutes the relief valve blew.

The investigators had physical evidence to support this scenario. After the accident, the local pressure gauge hole on tank 610 was still open and no plug had been inserted, as would have been normal for routine maintenance. When the MIC unit was examined, a crude drawing of the hose connection was found on the back of one page from that night's log book. Also, operators outside the MIC unit told the investigation team that MIC operators had told them about the hose connection that night. In addition, log entries had been falsified, revealing a crude cover-up effort. The major falsification was an attempt to hide the transfer of contents from tank 610.

Why did the supervisors and operators attempt a cover-up? The Carbide investigators gave this explanation.

> Not knowing if the attempted transfer had exacerbated the incident, or whether they could have otherwise prevented it, or whether they would be blamed for not having notified plant management earlier, those involved decided on a cover-up. They altered logs that morning to disguise their involvement. As is common in many such incidents, the reflexive tendency to cover up simply took over.[9]

[9] Ashok S. Kalelkar, "Investigation of Large-Magnitude Incidents: Bhopal as a Case Study," paper presented at the Instititution of Chemical Engineers conference on Preventing Major Chemical Accidents, London, England, May 1988, p. 27.

EXHIBIT 4   A Breakdown of the $470 million Settlement

The settlement was based on calculations about the number and size of payments in a range of categories.

Source: Kim Fortun, *Advocacy after Bhopal* (Chicago: University of Chicago Press, 2001), p. 38.

Amount	Medical Categorization
$ 43,500,000	$14,500 payments for 3,000 deaths
50,000,000	$25,000 payments for up to 2,000 victims with injuries of "utmost severity"
156,000,000	$5,200 payments to 30,000 permanently disabled
64,300,000	$3,215 payments to 20,000 temporarily disabled
140,600,000	Amount to cover 150,000 minor injuries, future injuries, property damage, commercial loss, and other claims
15,600,000	Medical treatment and rehabilitation of victims
$470,000,000	Total settlement

A SETTLEMENT IS REACHED

The theory of deliberate sabotage became the centerpiece of Carbide's legal defense. However, the case never came to trial. In 1989 a settlement was reached in which Carbide agreed to pay $470 million to the Indian government, which would distribute the money to victims (see Exhibit 4). In return, India agreed to stop all legal action against Carbide, UCIL, and their executives. India agreed to this settlement, which was far less than the $3.3 billion it was asking for, because a trial and subsequent appeals in the Indian court system would likely have taken 20 years. Carbide paid the settlement using $200 million in insurance and taking a charge of $0.43 per share against 1988 net earnings of $5.31 per share. Victims' groups were upset because they thought the settlement too small, and they challenged it. In 1992 the Indian Supreme Court rejected these appeals but permitted reinstatement of criminal proceedings against Warren Anderson and eight UCIL managers.[10]

In 1993 India issued an arrest warrant for Anderson on charges of "culpable homicide not amounting to murder," but it has never been served. At the trial of the remaining UCIL defendants Indian prosecutors argued the managers were criminally negligent because they knew of lax operating procedures but failed to improve them to avoid costs. After 18 years,

186 witnesses, and various delaying motions, the court convicted seven managers (one had died) of a reduced charge, "causing death by negligence."[11] They were sentenced to two years in prison, and fined the equivalent of $2,100. All appealed and were released on bail. Victims and the Indian public found the punishment outrageously modest.

Meanwhile, the Indian government was slow and inefficient in distributing settlement funds to gas victims. In 1993, 40 special courts began processing claims, but the activity was riddled with corruption. Healthy people bribed physicians for false medical records with which they could get compensation. Twelve court officials were fired for soliciting bribes from gas victims seeking payments. All told, 574,366 claims were paid, including 14,824 death claims, with average compensation about $1,280. Ninety percent of all claims were settled for $550, the minimum allowed.[12]

Because the claims process moved at a glacial pace for years, the settlement money accrued interest and, after all claims were paid, $325 million remained. The government wanted to use the interest

---

[10] *Union Carbide Corp. v. Union of India,* AIR 1992 (S.C.) 248.

[11] India Central Bureau of Investigation, "Eight Accused Sentenced in Bhopal Gas Tragedy Case," press release, New Delhi, June 7, 2010.

[12] Paul Watson, "Cloud of Despair in Bhopal," *Los Angeles Times,* August 30, 2001, p. A6; and Government of Madhya Pradesh, Bhopal Gas Tragedy Relief and Rehabilitation Department, "Facts and Figures," www.mp.gov.in/bgtrrdmp/facts.htm, accessed June 2010.

to clean up soil contamination at the plant. But in 2004 the Indian Supreme Court ordered it distributed to the victims and families of the dead in amounts proportionate to claims already paid.[13]

AFTERMATH

In the wake of Bhopal, Congress passed legislation requiring chemical companies to disclose the presence of dangerous chemicals to people living near their plants and to create evacuation plans. The chemical industry's trade association adopted a program of more rigorous safety standards that all major firms now follow.

In 1994 Union Carbide sold its 50.9 percent equity in UCIL to the Indian subsidiary of a British company for $90 million. It gave all of this money to the Indian government for a hospital and clinics in Bhopal. After the sale, the company had no presence or current legal obligations in India. Nevertheless, Bhopal had destroyed it. As it exited India, it was a smaller, less resilient company. Forced to sell or spin off its most lucrative businesses, it grew progressively weaker. In 1984, the year of the gas leak, Carbide had 98,400 employees and sales of $9.5 billion; by 2000 it had only 11,000 employees and $5.9 billion in sales. The end came when it merged with Dow Chemical Co. in 2001 and its workforce suffered the bulk of cost-reduction layoffs.[14]

The pesticide plant never reopened. According to a recent visitor, "The old factory grounds, frozen in time, are an overgrown 11-acre forest of corroded tanks and pipes buzzing with cicadas, where cattle graze and women forage for twigs to cook their evening meal."[15] Chemical waste at the site has contaminated the groundwater. In 1998 the state government took over the plant and made cleanup plans, but never carried them out.

In 2004 the United States again denied a request by the Indian government to extradite Warren Anderson. Anderson, who is now 91, has dropped from public view. In the unlikely event of extradition, he would face a long trial. Recently, his wife told a reporter that he had been "haunted for many years" by the accident.[16]

The struggle of gas victims for compensation spawned an activist movement that lives on after more than 25 years. The lead organization is the International Campaign for Justice in Bhopal, a coalition of gas victim groups and charities. Survivors complain of chronic medical conditions including headaches, joint pain, shortness of breath, and psychiatric problems. They believe that gas exposure and toxic wastes from the plant have caused birth defects.

NEW TARGET: DOW CHEMICAL

After Dow Chemical absorbed Union Carbide it became the victims' bull's-eye. Both victims and the Indian government now demand that Dow pay for cleaning up the contaminated plant site and further compensate injured survivors. In 2010 the Indian government filed a petition with the Indian Supreme Court seeking to overturn its 1989 settlement "to cure a miscarriage of justice." The petition, still pending, seeks to force Dow Chemical to pay another $1.1 billion to the victims.[17] This is justified, argues the government, because the full extent of the disaster was unknown in 1989.

Members of the victim's movement have repeatedly sued in U.S. courts seeking to overturn the $470 million settlement, accusing Union Carbide of human rights violations, and trying to hold it responsible for cleaning up groundwater pollution at the plant site. All their efforts have so far failed, although one case still drags on.[18]

Victims otherwise harass the company. They have joined with progressive religious orders and pension funds in the United States to picket its shareholder's meetings while inside, friendly shareholders introduce

---

[13] "Compensation for Bhopal Victims," *The New York Times*, July 20, 2004, p. A6.

[14] Susan Warren, "Cost-Cutting Effort at Dow Chemical to Take 4,500 Jobs," *The Wall Street Journal*, May 2, 2001, p. A6.

[15] Somini Sengupta, "Decades Later, Toxic Sludge Torments Bhopal," *The New York Times*, July 7, 2008, p. 1.

[16] Celeste Katz, "India Sez Bust Bhopal Yank," *Daily News*, August 2, 2009, p. 26.

[17] Geeta Anand and Arlene Chang, "Dow Chemical Hit Again on Bhopal," *The Wall Street Journal*, December 4–5, 2010, p. B5.

[18] The case is *Janki Bai Sahu, et al. v. Union Carbide Corp.*, No. 04 Civ. 8825, 2010 U.S. Dist. LEXIS 23860, February 11, 2010. Two previous long-running cases are *In re Union Carbide Corp. Gas Plant Disaster at Bhopal*, 634 F. Supp. 842 (S.D.N.Y. 1986) and *Bano v. Union Carbide Corp. and Warren Anderson*, No. 99 Civ. 11329, 2005 U.S. Dist. LEXIS 22871, October 5, 2005).

resolutions asking Dow to acknowledge its responsibilities. All such resolutions have been defeated, garnering only single-digit percentages of the vote. Activists tried to embarrass Dow with a brand of bottled water named B'eau Pal containing groundwater from near the old plant. Children of gas victims once went on a 22-city U.S. tour to promote congressional hearings on Dow's responsibilities. No hearings were held.

Dow never wavers in denying any obligation. "While we have sympathy for this situation," said a company representative recently, "it is not Dow's responsibility, accountability or liability to bear."[19] But the activists are resolute. "I will fight until my last breath against Dow," says one gas survivor. "I will not give up."[20] The fight also has ideological meaning. One movement leader believes that "[u]nless those responsible are punished in an exemplary matter, the message that goes out to the corporate world is that you can kill and maim people and carry on with business as usual."[21]

POSTSCRIPT

Despite the passage of time, Bhopal does not fade away. The library bookshelf on it keeps growing.[22] It has been the subject of at least seven films, including a drama that was a box office hit in India. A tendentious book of reality fiction based on Bhopal became a best seller in Europe.[23] Told as a tragedy, the story stirs basic emotions. A Canadian critic reviewing a play on Bhopal found it badly written and acted, but nevertheless "a touching tale of human suffering" raising "such imposing themes as the relative worth of a human life and the intersection of greed and development in the Third World."[24] Doubtless these themes will keep the story alive.

Questions

1. Who is responsible for the Bhopal accident? How should blame be apportioned among parties involved, including Union Carbide Corporation, UCIL, plant workers, governments in India, or others?

2. What principles of corporate social responsibility and business ethics are applicable to the actions of the parties in question?

3. How well did the legal system work? Do you agree with the decision to try the lawsuits in India? Were victims fairly compensated? Was Union Carbide sufficiently punished?

4. Did Union Carbide handle the crisis well? How would you grade its performance in facing uniquely difficult circumstances?

5. Does Dow Chemical Company have any remaining legal liability, social responsibility, or ethical duty to address unresolved health and environmental claims of Bhopal victims?

6. What lessons can other corporations and countries learn from this story?

[19] Quoted in Brian Bowling, "Group from Bhopal Says Gas Still Kills," *Pittsburgh Tribune Review,* May 1, 2009, p. 1.

[20] Hazara, a one-name activist, quoted in Mark Magnier, "Despair Lingers in Bhopal," *Los Angeles Times,* December 3, 2009, p. 28.

[21] Satinath Sarangi, quoted in Jim Gilchrist, "Bhopal Hero," *The Scotsman,* July 8, 2009, p. 18.

[22] A recent addition is *Surviving Bhopal: Dancing Bodies, Written Texts, and Oral Testimonials of Women in the Wake of an Industrial Disaster* (New York: Palgrave Macmillan, 2010).

[23] Dominique Lapierre and Javier Moro, *Five Past Midnight in Bhopal* (New York: Warner Books, 2002).

[24] Kamal Al-Solaylee, "Bhopal: A Chemical and Theatrical Disaster," *The Globe and Mail,* October 25, 2003, p. R17. The play is Rahul Varma, *Bhopal* (Toronto: Playwrights Canada Press, 2006).

Chapter Twelve

Globalization, Trade, and Corruption

McDonald's Corporation

Imagine an apparatus so colossal that it casts a shadow over most of the earth. At the back moves a stream of farmers pouring potatoes and lettuce through an opening, while beside them a line of cows, pigs, and chickens glides in and disappears. Inside, a uniformed crew of 385,000 works levers and pushes buttons. In front, a torrent of 694 meals a second, day and night, flies into endless waves of humanity. A side door opens regularly and bags of money drop out. Waste vents release bursts of paper and plastic. On top, the stars and stripes snap and weave against the sky. As you watch, the great machine expands and quickens.

It all started in 1948 when brothers Richard and Maurice "Mac" McDonald built several hamburger stands with golden arches in Southern California. One day a traveling salesman named Ray Kroc came by selling milkshake mixers. The popularity of their $0.15 hamburgers impressed him so much he bought the world franchise rights. In time, he stretched the golden arches across the globe. Today, McDonald's has 33,000 restaurants in 117 countries. More than half are outside the United States, accounting for 61 percent of revenues.[1]

The golden arches are now so ubiquitous that a British magazine, *The Economist,* prints a "Big Mac Index" using the price of a Big Mac in foreign currencies to assess exchange-rate distortions. McDonald's has the world's sixth most valuable brand, in part because of its ability to cross borders and cultures. Surveys show the golden arches are familiar to more people than the Christian cross; that 69 percent of three-year-old children recognize them, more than can state their own name; that after Santa Claus, the most-recognized person by children of the world is Ronald McDonald; and that in Beijing almost half of children under age 12 believe McDonald's is a Chinese company.[2]

---

[1] McDonald's Corporation, Form 10-K, February 25, 2011, pp. 10 and 16.

[2] Eric Schlosser, *Fast Food Nation* (Boston: Houghton Mifflin, 2001), p. 4; Jonathan Freedland, "The Onslaught," *The Guardian,* October 25, 2005, p. 8; "Big Mac's Makeover," *The Economist,* October 16, 2004, p. 64; and Randall E. Stross, "The McPeace Dividend," *U.S. News & World Report,* April 1, 2002, p. 36.

There are many views of McDonald's. For some it inspires spacious reasoning. A social critic finds profound meaning in the spread of "McDonaldization," a powerful force of global change based on principles of "efficiency, calculability, predictability, and control."[3] A prominent journalist popularized a "Golden Arches Theory of Conflict Prevention," observing that countries with McDonald's restaurants never war with each other.[4] Its validity was lost in less than a decade, when Russia invaded Georgia.

In developing nations, the arrival of a McDonald's signals modernization. It is often among the first foreign retail corporations to enter, and acts as "the canary in the coal mine of economic success" because it appears when disposable income rises and there is promise of sustained growth.[5] For consumers in emerging economies the Quarter Pounder is a connection with world culture, "an imagined global identity that they share with like-minded people."[6]

For leftists and jihadists, McDonald's symbolizes perceived evils of globalization, capitalism, and American values. Its restaurants have been targets of violence in more than a dozen countries. In France, a farmer upset with trade liberalization drove his tractor into a McDonald's. Bombs set by radical groups exploded in two other French restaurants, killing a worker. In Santiago and Guatemala City, restaurants were attacked to protest visits by President George W. Bush. Pakistani mobs in Islamabad and Lahore sought out golden arches when European newspapers published cartoons of the Prophet Mohammad.

In fact, McDonald's does transfer American culture and practices. A group of anthropologists documented its influence in east Asia. In Hong Kong and Taiwan its clean restrooms and kitchens set a new standard that elevated expectations throughout the country. In Hong Kong, children's birthdays had traditionally gone unrecognized, but McDonald's introduced the practice of birthday parties in its restaurants, and now birthday celebrations are widespread in the population. In Japan, *tachigui,* a centuries-old taboo against standing while eating, lost its strength after McDonald's opened restaurants in Tokyo with no tables or seats.[7]

On the other hand, many foreign customs are resistant to broad change based on what people eat for lunch. Years ago, when McDonald's first branched out from American soil, it learned to adapt, not conquer. It first moved into Canada in the 1960s, but faced popular rejection as a foreign business. The head of its Canadian operations then became a Canadian citizen. Most of McDonald's international restaurants are franchises, run as local businesses and managed to suit local custom. In Japan the company adds shrimp burgers to its menu. In India it subtracts beef. In

---

[3] George Ritzer, *The Globalization of Nothing* (Thousand Oaks, CA: Pine Forge Press, 2004), pp. 82–83. See also George Ritzer, ed., *McDonaldization: The Reader,* 3rd ed. (Thousand Oaks, CA: Pine Forge Press/ Sage Publishers, 2010).

[4] Thomas L. Friedman, *The Lexus and the Olive Tree* (New York: Farrar Straus Giroux, 1999), chap. 10.

[5] Jonah Goldberg, "The Specter of McDonald's," *National Review,* June 5, 2000, p. 30.

[6] Douglas B. Holt, John A. Quelch, and Earl L. Taylor, "How Global Brands Compete," *Harvard Business Review,* September 2004, p. 71.

[7] James L. Watson, ed., *Golden Arches East: McDonald's in East Asia* (Stanford, CA: Stanford University Press, 1997), pp. 103, 134, 178–79.

At a shopping mall in Riyadh, Saudi Arabia, women line up at the "ladies" sign and men at the "gentlemen's" sign. The mall is patrolled by Saudi religious police who enforce segregation of the sexes. Source: © AP Photo/Hasan Jamali.

globalization Growth in networks of economic, political, social, military, scientific, or environmental interdependence to span worldwide distances.

Taiwan it serves rice burgers, made with beef or crispy chicken, lettuce, and cabbage between two toasted rice "patties." At the world's largest McDonald's in Beijing, managers fly the Chinese flag and serve green pea pies. In Britain restaurants are painted green and serve rain-forest-friendly coffee, organic milk, and free-range eggs. In Saudi Arabia, restaurants close five times a day for prayers. Eating zones for men and women are segregated.

The McDonald's story illustrates the complexity of globalization. A small, local American business swelled into a far-flung multinational corporation with a radiant brand. It spread American business and cultural values, shaping both national cultures and an amorphous world culture. Yet its restaurants everywhere adapt to local tastes and customs.

GLOBALIZATION

Globalization occurs when networks of economic, political, social, military, scientific, and environmental interdependence grow to span worldwide distances. It can be viewed as both a process and an end state. As an end it is not inevitable. Universal forces advance only against the resistance of parochial forces. Even as cross-border forces gain momentum some nations and populations are bypassed or defy their dictates. As a process, globalization is ancient and enduring, at work since the first exchanges between human settlements. And it is not a solitary process, but a set of interacting forces. Here are a few illustrations.

- Technological advances have significantly increased the speed and reduced the costs of communications. In 1930, for example, the cost of a one-minute telephone call to London from New York was about $245. In 1990 it was $3.32. Today a fiber-optic voice or text communication costs only a fraction of a cent.

- Transportation costs and delivery schedules of goods have been substantially reduced. In the 1950s international shipping added as much as 25 percent to the cost of exports. In the 1960s the use of metal containers eliminated the need frequently to load and reload cargo, greatly reducing costs. In the 1970s a rising airfreight industry opened fast, intercontinental routes to fierce price competition.[8]

- International institutions created after World War II by the Allied powers to support a stable world economy have succeeded, for the most part, in their missions. Tariffs fell, setting the stage for spectacular growth in world trade. Exchange rates stabilized and restrictions on capital movement eased, leading eventually to explosive growth in investment to finance trade, acquire foreign assets, and speculate.

- Developing nations with low-cost labor have become the workshops of industrialized nations, spreading economic growth. In 1995 the output of developing nations was only 17 percent of world output, but by 2008 it had more than doubled and was almost a third of world output.[9] High income nations increased their output too, but at a far slower rate.

- Collapse of the Soviet Union and its socialist economy in 1991 brought greater receptivity to capitalism in developing countries. Free market ideas spread and flourished, opening previously insulated nations to global market forces.

- A vibrant civil society populated by thousands of nongovernmental organizations rose in the 1990s. Although its politics is richly diverse, its mainstream is united in defending the environment and the global poor against economic exploitation. It has created a web of principles for responsible economic activity and has growing power to enforce them with inventive forms of civil regulation.

- New institutions and networks rise to address pollution, species loss, disruption of natural chemistry cycles, and ecosystem deterioration, problems of the biosphere that threaten humanity across borders and cultures.

Figure 12.1 gives a more detailed summary of the main forces driving globalization. Although its extent and meaning are subject to interpretation, one snap-

---

[8] Marc Levinson, "Freight Pain: The Rise and Fall of Globalization," *Foreign Affairs,* November/December 2008), p. 134.

[9] Based on GDP figures in World Bank, *2010 World Development Indicators* (Washington, DC: International Bank for Reconstruction and Development, April 2010), table 4.2.

FIGURE 12.1 Main Forces in Globalization

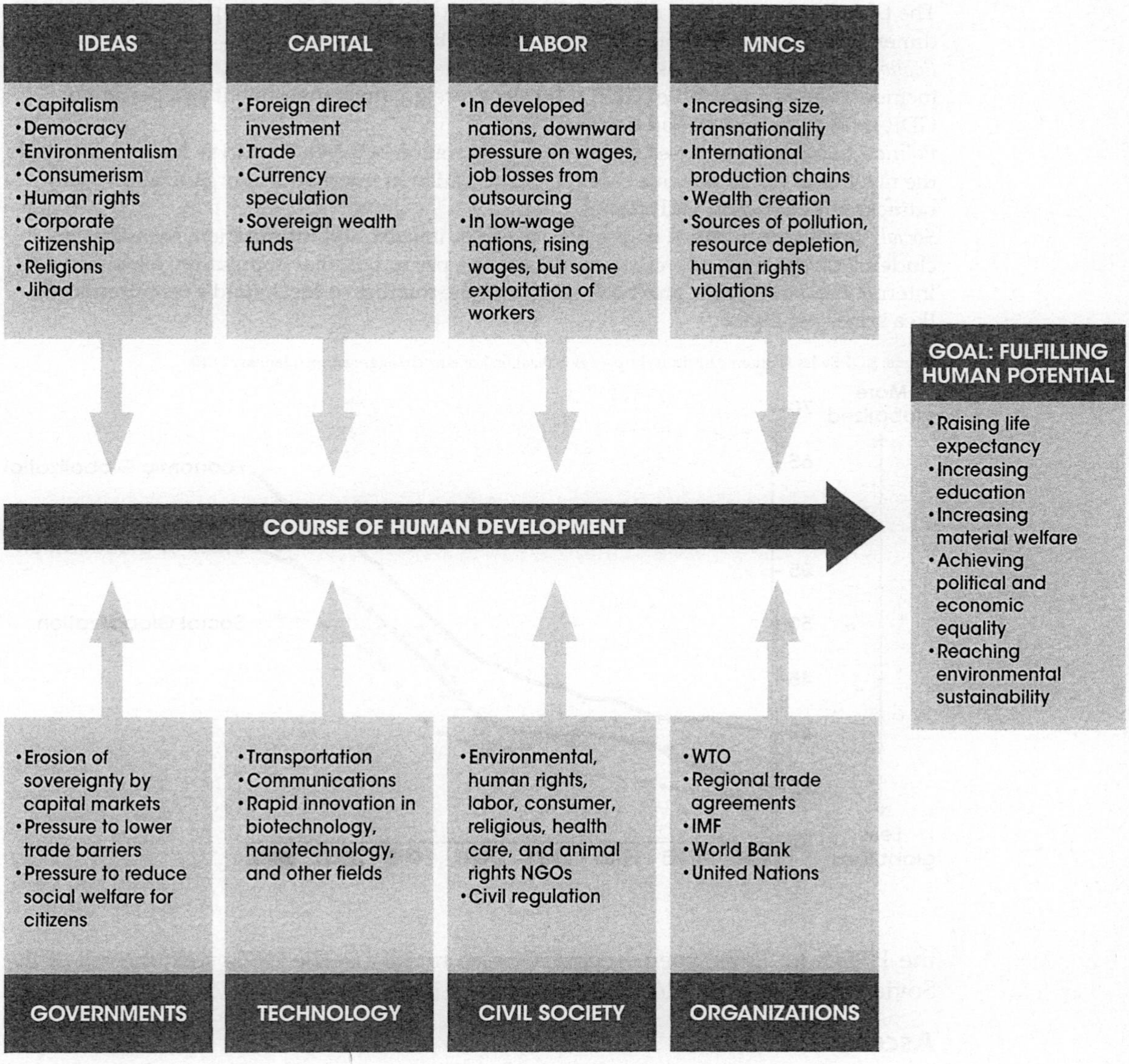

IDEAS	CAPITAL	LABOR	MNCs
•Capitalism •Democracy •Environmentalism •Consumerism •Human rights •Corporate citizenship •Religions •Jihad	•Foreign direct investment •Trade •Currency speculation •Sovereign wealth funds	•In developed nations, downward pressure on wages, job losses from outsourcing •In low-wage nations, rising wages, but some exploitation of workers	•Increasing size, transnationality •International production chains •Wealth creation •Sources of pollution, resource depletion, human rights violations

GOAL: FULFILLING HUMAN POTENTIAL

•Raising life expectancy
•Increasing education
•Increasing material welfare
•Achieving political and economic equality
•Reaching environmental sustainability

COURSE OF HUMAN DEVELOPMENT →

GOVERNMENTS	TECHNOLOGY	CIVIL SOCIETY	ORGANIZATIONS
•Erosion of sovereignty by capital markets •Pressure to lower trade barriers •Pressure to reduce social welfare for citizens	•Transportation •Communications •Rapid innovation in biotechnology, nanotechnology, and other fields	•Environmental, human rights, labor, consumer, religious, health care, and animal rights NGOs •Civil regulation	•WTO •Regional trade agreements •IMF •World Bank •United Nations

shot of its progress is captured by an index, the KOF Globalization Index, shown in Figure 12.2. This index combines three major dimensions of globalization—economic, political, and social—and shows their movement over almost 30 years. It compares 181 countries based on 24 variables of globalization across these three dimensions. Each country is scored on a scale of 0 (no integration) to 100 (a maximum score on each variable). The figure shows that overall, and in each of the three dimensions, the world has become more integrated. Global ties grew through

FIGURE 12.2   The KOF Index of Globalization and Subindexes: 1970–2010

The *Globalization Index* is a combination index. It combines economic, political, and social dimensions of globalization calculated as separate indexes.

Economic globalization is based on trade and investment flows and restrictions. Measures include trade as a percent of GDP, inflows of foreign direct investment as a percent of GDP, tariff rates, and import barriers.

Political globalization is based on political cooperation between countries. Measures include the number of embassies in a country, participation in international organizations, and ratification of international treaties.

Social globalization is based on the flow of ideas, images, and information. Measures include telephone traffic, foreign population as a percent of total population, television and Internet use, newspaper and book sales, and the number of McDonald's restaurants and Ikea stores per capita.

Source: KOF Swiss Economic Institute, http://globalization.kof.ethz.ch/aggregation/, January 2010.

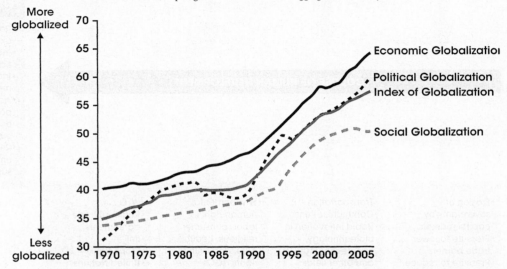

the 1970s and 1980s, then expanded more rapidly in the 1990s with the fall of the Soviet Union and the bloom of free market ideas.

Ascent and Inertia

For those who approve of globalization its great benefit is human progress. Some believe that never before in human history has there been anything approaching the improvement in welfare the world has recently witnessed. According to one economist, "The international economy has enabled countries to develop, alleviate poverty, improve social conditions, lengthen life spans and carry out social and political reform." To give one example, in the 1950s South Korea and Taiwan were "miserably poor countries whose very survival was in question: in the 1990s they graduated into the ranks of the world's advanced industrial nations."[10]

[10] Quotes are from Jeffrey A. Frieden, *Global Capitalism* (New York: W. W. Norton, 2006), p. 473.

TABLE 12.1
The Top 10 Most and Least Globalized Countries

Source: Swiss Federal Institute of Technology, "2010 KOF Index of Globalization," at http://globalization. kof.ethz.ch/static/ pdf/rankings_2010. pdf.

Rank	Country	Globalization Index	Rank	Country	Globalization Index
1	Belgium	92.95	172	Sao Tome and Principe	32.52
2	Austria	92.51	173	Tonga	31.63
3	Netherlands	90.90	174	Comoros	30.67
4	Switzerland	90.55	175	Bhutan	29.31
5	Sweden	89.75	176	Eritria	28.93
6	Denmark	89.68	177	Lao PDR	28.12
7	Canada	88.24	178	Equitorial Guinea	26.85
8	Portugal	87.54	179	Solomon Islands	26.35
9	Finland	87.31	180	Kiribati	25.45
10	Hungary	87.00	181	Myanmar	20.69

Since 1970, 155 countries with about 95 percent of world population have experienced rising incomes. World annual average per capita income in 2010 was $10,760, about 150 percent greater than in 1990. The fastest growth has been in developed countries, which averaged increases of 2.3 percent a year between 1970 and 2010. Income in developing countries rose more slowly at about 1.5 percent a year. Poverty has been reduced. In 1981, 52 percent of the world population lived on less than $1.25 a day, but by 2010 that figure had dropped to 21 percent.[11] In China the number tumbled spectacularly, from 84 percent to 15 percent over the same time. This material improvement is accompanied by gains in education, health, and other measures of social welfare.

Global progress is not uniform. Hidden in the rising lines of the indexes in Figure 12.2 is wide variation among countries. The very poorest countries are being left behind. Although they slowly expand their global connections, a huge gap has persisted for decades. Table 12.1 shows the 10 most and 10 least globalized countries and the yawning gulf between their index scores.[12] The consequence of this divide is a substantial difference in fortunes. The least globalized countries have stagnant economies. Thirteen of the world's poorest, least globalized countries, have lower per capita incomes today than in 1970.

Comparing two countries at opposite ends of the globalization index is instructive. Belgium is the world's most globalized country. Niger, with a similar size population, is one of the world's least globalized, ranking 165th of 181 countries. Belgium is closely joined to the world economy; Niger is not. In a recent year Belgium trade in goods totaled $721 billion.[13] The country attracted $100 billion in foreign investment. As a member of the European Union its average tariff was

[11] Figures in this paragraph are from World Bank, *World Development Indicators 2010;* and United Nations Development Program, *Human Development Report 2010* (New York: UNDP, 2010), various tables.

[12] The United States ranks 27th with an index score of 78.80.

[13] Figures in this section on Belgium and Niger are from World Bank, *World Development Report 2010* (Washington, DC: International Bank for Reconstruction and Development, April 2010), various tables for 2008; and World Trade Organization Statistics Database, "Time Series on International Trade," for 2009, at http:stat.wto.org.

only 1.6 percent. In Niger, the value of trade was $2.4 billion and it attracted $147 million in foreign investment, both figures just small fractions of the Belgian numbers. Its average tariff was a relatively high 13 percent.

The people of Belgium are exposed to a rich stream of cross-border information; the people of Niger are information-poor. Virtually everyone in Belgium has a telephone, 99 percent of households have a television, and 68 percent of adults use the Internet. The country received 7.2 million international tourists. In Niger, on the other hand, only 13 percent of the population has a telephone, 6 percent of households have televisions, and less than 1 percent of adults use the Internet. It was visited by only 48,000 international tourists.

The consequences of this divide are enormous for the citizens of the two countries. The average Belgian has 10.6 years of schooling, lives 80.3 years, and makes $34,873 a year. There are 42 physicians for each 10,000 citizens. Less than 1 percent of Belgians live below the United Nation's definition of poverty as less than $1.25 a day in income. The average Nigerian has a brief 1.4 years of schooling, lives only 52.5 years, and makes but $675 a year. If illness comes there is less than one physician per 10,000 citizens. Sixty-six percent of the population earns less than $1.25 a day.

TRADE

The mainspring of globalization is trade. Countries that open themselves to trade are more permeable to a wide range of other integrating influences. The current global trading system is a long-term, spectacular success. The total value of merchandise exports rose from $58 billion in 1950 to a high of $16.1 trillion in 2008.[14] To put this increase in perspective, if you had started measuring the value of trade at the stroke of the New Year in 2008 the value of all trade in 1950 would have been equaled by 9:42 a.m. on January 2. Modern growth in trade is one legacy of arrangements made by the victorious powers after World War II to rebuild the international economy. Here is the background story.

The Rise and Fall of Trade

The vicissitudes of global trade leading up to World War II are briefly told. Before 1800, growth of the world economy was slow and limited. International trade was restrained with barriers put up by governments. The richest European nations, the dominant traders of the time, ran their economies according to the theory of *mercantilism*. Their ruling monarchies sought to exploit weaker nations in far-flung empires by importing cheap raw materials, then selling more expensive finished goods back to the colonists. The wealth retained in the mother country from this lopsided exchange was used to increase national power by, for example, accumulating armaments and building gold reserves. Trade flowed through colonial empires, but not freely between them. The world of trade was a deeply divided world.

mercantilism
A policy of increasing national power by managing the economy to create a trade surplus. Exports were promoted, imports restricted.

---

[14] Ibid., "World, Total Merchandise Exports" series.

The Industrial Revolution undermined the logic of this system. As new technologies based on steam increased productivity, economies grew more rapidly. Industrialists and bankers, especially in Great Britain, were first to argue the potential gains from freer trade, and by 1850 the world's richest, most powerful country had lowered its protective barriers, opening itself to international markets. Others followed. Trade flourished. Technology in that era, as in the present one, shortened distances, expanding the reach of manufacturers to previously remote markets. Steamships and railroads sped shipping and lowered its cost. Mechanical refrigeration opened new markets for meat and foods. The telegraph, and later the telephone, connected traders. Although a long depression from 1873 to 1896 reduced trade, the world economy roared back and by the end of the century global trade was eight times greater than at the beginning.

The great run of free trade ended with World War I, which inflamed global markets with national conflicts. Trade barriers raised by the combatants remained after the armistice. Nations emerged from the war with wounded economies and high debts. Before trade could recover from this morass, the economic collapse of 1929–1934 crippled the world's leading economies with plunging output and high unemployment. Trade declined further. Around the world governments turned inward. Instead of seeking recovery through mutual benefit from trade exchanges, they sought to keep production at home and protect their struggling industries from foreign competition.

tariff
A tax or duty charged by a government on goods moved across a border. Tariffs raise the cost of imports, making them less competitive with similar domestic goods.

In the United States an isolationist, Republican Congress passed the remarkably unwise Smoot-Hawley Tariff Act in 1930. This law "added poison to the emptying well of global trade" by raising 890 *tariff* lines covering tens of thousands of items and increasing the average American duty on imported goods to 59.1 percent by 1932.[15] It also created nontariff barriers. For example, it required the country of origin be stamped on bottle corks, a process that more than doubled the cost of each.[16] Over the next two years imports into the United States dropped by 40 percent.[17] And other nations retaliated. Canada started an "egg war," putting such a high duty on American eggs that exports fell 99 percent.[18] France raised its tariff on American radios above 50 percent. Italy put a tariff of nearly 100 percent on American automobiles.

autarky
A policy of national self-sufficiency and economic independence.

In this downward spiral of retaliation and bitter national rivalries some governments moved in the direction of *autarky*, a policy of economic self-sufficiency in which a nation attempts to produce a full range of goods and services for itself, avoiding reliance on other nations. One example was Germany, where economic hardship led to the rise of an authoritarian leader, Adolf Hitler, who imposed stringent controls on the economy, cutting off capital flows, limiting trade, and building industrial and military power from within. Italy, Japan, and some developing

---

[15] "The Battle of Smoot-Hawley," *The Economist*," December 20, 2008, p. 125.

[16] William J. Bernstein, *A Splendid Exchange: How Trade Shaped the World* (New York: Grove Press, 2008), p. 351.

[17] "The Battle of Smoot Hawley," *The Economist*, p. 126.

[18] Douglas A. Irwin, "How 'Protectionist' Became an Insult," *The Wall Street Journal*, June 18, 2010, p. A15.

nations moved in the same direction. World trade fell further as political considerations eclipsed market forces. Soon the world plunged into the conflagration of World War II.

A New Postwar Order

During the war the United States and its allies started to plan a postwar order that would reopen nations to economic cooperation. Recent experience with self-defeating trade wars suggested that such cooperation was essential to lasting peace. After the war, representatives of the victorious nations met in the small town of Bretton Woods, New Hampshire, to forge an agreement. They created three institutions that began their work in 1947. A new World Bank would overcome shortages of private capital to make loans for rebuilding war-torn nations. Its funding would come from member nations. An International Monetary Fund (IMF) was started to stabilize exchange rates. During the era of trade wars countries had fought by devaluing currencies and limiting cross-border movement of funds. Now nations would join the IMF, fixing their currencies to the value of a dollar in gold, removing restrictions on capital flows, and contributing to a fund for rescuing countries with balance-of-payment emergencies.

A third institution, an International Trade Organization intended to promote freer trade, was fashioned, but never given life. However, as part of its design the Bretton Woods negotiators had included a General Agreement on Tariffs and Trade (GATT), intended to expand trade by eliminating discriminatory barriers. To activate the GATT, representatives from 23 countries met in Geneva in 1947 and agreed on rules for parties in trade negotiations. They set up policies for *multilateral trade negotiations*, or negotiations seeking consensus among all signatory nations.

These rules were built around two key principles. The first was the *most-favored-nation* principle, under which any duty, tariff, favor, or privilege granted to one signatory nation would be similarly granted to all others.[19] If, for example, Japan puts a 5 percent tariff on chewing gum imported from Brazil, it must levy the same tariff on chewing gum imports from any other nation in the multilateral agreement. The second principle was *national treatment*. Each nation was allowed to use trade restrictions such as tariffs as negotiated, but once inside a domestic market foreign goods would be given equal treatment with local goods. They would not be subject to additional taxes, licenses, or rules.[20] Then, in a series of more than 100 agreements GATT negotiators reduced tariffs on approximately 45,000 items making up about one-fifth the value of world trade.

Success and Evolution

After 1947 the Bretton Woods institutions evolved. When postwar recovery came more rapidly than predicted, the mission of the World Bank shifted from making reconstruction loans in war-ravaged Europe to making loans in developing nations

multilateral trade negotiation
A trade negotiation in which multiple nations seek consensus on an agreement that will apply equally to all.

most-favored-nation
A principle enacted in some trade agreements requiring that if one participant extends any benefit to another, that participant must extend the same benefit to all.

national treatment
Equal treatment for imported and local goods in a domestic market.

---

[19] General Agreement on Tariffs and Trade, *Text of General Agreement,* Geneva, July 1986, Article I, sec. 1.
[20] Ibid., Article III, sec. 2.

for dams, highways, hospitals, schools, and power plants.[21] Its now lends to promote long-term development in the poorest countries as a way to reduce poverty. Many of its loans are interest-free. In the late 1960s it began to raise most of its capital by selling AAA-rated bonds in world capital markets. In 2009 it had 187 country members and gave loans and grants of $47 billion to developing countries.

The primary mission of the International Monetary Fund has always been to promote international economic stability. Member nations pay "capital subscriptions" into a pooled fund based on the size of their economy. The money in this fund is then lent to countries with balance of payment problems. The IMF started with 29 member countries. By 2011 the number had grown to 187 and it had a fund of $340 billion. In the 1980s the IMF amplified its mission by using its power as a lender to promote the spread of free market ideas.

Both the World Bank and the IMF have always been dominated by the United States and the West. Both institutions are headquartered in Washington, D.C. Their governance mechanisms allocate votes based on financial contributions, which are in turn based on the output of national economies. Traditionally, the president of the United States nominates the president of the World Bank, and European nations nominate the managing director of the IMF. Important decisions in each organization can be made only by voting majorities of 85 percent in the governing bodies. The United States, with 16.7 percent of the vote in the IMF and 15.85 percent in the World Bank, has a veto power.

structural adjustment program
A set of economic policies prescribed to correct flaws in a national economy.

World Bank and IMF loans usually go to poor, indebted countries. Many loans are conditional. If the country accepts financial aid, it must agree to take actions that strengthen its economy. In the 1980s and 1990s the two organizations often required *structural adjustment programs*, or a set of policy prescriptions designed to reform perceived flaws in a nation's economy and put it on a road to growth. Because these policies were based on a philosophy of *liberalization*, deregulation, privatization, fiscal austerity, and tax reforms, they were criticized by global progressives as promoting a form of free market fundamentalism.

liberalization
An economic policy of lowering tariffs and other barriers to encourage foreign trade.

The conditions in World Bank and IMF loans were often said to be based on a *Washington Consensus*. This term was invented by a British economist, John Williamson. In a 1989 paper he set forth 10 policies that economists in the World Bank, IMF, and the U.S. Department of the Treasury prescribed as economic reforms for heavily indebted Latin American countries.[22] He believed there was a consensus among them that these policies would promote growth. Since all three institutions were headquartered in Washington, D.C., he called this set of 10 policies the Washington Consensus.

Washington Consensus
A set of free market policies imposed on developing nations by the IMF and the World Bank as loan conditions.

Soon critics of market fundamentalism and the spread of global capitalism broadened the meaning of the term to stand for a form of economic imperialism

[21] The World Bank consists of two institutions, the International Bank for Reconstruction and Development and the International Development Agency. It is part of the World Bank Group, which encompasses three additional institutions, the International Finance Corporation, the Multilateral Investment Guarantee Agency, and the International Centre for Settlement of Investment Disputes.

[22] See John Williamson, "From Reform Agenda to Damaged Brand Name: A Short History of the Washington Consensus and Suggestions for What to Do Next?" *Finance and Development,* September 2003, pp. 10–11.

pressed on developing countries by U.S.-dominated multilateral organizations to promote the interests of big multinational corporations. They were seen as "nothing more than U.S. imperial ambitions 'laundered' by law."[23] If nations accepted World Bank and IMF loans with *conditionalities*, they had to open their markets and turn themselves into capitalist clones. Sometimes IMF loans came with as many as 100 conditions, including lists of specific laws a nation's legislature had to pass. Rigid timetables might require a sequence of targeted actions every 30, 60, or 90 days.[24]

condition-alities
The conditions that accompanied World Bank and IMF loans, usually the adoption of new economic policies based on free market principles. Loans would be made in increments over time as conditions were met.

Although the fiscal and policy designs of the Washington Consensus sometimes worked, they sometimes did not. In Thailand they failed to curb rampant inflation. In Kenya an imposed policy on export incentives led to massive theft of public funds. Corrupt officials took payments of $400 million from the country's central bank—about 7 percent of the nation's money supply and 22 percent of its annual budget—for nonexistent shipments.[25] Many failures occurred because developing societies lacked the strong institutions needed to support free markets. Because of such failures loans are now less conditioned on growth policies and more on poverty reduction measures.

Although GATT was not a full-fledged international organization composed of member countries, it took on life as a "provisional" framework for trade negotiations among nations that became parties to it. As shown in Figure 12.3, between 1947 and 1994 the GATT parties, growing in number from 23 to 123, completed seven successive "rounds" of negotiation, each resulting in major tariff cuts. Over its life tariffs on manufactured goods in developed countries dropped from more than 40 percent right after World War II to only 3.8 percent in 1994.[26] At the conclusion of the last round, called the Uruguay Round because it was started at a meeting in that country, GATT was superceded by a new World Trade Organization (WTO), which was to continue the work of trade liberalization.

The World Trade Organization

The World Trade Organization began its work on January 1, 1995. Unlike GATT, the WTO is a formal international organization. It now has 153 members, including both countries and groupings such as the European Union. It is directed by the authority of a Ministerial Conference, a decision-making body consisting of all members that meets every two years. These "ministerials" are huge events attended by several thousand delegates from member nations. The WTO is administered by a secretariat in Geneva. Its structure also includes working groups and committees that are forums for year-round trade discussions.

Agreements reached under GATT were incorporated in the WTO. All member nations agree to abide by WTO rules and previously negotiated trade concessions.

---

[23] Jose E. Alvarez, "Contemporary International Law: An 'Empire of Law' or the 'Law of Empire'?" *American University International Law Review* 24 (2009), p. 826.

[24] Joseph E. Stiglitz, *Globalization and Its Discontents* (New York: W. W. Norton & Company, 2002), p. 44.

[25] "Kenya: Riches All Around," *The Economist,* August 14, 1993, p. 37.

[26] Kent Jones, *The Doha Blues: Institutional Crisis and Reform in the WTO* (New York: Oxford University Press, 2010), p. 43.

FIGURE 12.3
A History of Multilateral Trade Rounds
Eight rounds of multilateral trade negotiations were completed under the General Agreement on Tariffs and Trade. In 1995, GATT rules and agreements were incorporated in a new World Trade Organization. It launched a new Doha development round in 2001, which has not been successfully concluded.

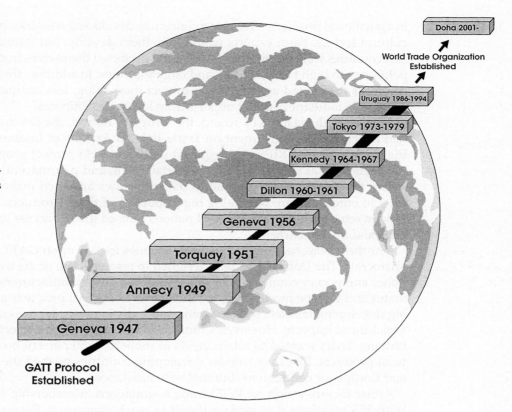

Doha 2001-

World Trade Organization Established

Uruguay 1986-1994

Tokyo 1973-1979

Kennedy 1964-1967

Dillon 1960-1961

Geneva 1956

Torquay 1951

Annecy 1949

Geneva 1947

GATT Protocol Established

New members go through an "accession" process, opening their markets to imports and extending most-favored-nation privileges to all other WTO members. In return, they gain reciprocal access to the other nation's domestic markets. When disagreements between nations arise, the WTO has a powerful dispute resolution mechanism. Under GATT the defendant in a dispute could veto a decision if it disagreed. But in the WTO the decision of a dispute body can be overturned only by the unanimous veto of all members, an unlikely event.

The WTO provides a framework for trade negotiations, but it has been unsuccessful in adding to the GATT legacy of trade liberalization. It has been unable to conclude a new trade round. It tried to launch a round in Seattle in 1999, but delegates failed to agree on an agenda as mass anti-globalization protests swirled around them in the streets. In 2001 it succeeded in launching a new round at meetings in Doha, Qatar, known as the Doha Development Agenda. However, the negotiations have since limped along through multiple breakdowns, growing so unproductive that one observer compared them to "watching paint that never dries."[27] Their failure can be traced to stubborn, unresolved conflicts lingering from the GATT rounds.

The GATT negotiations led to heavy reductions in tariffs for manufactured goods that liberalized trade between developed countries. Yet they failed to liberalize trade

[27] Sheila Page, quoted in "The Doha Round . . . and Round . . . and Round," *The Economist,* August 2, 2008, p. 71.

in agricultural products. This was a concern to developing countries with large agricultural sectors. Farm exports would help them develop, but farming interests in rich countries were politically powerful and protected themselves from import competition with high tariffs, quotas, and large subsidies. In addition, the industrialized countries negotiated agreements to protect their aging, less competitive clothing and textile industries against imports from low-wage countries.

Finally, in the last GATT round, the Uruguay Round, the developed countries had concluded an Agreement on Trade-Related Aspects of Intellectual Property Rights, known as TRIPS that required participants to protect property rights in products such as software, digital entertainment, and pharmaceuticals. Doing so meant that poorer countries had to pass new laws and then make expensive efforts to enforce them. Not being big importers of these products, they received little in return when the developed nations refused greater access to their agricultural and textile markets.

For these reasons, less developed economies looked upon GATT as a league of aristocrats. The Doha round was designed to resolve some of the tension between richer and poorer countries. The talks sought to give manufacturers in the United States and Europe more access to markets for industrial products and services in big developing markets such as China and India in return for lowering barriers to agricultural imports. However, China and India insisted on protecting their own farmers. India wanted to retain tariffs of more than 50 percent on some agricultural products. Blocks of smaller developing countries pushed the United States and Europe for concessions, but met with resistance.

Other factors weigh on WTO trade negotiations. Membership has expanded. With 153 members it is more difficult to reach consensus. Power relationships have changed. Trade negotiations are contests of power. Each nation seeks the advantage of opening another's markets to its domestic producers. But to do so it must give the other nation's industries access to some of its own markets. Influence in such negotiations is consistent with the comparative value of each nation's trade. During the GATT years the United States dominated world trade and gave strong leadership to a free trade agenda. Now, trade with developing nations such as China, India, and Brazil is a substantial fraction of world trade and they have more negotiating power. The United States and its World War II allies no longer can impose solutions.

For all these reasons the current WTO-led multilateral trading system has yet to produce a major advance in trade liberalization. Still, tariffs continue to fall and now stand at all-time lows. Since 1995 the world average for applied tariffs on goods has fallen by more than a third, from 13.65 percent to 8.76 percent. Between developed countries approximately 45 percent of all goods are traded under most-favored-nation rules with a zero percent tariff. Tariffs are higher in developing countries, averaging 12.27 percent in Sub-Saharan Africa, for example, compared with 4.47 percent in high-income countries.[28]

[28] World Bank Group, World Trade Indicators 2009/10, "Overtime Comparison: Applied Tariff, Simple Average, All Goods" and "MFN Applied Tariff, Simple Average, All Goods," at http://info.worldbank.org/etools/wti/4a.asp.

United States Free Trade Agreements

In 2010 the United States was a participant in free trade agreements with the following 17 countries. Agreements with three other countries—Colombia, Panama, and South Korea—were signed, but not yet approved by Congress.

- Australia
- Bahrain
- U.S.-Central America Free Trade Agreement
  Costa Rica
  Dominican Republic
  El Salvador
  Guatemala
  Honduras
  Nicaragua
- Chile
- Israel
- Jordan
- Morocco
- North American Free Trade Agreement (NAFTA)
  Canada
  Mexico
- Oman
- Peru
- Singapore

Source: Office of the United States Trade Representative

---

free trade agreement
A trade agreement in which member countries eliminate import duties and other barriers to trade with each other, but maintain them for imports from nonmembers.

customs union
A bloc of nations that form a free trade area and impose a common external tariff on imports from nonmember nations.

Regional Trade Agreements

The World Trade Organization is a singular, global trade institution. But it is not the only one. Nations also enter regional trade agreements with one or more other nations. Today there are 290 such agreements in force. Many of them are *free trade agreements*. In them, members of the group agree to eliminate import duties and other barriers to trade with each other, but maintain them for imports from non-members. The North American Free Trade Agreement (NAFTA) between Canada, Mexico, and the United States is an example. The nearby box lists free trade agreements that the United States has entered.

A few regional trade agreements are more precisely labeled *customs unions* because, along with creating a free trade zone among members, they impose common duties on nonmembers. The European Union and Mercosur are examples. Here, briefly, are the four largest regional trade agreements by trade volume. Most of the rest are bilateral agreements between two nations.

- The *European Union* (EU). On March 25, 1957, six European countries—Belgium, France, Italy, Luxembourg, the Netherlands, and West Germany—signed a treaty to establish the European Economic Community. Its objective was to prevent a recurrence of Europe's devastating wars. In 1993 this initial grouping was transformed into the European Union. Many national laws and policies affecting trade were annulled and replaced with hundreds of new rules and regulations to create a single national market allowing free movement of workers, capital, goods, and services. By 1999 the EU had adopted a uniform currency, the euro. In 2011 there were 27 member states, with a total population of 501 million and a GDP of $14.9 trillion. By both measures the EU is larger than the United States with its 311 million people and GDP of $14.3 trillion.

- The *North American Free Trade Agreement* (NAFTA). In 1987 the United States and Canada signed a free trade agreement. Then in 1994 that agreement was extended to Mexico, forming NAFTA. It has eliminated most but not all tariffs and barriers to trade in goods and services among the three countries. The average applied tariff for goods coming into NAFTA countries from nonmember countries is 8.76 percent.[29] Today this agreement unites countries with 457 million people and a combined GDP of $17.2 trillion. A major objective of the agreement was to increase trade among them. That has happened. From 1993 to 2008 trade among the three nations more than tripled, rising from $297 billion to $990 billion.[30]

- The *Association of Southeast Asian Nations Free Trade Area* (AFTA). The Association of Southeast Asian Nations (ASEAN) was formed in 1967 as a security alliance of Indonesia, Malaysia, the Philippines, Singapore, and Thailand to oppose the spread of communism. Since then Brunei, Cambodia, Laos, Myanmar, and Vietnam have joined. In 1992 the members formed a free trade area with the goal of gradually reducing tariffs to zero and removing other trade barriers. By 2003 tariffs had dropped more than 99 percent. All tariffs must be removed by 2015. Meanwhile, AFTA members can apply a tariff of up to 5 percent. Each member independently sets tariffs and trade rules with nonmembers. It has been especially difficult to dismantle trade impediments due to the economic divide between some AFTA members. Laos, Cambodia, and Myanmar are among the world's least developed nations, while Brunei and Singapore are highly developed. AFTA covers a population of 575 million in nations with a total GDP of $1.5 trillion. It has expanded its reach by entering into bilateral free trade agreements with China, Australia, New Zealand, India, Japan, and South Korea.

- The *Southern Common Market* (Mercosur). Mercosur is a customs union of Argentina, Brazil, Paraguay, and Uruguay with a common external tariff. Members are prohibited from entering free trade agreements with nonmember nations. It encompasses a population of 270 million and its members have a total GDP of $2.4 trillion. Its ultimate goal is to bring full economic integration to South America, but it has been hampered by feuding and tension among members. Some want to focus on economic development, while others want to make Mercosur a combined political and economic entity like the European Union. Some seek to promote trade with the United States, but others have strong anti-American feelings.

Regional trade agreements might better be called preferential trade agreements because they discriminate against nonmember countries. They undermine the

---

[29] World Bank Group, World Trade Indicators 2009/10, "Overtime Comparison: Applied Tariff, Simple Average, All Goods," at http://info.worldbank.org/etools/wti/4a.asp.

[30] International Trade Administration, *Top U.S. Export Markets: Free Trade Agreement and Country Fact Sheets: 2009* (Washington, DC: Department of Commerce, 2009), p. 26.

goal of a world trading system based on the most-favored-nation principle. Although WTO rules are guided by the principle of nondiscrimination among members, they leave loopholes that permit preferential agreements.[31] Some preferential trade agreements have existed for many decades, but they have proliferated since the early 1990s.

One observer compares these agreements with termites "eating away at the multilateral trading system relentlessly and progressively."[32] They now create a honeycomb of differential tariffs that divert trade from efficient producers in nonmember countries in favor of less efficient producers in member countries. With multiple free trade agreements any part or commodity in the global supply chain of a corporation can be subject to widely varying tariffs depending on its country of origin. Sourcing for lowest cost then requires navigating through a jumble of trade barriers, creating for any complex supply chain a chaotic tangle of routes akin to a "spaghetti bowl."[33] The proliferation of these agreements has bred concern about a global system marked by "incoherence, confusion, unnecessary business costs, instability, and unpredictability in trade relations."[34]

FREE TRADE VERSUS PROTECTIONISM

free trade
The flow of goods and services across borders unhindered by government-imposed restrictions such as taxes, tariffs, quotas, and rules.

Free trade, or the flow of goods and services over borders unhindered by government-imposed restrictions, has been the official policy of the United States since the end of World War II. It has taken the lead in creating international rules that advance free trade among nations. In practice, however, there have always been significant deviations from that policy due to protectionist pressures in domestic politics. Other nations that support free trade in principle also stray in practice.

Why Free Trade?

The case for free trade is straightforward. By virtue of geography, climate, labor conditions, raw materials, capital, management, or other considerations, some nations have an advantage over others in the production of particular goods. For example, Brazil can produce coffee beans at a much lower cost than the United States. Coffee beans could be grown in hothouses in the United States, but not at a price equal to what Brazilians can charge and make a profit. However, the United States has a distinct advantage over Brazil in producing coal because of its abundant deposits and highly developed railroads.

---

[31] See, for example, Article XXIV of GATT 1994, paragraphs 4–10, which allow customs unions and free trade agreements for trade in goods, and Article V, permitting regional trade agreements in services.

[32] Jagdish Bhagwati, *Termites in the Trading System* (New York: Oxford University Press, 2008), p. xii.

[33] Ibid., p. 61.

[34] Pascal Lamy, Director-General, World Trade Organization, "Foreword," in Richard Baldwin and Patrick Low, eds. *Multilateral Regionalism: Challenges for the Global Trading System* (New York: Cambridge University Press, 2009), p. xi.

**competitive
advantage of
nations**
The theory that
having a cluster
of similar pro-
ducers gives a
nation special
advantage over
other countries.

Professor Michael Porter has modified classical theory to fit the industrial world. He writes of a *competitive advantage of nations*. Porter asks: Why does a nation achieve global superiority in one industry? He answers that it is because "industrial clusters" are formed in the nation. These clusters are composed of firms and industries that are mutually supporting, innovative, competitive, low-cost producers, and committed to meeting demanding consumer tastes.

Why is it, he asks, that Switzerland, a landlocked country with few natural resources, is a world leader in the production of chocolates? Why is Japan, a country whose economy was in shambles after World War II, a global leader in low-cost, mass-produced, high-quality electronic products? Porter's answer lies in a congeries of factors that go beyond natural resources. Among the factors are a sizable consumer demand, an educated and skilled workforce, intense competition in the industry, and the presence of related and supporting suppliers. Government plays a part, but not a major one.

**law of
comparative
advantage**
Efficiency and
the general
economic wel-
fare are opti-
mized when
each country
produces that
for which it
enjoys a cost
advantage.

Resources are used most efficiently when each country produces that for which it enjoys a cost advantage. With free trade some industries will be less competitive. As they falter, resources shift to other industries that are more competitive, making them even more efficient and productive. Gain is maximized for all nations when one nation specializes in producing those products for which it has the greatest economic edge. This is what economists call the *law of comparative advantage*. It follows that maximum gain on a worldwide basis will be realized if there are no impediments to trade, if there is free competition in pricing, and if capital flows are unrestricted.

It is not always easy, however, to see just where a nation has a comparative advantage. At the extremes the case is clear, but not in the middle range. Differences in monetary units, rates of productivity of capital and labor, or elasticities of demand, for instance, obscure the advantage one nation may have over another at any time. Nevertheless, it is argued that free trade will stimulate competition, reward individual initiative, increase productivity, and improve national well-being. It will expand employment and produce for consumers a wider variety of goods and services at minimum prices and with higher quality.

This is the theory. It has been estimated that if all barriers to world trade were eliminated the global welfare gain would be $2.1 trillion. The benefit to the U.S. economy would be $497 billion, or about 4.5 percent of GDP.[35] In practice, this will not happen. All countries have at least some restraints on imports to protect their industries.

protectionism
The use of trade
barriers to
shield domestic
industries
from foreign
competitors.

Why Protectionism?

Most domestic businesses, whether engaged in foreign trade or not, feel pressures from foreign competitors, many with better products and lower prices. Some seek and get protection from the government. This is *protectionism*, or the practice of raising import barriers to shield domestic industries from foreign competitors. It exists in the trade histories of all nations. There are four basic reasons.

[35] Drusilla K. Brown, Alan V. Deardorff, and Robert M. Stern, "Multilateral, Regional, and Bilateral Trade-Policy Options for the United States and Japan," Research Seminar in International Economics, Paper No. 490, University of Michigan, December 16, 2002, p. 11.

trade deficit
A state in which the value of a country's total exports is less than the value of its total imports, either with a single trading partner or overall.

industrial policy
A government policy to shape the economy by promoting companies or sectors.

First, barriers help to lower unhealthy trade deficits. A *trade deficit* exists when, overall or in respect to a single trading partner, the value of total imports exceeds the value of total exports. In 1975 the United States enjoyed a small overall trade surplus. Since then, deficits have grown large. The trade deficit for goods and services in 2009 was $375 billion, including a surplus of $132 billion in services and a huge $507 billion deficit in goods. The largest trade deficit in goods with any country was with China, from which the United States imported $297 billion of goods but sent back only $70 billion. Other large deficits were $60 billion with the European Union, $50 billion with Mexico, and $45 billion with Japan.[36] Protectionists are concerned about the persistence and size of such deficits, believing they lead to loss of manufacturing capacity and jobs.

Second, some governments use an *industrial policy* to promote the growth of technologies, companies, or industry sectors. The chosen entities are often shielded from foreign competition, protected until they can compete on a global scale. China, for example, decided it was undesirable for its computer industry to depend on imported central-processing units. A state agency funded development of a new "Dragon" chip. Governments also subsidize the exports of favored industries. China plans to export its new chip.[37] A few sectors, such as munitions or armaments, are protected for reasons of national security.

Third, foreign countries sometimes use unfair trade tactics. Many have trade barriers to restrict American imports. In other cases they subsidize exports, which then enter the United States and sell at unfairly low prices, sometimes even below the cost of the same domestically produced item. In trade jargon this strategy is called *dumping,* and international trade rules allow countries to protect victimized industries and their workers by retaliating.

dumping
Exporting a product at a price below the price it normally sells for in its home market. This is usually done to build market share.

Finally, tariffs are important sources of revenue for some governments, particularly in low-income countries. While they account for only 7 percent of fiscal revenue in developed countries, they bring in about 25 percent in developing nations.[38] Markets do not register motives; if duties are imposed to support public services, they still distort prices for consumers and subsidize less efficient domestic producers.

The Politics of Protectionism

Protectionism is not solely, or even principally, an economic issue. There is an overriding political dimension. Although free trade benefits consumers with a wider selection of goods and services at lower prices, domestic industries that are less efficient than foreign producers lose financially and shed workers. Ideally, capital and labor should shift from these "losers" to industries more competitive in global markets. But when the diminished industries and their unions are large

[36] Figures in this paragraph are from U.S. Department of Commerce, Bureau of Economic Analysis, International Economic Accounts, table 2a, "U.S. Trade in Goods 2009"; and U.S. Bureau of the Census, "U.S. International Trade in Goods and Services," news release, September 2010, table on "Exports, Imports, and Balances."

[37] "Picking Winners, Saving Losers," *The Economist,* August 7, 2010, p. 70.

[38] Roumeen Islam and Gianni Zanini, *World Trade Indicators 2008: Benchmarking Policy and Performance* (Washington, DC: International Bank for Reconstruction and Development, 2008), p. xix.

and powerful, they seek to use the government to get protection. Although consumers get more aggregate economic gain in opening a market to international competition, each individual consumer gains only a small amount and does not find it worthwhile to mobilize and fight an industry's protectionist impulse. Here are two stories of American protectionism.

The first is about steel. When President George W. Bush took office in 2001, he made expanding free trade one of his highest priorities. In an early speech he was effusive about its benefits, saying, "When we negotiate for open markets we are providing new hope for the world's poor . . . and when we promote open trade we are promoting political freedom."[39] Why then, in his first major trade initiative, did he support substantial restrictions on imported steel?

His staff explained that the decision followed a thorough examination of the steel industry's problems and help was justified. For example, the industry employed only one-fifth the number of steelworkers it had in 1980, production had slumped, steel mills had closed, and the financial strength of companies had declined. The industry argued this was the result of lower-priced imports from many different countries.

Another reason for the president's decision was political. The industry and the United Steelworkers union have political strength. Consumers who paid just a little less for each automobile, refrigerator, filing cabinet, or wrench because of the foreign competition did not mobilize to lobby for the imports. On the other hand, the corporations contributed heavily to President Bush's campaign and their workers were concentrated in states with critical electoral votes such as Pennsylvania, Ohio, and West Virginia. In the close election of 2000, when the margin in the Electoral College was only 5 votes, President Bush would not have won without the 21 electoral votes of Ohio and the 5 electoral votes of West Virginia. In 2004 he again carried those states.

The second story is about tires. In 2008 the United Steelworkers petitioned to stop the import of low-cost tires from China by invoking a never-before-used "safeguard" in U.S. trade law. This provision allows action to stop "disruption" in markets that might "injure" domestic companies. The union claimed that over the past four years 5,168 rubber workers had lost their jobs and four U.S. plants had closed as China increased tire exports to the United States from 14.6 million to 46 million.[40] No tire companies joined the union in its petition. The nation's largest tire makers, Cooper Tire and Goodyear Tire & Rubber, had stopped making inexpensive tires in domestic plants. Instead, they were making them in China, some for export back to the United States.

President Barack Obama responded to the petition by raising tariffs on Chinese tires for three years.[41] In the first year the tariff would be 35 percent. It would fall

---

[39] Quoted in Joseph Kahn, "Bush Moves against Steel Imports: Trade Tensions are Likely to Rise," *The New York Times,* June 6, 2001, p. 1.

[40] Jonathan Weisman, "Obama Sets Tire Tariffs on China," *The Wall Street Journal,* September 12/13, 2009, p. A3.

[41] The President, "Proclamation 8484–To Address Market Disruption From Imports of Certain Passenger Vehicle and Light Truck Tires From the People's Republic of China," 74 FR 47861, September 17, 2009.

to 30 percent, then to 25 percent in subsequent years. At the time he did this he was working on a challenging legislative agenda, including a major health care reform law. The support of blue-collar workers and union leaders was critical. There were, however, costs to his action.

Low-income Americans would have to pay more for tires, perhaps driving longer on old tires at the risk of injury or death. There were fewer jobs for tire installers and dock workers unloading Chinese shipments.[42] And the Chinese government retaliated. It accused the United States of protectionism and calculated that the tire tariffs would cost China $1 billion a year in exports. To strike back, it targeted the $700 million import market for U.S. chicken. It announced that U.S. chicken growers had an unfair trade advantage because of federal subsidies for ingredients in chicken feed such as corn and soybeans. Then it imposed new tariffs of up to 31.4 percent on imported fresh or frozen whole chickens, chicken parts, and chicken by-products. Companies such as Pilgrim's Pride and Tyson Farms would pay these duties in amounts based on the level of feed subsidy in their products.[43]

Free Trade Responses to Protectionism

Free traders advance many arguments against protectionism. One main argument is the logic of overall benefit, as previously explained. Another is that a major cause of the rise in world trade—and with it globalization and human progress—is the widespread reduction in defensive barriers. Making a different point, former Sen. Phil Gramm of Texas once called impediments or hindrances to free trade an "immoral" violation of human rights. "They limit my freedom," he said. "If I want to buy a shirt in China, who has the right to tell me as a free person that I can't do it?"[44] And free traders are fond of quoting the practical John Stuart Mill, who wrote: "Trade barriers are chiefly injurious to the countries imposing them."[45]

Joseph Stiglitz and Andrew Charlton, in their book *Fair Trade for All,* conclude that rich countries should reduce tariff barriers but poor ones should be allowed to maintain them until reduction is comfortable.[46] They argue that some underdeveloped countries lack the infrastructure and institutions to open their markets. In many developing countries transportation systems are primitive, banks are fragile, educational systems are weak, and there is substantial unemployment. In brief, they are unable to take advantage of a liberalizing world. Each country, therefore, should be allowed to move to free trade on a suitable timetable. And rich nations should help poor ones to strengthen their institutions so they can move gradually to open markets.

[42] George F. Will, "The Cost of a Presidential Cave-In," *The Washington Post,* September 23, 2009, p. A29.

[43] Aaron Back, "China Adds to Tariffs on U.S. Chicken," *The Wall Street Journal,* April 29, 2010, p. A14.

[44] Quoted in Gerald F. Seib and John Harwood, "Disparate Groups on Right Join Forces to Make Opposition to China's Trade Status a Key Issue," *The Wall Street Journal,* June 10, 1997, p. A20.

[45] John Stuart Mill, *Essays on Some Unsettled Questions of Political Economy,* 2nd ed. (New York: Augustus M. Kelly, 1968), p. 38. Originally published in 1874.

[46] Joseph E. Stiglitz and Andrew Charlton, *Fair Trade for All* (New York: Oxford University Press, 2005).

U.S. Deviation from Free Trade Policy

Since World War II the United States has been the strongest global advocate of free trade. With the world's largest economy, it has offered access to its consumers as a lever for opening markets in other countries to foreign trade. However, all the while it has selectively used a range of defensive measures. Free trade rhetoric not withstanding, hundreds of examples of deviation from free trade theory and policy have added to the crazy quilt of world trade impediments. In a recent year, a trade watchdog group counted 69 actions taken by the United States that were "likely to harm" or "almost certainly discriminate" against foreign commercial interests.[47]

"buy American" laws
Laws that require or influence government agencies at all levels to purchase U.S.-made goods and services rather than foreign-made products.

Trade rules are marbled with *"buy American" laws*. The Federal Buy American Act of 1933, still in force, requires federal agencies to pay up to a 6 percent differential for domestically produced goods. Many states have similar laws covering a wide range of products. The Merchant Marine Act prohibits foreign vessels from plying domestic waterways. The Passenger Vessel Services Act requires ships going from one U.S. port to another to be U.S. flagged, U.S. built, and U.S. crewed. The $787 billion stimulus package of 2009 contained buy American provisions so strict that it forbade payment of money to a Maryland County for otherwise eligible wastewater plant equipment. The equipment required filters made by General Electric in Canada.[48]

U.S. average applied tariffs on all goods have declined significantly in recent years, from 4.62 percent to 2.54 percent between 1995 and 2009. But there are many exceptions. For example, there are relatively high tariffs on imports of sugar, peanuts, some types of glassware, motorcycles, and steel. To promote economic development the U.S. government allows duty-free entry of 4,650 products from 144 poorer countries. But in practice there are so many restrictions, exceptions, and limits on imported clothing, textiles, footwear, and agricultural commodities that poor nations, which are efficient producers of such items, wind up paying sizable duties. In a recent year, Cambodia and Bangladesh paid about $850 million in tariffs, roughly equal to the amount paid by France and the United Kingdom, although the value of imports from the two European countries was 15 times greater than that from the two Asian ones.[49]

Trade Barriers in Other Countries

Despite the benefits of free trade, all nations have some trade barriers. While tariffs have been steadily cut through the GATT rounds, especially on nonagricultural goods in developed countries, every country still uses them to raise revenue, protect industries, or bestow political favors. There are many examples of high tariffs designed to protect domestic producers. Japan has tariffs of 40 percent on cheese, 39 percent on beef, and 20 percent on cookies. China

---

[47] Simon J. Evenett, ed., *Tensions Contained . . . For Now: The 8th GTA Report* (London: Global Trade Alert, November 8, 2010), p. 218.

[48] Peter Fritsch and Corey Boles, "How 'Buy American' Can Hurt U.S. Firms," *The Wall Street Journal*, November 16, 2009, p. A5.

[49] Michael Gerson, "A Humane Trade Reform," *The Washington Post*, July 24, 2009.

imposes tariffs of 30 percent on motorcycles and video recorders and 35 percent on raisins. India shields its farmers with tariffs on agricultural products averaging 32 percent. It has tariffs of 100 percent on wine and 150 percent on distilled spirits. South Korea effectively halts imports of peanuts with a 230 percent tariff and of green tea with a 513 percent tariff. On other products it has low or zero tariffs, but sets import quotas and once they are exceeded further imports face astronomical tariffs; for example, 513 percent on mashed potatoes and 630 percent on popcorn.

nontariff barrier
Any impediment to merchandise imports aside from customs duties.

Even as nations' tariffs have generally fallen, nontariff barriers have multiplied. Common examples of *nontariff barriers* are bans, quotas, testing requirements, excessive inspection delays, and unreasonable health, safety, and quality standards. Unlimited and ingenious variations exist. Before it joined the World Trade Organization in 2001, China was one of the most resourceful countries. Since then it has removed impediments to meet WTO rules, but many remain. It allows only state-owned enterprises to import petroleum, sugar, theatrical films, music, newspapers, journals, and books. It bans foreign express companies such as FedEx and UPS from delivering certain documents inside its borders. It refuses to give nationwide trucking licenses to foreign companies. It requires importers of agricultural products to get an inspection permit before signing a purchase contract in China, but frequently, unpredictably, and with no explanation it slows or suspends issuance of the permits.

Elsewhere in the world, Saudi Arabia prohibits imports of alcohol, firearms, pork, and used clothing. Non-Islamic religious materials and radio-controlled model airplanes require special approval. El Salvador imposes a $0.04 tax on incoming telephone calls from the United States, but not on calls from other Central American countries. Russia requires that importers of alcohol pay customs duties in advance by depositing money in a bank. Since exact amounts are not known in advance, the government dictates a fixed fee that often exceeds what is owed. Refunds are delayed for up to seven months. France, Germany, Spain, and the United Kingdom subsidize Airbus aircraft to make them competitive with Boeing airliners in global markets. The giant Airbus A380 received more than $6 billion in subsidies, including $992 million spent by Germany to drain wetlands near Hamburg for its assembly site.[50]

We now turn to another major impediment to trade—corruption.

CORRUPTION

Corruption is a timeless trade barrier. Today, despite a limited but growing international effort to stop it, corruption remains widespread. In many countries it distorts markets, thwarts the efficient movement of goods, undercuts the honesty of customs and licensing decisions, and slows development. The World Bank estimates that corrupt expenditures are 5 percent of global GDP, or more than $2 trillion a year. In

[50] These illustrations are from Office of the United States Trade Representative, *2010 National Trade Estimate Report on Foreign Trade Barriers* (Washington, DC: USTR, March 2010).

corruption
The debasement of integrity for money, position, privilege, or other self-benefit.

developing countries where corruption is endemic it is the equivalent of a 10 percent tax and adds as much as 25 percent to the cost of government contracts.[51] In such nations public officials defraud the citizenry of an estimated $40 billion a year.[52]

Corruption is the debasement of integrity for money, position, privilege, or other self-benefit. Corrupt actions are efforts to gain an unfair advantage. They undermine markets by substituting dishonest exchanges for genuine competition based on price, quality, and service. They lead to inefficiencies and penalize honest conduct. And they violate maxims of distributive justice holding that results should be reached using impartial rules and criteria applied equally to all competitors.

A Spectrum of Corruption

facilitating payments
Small amounts of money demanded by minor officials to perform their regular duties.

Corruption has innumerable faces. Its universe is best illustrated on a spectrum, as in Figure 12.4. This spectrum is not hypothetical. Activity all across it is frequent and widespread. At one end are *facilitating payments*, or small amounts of money demanded by minor officials to do their duties, such as approving paperwork, clearing products through customs, or unloading cargo off docks. Facilitation payments violate anti-bribery laws in almost every nation but still are widely tolerated, especially in Africa, the Middle East, South America, and South Asia. They are sometimes justified as offsets to low salaries of public officials or union leaders. Their fundamental dishonesty is camouflaged by euphemisms such as "grease" or "tip," in English, and "baksheesh" (Egypt), "kumshaw" and "tea money" (parts of Asia), and "mordida" or "the bite" (Mexico) in other languages.

bribe
Anything of value improperly requested or given in exchange for a corrupt action.

Other forms of bribery span the rest of the spectrum, becoming larger toward the opposite end. A *bribe* is something of value improperly exchanged to induce corrupt behavior. A bribe can be either offered or solicited. Small bribes are endemic and routine in many less developed nations. A little farther along the spectrum are less trifling practices that pose subtle challenges to standards of integrity. An import expediter with family ties to government officials charges a fee slightly higher than usual. In a country where lavish entertainment is customary, officials draw out contract negotiations longer than seems necessary.[53] After a large forklift sale in Africa the manufacturer holds a program to train operators in a European city. Names of two ministry officials appear on the roster. A government

FIGURE 12.4 The Corruption Spectrum

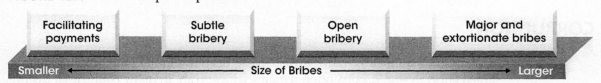

| Facilitating payments | Subtle bribery | Open bribery | Major and extortionate bribes |

Smaller ← — Size of Bribes — → Larger

[51] International Chamber of Commerce, et al., *Clean Business Is Good Business* (Paris: ICC, July 17, 2008), p. 1.

[52] U.S. Secretary of Commerce Gary Locke, "Remarks at OECD International Anticorruption Day," Washington, DC, December 9, 2009, p. 1.

[53] Kerry L. Pedigo and Verena Marshall, "Bribery: Australian Managers" Experiences and Responses When Operating in International Markets," *Journal of Business Ethics* 87 (2009), see pp. 64–65 for more examples.

procurement officer suggests that a company should donate some of its products to local schools.

Moving along the spectrum, bribes are more open and less modest. It is common for government or company officials to seek or be offered commissions, gifts, travel, and other improper benefits in return for their assistance. The following story is an illustration.

> Avery Dennison is a U.S. corporation that makes adhesives and labels. It does business in China through a wholly owned subsidiary, Avery Co. Ltd., with headquarters in Shanghai. This subsidiary wanted to sell reflective materials for road signs and vehicles to Chinese government agencies. To help win bids it engaged in bribery. One of its sales managers bought pairs of shoes for two officials with a combined value of approximately $500. Later, it hired an official from an agency, making him a sales manager. His wife supervised two projects at the agency on which the company wanted to bid.
>
> The company finally won two contracts to apply reflective graphics on 15,400 police cars. A manager agreed to inflate their price by 6 percent and kick back the added amount as a "consulting fee" for agency officials. It would have made a profit of $363,953 after kicking back $41,138.[54] However, the scheme was discovered by the U.S. parent before any payment was made. It reported the illegal activity to the Securities and Exchange Commission and paid a $200,000 fine. The Chinese government took no action against the bribe recipients.[55]

At the far end of the spectrum are extortion and outrageous bribery. In such cases high government officials demand large sums, percentages of contract value, campaign and "charitable" contributions, or lavish favors as a condition of acting. Such demands are often extortionate. *Extortion* occurs when a threat of lost business accompanies the solicitation of a bribe. If the bribe is not given, the needed official action does not occur. Here is one story of high-level corruption.

extortion
The act of accompanying the request for a bribe with a specific or implied threat of lost business.

> Frederic Bourke Jr. co-founded the Dooney & Bourke handbag and luggage company. Working with his next-door neighbor in Aspen, Colorado, he put $5 million into a brazen plot to take control of the State Oil Company of the Azerbaijan Republic, known as Socar. Azerbaijan is an impoverished but oil-rich nation with widespread corruption. The scheme required the nation's authoritarian president, Heydar Aliyev, to issue a special decree privatizing Socar. Then Bourke, his neighbor, and other investors would buy its assets in a rigged auction. Secretly, two-thirds of their profits would go back to President Aliyev, his family, and other officials.
>
> In pursuit of this plan Bourke and his neighbor bribed officials using payments with fictitious code names made through front companies and put $7 million into Swiss bank accounts for their children.[56] It was all uncovered by authorities in the United Kingdom, and Bourke was sentenced in the United States to a year and a day in prison and a fine of $5 million. His neighbor is a now a fugitive. Had this overgrown, shameless scheme succeeded, it would have defrauded the Azerbaijani people of a precious economic asset.

[54] *Securities and Exchange Commission v. Avery Dennison Corporation,* CV09-5493 (C. Dist. Calif., 2009), p. 4.

[55] Al Guo, "Call to Name and Shame Bribed Officials," *South China Morning Post,* August 12, 2009, p. 6.

[56] Brief for the United States in *United States v. Frederick Bourke Jr.,* 09-5149-cr(XAP), Second Circuit (2010).

TABLE 12.2

The Demand Side of Corruption
These countries are ranked as the public sector's perceived least and most corrupt in the world. The lower a country's score, the more likely foreign corporations are to face demands for corrupt payments.

The Corruption Perceptions Index 2010: Top 10 and Bottom 10

Rank	Country	Score	Rank	Country	Score
1	Denmark	9.3	169	Equatorial Guinea	1.9
1	New Zealand	9.3	170	Burundi	1.8
1	Singapore	9.3	171	Chad	1.7
4	Finland	9.2	172	Sudan	1.6
4	Sweden	9.2	172	Turkmenistan	1.6
6	Canada	8.9	172	Uzbekistan	1.6
7	Netherlands	8.8	175	Iraq	1.5
8	Australia	8.7	176	Afghanistan	1.4
8	Switzerland	8.7	176	Myanmar	1.4
10	Norway	8.6	178	Somalia	1.1

Source: Transparency International, *Corruption Perceptions Index 2010* (Berlin: TI, 2010), p. 3.

For corruption to exist there must be both demand and supply. In international markets the demand for corrupt payments and favors is highly variable. Table 12.2 shows rankings of the most and least corrupt countries based on surveys of business opinion. Possible scores range from 10 (very clean) to 0 (highly corrupt). Since corruption is often hidden and difficult to measure, the index reveals only perception. The United States ranked in a tie for 22nd place (with Belgium). Lower-ranking nations are the source of more demand for corruption. Typically, they have weak institutions. Flawed elections allow unrepresentative elites to retain power. Laws and regulations are complicated. Dishonest agencies and courts do not evenly enforce them. Graft overrides competition in local markets.

Table 12.3 shows that the supply of corruption is also highly variable. Here the 22 most developed countries are ranked on the likelihood that their companies will pay bribes when operating across borders. This ranking is based on several thousand interviews with managers in these and other countries. Here the United States is ranked in a three-way tie for ninth place.

The Fight Against Corruption

International efforts to reduce corruption have expanded with globalization. Though they make inroads, the problem abides and overwhelms their example. The first major plank in the anti-corruption framework was the Foreign Corrupt Practices Act (FCPA), passed in 1977 after Lockheed was caught trying to sell aircraft in Japan and the Netherlands by bribing high officials. An investigation found that more than 200 other U.S. firms routinely engaged in overseas bribery. It was an early effort that stood alone for two decades, lightly enforced, more symbolic than effective.

Corruption flourished as trade volume rose in the 1990s. Fighting it became a higher priority. In 1997 the Organisation for Economic Co-operation and

TABLE 12.3
The Supply Side of Corruption
These are the 22 industrialized countries evaluated in which companies are the least likely and the most likely to offer or to accede to corrupt demands in host nations.

Source: Transparency International, *Bribe Payers Index 2008* (Berlin: TI, 2008), p. 5.

The Bribe Payers Index 2008: Top 10 and Bottom 10

Rank	Country	Score	Rank	Country	Score
1	Belgium	8.8	13	Hong Kong	7.6
1	Canada	8.8	14	South Africa	7.5
3	Netherlands	8.7	14	South Korea	7.5
3	Switzerland	8.7	14	Taiwan	7.5
5	Germany	8.6	17	Italy	7.4
5	United Kingdom	8.6	17	Brazil	7.4
5	Japan	8.6	19	India	6.8
8	Australia	8.5	20	Mexico	6.6
9	France	8.1	21	China	6.5
9	Singapore	8.1	22	Russia	5.9
9	United States	8.1			

Development adopted an anti-bribery convention calling on its 33 member nations to make bribery of foreign officials a criminal offense, require corporate bookkeeping and internal controls to flag corrupt payments, and cooperate with each other, through extradition and other means, in prosecuting violators.[57] It also called on member nations to disallow tax deductions for bribes, which many permitted. This was a milestone because it committed the most industrialized nations to fight corruption. At about the same time regional anti-bribery conventions were adopted by the Organization of American States, the Council of Europe, and the African Union.

Multilateral organizations also engaged the problem. The United Nations passed an anti-bribery convention in 2003, calling on countries to enact domestic laws against corruption in business, elections, and government activity. In 2004 it added a tenth principle to the Global Compact requiring participating companies to adopt anti-corruption policies and controls. Both the World Bank and the IMF have rules that require loan recipients to take anti-bribery measures. Results have been mixed. For example, at the insistence of the World Bank the government of impoverished Chad agreed to use revenue from a new oil field for the public welfare. Though some money went to this end, Chad's president diverted $478,000 from the first payment to import European luxury cars for members of his regime.[58]

[57] Organisation for Economic Co-operation and Development, *Convention on Combating Bribery of Foreign Public Officials in International Business Transactions*, C(97)123/FINAL, May 23, 1997.

[58] Korinna Horta and Delphine Djiraibe, "Africa's Dangerous Treasure," *The Washington Post*, March 10, 2004, p. A29.

Progress in the fight against bribery is limited. According to the OECD only 13 of the 38 countries joining in its anti-corruption convention have imposed penalties in the 21 years since its adoption. Those 13 countries have sanctioned only 148 individuals and 77 companies.[59] Most enforcement comes from the United States.

However, the U.S. enforcement effort has been slow in coming. After passage of the FCPA in 1977 prosecutions averaged only three per year. There was little political will to apply the law strictly. Studies found massive business losses for U.S. multinationals in competition with firms from nations that did not prosecute foreign bribery. Most of this competition came from Europe. When the OECD adopted its new anti-bribery convention, it created a more level playing field. Then an amendment to the FCPA allowed the Department of Justice to act against foreign corporations if they did business in the United States.[60] After 2000, FCPA enforcement increased, and today as many as 30 criminal cases a year are brought forward.

This stepped-up enforcement chills bribery by the largest MNCs from Europe, Japan, Australia, and Canada that do business in U.S. markets. Yet U.S. companies continue to lose business, an estimated $450 billion over a 15-year period.[61] The reason is that MNCs from China, Russia, and some other developing nations now have the capital to compete in developing markets, but lack the scruples of MNCs from OECD countries. These "black knights" move in to meet demands for bribery.[62] Studies now show that as anti-bribery laws in developed nations are enforced, corrupt countries receive more foreign direct investment from MNCs headquartered in more corrupt countries.[63] This is one factor behind the growing investment of Chinese firms in Africa, Latin America, and East Asia. As anti-bribery laws are better enforced, world investment flows are distorted and a bifurcated world economy emerges in which more corrupt and less corrupt nations form separate trading blocs.

We now return to the Foreign Corrupt Practices Act to examine how this leading anti-bribery law works.

The Foreign Corrupt Practices Act

The Foreign Corrupt Practices Act (FCPA) makes it both a civil and a criminal offense to bribe an official of a foreign government or ministry, or a member of a foreign political party or candidate for office. It defines the act of bribery as making or offering to make a payment of money or anything of value with the "corrupt intent" to influence any official act or decision in favor of a company's business. The law applies to the actions of U.S. corporations and their executives anywhere in the world and to the actions of subsidiaries they control. It also

[59] Samuel Rubenfeld, "Corporate Anti-Corruption Effort Flagging as Enforcement Rises," *Dow Jones Corporate Governance,* June 30, 2010, p. 1.

[60] This was the International Anti-Bribery and Fair Competition Act of 1998, P.L. No. 105-366.

[61] U.S. Secretary of Commerce Gary Locke, "Remarks at OECD International Anticorruption Day," p. 1.

[62] Andrew Brady Spalding, "Unwitting Sanctions: Understanding Anti-Bribery Legislation as Economic Sanctions against Emerging Markets," *Florida Law Review,* April 2010, p. 44.

[63] Ibid., pp. 52–54.

applies to foreign corporations listed on U.S. stock exchanges and to foreign citizens who take actions in the United States or use interstate commerce to enable corrupt payments anywhere in the world.

For violations of the law's bribery provisions, companies can be fined up to $2 million and up to twice the pecuniary gain they derived. They can also be prohibited from bidding on government contracts. Individuals can receive up to a $100,000 fine and five years in prison, although application of federal sentencing guidelines has resulted in higher penalties.

Bribes paid by managers of one corporation to managers of another are legal under the FCPA, although they violate fraud statutes in almost every nation. However, if the bribe is given to a manager in a state-owned corporation, the recipient is legally a "foreign official, because employed by the government." Companies and individuals can defend themselves by showing that the bribe is legal under written laws of the foreign official's country. They are not allowed to claim extortion as a defense when the threat is lost business, only when they can prove "true extortion" involving threats of personal harm or property destruction.[64]

In addition, the FCPA requires companies and subsidiaries they control to keep accurate records of transactions and to use accounting controls for detecting corrupt entries. Corporations that violate these accounting provisions can be fined up to $25 million. Individuals can be fined up to $5 million and imprisoned up to 20 years.

The FCPA contains an exception for facilitating payments intended only to expedite "routine governmental action." The United States is one of only a few OECD countries that allow corporations to make such "grease" payments. The others are Canada, New Zealand, and South Korea. And in 2010 the OECD recommended that member nations ban the practice.[65] However, the FCPA allows U.S. companies to operate in business cultures where small sums are paid to obtain permits or licenses, connect utilities, speed inspections, or get police protection. Note that in the law illegal payments are not defined by their size, but by their purpose and the recipient. Even the smallest bribe to a government official, paid with the intent to corrupt, is illegal. Theoretically, a larger sum paid for obtaining a minor permit would be exempt from prosecution. In practice, no company or individual has been prosecuted for a single corrupt payment less than $1,000, except as part of a larger pattern of payments.

The FCPA is a powerful law with global reach. The stories of Siemens AG and Daimler AG, two of the world's largest transnational corporations, illustrate its strength. They also open a window into the vastness of the problem.

> Siemens is a giant. The German engineering firm has annual sales above $100 billion. Until caught, it used bribery freely to secure billions of dollars in government contracts. Investigators documented 4,283 bribes totaling approximately $1.4 billion

---

[64] See *United States v. Kozeny,* 664 F. Supp. 2d 369 (2009).

[65] Organisation for Economic Co-operation and Development, "Recommendation of the Council on Further Combating Bribery of Foreign Public Officials in International Business Transactions," C(2010)19 (amended) February 18, 2010, p. 3.

to government officials in many countries between 2001 and 2006. During this time Siemens shares were listed on the New York Stock Exchange and some bribes were paid from U.S. bank accounts.

A Russian subsidiary paid bribes of $55 million to get a hospital equipment contract. A subsidiary in Argentina paid $31 billion for a national identity card project. A Chinese subsidiary paid officials $25 million in pursuit of a high-voltage transmission line project.

Investigations in the United States and Germany revealed a tolerant corporate culture. High-level managers sometimes approved bribes. At lower levels managers held meetings about how to disguise them. Some considered it a matter of integrity to be "honest" with money in hidden accounts and slush funds, carrying cash in suitcases but never diverting it to personal use. Departments budgeted bribes along with other expenses.[66] Books were falsified. Internal controls were inadequate.

In the end, Siemens paid fines in the United States and Germany totaling $2.1 billion.[67] After disposition of legal actions in 2008, several managers were arrested in Germany. Siemens purged senior managers and adopted strict new policies. Its CEO resigned, but only to become the CEO of Alcoa, the big U.S. aluminum company that operates in 37 countries, including Russia and China.

Daimler AG is another German corporation caught in massive bribery and prosecuted in the United States using authority in the FCPA.

Vehicle manufacturer Daimler AG has annual sales of $110 billion. It is listed on U.S. stock exchanges. In 2010 the Department of Justice filed criminal charges against its German parent and three subsidiaries for making hundreds of corrupt payments worth tens of millions of dollars to officials in 22 countries. Bribes were approved by top management and identified in records as *nützliche Aufwendungen*, a phrase that translates into "useful payment."

To make these payments Daimler set up secret offshore bank accounts and routed money through shell corporations in the United States. For example, Daimler sent $75,000 to King Jack, Inc., a California company. Its owner, a man who lived in Texas, forwarded the money to managers of a state-owned Chinese company to further a sale of 28 trucks worth more than $2 million. King Jack did no other discernible business for Daimler.

In Turkmenistan managers who worried about losing a government contract gave an armored Mercedes-Benz S-Class automobile worth $400,000 to an official as a birthday gift. When a Nigerian diplomat approached Daimler employees about buying 10 buses, they inflated the price and paid him a "commission" of 11 percent or $60,000 when the deal went through. In Indonesia, a Daimler subsidiary paid $120,000 to a tax inspector, who reduced its tax payment by 18 percent.[68]

Daimler agreed to pay civil and criminal fines totaling $241 million. The Department of Justice attributed its problems to inadequate controls, a decentralized sales organization, a defective company culture, and complicity by top managers.

---

[66] Siri Schubert and T. Christian Miller, "Where Bribery Was Just a Line Item," *The New York Times*, December 21, 2008, p. 1.

[67] Department of Justice, *Steps Taken to Implement and Enforce the OECD Convention on Combating Bribery of Foreign Public Officials in International Business Transactions: United States* (Washington, DC: Department of Justice, Criminal Division, Fraud Section, May 28, 2010), pp. 43–44.

[68] Examples are in Department of Justice, *Information, U.S. v. Daimler AG*, 10-cr-00063 (Dist. of Col.) 2010, pp. 21, 43, and 66.

Corporate Actions to Fight Corruption

Managers at Siemens, Daimler, and other companies may have thought their bribes were necessary to do business. However, many companies resist illicit demands. They have a range of options when doing so. Consider the following hypothetical case.

> Your company is bidding for a large government project. Eventually, after two or three years of costly negotiations, it is awarded the contract. But just before the signing, you are solicited for a bribe by a member of the purchase committee. How can your company overcome this situation in a legally acceptable way without losing the contract?[69]

A company in this predicament is advised to look back and to look forward. Looking back, how could this demand have been prevented? The company could have included an anti-bribery clause in the contract. It could also have informed the purchasing agency at the beginning that its negotiation team had no authority to accede to requests beyond project specifications. Looking forward, how can the company respond? Its negotiating team should immediately report the request to management. The team might then go back to the soliciting person and, with one or more managers, advisers, or bank representatives present to witness the conversation, offer again to sign the contract, ignoring the request for a bribe. If the request is repeated, the person should be told that is unacceptable. The company can then threaten to reject the bid publicly, citing corruption. It can also go to the government agency sponsoring the bid and object to the solicitation. As a final step it could contact an anti-corruption authority elsewhere in the country's government.[70]

Here are basic actions multinational corporations can and do take to fight corruption. The list is distilled from advisory publications and company surveys.

- Set up an ethics and compliance program. Ensure it is supported by senior management and overseen by a senior manager.
- Establish appropriate policies. Set a zero-tolerance policy toward bribery in all its forms. If facilitation payments are unavoidable, make them more difficult by recording them with the official's name, limiting them to a set dollar amount, and making them one-time-only. Limit or avoid the use of petty cash funds and cash payments. Use electronic transfers in place of face-to-face payments. Write clauses in contracts to limit and clarify the amendment procedure.
- Publicize the anti-corruption program to establish a reputation for honesty. Make policies available to the public and to business partners.
- Train employees. Teach them to recognize how gifts, or charitable and political contributions can be subterfuges for bribery. Inform them about regulations and laws and of the risks of criminal prosecution.

---

[69] This story is in International Chamber of Commerce, et al., *Resist: Resisting Extortion and Solicitation in International Transactions: A Company Tool for Employee Training* (Paris: International Chamber of Commerce, 2010), p. 11.

[70] Ibid., p. 11.

- Assure confidential, rapid reporting of solicitations to management. Have a policy prohibiting retaliation against employees who report bribes. Have employees in positions with a high risk of receiving bribes or kickbacks sign periodic statements of compliance with company policies. Pay them competitive salaries to lessen temptation.
- Enforce penalties against violators.
- Use due diligence when hiring agents, consultants, and intermediaries or when taking on new business partners. Study the business climate of a country before entering its markets.
- Work with international organizations, industry groups, and other companies to share information about experiences with corruption, including the names of government agencies and individuals.[71]

Such efforts are effective, but also difficult to carry out. It is hard to monitor the behavior of agents and business partners. The difference between bribes and customary local practices of gift giving or entertaining can be ambiguous. And even within companies, conflicts exist about what constitutes bribery.[72]

CONCLUDING OBSERVATIONS

This chapter is a current snapshot of three timeless processes in human society—globalization, trade, and corruption. Each continues. There is much hyperbole about globalization. The integration of humanity is greater now, despite some resistance, because of new technologies. Economic globalization has led the way. It had a bumpy start in the 1800s and early 1900s, but the modern trading system created after World War II has led to explosive, widely based, and continuing growth.

One impediment to this growth is corruption. There is now much more widespread and effective effort by governments to control it. So far the results are limited. Laws that restrain Western multinational corporations from corrupt engagements are now better enforced. However, corporations from China, Russia, and other developing nations are less constrained. It seems unlikely that such a timeless phenomenon as corruption will be rapidly reduced.

---

[71] These points are compiled from International Chamber of Commerce, et al., *Resist,* "Annex: Guidance on Generic Good Practice Related to Extortion and Solicitation;" Organisation for Economic Co-operation and Development, *Convention on Combating Bribery of Foreign Public Officials in International Business Transactions* (Paris: OECD, 2010), annex II; World Economic Forum, *Partnering Against Corruption: Principles for Countering Bribery* (Geneva: World Economic Forum, 2005); and The Conference Board, *Resisting Corruption, an Ethics and Compliance Benchmarking Survey,* Research Report R 1397-06-RR, 2007.

[72] The Conference Board, *Resisting Corruption,* p. 27.

David and Goliath at the WTO

Jay Cohen, an American citizen, once had a lucrative job in San Francisco trading options and derivatives. However, he wanted to start his own business and make more money. Pursuing this dream, he and two friends moved to the island nation of Antigua and Barbuda. There, with the government's blessing, they set up an Internet sports betting site. Their business was successful, perhaps too successful, luring Americans to bet online and provoking opponents of gambling. When Cohen again set foot on American soil, he was arrested and imprisoned. Prosecuted by his own country, he asked Antigua and Barbuda for help. Obligingly, the tiny nation then challenged the United States in the arena of the World Trade Organization.

This is the story of that challenge. It begins in the balmy Caribbean, about 1,300 miles to the southeast of Florida.

ANTIGUA AND BARBUDA

Antigua and Barbuda (henceforth, simply Antigua) is a sovereign nation of two small islands. It is a former British colony that achieved independence in 1981. Antigua (an-TEE-ga) is the larger island with 108 square miles and is more developed. Barbuda (bar-BOO-duh) is smaller with 63 square miles. The two low-lying bumps of limestone and coral are separated by 25 miles of ocean. The little country has a population of 87,000 and a GDP of $1.1 billion.

The major industry in Antigua is tourism. It has been a minor thorn in the side of the United States as an offshore haven for tax evaders, money launderers, and illicit drug shippers. Another nuisance was added in 1994 when it created a free trade zone for bookmakers, allowing them to operate tax free. It expected that gambling activity would create jobs for Antiguans. All any gambling entrepreneur needed to set up shop was a license costing $100,000. The government used this revenue to fund computer training schools for Antiguans, teaching the skills needed to work for online bookmakers.[1]

JAY COHEN'S MISADVENTURE

Jay Cohen and his partners, all U.S. citizens, founded World Sports Exchange Ltd. (WSE) in 1996. It operated from the second floor of a strip mall on the island of Antigua. Cohen was president. It was one of roughly two dozen businesses doing telephone and online betting from the island. It lured American bettors with radio, newspaper, magazine, and television ads.

Customers set up accounts by making credit card payments, wiring money, or sending cashier's checks. Then they used passwords to access their accounts with a toll-free telephone number or by going online. Once signed in, they instructed WSE to place bets for contests in football, basketball, baseball, soccer, and other sports. If they won, the amount was credited to their account. If they lost, it was subtracted. Within two years, WSE had 2,000 customers. In one 15-month period it collected $5.3 million in funds wired from the United States. Its profits came from taking a 10 percent commission on each bet.[2]

WSE was exporting a service. Its actions would have been unlawful for a U.S. company. Sports betting is illegal in every state but Nevada. However, like other gaming sites in Antigua, WSE operated with a sense of legitimacy. It was licensed by the government and open about its operations. "People are more comfortable with us than with the illegal bookmakers," Cohen said, "They know that when they win, we pay."[3]

Meanwhile, opponents of gambling in the United States were angered by what they saw as brazen flaunting of the law. They thought that online gambling sites, flourishing where the trade winds blew, would seduce teenagers, ruin compulsive gamblers, and undermine American morality. Major sports leagues refused WSE and other offshore operators permission to use team names or use links to official league Web sites.

Soon the FBI started a sting operation. As part of it, agents placed bets through WSE. In 1998 federal

---

[1] Brett Pulley, "With Technology, Island Bookies Skirt U.S. Law," *The New York Times,* January 31, 1998, p. A1.

[2] *United States v. Jay Cohen,* 260 F.3d. 68, at 70.

[3] Quoted in Brett Pulley, "With Technology Bookies Skirt U.S. Law," p. A1.

prosecutors charged 14 offshore gambling site operators with illegal use of interstate phone lines to place bets. Jay Cohen was one of them and he was shocked. "We're licensed to do what we do here by a sovereign government," he told one reporter.[4]

Cohen volunteered to return to the United States, convinced that its laws did not apply to his business in Antigua. He thought common sense was on his side. He was so wrong. Federal officers arrested him on his arrival, charging him with one count of conspiracy to violate the Wire Wager Act of 1961 (the Wire Act) and seven counts of specific violations. The Wire Act reads, in part:

> Whoever being engaged in the business of betting knowingly uses a wire communication facility for the transmissions in interstate or foreign commerce of bets or wagers or information assisting in the placing of bets or wagers on any sporting event or contest, or for the transmission of a wire communication which entitles the recipient to receive money or credit as a result of bets or wagers, or for information assisting in the placing of bets or wagers, shall be fined under this title or imprisoned not more than two years, or both.[5]

Maintaining his innocence, Cohen refused to plead guilty or plea-bargain. He went to trial at the federal courthouse in Manhattan where anyone could have walked from the courtroom and bought a New York State Lottery ticket at a nearby store. At trial, Cohen claimed that his business was a foreign corporation engaged in legal activities that took place entirely in Antigua. He argued, somewhat cleverly, that customer calls and Internet messages from the United States were not bets, only instructions to place bets. All betting was done from Antigua. Based on the advice of an attorney he consulted, he believed he had acted in good faith, without criminal intent. Finally, he claimed that the Wire Act did not apply to the Internet, which did not exist in 1961 when it was passed.

Prosecutors argued that Cohen was violating the plain provisions of the Wire Act. His license to operate in Antigua was no defense, because the statute made bets over phone lines illegal unless gambling was legal in both their place of origin and their

Jay Cohen in a 2003 photograph taken at Nellis Federal Prison Camp in Nevada. Source: Photo Courtesy of *Las Vegas Sun.*

place of destination. Although he may have believed he was acting in good faith, ignorance of the law is no excuse. They also charged Cohen with aiding and abetting violations of the Wire Act because, even after his arrest, he never tried to stop his company's American operations and continued to receive a salary.

Cohen's arguments failed to persuade a federal jury, which convicted him on every count. In 2002 he was sentenced to 21 months in prison and went to a federal prison camp in the desert near Las Vegas.[6] Subsequent appeals were rejected.[7] He served 17 months and was released in 2004.

Cohen's partners still operate WSE. Although they live in the shadow of a criminal indictment they cannot be arrested on foreign soil, and Antigua refuses to allow their extradition to the United States. Enjoying the clement weather and graceful beaches of their tropical headquarters, these fugitives operate the business "to promote responsible gaming."[8] The business has done well, with profits rising to millions of dollars a year.

---

[4] Quoted in Benjamin Weiser, "14 Facing Charges in First U.S. Action on Internet Betting," *The New York Times,* March 5, 1998, p. A1.

[5] 18 U.S.C. §1084.

[6] Paul Blustein, "Against All Odds," *The Washington Post,* August 4, 2006, p. D1.

[7] See *United States v. Jay Cohen,* 260 F.3d 68 (2001) and *Jay Cohen v. United States* 122 S.Ct. 2587 (2002), and *Jay Cohen v. United States,* 128 Fed. Appx. 825 (2005).

[8] World Sports Exchange, "Social Responsibility Commitment," at www.wsex.com/, 2011.

GAMBLING IN AMERICA

Gambling has a long national history. It has moved through cycles of popularity and rejection. Today strong forces in favor and opposed are locked in battle.

In the colonial years the English settlers considered gambling harmless. The English Crown permitted lotteries to raise money for companies. In fact, the Virginia Company of London financed its Jamestown colony with a lottery. Later, the Colonists used lotteries to finance public works such as streets and harbors. Even churches, which would grow hostile to games of chance, were built with lottery funds. So were buildings at Harvard and Yale.

Gradually, however, taxation replaced lotteries as a source of public funding. By the 1860s only Delaware, Missouri, and Kentucky held state-authorized lotteries. Once gambling lost its civic justification, it was easy prey for moralists. State laws prohibiting various forms of gambling accumulated.

Gambling revived in the twentieth century and states began to reauthorize it in limited forms. A popular illegal game in the 1930s, the Irish sweepstakes, gave it new legitimacy. Ireland sold tickets that were smuggled into the United States. The proceeds were presumably used to finance hospitals in Ireland. Through the century gambling grew in popularity. Today only Hawaii and Utah prohibit it entirely. Other states' laws are inconsistent and vary widely. Playing online poker in Washington is a class C felony, putting it in the same category as rape.[9] But in Alabama or Massachusetts it is only a misdemeanor. Irrespective of this mix of rules, the country is awash in wagering. Many states that prohibit other kinds of gambling run state lotteries. And with the Internet, Americans gamble around the world from the comfort of their homes, though illegally.

Internet gambling attracts special ire from anti-gambling forces—including law enforcement organizations, church groups, conservative family groups, and sports leagues. They argue it is powerfully addictive and leads to bankruptcies, destruction of families, criminal activity, and a culture of betting that corrupts athletes. Especially alarming is the attraction of Internet gambling for young people, particularly adolescent males, who grew up on video games and are enticed by animated gaming sites. Without the maturity to predict the consequences, they are lured into a destructive habit.

ENTER THE WORLD TRADE ORGANIZATION

Jay Cohen believed that when the United States imprisoned him it might have violated international trade rules. He requested that Antigua challenge its actions in the World Trade Organization (WTO) and it did so. Thus, a speck of a nation took on the world's dominant superpower.

An important function of the WTO is to adjudicate trade disputes. These disputes are handled under an elaborate system of steps, procedures, and timetables, as shown in Exhibit 1. The first step is the consultation stage, in which members are given 60 days to resolve their dispute through discussions. If the parties cannot agree, an impartial panel of experts is formed to adjudicate the dispute. Panels are composed of three members chosen from lists of eligible participants agreed upon by all parties. Each is knowledgeable in the subject of the dispute. Panel members act independently of any government. Countries involved in a dispute can appeal a panel decision to a seven-member standing appellate body. Its members are appointed by the WTO for four-year terms. They cannot be government officials and must be broadly representative of WTO membership.

THE ANTIGUA COMPLAINT

In 2003 Antigua, which like the United States is a member of the WTO, started the dispute process by requesting a dispute settlement panel. Efforts by the two nations to settle their differences through consultations followed, but no agreement was reached and a panel convened to settle the dispute.

Antigua rejected the U.S. position that provision of gambling and betting services in the American domestic market by foreign companies was illegal. It argued that actions by the U.S. authorities to prevent or discourage cross-border gambling, including the imprisonment of Jay Cohen, violated U.S. obligations under a 1995 trade agreement known as the General Agreement on Trade in Services (GATS). Under this agreement, the United States had promised to open its borders to trade in a wide range of services, including online gambling.

[9] Michael Hiltzik, "Calling America's Bluff on Online Gambling," *Los Angeles Times*, October 19, 2009, p. B2.

EXHIBIT 1
The WTO Dispute Settlement Process

Source: Reprinted with permission of WTO Publications.

60 days

Consultations

(Art. 4)

During all stages

good offices, conciliation, or mediation (Art. 5)

---

by 2nd DSB meeting

Panel established

by Dispute Settlement Body (DSB) (Art. 6)

0-20 days

20 days (+10 if Director-General asked to pick panel)

Terms of reference	Composition
(Art. 7)	(Art. 8)

Panel examination

Normally 2 meetings with parties (Art. 12), 1 meeting with third parties (Art. 10)

Expert review group

(Art. 13; Appendix 4)

NOTE: a panel can be 'composed' (i.e. panellists chosen) up to about 30 days after its 'establishment' (i.e. after DSB's decision to have a panel)

Interim review stage

Descriptive part of report sent to parties for comment (Art. 15.1)
Interim report sent to parties for comment (Art 15.2)

Review meeting with panel

upon request (Art. 15.2)

---

6 months from panel's composition, 3 months if urgent

Panel report

issued to parties
(Art. 12.8; Appendix 3 par 12 (j))

... 30 days for appellate report

---

up to 9 months from panel's establishment

Panel report

issued to DSB
(Art. 12.9; Appendix 3 par 12 (k))

Appellate review

(Art. 16.4 and 17)

max 90 days

---

60 days for panel report unless appealed...

DSB adopts panel/appellate report(s)

including any changes to panel report made by appellate report
(Art. 16.1, 16.4 and 17.14)

TOTAL FOR REPORT ADOPTION:
Usually up to 9 months (no appeal), or 12 months (with appeal) from establishment of panel to adoption of report (Art. 20)

'REASONABLE PERIOD OF TIME': determined by: member proposes, DSB agrees; or parties in dispute agree; or arbitrator (approx 15 months if by arbitrator)

Implementation

report by losing party of proposed implementation within 'reasonable period of time' (Art. 21.3)

Dispute over implementation:

Proceedings possible, including referral to initial panel on implementation
(Art. 21.5)

90 days

In cases of non-implementation

parties negotiate compensation pending full implementation (Art. 22.2)

Retaliation

If no agreement on compensation, DSB authorizes retaliation pending full implementation (Art. 22)

Cross-retaliation:

30 days after 'reasonable period' expires

same sector, other sectors, other agreements
(Art. 22.3)

Possibility of arbitration

on level of suspension procedures and principles of retaliation (Art. 22.6 and 22.7)

The GATS is one achievement of the Uruguay round of trade negotiations conducted under the auspices of the General Agreement on Tariffs and Trade (GATT), an international framework for trade that predated the WTO. Previous rounds had focused on tariffs and trade in goods. Services were mainly domestic businesses. But by the mid-1990s advances in communications and transport meant that companies in one nation could supply services in another, even at great distances. Trade in services was growing and the GATS was negotiated to lower barriers.

During the GATS negotiations, each country created a schedule of commitments for opening various trade sectors. Once it obligated itself to exchange services in these sectors, it had to treat imported services "no less favorably" than domestic services.

During the GATS negotiations the United States and other countries worked from a common document that classified services in detailed categories. One of these categories was "sporting and other recreational services," which was subdivided into "sporting services" and "other recreational services." The latter included its own subcategories, one of which was "gambling and betting services."

As the GATS was hammered out, U.S. negotiators excluded "sporting services" from its schedule of commitments, but not "other recreational services." This may have been a careless mistake. But it meant the United States was formally obligated to accept imports of gambling services.

All WTO member nations are signatories to the GATS. So, like the others, the United States is required to meet GATS' commitments. Because it had formally agreed to exchange "gambling and betting services," Antigua believed it had violated the rules by imprisoning Jay Cohen. Not only did the United States try to obstruct those services, but in doing so it also failed to treat them "no less favorably" than domestic gambling services. This was because the United States allowed gambling in casinos, bingo parlors, card clubs, racetracks, and state lotteries. Horse racing bets were legally placed through U.S.-based Internet sites using the same telephone lines as Jay Cohen's company.

THE U.S. RESPONSE

The United States thought it had a strong defense on both legal and moral grounds. It claimed that Antiguan online operators plainly violated its domestic laws, notably the Wire Act. Some state laws

also prohibit illegal betting by wire, and two states, Utah and Hawaii, prohibit all gambling. These laws had been in existence for decades. The United States also alleged a sovereign right to ban goods and services that harmed its social fabric.

Unfortunately, argued the United States, when the GATS treaty was drafted in 1995, it failed to clarify that its market access provisions did not extend to "gambling and betting services." It had never meant to open its market to cross-border gambling and it should not now be forced to do so. Its government was obligated to protect public morals, including the protection of minors and other vulnerable groups. It cited evidence that Internet gambling was rapidly increasing in the United States, creating growing numbers of teenage gambling addicts.

PANEL DECISION

In late 2004 the WTO panel released its report.[10] The ruling favored Antigua. The panel held that application of U.S. gambling laws to offshore Internet gambling businesses was contrary to its GATS obligations, ruling that, whatever its current intentions, at the time the schedule of commitments was negotiated, the United States had clearly failed to exclude gambling services. U.S. laws that criminalized gambling were, therefore, a "disguised restriction on trade" constituting an "arbitrary and unjustifiable discrimination."[11] The United States denied offshore gambling operators the same freedom as domestic enterprises. The decision affirmed that the Antiguan businesses were lawful and entitled to enter the U.S. gambling market. Finally, the panel agreed that the restrictive gambling laws in question were designed to protect public morals, but ruled that the United States had failed to make a sufficient case that they indeed did so.

The United States quickly rebuffed the panel. A statement issued by the U. S. Trade Representative had this to say:

> This panel report is deeply flawed. In 1995 the [United States] clearly intended to exclude gambling from U.S. services commitments . . . Throughout our

[10] World Trade Organization, "United States—Measures Affecting the Cross-Border Supply of Gambling and Betting Services: Report of the Panel," WT/DS285R, November 10, 2004.
[11] Ibid., p. 270.

history, the United States has had restrictions on gambling . . . [I]t defies common sense that the United States would make a commitment to let international gambling operate within our borders.[12]

APPEAL

The United States appealed. In early 2005 an appellate body upheld most of the panel's decision.[13] It upheld the central finding that the United States acted inconsistently by barring cross-border online gambling while allowing domestic gambling companies to take Internet bets. It found particular significance in the Interstate Horseracing Act, which allows domestic betting services to take remote bets over the wires but prohibits foreign operators from taking the same bets. In such a situation, the moral justification raised by the United States lacked consistency and could not prevail.

However, the appellate body reversed the dispute panel's holding on the necessity of the U.S. laws for protecting public morals. It concluded that such laws could, in theory, be justified to protect the American public from immoral behavior. Nonetheless, it still agreed with the panel's finding that the United States violated terms of the GATS treaty requiring equal access for foreign operators.

NONCOMPLIANCE

WTO dispute settlement decisions are not binding. A sovereign nation cannot be forced to obey. However, if its members ignored the decisions, the multilateral trade regime, with all its mutual advantages, would crumble. The United States has generally, but not always, complied with WTO decisions. Between 1995 and 2007, for example, it encountered adverse rulings in 33 disputes. It complied with 26. It did not comply with seven.[14] The Antigua case would be one of these.

There was no further appeal. The Antiguan David had prevailed over the United States Goliath. The

[12] Office of the United States Trade Representative, "Statement from USTR Spokesman Richard Mills Regarding the WTO Gambling Dispute with Antigua and Barbuda," press release, November 10, 2004.

[13] World Trade Organization, "United States—Measures Affecting the Cross-Border Supply of Gambling and Betting Services: Report of the Appellate Body," WT/DS285R/AB/R, AB-2005-1, April 7, 2005.

[14] Bruce Wilson, "Compliance by WTO Members with Adverse WTO Dispute Settlement Rulings: The Record to Date," *Journal of International Economic Law* 10 (2007), p. 397.

appellate body gave the United States one year to comply with its holding before considering sanctions. Compliance required either of two actions. It could change its laws to permit cross-border online betting with foreign gambling services, bringing it in line with its GATS commitment. Or it could change its laws to ban all domestic online gambling, including online horse races, allowing it credibly to assert a moral corruption defense and close its market.

Domestic politics precluded both. A bill to legalize Internet betting would be blocked by a powerful anti-gambling coalition. A bill to outlaw any existing form of gambling would be frustrated by entrenched pro-gambling interests. Instead, Congress took a third path, passing the Unlawful Internet Gambling Enforcement Act of 2006, a law to stop most, but not all, online gambling.

The statute made it illegal to place, receive, or transmit a bet over the Internet if the bet violated any law in the state where it was initiated. Existing Internet gambling, such as betting on horse races, could continue. The law blocked the flow of gambling payments. It prohibited an online gambling business from taking payments from bettors using credit cards, electronic fund transfers, checks, or other means of financial transactions. Banks were responsible for enforcement. If they assisted such transactions or received funds from gambling, they could be prosecuted.

By enacting this law Congress defied the WTO. The United States then took a second action, making an end run around the ruling. It declared it was withdrawing the commitment to gambling services in its GATS schedule. In other words, it would rectify its earlier oversight by removing its obligation, allowing it to close its gambling market to foreign providers. This withdrawal was allowed under GATS. However, it would be very expensive.

When a withdrawn commitment causes lost revenues in other countries, they can request compensation. Antigua requested compensation of $3.4 billion a year, a figure based on its estimated losses from denial of access to the entire U.S. gambling services market. The United States disagreed with this sum and requested a WTO arbitration proceeding.

RETALIATION

Arbitration went forth. In it, the arbitrator calculated Antigua's losses as only those resulting from lack of access to U.S. betting on horse races. The arbitrator awarded it the right to retaliate by suspending its trade obligations with the United States in order to recover $21 million annually. Antigua was authorized to impose this $21 million penalty using trade preferences—tariffs or other barriers—that would ordinarily violate the most-favored-nation principle in WTO rules.

Retaliation has a place in the international trading system. It redresses an unfairly distorted trade relationship between a violator nation and its injured trade partner. It pays reparation to the harmed nation. And it encourages the violator to comply.[15] Ordinarily a country is awarded the right to retaliate in kind. That is, if the unfair trade practice is denial of services it is permitted to deny a like amount of services imported from the violating country.

At the time, Antigua imported about $102 million of services from the United States, mainly in transportation, insurance, travel, and telecommunications. In theory it could retaliate by suspending access or raising barriers in these areas. Yet that would be impractical. For example, it considered suspending telecommunications services from the United States, but calculated they were only worth about $5 million a year and doing so would subject Antiguans to much inconvenience.[16]

When a very small country imports relatively small dollar amounts of goods or services from a much larger one, the WTO sometimes allows a form of retaliation known as cross-retaliation, that is, it authorizes the injured nation to suspend its trade obligations in a different trade category from where the grievance arose. This is rare; it has happened only eight times in WTO disputes. However, the arbitrator thought it was justified and authorized Antigua to retaliate by suspending its obligation to protect U.S. intellectual property rights on copyrighted material up to the $21 million annual sum. This meant that companies in Antigua could request a license to copy and sell $21 million of U.S. music, films, and software each year without paying royalties or abiding by copyright protections.

For WTO members, intellectual property rights in trade are protected by the Agreement on Trade-Related Aspects of Intellectual Property (known as TRIPS), a companion agreement to the GATS that also was negotiated during the Uruguay round and went into effect in 1995. The arbitrator authorized Antigua to suspend its obligations under TRIPS. This was a highly unusual retaliation method. It had been used only once before under WTO rules when Ecuador was allowed to cross-retaliate against the European Union (EU) by suspending its TRIPS obligations and copying up to $201 million of sound recordings from EU countries.

Following Antigua's arbitration success, the European Union also requested compensation. Late in 2007 an agreement was negotiated. In it, EU nations were given new entries to service sectors in the U.S. economy including liquid natural gas storage, warehousing, and postal and courier services. No dollar figure was mentioned, but with this dramatic expansion of access the value of these concessions was "potentially massive."[17]

NO ENDING

Antigua has yet to exercise retaliation. It remains in confidential negotiations with the United States. In 2010 a Caribbean newspaper reported the United States had "apparently" offered Antigua $10 million a year if it agreed to shut down its online gaming businesses. A leader of the opposition party in Antigua urged rejection of the offer saying, "we must stand our ground . . . the U.S. government should not be allowed . . . to continue their casinos, horse and dog racing, [and] gambling sector while seeking to destroy our gaming sector."[18]

In the United States, the Motion Picture Association of America and the Recording Industry Association of America have pressed for a settlement before Antigua retaliates. They fear that if Antigua allows films and DVDs to be uploaded to the Internet, the economic harm would be far greater than the $21 million sanction. They also oppose setting a

[15] Gabriel L. Slater, "The Suspension of Intellectual Property Obligations Under Trips: A Proposal for Retaliating Against Technology-Exporting Countries in the World Trade Organization," *Georgetown Law Journal* 97 (2009), p. 1370–71.

[16] Ibid., note 35.

[17] Kevin F. King, "Geolocation and Federalism on the Internet: Cutting Internet Gambling 's Gordian Knot," *Columbia Science and Technology Law Review* 11 (2010), p. 56.

[18] "Deputy Opposition Leader Says that Antigua-Barbuda Should Not Bow to U.S. Pressure," *Caribbean News Now!*, November 16, 2010.

precedent for legalized "piracy" through a legitimate institution such as the WTO.[19]

A NEW DIRECTION?

The online gambling market is growing. In 2009 it generated global revenue of $26 billion.[20] According to some estimates at least half this revenue results from U.S. bettors gambling online illegally with offshore operators.[21] Internet gambling is still a small part, only 13 percent, of the $335 billion worldwide legal gambling market. However, it is growing rapidly and, as in other industries, it has the potential to be hugely disruptive. Already it is reducing revenues in horse racing because other sports events are opened for bets online. Operators of legal casinos and card clubs fear that gamblers may increasingly elect to stay home rather than visit brick-and-mortar establishments.

Technology now puts bookmaking in every living room and in every device with Internet access. At some point efforts to restrain consumers may be futile. In 2010 Rep. Barney Frank (D-Massachusetts) held hearings on a bill, the Internet Gambling Regulation, Consumer Protection, and Enforcement Act, that would legalize Internet gambling. It would require online operators in any country to obtain a federal license before accepting wagers from Americans. Federal and state tax revenues would increase as these operators reported customers' winnings to the government.

Advocates of the legislation argue that the existing situation of a broad ban is unworkable. It only pushes online gaming underground, turning otherwise law-abiding citizens into criminals and subjecting them to risks of criminal activity and fraud. With government licensing, online gaming sites would need to meet regulatory standards. In addition, a basic American value is the right of personal freedom. If millions of people want to gamble in the privacy of their homes, the government should not prevent them. Minors are an exception and licensed operators would have to use safeguards on their sites to restrict underage use.[22]

The bill's opponents disagree. Conservatives such as Rep. Spencer Bachus (D-Alabama), opine that creating a new "Federal right to gamble" will "open casinos in every home, dorm room, library, iPod, BlackBerry, iPad, and computer in America, many of which belong to minors."[23] Filtering technology is so flawed that young people will easily bypass it. And they are not the only ones who should, but will not, be blocked.

It is also persons who are alcoholics, sitting at home alone, drinking, gambling, and the person on the other end operating the Internet casino can't tell if that person is too drunk or not. A land-based casino operator can look at a person and say, gee, you are in too deep. It is time to stop . . .

Likewise, the person operating the Internet casino cannot tell if that person who is gambling on the other end is a drug user and has gotten high and is gambling away his fortune; if that person is mentally ill or not; if that person is developmentally disabled. How do we stop the developmentally disabled from losing their money, which is often government support money, through gambling?[24]

States rights advocates fear "the extreme step of refuting and jettisoning our national history and tradition of letting local and state governments decide what vices will be prohibited or permitted."[25] A conservative group, Concerned Women for America, sees the bill as "a policy that would inflict major social damages on American families."[26] And some law enforcement officials believe that expanded gambling will encourage more criminal behavior, including the use of gaming sites for money laundering.

---

[19] Gabriel L. Slater, "The Suspension of Intellectual Property Obligations Under TRIPS: A Proposal for Retaliating Against Technology-Exporting Countries in the World Trade Organization," *Georgetown Law Journal,* June 2009, pp. 1371–72.

[20] "Shuffle Up and Deal," *The Economist,* July 10, 2010, special report, p. 4.

[21] "U.S. Defers Bank Rules on Internet Gambling," *The Wall Street Journal,* November 28–29, 2009, p. A2.

[22] See, for example, "Statement of Annie Duke, Professional Poker Player, on Behalf of the Poker Players Alliance," in *H.R. 2267, the Internet Gambling Regulation, Consumer Protection, and Enforcement Act,* hearing, Committee on Financial Services, U.S. House of Representatives, 111th Cong., 2nd Sess., July 21, 2010, p. 6.

[23] Rep. Spencer Bachus, in ibid., p. 1.

[24] Michael K. Fagan, in ibid., p. 29.

[25] Ibid., p. 8.

[26] Ibid., p. 67.

Should the bill languish, the United States will abide, as before, with an inconsistent policy of privileges and prohibitions based on a patchwork of state laws predating Internet technology. This policy is increasingly out of step with public behavior. It is also awkward to maintain it under global trade rules.

Questions

1. Was Jay Cohen's conviction justified?
2. Do you concur with the dispute settlement decisions in the World Trade Organization in this case? The panel report? The appellate decision? The arbitration ruling?
3. Should Antigua and Barbuda have the right to retaliate against the United States by exporting copyrighted entertainment material? Is that a bad precedent?
4. Should the United States have abrogated its commitment to gambling services under the General Agreement on Trade in Services (GATS)? Did it have better alternatives?
5. How can the dispute between the United States and Antigua and Barbuda be resolved now?
6. Do you support the proposed Internet Gambling Regulation, Consumer Protection, and Enforcement Act? Why or why not?
7. Are current state and federal laws on gambling optimal? Should the nation move in the direction of stricter prohibition? Or should it move to more permissive laws, including those to legalize online gambling?

Chapter **Thirteen**

Industrial Pollution and Environmental Regulation

The Majestic Hudson River

Around 20,000 years ago temperatures fell and immense sheets of ice moved through the Appalachians, carving the valley for a great river. As temperatures warmed, meltwater from high elevations flowed south down a 315-mile passage to the sea. Rivulets became streams that converged in an exuberant, falling watercourse, a rush that finally slowed and widened to a majestic channel before mixing with the tides.

Thousands more years passed as the valley grew into an Eden of forests, wildlife, and native peoples. In 1609 Henry Hudson, an English navigator sailing for a Dutch corporation, journeyed far up its course, seeking a new trade route to China. It was not there, but he explored the river, which took his name. Dutch trading ports soon dotted its expanse. In the next century they supported a lively commerce in furs, fish, limestone, clay, and timber.

Over time, the Hudson River acquired a rich history. During the Revolutionary War, forts on its upper reaches blocked British armies. Later, its waters buoyed "a blooming old tub . . . propelled by water and fire" as Robert Fulton piloted his revolutionary device upriver at four miles per hour.[1] James Fenimore Cooper's characters darted in the region's wild forests. Washington Irving set "Rip Van Winkle" and "The Legend of Sleepy Hollow" on its banks. America's first native school of artists, the Hudson River School, painted its picturesque vistas.

Yet in America no purpose is as pressing as business. The delinquency that prowls free markets soon vandalized the river's natural glory. As the industrial age boomed on its shores, smoke from mills, ironworks, sawmills, and foundries filled skies where migrating birds once darkened the sun. Its forests were chopped for fuel. Its waters absorbed wastes. Inconvenient sandbars disappeared.

In 1929, far up the river, General Electric built two electrical equipment factories that used new chemicals called polychlorinated biphenyls, or PCBs. PCBs are a family

[1] Arthur P. Abbott, *The Hudson River Today and Yesterday* (New York: Historian Publishing Co., 1915), p. 75.

of artificial molecules having two rings of carbon atoms with chlorine atoms attached at one or more of 10 available sites. Depending on the number of occupied sites, they are light fluids, thick syrups, or waxy solids. Because they are inflammable and resist heat they made excellent lubricants and insulators.

At first PCBs were thought harmless, but decades later science associated them with cancer and other illnesses. In 1977 the Environmental Protection Agency (EPA) banned their use.[2] Meanwhile, the two GE factories, while obeying all existing laws, had released as much as 1,330,000 pounds of PCBs, mostly by hosing off equipment and letting the water drain to the river. There the PCBs collected in sediments. During spring thaws rushing currents scoured the bottom, covering and releasing PCBs unpredictably. Suspended PCBs rode downstream, infiltrating the food chain, contaminating drinking water, resettling, or passing as far as 200 miles down to the Atlantic Ocean.

Eventually the EPA calculated that the lifetime risk of cancer for a person who ate a half pound of fish from the river once a week was 1 in 1,000 and the risk of other diseases was 60 in 1,000.[3] These risks are very high compared with other industrial chemicals in the environment. The agency declared 197 miles of the river, from the GE plants down to New York Harbor, a high-priority *Superfund* site and developed a plan to dredge the PCBs out of the sediments. It asked GE to do the work and pay for it.

GE resisted, arguing that PCBs naturally degraded in the river or lay harmless, buried under layers of silt. Stirring up sediments would release more of them into the water. The EPA, however, believed only 10 percent of the PCBs would break down on their own. The rest would poison the river for centuries. It ordered GE to proceed. GE responded with a public relations campaign to turn the valley's residents against the plan. It also started a defiant lawsuit arguing that the agency's authority was unconstitutional.[4] Finally, the two antagonists negotiated an agreement. The cleanup would proceed.

The project was divided into two phases. Phase One was a test run to remove sediment from a six-mile "hot spot" just below the GE factories. If Phase One was successful, Phase Two would complete the project by removing PCBs along 30 more miles of river over five years.

Removal began after the spring thaw in 2009. Excavators sitting on flat barges did the dredging, dropping clamshell buckets to the bottom, scooping in contaminated mud, and emptying the contents in long hopper barges. Steel curtains were draped around the work to stop currents from spreading any stirred-up PCBs. Tugs moved the hopper barges upstream where the bottom muck and debris were unloaded, then sifted through successively smaller grates, screens, and filters. Filter presses squeezed out the water, which was treated to drinking water standards and returned to the river. PCB-contaminated residue was loaded on mile-long trains, taken to Texas, and entombed in clay-lined pits.

Superfund
A federal program set up in 1980 to clean up toxic waste sites. It takes its name from a fund holding money for the projects.

---

[2] The EPA classifies PCBs as a "probable human carcinogen." See "Polychlorinated Biphenyls (PCBs) (CASRN 1336-36-3)," Integrated Risk Information System at www.epa.gov/ncea/iris. Evidence of noncancer pathologies of the immune, reproductive, nervous, and endocrine systems is based primarily on animal studies. See "Araclor 1016 (CASRN 12674-11-2)."

[3] USEPA, Region 2, *Superfund Proposed Plan: Hudson River PCBs Superfund Site,* New York, December 2000, p. 11.

[4] It eventually lost the case. See *General Electric Company v. Lisa Jackson,* 595 F. Supp. 2d 8 (2009).

More than 100 vessels and 500 workers labored 24 hours a day, six days a week for six months. Although GE paid for it, the EPA exercised final authority. Each afternoon at 4 p.m. EPA and GE representatives met to discuss progress. The EPA had towering standards. It wanted more than 18,000 measurements of air and water quality and sound and light levels. Work slowed or stopped when limits were exceeded. It ordered repeated cuts into the riverbed until PCB concentrations dropped to 1 milligram per kilogram of sediment. To avoid propeller wash that stirred up PCBs it limited engine speeds on tugs to 1,000 rpm. Whenever "cultural resources" were raised, work stopped as archaeologists appraised sodden artifacts such as children's cribs and pieces of sunken boats.[5]

Eventually, 36,000 pounds of PCBs were removed from the river, only 80 percent of what had been hoped for. The price for Phase One was $451 million, including the cost of building a 110-acre processing facility and rail yard. Overall, GE has spent more than $1 billion on the Hudson River since the 1990s.

After Phase One GE and the EPA sharply disagreed on the results. GE thought that the EPA set impractical, unattainable standards. The agency predicted a resuspension rate of 0.13 percent of the PCBs dredged—the reality was 3 to 4 percent, about 25 times more. The EPA targeted 18 areas for dredging but only 10 could be done in the allotted time. Although 90 percent of PCBs were removed in two dredge passes, the EPA insisted on additional passes, each less and less productive. Samples showed more PCBs in the river water and in fish than before the bottom was disturbed. The company concluded that even "employing the best available dredging technology and controls, applying best management practices, and following all of EPA's directions," it could never meet the EPA's standards.[6]

Eventually, the EPA concluded that the dredging was effective enough to warrant proceeding with Phase Two. GE will comply, spending as much as another $500 million until work ends sometime between 2017 and 2019. It has little choice if it wants to continue its "ecomagination" strategy and call itself a socially responsible company.

The Hudson River story follows the line of exposition in this chapter. We first discuss the nature of industrial pollutants and the practices and social philosophies that allowed them to mar virgin ecosystems. We then explain how regulations such as Superfund developed to control and remedy offenses against nature, with limited success. Finally, we explore current prominences of regulation and how they affect corporations.

POLLUTION

pollution
The presence of substances in the environment that inconvenience or endanger humans.

Pollution is the presence of substances in the environment that inconvenience or endanger humans. Much of it comes from natural sources. Forest fires release particles and toxic metals such as mercury into the atmosphere. Water picks up asbestos as it flows over rocks, gravel, and sand. Natural background radiation in North

[5] USEPA Region 2, Oversight Team, *Phase 1 Observations Report: Hudson River PCB Superfund Site,* March 23, 2010.

[6] General Electric Company, *Phase 1 Evaluation Report: Hudson River PCBs Superfund Site,* March 2010, p. ES1.

America is about 300 millirem a year, the equivalent of 50 chest X-rays. Tons of oil seep from fissures in the ocean floor.

Human activity adds more contaminants. For millions of years, hunter-gatherer bands caused little pollution. However, a gradual revolution in agricultural methods beginning about 10,000 years ago led to more settled societies in which populations grew and people gathered in cities. Where they did, gases and particles from indoor fuel combustion for cooking and heating clouded the air. Significant death and disease rates are associated with exposure to the smoke of burning animal dung, wood, and charcoal, although this was unknown in those days.

Eventually, with the Industrial Revolution, cities swelled with workers. Spatially confined urban ecosystems were overwhelmed by concentrated pollution. City air was a haze of particles and gases from the innumerable wood or coal fires called for in daily life and work. A worse problem was huge amounts of human and animal waste. Dead animals, dung from beasts of burden, and entrails from butcher shops littered streets.[7] Water plant technology, widely introduced in the late 1800s, eventually ensured sanitary water supplies, but not soon enough to prevent a high death toll from waterborne disease. By this time, contaminants from fossil-fuel combustion and manufacturing activity were a serious added problem.

Most industrial pollution simply adds to background levels of natural substances, so that human exposures to metals, organic and inorganic compounds, radiation, and particles reach artificially high levels. For example, nearly all Americans over 20 years old carry elevated levels of cadmium in their bodies and about 10 percent carry levels high enough to cause kidney damage and decreased bone density.[8] Cadmium is a soft, bluish metal released into the environment by smelting, petroleum refining, and waste incineration. It settles onto soil, is taken up by plants, and then enters the food supply.

The rise of synthetic chemistry in the 1940s led to the creation and dispersal of persistent, complex artificial molecules used in plastics, pesticides, solvents, coolants, flame retardants, adhesives, cookware, and other products. The average person carries many of these substances in his or her tissues. One study detected 150 industrial chemicals, most of which did not exist 75 years ago, in the tissues of nine people. Their exposures could have come from any of 11,700 commercial products containing the chemicals.[9]

Industrial activity both harms human health and disturbs natural ecology. We will briefly discuss its impact in each area.

Human Health

Disease from industrial pollution is significant, but far less significant than disease caused by older, nonindustrial forms of pollution. Table 13.1 shows the estimated burden of disease caused by exposure to air, water, and lead pollution.

---

[7] Clive Ponting, *A Green History of the World* (New York: St. Martin's Press, 1992), p. 354.

[8] Centers for Disease Control and Prevention, *Fourth National Report on Human Exposure to Environmental Chemicals* (Atlanta, GA: National Center for Environmental Health, July 2009), pp. 199–203.

[9] Joseph W. Thornton et al., "Biomonitoring of Industrial Pollutants: Health and Policy Implications of the Chemical Body Burden," *Public Health Journal,* July–August 2002, p. 315.

TABLE 13.1   Percentages of Deaths and DALYs Attributable to Four Environmental Pollution Risks

Source: World Health Organization, Global Health Risk Summary Tables, October 2009 at www.who.int/evidence/bod. Figures are for 2004.

Risk	High income	Upper middle income	Lower middle income	Low income
Percentage of deaths				
Unsafe water and sanitation	0.1	0.5	1.4	6.1
Indoor air pollution from solid fuels	0.0	0.2	3.6	4.8
Urban outdoor air pollution	2.5	2.4	2.9	1.0
Lead exposure	0.0	0.2	0.3	0.3
Total	2.6	3.3	8.2	12.2
Percentage of DALYs				
Unsafe water and sanitation	0.3	0.9	2.2	6.3
Indoor air pollution from solid fuels	0.0	0.2	1.6	4.0
Urban outdoor air pollution	0.8	0.8	0.8	0.3
Lead exposure	0.1	0.4	0.7	0.6
Total	1.2	2.3	5.3	11.2

disability-adjusted life year (DALY)
A statistical measure combining in one number years lost to premature mortality and years lived with disability. One DALY equals one lost year of healthy life.

This burden is calculated as the percentage of deaths and *disability-adjusted life years*, or DALYs caused by four types of pollution. One DALY equals one lost year of healthy life.

As the table shows, exposure to four types of pollution causes 12.2 percent of deaths and 11.2 percent of DALYs in a group of 49 low-income nations but only 2.6 and 1.2 percent of deaths and DALYs in a group of 53 high-income nations. Most of the disease burden in developing nations is attributable to the centuries-old risks of unsanitary water and indoor combustion of wood and coal.[10] Urban air pollution from factories and vehicles causes only 1 percent of deaths and 0.3 percent of DALYs in low-income nations and 2.5 percent of deaths and 0.8 percent of DALYs in high-income nations.[11] Clearly, when nations industrialize, far from creating a deadly blizzard of pollution, they instead greatly reduce the overall burden of disease by lowering exposures to lethal nonindustrial pollutants. The main advances are access to water unpolluted by feces and the transition in homes from dirty solid fuels to electricity.

The Biosphere

Industrial activity also impinges on the biosphere, the slender margin atop the earth's surface that supports life, a space "so thin it cannot be seen edgewise from

[10] Mortality and morbidity from unsanitary water is caused by diarrhoeal diseases. Indoor smoke causes lower respiratory infections, cancers of the lung, bronchus and trachea, and chronic obstructive pulmonary disease.

[11] Morbidity and mortality from urban air pollution is caused by a wide range of respiratory infections, respiratory tract cancers, circulatory and heart diseases, asthma, and other respiratory diseases.

ecosystem
An animated, interactive realm of plants, animals, and microorganisms inhabiting an area of the nonliving environment.

ecosystem services
The productivity of natural ecosystems in creating food and fiber and in regulating climate, water, soil, nutrients, and other forms of natural capital.

an orbiting spacecraft."[12] The biosphere is home to multiple ecosystems. An *ecosystem* is an animated, interactive realm of plants, animals, and microorganisms inhabiting an area of the nonliving environment. Ecosystems may be tiny and short-lived, such as a pond in the hollow of a tree trunk, or as vast and enduring as the tropical forest that hosts it.

Ecosystems provide services that support human well-being. These *ecosystem services* are benefits that humanity derives from the dynamic work of nature. Ecosystems produce food, fiber, and water. They regulate climates; control flooding, pests, and disease; purify water; create soil; and cycle nutrients. Coral reefs, for example, absorb carbon, stabilize seabeds, provide plant and fish habitats, and nurture biodiversity. Ecological services are given away by nature, but if they were priced, one estimate is that they would equal world GDP, estimated at $65 trillion in 2010.[13]

Human economic and industrial activity capitalizes on ecosystem services. Recently, the United Nations commissioned a four-year effort by 1,300 scientists to study world ecosystems. Their report, *The Millennium Ecosystem Assessment*, finds that broad ecosystems are now degraded and under pressure.[14] Over the past two centuries remarkable advances in human well-being, including better nutrition, longer lives, and more material welfare, were achieved by exploiting ecosystems. Sometimes this exploitation damaged the ecosystem, reducing its capacity to continue providing services. Forests, for example, have been badly managed. While at the dawn of humanity forests covered 12.4 billion acres, they are now reduced to 9.9 billion acres and still shrink by 12.9 million acres a year, an area slightly larger than Costa Rica.[15] World forests provide about 5,000 commercial products, but as they shrink they are less able to support species diversity or regulate hydrological cycles.

The causes of ecosystem strain are multiple and complex, but they center on accelerating economic activity. Today ideologies of affluence support rising per capita consumption and spur global trade that exploits distant ecosystems. Pollution and waste increase. This creates a danger of exceeding natural limits and thresholds. For example, living coral reefs host intricate interactions among thousands of species. When they are bathed by even small amounts of pollution from nearby coastal cities, they undergo a rapidly cascading series of negative changes, ultimately becoming overgrown with algae. Already, about 20 percent of the world's coral reefs have been destroyed.[16] Similarly, when an area of habitat is reduced past a threshold point that a species requires to survive, the species is irreversibly doomed though it may be decades before the last member dies. The

---

[12] E. O. Wilson, "Hotspots: Preserving Pieces of a Fragile Biosphere," *National Geographic,* January 2002, p. 86.

[13] Edward O. Wilson, "That's Life," *The New York Times,* September 6, 2007, p. A25; and International Monetary Fund, *World Economic Outlook 2010* (Washington, DC: IMF, April 2010), table A1.

[14] Rashid Hassan, Robert Scholes, and Neville Ash, *Ecosystems and Human Well-being: Current State and Trends,* vol. 1 (Washington, DC: Island Press, 2006).

[15] Ibid., p. 16; and Food and Agricultural Organization of the United Nations, *Global Forest Resource Assessment: Key Findings* (Rome: Forestry Department, 2010), p. 3.

[16] Hassan, Scholes, and Ash, *Ecosystems and Human Well-being: Current State and Trends,* p. 515.

lesson is that economic activity is not now always, but must ultimately become, sustainable. Otherwise, deterioration in ecosystem services will limit human well-being.

INDUSTRIAL ACTIVITY AND SUSTAINABILITY

Some nations with ambitious development plans still put industry before environmental protection. Poor nations house the vast majority of the 2.6 billion people with purchasing power of less than $2 per day.[17] Their leaders see industrial growth as the only practical way of raising living standards and building national power. If these populous, underdeveloped nations take the path of the environmentally destructive eighteenth and nineteenth century Industrial Revolution in Europe, the United States, and Japan, the resulting pollution and resource depletion could lead to ecological disaster.

sustainable development
Nonpolluting economic growth that raises standards of living without depleting the net resources of the earth.

Much interest today is focused on the notion of *sustainable development*, that is, nonpolluting economic growth that raises standards of living without depleting the net resources of the earth. However, the modern industrial revolution, as it is currently unfolding in developing nations, bears little resemblance to this ideal. In fact, at least in its early stages, it promises to exceed the old-time industrial revolutions in generating pollution and depleting resources. The new industrialization is faster. Economic growth rates in countries such as Korea, Thailand, and China have compressed the transformation into less than two decades rather than the 100 years and more it took England and the United States. As growth skyrockets, a range of modern industries quickly appears, creating more varied and dangerous pollutants than were typical of eighteenth and nineteenth century factories.

environmental Kuznets curve
An inverted U-shaped curve illustrating that as gross domestic product rises in emerging economies pollution goes through stages of rapid increase, leveling off, and decline.

However, there is evidence that environmental quality in growing economies does not follow a path of long-term deterioration as in the old Industrial Revolution model. Studies suggest that developing economies now follow a sequence in which pollution rises in the early stages of growth when incomes are low. As per capita gross domestic product continues to rise, pollution reaches a peak and eventually decreases, even as GDP continues to rise. This phenomenon can be represented as an inverted U-shaped curve, known as an *environmental Kuznets curve*,[18] illustrated in Figure 13.1.

Researchers studying more than 50 countries found, for example, a rapid rise of sulfur dioxide emissions in the cities of countries undergoing economic development. Sulfur dioxide, a by-product of coal and oil combustion, is closely associated with industrialization. But this rise slowed and eventually leveled off when per capita GDP, measured as purchasing power parity with U.S. dollars, reached about $4,000. After that, emissions began to decline, even as incomes continued to rise. Particle emissions leveled off later, at a per capita GDP of around $8,000, and

---

[17] World Bank, *World Development Indicators: 2010* (Washington, DC: World Bank, April 2010), table 2.1.

[18] Simon Kuznets won the 1971 Nobel prize in economics for his studies of economic growth. He also said that, in addition to environmental quality, income inequality followed an inverted U-shaped relationship during development, first worsening, then leveling off, then declining.

FIGURE 13.1
The
Environmental
Kuznets
Curve

Source: Adapted
from Hakan Nord-
ström and Scott
Vaughan, *Trade and
Environment* (Geneva:
WTO Publications,
1999), p. 48.

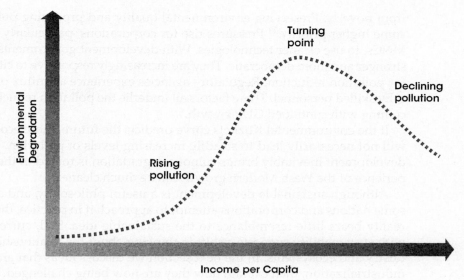

three types of water pollution leveled off at $7,500.[19] Other studies find that, for example, forest shrinkage stops and regrowth begins at a turning point of about $9,000 and asbestos use peaks between $10,000 and $15,000, then falls toward abandonment.[20]

These findings support the existence of an inverted U pattern for these pollutants. Although not all studies have arrived at the same figures and not all pollutants studied trace an inverted U pattern, there is general support for the theory.[21]

Many factors explain the environmental Kuznets curve. To begin, as countries industrialize, their economies change in composition. Early on, less capital-intensive agricultural and food processing sectors dominate. Pollution from them is quantitatively less and less toxic than from industries that come later. In the middle stages of industrialization, enough capital has accumulated to bring in more polluting industries such as cement, chemicals, and rubber. Other polluters that need even more capital and technical skill, including basic metals, paper and printing, and machinery, soon follow.[22] As the economy matures, however, the last structural shifts expand much cleaner technology and service industries.

Even as pollution rises, growth is bringing other changes. With greater affluence there is more education. Shifts in cultural values occur as the population ascends

[19] Gene M. Grossman and Alan B. Krueger, "Economic Growth and the Environment," *Quarterly Journal of Economics,* May 1995, p. 353.

[20] Ronald Raunikar, et al., "Global Outlook for Wood and Forests with the Bioenergy Demand Implied by Scenarios of the IPCC," *Forest Policy and Economics* 12 (2010); and Giang Vinh Le, et al., "National Use of Asbestos in Relation to Economic Development," *Environmental Health Perspectives,* January 2010.

[21] Michael J. Lamia, "Long-Run Determinants of Pollution: A Robustness Analysis," *Ecological Economics* 69 (2010).

[22] Richard M. Auty, "Pollution Patterns during the Industrial Transition," *The Geographic Journal,* July 1997, p. 206.

from poverty. Preserving environmental quality and protecting public health assume higher priority.[23] Pressures rise for corporations, particularly highly visible MNCs, to use cleaner technologies. With development governments tend to grow stronger and more democratic. They are increasingly responsive to citizen demands for pollution reduction. Regulatory agencies experience an influx of more technically skilled personnel. These factors all underlie the pollution reductions observed coming with continued GDP growth.

If the environmental Kuznets curve predicts the future, more economic growth will not necessarily lead to steadily increasing levels of pollution. The view that development inevitably brings ruinous degradation is rooted in the historical experience of the West. Modern growth can be much cleaner.

Although sustainable development is a useful philosophy, and as we will see, some nations and corporations attempt to approach it in practice, the broad global reality bears little resemblance to the sustainable idea. Still, current fascination with sustainability suggests a shift in thinking about the relationship between industry and ecosystems. In the next section we discuss ideas that arose to support industrialization, then explain how they are now being challenged.

IDEAS SHAPE ATTITUDES TOWARD THE ENVIRONMENT

What is the proper relationship between business and nature? In the past, and to some extent still, Western values that regard nature as an adversary to be conquered have legitimized industrial activity. These values were incubated in ancient Mediterranean society. Eventually they appeared in biblical text, giving them religious sanction and magnifying their influence. In the story of creation in Genesis, God creates first nature and then man and afterward instructs man on how to relate to nature.

> Be fruitful and multiply, and replenish the earth and subdue it; and have dominion over the fish of the sea, and over the fowl of the air, and over every living thing that moveth upon the earth. (Genesis 1:28)

This Judeo-Christian view laid the foundation for the conviction in Western civilization that humans were both separate from and superior to the natural world. It also incorporated the idea that humans must exercise wise stewardship over their dominion, but until recently the stewardship idea languished as a minor theme.

When church dogma began to lose its primacy during the Renaissance in Europe, secular philosophers did not reject the biblical doctrine of human superiority to nature but reinforced it with their own worldly thinking. Within the comparatively short span of 150 years, four new ideas appeared that, combined, determined how nature would be regarded and treated during the coming Industrial Revolution.

---

[23] Hoon Park, Clifford Russell, and Junsoo Lee, "National Culture and Environmental Sustainability: A Cross-National Analysis," *Journal of Economics and Finance,* Spring 2007.

dualism
The theory that humans are separate from nature because they have the power of reason and, unlike plants and animals, souls.

The theory of *dualism* held that humans were separate from nature. The French philosopher René Descartes (1596–1650) believed that nature operated like a machine, according to fixed laws that humans could study and understand. Humans were separate from nature and other living organisms because they alone had the power of reason and, unlike plants and animals, had souls. Descartes' perspective laid the foundation for modern experimental science but also established a dualism reinforcing the Judeo–Christian idea that humans were superior to and apart from nature.

progress
The belief that history is a narrative of improvement in which humanity moves from lower to higher levels of perfection.

The Renaissance brought improved living conditions, growth of cities, inventions, and the birth of industries. Such events kindled great optimism in European intellectuals who wrote about the idea of *progress,* or the belief that history was a narrative of improvement in which humanity moved from lower to higher levels on an inevitable march to perfection. This idea rejected the pessimism of previous civilizations that had looked back on past golden eras. Charles Darwin's theory of evolution supported the idea of progress in the popular mind. As industry expanded, the exploitation of nature for human welfare was soon entwined with the notion of progress.

capitalism
An economy in which private individuals and corporations own the means of production and, motivated by the desire for profit, compete in free markets under conditions of limited restraint by government. In this economy, nature is valued primarily as an input into the production process.

Then, during the early years of the Industrial Revolution in England, powerful doctrines of economics and ethics arose, which in additional ways justified the exploitation of nature. The theory of *capitalism,* based on principles set forth by Adam Smith in 1776, valued nature primarily as a commodity to be used in wealth-creating activity that increased the vigor, welfare, and comfort of society. As a practical matter, early capitalism in action largely ignored environmental damage. This tendency still exists. For example, the gross domestic product, the accounting system of capitalism, rises when goods and services are produced but does not fall when pollution damage occurs. Thus, the GDP rose because of the British Petroleum oil leak in the Gulf of Mexico in 2010, adding hundreds of millions of dollars spent on the cleanup but not subtracting the costs of dead fisheries and degraded estuaries.

utilitarianism
The ethical philosophy of the greatest good for the greatest number.

Finally, the doctrine of *utilitarianism,* or "the greatest good for the greatest number," arrived in England simultaneously with the rise of capitalism. It also was used to justify economic activity that assaulted nature. Industry made the utilitarian argument that, although pollution was noxious, the economic benefits of jobs, products, taxes, and growth outweighed environmental costs and were the "greatest good." Utilitarianism was an ethical worldview that rationalized the destructive side effects of commerce. It blinded Western societies to alternative, but less exploitive, views of nature.

In Eastern civilization, the values of Buddhism, Confucianism, and Taoism placed stronger emphasis on the interconnection of people and nature. They supported a more humble, less domineering role for humanity. However, their main impact was on interpersonal relations. Industrialization in Asia has been as destructive of the environment as in the West.

New Ideas Challenge the Old

In the second half of the twentieth century, an alternative, nonexploitive environmental ethic emerged. Naturalist Aldo Leopold pioneered the revised worldview. His

land ethic
A theory that humans are part of an ethical community that includes not only other human beings but all elements of the natural environment. It implies an ethical duty to nature as well as humanity.

seminal statement of a new *land ethic* in a 1949 book, *A Sand County Almanac,* inspired others to rethink traditional ideas about the man–nature relationship. He wrote:

> All ethics so far evolved rest upon a single premise: that the individual is a member of a community of interdependent parts . . . The land ethic simply enlarges the boundaries of the community to include soils, waters, plants, and animals, or collectively: the land . . . In short, a land ethic changes the role of *Homo sapiens* from conqueror of the land-community to plain member and citizen of it. It implies respect for his fellow members and also respect for the community as such.[24]

For Leopold, the conventional boundaries of ethical duty were too narrow. Expansion was merited to include not only duties toward fellow humans but also duties to nonhuman entities in nature, both living and nonliving.

In the early 1970s, a more radical form of this land ethic came from Norwegian philosopher Arne Naess. Naess argued that Leopold and mainstream environmentalists were too shallow in their thinking because they were conciliatory with the industrial age worldview. Naess said there were "deeper concerns" than how to compromise the protection of nature with ongoing economic activity. His position came to be called *deep ecology.* Naess argued that human domination of nature should cease. Philosophies of domination should be replaced by a "biospheric egalitarianism" in which all species had equal rights to live and flourish. Nature should no longer be valued only as inputs for factories, as in capitalist economics, because it has an intrinsic value that must not be compromised. In short, Naess rejected the four traditional ideas about the man–nature relationship that support industrial activity. He concluded that the present level of human interference in nature was excessive and detrimental and that drastic changes were needed.[25]

deep ecology
A theory that rejects human domination of nature and holds that humans have only equal rights with other species, not superior rights. Human interference with nature is now excessive and must be drastically reduced.

The views of Naess and other philosophers who share his thinking inspired anti-corporate environmental groups. Some, such as Earth First! and the Environmental Liberation Front, believe that extreme measures, including disregard for the law, are warranted by the moral obligation to end destruction of nature.

speciesism
Bias by humans toward members of their own species and prejudice against members of other species.

Other new philosophies justify the expansion of rights to nonhuman entities. For example, philosopher Peter Singer popularized the idea of *speciesism,* or "a prejudice or attitude of bias toward the members of one's own species and against those of members of other species," that is analogous to racism or sexism.[26] The racist and sexist believe that skin color and sex determine people's worth; the speciesist believes that the number of one's legs or whether one lives in trees, the sea, or a condominium determines one's rights. Traditionally, when *Homo sapiens* compete for rights with plants and animals, the latter have lost. Singer argues that humans, though superior in important ways, are simply one species among many. And the others have intrinsic value independent of any economic usefulness to *Homo sapiens.*

[24] Aldo Leopold, *A Sand County Almanac* (New York: Ballantine, 1970), pp. 239–40.

[25] Naess' basic arguments are in "The Shallow and the Deep, Long-Range Ecology Movement: A Summary," *Inquiry,* Spring 1973; and "A Defense of the Deep Ecology Movement," *Environmental Economics,* Fall 1984.

[26] Peter Singer, *Animal Liberation* (New York: Avon, 1975), p. 7.

Singer's arguments, like those of Naess, challenge the age-old view of human dominance and undermine the human-centered morality of industrial development—unless such development occurs in a way that respects nature. Recently, Singer has argued that because of modern scientific insights, traditional ethical values about the environment no longer conform to basic tenets of fairness. New ethical rules are needed. Our values evolved when the atmosphere, the forests, and the oceans seemed to be unlimited resources. Now, he writes, we know that "[b]y driving your car you could be releasing carbon dioxide that is part of a causal chain leading to lethal floods in Bangladesh."[27] Traditional values—for example, the sanctity of private property in capitalism—fail to impose adequate duties to protect assets that belong to all humanity.

ENVIRONMENTAL REGULATION IN THE UNITED STATES

The dominant approach to protecting the environment in the United States has been to pass laws that strictly regulate emissions, effluents, and wastes. Before the 1970s there was little environmental regulation; but by the 1960s the public had become frightened of pollution, and a strong popular mandate for controlling it emerged. As a result, during what came to be called the "environmental decade" of the 1970s, Congress passed a remarkable string of new laws, creating a broad statutory base for regulating industry.

Although more laws have been passed since the 1970s, the ones from that decade still form the basic regulatory framework. Most have been reauthorized and amended, some several times, and some of these revisions were so extensive they fundamentally altered the statute. To illustrate, the Clean Air Act of 1970 was 50 pages, but when Congress amended it in 1990 it ballooned to 800 pages. These 800 pages rolled out 538 specific requirements for new rules, standards, and reports.

The Environmental Protection Agency

The Environmental Protection Agency (EPA) is an executive branch regulatory agency. It was created in 1970 to consolidate environmental programs scattered throughout the federal government. Its mission is to protect human health and to preserve the natural environment. Although a few other agencies administer environmental laws, the EPA enforces more than 30 statutes making up the overwhelming bulk of regulation in this area. In 2010 it had more than 17,000 employees and a budget of $5.9 billion, making it the largest single regulatory agency in the federal government.

When Congress passes an environmental law, EPA employees write the detailed, specific rules needed to make it work. They have been prolific. Over the 30 years between 1970 and 2010 the agency issued 4,581 rules, 426 of which had an economic impact of $100 million or more.[28] The EPA can enforce these rules directly on corporations, but laws permit delegating enforcement to the states. State

[27] Peter Singer, *One World: The Ethics of Globalization* (New Haven, CT: Yale University Press, 2002), pp. 19–20.

[28] Office of Information and Regulatory Affairs, "Review Counts," May 26, 2010, at www.reginfo.gov/.

regulators, acting with federal funding and following EPA guidelines, now do most of the enforcement of the nation's environmental laws.

Although the EPA remains an aggressive agency imbued with a sense of mission, it suffers from a work overload. And since its founding it has been whipsawed by competing interests. Environmentalists and Democrats in Congress sometimes criticize its actions as too little. Industry and its Republican allies, on the other hand, are inclined to see many actions as too strong, imposing an unreasonable regulatory burden.

PRINCIPAL AREAS OF ENVIRONMENTAL POLICY

There are three media for pollution: air, water, and land. Here we give a brief overview of regulations that protect them from degradation. In each area, we describe laws, basic problems, central concerns for business, and progress.

Air

Air pollution is best described as a set of complex interrelated problems, each requiring different control measures. The Clean Air Act is the primary air quality statute. Although this law permits the use of some market incentives, these provisions depart from its core philosophy, which is to impose inflexible, draconian, command controls. We now discuss regulation of different air pollution problems.

National Air Quality

The Clean Air Act requires the EPA to set national standards for air pollutants at levels that protect public health and the environment. These standards are supposed to be set without regard for cost and must provide an "adequate margin of safety" that protects even the most sensitive people. To do this, the EPA has set standards to curb emissions of six substances, called *criteria pollutants* that are the primary threat to air quality because they are emitted in large quantities:

criteria pollutants Six natural substances in large quantities that cause substandard air quality— carbon monoxide, nitrogen dioxide, sulfur dioxide, ozone, particulates, and lead.

- *Carbon monoxide* (CO) is a gas produced from incomplete combustion of carbon in fuels such as gasoline. Its largest source is vehicle emissions. High concentrations of CO reduce the oxygen-carrying capacity of the blood and may aggravate cardiovascular disease.

- *Nitrogen dioxide* (NO_2) is a gas resulting from oxidation in the atmosphere of nitrogen oxide (NO), a pollutant formed during high temperature combustion. It comes mainly from vehicle exhaust and fuel combustion in industry. It is a lung irritant and aggravates respiratory disease.

- *Sulfur dioxide* (SO_2) is a colorless gas that comes primarily from the burning of fossil fuels, which releases trapped sulfur compounds. Two-thirds of SO_2 is emitted by electric utilities burning coal and oil. SO_2 contributes to acid rain and fine particle pollution. It is a lung irritant that triggers asthma attacks and is associated with heart attacks and cancer.

- *Ozone* (O_3) molecules are not directly emitted by industrial processes or vehicles. Instead, they form in the air by chemical reactions between nitrogen dioxide

volatile organic compounds
Gases that evaporate from liquid or solid carbon-based compounds such as gasoline or floor wax. In sunlight they react with other pollutants to form urban smog.

and carbon-based molecules known as *volatile organic compounds* (VOCs), gases that vaporize from a wide range of liquid or solid carbon-based compounds including petroleum fuels, solvents, paints, adhesives, pesticides, and waxes. These airborne reactions are promoted by the energy in sunlight, which is why urban smog is worse on sunny days. Industry accounts for about half of all VOC emissions and vehicles for the other half. Some VOCs, including benzine, toluene, vinyl chloride, and xylenes, cause cancer. Ozone is a bluish gas that irritates the lungs, and high concentrations damage lung tissue. Near ground level, ozone is considered a pollutant. High in the atmosphere, however, naturally occurring ozone absorbs solar radiation, making life possible on earth.

condensibles
Small particles formed in the atmosphere by photochemical reactions of gases found in urban smog.

- *Particulate matter* (PM) is composed of small particles suspended in the air. These particles are released by industrial activity and combustion. Coal-burning power plants emit massive numbers of particles because fly ash is not completely removed from stack gases by existing control methods. Diesel exhaust is filled with small carbon particles that can remain airborne for several days. Some particles, called *condensibles*, are created in the atmosphere by reactions of precursor gases including NO_2, SO_2, VOCs, and ammonia. The EPA regulates particles that are 10 micrometers in size, about one-seventh the diameter of a human hair, or smaller. Industry emits only about 15 percent of these particles, labeled PM_{10}. Most come from dust raised by the wind. Particulates pose the greatest health risks of all the criteria pollutants. They are associated with respiratory and cardiovascular disease. Hospitalizations and death rates for infants, the elderly, and the infirm rise during smog episodes primarily due to inhalation of these small particles. The World Health Organization estimates that each year PM_{10} in outdoor urban air is responsible for about 800,000 deaths worldwide.[29] Recently, the EPA introduced standards for very small particles of 2.5 micrometers or less, called $PM_{2.5}$, which are especially dangerous to human health because they go more deeply into the airways. The majority of $PM_{2.5}$ are condensibles.

parts per million (ppm)
The number of molecules of a chemical in 1 million molecules of a particular gas, liquid, or solid. It can also be expressed as the ratio of the molecules of a certain chemical to the total number of molecules in a gas, liquid, or solid.

- *Lead* (Pb) is a metal that causes seizures and mental retardation. With the elimination of leaded gasoline years ago, the problem of lead in urban air has ended. Airborne lead is now a danger only in a few areas near lead smelters and battery plants.

For each criteria pollutant, the EPA sets standards for maximum concentrations. The ground-level ozone standards, for example, are 0.75 *parts per million* (ppm) averaged over eight hours and 0.12 ppm for any one hour. This standard was barely met for the nation as a whole in 2008 with a mean of 0.74 ppm at 547 monitoring sites. Many sites were far above this number. The carbon monoxide standard, on the other hand, is 9 parts per million (ppm) averaged over eight hours, or 35 ppm for one hour. Despite being more than 10 times greater than the ozone standard, the eight-hour CO standard is met at every monitoring site and the national mean is 1.9 ppm.[30]

[29] United Nations Environmental Program, *Global Environmental Outlook 4* (Nairobi: Kenya, UNEP, 2007), p. 45.

[30] Figures in this paragraph are from Environmental Protection Agency, "Air Trends: Ozone" and "Air Trends: Carbon Monoxide," at www.epa.gov/airtrends/, May 2010.

FIGURE 13.2
**Declining
Emissions
of Criteria
Pollutants:
1970–2008**

Source: Adapted
from EPA, "Air
Quality Trends"
graphic, at
www.epa.gov/
airtrends/images/
comparison70.jpg.

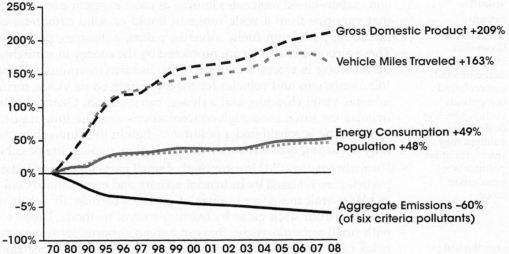

To suppress criteria pollutants, the Clean Air Act mandates a range of expensive actions including emissions controls on power plants, factories, smelters, and vehicles. Since controls began early in the 1970s, emissions have dropped 60 percent. Health benefits have been enormous. One study found that between 1980 and 2000 just the reduction of $PM_{2.5}$ alone increased average life expectancy in 51 American cities by 4.8 years.[31]

Figure 13.2 shows how aggregate emissions of the six pollutants fell over the 38 years following the 1970 Clean Air Act even as factors underlying emissions rose. Without the huge drop in lead emissions after lead was removed from gasoline in the early 1980s, the decline would be much less impressive. However, what remains is still a remarkable achievement against the backdrop of an expanding economy because, as shown in Table 13.2, business is the source of 47 percent of all emissions. Progress in meeting standards is slowed because the EPA must review its standards for each pollutant every five years and as scientific evidence of health dangers grows it makes the standards stricter. This ratchet effect means that, despite significant emission cuts over four decades, 127 million Americans, about 42 percent, still live in areas where one or more criteria pollutants exceed standards.[32]

**hazardous air
pollutants**
Chemical emissions that pose
a health risk of
serious illness
such as cancer
or birth defects
with small inhalation
exposures.

Hazardous Air Pollutants

Besides controlling the six criteria pollutants, the Clean Air Act mandates control of *hazardous air pollutants*. Hazardous air pollutants, sometimes called air toxics, cause cancer and other serious health effects such as brain damage or birth defects. The EPA has identified 650 air toxics. Examples are benzine, toluene, formaldehyde,

[31] C. Arden Pope III, et al., "Fine-Particulate Air Pollution and Life Expectancy in the United States," *New England Journal of Medicine,* January 22, 2009, p. 384.

[32] Environmental Protection Agency, *Our Nation's Air: Status and Trends Through 2008* (Research Triangle Park, NC: Office of Air Quality Planning and Standards, February 2010), p. 1.

TABLE 13.2
Estimated National Emissions of Criteria Pollutants by Source: 2008 (in thousands of short tons)

Substance	Industry[a]	Vehicles	Other[b]	Total
Carbon monoxide	27,088	38,866	11,731	77,685
Nitrogen oxides	10,873	5,206	260	16,339
Sulfur dioxide	11,280	64	85	11,429
Volatile organic compounds	11,177	3,418	1,332	15,927
Particulates (PM_{10})[c]	3,095	171	11,540	14,806
Particulates ($PM_{2.5}$)[d]	2,038	110	2,742	4,890
Lead[e]	2,164	185	11	2,360
Total	67,715	48,020	27,701	143,436
Percent	**47%**	**34%**	**19%**	**100%**

[a]Includes industrial fuel combustion, industrial processes, marine vessels, aircraft, and locomotives.
[b]Includes *inter alia*, residential wood burning, agricultural burning, forest wildfires, structure fires, and (for particulates) fugitive dust.
[c]Figures include condensable PM, or particles formed in the atmosphere from reactions of precursor gases.
[d]PM2.5 is included in PM10 and not added into totals.
[e]Figures are for 2005.

Source: EPA, *National Emissions Inventory Air Pollutant Emissions Trends Data: Current Emissions Trends Summaries*, www.epa.gov.ttn/chief/trends/, June 2010; for lead, www.epa.gov/air/emissions/pb.htm.

and xylenes, which come mostly from vehicles; and arsenic, chromium, dioxin, mercury, and hydrochloric acid, which come from industry. Combined emissions are between 4 million and 5 million tons per year, less than a thousandth of 1 percent of the six criteria pollutants, but the EPA estimates that the background presence of even these limited emissions poses a lifetime cancer risk of 36 in 1 million for average Americans. The noncancer risk is lower, but may exceed 10 in 1 million for some substances.[33]

maximum achievable control technology
A performance standard used by the EPA to control emissions of hazardous air pollutants. It requires control of toxic air emissions at least equal to that achieved by the top 12 percent of sources in the industry.

Large industrial sources such as electric utilities, oil refineries, chemical plants, steel mills, and paper plants are responsible for about 20 percent of air toxics releases. Of the remainder, about 41 percent come from vehicles, 30 percent from a range of small sources such as dry cleaners and gas stations, and 9 percent from fires.

The Clean Air Act requires the EPA to set emission standards for 187 air toxics at levels that prevent disease and requires industry to use the "maximum achievable control technology" to comply. In practice, *maximum achievable control technology* is emissions control equal to the control achieved by the best-performing 12 percent of sources in the industry. So far, the agency has set standards for 176 industrial sources. For example, the melting furnaces in iron and steel foundries emit hazardous air pollutants such as nickel, lead, chromium, and manganese. A recent rule limits these furnaces to 0.06 pounds of toxic metal air emissions per ton of metal melted (approximately one pound for every 17 tons melted).[34]

[33] Environmental Protection Agency, "National-Scale Air Toxics Assessment for 2002—Fact Sheet," June 24, 2009. For certain chemicals and areas the risk is as high as 110 in 1 million. See Chang-fu Wu, et al., "Cancer Risk Assessment of Selected Hazardous Air Pollutants in Seattle," *Environment International* 35 (2009), p. 516.

[34] Environmental Protection Agency, "National Emission Standards for Hazardous Air Pollutants for Iron and Steel Foundries Area Sources: Final Rule," 73 FR 230, January 2, 2008.

Hazardous air emissions have fallen 39 percent since 1993. Much of the decline is due to voluntary cuts by companies that do not want to report high emissions levels publicly and to reformulations of gasoline and diesel fuel intended mainly to cut criteria pollutants. The EPA's air toxics program is underfunded. It is now years behind on meeting most of its Clean Air Act deadlines. Within the agency it has low priority and action is taken mainly in response to lawsuits by environmentalists. Meanwhile, most Americans are exposed to cancer risks from these dangerous air pollutants far greater than the agencies' goal of 1 in 1 million over a lifetime.

Acid Rain

acid rain
Deposition of acids formed when sulfur and nitrogen compounds undergo chemical reactions in the atmosphere and return to earth in rain, hail, snow, fog, and dry fallout of acidic particles.

Acid rain is the deposition, in various forms of moist and dry precipitation, of highly acidic compounds from the atmosphere. It is caused primarily by two airborne pollutants, sulfur dioxide and oxides of nitrogen (NO_x). In the atmosphere, these gases undergo chemical reactions and return to earth as acids that alter the pH of water, degrading lakes and forests and causing buildings to deteriorate. Both also contribute to formation of $PM_{2.5}$, the fine airborne particles that cause regional haze and adversely affect human health.

When Congress amended the Clean Air Act in 1990, it responded to public alarm about acid rain by requiring the EPA to reduce emissions of these two key precursor substances. Profligate emissions of SO_2 and NO_x coming from coal-fired electric power-generating plants in the Northeast and Midwest were blamed for degrading sensitive Eastern lakes and forests downwind of emission plumes. These plants produce about two-thirds of the SO_2 and one-fifth of NO_x in the United States.

The EPA set up separate programs to reduce emissions of the two precursor gases. To control SO_2, it set a goal of capping aggregate emissions from power plants at 8.95 million tons per year in 2010. Rather than strictly regulating each plant and boiler, it issued permits to emit SO_2 equal to emissions in 1995, then slowly reduced the number of permits until their number limited emissions at the 8.95 million tons goal. Companies could reduce their emissions as fast as or faster than the permits were retired, or they could buy permits from other companies in an open market. This approach, which harnesses economic incentives to reduce pollution, is called cap and trade. How it works is discussed in more detail in the next chapter. The program has been a success. By 2008 SO_2 emissions fell to 7.6 tons, 15 percent below the goal and a 52 percent reduction from 1990 levels.[35]

To control NO_x emissions the agency first used command-and-control regulation, setting emission limits for boilers based on their type and heat output. A facility could comply with these limits for each boiler or could average emissions from two or more boilers to meet averaged limits. Later, the EPA added a NO_x cap-and-trade program. At the start of the effort in 1996 it set a goal of limiting NO_x emissions to 6.1 million pounds by 2010. This goal has been far exceeded. By, 2008 NO_x emissions had decreased 51 percent from 1995, falling to 3 million tons.

Figure 13.3 shows how aggregate emissions for power plants have fallen since the start of the acid rain program in 1995. As a result, wet sulfate and wet nitrate

[35] EPA, *Performance and Accountability Report: Fiscal Year 2009*, p. II-11.

FIGURE 13.3
Emission
Trends for
Electric
Power-
Generating
Plants in the
Acid Rain
Program

Source: Environmental Protection Agency, 2010.

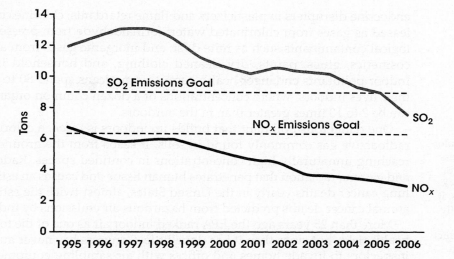

deposition have declined 35 percent and 15 percent, respectively. Still, problems remain. In the Northeast 18 percent of lakes are so acidic that near complete loss of fish is expected. In the Adirondack Mountains 33 percent of 565 streams remain chronically acidified.[36]

Acid rain control was estimated to cost $3.5 billion a year in 2010.[37] Most of this cost is borne by coal-burning utility companies. One study estimates that the equity value of coal-burning plants has declined by $28 billion due to investor fears of lower profits.[38] But while utility corporations and their shareholders are paying for acid rain control, the public reaps the benefits, which exceed costs by an astronomical margin. Recent estimates are that each year 21,400 deaths, 30,000 nonfatal heart attacks, 2.5 million lost workdays, and 910,000 lost school days are avoided due to the program's SO_2 and NO_x emission reductions. The overall monetized benefit is $4.1 billion a year.[39]

Indoor Air Pollution

Indoor air in developed nations contains a mixture of pollutants. These include carcinogens such as asbestos and tobacco smoke; combustion by-products from cooking such as carbon monoxide, fine particles, and nitrogen dioxides; suspected

[36] Environmental Protection Agency, *Air Trends,* p. 35; and Environmental Protection Agency, "Acid Rain and Related Programs: 2008 Environmental Results," October 2009, pp. 11–14, at www.epa.gov/airmarkt/progress/ARP_3.html.

[37] Testimony of Brian McLean, before the Committee on Energy and Commerce, Subcommittee on Energy and Air Quality, U.S. House of Representatives, 110th Congress, 1st Session, March 29, 2007, p. 7.

[38] Joshua Linn, "The Effect of Cap-and-Trade Programs on Firms' Profits: Evidence from the Nitrogen Oxides Budget Trading Program," *Journal of Environmental Economics and Management* 59 (2010), p. 2.

[39] These are lower-range estimates. Some studies contain significantly higher estimated benefits. See a review of estimates in Environmental Protection Agency, "Acid Rain and Related Programs: 2008 Emission, Compliance, and Market Analysis," September 2009, p. 4, at www.epa.gov/airmarkt/progress/arp08.html.

endocrine disrupters in plasticizers and flame retardants; chlorine compounds released as gases from chlorinated water; formaldehyde from pressed wood; biological contaminants such as mite dust; and inorganic gases from air fresheners, cosmetics, glues, paints, dry-cleaned clothing, and household insecticides.[40] Indoor pollutants endanger health because Americans spend 80 to 90 percent of their lives indoors, where concentrations of a dozen common organic pollutants can be 2 to 10 times greater than in the outdoors.

radon
An inert, colorless, odorless gas found in soil and rock formations. It is a naturally occurring decay product of uranium.

One dangerous pollutant that builds up indoors is *radon*, a colorless, odorless, radioactive gas commonly found in soils. It seeps from the ground into homes, reaching unnaturally high concentrations in confined spaces. Radon emits beta and gamma radiation that penetrates human tissue and causes an estimated 20,000 lung cancer deaths yearly in the United States, almost twice the estimated 10,800 annual cancer deaths predicted from hazardous air emissions by industry.[41]

More than 25 years ago the EPA ranked indoor air as one of the top five human health risks, but since then it has done little. Congress has never authorized EPA inspectors to invade homes and offices with air-sampling equipment and ticket books. Beyond modest and episodic spending on research, the agency has a voluntary radon measurement program for homes and provides pamphlets for schools. Overall, the hazards of specific indoor pollutants are largely an enigma, leaving one researcher to remark that "[g]iven the importance of this subject, it is striking how little directly measured . . . data exist on the kind and concentration of indoor pollutants."[42]

Ozone-Destroying Chemicals

While ozone in urban smog is regarded as a pollutant, ozone in the stratosphere screens out ultraviolet energy harmful to living tissue. Ozone (O_3) is a molecule of three oxygen atoms that forms naturally during chemical reactions with oxygen in the presence of sunlight. About 90 percent of all ozone forms in the stratosphere, which begins at 6 to 10 miles above earth and rises to about 31 miles. Even in its peak band high in the stratosphere it exists in very low concentrations of about 12,000 ozone molecules for every 1 billion air molecules. Yet it forms a critical barrier, reducing penetration of ultraviolet wavelengths in sunlight to levels that permit life on earth.

Emissions of manufactured gases containing chlorine and bromine threaten this delicate barrier. Examples of major sources are chlorofluorocarbon refrigerants, halons in fire extinguishers, solvents such as carbon tetrachloride, and pesticides containing methyl bromide. When released into the lower atmosphere they persist and eventually rise into the stratosphere, where they are converted by chemical reactions into more reactive gases that destroy ozone. In the catalytic processes that these reactive gases unleash, a single chlorine or bromine atom can destroy hundreds of ozone molecules.

[40] Ruth Barro, et al., "Analysis of Industrial Contaminants in Indoor Air," *Journal of Chromatography A* 1216 (2009).

[41] Department of Health and Human Services, Agency for Toxic Substances and Disease Registry, "Case Studies in Environmental Medicine: Radon Toxicity," ATSDR-HE-CS-2001-0006 (2001), p. 1.

[42] Charles J. Weschler, "Changes in Indoor Pollutants Since the 1950s," *Atmospheric Environment* 43 (2009), p. 167.

chlorofluoro-carbons
A family of gases containing the elements chlorine, fluorine, and carbon used as refrigerants, aerosol propellants, foams, and solvents. They are inert and exceptionally stable, but break down in the upper atmosphere in ozone-consuming reactions.

Many ozone-depleting gases are extremely long-lived. *Chlorofluorocarbons* (CFCs), for example, are large, tough molecules that defy natural breakdown processes. Typically, they survive 50 to 100 years in the atmosphere, and in one case 1,700 years.

In high latitudes, the ozone layer has thinned as much as 30 percent because of the action of these industrial gases. This exposes planetary life and ecosystems to more ultraviolet radiation, causing excess skin cancers, eye cataracts, weakened immune systems, lowered crop yields, and reduction of phytoplankton in oceans. Even the highest levels of ozone in urban smog are inadequate to protect humans from this radiation damage.

In 1987 a treaty called the Montreal Protocol set timetables to phase out worldwide use of 96 ozone-depleting chemicals. To meet treaty obligations the developed nations have phased out production of the most destructive gases. The last chemical, HCFC, is scheduled to be phased out by 2030. In the United States, the EPA enforces strict rules that phased out production of all but HCFC by 2005. Developing nations have had more extended timetables and are helped by a $2.5 billion fund to ease their transition.

The treaty has been so successful it is widely regarded as a "bureaucratic miracle." Under its terms 95 percent of the volume of ozone-depleting chemicals has gone out of production. Concentrations of ozone-depleting gases in the troposphere have declined since peaking in the mid-1990s and the depletion of stratospheric ozone observed since 1980 has been arrested, though not reversed. Ozone concentrations are now stable and are predicted to return to their 1980 levels between 2050 and 2075.[43] The EPA calculates this will reduce terrestrial radiation enough to save 6.3 million lives in the United States that would otherwise have been lost to skin cancers.[44] Without the treaty, scientists estimate that by 2050 only 30 percent of the ozone layer would have been left in higher latitudes and increased radiation would have caused more than 20 million additional skin cancers worldwide.[45]

Greenhouse Gases

greenhouse gases
Atmospheric gases that absorb energy radiated from the earth, decreasing its release into space.

The Industrial Revolution led to rising emissions of *greenhouse gases* that trap heat from the sun in the atmosphere instead of allowing it to radiate back into space at night. These gases include carbon dioxide, methane, nitrous oxide, and the fluorinated gases used in refrigerants and fire extinguishers. Energy from incoming solar radiation in ultraviolet wavelengths heats the earth. At night the earth cools when terrestrial radiation in infrared wavelengths passes out through the atmosphere into space. However, electrons in the atoms of greenhouse gas molecules are excited by the energy in infrared wavelengths and absorb it, causing atmospheric heating. Without them more infrared energy would radiate back into space and the earth would cool.

[43] World Meteorological Organization, *Scientific Assessment of Ozone Depletion: 2006,* Global Ozone Research and Monitoring Project, Report No. 50, February 2007, chap. 6.

[44] Environmental Protection Agency, *Achievements in Stratospheric Ozone Protection: Progress Report,* EPA-430-R-07-001, April 2007, p. 7.

[45] United Nations Environmental Programme, *Backgrounder: Basic Facts and Data on the Science and Politics of Ozone Protection* (Nairobi, Kenya: UNEP, October 5, 2001), p. 5.

FIGURE 13.4   Atmospheric Concentrations of Greenhouse Gases: 1750–2010
This chart shows observed concentrations of six greenhouse gases, including CO_2. Other gases are measured in terms of their CO_2 equivalents, or the amount of CO_2 that would have the same global warming potential. This is usually expressed as the number of tons of CO_2 that would have to be emitted to have the same potential for global warming as another gas. For example, one ton of methane is equal to 21 tons of CO_2, one ton of nitrous oxide is equal to 310 tons of CO_2, and one ton of HFC-23 (one of the fluorinated gases) is equal to 11,700 tons of CO_2. The CO_2 equivalent is expressed in parts per million, or the ratio of CO_2 molecules to air molecules.

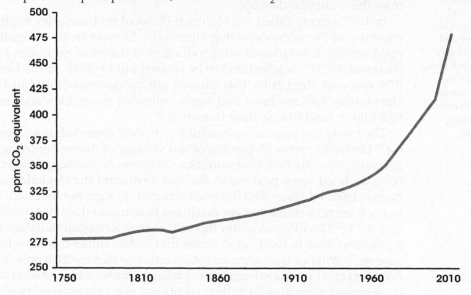

Source: Intergovernmental Panel on Climate Change, National Oceanic and Atmospheric Administration.

In their preindustrial atmospheric concentrations, greenhouse gases were part of the natural mechanism keeping a stable balance between heat buildup and heat loss so that global mean average temperature remained steady. Since the Industrial Revolution, however, human activity has raised atmospheric concentrations of these gases, as shown in Figure 13.4. The predominant greenhouse gas is carbon dioxide, which makes up about 85 percent of greenhouse gas emissions. Between 1750 and 2010, CO_2 resident in the earth's atmosphere rose from about 280 to 393 parts per million, an increase of 40 percent and a sudden upward departure from stable levels over 800,000 years.[46] Carbon dioxide is a product of complete combustion of carbon. Wood and fossil fuel combustion have released such huge amounts of carbon that natural processes of carbon absorption by oceans and forests are overwhelmed. Thus, more carbon remains in the atmosphere as CO_2.

Between 1850 and 2005 mean global surface temperature warmed an estimated 1.4 degrees Farenheit. The oceans have absorbed 80 percent of this warming with

[46] National Oceanic and Atmospheric Administration, "Mauna Loa Monthly Mean Data," at ftp://ftp.cmdl.noaa.gov/ccg/co2/trends/co2_mm_mlo.txt; and Dieter Lüthi, et al., "High-Resolution Carbon Dioxide Concentration Record 650,000-800,000 Years before Present," *Nature*, May 15, 2008, p. 379.

average temperatures increasing to depths of 9,800 feet. As oceans have warmed, the water has expanded, causing a global rise in sea level of about 6.7 inches through the twentieth century. A scientific consensus, though not a unity, emerged that these changes are caused by greenhouse gas emissions and that added warming of 3.2 to 7.2 degrees Farenheit and sea level rises of 7 to 23 inches could follow by 2100.[47] This consensus now drives global and U.S. policy.

Its major impact so far is an international treaty, the Kyoto Protocol, which went into effect in 2005. The treaty requires industrial nations to cut emissions of heat-trapping gases an average of 5 percent below 1990 levels by 2012. The United States, which emits 20 percent of global warming gases, is not a party to the Kyoto Protocol because of fears that its mandatory emissions reductions would hurt the economy. Of the 182 other countries that ratified the Kyoto Protocol, most are not required to reduce emissions. Developing nations, including big polluters such as China, India, Mexico, Brazil, and Nigeria, are not committed to emissions reductions under the treaty because of their fear that cuts would derail economic growth. This puts the entire burden of saving earth's climate on 37 more industrialized nations, including those of the European Union, but despite reduction efforts, their overall CO_2 emissions keep rising. The Kyoto Protocol expires in 2012 and international efforts to negotiate a new agreement are in progress.

The U.S. effort to limit warming gas emissions has come slowly. For two decades the main effort was a series of more than two dozen voluntary "climate programs" at the EPA. Together, these programs now reduce annual emissions by only about 1/100th of 1 percent.[48] Over this time the EPA refused to regulate CO_2, claiming it was not the kind of pernicious pollutant it had authority to reduce under the Clean Air Act. However, in 2007 the Supreme Court held that greenhouse gases, including carbon dioxide, are air pollutants within the meaning of the statute and should be regulated if the EPA determined they endangered public health or welfare.[49]

After study, the agency determined that six greenhouse gases caused climate change that threatened the public with temperature mortality, rising air pollution, water shortages, and other harms.[50] It was, therefore, justified in regulating them and issued a rule requiring new 2016 cars to average 250 grams of CO_2 per mile and 35.5 miles per gallon.[51] The EPA calculated it would cost automakers $52 billion to comply and they would pass most of the cost on to car buyers with price increases averaging $985. However, the overall benefits of fuel savings would be

[47] Susan Solomon et al., eds., *Climate Change 2007: The Physical Science Basis* (New York: Cambridge University Press, 2007), p. 13.

[48] Environmental Protection Agency, *Performance and Accountability Report: Fiscal Year 2009*, p. II-24; and "Summary Report for CO_2 Emissions," in Department of State, *U.S. Climate Action Report 2010* (Washington, DC: Department of State, 2010), p. 174.

[49] *Massachusetts v. EPA*, 549 U.S. 497 (2007).

[50] Environmental Protection Agency, "Endangerment and Cause or Contribute Findings for Greenhouse Gases Under Section 202(a) of the Clean Air Act; Final Rule," 74 FR 66496, December 15, 2009.

[51] Environmental Protection Agency and Department of Transportation, "National Highway Traffic Safety Administration: Light-Duty Vehicle Greenhouse Gas Emission Standards and Corporate Average Fuel Economy Standards: Final Rule," 75 FR 25324, May 5, 2010.

$185 billion.[52] It also issued another rule requiring the oil and auto companies and any facility emitting 25,000 tons or more of greenhouse gases a year to report the type and amount of emissions.[53] This rule does nothing to lower emissions, but it lays the groundwork for future command-and-control regulation that can. It also imposes 1.21 million hours of paperwork on an estimated 10,000 entities.[54]

Water

The basic statute for fighting water pollution is the Federal Water Pollution Control Act Amendments of 1972, usually called the Clean Water Act. Congress intended it to be a powerful measure that would stop the deterioration of the nation's lakes, rivers, streams, and estuaries. The act set a goal of eliminating *all* polluting discharges into these waters by 1985. However, the goal was not met and will not soon be met. The Clean Water Act is effective in reducing, but not eliminating, polluted factory outflows, or effluents. Every industrial plant uses water, and sources of pollution are numerous. In production processes, water is used as a washing, scrubbing, cooling, or mixing medium. It becomes contaminated with a variety of particles and dissolved chemicals. The Clean Water Act prohibits the release of any polluted factory discharge without a permit.

effluent
A treated or untreated wastewater discharge from an industrial facility.

point source
A discrete source of effluent such as a factory, mine, ship, or pipeline.

The EPA regulates industrial *effluents* from *point sources*, that is, sites that discharge from a single location, using a permit system called the National Pollution Discharge Elimination System (NPDES). Under the NPDES, each industrial facility must get a permit specifying the volume of one or more substances it can pour into a water body. Effluent limits are based on scientific estimates of how much of a substance the water body can absorb before deteriorating unacceptably and on the ability of available equipment to remove a particular pollutant.

The EPA sets water quality criteria for pollutants. Usually there are two standards, one for protecting human health and the other for aquatic life. To give examples, the chloroform standard prohibits chronic exposure of aquatic life to concentrations of more than 1,240 µg/l (micrograms per cubic liter) and exposure of humans to more than 470 µg/l. As noted, permit limits are also based on how much pollution the best control devices can remove from wastewater. These devices range from simple screens for large particles to intricate chemical and biological treatment systems.

For example, plants that make paperboard out of wastepaper have small amounts of the wood preservative pentachlorophenol (C_6HCl_5O) in their wastewater streams. C_6HCl_5O is so poisonous that swallowing one-tenth of an ounce, about a teaspoon, can be lethal. However, for this substance the EPA has defined the best control technology standard as effluent containing no more than 0.87 pound of C_6HCl_5O for each 1 million pounds of paperboard produced because the best control technology cannot remove more of it. In other words, a paperboard factory can drain almost

[52] "Report Under 5 U.S.C. § 801(a)(2)(A) on a Major Rule," in Government Accountability Office, GAO-10-739R, May 21, 2010, enclosure, pp. 1–2.

[53] Environmental Protection Agency, "Mandatory Reporting of Greenhouse Gases: Final Rule," 74 FR 56260, October 30, 2009.

[54] 74 FR 56366 and 56369.

14 ounces of C_6HCl_5O into a river or stream every time it makes a million pounds of paperboard. Currently, about 45,200 facilities operate under an NPDES permit.

While the EPA has limited factory discharges, "nonpoint" effluent, or runoff that enters surface waters from diffuse sources, is largely uncontrolled. Runoff from agriculture—animal wastes, pesticides, and fertilizers—is now the primary cause of impaired water bodies. Although general language in the Clean Water Act permits the EPA to act against any source of water pollution, the law avoided specific language aimed at farmers because of their political power. However, growing pollution from big animal feedlots and poultry farms led the EPA to place several thousand factory farms under permits.

Urban runoff is another major contributor to poor water quality. As urban areas increase in size, more water flows over their streets, collecting pollutants and carrying them to water bodies. The Clean Water Act empowers the EPA to require control measures by cities, including detention ponds, street sweeping, and public education programs. Nonpoint sources are now the biggest contributors to water pollution and efforts to control them are just beginning.

Overall, the quality of surface waters is marginally improved from 1972 when the Clean Water Act was passed. Then, it was estimated that only 30 to 40 percent of the nation's waters met the law's water quality goals.[55] Today, 64 percent of wetlands and 50 percent of rivers and streams meet these goals, but only 36 percent of bays and estuaries and 34 percent of lakes, including none of the Great Lakes.[56] Progress is slow, but without the EPA's strict hand of enforcement the nation's waters would be far more impaired. In a typical year the agency catches about 20,000 violations of its water rules.[57]

Recently, however, the Supreme Court called much of the EPA's activity into question. The Clean Water Act gave the agency jurisdiction over "navigable waters," which it had defined broadly to cover almost any rivulet, channel, wetland, ditch, or other body of water a polluter could sully, no matter how slight. But the Court decided that the words "navigable waters" mean "only those relatively permanent, standing or continuously flowing bodies of water 'forming geographic features' that are described in ordinary parlance as 'streams,' 'oceans, rivers, [and] lakes.'"[58] This decision probably puts thousands of major polluters outside the EPA's reach and it has pulled back its enforcement accordingly.

Land

After Congress passed air and water pollution control laws early in the 1970s, it became apparent that poor handling and disposal of solid hazardous wastes was a major problem. Also, devices that removed air- and waterborne poisons from

[55] Kevin Kane, *How's the Water? The State of the Nation's Water Quality,* Working Paper 171 (St. Louis: Center for the Study of American Business, January 2000), p. 3.

[56] Environmental Protection Agency, "Water Quality Assessment and TMDL Information: National Summary of State Information," at www.epa.gov/waters/ir/, accessed June 1, 2010.

[57] Charles Duhigg and Janet Roberts, "Rulings Restrict Clean Water Act, Hampering EPA," *The New York Times,* March 1, 2010, p. A1.

[58] *Rapanos v. United States,* 547 U.S. 715 (2006) at 739.

industrial processes under the new laws produced tons of poisoned sludge, slime, and dust that ended up in poorly contained landfills. Authority over the handling of hazardous waste was inadequate to prevent mismanagement. Responding to the menace, Congress passed two laws.

The Resource Conservation and Recovery Act (RCRA) of 1976 gave the EPA authority to manage hazardous waste "from cradle to grave," that is, from the moment it is created to the moment it is finally destroyed or interred. Firms must label, handle, store, treat, and discard hazardous waste under strict guidelines, keeping meticulous records all the while.

The RCRA is a difficult statute to administer and with which to comply. It demands that regulators keep track of all hazardous waste produced anywhere in the country—an exhausting job. It relies on smothering command-and-control regulation and prohibits balancing costs against benefits. One indication of the regulatory burden it imposes is that when it was first implemented, nearly 80 percent of the nation's waste disposal facilities elected to close rather than comply with it. Figure 13.5 illustrates a typical installation of wells required to monitor groundwater quality under a solid-waste disposal site.

FIGURE 13.5   RCRA Landfill Groundwater Monitoring Requirements
The EPA grants permits to all operators of hazardous waste dumps that comply with standards for physical layout, groundwater monitoring, and emergency planning. The drawing is a cross section of ground below a landfill illustrating minimal RCRA monitoring requirements. Water samples drawn from downgradient wells can detect chemical contamination seeping into the groundwater (saturated zone) from the landfill above.

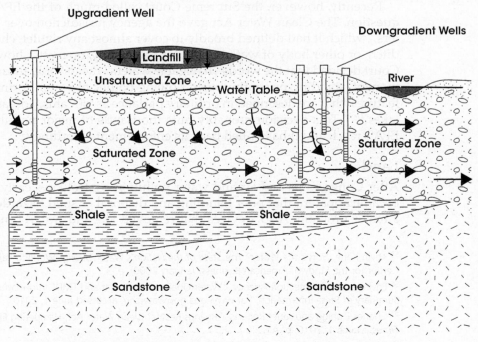

Source: Environmental Protection Agency.

RCRA regulations in the *Code of Federal Regulations* cover 1,763 pages of stupefying detail. For example, in monitoring wells, "[i]f an individual well comparison procedure is used to compare an individual compliance well constituent concentration with background constituent concentrations or a groundwater protection standard, the test shall be done at a Type I error level no less than 0.01 for each testing period."[59] If a pump begins to drip "a first attempt at repair shall be made no later than five calendar days after each leak is detected."[60] It is, in the words of one observer, "an amazingly inflexible law with extraordinarily detailed regulations, demanding controls, and a glacially slow permitting system."[61]

Because the law contains no requirement that the benefits of regulation exceed its costs, it has invited many lawsuits by industry. General Motors uses solvents to clean automobile spray painting guns when it changes colors, then recirculates them until, after repeated uses, they go to a waste tank. GM sued when the EPA tried to impose hazardous waste regulations on the recirculation piping. It argued that the solvents were not a waste while still in use during an industrial process. GM lost when the case was dismissed.[62] Strict enforcement invites litigation over such pinhead technicalities, but there is no question that hazardous waste is much better handled than before the RCRA.

While the RCRA ensured that existing facilities would operate at a high standard, it did nothing about thousands of abandoned toxic waste sites around the country. So Congress passed another law to clean them up. This law is the Comprehensive Environmental Response, Compensation, and Liability Act of 1980, better known as Superfund, so-named after the large trust fund it set up to pay for cleanups. At first, this fund was generated by a special tax on oil and chemical companies and a small—0.12 percent—addition to the corporate income tax. However, the taxes expired in 1995. Money in the fund now comes from congressional appropriations and from payments to cover the EPA's costs by the parties responsible for toxic waste sites, but there is not as much.

Congress intended Superfund as a temporary measure to be phased out when existing hazardous sites were cleaned. However, the number of sites is higher than predicted and the cleaning process more difficult and expensive than envisioned in 1980. So far, the EPA has identified about 47,000 sites. Early in the program it set up a priority list of sites posing the greatest risk to human health and the environment. These were mainly long-abandoned factories and waste dumps. Since then, 2,704 sites, about 5 percent of the total, have been listed. Most work has been completed at 1,132 sites, but only 341 have been fully restored and delisted.[63] When finished sites are taken off, new ones rotate in.

Far from receding in its activity, the Superfund program now confronts some of the most complex and expensive projects in its history. The average site cleanup costs $5.3 million, but about 130 priority sites are labeled "mega sites" where

[59] 40 CFR §258.53(h)(2), July 1, 2009.

[60] 40 CFR §61.242-2(c)(2), July 1, 2009.

[61] Robert J. Smith, "RCRA Lives, Alas," *Regulation,* Summer 1991, p. 14.

[62] *General Motors v. EPA,* 363 F.3d 442 (2003).

[63] USEPA, "NPL Site Totals by Status and Milestone," at www.epa.gov, April 9, 2011.

cleanup costs average $48 million and can go much higher.[64] The Hudson River site discussed at the beginning of the chapter is one example. Another is an old wood treatment plant in the town of Manville, New Jersey, population 10,000.

The American Creosoting Co.

In 1909 the American Creosoting Co. began treating railroad ties with creosote to resist insects and weather. For 47 years tons of creosote dripped and drained away, oozing into the soil. After the plant closed in 1956 its 50-acre site was sold to developers, who built 137 houses and a shopping mall. All was well until the late 1990s when a black, tar-like mass appeared to a repair crew at a sinkhole. In due course Superfund regulators were called.

Creosote is a derivative of coal tar, a mixture of as many as 300 chemicals, including at least seven that cause cancer. After taking 1,350 soil samples, Superfund sleuths warned the neighborhood's residents of a health risk, primarily from benzo[a]pyrene, one chemical in the creosote. The EPA classifies benzo[a]pyrene as a "probable human carcinogen."[65] Its levels in the soil posed a lifetime cancer risk of 4.4 in 10,000 for residents of the housing development.[66] In that tiny population this meant one expected cancer every 530 years, a time equal to that between the building of the Sistine Chapel and today.[67] For the EPA this was still too much. It acts when cancer risks exceed 1 in 10,000.

Methods of detoxifying soil differ from site to site. The EPA treats soils with chemicals, microorganisms, electric currents, solvents, and even vacuum devices that pull out vapors. Here it would remove the dirt. To achieve its goal of reducing cancer risk to 1 in 1 million it needed to lower concentrations of benzo[a]pyrene from as high as 130 parts per million in hot spots to an average of 0.66 parts per million over the 50 acres. It replaced 456,000 tons of soil, digging it out, trucking it away, and backfilling with new soil. The contaminated soil was treated by high-temperature incineration before disposal in a landfill. Figure 13.6 shows a diagram of an incinerator. At a rate of 20 tons per hour, excavated soil is moved through a giant revolving kiln, where temperatures as high as 2,200 degrees Farenheit break down organic molecules such as those in creosote into simple molecules of CO_2 and H_2O.

The project took nine years and cost $340 million, including $3.1 million in contractor fraud that led to several prison sentences.[68] The EPA believes a paint company in Oklahoma named Tronox must pay for the entire cleanup because, although it never operated the creosote plant, through a string of nine sales,

---

[64] Government Accountability Office, *Superfund: Litigation Has Decreased,* GAO-09-656, July 2009, p. 58.

[65] "Benzo[a]pyrene (BaP) (CASRN 50-32-8)," Integrated Risk Information System at www.epa.gov/ncea/iris.

[66] USEPA, Region II, *Record of Decision: Federal Creosote Superfund Site,* OU2, EPA/ROD/R02-00/526, September 2000, p. 15.

[67] Assuming a 70-year life span for 200 adults and 100 children.

[68] USEPA, Office of Inspector General, *Annual Superfund Report to Congress for Fiscal Year 2009,* EPA-350-R-10-001, February 2010, pp. 13–14.

FIGURE 13.6 Typical Rotary Kiln Incinerator at a Superfund Site

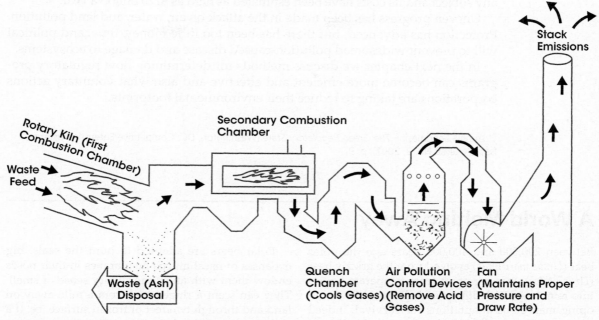

Source: EPA. From General Accounting Office, *Superfund: EPA Could Further Ensure the Safe Operation of On-Site Incinerators*, GAO/RCED-97-43, March 1997, p. 4.

mergers, and spin-offs going back more than 50 years it is the successor to the old American Creosoting Co.[69]

The law establishes harsh rules of liability for any company that has ever dumped hazardous waste in a Superfund site. In legal terminology, this liability is strict, retroactive, and joint and several. In practical terms, this means any company that ever dumped hazardous waste on a site can be responsible for the full cleanup cost even if it obeyed the law of years past, was not negligent, and dumped only a small part of the total waste. This liability cannot be washed away. It adheres to the assets of a company when they are sold. So far, Tronox refuses to pay and is facing legal action. By 2008, the EPA had spent more than $42 billion fixing contaminated sites across the nation, but it has recovered about $30 billion from polluting corporations.[70]

CONCLUDING OBSERVATIONS

Industrial processes damage the environment and cause serious local and global deterioration. The response in the United States and in most of the developed world has been to adopt a series of fairly rigid and expensive regulatory programs. In the United States it is now the largest and most expensive area of regulation.

[69] Tronox Incorporated, Form 8-K, September 12, 2008, attachment *United States v. Tronox*, No. 3:33-av-00001, U.S.D.C., D.N.J., pp. 3–6.

[70] GAO, *Superfund: Litigation Has Decreased*, pp. 11 and 31.

Environmental rules occupy 42 volumes of the *Code of Federal Regulations*, more than any subject and its costs have been estimated as high as $220 billion a year.[71]

Uneven progress has been made in the attack on air, water, and land pollution. Protection has advanced, but there has been too little money, time, and political will to prevent widespread pollution-caused disease and damage to ecosystems.

In the next chapter we discuss methods for determining how regulatory programs can become more efficient and effective and also what voluntary actions corporations are taking to reduce their environmental footprints.

[71] Angela Logomasini, *The Green Regulatory State* (Washington, DC: Competitive Enterprise Institute, Issue Analysis No. 9, 2007), p. 9.

A World Melting Away

Between 200,000 and 400,000 years ago the polar bear (*Ursus maritimus*) evolved from the grizzly bear (*Urus arctos*), moving north from temperate forests into remote Arctic latitudes and all the while developing marvelous adaptations for survival, indeed domination, in a cold, forbidding world. It now seems the great bear's venture will fail as the habitat to which it so carefully adapted falls apart over the current century, a time so short as to be only three-hundredths of 1 percent of its evolutionary journey. *Homo sapiens*, a fellow traveler of the bear in time and space, is aware that fate is closing in and is trying, but not very hard, to prevent the bad ending. This is the story.

THE POLAR BEAR

The polar bear is the largest species of bear. An adult male is two to three times the size of an adult female, weighing between 800 and 1,700 pounds and extending 8 to 10 feet in length. Females weigh only about 500 pounds, but can double their weight by gorging before they enter winter dens to give birth.

Polar bears are predators. Their main prey is the ringed seal (*Phoca hispida*), an elusive quarry because it is an excellent swimmer that can dive 300 feet and stay under water for as long as 45 minutes. Ringed seals venture farther offshore than other seals, living in areas of broken sea ice. They feed on shrimp and plankton in cold waters below the frozen surface, rising now and then to breathe through networks of holes in the ice they open with sharp claws.

Polar bears are adapted to hunt the seals. Big expanses of nasal mucus membranes in their noses endow them with an extraordinary sense of smell. They can scent a ringed seal from a mile away on land and through two feet of frozen surface ice. If a seal is resting on land, the bear will stalk it, creeping closer and closer, its white fur blending with the frozen landscape, finally charging at 25 miles per hour to disable its prey with the swat of a powerful foreleg. Polar bears are nimble on ice. Short curved claws and footpads that act like suction cups give them a foothold.

If a seal is on an ice flow, the bear may swim beneath, gliding under water for as long as two minutes, maneuvering its huge body with wide, paddle-like paws, then suddenly erupting from the water and grabbing the startled seal before it can plunge into the sea. Sometimes bears lie patiently at a breathing hole. When a seal rises there is an instant of violence when the bear smashes its paws through the ice, hooks the seal with short, sharp claws, and yanks it out of the water. The bear will rip the seal's body apart with sharp, curved teeth, gulping down chunks of blubber without chewing.

Bears also prey on other marine mammals including bearded seals, harp seals, and walrus pups. On land they will eat berries, bird eggs, grasses, and washed up whale carcasses. However, they cannot flourish without a diet rich in seal blubber. Polar bears store fat in their bodies. As mammals they need to maintain a constant body temperature and layers of fat up to five inches thick are excellent

A male polar bear on the shore of Hudson Bay in Canada. Note the slight ears, an evolutionary adaptation to avoid heat loss.
Source: AP Photo/The Canadian Press/Sean Kilpatrick.

insulation. Fat also adds buoyancy in water and can be metabolized to help the bear survive periods when food is unavailable. There are other protections from the intense cold as well. The bears have a wool-like undercoat and a dense outer layer of hairs up to six inches long. These hairs are impervious to moisture so the bear can shake off water before it freezes on the body. And their small ears and the small surface area to volume ratio of their bodies reduce heat loss.

Although there are stories of polar bears stalking humans, this is rare and commonly their actions are misinterpreted.[1] Having evolved as the top predator in Arctic regions the bears have no enemies in the animal kingdom. Therefore, they range freely without anxiety, approaching objects or movement with unalloyed curiosity. They wander up to campers, work sites, vehicles, villages, and roads. Ordinarily they do not see humans as food and will attack only if antagonized. However, oil companies hire bear monitors to watch for inquisitive ursine visitors at remote drilling pads.

[1] Richard Ellis, *On Thin Ice: The Changing World of the Polar Bear* (New York: Vintage Books, 2009), pp. 105–11.

EXHIBIT 1

The Arctic Polar Bear Population

These are estimates of polar bear numbers in the 19 populations studied by scientists. Many of the estimates go back to the 1990s. For some populations, as indicated, there are no reliable counts.

Population	Bears	Status	Current Trend
Arctic Basin	Unknown	Data deficient	Data deficient
Baffin Bay	2,074	Data deficient	Declining
Barents Sea	2,650	Data deficient	Data deficient
Chukchi Sea	Unknown	Data deficient	Data deficient
Davis Strait	2,142	Reduced	Declining
East Greenland	Unknown	Not reduced	Declining
Foxe Basin	2,197	Data deficient	Data deficient
Gulf of Boothia	1,592	Not reduced	Stable
Kane Basin	164	Reduced	Declining
Kara Sea	Unknown	Data deficient	Data deficient
Lancaster Sound	2,51	Data deficient	Declining
Laptev Sea	800–1,200	Data deficient	Data deficient
M'Clintock Channel	284	Reduced	Increasing
Northern Beaufort Sea	1,202	Not reduced	Stable
Norwegian Bay	190	Data deficient	Declining
Southern Beaufort Sea	1,526	Reduced	Declining
Southern Hudson Bay	900–1,000	Not reduced	Stable
Viscount Melville Sound	161	Data deficient	Data deficient
Western Hudson Bay	935	Reduced	Declining
Estimated global total	20,000–25,000		

Source: International Union for Conservation of Nature Polar Bear Specialist Group, "Summary of Polar Bear Population Status Per 2010," at http://pbsg.npolar.no/en/status/status-table.htmll, May 11, 2010.

The Northern Hemisphere circumpolar region where polar bears live is largely ocean. Frigid temperatures keep some surface waters frozen all year. This sea ice is the primary habitat of the polar bear. In the fall temperatures drop and areas of frozen ice enlarge. In the spring temperatures warm and the ice fields contract. This cycle of expansion and shrinkage creates dynamic conditions in which edges appear, cracks and spaces open and close, and sea currents shift ice floes around. All these movements create an arena where the bears can hunt seals.

Bears are powerful swimmers and travel easily in this environment. A mature bear may navigate a 600 to 1,000-mile journey over the winter as it hunts. As spring approaches the sea ice begins to break up and recede, and by summer polar bears move onto or close to land for four or five months, where they find less to eat and survive on their fat stores. When food is scarce, they conserve energy by sleeping and slowing their metabolism.

Polar bears have a low reproduction rate. Females have litters of one, two or, rarely, three cubs. The newborns are highly dependent on their mothers, staying with them for an average of 2.5 years before striking

out on their own. So females breed at best only once every three years. Breeding occurs in spring or summer, but embryos suspend their development until autumn, when the female bear will excavate a den in new fallen snow. The den is a thermal refuge from the winter cold and with the body heat of the mother it is 18 to 37 degrees warmer than the air outside.

The cubs are born in 195 to 265 days weighing about 1.3 pounds. They grow rapidly as the mother creates milk from energy in her fat stores and nurses them. With the arrival of spring they emerge from the den. Mortality of young cubs is high, but falls each year. Adults between 5 and 20 years old have a 90 percent annual survival rate.[2]

Polar bears were once decimated by hunting. For centuries native hunters killed them for meat, hides, and status. In the twentieth century the natives were joined by rich trophy hunters from the south who tracked bears from airplanes and set automatic gun

[2] U.S. Fish and Wildlife Service, "Endangered and Threatened Wildlife and Plants; Determination of Threatened Status for the Polar Bear (Ursus maritimus) Throughout Its Range," 73 FR 28214, May 15, 2008.

EXHIBIT 2
Distribution of the Polar Bear Populations
The 19 population groups are designated here by name or initials. As indicated by the shaded areas, the Chukchi Sea and Southern Beaufort Sea populations lie within or overlap U.S. territory.

Source: U.S. Fish and Wildlife Service.

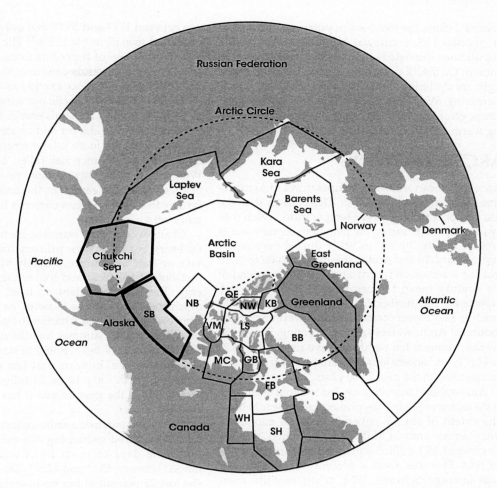

traps in remote locations. By the 1960s the bear population was only 5,000 to 10,000 individuals. However, in 1976 the five circumpolar nations—Canada, Russia, the United States, Denmark, and Norway—signed a conservation treaty limiting the harvest to subsistence hunting by natives and self-defense situations.

Russia and Norway now prohibit all hunting. Canada, the United States, and Greenland (a territory of Denmark) permit native hunting limited by strict annual quotas. Polar bears are still an important source of food, clothing, and income in native subsistence cultures, where polar bear hunts are an ageless source of prestige and cultural apprenticeship for young men.[3] The annual bear harvest is now

between 500 and 700 bears, a number thought to be sustainable.[4] Bear numbers have rebounded and the world population today is estimated at 20,000 to 25,000, yet the number has little precision and the bear's world may be falling apart. Scientists divide polar bears into 19 populations that live in distinct habitats. Exhibit 1 shows estimates of the numbers for each of these populations.

Exhibit 2 shows the area that constitutes the Arctic, which includes the Arctic Ocean and the territories of five nations above the Arctic Circle, an imaginary line hemming the earth at latitude 66 degrees, 33 minutes North. The dark bordered areas in

[3] George W. Wenzel, "Polar Bear Management, Sport Hunting and Inuit Subsistence at Clyde River, Nanuvut," *Marine Policy,* October 2010.

[4] International Union for Conservation of Nature, Polar Bear Specialist Group, "Polar Bear Hunting, Harvesting and Over-Harvesting," March 15, 2009 at http://pbsg.npolar.no/en/issues/threats/over-harvest.html.

Exhibit 2 show the two bear populations that live in or overlap U.S. territorial boundaries. For seven populations the data is deficient and trends are unknown. Of the 12 populations with adequate data, eight are declining, three are stable, and only one is increasing. Why? The answer lies in a series of anthropogenic insults to the bears, the primary one being warming of the Arctic ecosystem.

ARCTIC WARMING

Since 1875 mean annual air temperatures in Arctic regions have increased by 2.2°F.[5] This is faster than the rise in global mean average temperature, which rose by roughly 1.1°F during the twentieth century and is projected to rise by 3.6° to 10.8°F during the twenty-first century. In the Arctic, the decade 2000 to 2010 was the warmest on record since 1900.[6] By the end of the century mean temperatures in the region are expected to rise further, by 5.4° to 9°F overall and as much as 12.6°F over oceans if current warming trends continue.[7] Arctic waters are also warming. Since 1850 average summer temperatures have risen from 38.2° to 42.8°F, an "anomalous and unique" warming unprecedented in the past 2,000 years.[8]

Atmospheric warming has led to rapid shrinkage in the extent of sea ice, the primary polar bear habitat. The extent of sea ice coverage is at its maximum when winter ends in March, and in March 2010 sea ice covered 15.1 million square kilometers of the polar seas. This was about 4 percent less than the annual average between 1979, when satellite measurements began, and 2000. Sea ice shrinks to its minimum extent at the end of summer in September. In September 2010 it covered only 4.6 million square kilometers, or 31 percent less than the annual average between 1979 and 2000[9] and only about half that estimated to exist in the 1950s.[10] The sea ice has also thinned and less of it persists from one year to the next. If warming trends continue, studies project an Arctic free of seasonal ice as early as 2040.[11]

Ice loss accelerates Arctic warming. Light-colored ice reflects much of the sun's energy back into space. Sea water is much darker and as areas of ice shrink the oceans absorb more solar energy. Since 1979 polar surface reflectance has fallen by 11 percent.[12] With more heating there is more rain and less snow. Sea ice breaks up earlier in the season and moves farther from land. Ocean currents increase the distance between ice floes.

Changes caused by warming are bad news for polar bears. Sea ice is their primary habitat. They survive on land in summer, but only by lowering their metabolism, sleeping, and converting fat stores to energy. They are inefficient on land, using twice as much energy to walk as to swim. As ice floes recede from coasts, bears find it harder to find suitable hunting platforms. In summer months of low ice fewer than 10 percent of bears prefer to stay on land. Most seek floating ice. In years past late summer sea ice retreated north only 10 or 20 miles from Alaskan coasts, but in the past decade it has retreated more than 300 miles.

One recent summer a radio-collared female with a cub was tracked swimming 426 miles without rest over nine days to reach ice. Water temperatures ranged between 35.6° and 42.8°F. During her journey she lost 22 percent of her body weight and her cub succumbed to exhaustion. It was an incredible feat, but researchers noted it had abnormally "high energetic and reproductive costs."[13]

[5] U.S. Fish and Wildlife Service, "Endangered and Threatened Wildlife and Plants; Determination of Threatened Status for the Polar Bear (Ursus maritimus) Throughout Its Range," 73 FR 28214.

[6] J. Overland, et al., "Atmosphere," October 14, 2010, in J. Richter-Menge and J. E. Overland, eds., *Arctic Report Card 2010*, at www.arctic.noaa.gov/report card, p. 8.

[7] Center for Biological Diversity, *Extinction, It's Not Just for Polar Bears* (San Francisco: CBD, September 2010), p. 4.

[8] Robert F. Spielhagen, "Enhanced Modern Heat Transfer to the Arctic by Warm Atlantic Water," *Science*, January 28, 2011, pp. 452–53. Ancient water temperatures are calculated based on types and counts of microfossils from sediment cores.

[9] D. Perovich, et al., "Sea Ice Cover," October 15, 2010, in J. Richter-Menge and J. E. Overland, eds., *Arctic Report Card 2010*, p. 17.

[10] Leonard Polyak, et al., "History of Sea Ice in the Arctic," *Quaternary Science Reviews*, February 2010, p. 1759.

[11] Ibid., p. 1757.

[12] M. G. Flanner, et al., "Radiative Forcing and Albedo Feedback from the Northern Hemisphere Cryosphere between 1979 and 2008," *Nature Geoscience*, January 2011. The decline is from 3.95 watts per square meter to 0.45 watts per square meter.

[13] George M. Durner, et al., "Consequences of Long-Distance Swimming and Travel Over Deep-Water Pack Ice for a Female Polar Bear During a Year of Extreme Sea Ice Retreat," *Polar Biology*, January 2010, p. 9.

In Hudson Bay sea ice now breaks up more than two weeks earlier than it did in the 1970s, shortening the polar bear's feeding season. Over this time the average weight of female bears has declined almost 150 pounds, lowering their reproductive rate.[14] If future ice breakup occurs one month earlier, it is estimated that 40 to 73 percent of females will fail to reproduce. And if breakup occurs two months earlier the failure rate will be between 55 and 100 percent.[15] Litter sizes will decline as breakup times advance.

Warming also hinders reproduction of the bear's prey. Female ringed seals build snow lairs on surface ice to hide their pups during six weeks of nursing. With increased rainfall, areas of abundant snow have diminished. In fact, warming has broadly disrupted a web of dependencies in the Arctic ecosystem.

With spring coming earlier some species have advanced the timing of life events. Plants unfold and flower, birds lay their eggs, and insects come forth as much as a month sooner than a few decades ago. This creates mismatching life cycles when other species do not shift their activities. In Greenland, for example, moss and lichen begin to grow earlier now, but the caribou have not moved up their annual migration to coincide with this dietary availability.[16]

GLOBAL WARMING

Recent warming in polar regions is well documented. So is global warming over the past century. Although cycles of climate warming and cooling have occurred over millennia, recent warming is singularly abrupt and is attributed to human activity, particularly the emission of global warming gases through industrial activity. These gases alter the *greenhouse effect,* an atmospheric mechanism that insulates the earth's surface from the cold of space.

The atmosphere acts to maintain a delicate balance between energy gained by absorption of sunlight and energy lost when it is reradiated by the earth back into space. In retaining heat the molecules of the atmosphere are analogous to the glass in a common greenhouse where plants grow. Sunlight comes through the clear panes, and heat builds up inside. Actually, the analogy is flawed, since heat buildup in the greenhouse is due mainly to the blocking out of wind currents; the action of glass in blocking reradiated heat is trivial. The atmosphere, however, efficiently traps 85 percent of the heat radiated from the earth's surface. This planetary greenhouse is not caused by a barrier such as a pane of glass; it is created by a set of predictable interactions between radiant energy and atmospheric molecules. Here is how those interactions work.

Incoming Solar Radiation

The sun's radiation arrives at the edge of the thin atmospheric envelope surrounding the earth in energy waves. These waves are part of the *electromagnetic spectrum,* which is shown in Exhibit 3. Their length determines the amount of energy they carry, with shorter wavelengths having more energy than longer ones. Some solar radiation comes in very short, high-energy wavelengths of 0.01 to 0.4 micrometer.[17] This is called *ultraviolet radiation,* and its high energy makes it capable of disrupting chemical bonds in plants and animals. The emergence of life on earth in prehistoric times was delayed until a shield of ozone molecules formed in the upper stratosphere approximately 30 miles high. These molecules absorb the energy in ultraviolet radiation so dangerous levels never reach the planet's surface.

The bulk of solar radiation, however, arrives in wavelengths between 0.4 and 1.0 micrometer, which overlap the spectrum of visible light. The characteristic blue of the sky results from the scattering of solar radiation in the 0.4 to 0.5-micrometer wavelengths when it hits small molecules in atmospheric gases. The eyes of humans and animals evolved to register solar radiation within the so-called visible-light range that is prevalent in the planetary environment. The eyes convert different wavelengths of solar radiation into specific colors.

Incoming solar radiation, called *insolation* from a combination of the words "*in*coming *so*lar radi*ation,*" is absorbed when wave particles of light collide with

---

[14] U.S. Fish and Wildlife Service, "Endangered and Threatened Wildlife and Plants; Determination of Threatened Status for the Polar Bear (Ursus maritimus) Throughout Its Range," 73 FR 28254.

[15] Péter K. Molnár, et al., "Predicting Climate Change Impacts on Polar Bear Litter Size," *Nature Communications,* February 8, 2011, pp. 3–4.

[16] Center for Biological Diversity, *Extinction, It's Not Just for Polar Bears,* p. 30.

[17] One micrometer equals one-millionth of a meter.

**EXHIBIT 3
The Electro-
magnetic
Spectrum**
Ultraviolet
radiation from
the sun, visible
light, and the
infrared radia-
tion given off
by planet earth
are different
wavelengths
on the same
spectrum.

Source: Joe R.
Eagleman, *Meteorol-
ogy: The Atmosphere
in Action* (Princeton,
NJ: D. Van Nostrand,
1990).

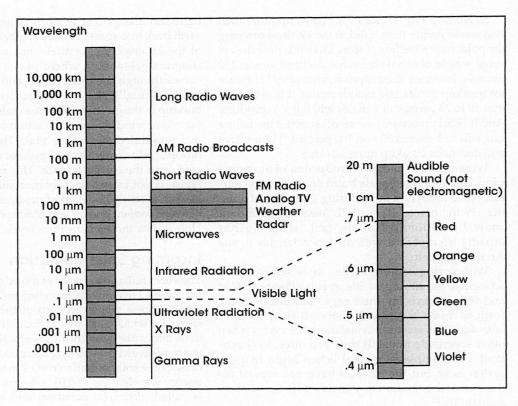

atmospheric molecules.[18] When collision occurs, energy in the light ruptures molecular bonds and moves electrons in the atoms into new orbitals; thus radiant energy in sunlight is converted to energy stored in these atoms. This conversion also causes a temperature rise in the upper atmosphere where it occurs. The process is analogous to making a space on a bus bench by shoving aside the person sitting where you want to sit. The bumped person is still there but in an angry, more energetic, agitated mood. The atom with an *excited electron* is more likely to combine with other atoms in the atmosphere to form a molecular compound. When, for example, ultraviolet radiation strikes ozone molecules in the stratosphere, they are broken down into excited oxygen atoms that tend to seek out other oxygen atoms and molecular oxygen to form ozone once again.

[18] A description of the precise nature of light is elusive. Light has some properties associated with waves, such as amplitude, wavelength, and velocity. It also has some properties associated with particles and has been described in terms of energy units called quanta.

The wavelengths of solar radiation that a molecule will absorb constitute its *absorption band*. Simply put, atmospheric molecules absorb wavelengths that carry an amount of energy roughly equal to that needed to excite an electron to higher energy levels. Molecular nitrogen and ozone in the atmosphere have strong absorption bands in the short wavelengths and block out insolation at wavelengths up to 0.3 micrometer. Beyond that, in the range of 0.3 to 0.5 micrometer, insolation is not absorbed before reaching the surface. Between 0.4 and 1.0 micrometer, the remaining range of the strongest insolation, water vapor in the air is strongly absorbent.

All told, the atmosphere absorbs 25 percent of insolation and reflects 5 percent back into space. Another 22 percent is absorbed or reflected by clouds. The earth's surface reflects about 3 percent back into space. Thus, only the remaining 45 percent of the sun's energy is absorbed by the surface.

Terrestrial Radiation

Solar energy absorbed by the earth's surface is retained as heat that is radiated back into the

EXHIBIT 4
Structure
of the
Atmosphere

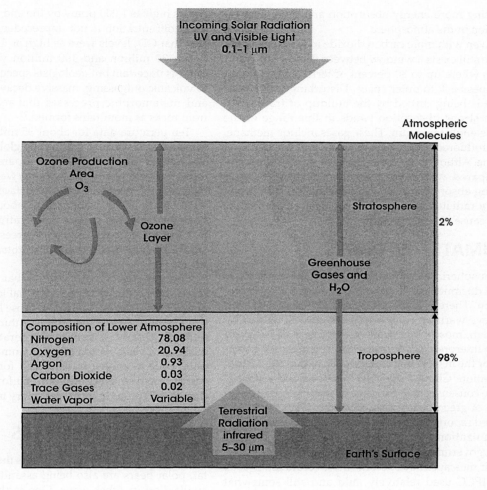

Incoming Solar Radiation
UV and Visible Light
0.1–1 μm

Atmospheric
Molecules

Ozone Production
Area
O_3

Ozone
Layer

Stratosphere

2%

Greenhouse
Gases and
H_2O

Composition of Lower Atmosphere	
Nitrogen	78.08
Oxygen	20.94
Argon	0.93
Carbon Dioxide	0.03
Trace Gases	0.02
Water Vapor	Variable

Troposphere   98%

Terrestrial
Radiation
infrared
5–30 μm

Earth's Surface

atmosphere. There is an important difference, however, between this outgoing *terrestrial radiation* and the incoming solar radiation. Radiation from the earth is given off in much longer wavelengths (see Exhibit 4). The reason is that the wavelength radiated by a body is inversely proportional to the temperature of that body.[19] The mean surface temperature of the sun is 5,800°F, so most of its energy is radiated in short wavelengths. The mean surface temperature of the earth, however, is a dramatically cooler 57.2°F, so radiation from its surface is in much longer wavelengths–from 5 micrometers to 30 micrometers, with peak radiation between 8 and 18 micrometers. This is *infrared radiation*.

[19] This is Wein's law.

Because their absorption bands are closely matched to infrared wavelengths, gases in the atmosphere absorb terrestrial radiation more efficiently than insolation; almost 85 percent of radiant energy from the surface is absorbed or reflected back to earth by the atmosphere. This absorption of radiated energy from the earth is the greenhouse effect. Infrared radiation is strongly absorbed between 0.5 and 7 micrometers and then upwards of 18 micrometers by water vapor. There is a "water window" between 7 and 18 micrometers through which outgoing radiation can escape. But it is partially closed in the wavelengths from 13 to 17 micrometers by atmospheric carbon dioxide. The growing concentrations of atmospheric carbon dioxide created by industrialization have increased the opacity of this window, causing more energy absorption and more heat retention in the atmosphere.

Even with more carbon dioxide in the atmosphere there still exists a window between 7 and 13 micrometers where up to 80 percent of terrestrial radiation escapes back to outer space. Disturbingly, this window is being dirtied by the buildup of trace gases with strong absorption bands in this range of the wavelength spectrum. These gases include methane, chlorofluorocarbons, nitrous oxide, and tropospheric ozone. Although the trace gases are small in quantity compared with carbon dioxide, because of their strong absorption bands in wavelengths that previously radiated into space freely, they are an important cause of heat retention.

CLIMATE HISTORY

Atmospheric warming in the twentieth century is well documented. Its meaning is subject to interpretation. There is conflict between climatologists who believe warming is *anthropogenic,* that is, caused by human, mostly industrial, activity, and disbelievers who interpret warming as either a temporary anomaly or the newest manifestation of a recurring natural variation. Climate scientists have reached a strong, wide consensus that the cause is anthropogenic emission of greenhouse gases. Since the 1970s they have issued reports and assessments through international organizations, most recently the United Nations Intergovernmental Panel on Climate Change (IPCC). Their messages have become more confident. In 1995 the IPCC used relatively mild and still somewhat tentative language when it said "the balance of evidence suggests a discernable human influence on climate."[20] In 2007 the IPCC issued a new report asserting that "warming of the climate system is now unequivocal" and "very likely due to anthropogenic [greenhouse gas] increases."[21]

Climate history is instructive. Atmospheric CO_2 has risen from about 270 parts per million by volume (ppmv) before the Industrial Revolution to 390 ppmv today. Absent actions to mitigate emissions it could rise as high as 1,000 ppmv by the end of the century. This concentration is not unprecedented. Data suggest that CO_2 levels were as high as 1,000 ppmv between 30 million and 100 million years ago. The cause is uncertain but geologists speculate it was due to volcanic outgassing, massive decay of vegetation, and metamorphic processes that released carbon from rocks as mountains formed.[22]

Temperature data for about 35 million years ago show a much warmer world. The global mean average temperature was 87.8°F compared with 57.2°F today.[23] Then, as today, warming was amplified in the polar regions. Tropical sea surface temperatures were 95° to 104°F compared to about 86°F today; however, polar sea surface temperatures were 68° to 77°F compared with only 40 degrees today, a temperature range that would mean total loss of Arctic sea ice.[24]

Study of past climates reveals that very high CO_2 levels were reduced to preindustrial levels over tens of millions of years. A return to those levels in a relative eye blink of less than three centuries is unprecedented. A slow, leisurely, temperature rise over millions of years would allow mammals such as the polar bear to evolve traits suited for survival in a warm, ice-free environment. Unfortunately, the change will occur in an evolutionary instant.

TWO OTHER THREATS

Just when Arctic warming threatens their sea ice habitat, polar bears are also being assaulted by modern civilization in other ways. One is the presence of industrial-age pollutants. Southerly winds and ocean currents transport molecular traces of flame retardants, solvents, surfactants, pesticides, metals, and other substances to the Arctic. Many of these chemicals are persistent, meaning their molecular bonds resist breakdown in nature.

[20] Intergovernmental Panel on Climate Change, *IPCC Second Assessment: Climate Change 1995* (Geneva and Nairobi: World Meteorological Organization and United Nations Environmental Programme, 1995), p. 22.

[21] Intergovernmental Panel on Climate Change, *Climate Change 2007: Synthesis Report* (New York: IPCC, 2007), p. 72.

[22] Paul N. Pearson, "Increased Atmospheric CO_2 During the Middle Eocene," *Science,* November 5, 2010, p. 763. Trace atmospheric CO_2 levels can be estimated using carbon isotope ratios in organic compounds found in marine algae taken from ancient sediments.

[23] Jeffrey Kiehl, "Lessons from Earth's Past," *Science,* January 14, 2011, p. 158; and National Aeronautics and Space Administration, "GISS Surface Temperature Analysis," at http://data.giss.nasa.gov/gistemp/abs_temp.html, February 20, 2011.

[24] Kiehl, "Lessons from Earth's Past," p. 158.

Of particular concern are dozens of organochlorine molecules, PCBs and DDT are two examples, because they bond with fat molecules. At the top of the Arctic marine food chain, polar bears that depend on fat-rich diets accumulate these organic chemicals in their adipose tissues. Their livers metabolize them, but the metabolites are biologically active and are suspected of interfering with the bear's immune, endocrine, and reproductive systems.[25]

A second intrusion into bear habitat is fossil fuel extraction. The Arctic is enormously rich in oil and natural gas, and activity is increasing. Most production now takes place on land, where networks of roads, pipelines, and well pads laid down in sparsely populated areas increase the number of bear–human interactions.

However, the outer continental shelf in seas north of Alaska holds as much $3 trillion of energy reserves, including 24 billion barrels of oil and 108 trillion cubic feet of natural gas.[26] Therefore, much future activity may move out to sea, bringing with it more noise, ship traffic, and oil spills with uncertain effect on the bears. Other nations will exploit Arctic oceans too. Russia already has a field of 113 trillion cubic feet of gas under development and estimates reserves of 586 billion barrels of oil in the Barents Sea.[27]

For a lease sale off the Alaskan north coast a federal agency estimated the chance of an oil spill of 1,000 barrels or greater was 11 percent. A few years later, for another lease sale, it estimated the chances in the range of 33 to 51 percent.[28] Oil spilled in the Arctic environment would persist. If it occurred in winter, oil might be trapped under the ice until summer thaw. Or oil might collect in cracks and open spaces between the ice floes where polar bears hunt seals. If a bear became coated with oil, its fur would mat and freeze, exposing it to catastrophic heat loss. If the bear ingested a large amount of oil in grooming itself, it would likely be poisoned.

Yet the Arctic holds huge reserves the world could use to meet its heavy energy demands. Nations are unlikely to forgo capitalizing on these reserves absent an as-yet undiscovered will to sacrifice economic welfare for even the most magnificent of species.

THREATENED, NOT ENDANGERED

In 2008 the Fish and Wildlife Service determined that the polar bear was threatened with extinction.[29] The Fish and Wildlife Service is a bureau of 9,000 employees in the Department of the Interior that enforces federal wildlife laws. Among them is the Endangered Species Act, a statute passed in 1973 setting forth procedures for designating, or "listing," such species. The act defines an *endangered* species as one "in danger of extinction throughout all or a significant portion of its range." It also permits listing of a *threatened* species that is "likely to become an endangered species in the future throughout all or a significant portion of its range." Once a species is listed in either category, it is entitled to a great deal of protection. Under threat of civil or criminal penalties, it is illegal to "harass, harm, pursue, hunt, shoot, wound, kill, trap, capture, or collect" any individual of the listed species on public or private lands.

The Fish and Wildlife Service listed the polar bear as a threatened species because its Arctic sea ice habitat was declining through its range and the decline was expected to continue. With a current population of perhaps 25,000 the species was not yet in danger of extinction; however, as the extent of sea ice contracted, it was likely to become an endangered species "within the foreseeable future," a time defined as 45 years, or three polar bear generations.

When a species is listed as threatened or endangered the Endangered Species Act requires designation of "critical habitat," a geographically defined area with features essential to its survival. In 2010 the Fish and Wildlife Service set aside 187,157 square miles

---

[25] See, for example, Melissa A. McKinney, et al., "The Role of Diet on Long-Term Concentration and Pattern Trends of Brominated and Chlorinated Contaminants in Western Hudson Bay Polar Bears, 1991–2007," *Science of the Total Environment* 408 (2010), p. 6211.

[26] U.S. Fish and Wildlife Service, *Economic Analysis of Critical Habitat Designation for the Polar Bear in the United States,* draft report (Cambridge, MA: Industrial Economics Incorporated, March 15, 2010), p. ES-2.

[27] Scott G. Borgerson, "Arctic Meltdown: The Economic and Security Implications of Global Warming," *Foreign Affairs,* March 2008, p. 63.

[28] U.S. Fish and Wildlife Service, "Endangered and Threatened Wildlife and Plants; Determination of Threatened Status for the Polar Bear (Ursus maritimus) Throughout Its Range; Final Rule," 73 FR 28289, May 15, 2008. The agency was the Bureau of Ocean Energy Management, Regulation and Enforcement.

[29] Ibid., at 73 FR 28212.

encompassing barrier islands and spits along the Alaskan coast, denning areas up to 20 miles inland, and sea ice extending out over the continental shelf to waters up to 1,000 feet deep.[30] About 95 percent of the habitat area is ocean, only 5 percent falls on land. This designated space, of course, protects only individuals of the two bear populations in U.S. territory.

There was major opposition to both the bear's listing and to setting aside critical habitat. Both the energy industry and the State of Alaska objected. Once critical habitat is defined, federal agencies, corporations, and individuals are prohibited from adversely modifying or destroying it. Although energy production can continue, oil and gas companies now have to take precautions not to disturb bears. They are required to study the areas they work in to see if bear habitat exists and make plans to avoid altering it. This requires hiring biologists to search for nearby bear dens and see if they are occupied. All this can delay or prevent production or require rerouting helicopters, pipelines, and roads. Biological assessments cost $50,000 to $300,000 per site. Energy companies also fear lawsuits by environmentalists. At the time critical habitat was designated, the State of Alaska estimated that for a hypothetical North Slope oil field a one-year delay would have a $203 million adverse regional economic impact and a five-year delay would cause a $2.6 billion loss.[31]

The Fish and Wildlife Service is required to set up a recovery plan for each listed species setting out the actions necessary to save it from extinction. For the polar bear this would mean actions to halt the loss of sea ice, nothing less than a massive global reduction in greenhouse gas emissions, and an immediate one, since many greenhouse gases will remain in the atmosphere for years, continuing to cause terrestrial heat buildup long after emissions cease. The agency recognizes that it has no legal authority to do this.

> While we recognize that climate change will negatively affect optimal sea-ice habitat for polar bears, the underlying causes of climate change are complex global issues that are beyond the scope of the [Endangered Species] Act.[32]

Obviously, most polar bear habitat lies outside the reach of the statute. The Fish and Wildlife Service has no jurisdiction over CO_2 emissions from a refinery in Lagos or a steel mill in Brussels. An international authority is required. So far the world has taken little action to reduce greenhouse gas emissions. Efforts to negotiate comprehensive regulations have repeatedly failed. The two most salient efforts, the Kyoto Protocol and a European emissions trading scheme, are better valued for their precedent than for their impact on atmospheric chemistry. The United States has avoided both international commitments and meaningful national reductions.

Nevertheless, a Fish and Wildlife Service field office in Alaska has a five-year conservation plan for polar bears in the critical habitat.[33] It protects maternal dens by prohibiting oil and gas drilling within one mile and setting a minimum altitude for airplane overflights. Barge operators who ply Alaskan waters are trained to avoid swimming bears. Other actions are designed to reduce lethal bear–human encounters. Town garbage dumps must be adequately fenced. Tourists are given safety guidelines. Funds are granted for village bear patrols by officers equipped with guns that fire crackershells and beanbags.

FADING AWAY

It is a small beginning indeed. Other nations have not galvanized themselves even this much. In Norway a law protects some land habitat from development. In Russia the bears are listed as a "protected" species when they are in areas with national park-like designations. And in Canada the bear is listed as a "species of special concern" under its Species at Risk Act, but this is a less urgent classification than the bear's "threatened" listing under the U.S. Endangered Species Act and requires no stringent measures.

Currently there are 1,372 species listed as threatened or endangered under the Endangered Species Act–579 animals and 793 plants. A listing is ominous. Only 46 species have ever been delisted despite

---

[30] U.S. Fish and Wildlife Service, "Designation of Critical Habitat for the Polar Bear (Ursus maritimus) in the United States; Final Rule," 75 FR 76086, December 7, 2010.

[31] Ibid., at 76104-76107.

[32] Ibid., at 76116.

[33] U.S. Fish and Wildlife Service, *Spotlight Species Action Plan: Polar Bear*, Anchorage, Alaska, RPN-5C, undated.

almost four decades of regulatory protection. Of these, nine species are extinct. Another 19 have recovered. The rest were taken off for a variety of reasons, most because they had been misclassified as a separate species.[34] The polar bear will be on the list for a long time. Eventually it will come off, for one reason or another.

[34] U.S. Fish and Wildlife Service, "Species Reports" Environmental Conservation Online System, at http://ecos. fws.gov/tess, February 15, 2011.

Questions

1. Do you believe that polar bears are endangered as a species now or in the future? Why or why not?
2. What is the value of the polar bear to the United States? To humanity?
3. Is it important that humanity act to save the polar bear? Why or why not?
4. Can the bear be saved? What actions are required?
5. Should more be done now? If so, what is feasible?
6. Would the economic and noneconomic benefits of saving the bear exceed the costs?

Chapter **Fourteen**

Managing Environmental Quality

The Commerce Railyards

Six miles east of downtown Los Angeles lies a busy, seven-square-mile city with a population of 13,435. On incorporation in 1962 it named itself Commerce to signal it was a business-friendly community. Over the years the city boomed, and today it is a vibrant jumble of factories, businesses, and residential neighborhoods, the whole bisected by two major freeways. Within its borders tight rows of older, modest homes abut industrial strips and railroad tracks.

The tracks bind four railyards sprawled over a land triangle four miles long and one mile deep. One is operated by Union Pacific Railroad and the other three by BNSF Railway. Together, these railyards constitute one of the world's largest inter-modal transport facilities. Approximately 40 percent of America's retail goods pass through them.

Around the clock trucks stream in through entrances three lanes wide. They arrive laden with imported goods in cargo containers from the ports of Los Angeles and Long Beach. Inside, cranes lift their loads onto trains that roll to every part of the country.

The area teems with locomotives. Every day, 40 long freights run through just the Union Pacific East Yard, pulled by line-haul diesels with 12 to 20 cylinders producing up to 6,000 horsepower. Smaller switch engines rove the metal arteries, building and breaking down the trains. Other locomotives sit being washed, fueled, serviced, and rebuilt.

The railyards saturate Commerce with diesel exhaust. A study by California regulators found that each year they pour out 40 tons of diesel particulate and another 113 tons comes from trucking activity in the vicinity.[1] Exhaust gases and soot billow forth, bred of innumerable explosions in the cylinders of locomotives, trucks, cranes, forklifts, and generators. They move on the breezes, infiltrating nearby homes. Residents inhale the vapors, and small poisons circulate in their blood.

---

[1] Ambreen Mahmood et al., *Draft Health Risk Assessment for the Four Commerce Railyards,* California Environmental Protection Agency, Air Resources Board, May 23, 2007, p. 7.

Diesel Exhaust

Diesel exhaust is a complex mix of gases and particles. It contains hundreds of substances, including at least 40 that cause cancer. Gases include carcinogens such as formaldehyde, acetaldehyde, acrolein, benzene, and 1,3-butadiene. The heat of combustion also forms particles, tiny spheres of elemental carbon 0.5 μm or smaller, so small it would take 1,270,000 put end to end to equal one inch. Other substances in the exhaust stream, including sulfuric acid, lead, mercury, hydrocarbons, and arsenic, adhere to these carbon spheres, coating them with toxins.

After emission, diesel exhaust undergoes complex reactions in the atmosphere. Its constituents degrade more rapidly during the day than at night. Most gases break down in a few hours to several days, although some have lifetimes of weeks to months. They contribute to acid rain, global warming, and urban smog. Organic compounds on the particles have half-lives of a few hours to two days. Black soot composed of carbon particles settles to earth over several days.[2] While suspended in the air it absorbs light and reduces visibility.

Inhaled specks of soot go deep into the airways. Toxic compounds on their surfaces come in contact with tissues and pass into the bloodstream. Acute exposure to diesel exhaust irritates the eyes, throat, and bronchial lining, causing phlegm production, coughing, headache, dizziness, chest tightness, bronchitis, and difficulty breathing. Chronic exposure can cause asthma. Based on studies of diesel exhaust exposure and lung cancer in truck drivers, locomotive engineers, and heavy equipment operators, the EPA characterizes diesel exhaust as a "likely" carcinogen.[3]

Calculating the Risk

California regulators recently studied the railyards, measuring diesel exhaust emissions, plotting winds, and calculating cancer risks to nearby residents. In a neighborhood of 400 people nestled between two of the railyards, they estimated a cancer risk elevation of 800 chances in a million. For another 4,800 people living just beside the railyards they estimated a risk elevation as high as 690 chances in a million. On two small residential islands within a half mile of railyard boundaries, another 13,000 people face an elevated risk of up to 500 chances in a million. Floating over the city limits of Commerce, the plume of diesel exhaust falls on another 1.3 million people. Their cancer risk is elevated by 100 chances in a million at roughly one mile, 50 chances in a million at two miles, 25 chances in a million at three miles, and 10 chances in a million at four miles and beyond.

Risk elevation from the railyards must be added to existing background levels. The background cancer risk in Los Angeles is roughly 250,000 per million. Additional risk

---

[2] National Center for Environmental Assessment, Office of Research and Development, *Health Assessment Document for Diesel Engine Exhaust* (Washington, DC: Environmental Protection Agency, EPA/600/8-90/057F, May 2002), table 2-20 and p. 2-93.

[3] Environmental Protection Agency, "Diesel Engine Exhaust (CASRN N.A.)," Integrated Risk Information System, at www.epa.gov/iris/, last revised February 28, 2003, I.B.

FIGURE 14.1
Average
Elevations
in Cancer
Risk for
Populations
near the
Commerce
Railyards

Source: Adapted
from Figure 11-4,
A. Mahmood et al.,
*Draft Health Risk
Assessment for the
Four Commerce
Railyards,* California
Environmental
Protection Agency,
Air Resources
Board, May 23, 2007.

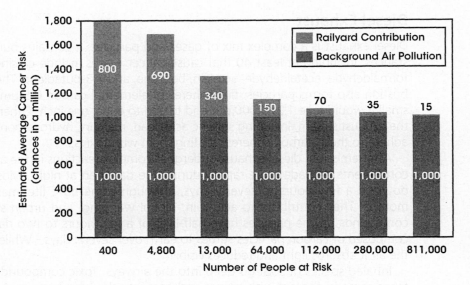

from inhaling toxic pollutants in the local air basin further elevates this risk by another 1,000 in a million. As Figure 14.1 shows, those living closest to the railyards have an overall risk elevation of 1,800 chances in a million. Public release of these estimates triggered anger in Commerce residents. In the words of one woman whose father died of cancer: "The railroads are a killer."[4]

Controlling the Risk

In 2008 the EPA adopted a rule to reduce particle emissions from locomotives 90 percent by 2030.[5] Railroads must use "catalyzed diesel particulate filters," effective, but so heavy that when they fill with particles cranes are needed to lift them from locomotives. The agency estimates that by 2030 its rule will prevent 1,100 premature deaths each year. But the most stringent emission standards begin only in 2015 and even by 2030 they apply only to new locomotives. According to one California air regulator, "It's too little too late. Every year they delay . . . is another year that Southern Californians die needlessly from air pollution from . . . locomotives."[6]

So families in Commerce live with an elevated cancer risk, one cost of filling big box stores across America with candles, furniture, school supplies, cell phones, printers,

[4] Rosa Zambrano, quoted in Bill Mongelluzzo, "Small Particles, Large Obstacle," *Journal of Commerce,* June 4, 2007, p. 44.

[5] Environmental Protection Agency, "Control of Emissions of Air Pollution From Locomotive Engines and Marine Compression-Ignition Engines Less Than 30 Liters per Cylinder; Republication," 73 FR 37096, June 30, 2008.

[6] Barry Wallerstein, executive officer of the South Coast Air Quality Management District, quoted in Janet Wilson, "Train, Ship Pollution Targeted by EPA," *Los Angeles Times,* March 15, 2008, pp. B1–B12.

and toys. They do not shoulder the burden cheerfully. "We call this cancer alley," says one resident, "[a]nd we're fed up."[7]

In this chapter we begin by explaining how pollution risks such as diesel exhaust are assessed to find out which are the most important to regulate. Then, we discuss alternative approaches to regulation with emphasis on new, more flexible initiatives. Finally, we illustrate ways that some innovative companies are seeking to reduce adverse environmental impacts.

REGULATING ENVIRONMENTAL RISK

Environmental regulation is very expensive. Estimates are imprecise, but past calculations have found its total national cost to be about 2 percent of gross domestic product. If so, the total amount for enforcement and compliance would have been $297 billion in 2010. This is a large sum. Is the money well spent? It seems to be. According to a government report, for the decade 1999 to 2009 the benefits of Environmental Protection Agency rules were estimated at between $82 billion and $553 billion while the costs were estimated to be only $26 billion to $29 billion.[8] Thus, every dollar spent returned between $3.15 and $19.07 in benefits.

risk
A probability existing somewhere between zero and 100 percent that a harm will occur.

If regulatory expenditures are to bring maximum benefit, they must be focused on the highest risks to human health and ecosystems. *Risk* is a probability existing somewhere between zero and absolute certainty that a harm will occur. The probability of any pollution risk can be studied scientifically; then regulators, politicians, and the public must decide what, if anything, should be done to lessen it.

Congress has added about 30 provisions in environmental laws requiring that regulatory decisions be based on risk assessments. Its goal is to focus limited dollars on the greatest hazards. The EPA does many risk assessments, and they have great significance for business. If the assessments show that a pollutant such as diesel exhaust poses relatively high risks, EPA rules can require enormous expenditures to reduce them. The railroad industry will spend an estimated $5.7 billion by 2040 to comply with the EPA's locomotive emissions rule. On the other hand, by 2020 benefits from cutting emissions will be $3.6 billion to $8 billion *each year* and by 2030 these annual benefits could be as much as $22 billion.[9]

ANALYZING HUMAN HEALTH RISKS

risk assessment
The largely scientific process of discovering and weighing dangers posed by a pollutant.

The basic model for analyzing human health risks is shown in Figure 14.2. It separates risk analysis into two parts represented by two circles. Circle A contains the elements of *risk assessment,* a largely scientific process of discovering and weighing

[7] Angelo Logan, quoted in Margot Roosevelt, "'We Call This Cancer Alley,'" *Los Angeles Times,* September 24, 2009, p. A1.

[8] Office of Management and Budget, *Draft 2010 Report to Congress on the Costs and Benefits of Federal Regulation* (Washington, DC: OMB, April 2010), table 1-1.

[9] Environmental Protection Agency, "Control of Emissions of Air Pollution From Locomotive Engines and Marine Compression-Ignition Engines Less Than 30 Liters per Cylinder; Republication," table V-13 and p. 37183.

FIGURE 14.2
Elements
of Risk
Assessment
and Risk
Management
and Their
Sequence

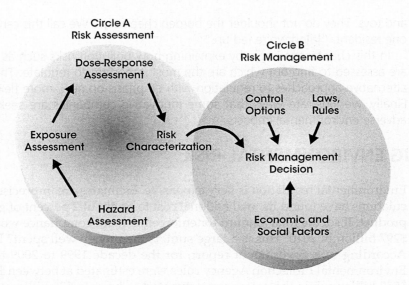

the dangers posed by a pollutant. Circle B contains the elements of *risk management*, the process of deciding which actions to take (or not take) regarding specific risks. We will explain the nature and interaction of these elements.

Risk Assessment

The four basic risk assessment steps used by the EPA are shown in Circle A of Figure 14.2.[10] This method has spread to environmental regulatory agencies in other nations and is now the standard worldwide. In theory, risk assessment is a scientific process leading to an objective, quantitative measure of the risks posed by a substance. As we will see, however, the EPA's method falls short of this ideal. So the agency makes a series of precautionary assumptions based on the fear that experimental results, which are often ambiguous or inconclusive, might understate risks to human health. As these precautionary assumptions pile one on top of another, the process grows less rigorous and, in the view of critics, begins to overstate risks. When risks are overstated, business regulation becomes more expensive and the nation's environmental regulation dollars are inefficiently spent. Nevertheless, risks are often overstated to ensure that public health is protected with a margin of safety.

Hazard Assessment

Hazard assessment establishes a link between a substance, such as a chemical, and human disease. When a substance is thought to pose a risk, the two basic methods of proving it dangerous are animal testing and epidemiological studies.

In animal tests, mice and rats are exposed to a substance through diet, inhalation, or other means for an appreciable part of their life span. A typical cancer

risk management The process of deciding which regulatory action to take (or not take) to protect the public from the risk posed by a pollutant.

hazard assessment The process of establishing a link between a substance, such as a chemical, and human disease. The link is established primarily by animal tests and epidemiological studies.

[10] The most recent statement of these guidelines is Risk Assessment Forum, Environmental Protection Agency, *Guidelines for Carcinogen Risk Assessment,* EPA/630/P-03/001F, March 2005. See also the recent evaluation of the guidelines by the National Research Council in *Science and Decisions: Advancing Risk Assessment* (Washington, DC: National Academies Press, 2009).

study has multiple groups of 50 rodents of both sexes six to eight weeks of age. One group is exposed to the maximum dose the animals can tolerate without dying. At least two other groups receive stepped-down doses. Another group is a control group with no exposure to the substance. At the end of the test, usually 24 months, the animals are dissected and tumors and other abnormalities in organs are counted. If the exposed animals have many tumors, the assumption is that the chemical is an animal *carcinogen*, and regulators make the precautionary assumption that the test is evidence of carcinogenicity in humans. However, several problems cast doubt on the validity of this assumption.

First, scientists rely heavily on strains of rats and mice genetically disposed to high rates of tumor production. This predisposition raises doubts about whether a substance is a complete carcinogen or simply a tumor promoter in an otherwise susceptible species. EPA guidelines call for summing benign and malignant tumors and basing the assumption of carcinogenicity on the total rather than only on the number of malignant tumors. This is another precautionary assumption that may exaggerate risk.

Second, in animals exposed to large amounts of a chemical, tumors can arise from tissue irritation rather than normal carcinogenesis. For example, rats forced to breathe extreme concentrations of formaldehyde exhibit nasal inflammation. Tumors appear in their noses, but some or all of them result from abnormally rapid cell division that magnifies chromosomal abnormalities, not from the carcinogenic properties of formaldehyde. It is scientifically uncertain if a substance that promotes cancer in high doses also promotes it in low doses. Humans, of course, have lower environmental exposures to chemicals than the prodigious doses given to test animals.

And third, animal physiology can be so different from that of humans that disease processes are unique. For example, gasoline vapor causes kidney tumors in male rats, but the biological mechanism causing these tumors is unique to rats; humans lack one protein involved. Even animals differ in their susceptibility to disease. Inhalation of cadmium dust, to which some factory workers are exposed, causes high levels of cancer in rats but no cancer in mice. Which result is appropriate for assessing risk to workers? Here EPA guidelines call for making the precautionary assumption that human risk calculations should be based on the reaction of the most sensitive species.

A second method of identifying hazards is the *epidemiological study*, a statistical survey of human mortality (death) and morbidity (sickness) in a sample population. Epidemiological studies can establish a link between industrial pollutants and health problems. To illustrate, recent studies show the following associations.

- Excessive hearing loss in workers exposed to toluene (TOL-you-een) and noise in a plant manufacturing adhesives. This hearing loss was not found in workers exposed to the same noise levels but without toluene inhalation.[11] Toluene is an inorganic compound used as a solvent in manufacturing paints and glues.

carcinogen
An agent capable of initiating cancer. There are 58 known human carcinogens and another 188 suspected human carcinogens.

epidemiological study
A statistical survey designed to show a relationship between human mortality (death) and morbidity (sickness) and environmental factors such as chemicals or radiation.

[11] Shu-Ju Chang et al., "Hearing Loss in Workers Exposed to Toluene and Noise," *Environmental Health Perspectives,* August 2006.

- A 6.5 percent reduction in the time it took to make decisions among workers exposed to 20 parts per million of styrene for eight years.[12] Styrene is used in making plastics, insulation, carpeting, and other products. Styrene inhalation also elevates the risk of losing color vision.
- Reduction in head circumference in babies born to mothers with exposure to chlorpyrifos and pyrethroids, ingredients in household pesticides.[13]
- Elevated mortality from lymphatic cancers among workers exposed to 1,3-butadiene (bue-ta-DIE-een), a chemical used to make synthetic rubber.[14]

Epidemiological studies have the advantage of measuring real human illness, but they have low statistical power and are riddled with uncertainties. In particular, people are exposed to literally thousands of substances, and individual exposures vary. For example, the study of synthetic rubber plant workers, noted above, showed four lymphatic cancers among 364 workers, more in a group that size than the 0.69 predicted by mortality tables for the area's general population. All 364 workers had been exposed to 1,3-butadiene by working at least six months at one of three Union Carbide synthetic rubber plants in West Virginia. The four lymphatic cancers are statistically significant but still a small number. Could exposure to multiple chemicals over the 39-year period covered by the study have caused these cancers?

There are difficulties with epidemiological studies beyond multiple, confounding exposures. Because cancers have latency periods of up to 40 years, these studies may not detect harm done by recent exposures. Death certificates and diagnoses of disease are frequently inaccurate. Multiple diseases contribute to many deaths. Past environmental exposures are difficult, if not impossible, to quantify. So epidemiology must resort to imprecise measures under less than ideal experimental controls. However, its use of human subjects overcomes weaknesses of animal tests, and when multiple studies reinforce a connection between exposure to a substance and elevated disease rates, it is compelling evidence of risk. Inorganic arsenic, for instance, does not cause cancer in lab animals; only epidemiology shows it to be a human carcinogen.

dose-response assessment
A quantitative estimate of how toxic a substance is to humans or animals at varying exposure levels.

Dose-Response Assessment

A *dose-response assessment* is a quantitative estimate of how toxic a substance is to humans or animals at increasing levels of exposure. The potency of carcinogens, for example, varies widely. Formaldehyde is a strong carcinogen that causes tumors in 50 percent of exposed lab animals at an inhalation dose of 15 parts per million (ppm). Vinyl chloride, on the other hand, is a very weak carcinogen that is

[12] Vernon A. Benignus et al., "Human Neurobehavioral Effects of Long-Term Exposure to Styrene: A Meta-Analysis," *Environmental Health Perspectives,* May 2005.

[13] Gertrud S. Berkowitz, "In Utero Pesticide Exposure, Maternal Paraoxonase Activity, and Head Circumference," *Environmental Health Perspectives,* March 2004. Paraoxonase is an enzyme that appears in the blood as a result of pesticide exposure.

[14] Elizabeth Ward et al., "Mortality Study of Workers in 1,3-Butadiene Production Units Identified from a Chemical Workers Cohort," *Environmental Health Perspectives,* June 1995.

FIGURE 14.3
**Alternative
Assumptions
for
Extrapolating
the Effects
of High Doses
to Lower-Dose
Levels**

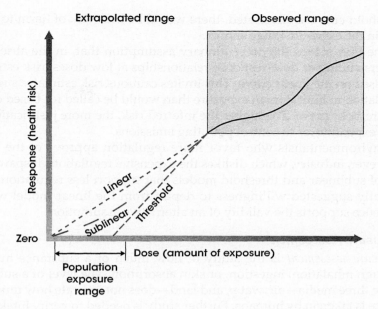

extrapolation
To infer the
value of an
unknown state
from the value
of another state
that is known.

**linear dose-
response rate**
A relationship
in which ad-
verse health
affects increase
or decrease
proportionately
with the amount
of exposure to a
toxic substance.

threshold
An exposure
point greater
than zero at
which a sub-
stance begins to
pose a health
risk. Until
this point, or
threshold, is
reached, expo-
sure to the sub-
stance poses no
health risk.

benign at less than 50 ppm and, even at the much higher dose of 600 ppm, causes tumors in less than 25 percent of animals.[15]

Public exposures to toxic substances are usually well below the exposures of workers. And the exposures of both workers and the public are far lower than the extreme exposures of animals in high-dose tests. For most chemicals, in fact, regulators use *extrapolation* from high doses to predict the effects on human populations at much lower doses. For many years, the EPA has used a model that assumes a *linear dose-response rate*—that is, that there will be a proportionate decrease in cancers from large exposures to small ones (if, for example, exposure decreases by 25 percent, then cancers will decrease by 25 percent).

Figure 14.3 illustrates the theory of extrapolation from high to low doses with respect to carcinogens. The shaded area covers an observed range of responses at relatively high doses. Epidemiological studies on workers and laboratory experiments with rodents typically produce such data in high-dose ranges. The linear extension moving down to zero from the observed range is a prediction made in the absence of experimental data, one that is conservative in protecting public health. It suggests that risks rise substantially over the range of exposure to a human population. Many carcinogens, on the other hand, are less dangerous at low doses, as represented by the sublinear curve extending from the observed range. And still other carcinogens have a *threshold*, that is, they do not produce tumors at very low exposure levels and pose no risk until some threshold exposure amount is exceeded. If the hypothetical substance in Figure 14.3 responded based on the

[15] Louis A. Cox, Jr., and Paolo F. Ricci, "Dealing with Uncertainty: From Health Risk Assessment to Environmental Decision Making," *Journal of Energy Engineering*, August 1992, p. 79.

threshold curve as illustrated, there would be little risk of harm to public health within the exposure range shown.

The EPA makes the precautionary assumption that, in the absence of a clear understanding of dose-response relationships at low doses, risk estimates should be based on the linear curve. This invites cautious risk estimates suggesting more regulation to limit human exposure than would be called for based on a sublinear or threshold curve. The higher the inferred risk, the more justification there is for high expenditures to control polluting emissions.

Environmentalists who favor more regulation approve of the linear model. However, industry, which dislikes the expensive regulations it spawns, favors the use of sublinear and threshold models that support less regulation. The EPA has recently suggested willingness to depart from the linear model when rigorous evidence supports the validity of an alternative assumption.

Exposure Assessment

exposure assessment
The study of how much of a substance humans absorb through inhalation, ingestion, or skin absorbtion.

Exposure assessment is the study of how much of a substance humans absorb through inhalation, ingestion, or skin absorption. The level of a substance in one of the three media—air, water, and land—does not indicate how much of that substance is taken in by humans. Further study is needed to verify intake and concentrations in body tissues.

An example is a study of people pumping gasoline. Gasoline contains five toxic organic compounds that evaporate easily.[16] Pumping gas displaces air in fuel tanks, exposing people to them. To measure this exposure, researchers took blood samples of 60 motorists, both before and after refueling. They found that blood concentrations of all five compounds rose after gas pumping. Benzene, for instance, rose from 0.19 parts per billion (ppb) to 0.54 ppb and toluene from 0.38 ppb to 0.74 ppb. The higher concentrations lasted no longer than 10 minutes. This study confirms that motorists have short-term exposure to carcinogens when they fill up.

risk characterization
A written statement about a substance summarizing the evidence from prior stages of the risk assessment process to reach an overall conclusion about its risk. It includes discussion of the strengths and weaknesses of data and, if the data support it, a quantitative estimate of risk.

To make exposure assessments, researchers measure activities that bring individuals in contact with toxic substances, including such things as how much water people drink, their length of skin contact with water, amounts of soil eaten by children at play, inhalation rates, and consumption of various foods. Because movements and activities differ among people in studied populations, regulators present their estimates as a distribution of individual exposures. The estimates include both a central estimate (based on mean or median exposure) of the average person's exposure and an upper-end estimate for the most highly exposed person.

Risk Characterization

Risk characterization is an overall conclusion about the dangers of a substance. It is a detailed, written narrative describing the scientific evidence, including areas of ambiguity. A risk characterization for a carcinogen, for example, discusses the

[16] These are benzene, ethyl benzene, *m-/p*-xylene, *o*-oxylene, and toluene. Lorraine C. Backer et al., "Exposure to Regular Gasoline and Ethanol Oxyfuel during Refueling in Alaska," *Environmental Health Perspectives,* August 1997, p. 850.

kinds of tumors promoted, human and animal data that suggest cancer causation for pertinent routes of exposure (oral, inhalation, skin absorption), and dose-response levels. Based on the weight of evidence, the narrative ultimately characterizes the risks in quantitative terms.

Benzene provides an example. Benzene is a liquid that evaporates on contact with air. It is produced from coal and petroleum and used as an industrial solvent, a chemical intermediate, and an additive making up 1 to 2 percent of the volume in unleaded gasoline. It is one of the most heavily manufactured chemicals in the United States.

Benzene is classified as a carcinogen based on strong epidemiological evidence showing that workers who inhale it in their occupations have a rising incidence of leukemias as the inhaled amounts increase. Studies with rats and mice show tumors in multiple sites rising in frequency as benzene exposures increase. Cellular research gives evidence of how benzene acts in the body to cause cancer. In the liver inhaled benzene is broken down into metabolites that alter DNA in pathological ways.

Everyone is exposed to benzene. The average American carries an infinitesimal amount, 0.39 nanograms per milliliter, in the bloodstream. Ambient concentrations of benzene rise in areas of heavy traffic and near filling stations. Benzene is also present in cigarette smoke. Based on a range of dose-response data from human and animal studies the EPA estimates a lifetime risk of leukemia from inhalation of benzene of 2.2 to 7.8 in one million for a person exposed to 1 $\mu g/m^3$ (microgram per cubic meter).[17] That is, in a hypothetically average population, 1 million 154-pound people inhaling 706 cubic feet of air each day and absorbing 50 percent of the benzene into their bloodstream, there will be over the average 70-year lifetime two to eight extra cases of leukemia. This risk is low compared with the risk from breathing some of the 58 other substances classified as human carcinogens. The inhalation cancer risk for 1 $\mu g/m^3$ is 4,300 in 1 million for inorganic arsenic, 12,000 in 1 million for chromium, and 67,000 in 1 million for benzidine, a textile dye.

Such quantitative risk estimates help to decide what level of abatement should be required of industry. There is no celestial law about how high a risk should be before regulators must act to reduce it. Years ago, the Supreme Court addressed the subject of when a risk became "significant" and required regulation. Its plain-spoken explanation has guided regulators ever since.

> Some risks are plainly acceptable and others are plainly unacceptable. If, for example, the odds are one in a billion that a person will die from cancer by taking a drink of chlorinated water, the risk clearly could not be considered significant. On the other hand, if the odds are one in a thousand that regular inhalation of gasoline vapors that are 2 percent benzene will be fatal, a reasonable person might well consider the risk significant and take the appropriate steps to decrease or eliminate it.[18]

At the EPA, a lifetime risk of contracting cancer from a chemical substance or radiation source greater than 1 in 10,000 is generally considered excessive and

---

[17] EPA, Integrated Risk Information System, "Benzene (CASRN 71-43-2)," April 17, 2003, II.C.1.1.

[18] *Industrial Union Department, AFL-CIO v. American Petroleum Institute,* 488 U.S. 655 (1989).

subject to regulation. The goal of regulation is to reduce such risks to 1 in a million or lower. Risks that fall between 1 in 10,000 and 1 in a million are usually considered acceptable. With benzene, the EPA estimates that long-term exposure to air concentrations of 0.13 to 0.45 $\mu g/m^3$ pose a 1 in 1 million risk, but when concentrations rise to 13 to 45 $\mu g/m^3$ exposed individuals face a 1 in 10,000 risk. In fact, the average ambient outdoor air concentration of benzene in the United States is 40 $\mu g/m^3$ (about 12.5 ppb), just below this level. If the EPA's unit risk factor is accurate this means that 27 to 78 of every 1 million exposed individuals will develop cancer over a 70-year lifetime. This risk characterization has led the EPA to regulate benzene emissions as a hazardous air pollutant under the Clean Air Act. The Occupational Safety and Health Administration also sets exposure benzene limits for workers (an eight-hour average of 1 ppm with peak exposures of 50 ppm lasting 10 minutes or less).[19]

Policy guidelines developed from quantitative risk estimates anger environmental activists. Asks one: "Would you let me shoot into a crowd of 100,000 people and kill one of them? No? Well, how come Dow Chemical can do it? It's OK for a corporation to do it, but the little guy with a gun goes to jail."[20] However, the alternative to accepting pollution risks between 1 in 10,000 and 1 in 1 million is to decide that virtually no level of risk is acceptable. Eliminating infinitesimal risks from chemicals in an industrial society is not possible. Efforts to reduce them much below the EPA's acceptable range are often prohibitively expensive.

Defenders of industry attack the EPA's risk estimates as arbitrary. A 2.8 in 1 million risk estimate appears precise, but it is based on a series of assumptions about the relevance of animal data, the validity of epidemiological studies, and the accuracy of dose-response curves never directly observed. According to one skeptic, the EPA uses its risk-assessment apparatus to "burden a nation and the world with regulations justified by arbitrary guesses of risk falsely disguised as science."[21] In fact, the agency admits uncertainty, as in its assessment of benzene, where it notes that "[a]t present, the true cancer risk from exposure to benzene cannot be ascertained . . . A range of estimates of risk is recommended, each having equal scientific plausibility."[22]

Risk Management

Risk management (see Figure 14.2, Circle B) encompasses regulation of pollutants and health risks. Whereas risk assessment in Circle A in Figure 14.2 is based on the natural sciences, risk management decisions are based on the social sciences—law, economics, politics, and ethics. We will discuss the elements of risk management.

---

[19] Statistics related to benzene in this section are in or calculated from unit risk and risk level-concentration estimates in EPA, Integrated Risk Information System, "Benzene (CASRN 71-43-2)," and Department of Health and Human Services, National Toxicology Program, *Report on Carcinogens, Eleventh Edition,* "Benzene CAS No. 71-43-2," 2005.

[20] Lois Gibbs, quoted in John A. Hird, *Superfund: The Political Economy of Environmental Risk* (Baltimore: Johns Hopkins University Press, 1994), p. 200.

[21] Gio B. Gori, "Regulating Unknown Risks," *Regulation,* Spring 2010, p. 18.

[22] EPA, Integrated Risk Information System, "Benzene (CASRN 71-43-2)," II.C.4.

Control Options

These are alternative methods for reducing most risks. For example, hazardous wastes can be stored in a landfill or broken down into harmless substances by high-temperature incineration. A spectrum of regulatory options also exists, ranging from strict enforcement to voluntary compliance. Later in the chapter these options are discussed.

Legal Considerations

Environmental laws may be more or less specific about risk reduction required and the methods of achieving it. The Clean Air Act, for example, sets forth the general guideline that regulators should develop criteria for urban air quality that are "reasonably anticipated" to protect public health with "an adequate margin of safety." Further on, the same statute requires the EPA to set standards for hazardous air pollutant emissions based on levels that can be achieved only by the most technologically advanced control devices on the market. The Endangered Species Act prohibits consideration of economic factors in the decision to list a species.

In general, environmental laws tend to dictate regulatory decisions, being so specific that one observer calls them "Congressional handcuffs."[23] However, there is usually some latitude for regulators when they set up the specific rules to carry out congressional mandates.

Economic and Social Factors

Risk decisions cannot always be based solely on science. Technical data, such as control device engineering, may open or limit options. Public opinion may define politically acceptable options. Cost–benefit studies can illuminate the economic consequences of regulatory alternatives. We will now discuss cost–benefit analysis.

COST–BENEFIT ANALYSIS

cost–benefit analysis
The systematic identification, quantification, and monetization of social costs and social benefits so they can be directly compared.

Cost–benefit analysis is the systematic calculation and comparison of the costs and benefits of a proposed regulation. Costs are reductions in human welfare. Benefits are increases in human welfare. Rigorous cost–benefit studies identify costs and benefits, quantify them, and then assign them monetary values so they can be compared using a common denominator. If benefits exceed costs, the regulation increases net social welfare and is desirable, other things being equal.

With environmental regulations, cost calculations typically include factors such as enforcement costs, capital and compliance costs to industry, potential job losses, higher consumer prices, and reduced productivity (for example, lower crop yields from restricting the use of a dangerous but highly effective pesticide). Benefits accrue from reduced injury to the environment and human health. Ecological benefits that are priced may include greater food and fiber production, recreation opportunities, beautiful scenery, and enhanced ecosystem services (for example,

---

[23] Kenneth W. Chilton, *Enhancing Environmental Protection while Fostering Economic Growth*, Policy Study No. 151 (St. Louis: Washington University, Center for the Study of American Business, March 1999), p. 22.

pollination by bees that increases honey yields or soil stability that reduces flooding). Health benefits may include reductions of death and illness, pain and suffering, absenteeism, lost wages, and medical costs.

All kinds of values are priced. The EPA once valued an episode of tightness in the chest from smog at $5.30.[24] In a rule that required mercury emission controls on power plants the EPA priced the value of one intelligence quotient (IQ) point at $8,807.[25] Coal-burning plants emit mercury, a toxic metal that settles on surface waters and travels up the food chain to fish. When pregnant women eat contaminated fish, their babies can suffer permanent mental deficits. Studies showed that a loss of one IQ point led to a 2.379 percent decrease in future lifetime earnings and a 0.1007 decrease in years of schooling. To arrive at the dollar value of an IQ point the agency calculated dollars lost in future earnings, then subtracted dollars saved by less time attending school.

Regulators must submit cost–benefit studies to justify any proposed rule with compliance costs of $100 million or more. In practice, these studies are recondite, expensive, and long, running to hundreds of pages. Although they are done to promote efficient decisions, one prominent effect is to complicate and slow regulation.

Advantages

Cost–benefit analysis has important advantages. First, it forces methodical consideration of each impact of a policy on social welfare. It disciplines thinking, though it does not always dictate choices. Calculations reveal the net social benefits (or costs) of a regulation in dollar terms, but other criteria can be equally or more important, including ethical duties and political consequences.

Second, cost–benefit analysis injects rational calculation into emotional arguments. Environmental risks are not always proportionate to public alarm. When people are fired up over a new menace, politicians, responding to the alarm, can be hasty to legislate. In some laws Congress has required that public health be protected without consideration of expense and this invites rules costing more than the social value they create. Emotional decisions are not necessarily wrong, but dispassionate ones may better match risks and limited dollars.

Third, cost–benefit analysis that reveals marginal abatement costs helps regulators find the most efficient level of regulation. Figure 14.4 illustrates the typical relationship between environmental regulation and changes in costs and benefits. Initially, at or near zero, pollution controls are very cost-effective. Control equipment rapidly cuts emissions and reduces risks to public health, creating rising benefits. However, as higher levels of control are reached, it is increasingly expensive to remove each additional increment of pollution. New control technologies need to be developed. More complex equipment that uses more energy must be installed. Yet even as this money is spent, the risk to public health is reduced less and less because falling concentrations of toxics pose fewer dangers. Costs begin

[24] Environmental Protection Agency, *The Benefits and Costs of the Clean Air Act: 1990 to 2010*, EPA-410-R-99-001, November 1999, p. 70.

[25] Environmental Protection Agency, *Regulatory Impact Analysis of the Final Clean Air Mercury Rule*, EPA-452/R-05-003, March 2005, p. 10–47.

FIGURE 14.4

Relationship Between Extent of Regulation, Costs, and Benefits in Environmental Regulation

Source: Kenneth W. Chilton, *Enhancing Environmental Protection while Fostering Economic Growth,* Policy Study No. 151 (St. Louis: Washington University, Center for the Study of American Business, March 1999), p. 8.

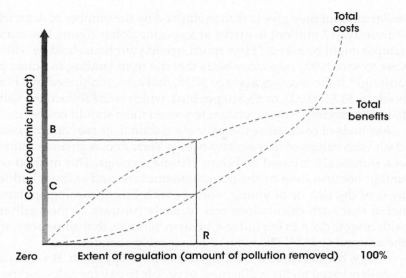

to rise more rapidly than benefits, ultimately exceeding them and eventually rising exponentially as 100 percent cleanup, a quixotic goal, is neared.

The ideal level of regulation is at point R in Figure 14.4, the point where benefits most exceed costs (B minus C). At this point, each dollar spent produces maximum benefit. In theory, dollars spent for regulation after point R could be better spent on reducing other, less-regulated environmental risks. In cases such as this, cost–benefit analysis can identify efficient regulatory goals to prevent skyrocketing expenditures for trivial benefits. It provides an artificial but valuable test of efficient resource allocation for regulators not subject to a market mechanism.

Criticisms

As attractive as cost–benefit analysis seems, it has critics. Here are their foremost concerns.

First, fixing precise values of costs and benefits is difficult and controversial. For the method to work, costs and benefits must be quantified and monetized so they can be measured using a common metric. Yet how can the value of a clear sky, fish in a stream, fragrant air, extra years of life, or preserving species for future generations be priced. Their worth is subjective. Assigning dollar amounts to untraded goods such as scenic beauty or human life invites discord. There are ways to do it, but critics dispute their accuracy.

One method of measuring the monetary value of ecosystem goods is *contingent valuation,* a polling process in which people are asked to put a dollar value on some aspect of nature. Contingent valuation prices natural features that are not traded in markets. One of its first uses was in pricing the value of ecosystems around Prince William Sound after the *Exxon Valdez* oil spill. Using surveys, people are asked what sum they would pay to protect or improve an ecosystem amenity. The average

contingent valuation
A method for assigning a price to ecological goods or services that are not traded in markets.

dollar amount they give is then multiplied by the number of American households (currently 117 million) to arrive at a specific dollar figure. For example, a survey sample might be asked, "How much would your household be willing to pay each year to save 5,000 migratory birds that die from landing in ponds polluted by oil drilling?" If the answers average $0.15, that sum, multiplied by 117 million households, is $17,550,000, or $3,510 per bird, which is the monetized value of the birds to human society. Any regulation to protect them should cost less.

value of a statistical life
The dollar amount that people exposed to a risk are willing to pay to reduce the risk of premature death.

Methods of calculating the *value of a statistical life* are controversial because they clash with values of fairness and equity. Years ago, regulators estimated the value of a statistical life based on future lifetime earnings. This method was attacked as unfair, because lives of the poor, homemakers, and retirees had less value than lives of the rich or of young workers with future earnings potential. One critic noted that such calculations run "directly contrary to the egalitarian principle, with origins deep in the Judeo-Christian heritage, that all persons are equal before the law and God."[26] The method was quickly abandoned.

Today, the EPA uses a "willingness to pay" approach. It values a statistical life in dollars based on the willingness of people to pay for reducing the risk of premature death. It estimates how much people will pay to reduce risk by combining values in a basket of more than two dozen studies. Of these, most are studies based on wage premiums that workers accept to do dangerous jobs. A few are contingent valuation studies that ask what people will pay to reduce certain risks of death or injury. If, for example, because of controls the risk of early death from an air pollutant is reduced by 1 in 1 million in a city of 2 million people, then two anonymous, or statistical, lives are saved each year. If data from wage studies and surveys show that individuals are willing to pay $5 to reduce their risk of premature death by 1 in 1 million, then the value of each statistical life saved in the town is $5 million.[27] Therefore, one benefit of the air pollution controls is $10 million a year, or the monetized value of two statistical lives.

As it turns out, the basket of studies used by the EPA values a statistical life at $7 million and that is now the default figure used by the agency. Critics believe the willingness-to-pay approach is flawed because workers are not always well informed about risks they face. And women, who are more risk-averse than men, are underrepresented in dangerous jobs.[28] Some opponents of life valuation reject all approaches, arguing that the very process of pricing human life mocks its extraordinary and sacred dignity.

Another criticism of cost–benefit approaches is that they compromise ecosystems deserving absolute, not conditional, protection. In American history, the Bill of Rights and the Emancipation Proclamation were never subject to cost–benefit

[26] Thomas O. McGarity, "Health Benefits Analysis for Air Pollution Control: An Overview," in John Blodgett, ed., *Health Benefits of Air Pollution Control: A Discussion* (Washington, DC: Congressional Research Service, February 27, 1989), p. 55.

[27] Environmental Protection Agency, *Guidelines for Preparing Economic Analysis*, EPA 240-R-00-003, September 2000, p. 87; and Environmental Protection Agency, *OAQPS Economic Analysis Resource Document*, Office of Air Quality Planning Standards, April 1999, p. 7–16.

[28] Frank Ackerman and Lisa Heinzerling, *Priceless: On Knowing the Price of Everything and the Value of Nothing* (New York: New Press, 2004), p. 75.

study; the moral rights they set forth were considered absolute. Now, according to some environmentalists, we have a duty to respect nature as we respect humanity, apart from money considerations. Such objections reject the need for efficiency and political compromise in regulation, substituting dogmatic principle in its place. However, it is correct that cost–benefit analysis implies that ethical duties can be balanced against utilitarian benefits to society.

Another difficulty with cost–benefit analysis is that the benefits and costs of a program often fall to separate parties. Purifying factory wastewater raises costs to businesses and consumers. Yet benefits from clean water accrue to shoreline property owners, real estate agents, and fish. In such cases, weighing diverse cost–benefit effects raises questions of justice.

In sum, there is validity in criticisms of cost–benefit analysis, but it may nonetheless bring more efficient regulation. Dollars for pollution abatement are limited. Decisions about where to spend them are required. One defender of the practice of monetizing human life puts it this way: "It's clearly not a winner when it comes to making yourself look good at public meetings, but it's the right thing to do from a public-safety standpoint."[29]

CONTROL OPTIONS

Legislators and regulators have many options for reducing risks to health and the environment. Figure 14.5 shows a spectrum of choices. Most regulation, by far, takes place on the far left. However, there is growing use of options to the middle and right based on evidence that a balance between control and freedom is most efficient. The regulatory alternatives discussed in this section can work in combination. They are not either/or options. They can reinforce each other as parts of an overall regulatory scheme.

command-and-control regulation
The practice of regulating by setting uniform standards, strictly enforcing rules, and using penalties to force compliance.

Command-and-Control Regulation

One cause of high pollution-abatement costs is heavy reliance on *command-and-control regulation*. Most statutes tell regulators to set uniform standards across industries, apply rigid rules to individual pollution sources, specify cleanup technology, set strict timetables for action, issue permits, and enforce compliance, all with limited or no consideration of costs.

Command-and-control regulation has advantages. It enforces predictable and uniform standards. There is great equity in applying the same rules to all firms in an industry. The record proves that it produces abatements and it comforts the

FIGURE 14.5
The Spectrum of Regulatory Options

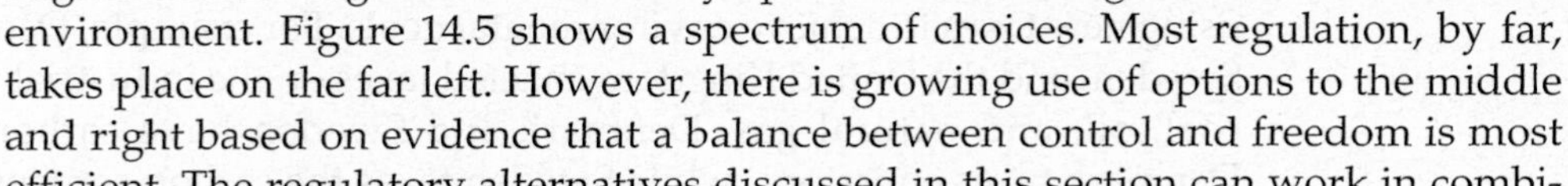

Command and control	Flexible enforcement	Market incentives	Required disclosure	Voluntary compliance
CONTROL				FREEDOM

[29] W. Kip Viscusi, quoted in John J. Fialka, "Balancing Act: Lives vs. Regulations," *The Wall Street Journal*, May 30, 2003, p. A4.

public to know that the EPA is there like an old-fashioned schoolmarm, watching companies like a hawk, slapping wrists, and putting polluters in the dunce's chair.

However, this approach can be inefficient and increase costs without commensurate increases in benefits. The lesson was learned in a milestone case study done by the EPA and Amoco. It focused on regulation at a single refinery. A key finding was that under the EPA's rigid command-and-control approach, cuts in air emissions cost an average $2,100 per ton, but if the refinery had more flexibility in how it achieved these cuts, 90 percent of reductions would cost only $500 per ton.[30] This study was a major stimulus for making regulation more flexible.

Market Incentive Regulation

market incentive regulation
The practice of harnessing market forces to motivate compliance with regulatory goals.

Market incentive regulation gives polluters financial motives to control pollution while also giving them flexibility in how reductions are achieved. This combination usually brings abatement at lower cost and with more creativity. Since the 1990s market incentives have grown in popularity, most of all in Europe, less in the United States. Here we discuss several market approaches.

Environmental Taxes

Taxes can be imposed on polluting emissions, fuels, or products. They were pioneered in Europe and are still most used there. As long ago as 1917 and 1920, Denmark and Sweden introduced the first taxes on gasoline and diesel fuel.[31] Then, the purpose was to raise revenue, but by the 1990s European nations were using new taxes to achieve environmental goals. For example, Denmark, Germany, Sweden, and the United Kingdom enacted taxes on the industrial use of electricity, coal, oil, and natural gas. Denmark and Sweden have carbon dioxide taxes. Denmark taxes emissions, while Sweden taxes the carbon content of fuels. Across Europe, environmental tax revenues average 2 to 2.5 percent of GDP. In the United Kingdom they are 7.2 percent.

The United States has never moved far down this path, but a few taxes are in place. For example, the EPA enforces an ozone-depletion tax on 20 chemicals. It is calculated by multiplying three factors, the number of pounds produced, the monetary tax rate, and a number representing the greater or lesser potential of the molecule for harming the ozone layer. This tax was first introduced in 1990 and since then rates have risen five times to discourage use of these chemicals.

"Green" taxes have important strengths as policy tools. Like command regulation they are an incentive for polluters to reduce emissions. And they are consistent with the "polluter pays principle," imposing costs directly on responsible companies. Unlike command regulation they allow polluters to forgo, change, or control production in any way that reduces compliance costs. For example, in 1991 Norway imposed a tax of $65 a ton on CO_2 emissions. At the time its largest oil and gas company, StatoilHydro, extracted natural gas with 9 percent CO_2 content from below the North Sea, then made a fuel for customers by reducing CO_2 to 2 percent. In the

---

[30] Caleb Solomon, "What Really Pollutes? A Study of a Refinery Proves an Eye-Opener," *The Wall Street Journal*, March 29, 1993, p. A1.

[31] Stefan Speck, "The Reality of Carbon Taxes in the 21st Century," *Vermont Journal of Environmental Law* 10 (2008), p. 32.

process it released the other 7 percent into the atmosphere. Rather than pay the tax this venting would entail, the company created a new technology for injecting the excess CO_2 back under the sea floor. Developing this process cost $200 million, but taxes to date would have totaled $840 million.[32]

Sometimes taxes are combined with incentives. An example is Sweden's tax on nitrogen oxide emissions from electric power plants. These plants pay a fixed, high charge for each kilogram of nitrogen oxides they emit. Then, except for a 1 percent administrative fee, the government rebates all the tax revenue to the power plants, but it does so based on the ratio of NOx emissions to the amount of energy each plant produces. This manipulates the plants into an emissions cutting competition. Plants with average emissions get a refund that matches their tax payment. Plants with worse than average emissions get less refunded than they paid in taxes. And plants with lower-than-average emissions get more refunded than they paid in taxes. In this scheme a plant is financially rewarded for lowering NOx emissions more or faster than other plants. It has worked. Since its introduction in 1992, NOx emissions in the largest plants have fallen from 407 to 205 kilograms NOx per gigawatt hour of energy produced.[33]

Environmental taxes can be very effective in changing corporate behavior. Their main drawback is the potential for hurting the competitiveness of a nation's firms in global markets. Because of this, European tax schemes are now riddled with exemptions. Sweden exempts manufacturing and agricultural firms from its fossil fuels tax and limits its CO_2 tax to no more than 2 percent of corporate annual sales. Denmark does not apply its energy tax to coal used in industrial processes. In fact, there are more than 1,150 such exemptions throughout Europe.[34]

environmental tax reform
The substitution of revenues from taxes on pollution for revenues from taxes on productivity.

Some European countries experiment with *environmental tax reform*, or the substitution of revenues from taxes on pollution for revenues from taxes on productivity. Traditionally, the bulk of government revenues comes from income, sales, revenue, and payroll taxes. Substituting revenue from green taxes for revenue from taxes on productivity pays a double dividend. The switch both penalizes ecological harm and eases the deadweight of taxation on wealth-creating activities.

Emissions Trading

cap and trade
A market-based pollution abatement scheme in which emissions are capped and sources must hold tradable permits equal to the amount of their discharges.

Emissions trading, an approach often called *cap and trade,* is an alternative to taxation. A cap-and-trade program begins by setting an initial, overall limit, or cap, on emissions of a specific pollutant. Then the cap is gradually lowered, trying to avoid a sudden compliance shock to industry. Each company is allocated a number of permits (also called credits or allowances) and allowed to release only amounts of pollution equal to those covered by the permits. Each permit equals a unit of pollution, for example, one pound or one ton, and is good for a year. Regulators then monitor emissions from each plant. At the end of the year, if a plant's emissions exceed the amount covered by its permits it is fined.

[32] Leila Abboud, "An Exhausting War on Emissions," *The Wall Street Journal,* September 30, 2008, p. A15.
[33] Lena Högland-Isaksson and Thomas Sterner, "Innovation Effects of the Swedish NOx Charge," Working Paper, Organisation for Economic Co-operation and Development, February 17, 2010, p. 6.
[34] "The Political Economy of Environmentally Related Taxes," *OECD Observer,* February 2007, p. 3.

Companies are allowed to trade permits at a market price. If they reduce emissions below their permit allowance, they can sell their unused permits. If emissions exceed their annual allowance, they must buy additional permits. In this way, polluting companies in effect pay a fine and the money goes to cleaner operators.

Total emission reduction comes when, at scheduled intervals, the government retires permits from the market. To reduce emissions by 50 percent over 20 years, for example, the government could eliminate 5 percent of the annual permits every two years. As the emissions cap lowers, companies either reduce their emissions or buy more and more permits at market prices.

If the scheme works, those plants that can cut emissions at the lowest cost will act earlier, do more abatement, and make money by selling excess permits to plants that can less cheaply cut emissions. Abatement costs vary for many reasons—type of fuel used, type of industrial process, age of equipment, and level of control already reached. In theory, a cap-and-trade program can achieve the same net reduction in pollution at lower cost than command regulations that ignore differences in marginal abatement costs from firm to firm.

The pioneering large-scale emissions trading scheme is a cap-and-trade program to cut sulfur dioxide emissions from electric generating plants in Eastern and Midwestern states. In 1995 the EPA capped annual SO_2 emissions from these facilities at 14 million tons per year and allocated one-ton permits totaling this amount to utility companies. Then the agency began yearly cap reductions by retiring permits, lowering the ceiling to 10 million tons in 2000 and 9.5 million tons in 2005 on the way to a final cap of 8.95 million tons in 2010. Over the life of the program about 200 million one-ton permits to release SO_2 have been traded on an auction market or directly between companies. Their price, set by market forces, rose from a low of $65 in 1996 to about $325 in 2008 with a brief peak of $1,600 in 2007. This is still far less expensive than the penalty of $3,464 the EPA assesses for each ton of SO_2 in excess of a generating unit's allocation.[35]

The acid rain program, described more in Chapter 13, worked so well it inspired other cap and trade schemes, notably in carbon dioxide and other global warming gases. Such schemes are a prominent response to the threat of climate change. In 2005 the European Union set up a cap-and-trade mechanism for tons of global warming gases measured as CO_2 *equivalents*, or CO_2e. The European Union Emission Trading Scheme covers 11,000 power plants, factories, mills, smelters, and airlines that altogether emit almost 50 percent of the CO_2e in EU countries. The European Union is required under the Kyoto Protocol (see Chapter 13) to reduce its emissions by 2012 to 8 percent less than they were in 1990. The plan is to reduce CO_2e allowances each year to meet this target. In 2010 an allowance to emit one metric ton of CO_2e traded for an average price of $18.70.

CO_2 equivalent (CO_2e)
A universal measure that uses the warming potential of CO_2 as a reference for the relative warming potential of the six greenhouse gases covered by the Kyoto Protocol—carbon dioxide, methane, nitrous oxide, hydrofluorocarbons, perfluorocarbons, and sulfur hexafluoride.

---

[35] Environmental Protection Agency, "Acid Rain Program: Notice of Annual Adjustment Factors for Excess Emissions Penalty," 74 FR 50962, October 2, 2009. Nitrogen oxide allowances, which are also traded in the program, were a little over $500 in 2008. The penalty for excess emissions is the same as that for SO_2.

So far, the European plan has brought 2 to 5 percent annual declines in overall CO_2e emissions.[36] Its most important contribution, however, is establishing a *carbon market*, or a mechanism in which a ton of CO_2e is a traded commodity with a price that fluctuates based on changes in supply and demand. There are other carbon markets but they are small. New Zealand is phasing in a national market. The United States has two. The first is the Chicago Climate Exchange, a voluntary allowance trading system. About 100 companies have agreed to make an annual 1 percent reduction in their emissions of CO_2e. After volunteering, they sign a legally binding contract to reduce emissions or, failing that, to purchase contracts equal to the shortfall at the exchange's market price. One contract, equal to 100 metric tons of CO_2e, sold for about $1.20 in 2010. This is a low price, voluntarily paid, and inadequate to force major emission reductions. The second is the Regional Greenhouse Gas Initiative, a program designed to trade CO_2e emissions from electricity plants in 10 Northeastern and Mid-Atlantic states. Its goal is to reduce CO_2e emissions 10 percent below 1990 levels by 2019. In 2010 an allowance for one ton of CO_2e sold for $3.30.

The global market for CO_2e allowances was $123 billion in 2009 and 97 percent of its value was in the European market.[37] Other markets have been slow to rise. Both Japan and Australia considered cap-and-trade systems but failed to pass the needed legislation. The United States is considering such a system. Political opposition is formidable due to fears that putting a cost on carbon will injure domestic industries, particularly those that are high energy users, in competition with industries in countries that put no price on carbon. Such fear will remain until there is a global carbon market. At present, no global institution is capable of setting up and enforcing a CO_2e permit system and cap.

In all the greenhouse cap-and-trade programs discussed here, companies are allowed to meet their reduction goals by paying for *carbon offsets*, or projects that compensate for all or part of a company's greenhouse gas emissions by eliminating the equivalent sum of those emissions from another source. Such projects include planting trees, preserving forests, paying farmers not to till their soil, and recovering methane from pig farms and landfills. In each case, the party buying the offset is credited with the CO_2e of the global warming gas that is never emitted or sequestered. Buying offsets may be less expensive than either direct reduction of factory or power plant emissions or purchase of market-priced allowances. A manager at Shell gives this illustration.

> Let's say the . . . cost [of CO_2e emission reductions] . . . could require a company to replace its diesel engines with natural gas driven engines at a cost of $50/ton, potentially impacting the cost of its products. If 20 percent of the reduction target is met using offsets, however, that company might reach the other 80 percent of the target by upgrading the diesel engine to improve its efficiency at a cost of $20/ton.[38]

carbon market
A mechanism in which an emission allowance for CO_2e is a traded commodity with a price set by forces of supply and demand.

carbon offsets
Projects that compensate for all or part of a company's greenhouse gas emissions by eliminating the CO_2 equivalent of those emissions from another source.

[36] Alexandre Kossoy and Philippe Ambrosi, *State and Trends of the Carbon Market: 2010* (Washington, DC: World Bank, May 2010), p. 6.

[37] Ibid, p. 1.

[38] Testimony of Graeme Martin, "Hearing on *The Role of Offsets in a Cap and Trade Program*," Subcommittee on Energy and the Environment of the Committee on Energy and Commerce, House of Representatives, 111th Congress 1st Session, March 5, 2009, p. 5.

Clean Development Mechanism
A carbon offset program set up under the Kyoto Protocol. It allows developed countries to meet greenhouse gas reduction pledges by paying for carbon offset projects in developing nations.

Worldwide expenditure for offsets under cap-and-trade programs was $3.4 billion in 2009. These offsets were claimed to equal 486 million metric tons of CO_2e. About 90 percent of this activity came under the auspices of the *Clean Development Mechanism* (CDM), a carbon offset program set up under the Kyoto Protocol.[39] The CDM allows countries in the developed world to meet their Kyoto pledges by funding offset projects in developing nations.

For example, the Netherlands built a modern landfill in Brazil to capture methane escaping from decomposition of urban rubbish. After capture the methane is simply burned, releasing CO_2 into the atmosphere. However, since methane is a much more potent global warming gas than CO_2, under Kyoto rules the Dutch receive emission reduction credits at a cost of only a little more than $4 a ton.[40] This is much cheaper than paying for allowances costing almost $19 on the European carbon market. In such faltering ways does the post-Kyoto world make progress toward its environmental goals.

Some environmentalists ridicule carbon offsets, comparing them with the sale of indulgences by the church. Catholics who committed a mortal sin owed God seven years of penance. Beginning in the fifteenth century sinners could instead pay a fee to the pope, who would forgive their sins. One pope, Sixtus IV, promised "complete absolution and remission of all sins" and "preferential treatment for their future sins."[41] Buyers were assured that the Holy Father's action would be accepted forthwith by God. An indulgence was convenient. It made the long work of humble contrition unnecessary. Critics charge that carbon offsets are "new indulgences" that allow polluters to "neutralize" their offense against nature without taking expensive steps to cut their own carbon discharges.[42]

In sum, cap-and-trade schemes open three ways for companies to meet carbon reduction goals. They can reduce emissions, pay for emissions with credits bought on carbon markets, or meet emissions goals using carbon offsets. All three impose costs but, as Figure 14.6 illustrates, market incentives allow flexibility. The major advantage of a cap-and-trade system is that, unlike a carbon tax, it can actually reduce overall emissions as the cap is lowered. Its current weakness is that it raises costs for companies under the cap, putting them at a competitive disadvantage when foreign competitors are outside the cap. In such circumstances, powerful economic interests oppose setting up carbon markets.

Information Disclosure

Information disclosure about environmental performance harnesses market forces by affecting consumer perceptions and equity prices. An example is the

---

[39] Kossoy and Ambrosi, *State and Trends of the Carbon Market: 2010.*, p. 1.

[40] Jeffrey Ball, "To Cut Pollution, Dutch Pay a Dump in Brazil to Clean Up," *The Wall Street Journal*, August 11, 2005, p. A1.

[41] William Manchester, *A World Lit Only by Fire* (Boston: Little, Brown, 1992), p. 133.

[42] Kevin Smith, *The Carbon Neutral Myth: Offset Indulgences for Your Climate Sins* (Amsterdam: Transnational Institute, February 2007), p. 6.

FIGURE 14.6 How a Cap-and-Trade System with Offsets Works

CAP-AND-TRADE MARKET
Say that company A is releasing more CO_2 than its assigned limit, whereas company B is emitting less than its allowance (*left*). Company A can pay company B for its unused permits and thus use them to meet its obligations (*right*).

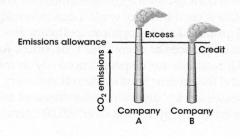
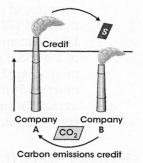

OFFSET EXCHANGE
Imagine that company A is over its emissions allotment. Through Kyoto's clean development mechanism, company A can invest in a carbon reduction project established by company C in a developing nation, which costs less than a similar project in the developed country (*left*). Company A gets the credits it needs at a reduced cost, and company C gets investment money it needs, while less total CO_2 enters the atmosphere than if the developing country had turned to a fossil-fuel energy source (*right*).

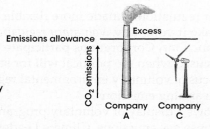
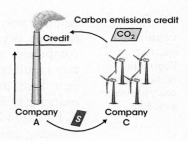

Source: David G. Victor and Danny Cullenward, "Making Carbon Markets Work," *Scientific American*, December 2007, p. 73. Reprinted with permission of illustrators Ann Sanderson and Logan Parsons.

Toxics Release Inventory
An EPA program that requires facilities handling any of 650 hazardous chemicals to disclose amounts each year that are released or transferred. The information is made public.

Toxics Release Inventory (TRI) compiled by the EPA.[43] Each year industrial facilities that release or transfer dangerous chemicals must report the amounts. The data is made public, and citizens can comb through it to learn what substances neighboring factories release. Overall, the numbers show massive use of toxic chemicals by industry, but they put more limited environmental releases into perspective.

In 2008 covered facilities used 23 billion pounds of the 650 toxic chemicals that must be reported. Out of these 23 billion pounds, 19 billion pounds were recycled, burned to produce energy, or detoxified through treatment. About 1.9 billion of the remaining 4 billion pounds were carefully isolated in regulated injection wells or landfills. Only 2.1 billion pounds of toxic chemicals, 9 percent of the total used, were released into the environment through air emissions, surface water discharges, and spills or leaks onto the ground. Of these polluting releases 382 million pounds were known or suspected human carcinogens.[44]

[43] TRI reporting is mandated by two laws, the Emergency Planning and Community Right-to-Know Act of 1986, a law passed after the 1984 gas leak in Bhopal to require that plants and factories report to the public amounts and types of chemicals they store or release; and the Pollution Prevention Act of 1990, a law that requires companies to report treating, recycling, and combusting toxic chemicals.

[44] Figures in this paragraph are derived from Environmental Protection Agency, "Toxics Release Inventory Reporting Year 2008 National Analysis: Summary of Key Findings," December 2009.

Companies dislike being listed as leading polluters by volume and there are many examples of reductions exceeding those required by law just to avoid attracting bad publicity. TRI data is used in many ways. Local newspapers report it to local citizens. Environmental groups identify corporate polluters. Researchers advance knowledge of the social consequences of chemicals. One study, for example, found that "risk producing [TRI] facilities are disproportionately in minority communities."[45] Another study found that in nine Southeastern states every 1 pound per person decrease in total TRI releases led to "an estimated increase of $3.72 in house value and a decrease of cancer mortality by 1 death over 100,000 persons."[46]

VOLUNTARY REGULATION

voluntary regulation
Regulation without legal compulsion or sanctions.

Another way that regulation is made more flexible, besides the use of market incentives, is to make it voluntary. *Voluntary regulation* is regulation without legal compulsion or sanctions. Corporations participate of their own free will. Voluntary regulation is used when the political will for stringent command rules is absent. Thus, the focus of voluntary environmental regulation in the United States is reducing global warming emissions.

Figure 14.7 shows a display of voluntary programs at the EPA oriented toward reducing greenhouse gas emissions. Climate Leaders is the centerpiece. Corporations that join it become "partners." They must inventory their emissions of the six major gases to create a baseline, set an "ambitious" 5- to 10-year emission-reduction goal at least 10 percent better than their industry average, and report their annual progress to the EPA. The agency gives its partners technical assistance

FIGURE 14.7
The Environmental Protection Agency's Climate Leaders Program

Source: Environmental Protection Agency.

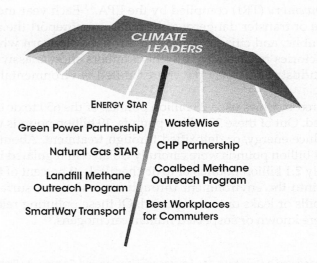

45 Heather E. Campbell and Laura R. Peck, "Justice for All? A Cross-Time Analysis of Toxics Release Inventory Facility Location," *Review of Policy Research* 27, no. 1 (2010), p. 21.
46 Chau-Sa Ho and Diane Hite, "The Benefit of Environmental Improvement in the Southeastern United States: Evidence from a Simultaneous Model of Cancer Mortality, Toxic Chemical Releases and House Values," *Papers in Regional Science*, November 2008, p. 602.

such as booklets with equations used to calculate gas emissions. Begun in 2002, Climate Leaders by 2010 had enrolled 195 corporations. Of these, 27 had already achieved their goals. For example, Anheuser-Busch cut emissions 10 percent, Bank of America 13 percent, Gap 20 percent, and Raytheon 33 percent. One partner, Shaklee, reduced its emissions 100 percent by purchasing alternative energy and buying emissions offsets.[47]

These emissions reductions are expensive, but companies have many reasons for making the effort. Most believe that more greenhouse gas regulation is imminent and want to advance control strategies. When they achieve their reduction goals, the EPA gives them awards and favorable publicity, for example, in full-page ads in magazines such as *Audubon, Forbes, Chemical Engineering,* and *Harvard Business Review* that reach various stakeholders.

Other programs under the Climate Leaders umbrella help reduce emissions in one way or another. WasteWise, for example, began in 1994 as a program to encourage waste reduction. Since then, 2,100 "partners" report eliminating 150 million tons of waste and with it millions of tons of warming gas emissions.[48] In the Green Power Partnership the EPA publicizes companies that buy renewable energy such as electricity from wind power. The Coalbed Methane Outreach Program simply provides technical assistance for mines trying to capture the methane released when underground coal deposits are disturbed.

These voluntary programs work only because there are strong pressures for companies to act sustainably. However, action under the Climate Leaders umbrella falls far short of profound. The EPA reports that since 2002 Climate Leaders claim to have eliminated 50 million metric tons of CO_2e emissions, but this is less than 1 ten-millionth of one percent of the nation's annual CO_2e emissions totaling more than 7 gigagrams. Also, oversight and reporting are not always rigorous. The Energy Star program identifies household and commercial products with high energy efficiency. To qualify, a manufacturer must submit information that its product is 10 to 25 percent above the minimum energy standards set by federal legislation. Yet when federal investigators submitted an application for a gasoline-powered alarm clock from a fictitious company, the EPA approved, never questioning its description as "sleek, durable, easy on your electric bill, and surprisingly quiet."[49] More than 40,000 products have qualified to use the Energy Star logo.

MANAGING ENVIRONMENTAL QUALITY

There are many pressures and incentives for corporations to sustain the natural environment. Although exploitation of nature is a core value of capitalism, some observers see "green management" emerging as an "imperative," a "megatrend,"

---

[47] Environmental Protection Agency, "2009 GHG Reduction Goal Achievers," at www.epa.gov/climateleaders/partner-recognition/2009achievers.html, updated June 17, 2010.

[48] Environmental Protection Agency, *WasteWise 2008 Annual Report,* EPA-530-08-015, p. 1.

[49] Government Accountability Office, *Energy Star Program: Covert Testing Shows the Energy Star Program Certification Process Is Vulnerable to Fraud and Abuse,* GAO-10-479, March 2010, p. 14.

Core Elements of an Environmental Management System

- An environmental policy
- Planning and strategy that include environmental factors
- Identification of impacts on the environment
- Development of goals and performance measures

- Monitoring and corrective action
- Formal stakeholder involvement
- Employee awards, incentives, and training
- A philosophy of continuous improvement

and a "fundamental and persistent shift in how companies compete."[50] Virtually every public company now devotes part of its Web site to statements of environmental goals and claims of stewardship, conservation, and pollution control.

For a few companies these claims are central. General Electric's "ecomagination" strategy repositioned it from an old-line manufacturing conglomerate to a supplier of clean energy and environmental hardware and services. Walmart's corporate emphasis on reducing its global environmental impact is changing its brand image from ruthless competitor to environmental champion. After activists settled on the theme of fresh water depletion as their main attack on Coca-Cola, the company adopted a goal of "water neutrality," promising no net depletion of watersheds in its business.

Environmental Management Systems

environmental management system
A set of methods and procedures for aligning corporate strategies, policies, and operations with principles that protect ecosystems.

Proactive companies establish an *environmental management system* (EMS), which is a set of methods and procedures for aligning corporate strategies, policies, and operations with principles that protect ecosystems. The core elements of these systems are shown in the accompanying box.

ISO 14001
A standard for an environmental management system created by an international standard setting body. Certification in this standard allows companies to claim state-of-the-art ecological responsibility.

The leading international model for such systems is *ISO 14001,* a standard for environmental management created by the International Organization for Standardization. The letters ISO reference this international body and the number 14001 indicates its place in a family of environmental standards. Some large companies, for instance, ExxonMobil, design their own systems, but typically firms base them on ISO 14001 and apply for certification by trained third-party auditors. This is especially attractive to smaller firms, because there is a trend for large multinationals to seek suppliers and vendors with a working EMS, and ISO 14001 certification verifies this. Matsushita Electrical Industries (Panasonic), for instance, has a procurement policy to consider a supplier's environmental record along with cost, quality, and delivery and gives priority to companies certified under ISO 14001.[51]

---

[50] David A. Lubin and Daniel C. Esty, "The Sustainability Imperative," *Harvard Business Review,* May 2010, p. 44.

[51] Matsushita Electric Group, *Green Procurement Standards,* rev. ed., ver. 5 (Osaka: Matsushita Electric Industrial Co., February 8, 2010), p. 5.

The green procurement trend is responsible for an explosion in worldwide ISO certifications from 257 facilities in 1995 to 223,149 in 2009.[52] Most certifications are in developing economies. More facilities in China or Africa have adopted ISO 14001 than in the United States. This is one example of the power of large corporations to extend environmental initiatives through global supply chains.

A Range of Actions

The universe of actions is very broad. Green management is not a fixed skill that can be dropped into a corporation like a module or part. It is an adaptive, singular modification of strategies, policies, goals, and processes that is unique for every company.[53] Nevertheless, there are patterns, as illustrated in the following broad and common categories of activity.

precautionary principle
When industrial activity poses a risk to human health or ecosystems, if that risk is poorly understood, then prudence calls for restraint.

- *Precautionary action.* An idea called the *precautionary principle*, which has taken root among environmentalists, holds that when industrial activity poses a risk, even if the threat is as yet poorly understood, prudence calls for restraint. Recently, advances in methods for detecting chemicals in living tissue led scientists to discover tiny amounts of the substance perfluorooctane sulfonate (PFOS) in human blood and animal tissue around the world. The source was 3M, which began using the chemical in Scotchgard fabric protector in the 1950s. Learning this, 3M scientists expressed surprise and disbelief. They examined health data on workers at Scotchgard plants, finding no adverse effects. However, 3M decided to take the product off the market in 2000 to avert any possible harm to life. Since it had no substitute for PFOS, it lost a $500 million-a-year business until 2006 when a reformulated Scotchgard was ready. Of course, the company anticipated government action and it was petrified by the lawsuit potential.[54] These pressures enforced the precautionary principle. Since production has ceased, blood levels of PFOS have fallen. Today they average 20 parts per billion in Americans.

- *Pollution prevention.* End-of-the pipe control equipment isolates or neutralizes pollutants after they are generated. Pollution prevention is the modification of industrial processes to eliminate contaminants before they are created. For example, many companies have stopped using solvents to clean production equipment, substituting soap or isopropyl alcohol in their place. This eliminates evaporation of hazardous compounds in solvents and often works just as well and at a lower cost. Simple forms of pollution prevention, such as putting a lid on a tank to stop evaporation or tightening valves to stop leaks, are used by many companies. After such easy steps, however, further progress usually requires complex redesigns of processes and products. These projects are

---

[52] International Organization for Standardization, *The ISO Survey of Certifications–2009* (Geneva: International Organization for Standardization, 2007), p. 25.

[53] Alfred A. Marcus and Adam R. Fremeth, "Green Management Matters Regardless," *Academy of Management Executive,* August 2009, p. 22.

[54] Both have come to pass. In 2006 the company paid an EPA fine of $1.5 million for 244 illegal releases of PFOS in violation of the Toxic Substances Control Act. Minnesota residents sued 3M for contaminating drinking water sources with PFOS, but a jury found the company innocent of negligence because it had obeyed existing laws. Bill McAuliffe, "3M Found Not Liable for Home Value Loss," *Star Tribune,* June 18, 2009, p. 1A.

expensive. At many firms they will not be approved, even if they reduce harmful emissions or reduce costs, unless they bring a return on capital invested equal to or greater than alternative investments.

- *Product analysis.* Products can be examined to reduce adverse environmental impacts. Eastman Kodak makes a life-cycle assessment. It looks at factors such as raw materials used, energy consumed, fugitive emissions, and potential for recycling. SC Johnson uses a "greenlist" to rate ingredients for household products. Its chemists have many raw material choices for the surfactants, solvents, propellants, fragrances, and other ingredients that go into brands such as Raid, Off!, Drano, Saran Wrap, and Windex. Before choosing one, they look at a scorecard ranking substances from 0 to 3 based on estimates of toxicity. A 0 means "restricted use" and requires higher management approval, 1 is "acceptable," 2 is "better," and 3 is "best." Chemists try to achieve higher scores as they formulate products. In 2001 the company had an average score of 1.23 and set a goal of raising its score to 2.0. By 2008 it had achieved a score of 1.62.[55]

- *Environmental marketing.* The presence of environmental risks creates markets. Sale of pollution control equipment is an old example. Innovative companies create new demand. Swiss Re, a colossus of the insurance industry, saw global warming as an opportunity. It now sells weather derivative contracts that work like put or call options, allowing buyers such as agricultural corporations to hedge against crop losses from warmer weather. It also sells catastrophe bonds that insure against disasters such as a giant U.S. hurricane or a major European windstorm. These bonds pay investors high interest rates, but if the catastrophe happens, they lose some or all of their principal.[56] Other companies find opportunities in their current business models. Walmart's mission is "saving people money so they can live better." It set a goal of selling 100 million compact fluorescent bulbs every year and achieved this by 2007. It estimates this saves customers $3 billion in annual electricity costs and it expects to get some of these savings back in customer purchases—in effect, stealing revenue from utility corporations.

- *Environmental metrics.* In the past, few companies had environmental goals. Activities that posed risks were largely unmeasured. That is changing. In 2003 a group of investors combined with the United Nations to measure CO_2e emissions in the largest 500 global corporations. Then a little more than 40 percent reported emissions; by 2009 the percentage had doubled to 82 percent. Today, companies measure environmental performance toward environmental goals. Office Depot uses a "dashboard" that matches objectives with key performance indicators. One of its objectives is to "increasingly be green" and a corresponding indicator is "CO_2 emissions from store deliveries." Since measurement started, these emissions have fallen from 91,300 tons in 2006 to 53,200 tons in 2009.[57]

[55] SC Johnson & Sons, *2009 Public Report: Doing Our Part* (Racine, WI: SC Johnson, 2009), p. 23.

[56] Bernard Belk and Roman Hohl, "Agribusiness Corporates Can Insure against Volatility in Grain Volumes," *Trade Finance*, February 2009, p. 6; and Ian McGugan, "Insuring Catastrophe," *Financial Post*, December 5, 2009, p. FP11.

[57] "2009 Office Depot Environmental Dashboard & Key Indicators," at www.officedepotcitizenship.com/ environmental_dashboard.php.

Dow Chemical issues quarterly updates of its performance on a set of environmental goals it intends to achieve by 2015. One goal is to cut the transportation of hazardous chemicals by 50 percent. By 2009 the number of ton-miles (one ton of freight moved one mile) dropped from 1,400 million to 851 million since 2005 when measurement began. Walmart has asked its 100,000 suppliers to calculate the full environmental costs of each product it sells. It plans to tag store items with a simple sustainability index.

CONCLUDING OBSERVATIONS

In the previous chapter we described how industrial activity harms the environment and explained major regulatory programs to mitigate the damage. In this chapter we looked more deeply into the methods underlying this regulation. We began with a story about railyard diesel exhaust to illustrate one molecular-level danger to human health in modern industrial society. Then we explained how such a danger is evaluated and how a regulatory approach is then chosen to mitigate it. We also give some illustrations of how companies are greening their operations.

The discussion emphasizes the strengths and weaknesses of both science-based risk assessment and a range of regulatory approaches. Command regulation is the most powerful, effective tool in the regulatory arsenal. Market approaches are more flexible and less expensive but have permitted companies to pay and continue polluting. Voluntary regulation is inexpensive, but often accomplishes little. Finally, voluntary corporate action can bring slow and modest, but widespread change. As thousands of companies around the world set out to measure their environmental impact and reduce it, their actions may be sufficient to slow the growth of pollution, if only in a small way.

In sum, much progress has been made in protecting both ecosystems and human health. Notwithstanding, the sum of human action is so far inadequate to avert rising global damage. The consequences of this failure will fill future chapters.

Harvesting Risk

This is the story of a scavenger. Ascending on shrewdness, Amvac Chemical Corporation has expanded from a small Los Angeles pesticide company into a multinational corporation with revenues of more than $200 million.[1] It keeps expanding. In the last several years it has added five new product lines, two foreign sales offices, and two factories.

Amvac's growth is based on a singular strategic vision. It stands apart from agrichemical industry giants as they create and market new pesticides. It waits while the big companies build brand names and markets for these molecules. Then, when a product has aged or become less attractive to the original owners, Amvac offers to buy it. Once Amvac has the brand rights, it pushes sales in remaining niche markets or, sometimes, opens new markets by registering additional crop applications or exporting to foreign customers. In this way, as the global behemoths shed shrinking, failing, dangerous, or obsolete products,

[1] Amvac operates as a wholly owned subsidiary of a holding company named American Vanguard Corporation and is the company's main business.

the opportunistic scavenger captures fresh streams of revenue.

Amvac's goal is to acquire one or two niche product lines every year and in recent years it has done so. Big agricultural chemical companies discard pesticides for many reasons. As they integrate businesses after mergers, they may decide to drop redundant brands. When Novartis and AstraZeneca merged their agribusinesses in 2000, Amvac got two vegetable crop insecticides and a herbicide used in cranberry fields. Sometimes big companies cast aside products when sales are inadequate. In the 1990s DuPont created a soil insecticide named Fortress that effectively controls corn rootworms, the most destructive cornfield pests. But sales missed targets. So Amvac bought Fortress in 2000 and with it entry into the Midwest corn market. It built a new sales team and within a year Fortress sales that would have disappointed DuPont were adding materially to Amvac's revenues.

In some cases products have matured or become outdated. Larger firms at the forefront of advancing biotechnology are shifting their focus from chemical poisons to genetic lines of insect-resistant seeds. As they do, Amvac has acquired older pesticides, including some organophosphates belonging to a family of pesticides that is on the way out in the industry.

Organophosphate molecules are effective pest killers and still widely used, but they are being superceded by both biotechnology products and by pesticides that better target pests and pose less risk. Some organophosphates are exceptionally dangerous to human health in terms of both acute and long-term exposures. A few are so toxic that they defy safe use, leading to personal injury lawsuits and regulatory crackdowns. Even in these instances Amvac sees opportunity. Faithful to the logic of its niche strategy, it has acquired rights to some of the most poisonous brands even as bigger companies cease their production. Then, it has sought new markets for them while defending them against alarmed regulators. Here are several stories about Amvac pesticides.

DIBROMOCHLOROPROPANE

Dibromochloropropane, or DBCP, is a chemical soil fumigant that kills parasitic worms feeding on fruit and vegetable crops (see Exhibit 1). It belongs to an aging class of organochlorine pesticides developed after World War II. Most of these molecules, which

EXHIBIT 1 Dibromochloropropane

Source: National Institutes of Health, http://ntp.niehs.nih.gov/ntp/htdocs/structures/2d/TR028.gif.

Chemical Formula: $C_3H_5Br_2Cl$

include DDT, are used now only in a few poor countries. They are stable molecules that linger in the environment and accumulate in human tissue. Beginning in the 1960s, DBCP was used in the United States and around the world on cotton, potato, banana, and pineapple crops. Dow and Shell manufactured it until 1977, when it was discovered to cause sterility in men at formulating plants.[2]

Regulators immediately banned DBCP in California. On the day of the ban, Dow and Shell suspended its production and marketing. Although the story of worker infertility got extensive media coverage, many farmers still wanted to use DBCP. So Amvac stepped in to fill the void and became its leading maker. Due to bad publicity, domestic sales had fallen, so Amvac supplied foreign markets. It replaced Dow and Shell as a supplier for Dole Fruit and other companies using DBCP on large banana plantations in Central America and the Caribbean.

By 1979 the EPA had gathered extensive data on DBCP and concluded it had no safe uses. The agency proposed a ban. Amvac disputed the evidence and finally persuaded regulators to allow an exception for Hawaiian pineapple crops. It agreed to promote safe application and to monitor local groundwater for contamination. In 1983 Amvac applied for a temporary exemption from the regulatory ban in South Carolina so that DBCP could be used in peach orchards. The EPA agreed, basing its decision on university research sponsored by Amvac. Outraged environmentalists stopped the exemption with a lawsuit.[3] Two years

[2] Helen Dewar, "Workers at Pesticide Plant Found Sterile in California Tests," *The Washington Post,* August 5, 1977, p. A3.

[3] Ward Sinclair, "The Return of DBCP," *The Washington Post,* February 1, 1983, p. A1.

later, Hawaiian wells for drinking water were found contaminated by runoff from pineapple fields and the EPA finally banned all applications of DBCP anywhere in the United States.

By this time evidence of DBCP's dangers was strong and before the end of the decade a substantial body of research backed up the agency's decision. DBCP causes sterility in both animals and humans. Studies showed that men who inhaled small concentrations produced fewer sperm and were more likely to father girls. With longer exposures their testicles atrophied and sperm production fell to zero.

DBCP is so dangerous that current regulations set safe inhalation exposure for workers at one part per billion over an eight-hour day. DBCP also causes cancer in rats and is classified as "reasonably anticipated" to be a human carcinogen. Like other molecules in the organochlorine family, it persists in the environment. After application it slowly evaporates from soil or surface water into the air, where it resides for up to three months before breaking down. In soil, it can linger for several years.[4]

DBCP bore a crop of lawsuits for Amvac. Villagers who drank contaminated water in Hawaii sued Amvac, along with Dow, Shell, and Dole Food Company, after researchers found unusual clusters of breast cancer, heart defects, learning disabilities, and infertility among them.[5] Amvac settled its part of the case for $500,000 in 1999. With the others, it was also named in multiple actions by Nicaraguan plantation workers charging that the companies continued to sell DBCP in developing nations after it was banned in the United States despite knowing it caused sterility, testicular atrophy, and other injuries.

These workers opened a broad legal war against Amvac and the others but it has fizzled. The last of the banana workers cases were dismissed in 2010 after the discovery that attorneys had engaged in widespread fraud, recruiting plaintiffs by sending men to labs that faked sperm tests to show sterility.[6] Another case, by banana and pineapple workers in the Ivory Coast, alleged the companies used DBCP for genocide and crimes against humanity. However, because the workers could not prove the companies intended to commit genocide they lost the decision.[7]

MEVINPHOS

Mevinphos (see Exhibit 2) is an insecticide developed by Shell in 1954.[8] It protects fruit and vegetable crops against aphids, leaf miners, mites, grasshoppers, cutworms, and caterpillars. It belongs to the organophosphate family of pesticides, which disrupt transmission of nerve impulses by blocking the action of critical enzymes. Organophosphates are unstable and break down rapidly in the environment so growers can use them to combat infestations that come just before harvest. Their drawback is an extreme and broad toxicity. They poison any living organism with a nervous system, including humans, fish, and animals. Consequently, large agrichemical companies are moving away from organophosphates to newer molecules that not only are less toxic but also more narrowly target pests.

EXHIBIT 2   Mevinphos

Source: Environmental Protection Agency, *Report on Tolerance Reassessment Progress and Risk Management Decision*, EPA 738-R-00-014, September 2000, p. 4.

Chemical Formula: $C_7H_{13}O_6P$

---

[4] U.S. Public Health Service, Agency for Toxic Substances and Disease Registry, *Toxicological Profile for 1,2-Dibromo-3-chloropropane* (Washington, DC: Public Health Service, September 1992); and Environmental Protection Agency, "1,2-Dibromo-3-chloropropane (DBCP) (CASRN 96-12-8), Integrated Risk Information System, at www.epa.gov/iris/, last revised October 28, 2003.

[5] Malia Zimmerman, "Water Quality Lawsuits Target Chemical and Agricultural Giants," *Pacific Business News*, October 8, 1999, p. 4.

[6] Steve Stecklow, "Fraud by Trial Lawyers Taints Wave of Pesticide Lawsuits," *The Wall Street Journal*, August 19, 2009, p. A1.

[7] *Abagninin v. Amvac*, 545 F. 3d 733 (2008).

[8] Mevinphos is technically an alpha or beta isomer of 2-carbomethoxy-1-methyl-vinyl dimethyl phosphate. Exhibit 2 shows alpha-Mevinphos. It has been sold under the trade name Phosdrin in at least four formulations. See Department of Pesticide Regulation, *Mevinphos: Risk Characterization Document* (Sacramento: California Environmental Protection Agency, June 30, 1994), p. 5.

After their introduction in the 1950s, organo-phosphates such as mevinphos were second choice pesticides. Growers preferred to use organochlorines until concerns about the inability of nature to break them down turned the market toward the shorter-lived organophosphates. By the late 1970s mevinphos was being sold in large quantities. DuPont held the rights to it. Amvac manufactured some mevinphos at its Los Angeles factory under contract for DuPont.

As mevinphos was used more widely, concerns about its safety grew. Multiple reports of farmworkers sickened by contact with it alarmed regulators. In 1978 the EPA restricted its use, so that only certified applicators could spray it on fields.

In 1988 the leader of the United Farm Workers, César Chávez, held a 36-day hunger strike to protest the use of organophosphate pesticides, including mevinphos, on grapes. He believed their use recklessly endangered the health of field hands. In fact, subsequent research confirms multiple effects in exposed farmworkers. For example, after prolonged exposure they show deficits in coordination, information processing, and other neurologic symptoms.[9] Children of Latina women in agricultural communities show impaired behavioral development.[10]

A few months after Chávez's hunger strike, DuPont ended mevinphos production. Amvac, however, was willing to embrace it. DuPont sold its exclusive rights to Amvac, which continued to sell mevinphos even as the EPA was gathering further evidence of its dangers. In early 1993 the agency called mevinphos one of the five most dangerous pesticides. It had reports of 600 poisonings and five deaths over the previous decade and calculated that the rate of poisonings was 5 to 10 times higher than for any other product.[11] Before banning mevinphos,

César Chávez, president of the United Farm Workers, receives a small piece of bread from Ethel Kennedy, widow of former Attorney General Robert Kennedy. Her symbolic action ended a 36-day hunger strike in 1988 undertaken to protest the exposure of grape pickers to mevinphos and other pesticides.
Source: © Bettmann/CORBIS.

however, it allowed Amvac to suggest risk-reduction measures that might allay its concerns.[12]

Meanwhile, Amvac saw a new market opportunity. Large agrichemical companies had taken several other organophosphate insecticides off the market to placate the EPA. Apple growers in Washington were concerned that they would be unable to fight off ruinous late-season aphid infestations. Amvac believed that mevinphos could be safely used, even though regulators in Washington allowed pesticides to be mixed in open vats before spraying. Other states, for example California, required closed-vat mixing. Amvac negotiated with Washington's regulators, promising to train workers in the use of respirators and safe application.

That summer there were immediate reports of mevinphos poisonings in Washington orchards. In all, there were 26 documented cases. No one died, but seven workers were hospitalized. Martin Martinez, who later sued Amvac, was told to mix a concentrate of mevinphos with water, load a sprayer, and apply it. "My vision started to get blurry," he said. "I started to get nauseous. I began to vomit."[13] These are classic symptoms of organophosphate poisoning. He was hospitalized for seven days.

[9] Joan Rothlein et al., "Organophosphate Pesticide Exposure and Neurobehavioral Performance in Agricultural and Nonagricultural Hispanic Workers," *Environmental Health Perspectives,* May 2006.

[10] Brenda Eskenazi et al., "Organophosphate Pesticide Exposure and Neurodevelopment in Young Mexican-American Children," *Environmental Health Perspectives,* May 2007.

[11] David Holmstrom, "Control of Farm Chemicals Needs Overhaul," *Christian Science Monitor,* October 6, 1994, p. 7; and *Andrews Litigation Reporter,* "Settlement Reached between Farm Workers and Pesticide Maker," May 31, 2002, p. 1.

[12] Environmental Protection Agency, *R. E. D. Facts: Mevinphos,* EPA-738-F-94-020, September 1994, p. 2.

[13] Arthur C. Gorlick, "Orchard Workers File Lawsuit," *Seattle Post-Intelligencer,* September 13, 1995, p. B4.

Martinez and others had been trained. They were supposed to wear respirators, face shields, and chemical-resistant clothing. However, mevinphos is so toxic that even a slight mistake is very dangerous. Some poisonings took place in hot weather, when applicators shed articles of clothing. Absorption through skin is rapid. Ten drops of concentrate spilled on flesh is a lethal exposure for a 150-pound person. Inhalation is also dangerous. A 150-pound person who failed to adjust a respirator properly would begin to show effects such as dilation of the pupils after breathing little more than one ten-thousandth of an ounce.[14]

Once inside the body, mevinphos interferes with the regulation of nerve impulses, disrupting the central nervous system and major organs. One of the earliest symptoms of exposure is compromised reasoning ability, which compounds the danger because a worker loses the ability to appreciate an urgent peril. High exposure eventually leads to irregular heart beat, convulsions, unconsciousness, and death. Breathing air with only 10 parts per million of mevinphos over one hour killed 50 percent of rats in one study.[15]

Three orchard workers, including Martinez, sued Amvac alleging that mevinphos was a defectively designed product. It was so unsafe, they argued, that it should never have been marketed for orchard use. At one point, the case went to the Supreme Court of Washington, which handed down a ruling on a point of product liability law. It noted that a pesticide, by its nature, was a dangerous product. Its costs to society could be eliminated only by sacrificing the lethal qualities that made it effective. The question was, when was a pesticide too dangerous, too lethal?

The court ruled that a pesticide could be sold as an unavoidably unsafe product if its advantages greatly outweighed the risks posed by its use.[16] It would be up to a lower court to decide if mevinphos passed this test. However, Amvac ended the lawsuit by settling with the orchard workers for approximately $750,000. According to one of their lawyers, Amvac "was willing to sacrifice farmworker's lives and safety for profits. It had to be held accountable."[17]

Meanwhile, Amvac defended mevinphos before the EPA but was unable to convince the regulators it could be safely used. All pesticides must have EPA registration for legal use. With the agency prepared to cancel registration of mevinphos, Amvac voluntarily requested its withdrawal.

The EPA now classifies mevinphos as hazardous waste and bans any agricultural use in the United States. Nevertheless, Amvac continued to sell it in Mexico, South Africa, and Australia.[18]

DICHLORVOS

Dichlorvos, or DDVP (see Exhibit 3), is another aging member of the organophosphate family abandoned by the big agrichemical firms but still sold by Amvac. It was synthesized in the late 1940s and first marketed by Shell in 1961. It targets a broad range of insect pests including flies, fleas, ticks, mites, cockroaches, chiggers, caterpillars, moths, and weevils. Like other members of the organophosphate family, it disrupts transmission of nervous impulses.

At first DDVP had many agricultural applications. It was used in silos, hoppers, and tobacco warehouses to protect stored crops. In feedlots it was sprayed over animals to control fleas and ticks. Farmers mixed it in feed to deworm horses and pigs. Canning and packing facilities applied it to control insects. It was sprayed over wide areas for mosquito control and used as the active ingredient in popular

EXHIBIT 3 **Dichlorvos**

Source: Environmental Protection Agency, *Interim Reregistration Eligibility Decision for Dichlorvos (DDVP)*, EPA 738-R-06-013, June 2006, p. 11.

Chemical Formula: $C_4H_7C_{12}O_4P$

---

[14] Based on a "no observable effect level" in humans of 0.025 mg/kg, see Department of Pesticide Regulation, *Mevinphos: Risk Characterization Document*, p. 1.

[15] Ibid., p. 1.

[16] *Guzman v. Amvac Chemical Corporation*, 141 Wn.2d 493, at 509–10.

[17] Co-lead counsel Richard Eymann, quoted in "Precedent-Setting Farm Worker Pesticide Poisoning Suit Settles," *Public Justice*, Summer 2002, p. 11.

[18] T. Christian Miller, "Pesticide Maker Sees Profit When Others See Risk," *Los Angeles Times*, April 8, 2007, p. A1.

household insecticides. Resin strips impregnated with DDVP were placed in homes, public buildings, buses, aircraft, and ships to control pests such as cockroaches.

By the late 1970s many companies manufactured it, including Amvac. Total annual output in the United States rose as high as 4.2 million pounds.[19] Then, scientific studies raised doubts about its safety and by the early 1980s annual use fell below 1 million pounds.

Like all organophosphate pesticides, dichlorvos poisons the nervous system. Acute exposure causes perspiration, nausea, vomiting, diarrhea, headache, and fatigue. Long-term, low exposures can also bring on these symptoms. Very high exposures cause convulsions and loss of consciousness. However, compared with similar pesticides, dichlorvos does not pose exceptional risks from contact during application. The main concern has been that it may cause cancer in humans.

Studies show it is an animal carcinogen. Rats and mice that inhale or ingest high doses of dichlorvos produce thyroid, adrenal, pituitary, and stomach tumors. Epidemiological studies suggest that dichlorvos can also cause cancer in humans. One showed a significantly elevated risk of leukemia among farmers in Iowa and Minnesota who used dichlorvos, even when they had used it as long as 20 years in the past. Another showed an elevated rate of non-Hodgkin lymphoma among Nebraska women who had used dichlorvos. Still a third found a "significantly increased risk" for brain cancer among children in homes using Amvac's No-Pest Strips.[20] The statistical power of these and similar studies is weak because they are based on small numbers of people with likely exposures to multiple pesticides. Nevertheless, they have ominous implications.

In 1980 the EPA initiated the first in a series of dichlorvos reviews. By law, the agency must regularly reassess whether a pesticide poses "unreasonable risk to man or the environment taking into account the economic, social, and environmental costs and benefits of [its] use."[21] With this criteria,

even very dangerous pesticides can stay on the market if their risks are controlled and outweighed by their utility.

After the first review in 1980, the EPA classified dichlorvos as a "suspected" human carcinogen that acted by mutating genetic material in cells. A second review seven years later led to its classification as a "probable" human carcinogen. This bad news caused the market for it to shrink even more. One by one, agrichemical firms stopped selling it until only Amvac was left. The company was determined to keep it on the market.

Amvac has a large budget for supporting the registration of its older pesticides in the face of doubts by increasingly skeptical regulators. In 1995 the EPA sought to cancel most uses of dichlorvos. Amvac responded by submitting supportive data, but the agency found it unpersuasive. So Amvac agreed to cancel almost two dozen applications, including aerial spraying and all uses in restaurants and food processing plants.[22]

Meanwhile, Congress in 1996 required the EPA to review pesticides under a new, tougher standard that required a "reasonable certainty of no harm."[23] The agency finally finished its dichlorvos review in 2006. It allowed continued marketing, but further restricted its uses. Amvac agreed to cancel registration for more applications, including all home uses except impregnated resin strips. In 2010 it agreed to cancel five additional fogging and spray applications.[24]

Dichlorvos can no longer be applied on lawns and turf, in cracks and crevices, and with handheld foggers. In addition, dichlorvos-impregnated pest strips in homes are limited in size. Larger strips containing more than 16 grams can be used only in garages, sheds, and crawl spaces occupied less than four hours a day. They can be used in vacation homes and cabins only if the dwellings are vacated for four months after use. Smaller strips and flea and tick collars for cats and dogs that contain less than 16 grams of dichlorvos are still in use. According to the EPA, the air concentration of dichlorvos in a room where a

[19] Renu Gandhi and Suzanne M. Snedeker, "Critical Evaluation of Dichlorvos' Breast Cancer Risk," *Program on Breast Cancer and Environmental Risk Factors in New York State,* Critical Evaluation #7, March 1999, p. 1.

[20] Ibid., p. 3.

[21] Federal Insecticide, Fungicide, and Rodenticide Act of 1947 (as amended), 7 U.S.C §136(bb)(1).

[22] Environmental Protection Agency, "Dichlorvos (DDV); Deletion of Certain Uses and Directions," 60 FR 19480-19581, April 19, 1995.

[23] This was the Food Quality Protection Act of 1996.

[24] Environmental Protection Agency, "Product Cancellation Order for Certain Pesticide Registrations," 75 FR 26227, May 11, 2010.

dog or cat is wearing one of these collars averages less than one-fortieth of the exposure level at which poisoning symptoms are detectable.[25] Recently, Amvac has targeted customers trying to control bedbugs with ads for hanging dichlorvos-impregnated strips that release vapors into a room.

Exposure of the U.S. population to dichlorvos is estimated as infinitesimal, 0.000007 milligrams per kilogram of body weight each day.[26] Even so, regulators believed that dichlorvos residues in food posed a cancer risk to the general population and that there were unacceptable risks to the nervous systems of those who mixed, handled, and applied it. The greatest danger is from skin contact. Based on animal studies, estimates are that short-term absorption of as little as 0.25 ounce of dichlorvos through the skin would cause death in 50 percent of applicators weighing 150 pounds.[27] This makes dichlorvos one of the most toxic pesticides in use.

Inhalation toxicity is lower, but still greater than most other pesticides. Current EPA estimates are that inhaling 198 parts per million over an eight-hour period would be fatal to 50 percent of exposed adults. Overall, the EPA believed that these risks outweighed the benefits for all but a few remaining applications.

Meanwhile, other countries have banned dichlorvos. In 2002, the United Kingdom rejected evidence submitted by Amvac and suspended all uses. Angola, Fiji, Denmark, and Sweden have also banned it. Amvac continued exporting dichlorvos to Australia, Canada, and Mexico.

COSTS AND BENEFITS OF PESTICIDES

Poisonous agrichemicals have high social and environmental costs. Their use on crops and in homes causes tens of thousands of acute exposure injuries each year. Long-term exposure from residues in foods, drinking water, and soil causes an unknown number of chronic illnesses including cancer, birth defects, liver poisoning, and neurological deficits. Many pesticides, especially the older organochlorines and organophosphates, do not discriminate between pests and other forms of life. They kill wildlife and pets along with target insects. An accurate calculation of monetary losses from such problems is infeasible.

Accidents increase the cost burden. Years ago a Southern Pacific freight train derailed on a steep curve above the Sacramento River north of Mt. Shasta in California. One tank car carried 13,000 gallons of metam sodium, a herbicide manufactured by Amvac. The resulting spill virtually sterilized a long stretch of the river, annihilating life right down to the moss on the rocks. It killed 200,000 fish and wiped out a celebrated trout-fishing area.[28] Lawsuits claimed that Amvac failed to identify properly and label its shipment, and it agreed to pay $2 million, although it bore no responsibility for the train's derailment.

A later mishap with metam sodium is more typical of accidental exposures. In Arvin, California, 72 workers processing carrots and 178 town residents were sickened when metam sodium manufactured by Amvac drifted from fields where it was being sprayed.[29] The applicator paid a $60,000 fine.

If the costs of pesticide use are great, so are the benefits. The major benefit is availability of a bountiful, affordable food supply. Pesticides control fungal infections, insects, and weeds that would otherwise decimate U.S. crop yields. Without control measures, 50 to 90 percent of fruit and vegetable crops would rot from fungal infections before harvest. To protect them, growers use about 100 million pounds of fungicides annually. Doing so saves an estimated $13 billion in crop value.[30]

---

[25] Ibid., p. 165. This figure is based on a margin of exposure of 39 for infants, who are presumed more sensitive to dichlorvos vapor than adults. Margin of exposure is the ratio of the dose at a "no observable adverse exposure level" to an observed or estimated dose.

[26] Environmental Protection Agency, *Interim Reregistration Eligibility Decision for Dichlorvos (DDVP)*, EPA 738-R-06-013, June 2006, app. J, p. 151. There are 31,000 milligrams in one ounce.

[27] Ibid., table 4.1a, Guideline No. 870.1200, p. 123.

[28] Scott Thurm, "Record Damages for 1991 Rail Spill Settlement," *San Jose Mercury News,* March 15, 1994, p. A1.

[29] Robert Rodriguez, "California Investigates Rise in Pesticide-Caused Illnesses in 2002," *Fresno Bee,* February 27, 2004, p.1; and Miller, "Pesticide Maker Sees Profit When Others See Risk," p. A25.

[30] Statement of Jay Vroom, in *Review of the EPA Pesticide Program,* Hearings before the Subcommittee on Conservation, Credit, Rural Development, and Research of the Committee on Agriculture, U.S. House of Representatives, 109th Congress, 2nd Session, September 28, 2006, p. 50.

Pesticides kill mosquitoes, ticks, rats, and other vectors that carry illnesses such as the plague, Lyme disease, and encephalitis. They make human habitations more comfortable by controlling cockroaches, mold, mildew, termites, ants, and spiders.

Herbicides reduce soil erosion, save water, and reduce fuel and labor costs for growers. Their use facilitates increasingly popular no-till agriculture in which farmers poison weeds rather than plowing them under. With less plowing there is less erosion, which means lower water treatment costs, less flood damage, and larger reservoir capacity.

Herbicides also kill unwanted growth that competes with crops for water. Without them, crop protection would require as many as 1.1 million hours of hand weeding in peak growing season. The labor force to employ at this job does not exist. Organic farmers, who cannot use herbicides, spend $1,000 per acre weeding their crops compared with only $50 for growers using chemical weed controls. One study estimated the overall benefits of herbicides at $26 billion in 2005.[31]

Finally, pesticides preserve wildlife habitats and protect endangered species. Without their use vastly expanded acreage would be required to grow necessary food crops. More land would be converted from its native state to farms, ranches, plantations, and orchards.

So pesticides clearly have both great costs and great benefits. There are other methods for controlling agricultural pests, but they complement pesticides rather than replace them. Cultivation techniques such as tilling and crop rotation make environmental conditions less favorable for destructive organisms. Biological control methods include release of insect predators such as wasps, lacewings, or lady bugs and the spread of friendly bacteria that compete with damaging strains. In the 1990s, big companies launched bioengineered seeds and their use has soared. Some crops are bred to have insect-resistant traits. Others are genetically manipulated to survive specific herbicides, giving farmers more alternatives for fighting weeds that over time become resistant to popular chemicals.

The rise of biological alternatives has not ended long-term growth in pesticide sales, which have risen an average of 11 percent a year since 1995 and reached a high of $10 billion in 2007.[32] For the time being, pesticides are still needed to protect the food supply and quality of life to which Americans are accustomed. In the words of an agricultural researcher:

> [S]ome people want a total ban on pesticides, but they must be ready to accept termites in their houses, fleas in their carpets, moldy vegetables, food-borne toxins, food shortages with soaring prices, and outbreaks of long-forgotten diseases.[33]

AMVAC MOVES AHEAD

Amvac now has more than 40 pesticide brands. It manufactures them at four plants in California, Idaho, Missouri, and Alabama and sells them in the United States and through foreign sales offices in Costa Rica, Mexico, Brazil, Switzerland, and the United Kingdom.

Amvac emphasizes profitability. Three directors—its two founding entrepreneurs and the son of one founder, now president and CEO—own 22 percent of its stock. Compensation of its president and CEO, which was $806,303 in 2009, is based on four factors: "achieving financial results that equal or exceed" targets, introducing new compounds, controlling manufacturing costs, and defining "a clear vision and strategy."[34] The ongoing shift to biological pest controls sustains its strategy. As industry giants continue to discard older pesticides, they create opportunities for Amvac.

Amvac adopted a seven-page Code of Conduct and Ethics in 2006. It states: "[O]ur efforts are focused on achieving the business and personal ethical standards as well as compliance with the laws and regulations that are applicable to our business." It intends its code to "ensure decisions that reflect care for all of

---

[31] Ibid., p. 50.

[32] Bureau of the Census, *Statistical Abstract of the United States: 2010*, 129th ed., table 813.

[33] Keith S. Delaplane, "Pesticide Usage in the United States: History, Benefits, Risks, and Trends," Cooperative Extension Service, University of Georgia College of Agricultural and Environmental Sciences, *Bulletin 1121*, November 2000, p. 1.

[34] American Vanguard Corporation, *Notice of Annual Meeting and Proxy Statement*, April 27, 2010, pp. 18 and 21.

our stakeholders."[35] The only mention of the environment is this brief section.

> The Company is committed to doing all that it can to assist in minimizing the degradation of our natural environment. Accordingly, employees should always take care in disposing of any waste materials or releasing any discharges into the air or water and comply with all applicable regulations and procedures required by law and by Company Code. If an employee is unclear about what is required, he/she must not dispose of any material or release any discharges until he/she has determined what procedures apply.[36]

A recessionary climate beginning in 2008 weakened Amvac. Sales dropped as farmers had difficulty getting credit and distributors cut their inventories. But by cutting costs, reducing long-term debt, and cutting its dividend, the company maintained a strong balance sheet, positioning itself for renewed growth and predicting rising pesticide demand when prosperity returned.

Amvac's presence is a lesson in capitalism. Legal opportunities for profit elicit the requisite effort. Actions are justified by their overall utility. Doubtless Amvac's strategic thinkers would be inspired by the words of a Robert Frost poem.

> But a crop is a crop,
> And who's to say where
> The harvest shall stop?[37]

Questions

1. Does Amvac have an ethical strategy? Does it pursue its strategy in an ethical manner?
2. Do you believe that Amvac is faithful to its ethics code? Does the code adequately address the consequences of its operations? What might be added or changed to improve it?
3. Should the law prohibit Amvac and others from exporting pesticides barred from use in the United States?
4. Is the value to society of pesticides such as dibromochloropropane, mevinphos, and dichlorvos great enough to warrant the risks they pose?
5. If economic and market conditions remain favorable for Amvac's strategy, would you buy its stock?

[35] American Vanguard Corporation, *Code of Conduct and Ethics,* adopted March 8, 2006, at www.amvac-chemical.com., p. i.

[36] Ibid., p. i.

[37] "Gathering Leaves," in Edward Connery Lathem, ed., *The Poetry of Robert Frost* (New York: Holt, Rinehart and Winston, 1969), p. 235.

Chapter **Fifteen**

Consumerism

Harvey W. Wiley

On a spring day in 1863 a tall thin lad of 18 left the family farm, walking five miles over dirt roads to a nearby town. There he would be the first in his family to attend college. Like the restless America of his era, he was leaving rural roots behind in a journey of hope and ambition. His name was Harvey Washington Wiley. He would become the first modern consumer crusader.

The example of his parents molded young Harvey's character. His father was a farmer, who through self-learning became an evangelical minister and part-time schoolteacher. A man of Christian virtue, principle, and independent mind, he stood against slavery despite the open anger of neighbors. His mother taught herself to read. Knowledge was so important in the Wiley home that the latest works of science, literature, and commentary were mail-ordered and read aloud to little Harvey.

Harvey got a bachelor's degree from Hanover College, then attended Indiana Medical College, graduating as a physician in 1871. Still hungry for formal education, he enrolled at Harvard and graduated in less than two years with a chemistry degree. He became a professor at the new Purdue University where he was soon absorbed in food chemistry and began working with Indiana state officials to detect adulteration in food products.

With industrialization, the nation's food supply was changing. As people moved from farms to cities they depended on businesses to prepare, can, bottle, package, and distribute edibles. It was a time of major advances in science, and the Victorian era had a childlike faith in the powers of modern chemistry. A large, highly competitive food industry applied new food chemistries using preservatives, colorings, flavorings, texturizers, and other additives. With few laws to police dishonorable operators, dangerous, fraudulent, and cheapened products made their way to market. Canned beef was preserved with formaldehyde. Strawberry jam was made from pulped apple skins, hayseeds, and glucose. Ground pepper was sometimes mostly nutshells.[1]

Working in his campus lab, Wiley pioneered the study of food adulteration. Using new techniques, he detected widespread fraud. His reputation grew and when he was offered the position of chief chemist at the Department of Agriculture in 1883, he accepted.

---

[1] W. E. Mason, "Food Adulteration," *North American Review,* April 1900, pp. 548–53.

Arriving in Washington, D.C., Wiley, now 39, took charge of the Bureau of Chemistry. This small entity had been set up in 1862 to hunt for contaminated agricultural commodities. He worked tirelessly, uncovering danger, dilution, mislabeling, and cheating in the nation's groceries. Yet he lacked the means to protect public health. Fewer than half the states had pure food laws and those were often contradictory—what was banned in one state was legal in another. Worse, no federal law existed to regulate foodstuffs in interstate commerce.

Wiley agitated for a national pure food law. For more than two decades he worked tirelessly, giving speeches, writing reports, convening meetings of scientists and food producers, and lobbying legislators.

As Wiley labored, 190 protective measures were introduced in Congress. None passed. Eventually he departed from the ordinary, staging a melodramatic experiment that captured the country's imagination. He believed that chemical preservatives harmed consumers, but lacked scientific proof, so he designed a series of "hygienic table trials" in which the participants would be fed suspect preservatives and monitored for signs of distress.

Wiley set up a kitchen, dining room, and laboratory in the basement of the Bureau of Chemistry building and advertised for volunteers. A dozen young men, all civil service employees from the Department of Agriculture, signed up. They pledged "on their honor" that while pursuing their regular work and sleep schedules they would take every meal in the basement dining room, eat or drink nothing (except water) that was not given as part of the trial, carry around jars for collection of urine and feces to be submitted for lab analysis, and submit to weekly doctors' exams.

Wiley first fed the men borax, a then-common preservative. He began by adding half a gram a day to their food. Over two years, he gradually added more. The routine was 10 days of healthy food followed by 20 days of food dosed with borax. At a dosage of two grams, appetites dropped off and some subjects had bowel problems. At four grams more serious problems emerged. The men had headaches and abdominal pain. Three took to their beds. Wiley stopped the test, believing he had evidence that borax was a human poison.[2]

A *Washington Post* reporter discovered Wiley's experiment, nicknamed the men the "poison squad," and wrote regularly about them. Whether or not Wiley intended the trials as partly grandstanding, the public was captivated. They inspired considerable levity, becoming the grist for comedians and minstrel shows. Yet they also put growing pressure on Congress to pass Wiley's pure food bill.

For five years Wiley tested other preservatives on new ranks of volunteers. He found signs of ill health caused by salicylic acid, formaldehyde, and copper sulfate, none of which are used as preservatives today. Years later, Wiley believed the experiments had permanently damaged the health of several poison squad members.

In 1906, even as the poison squad continued its work, Congress finally passed the Pure Food and Drug Act "preventing the manufacture, sale, or transportation of adulterated or misbranded or poisonous or deleterious foods, drugs, medicines, and

---

[2] Harvey W. Wiley, *The History of a Crime Against the Food Law* (Milwaukee: Lee Foundation for Nutritional Research, 1955), chap. II. Originally published in 1929.

Members of the "poison squad" dining in the basement of the old Bureau of Chemistry building. The Civil Service chef hired to cook their meals had once been chef to the Queen of Bavaria. Source: Courtesy of the Food and Drug Administration History Office.

liquors."[3] Opposition by the food industry yielded in the face of acute public indignation about meatpacking plants described in Upton Sinclair's novel *The Jungle*. Wiley's years of hard work and the theater of his poison squad, however, had prepared the ground. Recognizing this, Congress gave Wiley's Bureau of Chemistry the power to examine foods for adulteration or misbranding.

The press called the new law the Wiley Act. Its passage seemed to be the final victory in his crusade for public health. Yet appearance deceived. Wiley attempted vigorous enforcement, but his perfectionist standards often dictated overly strict rules. He was uneasy with compromise. Food makers resisted his severity and outflanked him by appealing to his boss, Secretary of Agriculture James Wilson, and to President Theodore Roosevelt. Both grew exasperated with him. Roosevelt thought him a vexing nag. At one White House meeting with Wiley and food manufacturers on the use of saccharine, the president became furious with the stubborn chemist. Only an idiot, he told Wiley, would be against all use of saccharine in food.

With time, Wiley's authority eroded. Secretary Wilson, with Roosevelt's approval, undermined Wiley's independence. Wilson appointed an assistant to Wiley who reported directly to him, not to Wiley. Then he set up a panel of scientists to look over Wiley's shoulder and review his decisions. Defeated and bitter, the aging warrior resigned his post in 1912. Yet he could not leave the field. He continued lecturing and writing about consumer causes. His new bride, a suffragette whom he had married in 1911 at age 66, was active in women's groups such as the Housekeepers' Alliance

[3] Pure Food and Drug Act of 1906, Sec. 1.

Harvey W. Wiley (1845–1930). Source: Redpath Chautauqua Collection, Special Collections Department, University of Iowa Libraries (Iowa City).

that fought for consumer causes. He wrote about food for *Good Housekeeping* magazine and set up the Good Housekeeping Seal of Approval standard. He died in 1930.[4]

Harvey Wiley's campaign for pure food came at the time when small, local markets for goods and services were expanding to national size. It was in this era that the idea of a class of people with a well-defined interest in safe, pure, and honest commodities emerged. This class came to be called consumers. Wiley's distinction is to have been its first national champion.

America's memory of Wiley has dimmed, but his work still touches our lives. The law he fought for is the foundation of modern food and drug regulation. The Bureau of Chemistry, by enforcing its provisions, evolved into the current Food and Drug Administration, a powerful agency that protects public health.

In this chapter we begin by defining and discussing the idea of consumerism. Then we describe the protective shield of statutes, regulations, and consumer law that has risen to protect consumers since Harvey Wiley's era.

CONSUMERISM

consumer
A person who uses products and services in a commercial economy.

consumerism
A term denoting (1) a movement to promote the rights and powers of consumers in relation to sellers and (2) a powerful ideology in which the pursuit of material goods beyond subsistence shapes social conduct.

A *consumer* is a person who uses products and services in a commercial economy. *Consumerism* is a word with two meanings. In common usage it refers to a movement to promote the rights and powers of consumers in relation to sellers of products and services. It also denotes an exceptionally powerful ideology of pursuit of material goods that shapes social conduct. We will discuss both these themes beginning with the second.

Consumerism as an Ideology

In this meaning, consumerism describes a society in which people define their identities by acquiring and displaying material goods beyond what they need for subsistence. Although small pockets of consumerism existed in the distant past, its spread through large populations is relatively recent, happening for the first time in Western Europe only about 300 years ago, then advancing from there.[5] Its appearance and success is explained by the rise of certain conditions.

[4] "Dr. H. W. Wiley Dies; Pure-Food Expert," *The New York Times,* July 1, 1930, p. 24.

[5] Peter N. Stearns, *Consumerism in World History: The Global Transformation of Desire* (London: Routledge, 2001), pp. ix–x.

Economic progress set the stage. By the 1700s, commercial economies based on currency exchange had replaced subsistence and bartering in Western Europe. As economies grew, modest affluence spread in classes below the aristocracy. Expanding overseas trade in colonial empires brought new products, including sugar from the West Indies, porcelain from China, and cotton fabrics from India. Slowly, average people began to spend more for goods and services beyond their basic needs.

As they did, the institutions necessary to support consumerism quickly appeared. Small shops selling goods sprang up in cities. Shopkeepers discovered that their customers' needs were not limited to necessities, but were infinitely expandable. Innovations such as window displays, sale pricing, loss leaders, and print advertising burst forth. Merchants encouraged producers to create a flow of new products, including toys, furniture, books, watches, perfumes, and household decorations.

However, the full bloom of consumerism came only when these economic developments interacted with cultural and social changes. One important change was the declining influence of religion. From the time of its rise in ancient Rome, Christianity sanctified the dignity of the poor and encouraged followers to forsake the life of this world for the goal of otherworldly salvation. This doctrine made no room for any soul living for material pleasure. It would have suffocated rising consumerism. But now this stricture was loosened by the great philosophical current of the *Enlightenment,* a wave of new, challenging ideas that arose early in the 1700s and ran through the century.

Enlighten-ment
A wave of new, challenging ideas based on human reason and scientific inquiry. It swept over Western Europe in the eighteenth century.

A key premise of Enlightenment thinking was that the use of human reason and scientific inquiry should supplant passive acceptance of religious dogma as the basis for understanding the world. This view elevated the importance of human ability, separated humanity from deity in a new way, and led to the rise of *individualism,* or the idea that human beings are ends in themselves. In the social realm it paved the way for consumerism as individual choice gained priority over duty to God and individuals could focus on material pleasures with less guilt.

individualism
The idea, arising in the Enlightenment, that human beings are ends in themselves.

Then, the Industrial Revolution put societies in flux. This was the final element in the alchemy of consumerism. Populations grew. People left ancestral homes in the country to live beside strangers in cities. New occupations emerged. Some merchants and traders became wealthy. Everywhere centuries-old class and status boundaries wore away. As they faded, people replaced them with displays of material goods intended to establish identity and standing in the social hierarchy. If a man no longer wore the insignia of a trade or guild, he could adorn himself with expensive, brilliantly dyed cotton garments to show that his current occupation made him affluent. A newly rich merchant could emulate the aristocracy by building a manor house of his own. People spent more time "shopping." The acquisition of material objects had a new centrality in their lives.

Consumerism Rises in America

Consumerism dawned in America when social and economic forces akin to those in Europe came into play. It took a century for the process to work. Beginning in the early 1800s, a commercial economy arose. The ascetic Puritan theology that oppressed individualism in the northern colonies was fading. Ambition for riches in the new land leapt the boundaries of the devout, solemn New England towns

FIGURE 15.1
Immigrants and others could display and feel a connection with American culture by using consumer products. This collage of tobacco advertising images from the late 1800s and early 1900s illustrates powerful symbolism for the ideals of liberty and freedom in American culture. Liberty Tobacco was an American Tobacco Company brand, George Washington Greatest American Cut Plug was made by R. J. Reynolds Tobacco Co., and Golden Eagle was made by T. C. Williams Co.

Source: Tobacco Collection-Database #D0321, D0347, D0363. Emergence of Advertising On-Line Project, John W. Hartman Center for Sales, Advertising & Marketing History. Duke University Rare Book, Manuscript, and Special Collections Library. http://library.duke.edu/digitalcollections/eaa/.

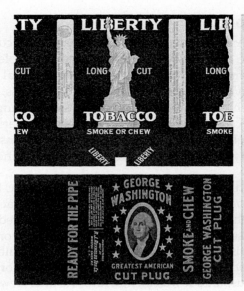

where it could not flourish. Wealth accumulated from foreign trade, and industrial development spread growing affluence in the last half of the century.

The full emergence of consumerism in America came with changes around the turn of the twentieth century. The railroads had knitted territory together, forming national markets. The great merger wave of 1896–1904 created businesses with the reach to serve them. Machines and assembly lines made possible mass production of consumer goods. Electricity and other new technologies led to a stream of new products, for example, autos, watches, refrigerators, vacuum cleaners, toasters, and radios. Simultaneously, in large numbers, people left cramped small-town societies and moved to cities with more fluid social currents. Waves of immigrants, people newly adrift from their cultural moorings, arrived.

In this open society characterized by loose social ties, high mobility, and cultural variation, people began to express role and status with the products they bought. Immigrants adopted American culture as they brewed Uncle Sam's Coffee, drank Coca-Cola, or ate a Baby Ruth candy bar, the latter named for the widely loved infant daughter of President Grover Cleveland.[6] Their children renounced old-country ways by wearing New World clothing styles. Advertising facilitated this social communication through products. It created new national brands and endowed them with social significance, allowing people to declare their membership in groups, their status, and their values by the goods they displayed (see Figure 15.1). The ads conferred on products meanings that were widely shared and understood, even by strangers, in a large and mobile population.

[6] Ruth Cleveland was born in 1891 when Grover Cleveland was out of office between his two nonconsecutive terms. A national mourning took place after her tragic death from diphtheria in 1904. The popular Democrat ran for the presidency three times and was elected in 1884, defeated in 1888, and elected again in 1892. The brand was created by the Curtiss Candy Company to honor the deceased "baby Ruth."

Consumerism in Perspective

Gary Cross, a historian of American commercial culture, defines consumerism as "the belief that goods give meaning to individuals and their roles in society."[7] According to Cross, consumerism, which has never been a formal philosophy, is now the dominant ideology in America. "Americans," says Cross, "define themselves and their relationships with others through the exchange and use of goods."[8] He believes that consumerism expresses a more powerful worldview than political ideologies, religions, or class and ethnic distinctions. If we are unable to appreciate this fully, it is because of its pervasiveness and the lack of a visible alternative.

Acquisitive desire is natural and inevitable in modern society. Purchased objects can fulfill needs beyond subsistence and beyond their practical function. One illustration comes in the story of a home interview conducted by marketers to learn how customers used household insecticides. At one woman's house a roach ran out during the visit. She cursed, sprayed until a puddle formed, then crushed it with the edge of the can, telling her wide-eyed visitors that roaches reminded her of her first husband. It was then, wrote one interviewer, we learned that "even a utilitarian product like bug spray can have deeply emotional, even primal meaning."[9]

Marketing research reveals a widespread, profound effort to find love, status, and self-expression in products. One researcher's studies for large corporations, for example, show evidence for the following conclusions.[10] The basic purpose of shopping is "reconnecting with life"; it is a social experience, not a hunt for necessities. People buy products to fulfill emotional needs rather than practical ones. For Americans, luxury products are like military stripes, a proof of success that confirms the "goodness" of a person. And, not surprisingly, cars are purchased to express identity, distinctiveness, and personality, not as practical conveyances.

These and similar insights invite condemnation by those who reject material possessions as the source of human happiness. *Materialism* is an emphasis on material objects or money that displaces spiritual, aesthetic, or philosophical values. Critics of materialism believe that pursuit of pleasure in external possessions is less worthy than concern for interior virtues, that buying a product creates only false satisfaction. True satisfaction comes from intellectual, artistic, and spiritual attainment. Real wisdom is in the cathedral, museum, or library, not the car lot. Despite lack of any objective evidence as to their inferiority, material values are subject to perennial ridicule and criticism.

One defining rejection of materialism in America came early from Henry David Thoreau. Thoreau was born in 1817 in a small Massachusetts town. As a boy he

materialism
An emphasis on material objects or money that displaces spiritual, aesthetic, or philosophical values.

---

[7] Gary Cross, *An All Consuming Society: Why Commercialism Won in Modern America* (New York: Columbia University Press, 2000), p. 1.

[8] Ibid., p. 4.

[9] Michael J. Silverstein, *Treasure Hunt: Inside the Mind of the New Consumer* (New York: Portfolio, 2006), p. xiv.

[10] Clotaire Rapaille, *The Culture Code: An Ingenious Way to Understand Why People around the World Buy and Live as They Do* (New York: Broadway Books, 2006).

Henry David Thoreau (1817–1862) was a naturalist, essayist, and early exemplar of plain living. He rejected the pursuit of money and material goods as "a fool's life." He preferred to seek "inner riches." Source: The Library of Congress.

showed a disposition to be an imaginative, independent observer. His mother once asked why he was staying awake long into the night. "Mother," he said, "I have been looking through the stars to see if I couldn't see God behind them."[11] At Harvard College he earned a degree but his real school was Nature. He was briefly a pencil maker, land surveyor, and schoolteacher but he preferred to spend his days in the woods where in idleness he felt freedom. He kept a lifelong journal and published his insights as articles, poems, and books.

In 1845 he built a crude cabin on Walden Pond near Concord, Massachusetts, where for two years he lived in solitude. At this remove from society he composed a shrewd, original critique of material values titled *Walden; or, Life in the Woods*. In nature, he wrote, God gives everyone the "necessaries of life" sufficient to satisfy basic needs for food, shelter, clothing, and fuel. Yet people are not satisfied. They want wealth and material objects. Working to possess these artificial satisfactions they toil away precious days, months, and years. Those who acquired farms, herds, and houses spent most of their hours getting money to pay for them, leaving too little time for the more rewarding tasks of perfecting mind and character. "The mass of men," he wrote, "lead lives of quiet desperation."[12] They are like serfs toiling to push before them loads of houses, barns, boats, and treasures and the endless task smothers their "better part."[13]

Thoreau poked fun at the pretenses of material life. He found one man overly concerned with his house, "how a few sticks are slanted over him or under him, and what colors are daubed upon his box."[14] He called household possessions "trumpery." He saw his neighbor's interest in fine clothes and noted "there is greater anxiety, commonly, to have fashionable, or at least clean and unpatched clothes, than to have a sound conscience."[15] He was particularly skeptical of anyone who wanted to be rich. "Money," he wrote, "is not required to buy one necessary of the soul."[16]

Thoreau was contrary. He was indolent. He did not work. He would not pay taxes. Yet he showed great integrity to the principle of simple living. His example became a beacon for the few in each succeeding generation who reject materialism.

---

[11] Quoted in Edward Waldo Emerson, *Henry Thoreau: As Remembered by a Young Friend* (Boston: Houghton Mifflin Company, 1917), p. 15.

[12] Henry David Thoreau, *Walden; or, Life in the Woods* (New York: Thomas Y. Crowell, 1910), p. 8.

[13] Ibid., p. 4.

[14] Ibid., p. 61.

[15] Ibid., p. 26.

[16] Ibid., p. 434.

But its light has a limited radius. Tourists now drawn to his Walden Pond homesite support three shopping malls within a mile as the crow flies.

A second defining attack on the values underlying consumerism came a half century later. It appeared in the caricature of material society by a maverick economist, Thorstein Veblen. In his 1899 book *The Theory of the Leisure Class,* Veblen challenged conventional economic wisdom that consumers bought goods for their functional utility, seeking the best value for their money. He argued that in the new industrial society people no longer earned their status by conquest in warfare or prowess in hunting. Instead, they acquired property to create what he called "invidious comparison" between themselves and their less successful neighbors.[17] They displayed their status through "conspicuous consumption," or the "unremitting demonstration of the ability to pay."[18]

In one illustration of his thesis, Veblen pointed out that a handcrafted sterling silver spoon does its job no better than a mass-produced base metal spoon of identical design. In fact, since silver requires polishing it is inconvenient and costly to own, making it less utilitarian. The most desirable quality of the silver spoon is its greater cost, which confers status on a display-conscious consumer. When the book appeared, it was received as only a satire, which disappointed Veblen. Now, a century later, this and other core insights are widely accepted.

Thorstein Veblen (1857–1929) wrote a satirical but penetrating account of modern consumer society. He outraged economists of his day with the insight that people bought products not for their utility, but to show off. Source: © Bettmann/CORBIS

[17] Thorstein Veblen, *The Theory of the Leisure Class* (New York: Penguin Books, 1979), p. 27. Originally published in 1899.
[18] Ibid., p. 87.

Since Veblen, consumerism has been a punching bag for social critics. Here are some general complaints. All are based on the belief that material values undermine other, "higher" values.

- Consumerism leads to commodification of all parts of life. Things are judged for their value on the market rather than by some intrinsic value. People are judged for their external possessions rather than their interior qualities.

- Consumption beyond practical needs for emotional reasons encourages unwise, irrational, and unproductive uses of money. In the 1920s a National Thrift Movement emerged to teach children the thrift ethic. It was inspired by the aphorisms of Benjamin Franklin, who cast industriousness and frugality as central character virtues. The movement had Congress declare that Franklin's birthday in January begin a National Thrift Week and its thrift classes were adopted by thousands of schools. Although its organized influence had withered by 1930, its notion of prudent buying lives on as a second-tier cultural value.

- Heavy consumption is profligate with natural resources and incompatible with sustainability. According to one critic, it even "threatens the collapse of human civilization" from long-term problems such as climate change.[19]

- Consuming beyond necessity, especially by purchasing luxury items, violates "the idea that God's world is already full and complete."[20] Those who consume beyond basic needs are guilty of the sins of gluttony and greed. Heavy consumption of frivolous and luxury goods diverts resources from more noble uses, such as ending world poverty.

- Consumerism distorts our values. It "favors laxity and leisure over discipline and denial," it replaces the work ethic with easy credit and compulsive buying.[21] It converts profligacy into social status. It encourages conspicuous, competitive, and imitative consumption in which people buy material goods to show off, outdo others, or try to fit in with peers. These are inferior motives.

- Consumerism is a pathology of corporate capitalism. Beginning with Lenin, socialists have argued that capitalist economies concentrate production in large firms that seek to expand and control their markets.[22] The continually rising returns necessary to satisfy investors require companies to create powerful marketing methods for manipulating consumers.[23] It is this corporate selling that promotes the false needs, thoughts, and values underlying consumerism.

[19] Erik Assadourian, "The Rise and Fall of Consumer Cultures," in Worldwatch Institute, *2010 State of the World: Transforming Cultures from Consumerism to Sustainability* (New York: W. W. Norton, 2010), p. 3.

[20] James B. Twitchell, *Living It Up: America's Love Affair with Luxury* (New York: Simon & Schuster, 2002), p. 56.

[21] Benjamin R. Barber, "Overselling Capitalism with Consumerism," *The Baltimore Sun,* April 15, 2007, p. A25.

[22] V. I. Lenin, *Imperialism: The Highest Stage of Capitalism* (New York: International Publishers, 1939), originally published in 1917, chap. 1. See also Harry Magdoff and Fred Magdoff, "Approaching Socialism," *Monthly Review,* July–August 2005, who write that consumerism, "the compulsion to purchase more and more, unrelated to basic human needs or happiness," is an "aspect of the culture of capitalism," p. 22.

[23] Michael Dawson, *The Consumer Trap: Big Business Marketing in American Life* (Champaign: University of Illinois Press, 2003).

Criticism of the values in modern consumerism is persistent. Ralph Nader and other leaders of the consumer's movement exhort Americans to be practical in their expenditures, to be vigilant against advertising that tempts them into extravagance, and to put function ahead of excitement in their purchases. From time to time eccentric souls do reject the embrace of consumer culture. A recent book, *Not Buying It: My Year without Shopping*, describes how the author and a companion elected to satisfy their needs without buying new products for a year.[24] In another book, *No Impact Man*, a New York City family tries to live for a year with zero environmental impact.[25] They do not fly, drive, or use taxis. They take stairs to their ninth-floor apartment since elevators use electricity. They live without electric lights or heat. They learn to produce no trash. Such examples come regularly, but they yield few converts. The alternative of simplified, utilitarian living in the mold of the Puritans, Benjamin Franklin, or Henry David Thoreau is now an impractical vision.

Attempts to create sanctuaries from consumerism in American society have also been losing efforts. Blue laws prohibiting stores from opening on Sundays, once pervasive, were an effort to rope off one day of the week and free it of commercialism. Such laws have little coverage now. When radio was new, pioneers of broadcasting such as David Sarnoff at RCA hesitated to air commercials. For the first time, sales pitches came right into the sanctum of the home. Would they offend listeners? Quickly, the answer came. The vast majority felt no affront.

More recently, consumer advocates have tried to fence off childhood from the blandishments of materialism. Battles are fought over ads in schools, school buses, children's television programs, video games, cell phones, and virtual worlds. Although there have been some victories with respect to specific products and locations, it is far too late to sequester children from advertising.

The Global Rise of Consumerism

Among young urban dwellers in Vietnam the "attitude of consumerism is now rampant."[26] In China, where "materialism is the new national ideology,"[27] Prime Minister Wen Jiabao warned that buyers of luxury goods could become "intoxicated with comfort" and sink "into depravity."[28] In Namibia, rising debt, excessive spending at Christmas, and a "growing culture of measuring people's success by material possessions" have caused concern.[29] Crossing the globe, the formula for consumerism is activated by economic growth and social change in one nation after another. The ideology has awakened in Russia, Asia, Latin America, the Middle East, and even sub-Saharan Africa. One historian speculates that it is "the most successful Western influence in world history."[30]

---

[24] Judith Levine, *Not Buying It: My Year without Shopping* (New York: Free Press, 2006).

[25] Colin Beavan, *No Impact Man* (New York: Farrar, Straus and Geroux, 2009).

[26] Roger Mitton, "Young Vietnamese Bitten Hard by Consumer Bug," *The Straits Times,* March 26, 2007.

[27] Noreen O'Leary, "The New Superpower: China's Emerging Middle Class," *Adweek,* January 1, 2007.

[28] Quoted in "If You've Got It, Don't Flaunt It," *The Economist,* June 2, 2007, p. 72.

[29] "Namibia: A Nation in Debt," *Africa News,* January 12, 2007.

[30] Stearns, *Consumerism in World History,* p. 73.

It may, however, be less a Western than a universal phenomenon. Rising like primordial life, it comes when human nature, economic progress, and cultural change interact at a certain moment in a modernizing society. For example, a report by the South African government expressed concern over the growing extent to which consumer goods have become yardsticks for self-identity in that nation. Its explanation is that racial hierarchy determined social status under the old apartheid system. With its end in the early 1990s, people turned to displays of material goods to communicate their social rank.[31]

Once it takes hold, consumerism seems irrepressible, but some resistance continues. Western colonialism in Africa left a persistent disdain for Western values and lifestyles, including consumerism. The presence of an Islamic fundamentalism that rejects Western materialism divides populations in the Middle East. And Catholicism still rejects a material focus. Pope John Paul II called the consumer life "improper" and "damaging" because it promotes "having rather than being" and subordinates "interior and spiritual" dimensions of human life to "material and instinctive dimensions."[32] His successor, Pope Benedict XVI, calls for modern society to switch from lifestyles of consumerism to lifestyles directed by a "quest for truth, beauty, goodness and communion with others for the sake of common growth."[33] Thoreau would have approved.

In Defense of Consumerism

Despite opposition in principle, the ideology of consumerism is triumphant in practice. This is evidence of important virtues. Products and services are designed to fill consumer's needs. Some of these needs are explicit. Others may be latent, waiting to be awakened by marketers. Fulfilling both explicit and latent needs with material objects has emotional benefits. If marketers create an aura of elegance for a brand of perfume, the woman who uses it may feel alluring. Though the chemicals in a $100-an-ounce fragrance may be worth only $0.10, her real purchase is the conviction that she is glamorous.

Successful products either create value for customers or they fail in competitive markets. Intense competition between corporations works to bring consumers more choices, higher quality, and lower prices. Proliferating choices stimulate consumption and economic growth. As prices fall consumer needs at lower income levels are met, in effect raising the standard of living.[34] Some nations adopt conscious policies of stimulating consumerism. After the end of a five-year United Nations embargo in 2003, the Libyan government took measures to reinvigorate its economy, including raising salaries of civil servants by 50 percent. They went shopping. Soon the streets of Tripoli filled with luxury cars going to

[31] Linda Nordling, "Chequered Future: Interview with Deborah Posel," *The Guardian*, May 5, 2009, p. 9.

[32] Ioannes Paulus PP.II, Encyclical Letter, *Centesimus annus* (May 1, 1991), no. 36.

[33] Benedict XVI, Encyclical Letter, *Caritas in veritate* (July 7, 2009), no. 51.

[34] These arguments are in John A. Quelch and Katherine E. Jocz, *Greater Good: How Good Marketing Makes for Better Democracy* (Boston: Harvard Business Press, 2008).

boutiques and malls. "Finally we can shop like everyone else," said one economic patriot.[35]

The most zealous critics of consumerism hold privileged and rare values. They argue that people can and should reject fulfillment in material objects or with money, instead meeting their inner emotional needs by memorizing Shakespeare, showing charity to the poor, communing with nature, or worshiping a deity. However, there is no evidence that happiness derived from a new sports car is less worthy than the joys of the opera.

Consumerism as a Protective Movement

The second basic meaning of consumerism is a movement to promote the rights and interests of consumers in relation to sellers. It arises because fraud, deception, and greed are universal in markets. In the United States, three national movements have sprung up to protect consumers. The first began in the 1870s when Populist farmers attacked railroads for unfair rates and bad service. The second was the Progressive movement. After 1900 both political parties capitalized on the political power of consumers as a class of citizens with similar interests and grievances. This led to passage of early consumer protection laws such as the Food and Drug Act of 1906. Then consumer issues receded until a new era of progressive activism in the 1960s and 1970s prompted a third wave of legislation to protect and expand consumer rights.[36]

There were several triggers for this modern movement. Popular critics accused business of manipulating consumers. In *The Waste Makers,* for example, Vance Packard attacked corporations for everything from using annual model changes to make automobiles obsolete to designing potato peelers that blended in with the peelings and got thrown away, thereby creating a need for another purchase.[37] Ralph Nader aroused the public about automobile safety in his book *Unsafe at Any Speed* and emerged as the leader of a national movement.[38] President John F. Kennedy responded to rising, widespread consumer discontent with a special message to Congress in 1962 in which he said that consumers had basic rights and these rights had been widely abridged.[39] He listed the rights to make intelligent choices among products and services, to have access to accurate information, to register complaints and be heard, to be offered fair prices and acceptable quality, to have safe and healthful products, and to receive adequate service.

Congress responded to President Kennedy's speech, over the next decade passing more than a dozen major consumer protection statutes that expanded the authority of existing agencies and creating four new agencies—the Federal

---

[35] Anonymous, quoted in Imed Lamloum, "Libyans Savour Joys of Consumerism," Agence France Presse, October 1, 2008.

[36] According to Elizabeth Cohen in *A Consumer's Republic* (New York: Knopf, 2003), after the Great Depression, politicians elevated the importance of consumers by defining consumer demand as the key to American prosperity.

[37] Vance Packard, *The Waste Makers* (New York: David McKay, 1960), pp. 40–41.

[38] Ralph Nader, *Unsafe at Any Speed* (New York: Pocket Books, 1966).

[39] See "Text of Kennedy's Message to Congress on Protections for Consumers," *The New York Times,* March 16, 1962.

FIGURE 15.2
Spending on Consumer Health and Safety by Federal Regulatory Agencies: 1960–2010
Figures are in constant (2000) dollars and include spending on a range of consumer protection programs by six departments and agencies. Included are regulation of food and drugs, product safety, and chemical safety. Figures do not include environmental regulation.

Source: Veronique de Rugy and Melinda Warren, *Regulators Budget Report 31* (Arlington, VA, and St. Louis, MO: Mercatus Center and Weidenbaum Center, October 2009), table A-2.

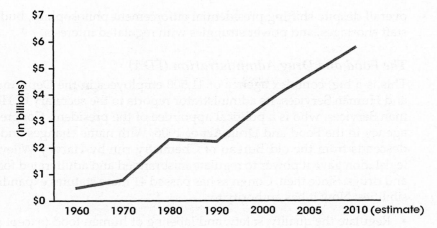

Highway Administration (1966) to set highway safety standards, the Federal Railroad Administration (1966) to regulate rail safety, the National Highway Traffic Safety Administration (1970) to protect the public from unsafe automobiles, and the Consumer Product Safety Commission (1972) to guard against unsafe products.

These legislative successes marked the crest of the modern consumer movement. By the mid-1970s business groups had mobilized to block the great dream of the movement's activists, which was to consolidate enforcement of consumer laws, then scattered among many agencies, into one superagency named the Consumer Protection Agency.

Instead, conservatives and business lobbies won a battle for public opinion, convincing Americans that their government was growing too powerful. They warned a rising tide of regulatory red tape created costs out of all proportion to benefits and handicapped corporations in international competition. In the changed political climate formed by these views, the Consumer Protection Agency bill was decisively defeated in 1976, never to rise again.

Since then, Congress has set up only one new consumer agency, the Bureau of Consumer Financial Protection, which is scheduled to begin its work in 2012. But over the years Congress has passed many new statutes expanding the authority of existing agencies, usually in response to a specific event or concern. The result is continuous growth in consumer regulation. Figure 15.2 shows a rise of spending by 14 consumer protection agencies from $485 million in 1960 to an estimated $5.8 billion in 2010.

The Consumer's Protective Shield

We now turn to the massive statutory shield that protects consumers from abuses, real and imagined. Every state and local government has consumer protection laws, More than 50 federal agencies and bureaus also work to protect consumers. We will focus on the four federal agencies that dominate this area of regulation. A description of their duties reveals the awesome responsibilities Congress has placed on them. While each is flawed, it is astonishing how effective their work is overall despite shifting presidential enforcement philosophies, budget restraints, staff shortages, and power struggles with regulated interests.

The Food and Drug Administration (FDA)

This is a big, complex agency of 11,500 employees in the Department of Health and Human Services. Its administrator reports to the secretary of Health and Human Services, who is a political appointee of the president. Congress created the agency in the Food and Drug Act of 1906. With name changes and relocations it descends from the old Bureau of Chemistry run by Harvey Wiley. The original legislation gave it power to regulate misbranded and adulterated food, beverages, and drugs. Since then, Congress has passed 41 more statutes expanding its responsibilities. Now it has authority to:

- Regulate the quality, safety, and labeling of human food (except poultry, meat, eggs, and alcoholic beverages), pet foods, animal feeds, and food additives.
- Approve human and veterinary drugs and medical devices.
- Set safety and effectiveness standards for over-the-counter drugs.
- Regulate the safety and labeling of cosmetics.
- Regulate the marketing, labeling, and ingredients of tobacco products.
- Set safety standards for radiation-emitting products including microwave ovens, televisions, X-ray machines, lasers, and sunlamps.

The agency's reach extends to economic activity comprising about 25 percent of the nation's GDP. Because its congressionally mandated duties have continuously grown, the FDA traversed the past several decades without suffering the steep declines in staffing and budgets experienced by the other three agencies discussed in this section. Between 1980 and 2010 its budget grew from $608 million to $2.4 billion and the number of employees rose from 8,045 to 11,756.

The FDA's main emphasis in terms of budget and staffing is drug regulation. It requires premarket testing of new prescription drugs to ensure their safety and effectiveness. Each year it approves more than 100 new drug applications. Until the 1990s the approval process was very cautious and took years. Then, AIDS activists challenged its conservatism, demanding fast access to drugs for treating HIV infection. The agency speeded its work and eventually approved the first in a new class of protease inhibitors in just three months. Congress then legislated streamlined procedures and the agency has been faster in recent years, blunting a main criticism against it.

Food regulation overwhelms the agency. One reason is the fundamental change in food markets with globalization. Imports are now 15 percent of America's food supply, including 60 percent of fresh fruits and vegetables and 80 percent of seafood. Each year 20 million shipments of imported food arrive, and the FDA inspects only 1 percent. It has the authority to inspect foreign food factories but the resources to visit only one-tenth of 1 percent of them.[40] Such undercapacity invites

---

[40] Government Accountability Office, *Food Safety: FDA Could Strengthen Oversight of Imported Food by Improving Enforcement and Seeking Additional Authorities,* GAO-1—669T, May 6, 2010, p. 1.

breaches. In 2007 a contaminated protein from China got into pet foods and cattle feed, causing hundreds of animal deaths and major economic losses from brand recalls and livestock quarantines.

Despite the agency's efforts since the days of Henry Wiley, it is unable to eradicate economically motivated contamination and counterfeiting in the food supply. Recently, it has discovered honey diluted with corn syrup, Mississippi paddlefish labeled as sturgeon caviar, rotten tomatoes sold as high-grade tomato paste, and wine made from a slurry of inexpensive grapes that was sold as pinot noir. One expert estimates that 5 to 7 percent of the food supply is dishonest.[41] Between 2006 and 2009 the agency confronted four outbreaks of salmonella from contaminated peanuts. One company, Peanut Corp. of America, ignored tests that showed contamination and shipped peanuts that killed eight people and sickened 575. More than 2,000 products had to be recalled.[42] When FDA inspectors went to the plant, it was the first visit in eight years. Subsequently, they discovered 20 facilities that, unknown to them, were making food with peanuts. These unregulated plants were found only because they bought peanuts from Peanut Corp.

In 2009 Congress gave the agency power to regulate cigarettes and smokeless tobacco. If cereals or soft drinks were as dangerous as these products, the FDA would prohibit their sale, but the new law forbids banning any tobacco product. It has the power to set nicotine levels but cannot reduce them to zero. It has broader powers over marketing and sales and has already banned the use of the words *light, mild,* or *low,* candy-flavored cigarettes, and free cigarette samples. The agency plans to build its tobacco division to 400 employees, making the division almost as large as two of the other agencies discussed in this section.

A federal agency with such importance and scope of responsibility, especially with limited resources, attracts critics. It is under constant pressure to speed its actions and reduce risks to the public. Observers suggest that the FDA needs a radical reorganization. Its jurisdiction comes from piecemeal legislation enacted over many decades. The laws have created internal bureaucratic overlaps and conflict. Repeatedly, however, proposals in Congress to consolidate and clarify FDA authority fail to pass. Some suggest dividing the agency in two, creating separate agencies for drugs and food.[43]

The Federal Trade Commission (FTC)

This venerable regulator was born in the Progressive era, a time of great alarm about the growth of big trusts. In 1914 Congress created it as an independent commission, giving it broad powers to protect the public from unfair competition. The president nominates its five commissioners, including one who is designated

[41] John Spink, Michigan State University, cited in Lyndsey Layton, "FDA Pressures to Combat Rising 'Food Fraud,'" *The Washington Post,* March 30, 2010, p. A1.

[42] Thomas H. Maugh II and Mary Engel, "FDA Says Firm Lied About Peanut Butter," *Los Angeles Times,* February 7, 2009, p. A1.

[43] Rob Stein, "Ailing FDA May Need a Major Overhaul," *The Washington Post,* November 26, 2008, p. A2.

chair, who are then approved by the Senate for seven-year terms. No more than three can be of the same political party. Once approved, they act independently of the executive branch. The FTC has broad duties to:

- Protect consumers from any practice that unfairly limits competition, including price-fixing, boycotts, conspiracies, and illegal agreements or combinations.
- Challenge mergers and acquisitions that reduce competition or innovation.
- Prevent false and deceptive advertising.
- Protect the public from fraudulent and deceptive sales practices.
- Prohibit discrimination by lenders based on race, sex, national origin, age, or marital status.

At its birth the agency was a fiery enforcer hurling antitrust actions at surprised cartels and trusts. But by the 1920s laissez-faire doctrines reasserted themselves in national politics, and the FTC lost support in Congress and the courts. It languished for decades until a new consumer movement rose in the 1960s, filling it with idealistic young attorneys who wanted to make markets honest. At its zenith in the 1970s it had a staff of 1,800. However, it was soon undercut again by a conservative philosophy, this time deregulation. Corporations annoyed by its actions got Congress to reduce its authority and cut its funding. By the late 1980s it was a demoralized entity with fewer than 900 employees. Now, 20 years later, the scars of deregulation still show, but it has expanded to 1,100 employees. It pursues two basic missions.

One mission is to promote fair competition in industries by enforcing antitrust laws. It seeks to prevent companies from hurting consumers by illegal actions that allow them to raise prices and stifle innovation. The FTC blocked a merger of Home Depot and Staples that would have created a dominant competitor in office supplies. It allowed Whole Foods Market to purchase its main competitor, Wild Oats Markets, only after Whole Foods sold 13 stores to restore competition in natural foods retailing. Recently it acted to deter collusion between Apple and Google. After an FTC investigation, Eric Schmidt, the CEO of Google, resigned from Apple's board, and Arthur Levinson, a biotechnology executive, resigned from Google's board but remained a director of Apple. Antitrust law prohibits *director interlock,* or the sharing of directors by two or more companies, when those companies compete in the same markets. Although Google is an online search and advertising company and Apple manufactures computers and portable electronics, the commission saw that both companies had some competing businesses. Both made mobile phones and both sold operating systems and browsers for mobile devices. It acted to break the director interlock.

director interlock
A situation arising when an individual sits on the board of directors of two or more corporations. This is illegal under the Clayton Act of 1914 if the corporations compete in the same market(s).

The FTC's second mission is to protect consumers from fraudulent or deceptive advertising and marketing. For example, Kellogg Company advertised that based on "clinical research" eating Frosted Mini-Wheats for breakfast improved the attentiveness of children three hours later by nearly 20 percent over children who ate no breakfast. Not so, said the FTC. In the study only about half the children who ate Frosted Mini-Wheats showed any improvement at all. Only 1 in

7 improved their attentiveness by 18 percent or more, and average improvement was only 10.6 percent.[44] Kellogg withdrew the ad. In another case a religious group called Daniel Chapter One marketed four herbal supplements it said would prevent or cure cancer. When the FTC filed a complaint the group argued the commission had no jurisdiction over a religious ministry and was attempting to censor its speech. The commission prevailed.

As part of its mission to protect consumers from deception the commission also regulates debt collection. After the economic downturn in 2008, Oxford Collection Agency began using illegal practices. Its agents called consumers before 8:00 a.m. and after 9:00 p.m., many times a day, and if they hung up, called back immediately. They used profane language and told employers, co-workers, relatives, and neighbors about the debtor's bills. Eventually, the commission levied a $1,060,000 civil fine against Oxford and four individuals.[45]

These stories only scratch the surface. Among its recent activities the FTC has also fought fraudulent green marketing claims, issued rules to reduce spam, published guidelines for bloggers who endorse products, and studied explicit sexuality and violence in online virtual worlds for children (it found instances of such in 19 of 27 worlds visited).[46] More than 175 million consumers have signed up for its do-not-call registry to stop unwanted telemarketer calls.

The Consumer Product Safety Commission (CPSC)

This agency was created by Congress in 1972. Its mission is "to protect children and families from unreasonable risks of injuries associated with consumer products."[47] It enforces 15 major statutes giving it power to:

- Set mandatory or encourage voluntary safety standards for more than 15,000 consumer products.
- Ban the sale of products that expose consumers to unreasonable risks.
- Require manufacturers to recall dangerous products.
- Investigate the extent and causes of deaths and injuries from consumer products.

The agency was set up at the crest of the third wave of consumer protection. Congress gave it considerable autonomy. It is an independent regulatory commission insulated from presidential control. Its five commissioners have staggered seven-year appointments. Yet from its creation it has faced political adversity. President Nixon, who established the agency, was unenthusiastic about it. President Reagan wanted to abolish it but could not. Instead, his allies in Congress drastically cut its budget and it has never been fully restored. Today it operates

[44] Complaint, *In the Matter of Kellogg Company,* Docket No. C-4262, Federal Trade Commission, July 27, 2009, p. 7.

[45] *United States v. Oxford Collection Agency,* CV 09 2467, District Court, E.D.N.Y., June 10, 2009, p. 6.

[46] Federal Trade Commission, *Annual Report: The FTC in 2010* (Washington, DC: FTC, April 2010), p. 45.

[47] Ibid., p. i.

with fewer than 400 employees, down from almost 1,000 in 1980. However, after a national dither over Chinese toys with lead in the paint, Congress in 2008 mandated an increase to 500 by 2013.

Over the years, as the CPSC languished, its regulatory realm dramatically changed. At its inception most consumer products were made in the United States. Now most are imported. Between 1998 and 2007 the value of consumer products entering the country increased by 101 percent to $638 billion. Products from China nearly quadrupled and now account for 43 percent of that total. The agency is required to stop the entry of unsafe consumer products but it is overwhelmed. While there are more than 300 ports of entry, it has only nine inspectors at seven locations. By contrast, the Food and Drug Administration has inspectors at 297 ports of entry.[48]

Despite a shortage of resources, the CPSC faces its massive regulatory task with a certain vigor. It regulates roughly 15,000 types of products, everything except alcohol, tobacco, food, drugs, cosmetics, pesticides, motor vehicles, flotation devices, firearms, and pesticides. It has set 38 mandatory safety standards for products as diverse as matchbooks, bicycles, and bunk beds and it has collaborated with industry to create another 390 voluntary standards. In almost 40 years it has banned only eight products including flammable glues and sharp lawn darts. However, each year it prods companies to carry out between 400 and 600 product recalls.

In one example, it requested that a company recall 1 million folding strollers made in China. It had received 15 reports of children catching fingers in a side hinge. Twelve suffered fingertip amputations.[49] In another case it pushed Mattel to recall 7.3 million Polly Pocket doll sets. Tiny magnets inside the toys could fall out and be swallowed by children. If more than one magnet was ingested, they could come together causing blocked, perforated, or infected intestines. By the time the recall was complete three children with perforated intestines needed surgery. The agency pushes recalls even when dangers seem not so grim. It announced that Ross Stores would recall 1,800 inexpensive plant stands. Two consumers were bruised when the stand's marble tops came loose and fell.[50]

The National Highway Traffic Safety Administration (NHTSA)

This is a small agency of about 550 employees in the Department of Transportation. Its administrator reports to the secretary of Transportation, who is a political

---

[48] Figures in this paragraph are from Government Accountability Office, *Consumer Safety: Better Information and Planning Would Strengthen CPSC's Oversight of Imported Products,* GAO-09-803, August 2009, pp. 1 and 12.

[49] Consumer Product Safety Commission, "Maclaren USA Recalls to Repair Strollers Following Fingertip Amputations," Release No. 10-033, November 9, 2009.

[50] Consumer Product Safety Commission, "Ross Stores Recalls Plant Stands; Marble Top Can Detach and Fall on Consumers," Release No. 09-292.

appointee of the president. Congress created it in 1966, giving it a mission of reducing motor vehicle deaths and injuries. It has authority to:

- Mandate minimum safety standards for automobiles, trucks, and their components, including tires.
- Set fuel economy standards for cars and light-duty trucks.
- Require manufacturers to recall cars and trucks with safety defects.
- Administer grants for states and cities to promote highway safety.

No other agency has such extensive controls over a single product. A short list of past rules just to protect occupants of an automobile includes rules on air bags, brakes, safety belts, energy-absorbing or collapsible steering columns, penetration-resistant windshields, recessed door handles, breakaway rearview mirrors, padded dashboards, collapsible front ends, crush-resistant passenger compartments, and tire standards. Over the years "more than 390 million cars, trucks, buses, recreational vehicles, motorcycles, and mopeds, as well as 46 million tires, 66 million pieces of motor vehicle equipment, and 42 million child safety seats have been recalled to correct safety defects."[51]

Since the agency's creation, highway fatalities per million vehicle miles have fallen from more than 3.5 to 1.4.[52] Although many factors led to this decline, including strict drunk driving laws, a major one is the safety standards NHTSA regulators impose on automakers. Yet critics believe the agency has become lax, slow, meek, ineffectual, even "sleepy."[53] Recently, lobbying by industry led it to relax a roof crush rule and drop a rule strengthening passenger seats. Although power windows have the force to strangle children, it has not required auto reverse features as are mandatory in Europe.

Sudden acceleration incidents in Toyota Motor Company automobiles put a spotlight on the agency in 2010 and it did not fare well. Over the previous decade it had received 3,400 complaints of sudden acceleration in the company's cars.[54] In three investigations the agency simply accepted the company's explanations and required a single recall replacing 55,000 floor mats. Toyota had hired former NHTSA enforcement officials who successfully lobbied the agency to avoid or narrow recall orders. Eventually, the agency ordered recall of 6.1 million Toyota and Lexus automobiles and imposed four fines totaling $49 million on Toyota for failing to notify it promptly of safety defects in brake pedals and floor mats. But by then there were reports of 34 deaths and hundreds of injuries from sudden acceleration crashes, and the agency was criticized for its slow response. The fines were the maximum the agency could give

51 National Highway Traffic Safety Administration, "Motor Vehicle Defects and Recalls Campaigns," www.nhtsa.dot.gov, accessed July 5, 2010.

52 Government Accountability Office, p. 11.

53 Ralph Nader, "Toyota's Enablers," *Los Angeles Times,* February 28, 2010, p. A27.

54 Opening Statement of Chairman Edolphus Towns, hearing on *Toyota Gas Pedals: Is the Public at Risk?* Committee on Oversight and Government Reform, House of Representatives, February 24, 2010, p. 2.

FIGURE 15.3

One Effect of Deregulation on Three Consumer Agencies

Staff reductions at three of the four consumer agencies discussed in this section reflect the philosophy of deregulation that gained strength in the 1970s. These agencies have yet to recover their former staffing levels. The exception is the FDA, which has steadily added employees due to expansion of its regulatory duties.

Source: Veronique de Rugy and Melinda Warren, *Regulators Budget Report 31* (Arlington, VA, and St. Louis, MO: Mercatus Center and Weidenbaum Center, October 2009), table A-3.

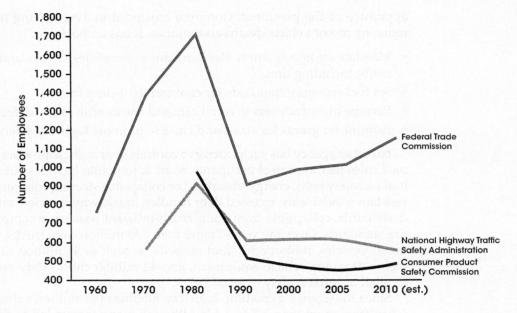

and came over a two-year period during which Toyota took in $452 billion in global revenues.

The Toyota episode bared agency shortcomings. Like other consumer agencies in this section, its staffing has languished with deregulatory trends over two decades (see Figure 15.3). In 2010 it had fewer employees than in 1970. Its enforcement budget is insufficient to conduct investigations, so it relies on manufacturers for information about defects. The product it regulates has changed dramatically. Since the 1960s automobiles have evolved from mechanical to electronic systems, becoming more complex. The agency was willing to accept Toyota's explanation that floor mats caused sudden acceleration because it did not employ a single electrical or software engineer with expertise on computerized acceleration systems.[55] Eventually, it hired outside consultants, including a NASA engineer, to improve its understanding.

Consumer Protection by Other Agencies

Other agencies add to the consumer's protective shield. The Environmental Protection agency defends consumers in many ways, for example, by setting drinking water standards. The Food Safety and Inspection Service in the Department of Agriculture inspects meat, poultry, and eggs. The Equal Employment Opportunity Commission acts against housing and loan discrimination. The Federal Deposit Insurance Corporation insures deposits in 4,900 banks. The new Bureau of Consumer Financial Protection created by Congress in 2010 will oversee all financial

[55] Statement of Joan Claybrook, hearing on *Toyota Gas Pedals: Is the Public at Risk?* Committee on Oversight and Government Reform, House of Representatives, February 24, 2010, p. 6.

FIGURE 15.4   Federal Agencies Responsible for Ensuring Safe Pizza

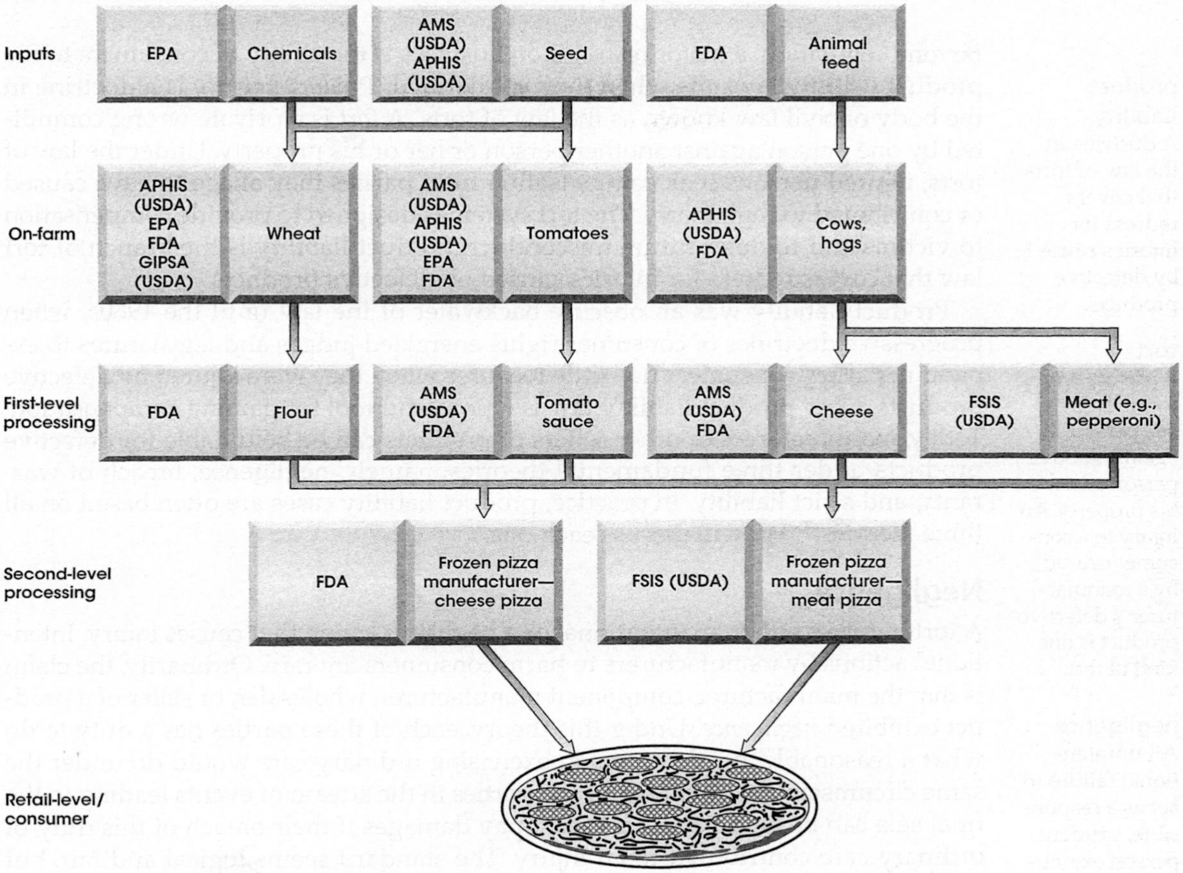

Source: Lawrence J. Dyckman, "Federal Food Safety and Security System," testimony before the Subcommittee on Civil Service and Agency Organization, Committee on Government Reform, House of Representatives, March 30, 2004, p. 5.

Note: AMS—Agriculture Marketing Service
       APHIS—Animal and Plant Health Inspection Service
       GIPSA—Grain Inspection, Packers and Stockyards Administration
       FSIS—Food Safety and Inspection Service

products, protecting consumers from hidden fees, abusive terms, and deceptive practices.

Dozens of other agencies and bureaus have protective duties. In fact, the protective shield, as forged piece by piece over many years, is fragmented, incomplete, and sometimes illogical. The EPA sets drinking water standards, but the FDA regulates bottled water. The FTC has oversight of deceptive marketing, but if the fraud involves a moving van the Federal Motor Carrier Safety Administration takes jurisdiction. And as Figure 15.4 shows, getting a safe pizza to the table is a bureaucratic jubilee. Despite all, consumers receive a great amount of benefit from agencies that struggle to keep up with the flood of work they are given by Congress.

PRODUCT LIABILITY

product liability
A doctrine in the law of torts that covers redress for injuries caused by defective products.

tort
A private wrong committed by one person against another person or her or his property. An injury to a consumer caused by a manufacturer's defective product is one kind of tort.

negligence
An unintentional failure to act as a responsible, prudent person exercising ordinary care.

privity
A relationship giving parties a common interest under the law, as in the relationship between parties to a contract.

Beyond regulation, a major restraint on business is the ability of consumers to file product liability lawsuits when they are harmed. *Product liability* is a doctrine in the body of civil law known as the law of torts. A *tort* is a private wrong committed by one person against another person or her or his property. Under the law of torts, injured persons seek compensation from parties they allege to have caused or contributed to their injury. The tort system is designed to provide compensation to victims and to deter future misconduct. Product liability is the branch of tort law that covers redress for injuries caused by defective products.

Product liability was an obscure backwater of the law until the 1960s, when progressive doctrines of consumer rights energized judges and legislatures to expand it. Earlier, consumers had little recourse when they were injured by defective products. Now product liability law is a powerful tool for gaining compensation. Today, manufacturers or other sellers of products can be held liable for defective products under three fundamental theories, namely, negligence, breach of warranty, and strict liability. In practice, product liability cases are often based on all three theories.[56] We will discuss each one.

Negligence

A tort involves either an intentional or a negligent action that causes injury. Intentional actions by manufacturers to harm consumers are rare. Ordinarily, the claim is that the manufacturer, component manufacturer, wholesaler, or seller of a product exhibited *negligence*. Under this theory, each of these parties has a duty to do what a reasonable, prudent person exercising ordinary care would do under the same circumstances. Thus, any of the parties in the stream of events leading to the final sale can be held liable and must pay damages if their breach of this duty of ordinary care contributed to an injury. The standard seems logical and fair, but early product liability law was not so generous to consumers.

As the United States turned into a consumer society in the late 1800s and early 1900s, manufacturers were well protected from liability suits brought by individuals who were injured by their products. An injured consumer trying to collect damages faced two formidable obstacles in the law.

One was the entrenched principle of *caveat emptor,* a Latin phrase meaning let the buyer beware. It imposed on buyers the responsibility to inspect carefully and skeptically items they purchased. If they failed to see dangerous defects, the legal presumption was that absent any specified remedy in a formal contract they were at fault, not the manufacturer or seller.

The other obstacle was a narrow interpretation of the doctrine of *privity,* which defined the legal relationship between a consumer and other parties to a sale.

---

[56] See, for example, the cases of a farmer who sued a herbicide manufacturer for marketing a chemical that stunted his sunflower crop, *Coleman v. Nufarm Americas,* 693 F. Supp. 2d 1055 (2010); a mother who sued a sperm bank over its product, sperm, that caused her daughter to be born with developmental problems, *Donovan v. Idant Laboratories,* 625 F. Supp. 2d 256 (2009); and a chicken-house worker who sued an equipment manufacturer after he lost a foot in a manure auger, *Vaughn v. Alternative Design Mfg. and Supply,* CV No. 6: 07-429-DCR, U.S.D.C. E.D.K, So. Div (2008).

Courts held that consumers could sue only the party that sold them the product. This restriction was based on English common law and may have been appropriate in an agrarian America where sellers and product makers were in face-to-face contact.[57] As the distribution chain lengthened and grew impersonal in industrial society, that experience became rare. Yet, under the law, injured buyers had no case against a manufacturer. They had to sue the retailer, the party with whom they had a direct relationship. If retailers lost a suit, they could sue the wholesaler, and the wholesaler, in turn, the manufacturer.

This legal wall protecting manufacturers was broken down by the milestone case of *MacPherson v. Buick Motor Co.* in 1916.[58] Donald MacPherson bought a Buick from a Schenectady dealer. While driving it at 8 miles per hour, defective wood spokes on one wheel disintegrated, causing its collapse. MacPherson was thrown out and injured. He sued Buick for negligence because it had sold the automobile without inspecting the spokes. Buick had purchased the wheel from a company that supplied it with 80,000 wheels, none of which had been defective before. Nevertheless, a future U.S. Supreme Court justice, Benjamin Cardozo, then sitting on the New York Supreme Court, affirmed a jury verdict for MacPherson, arguing that, as the manufacturer, Buick "was responsible for the finished product" and could reasonably have been expected to discover the defect by inspection. Furthermore, Buick "owed a duty of care and vigilance" that went beyond the immediate buyer, the dealer, to the driver. Because this extension of the negligence doctrine came in the large marketplace of New York, it spread to other states and became the foundation for a more consumer-friendly modern product liability law.

Over the years since *MacPherson* the negligence doctrine has been continuously stretched to favor consumers. For example, in a 1968 case General Motors made a car that was safe to operate, but was held negligent for not designing it to reduce injury in a collision. Erling Larsen had a head-on collision in a Corvair and suffered severe injuries when the steering wheel was pushed back into his head. He sued, arguing that the steering assembly was defective. Though it had not caused the crash, its design exposed him to greater harm than necessary. General Motors responded that its legal duty was to design a safe car, not a car that protected occupants during head-on collisions. In *Larsen v. General Motors* a federal court held that the design of the steering assembly was negligent because other practical designs could have stopped the wheel from moving back toward the driver after impact and it was foreseeable that there would be collisions.[59] Such expansions in the meaning of negligence have reversed the old *caveat emptor* doctrine. Now, let the manufacturer beware.

Warranty

warranty
A contract in which the seller guarantees the nature of the product. The seller must compensate the buyer if the warranty is not fulfilled.

A *warranty* is a contract in which the seller guarantees the nature of the product. If the product does not conform to the standards in the warranty, the buyer is entitled to compensation for any consequent loss or injury. A manufacturer or seller can be held liable for a breach of one or both of two kinds of warranties, express and implied.

[57] See *Winterbottom v. Wright*, 15 Eng. Rep. 402 (Eng. 1842) 177.
[58] 217 N.Y. 382 (1916).
[59] 391 F.2d 495 (8th Cir. 1968).

express warranty
An explicit claim made by the manufacturer to the buyer.

implied warranty
An unwritten warranty that a product is adequate to meet a buyer's reasonable expectations that it will fulfill its ordinary purpose and the buyer's particular purpose.

strict liability
The theory that liability exists, even in the absence of negligence, when an activity or product is inherently dangerous.

An *express warranty* is an explicit claim made by the manufacturer to the buyer. It can be a statement that the product will perform in a specified way, a description of the product, or a picture that shows a model product. In the past, manufacturers often put statements in warranties to limit their liability, but the courts have protected consumers by enlarging the idea of an *implied warranty*, or an unwritten, commonsense warranty arising out of reasonable expectations that a product will both fulfill its ordinary purpose and fulfill the particular purpose of the buyer.

Again, the landmark case involves the automobile industry. Claus Henningsen bought his wife, Helen, a new 1955 Plymouth as a Mother's Day gift. On the back of the purchase order he signed, buried in eight inches of fine print, was a statement that in case of a warranty claim for any defect the buyer must return the parts to Chrysler Corporation, postage paid, and that Chrysler would then decide "to its satisfaction" whether there was a defect. Ten days after getting the car, Mrs. Henningsen was driving about 20 miles per hour when a loud noise came from the front. The car veered at 90 degrees to the side, crashing into a brick wall. The steering mechanism in the front end was crushed, making evaluation of mechanical defects difficult. Both the dealer and Chrysler Corporation denied any obligation to pay for the damaged car and for medical expenses. In *Henningsen v. Bloomfield Motors* the court said the limitation on the express warranty was a "sad commentary" on industry practice and could not override an implied warranty that the car was "reasonably suited for ordinary use" by the purchaser.[60] Chrysler had to pay.

Strict Liability

The doctrine of *strict liability*, or liability without fault, arose in tort law many years ago in England.[61] There it was established that anyone who engaged in a dangerous activity, such as using explosives or keeping ferocious animals, is liable for damages to others, even if the activity is conducted with utmost care. The key to strict liability is that the injured person need not prove negligence to prevail in court. It is presumed that any person engaged in ultrahazardous activities is automatically liable for adverse consequences to society.

The theory of strict liability was gradually extended to product liability and by the 1960s it was firmly entrenched.[62] This furthered the trend toward expansion of manufacturers' liability because injured consumers no longer had to prove negligence or breach of warranty to prevail in cases where there was some inherent danger in the use of a product. The law transferred much of the risk of using such products from consumers to manufacturers.

A landmark case involved William Greenman, who was turning a piece of wood when it flew off the machine, hitting him in the forehead, and causing serious injury. Greenman found evidence that the machine's design was defective and sued the manufacturer, Yuba Power Products, alleging negligence and breach of warranty. A lower court found no evidence of negligence or breach of express warranty, but a jury awarded Greenman $65,000 for breach of implied warranty. On appeal, the manufac-

[60] *Henningsen v. Bloomfield Motors, Inc,* 32 N.J. 358 at 374 and 384.
[61] See *Rylands v. Fletcher,* L.R. 3 H.L. 330 (1868).
[62] See American Law Institute, *Restatement of the Law of Torts,* 2d, ed. vol. 2 (Washington, DC: American Law Institute Publishers, 1965), sec. 402A, pp. 347–48.

turer raised serious issues that might have overturned the verdict, but the California Supreme Court imposed strict liability on the company, holding that all Greenman had to prove was that he was injured by the defective product while using it as it was intended to be used. Proving negligence or breach of warranty was not necessary.[63]

Under strict liability an injured plaintiff must prove only that the manufacturer made a product in a defective condition that made it unreasonably dangerous to the user, that the seller was in the business of selling such products, and that it was unchanged from its manufactured condition when purchased. The "defect" can exist because of poor design, insufficient warning, or even hazards unknown to the manufacturer. It is an inherent danger not anticipated by the buyer and can exist even though the product was carefully made.

This is the legal doctrine that dismantled the asbestos industry. When strict liability was accepted by the courts, sick asbestos workers no longer had to prove that Johns Manville or other companies were negligent because they already knew about asbestos hazards. All they had to prove was that asbestos was "defective," that is, that it contained an inherently dangerous quality. The asbestos companies were then liable to compensate workers having asbestos disease. As the court stated in *Greenman v. Yuba Power Products,* "The purpose of [strict] liability is to insure that the costs of injuries resulting from defective products are borne by the manufacturers that put such products on the market rather than by the injured persons who are powerless to protect themselves."[64] This idea, now embedded in the law, was another big step away from *caveat emptor.*

Costs and Benefits of the Tort System

Product liability suits are filed in every state and in federal courts. There is no central reporting of them. Comprehensive statistics about their number, disposition, and jury awards do not exist. However, they are a significant part of an overall tort system that imposes massive costs on business.

The tort system is designed to compensate injured parties and deter future wrongdoing by imposing the cost of injuries on persons or corporations whose behavior caused harm. A recent estimate is that this system inflicts an annual economic cost of $835 billion on American society, about 2.2 percent of GDP. This is the highest in the world and more than double the 1 percent average of other industrial nations.[65] About a third of this cost is from personal torts, most related to auto accidents; the rest is for commercial torts against businesses including product liability, medical malpractice, and workers compensation.

Much of the cost may be worth it. Because of product liability suits, dangerous products such as asbestos, cigarettes, flammable children's pajamas, and some birth control devices have been either taken off the market, had their sales restricted, or been redesigned. Those injured by them have been compensated. While the public may benefit from such lawsuits, others are more problematic. Lawsuit threats and expensive liability insurance regularly cause companies to

[63] *Greenman v. Yuba Power Products, Inc.,* 59 Cal. 2d 57 (1963).

[64] Ibid., at 63.

[65] Lawrence J. McQuillan and Hovannes Abramyan, *U.S. Tort Liability Index: 2010 Report* (San Francisco: Pacific Research Institute, 2010), pp. 17–18.

drop high-risk products such as off-road vehicles, medical implants, football helmets, drugs, and vaccines, some of which are valuable to society. An unknown number of new products and innovations never come to market because their liability potential scares manufacturers. In the pharmaceutical industry, funds that might go into developing new drugs are regularly diverted to litigation expenses. In other cases, liability insurance and litigation costs are simply passed on to consumers—like an extra tax on the products they buy. Sometimes liability costs even have the perverse effect of reducing safety. Extension ladders for home use now carry such a high price premium for product liability costs that many people just go on using deteriorating older ladders.[66]

CONCLUDING OBSERVATIONS

Consumerism is a word with two meanings. It refers both to an ideology and to a protective movement. In this chapter we discuss trends related to both meanings. First, consumerism as a way of life is spreading around the world because the conditions that support it are becoming more common. Where it is already established, it is strengthening its grip. Second, consumers in the United States are now more protected from injury, fraud, and other abuses than in the past because of stronger government regulation and more consumer-friendly common law doctrines.

These trends seem likely to continue. As the ideology of consumerism tightens its hold, responsible governments will expend more resources on issues raised by shopping for, purchasing, using, and displaying material objects. These issues will be more complex as populations grow, product choices expand, new technologies change products, and marketing becomes more amplified and pervasive.

[66] Michael Krauss, "Tort-Eating Contest," *The Wall Street Journal,* May 2, 2007, p. A20.

Alcohol Advertising

Anheuser-Busch had high hopes for Spykes. When the product was introduced in 2005, the giant brewer was losing market share to distilled spirits. In 2001 spirits makers had ended a long-standing voluntary policy against aggressive advertising. Liquor ads filled cable channels, then appeared on network affiliates. At NASCAR races lettering for Jim Beam and Jack Daniels appeared on the cars. More drinkers, notably young adults between 21 and 30 years old, found novelty in new brands, drinks, and mixes marketed by the distillers. Drinking tastes were changing. The trend in bars and clubs was moving away from domestic beers such as Anheuser-Busch's Budweiser.

Chairman August A. Busch III thought the company needed something "fun and new and innovative" to put into the hands of young drinkers.[1] That product was Spykes, a caffeinated malt liquor beverage that was 12 percent alcohol. It came in a 1.7-ounce bottle for $0.75 or a 2-ounce bottle for $1. Spykes included caffeine to capitalize on the popularity of mixing energy drinks with alcohol and it came in multiple flavors—Spicy Lime, Spicy Mango, Hot Melons, and Hot Chocolate. Drinkers could down it as a shot or experiment by mixing the flavors in beer or cocktails.

Anheuser-Busch tried to build the brand slowly through word of mouth at the local level. It set up a

[1] Quoted in Victor Reklaits, "Anheuser-Busch Unveils Product Aimed at 21- to 30-year Olds," *Daily Press-Newport,* December 2, 2005, p. 1.

brightly colored Web site with recipes for Spykes. "Try it as a shot. Spice up your beer. Invent a new cocktail. Mix two or more together for a new flavor."[2] Visitors downloaded music mixes, ringtones, and screen savers. A message board let users interact with the site. One exchange of ideas was, "I wonder if it still tastes good if you heat it up lol," followed by, "I'm gonna try putting one in the microwave . . . lol."[3]

By early 2007 Spykes had been rolled out in 32 states. Then a mighty eruption rose from the precincts of those self-appointed to protect the public from the evils of alcohol. It began with a press release from the Center for Science in the Public Interest, a watchdog group founded by Ralph Nader. In it, George A. Hacker, head of the group's alcohol campaign, unloaded a vicious attack on Spykes, calling it "the latest attempt by Anheuser-Busch to get children interested in alcohol." "This is a shameful ploy to market malt liquor to the Lunchables set," he said. "It's hard to imagine an adult purchasing this beverage, unless they were bringing it for a surprise date with Chris Hansen on Dateline NBC."

The evidence that Spykes targeted underage drinkers included its sweet flavors, the lack of age-verification and "teen-friendly" attractions on its Web site, and its caffeine (because energy drinks are popular with teenagers). Hacker called on the company to "immediately pull Spykes off of shelves, apologize to parents, and hope that in the meantime, no young person wraps his or her car around a tree after being Spyked once too often at the prom."[4]

The Center for Science in the Public Interest is at the forefront in a coalition of antialcohol groups that faults the alcoholic beverage industry for social problems caused by drinking. Others in this coalition piled on. Project Extra Mile, which fights underage drinking, expressed concern that minors could hide small Spykes bottles in pockets and purses.[5] Another

leading antialcohol group, the Marin Institute, called the product "egregious."[6]

Anheuser-Busch was taken by surprise. "Frankly," said a spokeswoman, "we're perplexed at this criticism. These professional critic groups need to stop the fear mongering and focus on reality."[7]

Concern spread. The Michigan State Police put its officers on alert for small bottles of Spykes, especially in women's purses. A county coroner in Illinois warned parents to "check your teen on prom night" because Spykes can "fit easily into a tux jacket pocket or . . . a purse for prom night 'fun.'"[8] The attorneys general of 28 states wrote to Anheuser-Busch expressing "serious concern" about Spykes and its marketing. Soon after receiving this letter, the company gave up. Due to what it called "unfounded criticism" by "perennial anti-alcohol groups" it announced the end for Spykes.

In fact, Spykes was just the opening skirmish in a war over caffeinated alcoholic beverages. It was an important product innovation in a highly competitive industry. Its success had illuminated a lucrative niche market. In fact, Anheuser-Busch had two similar caffeinated brands, Tilt and Bud Extra. MillerCoors was readying a brand named Sparks. And by 2008 more than two dozen smaller companies marketed products with colorful names such as Liquid Charge, Max Fury, Evil Eye, Joose, Four Loco, and Moonshot.

This proliferation was a red flag for antialcohol activists who felt caffeinated alcoholic beverages posed serious risks. These drinks contained less caffeine than a cup of coffee and met federal guidelines of 200 parts per million or less for caffeine in soft drinks. Nonetheless, the critics believed that caffeine stimulated drinkers, leading them to drink more and leaving them less aware they were impaired by alcohol. Studies confirm this. A professor in Florida, for example, found that patrons in a college bar district who consumed alcohol mixed with energy drinks were three times more likely to leave a bar highly

[2] Donna Leinwand, "Beermaker Urged to Pull Spykes," *USA Today,* April 10, 2007, p. A3.

[3] Quoted in Kari Huus, "A Booze Buzz for Teenyboppers?" MSNBC, April 3, 2007 at www.msnbc.msn.com/id/17862137/37273872.

[4] "CSPI Urges Nationwide Recall of Spykes 'Liquid Lunchables,'" Center for Science in the Public Interest, April 4, 2007, at www.cspinet.org.

[5] Jim Osborn, "Tiny Flavored Drink a Worry," *Columbus Telegram,* May 4, 2007, p. 1.

[6] David Lazarus, "Spykes Is No Longer Buzzing," *San Francisco Chronicle,* May 27, 2007, p. G1.

[7] Francine Katz, Anheuser-Busch vice president of communications, quoted in "Anheuser-Busch Product Criticized," *AFX News Limited,* April 6, 2007.

[8] Blog of Dr. Richard Keller, "Live from the Coroner's Office: Spykes, May 4, 2007, at http://coronerlakecountyil.blogspot.com/.

intoxicated and four times more likely to drive home.[9] Critics thought marketing claims duped young drinkers into complacency and they engaged in more risky behavior, from sexual aggression to drunk driving. The products were dangerous, their marketing execrable.

After Spykes, Anheuser-Busch was an easy target. In 2008 it was attacked by 11 state attorneys general who alleged that the labels on Tilt and Bud Extra failed accurately to disclose health risks and that ads for the products illegally targeted minors. The company agreed to reformulate the products, removing caffeine. MillerCoors was next. The attorneys general subpoenaed documents on Sparks, a new caffeinated brand MillerCoors was prepared to market. The Center for Science in the Public Interest sued the company, alleging it used unapproved ingredients that posed health and safety risks for consumers. Eventually MillerCoors gave in and agreed to remove caffeinated ingredients from Sparks.

Next in line was Constellation Brands, which sold a caffeinated schnapps, named Wide Eye. It was advertised with images of a woman boxer. One ad said, "this is your wake-up call." Another stated: "When you party with the world's first caffeinated schnapps it'll seem like the rest of the world is sleepwalking through life."

After receiving complaints from "consumers," the Federal Trade Commission issued a complaint against Constellation Brands, accusing it of saying "expressly or by implication, that consumers who drink Wide Eye will remain alert when consuming alcohol," and charging the statements were "false and misleading."[10] In a settlement the company agreed to stop making misleading claims. In fact, it had already stopped producing the brand.

Late in 2009 the Food and Drug Administration, responding to pressure from activists, sent a letter to 27 companies still making caffeinated alcoholic beverages asking them to explain why they believed caffeine is a safe ingredient. The agency reminded the companies that the Federal Food, Drug, and Cosmetic Act gave it jurisdiction over ingredients added to drinks and that unless the companies provided data showing caffeine was "generally recognized as safe," it had the power to ban its use.[11]

They failed to do so and a year later the FDA notified them that the caffeine added to their beverages was an "unsafe food additive." The agency cautioned consumers to avoid caffeinated brands. Some of the companies continued to market them anyway, inviting the FDA to proceed toward a ban. If it does, it will write the final chapter in the caffeinated alcoholic brand story.

No matter, the industry and its opponents carry on a ceaseless cat-and-mouse game in which companies find new product and marketing innovations to replace initiatives blunted by critics and regulators. A new fight will emerge.

THE ATTACK ON ALCOHOL MARKETING

In the late 1800s temperance groups launched a noble crusade against the evils of alcohol. Eventually, they dragged the nation into a brief Prohibition era. In 1919 the Eighteenth Amendment banned production and sale of "intoxicating liquors," but the widely evaded ban lasted only until 1933, when the Twenty-First Amendment repealed it. Since then, prohibition attitudes have faded, but not vanished.

Since the end of Prohibition the majority of Americans have been drinkers. In a 1939 Gallup poll 58 percent of adults reported they drank alcohol. The number is a little higher today, 64 percent in a 2010 Gallup poll, and virtually unchanged over a decade.[12] Of the 33 percent who abstain about a third are neoprohibitionists who believe that drinking alcohol "can never be justified."[13]

The alcoholic beverage industry must live with these opponents. Although prohibition is a moribund idea, a strong, well-organized antialcohol movement marches on. Its strength lies in dozens of church,

---

[9] Dennis L. Thombs, et al., "Event-Level Analysis of Energy Drink Consumption and Alcohol Intoxication in Bar Patrons," *Journal of Addictive Behaviors* 11, no. 4 (2009).

[10] Federal Trade Commission, Complaint in the matter of Constellation Brands, Inc., No. C-4266, (2009), pp. 2–3.

[11] See, for example, the letter to City Brewing, undated, at www.fda.gov/Food/FoodIngredientsPackaging/ucm190387.htm.

[12] Gallup Poll, "Alcohol and Drinking," July 8-11, 2010, at http://www.gallup.com/poll/1582/alcohol-drinking.aspx.

[13] Princeton Survey Research Associates International, "Pew Forum 10 Nation Survey of Renewalists," USPSRA, 100506RENEW R29F, November 7, 2006.

Polygamy
Porter, a brand
marketed by
Wasatch
Brewing Co.,
is a parody of
the Mormon
custom, now
banned, of
taking multiple
wives. The ad
campaign fea-
tures the slogan
"Why have just
one!" This kind
of appeal is
condemned by
the antialcohol
movement for
encouraging
more consump-
tion. Source:
Courtesy of
Wasatch Brew
Pub.

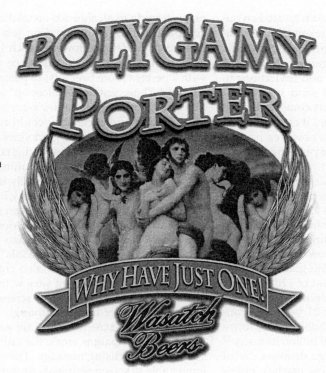

health, consumer, and citizens' groups such as Mothers Against Drunk Driving. Its greatest successes
have been getting all states to raise the legal drinking
age to 21 and establishing a national drunken-driving
standard of .08 blood alcohol content. It persists in
trying to ban or restrict alcoholic beverage advertising. The movement's indictment against alcohol ads
is based on four beliefs.

First, advertising increases consumption. Many ads
are designed to attract new drinkers and promote
additional drinking. Miller Lite's classic "Tastes
Great–Less Filling" spots attempted to reposition
beer as a competitor to soft drinks, telling consumers that light beer is a low-calorie drink that can be
consumed more often than regular beer. The Mich-
elob beer campaign based on the slogan "Put a little
weekend in your week" encouraged weekend social drinkers to think of all days of the week as
drinking occasions. And Polygamy Porter states,
"Why Have Just One!"

Studies of the effect of advertising on consumption produce mixed evidence. Generally, national
studies find no correlation between overall spending

for alcohol ads and consumption.[14] The number of
drinkers in the United States reached an all-time high
of 71 percent in 1976, and per capita consumption
reached its all-time high of 28.8 gallons a year in
1981. Although ad spending by the industry has
steadily risen since then, the percentage of drinkers
and per capita consumption have fallen. Some studies of local areas and small groups show that increased advertising does raise consumption. For
example, a study of 139 women in Central Harlem
found that alcohol dependence and abuse were associated with the density of outdoor alcohol ads in
their neighborhoods.[15] Specific ad campaigns may

[14] See Henry Saffer, "Studying the Effects of Alcohol
Advertising on Consumption," *Alcohol Health & Research
World* 20, no. 4 (1996); and Hae-Kyong Bang, "Analyzing the
Impact of the Liquor Industry's Lifting of the Ban on Broadcast
Advertising," *Journal of Public Policy & Marketing,* Spring 1998.

[15] Naa Oyo A. Kwate and Ilan H. Meyer, "Association Between
Residential Exposure to Outdoor Alcohol Advertising and
Problem Drinking Among African American Women in New
York City," *American Journal of Public Health,* February 2009.

also be successful. Recently, Heineken created an online virtual universe named Heineken City. Participants could buy apartments there with awards earned from playing branded games. Apartment owners received "keys" by mail and invitations to special events. They also could send free e-mail through a special domain, @heicity.com. According to the agency behind the campaign, it created 10,000 new Heineken drinkers.[16] Overall, however, no firm conclusion about the effect of advertising on consumption is warranted.

Second, ads encourage underage drinking. Underage alcohol consumption is a serious problem. Survey data show that by the 12th grade 72 percent of students have experimented with alcohol and 55 percent have been drunk at least once. Binge drinking, defined as five or more drinks in a row in the previous week, is reported by 8 percent of 8th graders, 16 percent of 10th graders, and 25 percent of 12th graders. About 40 percent of college students report binge drinking.[17] Overall, youth under 21 years old consume about 20 percent of all alcoholic drinks, forming an $8 billion market for the $40 billion industry.[18]

Each year some 5,000 underage drinkers die of alcohol-related injuries, most in car crashes, homicides, and suicides. Underage drinking is associated with academic failure, risky sexual behavior, and illicit drug use. New evidence shows that alcohol has pernicious effects on the developing adolescent brain.[19]

There is little proof that alcohol advertisers target minors in a calculated way, but there is enough evidence on which to base at least some suspicion. For example, all three segments of the alcohol industry—beer, wine, and distilled spirits—have agreed to voluntary media guidelines that require companies to buy ad placement only when at least 70 percent of the audience is expected to be 21 years of age or older. A study of alcohol ads on television found that companies did an outstanding job following the 70 percent guideline. However, each 1 percent rise in adolescent viewers in the audience was associated with 7 percent more beer ads, 15 percent more spirits ads, and 22 percent more "alcopop" ads, suggesting that some alcohol companies were seeking at least the youngest audiences they could reach while still complying with the media guidelines.[20]

In addition, expenditures for digital marketing are rising. Alcohol companies are putting more alcohol ads on the Internet, a realm heavily trafficked by an underage audience. There are many Internet marketing tactics. Viral marketing has been used for Miller Lite, Bud Light, Absolut, Captain Morgan, Smirnoff, and other brands. A YouTube video titled "Banned Super Bowl 2007 Bud Commercials" had 9 million views.[21] Alcohol advertisers also create sponsored sites and social networking sites with games, applications, widgets, blogs, music, screen savers, drink recipes, and other hooks. Although they often use age verification screens, these are easily bypassed. When viral campaigns work, the online community sends the advertising message. The advertiser is no longer able to screen recipients for age.

Activists claim that companies target underage drinkers not only with advertising but also with products designed to attract youth. These include flavored malt beverages like Spykes, often called "alcopops," single-serving vodka and tequila cocktails with names such as Yellin Melon Balls and Blue-Dacious Kamikaze, and novelty products such as cups of strawberry gelatin containing vodka. Other questionable marketing gimmicks include spring break promotions, brand placements in films seen by children, and brand logos on T-shirts and toys. A recent study showed that elementary school children who played with alcohol-themed toys tended to start drinking earlier.[22]

[16] "Heineken: "Heineken City," *Advertising Age*, September 15, 2008, p. S4.

[17] Figures are from Lloyd D. Johnson, et al., *Monitoring the Future: National Survey Results on Drug Use, 1975–2008*, Vol. II (Bethesda, MD: National Institutes of Health, 2009), pp. 22–23.

[18] Leslie B. Snyder, et al., "Effects of Alcohol Advertising Exposure on Drinking among Youth," *Archives of Pediatric and Adolescent Medicine*, January 2006, p. 18.

[19] Department of Health and Human Services, *The Surgeon General's Call to Action to Prevent and Reduce Underage Drinking: 2007* (Rockville, MD: Office of the Surgeon General, pp. 1–11 and 19–20.

[20] Paul J. Chung, et al., "Association Between Adolescent Viewership and Alcohol Advertising on Cable Television," *American Journal of Public Health*, March 2010, p. 555.

[21] Jeff Chester, Kathryn Montgomery, and Lori Dorfman, *Alcohol Marketing in the Digital Age* (Oakland, CA: Public Health Institute, May 2010), p. 10.

[22] Erica Weintraub Austin, "Why Advertisers and Researchers Should Focus on Media Literacy to Respond to the Effects of Alcohol Advertising on Youth," *International Journal of Advertising* 25, no. 4 (2006), p. 542.

Research about the effect of alcohol advertising on youth points to caution. A review of seven studies following the drinking behavior of 13,000 subjects aged 10 to 26 found that "exposure to alcohol advertising in young people influences their subsequent drinking behavior" and the greater the exposure the greater the frequency of drinking. Yet the study counseled that the effect of advertising was "generally modest."[23] Another study of 200 adolescents found that exposure to advertising influenced subsequent drinking frequency, but very little. It was responsible for only about 1 percent of variation. Peer influence was the strongest factor in drinking behavior, followed by parental influence.[24]

Third, sophisticated lifestyle advertising used by alcohol makers is manipulative because it locks into inner drives. Informational advertising presents details about a product, for example, its price, availability, and quality. In contrast, lifestyle advertising positions a product to fulfill emotional needs. Pictures and copy associate alcohol with fulfillment of desires for popularity, success, sophistication, rebellion, romance, and sexual conquest. The ads endow commodity products such as vodka or lager beer with brand images. Then by drinking that brand, the consumer adopts and projects the brand image. These ads convey little or no objective information about the beverage, only an emotional theme. Sexual images are a stable of alcohol marketing. However, one study of alcohol ads in magazines during a 14-year period found that other appeals predominated over sexual imagery. In *Life,* for example, prestige and social acceptance were more frequent themes.[25] Whatever the image, critics believe that since lifestyle ads play on emotion, they are highly manipulative. Consumers who respond to them are being tricked into fulfilling inner needs by drinking.

Fourth, alcohol advertising is targeted not only at young drinkers but, sometimes inappropriately, at other groups too. Critics object, for example, to endless ads for malt liquors in inner-city black neighborhoods and in black media. Malt liquor has a higher alcohol content than regular beer, and advertisements for it appeal to drinkers seeking inebriation. United States Beverage Company faced this criticism when it introduced a new brand named Phat Boy with graffiti-style ads for a "new malt liquor with an attitude." Phat Boy came in 40-ounce bottles, each having as much alcohol as a six-pack of regular beer. After an outcry by activists, the company dropped the brand. Hispanics are also targets. Perhaps because 40 percent of Hispanics in the United States are under 21 years old, Hispanic neighborhoods are filled with beer billboards. In Chicago, neighborhoods of elementary schools with more than 20 percent Hispanic children have 6.5 times more alcohol advertising than those with lower percentages.[26]

Young women are also targeted. Companies have introduced sweet-flavored drinks appealing to their tastes. Barton Brands sells a brand of vodka martini called Cocktails by Jenn in Blue Lagoon, Lemon Drop, and Appletini flavors. The drinks come in four-packs instead of six packs because they are lighter and easier for women to carry. Around their necks, the bottles have small metal charms such as a high-heeled shoe, diamond ring, or perfume bottle.[27] Only about 25 percent of women drink beer, so they are a huge growth market for brewers, who target them with lighter and flavored malt beverages such as Molson Coors' orange-flavored wheat beer Blue Moon and Anheuser-Busch's blueberry-flavored Wild Blue.

ALCOHOL MARKETERS DEFEND THEIR ADVERTISING

Alcoholic beverages are a mature industry. Due to population aging and health consciousness, per capita consumption is in a slow, long-term decline, dropping by an average 4 percent a year from 1998 to 2008. Still, Americans today drink a lot of alcohol,

[23] Lesley A. Smith and David R. Foxcroft, "The Effect of Alcohol Advertising, Marketing and Portrayal on Drinking Behavior in Young People: Systematic Review of Prospective Cohort Studies," *BMC Public Health,* February 2009, p. 11.

[24] Brian R. Kinard and Cynthia Webster, "The Effects of Advertising, Social Influences, and Self-Efficacy on Adolescent Tobacco Use and Alcohol Consumption," *Journal of Consumer Affairs,* March 2010, p. 39.

[25] Geng Cui, "Advertising of Alcoholic Beverages in African-American and Women's Magazines: Implications for Health Communication," *Howard Journal of Communications,* October 2000, p. 288.

[26] Keryn E. Pasch, et al., "Does Outdoor Alcohol Advertising Around Elementary Schools Vary by the Ethnicity of Students in the School?" *Ethnicity & Health,* April 2009.

[27] "Welcome to the World of Cocktails by Jenn," at www.oropesacreative.com/cbj/cocktails_750_d.htm.

about 26 gallons per capita in recent years, compared with 24 gallons of coffee and 21 gallons of milk.[28] And because the population is growing, industry sales grew from $29 billion in 1998 to $40 billion in 2008, a 39 percent increase.[29]

Amid overall market growth, industry segments compete fiercely for market share. Beer dominates, but since 1998 its sales have dropped from 63 percent of all alcoholic beverages to 49 percent. The wine sector picked up 10 percentage points to 34 percent and distilled spirits added 4 percentage points, rising to 17 percent.[30] Two implications of these figures for advertising are clear. First, if per capita consumption is stagnant but the overall population is growing, ads to recruit new and younger drinkers pay off. Second, if sales of industry segments are in flux, ads that promote brand loyalty can be used to protect or seize market share. Both conclusions lie behind the industry's heavy advertising. It defends its ads against the attacks of critics with these basic arguments.

First, ads are not the cause of alcohol abuse. As noted, studies fail to show that advertising increases consumption. So commercials and billboards cannot be blamed for car accidents, teen suicides, sexual aggression, spousal abuse, binge drinking, and alcoholism. Alcoholism, for example, is a complex disease caused by personality, family, genetic, and physiological factors rather than by viewing ads. Restraints would only deprive moderate drinkers of product information, not relieve social problems. As one advertising executive noted, trying to stop problem drinking with an ad ban "makes as little sense as trying to control the Ku Klux Klan by outlawing bed linens."[31] Ad restrictions would also muzzle a competitive weapon. Without advertising, starting a new national brand would be almost impossible and established brands would have an insurmountable advantage.

Second, antialcohol groups assume the public is too stupid to decide responsibly. The idea of curbing ads is condescending. Consumers are intelligent and skeptical. They are not duped by the association of alcohol with attractive images. Does anyone expect brewers and vintners to associate their products with root canals, traffic congestion, or taxes? The rejection of lifestyle advertising is also condescending. If a marketer positions a brand to satisfy emotional needs for sophistication, popularity, or sexual attractiveness, who is to say the consumer who finds gratification in the brand is wrong? No one would criticize a woman for feeling glamorous while she is wearing perfume, though the perfume is simply a chemical, nonessential to healthy life, and the glamour is created by imagery. Advertising also has the power to endow alcoholic beverages with emotional benefits for drinkers. The critics assume there is no merit to a product beyond its utilitarian qualities. What a dull world it would be if all products were marketed and used on this basis.

Third, the beer, wine, and spirits industries have voluntary codes to regulate advertising behavior. The policies in these codes are extensive and specific. For example, the Beer Institute's Advertising and Marketing Code prohibits depictions of excessive consumption, intoxication, and drinking while driving. Models in beer ads must be over 25 and "reasonably appear" to be over 21 years old. Beer ads should never have "any symbol, language, music, gesture, or cartoon character intended to appeal primarily to persons below the legal purchase age." No depictions of Santa Claus or sexual promiscuity are permitted.[32] The Wine Institute's Code of Advertising Standards has similar guidelines. It also prohibits showing the Easter bunny.[33] The Distilled Spirits Council of the United States' *Code of Good Practice for Distilled Spirits Advertising and Marketing* is similar to the two other codes. It allows advertisers to "depict affection or other amorous gestures," but forbids them to "rely upon sexual prowess or sexual success as a selling point," perhaps a fine distinction.[34]

[28] Department of Agriculture, Economic Research Service, "Data Sets: Beverages," February 1, 2010, at www.ers.usda.gov/Data/FoodConsumption/Spreadsheets/beverage.xls. Figures are for 2008.

[29] Department of Commerce, *Annual Survey of Manufactures, 2002 and 2009* (Washington, DC: Bureau of the Census, 2002 and 2009), sector 31.

[30] Ibid., sector 31.

[31] James Kuras of McCann-Erickson, quoted in Eric Clark, *The Want Makers* (New York: Viking Press, 1988), p. 285.

[32] At www.beerinstitute.org/tier.asp?bid=249, January 2006 edition.

[33] At www.wineinstitute.org/initiatives/issuesandpolicy/adcode, revised September 2005.

[34] At www.discus.org/pdf/61332_DISCUS.pdf, January 2009, p. 8.

DISTINCTIVE SINCE 1953

DISTINCTIVE SINCE 1930

Tanqueray
IMPORTED

He says drink responsibly

IMPORTED LONDON DRY GIN 47.3% ALC/VOL, 100% GRAIN NEUTRAL SPIRITS, SCHIEFFELIN & SOMERSET CO., NEW YORK, N.Y. © 2002 GUINNESS UNITED DISTILLERS & VINTNERS AMSTERDAM B.V.

www.tanqueray.com

Although the distiller's advertising code warns advertisers not to "rely upon sexual prowess or sexual success as a selling point," this ad links a brand of gin with Hugh Hefner, mastermind of the *Playboy* philosophy.
Source: © The Advertising Archives.

All three codes are backed by mechanisms to investigate possible violations. The Distilled Spirits Council, for example, convenes a 10-member Code Review Board to look at complaints. All the board members are industry executives and its rulings can be gentle, but it raps knuckles too. Recently it received a complaint from a company about a vodka print ad run by White Rock Distilleries. The ad depicted a man in a rabbit costume and two women in bikinis around a card table drinking vodka and playing strip poker. As the man smiled one woman removed her top. The complaint alleged that the ad violated the industry code's prohibition against using "sexual prowess or sexual success as a selling point." The board decided the ad violated the code "insofar as the female models are either partially clad or completely unclad in a strip poker game where the male model is fully

clad in a rabbit costume with a lascivious facial expression."[35] White Rock Distilleries stopped running the ad.

Fourth, alcohol makers promote responsible consumption. Companies broadcast public service announcements to preach moderation and safe driving. They sponsor designated-driver programs such as Anheuser-Busch's Alert Cab, which gives free taxi rides to restaurant and bar patrons who have been drinking. The Distilled Spirits Council funds college programs in which students teach other students about moderation. It also trains bartenders to serve drinks responsibly. These efforts, while important, do not get nearly the funding of brand advertising.

[35] Distilled Spirits Council of the United States, *Semiannual Code Report*, 10th ed. (Washington, DC: DISCUS, September 2009), p. 9.

According to one study by an activist organization, responsibility ads are only 2 percent of the alcohol advertising budget and youths see 239 product ads for every message about safe driving.[36]

Finally, targeting respects diverse audiences. The industry agrees that it targets younger drinkers, minorities, women, and other groups with advertising themes. Young adult drinkers find value in advertising that informs them of new products and creates images that fulfill their emotional needs. The puzzle faced by companies is that young adults aged 21 to 25 share many interests and behaviors with those just below the legal drinking age. Some spillover appeal is inevitable. Ads aimed at minorities are also legitimate. Market segmentation and the targeted advertising that makes it work are standard in many industries. When toy companies make black or Latina dolls, social critics applaud, but when alcohol companies make products that appeal to minority communities, critics argue that these consumers are too gullible to withstand manipulation. The implication is that Hispanic or black consumers are not as astute as white consumers. The real problem is that the product is alcohol, not that the ads have ethnic or racial appeal. Finally, there is no evidence that targeting raises consumption. Despite concerns over targeting young women, a large national study found that the percentage of female 12th graders having a drink in the past 30 days declined from 47 percent in 1998 to 41 percent in 2008 and the number of young women aged 19 to 28 who drank a flavored alcohol beverage in the past 30 days declined from 30 percent in 2004 to 27 percent in 2008.[37]

RESTRICTING ALCOHOL ADVERTISING

Alcohol advertising is highly regulated. Companies must navigate a labyrinth of restrictions. Approximately half the states restrict ad placements. Arizona prohibits it on school buses. Ohio bans it near churches, schools, and playgrounds. Many cities also restrict it. San Diego bans billboard ads within 500 feet of playgrounds, child care centers, schools, and libraries. San Jose bans beer and wine ads on fueling islands at gas stations. San Francisco prohibits alcohol ads on public transit.[38]

Three federal agencies have the power to regulate marketing claims. The Food and Drug Administration approves ingredients in alcoholic beverages for safety. The Federal Trade Commission has the authority to stop advertising that is false, deceptive, misleading, or unfair. The Department of Treasury's Alcohol and Tobacco Tax and Trade Bureau enforces labeling requirements and monitors advertising for compliance with certain requirements under a 1935 law. For example, if the words "Scotch whisky" are used, the product must be manufactured in Scotland. Labels cannot resemble a postage stamp. Depictions of the American flag cannot appear on labels or in ads. Advertisers cannot use subliminal means, defined as "any device or technique that is used to convey, or attempts to convey, a message to a person by means of images or sounds of a very brief nature that cannot be perceived at a normal level of awareness."[39]

Originally, the law prohibited statements of alcohol content on labels so that companies could not start strength wars. However, in 1995 the Supreme Court held that censoring this information violated bottlers' speech rights, so alcohol content can now be printed on labels and is required on distilled spirits labels.[40]

Altogether, the body of government regulation covering alcohol advertising imposes significant restraints. But critics want stronger, more uniform measures. In the 1990s several bills were introduced in Congress to limit alcohol ads, for example, by banning them near schools and playgrounds, in publications with large youth readerships, on college campuses, and during prime-time television hours.[41] The prospect for such measures faded after

[36] Center on Alcohol Marketing and Youth, *Drowned Out: Alcohol Industry 'Responsibility' Advertising on Television,* 2001–2005 (Washington, DC: CAMY, 2005), p. 1.

[37] Lloyd D. Johnson, et al., *Monitoring the Future: National Survey Results on Drug Use,* 1975–2008, vol. I, table D-70 and vol. II, table 5-3.

[38] Marin Institute, *Out of Home Advertising: A 21st Century Guide to Effective Regulation* (San Rafael, CA: Marin Institute, March 2009), pp. 9–11.

[39] 27 CFR §5.65(h), 2010.

[40] *Rubin v. Coors Brewing Company,* 514 U.S. 618 (1995).

[41] See, for example, the "Voluntary Alcohol Advertising Standards for Children Act," H. R. 1292, 105th Congress, 1st Sess. (1997), introduced by Rep. Joseph P. Kennedy II (D-Massachusetts).

a Supreme Court decision that struck down a federal ban on broadcast ads by casinos.[42]

The court also chipped away at other restrictions. Until 1996 Rhode Island banned price advertising for alcoholic beverages, claiming it was justified in doing so to promote temperance. However, the justices struck the ban down, saying price advertising is protected by the First Amendment's free speech guarantee.[43]

Other initiatives by antialcohol forces have failed. A series of lawsuits sought to regulate the alcohol industry using product liability law. Parents of underage drinkers accused more than 100 companies of defrauding them by attracting their sons and daughters to spend family money illegally on alcohol. The parents alleged injury from a complicated scheme including marketing "alcopops" with themes that appeal to youth, distributing promotional items, using cartoons, sponsoring spring break events, and setting up sham regulatory codes. They sought to recover the money their underage children spent and to stop the ongoing seduction of youth. However, courts dismissed these lawsuits for insufficient evidence that company actions caused underage alcohol abuse.[44]

Some countries go further than the United States in national restrictions. India and Thailand ban all alcohol advertising. Ireland prohibits distilled spirits ads on television and radio and prohibits beer and wine ads before sports events. France bans alcohol ads on television and restricts ad content in other media. Norway, Sweden, Denmark, and Finland prohibit advertising beverages with more than a certain alcohol content ranging from 2.2 to 3.5 percent, less than regular beer or wine. Italy, Spain, and Portugal restrict televised alcohol ads before 8:00, 9:00, and 10:00 p.m., respectively. Greece limits the number of broadcast ads per brand per day. Russia prohibits the appearance of people and animals in television ads. When alcohol companies skirted these rules with off-screen voices and animated bottles, it banned that too. Such restrictions might not work in the United States due to constitutional protections for free speech.

---

[42] *Greater New Orleans Broadcasting Association, Inc., v. U.S.*, 527 U.S. 173 (1999).

[43] *44 Liquormart v. Rhode Island*, 517 U.S. 484 (1996).

[44] See, for example, *Hakki v. Zima Company*, 03-0009183 (Sup. Ct. Dist. Col., November 14, 2003); and Eisenberg v. Anheuser-Busch, Inc., *1:04 CV 1081* (N.D. Ohio, February 1, 2006).

ARE RESTRICTIONS ON ALCOHOL ADS CONSTITUTIONAL?

Images and statements in advertising are speech. Therefore, proposals for muzzling liquor, beer, and wine companies raise constitutional issues. The First Amendment protects all speech from government curbs, but courts have distinguished *noncommercial* speech from *commercial* speech. The former is speech in the broad marketplace of ideas, encompassing political, scientific, and artistic expression. Such speech is broadly protected. The latter is speech intended to stimulate business transactions, including advertising. This kind of speech receives less protection.

The right of free speech is assumed to be a fundamental barrier against tyranny and is not restricted lightly. Courts will not permit censorship of noncommercial speech unless it poses an imminent threat to public welfare, as it would, for example, if a speaker incited violence or a writer tried to publish military secrets.

With respect to commercial speech, however, various restrictions are allowed. For example, ads for securities offerings can appear only in the austere format of a legal notice and tobacco ads are barred on radio and TV. Would courts approve additional restrictions on alcoholic beverage advertising?

The most important legal guidelines for weighing restraints on commercial speech are those set forth by the Supreme Court in 1980 in the *Central Hudson* case.[45] Here the Court struck down a New York regulation banning advertising by public utilities, a regulation intended to help conserve energy. Justice Lewis Powell, writing for the majority, set forth a four-part test to decide when commercial speech could be restricted.

- The ad in question should promote a lawful product and must be accurate. If an ad is misleading or suggests illegal activity, it does not merit protection.

- The government interest in restricting the particular commercial speech must be substantial, not trivial or unimportant.

---

[45] *Central Hudson Gas & Electric Corp. v. Public Service Commission*, 447 U.S. 557.

- The advertising restriction must directly further the interest of the government. In other words, it should demonstrably help the government reach its public policy goal.
- The suppression of commercial speech must not be more extensive than is necessary to achieve the government's purpose.

All government actions to ban or restrict alcohol ads could be challenged by industry and would have to pass the four-part *Central Hudson* test to survive.

ALCOHOL ADVERTISING IN PERSPECTIVE

The mainstream antialcohol campaign today is to restrict advertising more. The Prohibition Party argument that alcohol is immoral, sinful, and unhealthy has few advocates now. But those who still believe it have seized on underage drinking as a weapon to attack the alcohol industry. Since underage drinking is a genuine social problem, antialcohol activists find many allies.

Alcohol advertising is creative, witty, and clever. Evidence is strong that children and teenagers are attracted to alcohol ads and increasing exposure is associated with more future drinking. Some of this drinking leads to tragedy for families. Such serious concerns are to be weighed against other factors.

Some studies show the influence of ads is very modest. Most Americans drink alcoholic beverages. Advertising limits would reduce information about products. And the constitution, while permitting restrictions, protects advertisers from needless and sweeping government actions. What dangers of alcohol ads justify what restrictions?

Questions

1. Were Spykes and Wide Eye bad products? Do you think they were marketed in objectionable or misleading ways? Do you think companies should be allowed to market other caffeinated alcoholic beverages?
2. Do alcoholic beverage companies fulfill their ethical duty to be informative and truthful in advertising? Do they generally uphold their ethical duty to minimize potential harm to society from underage drinking?
3. Are some beer, wine, or spirits ads misleading? What examples can you give? What is misleading in them? Do some ads contain images and themes that go too far in appealing to an audience under the legal drinking age? Can you give examples?
4. Do you believe there is a need for more restrictions on alcohol advertising? If so, what limits are needed? Explain how a ban or any restrictions could meet the *Central Hudson* guidelines.

Chapter Sixteen

The Changing Workplace

Ford Motor Company

The history of the Ford Motor Company is told in the changing experiences of its workers. Their story illustrates how powerful forces discussed in this chapter act to change the workplace.

Henry Ford (1863–1947) was a brilliant inventor. After incorporating the Ford Motor Company in 1903, he designed one car after another, naming each chassis after a letter of the alphabet. In 1908, he began selling the Model T, a utilitarian, crank-started auto that came only in black. An early Model T cost $850, but Ford introduced the first moving auto assembly line and, by 1924, mass output lowered the price to $290. The assembly line was a new, revolutionary technology that changed work at Ford, turning assemblers from craftsmen into interchangeable parts like those in the cars they put together.

Ford sold 15.5 million Model Ts before production ended in 1927. Despite a warning in the form of fast-dropping market share in the mid-1920s, Ford failed utterly to anticipate a sea change in the auto market. The company clung to the spartan Model T even as consumers turned to the styling changes, closed body design, and brand hierarchy offered by General Motors. Finally, Ford had to suspend production, stilling its great River Rouge assembly plant for seven months while the Model A was hurriedly designed. More than 100,000 idled workers felt the sting of hardship that came from competition not well met.

Henry Ford was an obstinate man, obsessed with power, iron-willed, dictatorial, and cynical about human nature. He spied on his employees in their homes to see if they smoked or drank. Believing that workers were motivated by fear, he created a tense atmosphere marked by arbitrary and capricious dismissals. Managers knew they had been fired when they came to work and found their desks chopped into splinters. Sometimes two managers were given the same duties and the one failing to thrive in the competition was fired. In his autobiography, Ford wrote that a "great business is really too big to be human."[1] As the firm grew, his authoritarian style

[1] Henry Ford, *My Life and Work* (Garden City, NY: Doubleday, 1923), p. 263.

Model Ts pass along the first moving assembly line at Ford Motor Company's Highland Avenue plant in Detroit. The photograph was taken in 1913. Source: © National Archives/CORBIS.

became embedded in its informal culture. Independent managers left, and he was surrounded by sycophants who would have jumped into the Detroit River had he asked. They, in turn, were ruthless and autocratic with their subordinates.[2]

This atmosphere made conditions attractive for early labor organizers. The first efforts came in 1913. Ford fought unions, calling them "the worst things that ever struck the earth."[3] He hired thugs and underworld figures to work at his plants, spying on workers and intimidating anyone who abetted the union cause. This strategy was successful until Congress passed the landmark National Labor Relations Act in 1935, protecting the right of unions to organize. Under the new law, Ford Motor Company was found guilty of unfair labor practices at nine plants. Ford's lawyers delayed the inevitable for a few years, but in 1941 its workers, by a vote of 97 percent to 3 percent, voted to unionize. Federal regulation had been too powerful a force for Ford's campaign of fear to overcome.

Even after the unions, authoritarianism remained firmly entrenched. In 1945 Henry Ford himself felt its barb when he was ousted in a coup engineered by family members. He was replaced by his grandson, Henry Ford II, who also proved to be an autocrat. In the early 1980s Ford again suffered the harsh discipline of the market. Three years of disastrous losses awakened it to heightened international competition. Japanese auto companies had captured 20 percent of American sales. The company studied the Japanese and decided to emulate their focus on work teams and continuous quality improvement. Ford set out to make a world-class sedan using the Japanese carmakers' methods.

[2] Anne Jardim, *The First Henry Ford: A Study in Personality and Business Leadership* (Cambridge, MA: MIT Press, 1970), pp. 114–15.

[3] Quoted in Keith Sward, *The Legend of Henry Ford* (New York: Rinehart & Company, 1948), p. 370.

In Japanese management philosophy, competing personalities and individualism are thought to hamper productivity. So Ford tried to change its corporate culture. Over the years, it had tended to select autocrats for management positions. A study of 2,000 Ford managers classified 76 percent as "noncreative types who are comfortable with strong authority" (as compared with 38 percent of the population).[4] To bring change, thousands of managers went to workshops on participative management.

Ford was rewarded for its efforts with the new Taurus sedan in 1985. It was a quick success and became the best-selling car in America between 1993 and 1995. In 1994 the company made an extraordinary profit of $5.3 billion. Yet this prosperity was deceptive. Two underlying problems rooted in the legacy of Henry Ford would cripple the company.

First, its relations with its workers had been poisoned by the pitched battles to organize many years before. Since then the powerful United Auto Workers (UAW) had bargained with the company in an adversarial way. During the postwar years when Ford was very profitable, the union negotiated rising wages, generous benefits, and rigid work rules. By the early 1980s more than 100 job classifications existed in Ford plants. When a machine broke on an assembly line, even if a nearby worker could fix it, the line stopped while a skilled worker in the appropriate classification was found to come and do the repair.

When Japanese car companies began to make inroads into Ford's sales, the UAW demanded more job security. In 1984 it negotiated a Jobs Bank in which Ford agreed to place laid-off workers, paying them their full salaries and benefits for up to two years. All these union gains were expensive for Ford.

The second problem was a corporate culture resistant to innovation. The success of the Taurus aside, as Japanese automakers stormed the domestic market, Ford management allowed vehicle quality to deteriorate, then used rebates to push sales, a tactic that cheapened car brands in the eyes of consumers. Ford also emphasized production of sport-utility vehicles and trucks when gas prices were low. Because margins were higher on these vehicles, it could profitably make them with its high-wage auto workers. However, when gas prices rose above $4 a gallon in 2008, demand for gas guzzlers collapsed, exposing the flaw in Ford's truck-heavy product strategy.

In 2006 Ford brought in a new chief executive, Alan Mulally from Boeing. As an outsider Mulally took a fresh look at Ford and initiated a strategy of broad restructuring. He sold Jaguar, Aston-Martin, Land Rover, and Volvo to focus on the Ford brand. He further reduced brand nameplates from 97 to 25 and the number of car chassis from 20 to 8. He closed eight plants to match production more closely with demand. To finance Ford's transformation, he borrowed $23.5 billion, using the company's assets as collateral. It was a tremendous gamble.

Still, the UAW refused to make concessions. By 2007 Ford's hourly workers received an average $70 to $75 an hour in wages and benefits, while Toyota and Honda made cars in Southern states with nonunionized workers making only $40 to

[4] Melinda G. Builes and Paul Ingrassia, "Ford's Leaders Push Radical Shift in Culture as Competition Grows," *The Wall Street Journal,* December 3, 1985, p. A1.

$45. Ford offered comparatively higher health care benefits to its workers and retirees. Although the company lost an average $5,234 on every vehicle made in 2007, the UAW, by threatening a strike, negotiated average gains of $12,904 in pay and benefits for hourly workers. Its new contract extended the Jobs Bank. And it prohibited the company from deciding to close more plants or send more jobs to another country.[5]

Mulally forged ahead. With a deep recession in 2008, auto sales declined from almost 17 million a year to 11 million. Financial markets froze. Both General Motors and Chrysler were forced into bankruptcy, but Ford escaped this fate because it had borrowed money for its restructuring earlier. Still, it was in precarious condition. While GM and Chrysler had shed most of their debt in bankruptcy proceedings, Ford carried almost $27 billion in debt and had 1,400 laid-off workers in the Jobs Bank costing an average of $130,000 a year.

Finally, in 2009, the UAW granted major concessions. It agreed to a two-tier wage system allowing Ford to hire new workers at half the hourly pay of current employees, reduction in the number of job classifications, suspension of cost-of-living increases and bonuses, and an end to the Jobs Bank. It also let Ford cap spiraling health care costs by allowing it to make a onetime $7 billion payment into a health care trust fund that the union would manage. Now, Ford's cost for hourly workers averaged only about $50 an hour, very close to the wages at competitors' nonunion plants.

The basic problem at Ford is the relentless pressure of global competition on a dysfunctional culture that defied change until an economic crisis left no other choice. The antagonism between workers and management has been hard on both. It led the union to negotiate worker protections that reduced Ford's strategic flexibility and that, in the end, may not have been in the workers' best interest. In 1984 Ford had 179,000 employees in the United States. Today it has only 71,000. Now, for the first time in several decades, Ford has a chance to overcome the two weaknesses—high costs and lack of innovation—that brought it to its knees.

In this chapter we take a more systematic look at some of the forces that sealed the fate of those roughly 108,000 workers shed by Ford. We start by looking at six external forces shaping workplaces, including Ford's. Then we discuss how government protects workers, not only in the United States but in other countries as well. Finally, we explain the universal tension between protecting workers and preserving flexible labor markets.

EXTERNAL FORCES SHAPING THE WORKPLACE

Those who work today are caught up in turbulence created by six environmental forces: (1) demographic change, (2) technological change, (3) structural change, (4) competitive pressures, (5) reorganization of work, and (6) government intervention. These forces are interconnected. A discussion of each follows.

---

[5] "UAW Ford Bargainers Preserve Jobs, Protect Wages and Benefits," *UAW Ford Report,* November 2007, p. 1.

Demographic Change

Population dynamics slowly but continuously alter labor forces. Out of a 2010 population of 310 million Americans, about half, or 154 million, made up the civilian labor force as either working or unemployed (the rest are retired, disabled, students, homemakers, children under age 16, or not counted because they received unreported wages). This is the third-largest labor force in the world, though it pales in comparison to China's 814 million and India's 467 million.[6]

baby-boom generation
A large cohort of workers born between 1946 and 1964.

replacement fertility rate
The number of children a woman must have, on average, to assure that one daughter survives to reproductive age.

Table 16.1 gives three snapshots of the American labor force, showing its size and composition in 2008, then a medium-range 2018 and a long-range 2050 projection. The figures reveal three important trends.

First, growth is slowing. Historically, the American labor force grew rapidly and continuously. It continues to grow, but more slowly now because the population is growing more slowly. In the 1970s, as the *baby-boom generation* entered, labor force growth peaked at 2.6 percent a year, but by 2008 growth fell to 1.1 percent, and the deceleration is projected to continue, with annual growth falling to 0.8 percent by 2018 and 0.6 percent by 2050.[7] This slowing is caused by a fall in the fertility rate of American women. The rate is now about 2.09, just below the *replacement fertility rate* of 2.1. Growth in the population, which is eventually reflected in the labor force, continues because of reductions in mortality and net international immigration.

Second, the labor force is growing more diverse in gender, race, and ethnicity. This is a long-term trend. Table 16.1 shows that all components of the labor force are projected to increase in numbers. Yet they are increasing at different rates and

TABLE 16.1
Three Snapshots of the American Labor Force (in thousands)

Source: Bureau of Labor Statistics.

	2008		2018		2050		Percentage Point Change 2008–2050
Total labor force	154,287		166,911		210,427		
Men*	82,520	53.5%	88,682	53.1%	110,365	52.5%	−1.0
Women	71,767	46.5	78,229	46.9	100,061	47.6	1.1
White	125,635	81.4	132,490	79.4	156,775	74.5	−6.9
Black	17,740	11.5	20,244	12.1	26,083	12.4	0.9
Hispanic	22,024	14.3	29,304	17.6	64,025	30.4	16.1
Asian	7,202	4.7	9,345	5.6	17,989	8.6	3.9
Other groups†	3,710	2.4	4,832	2.9	9,502	4.5	2.1
Median age	41.2		42.3		41.6		

*Numerical and percentage totals exceed 100 percent because Hispanics may also be classified in other racial categories.
†Includes American Indians, Alaska Natives, Native Hawaiians, Pacific Islanders, and those reporting two or more races.

[6] Central Intelligence Agency, *World Factbook,* "China" and "India," at www.cia.gov/library/, updated August 3, 2010.

[7] Mitra Toossi, "Labor Force Projections to 2018: Older Workers Staying More Active," *Monthly Labor Review,* November 2009, table 1; and Mitra Toossi, "A New Look at Long-Term Labor Force Projections to 2050," *Monthly Labor Review,* November 2006, table 2.

their relative proportions will change. Decade by decade the ebbs and flows of these differential movements create modest changes, but as the right-hand column shows, by 2050 cumulative changes in race and ethnicity will be dramatic, with changes in gender less so.

By 2050 whites will decline as a percentage of the labor force by 6.9 percentage points and men by 1 percentage point. The largest increase will be the 16.1 percentage point expansion of Hispanics. Asians will increase at a rapid rate, more than doubling their numbers and rising by 3.9 percentage points. However, their overall numbers will remain small. Blacks will increase a slight 0.9 percentage point. The proportion of the sexes will change little. Since the 1950s women have increased their participation more rapidly than men. Now this trend is slowing and although it will continue through 2050 the percentage of women in the labor force will rise by only 1.1 percentage point.

Third, the workforce is aging. High fertility rates following World War II created the baby-boom generation. As this generation entered the labor market in the 1970s, the median age of the workforce dropped, reaching a low of 34.6 years in 1980. The baby boomers are now a bulge of workers in their late 40s to early 60s. As they age, the median age of the workforce rises, and it is predicted to reach 42.3 years in 2018, then fall only slightly after 2020 as baby boomers retire.[8] Because the nation's fertility rate has declined since the baby-boom years, generational cohorts of workers following the baby boomers are smaller and the average age will decline only slightly as these aging mainstays of the labor force retire during the 2010s and 2020s. As they leave, shortages of skilled and experienced workers may arise.

Graying of the workforce is more rapid in other developed nations. It is caused by increases in life expectancy combined with declines in fertility. Life expectancy has increased markedly in most nations. In the United States it rose from 47 in 1900 to 79 in 2010.[9] Birthrates have fallen in the developed world and are now below the replacement rate in many nations. In Japan, for example, the fertility rate of 1.3 births per woman is far below the replacement rate of 2.1.[10] The populations of these nations are predicted to experience long-term decline. The Japanese labor force began to shrink in 1996 and is expected to fall 17 percent from its current levels by 2013.[11]

While Japan and Europe confront population declines and aging labor forces, many developing countries have explosively growing, youthful populations. Over the past 20 years the United States has absorbed a huge wave of immigrants, most from these nations, including 8.7 million unauthorized entrants, some of whom are among the 20.1 million people who became legal permanent residents over those

---

[8] Toossi, "Labor Force Projections to 2018: Older Workers Staying More Active," table 6.

[9] Robert A. Rosenblatt, "U.S. Not as Gray as 31 Other Countries," *Los Angeles Times,* December 15, 2001, p. A17; and United Nations, "World Population Prospects: The 2008 Revision Population Database," http://esa.un.org/unpp, extracted August 2010.

[10] United Nations Department of Economic and Social Affairs, *Statistical Yearbook* (New York: United Nations, June 2008), table 9.

[11] Michiyo Nakamoto, "A Labor Force in Decline," *Financial Times,* November 6, 2006, p. 3.

years.[12] The influx of immigrants shapes the American labor force by accelerating its growth, increasing its diversity, and slowing the rise in average age.

Since the fertility rate in the United States has fallen below the replacement rate, continued immigration will prevent the population declines facing Europe and Japan. Immigration gives the United States a long-run competitive advantage in labor costs. Japan and some European countries have tight immigration laws. The Japanese want to preserve racial purity and have difficulty integrating non-Japanese into their workplaces.[13] Many European nations are strongly ethnocentric and do not welcome immigrants. Immigration, however, brings an influx of younger workers who are less costly and more adaptable.

Technological Change

The greatest story of technology shaping the American labor force is not about the computer, but the mechanical harvester. When the United States was an agrarian nation, fall harvests absorbed heroic investments of labor. Gangs of men crossed grain fields swinging sickles and scythes. Behind them came women and children to bundle the cuttings. In the 1850s Cyrus McCormick (1809–1884) began to manufacture horse-drawn mechanical harvesters, each ridden by a single farmer that mowed and mechanically baled tall crops. Over the last three harvests of the Civil War, farmers bought 160,000 of McCormick's harvesters. The commissioner of Agriculture estimated that each reaper freed five men for service in the Union Army, a factor in its victory.[14] With the war over, the men returned to work in factories, not fields, a sudden, unprecedented conversion of 7.6 percent of the labor force that stimulated industrial growth.[15]

Technological change has many impacts on work. It affects the number and type of jobs available. Invention of the airplane, for example, created new job titles such as pilot and flight attendant. Webmasters, or employees who design and update Web sites, emerged with the rise of the Internet. New machines are used by management to raise productivity and reduce costs. Robots in auto manufacturing made American companies more competitive in cost and quality with Japanese automakers. Computers have reduced the need for clerical workers and middle managers who existed primarily to collect, analyze, and report information.

Automation has a turbulent impact on employment. It has long been feared. When running for president in 1960, John F. Kennedy warned that automation posed "the dark menace of industrial dislocation."[16] Two years later an industry

---

[12] Daniel Hoefer, Nancy Rytina, and Brian C. Baker, "Estimates of the Unauthorized Immigrant Population Residing in the United States: January 2009," *Population Estimates,* Office of Immigration Statistics, January 2010, table 1; and Department of Homeland Security, *Yearbook of Immigration Statistics:* 2009 (Washington, DC: DHS, 2010), table 1.

[13] Chico Harlan, "Strict Immigration Rules May Threaten Japan's Future," *The Washington Post,* July 28, 2010, p. A1.

[14] T. A. Heppenheimer, "Cyrus H. McCormick and Company," *American Heritage,* June 2001, p. 10.

[15] Based on an estimate of 800,000 agricultural workers as a percentage of the 1860 labor force of 10,532,750.

[16] Quoted in Brink Lindsey, "10 Truths about Trade," *Reason,* July 2004, p. 31.

labor group compared automation's effects on the economy to that of a hydrogen bomb. It displaces jobs in traditional occupations. Yet, the number of jobs available in the United States, except in recessionary periods, has continuously increased to absorb new entrants into a growing labor force.

Automation causes significant job loss in less-skilled manufacturing and service occupations. In coal mining, for example, mechanization has eliminated 319,400 jobs, 88 percent, since 1950 while over the same period output of coal has increased 404 percent.[17] The movement to robotics in the 1980s put almost 40,000 robots on U.S. assembly lines and eliminated two-thirds of all assembly-line jobs by 1990. In service industries, the blows have been equally telling. Automated calling has eliminated the jobs of more than 250,000 telephone operators since 1950. Between 1987 and 1998, 20 percent of these jobs were lost, even as the average number of daily conversations increased by more than 600 percent.[18]

structural change
Any shift in the proportions of agricultural, goods-producing, and service occupations in an economy.

agricultural sector
The sector that includes farming, fishing, and forestry occupations.

Structural Change

Structural change is caused by processes of job creation and job destruction that continuously alter the mix of productive work in every economy. The American job landscape is shaped by the three long-term structural trends shown in Figure 16.1. Their action is similar in all industrialized nations.

First, the *agricultural sector* has declined from predominance to near insignificance in numbers of workers. In colonial America, farming occupied 90 percent of Americans. By 2008 it employed only 1.4 percent as fewer and larger

FIGURE 16.1 **Historical Trends for Employment by Major Industry Sector: 1800–2018 (Projections)**

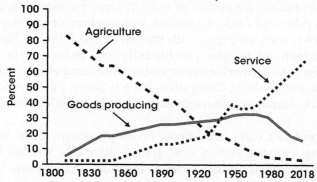

Source: Bureau of Labor Statistics; U.S. Census Bureau; and Herman E. Kroose, *American Economic Development*, 2nd ed. (Englewood Cliffs, NJ: Prentice Hall, 1966), p. 27. Post-1985 figures reflect some reclassification of industries.

[17] Figures for coal mining are from Bureau of the Census, *Statistical Abstract of the United States, 1956,* 77th ed. (Washington, DC: Government Printing Office, 1956), tables no. 257 and 910; and Census Bureau, *Statistical Abstract of the United States: 2010,* 129th ed. (Washington, DC: Census Bureau, 2009), tables 102 and 870; and the Bureau of Labor Statistics, "May 2009 Occupational Employment and Wage Estimates," at www.bls.gov/oes/tables.htm.

[18] Stephen Franklin, "Telephone Operators are Among Those Being Displaced by Technology," *San Jose Mercury News,* September 6, 1998.

farms delivered the nation's food supply using automated methods to grow crops and raise animals.[19] The Bureau of Labor Statistics predicts that the number of agricultural workers will fall a little more, to 1.2 percent of the labor force, by 2018.

goods-producing sector
The economic sector that includes manufacturing, mining, and construction.

Second, the percentage of workers employed in the *goods-producing sector*, which rose through most of the nation's early history, is now in long-term decline. In 1950 goods-producing jobs occupied 34 percent of workers, but by 2008 they occupied 14.2 percent of the labor force. By 2018 these occupations are predicted to contract further to 12.9 percent. There are many reasons for the decline of goods-producing work as a percentage of the overall labor force, but the two most significant are productivity growth, primarily through automation, and movement of work to lower-wage countries. Though fewer people are employed in goods-producing occupations today than in the past, it is a myth that the United States is losing its productive capacity. Over the decade between 1998 and 2008 employment in manufacturing fell by 24 percent in absolute numbers. At the same time, the value of manufacturing output increased by 32 percent, from $3.9 trillion to $5.2 trillion.[20] So, even as fewer Americans go to work in factories their output is surging.

service sector
The sector of occupations that add value to manufactured goods.

Third, there is explosive growth in the *service sector*, which includes jobs in retailing, transportation, health care, and other occupations that add value to manufactured goods. For example, a surgeon adds value to a scalpel, a desk clerk to the mattress in a hotel room. Growth in this sector is caused by growth in goods production and trade. Service jobs have risen from 40 percent of the workforce in 1950 to 77 percent in 2008 and are predicted to rise to 79 percent by 2018.

The direction of these three trends is remarkably similar in all nations as they develop. Table 16.2 shows how occupational structures reflect development stages elsewhere. The 12 nations in the table illustrate how development brings long-term job losses in agriculture and industry and steep growth in service-sector employment. Nations that have not yet industrialized tend to have large agricultural sectors. Among low-income countries, the agricultural sector averages 25 percent of GDP as opposed to just 1 percent in developed countries.[21]

Structural change is a critical factor in the fortunes of labor unions. Before the wave of protective legislation passed in the 1930s, unions represented only 5 percent of industrial workers, but this tripled to 15 percent by 1940 and reached a peak of 25 percent in the 1950s.[22] Unions raised wages and increased benefits for blue-collar workers. These improvements rippled through the entire manufacturing

---

[19] Historical sector employment figures in this section are from Bureau of the Census, *Statistical Abstract of the United States: 1956,* table 987. Current figures and projections are from Rose A. Woods, "Industry Output and Employment Projections to 2018," *Monthly Labor Review,* November 2009, tables 1 and 2. Sector employment percentages do not total 100 percent; the missing remainder includes private household wage and salary earners and nonagricultural self-employed not included in the three sectors by the Bureau of Labor Statistics.

[20] Rose A. Woods, "Industry Output and Employment Projections to 2018," tables 1 and 2.

[21] World Bank, *World Development Report 2010* (Washington, DC: World Bank, 2009), table 4. Figures in this paragraph are value-added as a percent of GDP in 2008.

[22] U.S. Bureau of the Census, *Statistical Abstract of the United States: 1956,* table 271.

TABLE 16.2		Agriculture	Goods Producing	Service
Comparative Employment Structures in Nations at Varying Stages of Development	**Less Developed**			
	Ethiopia	85	5	10
	Zambia	85	6	9
	Mozambique	81	6	13
Source: Central Intelligence Agency, *World Factbook 2010* at www.cia.gov/library/publications/, "Economy: Labor Force by Occupation," extracted August 7, 2010. Percentages are for 2009 with the exceptions of France (2005), Sweden (2007), and the United Kingdom (2006).	**Developing**			
	India	52	14	34
	China	40	27	33
	Brazil	20	14	66
	Russia	10	32	58
	Developed			
	Australia	4	21	75
	France	4	24	72
	Japan	4	28	68
	Sweden	1	28	71
	United Kingdom	1	18	81

sector because nonunionized companies had to approximate the welfare levels of union workers if they wished to keep unions out, as most did.

In the 1970s, however, union membership in the private sector began a long slide as structural change eroded its base of factory workers. Employment shifted to service industries and to industries employing knowledge workers, who are difficult for industrial unions to organize, and to low-wage countries where unions are illegal or weak. By 2009 unions represented only 7.2 percent of private-sector employees in the United States.[23] The upward push on wages and benefits they provided for both members and nonmembers has weakened commensurately.

Today, the United States has lower union representation of the private labor force than most other developed economies. In Western Europe, although union membership has declined for decades, roughly a quarter of all workers remain unionized and more than half in some countries.[24] This is one reason that labor costs are much higher in many European nations than in the United States.

Competitive Pressures

Recent trends have intensified competition for American companies. Customers demand higher quality, better service, and faster new-product development. In the United States deregulation of large industries such as airlines, telecommunications, trucking, and electric utilities has stirred formerly complacent rivals. In both domestic and foreign markets, corporations are increasingly challenged by global

[23] Bureau of Labor Statistics, "Union Members in 2009," BLS news release, January 22, 2010, p. 1.

[24] Organisation for Economic Co-operation and Development, "Trade Union Density (%) in OECD Countries: 1960–2008, Employment Database, www.oecd.org/dataoecd/25/42/39891561.xls, panels A and B, August 16, 2010.

competitors. Foreign trade grew from just 9 percent of the U.S. economy in 1960 to 29 percent in 2008 and is predicted to rise to 35 percent by 2018.[25] Foreign competitors have many advantages, including lower labor costs, favorable currency valuations, and, sometimes, higher worker productivity.

In a global labor market, workers in developed countries are exposed to competition from pools of low-cost workers. In less affluent, less industrialized countries, wages are lower for many reasons, including oversupply of labor compared with demand, low living standards, local currency valuations, labor policies of regimes where workers have limited political power, and wage competition among countries seeking to attract jobs.

By global standards, American workers are very expensive. In 2009 the average hourly compensation for a U.S. manufacturing worker was $33.53. This was not the highest in the world. That distinction went to heavily unionized workers in Norway making $53.89 an hour. Average compensation in Europe was $39.73.[26] However, in the industrializing economies of Asia and Latin America an hour of labor costs far less. Table 16.3 shows the huge wage gap between developed and developing economies.

Given this wage variation, companies in some industries can no longer afford to do low-skilled manufacturing in the United States; instead they contract to have it done in a foreign country. Or they find ways to increase the productivity of domestic labor by reducing employees to a minimum and applying technology to enlarge their output. Either way, there are generally fewer jobs for American workers in the occupation affected. Similar wage competition now exists in globalizing service industries.

TABLE 16.3
International Wage Comparison
The table shows hourly compensation of manufacturing workers in U.S. dollars. Compensation includes wages, insurance, labor taxes, and paid leave. Figures are for 2009, except China and Sri Lanka (2008) and India (2007).

Source: Bureau of Labor Statistics.

Norway	$53.89
Germany	46.52
France	40.08
United States	**33.53**
United Kingdom	30.78
Japan	30.36
Singapore	17.50
South Korea	14.20
Brazil	8.32
Taiwan	7.76
Mexico	5.38
Philippines	1.50
China	1.36
India	1.17
Sri Lanka	0.68

[25] Ian D. Wyatt and Kathryn J. Byun, "The U.S. Economy to 2018: From Recession to Recovery," *Monthly Labor Review*, November 2009, table 2. Foreign trade is the sum of imports plus exports.

[26] Bureau of Labor Statistics, "International Comparisons of Hourly Compensation Costs in Manufacturing, 2009," BLS news release, March 8, 2011, table 1.2.

Reorganization of Work

business process
Any sequence of actions that adds value to a product or service.

Corporations alter *business processes*—sequences of actions that add value to products and services—as they adjust to environmental changes, primarily competition. A key driver of competition, and, therefore, change in business processes, is a changing relationship with time and space. Digitized communication and modern transport are both faster and cheaper than in the past. Both factors lead companies to reorganize their work flows to cut costs, speed product cycles, and increase productivity. These reorganizations cause workforce turbulence. This turbulence, which is the creative force of the economy on display, is widely feared by workers who lose jobs.

For most of the twentieth century, manufacturing occurred near markets for products. As transport costs have fallen, manufacturers more often separate production from consumption by sending their manufacturing to low-cost countries, then shipping products back to customers. There are many examples. One story is how the prime contractor on a new six-story Salt Lake City public library underbid its competitors by sending part of the construction work to Mexico. It hired a Mexico City company with lower labor costs to manufacture 2,000 massive concrete panels that make up the building, saving $1 million although the panels had to be trucked 2,350 miles to the job site.[27]

Because of abundant and inexpensive bandwidth in fiber-optic cable, service work that formerly had to be done within companies can now also be sent to low-cost foreign locations. At first, only simple, routine tasks such as customer service, telemarketing, accounting, and document management were outsourced. But increasingly complex tasks such as software development, financial analysis, and marketing research are going offshore. The redesign of the 10,200-room Tropicana Casino & Resort in Las Vegas was done 8,000 miles from Las Vegas by dozens of Indian architects making about $15,000 a year.[28] DuPont sends much of its legal work to the Philippines, where attorneys with years of experience handle it for $30,000 annual salaries. A newly hired attorney in New York doing the same work would make $150,000 a year.[29]

outsourcing
The transfer of work from within a company to an outside supplier.

Trade between nations is growing, creating fears about job loss from *outsourcing*. Outsourcing occurs when a company sends work of any kind to an outside supplier rather than have its own employees do it. It may be manufacturing or service work. Usually, outsourcing is done to cut labor costs, although outside suppliers may have expertise or achieve economies of scale that a company would find expensive to duplicate. Outsourcing can move work to either a domestic or a foreign contractor. When work moves to a foreign country, this is called *offshoring*. Offshoring occurs when reorganized work remains within the company but moves from the home country to a foreign location or when work is outsourced to a foreign company.

offshoring
The transfer of work from a domestic to a foreign location or to a foreign supplier.

Offshoring has fueled attacks on corporations for destroying well-paying jobs in developed nations out of greed. In fact, there are many reasons for it.

---

[27] Joel Millman, "Blueprint for Outsourcing," *The Wall Street Journal*, March 3, 2004, p. B1.

[28] Pete Engardio, "Blueprint from India," *BusinessWeek*, April 2, 2007, p. 44.

[29] Pete Engardio, "Let's Offshore the Lawyers," *BusinessWeek*, September 18, 2006, p. 42.

The fundamental one is lowering cost. Manufacturing in the United States is often more expensive than in less developed nations, not only because of high worker compensation, but also due to higher costs of regulatory compliance, lawsuits, and taxes. But there are other reasons for offshoring. In return for access to its domestic market, for example, China sometimes requires foreign corporations to build factories there.

Statistics on offshoring lack the precision to reveal its full extent. In 2004 the Bureau of Labor Statistics began measuring the number of jobs that left the country because of mass layoffs, defined as 50 or more employees. Since then, the figures record only slight job loss from offshoring. Between 2004 and 2009 a total of 11.4 million private-sector workers lost their jobs in mass layoffs, but only 75,259 of those jobs left the country, less than 0.7 percent.[30] These figures understate offshoring. They do not measure job losses from smaller layoffs. Nor do they measure jobs that were never created because a company never started.

Some predict that the current trickle of offshoring will grow to a flood. One scholar analyzed 817 occupations for susceptibility to foreign migration and concluded that 22 to 29 percent of all jobs are in danger of being lost to other countries the next decade.[31] Several economists in the Bureau of Labor Statistics found that 26 percent of service jobs were vulnerable to offshoring, a total of 30.3 million workers.[32] Nevertheless, outsourcing is so far a minor eddy in the churning tides of job gain and job loss that wash over American workers. It has yet to turn into a flood. Even with cost savings there are advantages to keeping jobs in the country. An interview with an executive at a machine tool company in California explains why. One customer returned its work to the United States after a harbor strike disrupted shipping. Another did the same to avoid the volatility of shipping prices and material costs in a foreign country. It wanted prices to remain stable over a one-year contract period. Finally, having a relationship with a vendor "who knows the names of your children" can be important.[33]

Figure 16.2 shows that between 1993 and 2010, except during periods of recession and recovery, each year more jobs were created than lost. Each year the economy, whatever its state, created millions of new jobs while eliminating millions of old ones, but averaged an annual gain of about 1.5 million jobs. This dynamic of job creation and job loss is what reshapes the structure of the economy.

[30] Figures in this paragraph are from Bureau of Labor Statistics, "Mass Layoff Statistics Database," at www.bls.gov/mls/#data, August 2010.

[31] Alan S. Binder, "How Many U.S. Jobs Might Be Offshorable?" Working Paper No. 142, Center for Economic Policy Studies, Princeton University, March 2007, pp. 34–35.

[32] Roger Moncarz, Michael G. Wolf, and Benjamin Wright, "Service-Providing Occupations, Offshoring, and the Labor Market," *Monthly Labor Review,* December 2008.

[33] Patricia Szczuka, vice president, Computed Tool & Engineering, quoted in William B. Cassidy, "Cushioning the Blow," *Journal of Commerce,* May 31, 2010, p. 59.

FIGURE 16.2   Quarterly Private Sector Job Gains and Job Losses: 1993–2010

Source: Bureau of Labor Statistics, "Business Employment Dynamics," series at www.bls.gov/bdm/#data, extracted March 16, 2011. Figures are gross job gains, seasonally adjusted.

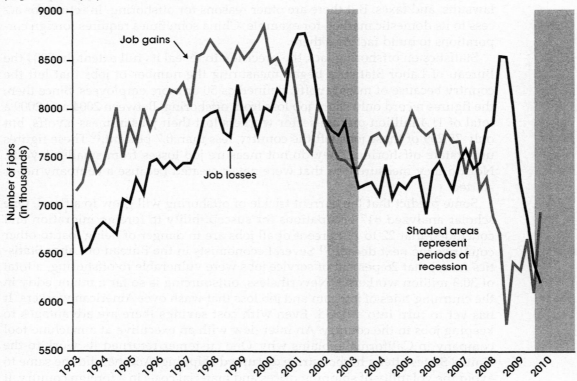

GOVERNMENT INTERVENTION

employment contract
The agreement by which an employee exchanges his or her labor in return for specific pay and working conditions. It is an abstract concept, but may also be set forth in writing.

All governments intervene in labor markets, but there is wide variation. We first discuss how labor regulation has developed in the United States. Then we explain the alternative model in Japan and Europe. Last, we explain the trade-offs in labor regulation that all governments face.

Development of Labor Regulation in the United States

Historically, a strong laissez-faire current in American economic philosophy made governments at all levels reluctant to interfere with the *employment contract*, or the agreement by which an employee exchanges his or her labor in return for specific pay and working conditions. Today, government intervention is extensive and growing, but this is a twentieth century trend.

Before 1860, the number of persons employed as wage earners in factories, mines, railroads, and other workplaces was relatively small. With industrialization, the number rapidly grew. Between 1860 and 1890, the number of wage earners rose

liberty of contract
The freedom of employers and workers to negotiate the employment contract, including wages, hours, duties, and conditions, without government interference.

from 1.33 million to 4.25 million, a 320 percent increase.[34] This rise, which would continue into the 1930s, created a new class interest, and it was an aggrieved one. In the hardhearted wisdom of the day, employers treated workers as simply production costs to be minimized; there was relentless downward pressure on wages and reluctance to improve working conditions.

Liberty of Contract

Before the 1930s, government intervention on behalf of workers was very limited, consisting mostly of feeble state safety regulations and laws to limit working hours. In the late 1800s and early 1900s, strong majorities on the Supreme Court upheld the *liberty of contract* doctrine. This doctrine was that employers and workers should be free of government intervention to negotiate all aspects of the employment contract, including wages, hours, duties, and conditions.[35] For many

Turn-of-the-century cartoonist Art Young drew this cynical view of the lopsided employment contract in the days before labor unions and laws protecting worker rights.
Source: Cartoon by Art Young.

[34] Arthur M. Schlesinger, *Political and Social Growth of the United States: 1852–1933* (New York: Macmillan, 1935), p. 203.

[35] The liberty of contract majority first emerged in *Allgeyer v. Louisiana*, 106 U.S. 578 (1897), where Justice Rufus W. Peckham grounded it in the due process clause of the Fourteenth Amendment, which says no state can "deprive any person of life, liberty, or property, without due process of law."

years, the Court struck down state and federal laws inconsistent with this theoretical freedom. Such laws were regarded as "meddlesome interferences with the rights of the individual."[36]

The great flaw in the liberty of contract doctrine was that it assumed equal bargaining power for all parties, whereas employers unquestionably predominated. For employers, liberty of contract was the liberty to exploit. Employees could be fired at will and had to accept virtually any working conditions. Unchallenged dominion of employers opened the door to the negligent treatment of workers that fueled the labor union movement, a social movement to empower workers. Employers resisted demands for kinder treatment of workers and bitterly fought the rise of unions.

Waves of Regulation

It was not until the 1930s that government regulation of the workplace began to redress the huge power imbalance favoring employers. One major step was the Norris-LaGuardia Anti-Injunction Act of 1932, which struck down a type of employer–employee agreement called, in the colorful language of unionists, a "yellow dog contract." These were agreements that workers would not join unions. Employers virtually extorted signatures on them when workers were hired, and hapless applicants had little choice but to sign if they wanted the job—and jobs were scarce in the 1930s. If union organizing began, companies went to court, where judges enforced the agreements. The Norris–LaGuardia Act outlawed yellow dog contracts, overturning a 1908 Supreme Court decision that upheld them under the liberty of contract doctrine.[37]

The new law encouraged unions. It was soon followed by the National Labor Relations Act of 1935, which guaranteed union organizing and bargaining rights, and by other laws that fleshed out a body of rules for labor relations. After the 1930s, employers still dominated the employment contract, but unions increasingly checked company power over wages and working conditions.

Figure 16.3 shows how this first wave of federal workplace regulation in the 1930s, which established union rights, was followed by two subsequent waves. A second wave, between 1963 and 1974, moved federal law into new areas, protecting civil rights, worker health and safety, and pension rights. A third wave, between 1986 and 1996, broadened federal authority to address additional, and somewhat narrower employment issues, such as when employers may use polygraphs and when they can test for drug use. The most broadening statute of this period was the Americans with Disabilities Act of 1990, which prohibits discrimination against the disabled and requires employers to make reasonable accommodations for people with substantial physical or mental impairments. Other laws defined rights to health care coverage, mandated equal treatment based on citizenship status, required warnings before layoffs, and gave workers up to 12 weeks of unpaid leave for family reasons.

---

[36] Justice Peckham, writing for a 5–4 majority in *Lochner v. New York*, 198 U.S. 61 (1905). The decision struck down an 1897 New York State law limiting bakery employees to 60-hour weeks.

[37] *Adair v. United States*, 291 U.S. 293 (1908).

FIGURE 16.3 A Chronology of Major Workplace Regulations

This figure shows the historical march of major statutes (and one executive order) regulating labor–management and employer–employee relations. Note the existence of three rough clusters or waves of intervention.

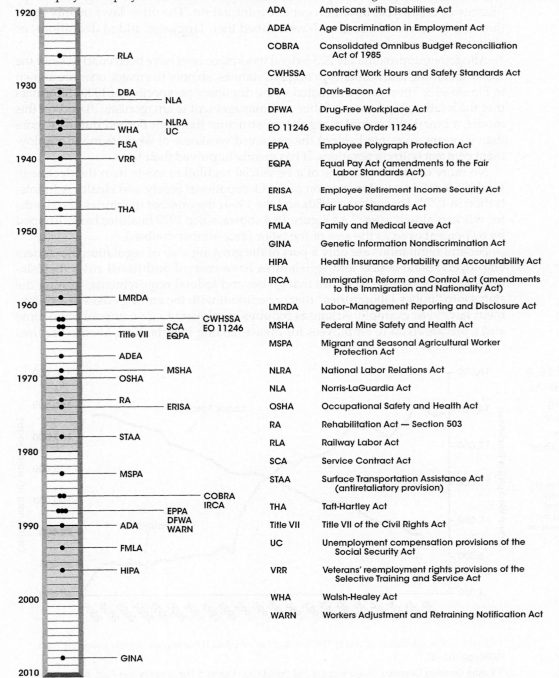

ADA	Americans with Disabilities Act
ADEA	Age Discrimination in Employment Act
COBRA	Consolidated Omnibus Budget Reconciliation Act of 1985
CWHSSA	Contract Work Hours and Safety Standards Act
DBA	Davis-Bacon Act
DFWA	Drug-Free Workplace Act
EO 11246	Executive Order 11246
EPPA	Employee Polygraph Protection Act
EQPA	Equal Pay Act (amendments to the Fair Labor Standards Act)
ERISA	Employee Retirement Income Security Act
FLSA	Fair Labor Standards Act
FMLA	Family and Medical Leave Act
GINA	Genetic Information Nondiscrimination Act
HIPA	Health Insurance Portability and Accountability Act
IRCA	Immigration Reform and Control Act (amendments to the Immigration and Nationality Act)
LMRDA	Labor–Management Reporting and Disclosure Act
MSHA	Federal Mine Safety and Health Act
MSPA	Migrant and Seasonal Agricultural Worker Protection Act
NLRA	National Labor Relations Act
NLA	Norris-LaGuardia Act
OSHA	Occupational Safety and Health Act
RA	Rehabilitation Act — Section 503
RLA	Railway Labor Act
SCA	Service Contract Act
STAA	Surface Transportation Assistance Act (antiretaliatory provision)
THA	Taft-Hartley Act
Title VII	Title VII of the Civil Rights Act
UC	Unemployment compensation provisions of the Social Security Act
VRR	Veterans' reemployment rights provisions of the Selective Training and Service Act
WHA	Walsh-Healey Act
WARN	Workers Adjustment and Retraining Notification Act

Source: Adapted from General Accounting Office, "Testimony: Rethinking the Federal Role in Worker Protection and Workforce Development," 1995, p. 5.

Since the late 1990s Congress has passed at least 20 more laws to secure employee rights, but only one, the Genetic Information Nondiscrimination Act of 2008, breaks new ground. It prohibits employers from discriminating against applicants or employees based on genetic information. The other laws mainly reauthorized or amended previous laws, refined their language, added definitions, or shifted requirements.

Altogether, approximately 225 federal workplace laws have been enacted since the 1930s, including amendments to original statutes, so only the major ones are shown in Figure 16.3. These laws are rooted in the dominant perspective of 1930s reformers that the relationship between labor and management is antagonistic. Based on this model, a broad and complex regulatory structure has been fleshed out over more than 90 years to counterbalance the perceived weakness of workers in the employment contract with corporations. It has greatly improved their lives.

No more dramatic example of a beneficial regulation exists than the decline in workplace fatalities after creation of the Occupational Safety and Health Administration in 1970. Through the 1950s and the 1960s the number of injuries and deaths for workers slowly rose.[38] As Figure 16.4 shows, since 1970 fatalities have dropped by 69 percent even as the size of the labor force almost doubled.

Federal regulations are only a part of the growing web of regulation that fetters employers. State courts and legislatures have created additional rules. Legislatures in many states enact laws that go beyond federal requirements, turning the states into "policy laboratories" that experiment with the cutting edges of employment law.[39] For example, Arkansas requires employers to give unpaid break time and a private room to employees for breast-feeding infants. New Mexico requires

FIGURE 16.4
After OSHA: Declining Workplace Fatalities, Rising Labor Force

Source: Bureau of Labor Statistics, Census of Fatal Occupational Injuries and *Employment and Earnings*.

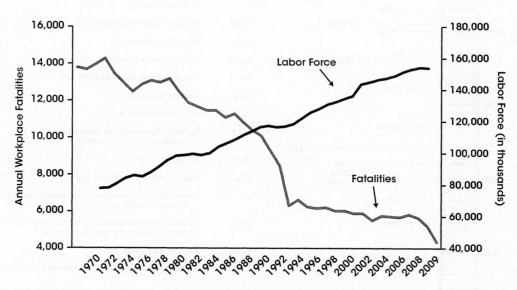

[38] Charles Noble, *Liberalism at Work: The Rise and Fall of OSHA* (Philadelphia: Temple University Press, 1986), pp. 61–63.
[39] Kirstin Downey Grimsley, "New Test Labs of Social Law: States," *The Washington Post,* August 13, 2000, p. H1.

employers to grant up to 14 days' leave for victims of domestic abuse to get protection orders. And Oregon prohibits required religious or political meetings at work unless they are management meetings where religious or political ideas are discussed.

State courts have added more worker protections. While federal courts often decide issues of constitutionality and statutory interpretation, they have not expanded workplace rights beyond the statutes. State courts, on the other hand, have used doctrines of common law to establish new employee rights in the absence of legislation. A leading example of the power of state courts is how, in recent years, they have revised the doctrine of employment-at-will, shriveling perhaps the most fundamental right of an employer—the right to hire and fire.

Erosion of Employment-at-Will

In the United States, a body of common law, or law derived from judicial decisions, governs employer–employee relationships. In general, this law holds that employers and employees may enter voluntary employment contracts and that either party may freely end these agreements anytime.

While employed, an employee must act "solely and entirely" for the employer's benefit in all work-related matters or be liable for termination and damages. Furthermore, when a conflict arises between an employee and an employer, the employee must conform to the employer's rules. The common law in this area is derived from paternalistic English common law that, in turn, was influenced by Roman law that framed employment in terms of a master–servant relationship. Under this body of law, employers have had extensive rights to restrict employee freedom and arbitrarily fire workers.

Until recently, an extreme interpretation of the employment contract prevailed. It resounds in the oft-quoted statement by a Tennessee judge in 1884: "All may dismiss their employees at will be they many or few, for good cause, for no cause, or even for cause morally wrong without being thereby guilty of legal wrong."[40]

employment-at-will
A theory in law that an employment contract can be ended by either the employer or the employee without notice and for any reason.

Employment-at-will, therefore, was traditionally defined as an employment contract that could be ended by either party without notice and for any reason—or for no reason.

With the rise of government intervention since the 1930s, absolute discharge rights have eroded. Federal and state laws take away the right to fire employees for many reasons, including union activity, pregnancy, physical disability, race, sex, national origin, and religious belief. In addition, state courts have introduced three common-law exceptions to firing at will.

First, employees cannot be fired for complying with public policy. In *Petermann v. International Brotherhood of Teamsters*, a supervisor requested a California worker to dissemble in testimony before a legislative committee probing unions.[41] The worker answered questions honestly anyway and was fired. The court struck down the firing, declaring an overriding public interest in ensuring truthful testimony to lawmakers. In another case, *Sabine Pilot Service, Inc. v. Hauck*, a deckhand

[40] *Payne v. Western & Atlantic R.R. Co.*, 81 Tenn. 507 (1884).
[41] *Petermann v. International Brotherhood of Teamsters*, 344 Cal. App. 2d 25 (1959).

was ordered to pump oily bilge water into the ocean off the Texas coast. The worker read a placard posted on the ship stating that this was illegal, phoned the Coast Guard for confirmation, and refused to do it any more. He was fired. A Texas court held that an employer could not fire a worker for refusing to disobey the law.[42] This exception to firing at will is recognized in 43 states.[43]

A second check on freedom to fire is recognized where an implied contract exists. Daniel Foley worked at Chase Manhattan Bank, and his superiors made oral statements that his job was secure. For seven years he got regular promotions and raises. One day, Foley learned that the FBI was investigating his supervisor for embezzling money at a former job, so he told a vice president. Shortly, the supervisor fired Foley. However, a California court ruled that Foley had been promised permanent employment if his performance was satisfactory. It held, in *Foley v. Interactive Data Corp.*, that the company had violated an implied contract.[44] Following this decision, companies began to avoid hinted promises of job tenure, such as references to "permanent" employees in brochures and handbooks. Courts in 38 states have adopted this exception.

Third, courts in 11 states limit the employer's ability to fire when an implied covenant of good faith is breached. These courts accept that such a covenant is present in all employer–employee relations. The test of any firing is whether it meets an implied duty to be fair and just. Unfair and malicious dismissals fail to pass. In *Cleary v. American Airlines*, for example, the company fired an 18-year employee, giving no reason.[45] Although company policy contained a statement that the firm reserved the right to fire an employee for any reason, a California court was convinced that the purpose of the firing was to avoid paying Cleary a sales commission. It awarded him punitive damages.

Of the three exceptions to employment-at-will, the implied covenant of good faith exception departs most from the vision of unrestricted dismissal. Indeed, it defies the amoral core of employment-at-will. Those courts adopting it reject the old notion of employer–employee equality, believing that employers overmatch the power of employees and have a duty of fairness in actions that determine the livelihoods of their workers. In a case where Kmart Corporation fired an employee to avoid paying retirement benefits, a Nevada court, holding the firing in "bad faith," noted:

> We have become a nation of employees. We are dependent upon others for our means of livelihood, and most of our people have become completely dependent upon wages. If they lose their jobs they lose every resource except for the relief supplied by the various forms of social security. Such dependence of the mass of the people upon others for all of their income is something new in the world. For our generation, the substance of life is in another man's hands.[46]

---

[42] *Sabine Pilot Service, Inc. v. Hauck,* 687 S.W.2d 733 (Tex. 1985).

[43] Charles J. Muhl, "The Employment-at-Will Doctrine: Three Major Exceptions," *Monthly Labor Review,* January 2001, p. 4.

[44] *Foley v. Interactive Data Corp.,* 205 Cal. App. 3d 344 (1985).

[45] *Cleary v. American Airlines,* 168 Cal. Reptr. 722 (1980).

[46] Quoted in Muhl, "The Employment-at-Will Doctrine: Three Major Exceptions," p. 10, citing 103 Nev. 49, 732 P.2d 1364 (1987).

Only three states fail to take up any of the new exceptions, and only six states embrace all of them. The great majority have adopted one or two, and the overall trend is toward greater restriction on the employer's ability to fire. One state, Montana, now has a law that permits employers to discharge workers only for "good cause."

WORK AND WORKER PROTECTION IN JAPAN AND EUROPE

The U.S. labor model is singular, a unique outgrowth of historical circumstance and social values. It evolved out of an early hostility between workers and employers, was shaped by a militant union movement, and is now enforced by a mature body of law and regulation. The U.S. model combines strong rights and protections for workers with a high degree of flexibility for employers who want to adjust labor costs when business conditions change. Elsewhere in the developed world, workers benefit from comparable and sometimes greater welfare guarantees. Where protections for workers are stronger, employers sometimes have less ability to adjust the size, pay, and benefits of their workforces to economic conditions. Other labor models have also grown out of distinct cultural experiences. Both Japan and Europe provide examples.

Japan

Many workers in Japanese companies receive lifetime employment contracts, steadily rising salaries, company housing, children's education expenses, and paid vacations. Japanese history and culture explain why companies are so generous. Japan's long feudal period shaped cultural patterns based on values derived from the spread of ancient Chinese culture to the islands, including belief in rigid status hierarchies, strong duties of loyalty owed to rulers, emphasis on group rather than individual welfare, and the belief that a paternalistic government should provide for citizen welfare. Later, these values molded the relationship between workers and industrial corporations.

community firm
A Japanese company that operates on a model analogous to a family. The company offers lifetime employment and rising income in return for hard work and loyalty from employees.

Just as the feudal Japanese vassal owed fealty to a lord, workers were asked to give loyalty to their company and place work group interests above individual interests. A strongly hierarchical and paternalistic form of management emerged during the early 1900s as Japanese industry developed. It was based on a fiction in which the corporation was analogous to a family. The *community firm* was a benevolent parent that took care of its employee children. In return, it demanded strenuous effort and complete loyalty from its workers. Although a labor union movement arose in the early 1900s, in this business culture any fundamental clash with an employer was insubordinate. Unions never consolidated into national entities with deeply antagonistic goals. They remained smaller, attached to individual companies, and inclined to be cooperative. In return, the companies gave generous benefits and protections to workers that unions in other nations fought for over decades. In Japan there were no bloody labor wars.

As the system works today, Japanese firms hire young college graduates with the promise of lifetime employment, usually until retirement at age 60. It pays

nenko curve
A slowly rising wage scale based largely on seniority that allows for small differentials based on ability and provides a comfortable income fitting various stages of life.

them on the *nenko curve,* a slowly rising wage scale with many small steps predicted largely on seniority. This pay system allows for subtle differences based on ability, but employees of like age and seniority have very similar salaries.[47] It is designed to provide a comfortable income fitting various stages of life.

In return for these employment and wage guarantees, the community firm requires absolute loyalty and strenuous effort. Regular employees, often called salarymen, are expected to remain with the firm. They do not shop for better opportunities or salaries at other companies. Within the firm they are trained, moved, and constantly pushed to enhance their performance. They also must work long hours.

Most salarymen will not leave the office at night until their boss does and the boss is reluctant to leave before his subordinates. Vacations are often neglected and holiday credits accumulate. Sick leave is seldom used. Salarymen sometimes work themselves to illness or death. A stereotypical case is that of 30-year-old Kenichi Uchino, a Toyota team leader in an assembly plant. He was still at his desk at 4:30 a.m. doing paperwork when he suffered sudden heart failure and collapsed. He had been working 14-hour days and in the previous month put in 144 hours of unpaid overtime, a practice called "service to the company." "I'm tired," he told his wife, "but what can I do?"[48] Such overwork is not blamed on unreasonable employers. It is regarded as exceptional dedication and as a duty called forth by the beneficence of the company toward its workers.

karoshi
A Japanese word for death from the stress of overwork.

Estimates of incidents of mortality from working too hard range from 1,000 to 10,000 each year. Such deaths are so common that a word, *karoshi,* appeared in the Japanese language to denote death from the stress and fatigue of overwork. The Japanese workers' compensation system defines karoshi as a syndrome marked by emotional and physical stress accumulated during six months or more of overwork.

When the Japanese economy entered a long recession in the 1990s the community firm model came under pressure. However, it has survived. These firms were able to compensate for the lifetime employment and generous benefits given to regular employees by cutting salaries and reducing paid working hours to avoid layoffs. In some cases they asked for early retirements, offering generous sums to volunteers, and loyal workers sacrificed themselves. Companies also hired many more part-time and contract workers. Today the average tenure of workers in Japanese companies is 12.2 years compared with 6.6 years in the United States.[49]

Europe

Industrialized nations in Europe also give high wages and comprehensive benefits to workers. This is reflected in average hourly compensation for manufacturing

---

[47] Takeshi Inagami, "The Japanese Flexicurity System and the Community Firm," *Comparative Labor Law & Policy Journal,* summer 2010, p. 779; and Toyohiro Kono and Stewart Clegg, *Trends in Japanese Management: Continuing Strengths, Current Problems and Changing Priorities* (New York: Palgrave, 2001), p. 280.

[48] John M. Glionna, "Workers Warned of Dangers at Toyota," *Los Angeles Times,* March 8, 2010, p. A1.

[49] Thomas Bredgaard and Flemming Larsen, "External and Internal Flexicurity: Comparing Denmark and Japan," *Comparative Labor Law & Policy Journal,* Summer 2010, p. 752.

social welfare model
A form of industry–labor–government cooperation in which government strongly regulates the labor market to secure expansive rights and generous benefits for workers.

workers of $39.73 across Europe, including $53.89 in Norway, $49.56 in Denmark, and $49.40 in Belgium.[50] In the aftermath of World War II, these countries and others in Europe adopted, in similar versions, a *social welfare model* of industrial relations to protect their populations against any repeat of the ravages of depression and unemployment experienced in the 1930s. Some governments took over major industries and ran them to ensure full employment. Lavish welfare packages for workers were legislated in European parliaments. Socialist parties supported the creation of powerful unions that could negotiate wages and benefits over entire industries.

Germany is an example. The benefits and protections achieved by German workers are exceptional. The average German worker gets 35 vacation days a year, compared with 16 for an American counterpart. Most retail stores must close on Sundays to give employees the day off. Workers are entitled to generous government pensions, health insurance, annual sick leave of up to four weeks, a six-month notice before firing, and unemployment checks of up to 60 percent of their previous wages for 70 weeks.[51] The average payroll tax to support federal programs is 20 percent of a paycheck. By law, workers' spouses who get a job are taxed at an even higher rate. Germany's detailed, voluminous labor laws are enforced by a huge bureaucracy, the Bundesagentur für Arbeit, which at 90,000 employees is the country's largest federal agency.

Forces of global competition have strained the German model, but because of high productivity Germany is able to maintain a strong export trade. When global recession added further strain in 2008, the German government rejected the politically deadly task of reducing worker welfare. Instead, it set up a massive program of *kurzarbeit*, or government subsidy of salaries for workers who lacked enough work. Instead of yielding to companies laying off workers, the government paid two-thirds of a worker's salary if he or she remained employed. Daimler-Mercedes, for example, put workers on three-day weeks.[52] Within a year more than 1.5 million workers were on *kurzarbeit*. Even as unemployment rose in the United States and elsewhere, it actually fell in Germany.

kurzarbeit
A German term, meaning literally "short-work," for a program in which the government subsidizes worker pay to promote employment.

Other European nations are equally or more generous. Between 2000 and 2002 a socialist government in France, over the objections of employers, established a 35-hour workweek. Its purpose was to create more jobs by mandating shorter hours, forcing companies to hire more people to maintain output. Like their German counterparts, French employees are expensive. In France, a motorman on the state railway gets $90,000 a year and free health care for working a 25-hour week and can retire at age 50.[53] French employers pay an average of 47 percent of

---

[50] Bureau of Labor Statistics, "International Comparisons of Hourly Compensation Costs in Manufacturing, 2009," BLS news release, March 8, 2011, table 1.2.

[51] Mark Landler, "Where to Be Jobless in Europe," *The New York Times,* October 9, 2005, p. 4.

[52] Doug Saunders, "The Maintenance of Hope: Germany's Secret to Recovery," *The Globe and Mail,* August 2, 2010, p. A1.

[53] Sebastian Rotella, "France's Economic Model Showing Signs of Stress," *Los Angeles Times,* October 17, 2005, p. C1.

social welfare costs
Nonwage costs, including payments for social security, health insurance, and payroll taxes that employers must pay to cover disability, unemployment, maternity leave, and similar benefits.

each employee's wages in *social welfare costs*, the second-highest total in the world (Belgium is the highest at 55 percent, and the rate in the United States is 8 percent).[54] Laid-off workers must be paid by their former employers for eight months while they seek new jobs.

As a result of the global recession beginning in 2008 there are many proposals for reform of such policies. However, in the face of widespread protests, European governments have had little success in rolling back social benefits for workers. When French President Nicolas Sarkozy considered raising the legal retirement age from 60 to 62, workers staged mass rallies in the streets. When Caterpillar tried to lay off 733 workers at a French plant in 2009, the workers held four managers in their offices overnight. The company then offered to fire only 600 workers if the rest would give up free cafeteria food and free rides to work. The union refused.[55] Faced with such defiance, governments across the continent usually lack the political will to act. Jean-Claude Juncker, prime minister of Luxembourg, once said, "We all know what to do, but we don't know how to get re-elected once we have done it."[56]

LABOR REGULATION IN PERSPECTIVE

core labor standards
Four fundamental standards to protect basic worker rights on which there is broad international agreement.

The bare minimum for labor market regulation is compliance with four *core labor standards* set forth in international labor conventions. These standards are distilled from 188 conventions adopted between 1919 and 2007. They call on nations at any stage of economic development to (1) eliminate all forced or compulsory labor, (2) abolish child labor, (3) eliminate employment discrimination, and (4) guarantee the right of collective bargaining.[57] These standards are widely accepted, though not yet universally enforced. Most nations move beyond them, providing added rights and protections for workers.

Worker welfare is an important goal, but experience teaches that nations must strike a balance between protecting workers from unfair treatment and allowing labor market flexibility. When Slovakia turned over state-run enterprises to private owners, it tried to protect workers by adopting a labor code that made firings nearly impossible. The new owners promptly moved operations across the border to the Czech Republic where labor laws made separating employees easier.[58]

---

[54] World Bank, *Doing Business 2008: OECD High-Income* (Washington, DC: World Bank, 2007), pp. 11 and 12.

[55] Steven Erlanger, "French Strikers Hang on to Threads of a Worldview," *The New York Times,* April 17, 2009, p. 13.

[56] Quoted in "Can Anything Perk Up Europe," *The Economist,* July 10, 2010, p. 11.

[57] See *ILO Declaration on Fundamental Principles and Rights at Work,* General Conference of the International Labor Organization, 86th Session, Geneva, June 1998, §2(a)-(d).

[58] World Bank, *Doing Business 2007: How to Reform* (Washington, DC: World Bank, 2006), p. 20.

FIGURE 16.5
The Trade-off in Labor Regulation

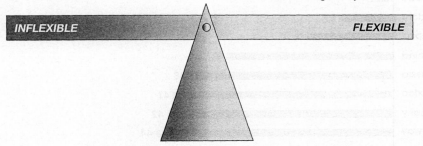

Worker Protection Goals
- Job security
- Collective bargaining
- High wages
- Limited hours
- Pensions
- Health and safety
- Nondiscrimination

Competitiveness Goals
- Create jobs
- Allow restructuring
- Adopt new technology
- Adjust to changing demand
- Encourage investment
- Allow turnover
- Reduce regulatory burden

INFLEXIBLE   FLEXIBLE

Workers must be protected, but they are hurt in the end if companies cannot allocate labor to its most productive uses. Firms must respond quickly to changing technologies and competition. If they are slowed by rules that obstruct the reorganization of work they grow less competitive and, in the long run, hire fewer workers at lower wages. Research suggests that in heavily regulated labor markets job growth is slower, unemployment lasts longer, companies invest less in new technology, firm size is smaller, and the labor force is less skilled.[59]

Figure 16.5 illustrates trade-offs in labor regulation and suggests that a balance must be struck between worker welfare and competitiveness. When a nation puts more weight on the left side of the balance by protecting workers, its labor market gets more inflexible. When it moves to the right, by loosening constraints on employers, its labor market grows more flexible. *Labor flexibility* is the ability to make quick and smooth shifts of workers into and out of jobs, companies, or industries as business conditions change.

Trade-offs are unavoidable. If a nation tries to create good jobs for low-skilled workers by adopting a high minimum wage, employers will hire fewer unskilled workers, leaving many without any job. As the minimum wage drops, more jobs appear, but the workers' standard of living falls. In some nations expensive safety regulations discourage hiring and leave many workers in the informal sector where they are not protected by any rules at all. If rules are too strict, they will be bypassed, frustrating both workers and employers. Similar trade-offs are present with rules that set work hours, limit dismissals, mandate union participation in company decisions, and tax employers for social benefits provided by the government.

labor flexibility
The ability to make quick and smooth shifts of workers into and out of jobs, companies, or industries as business conditions change.

[59] See, for example, Rita Almeida and Pedro Carneiro, "Enforcement of Regulation, Informal Labor, Firm Size, and Firm Performance," Working Paper, World Bank, January 13, 2006.

FIGURE 16.6   Country Scores on the World Bank Rigidity of Employment Index

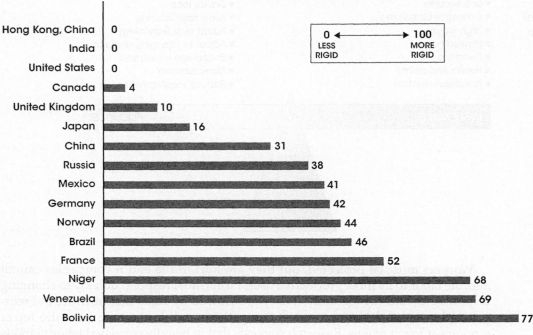

Source: World Bank, 2010.

Around the world countries differ greatly in labor market flexibility. Figure 16.6 shows how selected countries rank on the World Bank's Rigidity of Employment Index, a composite of 16 measures of labor regulation that runs from 0, highest flexibility, to 100, least flexibility. A score of 0 is consistent with a country's minimal adherence to the four fundamental core labor standards. The figure shows that the United States, with a score of zero, has one of the most flexible labor markets. Least flexible of all are some less developed economies, including Venezuela and Bolivia, which have the most rigid labor codes anywhere. When countries pass new labor laws, the World Bank adjusts their scores.

In theory, greater labor flexibility benefits both workers and employers by making industries competitive in global markets. "The best protection for workers," argues the World Bank, "is to make labor rules flexible so that the economy will have more jobs . . . and transitions from one job to another are easy."[60] In practice, its Rigidity of Employment metric rewards countries for reducing labor regulation in the direction of zero, the minimum. As worker protections loosen, scores are recalculated downward, making the country seem more attractive to employers and investors. When Argentina reduced severance payments for workers with

[60] World Bank, *Doing Business 2007: How to Reform*, p. 22.

20 years of seniority from 30 months to 20 months, its score moved from 41 to 35. When Australia passed a reform law abolishing limits on overtime and night work and freeing companies with 100 or fewer workers from unfair dismissal laws, its score improved from 17 to 3. Such flexibility reforms lessen worker protections and weaken unions, which naturally oppose them. An editorial in the pro-labor *Multinational Monitor* argued that "flexibility is all for employers, not workers," calling it "a corporate con" that should be seen "as a fancy and obscure term for enhanced employer power over workers."[61]

CONCLUDING OBSERVATIONS

Six forces are changing the workplace—demography, technology, structural shift, competition, reorganization of work, and government regulation. All have a profound affect on the fortunes of millions of workers around the globe. In the United States demographic change is creating more diverse, less discriminatory workplaces. Structural change and automation are moving more workers into service occupations. Global competition in labor markets and reorganization of work has reduced the job security of American workers. However, government regulation in the United States gives workers many protections.

Every nation must strike a balance between worker protection and employer flexibility. After nearly 100 years of labor strife and legislation the United States seems to have found its way to a balance that protects a broad range of worker rights while leaving employers relatively free to hire and fire for economic reasons. In the next chapter we will explore in more depth one of the most fundamental of workers' rights—civil rights.

[61] "The Labor Flexibility Con," *Multinational Monitor,* July/August 2006, p. 6.

A Tale of Two Raids

Migration, or the resettlement of people, is as old as humanity. It often has shaped history, as it did when migrants from Europe to the New World formed an American civilization. Migrants are driven by the opportunity to improve their lives. Costs of migrating are very high, but individuals who leave less developed countries on average double their educational attainment and increase their income by 15 times.[1]

Today, migrants make up about 3 percent of the world population. In the U.S. population the figure is higher, 8.1 percent, or 25.1 million people. Of these, 12.6 million are legal permanent residents, 0.9 million are authorized temporary workers, and 11.6 million are unauthorized entrants. Each year 750,000 of these migrants become U.S. citizens. Another 1.2 million leave the country voluntarily or are removed.[2]

[1] United Nations Development Programme, *Human Development Report 2009, Overcoming Barriers: Human Mobility and Development* (New York: UNDP, 2009), p. 24.

[2] Figures in this paragraph are from Department of Homeland Security, Office of Immigration Statistics, at www.dhs.gov/files/statistics/immigration.shtm, August 4, 2010.

EXHIBIT 1 Number of Persons Obtaining Legal Permanent Resident Status: 1820–2009

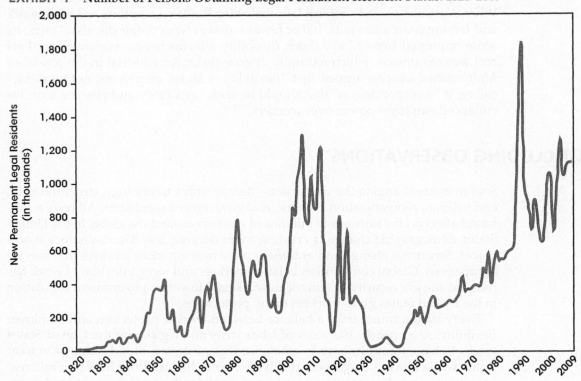

Source: Department of Homeland Security. Figures are for fiscal years.

The United States has attracted many immigrants over time (see Exhibit 1). Although they come for many reasons, jobs are the principle motivating factor. To control the influx of people across the borders Congress has made it illegal to hire aliens lacking official authorization to work. This is the story of how that prohibition works in practice.

OPERATION WAGON TRAIN

December 12 is Feast Day of Our Lady of Guadalupe, one of the most important cultural and religious dates on the Mexican calendar, a day of prayer and fiestas. It celebrates a day, almost 500 years ago, when an image of the Virgin Mary miraculously appeared on a peasant's ragged cloak.

On this day in 2006, a Tuesday, the morning shifts at Swift & Company processing plants in six states reported for work at 7:00 a.m. Swift & Company is one of the world's largest beef and pork processing corporations. It traces its beginning to Gustavus Swift, who opened a meat store near Boston in 1859. Swift had exceptional ambition. As his business grew, he revolutionized the industry with conveyor lines on which livestock carcasses were cut apart into products and shipped on railroads. These disassembly lines required plenty of workers willing to take low wages for hard, dangerous labor. The 7,000 workers who reported for the morning shift more than 100 years later were still doing the jobs the founder created. As in the past, most were immigrants doing work spurned by more affluent Americans.

It may have been a holy day, but no miraculous images would appear. Instead, just as shifts began uniformed Immigration and Customs Enforcement (ICE) agents swarmed the six plants in a coordinated raid, the largest ever conducted before or since. They sealed entrances and exits. Inside, they sought out individuals suspected of working illegally under false identities.

Monica Salazar, 26, stood with this sign outside the Swift plant in Greeley, Colorado.
Source: © AP Photo/Ed Andrieski.

Panic followed. In Grand Island, Nebraska, people started running and yelling. They tried to hide in lockers and broke windows to get out. Buses came to the plant and drove 240 workers to detention centers for deportation processing. They rolled past knots of family members at the fences waiting for word of loved ones inside.[3] Guards handed out leaflets with a toll-free, bilingual phone number to call for information.

In Greeley, Colorado, some workers hid in cattle pens. Veronica Perez and her husband were pulled apart. "He tried to give me a kiss on the forehead," she said, "but they would not let us talk to each other. They made him and myself seem like criminals."[4] A woman in tears asked a co-worker to adopt her child, saying she had no one else in the area.[5] ICE agents handcuffed 261 workers and assembled them in the plant cafeteria. One, Sergio Rodriguez, was working legally, but did not have his resident alien card. His wife brought it to the plant but was not allowed in. He was bused to a detention center near Denver and held until 8:30 p.m. before being released. Around this time another detainee, Gabriela Terrazas, was allowed to call and ask a brother to pick up her daughter from the babysitter.

And so it went. Another 230 workers were arrested in Worthington, Minnesota; 275 in Cactus, Texas; 196 in Marshalltown, Iowa; and 95 in Hyrum, Utah, for a total of 1,297. All were charged with immigration status violations and 274 were also charged with criminal offenses. Families were torn apart. When Juan Ramirez was taken in Greeley, he left behind his wife, Isabel, and three children, two of whom had been born in the United States. Juan brought in the family's only income. Now his wife, who also was in the country illegally, had no way to pay the bills. Church officials in Greeley said more than 100 children were left without one or both parents.[6]

Communities were challenged. On the day of the raid nearby schools saw attendance plummet and sales at local stores fell off as immigrant families stayed in their homes. Some would hide for days. A woman in Worthington, Minnesota, took in 24 immigrants too afraid to go back to their homes.[7] In Cactus, Texas, hundreds appeared at an evening mass offering prayers for divided families.[8] Swift & Company made contributions to the United Way to help people affected by the raids. However, distrust of authority kept most families from approaching social service and welfare agencies for aid. Many turned to their churches instead.

Operation Wagon Train, the agency's code name for the raids, left Swift & Company in disarray. Nearly 20 percent of its morning shift was gone. Hundreds more employees failed to show up for the

[3] Leslie Reed, "'Terrible' Day Separates Families," *Omaha World Herald,* December 13, 2006, p. 1A.

[4] Quoted in Julia Preston, "Immigrants' Families Figuring Out What to Do after Federal Raids," *The New York Times,* December 16, 2006, p. 13.

[5] Bruce Finley, "Fractured Families," *Denver Post,* December 14, 2006, p. A1.

[6] ICE policy is not to detain or arrest sole caregivers for small children. Its agents worked with Swift to identify and release them. Julie L. Myers, U.S. Immigration and Customs Enforcement, speech to the American Immigration Lawyers Association, June 14, 2007, pp. 3–4.

[7] Maricella Mirand and John Brewer, "Worthington Still Reeling After Raid," *St. Paul Pioneer Press,* December 14, 2006, p. A1.

[8] Frank Trejo and Isabel Morales, "Raid, Fear Tear Apart Families," *Dallas Morning News,* December 13, 2006, p. A21.

second shift. It was unsure exactly how many employees it had. In the end it estimated the raid cost it $30 million.[9] When the company criticized ICE for a heavy-handed operation, it got a curt response. "ICE is not responsible for Swift's illegal alien workforce, nor did ICE create this problem for Swift," said an agency statement. "Any company with illegal aliens on its payroll should not be surprised to see ICE agents at its door."[10]

In fact, the company knew the raid was coming. Ten months earlier ICE had opened a review of its employment records. Its investigation was started by tips from local police and anonymous calls from individuals suggesting that hundreds of illegal aliens, aided by document rings, were using identities stolen from U.S. citizens to work at Swift plants.[11] Soon the agency's investigators suspected that up to 30 percent of Swift's employees were unauthorized workers. It decided to obtain search warrants for raids.

When Swift learned this, it asked to work with ICE to reduce disruption. Instead of a one-day raid it proposed a step-by-step action in one plant at a time over four months. ICE rejected the idea because it would alert unauthorized workers who would vanish and use their stolen documents to get jobs elsewhere.

Then Swift suggested doing its own voluntary review of employees. At first ICE restrained the company, but finally gave it permission. Swift hired immigration experts, identified suspect employees, and scheduled interviews with them. As a result, more than 400 workers were fired, quit, or failed to show up for the interviews. At that point ICE ordered Swift to end its self-review because many unauthorized workers were disappearing before they could be taken into custody and deported.

Finally, Swift tried to stop the raids with a court order, arguing they would "irreparably harm Swift by interfering with its legal business operations and by damaging its reputation" in violation of its constitutional property rights.[12] ICE countered: "Put simply, there is no constitutional or statutory right for anyone to continue violating the law, and the government need not work on a potential violators' timetable . . ."[13] A federal judge allowed the raids to proceed.[14]

The enforcement philosophy at ICE is to focus on employers suspected of egregious violations. It seeks out those who "knowingly" violate immigration law by trafficking in illegal laborers, harboring illegal aliens, or participating in identity fraud. Swift & Company did not seem to fit these characteristics of an egregious violator. In many ways it exemplified compliance with the law.

It did not exploit unauthorized laborers. It paid its packing plant employees more than twice the federal minimum wage. It offered them comprehensive health plans that 80 percent joined. Its accident rate was lower than the industry average. When Congress passed the Immigration Reform and Control Act in 1986, it complied strictly with the law's requirement that every newly hired employee fill out a Form I-9.

FORM I-9

The Immigration Reform and Control Act was a compromise. In return for granting amnesty to 3 million unauthorized residents Congress promised to curtail further illegal entry. A major lure for illegal entrants was the ease of finding work. To attack this problem, Congress flourished a sword of paperwork called the Employment Eligibility Verification Form, or Form I-9, and drafted the nation's employers to wield it.

Hiring an alien worker is illegal if the employer knows that person is not authorized to work in the United States. The employer must complete Form I-9 to check on the status of every employee hired.[15] It is a one-page form with three sections (see Exhibit 2).

[9] Testimony of John Shandley, senior vice president for human resources, Swift & Company, Hearing on *Problems in the Current Employment Verification and Worksite Enforcement System,* Subcommittee on Immigration, Citizenship, Refugees, Border Security, and International Law of the Committee of the Judiciary, U.S. House of Representatives, 110th Congress, 1st Session, April 24, 2007, p. 4.

[10] Quoted in Christine Tatum, "Raid on Swift Leaves Staffing in Disarray," *Denver Post,* December 15, 2006, p. C1.

[11] Julie Myers, assistant secretary, Department of Homeland Security, "Remarks at a News Conference Announcing a Worksite Enforcement Operation at a Nationwide Meat Processor," Washington, D.C., December 13, 2006, p. 2.

[12] S&C Holdco 3, Inc., Form 8-K, December 13, 2006, p. 5.

[13] Christine Tatum, "Swift Tried to Block Raid," *Denver Post,* December 14, 2006, p. C1.

[14] *Swift & Company v. Immigration and Customs Enforcement,* No. 2-06-CV-314-J, N. Dist. Texas, order entered December 7, 2006.

[15] There are very limited exceptions, for example, for householders hiring domestic workers and for employees who will not be working on U.S. soil.

EXHIBIT 2 Form I-9

Department of Homeland Security
U.S. Citizenship and Immigration Services

OMB No. 1615-0047; Expires 08/31/12

Form I-9, Employment Eligibility Verification

Read instructions carefully before completing this form. The instructions must be available during completion of this form.

ANTI-DISCRIMINATION NOTICE: It is illegal to discriminate against work-authorized individuals. Employers CANNOT specify which document(s) they will accept from an employee. The refusal to hire an individual because the documents have a future expiration date may also constitute illegal discrimination.

Section 1. Employee Information and Verification *(To be completed and signed by employee at the time employment begins.)*

Print Name: Last | First | Middle Initial | Maiden Name

Address *(Street Name and Number)* | Apt. # | Date of Birth *(month/day/year)*

City | State | Zip Code | Social Security #

I am aware that federal law provides for imprisonment and/or fines for false statements or use of false documents in connection with the completion of this form.

I attest, under penalty of perjury, that I am (check one of the following):
- [ ] A citizen of the United States
- [ ] A noncitizen national of the United States (see instructions)
- [ ] A lawful permanent resident (Alien #) _____
- [ ] An alien authorized to work (Alien # or Admission #) _____ until (expiration date, if applicable - *month/day/year*) _____

Employee's Signature | Date *(month/day/year)*

Preparer and/or Translator Certification *(To be completed and signed if Section 1 is prepared by a person other than the employee.)* I attest, under penalty of perjury, that I have assisted in the completion of this form and that to the best of my knowledge the information is true and correct.

Preparer's/Translator's Signature | Print Name

Address *(Street Name and Number, City, State, Zip Code)* | Date *(month/day/year)*

Section 2. Employer Review and Verification *(To be completed and signed by employer. Examine one document from List A OR examine one document from List B and one from List C, as listed on the reverse of this form, and record the title, number, and expiration date, if any, of the document(s).)*

List A	OR	List B	AND	List C

Document title:
Issuing authority:
Document #:
Expiration Date *(if any)*:
Document #:
Expiration Date *(if any)*:

CERTIFICATION: I attest, under penalty of perjury, that I have examined the document(s) presented by the above-named employee, that the above-listed document(s) appear to be genuine and to relate to the employee named, that the employee began employment on *(month/day/year)* _____ and that to the best of my knowledge the employee is authorized to work in the United States. (State employment agencies may omit the date the employee began employment.)

Signature of Employer or Authorized Representative | Print Name | Title

Business or Organization Name and Address *(Street Name and Number, City, State, Zip Code)* | Date *(month/day/year)*

Section 3. Updating and Reverification *(To be completed and signed by employer.)*

A. New Name *(if applicable)* | B. Date of Rehire *(month/day/year)* *(if applicable)*

C. If employee's previous grant of work authorization has expired, provide the information below for the document that establishes current employment authorization.

Document Title: | Document #: | Expiration Date *(if any)*:

I attest, under penalty of perjury, that to the best of my knowledge, this employee is authorized to work in the United States, and if the employee presented document(s), the document(s) I have examined appear to be genuine and to relate to the individual.

Signature of Employer or Authorized Representative | Date *(month/day/year)*

In Section 1 the employee fills in a name, address, date of birth, and Social Security number, checks a box regarding authorization to work in the United States, and signs with the date.

In Section 2 the employer certifies a review of documents that show the new employee is authorized to work. The employer must verify this review by writing down which of a combination of 26 different documents from three "Lists of Acceptable Documents" has been reviewed. These documents must establish both identity and employment authorization. Some documents, such as a U.S. passport or a permanent resident card (commonly called a "green card"), establish both. Other documents establish one or the other and must be presented in combination.

Some combinations work. Others do not. For example, the employee might use a driver's license to establish identity and a Social Security card to establish work authorization. Another sufficient combination is a school identification card (for identity) and a birth certificate issued in the United States (for work authorization). However, a Social Security card and a birth certificate in tandem are not acceptable because neither establishes identity.

The company must examine the documents to make sure they are current and "reasonably appear on their face to be genuine."[16] It is not required to investigate their authenticity. However, it must teach its staff such arcana as when to expect watermarks, where seals appear, and how designs changed in certain years. If documents are stolen or skillfully counterfeited the employer is not expected to detect the fraud. Simply taking a good faith look shields companies from prosecution.

Section 3 is for updating. If an employee's work authorization had an expiration date, the employer must ask the employee for new documents to verify reauthorization, then attest that they appear genuine.

Form I-9 has to be completed within three days after a new employee first reports for work. An employee who does not produce the required documents within that time can be fired.

Violation of this paperwork regime invites serious penalties for corporations and their managers. Failure to properly complete Form I-9 can lead to civil penalties of up to $1,100 for each violation. If a company knowingly hires an unauthorized alien, it can receive a civil fine of up to $16,000 per alien hired. Where there is a "pattern or practice" of knowingly hiring unauthorized workers, managers and companies face criminal fines of up to $3,000 per hire and six months in prison. Aliens who use counterfeit or stolen documents or falsely attest their work eligibility on a Form I-9 can be fined and sentenced to a maximum of five years in prison.[17]

Employers must be careful how they handle the Form I-9 process. It is unlawful to discriminate against job applicants or employees based on national origin, race, ethnicity, citizenship, or immigration status. A company cannot require job applicants to complete Form I-9 and reveal their citizenship status before hiring. It cannot decide to hire only citizens. It cannot treat applicants or workers differently because they look or sound "foreign." A job requirement for fluent English is only permitted if it is required to do the job effectively or essential to safety. Employers cannot dictate the specific documents workers offer or ask for documents beyond the minimum required. It was here that Swift & Company ran into trouble.

After passage of the 1986 immigration law the company decided to exercise great caution. It tried to avoid hiring unauthorized workers by taking extra care to screen individuals who looked or acted "foreign," asking these persons for extra documentation not required of others. It may have hired fewer unauthorized workers this way, but it also subjected some U.S. citizens and lawful immigrants to greater scrutiny, thus violating their civil rights. In 2002 it was sued for $2 million by the Department of Justice for engaging in "a pattern or practice of citizenship status discrimination . . . against U.S. citizens" and lawful immigrants.[18] Swift paid a settlement of $174,088, a record sum, and agreed to retrain its hiring staff. It was a lesson that there were limits in its ability to screen its workers.

---

[16] U.S. Citizenship and Immigration Services, *Handbook for Employers: Instructions for Completing Form I-9* (Washington, DC: Department of Homeland Security, July 31, 2009), p. 6.

[17] These prosecutions are, however, difficult because the Supreme Court has required the government to prove the worker used counterfeit documents knowing the numbers on them belonged to other people. See *Flores-Figueroa v. United States*, 129 S. Ct. 1886 (2009).

[18] Department of Justice, "Department of Justice Announces Settlement Agreement with Swift & Company," press release 630, November 4, 2002.

E-VERIFY

Swift always prided itself on its diligent hiring. In 1997 it volunteered to be one of the first companies using a pilot program for electronic screening set up by the government. This program, which is now called E-Verify, allows the employer to enter the employee's name and Social Security number in a government Web portal. That information is then compared with databases at the Department of Homeland Security and the Social Security Administration.

If the employee's information matches entries in the databases, within seconds the company receives a certification that the employee is eligible to work. If there is no match, the employer has a chance quickly to check for typographical errors. If there still is no match, the employee's information is referred to staffs of verifiers who check other databases. If they cannot confirm eligibility then the system issues a tentative nonconfirmation. The employee has eight working days to correct any errors by calling toll-free Social Security Administration or United States Customs and Immigration Service numbers or by visiting these agency's local offices.

Some errors are simple to correct, for example, a name change. If the employee does not correct an error during this eight days the E-Verify system issues a final nonconfirmation to the employer who must then either discharge the employee or continue employment only for a brief time if it seems likely an error will be corrected.

Participation in E-Verify has grown to more than 200,000 employers. It is now mandatory for federal contractors, and 12 states require its use by some or all businesses. One mark of its effectiveness is that when a company announces it uses E-Verify it can work just like drug testing to deter unacceptable applicants. Marcelino Garcia owns a chain of Mexican restaurants. When he started using E-verify, he immediately began having trouble finding kitchen help. "It's been very, very tough," he says. "We can interview 20 people and maybe only one person" can legally work.[19] Ironically, Garcia entered the country years ago by swimming the Rio Grande River and traveling in a car trunk. He worked hard, was naturalized, and now employs 500 people.

According to the Department of Homeland Security, E-Verify works well. About 96 percent of initial responses are consistent with the employee's work authorization status. Of the 4 percent that are in error, about 0.7 percent reflect database or keyboarding errors and the other 3.3 percent are cases of successful identity fraud.

Yet E-Verify has major weaknesses, as the experience at Swift & Company showed. Only 6.2 percent of E-Verify inquiries are for unauthorized workers and that 3.3 percent error rate balloons into a 53 percent failure rate when it is applied only to the 6.2 percent of inquiries about unauthorized individuals.[20] If such persons submit real Social Security numbers with matching names of persons qualified to work in the United States, E-Verify issues certifications. E-Verify has encouraged a widespread identity theft industry that helps its customers to appropriate real numbers and names to qualify for work.

THE OUTCOME FOR SWIFT

In the end, Swift was never charged with any crime. That did not mean it went unpunished. On the day of the raid the company issued a press release in which Sam Rovit, its president and CEO, said, "Swift has played by the rules and relied in good faith on a program explicitly held out by the President of the United States as an effective tool to help employers comply with applicable immigration laws."[21]

It had taken on the administrative burden of helping the government detect and police illegal immigration. It had made a good faith effort as required by law to verify the status of all its employees. It had volunteered to go beyond legal requirements by participating in the E-Verify program. It paid large sums for training, software, record keeping, consultants, and attorneys.

These efforts were rewarded with the largest civil fine ever levied for national origin discrimination and the largest worksite raid ever conducted. Another Swift executive, reflecting on these events, said, "It is particularly galling to us that an employer who played by all the rules and used the

---

[19] Quoted in Thomas Burr, "Employment Screening: Here It Comes, Ready or Not," *Salt Lake City Tribune*, June 19, 2010, p. 1.

[20] Westat, *Findings of the E-Verify Program Evaluation* (Rockville, MD: Westat, December 2009).

[21] Swift & Company, "U.S. Immigration Officials Commence Employee Interviews at Six Swift & Company Facilities," press release, December 12, 2006, p. 1.

only available government tool to screen employee eligibility would be subjected to adversarial treatment by our government."[22]

A NEW ENFORCEMENT PHILOSOPHY

The departure of the George W. Bush administration altered the enforcement philosophy at ICE. Although President Obama vowed not to "look the other way as a significant portion of our economy operates outside the law" and promised to "step up enforcement against the worst workplace offenders," there have been fewer workplace raids.[23] Only 765 undocumented workers were arrested at their jobs in fiscal year 2010 versus 5,184 in 2008.[24] Instead of raids, the Obama administration emphasizes another enforcement tool—the employer audit.

Some employers call these audits "silent raids." Employers are required to keep Form I-9 for all current employees on file. If a company is targeted for enforcement, ICE auditors scrutinize these forms, photocopies of employee documents, and payroll records.

Audits are efficient. Small numbers of ICE auditors quietly check immigration status without the confrontation and disruption of a worksite raid. When the audit is complete, ICE gives the employer the name of each employee it suspects is unauthorized to work. The employer and employee then have an opportunity to correct any error. However, if ICE is correct, the company is put on notice that some workers are unauthorized to work. It now "knowingly" employs these workers, which breaks the law. If it continues it risks fines and prosecution of managers.

GEBBERS FARMS

Although audits lack the sudden drama of a worksite raid, they can be harsh enforcement tools as the story of Gebbers Farms illustrates. A century ago the Gebbers family settled in Brewster, Washington, a small community in the eastern part of the state where the cool nights, sunny days, and dry atmosphere make conditions just right for growing apples and cherries. For five generations the family tended its orchards until its privately held company became the third-largest grower in the country. Other growers sprang up nearby.

The town of Brewster, population 2,189, prospered with stores and services for the area's field hands. Apples are hand-picked and apple trees have to be pruned and thinned by hand. To avoid bruising, cherries are also picked by hand. This is hard work. It pays low wages and the only willing workers are immigrants. Spanish now prevails on the streets of Brewster and 90 percent of the students in its school district are Hispanic.[25]

In 2009 ICE targeted Gebbers Farms for an audit. When it checked Form I-9s for field hands and warehouse workers against Social Security and legal immigration databases, it found 550 employees lacking work authorization. As a result, two days before Christmas the company hand-delivered brief letters to workers explaining that those without proper documents were fired. It gave them three months to vacate company housing.

No one was handcuffed. No one was arrested. No families were separated. No one went into hiding. Still, there was trauma. Some fired workers had been with Gebbers Farms for up to 20 years. Many owned homes and had stable lives in Brewster.

In the town, business dropped off. People stopped making car and rent payments. At the La Moderna clothing store sales dropped 30 percent. The owner of the taco truck named Taqueria el Tapatio No. 4 reported "fewer people are coming to eat."[26] A few families returned to Mexico, others wanted to stay. Antonio Sanchez, a 51-year-old orchard worker, thought he might buy a new Social Security number and reapply for his old job.[27] Most

[22] Testimony of John W. Shandley, p. 4.

[23] President Barack Obama, "Getting Past the Two Poles of This Debate," speech at American University, July 1, 2010, at www.whitehouse.gov.

[24] Peter Slevin, "Deportation of Illegal Immigrants Increases Under Obama Administration," *The Washington Post,* July 26, 2010, p. A1; and Immigration and Customs Enforcement, "Worksite Enforcement Overview," at www.ice.gov/pi/news/factsheets/worksite.htm.

[25] Julia Preston, "Illegal Workers Swept from Jobs in 'Silent Raids,'" *The New York Times,* July 10, 2010, p. 1.

[26] Jose Antonio, quoted in Rochelle Feil Adamowsky, "Layoffs Leave Brewster Waiting, Worrying," *The Wenatchee World,* January 9, 2010, p. 1.

[27] Melissa Sanchez, "Massive Firings in Brewster," *Yakima Herald-Republic,* February 14, 2010, p. 1.

bought new documents and fanned out for work at other orchards, but because of the audit, employers in the area were wary of hiring them. Within months, Brewster lost a sizable part of its population.

Operations at Gebbers Farms were disrupted. It immediately advertised hundreds of jobs, but had trouble filling them. Eventually it brought in about 100 temporary guest workers from Jamaica, not enough to replace its lost hands, but all it could legally get.[28] The Jamaicans spend little in local stores, preferring to send their pay back home. Meanwhile, groups of Hispanics from Los Angeles appeared in town. One man asked a reporter if there would be more audits, saying he might need a better Social Security number.[29]

Many in the area believed this kind of immigration enforcement was unreasonable and unfair. Daniel Aguilar, who had been fired along with his wife, pointed out that during "the cherry-picking season, there's maybe 2,200 of us working in the orchards. Of those, there wasn't a single white American. Why does it bother them that we're doing the work they don't want to do?"[30] Tracy Warner, an editor at *The Wenatchee World*, a local paper, elaborated on the theme.

> [Y]ou wonder exactly what this "enforcement" accomplishes, by forcing people out of productive employment due to suspect paperwork. If indeed they are illegal aliens they are still illegal aliens. Presumably they will resume life in the shadows and find other work, somewhere. Meanwhile, a community will be struck an economic blow. These workers were producing wealth in a mutually beneficial pact with their employer . . . For a community to lose perhaps hundreds of hardworking people overnight will have a profound effect, and belie the false notion that immigrants make no contribution . . . But the law is the law.[31]

---

[28] These workers were brought in under the H-2A Temporary Agricultural Worker Program. Employers must certify that no U.S. workers are available in their area and three federal agencies—the Department of Labor, the Department of Homeland Security, and the Department of State—must approve. In recent years only 50,000 to 80,000 workers have been admitted under the program.

[29] Melissa Sanchez, "Massive Firings in Brewster," p. 1

[30] Ibid.

[31] Tracy Warner, "Immigration Reform Soon," *The Wenatchee World*, January 7, 2010.

UNAUTHORIZED WORKERS: RIGHTS AND ABUSES

The 11.6 million illegal immigrants in the United States fill many jobs Americans are unwilling to take. Every year the economy creates more of these lowly jobs than the number of immigrants who legally enter the country. Those who enter without authorization are often victims of human trafficking and fraudulent recruiting. Some die on the journey.

However, once in the country they are entitled to the same civil rights protections against discrimination and sexual harassment in the workplace as American citizens. They are also entitled to protection under labor laws. For example, when six Hispanic employees at Wok Teriyaki restaurant in Gig Harbor, Washington, lied about their work authorization, its owners fired them and refused to pay their final wages. These migrants got a lawyer and sued not only for their final wages, but for failure to pay overtime and the minimum wage. A federal judge ruled their immigration status was "irrelevant" and ordered a judgment based on the Fair Labor Standards Act, a 1938 law that establishes wage standards for all employees.[32]

Despite such entitlements, unauthorized workers often face labor law violations. A study of low-wage industries in the three largest U.S. cities—Chicago, Los Angeles, and New York—found that foreign-born unauthorized workers were frequently victimized. Among those working as cooks, dishwashers, sewing machine operators, car wash attendants, child care workers, and in similar low-wage occupations, 38 percent were paid less than the federal minimum wage and 85 percent worked unpaid overtime.[33]

When unauthorized workers are found on payrolls, they can be arrested and torn from homes and families. Businesses and corporations then use a flawed verification system to fill the job vacancies, inevitably hiring more unauthorized workers. But they must walk a very thin line between being caught by ICE for "knowingly" harboring unauthorized

---

[32] *Bailon v. Soek Am #1 Corp.*, U.S. Dist. LEXIS 114744 (2009) at 14. No. C09-05483JRC, W. Dist. Washington (2009).

[33] Annette Bernhardt, et al., *Broken Laws, Unprotected Workers: Violations of Employment and Labor Laws in America* (Chicago: Center for Urban Economic Development, 2009), pp. 42 and 44.

workers and being prosecuted by the Department of Justice for citizenship status discrimination. If they are successful, the profits that come from the illegal toil are protected.

Questions

1. Is the current employment verification system fair to employers?
2. Was Swift & Company socially responsible in its hiring and verification practices? Could it have done more? Was it treated fairly by ICE?
3. Is the work authorization audit a better enforcement tool than the worksite raid? What are the advantages and disadvantages of each?
4. Is the current verification system fair to job applicants and employees? Does it allow companies to exploit unauthorized workers?
5. Do you believe that unauthorized workers should have the same protections against discrimination, sexual harassment, and wage and hour violations as authorized workers?
6. Does current enforcement of workplace immigration rules invite disrespect for the law? Should the government step up enforcement? Should U.S. immigration policy be reformed? If so, how should it be changed?

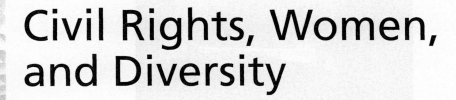

Chapter Seventeen

Civil Rights, Women, and Diversity

The Employment Non-Discrimination Act

Anyone, even a noncitizen, who works in a corporation on American soil, or any American who works for an American corporation on foreign soil, is broadly protected against workplace discrimination. It is unlawful for a company to discriminate against or allow harassment of workers based on race, color, national origin, sex, or religion. Women are protected against unfair job actions based on pregnancy. Employers must make reasonable accommodations for physical and mental disabilities. Persons over 40 years old are shielded from age bias.

These legal protections are remarkable, even astonishing, in their extent. A citizen of China or Mexico working unauthorized in a New York garment factory is protected against ethnic jokes and teasing about accents or English fluency. A deaf person or a person blind in one eye must be given a chance to work as a truck driver. A person cannot be fired simply for being diagnosed with paranoid schizophrenia. A woman who has just delivered a baby cannot be told to take time off from work. Overall, the laws prohibit *almost* all kinds of workplace discrimination.

Brooke Waits was hired by Cellular Sales of Texas. Her job was to track inventory in stores. She worked hard, arriving early and putting in extra hours before the office opened. In her words, "I went to work to be a rock star."[1] Her supervisor regularly praised her. Yet she was anxious.

Men in the office joked about gay and lesbian people. A co-worker said her walk was masculine. Away from work, Waits was open about being a lesbian, but she sensed that revealing herself would estrange her from others. She wavered, then hesitation turned to hiding and she was caught in a game of daily deceptions. She avoided telling personal stories. She sidestepped pronouns. When others spoke of husbands and wives, she called her girlfriend her "better half."

---

[1] Testimony of Brooke Waits, Hearing on *The Employment Non-Discrimination Act of 2007 (H.R. 2015),* U.S. House of Representatives, Health, Employment, Labor, and Pensions Subcommittee, 110th Congress, 1st Session, September 5, 2007, CQ Transcriptions, p. 31.

Congressman Barney Frank (D-Mass.), a multiyear sponsor of the Employee Non-Discrimination Act. Source: © AP Photo/ Susan Walsh.

Almost a year passed. One morning, her supervisor picked up Waits' cell phone and saw a picture of her kissing her girlfriend. That day the atmosphere froze.

> I dreaded coming to work the next day and, to my dismay, my manager was already there three hours earlier than she usually arrived. As I passed her office door, she called me in, stood up, and without the slightest hesitation, told me that she was going to have to let me go. When I asked why, she told me that they needed someone more dependable in the position . . . When I defended myself, she simply repeated, "I'm sorry. We just need to let you go."[2]

Testifying before Congress, Waits said, "I do not believe that anyone should be exposed to a workplace where they have to worry about being who they are costing them their livelihood."[3]

In fact, the federal laws that forbid so many acts of bias lay useless and silent in the face of Waits' humiliation. Twenty-two states protect gay, lesbian, and bisexual workers against workplace discrimination for sexual orientation. Thirteen states also protect transsexuals against gender identity bias.[4] Her misfortune was to work in Texas, a state offering no such protections.

Since 1994 a bill to protect workers like Brooke Waits has been introduced in almost every Congress. The latest effort was a bill entitled the Employment Non-Discrimination Act of 2009, which would have made it illegal to refuse to hire, to fire, or to take any adverse action against a person based on sexual orientation or gender identity. According to its lead sponsor, Rep. Barney Frank (D-Massachusetts), "An American who would like to work and support himself or herself ought to be allowed to do that judged solely on their work ethic and talents."[5] Although a similar bill

[2] Ibid., p. 32.

[3] Ibid.

[4] Government Accountability Office, *Sexual Orientation/Gender Identity Employment Discrimination,* GAO10-135R, October 1, 2009, p. 2.

[5] Testimony of Rep. Barney Frank, Hearing on *H.R. 3017, Employment Non-Discrimination Act of 2009,* Committee on Education and Labor, 111th Congress, 1st Session, September 23, 2009, p. 1.

passed the House in 2007, it failed in the Senate. At the end of the 111th Congress in 2010 the successor bill had failed even to come to a vote in either chamber.

The Employment Non-Discrimination Act will likely be reintroduced. If passed, it would be a landmark achievement but a relatively weak law. It exempts religious organizations such as churches, schools, broadcasters, and bookstores that might object on scriptural grounds to hiring a gay, lesbian, bisexual, or transsexual employee. It prohibits use of quotas or affirmative action. It does not require extending benefits to domestic partners. And it lets employers enforce dress and grooming codes they consider inoffensive.

Its subdued, minimal requirements are necessary to give it a chance against strong opposition. Some religious critics believe that homosexuality affronts God and oppose creating a new protected class, then helping its members to promote a sinful lifestyle. Although religious organizations are exempt, devout Christian, Jewish, and Muslim owners of private businesses would be compelled, in the words of one opponent, "to leave sincerely held religious beliefs at the workplace door and submit to the demands of the homosexual activist lobby."[6] Moral conservatives also oppose the law, refusing to equate criticism of sexual behavior with racism because they see gay, lesbian, bisexual, or transsexual behavior as voluntary, unlike race, which is fixed and unchangeable.[7]

Advocates of the bill believe it is the constitutional right of every American to have equal protection under the law. One civil rights advocate has "a dream that we will one day live in a nation where people will be judged not by whom they love but by the content of their character."[8] And Rep. Frank has this to say:

> People have their rights to their opinions. People have a right to be racist. People have a right to dislike certain religions. What you don't have a right to do . . . is, in your economic interactions with people, be prejudiced against them on that.[9]

This fight is part of the long history of struggle for civil rights protections in the workplace. In this chapter we discuss this history, explaining the evolution of laws and methods used to fight employment discrimination over the years. We then explain how these laws function today. The chapter also explores the topics of women in management and diversity in organizations.

A SHORT HISTORY OF WORKPLACE CIVIL RIGHTS

The American nation was founded on noble ideals of justice, liberty, and human rights. Yet for most of the country's history, business practice openly diverged from these ideals and discrimination based on race, color, sex, national origin, religion, and other grounds was common and widespread. Significant protection

[6] J. Matt Barber, "Barney and Barack's Anti-Religion Agenda," *Washington Times,* April 15, 2010, p. B3.

[7] See, for example, Kevin J. Jones, "ENDA Would Only Add 'Thought Police,'" *Washington Times,* April 29, 2010, p. B2.

[8] Julian Bond, "Rights Still to Be Won," *The Washington Post,* October 9, 2009, p. A23.

[9] Testimony of Rep. Barney Frank, Hearing on *The Employment Non-Discrimination Act of 2007 (H.R. 2015),* House of Representatives, Health, Employment, Labor, and Pensions Subcommittee, 110th Congress, 1st Session, September 5, 2007, CQ Transcriptions, p. 21.

from employment discrimination has existed for less than 50 years of the 235 years since independence.

The Colonial Era

Employment discrimination in America can be dated from 1619 when European slave traders first brought African natives to the New World's shores. When the colonies declared their independence from England in 1776, there were 500,000 slaves, mostly in the southern colonies. In the northern colonies, there was considerable anguish about slavery because it clashed with the ideals of those who had recently escaped from religious persecution and government tyranny in Europe. The Declaration of Independence expresses the founders' ideals.

> We hold these truths to be self-evident, that all men are created equal, that they are endowed by their Creator with certain unalienable Rights that among these are Life, Liberty, and the pursuit of Happiness.

natural rights
Rights to which all human beings are entitled. Governments cannot grant them or take them away.

These "unalienable" rights are *natural rights*, that is, rights to which a person is entitled simply because he or she is human and that cannot be taken away by government. Natural rights exist on a higher plane than *civil rights*, which are rights bestowed by governments on their citizens. Natural rights are a standard against which the actions of governments and employers must be measured and can be found wanting.

civil rights
Rights bestowed by governments on their citizens.

This statement in the Declaration of Independence distills a body of doctrine known as the American Creed, which historian Arthur M. Schlesinger, Jr., defines as incorporating "the ideals of the essential dignity and equality of all human beings, of inalienable rights to freedom, justice, and opportunity."[10] In the language of the time, the phrase "all men" was a reference to free, white males. Thomas Jefferson included in the original draft a strong statement condemning slavery as a "cruel war against human nature itself, violating its most sacred rights of life & liberty."[11] But this offended slave owners and had to be deleted to preserve unity in the coming revolution against England.

Despite the limited inclusiveness of the Declaration's language, its statement of natural rights, notes Schlesinger, challenged whites to live up to its ideals and, if anything, "meant even more to blacks than to whites, since it was the great means of pleading their unfulfilled rights."[12]

The U.S. Constitution reflected this bifurcated view of civil rights. When it was ratified in 1789, it sanctioned the practice of slavery in five clauses. Article 1, section 2, for example, counted slaves as three-fifths of a person for purposes of apportioning seats in the House of Representatives.[13] Yet the Bill of Rights contained ringing phrases protecting a wide range of fundamental rights.

---

[10] Arthur M. Schlesinger, Jr., *The Disuniting of America* (New York: Norton, 1992), p. 27.

[11] Edward S. Corwin and J. W. Peltason, *Understanding the Constitution,* 4th ed. (New York: Holt, Rinehart and Winston, 1967), p. 4.

[12] Schlesinger, *The Disuniting of America,* p. 39.

[13] See also Article I, section 9, limiting taxation of slaves; Article I, section 9, prohibiting Congress from ending the slave trade before 1808; Article IV, section 2, requiring return of fugitive slaves to owners; and Article V, prohibiting amendment of Article 1, section 9, before 1808.

Civil War and Reconstruction

Beginning about the time the Constitution was ratified, an antislavery movement originated in a small sect within the Church of England. This movement grew rapidly, and in a century's time, its moral arguments largely swept slavery from the world stage.[14] In the United States, the issue of slavery rose to a crisis in the Civil War fought between 1861 and 1865. In 1863 President Abraham Lincoln issued the Emancipation Proclamation that freed an estimated 4 million slaves. Following the war, Congress passed three constitutional amendments designed to protect the rights of former slaves, especially in the South.

- The *Thirteenth Amendment* in 1865 abolished slavery.
- The *Fourteenth Amendment* in 1868 was intended to prevent Southern states from passing discriminatory laws. It reads, in part: "No State shall make or enforce any law which shall abridge the privileges or immunities of citizens of the United States; nor shall any State deprive any person of life, liberty, or property, without due process of law; nor deny to any person within its jurisdiction the equal protection of the laws."
- The *Fifteenth Amendment* in 1870 prohibited race discrimination in voting.

These amendments were supplemented by a series of civil rights acts passed by Congress, most notably one in 1866 to protect blacks against employment discrimination and another in 1875 to protect them from discrimination in transportation and accommodations. Altogether, these amendments and statutes created a formidable legal machinery to implement the rights to which blacks were entitled under the American Creed. If this machinery had been allowed to function, a century of painful employment discrimination against blacks and other groups might have been prevented. But it was not to be.

There was tremendous resistance to the new laws in the South, but at first much enforcement was possible because of the continuing presence of the Union Army, an occupying force that kept a temporary lid on Southern resistance to black rights, which was formidable and violent. Because the troops protected voting rights, for example, 16 blacks were elected to Congress and about 600 to state legislatures. But the presidential election of 1876 ended the era of Southern rehabilitation.

In the race, the Republican candidate, Rutherford B. Hayes, lost the popular vote to his Democratic opponent, Samuel J. Tilden, but the vote was close in the Electoral College and returns from three Southern states were contested. Hayes agreed to an "understanding" that if the electoral votes from these Southern states were cast for him, he would withdraw the remaining federal troops. History records that Hayes won the election and the soldiers left. An important check on racism went with them.

White racism reasserted itself in the South in many ways. *Racism*, defined broadly, is the belief that each race has distinctive cultural characteristics and that one's own race is superior to other races. It persists when myths and stereotypes about inferiorities are expressed in institutions of education, government, religion,

racism
The belief that each race has distinctive cultural characteristics and that one's own race is superior to other races.

---

[14] Thomas Sowell, *Race and Culture: A World View* (New York: Basic Books, 1994), pp. 210–14.

and business. Racism leads to social discrimination, or the apportioning of resources based on group membership rather than individual merit. It insulates the power of a privileged group—for example, white Americans—from challenge.

Southern states adopted segregationist statutes called *Jim Crow laws*. These laws institutionalized the idea that whites were superior to blacks by creating segregated schools, restrooms, and water fountains; in literacy tests that disenfranchised blacks; in restrictive deeds that prevented whites from selling property to blacks in certain neighborhoods; and in discriminatory hiring that kept blacks in menial occupations.

Jim Crow laws
Measures enacted in the South from 1877 to the 1950s legalizing segregation in public places, buses, trains, restaurants, schools, and businesses. The term *Jim Crow*, taken from a song in a nineteenth century minstrel show, came to stand for the practice of discrimination or segregation.

Other Groups Face Employment Discrimination

Other groups in the United States faced extensive and institutionalized employment discrimination as well. Native Americans were widely treated as an inferior race. In the nineteenth century, the federal government spent uncounted millions of dollars to destroy their societies and segregate them on reservations.

A large population of roughly 90,000 Hispanics suddenly became residents of United States territory when Mexico ceded Texas in 1845 and other tracts of Southwestern land in 1848. Soon these Mexican Americans were victims of a range of discriminatory actions. They were legally stripped of extensive land holdings and exploited in a labor market where discrimination confined them to lesser occupations. They suffered great violence; more Hispanics were killed in the Southwest between 1850 and 1930 than blacks were lynched in the South.[15]

Beginning in 1851, Chinese laborers began to enter the country. They settled in Western states and many owned placer mines. In 1863 several thousand began working on the construction of the Central Pacific Railroad. Some started businesses such as laundries and restaurants. By the 1870s there were 100,000 Chinese in Western states; in California there were 75,000, about 10 percent of the population. Although they faced prejudice, their presence was tolerated until economic depression set in and the white majority felt they were competing for jobs and customers. Then economic and racial discrimination began in earnest.

Special taxes passed by state legislatures were used to confiscate their mines and ruin their commercial businesses. Some towns ordered all Chinese to leave. San Francisco passed an ordinance requiring city licenses for all laundries, then denied licenses to Chinese laundries.[16] The California state constitution, adopted in 1874, prohibited Chinese from voting and made it illegal for corporations to hire them. Finally, Congress banned the immigration of Chinese laborers in 1882.

The earliest Japanese immigrants found similar inhospitality. By 1880 there were only 124 Japanese in the United States, but their numbers increased rapidly as employers sought replacements for the cheap Chinese labor supply that had been cut off. By 1890 about 100,000 Japanese immigrants had arrived, most in California. Japanese laborers were typically paid 7 to 10 cents an hour less than

---

[15] John P. Fernandez, *Managing a Diverse Work Force* (Lexington, MA: Lexington Books, 1991), p. 165.

[16] In *Yick Wo v. Hopkins*, 118 U.S. 356 (1886), the Supreme Court struck down the ordinance as a violation of the equal protection clause of the Fourteenth Amendment. Had the Court followed up on this precedent, it could have struck down Jim Crow laws in the South.

whites. Like the Chinese, they ultimately threatened white labor and soon faced violent prejudice in cities. They turned to agricultural work in California's fertile inland valleys, but powerful white farmers resented their presence. California passed laws prohibiting Japanese land ownership, and in 1924 Congress banned further Japanese immigration.

Although employers wanted to utilize Japanese labor, social attitudes frequently made this impossible. For example, in 1925 Pacific Spruce Corporation brought 35 Japanese to the small lumber town of Toledo, Oregon, to work in its sawmill. A mob of 500 men, women, and children swarmed the mill, and the company had to load the Japanese on trucks that took them to Portland.[17]

As this brief sketch on nineteenth and early twentieth century employment discrimination shows, neither the American Creed nor the fine legal mechanism put in place after the Civil War worked to stop racism. Why not? The former was eclipsed by broad public prejudice. The latter had to be enforced against the grain of Southern racism and was, in any case, soon dismantled by the Supreme Court in two landmark cases—the *Civil Rights Cases* and *Plessy v. Ferguson.*

The *Civil Rights Cases*

The Civil Rights Act of 1875 was passed to prevent racial discrimination in "inns, public conveyances on land or water, theaters and other places of public amusement."[18] The law set a fine of up to $1,000 or imprisonment up to one year for violation. Still, there was widespread discrimination against freed slaves by business and soon a series of cases reached the Supreme Court. Two cases involved inns in Kansas and Missouri that had refused rooms to blacks. And in one case, the Memphis and Charleston Railroad Company in Tennessee had refused to allow a woman "of African descent" to ride in the ladies' car of a train. These cases were consolidated into one opinion by the Supreme Court in 1883 and called the *Civil Rights Cases.*[19]

The Civil Rights Act of 1875 was based on the Fourteenth Amendment, and in the Court's opinion, Justice Joseph P. Bradley focused on its wording. Because the amendment reads that "no state" shall discriminate, Bradley held that it did not prohibit what he referred to as a "private wrong." If race discrimination was not supported by state laws, it was a private matter between companies and their customers or employees and the Fourteenth Amendment did not prohibit it. For this reason, Congress lacked the authority to regulate race bias among private parties; therefore, the Civil Rights Act of 1875 was unconstitutional.

The *Civil Rights Cases* so narrowed the meaning of the Fourteenth Amendment that it became irrelevant to a broad range of economic and social bias. Congress and the courts could no longer use it to strike down much of the most brazen race discrimination. It was not necessarily a wrong decision; in fact, many constitutional scholars believe that the Court made a reasonable decision for that day given the clear reference to state action in the Fourteenth Amendment. But in

---

[17] Herman Feldman, *Racial Factors in American Industry* (New York: Harper, 1931), pp. 89–90.

[18] An Act to Protect all Citizens in their Civil and Legal Rights, 18 Stat. At L., 335, section 1.

[19] *Civil Rights Cases,* 109 U.S. 835 (1883).

dissent, Justice John Marshall Harlan argued that "the substance and spirit of the recent Amendments of the Constitution have been sacrificed by a subtle and ingenious verbal criticism."[20]

Plessy v. Ferguson

Southern states had passed so-called Jim Crow laws that sanctioned race segregation. If the Fourteenth Amendment could not prohibit private individuals from depriving each other of basic rights, did it not still clearly prohibit states from enacting laws that abused the former slaves? The answer was no.

One such law was the Separate Car Act passed by Louisiana in 1890. This statute required all Louisiana railroads to "provide equal but separate accommodations for the white, and colored races, by providing two or more passenger coaches for each passenger train, or by dividing the passenger coaches by a partition so as to secure separate accommodations."[21] This law, like other Jim Crow laws, was based on the *police power* of the state, a presumed power inherent in the sovereignty of every government, to protect citizens from nuisances and dangers that might harm public safety, health, and morals.

On June 7, 1892, Homer Plessy, who was seven-eighths Caucasian and one-eighth African, bought a first-class ticket on the East Louisiana Railroad to travel from New Orleans to Covington. Boarding the train, he took a vacant seat in the white coach. He was asked by the conductor to move to the "nonwhite" coach. Plessy refused and was taken to a New Orleans jail.

Plessy brought suit, claiming he was entitled to "equal protection of the laws" as stated in the Fourteenth Amendment. In 1896, in *Plessy v. Ferguson*, the Supreme Court disagreed, holding that as long as separate accommodations for blacks were equal to those of whites, blacks were not deprived of any rights. Justice Henry B. Brown, writing for the majority, argued that laws requiring race separation "do not necessarily imply the inferiority of either race to the other" and were a valid exercise of police power by state legislatures because they enhanced "comfort, and the preservation of the public peace and good order."[22]

This ruling completed the destruction of the Fourteenth Amendment as a mechanism to guarantee civil rights. The Court's interpretation legitimized the *separate but equal* doctrine, or the belief that segregation of races was not inherently unequal. The separate but equal doctrine, which became the foundation for legal apartheid in the South, stood for 58 years until reversed in 1954 by the Court in its famous school desegregation case, *Brown v. Board of Education*.[23]

Plessy is in retrospect notorious and some say one of the worst decisions ever made by the Court because of its consequences. The justices missed an opportunity to read the Fourteenth Amendment in a way that would protect blacks from

police power
An inherent power of state governments to regulate economic and social relationships for the welfare of all citizens.

separate but equal
The belief, prevalent in the South, that racially segregated facilities were not inherently unequal.

[20] 109 U.S. 844.

[21] Act 111 of 1890, quoted in Richard Epstein, *Forbidden Grounds: The Case Against Employment Discrimination Laws* (Cambridge, MA: Harvard University Press, 1992), pp. 99–100.

[22] *Plessy v. Ferguson*, 163 U.S. 540 (1896), at 544 and 550. John H. Ferguson was the judge who denied Plessy's constitutional claim in the New Orleans Criminal Court.

[23] *Brown v. Board of Education*, 347 U.S. 483.

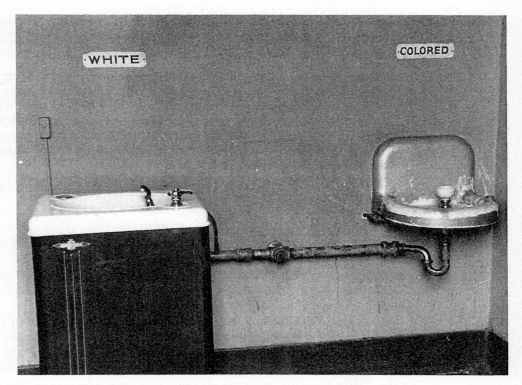

After the *Plessy* decision, Jim Crow laws became entrenched throughout the South. The water fountains in this photograph taken in North Carolina in 1950 symbolize a much larger universe of discrimination, including employment discrimination. Source: © Elliott Erwitt/Magnum Photos.

the schemes of white racists. They must have thought that a decision striking down Jim Crow would be unpopular and widely disobeyed and may have sought to prevent the Court from being weakened by disregard for its opinions. As in the *Civil Rights Cases*, Justice Harlan was a lone dissenter who kept the light of the American Creed flickering by lecturing the majority. He wrote:

> Our Constitution is color-blind and neither knows nor tolerates classes among citizens. In respect of civil rights, all citizens are equal before the law. The humblest is the peer of the most powerful. The law regards man as man, and takes no account of his . . . color when his civil rights as guaranteed by the supreme law of the land are involved.[24]

Long Years of Discrimination

The nation's civil rights laws were now hopelessly crippled. Southern legislatures were emboldened by *Plessy*. Now needing no special moral justification, Jim Crow laws spread. Black workers faced the most blatant discrimination. They were not allowed to hold jobs such as streetcar conductor or cashier where they would have any authority over whites. Labor unions refused to admit blacks, and a few that did limited them to low-pay occupations. The Brotherhood of Locomotive Engineers, for example, barred blacks from being locomotive engineers. In South Carolina, a law prohibited blacks and whites from working in the same room or

[24] 163 U.S. 537.

using the same plant entrances in the cotton textile industry. Such customs spread to the North. A study of economic opportunity for blacks in Buffalo, New York, told the following tale.

> A [black] man tells of being made a moulder in a foundry, later to be replaced by a white worker and reduced to the grade of moulder's helper, and finally dismissed when he made a complaint. Another man was given a chance to try out for a skilled-labor job in a stone-cutting concern and, having made good, was given the position temporarily, losing it, however, a few days later when the superintendent "came down through the shop" and, seeing him so employed, told the foreman to put another man on the work.[25]

THE CIVIL RIGHTS ACT OF 1964

This kind of open discrimination continued in the South. A study of 175 firms in New Orleans in 1943 found that almost all of them hired blacks, but then 93 percent segregated their workforces and 79 percent segregated job categories.[26] In the North, many companies refused to hire blacks at all. A study of 14 plants in Chicago in 1952, for example, found that 10 of them excluded blacks.[27]

In the late 1950s and early 1960s, a new civil rights movement arose. Under the leadership of blacks such as Martin Luther King, this movement was nonviolent and again focused on making America live up to the ideals in the American Creed. "The American people are infected with racism—that is the peril," said King. "Paradoxically, they are also infected with democratic ideals—that is the hope."[28]

The pressures of this movement led to many social reforms, among them passage of the Civil Rights Act of 1964, which is today the cornerstone of the structure of laws and regulations enforcing equal opportunity. Its Title VII prohibits discrimination in any aspect of employment. It reads, in part:

> It shall be an unlawful employment practice for an employer:
>
> 1. To fail or refuse to hire or to discharge any individual, or otherwise to discriminate against any individual with respect to his compensation, terms, conditions, or privileges of employment, because of such individual's race, color, religion, sex, or national origin.
> 2. To limit or classify his employees or applicants for employment in any way which would deprive any individual of employment opportunities or otherwise adversely affect his status as an employee, because of such individual's race, color, religion, sex, or national origin. [Section 703(a)]

[25] Quoted in Feldman, *Racial Factors in American Industry*, p. 36.

[26] Logan Wilson and Harlan Gilmore, "White Employers and Negro Workers," *American Sociological Review*, December 1943, pp. 698–700.

[27] Lewis M. Killian, "The Effects of Southern White Workers on Race Relations in Northern Plants," *American Sociological Review*, June 1952, p. 329.

[28] Quoted in Lani Guinier, "[E]racing Democracy: The Voting Rights Cases," *Harvard Law Review*, November 1994, p. 109.

Title VII also created the Equal Employment Opportunity Commission (EEOC), an independent regulatory commission, to enforce its provisions. All companies with 15 or more employees fall under the jurisdiction of Title VII and must report annually to the EEOC the number of minorities and women in various job categories.[29] If bias exists, employees can file charges with the EEOC. The agency then attempts to resolve charges through conciliation or voluntary settlement, but if that fails, it can sue in a federal court. In 2010 there were 73,058 charges filed under Title VII leading to the recovery of $230 million in monetary benefits to workers suffering discrimination.[30]

The overall purpose of Title VII, which is clear from the congressional debates that preceded its passage, was to remove discriminatory barriers to hiring and advancement and create a level playing field for all workers. As originally enacted, it did not require that minority workers be hired simply because they belonged to protected groups. It did not require employers to redress racially imbalanced workforces or change established seniority systems. No whites would be fired, lose their seniority, or be adversely affected. Simply put, from the day the law went into effect, all bias was to end. Job decisions could be made only on merit.

Disparate Treatment and Disparate Impact

disparate treatment
Unequal treatment of employees based on race, color, religion, sex, or national origin.

Title VII made overt, blatant employment discrimination illegal. It enforced a legal theory of *disparate treatment*. Disparate treatment exists if an employer gives less favorable treatment to employees because of their race, color, religion, sex, or national origin. For example, a retail store that refused to promote black warehouse workers to sales positions, preferring white salespeople to serve predominantly white customers, would be guilty of this kind of discrimination. Disparate treatment violates the plain meaning of Title VII.

Although the intention of Title VII was to create a level playing field by prohibiting all discrimination, given the entrenched prejudices of employers in the 1960s, expecting that bigotry would instantly vanish was futile. The statute would need to evolve, and it did.

When Title VII went into effect, employers could no longer engage in outwardly visible displays of discrimination. "Whites only" signs came down from windows and discrimination went underground where it was disguised but just as invidious. Instead of openly revealing prejudicial motives, employers hid them. Minority job applicants were simply rejected without comment or were found less qualified in some way. Or employers introduced job requirements that appeared merit based but were in fact pretexts for discrimination. Female applicants had to meet height, weight, and strength requirements that favored men. Southern blacks were given tests that favored better-educated whites.

---

[29] A 1972 law extended coverage of Title VII to federal, state, and local government employees, so today Title VII covers most workers. Workers at firms with fewer than 15 employees can sue under state and local civil rights laws or, for race discrimination, may seek remedy under the Civil Rights Act of 1866.

[30] U.S. Equal Employment Opportunity Commission, "Title VII of the Civil Rights Act of 1964 Charges: FY 1997–FY 2010," www.eeoc.gov/eeoc/statistics/enforcement/titlevii.cfm.

This kind of discrimination was hard to eradicate under the existing provisions of Title VII because employers would not admit a discriminatory motive and claimed that their job criteria were neutral and merit based. The flaw in Title VII was that it contained no weapon to fight *disparate impact*. Disparate impact exists where an employment policy is apparently neutral in its impact on all employees but, in fact, is not job related and prevents individuals in protected categories from being hired or from advancing.

To combat disparate impact, the court initially used a case-by-case judicial test for discrimination. First, the applicant or employee made a charge alleging bias. Then the employer had to set forth a reason why it was a *business necessity* to engage in the practice. Then the burden of proof shifted back to the employee to prove that the employer's reason was phony, which was frequently hard to do.[31] This back-and-forth dance in which each individual case was separately considered was awkward and time consuming for the courts and placed the difficult burden of proving the employer's secret motive on individual plaintiffs who lacked the legal resources of corporations. Some other way to fight hidden employer racism was needed. The Supreme Court would create it.

The *Griggs* Case

At the Duke Power Company steam-generating plant in Draper, North Carolina, workers had always been segregated by race. The plant was organized into five departments, and blacks were allowed to work only in the lowest-paying labor department. Whites hired in the labor department could advance to jobs in other departments, provided they had a high school diploma. Blacks could not advance, no matter how well educated.

When Title VII took effect, the company ended its policy of race discrimination. All jobs were opened to blacks. As had been the case with whites, black workers now needed a high school diploma to move up from the labor department to the coal-handling, operations, maintenance, or laboratory departments. Alternatively, they could take an intelligence test and a mechanical aptitude test, and if they scored at the level of an average high school graduate, they could meet the high school diploma requirement.

However, blacks in the area were less educated. Segregated black schools had been inferior. Black students from poor families were more likely to drop out early. The diploma requirement, despite being enforced in an evenhanded way, frustrated their ambitions. Instead of rejecting blacks for being black, Duke Power now rejected them for being unschooled. Black workers filed suit, alleging that the education and testing requirements were simply a different face of the old bigotry and were, in any case, unrelated to fitness to, for example, shovel coal in the coal-handling department.

In *Griggs v. Duke Power*, decided in 1971, the Supreme Court held that diploma requirements and tests that screened out blacks or other protected classes were illegal unless employers could show they were related to job performance or

disparate impact
Discrimination caused by policies that apply to everyone and seem neutral but have the effect of disadvantaging a protected group. Such policies are illegal unless strongly job related and indispensable to conduct of the business.

business necessity
A legal defense a company can use to fight a disparate impact charge. It must show the practice in question was job-related and essential. To rebut this defense, a plaintiff can show that another practice was equally good and less discriminatory.

---

[31] This sequence was set up in *McDonnell Douglas v. Green*, 411 U.S. 792 (1973).

justified by business necessity.[32] They were unlawful even if no discrimination was intended. The *Griggs* decision and the legal theory of disparate impact it created were necessary for Title VII to work. If employers had been permitted to use sinuous evasions and substitute proxies for direct racial bias, Title VII would have been ineffective.

In 1978 the EEOC defined illegal disparate impact for employers with a guideline known as the *80 percent rule.*

80 percent rule
The statistical test for disparate impact. The test is failed when, for example, blacks or women are selected at a rate less than 80 percent of the rate at which white male applicants are selected.

> A selection rate for any race, sex, or ethnic group which is less than four-fifths (4/5) or (eighty percent) of the rate for the group with the highest rate will generally be regarded . . . as evidence of adverse impact.[33]

This rule is met if a company has hired minorities at the rate of at least 80 percent of the rate at which it hires from the demographic group (usually white males) that provides most of its employees. If, for example, it hires 20 percent of all white applicants, it must then hire at least 16 percent (80 percent of 20 percent) of black applicants. If it hires less than 16 percent of blacks, this statistical evidence defines unlawful disparate impact. The company is now on the defensive. It must show that the employment practices it uses, such as tests or applicant screening criteria, are a business necessity. Using the business necessity defense, it must prove that the test or practice is "essential," and the need for it is "compelling."[34]

With the addition of the theory of disparate impact by the judiciary, Title VII had evolved beyond its original meaning and could be used to strike down a broader range of discrimination. Title VII finally gave blacks and others a potent legal mechanism to get the civil rights on the job that Congress had tried to give them during the Reconstruction era. In a sense, broken promises were repaired. There is little in Title VII that would have been needed if, a century before, the Supreme Court had given good-faith construction to Reconstruction era laws.

AFFIRMATIVE ACTION

affirmative action
Policies that seek out, encourage, and sometimes give preferential treatment to employees in groups protected by Title VII.

Affirmative action is a phrase describing a range of policies to seek out, encourage, and sometimes give preferential treatment to employees in the groups protected by Title VII. The broad use of affirmative action was rejected when Title VII was drafted and its congressional backers assured the business community that blacks and others would not have to be given preference over whites. Title VII was designed as a stop sign to end discrimination, not as a green light to engineer racially balanced workforces. Yet no sooner had President Lyndon Johnson signed it than civil rights groups argued that its philosophy of equal opportunity was too weak; blacks and others were so disadvantaged by past rejection that they lacked the seniority and credentials of whites. They could

---

[32] *Griggs v. Duke Power Co.,* 401 U.S. 424.

[33] U.S. Department of Labor, "Uniform Guidelines on Employee Selection Procedures," 43 FR 38295, August 25, 1978.

[34] Epstein, Forbidden Grounds, p. 212, citing *Williams v. Colorado Springs School District,* 641 F2d 835 (1981), at 842.

not compete equally in a merit system, and preferential treatment was needed to get justice.

Executive Order 11246

The origin of most affirmative action in corporations is Executive Order 11246, issued by President Johnson in 1965.[35] It requires all companies with federal contracts of $50,000 or more and 50 or more employees, criteria that include almost every Fortune 500 company, to have a written affirmative action plan. This plan must specify the policies, procedures, and actions being used to recruit minorities and women and eliminate discrimination.

Each company must analyze its workforce at every major location, using census data to learn if it is employing minorities and women in the same proportion as they are present in the area labor force. American Indians, Alaskan Natives, Asians, Native Hawaiians or other Pacific Islanders, blacks, Hispanics, or persons of "two or more races" are considered minorities. The analysis focuses on employment in 10 major job categories to see if, in each one, minorities and women are employed in the same proportion as they are present in the local population.[36] If protected groups are underrepresented, companies must set up goals and timetables for hiring, retention, and promotion.

Executive Order 11246 is enforced by the Office of Federal Contract Compliance Programs (OFCCP), an agency in the Department of Labor. The OFCCP, with one exception, does not establish rigid hiring goals for companies. The exception is in the construction industry, where, since 1980 it has mandated a goal of 6.9 percent females. In other industries, however, it requires contractors to set hiring goals and make a "good faith" effort to achieve them. Adequate progress is usually defined as a final hiring total that meets the 80 percent rule.

The OFCCP conducts zealous compliance reviews. It uses statistical tools to target companies where discrimination is most likely to be uncovered. Then, teams descend on a facility, looking around, interviewing employees and managers, and auditing all kinds of records from interview notes to payroll slips. It is common for inspections to uncover technical violations. They also uncover a surprising number of *systemic discrimination* cases, 77 in fiscal year 2009 involving 21,820 workers.[37] An example of such an offender is Tyson Foods. At a bacon plant in Texas it turned down 530 black and Caucasian applicants to favor Hispanics, at a packing plant in Illinois it rejected more than 750 women applicants in favor of men, and at a plant in Wisconsin it discriminated against Latino applicants.

systemic discrimination
A pattern or practice of individual acts or rules in a corporate culture that permits or condones discrimination.

---

[35] "Equal Employment Opportunity," 30 FR 12319, September 24, 1965.

[36] These job categories are executives and senior officials, first- and mid-level managers, professionals, technicians, sales workers, administrative support workers, craft workers, operatives, laborers and helpers, and service workers.

[37] Department of Labor, *Performance and Accountability Report FY 09* (Washington, DC: Department of Labor, 2009), p. 109.

THE SUPREME COURT CHANGES TITLE VII

From the beginning, affirmative action was controversial. Philosophically, it challenges the American Creed in several ways. It affronts the ideal of equality of opportunity by substituting equality of result. It affronts the ideal of achievement based on merit. And it affronts the ideal of individual rights before the law by substituting group preferences. When affirmative action first started, it posed more than a philosophical problem. Corporations were alarmed by its potential for generating lawsuits. If they failed to remedy race and sex imbalances in their workforces, they faced penalties for violating federal laws. If they used affirmative action to increase numbers of minorities and women, they feared reverse discrimination suits by white males.

Affirmative action was bound to provoke fierce legal challenges, and the Supreme Court used these attacks to read revolutionary changes into Title VII. The first high-profile challenge came from Allan Bakke, a white male denied admission to the medical school at the University of California at Davis. In the entering class, 16 places out of 100 had been reserved for minority students. Bakke argued that he was better qualified than some minority students admitted and he had suffered illegal race discrimination under Title VII because he was white. In *Regents of the University of California v. Bakke*, the Supreme Court ruled in his favor. In a muddled, divided, and verbose opinion, the justices forbade strict quotas. Yet they also held that race and ethnicity could be one factor considered in admissions. This kept affirmative action alive but failed to resolve the dilemma of employers, who still feared reverse discrimination lawsuits.

Then a second case arose from a Kaiser Aluminum and Chemical Corporation plant in Louisiana. The Kaiser plant was near New Orleans where 39 percent of the workforce was black. Few blacks worked at the plant before passage of Title VII, and even with it, by 1974, only 18 percent of the plant's workers were black. Moreover, less than 2 percent of skilled crafts workers were black because Kaiser required previous craft experience and seniority. Blacks had little of either since crafts unions excluded them. Kaiser had federal contracts and, to comply with Executive Order 11246, it adopted an affirmative action plan in 1974 to raise percentages of black workers. One goal was to bring blacks into skilled craft positions, so the plan reserved 50 percent of crafts-training openings for them. This was clearly a race-based quota.

In 1974 a white laboratory analyst, Brian Weber, who had worked at Kaiser for 10 years, applied for a crafts-training program that would place him in a more skilled job and substantially raise his yearly pay. To select the trainees, Kaiser set up dual seniority ladders—one for blacks and another for whites. Names were picked alternately in descending order from the top of each ladder, starting with the black ladder, until positions were filled, with the result that seven blacks and six whites were chosen. Weber was too low on the white ladder and was not selected, whereas two blacks with less seniority than Weber were chosen (see Figure 17.1). This was a classic case of reverse discrimination.

FIGURE 17.1

Selection of Crafts Trainees at Kaiser

Kaiser and the union selected 13 crafts trainees. All candidates met minimum qualifications, but black applicants number 6 and 7 had less seniority than whites number 7, 8, and 9.

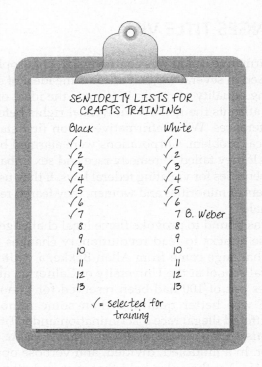

SENIORITY LISTS FOR
CRAFTS TRAINING

Black	White
✓1	✓1
✓2	✓2
✓3	✓3
✓4	✓4
✓5	✓5
✓6	✓6
✓7	7 B. Weber
8	8
9	9
10	10
11	11
12	12
13	13

✓ = selected for training

Weber brought suit, claiming that the selection procedure violated the clear language in Title VII that prohibited making employment decisions based on race. He claimed that his Fourteenth Amendment right to equal treatment under the law had been abridged. Justice William J. Brennan delivered the opinion of the Court in 1979 in *United Steelworkers of America v. Weber,* ruling that Kaiser's affirmative action plan embodied the "spirit of the law," which was to overcome the effects of past discrimination against blacks.[38]

The *Weber* decision added an entirely new meaning to Title VII. Henceforth, Title VII no longer stood guard over a neutral playing field. Now, it permitted the very thing its drafters assured the nation it would not do—it permitted race-conscious preferential treatment for members of protected groups. A strong dissent in *Weber* by future Chief Justice William Rehnquist attacked the majority for adding this meaning to Title VII in contravention of its language, which clearly forbade *all* race discrimination, including that against whites. He referred to Brennan's opinion as "a tour de force reminiscent not of jurists such as Hale, Holmes, or Hughes, but of escape artists such as Houdini."[39]

The *Weber* case squarely raised the issue of reverse discrimination and confirmed that affirmative action plans were legal even if they adversely affected whites. After *Weber,* companies no longer worried about lawsuits by angry white workers. Affirmative action spread.

---

[38] *United Steelworkers of America v. Weber,* 443 U.S. 193.

[39] 443 U.S. 222..

In the decade after *Weber* a liberal majority on the Court expanded the boundaries of affirmative action and upheld it against all challenges.[40] Throughout, a minority of conservative justices vigorously dissented. And by the late 1980s a conservative bloc of five justices formed to dominate the liberals on affirmative action cases. As cases came to the court, this group whittled away at race-conscious preferences, making affirmative action more difficult to carry out. Advocates of the policy were infuriated, and soon Congress sent a clear message to the Supreme Court in the Civil Rights Act of 1991. This statute reversed several decisions and restored broader grounds for affirmative action.

Since 1991, through retirements and appointments, a conservative majority with a jaundiced view of affirmative action has abided. Yet the policy survives every major test. In *Adarand v. Peña*, a cobbled-together majority saved the day by setting up a "strict scrutiny" test that made affirmative action more difficult to justify.[41] In *Grutter v. Bollinger*, a bare five-to-four majority agreed that the University of Michigan Law School's affirmative action program met this test.[42] The future is uncertain, but if the conservative bloc retains its strength, a decision that racial preferences in employment violate the Equal Protection Clause in the Fourteenth Amendment is likely. And that will be the end of it.

The Affirmative Action Debate

The legal debate about affirmative action parallels a broader debate in society. This debate revolves around three basic ethical considerations.

First, there are *utilitarian* considerations. Utilitarian ethics require calculations about the overall benefit to society, as opposed to the costs, of affirmative action. Advocates argue that preferential treatment policies benefit everyone by making fuller use of talent. Critics say that affirmative action has been ineffective or that its meager benefits are outweighed by the fairness problems it raises.

Research on the effectiveness of affirmative action is mixed, but suggests that, overall, it works. A recent study of 708 companies over 31 years found that after they set up a plan "the odds for [the presence of] white men in management decline by 8 percent; the odds for white women rise by 9 percent; and the odds for black men rise by 4 percent."[43] However, such statistics cannot resolve the utilitarian argument about whether affirmative action, on the whole, is a net benefit or cost to society.

Second, ethical theories of *justice* raise questions about the ultimate fairness of affirmative action. Norms of distributive justice require that fair criteria be used to assign benefits and burdens. It is widely believed that economic rewards should

---

[40] See, for example, *Local 28 v. EEOC*, 478 U.S. 421 (1986) and *United States v. Paradise*, 480 U.S. 149 (1987) upholding hiring quotas for blacks; and *Johnson v. Transportation Agency, Santa Clara County, California*, 480 U.S. 616 (1987) permitting affirmative action to increase the percentages of women in skilled crafts.

[41] *Adarand v. Peña*, 515 U.S. 200 (1995).

[42] *Grutter v. Bollinger*, 539 U.S. 306 (2003).

[43] Alexandra Kalev, Frank Dobbin, and Erin Kelly, "Best Practices or Best Guesses? Assessing the Efficacy of Corporate Affirmative Action and Diversity Policies," *American Sociological Review*, August 2006, p. 604.

be distributed based on merit, not on race, ethnicity, or sex. On the other hand, norms of compensatory justice require that payment be made to compensate for past wrongs. Past and current discrimination has handicapped women and minorities and placed them at a disadvantage. Thus, discrimination in their favor may be justified to compensate for past deprivation. In 1963 President Lyndon Johnson used a colorful analogy to make this point.

> Imagine a 100-yard dash in which one of the two runners has his legs shackled together. He has progressed 10 yards, while the unshackled runner has gone 50 yards. How do they rectify the situation? Do they merely remove the shackles and allow the race to proceed? Then they could say that "equal opportunity" now prevailed. But one of the runners would still be 40 yards ahead of the other. Would it not be the better part of justice to allow the previously shackled runner to make up the 40-yard gap or to start the race all over again?[44]

With affirmative action, however, the penalty for past injustices falls on the current generation of white males—the least racist of any generation. Retributive justice requires that punishment be proportional to the crime committed. By what proof can it be shown that this generation should inherit the guilt of past generations?

And third, affirmative action may be debated in light of ethical theories of *rights*. Advocates of affirmative action argue that it is appropriate to mint a new civil right for women and minorities, the right to preferential treatment, and to exercise it until equality prevails. Discrimination in favor of protected groups is benevolent of intention, unlike the evil race discrimination of bigoted whites in the past. Opponents of the right to preferences argue that they destroy a more fundamental right—the right of all individuals to equal treatment before the law. Affirmative action can result in rewards being taken from persons who did not discriminate and given to persons who suffered no discrimination.

There is no easy solution to the contradictory appeals of these ethical arguments. Affirmative action is a complex policy with important benefits but also highly visible drawbacks. As a broad public policy, it is aging and past its prime.

WOMEN AT WORK

Around the world more women work than ever before. In 2009 there were 1.3 billion women in a global labor force of 3.2 billion, making them 40 percent of the total. Everywhere they face social and cultural barriers to economic equality with men. These barriers are wearing away now, but slowly.

Women participate in paid labor at a lower rate than men. Worldwide only 52 percent of females work outside the home compared with 78 percent of males.[45]

[44] Quoted in Robert A. Fullinwider, *The Reverse Discrimination Debate: A Moral and Legal Analysis* (Totowa, NJ: Rowman and Littlefield, 1980), p. 95.
[45] International Labour Office, *Women in Labor Markets: Measuring Progress and Identifying Challenges* (Geneva: ILO, March 2010), tables 2A and 2B. Figures are for 2009.

Other Key Employment Discrimination Laws

Besides **Title** VII of the Civil Rights Act of 1964 and Executive Order 11246, other laws protect Americans from discrimination. They include the following, set forth in the order of their enactment.

The Civil Rights Act of 1866 was passed after the Civil War to protect the employment rights of freed slaves. It provides that "All persons . . . shall have the same right . . . to make and enforce contracts . . . as is enjoyed by white citizens."[46] Soon after its passage, the Supreme Court narrowly interpreted it to protect only state employees. For nearly a century, it remained on the books as an emasculated law, but it was revived by the Supreme Court in 1968.[47] Since then, it has been widely used by civil rights attorneys. It protects millions of workers in firms with fewer than 15 employees against all forms of racial discrimination in employment. Employees of such small firms are not covered by Title VII.

The Equal Pay Act of 1963 prohibits pay differentials between male and female employees with equal or substantially equal duties in similar working conditions. It does not override pay differences that stem from legitimate seniority or merit systems. It also covers nonwage benefits.

The Age Discrimination in Employment Act of 1967 protects people over age 40. After that age, it is illegal to discriminate against people in hiring and job decisions because of their age. As the workforce ages, age bias complaints are the fastest-growing kind of discrimination charge. The average charge is brought by a white male in his fifties, dismissed in corporate downsizing, believing that his age was the reason.

The Pregnancy Discrimination Act of 1978 prohibits employment discrimination based on pregnancy, childbirth, or related medical conditions. If a woman can still work, she cannot be made to resign or go on leave for any pregnancy-related condition, including having an abortion. If she is temporarily unable to perform her regular duties, the employer must try modifying her work assignments or grant leave with or without pay.

The Americans with Disabilities Act of 1990 protects workers with mental and physical impairments, including those with AIDS, from job discrimination and extends to them the protections granted to women and ethnic, racial, and religious minorities in Title VII. In interviews, employers can ask only about the ability to do specific work. Companies must make "reasonable accommodations" for disabled workers, including, for instance, provision of devices that allow deaf workers to communicate visually and readers for blind workers. Companies must also try to accommodate persons with mental illnesses such as major depression, manic depression, schizophrenia, and obsessive compulsive disorder. For example, employers have been required to install soundproofing and set up room dividers for schizophrenic workers who have heightened sensitivity to noise and visual distractions. However, companies are not required to make accommodations imposing an "undue burden" on the business.

The *Genetic Information Nondiscrimination Act of 2008* makes it illegal to discriminate against applicants or employees or to make decisions about employees based on genetic information. Insurance companies cannot use such information regarding health insurance eligibility, coverage, or premiums. It is an unusual law. Every other antidiscrimination statute was passed to stop a long history of bias. This law is preemptive; there is almost no record of genetic information discrimination.[48] It was passed because employers and insurers can now know who is at risk for diseases such as breast cancer, sickle cell anemia, or Huntington's Disease. There are now more than 1,000 genetic tests. Congress intended to prevent genetic risk discrimination before it began.

---

[46] 42 U.S.C. Sec. 1981, rev. stat. 1977.

[47] *Jones v. Alfred H. Mayer Co.*, 392 U.S. 409 (1968). This case overturned the *Civil Rights Cases* of 1883.

[48] Jessica L. Roberts, "Preempting Discrimination: Lessons from the Genetic Information Nondiscrimination Act," *Vanderbilt Law Review,* March 2010.

Participation rates are highest in the least-developed countries, where poverty pushes women into paid labor. The rate averages 64 percent in East Asia and 60 percent in Sub-Saharan Africa, where Rwanda and Tanzania have the world's highest rates at 86 percent each.[49] At 59 percent the United States has a relatively high participation rate for a developed nation. Among these the highest rate is New Zealand's 62 percent.

The lowest rates are in the Middle East and North Africa, where patriarchal religious and cultural values discourage women from paid employment. In Oman, only 23 percent of women enter the labor force, in Egypt and Jordan, only 22 percent. Saudi Arabia, at 21 percent, has the world's lowest participation rate. The main barrier in that country is a requirement, enforced by moral police, that women be segregated from men to prevent immorality. The Prophet Muhammad is quoted as saying, "A man is not secluded with a woman but that Satan is the third party to them." Women cannot drive to work. They cannot get on elevators with unrelated men. Employers must set up separate rooms for them. At a three-story mall in Riyadh women work as salespersons, but they are confined to a single floor for women shoppers. The inefficiencies of such rules for employers reduce women's access to the labor market.

A supermarket in Riyadh recently hired 16 women as cashiers. They worked at their registers draped in concealing black abayas with face veils, separated from male cashiers by a glass divider. Only women and families could go through their lines. Nevertheless, a committee of Islamic scholars issued a fatwa, or an official ruling that: "It is not permitted for a Muslim woman to work in a mixed environment with men who are not related to them."[50]

Wherever women work, they are more likely than men to be in low-productivity jobs in agriculture and services and to be paid less, even in the same jobs as men. They are more likely to be unemployed. And they are less likely to reach positions of high power, status, and income. Their subordination is caused by cultural values that give higher status to men, leading to women getting less education, owning less land, having fewer legal rights, and facing unequal distribution of household responsibilities.

Gender Attitudes at Work

Historically, men and women have been socialized into distinct sex roles. Men were traditionally thought to be aggressive, forceful, logical, self-reliant, and dominant; they were the warriors and breadwinners. Women were objects of sexual desire and homemakers; they were expected to be kind, helpful, submissive, and emotional. For centuries, these stereotypes prevailed. With the rise of organizations they were carried from family and social life into the modern workplace, where they defined male–female relationships.

[49] Participation rate figures in this section are from World Bank, *World Development Indicators 2010* (Washington, DC: International Bank for Reconstruction and Development, April 2010), table 2.2.
[50] Rima al-Mukhtar, "Saudi Fatwa Bans Women from Working as Supermarket Cashiers," *Arab News,* November 1, 2010, at www.arabnews.com.

In the 1960s, however, an international women's movement stood up to challenge male domination. Arguing that women could do men's jobs, its advocates attacked cultural impediments to equality. Because of this movement, two competing values began to clash in the workplace. The feminist perspective asserted that women were entitled to the same jobs, rights, ambitions, and status achievements as men. Yet deeply rooted traditional sex-role stereotypes remained. Men who believed in them still thought women were too emotional to manage well; lacked ambition, logic, and toughness; and could not sustain career drive because of family obligations.

In the United States, as in much of the developed world, belief in the traditional stereotype has eroded but proves durable. In 1965 only 27 percent of male executives in a survey said they "would feel comfortable working for a woman." Twenty years later, when the survey was given again, that number rose to 47 percent. And given again after passage of still another 20 years, it rose further to 71 percent.[51] Thus, in 2005 almost a third of the men still felt uneasy about a female boss. The persistence of such attitudes shapes work environments that slight and hinder women in many ways.

Subtle Discrimination

Most workplace cultures are based on masculine values, and women can find them difficult to navigate. For one thing, many men still expect women to behave according to traditional male–female stereotypes. Men holding these attitudes are conditioned to see women in the role of mothers, lovers, wives, or daughters; they consciously or unconsciously expect female co-workers to act similarly. One female executive explains how this hurts women.

> Women are put into this box that I call the four-H club. What the four H's stand for are a woman's hair, hips, hemline, and husband. You rarely hear any of these for a man—and of course you expect his wife to be at home. So there's this unconscious bias stuff swimming around when people are interviewing others for positions. They think to themselves, "This woman can't travel," or "She's married, she's not going to want to move," or "She's going to want to have kids so therefore won't be available."[52]

In blue-collar settings, sexism can be more blatant; some men openly express biases. In managerial settings, it is usually subtle, even unintentional. Men may assume that women are secretaries. One woman CEO, invited to participate in a meeting of business and political leaders in Washington, describes being repeatedly skipped over in the conversation because the men at the table assumed she was an office assistant. "Happens all the time," she noted.[53] Men also discount or

---

[51] Dawn S. Carlson, K. Michele Kacmar, and Dwayne Whitten, "What Men Think They Know about Executive Women," *Harvard Business Review,* September 2006, p. 28.

[52] Michele Coleman Mayes, senior vice president, Allstate Corp., quoted in "View From the Top," *The Wall Street Journal,* November 19, 2007, p. R6.

[53] Carol Bartz, former CEO of Autodesk, quoted in Julie Creswell, "How Suite It Isn't: A Dearth of Female Bosses," *The New York Times,* December 17, 2006, sec. 3, p. 1.

ignore women's ideas. They make women uncomfortable with locker-room humor and macho behavior.

> EMC Corp. sells software and data-storage devices to corporations. It favors former college athletes in its sales force, but there are some women. Sales tactics are very aggressive. Over time a sales culture of masculine recreation and entertainment with clients formed. The entertainment included frequent trips to strip clubs. One saleswoman was told that she was unqualified to work on a big Motorola account because she did not "smoke, drink, swear, hunt, fish and tolerate strip clubs."[54]

Masculine cultures underlie many kinds of differential treatment. The norms in these cultures are not openly sexist. They can be nearly invisible, manifest only as practices that seem innocent and neutral. The problems they cause are often unintended. One main problem for women is the traditional career path. According to one study, men typically rise in a smooth trajectory, making especially rapid progress in their thirties. Their success in achieving promotions and their rising status is based on uninterrupted hard work. Women, on the other hand, achieve progress roughly equal to men's in their twenties, but face a deepening conflict in their thirties, the peak childbearing and child-rearing years. Many women interrupt their progress with leaves that average 1.2 years.[55] Throughout their careers, women also do more of the routine work in the home than men.

> At one global retailing corporation dominated by men in the top ranks, a culture of flexible operations had grown up in which meetings were held spontaneously, often at the last minute or late in the day. Important decisions were made quickly. This culture was highly successful because it facilitated fast reaction to markets and minimized bureaucratic inefficiencies. However, it was hard on women who bore heavier responsibilities for households and children than the men. When a meeting suddenly was called for the early evening, some women could not stay, and if they did not they were left out of critical decisions and unable to defend their turf.[56]

Success in this kind of workaholic atmosphere requires the ambitious to invest in face time at the office and not divide their time with responsibilities away from work. Thus, flexible working hours and telecommuting, often introduced for working mothers, may fail because they violate workplace norms. At one firm telecommuting was "jokingly referred to as 'Mom's day off,'" and women were afraid to sign up for fear of career damage.[57]

Deborah Tannen studied the linguistic styles of men and women at work.[58] According to Tannen, men and women learn different ways of speaking in

---

[54] Quoted in William M. Bulkeley, "A Data-Storage Titan Confronts Bias Claims," *The Wall Street Journal*," September 12, 2007, p. A16.

[55] Sylvia Ann Hewlett and Carolyn Buck Luce, "Off-Ramps and On-Ramps: Keeping Talented Women on the Road to Success," *Harvard Business Review*, March 2005, p. 46.

[56] Debra E. Meyerson and Joyce K. Fletcher," "A Modest Manifesto for Shattering the Glass Ceiling," *Harvard Business Review*, January–February 2000, pp. 128–29.

[57] Louise Marie Roth, "Women on Wall Street: Despite Diversity Measures, Wall Street Remains Vulnerable to Sex Discrimination Charges," *Academy of Management Perspectives*, February 2007, p. 31.

[58] Deborah Tannen, "The Power of Talk: Who Gets Heard and Why," *Harvard Business Review*, September–October 1995.

childhood. Boys are taught by peers and cultural cues to use words in ways that build status and emphasize power over other boys. Girls, on the other hand, use language to build rapport and empathy with their playmates. Unlike boys, girls will ostracize a playmate who brags and asserts superiority in a group.

Later in life, these conversation styles carry over into the workplace, where they can place women at a disadvantage. In meetings, women may be reluctant to interrupt or criticize the ideas of another, whereas men push themselves into the conversation and engage in ritual challenges over the validity of ideas. Men hear women make self-effacing or apologetic remarks and conclude that they lack self-confidence. Tannen thinks that the female linguistic style makes it harder to make a firm impression in male-dominated groups, so women are more often interrupted in meetings and their ideas may be pushed aside. Tannen recommends demonstrative speech, but many women report that men can react negatively to an "unfeminine," assertive tone. A former prime minister of Canada explains:

> I don't have a traditionally female way of speaking . . . I'm quite assertive. If I didn't speak the way I do, I wouldn't have been seen as a leader. But my way of speaking may have grated on people who were not used to hearing it from a woman. It was the right way for a leader to speak, but it wasn't the right way for a woman to speak.[59]

Studies also suggest some hesitance of women in management to engage in competition, show ambition, or negotiate for salary.[60] And they seem to get a slow start. One study of 4,100 MBA graduates from elite universities found that the women lagged behind the men at every stage of their careers. The reason was that they started at lower-level positions, having less responsibility and making on average $4,600 less in their first salary. These "fate-sealing first jobs" set the stage for long-term shortfall.[61] The same study also found that mentoring was less beneficial to these women. Although they received more mentoring than men, their mentors had lower status than those assigned to men and the men's mentors more often went beyond advising them and used their influence to advance them. As a result, the men were more rapidly promoted.

Sexual Harassment

sexual harassment Annoying or persecuting behavior in the workplace that asserts power over a person because of their sexual identity. It is illegal under Title VII of the Civil Rights Act of 1964.

Many women experience *sexual harassment* at some time in their careers. In a landmark book, *Sexual Shakedown*, Lin Farley defined this form of harassment as "unsolicited nonreciprocal male behavior that asserts a woman's sex role over her function as a worker."[62] Various forms of harassment exist, including women harassing men and same-sex harassment; however, the strong, background presence

[59] Kim Cameron, quoted in Alice H. Eagly and Linda L. Carli, "Women and the Labyrinth of Leadership," *Harvard Business Review,* September 2007, pp. 65–66.

[60] See, for example, Uri Gneezy et al., "Performance in Competitive Environments: Gender Differences," *Quarterly Journal of Economics,* August 2003; Anna Fels, "Do Women Lack Ambition?" *Harvard Business Review,* April 2004; and Linda Babcock and Sara Lashever, *Women Don't Ask: Negotiation and the Gender Divide* (Princeton, NJ: Princeton University Press, 2003).

[61] Nancy M. Carter and Christine Silva, "Women in Management: Delusions of Progress," *Harvard Business Review,* March 2010, p. 21.

[62] Lin Farley, *Sexual Shakedown* (New York: McGraw-Hill, 1978), pp. 14–15.

of gender stereotypes assures that the major workplace problem is sexual harassment of women by men.

Sexual harassment of women encompasses a wide range of behaviors. It can be very subtle, as when older men treat younger women like daughters, an approach that diminishes the authority of a female manager. More direct forms of harassment are staring, touching, joking, and gratuitous discussions of sex. The most serious forms include demands for sexual favors or physical assaults.

Men are motivated to harass by gender distinctions. Some harassment is based on romantic motives, but this is uncommon. More often it is intended to reinforce male power and status in work settings. Hostile, intimidating behavior based on sex-role distinctions is designed to frighten or humiliate a woman, putting her in the stereotyped role of submissive female, thereby subordinating her. The message is, "You're only a woman, that's the way I see you. And at that level you're vulnerable to me and any man."[63]

Research by social psychologist Jennifer Berdahl suggests that the women most likely to be harassed are those that violate traditional gender ideals by exhibiting masculine behaviors. Women who have more typically feminine behaviors are less likely targets.[64] According to Berdahl, men use sex-based harassment to maintain their social status, which is based on being male. In every society, and in male-dominated corporate cultures, "being male is associated with higher status than being female."[65] Maintaining social status is a deep drive because such status is the basis for self-esteem, income, influence, and job security.

quid pro quo
A situation, defined as illegal, when submission to sexual activity is required to get or keep a job.

hostile environment
A situation, defined as illegal, where sexually offensive conduct is pervasive in a workplace, making work unreasonably difficult for an affected individual.

Men use sex-based harassment to define and enforce gender distinctions, doing so to defend against threats to their status by women who display masculine qualities. When, for example, a woman becomes an assertive leader, a man may devalue her to subordinate female status by calling her a "bitch." A woman in a traditionally male job may threaten men who define their status by their ability to do strenuous or skilled labor. Male co-workers may try to reassert their superior male status by sex-based intimidation as with a woman at a Chrysler plant who found crude phalluses made of rubber sealant coming down the assembly line to her station.[66] Similar race- or ethnicity-based harassment is used to defend white status against the perceived incursions of minority workers.

In 1980 the EEOC issued guidelines (see Figure 17.2) making sexual harassment a form of sex discrimination under Title VII. The guidelines define two situations where harassment is illegal. One is the *quid pro quo,* when submission to sexual activity is required to get or keep a job. The other is a *hostile environment,* where sexually offensive conduct is so pervasive that it becomes unreasonably difficult to work.

[63] Cynthia Cockburn, *In the Way of Women: Men's Resistance to Sex Equality in Organizations* (Ithaca, NY: ILR Press, 1991), p. 142.

[64] Jennifer L. Berdahl, "The Sexual Harassment of Uppity Women," *Journal of Applied Psychology 92,* no. 2 (2007), p. 433.

[65] Jennifer L. Berdahl, "Harassment Based on Sex: Protecting Social Status in the Context of Gender Hierarchy," *Academy of Management Review,* April 2007, p. 645.

[66] *Donnie M. Wilson v. Chrysler Corporation,* 172 F.3d 500 (1999).

FIGURE 17.2
The EEOC
Guidelines
on Sexual
Harassment

Source: 29 CFR
1604.11(a).

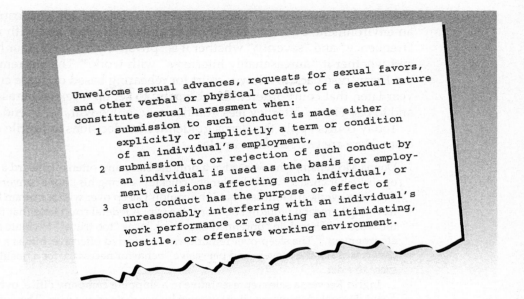

Unwelcome sexual advances, requests for sexual favors,
and other verbal or physical conduct of a sexual nature
constitute sexual harassment when:
1 submission to such conduct is made either
   explicitly or implicitly a term or condition
   of an individual's employment,
2 submission to or rejection of such conduct by
   an individual is used as the basis for employment decisions affecting such individual, or
3 such conduct has the purpose or effect of
   unreasonably interfering with an individual's
   work performance or creating an intimidating,
   hostile, or offensive working environment.

While the definition of *quid pro quo* harassment was straightforward, the courts struggled to clarify the range of conduct that created a hostile environment. However, in 1993 the Supreme Court set up a definitive test. Teresa Harris, a manager in a Nashville company that rented forklifts, filed an EEOC complaint about the behavior of its president, Charles Hardy. Over several years, Hardy had engaged in a pattern of vulgar and demeaning behavior that targeted Harris as a woman. He made derogatory remarks such as "You're a woman, what do you know?" and "We need a man as the rental manager." He made her serve coffee in meetings. He asked Harris and other female employees to fish coins out of his front pants pockets and sometimes threw objects on the floor, asking the women to pick them up while he commented on their breasts and clothing. He proposed negotiating Harris' raise at a Holiday Inn and suggested she try giving sexual favors to get forklift rentals. When Harris complained and threatened to quit, Hardy apologized and she stayed, but his boorishness resumed.

Other women at the company testified that Hardy's behavior was all part of a ribald, joking atmosphere that everyone understood and enjoyed. Did Forklift Systems contain a hostile working environment? A lower court did not think so, ruling that although it was a close call and Hardy was a vulgar man, there was no proof his conduct created a situation so intimidating that it interfered with Harris' ability to do her job.[67] However, when the case reached the Supreme Court, the justices created new criteria for defining a hostile environment.

In *Harris v. Forklift Systems*, they held that the guideline was whether sexual harassment created "an environment that a reasonable person would find hostile

[67] *Harris v. Forklift Systems, Inc.*, No. 3-89-0557 (M.D. Tenn. 1990).

or abusive." There was no "mathematically precise test" for what constituted such an environment, but harassing conduct should be examined with respect to its "frequency" and "severity," whether it is "physically threatening or humiliating," and whether it "unreasonably interferes" with work.[68] The Supreme Court sent the *Harris* case back to a lower court for rehearing based on these criteria, and, a year later, that court ordered the company to set up a sexual harassment policy and to pay Harris' attorney fees. It ultimately settled with her to end the case.

Today courts apply the *Harris* guidelines for decisions in hostile environment cases. Here are two recent examples.

> Donna McGullam, who worked at a printing company, often overheard a salesman opposite her cubicle wall call women "chickies" during his phone conversations. Once she overheard him say that if he couldn't sleep over with a woman he was traveling to meet it wouldn't be worth the trip. A federal court held that the use of the word *chickies* while "unrefined or uncivil," was "too trivial" to create a hostile environment.[69] The sleep-over remark was considered offensive, but as a sole incident it was not the "severe and pervasive" behavior necessary for a hostile environment to exist.

> Ingrid Reeves, a sales representative in a shipping company office, overheard frequent derogatory remarks about women by her male co-workers. They used derogatory terms such as *bitch* and crudely discussed female anatomy. Each morning the office radio was on for a show filled with sexual jokes and degrading language. When the woman complained, she was told to wear earplugs or "to learn to ignore it." A federal appeals court held that while "Title VII is not a civility code" the behavior, taken "cumulatively," was sufficient to create a hostile environment, "a workplace that exposed [the woman] to disadvantageous terms or conditions of employment to which members of the other sex were not exposed."[70]

After the *Harris* decision, the Supreme Court expanded the liability of corporations for sexual harassment, making them liable for the actions of their employees.[71] They can escape this liability only if management proves it tried hard to prevent and remedy harassment and, in addition, that the aggrieved employee neglected to make a complaint.[72] Now, most companies have formal policies prohibiting sexual harassment and set up formal complaint channels.

Occupational Segregation

Women are more likely to work in some jobs than others. Within corporations and in the economy as a whole, traditionally female jobs generally are lower in status and pay than typically male jobs. Women also have less occupational diversity than do men.

Fifty years ago, in the 1960s, two-thirds of women worked in clerical, sales, or low-level service occupations such as domestic worker. Another 15 percent

---

[68] *Harris v. Forklift Systems, Inc.,* 510 U.S. 17 (1993).

[69] *Donna L. McGullam v. Cedar Graphics,* 609 F.3d 70 (2010).

[70] *Ingrid Reeves v. C. H. Robinson Worldwide,* 594 F.3d 798 (2010), at 813.

[71] See *Burlington Industries v. Ellerth,* 524 U.S. 742 (1998); and *Faragher v. City of Boca Raton,* 524 U.S. 775 (1998).

[72] See *Pennsylvania State Police v. Suders,* 124 S. Ct. 2342 (2004).

**TABLE 17.1
The Top and
Bottom 10
Occupations
in Percentages
of Women**

Source: Department
of Labor, *Women in
the Labor Force: A
Databook* (Washington,
DC: Bureau of Labor
Statistics, December
2010), table 11.

Highest Percentage of Women*		Lowest Percentage of Women*	
Preschool and kindergarten teachers	97.8%	Brick and stone masons	0.1%
Dental assistants	97.6	Roofers	0.5
Secretaries and administrative assistants	96.8	Small engine mechanics	0.5
Dental hygienists	96.6	Cement masons	0.6
Speech language pathologists	95.8	Loggers	0.7
Child care workers	95.0	Air-conditioning mechanics	0.7
Bookkeepers	92.2	Diesel mechanics	0.8
Typists	92.2	Tool and die makers	0.8
Registered nurses	92.0	Crane and tower operators	1.1
Teacher assistants	91.5	Pipelayers and steamfitters	1.5

*Refers to women as a percentage of all workers in the specific occupation for occupations with more than 50,000 workers in 2009.

worked in the professions, mainly as teachers and nurses. Since then, women have entered nontraditional occupations. They flow most freely into growing occupations where demand for labor reduces barriers to entry, including sex discrimination. They have moved in large numbers into management positions in service industries becoming, for example, 70 percent of managers in health care organizations. They are now 57 percent of the workforce in financial occupations, and 58 percent in professional occupations. Because jobs in the goods-producing sector have not been expanding since the 1960s, women have had far less success moving into blue-collar occupations. They are only 2.6 percent of construction workers and 4.2 percent of maintenance and repair occupations.

Table 17.1 shows specific occupations with the largest and smallest percentages of women. The 10 female-dominated job categories on the left have the largest ratio of women to men. The 10 jobs on the right are the least feminized among 93 traditionally male occupations in manufacturing, construction, and precision craft work tracked by the Bureau of Labor Statistics. Of these, 53 occupations, or 57 percent, have fewer than 5 percent women.[73] Although women move into these nontraditional occupations, they do so in very small numbers.

About 5.8 million women work in management occupations, where they are 37 percent of all managers. Yet they have not moved into the highest-paying, most prestigious positions in comparable numbers. Within all corporations women are only 25 percent of chief executives and 30 percent of general managers. However, even this proportionately low upper-echelon presence falls precipitously within the aristocracies of the Fortune 500. There, in 2010, women were only 15.7 percent of directors, 7.6 percent of officers in the top-five highest-paying positions, and 2.6 percent of CEOs.[74]

glass ceiling
An invisible
barrier of sex
discrimination
thwarting the
advance of
women to top
corporate
positions.

These numbers lead some to say that women have hit a *glass ceiling*, or an invisible barrier of sex discrimination thwarting career advancement to the highest

[73] These and other occupational percentages are from Department of Labor, *Women in the Labor Force: A Databook* (Washington, DC: Bureau of Labor Statistics, December 2010), table 11, pp. 205–11.
[74] Catalyst, "U.S. Women in Business," December 2010, at www.catalyst.org.

levels. Although the image of a glass ceiling is now conventional, to the extent it implies a single barrier stopping women's promotion to the highest levels, it is misleading. In fact, the low representation of women at the top is the cumulative result of a series of abrasions, impediments, and disadvantages that complicate women's careers from the beginning. It has been suggested that the metaphor of a glass ceiling should be replaced by that of a labyrinth, or a "complex journey toward a goal" filled with twists, turns, blind alleys, and obstacles in which "the odds are stacked higher against women with each step."[75]

Compensation

Women earn less than men; however, the gap is narrowing. Before the Equal Pay Act of 1963, newspapers openly ran help-wanted ads with separate male and female pay scales for identical jobs, and in that year, across all occupations, the average woman earned only 59 cents for every dollar earned by a man. Since passage of the Equal Pay Act, which forbids pay differences based on sex, the gap has steadily narrowed. By 2010 women earned 81.4 cents for every dollar earned by a man.[76]

As the gap has narrowed, women's earnings have steadily grown, while men's have stagnated. Figure 17.3 shows the long-term trend in average weekly earnings in all occupations for both men and women. Adjusted for inflation, men's earnings in 2010 were only $9 a week more than they were 31 years ago, while women made $161 a week more, an increase of 32 percent. An underlying factor that explains the better fortune of women is long-term structural change in the

FIGURE 17.3
The Narrowing Gap in Weekly Earnings

Source: U.S. Department of Labor, *Highlights of Women's Earnings in 2009* (Bureau of Labor Statistics, June 2010), tables 12 and 13.

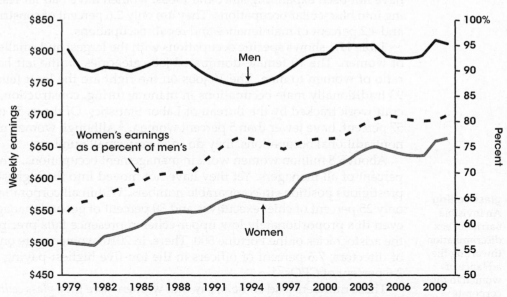

Note: Earnings trend lines represent median weekly earnings of full-time wage and salary workers over 16 years old between 1979 and 2009. Trend lines for men and women are in current (2009) dollars.

[75] Eagly and Carli, "Women and the Labyrinth of Leadership," pp. 64–65.

[76] Bureau of Labor Statistics, "Usual Weekly Earnings of Wage and Salary Workers," *Economic News Release,* October 19, 2010, table 2. The figure is for third quarter 2010.

economy. Women hold a higher percentage of jobs in rapidly growing service occupations, while men predominate in static manufacturing and construction sectors, which lack job growth. Other factors are gains in women's educational levels
and their progress toward equal opportunity because of new laws and ebbing
sexism. Although slowly closing, the gender wage gap is persistent. There are
several reasons.

First, occupational segregation places many women in female-dominated
occupations that tend to be lower paying than male-dominated ones. Women
continue to choose these female-dominated occupations because they see other
women in them, because cultural stereotyping feminizes certain occupational
roles, because some traditionally female jobs better accommodate career interrup-
tions, and because barriers to entry are low.

Second, women pay a heavy earnings penalty for childbearing and child rear-
ing, activities that interrupt careers. Because women in their twenties and thirties
often leave work, employers sometimes hesitate to invest heavily in training them,
their seniority lags, and men leap ahead. The statistic that women now make 81.4
percent of men's earnings is based on comparisons of earnings for men and
women working full time for a year. It does not account for women who work
only part time or part of the year. An analysis of the actual earnings histories for a
group of 2,826 similar men and women aged 26 to 59 over 15 years revealed that
the women made only 38 percent of what the men did.[77] So the yearly estimates of
an earnings gap reported by the government fail to tell the story of a deeper gap
that grows over careers.

Finally, the earnings gap reflects elements of sex discrimination. Nothing in the
statistical analysis of key factors that affect earnings, besides gender, fully accounts for shortfalls. Even when men and women of similar age, occupational experience, and educational background are compared, a mysterious increment of
salary lag remains. Even in the most heavily female occupations men still earn
more than women. For example, women's earnings are only 95 percent of men's
for registered nurses, 86 percent for elementary school teachers, and 84 percent for
maids and housekeepers.[78]

The pay gap between men and women is worldwide. According to the International Labor Organization it is between 10 and 30 percent in most countries.[79]
In the European Union it is 15 percent, but this average disguises a broad range
from 5.4 percent in Poland to 25.4 percent in the United Kingdom.[80] Although
globalization has narrowed gender wage differentials, especially in low-skill
occupations, they persist due to cultural traditions that shape labor market

[77] Stephen J. Rose and Heidi Hartmann, *Still a Man's Labor Market: The Long-Term Earnings Gap*
(Washington, DC: Institute for Women's Policy Research, 2004), p. 10.

[78] Bureau of Labor Statistics, *Highlights of Women's Earnings in 2009,* table 2.

[79] International Labour Office, *Global Employment Trends for Women* (Geneva: International Labour
Organization, 2009), p. 19.

[80] European Commission, *Equal Pay: Exchange of Good Practices* (Luxembourg: Office for Official
Publications of the European Communities, January 2007), p. 5; and International Labour Office, *Women
in Labour Markets: Measuring Progress and Identifying Challenges* (Geneva: International Labour
Organization, March 2010), table 4.

characteristics and to discrimination. In many countries women are segregated into low-paying, informal jobs. Worldwide they make up most of part-time workers.

DIVERSITY

diversity management
Programs to recruit from diverse groups, promote tolerance, and modify cultures to include nonmainstream employees.

Workplaces are increasingly diverse. Many companies, particularly the largest, engage in *diversity management,* or systematic efforts to recruit from diverse groups, promote tolerance, and modify corporate cultures to include nonmainstream employees.

Categories of diversity are numerous. They include race, gender, social class, ethnicity, language, religion, disability, sexual orientation, age, generation, national culture, language, place of origin, profession, and political affiliation. All these categories, where they are in some aspect disfavored by the mainstream, can be divisive, leading to discrimination, exclusion, and constricted opportunity. Not all types of diversity have equal significance in every work setting. Some can subject the person with that characteristic to negative consequences. Others can have favorable implications. Managing diversity means removing exclusionary barriers that rise due to attitudes about disfavored groups.

The identity of disfavored groups varies among societies. Those who face barriers in the work environment include Turks in Germany, Moroccans in Belgium, Koreans in Japan, Catholics in Northern Ireland, ethnic Malays with Chinese companies in Malaysia, and members of lower castes in India. In Italy and China migrants from rural areas face stereotypes of laziness and ineptness. In the United States diversity efforts focus on inclusion of blacks, ethnic minorities, women, older workers, gays, lesbians, transsexuals, Muslims, and the disabled into corporate cultures dominated by white males.

Workforce diversity creates many kinds of tensions. Attitudes of racism, sexism, and ethnic bias are the most pernicious and are as well known as they are difficult to control. But there are many other tensions. For example, national cultures instill remarkably opposite values that bear on basic elements of work life. In the so-called "masculine" cultures of Japan, Mexico, and the United States, assertiveness and ambition are highly valued. But in the "feminine" cultures of Scandinavia cooperation and compromise have much higher priority.[81] When workers from these cultures mix, they may misunderstand or condescend to behavior outside the mainstream. In new technology companies the generations have clashed, as in the following story.

> Brian Reid was 52 when he was hired by Google as its director of operations and director of engineering. Before going to Google, he had been a faculty member at Stanford University with a doctorate in computer science. Reid set to work.
>
> An early performance review described him as having "an extraordinarily broad range of knowledge" and projecting "confidence when dealing with fast changing situations." His attitude was described as "excellent" and he was said to be

---

[81] See, for example, the discussion of national cultures in Michálle E. Mor Barak, *Managing Diversity: Toward a Globally Inclusive Workplace* (Thousand Oaks, CA: Sage Publications, 2008), chap. 8.

"creative" and "a problem solver." Yet the review also noted that: "Adapting to the Google culture is the primary task for the first year here . . . Right or wrong, Google is simply different: Younger contributors, inexperienced first line managers, and the super fast pace are just a few examples of the environment."[82]

This was prophetic. A 38-year-old executive who dealt with Reid began making comments that his views were "obsolete" and "too old to matter," that he was "slow," "fuzzy," "sluggish," and lacked "a sense of urgency." Others at Google called him an "old man," and an "old fuddy-duddy." A running joke was that the CD label on a case in his office should read LP instead.

Less than two years after being hired, Reid was told he was not a "cultural fit," and terminated.

The causes of diversity-based tensions are often elusive. Without insight they are invisible. And without intervention they persist. They cannot be eliminated as long as people bring divergent attitudes to work. However, managers can act to reduce them. One example is the story of a woman raised in Taiwan who was hired by General Electric. Growing up, she was taught to be modest and never boast, in keeping with the Chinese proverb that "the loudest duck gets shot." At GE she entered an atmosphere charged with ambition and competition. As part of the company's diversity program she was coached on how to be aggressive.[83] Such efforts are the sign of a well-developed program.

Diversity management practice has evolved. Initially, after passage of Title VII in 1964, corporations promoted numerical diversity, using affirmative action and outreach to hire more individuals from underrepresented and previously disfavored groups. This increased numbers, but did nothing to resolve tensions and conflicts among employees. So companies then extended their efforts beyond hiring, mainly to include sensitivity training for employees. The theory was that if workers understood and appreciated differences they would follow the Golden Rule, accepting variance, being inclusive, and working productively. However, this well-intentioned approach failed to resolve multiple problems. It is still used, but women, minorities, and others from nonmainstream groups continue to perceive prejudice, disfavor, and exclusion.

Most often the core problem is that individuals from disfavored groups have difficulty assimilating into work cultures that evolved from mainstream, usually white and male, values. There are many illustrations. More than 100 Muslim employees at the JBS Swift meatpacking plant in Greeley, Colorado, asked to have their dinner break moved up during the holy month of Ramadan so they could make religious observances at sunset. Management was uncooperative. Supervisors interrupted them when they knelt or prayed.[84]

At another company a woman had advanced to be chief financial officer. Yet at meetings of top managers the men continued discussions while they walked to and from and were in the restroom. When she finally objected, they were blind to

---

[82] Quotations are in *Brian Reid v. Google, Inc,* 2010 Cal. LEXIS 7544 (Cal., August 5, 2010) at 5-10.

[83] Lisa Takeuchi Cullen, "Pathways to Power," *Time,* December 2005, p. A3.

[84] Vickie Elmer, "Muslims File EEOC Suits Against Meatpacking Plants," *The Washington Post,* September 7, 2010, p. A13.

her concern and counseled her it was nothing at all.[85] A black executive felt anger that he was addressed in more familiar ways than his white counterparts.[86] An Asian woman complained that co-workers talked only about "American culture stories." She began to avoid having lunch with them and they invited her to join them less frequently.[87] A Hispanic manager complained that colleagues held stereotyped attitudes toward Mexican workers and assumed that she would take siestas and be lazy.[88]

Such conflicts have been extremely difficult to eradicate. Diversity experts suggest that underlying, unspoken assumptions in the corporate culture are the culprits. Only major culture change efforts will bring about inclusive work environments. If the mainstream is, for example, a white and male culture, it is unrealistic to predict that blacks, women, Asians, Hispanics, and lesbians will be fully included no matter how much affirmative action or sensitivity training is used. Only if the mainstream itself is altered by deep culture change can it become a new mainstream that shares the values of previously excluded minorities.[89]

Elements of Diversity Programs

Leaving aside multiyear culture-change projects, which are uncertain in result and rarely used, diversity management relies on common elements such as these.

1. *Leadership from the top* is critical. Without it, diversity efforts are not seen as central to business strategy. Taylor Cox, Jr., a diversity management consultant, tells how leaders go wrong. Managers commit to attending meetings about diversity but change their plans when operations compete for their time. A manager picked to open a diversity training session welcomed attendees and then said, "I'm sorry you have to be here today and sit through all of this."[90] When asked at a diversity meeting whether anyone in the company had been promoted or passed over because of performance on diversity, a senior vice president of human resources could not think of anyone. Glen Hiner of Owens Corning, Inc., set a different example. When he came into the company, he stated at the first meeting with senior executives, "We are too white and too male, and that will change."[91] He followed this by taking large and small actions, from appointing women and minorities to high positions to requiring a statement about the dignity of all individuals printed on business cards.

[85] Barak, *Managing Diversity: Toward a Globally Inclusive Workplace,* p. 149.

[86] Robin J. Ely, Debra E. Meyerson, and Martin N. Davidson, "Rethinking Political Correctness," *Harvard Business Review,* September 2006, p. 81.

[87] Catalyst, *Advancing Asian Women in the Workplace: What Managers Need to Know* (New York: Catalyst, 2003), p. 14.

[88] Catalyst, *Advancing Latinas in the Workplace: What Managers Need to Know* (New York: Catalyst, 2003), p. 15.

[89] See, for example, R. Roosevelt Thomas, Jr., *World Class Diversity Management* (San Francisco: Berrett-Koehler, 2010), pp. 116–17.

[90] Taylor Cox, Jr., *Creating the Multicultural Organization* (San Francisco: Jossey-Bass, 2001), p. 41.

[91] Quoted in Marc Bendick, Jr., Mary Lou Egan, and Suzanne M. Lofhjeim, "Workforce Diversity Training: From Antidiscrimination Compliance to Organizational Development," *Human Resource Planning,* January 2001, p. 10.

2. *Change in the organization structure* creates focal points for diversity efforts. Leadership can come from steering committees or task forces. Many companies now have chief diversity officers who manage diversity coordinators in business units. Larger firms encourage *affinity groups,* or networks of employees based on race, culture, ethnicity, gender, sexual orientation, age, disability, or other identity grouping. Participation in such groups can reduce an individual's sense of isolation in a work culture. Affinity groups are a forum for mentoring, coaching, exchanging ideas, and advising the company. At IBM locations around the world there are 181 such groups ranging from aboriginal employees to Latinas with MBAs. Among multiple groups at PepsiCo, a company with a major diversity effort, there is even a "white male inclusion" group.

affinity group
A support network formed by employees who personify an attribute associated with discrimination, stereotyping, or social isolation.

3. *Training programs* are very popular. They are designed to overcome stereotypes and biases by teaching employees to respect differences. Often they feature short cases or videos to invite discussion of misunderstandings and coach more sensitive behavior. Some studies suggest that training is effective in shifting values.[92] Others have found it can awaken biases rather than softening them. A long-term evaluation of diversity training in hundreds of corporations concluded that it was the least effective of seven methods for increasing diversity.[93]

4. *Mentors* can be assigned to women and minorities to overcome isolation in firms where the hierarchy is predominantly white and male. At General Electric diversity officers assign not just one mentor but a "personal board of directors" to advise individuals. One study of successful managers in large companies found that high-potential minorities were often demoralized by midcareer. They moved up more slowly than high-potential whites, who were put on fast tracks earlier. As whites got key assignments and promotions, the minority managers grew discouraged. A key to their ultimate success was the support of mentors who opened doors for them.[94] Mentoring requires sensitivity to cultural backgrounds. Some blacks want to advance solely on merit and see mentoring as selling out. Latinos and women may see it as phony because they have been socialized to value relationships for their intrinsic good, not for some instrumental value.[95]

5. *Data collection* is needed to define issues and measure progress. Because of the business dictum that what gets measured gets done, many companies quantify the practice of diversity. One of the more imaginative examples is the "best-practices index" used by the Quaker Oats Company before it was acquired by PepsiCo. The index registered points for every program and action taken at each of its plants. Its diversity administrator explained: "Most CEOs may not

---

[92] Kenneth P. DeMeuse, "A Longitudinal Evaluation of Senior Managers' Perceptions and Attitudes of a Workplace Diversity Training Program," *Human Resource Planning* 30, no. 2 (2007).

[93] Kalev, Dobbin, and Kelly, "Best Practices or Best Guesses? Assessing the Efficacy of Corporate Affirmative Action and Diversity Policies," p. 602. See also Drake Bennett, "Who's Still Biased?" *Boston Globe,* March 7, 2010, p. A1.

[94] David A. Thomas, "The Truth about Mentoring Minorities: Race Matters," *Harvard Business Review,* April 2001.

[95] Kathryn Tyler, "Cross-Cultural Connections," *HR Magazine,* October 2007, p. 77.

know a lot about diversity, but they understand numbers. They can tell the difference between a facility with 1,000 points on the best-practices index, and a facility with 500 points."[96] Today at PepsiCo the CEO chairs a high-level diversity council and the company collects data from a worldwide, biennial survey of all employees designed to reveal diversity issues.

6. *Policy changes* establish new rules. South African mines, where workers come from many countries and tribes, are a cacophony of languages. To avoid confusion in dangerous work the miners speak Fanagolo, a simplified language that fuses Zulu, the language of the dominant South African tribe, with English and Afrikaans, the language spoken by the country's white settlers. When the large mining company Anglo American learned that younger black miners regard Fanagolo as a racist affront, it decided to convert to English. Accordingly it has enrolled miners in English classes.

7. *Reward systems* encourage managers to achieve diversity goals. Diversity can be one element of performance reviews. Division managers at ExxonMobil are required at annual reviews to present career development plans for 10 females and 10 minority males. At Lockheed Martin each business unit is ranked using a mathematical "diversity maturity model" that includes surveys of employees. Part of each manager's bonus is tied to the unit's score.[97]

Despite decades of efforts to manage diversity tensions remain. There are many reasons. Problems related to diversity are complex. Attitudes and prejudices are deep rooted. Being resistant to change based on short training sessions, they linger. Diversity programs are now institutionalized in large corporations, but that has often turned them into empty rituals lacking any special support from top management. They are also resisted by employees who feel a threat to their status. Corporate cultures change very slowly; in fact, it is difficult to make them change at all. One diversity management practitioner with long experience suggests that even in the best of circumstances "only so much harmony is possible" and that as workplaces become more diverse those in them should learn to accept "eggshell situations" as inevitable.[98]

CONCLUDING OBSERVATIONS

This chapter covers four civil rights eras in American history, as shown in Figure 17.4. Workplace discrimination has existed through all of them. It began with a long era of slavery extending 244 years and ending when President Abraham Lincoln signed the Emancipation Proclamation. It was followed by a short post-Civil War era in which the liberated slaves were protected by new laws and constitutional amendments extending "equal protection" to all citizens. For a brief,

---

[96] I. Charles Mathews, vice president of diversity management, cited in Margaret A. Hart, *Managing Diversity for Sustained Competitiveness* (New York: The Conference Board, 1997), p. 8.

[97] Jill Dutt, "Taking an Engineer's Approach at Lockheed Martin," *The Washington Post*, May 1, 2006, p. D1.

[98] Thomas, *World Class Diversity Management*, p. 80.

FIGURE 17.4   Four Civil Rights Eras

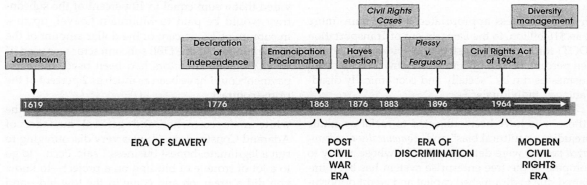

incandescent hour the freed slaves enjoyed extensive federal protection of their liberties.

Unfortunately, these liberties, particularly the right to vote, could no longer be protected after President Rutherford B. Hayes removed federal troops from the South in a corrupt bargain to secure his election. And the climate of civil rights deteriorated further as the Supreme Court eviscerated the Fourteenth Amendment in the *Civil Rights Cases* and the *Plessy* decision. The nation now entered a third era, a long spell of widespread discrimination that spread across both North and South.

After 88 years that era ended with the Civil Rights Act of 1964. Its passage began a fourth era, lasting now almost 50 years, during which the climate of civil rights in society and in the workplace has greatly and continuously improved. Now, the accumulated corpus of antidiscrimination law is massive, complex, and well enforced.

Although there is far less blatant discrimination today than in the past, it is not eradicated. Every year tens of thousands of workers still file claims against their employers. Nevertheless, it has receded enough that attention has turned to more finely grained, indirect forms of exclusion that many corporations now address with efforts such as diversity programs.

Adarand v. Peña

This is the story of an affirmative action case that made its way to the U.S. Supreme Court. When the Court announced it would hear *Adarand v. Peña*, there was considerable speculation about the outcome. The plaintiff, a white male, argued that preferential treatment for minority and female contractors was unconstitutional. Would the justices agree?

In due course, the nine-member Court issued a lengthy (21,800 words) split decision, showing itself to be as fractured as the public in its thinking. It divided five to four, with six separate opinions—a majority opinion, two concurring opinions, and three dissents. The result? Affirmative action lived on but became harder to justify. With the support of affirmative action foes in the legal community, Adarand Constructors tried to carry the case further; refusing to give up until the Court killed affirmative action in all its forms. The case bounced around the federal court system for another six years until fizzling out in 2001 when the Supreme Court dismissed it.

THE GUARDRAIL SUBCONTRACT

In 1987 Congress appropriated a huge sum, more than $16 billion, to the Department of Transportation (DOT) for highway construction across the nation.[1] Ten percent, or $1.6 billion, was earmarked for small businesses run by "socially and economically disadvantaged individuals."[2]

Socially disadvantaged persons were defined as "those who have been subjected to racial or ethnic prejudice or cultural bias" and *economically disadvantaged persons* were defined as those "whose ability to compete in the free enterprise system has been impaired due to diminished capital and credit opportunities as compared to others in the same business area who are not socially disadvantaged."[3]

It was to be presumed that black, Hispanic, Asian Pacific, subcontinent Asian, and Native American persons and women were both socially and economically handicapped. Any small business with 51 percent or greater ownership by persons in these categories could be certified as a *disadvantaged business enterprise*, or DBE. Then, Congress put monetary incentives to hire DBEs into the highway construction law. The story here illustrates how these incentives worked.

In 1989 Mountain Gravel & Construction Company received a $1 million prime contract to build highways in the San Juan National Forest of southwest Colorado. It requested bids from subcontractors to install 4.7 miles of guardrails. Two small companies that specialize in guardrail installation responded. Adarand Constructors, Inc., a white-owned company, submitted the low bid, and Gonzales Construction Company, a firm certified as a DBE, submitted a bid that was $1,700 higher.

Ordinarily, Mountain Gravel would have chosen the low bidder, but the prime contract provided that it would be paid a bonus, up to 10 percent of the guardrail subcontract, if it picked a DBE.

On this subcontract, the bonus payment was approximately $10,000, so even by accepting a bid $1,700 above the low bid, Mountain Gravel came out $8,300 ahead. Gonzales Construction got the nod.

The part of the prime contract that caused Mountain Gravel to reject Adarand Constructors' low bid was called a *subcontractor compensation clause*. It provided that a sum equal to 10 percent of the subcontract would be paid to Mountain Gravel, up to a maximum of 1.5 percent of the dollar amount of the prime contract, if one DBE subcontractor was used. If two DBE subcontractors had been used, the extra payment could have been as much as 2 percent of the prime contract.

Losing the guardrail job angered Randy Pech, the white male co-owner and general manager of Adarand Constructors. "It was very discouraging to run a legitimate, honest business," said Pech, "to go to a lot of trouble of bidding on a project—to know you did a great job and come in the low bid—and then find out they can't use you because they have to meet their 'goals.'"[4] Pech's lawyer, William Pendley, spoke more bluntly about the subcontractor compensation clause. "It works like a bribe," he said.[5]

This was not the first time Adarand Constructors had faced this situation. It was one of only five Colorado contractors specializing in guardrails. The other four, Cruz Construction, Ideal Fencing, C&K, and Gonzales Construction, were minority-owned and, by virtue of that, designated as DBEs. These four competitors were all stable businesses at least 10 years old, and on nonfederal highway projects, they sometimes beat Adarand Constructors with lower bids. Yet when federal highway dollars were being spent, Adarand Constructors frequently lost— even with the lowest bid.

Later it would be documented that because of the subcontractor compensation clause, prime contractors had rejected the company's low bids five times to favor its DBE competitors. Mountain Gravel's bid estimator verified that Adarand Constructors' low bid on the 4.7-mile guardrail job would have been accepted if the extra payment had not existed. Fed up, Randy Pech sued the federal government.

In his suit, Pech claimed that the subcontractor compensation clause violated his constitutional right to equal treatment under the law. This right is found in the Fifth Amendment, which reads: "No person shall . . . be deprived of life, liberty, or property, without due process of law." Although this wording does

---

[1] The Surface Transportation and Uniform Relocation Assistance Act of 1987, P.L. 100–17.

[2] Section 106(c)(1).

[3] Section 106(c)(2)(B).

[4] Marlene Cimons, "Businessman Who Brought Lawsuit Praises Ruling by Justices," *Los Angeles Times,* June 13, 1995, p. A15.

[5] David G. Savage, "'Colorblind' Constitution Faces a New Test," *Los Angeles Times,* January 16, 1995, p. A17.

not literally state that citizens are entitled to equal treatment, the Supreme Court has held that its meaning protects citizens from arbitrary or unequal treatment by the federal government in the same way that the Fourteenth Amendment prohibits states from denying "equal protection of the laws" to their citizens. Pech did not seek monetary damages, but requested an injunction, or a court-ordered halt, to any future use of contract clauses providing extra payments on subcontracts given to DBEs.

Things got off to a bad start for Pech when the U.S. District Court for the District of Colorado ruled against him.[6] The court held that it was within the power of Congress, when it enacted the highway bill, to use race- and gender-based preferences to compensate for the harmful effects of past discrimination. Pech appealed to the Tenth Circuit Court of Appeals, but, two years later, it affirmed the district court's decision.[7] Pech then took the next step and appealed to the Supreme Court, which agreed to decide the case. Because the lawsuit named Transportation Secretary Federico Peña as a defendant, it was entitled *Adarand v. Peña.*

THE CONSTITUTION AND RACE

The Court was being asked to decide whether classifying citizens by race in order to treat them differently was constitutionally respectable. This was not a new question; neither was it one that has ever been resolved with clarity. Affirmative action has deeply divided the Court, but it is not the first race-based classification scheme to raise constitutional problems.

Between 1884 and 1893, the Court decided a series of challenges to exclusionary laws passed by Congress stopping the immigration of Chinese laborers and restricting the civil rights of resident Chinese. At first, the justices struck down laws that treated Chinese differently from American citizens.[8] Eventually, however, the Court went along with a wave of

public hysteria over the Chinese and in key decisions upheld laws that denied them equal treatment.[9]

A few years later, in 1896, the Court had an opportunity to strike down the Jim Crow laws of the old South in *Plessy v. Ferguson* but failed to do so. Instead, it upheld the Louisiana statute requiring segregation of whites and nonwhites in separate railroad cars and fixed in place the infamous "separate but equal" doctrine. In a lone dissent that rang across decades, Justice John Marshall Harlan called the Constitution "colorblind" and said that race was not a valid criterion for making law.

> In respect of civil rights, common to all citizens, the Constitution of the United States does not, I think, permit any public authority to know the race of those entitled to be protected in the enjoyment of such rights . . . [T]he common government of all shall not permit the seeds of race hate to be planted under the sanction of law.[10]

During World War II, the Court was once again called upon to decide the question of a race-based government action. In early 1942, President Franklin Roosevelt issued an executive order, which Congress ratified, requiring the relocation of 70,000 persons of Japanese descent, both American citizens and resident aliens, from homes on the West Coast to inland evacuation camps.

This policy was challenged as depriving the Japanese Americans of their Fifth Amendment guarantee of equal protection of the laws. However, the Court once again upheld a racial classification scheme. In the majority opinion, Justice Black conceded that "all legal restrictions which curtail the civil rights of a single racial group are immediately suspect" and must be subjected "to the most rigid scrutiny."[11] Nevertheless, the evacuation order passed this "rigid scrutiny," because the president and Congress were taking emergency actions in time of war to prevent sabotage and avert grave danger. In dissent, Justice Frank Murphy argued that the evacuation "goes over 'the very brink of constitutional power' and falls into the ugly abyss of racism."[12]

In 1954 the Court finally reversed its decision in *Plessy.* In the landmark school desegregation case *Brown v. Board of Education,* it agreed that under the

---

[6] *Adarand Constructors, Inc. v. Samuel K. Skinner,* 790 F. Supp. 240 (D.Colo. 1992). Then-Secretary of Transportation Skinner was named as the defendant.

[7] *Adarand Constructors, Inc. v. Federico Peña,* 16 F.3d 1537 (10th Cir. 1994). By this time, Peña was secretary of Transportation.

[8] *Chew Heong v. United States,* 112 U.S. 536 (1884); and *United States v. Jung Ah Lung,* 124 U.S. 621 (1888).

[9] *Lee Joe v. United States,* 149 U.S. 698 (1893).

[10] 163 U.S. 554, 560.

[11] *Korematsu v. United States,* 323 U.S. 214.

[12] 323 U.S. 242.

"separate but equal" doctrine, the states had provided grossly unequal schools for blacks.[13] During oral arguments in the case, Thurgood Marshall, destined to be the first black Supreme Court justice, invoked the principle of a color-blind Constitution. A unanimous Court struck down "separate but equal" as a violation of the Equal Protection Clause in the Fourteenth Amendment.

The *Brown* decision, however, did not mean that the Court saw a completely color-blind Constitution. In the 1970s, suits by whites who had suffered reverse discrimination as a result of affirmative action began to reach its docket. In the first such cases, a divided Court upheld affirmative action, but was obviously troubled by it and tried to define its limits. There was also an ideological split among the justices, with a liberal bloc condoning race-based affirmative action and a conservative bloc inclined to severely limit or prohibit it.

THE FULLILOVE CASE

In 1980 the Court heard for the first time a challenge to a set-aside program for minority businesses. In the Public Works Employment Act of 1977, Congress authorized $4 billion for public works projects such as dams, bridges, and highways. At least 10 percent of this sum was set aside for businesses owned by "minority group members," who were defined as "Negroes, Spanish-speaking, Orientals, Indians, Eskimos, and Aleuts."[14]

The law was challenged by several associations of white contractors, who claimed to have lost business and argued that the set-aside violated their constitutional rights to equal protection. But in *Fullilove v. Klutznick,* the Court held that Congress could use racial classification schemes to strike at racist practices used by prime contractors on federal projects.[15]

Over the years, courts have developed standards for testing the constitutional validity of laws that classify citizens. All such laws must withstand one of three levels of scrutiny by a skeptical judiciary.

The lowest level is *ordinary scrutiny,* which requires that government prove its classification scheme is "reasonably" related to a "legitimate interest." For example, classifying citizens by income for purposes of tax collection would pass this minimum test.

The second level is *intermediate scrutiny,* a heightened standard requiring that the law be "substantially related" to an "important government objective." In the past, intermediate scrutiny was typically used for laws related to gender, for example, the law drafting men for military service but not women.

The final, and most exacting, level of scrutiny, called *strict scrutiny,* is reserved for racial classifications regarded as pernicious and undesirable. When strict scrutiny is used, it is presumed that the law in question is unconstitutional unless it passes a specific two-part test. The government must prove that it (1) serves a "compelling" government interest and (2) is "narrowly tailored," that is, not more extensive than it needs to be to serve its purpose.

There are no fixed definitions of the words "reasonably," "substantially related," and "compelling," but they represent an escalating standard of proof.

The majority opinion in *Fullilove* showed that neither Chief Justice Warren Burger nor the five other justices who joined and concurred with him were particularly alarmed about race-based set-asides for minority contractors. The chief justice subjected the minority business program in the Public Works Employment Act to only an intermediate level of scrutiny.

THE CROSON AND METRO CASES

After *Fullilove,* nine years passed before the Court looked at set-asides again. In 1989 the Court struck down an affirmative action plan used by the city of Richmond, Virginia, requiring that 30 percent of construction work be awarded to minority contractors. In *Richmond v. Croson,* the Court held that because the city's plan was a suspect racial classification, it should be subject to strict scrutiny.[16] And when the two tests required by strict scrutiny were applied, the plan could not pass constitutional muster.

First, although the population of Richmond was 50 percent black and less than 1 percent of city contracts were awarded to black firms, the city had not proved a "compelling" interest because it had never conducted studies to show that this statistical discrepancy was caused by race discrimination. Without proof of past discrimination, no "compelling" justification for raced-based remedial action existed.

---

[13] *Brown v. Board of Education,* 347 U.S. 483.

[14] Public Works Employment Act of 1977, Section 103(f)(2).

[15] 448 U.S. 448.

[16] *City of Richmond v. J. A. Croson Co.,* 488 U.S. 469 (1989).

And second, the plan was not "narrowly tailored"; in addition to giving preference to black contractors, it entitled Hispanic, Asian, Native American, Eskimo, and Aleut contractors located anywhere in the United States to take advantage of preferential bidding rules. This scheme of inclusion was too broad. The Court ruled that for white contractors, the Richmond plan violated the Fourteenth Amendment guarantee of equal protection under the law.[17]

In the wake of the *Croson* decision, more than 200 set-aside plans around the country were dropped or changed for fear that they would be challenged and struck down. In Richmond, the percentage of contract dollars awarded to minority businesses plummeted from 30 percent to "the low single digits."[18]

A year later, in 1990, the Court confronted a case in which white-owned broadcasters challenged a congressional statute requiring that the Federal Communications Commission give certain preferences to minority radio and television companies when it issued broadcast licenses. Congress declared that its purpose was to promote diversity in programming. In *Metro Broadcasting v. FCC*, a five-member majority of the Court composed of four remaining liberals and the usually conservative Justice Byron White held that "benign race-conscious measures" undertaken by Congress to compensate victims of discrimination need be subject only to the standard of "intermediate scrutiny."[19] Creating diversity in broadcasting was an "important governmental objective," and preferences for nonwhite and female broadcasters were "substantially related" to achieving this objective. In dissent, Justice Anthony M. Kennedy sought to refocus the Court on the mistake made in the *Plessy* case. "I regret," he wrote, "that after a century of judicial opinions we interpret the Constitution to do no more than move us from 'separate but equal' to 'unequal but benign.'"[20]

[17] The Fourteenth Amendment protects American citizens from unjust actions by state governments. It reads: "No State shall . . . deny to any person within its jurisdiction the equal protection of the laws." The City of Richmond, being chartered by the state of Virginia, was therefore a governmental actor falling under the reach of the Fourteenth Amendment.

[18] Paul M. Barrett and Michael K. Frisby, "Affirmative-Action Advocates Seeking Lessons from States to Help Preserve Federal Programs," *The Wall Street Journal*, December 7, 1994, p. A18.

[19] *Metro Broadcasting v. FCC*, 497 U.S. 547.

[20] 497 U.S. 637–38.

TWO LINES OF PRECEDENT

This was where matters stood until 1994, when *Adarand* came before the Court. The Supreme Court likes to follow precedent and generally adheres to the rule of *stare decisis* (STARE-ray da-SEE-sis), a Latin term meaning to stand as decided. The judicial system is based on the principle that once a matter of law is settled, courts should follow the established path. Judges believe that this should be the case even though a court would decide the question differently if it were new. *Stare decisis* preserves one of the law's primary virtues, its predictability.

However, two different precedents had been established for minority preferences in contracting. In *Croson,* the Court had applied strict scrutiny to a city plan and declared it unconstitutional. But *Adarand* was not about a city plan; it involved a plan enacted by Congress. Traditionally, the Supreme Court recognizes that Congress represents the will of the American people and thus its actions deserve great deference. The line of precedent closest to the issue in *Adarand* was that emerging from *Fullilove* and *Metro.* In both cases, the Court had applied only intermediate scrutiny to congressional affirmative action plans and in both cases the plans were upheld. This result was consistent with the Court's studied deference toward Congress.

THE DECISION

Attorneys for each side in *Adarand v. Peña* presented 30 minutes of oral argument before the nine justices on January 17, 1995.[21] On June 12, 1995, the Supreme Court released a five-to-four decision in favor of Adarand Constructors.[22] The majority opinion, written by Justice Sandra Day O'Connor, departed from the line of precedent running from *Fullilove* and *Metro* and instead returned to *Croson* and ruled that the Department of Transportation plan giving preferences in bidding to minority subcontractors would have to withstand the test of strict scrutiny. It held that the plan was a race classification and presumed to be unconstitutional unless it was "narrowly tailored"

[21] Listen to this oral argument by visiting the Oyez Project Web site at www.oyez.org/cases/1990-1994/1994/1994_93_1841.

[22] *Adarand v. Peña*, 132 L. Ed. 2d 158, 515 U.S. 200 (1995).

to meet a "compelling government interest." Justice O'Connor wrote as follows.

> [W]e hold today that all racial classifications, imposed by whatever federal, state, or local governmental actor, must be analyzed by a reviewing court under strict scrutiny. In other words, such classifications are constitutional only if they are narrowly tailored measures that further compelling governmental interests. To the extent that *Metro Broadcasting* is inconsistent with that holding it is overruled.[23]

She justified departing from the *Fullilove* and *Metro* precedents by citing Justice Felix Frankfurter, who 55 years earlier had written that "*stare decisis* is . . . not a mechanical formula of adherence to the latest decision, however recent and questionable, when such adherence involves collision with a prior doctrine more embracing in its scope, intrinsically sounder, and verified by experience."[24] The Court's longstanding, deep suspicion of any race classification, wrote O'Connor, should override the recent efforts of some liberal justices to apply more lax scrutiny to forms of discrimination they called "benign."

However, the majority was unwilling to say that no scheme of race-conscious preferences could withstand strict scrutiny. Using affirmative action might still be possible for the government. O'Connor wrote:

> Finally, we wish to dispel the notion that strict scrutiny is "strict in theory, but fatal in fact . . ." The unhappy persistence of both the practice and the lingering effects of racial discrimination against minority groups in this country is an unfortunate reality, and government is not disqualified from acting in response to it.[25]

This completed the majority opinion. The Court did not uphold or strike down the Transportation Department's subcontractor bidding clauses. Instead, it remanded, or returned, the case to the Tenth Circuit to be redecided using the strict scrutiny test instead of the lesser test of intermediate scrutiny.[26] The result of this tougher review would determine whether the equal protection rights of Randy Pech at Adarand Constructors had been violated. Thus, as in

many cases that come before the high court, the justices avoided deciding the specific question and decided only matters of law.

JUSTICE SCALIA CONCURS

Justice Antonin Scalia, a conservative and longtime foe of affirmative action, wrote a concurring opinion in which he agreed with the application of strict scrutiny but took the extreme position that "government can never have a 'compelling interest' in discriminating on the basis of race in order to 'make up' for past racial discrimination in the opposite direction."[27] He elaborated:

> Individuals who have been wronged by unlawful racial discrimination should be made whole; but under our Constitution there can be no such thing as either a creditor or a debtor race. The concept of racial entitlement—even for the most admirable and benign of purposes—is to reinforce and preserve for future mischief the way of thinking that produced race slavery, race privilege and race hatred. In the eyes of government, we are just one race here. It is American.[28]

Justice Scalia concluded that it was very unlikely and probably impossible that the Department of Transportation program could pass the strict scrutiny test.

JUSTICE THOMAS CONCURS

Justice Clarence Thomas, the Court's only black member, agreed with the majority opinion, but wrote separately to underscore the principle that the Constitution requires all races to be treated equally. In his eyes, there was no moral difference between a law designed to subjugate a race and a law passed to give it benefits.

> That these programs may have been motivated, in part, by good intentions cannot provide refuge from the principle that under our Constitution, the government may not make distinctions on the basis of race. As far as the Constitution is concerned, it is irrelevant whether a government's racial classifications are drawn by those who wish to oppress a race or by those who have a sincere desire to help those thought to be disadvantaged.[29]

---

[23] 132 L. Ed. 2d 182.

[24] 132 L. Ed. 2d 184, citing *Helvering v. Hallock*, 390 U.S. 106, at 119.

[25] 132 L. Ed. 2d 188.

[26] 16 F.3d 1537, vacated and remanded.

[27] 132 L. Ed. 2d 190.

[28] Ibid.

[29] Ibid.

The nine Supreme Court justices who decided the *Adarand* cases. Front row, left to right, are Antonin Scalia, John Paul Stevens, William Rehnquist (Chief Justice), Sandra Day O'Connor, and Anthony Kennedy. Back row, left to right, are Ruth Bader Ginsburg, David Souter, Clarence Thomas, and Stephen Breyer.
Source: © Reuters/CORBIS.

Thomas also argued that affirmative action degrades the very individuals it tries to help.

> So-called "benign" discrimination teaches many that because of chronic and apparently immutable handicaps, minorities cannot compete with them without their patronizing indulgence. Inevitably such programs engender attitudes of superiority or, alternatively, provoke resentment among those who believe that they have been wronged by the government's use of race. These programs stamp minorities with a badge of inferiority and may cause them to develop dependencies or to adopt an attitude that they are "entitled" to preferences.[30]

THE DISSENTERS

Three separate dissenting opinions were written, joined in by four justices. In the first, Justice Stevens, joined by Justice Ginsburg, objected to the departure of the majority from established precedent and argued that the Court had a duty to uphold the intermediate scrutiny standard. Stevens also disagreed with the majority that all discrimination was the same in principle.

> There is no moral or constitutional equivalence between a policy that is designed to perpetuate a caste system and one that seeks to eradicate racial subordination. Invidious discrimination is an engine of oppression, subjugating a disfavored group to enhance or maintain the power of the majority.

[30] 132 L. Ed. 2d 191.

Remedial race-based preferences reflect the opposite impulse: a desire to foster equality in society. No sensible conception of the Government's constitutional obligation to "govern impartially" . . . should ignore this distinction . . . The consistency that the Court espouses would disregard the difference between a "No Trespassing" sign and a welcome mat.[31]

A second dissent by Justice Souter, in which Justices Ginsburg and Breyer joined, objected to the Court's departure from the *Fullilove* and *Metro* precedents. He argued that more deference was owed to Congress and affirmed his approval for laws that try to redress persistent racism.

The third dissenting opinion came from Justice Ginsburg, joined by Justice Breyer. She wrote to underscore the lingering effects of "a system of racial cast" in American life. According to Ginsburg:

> White and African-American consumers still encounter different deals. People of color looking for housing still face discriminatory treatment by landlords, real estate agents, and mortgage lenders. Minority entrepreneurs sometimes fail to gain contracts though they are the low bidders, and they are sometimes refused work even after winning contracts. Bias both conscious and unconscious, reflecting traditional and unexamined habits of thought, keeps up barriers that must come down if equal opportunity and nondiscrimination are ever genuinely to become this country's law and practice.
>
> Given this history and its practical consequences, Congress surely can conclude that a carefully designed affirmative action program may help to realize, finally, the "equal protection of the laws" the Fourteenth Amendment has promised since 1868.[32]

THE CASE MOVES ON

The Supreme Court elected to decide principles of law. It declined to settle the specific question of whether the subcontractor compensation clause was constitutional. Therefore, it sent the case back to the Tenth Circuit, with instructions to decide the constitutionality question. The Tenth Circuit, in turn, sent the case down to the U.S. District Court in Colorado where it had originated in 1992.

In 1997, almost two years after the Supreme Court's decision, the district court issued an opinion. Judge John L. Kane Jr. applied the strict scrutiny test to the subcontractor compensation clause, and the

[31] 132 L. Ed. 2d 192, 193.
[32] 132 L. Ed. 2d 212.

result invalidated the clause. The clause passed the part of the test requiring the government to show a compelling interest. Judge Kane stated that there was sufficient evidence of bias in contracting before Congress when it passed the law.

However, the clause failed the test of narrow tailoring. Judge Kane held that basing social and economic disadvantage solely on race was unfair. Under the existing criteria for selecting DBEs, a multimillionaire who immigrated from Hong Kong and became a U.S. citizen one day before applying would automatically qualify, but a poor white man who had lived in the United States his entire life could not. So the set-aside program was overinclusive and unconstitutional. Since Colorado was administering the program for the federal government, Judge Kane issued an injunction ordering the state to stop using the objectionable regulation.[33]

Pech and his company had won, but defenders of affirmative action wanted to put up a fight. The Department of Transportation appealed the decision back to the Tenth Circuit. Then Colorado refused to comply with Judge Kane's ruling. Governor Roy Romer argued, disingenuously, that a federal court order did not apply to a state government.

Adarand Constructors immediately sued the state to force its obedience. When the case came before Judge Kane, Colorado argued that it had changed its contracting program. It no longer used the subcontractor compensation clause, and it allowed all contractors, including white males, to get DBE status if they could show disadvantage.

Judge Kane was furious at the recalcitrance of Colorado officials. Instead of retrying the entire issue, he declared that Adarand Constructors had suffered years of discrimination and financial hardship at the hands of a government enforcing an unfair, unconstitutional law. He decreed that the company was eligible for DBE status.[34] Pech applied for it, and it was granted by Colorado in 1998.

Meanwhile, the *Adarand* decision sparked a national debate. The federal government had approximately 160 preference programs for businesses certified as disadvantaged. In the year that *Adarand* was decided, $10 billion in contracts earmarked for minority and female vendors was distributed through various preference schemes. Opponents of affirmative action felt that, because of the decision, such practices should cease.

There was no doubt that *Adarand* cast a shadow over these arrangements, but their supporters had no intention of conceding defeat. Instead, President Bill Clinton promised to "mend, not end" affirmative action. What he had in mind was revising preferential treatment rules so that the programs would withstand legal challenge.

Congressional opponents of affirmative action started a floor fight trying to kill the 10 percent set-aside provision in a new highway funding bill. In March 1998 strident debate erupted in the Senate over an amendment to delete the set-aside, but the amendment was defeated, leaving more than $17 billion of new highway funds earmarked for DBEs.[35]

In 1999 the Department of Transportation issued revised rules for awarding federal highway contracts to DBEs.[36] They stated that the 10 percent of highway funding reserved for DBEs was not a "quota" or a "set-aside" but an "aspirational goal at the national level." The DBE participation level in each state receiving highway funds could be higher or lower. To meet DBE goals, the states were required to first use "race-neutral" measures, that is, to do things to help all small businesses, including both DBEs and white-male-owned companies.

These measures did not require race–gender classifications and included, for example, training and advice in bidding and contract work, bonding assistance, and breaking large contracts into pieces that small businesses could more easily handle. However, if such methods did not fully achieve DBE goals and "egregious" discrimination existed, then "race-conscious" methods that gave preferences to DBEs, including set-asides on which only DBEs could bid, could be used.

The states were required to do studies pinpointing discrimination, so that there would be a compelling rationale for race-conscious actions if they were needed. The rules also tightened qualifications for persons designated as "economically disadvantaged." This

---

[33] *Adarand Constructors, Inc. v. Peña,* 965 F. Supp. 1556 (D. Colo. 1997).

[34] *Adarand Constructors, Inc. v. Romer,* Civ. No. 97–K–1351 (June 26, 1997).

[35] Amendment No. 1708, 144 Cong. Rec. S1395.

[36] Department of Transportation, "Participation by Disadvantaged Business Enterprises in Department of Transportation Program," 64 FR 5096–5148, December 9, 1999.

Who Is Disadvantaged?

Any person who is a citizen and falls into one of the following categories is presumed to be socially and economically disadvantaged (beginning in 1999, persons with a net worth of $750,000 or more were disqualified). If the person has 51 percent ownership or greater in a company applying for a federal highway construction contract, that company qualifies as a "disadvantaged business enterprise" and can receive preferential treatment on federal highway contracts.

Black Americans. Includes persons having origins in any black racial groups in Africa.

Hispanic Americans. Includes persons of Mexican, Puerto Rican, Cuban, Dominican, Central or South American, or other Spanish or Portuguese culture or origin, regardless of race.

Native Americans. Includes American Indians, Eskimos, Aleuts, or Native Hawaiians.

Asian-Pacific Americans. Includes persons whose origins are from Japan, China, Taiwan, Korea, Burma (Myanmar), Vietnam, Laos, Cambodia (Kampuchea), Thailand, Malaysia, Indonesia, the Philippines, Brunei, Samoa, Guam, the U.S. Trust Territories of the Pacific Islands (Republic of Palau), the Commonwealth of the Northern Marianas Islands, Macao, Fiji, Tonga, Kirbati, Juvalu, Nauru, Federated States of Micronesia, or Hong Kong.

Subcontinent Asian Americans. Includes persons whose origins are from India, Pakistan, Bangladesh, Bhutan, the Maldives Islands, Nepal, or Sri Lanka.

Women. All women are included.

Source: 49 CFR §26.5 and §26.67 (2000); 64 FR 5126, Feb. 2, 1999, as amended at 64 FR 34570, June 28, 1999; 68 FR 35553, June 16, 2003. Current as of January 2011.

status was from now on denied to persons with a net worth of $750,000 or more (calculated as personal net worth minus the value of a primary residence and the ownership interest in the contracting business). The rules allowed white males to apply for socially or economically disadvantaged status. However, unlike minorities and women who are still automatically included (unless worth more than $750,000), the burden is on white males to prove that they have suffered financial hardship from discrimination.

These changes significantly scaled back affirmative action in highway programs. Later, President Clinton issued an executive order introducing similarly constricted affirmative action methods in all federal contracting.[37]

ADARAND KEEPS GOING

Although the use of preferences was being scaled back, through it all Pech persisted in the belief that any race- and sex-based preferences at all were

unconstitutional. The case continued its odyssey through the federal courts.

The Department of Transportation had appealed Judge Kane's 1997 ruling that the subcontractor compensation clause was unconstitutional. In 1999 the Tenth Circuit ruled that the case was now moot because Colorado had changed its contracting guidelines and no longer used the bonus clause. In addition, the court noted that Colorado had classified Adarand Constructors as a DBE.[38] Adarand, which argued that the Colorado guidelines were still unconstitutional, appealed to the Supreme Court. In 2000 the Supreme Court reversed the Tenth Circuit's decision and sent the case back with instructions to decide the constitutionality of the Colorado contracting guidelines.[39]

Later that year, the Tenth Circuit responded, deciding that although the original Colorado highway contracting rules had been unconstitutional, the states' new rules were narrowly tailored to meet a compelling

[37] Executive Order 13170, "Increasing Opportunities and Access for Disadvantaged Businesses," October 6, 2000.

[38] *Adarand Constructors, Inc. v. Slater,* 169 F.3d 1292 (10th Cir. 1999).

[39] *Adarand Constructors, Inc. v. Slater,* 528 U.S. 216 (2000).

EXHIBIT 1 The *Adarand* Odyssey.

This diagram shows the path of the case as it moved through levels of the federal court system over nine years. Twice the Supreme Court remanded the case, that is, sent it back to a lower court for deliberation consistent with legal principles it set forth. Name changes occurred as each new Secretary of Transportation was named as the defendant.

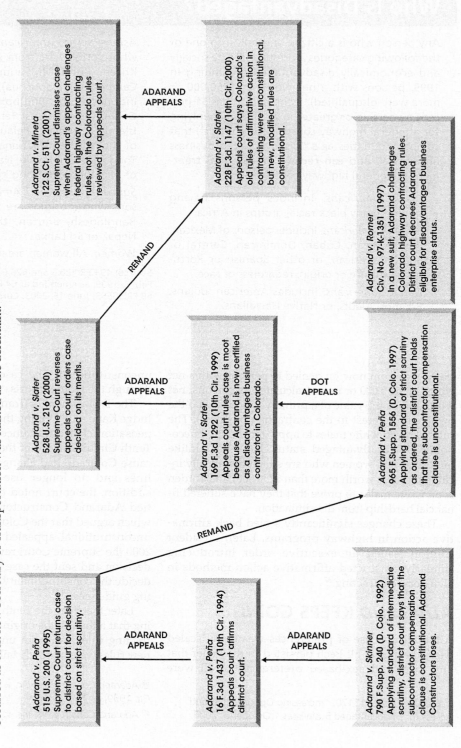

Adarand v. Mineta
122 S.Ct. 511 (2001)
Supreme Court dismisses case when Adarand's appeal challenges federal highway contracting rules, not the Colorado rules reviewed by appeals court.

← ADARAND APPEALS

Adarand v. Slater
228 F.3d. 1147 (10th Cir. 2000)
Appeals court says Colorado's old rules of affirmative action in contracting were unconstitutional, but new, modified rules are constitutional.

REMAND

Adarand v. Romer
Civ. No. 97-K-1351 (1997)
In a new suit, Adarand challenges Colorado highway contracting rules. District court decrees Adarand eligible for disadvantaged business enterprise status.

Adarand v. Slater
528 U.S. 216 (2000)
Supreme Court reverses appeals court, orders case decided on its merits.

← ADARAND APPEALS

Adarand v. Slater
169 F.3d 1292 (10th Cir. 1999)
Appeals court rules case is moot because Adarand is now certified as a disadvantaged business contractor in Colorado.

← DOT APPEALS

Adarand v. Peña
965 F.Supp. 1556 (D. Colo. 1997)
Applying standard of strict scrutiny as ordered, the district court holds that the subcontractor compensation clause is unconstitutional.

REMAND

Adarand v. Peña
515 U.S. 200 (1995)
Supreme Court returns case to district court for decision based on strict scrutiny.

← ADARAND APPEALS

Adarand v. Peña
16 F.3d 1437 (10th Cir. 1994)
Appeals court affirms district court.

← ADARAND APPEALS

Adarand v. Skinner
790 F.Supp. 240 (D. Colo. 1992)
Applying standard of intermediate scrutiny, district court says that the subcontractor compensation clause is constitutional. Adarand Constructors loses.

government interest and, therefore, constitutional. Again, Adarand Constructors appealed the decision to the Supreme Court, which took the case under review. Adarand argued that the Tenth Circuit had erred in its constitutional analysis because no rules that used race or sex as a criterion for awarding government funds could pass the strict scrutiny standard. In its brief, it argued the arbitrariness of the rules:

> [E]very single legally admitted permanent resident or citizen of the United States who happens to be female or who can trace his origins to any of 42 specifically designated countries is automatically presumed to have attempted to enter the American highway construction business and to have experienced racial prejudice that somehow hindered that attempt.[40]

Adarand Constructors urged the Court to adopt the position of Justice John Marshall Harlan that the Constitution is color-blind. It believed that both Congress and the states continued to "trample the constitutional rights of countless innocent individuals."[41] Conservative foes of affirmative action cheered the case on. John O'Sullivan, writing in *National Review,* articulated their view.

> Today . . . preferences bestow benefits on something like 65 percent of Americans by extracting a sacrifice from the remaining 35 percent who happen to be white males. Their injustice is now real and concentrated. In other words, they are now plainly and undeniably [victims of] an official program of negative discrimination against a minority: the sole remaining example of institutionalized racism in the United States.[42]

Adarand was a major challenge to affirmative action, but there would be no decision on it. In late 2001 the Supreme Court, after hearing oral arguments, dismissed the case without a decision, saying it should never have accepted it in the first place. The reason was something of a technicality. In an unsigned opinion, a unanimous Court explained that, in the case, Adarand Constructors was not challenging the Tenth Circuit's decision about Colorado's contracting rules. Instead, it was arguing that federal guidelines were unconstitutional. The Tenth Circuit

decision had not addressed federal guidelines. Therefore, since the Supreme Court was "a court of final review and not first review," it declined to take up the merits of Adarand's arguments and the case was "dismissed as improvidently granted."[43]

With this dismissal the litigation epic of the *Adarand* case, shown in Exhibit 1, came to sudden end. The merits of its final appeal are still up for debate, if not for a formal decision.

While the *Adarand* decision lives on, making affirmative action in government contracting harder to justify, minority contractors continue to struggle. For example, in 1996 California voters passed a proposition banning affirmative action in state contracting. Over the next 10 years, the dollar amount of contracts awarded to minority-owned contractors by the California Department of Transportation fell more than 50 percent and two-thirds of these contractors went out of business.[44]

Questions

1. What constitutional issue is raised in the *Adarand* litigation?
2. After the Supreme Court's 1995 decision in *Adarand v. Peña* what requirements did an affirmative action program have to meet to be constitutional?
3. Was the decision of the Court majority correct? Why or why not?
4. In a concurring opinion, Justice Scalia said that race classifications by government were never legitimate. In dissenting opinions, Justices Stevens, Souter, and Ginsburg argued that race-conscious remedies were justified. What were their arguments? With whom do you agree? Why?
5. Following *Adarand v. Peña,* the district court held that the affirmative action program in federal highway contracts was unconstitutional. Do you agree with this decision? Why or why not?
6. Do you believe that the Department of Transportation's current rules for helping DBEs get highway construction contracts pass the strict scrutiny requirement?

[40] Petitioner's Brief on the Merits, June 11, 2001, p. 11.

[41] Ibid., pp. 19–20.

[42] John O'Sullivan, "Preferred Members," *National Review,* September 3, 2001, p. 20.

[43] *Adarand Constructors, Inc. v. Mineta,* 122 S. Ct. 511, at 514 and 515. Norman Mineta, a new secretary of Transportation, was now the respondent.

[44] Monique W. Morris et al., *Free to Compete: Measuring the Impact of Proposition 209 on Minority Business Enterprises* (Berkley, CA: Discrimination Research Center, 2006), p. 42.

Chapter **Eighteen**

Corporate Governance

Mark Hurd

Mark Hurd arrived as the chief executive officer at Hewlett-Packard in 2005. The company's board of directors, a body of strong and conflicted personalities, had just fired Carly Fiorina, the first woman ever to lead a corporation as big as HP. Her dual sins were trying to dominate the board and allowing the stock price to languish. Her story is the subject of the case study at the end of this chapter.

Hurd got along with the board and got results. He was diligent and relentless, dictating a regimen of cost-cutting, wringing waste from every department, forcing managers to justify every dollar in their budgets. Soon he eliminated 14,500 jobs, about 10 percent of the company's workforce. His severities were resented by some, but share prices climbed. He also had strategic vision. Major acquisitions moved HP into growing markets. He acquired Electronic Data Systems (EDS), then shed another 24,600 workers in the consolidation. He acquired 3Com, then Palm Inc. In five years he turned HP into the world's largest information technology company. Its share price, shown in Figure 18.1, more than doubled.

Then, on June 29, 2010, Hurd opened a letter from celebrity lawyer Gloria Allred. It accused him of sexually harassing an HP marketing contractor named Jodi Fisher by touching her body suggestively and speaking of intimate personal matters. It also said he had breached his duty of confidentiality in telling her about HP's pending purchase of EDS in 2008. An eight-page chronology of his contacts with Fisher was enclosed. The letter ended with an offer to settle. He immediately gave it to an HP attorney, who forwarded it to the board of directors.[1]

In 2007 Hurd had begun a series of "executive summits" held around the world to meet important customers. An assistant recommended Jodi Fisher as a consultant who could help at the events by briefing him on people, making introductions, and steering him around the room. Her qualifications were elusive. After graduating from Texas Tech University with a political science degree, she moved to Los Angeles seeking her fortune as an actress. Her subsequent portfolio included nude *Playboy* photos, roles in a string of erotic films such as "Intimate Obsession" and "Blood

---

[1] Robert A. Buth, Ben Worthen, and Justin Scheck, "Accuser Said Hurd Leaked an H-P Deal," *The Wall Street Journal,* November 6–7, 2010, p. A1.

FIGURE 18.1
Hewlett-
Packard
Share Price:
2005–2011

Source: Yahoo!
Finance, Historical
Prices.

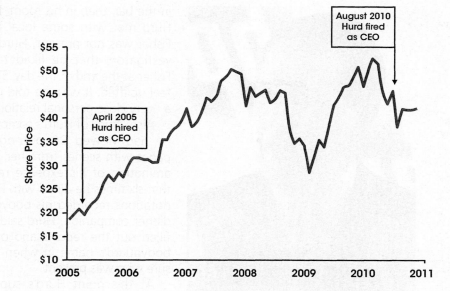

Dolls," and a reality television show appearance. Along the way, she married, divorced, and managed apartments.[2]

Hurd first interviewed Fisher in Los Angeles. Then she was flown to Denver, where they had a three-hour dinner. He hired her and between 2007 and 2009 they worked a dozen meetings together at luxury hotels around the world. Often they dined after the day's event. She was paid between $1,000 and $10,000 each time.

The 10 members of HP's board were concerned about the letter. That weekend they conducted a conference call to talk with him. Hurd said he and Fisher had dined several times but were not closely acquainted. He denied any sexual relationship with her.[3] Later she would say the same. He assured them her accusations were false. Some directors had done searches of her name, discovering her background in adult films. Hurd said he was unaware of this. The board was supportive. It wanted to keep a talented chief executive.

Shortly, Hurd suggested to the board that HP pay to settle the allegations. It did not agree. It also was unsure of its obligation to disclose events to shareholders. If the tale of a CEO and an adult actress came out, tabloid journalism would damage HP's reputation. That could affect the share price. If the claims were groundless, however, was there any duty to reveal them?

The board also hired a law firm to investigate Hurd's actions. That investigation revealed a series of prevarications. While Hurd had denied a close relationship with Fisher, a different picture emerged. The two had often dined together. They met at times when she did not work at an HP event. One night HP flew Fisher to a luxury hotel in Boise, Idaho, where she and Hurd had dinner. They watched a football game

[2] Alexandra Berzon, Ellen Byron, and Ben Worthen, "Far From H-P, A Job in Jersey," *The Wall Street Journal,* August 12, 2010, p. B1.

[3] Robert A. Guth, "Former H-P CEO Defends His Acts," *The Wall Street Journal,* October 19, 2010, p. B3.

Mark Hurd, chief executive officer, chairman of the board, and president of Hewlett-Packard is shown here speaking at a 2010 company event. Source: AP Photo/Danny Johnston.

in the bar, then in his room. The next day Hurd met with some local officials, but Fisher was not present. Hurd told the investigators that he liked to relax with Fisher at the end of the day. She made him feel uplifted. It was, he told investigators, a "very close personal relationship."[4]

Also, study of Hurd's computer revealed he had viewed 30 pornographic Web pages with scenes from her films. An examination of his expense reports found that six times he dined with Fisher but the notations recorded his bodyguard as the dinner companion. Hurd said his assistant filled out the reports and often put the bodyguard's name in when she was unsure who was present.

At this point Hurd's support on the board ebbed. Some directors favored firing him, but at least two holdouts wanted to avoid losing such an effective CEO. If the sexual harassment claims were groundless, the rest was of small concern. The directors scheduled a meeting with Gloria Allred to review the allegations. Hurd offered to repay the company for contested expense claims amounting to about $20,000. This was a minor amount to him and to the company. Since arriving he had received $146 million in compensation.

Other directors were unpersuaded. "He lied to my face and he's lying to you," one said.[5] He had violated HP's conduct code, which requires "uncompromising integrity" from every employee in a "company known for its ethical leadership." Part of the code sets forth a "Headline Test," to distinguish right from wrong by asking how actions would look if they came out in a news story or were reviewed by respected colleagues. It also admonishes employees to "[c]reate business records that accurately reflect the truth."[6] At HP a fabricated expense account was grounds for firing.

Early in August, Hurd reached an undisclosed financial settlement with Fisher that prohibited her from discussing the allegations. She released a statement saying there were many inaccuracies in her letter. Hurd explained he had settled because the amount was small compared with going to court.[7] The board was furious. Now it would have no chance to hear from Fisher and her lawyers. Hurd's remaining supporters gave up and agreed to a unanimous vote calling for his resignation. He complied.

[4] Guth, Worthen, and Scheck, "Accuser Said Hurd Leaked an H-P Deal," p. A10.

[5] Lucille S. Salhany, quoted in ibid., p. A10.

[6] Hewlett-Packard Company, *Our Standards of Business Conduct* (Palo Alto, CA: Hewlett-Packard Company, 2010 revision), front cover and pp. 3, 8, and 11.

[7] Guth, "Former H-P CEO Defends His Acts," p. B3.

His severance package was worth approximately $40 million. HP's share price dropped 14 percent over the next weeks and did not fully recover for six months. Fisher released a statement that she was "saddened" by his downfall.[8]

Not everyone agreed with the decision. A *Wall Street Journal* columnist called Hurd's offenses "piddling."[9] A *Los Angeles Times* business writer suggested "maybe it's the board that should have gone, not Hurd."[10] Larry Ellison, founder and CEO of Oracle Corporation, spoke for many.

> The HP board just made the worst personnel decision since the idiots on the Apple board fired Steve Jobs many years ago . . . In losing Mark Hurd, the HP board failed to act in the best interest of HP's employees, shareholders, customers and partners.[11]

Ellison then hired Hurd as a co-president of Oracle. HP filed a trade secrets lawsuit because Hurd had signed a confidentiality agreement. He was intimately familiar with the pricing details and component costs of HP products in areas where HP and Oracle directly competed. To settle the suit, Hurd waived his rights to $14 million of stock options in his severance package. He stayed at Oracle.

The Mark Hurd story is a story of corporate governance in action. The duty of every company's board is to watch over management in the interest of shareholders. What was the board's duty here, to maximize shareholder wealth or to uphold the integrity of management? In this chapter we define corporate governance and explain how it works. We also discuss its flaws. An unusual part of the Mark Hurd story is that, unlike many corporate boards, this one had the courage to fire a CEO. As we will show, many do not.

WHAT IS CORPORATE GOVERNANCE?

corporate governance
The exercise of authority over members of the corporate community based on formal structures, rules, and procedures.

Corporate governance is the exercise of authority over members of the corporate community based on formal structures, rules, and procedures. This authority is based on a body of rules defining the rights and duties of shareholders, boards of directors, and managers. These parties form a power triangle, shown in Figure 18.2, that controls the corporation. Steady tension exists between them, and the rules are designed to align their interests, distribute power, and settle disputes. The rules come from multiple sources, including state charters, state and federal laws, stock exchange listing standards, and corporate governance policies.

Corporate governance practice has changed dramatically over time. From the rise of market economies in the early 1700s until the mid-1800s most companies were small and run by their owners. However, with industrial capitalism some small companies grew very large and could no longer be capitalized or managed by one or two owner-proprietors. Soon ownership was dispersed in a stockholder

[8] Quoted in Ben Worthen and Joann S. Lublin, "Mark Hurd Neglected to Follow H-P Code," *The Wall Street Journal*, August 9, 2010, p. B1.
[9] Holman W. Jenkins, Jr., "The Mark Hurd Show," *The Wall Street Journal*, August 18, 2010, p. A15.
[10] Michael Hiltzik, "Ouster of HP Chief Has Look of Panic," *Los Angeles Times*, August 11, 2010, B6.
[11] Quoted in Ashlee Vance, "Oracle Chief Faults H.P. Board for Forcing Hurd Out," *The New York Times on the Web*, August 10, 2010.

FIGURE 18.2

The Power Triangle

Corporate governance is the exercise of authority over members of the corporate community. It is based on rules that define power relationships between shareholders, boards of directors, and managers.

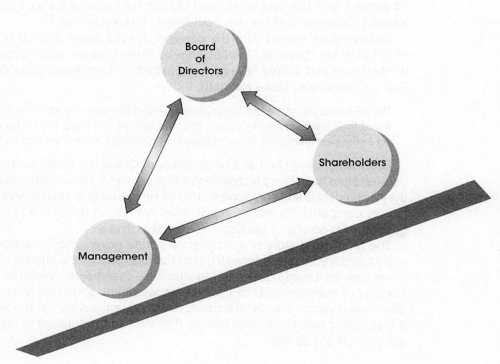

multitude where each person had only a small, fractional investment and most had little knowledge of the business. In this situation, power passed to expert managers who ran companies for the unorganized, inarticulate crowd of owners.

With the transition, boards of directors formed to monitor management for the shareholders. Shareholders were largely unqualified to manage what they owned. Hired managers had the competence to run a complex corporation, but they needed day-to-day freedom from a crowd of meddling owners. Yet they still needed supervision, because as salaried employees they lacked the same incentive to maximize profits as the owners. They might even be tempted to make their continued employment and larger salaries the top priority. It became the board's job to balance, mediate, and reconcile the competing powers and interests of owners and managers. Thus emerged the basic structure of modern corporate governance.

THE CORPORATE CHARTER

corporate charter
A document issued by a state government to create a corporation.

A *corporate charter* is the document that creates a corporation. Charters are also called articles of incorporation. U.S. corporations are chartered by the state in which they incorporate.[12] All 50 states and the District of Colombia charter corporations. When a corporation is formed in a state, it is then governed by that

---

[12] A few quasi-public enterprises chartered by the federal government, such as the Tennessee Valley Authority, are exceptions.

state's laws. At the Constitutional Convention of 1787, the founders debated a federal chartering power but decided that state controls were appropriate to regulate the more geographically limited corporate activity of that era. Their judgment was eventually outdated. As corporations expanded in size and power, states were unable to control their excesses and, as we will see, the federal government has slowly added layers of corporate law above state laws. However, all corporations are still chartered by a state.

fiduciary responsibility
The legal duty of a representative to manage property in the interest of the owner.

Corporate charters specify the purpose of the corporation, usually "any lawful act for which a corporation may be organized," and specify basic rights and duties of stockholders, directors, and officers. Fundamentally, they lodge control over the enterprise in stockholders who own shares of stock with voting rights in corporate matters. State corporation laws then give directors a *fiduciary responsibility* to shareholders, that is, as the entity entrusted with oversight of the owner's property, they are legally bound to care for that property in the owner's interest. They are responsible for appointing the managers who run the day-to-day affairs of the company.

bylaws
Rules of corporate governance adopted by corporations.

Charters may also include provisions about numbers of shares and classes of stock authorized, dividends, annual shareholder meetings, the size of boards, and procedures for removing directors. They are brief documents, usually no more than 10 or 20 pages even for the largest companies. They are supplemented with *bylaws,* or rules the company writes to clarify in detail how broad provisions of its charter will work. These bylaws resolve such ordinary matters as who presides over shareholder meetings and whether directors can hold a meeting over the telephone.

States compete to attract the incorporation fees and tax revenues of corporations. For more than a century tiny Delaware has been the victor in this competition. It charters about half of all public corporations in the United States. About 17 percent of its state tax revenues, far more than any other state, come from chartering fees. Although costs of incorporating in Delaware are high, its corporate laws are friendly toward directors and managers. To maintain its addiction to corporate tax revenue the state has repeatedly innovated more flexible and enabling rules. Other states must match or approach its standards to remain competitive.

Delaware refuses to be underregulated. For example, when the personal liability of directors began to expand in the 1980s, several states experimented with tentative limits to such exposure. Delaware reacted by limiting director liability for all but the most witless and negligent acts. Within a year, 35 states matched its leniency.[13] In this race to the bottom "no one in Delaware is willing to play hare while some other state tortoise gains ground."[14] In addition, Delaware also has a special Chancery Court that handles only business cases and is very friendly to boards and managers. It is expensive and difficult for all but the wealthiest shareholders of a Delaware corporation to prevail in a lawsuit against directors or managers.

---

[13] Roberta Romano, "The States as a Laboratory: Legal Innovation and State Competition for Corporate Charters," *Yale Journal on Regulation,* Summer 2006, p. 212.

[14] Delaware attorney Lawrence A. Hamermesh, quoted in Mark J. Roe, "Delaware's Shrinking Half-Life," *Stanford Law Review,* December 2009, p. 129.

Shareholder activists, who believe that boards and top executives have too much power in corporate governance, are provoked by Delaware. They lobbied North Dakota to pass a new, model law with provisions that strengthen the powers of stockholders and make boards more independent of management.[15] Corporations such as Whole Foods Markets that emphasize social responsibility in their strategies have been pressured to reincorporate in North Dakota. There has been no rush.

POWER IN CORPORATE GOVERNANCE: THEORY AND REALITY

The legal line of power in state charters and incorporation laws runs from the state, to shareholders, to directors, to managers. However, this legal theory diverges from the reality as widely practiced. The theory is shown on the left side of Figure 18.3. The reality, as shown on the right, is that CEOs often dominate boards of directors and both together dominate shareholders.

Stockholders

Stockholders are said to be owners of corporations. However, rather than owning an identifiable part or fraction of the corporation as property they own only a

FIGURE 18.3   Flow of Authority in Corporate Governance

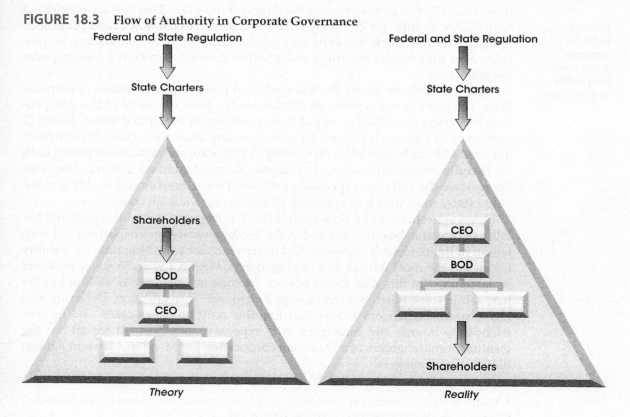

[15] The Publicly Traded Corporations Act (2007).

stock certificate. Owning this certificate gives them certain limited, but important, rights. A basic reason their rights are limited is that under state laws common stockholders are free of liability for the corporation's actions, therefore, their control of those actions is diminished.

Stockholders' rights are given in corporate charters, bylaws, and state and federal laws. Their basic entitlements are to (1) sell their stock, (2) vote to elect directors and on other corporate issues, (3) receive information about the corporation, (4) receive dividends, (5) sue the corporation if directors and officers commit wrongful acts, and (6) acquire residual assets in case of bankruptcy, but only after payment of creditors and bondholders.

If stockholders are dissatisfied with corporate management, they can sell their shares. Otherwise, they influence management by voting in corporate elections. In large public companies stockholders receive notice of elections to be held at annual meetings. Such elections typically ask for a vote on director nominees, management's choice of auditors, charter amendments or changes in bylaws, stock issuances, and nonbinding resolutions. Stockholders are invited to attend an annual meeting and vote their shares. Or, if they do not attend, they can fill out a ballot-like *proxy card* that gives management the authority to cast votes for them as they indicate. The proxy card is accompanied by a *proxy statement* with legally mandated information about the matters up for a vote, including biographies of director nominees and their qualifications, a detailed analysis of executive compensation, and the text of other proposals.

The annual meeting itself is a formal, ritualized event usually held in the spring. Its purpose is to allow voting and interaction between stockholders, directors, and officers. A typical meeting has several parts, a business meeting where agenda items are raised and voting results announced, a presentation by the chief executive about the company's outlook, and a question-and-answer session for stockholders. When the floor is opened for questions at a big company meeting, meaningful exchanges are rare. A few stockholders may praise the CEO for doing a good job. Activists, who have purchased a few shares to gain entry, harangue management for irresponsible behavior. Most are respectful, but some are not. At a recent Chevron Corp. meeting an energy activist started a protest chant and was arrested.[16] Every spring a few others require security escorts to leave. Employees may rise to express grievances. At one FedEx meeting a freight handler stated that while the company was making millions of dollars in profits he and others were not paid enough to "have a decent life."[17]

Shareholder Resolutions

Shareholders, either individuals or funds, can propose resolutions for a vote at the annual meeting. These resolutions are printed in the proxy statement. Securities

proxy card
A form stockholders mark giving management the right to vote their shares as indicated. It is also called simply a proxy or a proxy form.

proxy statement
A booklet of information sent to stockholders before annual votes on directors, executive pay, and other matters.

---

[16] John Letzing, "Activist Faces Charges in Chevron Outburst," *The Wall Street Journal*, September 29, 2010, p. B4.

[17] Comments of Ray Mercado, FedEx Corp., *FedEx 2010 Shareowners Meeting Transcript*, September 27, 2010, pp. 10–11.

and Exchange Commission (SEC) regulations set forth the requirements they must meet, including the following.[18]

- Sponsors must own $2,000 or more of the company's shares for at least one year.
- They may not submit more than one resolution a year.
- The resolution cannot exceed 500 words and must be sent to the company for approval at least 120 days before the annual meeting.
- The shareholder must appear at the meeting to present the resolution.
- The resolution must get 3 percent of the vote to be resubmitted the next year, 6 percent to be resubmitted a third year, and 10 percent for the fourth year and after.

Under SEC rules, a company can reject a proposed resolution for any of 13 reasons. For example, it can reject a proposal if it is a personal grievance, contains false or misleading statements, or deals with matters beyond the company's influence. The SEC must approve each rejection. In 2009 a Catholic investor group wanted to introduce a proposal about sensitivity to American Indian peoples at the FedEx annual meeting. The resolution required FedEx to "identify and dissociate with any names, symbols and imagery that disparage American Indian peoples" and to report on whether its diversity training for management was "sensitive to Native American rights, histories and cultures." FedEx contacted the SEC, seeking to omit the proposal because it dealt with "ordinary business operations." Proposals can be excluded under this exception if they constitute shareholder micromanagement of fundamental, day-to-day tasks in running the company. FedEx argued this one sought oversight of advertising and training, both "ordinary" functions that shareholders were unqualified to oversee. The SEC agreed and the proposal was omitted.[19]

Each year hundreds of shareholder resolutions qualify to appear on proxy statements. In 2010, 507 resolutions were voted on. Most, 342, wanted corporate governance reforms such as allowing shareholders to convene special meetings, splitting the chairman and CEO positions, and forcing managers to hold stock awards until two years after their employment ended. Ninety got a majority of votes cast. Another 165 resolutions focused on social issues, including concerns such as political spending, carbon emissions, toxic chemicals, diversity, and animal welfare. There was little support for them. Only two had a majority vote, both requesting the company prepare a report on sustainability.

Almost universally, shareholder proposals are followed by the statement, "The Board of Directors recommends a vote AGAINST this proposal." This is accompanied by an explanation of why the board urges rejection. Its opposition is usually fatal. Even when a proposal receives a majority vote, it is not binding. However, its success puts pressure on the company and often results in change.

---

[18] "Shareholder Proposals," 17 CFR §240.14a-8 (2011).

[19] Securities and Exchange Commission, Office of Chief Counsel, Division of Corporation Finance, FedEx Corporation No Action Letter, July 14, 2009.

Assessing Shareholder Influence

Although in theory shareholders have the voting power to influence or even replace management, they rarely exercise it. First, corporate elections are not fully democratic. They have several elements of democracy. Shareholders are at liberty to vote. Their votes count equally.[20] And the majority rules. However, as in old-style communist elections there is often no contest. Directors usually run unopposed. Stockholders can vote for or against them (or abstain), but they cannot vote for another candidate. Stockholders can submit nominees to board nominating committees, but the directors do not have to pick them. Occasionally a large shareholder tries to challenge the election of one or more directors, but this is hugely expensive and rarely successful.

Management also has other advantages. It is united, while stockholders are fragmented. Among such a large group of passive individuals it is hard for opposition to coalesce. Most shareholders follow management's voting recommendations. And as proxies come in, management can see how the vote is going and, if necessary, call on large shareholders, including brokers or pension funds, to change their votes. In sum, the influence of shareholders is very weak. In 1949 one perceptive investor summed up the contradiction of stockholder power this way. The words are as apt today as then.

> In legal rights and legal machinery . . . stockholders as a class are king. Acting as a majority they can hire and fire managements and bend them completely to their will. Though ownership may be widely scattered, there is no legal obstacle to many stockholders' joining forces so as to create an effective majority voice on any issue that may arise . . .
>
> [I]n practice . . . the stockholders are a complete washout. As a class they show neither intelligence nor alertness. They vote in sheep-like fashion for whatever the management recommends and no matter how poor the management's record of accomplishment may be.[21]

FEDERAL REGULATION OF GOVERNANCE

For more than 150 years state incorporation statutes, laws, and court decisions defined the requirements of corporate governance. At first this worked well. Most corporations were small. Their activities were confined within state boundaries. However, in the late 1800s and early 1900s mergers and firm growth created much larger firms that served national markets. These firms required more capital. Before the 1890s only a small number of very wealthy individuals held stock. But larger firms issued stock freely and their ownership was dispersed among small investors in many states.

---

[20] An exception is when companies have dual classes of stock. An example is Ford Motor Company, where members of the Ford family own Class B shares, which are given greater weight than common shares in company elections.

[21] Benjamin Graham, *The Intelligent Investor* (New York: HarperCollins, 2005), p. 207. Originally published in 1949.

Now both business activity and stock ownership crossed state lines. State corporation laws proved less and less adequate for oversight, especially since corporations sought charters in those states with the most flexible and permissive rules. Perhaps the greatest defect of state governance laws was inability to prevent fraud and manipulation in national capital markets.[22]

This deficiency eventually had catastrophic consequences. Prosperity in the 1920s led to a stock market boom. After 1927, buying in then-unregulated securities markets reached a frenzy. Entrepreneurs set up hollow empires of companies just to issue stock. Brokers allowed investors with very modest incomes to buy shares on margins as low as 10 percent. The buyers often knew little or nothing about the companies behind their shares. When a speculative bubble burst in October 1929, prices collapsed in days of extreme panic. People lost their savings. The nation advanced into depression.

In response to this catastrophe the federal government intervened to protect stockholders and bring integrity to capital markets. Congress passed the Securities Act of 1933 requiring companies to register securities and provide financial statements and other information to buyers before their sale. It then passed the Securities Exchange Act of 1934 giving birth to a regulatory agency, the Securities and Exchange Commission that would police securities markets. The 1934 law also required companies to file periodic reports, including annual reports called 10-Ks, quarterly reports called 10-Qs, and reports known as 8-Ks that quickly update investors on significant events such as votes in annual meetings.

These initial statutes added a layer of governance law above state laws. Since then, this layer has expanded. The Securities and Exchange Commission (SEC) is an independent regulatory commission with five members, one of whom serves as chairman, appointed by the president for five years. Since 1934 Congress has passed 38 more statutes adding to the SEC's powers. It now has a staff of 3,500 and an annual budget of approximately $900 million. Other entities, including the Treasury Department and the Federal Reserve System, also regulate securities markets.

Despite proliferation, federal and state governance laws have not always been a match for situations that arise. The stories of Enron and Lehman Brothers teach how governance reforms still play catch-up with governance abuses.

Enron Corp.

Spectacular business scandals are recurrent in American history. However, not since the epic corporate misdeeds of the 1930s had there been such a wave of business scandals as at the turn of the twenty-first century. Enron's amazing disintegration in 2001 was the supernova in a field of frauds where executives looted shareholder wealth while directors slept. In multiple instances corporate governance failed.

Enron was an energy company headquartered in Houston, Texas, and incorporated in Oregon. Until the 1990s it was a staid natural gas, oil, and electricity

---

[22] Jack B. Jacobs, "The Reach of State Corporate Law Beyond State Borders: Reflections Upon Federalism," *New York University Law Review,* November 2009, pp. 1151–55.

producer. Then it radically changed its business model to become the world's largest online energy trading company. Its apparent success earned the admiration of investors, academics, and the public.

As it grew it created a structural maze of limited partnerships and other financial entities, numbering in the hundreds, to carry out exotic financial transactions. It all seemed to work. Enron's profits went from $1 million in 1996 to $1.1 billion in 2000. Investors, few of whom understood the puzzling structure and hedging activities, romanticized its prospects and drove share prices skyward. They delighted in a 1,415 percent return between 1990 and 2000, a period ending in speculative frenzy as the stock shot from $19.10 in 1999 to a high of $90.80 in 2000.

This bright picture clouded late in 2001 when the company announced a $554 million after-tax charge against revenues. Soon it revised its financial statements from 1997 to 2001, reducing net income more than $1 billion. The reason was it had reported false income from suspicious trading arrangements. Markets turned against Enron. It could not borrow to meet its obligations and late in 2001 it filed for bankruptcy. About $60 billion in market value was wiped out.

Enron had a board of distinguished directors (see the box on the next page). Following the bankruptcy it set up a special committee to investigate its actions. One focus was on a series of off-balance-sheet partnerships created by Andrew S. Fastow, the company's chief financial officer. The board had approved them although they created a conflict of interest.[23] In some partnerships Fastow was both a manager for Enron and an investor in an outside entity that engaged in financial transactions, such as the buying and selling of assets, with Enron. Which interest would be his priority, Enron's or his own? Unfortunately, Fastow was using the partnerships to enrich himself.

Another problem was that the partnerships concealed Enron's true financial state. Accounting rules were that if an outside investor, here Fastow, put in 3 percent or more of the capital in a partnership, the corporation, even if it provided the other 97 percent, did not have to declare it a subsidiary. Therefore, its assets and debt could be withheld from the corporation's balance sheet.[24] Using this loophole, Enron's directors eventually approved removing almost half Enron's assets from its balance sheet, hiding losses and debt totaling hundreds of millions of dollars.

The directors recognized it was a conflict of interest for Fastow to be an outside investor in the partnerships, but rationalized it was a modest risk considering the great possible gain for Enron. They thought it could be handled with controls specified by the board. They were mistaken. Their policy gave a green light to expansion of the partnerships beyond anything they ever envisioned. In fact, this partnership proliferation exposed the company to fatal risks. Simultaneously, Fastow orchestrated side deals netting him more than $30 million as an individual.

---

[23] William C. Powers, Jr., chair; Raymond S. Troubh; and Herbert S. Winokur, Jr., *Report of Investigation by the Special Investigative Committee of the Board of Directors of Enron Corp.*, February 1, 2002. Powers was dean of the University of Texas School of Law. Powers and Troubh were appointed to the board after the committee was formed. Winokur had been a member of the board at the time of bankruptcy.

[24] John R. Emshwiller and Rebecca Smith, "Murky Waters: A Primer on Enron Partnerships," *The Wall Street Journal*, January 21, 2002, p. C14.

Enron's Board of Directors

In 2001, the year that Enron filed for bankruptcy, its board consisted of the 14 members below, including one female, one black, and two Asian directors. Two members, Lay and Skilling, were officers of Enron. The other 12 were nonemployee directors.

ROBERT A. BELFER, 65
Chairman and CEO
Belco Oil & Gas Corp.

NORMAN P. BLAKE, JR., 59
Chairman, President, and CEO
Comdisco, Inc.

RONNIE C. CHAN, 51
Chairman
Hang Lung Group

JOHN H. DUNCAN, 73
Investor

DR. WENDY L. GRAMM, 56
Director, Mercatus Center Regulatory Studies
Program, George Mason University and wife of
U.S. Senator Phil Gramm (R-Texas)

DR. ROBERT K. JAEDICKE, 72
Professor (Emeritus) of Accounting
Stanford University

KENNETH L. LAY, 58
Chairman of the Board

CHARLES A. LeMAISTRE, 77
President (Emeritus)
University of Texas M.D. Anderson Cancer Center

JOHN MENDELSOHN, 64
President
University of Texas M.D. Anderson
Cancer Center

PAULO V. FERRAZ PEREIRA, 46
Executive Vice President
Group Bozano

FRANK SAVAGE, 62
Chairman
Alliance Capital Management International

JEFFREY K. SKILLING, 47
President and CEO
Enron Corporation

JOHN WAKEHAM, 68
United Kingdom Secretary of State (ret.) and
former Member of Parliament

HERBERT S. WINOKUR, JR., 57
Chairman and CEO
Capricorn Holdings, Inc

In the previous year, each nonemployee director received an average cash payment of $79,107, including an annual fee and additional fees for attending meetings or chairing one of the five board committees (executive, audit, finance, compensation, or nominating). In addition, each nonemployee director received grants of Enron stock and stock options valued at $836,517. At the time of the 2001 annual shareholders' meeting the nonemployee directors owned a total of $670 million in Enron shares. The 14 directors also served on the boards of 25 other companies.

Source: Enron Corp., *Proxy Statement,* March 27, 2001, pp. 1–12.

Controls on Fastow were never properly implemented. The board's audit committee was supposed to conduct annual reviews of all partnerships, but it failed to probe deeply into the bizarre transactions being generated. The board also made Enron's chief accounting officer responsible for reviewing and approving all transactions between the company and its partnerships. The review was inadequate because, said the investigating committee, top management was "not watching the store."

Indeed, a fundamental cause of the catastrophe was a change in culture wrought by the two top officers, Chairman of the Board Kenneth L. Lay and CEO Jeffrey K. Skilling. They fostered and permitted a freewheeling climate that tolerated junior officers engaging in illegal activities. Enron became the classic illustration of a Wild West corporate culture characterized by reckless financial deals, avarice, and deceit. It lacked an emphasis on integrity. With Lay as its chairman and Skilling a member, the board failed in its duty to maintain norms of ethics and compliance.

The investigative committee absolved Enron's board of sole blame for the bankruptcy, but accused it of failing to exercise its oversight responsibility. It found that board members "were severely hampered by the fact that significant information was withheld from them," but also that the board "did not fully appreciate the significance of some information that came before it."[25] Partnership arrangements involving substantial sums and risk were presented to the board and it failed to give them the scrutiny they deserved. Some intricate deals received only 10 or 15 minutes of attention. Fastow's first partnership was one of six agenda items in a board meeting that lasted just an hour. One director attended by calling in from a pay phone in Virginia and could not clearly hear the discussion.[26] While the investigating committee felt the board could not be faulted for not acting if it had no or insufficient information, it could be faulted for limited scrutiny and probing.

An investigation by the U.S. Senate was harder on the board. Interviews with board members revealed many conflicts of interest. For example, Enron was paying director John Wakeham $6,000 a month in consulting fees. The current and prior presidents of the M.D. Anderson Cancer Center in Texas were both board members. In the previous five years Enron and Ken Lay had given $600,000 to this institution. Director Wendy Gramm's husband, Senator Phil Gramm, received campaign contributions from Enron.[27] These and several other financial ties undermined the independence of the directors.

The Senate investigation also concluded that the board had authorized excessive compensation of Enron executives. One year the board approved a compensation plan in which executives received $430 million in bonuses when the company's

[25] Powers, Troubh, and Winokur, *Report of the Special Investigative Committee of the Board of Directors of Enron Corp.*, pp. 159 and 148.

[26] The director was Wendy Gramm. In John Gillespie and David Zweig, *Money for Nothing* (New York: Free Press, 2010), pp. 67–68.

[27] Report of the Permanent Subcommittee on Investigations, Committee on Governmental Affairs, U.S. Senate, *The Role of the Board of Directors in Enron's Collapse,* 107th Congress, 2nd Session, Report 107-70, July 8, 2002, pp. 54–56.

entire net income was only $975 million. In 2000 Ken Lay earned $140 million. One of his subordinates received $265 million in the same year. The board also approved a line of credit for Lay, who withdrew $77 million in cash from Enron, then replaced it with Enron stock! Overall, concluded the Senate report, "the Enron Board failed to provide the prudent oversight and checks and balances that its fiduciary obligations required and a company like Enron needed."[28]

In 2006, a federal jury found Lay and Skilling guilty of conspiracy and fraud in the Enron collapse. Jurors believed both had lied publicly about the company's financial health while all along profiting from the sale of millions of shares of their Enron stock.[29] Lay's death voided his conviction, but Skilling was sentenced to 24 years and four months in jail. Fastow pleaded guilty to conspiracy and fraud charges. Because of his willingness to testify against former top executives he was given a comparatively light six-year sentence. None of Enron's outside directors faced criminal indictments. However, 10 members of the board agreed to pay $13 million from their own pockets to settle a civil suit by Enron employees charging they had failed in their oversight of company retirement plans.[30]

Other Failures of Governance

The failures of the Enron board were echoed in other fraud scandals at about the same time. Among the most prominent are these.

- At Tyco International the board slumbered while CEO L. Dennis Kozlowski took as much as $125 million in corporate funds for his personal use and conspired with his CFO Mark H. Swartz to misrepresent the company's financial condition and boost its stock price. On conviction for grand larceny, falsifying accounting records, and conspiracy, both received prison sentences of 8 to 25 years. Kozlowski was ordered to pay $97 million in restitution and a $70 million fine. His wife visited him only once in prison, coming to tell him she wanted a divorce.[31] Tyco's directors, who failed to exercise adequate oversight, suffered no formal penalty.

- At Adelphia Communications the directors dozed as founder John J. Rigas and his son Timothy concealed $2.3 billion in off-balance-sheet debt, stole $100 million from the company, and lied to investors about its financial condition. At sentencing, the judge told the elder Rigas that he had "set Adelphia on a track of lying, of cheating, of defrauding," then heard Rigas respond that "in my heart and conscience, I'll go to my grave really and truly believing I did nothing."[32] He was sentenced to 15 years in federal prison, his son Timothy to 20 years, and another son, John, Jr., to 10 months' home confinement. The Adelphia directors were never penalized for their limp oversight.

[28] Ibid., p. 59.

[29] *United States v. Jeffrey K. Skilling and Kenneth W. Lay,* Cr. No. H-04-025, S. Dist. Tex. (2006).

[30] *Newby, et al., v. Enron Corp.,* 235 F. Supp. 2d 594 (2002).

[31] Steve Dunleavy, "On Her First Prison Visit, My Wife Told Me, 'I Want a Divorce' Koz," *New York Post,* October 30, 2006, p. 6.

[32] Quotations are in Dean Starkman, "Rigases Given Prison Terms," *The Washington Post,* June 21, 2005, p. D1.

- At WorldCom, in a story told more fully in Chapter 7, the board napped while CEO Bernard J. Ebbers and CFO Scott D. Sullivan concealed falling revenues and rising expenses in an $11 billion accounting fraud. Ebbers was sentenced to 25 years in prison, Sullivan to 5 years. Accused of negligent oversight, 11 WorldCom directors agreed to pay 20 percent of their aggregate net worth, about $20.3 million, in restitution to defrauded investors.[33] As with the Enron directors, this came from their own pockets.

Each of these corporations declared bankruptcy. Jobs and life savings were lost. In each case the directors failed in their duty to protect shareholders from self-interested, predatory managers. Their failure inspired a range of corporate governance reforms aimed at sharpening boardroom vigilance. The centerpiece was the Sarbanes-Oxley Act of 2002.

The Sarbanes-Oxley Act

Sarbanes-Oxley Act of 2002
A statute enacted to prevent financial fraud in corporations. It mandated stricter financial reporting and greater board oversight.

On signing the *Sarbanes-Oxley Act of 2002* into law President George W. Bush said it embodied "the most far-reaching reforms of American business practice since the time of Franklin Delano Roosevelt."[34] There was little disagreement. The law's primary focus is on accounting rules. It also puts devices in place to hold management responsible for accurate financial reports and it increases the oversight responsibilities of boards of directors. Here are its main provisions.

- It creates a Public Company Accounting Oversight Board to oversee accounting firms and improve the accuracy of their audits.
- Audit firms are prohibited from doing consulting work for corporations while also auditing their books. Audit firms must rotate every five years. This broke a long-standing conflict of interest situation where auditors were tempted to please their clients in order to pursue lucrative consulting contracts.
- Companies must tell whether they have a code setting forth "standards of honesty and ethical conduct" for senior financial officers or, if not, why not.
- Every board of directors must create an audit committee to oversee the firm's accounting policies and controls. It must consist of independent directors who do not receive fees from the company other than their director's compensation. One member of this committee must be a "financial expert."
- The CEO and the CFO must sign and certify the accuracy of annual and quarterly financial reports. If the statements are false, they face criminal penalties up to $5 million and 20 years in prison.
- Companies must reveal off-balance-sheet transactions such as those used by Enron.
- Boards of directors are prohibited from approving personal loans for company executives.
- Directors (and managers) are subject to heavy penalties. Civil violations can lead to fines of up to $100,000. Criminal violations can lead to fines of up to $50 million and lengthy prison terms.

[33] Daniel Akst, "Fining the Directors Misses the Mark," *The New York Times,* August 21, 2005, sec. 3, p. 6.
[34] Quoted in Stephen M. Bainbridge, "The Creeping Federalization of Corporation Law," *Regulation,* spring 2003, p. 28.

The business community complained that the law was burdensome. A 2005 survey found the average cost of implementing it in 90 companies ranged from a few hundred thousand dollars for small firms to $7.8 million for the largest.[35] Large corporations now spend millions of dollars a year in complying and complain that its costs may exceed its benefits.[36]

Enron's failure shook up the governance system everywhere. Corporate groups, accountants, credit rating agencies, securities analysts, and stock exchanges all came out with sets of reforms to strengthen boards. The New York Stock Exchange is an example. It maintains rules that all listed companies must follow. Soon after the enactment of Sarbanes-Oxley it revised these rules to conform with and go beyond the new law. It required a majority of independent directors on the boards of all listed companies. In addition, it required every board to have three committees—audit, compensation, and governance (or nominating)—each composed entirely of independent directors.

Did all this rulemaking work to awaken and empower boards? The answer is no. While it may have prevented an unknown number of frauds and scandals, it failed to prevent widespread board somnolence, a curiosity at the center of a near systemwide financial collapse in 2008. The story of Lehman Brothers is exhibit A.

Lehman Brothers

Lehman Brothers Holdings began in 1850 as a cotton broker and grew into the nation's fourth-largest investment bank. Since 1994 it had been run by a CEO named Richard S. Fuld, Jr. Intense, intimidating, and impatient, Fuld had a confrontational manner and, according to one colleague, gave off "little physical cues" hinting any disagreement could turn to physical violence.[37] Once, when a manager asked him to wait, he cleared the person's desk with a sweep of his hand. Fuld referred to Lehman as "the mother ship" and demanded total loyalty. He saw each day, each situation as a battle. You were either on the team or off it. In keeping with this worldview, he made Lehman stock a large part of compensation and required employees to hold it as long as five years before selling. This motivated everyone so long as the stock price rose.

In 2006, Fuld decided that the way to keep share prices rising was to make Lehman grow faster. He introduced an aggressive strategy requiring more risk and increased leverage on capital. Lehman invested its assets in subprime mortgages, commercial real estate, high-yield bonds, leveraged loans, and mortgage-backed securities. This reduced its liquidity and raised firmwide risk. It did grow, to $691 billion in assets by 2007. Its leverage ratio eventually reached 39 to 1, that is, it had borrowed $39 for every dollar in its accounts.

---

[35] Deborah Solomon, "At What Price?" *The Wall Street Journal*, October 17, 2005, p. R3.

[36] One 2007 survey found average annual compliance costs of $5 million and only 31 percent of directors of surveyed firms who thought benefits exceeded costs. Korn/Ferry Institute, *34th Annual Board of Directors Study* (New York: Korn/Ferry International, 2007), p. 16.

[37] Anonymous, quoted in Steve Fishman, "Burning Down His House," *New York Magazine*, December 8, 2008, p. 1.

Richard S. Fuld at a 2010 hearing of the Financial Crisis Inquiry Commission where he testified on the bankruptcy of Lehman Brothers.
Source: AP Photo/ Carolyn Kaster.

repurchase agreement
A financing transaction in which one firm lends assets to another firm in exchange for cash with a simultaneous agreement to purchase the assets back.

To fund its operations, Lehman depended on borrowing tens of billions of dollars each day in financial markets. Its ability to do so turned on the confidence of others in its liquidity. When the subprime mortgage crisis materialized in 2007, lenders began to lose confidence in Lehman and required more collateral, even for routine financing. To shore up confidence Lehman resorted to an accounting trick its employees called "Repo 105." Ordinarily, Lehman raised cash using *repurchase agreements* in which it sold assets to a counterparty and agreed to repurchase them in the next 24 to 72 hours. During these brief, routine financing transactions the assets stayed on Lehman's balance sheet. But with the Repo 105 technique, Lehman sold assets equal to 105 percent or more of the cash it received, which, under a strained interpretation of accounting rules, allowed it to treat the asset transfer as a sale.

Using Repo 105, Lehman briefly removed up to $50 billion of assets from its balance sheet precisely at the end of the first and second quarters in 2008, allowing it to reduce its net leverage ratio from 13.9 to 12.1. With this sleight of hand Lehman ended reporting periods with a stronger-looking, but misleading, balance sheet. It was not a clear violation of accounting rules, yet Lehman never disclosed its use to lenders, investors, analysts, or its own board of directors. Thus, it concealed the firm's real debt level from interested parties. Not everyone at Lehman accepted the legitimacy of Repo 105. Some of its accountants called it a gimmick. A senior vice president wrote to the firm's controller complaining of "balance sheet manipulation" and reported the use of Repo 105 to Lehman's external auditor Ernst & Young.[38] Nobody acted.

Repo 105 was not enough to save Lehman Brothers. In September 2008, as credit markets began to freeze, another investment bank, Bear Stearns, almost failed and was rescued at the last minute by a government-arranged merger with JP Morgan Chase. Attention then turned to Lehman Brothers, which was viewed as the next most vulnerable investment bank. It faced a run on its assets, was no longer able to borrow, and filed for bankruptcy September 15. It set a new record for the size of a bankruptcy, besting WorldCom and, before it, Enron.

Lehman's bankruptcy caused panic in the markets. That day the Dow Jones average fell 504 points. The next day insurer AIG faced imminent collapse. Prime Fund, a money market fund that held Lehman's notes, was no longer able to maintain its shares at $1 of face value. Both had to be bailed out by an infusion of billions of dollars from the Federal Reserve System. And within a month Congress passed an emergency rescue plan, the $700 billion Toxic Assets Relief Program intended to shore up the nation's "too-big-to-fail" institutions. Fuld would later argue that "Lehman's demise was caused by uncontrollable market forces," but admit that "I, myself, did not see the depth and violence of the crisis. I did not see the contagion. I believe we made poor judgments . . ."[39]

Lehman's shareholders lost almost everything. Its stock fell from a high of $62.19 that January to $3.65 at bankruptcy, a 94 percent decline. Where was the firm's board of directors, the entity charged with monitoring management for them? Lehman had an 11-member board including 10 independent directors and one insider, Richard Fuld, who was both chairman of the board and CEO (see the box). Fuld dominated the selection of directors, and they were a congenial group, unlikely to challenge him. There was little board turnover. And directors were generous in compensating Fuld. Between 2000 and 2008 his average pay was $46 million a year.[40]

Only 1 of the 10 outside directors, Jerry A. Grundhofer, had any recent banking experience and he had served only for five months. Another, 80-year-old Henry Kaufman, had retired from investment banking 20 years earlier. Others included current and retired executives from nonfinancial industries. It was not a group selected for keen insight into financial transactions.

During the year preceding bankruptcy the board met eight times and its members earned between $325,038 and $397,538. The directors were informed that Lehman was taking increased risk to create firm growth. At every board meeting they received a risk report, including a numeric representation of the firm's "risk appetite." Managers told the board they were taking precautions to monitor and limit overall risks. They did not, however, fully inform it about all

[38] *Report of Anton R. Valukas, Examiner, In re Lehman Brothers Holdings Inc.*, Chapter 11 Case No. 08-13555, S. Dist. N.Y., March 11, 2010, vol. 1, p. 21.

[39] Testimony of Richard S. Fuld before the Financial Crisis Inquiry Commission hearing on "Too Big to Fail: Expectations and Impact of Extraordinary Government Intervention and the Role of Systemic Risk in the Financial Crisis," Washington, DC, September 1, 2010, p. 203.

[40] Scott Thurm, "Oracle's Ellison: Pay King," *The Wall Street Journal,* July 27, 2010, p. A16.

Lehman Brothers' Board of Directors

These were the 11 members of the Lehman Brothers board of directors in 2008 when the firm filed for bankruptcy. Only Richard S. Fuld was a Lehman Brothers executive. The other 10 were nonemployee directors who qualified as independent under the rules of the New York Stock Exchange.

MICHAEL L. AINSLIE, 64
Private Investor and Former President and
Chief Executive Officer of Sotheby's Holdings

JOHN F. AKERS, 73
Retired Chairman of International Business
Machines Corporation

ROGER S. BERLIND, 77
Theatrical Producer

THOMAS H. CRUIKSHANK, 76
Retired Chairman and Chief Executive Officer of
Halliburton Company

MARSHA JOHNSON EVANS, 60
Rear Admiral, U.S. Navy (Retired)

RICHARD S. FULD, JR., 61
Chairman and Chief Executive Officer,
Lehman Brothers Holdings Inc.

SIR CHRISTOPHER GENT, 59
Non-Executive Chairman of GlaxoSmithKline Plc.

JERRY A. GRUNDHOFER, 63
Chairman Emeritus and Retired Chief Executive
Officer of U.S. Bancorp

ROLAND A. HERNANDEZ, 50
Retired Chairman and Chief Executive Officer of
Telemundo Group, Inc.

HENRY KAUFMAN, 80
President of Henry Kaufman & Company, Inc.

JOHN D. MACOMBER, 80
Principal of JDM Investment Group

In the previous year, each nonexecutive director received an annual cash retainer of $75,000 plus fees for chairing and attending meetings of board committees. Each also received grants of Lehman Brothers stock or stock options valued at $245,038. The 10 nonexecutive directors served on the boards of 16 other companies.

Source: Lehman Brothers Holdings Inc., *Proxy Statement,* March 5, 2008, pp. 6–18.

the dangers. For example, they neglected to mention periodic shortcomings in liquidity tests. And they failed to inform the directors that the firm sometimes exceeded its risk limits. At one board meeting, when the firm had exceeded these limits, the CFO edited a standard chart to remove the risk appetite numbers that ordinarily appeared.[41]

Another time, Lehman's president told a manager not to give the board much detail about risky subprime mortgages because the directors were "not

[41] *Report of Anton R. Valukas, Examiner, In re Lehman Brothers Holdings Inc.,* Chapter 11 Case No. 08-13555, S. Dist. N.Y., March 11, 2010, vol. 1, pp. 21 and 141.

sophisticated."[42] The board did have a risk committee, but it met only twice in the year before Lehman's bankruptcy. It was chaired by the octogenarian Henry Kaufman. Its other members included a retired admiral who had been head of the Girl Scouts, the retired chairman of IBM, a theatrical producer, and the retired chairman of a Spanish-language television company. It was not a group with much background for judging such esoterica as the single tranche collateralized debt obligations that Lehman used to hedge risks.

Lehman's management made serious errors of judgment. Senior officers, including Fuld, certified deceptive financial statements based on accounting tricks. The board failed to detect trouble and rein in extreme risk. Corporate governance let the firm's shareholders down. Although Lehman's headquarters were in New York, it was incorporated in Delaware. A special examiner appointed by the court in Lehman's bankruptcy case found that neither company officers nor directors had breached their fiduciary duty to shareholders under Delaware law. They were protected by its lenient "business judgment" rule, which rejects personal liability absent "reckless indifference," "deliberate disregard," or actions "without the bounds of reason."[43]

Since Lehman had risk policies in place and the directors had discussed risk, their bank accounts were safe from angry shareholders. However, as a group, directors and managers lost considerable wealth. Fuld was Lehman's largest individual shareowner with 12.6 million shares. He held them until the end and, based on price decline from a 2008 high, lost approximately $738 million. The directors held a combined 1.1 million shares that lost about $60 million in value.

The Dodd-Frank Act

Dodd-Frank Act
A statute to reform financial regulation and prevent a recurrence of the 2007–2008 financial crisis.

In the aftermath of Lehman's failure and the financial disaster in its wake, Congress responded with another repair statute, the 849-page *Dodd-Frank Wall Street Reform and Consumer Protection Act of 2010* (the Dodd-Frank Act). At its core it was a huge dose of new financial regulations targeting root causes of the recent crisis. It mandated five new agencies and 330 new rulemakings.[44] There were new powers over banks and financial markets, restraints on risk-taking, limits on hedging and the use of novel financial products, mortgage lending reforms, and strengthened mortgage lending criteria.

While the law's main focus was financial reform, it did not neglect governance failures observed at Lehman and other companies that survived the crisis only with government assistance. The public believed investment bankers were overpaid, and so the Dodd-Frank Act moved to strengthen checks on executive compensation.

- At least once every three years companies have to submit their executive compensation packages to a stockholder vote. The stockholders may approve or disapprove; however, the vote is not binding.

[42] Ibid., p. 90.
[43] Ibid., pp. 47–48 and pp. 54–55.
[44] Curtis W. Copeland, *Rulemaking Requirements and Authorities in the Dodd-Frank Wall Street Reform and Consumer Protection Act,* Congressional Research Service, Report No. R414722, November 3, 2010, p. 8.

- If an executive is entitled to special compensation in case of merger, buyout, or other change of control, the stockholders must have a chance to vote their approval or disapproval. Again, the vote is not binding.
- All members of the board committee that sets executive compensation must be "independent," that is, free of any conflict of interest coming from any paid connection to the company apart from being a director.
- In proxy statements companies must disclose the relationship between executive compensation and their financial performance, including changes in stock values. They must also disclose the ratio of the median pay of all the firm's employees to that of the chief executive.
- If a company issues an accounting restatement, it must recoup any compensation paid to an executive based on financial performance.

It is too early to tell whether and how these requirements will affect executive pay. They attempt to empower stockholders, a notoriously apathetic lot. An additional effort to strengthen stockholders is a requirement that they can submit the names of director nominees and have them included in the proxy materials sent out by companies. This is a big change. In the past shareholders who wanted to run a board candidate had to contact other shareholders at their own very high expense. Now, the company would be forced to put opposition names on its own proxy forms. However, implementation of this procedure is uncertain. When the SEC wrote a new rule giving stockholders who owned 3 percent of the companies' shares access to the proxy, big corporations sued to stop it.[45] They feared that dissident groups, for example, union pension funds or activist coalitions, would be empowered to undermine and distract management by triggering election battles.

BOARDS OF DIRECTORS

The stories of the boards at Enron and Lehman Brothers are singular, but they illustrate widespread tendencies and shortcomings. In fact, the boards of American corporations are marbled with pathologies that enervate them in performance of their watchdog function.

They are often hand-picked by powerful CEOs who fill them with friends and retired CEOs having reputations for congeniality. They depend on management for information and allow management to control agendas. They are unwilling to confront CEOs to whom they owe their selection and compensation. In the harmonious board cultures of most corporations, an abrasive director faces ostracism. Not all directors work hard. Some see their service as largely honorific. Others who are top executives at other companies are preoccupied. A few divide their attention by serving on too many other boards. Many CEOs see their boards as

[45] Securities and Exchange Commission, "Facilitating Shareholder Director Nominations; Proposed Rule," 74 FR 29024, June 18, 2009.

unproductive; in a recent survey only 16 percent rated them "highly effective."[46] One described his board as "an aquarium full of dead fish."[47]

Despite pronounced flaws, governance reforms are having an effect. Today boards of directors are in transition, evolving from a collegial, largely honorific group to an assertive watchdog of management. The transition is incomplete, perhaps even preliminary, but that is the direction of change.

Duties of Directors

State incorporation laws require boards of directors. They impose two lofty duties on them, first, to represent the interests of stockholders by conducting a profitable business that enhances share value, and second, to exercise due diligence in supervising management. Directors violate these duties if they put their own self-interest ahead of the shareholders or if they are unreasonably neglectful in their oversight. In practice, directors do not make day-to-day management decisions. Instead, they exercise a very broad oversight, taking responsibility for "the overall picture, not the daily business decisions, the forest, not the trees."[48]

Here is a short list of specific board functions.

- Approve the issuance of securities and the voting rights of their holders.
- Review and approve the corporation's goals and strategies.
- Select the CEO, evaluate his or her performance, and remove that person if necessary.
- Give advice and counsel to management.
- Create governance policies for the firm, including compensation policies.
- Evaluate the performance of individual directors, board committees, and the board as a whole.
- Nominate candidates for election as directors.
- Exercise oversight of ethics and compliance programs.

Board Composition

The average board has 11 members and this has not changed for many years. Most state incorporation laws require a minimum of three, but companies typically have between 7 and 15. The number is often specified as a range in corporate charters. For example, in its Delaware charter Walt Disney Corporation specifies a board of "not less than nine directors or more than twenty-one."[49] Directors are elected by shareholders, usually for terms of one year. Under Delaware law, once

[46] The 2009 National Association of Corporate Directors *Public Company Governance Survey,* cited in Beverly Behan, "Wise Counsel? How to Get Your Board Back on Track," *The Conference Board Review,* Summer 2010, p. 46.

[47] Anonymous, quoted in Ibid., p. 44.

[48] Robert A. G. Monks and Nell Minow, *Corporate Governance,* 3rd ed. (Malden, MA: Blackwell Publishing, 2004), p. 201.

[49] *Restated Certificate of Incorporation of the Walt Disney Company,* Office of the Secretary of State of Delaware, November 17, 1999, Article V(1).

elected they cannot be removed by their fellow directors. Some have terms of two or three years. In such cases only half or a third of the directors are elected each year. Some shareholders dislike such staggered terms, arguing that they insulate directors from frequent accountability.

Directors are most often current or retired executives of other corporations who are sought out for their business acumen. Others include former government officials, politicians, athletes, entertainers, and university presidents or professors. There is growing but limited demographic diversity. In a survey of the largest 100 public corporations 16 percent of directors were female and 15 percent were minorities. Directors are also older; 42 percent were 65 or over.[50] Those who are officers of the company are *inside directors*. They usually come from the ranks of top executives. Those who are not employed by the company are *outside directors*. These directors are also called nonexecutive directors. When outside directors have no important business dealings with the company other than being on its board, they are called *independent directors*.

Standards of independence have tightened. Since recent regulatory and listing rules require a majority of independent directors on the full board and on several committees, they now dominate in numbers. The typical board of 11 has only 1 inside director, the CEO, usually acting as chairman of the board. Overall, outside directors now hold 87 percent of board seats and insiders only 13 percent.[51] The average director serves on only one or two boards; less than 2 percent serve on five or more.[52]

Boards do much of their work in committees. Federal law and stock exchange rules mandate at least three, each composed entirely of independent directors. An *audit* committee oversees auditing and financial reports and assesses financial risks in the company's strategy. A *compensation* committee reviews the performance of top executives and sets their compensation. It also sets the director's pay. The average director of a large public company puts in about 20 hours a month and earns $213,000 a year in retainers and company stock. Shareholders do not approve director's pay packages.[53] And a *nominating* committee identifies candidates for election to the board. Additional committees sometimes found are executive, corporate governance, finance, succession planning, sustainability, science and technology, and investment committees. Board committees usually have three to five members.

Board Dynamics

The average board meets eight times a year, although many meet monthly. In advance, the directors receive "board books" of materials, often voluminous, for their review. Then they travel to corporate headquarters. The day before the meeting is occupied with committee meetings, most of which last two to four hours, followed in the evening by a dinner for directors and company executives.

inside directors
Directors who are employees of the company.

outside directors
Directors who are not company employees.

independent directors
Outside directors of a corporation who, aside from their directors' duties, do not have business dealings with it that would impair their impartiality.

---

[50] Korn/Ferry Institute, *The Korn/Ferry Market Cap 100: Board Leadership at America's Most Valuable Public Companies* (New York: Korn/Ferry, 2010), pp. 10–12.

[51] PwC, *Annual Corporate Directors Survey: The 2010 Results* (New York: PwC, 2010), p. 30.

[52] Ibid., p. 32.

[53] Colin Leinster, "Are Board Members Paid Enough? 'Definitely Not,'" *Corporate Board Member,* Third Quarter 2010, at www.boardmember.com; and Robert C. Pozen, "A New Model for Corporate Boards," *The Wall Street Journal,* December 30, 2010, p. A15.

The full board meets the next day for an average of four to six hours.[54] Agendas include committee reports, mandatory governance matters, and presentations by company executives. Sometimes a favored senior manager comes to give a Power-Point presentation. Much is routine. The agenda is often crowded and rushed, leaving no time for probing discussions of strategy or risks.[55] In a recent survey a majority of directors said they would like "much more" time devoted to these two subjects.[56] Even if there is meaningful dialogue, conflict and discord are rare. For example, Enron directors who had served for many years described an atmosphere of amity and consensus. They recalled only two instances of a dissenting vote.[57]

The chairman of the board presides over meetings. At most companies this title is held by the CEO, giving him or her a dual role. From this position CEOs can dominate their boards by deciding what information to circulate and by fixing agendas. CEO influence often extends to the selection of supportive directors. In the past CEOs simply suggested new names to compliant boards that then approved nominees who were virtually assured of election by shareholders. Stock exchange rules now require that names be approved by nominating committees of independent directors. These committees have the power to hire search firms to find candidates. However, the CEO is still a source of nominations; few boards will act on a nominee over the objection of a CEO, giving the CEO, in effect, a veto power.

In 2003 the New York Stock Exchange modified its listing standards to require that independent directors meet regularly absent members of management. This is intended to allow outside directors to express concerns that might be suppressed for reasons of collegiality or intimidation in the presence of management. Most large company boards elect a *lead director* from the ranks of independent outside directors to create agendas and preside over such sessions. In practice, however, a lead director operating in the shadow of a combined chairman and CEO lacks substantial power to reshape a board.[58]

lead director
An independent director who presides over meetings of nonmanagement directors.

Advocates of greater board independence believe that a better solution for strengthening the board is to split the roles of chairman and CEO. They argue that if the board is supposed to appoint, monitor, evaluate, and compensate the CEO it is a conflict of interest to put the CEO in charge. Having a chairman other than the chief executive would diminish that conflict even if the CEO still sat on the board. Thus, many companies have separated the two roles, appointing a *nonexecutive chairman* to lead their boards. Most still combine the two roles, but the trend is toward a split. After the financial crisis in 2008, given the example of Richard S. Fuld's reign over a

nonexecutive chairman
A chairman of the board who is not an executive of the corporation.

54 Ibid., pp. 8 and 14.

55 Gillespie and Zweig, *Money for Nothing,* pp. 107–08.

56 PwC, *Annual Corporate Directors Survey: The 2010 Results,* pp. 8–9.

57 Report of the Permanent Subcommittee on Investigations, Committee on Governmental Affairs, U.S. Senate, *The Role of the Board of Directors in Enron's Collapse,* p. 8.

58 Ira M. Millstein and Stephen Davis, eds., *Chairing the Board: The Case for Independent Leadership in Corporate North America,* Policy Briefing No. 4, Millstein Center for Corporate Governance and Performance, Yale School of Management, 2009, p. 20.

weak Lehman Brothers board, Congress stopped short of requiring separation, but the Dodd–Frank Act requires companies to tell their shareholders once a year why they choose to combine or separate the two roles.[59]

Management often opposes separation. One fear is compromising clarity in the chain of command. According to Jack Welch, former chairman and CEO of General Electric, splitting the roles encourages "decision shopping" by managers who seek out the leader most likely to support them. "When there are two bosses," he says, "you can often get two messages, and that's too bad."[60] It can also be harder for the CEO to make quick decisions if the chairman must be consulted. Another fear is that split roles might threaten a collegial board environment by provoking "mindless animosities and ego contests" between the two leaders.[61] To avoid this, advocates of separation advise that the chairman be someone without ambition to run the company, perhaps a retired chief executive. Despite doubts and resistance, the trend is to move to nonexecutive chairmen; about 40 percent of companies on the Standard & Poor's 500 index have done so.[62]

EXECUTIVE COMPENSATION

Top executives are not simply given paychecks. Instead they are compensated using arcane schemes, mysterious in their complexity that can baffle untutored bystanders. When the schemes are well devised, pay follows performance. When poorly devised they result in excessive pay unrelated to performance. In this section we discuss the components, dynamics, and problems of executive compensation.

Components of Executive Compensation

The pay of top corporate officers is set by the board of directors. In keeping with stock exchange rules, each board must have a compensation committee composed entirely of independent directors. Its members, of course, may be cronies of the CEO. Nevertheless, the committee must create a defensible written plan. At most companies the compensation scheme reflects three beliefs. First, to attract and retain managerial talent, compensation must be competitive. Second, it should be based on both individual and company performance. And third, it should align the interests of executives with the interests of shareholders. These goals are typically achieved using some combination of the following elements.

Base Salary

The annual base salary is usually set near the median salary for leaders of similar firms. At Sherwin-Williams, for example, the salaries of the top five executives are based on a survey of the base salaries of executives with similar

[59] Section 972, "Disclosures Regarding Chairman and CEO Structures," 15 USC 78a, sec. 14B.

[60] Jack Welch and Suzy Welch, "A Week of Blows to Business," *BusinessWeek,* May 18, 2009.

[61] Millstein and Davis, *Chairing the Board,* p. 19.

[62] Joann S. Lublin, "Chairman-CEO Split Gains Allies," *The Wall Street Journal,* March 30, 2009, p. B4.

stock option
The right to buy shares of a company's stock at a fixed or *grant price* in the future and under conditions determined by the board of directors.

grant price
The price at which a specified number of shares can be purchased in the future by executives who hold options.

vesting date
The date when stock options can be exercised by purchasing shares at the grant price.

expiration date
A future date, after the vesting date, when shares can no longer be bought at the grant price.

performance shares
Shares of company stock awarded after a fixed period of years if individual and company performance goals are met.

responsibilities at 18 peer companies, all similarly sized industrial firms.[63] Companies use such peer group comparisons as a measure of the market for executive talent. Base salaries for CEOs stay around $1 million, the amount that the Internal Revenue Service allows as tax deductible.[64] At Sherwin-Williams the CEO received $1.3 million in 2009. Its other top executives received between $488,000 and $733,000.

Annual Cash Incentives

Most large companies make an annual bonus part of the compensation package. Criteria for earning the bonus vary. At McGraw-Hill the CEO's incentive pay is based on meeting net income (weighted 75 percent) and revenue (weighted 25 percent) goals.[65] At Abbott Laboratories the CEO's yearly bonus is based on whether the company hits multiple financial goals including profitability, sales, returns, and earnings per share. This resulted in an award of $3.9 million in a recent year.[66] Annual cash incentives are typically based on meeting financial targets. If targets are missed bonuses go down and, when companies do poorly, the bonus columns in compensation tables often contain goose eggs.

Long-Term Stock-Based Incentives

Compensation in stock is designed to align managers' incentives with the interests of stockholders. There are several frequently used types of stock awards.

First, *stock options* give an executive the right to buy the company's stock at a fixed or *grant price* in the future and under conditions determined by the board of directors. Options are usually priced at the closing market price on the day they are granted. The holder of the options then can buy these shares from the company at a specified future date, called the *vesting date*. The holder must buy them before a later *expiration date* when the options can no longer be exercised. At Johnson & Johnson, for example, options vest and can only be exercised (purchased) three years after they are granted and must be exercised within 10 years or they expire.[67] Thus, if Johnson & Johnson grants 1,000 options to an executive at $70 a share and the price rises to $100 after five years, the executive may buy them from the company for $70,000, then sell them for $100,000, making a $30,000 profit (minus taxes and fees). However, if after three years the shares have fallen to $50, they are said to be "under water" and they are worthless. The executive will not exercise the options.

Second, *performance shares* are shares awarded after a fixed period of years only if individual or company performance goals are met. These shares may be awarded in part or not at all depending on how closely performance matches goals. Typically, the time from grant to award is at least three years. General Electric awards its top executives "performance share units" that convert into shares of GE stock after five years. Half the shares are awarded if cash flow from operating activities grows

[63] Sherwin-Williams Company, *Proxy Statement,* March 9, 2007, pp. 24–25.
[64] See 26 USC §162(m)(1) 2010.
[65] McGraw-Hill Companies, *Proxy Statement,* March 23, 2010, p. 38.
[66] Abbott Laboratories, *Proxy Statement,* March 15, 2010, pp. 14 and 18.
[67] Johnson & Johnson, *Notice of Annual Meeting and Proxy Statement,* March 17, 2010, p. 29.

an average of 10 percent a year during the interim.[68] The other half of the shares are awarded if total return to shareholders exceeds that of the Standard & Poor's 500 index. If these goals are not met, the "units" are canceled, unlike options that can be exercised any time between vesting and expiration.

restricted stock
A grant of stock with restrictions. It cannot be sold until certain conditions are met, most often the lapse of time or meeting a performance goal.

Third, *restricted stock* is a grant of stock with restrictions on transaction that are removed when a specified condition is met. Usually, the recipient receives dividends and can vote the shares but cannot sell them until the restriction is lifted. Any specified condition can be a restriction. Often, it is tenure at the company. In this way, restricted stock is used to lock in promising talent or key executives. If, for example, the shares vest in 10 years, then the executive must stay on the job that long to realize their value.

IBM uses restricted stock to retain the loyalty of its "senior leadership team" in what it believes is a highly competitive market for executive talent. Awards are typically for five years and are forfeited if the person leaves. In 2010 the top five most compensated executives at IBM held a little more than 14 million restricted stock units worth approximately $2.2 billion.[69] At ExxonMobil 50 to 75 percent of senior executive's pay is in restricted shares. Of these, half are restricted for 5 years and half for 10 years or until the executive retires, whichever is *later*. If the person leaves, the grants are canceled. Its compensation committee argues for such lengthy time restrictions because in the oil and gas industry the wisdom of investments may not be known for many years.[70] Unlike stock options, restricted shares are not worthless if their market price is below the grant price when they vest.[71]

Options, performance shares, and restricted stock are all used to create a long-term performance incentive. They also align manager and shareholder interests by promoting stock ownership of top executives.

Retirement Plans

Companies provide generous pensions for top executives. Each year they credit pension funds with a sum calculated as a percent of the person's salary. This sum is held by the company to cover future pension payments; however, it is reported as part of the executive's total compensation. For large companies with highly paid CEOs the increased value of a pension can be significant. In a recent year it added $1.9 million for Samuel J. Palmisano of IBM, $1.9 million for Jeffrey Immelt of GE, and $4.4 million for Andrew Liveris of Dow Chemical Company.

Perquisites

Acknowledging the needs and lifestyles of top executives, companies often provide extra benefits. Among the most common are annual physical exams, travel on

---

[68] Performance share units granted after 2009 convert if adjusted cumulative industrial cash flow from operating activities is $70 billion or higher. General Electric Company, *Notice of 2010 Annual Meeting and Proxy Statement,* March 9, 2010, p. 24.

[69] IBM *Notice of 2010 Annual Meeting and Proxy Statement,* March 8, 2010, p. 44.

[70] ExxonMobil Corp., *Notice of 2010 Annual Meeting and Proxy Statement,* April 13, 2010, pp. 29–30.

[71] As an example, suppose a manager is awarded both options and restricted stock on a day when shares sell at $20. Five years later, on a day when the price is $18, both the options and the restricted shares vest. The options are worthless, because to exercise them the manager must buy the shares at $20. The restricted stock, on the other hand, is transferred to the manager at its current value. It can be sold immediately for $18 a share.

FIGURE 18.4   How Emerson Electric Uses Elements of Compensation

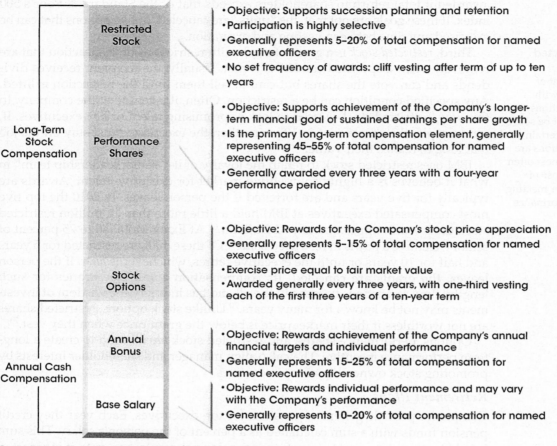

Source: Emerson Electric Co., *Definitive Proxy Statement*, December 10, 2010, p. 18.

company jets, home alarm systems, bodyguards, leased autos, club memberships, personal financial planning, and life and health insurance. SEC rules require that the dollar value of such extras be disclosed to shareholders. A few examples of reported perks are $38,272 in premiums on a medical plan with no deductibles or co-payments for the chief executive at TRW Automotive, $49,440 for a "weekend driver" for Martha Stewart at Martha Stewart Living Omnimedia, $391,000 for personal financial planning for the CEO of Occidental Petroleum, and $3.7 million to a division president at Microsoft for a loss on the sale of his home when he relocated.[72]

At each company, compensation committees choose among these basic elements of executive pay, picking combinations that fit their compensation philosophy. Figure 18.4 shows how Emerson Electric Co. uses a flexible combination of

---

[72] Joann S. Lublin, "Shareholders Hit the Roof Over Home-Loss Subsidies," *The Wall Street Journal*, October 25, 2010, p. B1; and Daniel Fisher, "The Perk Game," *Forbes,* June 7, 2010, p. 36.

pay elements to reward and retain its top executives. Each executive is compensated based on factors such as level of responsibility, promise, performance, and length of service.

Although the base pay of top executives can be generous, astronomical payouts are usually the fruition of earlier incentive awards. With stock-based awards the bonanza can come as long as 10 years after the shares are awarded, sometimes making it seem that compensation is out of step with current performance.

Problems with CEO Compensation

There are multiple shortcomings of CEO compensation. Here are some of the most important.

First, critics are outraged by extraordinary payouts. The perception of widespread, excessively generous remuneration is an old story. President Franklin D. Roosevelt railed against the "entrenched greed" of executives. Yet pay in his era was modest compared with today. For example, in 1929 Eugene G. Grace, president of Bethlehem Steel, the highest-paid top executive, received a salary of $12,000 and a bonus of $1.6 million. Translated into current dollars this is $20 million. If that sum astonished the nation, it would no longer. The highest paid executive in the decade 2000 to 2010, Larry Ellison, the CEO of Oracle, averaged $184 million a year and took home $700 million in 2001 alone.[73] In 2009 average CEO pay at 456 of the largest companies was $7.23 million and eighteen companies went over the $20 million mark.[74]

The source of outrage about CEO pay is a sense of unfairness. In 2010 the average S&P 500 CEO made 267 times the wages of the least-paid company worker.[75] The CEO is only one person, but hundreds or thousands of employees labored to make the firm profitable. Usually, however, CEO pay is determined by market forces in the competition for managerial talent.[76] And most managers never get the dramatically high salaries that attract criticism. Indeed, some argue that more than a few top executives are underpaid. This is especially true in smaller businesses. However, spectacular excesses define public perception of pay in corporate America.

Second, compensation is not always aligned with performance. While total compensation is higher in larger firms and mostly follows share price performance, there are notable exceptions. Between 2000 and 2009 Barry Diller of IAC/InterActive and Expedia.com received $1.1 billion while the share price declined 12 percent. Over the same years Richard D. Fairbank of Capital One Financial received $569 million while the share price declined 14 percent. From 1999 to 2009 John T. Chambers of Cisco Systems received $393 million while the share price

[73] Thurm, "Oracle's Ellison: Pay King," p. A16.

[74] Joann S. Lublin, "Paychecks for CEOs Climb," *The Wall Street Journal,* November 15, 2010, p. A1; and Joann S. Lublin, "A Closer Look at Three Big Paydays," *The Wall Street Journal,* November 15, 2010, p. B5.

[75] Rana Foroohar, "Stuffing Their Pockets," *Newsweek,* September 13, 2010, p. 20.

[76] Steven N. Kaplan, "Are U.S. CEOs Overpaid?" *Academy of Management Executive,* May 2008.

declined 29 percent.[77] Robert Nardelli, who abruptly resigned as CEO of Home Depot in 2007, received exit pay of $210 million on top of his previous year's pay of $33 million. Nardelli, who was reputed to be a despot, failed over six years to raise the company's share price.

Nevertheless, defenders of CEO compensation say many large compensation packages are justified by stockholder gains. This clearly applies to former CEOs Lee Raymond of ExxonMobil and Jack Welch of General Electric. The price of their companies' stock rose significantly over long periods while they were in office. Steven Jobs of Apple received more than $700 million in compensation over the past decade, most in the vesting of restricted shares, but in that time shareholder value increased more than 1,000 percent. Arguably, these executives, and others, devised and executed the strategies responsible for rising equity. Their achievements were rewarded accordingly.

Third, some compensation committees fail to design and execute adequate compensation plans. Such plans are a complex mixture of art and science involving many choices and judgments.[78] Not a few committees choose badly. For example, when they base salaries and bonuses on median levels in a group of peer companies they often choose larger peers. Compensation tends to increase with company size. Since most committees set executive compensation at or above the median in the peer group, choosing larger peer companies increases pay. One study of 429 firms found that more than 96 percent set their CEO's median salary and bonus at or above the peer group benchmark. Because firms chose larger companies in their peer groups, this had the effect of raising chief executive total compensation an average of $1,191,020 over what it would have been if peer groups contained similarly sized companies.[79]

An example is Tootsie Roll Industries, which uses a peer group of 16 companies, all larger than Tootsie Roll, most substantially (see the box). Four have between 20 and 30 times Tootsie Roll's revenues. Using median compensation in the peer group as one element of compensation, Tootsie Roll paid its 90-year-old CEO Melvin Gordon $2.6 million in 2009.[80] Its board has only five directors, including Melvin Gordon and his wife, President Ellen Gordon, who was paid $2.5 million. The remaining three independent directors sit on the compensation committee.

Some compensation committees fall under the spell of a powerful CEO. Imagine a situation in which a committee with a well-constructed compensation plan is approached by such a CEO during a recession. The CEO's pay, which is based on incentives to achieve revenue growth, has fallen. "I'm working harder than ever," argues the CEO. "The economy is beyond my control and I deserve more than the current plan allows." The committee then gives in, making a onetime departure

---

[77] Thurm, "Oracle's Ellison: Pay King," p. A16.

[78] Robin A. Ferracone, *Fair Pay, Fair Play: Aligning Executive Performance and Pay* (San Francisco: Jossey-Bass, 2010), p. 35.

[79] Michael Faulkender and Jun Yang, "Inside the Black Box: The Role and Composition of Compensation Peer Groups," *Journal of Financial Economics,* May 2010, p. 268.

[80] Tootsie Roll Industries, Inc., *Proxy Statement,* March 26, 2010, pp. 11 and 16.

Tootsie Roll Industries Peer Group

Tootsie Roll Industries uses a study of compensation levels in other companies as a basis for determining the compensation of its top executives. In 2009 it picked these 16 companies as its peers in the snack and confectionary industries. Tootsie Roll had revenues of $496 million.

Peer Company	Annual Revenues (in millions)
Campbell Soup Company	$7,586
Dean Foods Company	$11,158
Del Monte Foods Company	$3,627
Diamond Foods, Inc.	$571
Flowers Foods, Inc.	$2,601
General Mills, Inc.	$14,691
H. J. Heinz Company	$10,148
Hershey Company	$5,299
J&J Snack Foods Corp.	$653
Kellogg Company	$12,587
Lancaster Colony Corp.	$1,051
Lance, Inc.	$918
McCormick & Company, Inc.	$3,192
Ralcorp Holdings, Inc.	$2,892
The J. M. Smucker Company	$3,758
TreeHouse Foods, Inc.	$1,512

Source: Tootsie Roll Industries, *Proxy Statement*, March 26, 2010, p. 11 and Tootsie Roll Industries, *Annual Report*, Form 10-K, March 1, 2010, exhibit 13, p. 2.

from its formal plan, and approves an award of several million stock options, currently of modest value, to the unhappy CEO. Years down the road, when the economy is better, this exception might result in princely sums that are wildly inconsistent with current performance. If pay is to correlate with performance, compensation policies must not only be designed well, but they must be consistently implemented.

Fourth, executives can manipulate their compensation. When annual salary and bonus are based on accounting measures such as net income, the CEO can take actions to maximize short-term profits. When compensation is based on stock options, the CEO can delay taking profits until a future year when options vest. Another problem with options has been *backdating*, or setting the exercise price of options at the price on a date before the date they were granted. As explained, an option gives the owner the right to buy stock in the future at a set price. Normally that price is the closing stock market price on the day of the grant. Backdating occurs when the company, at the time of the grant or retroactively, fixes the grant

backdating
Setting the exercise price of stock options at the price on a date before the date they were granted.

Backdating: A Hypothetical Example

1. On June 1, 2008, a CEO gets an option grant to purchase 1,000 shares of his company's stock which can be exercised in two years. The shares are priced at $30, the closing price on the New York Stock Exchange that day.

2. On June 1, 2010, when the options vest, the stock is selling for $29 a share. At this point the stock option is worthless.

3. The company decides to backdate the options to May 1, 2008, when the shares closed at $22.

4. The executive now decides to exercise the options, buying 1,000 shares from the company at $22 for $22,000, then selling them on the open market for $29 a share or $29,000. This nets a profit before taxes and brokerage fees of $7,000.

5. The value of the options is reported by the corporation as a cost, reducing net income. The lost value, in theory, reduces shareholder value.

date as a past date when the price of the stock was lower. In plain terms, companies search the past for troughs in share prices, then pretend the options were granted at these low points (see the above box).

A statistical analysis of options published in *The Wall Street Journal* found that at some companies they were granted repeatedly on days when share prices hit historic lows.[81] One example was a striking series of favorable coincidences at UnitedHealth Group, where 12 separate option grants went to William W. McGuire, its chairman and chief executive, on days when the stock fell to yearly or quarterly lows. According to the *Journal*, the odds against picking this series of dates by chance were 1 in 200 million, lower than the odds for winning the Powerball lottery. Further investigation found that over time McGuire received 44 million options, most of which were illegally backdated. He was forced to resign and return more than $600 million to the company.[82]

And fifth, disclosures of compensation policy are difficult to understand. Companies must disclose their compensation plans and the annual compensation of the top five executive officers to shareholders. They do this in the proxy statements mailed before annual meetings. The sections on compensation are lengthy. An average "discussion and analysis" is 25 to 30 pages of challenging prose filled with charts, columns of figures, and footnotes that invite a magnifying glass. IBM's most recent compensation discussion covered 53 pages with 30 charts and tables.

These discussions became more complex in 2006 when the SEC imposed more than 100 pages of new rules for their contents.[83] Although the rules were

[81] Charles Forcelle and James Bandler, "The Perfect Payday," *The Wall Street Journal*, March 18, 2006, p. A1.

[82] Eric Dash, "Former Chief Will Forfeit $418 Million," *The New York Times*, December 7, 2007, p. C1.

[83] See Securities and Exchange Commission, "Executive Compensation and Related Person Disclosure; Final Rule and Proposed Rule," 71 FR 53158, September 8, 2006; Securities and Exchange Commission, Executive Compensation Disclosure; Interim Final Rule," 71 FR 78338, December 29, 2006; and subsequent conforming amendments, RIN 3235-AI80.

intended to give stockholders more "clear, concise and meaningful information," they may have had a reverse effect.[84] Most companies now design their discussions to satisfy regulators rather than as a communication to the average shareholder, who might be inclined to stop reading after sentences such as the following.

> *United States Steel* The 2006 performance award vested in 2009 at a rate of 53.84 percent of the target based upon U.S. Steel's total shareholder return ranking at nearly the 27th percentile of the peer group for the preceding three-year performance period.[85]

> *Target Corporation* The amounts reported have been adjusted to eliminate service-based forfeiture assumptions and exclude reversals of amounts expensed but not reported in prior years' Summary Compensation Tables, both of which are used for financial reporting purposes.[86]

> *Suncor Energy* Cash payments are provided for annual remuneration during the notice period, for ESP options which, but for the Termination Event, would have become exercisable during the notice period, and for PSUs and RSUs that would pay out during the notice period based on a performance factor calculated at the date of termination, if applicable.[87]

Despite such examples, there is also some clarity in compensation discussions. A required "summary compensation table" gives the sum of annual salaries, bonuses, stock awards, pension value, and perquisites. However, a CEO's true compensation is a stream of value extending into the future that expands or contracts depending on periodic vesting of stock awards, the market value of those shares, incentive payments based on future corporate performance, and unusual events such as hostile mergers, which can trigger special "golden parachutes" for ousted executives. In such a living equation, a precise dollar figure for compensation is an elusive, moving target.

CONCLUDING OBSERVATIONS

In this chapter we discuss how shareholders, boards of directors, and managements interact in an imperfect system of corporate governance. Shareholders have the power to control managers, but they are scattered, passive, and largely absent any influence in practice. Boards of directors exist to monitor management for the shareholders, but they are frequently watchdogs without a bark, content to rubber-stamp the actions of management. Fortunately, most of the time management is trustworthy and proficient, giving stockholders a fair return on their investment.

[84] Securities and Exchange Commission, "Executive Compensation and Related Person Disclosure," 71 FR 53158, September 8, 2006, at 53160.

[85] United States Steel Corporation, *Notice of Annual Meeting of Stockholders and Proxy Statement*, April 27, 2010, p. 57.

[86] Target Corporation, *Proxy Statement*, April 23, 2009, p. 35.

[87] Suncor Energy Inc., *2010 Management Proxy Circular*, p. 29.

Recently, as in the cases of Enron and Lehman Brothers, failures of governance have had awful consequences. As in the past, Congress responded with new rules to strengthen governance by making directors more independent of management and giving shareholders a more powerful voice. So the governance system is evolving. Its formal checks and balances, having been slightly recalibrated, may now better protect corporate stakeholders.

High Noon at Hewlett-Packard

In the beginning there was a garage. As legend has it, this humble structure in Palo Alto, California, gave birth to giant Hewlett-Packard Company. It was there that Bill Hewlett and David Packard, both recent graduates of Stanford University, spent years tinkering before coming up with their first successful product, a precision oscillator. The two partners went public with their company in 1949.

As it grew they ran it using a homegrown philosophy called the HP Way. At its core the HP Way emphasized the worth of each employee. It inspired a nonhierarchical, decentralized, and participative company in which the creativity of each scientist and engineer was freed.

For many years Hewlett-Packard was the bright star in the Silicon Valley firmament. But as the twentieth century approached, it no longer blazed with innovation. Its aging co-founders' hands had lifted from the controls. Despite booming markets, its earnings were lackluster, its share price stagnant. Eventually, its board of directors saw the need for a new CEO.

CARLY FIORINA

The choice was Carleton S. Fiorina, called Carly by friends and associates. Fiorina was the first woman to head a corporation as large as Hewlett-Packard. She came from a position as a group president at Lucent Technologies. Her mandate from the HP board was to shake things up.

Immediately, Fiorina was a celebrity. It frustrated her when the media categorized her as "Carly Fiorina, female CEO" and reporters focused on her as a woman rather than on her mission at HP.[1]

> From the first . . . both the language and the intensity of the coverage were different for me than for any other CEO. It was more personal, with much

commentary about my personality and my physical appearance, my dress, my hair or my shoes . . . There was a persistent rumor . . . that I'd built a pink marble bathroom in my office.[2]

She learned that her actions would be interpreted through a gender lens. After taking the helm at HP in 1999 she was called both a "bimbo" and a "bitch" in Silicon Valley chat rooms. When male CEOs fired people, they were called firm and commanding; she was labeled vengeful. Such interpretations made her job "infinitely more difficult."[3]

Fiorina believed that HP had been poorly managed for years. She set to work galvanizing its managers. One problem was that in the HP culture, decisions were decentralized. This was faithful to the HP Way, which taught that employees were the primary source of wisdom. But it slowed operations. Fiorina began to restructure processes so that everything went through her.

The first sign of trouble came in November 2000, when Lewis Platt, the former CEO who continued as chairman of the board, requested that Fiorina leave a board meeting so the other directors could talk.[4] He told them she was moving too fast with her plans for change.

Although the board affirmed its support for her, Fiorina was troubled. She responded by regularly inviting the directors to management meetings and setting up a Web site where they could find any data available to other HP employees. At board meetings she started going around the table asking each director to speak and state what action they would take on important issues. After each meeting she summarized points of agreement and disagreement in writing,

---

[1] Carly Fiorina, *Tough Choices: A Memoir* (New York: Portfolio, 2006), p. 171.

[2] Ibid., p. 172.

[3] Ibid., p. 173.

[4] Platt's resignation as CEO had been amicable. He would resign as chairman and retire from the company on December 31, 1999. Fiorina was then elected chairman.

EXHIBIT 1
The Hewlett-Packard Board in 1999

When Carly Fiorina arrived at Hewlett-Packard this was the board of directors. There were 13 members, 9 outside directors and, including herself, 4 inside directors. Four of the outside directors were related to the cofounders by birth or marriage. The board had five committees: Audit, Compensation, Executive, Finance and Investment, and Organization Review and Nominating. Each director was paid a $100,000 retainer, of which 75 percent was paid in HP stock. Individual directors were paid $5,000 for serving as committee chairs and a fee of $1,200 for each full board meeting attended.

Philip M. Condit, 57
Chairman and CEO, Boeing Company

Patricia C. Dunn, 46
Chair, Barclays Global Investors

John B. Fery, 69
Retired Chairman and CEO, Boise Cascade

Carleton S. Fiorina, 45
CEO, Hewlett-Packard Company

Jean-Paul G. Gimon, 63
General Representative, Credit Lyonnais and
son-in-law of HP cofounder William R. Hewlett

Sam Ginn, 62
Chairman, Vodafone AirTouch

Richard A. Hackborn, 62
Retired Executive Vice President, Hewlett-Packard

Walter B. Hewlett, 55
Chairman, The William and Flora Hewlett Foundation

George A. Keyworth, 60
Chairman, Progress & Freedom Association

Susan Packard Orr, 53
Chair, The David and Lucile Packard Foundation

David Woodly Packard, 58
Founder, Packard Humanities Institute

Lewis E. Platt, 58 (Chairman)
Former CEO, Hewlett-Packard

Robert P. Wayman, 54
Executive Vice President and Chief Financial Officer, Hewlett-Packard

along with action steps. This detail mentality may have irritated some directors.

TENSION ON THE BOARD

Fiorina had a strong view about the board's role in corporate governance. The directors were there to watch over management. Their duty was to see the big picture and ensure that major strategies were aligned with the stockholders' interests. However, the day-to-day work of running the enterprise was management's job—her job.

> The management team's job is to manage the company and produce results. A board meets six or eight times a year and cannot possibly know enough of the details of a business to manage it. And yet a board must represent the company's owners and this means knowing enough to ask the right questions.[5]

[5] Fiorina, *Tough Choices*, p. 210.

As time went on, she believed that some influential board members failed to draw a line between their broad oversight role and her daily management role. One was Richard Hackborn, a retired HP executive who had worked closely with the co-founders over the years. Another was George Keyworth, a former science adviser to President Ronald Reagan with a doctorate in physics. Both were technologists who, she felt, lacked appreciation for problems of execution. They were filled with suggestions and sometimes wanted to change projects and budgets in midstream. They met with employees. They even suggested that Fiorina fire certain managers.

Among other ideas, they proposed the acquisition of Compaq Computer Corporation. This was an opportunity to expand market share and achieve operating economies, but the combination would be difficult. It would require laying off tens of thousands of people in both companies and blending distinctive cultures.

After considerable debate, the full HP board unanimously agreed to the $22 billion acquisition. Just before the announcement in late 2001, HP's intentions were leaked to the media, obviously by a well-informed insider. Now HP was placed on the defensive. Reaction in the business press and among investors was immediately hostile due to the conventional wisdom that such huge combinations usually failed. HP's share price fell. The identity of the leaker was never discovered.

Then board member Walter Hewlett, the co-founder's son, surprised Fiorina by changing his mind and opposing the acquisition. He was soon joined by David Packard, son of the other co-founder. Together, the two controlled more than 16 percent of HP shares. Both disliked the dilution of their ownership in the company that would come from issuing millions of new shares for the acquisition.

Hewlett stopped attending board meetings and, with Packard, launched a battle to garner enough votes to stop the deal. He persuaded one board member, Sam Ginn, to change his mind. Ginn then came to a board meeting and pressed the other directors to reverse course. They held firm. Finally, after a bitter fight, HP's shareholders approved the acquisition by a slight 3 percent margin.[6] The merger was completed;

Carly Fiorina discusses the plan to buy Compaq at a 2001 news conference. Source: © AP Photo/Paul Sakuma.

however, a consequence of the internecine battle was that investors remained skeptical about it for years.

Fiorina's problems with the board continued. As time passed, expectations from the Compaq merger were far from being met. Earnings targets were missed. HP's share price languished. The board was unhappy. Fiorina continued to believe that the board was intruding on her role as chief executive by nosing into operational details.

A change on the board came when two CEOs, Sam Ginn and Phil Condit, retired in early 2004. That left only two other CEOs with operating experience. These were the kind of board members most valued by Fiorina because she felt that they respected her management prerogatives. It proved difficult to recruit others in their mold, however, because after the passage of the Sarbanes-Oxley Act in 2002 the leaders of large corporations cut back on outside board memberships to focus more on time-consuming governance requirements in their own firms.

Then there was the abrasion of the board's technology committee. It was formed in 2002 at the suggestion

[6] A week after the meeting Walter Hewlett filed a lawsuit in the Delaware Chancery Court alleging that HP had bought the vote of Deutsche Bank. In April, the court dismissed the lawsuit and Hewlett did not further contest the vote.

of director Tom Perkins. Perkins had moved to the HP board from the Compaq board in 2001. He was a formidable presence, combining a long history at HP with a keen mind for strategy. He had been hired by Hewlett and Packard in 1957 and ran the company's research labs for more than a decade until they put him in charge of the new computer division. Perkins built the HP computer business, then left in 1972 to co-found what became the nation's leading venture capital firm, Kleiner, Perkins, Caufield & Byers.

This partnership provided seed capital for Silicon Valley start-ups. Its spectacular successes were Genentech, AOL, Netscape, Amazon, and Google. Perkins became a billionaire, soon adopting an extraordinary lifestyle of mansions and fast cars. His sailing ship, the *Maltese Falcon* is, at 289 feet, the longest private yacht in the world. After his first wife died of cancer, he married, then divorced, celebrity romance novelist Danielle Steel. According to Perkins, they remain deeply in love, but they cannot live together because "it would be easier to merge General Motors and General Electric. You know, we lead big, complicated lives."[7]

Perkins was joined on the technology committee by George Keyworth and Dick Hackborn, the inventor of laser printing. All three were fascinated with scientific details and soaring possibilities for new products. All three were dominating directors. Under their lead, the committee began to function as a board-within-a-board. It often met the day before a regular board meeting, and its agenda ranged over all aspects of HP's business. It was a breeding ground for projects and suggestions. Most of them were rejected by Fiorina, who believed that the "disruptive" technologists lacked appreciation for the obstacles to achieving financial results from their ideas. In her view, "They thought because they understood technology, they understood everything."[8] As their suggestions were spurned, the committee members grew restive.

Another conflict also arose. The technologists became impatient with director Patricia Dunn's leadership of the audit committee. Dunn was a determined force. The proof was in her career. She grew up in Las Vegas, where her mother was a model and showgirl and her father booked entertainment at hotels. When she was 11, her father died. When the time for college

HP Director Tom Perkins at the window of his San Francisco office in 2006. Source: © AP Photo/Eric Risberg.

came, she won a scholarship to the University of Oregon, but had to drop out and work as a cook and housekeeper to support herself and her mother. Later she attended the University of California, Berkeley on a scholarship, making a daily three-bus commute and graduating with a journalism degree.[9]

Soon she took a temporary secretarial position at Wells Fargo Bank in San Francisco. After the bank was acquired by Barclays Global Investors, she rose to become that company's CEO from 1995 to 2002. She came to the HP board in 1998. In 2001 she was diagnosed with breast cancer and a year later with melanoma, causing her to step down as CEO. She retained her position as chairman of the board at Barclays.

On the audit committee she focused on governance procedures. She was methodical and organized. Keyworth and others saw an obsession with details that blocked her appreciation of the big picture. Her strength was the minutia of legal compliance, not the spirited, freewheeling strategy debate the technologists thrived on. They worried that the board was moving in the wrong direction. It needed an infusion of imagination.

Perkins felt it had become what he called a "compliance board," or a board focused on obeying laws

[7] "Conversation with Tom Perkins," *The Charlie Rose Show,* December 5, 2007, transcript, p. 12.

[8] Fiorina, *Tough Choices,* p. 280.

[9] George Anders and Alan Murray, "Inside Story of Feud That Plunged HP into Crisis," *The Sunday Times,* October 15, 2006, p. B18.

and rules, where meeting time was consumed with boring hours of reports by lawyers and committees. In contrast, Perkins wanted a "guidance board," or a board of knowledgeable insiders and industry experts that takes an active role in the company, not only reviewing strategy, but becoming deeply involved in its management.[10] A compliance board plodded along checking boxes. A guidance board could better jolt HP from its slumber.

Perkins and his technology committee colleagues wanted to add Silicon Valley friends with scientific and entrepreneurial backgrounds to the board. Fiorina resisted these nominations. She continued to favor candidates with big-company operating experience, ideally, CEOs of other large corporations who were more likely to share her view that the board should stay at arms' length from management. Tension over the role of the board and its composition hung in the air. It did not ease when Tom Perkins retired in 2003 after reaching the mandatory retirement age for HP directors of 72.

Over the next year the directors grew more troubled by Fiorina's performance. Revenues and profits were climbing, largely because the Compaq merger made HP much bigger. However, the merger was not living up to expectations. Fiorina continued to be a media celebrity. She frequently traveled for speeches and appearances. Keyworth, Dunn, and others believed she was distracted from, even unattracted to, the relentless, draining hard work of running a big company. Her subordinates were frustrated. Talented managers were quitting. HP had lost market share in computers to Dell and in network servers to both Dell and IBM. Its profit margins in key business segments were falling. HP's share price was just over $40 when Fiorina was named CEO in 1999. Through 2004 it traded below $20. She had centralized management so that almost every decision went through her, and she resisted efforts by board members to reach into the management process. She failed to communicate with them except at regularly scheduled meetings. They regarded her as imperious.[11]

Late in the year, Keyworth led a movement to bring Perkins back, arguing that the board needed

another member with technology expertise. He told Fiorina that Perkins missed being on the board. She countered that his return was a breach of HP's governance policy. In the post-Enron climate of reform, disregard of the retirement rule would look bad. Moreover, what the board really needed was another big-company chief executive with operating expertise. Yet in a momentary lapse of resolve, she agreed to Perkin's return. It was a slip she would regret.

FIORINA'S FALL

Perkins was invited to attend a January 2005 board meeting as a visitor. His official reappointment would take longer to meet the letter of HP's governance policy. However, several members requested that the board vote immediately to appoint him. Fiorina countered that his formal confirmation must wait. He had not studied statements of operating results that needed approval that day. If all voting directors were not well versed on the financials, requirements of the Sarbanes-Oxley Act would be sacrificed. She got her way.

Although not yet officially appointed, Perkins nevertheless stayed in the meeting and was immediately outspoken. He suggested specific actions, including acquisition of another software firm and altering the roles of certain top executives. Fiorina rebuffed the advice, telling Perkins and his allies that it was her prerogative as CEO to make such decisions. According to Perkins, "She made it very clear . . . that our opinions were less than welcome on operational and organizational specifics."[12]

As the meeting wore on, the board proposed a reorganization to delegate some of Fiorina's duties to other executives. She opposed the plan. If the board held her accountable for results, then it should let her make her own decisions about how to achieve them. But by the end of the meeting she had agreed to combine two product groups under a new manager and yielded to ground rules for evaluating other changes over the coming months.

Days later, *The Wall Street Journal* published a front-page story about the meeting quoting "people close to the situation," phrasing that could refer only to two or more directors.[13] According to the article,

[10] Tom Perkins, "The 'Compliance' Board," *The Wall Street Journal*, March 2, 2007, p. A11.

[11] Anthony Bianco, *The Big Lie: Spying, Scandal, and Ethical Collapse at Hewlett-Packard* (New York: Public Affairs, 2010), pp. 105–06.

[12] Tom Perkins, *Valley Boy: The Education of Tom Perkins* (New York: Gotham Books, 2007), p. 4.

[13] Pui-Wing Tam, "Hewlett-Packard Board Considers a Reorganization," *The Wall Street Journal*, January 24, 2005, p. A1.

the HP board was still supportive of Fiorina, but very concerned about the company's ragged financial performance, an exodus of managers to competing firms, and weak market performance. Of Fiorina, one source said she "has tremendous abilities," but "she shouldn't be running everything every day. She is very hands on and that slows things down."[14]

"It is hard to convey how violated I felt," said Fiorina.[15] This leak was a profound breach of confidentiality. If directors are to fulfill their oversight role, they must be able to trust the others present. If they fear that remarks will become public they might not engage in the open, honest, and unreserved deliberations that best serve stockholders. She immediately convened a conference call with the entire board. After scolding them for the breach, she asked the board's nominating and governance committee to investigate. It engaged an attorney to interview each board member, not only to ask about the leak, but to solicit their views about the overall effectiveness of the board and how to improve its functioning.

Fiorina was certain that Tom Perkins and his technology committee friend Keyworth were the leakers because they were the ones pushing hardest for the reorganization described in the article.[16] In the investigation, only Perkins admitted speaking to a reporter, insisting that he had not initiated the story, but responded only when he was called to confirm its contents. He claimed he had only tried to ward off some damaging details. No other director admitted involvement. The attorney's report also described the board as "dysfunctional" due to personality conflicts and the tendency of a few dominating members to divert the agenda to long discussions on side topics.

After this, the directors stopped communicating with Fiorina. A special February 8 board meeting was set up in a hotel to keep it out of the media. When Fiorina arrived Patricia Dunn immediately called the group to order, though Fiorina, as chairman of the board, would ordinarily preside. Dunn asked if Fiorina had anything to say. Fiorina read a 30-minute statement defining and defending her role as CEO. It was met with silence. According to Dunn, "The basic message the board took from it was, 'You guys don't

know what you're doing.'"[17] She was asked to leave the room.

After she left, the directors broke into "turbulent" debate, with Perkins and Keyworth pushing hard for her removal.[18] Three hours later, a majority formed behind Fiorina's immediate replacement. She was summoned. On her return, only two board members remained at the conference table, Dunn and Robert Knowling, the retired CEO of Simdesk Technologies. "The Board has decided to make a change," said Knowling. "I'm very sorry, Carly."[19] She left with a bonus package of $21 million, HP shares worth $18.2 million, and a pension of $200,000 a year.[20] Yet in that hour her star fell to earth. She felt devastated.[21]

PATRICIA DUNN ASCENDANT

In the following days, the board named Robert P. Wayman, HP's long-time chief financial officer, to be interim CEO and picked Patricia Dunn to be its non-executive chairman. In this position Dunn would preside at board meetings but would not play an active role in managing the company. Separation of the board chairmanship from the CEO position was Tom Perkins' idea and reflected his belief that a strong board should not be dominated by the same person who is the company's top manager. It also gave the board more power over management.

Dunn's influence had risen during the period when Perkins and Keyworth emerged as the leading antagonists toward Fiorina. At first Dunn was neutral, but at some point she moved over to join the two in their campaign for change.[22] In addition, Dunn had been diagnosed the year before with advanced ovarian cancer and endured surgery and chemotherapy. Both Perkins and Keyworth had lost wives to cancer. They were sympathetic and liked her fortitude. Perkins even proposed that Dunn receive an

[14] Ibid., p. 1.

[15] Fiorina, *Tough Choices,* p. 290.

[16] James B. Stewart, "The Kona Files," *The New Yorker,* February 19–26, 2007, p. 155.

[17] Quoted in Bianco, *The Big Lie: Spying, Scandal, and Ethical Collapse at Hewlett-Packard,* p. 120.

[18] Perkins, *Valley Boy,* p. 6.

[19] Fiorina, *Tough Choices,* p. 303.

[20] Pui-Wing Tam and Joann S. Lublin, "H-P Gave Fiorina $1.57 Million in Bonus Payments Last Year," *The Wall Street Journal,* February 14, 2005, p. B2; and Carol J. Loomis, "How the HP Board KO'd Carly," *Fortune,* March 7, 2005, p. 99.

[21] Fiorina, *Tough Choices,* p. 303.

[22] Stewart, "The Kona Files," p. 156.

EXHIBIT 2
The Hewlett-Packard Board in Early 2005

This is the board that fired Carly Fiorina on February 8. One director, Sanford Litvak, had abruptly resigned on February 2. He was replaced on February 7 by Tom Perkins. Since 1999 the board had shrunk to nine members due largely to resignations by representatives of the Hewlett and Packard families in protest over the Compaq merger. Finding replacements in the new governance climate created by the Sarbanes-Oxley Act proved difficult. By now each director was paid a $200,000 retainer. The board had voted in 2004 to double its compensation. Directors who chaired committees were paid an additional $10,000.

Lawrence T. Babbio, Jr., 60
Vice Chairman and President, Verizon Communications

Patricia C. Dunn, 51 (Non-executive Chairman)
Chair, Barclays Global Investors

Richard A. Hackborn, 67
Retired Executive Vice President, Hewlett-Packard

George A. Keyworth, 65
Chairman, Progress & Freedom Association

Robert E. Knowling, Jr., 49
Former Chairman and CEO, Simdesk Technologies

Thomas J. Perkins, 73
Partner, Kleiner Perkins Caufield & Byers

Robert L. Ryan, 61
Senior Vice President and CFO, Medtronic

Lucille S. Salhany, 58
President and CEO, JHMedia

Robert P. Wayman, 59
Interim CEO, Hewlett-Packard

---

additional $100,000 for serving as chairman. She declined to accept it.

The immediate task for the board was to find a new CEO. Dunn, Perkins, and Keyworth headed the search. Within two months they hired Mark Hurd from NCR Corporation. Meanwhile, seven directors had approached Dunn, telling her that identifying the source of leaks and ending them was critical to maintaining trust and integrity on the board. All told, there had been 10 unauthorized leaks. They asked her to make renewed investigation a top priority.[23] She opened a new one and named it Project Kona after a spot in Hawaii where she and her husband own a vacation home.

[23] U.S. House of Representatives, Subcommittee on Oversight and Investigations of the Committee on Energy and Commerce, *Hewlett-Packard's Pretexting Scandal*, 109th Congress, 2d Sess., September 28, 2006, pp. 90, 129.

As the investigation began, other events eroded the comity between Dunn and Perkins. Perkins believed that since he had initiated her elevation to the chairmanship she would be deferential toward him. In this he erred. Early on he came to a board meeting with a sweeping agenda of strategy issues he wanted discussed. Dunn, however, had retreated into her armor of focus on details. She announced her discovery of many inconsistencies between HP's director's handbook and its bylaws. The meeting would be about harmonizing the two. Perkins was taken aback. This button-down approach assaulted his venture capitalist DNA. He had not even read the handbook and had no intention ever of doing so.

Vacancies existed on the board. As chairman of the nominating and governance committee Perkins found nominees, but Dunn was lukewarm. Again a difference of philosophy was the cause. Perkins submitted the names of Silicon Valley comrades who shared his values. Dunn wanted top executives from large, established corporations. When she suggested the president of PepsiCo, Perkins mocked him as "Sugar Daddy."[24]

Other abrasions angered Perkins, including a comment by Dunn in the presence of Hewlett-Packard managers that his new novel, *Sex and the Single Zillionaire,* was not her kind of reading.[25] The two frequently quarreled. However, he thought they had an agreement that if the leak investigation bore fruit, the matter would be handled by the two of them talking privately with the offending director. He wanted to extract an apology and a promise never again to talk with the press, then close the matter and go on. Again, he misjudged.

In the background, the leak investigation continued. One day the head of the Boston security firm told Dunn and HP's general counsel that his investigators had gotten the phone numbers of reporters who had written stories based on leaks. They were now going to obtain phone records using a technique called "pretexting." Investigators would call phone companies, pretending to be the reporters, and ask for records of their calls. Then they would get the directors' phone records the same way and check for calls back and forth. The HP counsel asked if this was legal. The security firm manager said yes. When the phone records were obtained, however, no evidence incriminated any director. The investigation had failed.

Nothing further was done until early in 2006 when another leak appeared. A CNET reporter published a story about the company's annual management retreat in January 2006. In it "a source" was quoted as saying that "[b]y the time the lectures were done at 10 p.m., we were pooped and went to bed."[26] The story also revealed that HP was considering certain kinds of software acquisitions.

Because of this new leak, Dunn launched a second round of investigation labeled Kona II. This time it was run by an HP lawyer with in-house investigators. Again, pretexting was used to obtain the phone records of both reporters and HP directors.

Patricia Dunn at a 2005 news conference. Source: © AP Photo/Paul Sakuma.

Comparing these phone records, they discovered two brief calls between Dawn Kawamoto, the reporter who wrote the January story, and director George Keyworth.

Trying to catch the conspirators in the act, they launched a sting operation. They fabricated a disgruntled HP manager who sent Kawamoto fake e-mails offering to reveal something sensational. A tracking program was embedded, so that if she sought to forward them to Keyworth or another director for confirmation the investigators would know. However, she simply invited the employee to call her. The HP investigators also staked out the homes of Kawamoto and Keyworth. No contact between them was observed.

In weekly meetings the investigative team kept Dunn informed. Questions about the legality of the tactics being used were raised by former police officers in HP's security department, but company attorneys told Dunn that all actions were legal. She said, "Throughout the process I asked and was assured—by both H-P's internal security department and the company's top lawyers, both verbally and in writing—that the work being undertaken to investigate and discover these leaks was legal, proper and consistent with the H-P way of performing investigations."[27]

[24] Stewart, "The Kona Files," p. 157.

[25] Tom Perkins, *Sex and the Single Zillionaire* (New York: Harper, 2007). Perkins had given Dunn an early draft of the book.

[26] Dawn Kawamoto, "HP Outlines Long-Term Strategy," CNET News.com, January 23, 2006.

[27] Patricia Dunn, "The H-P Investigation," *The Wall Street Journal,* October 11, 2006, p. A14.

Dunn and Perkins continued to abrade each other. After the regular board meeting in March, Dunn requested that Perkins and two others remain in the meeting room for a moment. The two disagree on what happened next. According to Perkins, Dunn told the others that he was out to get her and burst into tears. Dunn denies the statement, saying she told Perkins that his disruptive outbursts in meetings were counterproductive.[28]

Results of the leak investigation were revealed at the May 18, 2006, board meeting. That morning, just before the board convened, director Robert Ryan, an executive with Medtronic, who was now chair of the audit committee, met with Keyworth. When asked about Kawamoto's CNET article, Keyworth admitted to having lunch with her and discussing the retreat. He considered it a friendly lunch, not a press contact, and said he was surprised by the article. He felt that it was positive and harmless and told Ryan that if anyone had just asked him, he would have divulged the conversation. He was amazed to learn that this piece was the focus of a major investigation.

Meanwhile, Dunn took Perkins aside moments before the meeting and informed him about Keyworth. When she said the matter had to go before the full board, he was startled and irate. In the meeting, Ryan summarized a report from the HP lawyer in charge of the investigation. Keyworth was contrite. "I apologize for any discussion I had with the reporter in question that may have resulted in any of my colleagues on this board losing trust with me."[29] He added, "I would have told you all about this. Why didn't you ask? I thought I was just helping the company through a rough patch with the press. Aren't directors supposed to do that?"[30] He was asked to leave the room.

With Keyworth outside, Perkins spoke up. He argued that his friend's intention was innocent and the leak inconsequential. He believed that once again Dunn was focused on the trivia of process, "the 'sin' of the leak itself," rather than its substance.[31] When a motion was made to ask for Keyworth's resignation, Perkins grew "incandescent," and directed most of his fury at Dunn. After 90 minutes of dispute a vote was taken by secret ballot. The motion passed. At

that, Perkins said simply, "I resign," and walked out.[32] When Keyworth reentered he was asked to resign, but refused, noting that he had been elected by HP share owners and his legal obligation was to serve until they removed him.

THE END OF DUNN

It was Perkins' final meeting as an HP director, but he was not through with the company. He sought to have the minutes of the meeting rewritten to include his remarks that the investigatory tactics were illegal. When he discovered that his home telephone records had been deceitfully obtained, he wrote a letter to the board saying the investigation had violated the law. He demanded that it forward a copy of the letter to the Securities and Exchange Commission. When his demands were rejected, he instructed his lawyer to contact not only the SEC, but U.S. Attorney's offices in Manhattan and San Francisco, the California Attorney General, the Federal Communications Commission, and the Federal Trade Commission. This caused an explosion in the press, removing the cloak from an investigation that could not survive the light.

Within months, Dunn agreed to step down as chairman. Individual board members told her they did not believe she was involved in anything improper or illegal. But she had become a lightning rod for criticism of HP and its board.

CEO Mark Hurd and other directors urged her to remain on the board as a member. Soon, however, it was plain that she would be a major distraction. Finally, the board asked her to resign and she did so on September 22. She was asked not to speak at the press conference where her retirement was announced. Two HP attorneys who played a leading role in the investigations also resigned.

The next week, Dunn testified at a congressional hearing where she was flayed by members of the House Committee on Energy and Commerce. "What were you thinking?" asked Rep. John Dingell (D-Michigan).[33] "[I]s all of this really the HP way?" inquired Rep. Jan Schakowsky (D-Illinois).[34] In her testimony Dunn repeatedly fell back on assurances by

---

[28] Stewart, "The Kona Files," p. 162.

[29] Ibid, p. 163.

[30] Perkins, *Valley Boy*, p. 15.

[31] Ibid., p. 15.

[32] Ibid., p. 16.

[33] U.S. House of Representatives, Subcommittee on Oversight and Investigations of the Committee on Energy and Commerce, *Hewlett-Packard's Pretexting Scandal*, p. 13.

[34] Ibid., p. 96.

HP lawyers and managers that the investigation was legal, at one point saying, "I do not accept personal responsibility for what happened."[35]

On October 4, she was charged by the State of California with four felony counts of wire fraud, identity theft, and conspiracy, charges that carried a potential sentence of 12 years in a state prison. Three investigators were also charged. All pleaded not guilty. Dunn's defense was that she had consistently questioned investigation tactics and been assured that they were legal. Therefore, state prosecutors could not prove she intended to commit a crime, a necessary factor for conviction. Moreover, no federal or state law was specific in making pretexting a crime.[36] Five months later a California Superior Court judge dropped the case against her and agreed to dismiss charges against the others in exchange for 96 hours of community service.[37] Dunn's health was a factor in the judge's decision, but the main reason was the tenuous nature of the charges.

Whether Dunn intended to commit a crime or not, Perkins is convinced that she pursued the investigation on the likelihood that he and Keyworth would be incriminated and forced to resign, thereby removing two of her political enemies. He states that at one point he decided to seek her resignation as chair, but claims he was talked out of it by Keyworth.[38] In the end he brought her down, doing on the outside what he did not do on the inside. His actions put Hewlett-Packard at the center of a scandal, made it the subject of late-night jokes, and ended careers. As a director, he was unruly, challenging, and stubborn. Those who would condemn him, however, should entertain this question. What would happen if he were put in a time machine and returned to the 1990s for service on Enron's board?

Questions

1. Over the time covered here, did Hewlett-Packard's board of directors fulfill its duties to the company's share owners? Explain how it met or did not meet basic duties.

2. What different perspectives on the role of the board are revealed in this story?

3. Was Carly Fiorina treated fairly by the board? Why or why not?

4. Were the leak investigations overseen by Patricia Dunn useful and important? Were they ethical?

5. Should George Keyworth have been asked to resign? Why or why not?

6. How do you appraise the behavior of Tom Perkins? Was he a model director or a renegade?

7. What actions could have been taken to improve the functioning of the HP board?

8. Did gender play any role in the fortunes of Fiorina and Dunn?

[35] Ibid., p. 120.

[36] As a result of the scandal, Congress passed the Telephone Records and Privacy Protection Act of 2006 (P. L. 109-476) to criminalize pretexting. More than a dozen states have passed similar laws.

[37] Matt Richtel, "H.P. Chairwoman and 3 Others Cleared in Spying Case," *The New York Times,* March 15, 2007, p. C1.

[38] Perkins, *Valley Boy,* p. 15.

Index

Page numbers followed by n refer to notes.